Comparative Oriental Manuscript Studies

An Introduction

Comparative Oriental Manuscript Studies

An Introduction

Edited by

Alessandro Bausi (General Editor)
Pier Giorgio Borbone
Françoise Briquel-Chatonnet
Paola Buzi
Jost Gippert
Caroline Macé
Marilena Maniaci
Zisis Melissakis
Laura E. Parodi
Witold Witakowski

Project editor

Eugenia Sokolinski

COMSt
2015

Review body: European Science Foundation, Standing Committee for the Humanities

Typesetting, layout, copy editing, and indexing: Eugenia Sokolinski

Contributors to the volume:

Felix Albrecht (FA)
Per Ambrosiani (PAm)
Tara Andrews (TA)
Patrick Andrist (PAn)
Ewa Balicka-Witakowska (EBW)
Alessandro Bausi (ABa)
Malachi Beit-Arié (MBA)
Daniele Bianconi (DB)
André Binggeli (ABi)
Pier Giorgio Borbone (PGB)
Claire Bosc-Tiessé (CBT)
Françoise Briquel-Chatonnet (FBC)
Paola Buzi (PB)
Valentina Calzolari (VC)
Alberto Cantera (AC)
Laurent Capron (LCa)
Ralph M. Cleminson (RMC)
Marie Cornu (MCo)
Marie Cronier (MCr)
Lorenzo Cuppi (LCu)
Javier del Barco (JdB)
Johannes den Heijer (JdH)
François Déroche (FD)
Alain Desreumaux (AD)
Arianna D'Ottone (ADO)
Desmond Durkin-Meisterernst (DDM)
Stephen Emmel (SE)
Edna Engel (EE)
Zuzana Gažáková (ZG)
Antonia Giannouli (AGi)
Jost Gippert (JG)
Alessandro Gori (AGo)
Oliver Hahn (OH)
Paul Hepworth (PH)
Stéphane Ipert (SI)
Grigory Kessel (GK)
Dickran Kouymjian (DK)
Paolo La Spisa (PLS)
Isabelle de Lamberterie (IL)
Hugo Lundhaug (HL)
Caroline Macé (CM)
Marilena Maniaci (MMa)
Michael Marx (MMx)
Alessandro Mengozzi (AM)
Manfred Mayer (MMy)
Joseph Moukarzel (JM)
Sébastien Moureau (SM)
Mauro Nobili (MN)
Renate Nöller (RN)
Denis Nosnitsin (DN)
Maria-Teresa Ortega Monasterio (MTO)
Bernard Outtier (BO)
Laura E. Parodi (LEP)
Tamara Pataridze (TP)
Irmeli Perho (IP)
Delio Vania Proverbio (DVP)
Ira Rabin (IR)
Arietta Revithi (AR)
Valentina Sagaria Rossi (VSR)
Nikolas Sarris (NS)
Karin Scheper (KS)
Andrea Schmidt (AS)
Denis Searby (DSe)
Lara Sels (LS)
David Sklare (DSk)
Wido van Peursen (WvP)
Annie Vernay-Nouri (AVN)
François Vinourd (FV)
Sever J. Voicu (SV)
Witold Witakowski (WW)
Jan Just Witkam (JJW)
Ugo Zanetti (UZ)

Printed by: Tredition, Hamburg
ISBN 978-3-7323-1768-4 (Hardcover)
ISBN 978-3-7323-1770-7 (Paperback)
ISBN 978-3-7323-1769-1 (Ebook)

Table of Contents

Contributors

Felix Albrecht, Georg-August-Universität – Akademie der Wissenschaften zu Göttingen, Germany
Per Ambrosiani, Umeå universitet, Sweden
Tara Andrews, Universität Bern / Université de Berne, Switzerland
Patrick Andrist, Universität Basel – Université de Fribourg, Switzerland
Ewa Balicka-Witakowska, Uppsala universitet, Sweden
Alessandro Bausi, Universität Hamburg, Germany
Malachi Beit-Arié, Hebrew University of Jerusalem – Israel Academy of Sciences, Israel
Daniele Bianconi, Sapienza Università di Roma, Italy
André Binggeli, Centre national de la recherche scientifique, Paris, France
Pier Giorgio Borbone, Università di Pisa, Italy
Claire Bosc-Tiessé, Centre national de la recherche scientifique, Paris, France
Françoise Briquel-Chatonnet, Centre national de la recherche scientifique, Paris, France
Paola Buzi, Sapienza Università di Roma, Italy
Valentina Calzolari, Université de Genève, Switzerland
Alberto Cantera, Universidad de Salamanca, Spain
Laurent Capron, Centre national de la recherche scientifique, Paris, France
Ralph M. Cleminson, Winchester, United Kingdom
Marie Cornu, Centre national de la recherche scientifique, Paris, France
Marie Cronier, Centre national de la recherche scientifique, Paris, France
Lorenzo Cuppi, Katholieke Universiteit Leuven, Belgium
Javier del Barco, Consejo superior de investigaciones científicas, Madrid, Spain
Johannes den Heijer, Université catholique de Louvain, Belgium
François Déroche, École Pratique des Hautes Études, Paris, France
Alain Desreumaux, Centre national de la recherche scientifique, Paris, France
Arianna D'Ottone, Sapienza Università di Roma, Italy
Desmond Durkin-Meisterernst, Berlin-Brandenburgische Akademie der Wissenschaften, Germany
Stephen Emmel, Westfälische Wilhelms-Universität Münster, Germany
Edna Engel, The Hebrew Paleography Project, Jerusalem, Israel
Zuzana Gažáková, Univerzita Komenského v Bratislave, Slovak Republic
Antonia Giannouli, Πανεπιστήμιο Κύπρου / University of Cyprus, Nicosia, Cyprus
Jost Gippert, Goethe-Universität, Frankfurt am Main, Germany
Alessandro Gori, Københavns Universitet, Denmark
Oliver Hahn, Universität Hamburg – Bundesanstalt für Materialforschung und -prüfung, Berlin, Germany
Paul Hepworth, Istanbul, Turkey
Stéphane Ipert, Arles, France
Grigory Kessel, Philipps-Universität Marburg, Germany
Dickran Kouymjian, California State University, Fresno, USA – Paris, France
Paolo La Spisa, Università degli studi di Genova, Italy
Isabelle de Lamberterie, Centre national de la recherche scientifique, Paris, France
Hugo Lundhaug, Universitetet i Oslo, Norway
Caroline Macé, Katholieke Universiteit Leuven, Belgium
Marilena Maniaci, Università degli studi di Cassino e del Lazio meridionale, Italy
Michael Marx, Berlin-Brandenburgische Akademie der Wissenschaften, Germany
Manfred Mayer, Karl-Franzens-Universität Graz, Austria

Alessandro Mengozzi, Università degli studi di Torino, Italy
Joseph Moukarzel, Université Saint-Esprit de Kaslik, Lebanon
Sébastien Moureau, F.R.S. (FNRS) – Université catholique de Louvain, Belgium
Mauro Nobili, University of Illinois at Urbana-Champaign, USA
Renate Nöller, Bundesanstalt für Materialforschung und -prüfung, Berlin, Germany
Denis Nosnitsin, Universität Hamburg, Germany
Maria-Teresa Ortega Monasterio, Consejo superior de investigaciones científicas, Madrid, Spain
Bernard Outtier, Centre national de la recherche scientifique, Paris, France
Laura E. Parodi, Genoa, Italy
Tamara Pataridze, Université catholique de Louvain, Belgium
Irmeli Perho, Det Kongelige Bibliotek, Copenhagen, Denmark
Delio Vania Proverbio, Biblioteca Apostolica Vaticana, Vatican
Ira Rabin, Bundesanstalt für Materialforschung und -prüfung, Berlin – Universität Hamburg, Germany
Arietta Revithi, Βιβλιοθήκη της Βουλής των Ελλήνων / Hellenic Parliament Library, Athens, Greece
Valentina Sagaria Rossi, Accademia Nazionale dei Lincei, Rome, Italy
Nikolas Sarris, Τεχνολογικό Εκπαιδευτικό Ίδρυμα Ιονίων Νήσων / TEI of the Ionian Islands, Zakynthos, Greece
Karin Scheper, Universiteit Leiden, The Netherlands
Andrea Schmidt, Université catholique de Louvain, Belgium
Denis Searby, Stockholms universitet, Sweden
Lara Sels, Katholieke Universiteit Leuven, Belgium
David Sklare, Ben-Zvi Institute, Jerusalem, Israel
Eugenia Sokolinski, Universität Hamburg, Germany
Wido van Peursen, Vrije Universiteit Amsterdam, The Netherlands
Annie Vernay-Nouri, Bibliothèque nationale de France, Paris, France
François Vinourd, Centre de conservation du livre, Arles, France
Sever J. Voicu, Augustinianum, Vatican
Witold Witakowski, Uppsala universitet, Sweden
Jan Just Witkam, Universiteit Leiden, The Netherlands
Ugo Zanetti, Chevetogne, Belgium

Preface

The present introductory handbook on comparative oriental manuscript studies is the main achievement of the Research Networking Programme 'Comparative Oriental Manuscript Studies' (COMSt), funded by the European Science Foundation from June 2009 to May 2014. Within the framework of the five-year programme, several hundred scholars from 'central' as well as 'marginal' fields related to manuscript study and research had the opportunity of exchanging ideas and discussing diverse approaches, looking for common ground and a better understanding of the others' reasons and methodology in manuscript studies: from codicology to palaeography, from textual criticism and scholarly editing to cataloguing as well as conservation and preservation issues, and always taking into account the increasing importance of digital scholarship and the natural sciences.

Out of the larger community of COMSt members and associates, a smaller group of scholars and experts have enthusiastically accepted the challenge of contributing one or more pieces to this handbook, being convinced of the importance of presenting in a compact form not only the state of the art but a coordinated reflection on a wide range of selected themes on comparative manuscript studies. Working together, sometimes in unpredictable grouping constellations, they carried out their task to the best of their abilities. For all this, all those who have *volunteered* to contribute to this enterprise deserve the deepest gratitude.

The handbook is the result of joint and cooperative work both within each of the five Teams of the programme and across the Teams. Each Team was directed and coordinated by a Team-Leader (and in some cases by a Co-Leader) who assumed the major responsibility of the work. The central management of the project was provided by the Project Coordinator in Hamburg, and the general supervision, by an international Steering Committee representing the countries and their respective funding institutions (national research councils and/or academies as well as single universities in some cases) which made the COMSt project possible through the European Science Foundation. They are, in alphabetical order, Belgium, Cyprus, Denmark, France, Germany, Greece, Israel, Italy, the Netherlands, Norway, Slovakia, Sweden, and Switzerland. It has been my honour to chair the Steering Committee since December 2009, when my predecessor and co-applicant for the COMSt project, Siegbert Uhlig, resigned. During the second phase of the project, which was more directly focused on the preparation of the handbook, an Editorial Board composed of the Team Leaders and a few members of the Steering Committee took the most important decisions related to this task. Throughout the project runtime, the organizational umbrella was provided by the European Science Foundation as the funding institution and by its Standing Committee for the Humanities.

Peer reviewing was a major asset of the network. Besides undergoing the obligatory mid-term and final evaluations by the European Science Foundation, the COMSt programme continuously subjected itself to an internal review process. It is now time to face a more crucial trial, namely the verdict of our readers as to whether the cooperative and comparative approach is indeed so sound, fruitful and useful that it might set standards for future research. What is certain even now is that many people who have taken part in COMSt share the feeling that the scholarly and human experience acquired during this project will last a long time.

Some explanation is due to the larger community of all those who have participated in COMSt activities in the last few years on how the work was actually conducted. We may certainly state that neither the Steering Committee nor the Editorial Board have ever reduced 'formalities' in the technical sense to 'simple formalities'. In projects such as COMSt, formalities are matters of substance indeed, and they were approached accordingly. Every application for a workshop or a travel grant, report, minutes, every draft submitted for the present volume, all were openly and thoroughly discussed, without any pre-determined result. There may be projects where any question is settled in a two-minute discussion, or even without any discussion at all. In the case of COMSt, this was never the case—even if in some cases this might have caused some inconvenience. True collegiality—sharing responsibilities, the search for unanimity wherever possible or at least for widely shared compromises, without concealing divergences and open questions—has always been the leading work principle in COMSt.

The community of scholars that cooperated in the Comparative Oriental Manuscript Studies Research Networking Programme was inspired right from the beginning by the common expectation that an agreed approach can provide a significant contribution to progress in manuscript research, both on a general, interdisciplinary level and with regard to the individual disciplines of manuscript book culture; this community has therefore volunteered to accomplish a common task deemed important and urgent. The academic backgrounds of the COMSt members are different but, along with their respective differences and various ideas and attitudes, they have shared some basic convictions, which in some cases were challenged or looked upon in a new or different light in the course of these years. The intensive activity of exchanging ideas, experiences and points of view has eventually served to create a common language and to focus on the topics that were selected as relevant and crucial in the comparative perspective. The many core-points where the practice of the COMSt activity and interchange deployed its fruitful results with regard to achievements and contents, reveal themselves in the chapters of the present manual.

Not only do COMSt associates come from different nationalities and research disciplines, they differ also in regard to their formal academic role and status: there are full professors, *professores emeriti*, even *honoris causa laureati*, members of venerable academies, side by side with young emerging researchers, as well as non-academic professionals who mostly work outside the narrower university circles. As a result, new ideas and research concepts have been developed by many, if not all, participants and contributors. Moreover, some of the early stage researchers involved may even have acquired better career chances thanks to their active participation and to the contacts established through the programme.

The differences regarded also the degree of challenge involved, even for people with the same or similar academic status. For some of them, being involved in a project with a comparative perspective of this type may have been just one more among many contributions already delivered within the framework of international and cooperative endeavours. This is true for all those whose discipline was well advanced before in terms of available handbooks, comprehensive syntheses, introductory works, as well as methodological standardization, or first-hand work carried out in the field—for example, some codicologists who were in the forefront of our work, and generally participants coming from fields with a stronger methodological orientation. For them, contributing might have meant mainly a question of selection, or of putting new accents and fine-tuning. For those who best interpreted their project role, the COMSt project was another intriguing challenge. Others, however, had to start from next to nothing in some cases, building upon scant information available only in less accessible languages, or upon very elementary previous research, or working with a highly restricted profile and with special linguistic prerequisites. The COMSt undertaking was anything but a minor task. Contributing to this endeavour meant the collecting of data scattered across a number of publications and selecting and narrowing down all essential data to a concise synthesis, in a clear and comprehensible form of presentation and, what was even more crucial, in a comparative perspective. In many cases this implied undertaking first-hand research *ad hoc*, starting from catalogues or, in some cases, from the manuscripts themselves, sometimes even from still unexplored collections requiring hard field work.

Another important factor to be considered was the need, agreed by the members, to produce an introductory handbook that could be used by a wide audience, by students as well as by established scholars on manuscripts in different fields looking for reliable and up-to-date information. The profile of the handbook therefore remains that of a didactic and elementary work, with the ambition to cover, with a consistency and coherence never attempted before, the whole spectrum of manuscript cultures envisaged by COMSt (see below for this). Starting from the example of some comprehensive comparative handbooks of the last decade, each one with its own merits (for example Maniaci 2002a; Agati 2003; Géhin 2005; Agati 2009), our intention was to go beyond them in focusing on oriental manuscript cultures in an unrestricted perspective, where the consideration of 'materiality' is not intentionally regarded as opposed or detrimental or alternative to textual investigation, and vice versa, and where everything is put at the service of a better 'understanding' of manuscript cultures (including the textual heritage they carry).

This handbook is neither intended to be exclusively a *Nachschlagewerk* nor a *Sachlexikon* nor an *Encyclopaedia*. Articulated in chapters, it still aims at being, especially in its introductory sections, a book that can be read from the beginning to the end. As we all well know from our own experience, it is anything but a simple task to avoid specialisms and, at the same time, not to miss the most essential data. Since the very beginning of our work, we have attempted not to include and consider in our handbook every single detail for every manuscript culture considered, but only and precisely those which appeared important in the light of our comparative (or even contrastive) perspective, aiming at a comparison against a vast and various background.

Thinking more broadly, our project was also a serious attempt to defend and preserve the COMSt-related fields within the academic world. We know that disciplines and fields are often determined and justified by the mere existence of an easily accessible handbook or, in the better cases, sets of handbooks, textbooks, series and journals. The lack of comprehensive introductory works which are reliable, up-to-date, of broad interest and accessible to a wide audience and might be used in teaching, has a direct impact on the survival of the 'small subjects' most of the COMSt-related disciplines pertain to. The decision to make the COMSt handbook freely accessible online and printable on demand in a paper version at an affordable price was strategic in this respect, and not just meant to meet the prescriptions of the European Science Foundation. We deliberately declined to produce an extremely expensive work that might be bought only by a few libraries and research institutions; on the other hand, a plain electronic edition only to be accessed and downloaded as a PDF file was not regarded as a desirable solution either. Dealing with two millennia of manuscripts and codices, we did not want to dismiss the possibility of circulating a real book in our turn.

It remains, hopefully, only to say,

Lector intende: laetaberis.

Alessandro Bausi

Acknowledgements

There are many persons and institutions who must be thanked for their work in the COMSt project, including people who advised early in the application phase. The first is Siegbert Uhlig, who was the main applicant in the earliest phase of the project, doing everything to prepare and submit a successful application. He also acted at the very beginning as the Chair of the Steering Committee. At the very beginning, and in all subsequent phases of the project, in her new capacity of COMSt Coordinator, Eugenia Sokolinski displayed her skills and dedication: she must be deeply thanked for her competence in all matters of the managing of the project, from practical organization to the redaction of minutes, reports and budget planning, and for editing and typesetting all COMSt publications, including all the issues of the *COMSt Newsletter* as well as this handbook.

Some of the COMSt members volunteered beyond the limit of their individual contributions to the manual. Besides the general and chapter editors, the language tradition editors Bernard Outtier and Lara Sels deserve a particular mention. I am deeply grateful to Stephen Emmel and Ralph Cleminson for the thorough English language revision and to Sever Voicu for the control of the final bibliography to this volume. I would also like to thank Cristina Vertan for setting up the bibliographic database and Sophia Dege for her assistance in the consistency checking of the bibliography.

Several European Science Foundation science and administrative officers helped us in keeping fruitful relationships with the funding institution, at times when restriction of funding also caused serious inconveniences and disappointment. We would like to thank in particular the administrative officers Madelise Blumenroeder and Marie-Laure Schneider and the science officers Arianna Ciula, Barry Dixon, Rifka Weehuizen and Etienne Franchineau. In particular, Arianna Ciula played a special role from the very beginning of the network, and her involvement lasted beyond her employment with the European Science Foundation.

The national funding bodies who provided the European Science Foundation with the necessary funds must be thanked here: in Belgium, Funds for Scientific Research Flanders (FWO, Fonds Wetenschappelijk Onderzoek – Vlaanderen), in Cyprus, the Research Promotion Foundation (RPF, Ἵδρυμα Προώθησης Έρευνας), in Denmark, the Danish Agency for Science, Technology and Innovation (DASTI, Styrelsen for Forskning og Innovation), in France, the National Centre for Scientific Research (CNRS, Centre national de la recherche scientifique), in Germany, the German Research Foundation (DFG, Deutsche Forschungsgemeinschaft) and the University of Hamburg (Universität Hamburg), in Greece, the National Hellenic Research Foundation (NHRF, Εθνικό Ἵδρυμα Ερευνών), in Italy, the Sapienza University of Rome (Sapienza Università di Roma) with the Department of History, Cultures and Religions, the University of Cassino and Southern Latium (Università degli studi di Cassino e del Lazio meridionale) with the Dipartimento di Lettere e Filosofia, and the University of Pisa (Università di Pisa) with the Dipartimento di Civiltà e Forme del Sapere, in Israel, the Israel Academy of Sciences and Humanities (האקדמיה הלאומית הישראלית למדעים), in the Netherlands, the Netherlands Organisation for Scientific Research (NWO, Nederlandse Organisatie voor Wetenschappelijk Onderzoek), in Norway, the Research Council of Norway (RCN, Norges forskningsråd), in the Slovak Republic, the Slovak Research and Development Agency (SRDA, Agentúra na podporu výskumu a vývoja), in Sweden, the Swedish Research Council (VR, Vetenskapsrådet), in Switzerland, the Swiss National Science Foundation (SNSF, Schweizerische Nationalfonds zur Förderung der wissenschaftlichen Forschung / Fonds national suisse de la recherche scientifique).

Of these institutions, the University of Hamburg must be thanked in particular, since it not only supported the programme financially, contributing the missing sum necessary to launch the programme back in 2009, but it also provided the headquarters, offering offices for the Chair and the Coordinator, server space for the web applications as well as logistic support in the organization of the two major programme conferences (the Launching in 2009 and the Final in 2014).

I have certainly forgotten or unwittingly omitted too many important points, and for this I sincerely apologize.

Alessandro Bausi

Notes to the reader

A series of editorial choices have shaped the present handbook. While most are clear and transparent, some may need explanation.

The language of the book is British English, in the standard suggested by the *New Oxford Style Manual* (Oxford: Oxford University Press, third impression, 2012). The style is reflected in the orthography (including capitalization) and punctuation throughout the volume.

Some exceptions to the Oxford style have been necessary. A notable exception is the bibliographic format: for the sake of clarity and economy, we have adopted the author–date referencing method in the text; the works cited are listed alphabetically by author in the general bibliography at the end of the volume. For works with three or more authors, citations have been abbreviated to the name of the first author followed by 'et al.'; in the final bibliography, the names of the co-authors are provided between a pair of curly brackets. In order to keep works by the same author together in the bibliography, the spelling of names has been standardized, with the variants provided in square brackets. Authors bearing the same surname appear separately in the final bibliography; in order to help the readers identify the right title, the initial or, if this is not sufficient for the disambiguation, an abbreviation of the first name is supplied after the surname whenever the work is cited in the handbook.

In order to increase the readability of the volume, and underline its handbook character, it has been decided not to use footnotes, with the exception of acknowledgements at the beginning of some chapters or sections. Usability was also the reason behind the decision to keep the number of abbreviations to a minimum; the list of abbreviations used can be found on p. xxi. Practical use is further facilitated by a number of internal cross-references to paragraphs or chapters within the handbook.

The authors and editors have tried hard to illustrate aspects that may be difficult to put in words by appropriate figures and tables. The overwhelming majority of images in this volume are previously unpublished. The illustrations are numbered continuously, the designation always beginning with the number of the chapter and the subchapter in which the figure is to be found (for example the first figure in Chapter 1, subchapter 9, is referred to as fig. 1.9.1, etc.). The maps showing the approximate extent of the individual manuscript traditions in the General introduction § 3 are numbered continuously as Map 1, Map 2, etc. A list of all figures, tables, and maps is included on p. xxiii.

The readers are further assisted by the indexes of languages and traditions, place names, persons and works, institutions and projects, and manuscripts and manuscript collections. The general index concludes the volume.

Abbreviations

AG	Georgian era	fig. (figs.)	figure(s)
AH	*anno Hegirae*	i.e.	*id est*, that is
BCE	Before Common Era	l. (ll.)	line(s)
c.	circa	lit.	literally
C	Celsius (degrees centigrade)	m	metre(s)
CE	Common Era	mm	millimetre(s)
Ch.	Chapter	MS (MSS)	manuscript(s)
cf.	confer	n. (nn.)	note(s)
cm	centimetre(s)	nm	nanometre(s)
cp.	compare	no. (nos.)	number(s)
d.	died	p. (pp.)	page(s)
ed.	editor, edited	pl. (pls)	plate(s)
e.g.	*exempli gratia*, for example	r	*recto*
et al.	*et alii*, and others	š.	*Šamsī* (solar Hegira)
etc.	*et cetera*, and so on	v	*verso*
f. (ff.)	folium (folia)	vs.	versus

For the abbreviations of the names of contributors see Copyright page.

For the abbreviations of libraries and collections, see Indexes: Collections and manuscripts.

Tables, figures, and maps

Maps

(Unless specified otherwise, the schematic maps in the General introduction show the places mentioned in the text as well as some other sites considered relevant by the authors and the editors of the Handbook)

Tables

Figures

Introduction

Chapter 1

Fig. 1.7.8 Tbilisi, National Centre of Manuscripts, A-648, of 1030, f. 2r, with the image of John Nesteutes, photograph courtesy of the National Centre of Manuscripts.

Fig. 1.7.9 Sinai, St Catherine, georg. 15, of 978, back cover of a later binding, photograph by JG, 2009.

Fig. 1.7.10 Tbilisi, National Centre of Manuscripts, Q-907 (Çq̇arostavi Gospels), of 1195, front cover.

Fig. 1.8.1 Athens, National Library of Greece, 223, palimpsest, lower uncial script (*ogivale inclinata*) in two columns, upper script: 28 April 1195 CE, Basil of Caesarea, *Ascetica*; lower script: eight/ninth century, Basil of Caesarea, *Homilies in Hexaemeron*; *Ascetica*, f. 268r, detail.

Fig. 1.8.2 Athos, Pantokrator, 84, dated by the colophon 6 May 1362 CE, Collection of sermons by various church fathers (*Panegyricon*), ff. 424v-425r.

Fig. 1.8.3 Tirana, Albanian National Archives, 93, first half of the tenth century, Four Gospels, f. 224v: St John the Evangelist, photograph courtesy of the Centre for the Study of New Testament Manuscripts, <http://www.csntm.org>.

Fig. 1.8.4 Rome, Biblioteca Vallicelliana, G70, end of the twelfth century, the liturgy of St John Chrysostom.

Fig. 1.8.5 *Codex Sinaiticus*, London, BL, Add. 43725, *c.*360 CE, f. 153r, Wisdom of Solomon 6.10.

Fig. 1.8.6 Rome, Biblioteca Vallicelliana, B16, early eleventh century, a collection of works by St John Chrysostom, f. 70r, detail showing pricking, ruling for a two-column text layout and a quire signature in the upper right corner.

Fig. 1.9.1 Vatican City, BAV, Vat. ebr. 468, La Rochelle, 1215; colophon.

Fig. 1.9.2 Paris, BnF, Hébreu 1221, copied in Italy, 1285–1287, ff. 185v–186r, showing pricking on the outer margins.

Fig. 1.9.3 A student's model of ruling board (*misṭara*) preserved in the Cairo Geniza, Cambridge, University Library, Taylor-Schlechter K11.54.

Fig. 1.9.4 Signatures at the head of quires, MS Jerusalem, NLI, Heb. 8°2238, (Iran), 1106/1107, ff. 16v–17r.

Fig. 1.9.5 Double pricks for special lines (through lines), Vatican City, BAV, Vat. ebr. 438, f. 107v.

Fig. 1.9.6 Marking the openings of the central bifolium of the quires, Oxford, Bodleian Library, MS. Huntington 372, ff. 205v–206r.

Fig. 1.9.7 Manuscript measurements in a snapshot from the *SfarData* database.

Fig. 1.9.8 Micrographic 'carpet' page of Masoretic notes in a manuscript of the *Prophets*, the Hebrew codex with the earliest dated colophon, Tiberias (Palestine) 894/895 (copied about a century later). Cairo, Karaite Synagogue, photograph courtesy of MBA.

Fig. 1.10.1 *Codex Suprasliensis*, eleventh century, f. 8r, photograph courtesy of the Ljubljana University Library.

Fig. 1.10.2 Ostromir Gospels, eleventh century, f. 2r, photograph courtesy of the Russian National Library.

Fig. 1.10.3 Birch-bark document, fourteenth century, Novgorod, State Historical Museum, gramota 366, photograph courtesy of V.L. Janin, <http://www.gramoty.ru>.

Fig. 1.10.4 Kiev Missal, tenth century, Kiev, Ukrainian National Library, 19264, f. 3r, photograph Ukrainian National Library.

Fig. 1.10.5 *Codex Zographensis*, tenth/eleventh century, St Petersburg, RNB, Glag. 1, f. 1r.

Fig. 1.10.6 *Codex Assemanianus*, eleventh century, Vatican City, BAV, Vat. slav. 3, f. 81v, from Ivanova-Mavrodinova – Džurova 1981.

Fig. 1.10.7 The Anikievo Gospel Book, early fifteenth century, Library of the Russian Academy of Sciences 34.7.3, ff. 92v–93r, miniature showing St Mark and the *incipit* of the Gospel of Mark, photo from Sarab'janov – Smirnova 2007, 457.

Fig. 1.10.8 *Codex Rilensis* 4/14, copied by Vladislav Grammaticus in 1456 (*Hexaemeron*), f. 1r, photograph courtesy of the abbot and the monks of the Monastery of St Ivan of Rila, Bulgaria, and the Virtual Library and Digital Archives of the Rila Monastery manuscript collection, Sofia University.

Fig. 1.11.1 London, BL, Rich. 7174, dated 1499, Four Gospels, ff. 94v–95r.

Fig. 1.11.2 Charfet, Bibliothèque patriarchale syro-catholique, Rahmani 79, of 1901, f. 40v, courtesy of Bibliothèque patriarcale syro-catholique, Charfet, Lebanon.

Fig. 1.11.3 Kaslik, Ordre Libanais Maronite, 983, dated 1673, lectionary, f. 93r, detail.

Fig. 1.11.4 Dublin, Chester Beatty, Syr. 3, eleventh century, Four Gospels, ff. 2v–3r.

Fig. 1.11.5 Berlin, Staatsbibliothek, Sachau 304, dated thirteenth century, Four Gospels, f. 90v.

Fig. 1.11.6 Jerusalem, Biblioteca Generale della Custodia di Terra Santa, Syr. 6, seventeenth century.

Chapter 2

Fig. 2.2.1 *Dīnār* of 'Abd al-Malik, dated 77 AH / 696–697 CE. Diameter: 19 mm; Weight: 4.25 g. London, British Museum, CM 1874 7–6 1, © Trustees of the British Museum.

Fig. 2.2.2 Detail of a papyrus from the chancellery of Qurra b. Šarīk, eighth century. Heidelberg, Institut für Papyrologie der Ruprecht-Karls-Universität Heidelberg, *P.Heid.inv.* Arab. 1.

Fig. 2.2.3 Islamic seal, 2 lines of angular script, eighth/ninth century. London, British Museum, no. 1892,0328.94, © Trustees of the British Museum.

Fig. 2.2.4ab Engraved sapphire and its impression, cursive script, tenth to thirteenth century CE (and later). London, private collection.

Chapter 3

Chapter 4

Chapter 5

Fig. 5.4.2 Mould: The stain on the paper indicates that it was once wet in this area, and the associated purplish colour is the result of mould attack. Private collection, Istanbul, photograph by PH.
Fig. 5.4.3 Insects: The visible channels and holes in the text block are created by insects as they eat their way through the support. Private collection, Istanbul. Photograph by PH.
Fig. 5.4.4 Rodent damage in an Ethiopic manuscript. Bite marks on parchment are clearly visible; the leaves have been partially destroyed. Northern Ethiopia, 2011, photograph by EBW.
Fig. 5.4.5 Iron gall ink: Characteristic browning of the support behind where ink was applied on the other side of the leaf indicates the deterioration of the paper in these areas. When the manuscript is used, cracks and breaks can occur in the weakened and brittle support and result in losses over time. Private collection, Istanbul, photograph by PH.
Fig. 5.4.6 Copper corrosion: Browning of the support is visible behind a framing line drawn on the other side of the leaf with copper-containing paint. When the leaf was turned, the paper cracked along this weakened line. Small losses have been sustained along the edge of the break and eventually the whole section framed by the painted line may break out of the leaf and be lost. Private collection, Istanbul, photograph by PH.
Fig. 5.4.7 Bleed: Many inks or paints can be reactivated by water in liquid form or high environmental humidity which causes them to spread across the support. Private collection, Istanbul, photograph by PH.
Fig. 5.4.8 Transfer: The binder which causes ink or paint to adhere to the support can be softened by high environmental humidity, causing it to adhere to another object when it is pressed against the softened media. In this case, the painted red circle across some of the letters was transferred from an illumination on the facing page in the manuscript. Private collection, Istanbul, photograph by PH.
Fig. 5.4.9 Flaking media: Ink (and paint) made with insufficient binder or binder that has weakened with age is prone to flaking losses, as can be seen in the letters in this sample of calligraphy. Private collection, Istanbul, photograph by PH.
Fig. 5.4.10 Multiple damage: As is typical, a single page in a manuscript often shows many different types of damage. In this case, from a manuscript on a paper support, some of the damage that is apparent includes water and mould stains, transfer of ink from the opposite page, and insect damage and old repairs near the gutter. Leiden, Leiden University Library, Or. 107, photograph by KS.
Fig. 5.7.1 Opening a manuscript on a support created from soft foam cushions, photograph by MMy.
Fig. 5.7.2 Opening a manuscript with a damaged spine, photograph by MMy.
Fig. 5.7.3 Coding the preservation state of manuscripts by signal stripes, photograph by MMy.
Fig. 5.7.4 One and the same page photographed with raking light (above) and balanced light (below), photograph by MMy.
Fig. 5.7.5 The prism effect, photograph by MMy.
Fig. 5.7.6 Digitization protocol.
Fig. 5.7.7 Digitization workflow chart.
Fig. 5.7.8 Digitization studio set up in a cave. Northern Ethiopia, 2011, photograph by EBW.
Fig. 5.7.9 Keeper of a church's manuscript collection instructed by a book conservator. Northern Ethiopia, 2013, photograph by EBW.

General introduction

edited by Alessandro Bausi and Jost Gippert[*]

1. Scope of COMSt (ABa)

1.1. The background of COMSt

Work with manuscripts in both an academic, i.e. scholarly, and a non-academic context involves a huge number of aspects to be considered. It has not been a goal of the COMSt project to work on a theoretical definition of the *manuscript*, namely to define *what a manuscript is*. Instead of such a theoretical and comparative typological approach, the object of COMSt was, right from the beginning, *manuscript studies* as a conglomeration of already existing disciplines spread among various fields that were to be put in dialogue with each other. For the sake of convenience, a recent definition might be provided as a starting point here, according to which a 'book' is 'a transportable object intended for hosting, sharing and transmitting immediately readable contents in an ordered and lasting way' (Andrist et al. 2013, 46, my translation). The focus of the COMSt handbook, however, is on a peculiar subtype of the 'book', namely *handwritten book forms* of the *codex* area, including the horizontal and vertical roll and rotulus, all of them seen in their historical development *in a definite historical and geographical area* here styled 'oriental' (see below). Other types of handwritten artefacts that are often subsumed under the term 'manuscript'—such as *ostraca* or inscriptions on other solid or soft supports—are considered and mentioned only in cases where they overlap to some extent in use and function with codex-like book forms in a given manuscript culture (typically in the case of the Coptic manuscript culture (see Ch. 1 § 5.1) and, in general, that of papyrology (see Ch. 3 § 3.16), where *ostraca* are rightly assimilable to manuscripts).

Some basic principles and shared assumptions of COMSt should be introduced here.

(1) COMSt deals with manuscripts as intellectual products of written cultures in the ancient, mediaeval and pre-modern period, before the introduction of printing; it considers manuscripts as products of literary activity, as opposed, as a rule, to purely archival or documentary materials.

(2) COMSt deals with manuscripts written in less-taught languages that are mostly considered ancillary, or somehow exotic in the present-day academic landscape of Europe (with the exception of Greek, for reasons that will be explained below); they are opposed to and compared with:
(a) languages or clusters of languages which by themselves define disciplinary fields (typically, the classical languages and literatures, namely Greek and Latin, the Romance languages and literatures, the Germanic languages and literatures, the Mediaeval Latin language and literature, and so on);
(b) mainstream disciplines and fields which are not defined linguistically, yet traditionally related to some linguistic spheres, even where this is not explicitly declared, as in the cases of codicology and palaeography, which are mainly and usually associated in the European academic environment with Greek, Latin, or Mediaeval European languages and literatures, with a focus thus limited from the very beginning to manuscripts from precise areas. These mainstream fields (either linguistically or methodologically oriented) can look back upon a long tradition of research and standard practices manifesting themselves in a number of handbooks, series, journals, scholarly tools, and scholarly associations: for most of the disciplines in the COMSt spectrum, such an infrastructure is not yet available.

(3) COMSt deals with manuscripts not only as testimonies of the history of a literate civilization, objects of textual criticism, or cataloguing. They can also be the object of scholarly interest independently of their linguistic domain, in particular when we speak of material (physical, chemical, biological) and digital analysis, as well as conservation, preservation, and restoration.

(4) COMSt does not focus on the contents as such, even if the textual and figurative constituents are in most cases—yet not always—the ultimate reason for the emergence of a manuscript. Contents have been considered only insofar as they were strictly functional, to illustrate issues concerning codicology, principles of text editing, cataloguing, conservation, preservation and restoration. To deal with the contents of the texts would have meant dealing with the unmanageable mass of knowledge

* The editors thank Stephen Emmel for his invaluable help, as well as for proofreading and revising the English, and Laura E. Parodi for her fruitful contribution in editing § 4.

transmitted in the manuscripts, that is of the entire knowledge of a good portion of the ancient, mediaeval and pre-modern cultures of the world. At the same time, limiting the content to be considered to pictorial matters would not be justifiable either, since this is subject of yet another well-defined discipline, namely art history.

As mentioned above, most of the COMSt disciplines have not (yet) reached the recognition of the 'major' fields. Besides, it is anything but easy to overcome the confines of many national or even European and Occidental scholarly traditions, especially in some fields where the echo of harsh debates is still heard. Just to give an example, in textual criticism, the trend towards a 'New Philology' was initially accepted enthusiastically in the United States and France (where Bernard Cerquiglini's *Éloge de la variante*, 1989, was considered a milestone in the field). While much less popular in those countries now, and considered largely irrelevant—superfluous and misleading—in many others (e.g. Italy), this trend has been still attracting adepts in Germany in recent years (as an understandable reaction to a sort of divinization of the 'old' *Philologie*) and in the countries that are relatively new to the field of philology in general.

The same can be said of the varying and asymmetric constellations in which the minor COMSt-relevant fields are accommodated within the narrow academic scene of Europe. Some find themselves within (Christian) theology—with religious history, biblical (Old and New Testament) criticism, and patristic studies—or classical studies, with an 'extended' look at one or more parallel oriental traditions (for example, Syriac, as already in the case of some of the greatest philologists of the twentieth century, such as Eduard Schwartz or Wilhelm Frankenberg, the editor of the Syriac *Pseudo-Clementines*, who used to retrovert Syriac into Greek; also Coptic, Armenian, and other languages, all the more after the explosion of Late Antique studies in the last decades). Some are addressed within general Islamic studies and history, including Arabic, Persian and Turkish literature. Some are at times accommodated within comparative linguistics, in particular Afro-Asiatic (for the Semitic and Coptic traditions), Indo-European (for the Armenian, Slavonic or Iranian languages), Altaic (for Turkic), and Kartvelian studies (for Georgian); they can also be found as particular area studies; subfields of comparative literature; mediaeval history, etc.

To try to overcome the barriers between the disciplines and the various scholarly traditions was among the most prominent tasks of the COMSt programme. It meant comparing the methods used and, eventually, seeking a shared approach, taking into very serious consideration the achievements of the mainstream disciplines, but also giving due importance to the specifically 'oriental' features wherever these became apparent.

1.2. The notion of 'oriental' in the COMSt perspective

The first and most engaging aspect that has been used to identify 'oriental' fields of research is definitely the languages involved. We may state with conviction that there is practically no 'oriental' study imaginable that is not multilingual, and therefore multilingualism is in a way consubstantial with 'oriental studies'. However, this is not necessarily true for 'oriental' manuscript and textual traditions in themselves.

In her recent book, *German Orientalism in the Age of Empire* (a well-informed book indeed, yet not from the point of view of oriental studies, but much more from that of the history of European culture), Suzanne L. Marchand (2009, xxiii) defines Orientalism as a '*set of practices* that were bound up with Central European institutional settings in which the sustained and serious study of the languages, histories, and cultures of Asia took place'. Taking this definition as a basis, the determining feature of an 'orientalist' is—at least historically—to be able to read texts of a culture from Asia (extending to other regions and areas assimilated to it, typically the whole Islamic World, including Egypt, North Africa, and Ethiopia), in the original language.

The definition of what is 'oriental' in the view of COMSt was obviously among the tasks of the project, but it pertained by necessity also to its very preliminary choices, and the ongoing activities of the project have in fact positively contributed to the point. 'Oriental' in the COMSt perspective actually embraces *all non-Occidental (non-Latin-based) manuscript cultures which have an immediate historical ('genetic') relationship with the Mediterranean codex area*. This definition first excludes all East-Asian manuscript cultures, which are also 'oriental' in a broader sense but which do not share the relationship with the Mediterranean codex area. As a working definition, this delimitation geographically largely corresponds to an alternative one which builds upon the concept of the *area of monotheistic cultures* (Jewish, Christian, and

Islamic). However, the ancient Near Eastern and classical civilizations, especially the Graeco-Roman one, have played a decisive role in the *uninterrupted development of manuscript cultures manifesting themselves in a Mediterranean 'codex area'*, and in this respect, the former definition appears by far superior, all the more since it stresses the basically and intrinsically historical character—be it of structural codicology, textual criticism, or comparative scientific analysis—of all research on manuscripts.

Members of the COMSt community are well aware that the delimitation and selection of an area of study focusing on 'oriental codex cultures' defined as above still remains arbitrary, at least to some extent. More than the exclusion of non-related Central and East Asian manuscript cultures, which has mainly typological implications, the main limitation of this choice consists in the disregarding of the Ancient Near Eastern civilizations, notably the Ancient Egyptian and the cuneiform script cultures, which are nevertheless crucial to understanding the origin of practices still observable in the 'codex cultures'. An example here can be the phenomenon of the colophon, not to mention the impressive results that the application of text-critical 'genealogical' principles to cuneiform texts has brought about recently (see Worthington 2012 on Akkadian textual criticism).

The delimitation of the COMSt focus area has had a substantial consequence: it has distinguished the COMSt enterprise from other 'manuscriptological' projects and research initiatives which pursue more theoretical issues that are inspired by the necessity, in their case unavoidable, of a more typologically than historically oriented comparison. The specific ambition of the COMSt network has been to demonstrate that a strict cooperation between comparative typological and historical approaches can uniquely enhance our understanding of the cultures involved and the relevant phenomena—in terms of codicology, textual criticism, cataloguing, preservation and conservation practices, and, across all these different fields, of digital and technical approaches—and thus establish a sounder basis for an eventual broader comparative perspective.

The geographical and cultural spectrum of COMSt embraces the Greek manuscript culture, from Classical Antiquity down to the Late Byzantine period, as one of the main cultures that were responsible for the emergence and the further development of the codex in Graeco-Roman times and in Late Antiquity, but also in consideration of the quality of the evidence it provides in continuous documentation, starting with papyri and *ostraca*, and of the unparalleled cultural interconnexions it has always had with most of the other manuscript cultures considered. As a matter of fact, all other COMSt-related manuscript cultures have a relation to Greek, manifesting itself in translations from and/or into Greek. What is more, Greek is also essential in terms of the methodology applied and of the scholarly work carried out in manuscript studies. This is true not only for recent developments in codicology, but even more so for the centuries-long expertise in textual criticism, the very invention of palaeography as an autonomous discipline three centuries ago (at the time basically including what is styled codicology today), and the development of scientific practices of cataloguing. It is true that the scholarly work on Latin and western European manuscript traditions offers no lower standard, but it was not considered in COMSt in consideration of its vastness and because, to some extent, its link to the 'oriental' cultures is weaker and more indirect. However, dialogue with specialists in the field was continuously entertained by the COMSt network, and some of the sections take the 'western' studies into consideration.

For evident reasons, the study of the Hebrew manuscript culture, one of the major manuscript cultures that adopted the codex book form at a certain time, has likewise been central for COMSt; not only because it pervaded at large the Mediterranean area and beyond, into Occidental Europe to the North, to Yemen southward, and to Iran eastward, but also because of its exceptional and huge interrelationship with the Graeco-Roman culture and with the Christian and the Islamic civilizations, and moreover, because of the exceptionally high state of the art in the field of codicology it has achieved (Beit-Arié 2014).

The Arabic manuscript cultures, meaning the manuscript cultures that use Arabic characters in writing—Arabic, Turkish, Persian, and the large spectrum of *ʿağamī* literate civilizations—provide by far the largest amount of manuscripts covered by the COMSt spectrum, also embracing the largest geographical area, which extends well beyond the Mediterranean area. It is not only its central place and its vastness, but also its comprehensiveness, the hegemonic role it played for many centuries in the 'Orient' above almost all other manuscript cultures here considered, and the quality, variety and importance of the relevant scholarly tradition that makes it one more major domain in COMSt (see Gacek 2001; Déroche 2006; Gacek 2009; Déroche – Sagaria Rossi 2012).

The Zoroastrian and Manichaean manuscript cultures represented by Avestan, Middle Persian, Parthian, Sogdian, and other mostly Iranian-speaking traditions, are a peculiar case in that they illustrate the easternmost diffusion of the codex book form towards India and Central Asia, with a scholarly tradition that has remained extremely specialized. In accordance with the relative scarcity of relevant materials, they have only been touched upon casually in the present handbook.

The remaining oriental manuscript cultures considered in this handbook are part of a consistent, even though very varied field in terms of languages, scripts, typology of contents, quantity of manuscripts, chronological distribution, and state of the art, which may be subsumed under the heading of the 'Christian Orient'. Traditionally, Greek is also included (*ex professo* or *de facto*) in this area. The Slavonic manuscript culture holds a place of its own in it, due to its strict relationship to the Byzantine civilization. Within this group, we may distinguish various clusters: a Syro-Palestinian one (including Syriac and Palestinian Aramaic, often in close connexion with Hebrew and Jewish Aramaic manuscript cultures, later continued by Christian Arabic), an Egyptian one (including Coptic, Nubian, too scarcely attested to be considered *in extenso* in our handbook, again Christian Arabic and Ethiopic), and a Caucasian one (with Armenian, Georgian, and Caucasian Albanian, the latter attested only in palimpsest form). The Christian Oriental tradition is indeed one for which we have extensive studies that might be considered 'comparative' (with investigations into parallel literary, liturgical, or church historical traditions across several languages), but, to be honest, there is still very little and very poor methodological consistency in these studies, especially as far as the editorial practices are concerned (in the series *Patrologia Orientalis* and *Corpus Scriptorum Christianorum Orientalium*; in several journals, the *Revue de l'Orient Chrétien*, *Oriens Christianus*, *Le Muséon* etc.; and in introductory works such as Assfalg – Krüger 1975; Albert et al. 1993; see also Ch. 3 §§ 1.3B and 3.17). This situation has partially changed only in the last years, with a new editorial policy in some of the most important series (notably, the *Corpus Scriptorum Christianorum Orientalium*) and some important projects in specific fields; we may quote, for example, the editorial activity carried out in the field of Christian Apocrypha by the AELAC (Association pour l'étude de la littérature apocryphe chrétienne), which has introduced a systematic consideration of all available manuscript witnesses to the texts considered, from Western European languages to Sogdian.

1.3. Oriental studies and the role of 'orientalism'

A history of oriental manuscript studies has not yet been sketched from the inside so far, or only very partially, at least in the perspective of the methodologies and critical approaches the COMSt project has tried to apply. However, when talking of current practices, especially in text editing and cataloguing, we will immediately realize that a whole range of orientations and choices—arbitrary at times and often completely divergent for the different fields—can only be explained by looking at the history of the research in the respective fields.

The work in COMSt, to everyone's surprise, has revealed that the perception of what is the 'normal' approach in a given field (for example, in the case of cataloguing practices) is often a matter of dispute. For many people, the 'normal approach' is simply the one they regard as 'the only possible one'; this, however, may be very different in its contents and its methodology for each field. Comparing the various 'normal approaches' has revealed the huge range of methodological differences between the individual disciplines within oriental studies and has resulted in questions such as 'what should be introduced into my own field that is normal in others?' or 'why have the 'normal' approaches of others been so far ignored in my own field?' The different 'normal' approaches are often unconnected with each other, being the result of early choices and traditions no longer scrutinized today, rather than the effect of continuous reasoning. This sound criticism should always be preferred to thinking that there is only one way (I am thinking for example of text editing) and to looking for a 'unique solution' (for example a fixed, immovable set of 'fields' to be filled in in cataloguing). Conversely, in keeping with the comparative approach, similar cases evidenced in other disciplines and fields should not be considered in principle as unrelated ones for which something new and unique must be invented every time, and no single problem can be solved with a vague 'good sense'.

If we try to have a general view of the development of oriental studies, from the perspective of how this term has been and still is used in the academic occidental environment, we may distinguish the following features.

(a) The so-called *philologia sacra* ultimately rooted in ancient Hellenistic philology, through the example of Origen and his *Hexapla* (see Ch. 3 § 3.21) obviously made no distinction whatsoever between 'oriental' and 'non-oriental' texts and manuscripts, since no such distinction existed. This functional consideration of the material evidence to be used for the study of the divine revelation, characterized by a strict interrelationship between classical philology and oriental studies, has somehow remained—with all possible caution—a continuum up to the present day in the western scholarly tradition. Relying on a knowledge deriving from pilgrimages, crusades, long-distance trade (Marco Polo) or legendary travels (John Mandeville), the Orient was located before the modern age in the Ancient and Near East, as the birthplace of some of the most important world religions and religious texts. Some cases remain exceptional, such as that of the Florentine Riccoldo da Monte di Croce (*c.*1243–1320), who learnt Arabic, visited the Orient (Baghdad around 1290), and also authored a detailed analysis of the Qurʾān based on the Arabic text. On the eve of modernity this interest was renewed with the flowering of Greek studies, when Europe was invaded by a flood of Greek as well as oriental manuscripts after the fall of Byzantium (1453). Before the Renaissance, already during early Humanism, the knowledge of Hebrew, besides Latin and Greek (consider Giannozzo Manetti, 1396–1459), sometimes also of Aramaic and Arabic (Giovanni Pico della Mirandola, 1463–1494), was not a rare exception but something envisaged by the scholarly and humanistic ideal of the *vir trilinguis*. In addition, the role played by the Jewish as well as by the Christian oriental communities at the pilgrimage sites and even in Europe must not be underestimated. For example, the Ethiopian community in Rome played a decisive rôle in the development of Ethiopian studies, and the ecumenical councils of the west which saw the participation of oriental delegations, such as the Council of Basle–Ferrara–Florence of 1431–1445 promoted the interest in the east. This went together with the curiosity and interest in the 'oriental face' of the syncretistic traditions of Late Antiquity and the appreciation of Jewish cabalistic traditions, Hermetism, Egyptian and neo-Platonic traditions, as they were perceived at the time. But even earlier, for example in Spain, the relationships of Arabic-speaking, Jewish and Romance communities gave birth to a variety of contacts and exchanges, the importance of which must not be disregarded. Translations from Arabic into Hebrew, from Hebrew into Spanish, from Spanish into Latin, and so on were often the way through which lost Greek texts, once translated into Arabic, survived and were circulated (see Ch. 3 § 3.18). (For a first elementary sketch of the forerunners of oriental studies in Europe, see at least Richard [J.] 2001, and for Italy some of the essays included in Spina 2013, 9–20, preface by Franco Cardini, and Galletti 2013).

(b) The early modern period, with a broadening of the concept of the 'Orient' beyond the Near Eastern biblical horizon (see Irwin 2006), still kept the same interest in *philologia sacra* unchanged. Humanists and scholars such as Guillaume Postel (1510–1581), Josephus Justus Scaliger (1540–1609), Giovanni Battista Raimondi (1536–1614), the brothers Giambattista (d.1619) and Girolamo Vecchietti (d. after 1635) or Nicolas-Claude Fabri de Peiresc (1580–1637), or later Hiob Ludolf (1624–1704) had strong interests in the oriental cultures, and some of them in oriental manuscripts in particular (Scaliger's manuscripts are preserved in Leiden University Library; Peiresc tried, in vain, till the last days of his life, to acquire a copy of the Ethiopic *Book of Enoch*; and Ludolf tried to acquire Ethiopic manuscripts through his pupil Johann Michael Wansleben, who failed then, yet succeeded later in providing Jean-Baptiste Colbert with hundreds of Greek and oriental manuscripts, which are now kept in the Bibliothèque nationale de France). Frequently they relied on Levantines who supplied them with oriental manuscripts and information on the Orient. The situation did not change with the Protestant and Catholic Reformations, quite the opposite (see Wilkinson 2007a): the study of the Bible became even more important and it had to be done in the original language in Protestant Churches, thus being a continuous source of impetus to oriental studies. Hebrew was completely integrated into biblical scholarship. The sixteenth and the seventeenth centuries are also the period of the absolutely remarkable intellectual, technical and editorial enterprises of the polyglot Bibles (from 1514 to 1657; see Wilkinson 2007b).

(c) On the other hand, political events and other factors (for example, the missionary activity in the Orient by the Jesuits) strongly contributed to the condescending view characterizing Islam in derogatory terms, even though in the sixteenth and seventeenth centuries there are still several examples of Arabic being considered a key instrument to access Greek mathematics, as appears from the numbers of miscellaneous manuscripts preserved, not a few from a Jewish milieu, containing mediaeval translations; and the edition (1663) by Edward Pococke (1604–1691) of the *Taʾrīḫ muḫtaṣar al-duwal* by Ibn al-ʿIbrī shows the interest in Arabic as a source for historical research, with the paradoxical result that the first ever printed Arabic historiographical work is one authored by a Christian. It was only in the second half of the eighteenth century, with the gradual decrease of the power of the 'Turks', that a more scientific and less suspicious interest in Islam grew (it is needless to mention the importance of Galland's 'translation' of the *Thousand and One Nights*, 1704–1717). Yet, Arabic still tended to be considered an auxiliary language for theology (biblical and Christian studies), since this language had for centuries mainly been cultivated for Christian theological interests and selected manuscripts had been acquired for European collections accordingly (on Arabic studies in England, see Toomer 1996).

(d) The Age of Enlightenment saw the discovery of further oriental cultures, mostly the Indian, with the publications of the first Indian texts in the late eighteenth century by William Jones (1746–1794). The growing interest in Far Eastern cultures provoked a diminution of interest in the Near East; in particular, the interest in Islam, perceived as a 'late', definitely not an '*Ur*-culture', decreased, while the charm and fascination of ancient civilizations still grew.

(e) The institutionalization of oriental studies, at least at some European universities (in Germany at Göttingen, for example), also dates from the last decades of the eighteenth century. It happened in close connexion with the extraordinary development of classical philology, and still within the framework of Old Testament and generally biblical criticism. Theology still kept all its importance for oriental studies, and theologians, for example in the Protestant tradition, had to learn Greek and Hebrew. Besides the interest in the biblical text, the interest in ancient Judaism played a major role in keeping this ultimately humanistic Christian oriental tradition alive.

(f) It is extremely important to observe that it is from within this tradition that those philological and text-critical innovations emerged that provoked—applied to the text of the New Testament—a revolution in philological studies. Johann Albrecht Bengel (1687–1752) tried to establish a relationship between the manuscripts on the basis of similar readings. He did not yet distinguish between errors and correct readings; he did realize, however, that it is the majority of the families that is important, and that the authenticity of a reading is proved by the agreement of codices of different families. Johann Jacob Wettstein (1693–1754) claimed that it was important to use the codices and not the *textus receptus*, that is the Greek text of the New Testament as first established by Erasmus and then accepted by the Protestant Churches, even in minor details. He did not understand the criterion of the majority of the families but preferred, like Bengel, the use of internal criteria, and only when two readings were equivalent, he turned to the codices—unlike Karl Lachmann (1793–1851), who used *iudicium* only when two readings had the same authority. Johann Salomo Semler (1725–1791) distinguished between the external and internal age (*äusserliches* and *inneres Alter*) of a reading. Johann Jacob Griesbach (1745–1812) summarized what his predecessors had proposed.

(g) We may say that up to the end of the eighteenth century most of the orientalists working and dealing with manuscripts had shared substantially the same methods and approaches as were used in classical philology: orientalists and classicists belonged to the same academic milieu and their attitudes overlapped at large. Between the last decades of the eighteenth century, still in the Age of Enlightenment, and the mid-nineteenth century, a text-critical method emerged in classical studies; this is the reconstructive method connected with the name of Lachmann. A century earlier, Johann August Ernesti (1707–1781) and, above all, Friedrich August Wolf (1759–1824) had already taken systematic recourse to manuscript witnesses for their philological work, and it was Wolf who stressed the unparalleled superiority of classical, and Greek philology in particular, as the best way to interpret humanistic culture, and who consistently disparaged the importance of the *philologia sacra*. As a result, philological studies focused exclusively on classical Greek, and oriental studies still followed their own traditional way, in theological studies or biblical criticism, or even, at the other end, in the current of a more explicitly 'orientalist' approach in the Saidian sense. It is important to remark here that a great deal of oriental studies was completely underestimated by Edward Said in his celebrated, yet misleading and definitely one-sided analysis of European orientalism, the birth of which he locates in the age of Imperialism (see Said 1978) and which he substantially restricts to British and French orientalism. Mallette (2010) has provided a completely new perspective on orientalism from a Mediterranean perspective, with much stronger consideration of the phenomena of interchange and cultural continuity in the Mediterranean basin, where, for example, such figures as the scholar and colonialist Enrico Cerulli (1898–1988), who animated the intellectual debate on cross-Mediterranean cultural interconnexions and relationships for fifty years, is portrayed as one of the most emblematic figures (see also Fiaccadori 2011).

Still in the nineteenth century, while classical philology became more and more elaborate, oriental studies tended to become weaker and gradually less up-to-date and less methodologically oriented, since the mainstream was dictated now by classical and particularly Greek studies, as Marchand (2009, 73) states:

> In the early modern period, oriental philologists had pioneered many of these text-critical skills, but nineteenth-century orientalists almost by definition could not concentrate on one language; nor could they secularize their field with equal alacrity.

The end of the eighteenth century—*c.* 1780—is the period to which the beginning of scientific secularized oriental studies is usually fixed, but also exactly the period when oriental studies ceased to follow the development of the mainstream humanistic disciplines. We may say that this was also due to some intrinsic features of the respective fields. Classical studies were based upon an intensive scholarly tradition extending over several centuries, with a huge number of printed editions of texts, where often manuscripts did not play the most important role in editing (yet this was again one of the important contributions by Wolf and Lachmann). Besides, the needs of oriental studies were completely different, the majority of texts remaining unpublished (somewhat similar to mediaeval Latin and Byzantine studies). For a long time, 'to publish a manuscript' (one manuscript, the most accessible, not necessarily the best, or only 'the best', etc.), rather than to edit a text, was the 'normal' working condition, and this trend has in many cases survived to the present. In oriental studies, the content of a single manuscript—*understood exclusively as a text-carrier*—has remained for much longer a self-justified object of study and research.

(h) One more factor to be considered is the development of comparative and historical linguistics in the nineteenth century. Unlike Romance studies, where the link between linguistics, philology as textual criticism, and, in a way, the whole spectrum of manuscripts and literary studies, was not broken and interrupted, certain fields of oriental studies, for example in the Neo-Grammarians' approach, were absorbed by and reduced to comparative linguistics, implying a disregard of non-linguistic aspects, including material carriers, but also text-critical methodology.

(i) As said before, we do not have any history of oriental studies from a proper methodological perspective: we only have very sectorial approaches that are based upon all-embracing empty and almost meaningless labels. One may quote two examples, among possibly many others, of orientalists who were well aware of the methodological questions discussed at their time (it is a pity that neither of them has received any attention in this respect in Marchand 2009).

(1) The first is the very remarkable antiquarian—or, better, classicist and orientalist—and, above all, coptologist, Georg Zoëga (1755–1809). Like Wolf, who was only a few years younger, he was a pupil of Christian Gottlob Heyne (1729–1812) at Göttingen. Wolf dealt with Homer and classical texts, whereas Zoëga, besides the bas-reliefs of Rome, also worked with coins, obelisks, and Coptic parchments. Zoëga applied principles that were very similar to those proposed by Wolf, which he developed independently and in parallel. The study of Coptic and of the special kind of documentation represented by dismembered codices oriented his research in a decisive way. As elsewhere, in countries such as Italy, the knowledge of Greek was at the time in the hands of the orientalists, who were somehow its 'custodians'. Moreover, the documentation of Coptic, dispersed and fragmentary, implied and required an extremely careful and absolutely new type of material philology and cataloguing, in an extremely modern sense, which was radically different from the purely formal textual analysis (see Ch. 4 § 2.3). One more important element to consider is that Zoëga did not feel the need to dispose of *philologia sacra*—probably he could not and did not want to do so, for various reasons, some of them obvious (he worked at the papal court). Rather he understood the potential interest of the almost virgin field of oriental Christian apocrypha, which he started to explore.

(2) The other remarkable example to be mentioned, although outside the COMSt spectrum, is that of August Wilhelm Schlegel (1767–1845). While Sanskrit linguistics was rapidly developing,

> it was he who understood, even better than his British contemporaries or predecessors, that besides a pure Sanskrit *linguistics* also a real Sanskrit philology had to be established, furnished with text editions and commentaries carried out according to those principles of textual criticism and exegesis which were being developed by the scholars of Greek and Latin philology. He planned a very clear programme of this activity, which he also began to implement, and he also had a pupil and collaborator of exceptional value: Christian Lassen (1806–1876; Timpanaro 1973, 61–62, translation ABa; see also nn. 8–9 for reference to Schlegel's method and philological activity).

Note that besides being a pioneer in Sanskrit philology, Christian Lassen was also a remarkable Arabist.

In the course of the nineteenth century, philological discourse and methodologies were developed in the field of classical, New Testament, and Romance studies, and the names of Karl Lachmann and Gaston Paris (1839–1903; see Ch. 3 § 3.13) can be mentioned as exemplary for the critical, reconstructivist methodology. It is a matter of fact that with very few exceptions—usually due to a stronger connexion to biblical scholarship or classical studies—at the beginning of the twentieth century and later on, oriental studies in the COMSt spectrum still practised by and large the method of the 'base manuscript'. This practice had little to do with Joseph Bédier's (1864–1938) rethinking of the reconstructive Lachmannian method—a rethinking that might have had its reasons, although the solution is always questionable (see Ch. 3 § 2.3)—and had much more to do with the continuation of a previous practice current in oriental studies, corresponding to what might be termed 'the simple normal way'. In pre-Lachmannian classical studies, the editor 'normally' started from the *textus receptus* and an existing edition which he emended, and the recourse to codices was occasional and optional; in oriental studies, however, the editor usually started from one manuscript, since most of the time the text in question was to be published for the first time. Not much more attention was paid in oriental studies to the application of the so-called 'neo-Lachmannian' approach which was elaborated in Classics by Giorgio Pasquali (1885–1952) and his pupils, and in Romance studies by Gianfranco Contini (1912–1990)—even though they did take into account cases and questions that would also be relevant for some oriental traditions, the latter not being affected by a special status of their own (Witkam 1988). For the Christian Near East in particular, René Draguet's (1896–1980) credo of the 'base manuscript' method has dominated for long, even before being canonized in a controversial contribution (Draguet 1977; see Ch. 3 § 3.17), a major part of which was dedicated to technical concerns of layout and printing, and very little to methodological concerns. It recommended a simple reproduction of the best manuscript's text—taking into consideration its age and legibility—with all its errors included. Draguet's 'best manuscript' is thus simply the most suitable for the representation of the form; it is not even the 'best manuscript' *a posteriori*, i.e. the manuscript most similar to the critically established text (see Bausi 2006a, 2008b). It is therefore different, one might even say, worse, than the *codex optimus*, *codex vetustissimus*, etc. of pre-Lachmannian philology, which was a 'base manuscript' whose errors could be corrected *ope codicum* and *ope ingenii*.

Exceptions to this trend can be probably traced in every field. One example is Bernard Botte (1893–1980), the investigator of Christian oriental canonico-liturgical texts, who pleaded for the consideration of versions as textual witnesses, *when undertaking the search for an original*:

> The principles I have set out are not new... I do not think one can proceed in any other way, without risking falling into fantasy. One cannot blindly trust any version. The question is not that of finding 'the right version', any more than in a critical edition of a Greek text one must look for 'the right manuscript'. What is important is to make a good use of all the witnesses (Botte 1955, 168, translation ABa; see also Botte 1966, 177–179).

Earlier in 1922, Albrecht Götze (1897–1971), later the great Hittitologist, examined the manuscript tradition of the Syriac *Cave of Treasures*, and on the basis of the extant manuscripts he supposed the existence of an archetype, reconstructed its physical structure (columns and number of lines), as well as that of a subarchetype; he established subgroups on the basis of mechanical errors (loss of folia), and corroborated all this evidence by that of 'various readings and shared innovations' ('verschiedene Lesungen und gemeinsame Neuerungen'), giving also a complex but clear *stemma codicum* (Götze 1922, 5–12).

A third even earlier example is that of the Syriacist Arthur Amiaud (1849–1889). In the year of his death, 1889, following in the footsteps of Gaston Paris both in contents and method, he published a reconstructivist edition of the Syriac Alexis legends, stating in his introduction:

> We do not deal... with personal compositions... If one undertook the publication of a family of such works, where every author respecting only the general features of the legend has dealt with all other features with absolute freedom..., all that one could do would be to present each one entirely and separately. But here, where we have only more or less precise copies of the same text, the duty of the editor is to try to trace the original or to restore it as far as possible, and this is the target we are aiming at now through the comparison and the classification of our manuscripts (Amiaud 1889, ix, with an explicit reference to Paris 1872 on p. x, n. 1; translation ABa).

It is quite remarkable then to note that while little has been proposed on a methodological level for the scholarly editor, the respective 'traditional philologies' of the individual oriental cultures have, in some cases, been investigated widely and in-depth: this is definitely the case of the Islamic one, starting from Franz Rosenthal's classic work *The technique and approach of Muslim scholarship* (Rosenthal 1947), and all handbooks of Arabic codicology devote some sections to the question of *iǧāza* (certificates of transmission) and related phenomena (Gacek 2001, 256–261; Déroche 2006, 332–334; Gacek 2009, 266–268).

Among the few attempts at applying a consistent text-critical methodology in oriental studies, one may mention the work conducted on Ethiopic texts by Paolo Marrassini (1942–2013), who used with full awareness a 'neo-Lachmannian' approach in a number of critical editions of Ethiopic texts, both original (hagiographical and historiographical ones) and translated (apocryphal writings, for example the Ethiopic version of the *Apocalypse of Peter*; Marrassini 2009).

1.4. The comparative approach

The COMSt handbook is a comparative manual. We can distinguish at least two meanings of 'comparative' in the COMSt perspective. In the field of codicology in particular, the necessity of a comparative approach has become the watchword of the most progressive trends in the last decades. A broader scope of interests has actually been encouraged and applied by codicologists starting from the 1980s at least, in a series of conferences that have focused on book forms and cultures in the Byzantine, Near Eastern and Islamic areas, yet these at times have assembled views from different fields rather than pursuing a real comparative work, which was hardly possible because of the uneven state of the art and consequent lack of data (see Déroche 1989; Cavallo et al. 1991; Maniaci – Munafò 1993; Condello – de Gregorio 1995; Déroche – Richard 1997; Hoffmann [P.] 1998). The importance of the most recent trend is well declared by J. Peter Gumbert in his preface to Agati's manual (Agati 2009, 14), stating that 'comparative codicology and quantitative codicology' are 'the two most striking modern developments' in the field (see for example Gumbert 2011, for a keen application of the comparative approach in codicology).

While a generally applied quantitative approach is still to come for most of the fields concerned with the manuscript traditions considered in this handbook, with a few notable exceptions (mainly, Hebrew and Greek codicology), we can confidently say that each chapter displays a comparative approach, yet in different ways. Moreover, it is the first time that such a systematic attempt of overall comparison has been carried out in a handbook on such a scale. In Chapters 1 ('Codicology') and 4 ('Cataloguing'), the manuscript traditions compared alternate, whenever applicable and possible, according to a common scheme of themes and topics corresponding to the intrinsic features of the manuscripts as objects of investigation and the studies carried out, whereas a comprehensive and synthetic overview of the main common points is outlined in the relevant chapter introductions. Chapter 2 ('Palaeography' in the narrow sense) is less comparative in fact, since it answers to the need of providing basic information on the scripts featuring in the handbook and their history. Of a broadly unitary character is Chapter 5 ('Conservation and preservation'), where methods, practices, and questions revolve around material aspects that largely transcend the individual manuscript traditions. Quite different is the case of Chapter 3 ('Textual criticism and text editing'), the first section of which assumes the text as an absolute reference point independently of the individual manuscript cultures, while the comparative perspective is delegated to a series of detailed case studies, not necessarily representative of a linguistic or manuscript culture, but rather of a method, a typology, or a problem to be approached.

Obviously, even in the extended COMSt perspective, a total comparative view was limited by the availability and accessibility of data and was only possible in terms of goals to be pursued and issues to be discussed. Moreover, as stated above, the comparison was applied to a coherent or in any case defined historical and cultural area of the 'codex' cultures. (As to a more general definition of 'codex' that to some extent seems to go beyond the usual understanding, see Andrist et al. 2013, 47, 'a book consisting of a series of folia' (translation ABa): yet the authors do not consider cases beyond the COMSt spectrum, and actually focus only on the Greek codex).

1.5. Structure of the book

1.5.1. Structure and approach

Needless to say, any structuring is arbitrary, at least to a certain extent, like every cutting of a continuum of documentation and questions. The chapters of the present handbook follow five thematic focuses that were originally selected as relevant and most appropriate for the work to be carried out in the COMSt research networking programme. These focuses correspond to the work done by, and within, the respective work teams, namely, 'Codicology' (Chapter 1 and in part Chapter 2), 'Textual criticism and text editing' (Chapter 3), 'Cataloguing' (Chapter 4 and in part Chapter 2), and 'Conservation and preservation' (Chapter 5, and the part of the *General introduction* dedicated to ethical and legal issues). The work of the team 'Digital and instrumental approaches to manuscript studies' has been distributed in the General introduction and every chapter wherever applicable.

The structure of the handbook has been conceived in order to provide a reasonable balance between a strictly focused presentation of the topics on the one hand, and a comfortable readability on the other hand, the latter necessarily implying some repetition in providing background information. In order to limit repetitions and redundancies, cross-references to the relevant chapters and paragraphs have been provided wherever possible. In a few cases redundancies are dictated by the uneven state of the art in the single fields, which also implied the consideration of different points of view. This is not always a matter of the state of the art, but also of the specific internal features of each single tradition. For example, arranging single codicological features chronologically, usually done in order to date precisely undated manuscripts, is a practice little developed in Armenian codicology, since Armenian manuscripts can be so precisely dated, almost without exception, by colophons, that it was never necessary to establish such correlations. This is definitely not the case for most of the other manuscript traditions, some of which (Hebrew, to a lesser extent Greek) successfully developed refined codicological and palaeographical dating systems. Some very particular issues (for example, manuscripts with musical notation) could not be dealt with within the limited time frame and the physical space allotted. The same applies, as already said, to art-historical issues, which were to some degree considered as aspects of codicology / book production.

Finally, I cannot stress enough that the COMSt approach tends to consider manuscript studies in a global perspective, and that every attempt has been made to take advantage of the fruitful interrelationship established between methodologies, in a real interdisciplinary approach, where the more precisely focused single disciplines are, the better they can reveal their potential—which is the opposite of an all-embracing interdisciplinary approach, where disciplines tend to merge and methodological clearness disappears.

1.5.2. Questions of terminology

The question of terminology is extremely sensitive in a comparative approach, since comparing necessarily entails defining exactly *what* is compared. The COMSt manual has approached this difficult question with a practical attitude. The redaction of a detailed, extensive terminology for the whole area encompassed by COMSt would have been a research project in itself. The present handbook has considered throughout the work carried out in major fields that investigate the codex manuscript cultures (see for example Muzerelle 1985; Maniaci 1996; Ostos et al. 1997); however, as a matter of fact, it appeared that the construction of a common and satisfactory English terminology, also in main-stream disciplines, is still in its very beginning (see Beal 2008; and above all, Gumbert 2010b; see also Andrist et al. 2013 for a detailed critical discussion of some of Gumbert's proposals, starting from Gumbert 2004).

Carrying out a complete standardization of terminology has therefore been impossible at this stage of research. Consequently, terminology specific to certain fields has sometimes been retained when the relevant scholarly tradition had established practices that did not entail methodological consequences. Yet due explanation has always been provided. Book forms, *Realien*, all phenomena related to codicology, palaeography, textual criticism, cataloguing, and digital and scientific approaches, have been defined as clearly as possible when first introduced (typically for book forms such as 'roll' versus 'scroll' versus 'rotulus', respectively defined as horizontal or vertical rolls/scrolls; 'accordion book' has been adopted for the alternative terms 'concertina' or 'leporello book'; and 'painting', 'illumination', 'illustrator', and 'decoration' with the relevant *nomina agentis*, that is 'painter', 'illuminator', 'illustrator', and 'decorator' are all used and as carefully as possible distinguished, instead of the often comprehensively and extensively used 'illumination' and 'illuminator', or even simply 'artist'). In particular in Chapter 3 ('Textual criticism and text editing'), case studies show the variety of traditions and theoretical and practical approaches, and consequently of terminology, which is precisely what was intended to be surveyed and displayed in that part of the chapter.

We must not disregard, however, that the parallel presentation of the single manuscript traditions in the single chapters has *de facto* enforced a tendentially uniform, consistent, common and shared terminology, and even in this respect the COMSt manual definitely marks a substantial progress.

On the other hand, no attempt has been undertaken to collect or systematically take into account the traditional terminology used by the single manuscript traditions. Except for a few fields, where much research has been done and the tradition itself has developed a special interest in terminological taxonomy (for example, the Arabic and Islamic manuscript tradition, see Gacek 2001, 2008), basic research is still very much needed in most of the fields (for a first attempt and with a degree of caution, see for example Mersha Alehegne 2011 on Ethiopic manuscript culture terminology). In very few cases, however, local terminology has been introduced or quoted to describe specific phenomena.

References

Agati 2003, 2009; Albert et al. 1993; Amiaud 1889; Andrist et al. 2013; Assfalg – Krüger 1975 (1991); Bausi 2006a, 2008b; Beal 2008; Beit-Arié 2014; Botte 1955, 1966; Cavallo et al. 1991; Cerquiglini 1989; Condello – de Gregorio 1995; Déroche 1989, 2006; Déroche – Richard 1997; Déroche – Sagaria Rossi 2012; Draguet 1977; Fiaccadori 2011; Frankenberg 1937; Gacek 2001, 2008, 2009; Galletti 2013; Géhin 2005; Götze 1922; Gumbert 2004, 2010b, 2011; Hoffmann [P.] 1998; Irwin 2006; Mallette 2010; Maniaci 1996, 2002a, 2008; Maniaci – Munafò 1993; Marchand 2009; Marrassini 2009; Mersha Alehegne 2011; Muzerelle 1985; Ostos et al. 1997; Paris 1872; Pfeiffer – Kropp 2007; Richard [J.] 2001; Rosenthal 1947; Said 1978; Spina 2013; Timpanaro 1973; Toomer 1996; Wilkinson 2007a, 2007b; Witkam 1988; Worthington 2012.

2. Digital and scientific approaches to oriental manuscript studies (JG–IR–FA)

2.1. Digital approaches to oriental manuscript studies (JG)

With the spread of personal computers in the 1980s and early 1990s, studies concerning manuscripts and their contents started to change in both their aims and their methods, and the 'digital turn' has meanwhile embraced nearly all relevant fields. It seems therefore appropriate first to outline the essentials of digital approaches to oriental manuscript studies here; more detailed treatments will be found in the individual chapters following. The present survey focuses on questions of the representation of different scripts (original and transcriptional) and the encoding of characters; the conception of electronic texts, their structuring and their processing; the arrangement of databases, their layout and their handling; and the basics of digital imaging including special relevant methods of photography.

2.1.1. The representation of oriental scripts and the encoding of characters

In the early times of the digital age, attempts to store and process data in oriental languages were for many years hampered dramatically by the fact that computers were not yet able to deal with scripts other than Latin, and even the correct treatment of extra characters such as the 'umlaut vowels' of German or the accented letters of French was anything but guaranteed. The reason was that in a digital environment, the encoding of written text must be based on a given set of correspondences of characters with numerical values, every character being represented by one unique value. To encode the two times 26 letters (lower and upper case) of the Latin alphabet plus the digits from 0 to 9, the punctuation marks, parentheses, and the like, a set of less than 100 unique values is necessary, and this is why the 'stone age' mainframe computers of the 1960s to 1970s were based on a so-called 7-bit encoding: with 7 bits, $2^7 = 128$ characters can be encoded uniquely. The most popular standard developed on this basis is the so-called ASCII standard ('American Standard Code for Information Interchange', see Table 0.2.1), which prevailed in the first personal computers.

It is clear that on the basis of this encoding scheme, English texts could easily be digitized, but German, French, or Spanish texts could not, let alone Greek, Russian, or Arabic texts in their original scripts. This does not mean, however, that it was impossible then to process texts in more 'exotic' languages. What was necessary was the invention of encoding schemes that used more than one 'code point' to represent certain characters. One such scheme, the so-called 'BETA-Code', was applied to encode the ancient Greek texts that are comprised in the 'Thesaurus Linguae Graecae' (TLG), a huge database attempting to cover the complete textual heritage from Homer down to the Middle Ages. Cf. Table 0.2.2 which shows the 7-bit adaptation of the beginning of Hesiod's *Theogony*, contrasted with the 'traditional' rendering in Greek script. It is clear that the 7-bit encoding had at least two disadvantages: it was hardly possible to visualize the text as it should be on a computer screen, and the encoding was not transparent (or 'self-explaining') in the sense that the individual items (letters, diacritics, accent marks) could be easily determined by people who were not involved in the encoding process themselves. It is true that this encoding met the condition of being consistent in that a given sequence of codes always represented the same character, and this is why these texts can be used and analysed even today (and the TLG website still supports it); however, it will be clear that it remains clumsy and hard to handle.

With the extension of the ASCII encoding basis to 8 bits, this problem was at least partially overcome. On an 8-bit (= 1-byte) basis, $2^8 = 256$ characters can be encoded uniquely, and since the early 1980s, many 8-bit encoding schemes were developed and applied, adding 'special' characters such as those representing German *ä*, *ö*, *ü*, the accented vowels *é*, *à*, *ô*, etc. of French, or the Spanish palatal nasal *ñ* to the inventory. Unfortunately, this was not done in an equal, 'standardized' way right from the beginning; instead, several leading computer companies developed their own individual schemes, which resulted in serious problems whenever data were to be exchanged between systems. Tables 0.2.3–5 show the encoding systems used in IBM/DOS computers, Mac computers, and MS-Windows—only the latter one is more or less identical with the 8-bit standard used in many applications up till now, the ANSI standard ('American National Standards Institute') also known as ISO standard no. 8859-1 (the special MS-Windows characters are displayed on a grey background within Table 0.2.5).

Still, these encoding systems were not sufficient for the immediate encoding of other scripts such as Greek, Cyrillic, or Chinese. This is why from the middle of the 1980s on, so-called 'code pages' were

Table 0.2.1 ASCII encoding standard (7-bit)

	0	1	2	3	4	5	6	7	8	9	0	1	2	3	4	5	6	7	8	9
000																				
020														!	"	#	$	%	&	'
040	(	)	*	+	,	-	.	/	0	1	2	3	4	5	6	7	8	9	:	;
060	<	=	>	?	@	A	B	C	D	E	F	G	H	I	J	K	L	M	N	O
080	P	Q	R	S	T	U	V	W	X	Y	Z	[	\	]	^	_	`	a	b	c
100	d	e	f	g	h	i	j	k	l	m	n	o	p	q	r	s	t	u	v	w
120	x	y	z	{	|	}	~													
	0	1	2	3	4	5	6	7	8	9	0	1	2	3	4	5	6	7	8	9

Table 0.2.2 Greek text with its BETA-Code representation (Hesiod, *Theogony*)

*MOUSA/WN *(ELIKWNIA/DWN A)RXW/MEQ' A)EI/DEIN,
AI(/ Q' *(ELIKW=NOS E)/XOUSIN O)/ROS ME/GA TE ZA/QEO/N TE,
KAI/ TE PERI\ KRH/NHN I)OEIDE/A PO/SS' A(PALOI=SIN
O)RXEU=NTAI KAI\ BWMO\N E)RISQENE/OS *KRONI/WNOS:
KAI/ TE LOESSA/MENAI TE/RENA XRO/A *PERMHSSOI=O
H)' *(/IPPOU KRH/NHS H)' *)OLMEIOU= ZAQE/OIO
A)KROTA/TW| *(ELIKW=NI XOROU\S E)NEPOIH/SANTO,
KALOU\S I(MERO/ENTAS, E)PERRW/SANTO DE\ POSSI/N.
E)/NQEN A)PORNU/MENAI KEKALUMME/NAI H)E/RI POLLW=|
E)NNU/XIAI STEI=XON PERIKALLE/A O)/SSAN I(EI=SAI,

Μουσάων ῾Ελικωνιάδων ἀρχώμεϑ' ἀείδειν,
αἵ ϑ' ῾Ελικῶνος ἔχουσιν ὄρος μέγα τε ζάϑεόν τε,
καί τε περὶ κρήνην ἰοειδέα πόσσ' ἁπαλοῖσιν
ὀρχεῦνται καὶ βωμὸν ἐρισϑενέος Κρονίωνος·
καί τε λοεσσάμεναι τέρενα χρόα Περμησσοῖο
ἠ' ῞Ιππου κρήνης ἠ' ᾿Ολμειοῦ ζαϑέοιο
ἀκροτάτῳ ῾Ελικῶνι χοροὺς ἐνεποιήσαντο,
καλοὺς ἱμερόεντας, ἐπερρώσαντο δὲ ποσσίν.
ἔνϑεν ἀπορνύμεναι κεκαλυμμέναι ἠέρι πολλῷ
ἐννύχιαι στεῖχον περικαλλέα ὄσσαν ἱεῖσαι, …

Table 0.2.3 Non-standard 8-bit encoding (‘DOS/IBM’, ‘Extended ASCII’, ‘Codepage 437’)

	0	1	2	3	4	5	6	7	8	9	0	1	2	3	4	5	6	7	8	9
000		☺	☻	♥	♦	♣	♠	•	◘	○	◙	♂	♀	♪	♫	☼	►	◄	↕	‼
020	¶	§	▬	↨	↑	↓	→	←	∟	↔	▲	▼		!	"	#	$	%	&	'
040	(	)	*	+	,	-	.	/	0	1	2	3	4	5	6	7	8	9	:	;
060	<	=	>	?	@	A	B	C	D	E	F	G	H	I	J	K	L	M	N	O
080	P	Q	R	S	T	U	V	W	X	Y	Z	[	\	]	^	_	`	a	b	c
100	d	e	f	g	h	i	j	k	l	m	n	o	p	q	r	s	t	u	v	w
120	x	y	z	{	|	}	~	⌂	Ç	ü	é	â	ä	à	å	ç	ê	ë	è	ï
140	î	ì	Ä	Å	É	æ	Æ	ô	ö	ò	û	ù	ÿ	Ö	Ü	¢	£	¥	₧	ƒ
160	á	í	ó	ú	ñ	Ñ	ª	º	¿	⌐	¬	½	¼	¡	«	»	░	▒	▓	│
180	┤	╡	╢	╖	╕	╣	║	╗	╝	╜	╛	┐	└	┴	┬	├	─	┼	╞	╟
200	╚	╔	╩	╦	╠	═	╬	╧	╨	╤	╥	╙	╘	╒	╓	╫	╪	┘	┌	█
220	▄	▌	▐	▀	α	ß	Γ	π	Σ	σ	µ	τ	Φ	Θ	Ω	δ	∞	∅	∈	∩
240	≡	±	≥	≤	⌠	⌡	÷	≈	°	·	.	√	^{n}	^{2}	■					
	0	1	2	3	4	5	6	7	8	9	0	1	2	3	4	5	6	7	8	9

Table 0.2.4 Non-standard 8-bit encoding (Mac OS)

	0	1	2	3	4	5	6	7	8	9	0	1	2	3	4	5	6	7	8	9
000																				
020														!	"	#	$	%	&	'
040	(	)	*	+	,	-	.	/	0	1	2	3	4	5	6	7	8	9	:	;
060	<	=	>	?	@	A	B	C	D	E	F	G	H	I	J	K	L	M	N	O
080	P	Q	R	S	T	U	V	W	X	Y	Z	[	\	]	^	_	`	a	b	c
100	d	e	f	g	h	i	j	k	l	m	n	o	p	q	r	s	t	u	v	w
120	x	y	z	{	|	}	~		Ä	Å	Ç	É	Ñ	Ö	Ü	á	à	â	ä	ã
140	å	ç	é	è	ê	ë	í	ì	î	ï	ñ	ó	ò	ô	ö	õ	ú	ù	û	ü
160	†	°	¢	£	§	•	¶	ß	®	©	™	´	¨	≠	Æ	Ø	∞	±	≤	≥
180	¥	µ	∂	Σ	Π	π	∫	ª	º	Ω	æ	ø	¿	¡	¬	√	ƒ	≈	∆	«
200	»	…		À	Ã	Õ	Œ	œ	–	—	"	“	‘	’	÷	◊	ÿ	Ÿ	⁄	¤
220	‹	›	ﬁ	ﬂ	‡	·	‚	„	‰	Â	Ê	Á	Ë	È	Í	Î	Ï	Ì	Ó	Ô
240		Ò	Ú	Û	Ù	ı	ˆ	˜	¯	˘	˙	˚	¸	˝	˛	ˇ				
	0	1	2	3	4	5	6	7	8	9	0	1	2	3	4	5	6	7	8	9

Table 0.2.5 Standardized 8-bit encoding (ANSI / ISO 8859-1 plus MS-Windows / Codepage 1252)

	0	1	2	3	4	5	6	7	8	9	0	1	2	3	4	5	6	7	8	9
000																				
020														!	"	#	$	%	&	'
040	(	)	*	+	,	-	.	/	0	1	2	3	4	5	6	7	8	9	:	;
060	<	=	>	?	@	A	B	C	D	E	F	G	H	I	J	K	L	M	N	O
080	P	Q	R	S	T	U	V	W	X	Y	Z	[	\	]	^	_	`	a	b	c
100	d	e	f	g	h	i	j	k	l	m	n	o	p	q	r	s	t	u	v	w
120	x	y	z	{	|	}	~				‚	ƒ	„	…	†	‡	ˆ	‰	Š	‹
140	Œ					‘	’	“	”	○	—	–	˜	™	š	›	œ			Ÿ
160		¡	¢	£	☼	¥	|	§	¨	©	ª	«	¬	-	®	¯	°	±	²	²
180	’	µ	¶	-	¸	¹	º	»	¼	½	¾	¿	À	Á	Â	Ã	Ä	Å	Æ	Ç
200	È	É	Ê	Ë	Ì	Í	Î	Ï	Ð	Ñ	Ò	Ó	Ô	Õ	Ö	×	Ø	Ù	Ú	Û
220	Ü	Ý	Þ	ß	à	á	â	ã	ä	å	æ	ç	è	é	ê	ë	ì	í	î	ï
240	ð	ñ	ò	ó	ô	õ	ö	÷	ø	ù	ú	û	ü	ý	þ	ÿ				
	0	1	2	3	4	5	6	7	8	9	0	1	2	3	4	5	6	7	8	9

developed for 8-bit based computers, in which, just as in the examples shown above, the ‘upper’ area exceeding the basic ASCII plain (values above 128) was used to encode various other character sets. Some of these code pages have been standardized within the ISO standard 8859 (see, for example, Table 0.2.6 contrasting the Cyrillic code page ISO 8859-5 with the ANSI standard, ISO 8859-1), and some of them are still used in web pages.

Apart from these ‘official’ extensions, an unknown amount of local or even personal 8-bit encoding systems were developed in the 1980s and 1990s to meet the needs of philologists dealing with oriental languages. As a matter of fact, whenever someone developed and applied a certain font, the encoding of which did not match one of the standardized code pages, a new encoding system was created from scratch. Applying the method of ‘font mapping’, one could thus meet, for example, the requirements of Ancient (‘Polytonic’) Greek to be noted in original characters as well as Iranian languages to be rendered in a scholarly Latin transcription (see Tables 0.2.7–8).

Table 0.2.6 Standardized 8-bit mapping: ISO 8859-1 vs. ISO 8859-5

ISO 8859-1																	
32		!	"	#	$	%	&	'	(	)	*	+	,	-	.	/	47
48	0	1	2	3	4	5	6	7	8	9	:	;	<	=	>	?	63
64	@	A	B	C	D	E	F	G	H	I	J	K	L	M	N	O	79
80	P	Q	R	S	T	U	V	W	X	Y	Z	[	\	]	^	_	95
96	`	a	b	c	d	e	f	g	h	i	j	k	l	m	n	o	111
112	p	q	r	s	t	u	v	w	x	y	z	{	|	}	~		127
160		¡	¢	£	¤	¥	¦	§	¨	©	ª	«	¬		®	¯	175
176	°	±	²	³	´	µ	¶	·	¸	¹	º	»	¼	½	¾	¿	191
192	À	Á	Â	Ã	Ä	Å	Æ	Ç	È	É	Ê	Ë	Ì	Í	Î	Ï	207
208	Ð	Ñ	Ò	Ó	Ô	Õ	Ö	×	Ø	Ù	Ú	Û	Ü	Ý	Þ	ß	223
224	à	á	â	ã	ä	å	æ	ç	è	é	ê	ë	ì	í	î	ï	239
240	ð	ñ	ò	ó	ô	õ	ö	÷	ø	ù	ú	û	ü	ý	þ	ÿ	255

ISO 8859-5																	
32		!	"	#	$	%	&	'	(	)	*	+	,	-	.	/	47
48	0	1	2	3	4	5	6	7	8	9	:	;	<	=	>	?	63
64	@	A	B	C	D	E	F	G	H	I	J	K	L	M	N	O	79
80	P	Q	R	S	T	U	V	W	X	Y	Z	[	\	]	^	_	95
96	`	a	b	c	d	e	f	g	h	i	j	k	l	m	n	o	111
112	p	q	r	s	t	u	v	w	x	y	z	{	|	}	~		127
160		Ё	Ђ	Ѓ	Є	Ѕ	І	Ї	Ј	Љ	Њ	Ћ	Ќ	·	Ў	Џ	175
176	А	Б	В	Г	Д	Е	Ж	З	И	Й	К	Л	М	Н	О	П	191
192	Р	С	Т	У	Ф	Х	Ц	Ч	Ш	Щ	Ъ	Ы	Ь	Э	Ю	Я	207
208	а	б	в	г	д	е	ж	з	и	й	к	л	м	н	о	п	223
224	р	с	т	у	ф	х	ц	ч	ш	щ	ъ	ы	ь	э	ю	я	239
240	№	ё	ђ	ѓ	є	ѕ	і	ї	ј	љ	њ	ћ	ќ	§	ў	џ	255

Table 0.2.7 Non-standard 8-bit encoding: Ancient ('polytonic') Greek

	0	1	2	3	4	5	6	7	8	9	0	1	2	3	4	5	6	7	8	9
000		᾿	῎	῏	῾	῞	῟	·		°										
020		§			῍	῝	΄	`	΄ͺ	F	ϟ	ϡ		!	"	ἥ	ῄ	ῂ	ῇ	'
040	(	)	*	†	,	-	.	/	0	1	2	3	4	5	6	7	8	9	:	;
060	ή	ἧ	ὴ	?	ς	A	B	C	D	E	F	G	H	I	J	K	L	M	N	O
080	P	Q	R	S	T	U	V	W	X	Y	Z	[	ῃ	]	ἣ	·	`	a	b	c
100	d	e	f	g	h	i	j	k	l	m	n	o	p	q	r	s	t	u	v	w
120	x	y	z	ἡ	|	ἠ	ἦ	ἅ	ἄ	ü	έ	ἃ	ä	ὰ	ᾶ	ἶ	ἓ	ἕ	ὲ	ϊ
140	ἳ	ὶ	Ä	ἵ	ὅ	ὕ	ἒ	ὃ	ὄ	ὸ	ὓ	ὺ	ὒ	Ö	Ü	ἂ	ἒ	ἲ	ὂ	ὒ
160	ά	ί	ό	ύ	ῴ	ῲ	ῷ	ᾠ	ᾤ	ᾥ	ᾦ	ᾧ	ἴ	ὔ	ἆ	ᾐ	ᾔ	Γ	Δ	ἧ
180	ἤ	ἦ	Θ	ώ	ὼ	Λ	ῶ	ὠ	Ξ	ὡ	Π	ὤ	Σ	ὢ	ὦ	Φ	ὥ	Ψ	Ω	ᾷ
200	ἷ	ὗ	ᾴ	ᾄ	ἥ	ἣ	ἧ	ἀ	ἐ	ἰ	ὀ	ὐ	ᾀ	ᾅ	ἇ	α	ὥ	γ	δ	ε
220	ζ	η	ϑ	ι	κ	β	λ	μ	ν	ξ	ὧ	π	ρ	σ	τ	υ	φ	χ	ψ	ω
240	ϱ	ἷ	ὗ	ᾇ	ᾆ	ῃ	ῳ	ᾳ	ἁ	ἑ	ἱ	ὁ	ὑ	ὖ	ὅ					
	0	1	2	3	4	5	6	7	8	9	0	1	2	3	4	5	6	7	8	9

Table 0.2.8 Non-standard 8-bit encoding: Latin font with diacritics for Iranian languages

	0	1	2	3	4	5	6	7	8	9	0	1	2	3	4	5	6	7	8	9
000		.	˙	¯	˘	ˇ	´	`	¨	^	˝	.	˙	˘	˘	ˇ	´	`	¨	"
020	"	§	ˆ	ʻ	,	Ł	Þ	ʰ	ᵘ	°	'	'		!	"	#	†	°	+	'
040	(	)	*	+	,	-	.	/	0	1	2	3	4	5	6	7	8	9	:	;
060	<	=	>	?	√	A	B	C	D	E	F	G	H	I	J	K	L	M	N	O
080	P	Q	R	S	T	U	V	W	X	Y	Z	[	\	]	^	¯	`	a	b	c
100	d	e	f	g	h	i	j	k	l	m	n	o	p	q	r	s	t	u	v	w
120	x	y	z	{	|	}	~	≈	ž́	ü	é	â	ä	à	å	ç	ê	ë	è	ï
140	î	ì	Ä	ø	ė	æ	œ	ô	ö	ò	û	ù	ẏ	Ö	Ü	ã	ẽ	ĩ	õ	ũ
160	á	í	ó	ú	ñ	ŋ	ā	ē	ī	ō	ū	ā́	ǰ	ī́	ł	ū́	ā̀	ě	ī̀	ı
180	ū̆	ą̇	ā̊	x́	xᵘ	ž	ŋᵘ	ṛ̇	ī̆	r̄	ŭ	ą	ę	į	ǫ	ų	i̯	u̯	ə	ə̄
200	ə̣	ą̃	ą́	ę̃	ę́	ē̃	ḗ	į̃	į́	ų̃	ų́	ū̃	ỹ̄	ý	β	ƀ	č	ḍ	đ	δ
220	ǵ	ġ	g̲	γ	ḫ	ß	ḥ	ƕ	ḱ	ḷ	ḷ́	ḹ	l̥̃	ṃ	m̃	m̊	m̨	ṅ	ń	ŋ́
240	ṇ	ṛ	ṛ́	ṝ	ṝ́	r̃	ś	ṣ	š	š́	ṣ̌	ṯ	ṭ	ϑ	þ					
	0	1	2	3	4	5	6	7	8	9	0	1	2	3	4	5	6	7	8	9

The problem about all this is that whenever 'font mapping' is applied, the basic requirements of consistent encoding, namely the recoverability and exchangeability of data, cannot be guaranteed as there is no unique one-to-one-relation between a character to be encoded and a given digitized value. If, for example, we applied the Greek 8-bit font illustrated in Table 0.2.7, the value of 231 would represent a Greek lower case letter *pi* (π); the same value would stand for a Cyrillic *ča* (ч), however, if we used a font matching the standard codepage ISO 8859-5, and it would represent a Latin *c* with cedilla (ç) if we used the plain ANSI standard. This means that whenever an 8-bit encoding was applied in the encoding of tex-

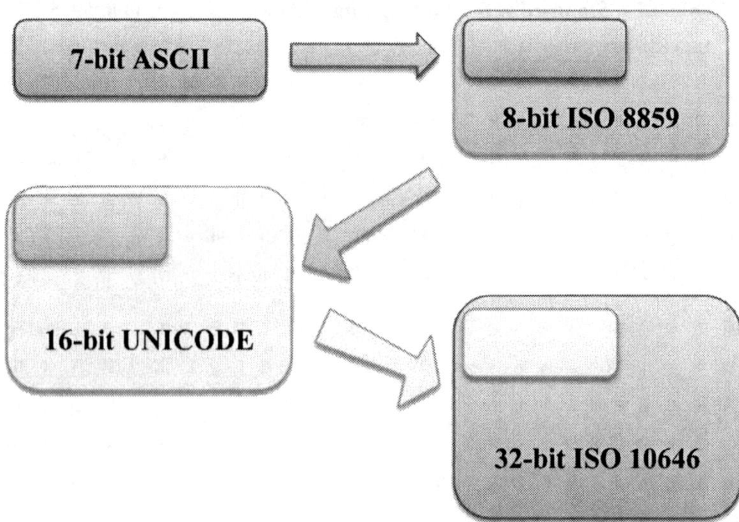

Fig. 0.2.1 From 7-bit to 32-bit encoding

tual materials, additional information had to be stored as to what code page or font encoding was valid for a given character. This information, however, was not encodable as such in a standardized way, being dependent on the idiosyncrasies of word processing programs such as Microsoft Word, and it was lost all too easily when data were transferred across systems. This is all the more true so for scripts with right-to-left direction such as Arabic, which required special encoding solutions in all cases. This is why many textual materials in oriental languages stored electronically in the twentieth century (sometimes even later) in transcribing manuscripts or editing their contents are no longer usable today—or at least hard to process.

To be able uniquely to encode all characters that have been used in writing down human languages including both 'original' scripts and alphabets and linguistic 'transcriptions', the basis of encoding had to be extended far beyond the 1-byte (8-bit) standard. This is exactly what has been undertaken since the early 1990s when the so-called 'Unicode' standard was created: based on 16 bits (or 2 bytes), this standard comprises $2^{16} = 65536$ basic 'code points' used for the 'unique' encoding of characters. Considering that for the Chinese script alone, far more than 65,000 different characters have been used throughout history, it is clear that even this standard is not yet sufficient to cover all characters used by mankind at all times. This is why a further extension has been conceived, in the 32-bit standard ISO 10646 which provides a total of (2^{32} =) 4,294,967,296 code points; as a matter of fact, the Unicode standard is but one subset of this near to 'infinite' inventory, just as the ANSI standard (ISO 8859-1) is a subset of Unicode, and the ASCII standard a subset of ANSI (see fig. 0.2.1).

Along with the expansion of the World Wide Web, Unicode encoding has become more and more prominent since the late 1990s, and it is the encoding basis of practically all up-to-date operating systems and word processors today. There can be no doubt that this is a huge advantage for the purposes of oriental manuscript studies. Cf., for example, Table 0.2.9 which shows a few of the 'blocks' of Unicode characters: the distinction of a Cyrillic *ča* (ч) and a Latin *c* with cedilla (ç) is now guaranteed by their different code points (hexadecimal number 0447 = decimal 1095 vs. hexadecimal 00E7 = decimal 231), and various Latin-based characters used in transcription systems can now as well be encoded as characters of the Greek, Coptic, or Georgian scripts. In addition, the Unicode standard even comprises information on the directionality of a given character so that Hebrew, Arabic, or Syriac texts can be encoded (and exchanged!) without further programming—provided the system used has implemented the relevant 'blocks' and the rules pertaining to them.

However, even Unicode encoding is not without problems. First of all, it builds upon the so-called character/glyph distinction. According to the definition provided by the Unicode Consortium, a 'glyph is a particular image which represents a character or part of a character', and it 'may have very different shapes' as illustrated by the set of six 'sample glyphs' for the Latin 'character' *a* in Table 0.2.10 (modelled after the diagram in General introduction § 2.1 at <http://www.unicode.org/reports/tr17/tr17-3.html>, accessed March 2014). It will be clear from the example that a 'character', which is what is to be encoded, is an abstraction of all the possible actual forms of a 'letter' that may appear in handwritten or printed

Table 0.2.9 16-bit encoding: Unicode blocks Latin and Cyrillic

Latin

	0	1	2	3	4	5	6	7	8	9	A	B	C	D	E	F
000																
001																
002	?	!	“	#	$	%	&	'	(	)	*	+	,	-	.	/
003	0	1	2	3	4	5	6	7	8	9	:	;	<	=	>	?
004	@	A	B	C	D	E	F	G	H	I	J	K	L	M	N	O
005	P	Q	R	S	T	U	V	W	X	Y	Z	[	\	]	^	_
006	`	a	b	c	d	e	f	g	h	i	j	k	l	m	n	o
007	p	q	r	s	t	u	v	w	x	y	z	{	|	}	~	
008																
009																
00A		¡	¢	£	¤	¥	¦	§	¨	©	ª	«	¬		®	¯
00B	°	±	²	³	´	µ	¶	·	¸	¹	º	»	¼	½	¾	¿
00C	À	Á	Â	Ã	Ä	Å	Æ	Ç	È	É	Ê	Ë	Ì	Í	Î	Ï
00D	Ð	Ñ	Ò	Ó	Ô	Õ	Ö	×	Ø	Ù	Ú	Û	Ü	Ý	Þ	ß
00E	à	á	â	ã	ä	å	æ	ç	è	é	ê	ë	ì	í	î	ï
00F	ð	ñ	ò	ó	ô	õ	ö	÷	ø	ù	ú	û	ü	ý	þ	ÿ
	0	1	2	3	4	5	6	7	8	9	A	B	C	D	E	F

Cyrillic

	0	1	2	3	4	5	6	7	8	9	A	B	C	D	E	F
040	Ѐ	Ё	Ђ	Ѓ	Є	Ѕ	І	Ї	Ј	Љ	Њ	Ћ	Ќ	Ѝ	Ў	Џ
041	А	Б	В	Г	Д	Е	Ж	З	И	Й	К	Л	М	Н	О	П
042	Р	С	Т	У	Ф	Х	Ц	Ч	Ш	Щ	Ъ	Ы	Ь	Э	Ю	Я
043	а	б	в	г	д	е	ж	з	и	й	к	л	м	н	о	п
044	р	с	т	у	ф	х	ц	ч	ш	щ	ъ	ы	ь	э	ю	я
045	ѐ	ё	ђ	ѓ	є	ѕ	і	ї	ј	љ	њ	ћ	ќ	ѝ	ў	џ
046	Ѡ	ѡ	Ѣ	ѣ	Ѥ	ѥ	Ѧ	ѧ	Ѩ	ѩ	Ѫ	ѫ	Ѭ	ѭ	Ѯ	ѯ
047	Ѱ	ѱ	Ѳ	ѳ	Ѵ	ѵ	Ѷ	ѷ	Ѹ	ѹ	Ѻ	ѻ	Ѽ	ѽ	Ѿ	ѿ
048	Ҁ	ҁ	҂	҃	҄	҅	҆	҇	҈	҉	Ҋ	ҋ	Ҍ	ҍ	Ҏ	ҏ
049	Ґ	ґ	Ғ	ғ	Ҕ	ҕ	Җ	җ	Ҙ	ҙ	Қ	қ	Ҝ	ҝ	Ҟ	ҟ
04A	Ҡ	ҡ	Ң	ң	Ҥ	ҥ	Ҧ	ҧ	Ҩ	ҩ	Ҫ	ҫ	Ҭ	ҭ	Ү	ү
04B	Ұ	ұ	Ҳ	ҳ	Ҵ	ҵ	Ҷ	ҷ	Ҹ	ҹ	Һ	һ	Ҽ	ҽ	Ҿ	ҿ
04C	Ӏ	Ӂ	ӂ	Ӄ	ӄ	Ӆ	ӆ	Ӈ	ӈ	Ӊ	ӊ	Ӌ	ӌ	Ӎ	ӎ	ӏ
04D	Ӑ	ӑ	Ӓ	ӓ	Ӕ	ӕ	Ӗ	ӗ	Ә	ә	Ӛ	ӛ	Ӝ	ӝ	Ӟ	ӟ
04E	Ӡ	ӡ	Ӣ	ӣ	Ӥ	ӥ	Ӧ	ӧ	Ө	ө	Ӫ	ӫ	Ӭ	ӭ	Ӯ	ӯ
04F	Ӱ	ӱ	Ӳ	ӳ	Ӵ	ӵ	Ӷ	ӷ	Ӹ	ӹ	Ӻ	ӻ	Ӽ	ӽ	Ӿ	ӿ
	0	1	2	3	4	5	6	7	8	9	A	B	C	D	E	F

Table 0.2.10 Example of the character/glyph distinction in Unicode

Character	**Sample glyphs**					
a	a	a	a	a	a	a

form, while every single appearance of the letter is regarded as a ‘glyph variant’. This distinction, then, is crucial indeed for manuscript studies, as the assignment of individual ‘letter shapes’ occurring in handwritten sources to ‘abstract’ character values may always be a matter of dispute, especially in a diachronic perspective: we may think, for example, of the emergence of minuscules from majuscules over time, or of ‘new letters’ from former ligatures. As a matter of fact, the decision of the Unicode Consortium to treat the ‘minuscule’ *a* as a character in its own right, with a unique code point, and not to treat all the ‘minuscule’ variants of *a* as glyphs of the one (‘majuscule’) character *A*, which has another code point, may be justified for practical (and traditional) reasons, but it may be problematical indeed for manuscript studies concerning the first millennium. It may be even more problematical when it comes to scripts that are less ‘fixed’ than Latin.

To be sure, the problem of assigning letter forms as appearing in a handwritten context to ‘abstract’ units is not intrinsically determined by digitization, and it is by no means confined to it: just like a scholar of today, who has to decide by what code point he would represent the glyph he ‘reads’ in a manuscript, a scholar using pen or pencil in transcribing a manuscript would have had to decide for an ‘abstract’ character, too, at least when handing his transcript over to a typesetter. There is indeed an important difference, however, in that the purpose of typesetting was limited to a reproduction in print, whereas a digital encoding can be used for other purposes such as automatic indexation as well; here, the consistency of the encoding becomes crucial indeed (cf. below). Another difference concerns the way restrictions could be overcome when necessary, those of a typesetter’s letter case of old and those of an encoding standard of today: the typesetter may have resorted to the production of new types if this was deemed unavoidable (cf. the approaches summarized in the case study on the edition of the Berlin Turfan manuscripts, Ch. 3 § 3.9), and the ‘digital’ scholar, to the tedious process of convincing the Unicode Consortium that a character (not a glyph!) is missing in their standard (cf. the problem of a ‘different letter for *q* and initial *y*’

Table 0.2.11 16-bit font mapping: The 'Private Use Area' of Unicode

Font 'a'

	0	1	2	3	4	5	6	7	8	9	A	B	C	D	E	F
E80	.	!	(	)	«	»	'	ـ	[illegible]	[illegible]	.	[illegible]	[illegible]	ـ	ـ	ـ
E81	[illegible]	[illegible]	[illegible]	[illegible]	[illegible]	[illegible]	[illegible]	[illegible]	[illegible]	[illegible]	[illegible]	[illegible]	[illegible]	[illegible]	[illegible]	[illegible]
E82	[illegible]	[illegible]	[illegible]	[illegible]	[illegible]	[illegible]	[illegible]	[illegible]	[illegible]	[illegible]	[illegible]	[illegible]	[illegible]	[illegible]	[illegible]	[illegible]
E83	ٿ	ٿ	ڐ	ڐ	ڃ	ڃ	ڄ	ڄ	خ	خ	ځ	ځ	ٻ	ٻ	ٻ	ٻ
E84	ڌ	ڌ	ڙ	ڙ	ڒ	ڒ	ژ	ژ	ڔ	ڔ	ڕ	ڕ	ښ	ښ	ښ	ښ
E85	ۼ	ۼ	ۼ	ۼ	ڬ	ڬ	ک	ک	ڰ	ڰ	ڲ	ڲ	ګ	ګ	ڴ	ڴ
E86	ڳ	ڳ	ڳ	ڳ	ڵ	ڵ	ڵ	ڵ	ڵا	ڵا	ڽ	ڽ	ڽ	ڽ	ۊ	ۊ
E87	ۋ	ۋ	ۑ	ۑ	ێ	ێ	ې	ې	ٻ	ٻ	ٽ	ٽ	ٽ	ٽ	ێ	ں
E88	ڵا	ڵا	ڵا	ڵا	ڹ	ڹ			ڿ							
E89																
E8A																
	0	1	2	3	4	5	6	7	8	9	A	B	C	D	E	F

Font 'b'

	0	1	2	3	4	5	6	7	8	9	A	B	C	D	E	F
E80	·	ו	ך	ך	ל	ל	·	·	·	·	·	·	·	·	·	·
E81	·	·	·	·	·	□	ナ	⺈	[illegible]	□	□	□	□	□	⺅	□
E82	□	□	□	□	□	□	手	□	□	□	□	丰	廾	□	□	□
E83	□	夫	艸	□	□	□	□	□	□	□	□	戋	□	□	□	□
E84	□	□	□	共	□	□	□	□	□	□	□	□	□	□	□	□
E85	□	□	□	□	卓	幽	□	□	□	□	□	□	□	□	□	□
E86	□	□	□	□	٢	·	·	<	·	·	·	·	·	·	·	·
E87	·	·	·	·	·	·	·	·	·	·	·	·	·	·	·	·
E88	·	·	·	·	·	·	·	·	·	·	·	·	·	·	·	·
E89	ڎ	·	·	·	·	·	·	·	·	·	·	·	·	·	·	·
E8A	·	·	·	·	·	ۏ	ۏ	ڥ	·	·	·	·	·	·	·	·
	0	1	2	3	4	5	6	7	8	9	A	B	C	D	E	F

in Indian and Iranian manuscripts of the *Avesta*, thematized in case study Ch. 3 § 3.5). Be that as it may, the problem of distinguishing abstract 'characters' from 'glyphs' as their 'representations' is actually one of the history of scripts, their analysis and their usage in general, not of digitization. The development of the Unicode standard has contributed a lot to this question by enforcing thorough investigation, and many of us have been involved in the process of its extension. However, it is a pity that this has often not been determined by scientific reasoning alone but by practical (or even economic) considerations, thus leaving inconsistencies and shortcomings that we still have to cope with.

One such inconsistency lies in the fact that the encoding facilities Unicode provides are not always 'unique'. This is especially true for the huge amount of combinations of (Latin, Greek, Cyrillic etc.) characters with diacritics it intends to cover, many of which can be encoded 'as such', that is as so-called 'precomposed characters', or as combinations of the respective 'basic character' and the diacritic(s) it carries. For example, the German *ä* can be encoded as the Unicode character no. 226 (U+00E4) or as a sequence of *a* = no. 97 (U+0061) and the 'umlaut' diacritic ('diaeresis', U+0308); in a similar way, *r* with a macron above and a dot below (*ṝ*) can be encoded as such as no. 7773 (U+1E5D) or as a sequence of *r* (U+0072), macron above (U+0304), and dot below (U+0323), or even as a sequence of *r* with a dot below (*ṛ*, U+1E5B) and a macron above (U+0304). It is true that the different ways of encoding the same 'composed character' are essentially equivalent according to the definition of the standard—with the 'precomposed' units being considered as the first choice—and should be treated as such by Unicode-based systems; however, users cannot rely upon this in all cases yet, depending on system or software peculiarities.

A similar problem is posed, for example, by Arabic characters, given that Unicode provides code points for both the different 'surface' forms they may appear in within words (isolated, final, initial, medial, for example ﻍ, ﻎ, ﻏ, ﻐ; U+FE81 to FEF4) and an 'idealized' representation of the underlying 'abstract' character (identical in shape with the 'isolated' variant) which is meant to be adapted automatically to the context (for example غ, U+062A). Here, too, the different ways of encoding the same character are essentially equivalent according to the definition of the standard, with the 'idealized' representations to be used preferably wherever possible.

Another problem that may be crucial in the application of Unicode is the persistence of at least one area that is designed for font mapping. This is the so-called 'Private Use Area' (PUA), which comprises 6144 code points for non-predefined characters (in the blocks U+E000–EFFF and F000–F7FF). This area can be assigned *ad libitum* by companies, user groups, or individuals, with the result that additional information is again necessary to distinguish the characters 'encoded' in it. Table 0.2.11 shows what can happen when different fonts are applied to visualise PUA encoded characters; in the worst case, the intended information will again be lost. The use of the 'Private Use Area' should therefore be avoided wherever possible.

2.1.2. Electronic texts and their structuring

Depending on their envisaged use, electronic texts to be produced and used in oriental manuscript studies require special attention as to their structuring beyond character encoding, too. To clarify what this means, it is helpful to look again at the Greek text we have dealt with above (see Table 0.2.2). Even without any knowledge of the language and script, we will immediately have the impression that this text consists of verses. This is clearly indicated by two signals we are used to in reading poetical texts, namely the relative shortness of lines (with no full justification), and the numbers 1, 5, and 10 attached to the respective lines (in the Greek rendering). There are many further elements of textual structure involved, however. First, we will easily guess that the text consists of several sentences, partially extending across verses and partially consisting of subordinate clauses and phrases: this is indicated by the punctuation marks used. Then, we will be able to state that the text consists of 51 words, in their turn indicated either by empty spaces between them or by punctuation marks adjoining their first or last characters. This may all sound trivial, but as a matter of fact, it can be crucial indeed for textual materials to consider the function of their internal elements and to 'mark them up' accordingly when preparing them for further usage; and this should be done as consistently as the encoding of the characters appearing in words.

So what elements are we talking about? Among the basic elements of every kind of text, we have already mentioned words (consisting of characters when written down), phrases, clauses, and sentences; on a higher level, we will have to deal with sections, paragraphs, chapters, text parts, and the like. For many of these elements, we intuitively adapt signals we have been used to since we were at school, such as spaces indicating word boundaries, full stops indicating sentence breaks, or 'hard' line breaks indicating the end of a section or paragraph. For a consistent encoding of a digital text to be used in a (critical or diplomatic) edition, in an electronic corpus, or for other purposes, this may not be sufficient, though, especially when the contents of oriental manuscripts are concerned. An appropriate example may suffice to illustrate why.

Fig. 0.2.2 shows the upper half of the front fly-leaf of the codex Vienna, ÖNB, Cod.Vind.georg. 2, a Georgian palimpsest manuscript stemming from the Monastery of the Holy Cross at Jerusalem. The leaf in question originally pertained to another codex from the same site, which is kept today in the Dumbarton Oaks Research Library in Washington, DC (MS WAS.1.2), and which represents a menaion covering the months of December to February, starting, in accordance with the Greek Synaxarion, with the commemoration of St Ananias of Persia and SS Onesimus and Solomonus (Solochonus) of Ephesus (see Gippert et al. 2007a, xii–xvii). Even without any knowledge of Georgian, and even neglecting the bad state of preservation especially of the upper part of the page, people experienced with mediaeval manuscripts will easily recognise that there are two different scripts used side by side in it, a majuscule and a minuscule, the former mostly appearing in the four red lines under the ornamental braid of the top, and the latter, mostly in the black text below. A closer look will reveal that even within the black text, there are some red elements, mostly dots accompanying other dots in black, but also some (majuscule) letters (in the fourth line); on the other hand, the first line contains a black letter in a red environment. One might further guess that lines five and ten contain a majuscule letter extending into the left margin, the first in red and the second in black; beyond that, the first text line shows a hanging initial in black, in its turn enclosed by an ornamental structure that might represent another majuscule letter. The colour of the latter is neither red nor black but the same (purple) colour as that of the ornamental heading on the top, and this very colour also appears in an attention mark in the shape of a shaft cross in the left margin; different from the text characters, it is only the contour-lines of these elements that are coloured, not their solid bodies.

As a matter of fact, none of these features is accidental, all of them being related to the meaning and the functions of the textual elements they pertain to. To start with, the four lines in red represent what we might call a heading (actually, it is exactly this use of red ink that has led to the emergence of the word 'rubric'). It begins with the indication of 1 December as the date the following text relates to; the (dative-locative) case form of the month name, *deḳembersa*, appears written in red, while the single character following it in black with an overbar attached to it is the letter *a* in its numerical value, '1', denoting the day of the month. The same letter appearing enclosed at the beginning of the line represents the word-final vowel of *ttuesa*, the word for 'month' in the dative case form corresponding to *deḳembersa*, 'in the month of December'; and its ornamentally-shaped enclosure in violet colour is the word-initial letter of the same word, *t*. The overbar above the *a* here marks the suspension of the characters between *t* and *a* in *t*(*towes*)

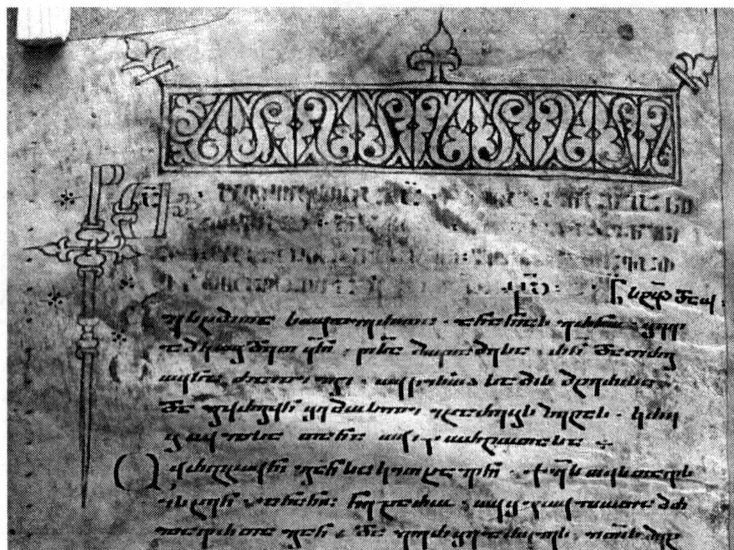

Fig. 0.2.2 Vienna, ÖNB, Cod.Vind.georg. 2, front fly-leaf (excerpt)

a, not the numerical use of *a* = '1' as in the indication of the day; as a matter of fact, the two overbars seem not to be identical, both being curved a bit differently. Note that between the abbreviated word form and the month name, and also on both sides of the numerical *a* and elsewhere within the rubric, we can detect double dots in black, always used as separators but not necessarily in the same way as a colon (or any other punctuation mark) would be used in modern European languages (including modern Georgian); they simply serve to denote boundaries between major meaningful elements (words, phrases, or clauses).

The text of the rubric continues with the names of the saints commemorated, all in the genitive case as if depending on a head noun like 'commemoration': *çmidisa : ananiasi sṗarsisay : da çmidata : ʒmata : onisime : da solomonisi : epesis mtavarepisḳoṗostay* 'of Saint Ananias the Persian and of the Saints, the brothers Onesimus and Solomonus, the archbishops of Ephesus'. Note that the word for 'saint' in its singular and plural forms appears abbreviated here, with a similar overbar marking the suspension (*ç̃isa / ç̃ta*), as do many other common words in both the rubric and the main text. What follows in the fourth line of the heading, are elements of prayers (*upalo čueno* 'our Lord', again abbreviated: *õo č̃no*; and *šeiçqalen* 'have mercy', written *š̃n* with the first character in red and the second together with the abbreviation mark, in black); between them we find the indication of a 'mode' to be used in singing (*: q̃y :* = *qmay ã*, lit. 'tone (or voice) 1', with the noun written in black), and, as the first textual elements written in minuscules, the (abbreviated) *incipit* of the master hymn (*heirmos*) sung in that 'mode' (*sṭ̃q̇y dau:* = *siṭq̇uay dausabamoy*, 'the boundless word').

The main text block then consists of hymns of praise addressed to the commemorated saints, with the initial letters of the individual strophes extending into the margin, as majuscules; the first initial is in red, the others in black. The red dots (or combinations of red and black dots) denote boundaries between individual verses while the end of strophes is indicated by more complex arrangements of punctuation marks (:·, ÷, and the like, in black). The most complex arrangements of dots, quincunxes (⁙) in black with a red cross overlaid, are found in the left margin, encircling the long-shaft cross in purple; as a matter of fact, the latter is likely to represent a character rather than the cross, namely the Georgian majuscule letter *k* (Ⴕ) standing for 'Christ', *krisṭe*, or even its Greek equivalent, the *Chi-Rho* symbol, adapted in shape to the Georgian *k*.

With up-to-date computer systems and text processing software, it may well be attempted to reproduce the contents of a manuscript page of this complexity as it is, both on the screen and on a (colour) printer; Table 0.2.12 shows to what extent the 'WYSIWYG' principle ('what you see is what you get') can be achieved having appropriate fonts at hand. It must be stressed here, however, that some of the characters implied are not yet represented in Unicode (as of January 2014) so that the encoding remains arbitrary to a certain extent. This is true, for example, for the peculiarly shaped *k* symbol (with a loop to the right at its top) standing for *krisṭe*, which is replaced by a mere *k*-letter here (Unicode does provide a code point for the *Chi-Rho* symbol, U+2627, which might as well have been used). It is also true for the combinations of a quincunx with an overlaid cross (the former does have a code-point, U+2059, but the latter has none);

Table 0.2.12 Near-to-facsimile rendering of MS Vienna, ÖNB, Cod.Vind.georg. 2, front fly-leaf (excerpt)

[illegible]

what is more, the co-occurrence of two colours within the combinations makes it impossible to encode them as 'precomposed' characters. A more important deficiency of the Unicode standard of today is the lack of code-points for the different types of overbars appearing in numerical notations and abbreviations (over one character, over two characters, etc.) in mediaeval manuscripts, not only of Georgian provenance.

It must be stated off-hand that such a near-to-facsimile representation of the contents of a manuscript has only a very limited use as it can only be deployed as part of a 'diplomatic' edition (see Ch. 3 § 3.11 for this type of editions). For most other purposes, the 'surface-oriented' aim to reproduce the visual appearance of a given manuscript page will be deemed subordinate to a consistent registration of the meaningful elements contained in the texts and their functions. This is true, first of all, for the preparation of 'critical' editions that are based on the collation of several manuscripts. In this process, described in more detail in Ch. 3 of the present handbook, one would typically ignore the distinction of majuscules and minuscules as well as the different colours and sizes as appearing in our example. Words written across line breaks (with or without hyphenation marks, as usual in Georgian manuscripts) would be re-joined; in addition, one would resolve the abbreviations and, possibly, also the values of numerically used letters. Depending on the specific conventions of the individual scholarly traditions, one might further adapt the system of punctuation appearing in the manuscript with that used in modern orthography, including the corresponding division into sentences (or, in the case of metrical texts, verses) and the use of a modern script. For the fly-leaf of the Vienna codex, we should thus arrive at a rendering like that displayed in Table 0.2.13a. For the purpose of illustration, the Table contains the same text in both the modern Georgian *mxedruli* script and in a Roman transcription; note that the Old Georgian digraph ႭჃ (lit. *ow*), which represents the plain vowel *u*, is rendered by the single letter უ = *u* here as usual in modern Georgian editions.

The rendering thus achieved consists only of the most basic elements of textual contents, namely words (separated by spaces), clauses and sentences (separated by punctuation marks), and paragraphs (separated by hard line breaks). A 'plain text' of this type can indeed be used for several purposes, as the basis for a 'critical' text edition to be produced, as the basis of collation with other witnesses (automatic or manual, see Ch. 3 § 2.2), or as the basis for (automatic) indexation (Ch. 3 § 2.6.5). For the latter purpose, however, the 'annotation' of some more information will be required, depending on what kinds of indexes are to be generated. For a mere word index that ignores the affinity of a given (inflectional) word form to the corresponding lexicon entry (the lemma), it will still be necessary to apply a system of reference to the individual units of the text, that is chapters, paragraphs, sentences and the like if the indexation is meant to refer to its 'internal' structure, or production units, folia / pages, columns, lines and so on if it is meant to refer to its 'external' representation in a given manuscript—without such a referencing system, the index would be a mere assemblage of all word forms occurring, which would be rather worthless, especially if the text has a considerable length. The establishment and application of a consistent referencing system may also be helpful for later comparison of a given text with parallel sources. A good example for this is the referencing system used for Biblical texts today, which consists of the indication of a given book, chapter, and verse, and which has substituted older systems such as that of the Ammonian section numbers. In an ideal case, the different systems of reference relevant to a given text should be combined with

Table 0.2.13 Rendering of Vienna, ÖNB, Cod.Vind.georg. 2, f. 1a (excerpt)

(a) Plain text rendering

თთუესა დეკემბერსა 1.	*ttuesa deḳembersa 1.*
წმიდისა ანანიასი სპარსისაჲ და წმიდათა ძმათა ონისიმე	*çmidisa ananiasi sṗarsisay da çmidata*
და სოლომონისი ეფესის მთავარეპისკოპოსთაჲ.	*ʒmata onisime da solomonisi epesis*
	mtavarepiskopostay.
უფალო ჩუენო! შეიწყალენ!	*upalo čueno! šeiçq̇alen!*
ჴმაჲ 1: სიტყუაჲ დაუსაბამოჲ...	*qmay 1: siṭq̇uay dausabamoy...*
შესხმითა სულიერითა, ანანიას ერნო, შევამკუდეთ	*šesxmita sulierita, ananias erno, ševamḳudet q̇ovelni*
ყოველნი წმიდასა მოწამესა, რომელმან დათრგუნა ძალი	*çmidasa moçamesa, romelman datrguna ʒali igi*
იგი უჩინოჲსა მის მტერისა და გჳრგჳნ-შემოსილი	*učinoysa mis mṭerisa da gwrgwn-šemosili ixarebs*
იხარებს ზეცას კრებულსა თანა უჴორცოთასა.	*zecas ḳrebulsa tana uqorcotasa.*
ურიცხუნი განსაკითხავნი...	*uricxuni gansaḳitxavni...*

(b) Overlapping hierarchies (non-compliant)

<line n='5'><hymn n='1'><strophe n='1'><verse n='1'>*šesxmita sulierita, ananias erno,*</verse> <verse n='2'>*šev*</line><line n='6'>*amḳudet q̇ovelni çmidasa moçamesa,*</verse> <verse n='3'>*romelman datrg*</line><line n='7'>*una ...*</verse>

(c) Overlapping hierarchies (compliant)

<line n='5' /><hymn n='1'><strophe n='1'><verse n='1'>*šesxmita sulierita, ananias erno,*</verse> <verse n='2'>*šev*<line n='6' />*amḳudet q̇ovelni çmidasa moçamesa,*</verse> <verse n='3'>*romelman datrg*<line n='7' />*una ...*</verse>

each other as in the online edition of one of the oldest Georgian codices, the so-called 'Sinai Lectionary' of the Universitätsbibliothek Graz (Austria), provided by the TITUS project (Graz, UBG, 2058/1; Gippert et al. 2007b), which provides the references both to the position in the manuscript ('Manuscript page' and 'line') and to that of the Gospel passage concerned ('Book', 'Chapter', 'Verse') side by side (see fig. 0.2.3). In addition, the online text contrasts the 'diplomatic' rendering of the manuscript text (in Old Georgian majuscules) with a transcript into 'modern' style (*mxedruli*). The index produced on this basis is incorporated in a search engine which can be accessed, for example, by clicking upon ą word form (in *mxedruli*), which will yield a list of all occurrences of the given word form within the same text, with clear indication of their position (see <http://titus.uni-frankfurt.de/texte/textex.htm> for a description of the applicable methods of use of the TITUS search engine, and fig. 0.2.4 for the output of the query for Georgian *çigni* 'book, epistle, letter').

More sophisticated types of annotations must be applied if an index is to subsume word forms under their respective lemmas and if it is meant to differentiate common nouns from several types of proper names (personal names, toponyms, ethnonyms etc.), as usual in modern text editions. In this case, the word forms in question must be 'marked up' in a special way, with the corresponding information being added in an underlying structure. This is the approach taken by the 'Text Encoding Initiative' (TEI), a 'consortium which collectively develops and maintains a standard for the representation of texts in digital form' (see <http://www.tei-c.org>) and which comprises, among others, a 'Special Interest Group' concerning manuscripts (see <http://www.tei-c.org/Activities/SIG/Manuscript/>). The foundation of the TEI approach, outlined in extensive 'Guidelines for Electronic Text Encoding and Interchange' (present issue: 'P5'; <http://www.tei-c.org/release/doc/tei-p5-doc/en/html>), is the application of the so-called 'eXtensible Markup Language' (XML), an extremely flexible markup system developed by the 'World Wide Web Consortium' (W3C; <http://www. W3.org/XML/>) since the 1990s in extension of former standards such as SGML ('Standard Generalized Markup Language') and HTML ('Hypertext Markup Language', the markup system used predominantly in web pages to this day). The basic structural element of these markup languages consists of so-called 'tags', i.e. information units stored, in angle brackets, either on both sides of a text element to be marked up ('start-tag' and 'end-tag') or as independent entries ('empty-element tag'); these tags will usually not be rendered as such on the screen or in print but serve the purpose of controlling the output 'from behind'. To mark, for example, that a given word in a text is meant to be output in bold characters in an HTML-based web page, it has to be enclosed in two corresponding tags, which are <b> and </b> respectively, denoting the beginning and the end of the bold-faced area. With an empty-element tag, one can add the information that there is a line-break at a given position; the corresponding HTML tag is <br>. In contrast to this, XML exhibits two differences. First, empty-element tags must here be terminated by a slash within the brackets (<br />), thus distinguishing them from start-tags, which have no slashes. Second, and this is the major advantage of XML, the tags to be used can be chosen *ad libitum*, provided the choice is declared in either a 'Document Type Definition' (DTD)

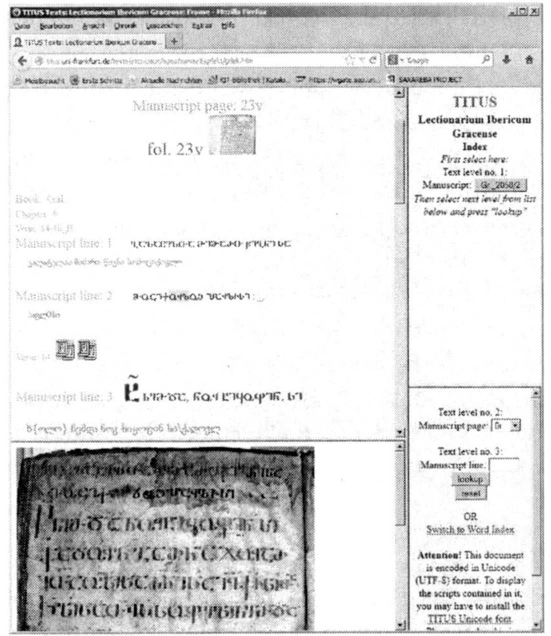

Fig. 0.2.3 Online edition of the Graz Sinai Lectionary

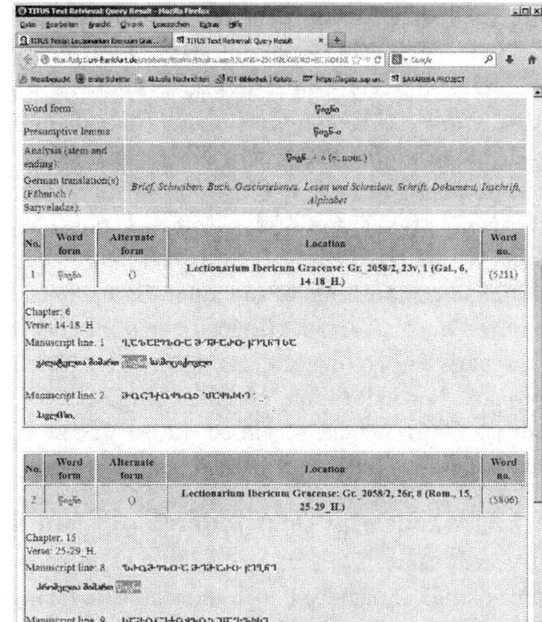

Fig. 0.2.4 Search engine output (*çigni* 'book')

or an 'XML Schema Definition' (XSD). This allows, for example, the use of a more explicit <bold> tag instead of <b>, or <line-break /> instead of <br />. Unlike the fixed set of tags acknowledged by the HTML standard, which was mostly addressed towards screen output and did not therefore contain many content-related tags, XML can thus be conceived to further distinguish several types of meaningful text elements such as indications of dates (in our Georgian menaion example, <date>*ttuesa dekembersa* 1</date>), personal names (for example, <anthroponym>*ananiasi*</anthroponym>), ethnonyms (<ethnonym>*sparsisay*</ethnonym>), hymn incipits (<incipit>*siṭq̇uay dausabamoy*</incipit>), or verses (<verse>*šesxmita sulierita, ananias erno*</verse>), with a view to a particular rendering in the output, to proper indexation, or to other purposes.

An even more powerful feature of the markup languages is the possibility of adding 'attributes' to the tags, consisting of a denominator and a value. These can be output-oriented as in the case of the HTML 'font' tag which can imply information as to the size, colour, and other features of the font the marked-up text is to be displayed in (in our manuscript, for example, <font size='12' colour='red'>*deḳembersa*</font>). Beyond this, an appropriate XML tag may contain lexical, grammatical, or other content-related information (for example, <word lemma='deḳemberi' morph='dat_sg'>*deḳembersa*</word>). The flexibility of XML even allows for a combination of both types of information (<word lemma='deḳemberi' morph='dat_sg' fonttype='mrglovani' fontsize='12' fontcolour='red'>*deḳembersa*</word>). By the way, it is true that much 'markup' information that is linguistic can be added automatically, by applying so-called 'parsers' that analyse the given text on the basis of programmed grammatical rules and lexicons; however, in the field of oriental manuscript studies and the languages relevant to them, the development of tools for these purposes is not yet very much advanced.

Another important feature of XML is that taggings can further be nested, thus allowing, for example, to account for the change of the font colour in the abbreviated imperative form *šeiçq̇alen* 'have mercy' in our text, which might be tagged as <word expanded='šeiçq̇alen' lemma='šeçq̇aleba' morph='impv_aor'><chunk fontsize='14' fontcolor='red'>*š*</chunk><chunk fontsize='14' fontcolor='black'>*˜n*</chunk></word>. (As a matter of fact, several more sophisticated ways of annotating abbreviated word forms have been designed in the TEI-P5 guidelines.)

A peculiar problem of XML is that hierarchically organized taggings must not overlap in the sense that a start tag Y must not fall between a superior sequence of a start tag X and an end tag X if the end tag corresponding to Y does not (schematically: <X> … <Y> … </X> … </Y>). This is especially crucial for the parallel markup of different referencing systems ('internal' and 'external' references in the sense outlined above). If in our Georgian example, we wanted to mark up both the units of the text structure (for example, verses) and their distribution on the manuscript page, we should arrive at exactly this problem right from the second verse on; what is more, there are line breaks within words that would have to be accounted for. Table 0.2.13b shows the resulting picture for the first three lines of the hymnal text, which would not be XML-compliant. A possible way out of this is the use of empty-entity tags for one of the overlapping hierarchical referencing systems; in Table 0.2.13c, it is the ('external') line referencing that is treated this way, with an XML-compliant result (note that font colours and other similar parameters are ignored here).

Taking all the features of XML together, it is conceivable that the contents of a manuscript can be electronically annotated with them in such a way that both different forms of editions ('diplomatic' and 'critical', printed and online) and several kinds of indexes can automatically be derived from the annotated text (cf. Ch. 3 § 3.1 for relevant considerations). For the former purpose, this presupposes the design and application of so-called 'Extensible Stylesheet Language Transformations' (XSLT), which can be used to transform XML documents into HTML web pages, plain text files, or 'Extensible Stylesheet Language Formatting Objects' (XSL-FO) which can subsequently be converted to PDF or other output formats. For indexation, one may still have to rely upon special tools that are conceived to extract the targeted information. The more scholars show interest in these kinds of tools and methods, the more it is likely that we shall have them at hand for usage in the foreseeable future.

2.1.3. Manuscript related databases and their structuring

In recent years, XML has gained more and more ground in yet another domain that is relevant for manuscript studies, namely the structuring of databases. If we leave indexes used for the search of words or word forms in textual contexts aside, the typical field of application for databases concerning manuscripts is cataloguing. More and more manuscript catalogues are being conceived and compiled electronically today, both as a basis for printed output and for the integration in online search engines, portals, and the like (see Ch. 4 § 6), and the question of how to structure them may therefore be crucial. As in other fields of application, XML-based structures are in competition with so-called 'relational' databases here, and the decision in favour of one or other of them may not be easy to take.

The main difference between the two types of database consists in the fact that XML yields more flexible structures than relational databases, which are characterized by a consistent setup of 'records', that is entries. Typically, a record in a relational database comprises a fixed set of 'fields' that are identical throughout the whole collection of data of the same structure. The interrelation of these elements can easily be visualized in form of a table, with the rows representing records and the columns, fields; see Table 0.2.14 for an arbitrary example that is derived from the description scheme developed for the 'Union Catalogue of Oriental Manuscripts in German Collections' of the Göttingen Academy of Sciences (see Ch. 4 § 6.1 for more details). It is true that such a scheme can be extremely helpful to ascertain that no item of information is overlooked and that the data are kept consistent, for example, in their orthographical representation, throughout the records; there is a clear disadvantage, however, in that it may be difficult, if not impossible, to deal with manuscripts of mixed content, written by different scribes and/or at different times and places, etc. In other words, as soon as we take codices into account that consist of several 'production units' (see Ch. 4 § 4 for the concept underlying this term), the given scheme may all too soon prove to be too rigid to be expedient.

If we conceive the same database in an XML structure, we may indeed 'spread' the scheme much more easily according to the peculiarities of our objects. The 'shelf number' may still be the governing information, but we may insert any number of 'production units' below it, each with its own record of data. In addition, there is no limit as to the amount of data to be stored within a given field, different from relational databases where this may lead to problems. Table 0.2.15 may give an idea of such an approach, building upon the arbitrary example introduced above.

It will be clear from this example that an XML database has a certain disadvantage, too. This is the amount of data that has to be stored and processed in a clear-text structure of this type. This may be un-

Table 0.2.14 Relational database structure used in cataloguing (example)

shelf number	material	state of preservation	pages	format	lines	writing style	decoration	scribe	date	origin	author	title
1	parch.	III	142	17 × 23	26	maj.	+	Io.Zos.	981	Sinai	anon.	Gospels
2	paper	II	255	16 × 24	29	min.	–	unknown	1231	Šaṭberdi	Mi.Mo.	Hymn.
3	parch	IV	183	18 × 23	25	maj.	+	Io.Xax.	X	Ṭao	anon.	Hagio.

Table 0.2.15 XML database structure used in cataloguing (example)

```
<shelfnumber n='1'>
  <productionunit n='1'>
    <material>parchment</material>
    <stateofpreservation>III</stateofpreservation>
    <pages>1r-126v</pages>
    <format>17 × 23</format>
    <lines>26</lines>
    <writingstyle>majuscules</writingstyle>
    <illumination n='1' page='3r'>Matthew</illumination>
    <illumination n='2' page='38r'>Mark</illumination>
    <illumination n='3' page='64v'>Luke</illumination>
    <illumination n='4' page='101r'>John</illumination>
    <scribe>Ioane Zosime</scribe>
    <date>981</date>
    <origin>St. Catherine's Monastery, Mt. Sinai</origin>
    <author>anonymous</author>
    <title>Gospels</title>
  </productionunit>
  <productionunit n='2'>
    <material>parchment</material>
    <stateofpreservation>III</stateofpreservation>
    <pages>127r-139v</pages>
    <format>17 × 22.5</format>
    <lines>28</lines>
    <writingstyle>majuscules</writingstyle>
    <scribe>Ioane Zosime</scribe>
    <date>981</date>
    <origin>St. Catherine's Monastery, Sinai</origin>
    <author>anonymous</author>
    <title>Lection index</title>
  </productionunit>
  <productionunit n='3'>
    <material>parchment</material>
    <stateofpreservation>IV</stateofpreservation>
    <pages>140r-142v</pages>
    <format>17 × 22.5</format>
    <lines>29</lines>
    <writingstyle>minuscules</writingstyle>
    <scribe>Ioane Zosime</scribe>
    <date>981</date>
    <origin>St. Catherine's Monastery, Sinai</origin>
    <author>Ioane Zosime</author>
    <title>Colophon</title>
  </productionunit>
</shelfnumber>
<shelfnumber n='2'>
  <productionunit n='1'>
    <material>paper</material>
    <stateofpreservation>II</stateofpreservation>
    <pages>1r-255v</pages>
    <format>16 × 24</format>
    <lines>29</lines>
    <writingstyle>minuscules</writingstyle>
    <scribe n='1'>unknown</scribe>
    <scribe n='2'>Giorgi</scribe>
    <date>1231</date>
    <origin>Šaṭberdi</origin>
    <author>Mikael Modreḳili</author>
    <title>Hymnary</title>
  </productionunit>
</shelfnumber>
...
```

problematic if the database is only meant to be the basis for printed or online output; for other purposes such as, for example, retrievability via hypercatalogues (see Ch. 4 § 6.2), relational databases may still be regarded as superior, given that they can be accessed much faster due to preindexation. However, with the steadily increasing storage capacity and processing speed of modern computers, this advantage may vanish soon.

2.1.4. Digital imaging

No field relevant to oriental manuscript studies has profited more from technological progress in the digital age than imaging. A clear witness to this is the fact that the amount of high-quality images of manuscripts that are available online has been increasing exponentially since the late 1990s, and many of us use such images every day without thinking too much about their structural properties. Nevertheless, it may be worthwhile here to summarize a few basics concerning the processes involved.

No matter what quality is to be achieved, digital imaging presupposes the dissolution of the visual appearance of a given object into a bulk of tiny dots, so-called pixels, each of them characterized by a certain degree of light intensity of different colour components, mostly red, green, and blue, exposed either individually or in groups (stacks). The number of picture cells (pixels) available on the camera sensor is the basis for the calculation of the data a digital image comprises, usually called its 'resolution': while by the end of the twentieth century, an amount of two megapixels (1,600 × 1,200 pixels, with an aspect ratio of 4:3) was still beyond reach, cameras with a resolution of 50 megapixels (8,176 × 6,132 pixels with the same ratio) are no longer exceptional today. With such a resolution, even an extremely large manuscript page of 82 × 61 cm could be photographed and reproduced in printed form without any visible loss of information, the resolution still yielding 10 pixels per millimetre in printing. For the complete rendering of the same page on a computer screen, much lower resolutions would be sufficient, given that a normal screen resolution of 1280 × 960 pixels equals to no more than 1.23 megapixels; however, the great advantage of large-resolution digital images is that they can be enlarged in screen output so that individual sectors of the manuscript page can be displayed in even much larger size than that of the original.

The calculation by pixels (or dots) per centimetre (or per inch, differentiated by a factor of 2.54) may be misleading, however. In the early years of manuscripts digitization, when the resolution of digital cameras was not yet sufficient for this purpose, attempts were made to achieve the same goal by applying optical scanners with much lower resolutions; for example, a flatbed scanner with a surface of 21 × 29.7 cm (the measure of A4 paper) and a resolution of 600 dots per inch (dpi; the metrical equivalent would be 236 dots per centimetre) yielded a digital image of (4960 × 7015 =) 34.8 megapixels, and even with 300 dpi the image still had (2480 × 3057 =) 8.7 megapixels. However, the application of flatbed scanners for the digitization of manuscripts was not always possible due to conservation concerns, either because of the extreme light exposure those scanners work with or because of the threat of damaging the binding of the codices etc. Therefore, an intermediate solution was sought in the application of a hybrid approach which made use of traditional (film) photography by producing colour slides as the basis for digitization; this approach was, for example, applied in one of the earliest projects aiming at an online edition of manuscripts comprising colour images of the originals, namely the project concerning the Tocharian manuscripts of the Berlin Turfan collection, which have been published on the TITUS server since 1999 (see <http://titus.fkidg1.uni-frankfurt.de/texte/tocharic/tht.htm>). The resolution that could be achieved on this basis in the late 1990s was 2700 dpi, a value seeming much higher indeed than the 600 dpi of a flatbed scanner; however, we must consider that the surface of the underlying colour slides was much smaller than that of any manuscript page and that the scanner resolution is always relative to the size of the scanned object: when a colour slide of 24 × 36 mm containing an image of an A4-sized manuscript page was scanned at the resolution of 2700 dpi, the resulting image comprised (2551 × 3827 =) 9.7 megapixels, which was not much more than the resolution of a 300 dpi scan of the same page on an A4 flat-bed scanner or a digital image of it with a resolution of 10 megapixels (Table 0.2.16 lists some noteworthy figures concerning the digitization of an A4-sized manuscript page). Still, the production of colour slides had a big advantage, given that they can be used as a secondary ('analog') storage medium in order to preserve the contents of a large amount of manuscripts and that they remain available for scanning with higher-resolution scanners for a long time, with no need to touch (and contaminate) the original documents. It must be underlined though that all this depends on the quality of the film used and that only a few colour slide films have proven to sustain the quality of the images they contain over a longer period of time.

The same holds—and even more so—for the digitization of microfilms, an approach that has been undertaken with great effort until the present day (for example, the digital collections of manuscripts at the Bayerische Staatsbibliothek, Munich, are partly based on microfilms 'in a bitonal or grey-scale quality' instead of 'full colour copies' of the original manuscripts; see <http://www.digitale-sammlungen.de/index.html?c=sammlungen&kategorie_sammlung=1&l=en>). This may be acceptable in cases where the original manuscripts have been lost or are no longer or not easily accessible for other reasons, as in the case of the microfilms of the manuscripts of St Catherine's Monastery on Mount Sinai which were produced in the 1940s on behalf of the Library of Congress and parts of which have now been digitized for online retrieval (see, for example, the collection 'Microfilms des manuscrits géorgiens du Mt Sinai' provided by the Université Catholique de Louvain, Belgium, <http://www.e-corpus.org/eng/notices/96559-Micro-films-des-manuscrits-g%C3%A9-orgiens-du-Mt-Sinai.html>). In other cases, however, the quality of microfilms, especially those produced during extensive microfilming campaigns as in the case of the Sinai manuscripts, is hardly sufficient to meet the requirements of in-depth manuscript studies. This is all the more true since the microfilms used in such campaigns were usually monochrome, thus obscuring information on the use of different (coloured) inks, which may be crucial as a text structuring element in many cases (see above). In any digitization project, the question of whether and to what extent microfilms may be a usable basis should therefore be pondered seriously. The production of new digital images directly from the original manuscripts will nearly always yield much better results today (see also Ch. 5 § 7 for a detailed treatment of the processes involved).

In the recent past, special methods of digital imaging have gained importance in oriental manuscript studies, especially in the analysis of palimpsests. Based on the fact that parchment as the typical support material of palimpsests fluoresces in ultraviolet (UV) light (see General introduction § 2.3), it was mostly UV photography that was used until the end of the twentieth century to enhance the contrast between the parchment surface and the ink of the underwriting, with more or less satisfying results. By the beginning of the twenty-first century, UV photography has been superseded by so-called 'multispectral imaging', a process that builds upon the production of several images that are restricted to a certain wavelength of the visible and the invisible light (ultraviolet and infrared), and the digital comparison of these images. The main principle of multispectral imaging consists in the fact that the resonance of any object differs with

Table 0.2.16 Digitizing a manuscript page of A4 size

A4-page	11,69 × 8,27 inch	29,7 × 21,0 cm
colour slide / microfilm image	1,42 × 0,94 inch	3,6 × 2,4 cm
Microfilm / slide scanner, 1200 dpi	1704 × 1132 pixels	2 megapixels
Flatbed scanner, 300 dpi	3507 × 2480 pixels	8.7 megapixels
Microfilm / slide scanner, 2700 dpi	3834 × 2538 pixels	9.7 megapixels
Digital camera, 12 megapixels	4200 × 2800 pixels	11.7 megapixels
Microfilm / slide scanner, 4000 dpi	5680 × 3760 pixels	21.35 megapixels
Flatbed scanner, 600 dpi	7014 × 4960 pixels	34.8 megapixels
Flatbed scanner, 1200 dpi	14028 × 9920 pixels	139.2 megapixels

respect to different wavelengths, depending on the consistence of its colour. By applying a photographing method that is restricted to a certain range of the spectrum, a specific resonance may be retained or suppressed. In the case of palimpsest manuscripts, the effect that can be gained from this predisposition depends on three factors: the colour resonance of the upper script, that of the lower script, and that of the background, i.e. the parchment surface. One might expect that the first two are the most decisive factors in this constellation, as in many cases it will be desirable to 'enhance' the lower script in contrast to the upper script covering it. This, however, is not always possible in parchment palimpsests of oriental provenance as both the lower and the upper scripts were usually written with the same type of inks, which results in similar resonances. Thus the application of multispectral imaging must concentrate upon two aims, a) increasing the contrast between the (erased) lower script and the background, and b) exploiting the difference of several images showing the same object to reduce the preponderance of the upper script. Normally, a set of three images (one in the UV or violet range, at a wavelength of less than 440 nm; one in the yellow or green range, at a wavelength of between 500 and 600 nm, and one in the red or near-infrared range, at a wavelength of above 700 nm) will be sufficient for this purpose. Several projects concerning oriental palimpsests have successfully adapted multispectral imaging since 2002 (see General introduction § 2.4), and the methods and facilities implied are steadily developing.

References

Gippert et al. 2007a. Web sources: Gippert et al. 2007b; <http://www.digitale-sammlungen.de/>, last access October 2014; <http://www.e-corpus.org>, last access October 2014; <http://www.tei-c.org/>, last access October 2014; <http://www. W3.org/XML/>, last access October 2014; <http://titus.fkidg1.uni-frankfurt.de>, last access October 2014

2.2. Instrumental analysis in manuscript studies (IR)

Physico-chemical analyses of writing materials offer insight into various questions associated with historical, cultural and conservation aspects of manuscript studies. The catalogue of questions includes authenticity, dating, or attribution of various parts of the text to different scribes, relation between primary and secondary texts, and so on. Similarly, preservation of the manuscripts requires knowledge of the composition of the original materials vs. old repairs, identification of damage, as well as recognition of natural ageing and degradation processes. The material sciences can contribute data about the chemical compositions of the writing materials, elucidation of the techniques of their production and the absolute age of organic components, as well as characterization of corrosion effects, evaluation of conservation treatment, and monitoring of the preservation state.

It is probably impossible now to pinpoint the first analytical studies of objects of historical interest. It seems, however, that metal studies of pre-historic finds in the 1870s belong to the earliest documented chemical investigations. In 1888 the first chemical laboratory, today known as Rathgen Research Laboratory, was opened in Berlin to assist conservation. Within the following fifty years scientific studies in archaeology and conservation became established mostly within the frame of Egyptology, as witnessed by numerous editions of the standard textbook *Ancient Egyptian Materials and Industries* first published by Alfred Lucas in 1926 (1962[4]).

In 1946 Willard Libby published the first paper on the decay of radiocarbon, which can be viewed as a revolution in the studies of organic artefacts: he showed that organic matter carries an internal clock and, therefore, can be dated within the range of approximately fifty thousand years. It took some forty years to improve the measurements methods that allow for reduction of the material tested, to standardize and to calibrate this technique (<http://www.c14dating.com/>). Despite the fact that it is an inherently destructive analysis, it is universally accepted in the studies of manuscripts.

In the 1990s another scientific breakthrough—DNA sequencing—looked very promising not only for identification of the precursor species for parchment but for a range of historical questions such as relation between the species and their geographical origin. This technique is, however, still under refinement and is not routinely employed in the field of manuscript studies (Bower et al. 2010). Recently, researches from the department of archaeology at the University of York developed a radically new method that requires only minute amounts of collagen to determine the species of animal used in parchment production (Fiddyment et al. 2014). We hope that this technique will find a broad application in the field of cultural heritage.

One of the great shortcomings of the radiocarbon and DNA methods is their sensitivity to contaminations. Radiocarbon analysis of a contaminated sample can easily result in an error of hundreds of years. Therefore, both techniques should be coupled with non-destructive material analysis to reduce the chance of sampling contaminated material.

Over the last two decades, the impact of material studies has increased enormously with the industry-driven development of so-called 'non-destructive technology' (NDT) that does not require extracting samples for testing. Further technological developments have led to the invention of NDT methods using extremely small measurement spots. Alongside their advantages, however, these methods have obvious limitations when deployed to analyse objects whose composition displays heterogeneity of the same order of magnitude as the measurement spot. Therefore their application as a random single-shot measurement should be avoided. Since protocols for routine measurements pertaining to X-ray intensity, measurement time and minimal signal-to-noise ratio similar to those current in the medical sciences have yet to be established, presently available results must be interpreted with extreme caution. Denker et al. (2006) offer a good introduction to relevant technical investigations in the field of arts and cultural heritage.

The most popular non-destructive techniques can be roughly subdivided into optical and vibration spectroscopy for the identification of chemical compounds, and X-ray emission techniques for the identification of elemental composition. Other techniques such as electron microscopy to study surface morphology and X-ray diffraction (XRD) to identify pigments are traditionally used when extracting samples is allowed. XRD is a method based on the fact that X-rays' interaction with crystals results in patterns that are specifically characteristic of the crystal structure of the material tested.

Optical properties reflect the interaction of a material with light from ultraviolet (UV), visible (VIS), and infrared (IR) regions of the electromagnetic spectrum. IR reflectography has been traditionally used to study soot-based pigments or carbon inks: the colour of soot inks is independent of the illumination wavelength in the range 300–1,700 nm; plant inks lose opacity between 750 and 1,000 nm, whereas iron-gall inks become transparent only at a wavelength > 1,000 nm. Similarly, multispectral imaging for the visualization of palimpsests can allow one to differentiate between soot-based and tannin-based inks, since only the latter become transparent in the infrared region of the spectrum. A conventional multispectral imaging set-up employs LED illumination with up to thirteen different wavelengths ranging from UV to near IR region (Christens-Barry et al. 2011). To incorporate ink differentiation into routine manuscript digitization workflows, one could adopt a simplified 2- or 3-wavelength reflectography, since the main goal is to investigate the opacity in the spectral range 700–1000 nm. An easy way to add such functionality to the routine inspection of manuscripts by scholars is to use a hand-held USB microscope equipped with a 940 nm light source, or a pocket multispectral camera. It should be stressed, however, that pure soot inks can be unambiguously identified by reflectography at a wavelength > 1,000 nm. It is distinguishing between plant and iron-gall inks that is challenging and requires additional tests in the range 750–1000 nm. It has become customary to refer to this range as 'near infrared' since commonly used digital cameras are equipped with silicon detectors that lose sensitivity around 1,000 nm.

Vibration spectroscopy (IR and Raman) allows identification of molecules and their structure by supplying specific information on vibrations of atoms in the molecules and is therefore routinely applied in order to screen unknown materials. In the first technique, a molecule absorbs a portion of the irradiated infrared light, hence its name, IR spectroscopy. In the second technique, Raman spectroscopy—named after the Indian physicist Sir Chandrasekhara Venkata Raman—monochromatic light in the ultraviolet, visible, or near infrared ranges of the electromagnetic spectrum hits the sample and loses part of its energy. The difference in energy corresponds to the molecule vibration. Since the mechanisms of the interaction between light and matter differ from one technique to the other, these techniques complement each other. Historically, IR spectroscopy has been commonly used for the investigation of organic materials. It is a well-established method for classifying binding media in inks and pigments, surface treatments, and adhesives. To perform a conventional measurement (in so-called 'transmission mode'), a thin or powdered sample is placed in the beam pass, and the amount of transmitted light is detected as a function of wavelength or frequency, resulting in an infrared spectrum. Hence, this method requires samples to be extracted from an object. To reduce the sample size, special diamond cells to be placed in the beam path were developed. Rapid technological progress in this field led to the appearance of non-destructive methods based on the detection of the IR-radiation reflected by the sample, thus eliminating the need to extract samples from the object. Examples of these techniques are Attenuated Total Reflection Fourier Transform Infra-Red (ATR-FTIR) spectroscopy (Marengo et al. 2005) to study surfaces, fibre-optic FTIR in reflection (Miliani et al. 2007), and synchrotron-based FTIR spectroscopy (Salvadó et al. 2005; Bartoll et al. 2008). The miniaturization of infrared light sources and detectors brought a new generation of portable FTIR spectrometers, for example a hand-held Exoscan (*A2 Technologies* 2011).

Raman spectroscopy has proved useful in studies of decorated manuscripts, since tabulated Raman data for inorganic salts and minerals allow for a quick and unequivocal identification of (inorganic) pigments (Brown – Clark 2004; Baraldi et al. 2009). Reliable Raman identification of mediaeval black inks started to emerge only during the past decade (Lee et al. 2008). Raman studies of the inks show that soot, plant and iron-gall inks have characteristic Raman spectra that provide a recognition pattern (Bicchieri et al. 2008). Unfortunately, mobile tools designed for on-site use by non-specialists are not yet available. Nevertheless it is to be hoped that the ongoing analysis of historical ink samples by means of conventional techniques will ultimately lead to improvements in the mobile equipment and the establishment of a database of different inks.

Elemental analysis by X-ray emission techniques relies on the study of characteristic patterns of X-ray emissions from atoms irradiated with high-energy X-rays or particles: X-ray Fluorescence (XRF), Particle Induced X-ray Emission (PIXE), and Energy-dispersive X-ray spectroscopy (EDX). When the external excitation beam interacts with an atom within the sample, an electron of the inner shell is ejected, creating a vacancy. In the next step, another electron from an outer shell fills the vacancy. The energy of the emitted X-ray fluorescence is characteristic for a certain element, whereas the signal intensity allows one to determine the amount of the element in the sample. It is noteworthy that each technique has its applicability limits and different penetration depths, so that excitation by electrons (EDX), conventionally used with electron microscopy, is limited to the study of surfaces (but capable of detecting light elements), whereas excitation by X-rays (XRF) has a greater penetration power and allows one to detect elements with $n > 13$, that is elements heavier than aluminium. Though XRF is one of the most suitable methods for obtaining qualitative and semi-quantitative information (relative to the major element) concerning a great diversity of materials, it should be remembered that it is not suitable for the determination of the elemental composition of organic materials since their main constituents (carbon, oxygen, nitrogen, and hydrogen) cannot be detected with this technique. Therefore, it is advisable to use both XRF and EDX techniques for such studies. Indeed, new scanning electron microscopes are often equipped with both instruments.

Today XRF is undoubtedly one of the most popular techniques used on-site because it benefits from the availability of a variety of transportable instruments ranging from single-spot to high-resolution scanning equipment, as well as from a wealth of knowledge and experience that has been accumulated in the characterization of various writing materials. Recently, I compared three mobile XRF (Bruker) spectrometers used for manuscript studies (Rabin 2014).

The low-resolution, portable instrument TRACER SD-III is relatively cheap, light and easy to operate. In many cases it provides one-shot analysis, and it is best used with homogeneous materials. Its major shortcomings are low sensitivity and low spatial resolution.

ARTAX (Bronk et al. 2001) was specially designed for the study of art objects and has proved its efficiency for a decade now. It is a robust device that weighs some 80 kg but can be transported to the site where the objects must be studied. Its 70 μm X-ray beam and scanning facility enables the study of fine differences when a heterogeneous or degraded object is the object of investigation.

The Jet Stream M6 instrument presents a further development in the XRF field. Fast scanning in combination with two microscopes and a variable X-ray excitation spot allow one to obtain large images accompanied by spatial elemental distributions that are presented graphically during measurement. In this way, one area scan provides information about all the materials simultaneously, including degradation patterns of each material. Since the device is rather new on the market, its full capabilities have not yet been explored. In the future, a small optical multispectral camera will be integrated into XRF equipment, leading to the possibility of making a simultaneous test of the optical properties of the object under study.

A note on the classification of inks

Soot, plant, and iron-gall inks form different typological classes of historical black writing materials used in manuscript production. Soot ink is a fine dispersion of carbon pigments in a water-soluble binding agent; plant-based ink consists of tree bark (tannin) solution; iron-gall ink, produced by mixing iron(II) sulphate with a tannin extract from gall nuts, presents a boundary case between soot and plant ink—a water soluble preliminary stage (similar to inks from the second group) oxidizes and evolves into a black, insoluble material (similar to the carbon pigments of the first group) when the writing is exposed to air. Each ink class has distinct properties that would readily permit their easy differentiation, if only the inks used throughout history always belonged to just one of these classes. Carbon inks do not penetrate the substrate (whether papyrus, parchment or paper) and stay well localized on the surface. In contrast, plant inks and iron-gall inks are absorbed by the substrate, and the degree of their absorption depends to a great extent on the nature of the substrate.

Iron-gall inks are best studied by the means of the XRF technique. Natural vitriol, the main component of the historical iron-gall inks, consists of a mixture of metallic sulphates (iron sulphate, copper sulphate, manganese sulphate, and zinc sulphate) with relative weight contributions characteristic of the vitriol source or purification procedure (Krekel 1999). One uses this very property of the iron-gall inks to compare them and to distinguish among them. Specifically, the development of the fingerprint model based on the qualitative and quantitative detection of inorganic components of iron-gall inks allows their reliable classification (Hahn et al. 2004, 2008b).

In addition to inks of pure classes, mixed inks containing components of different classes are well known. In such cases, the ink usually has a type-defining component and 'picture smearing' additives. In this respect, a recipe from Dioscorides is remarkable among ancient Roman recipes for the production of soot inks. Along with soot ('condensed smoke') and gum, the recipe mentions a copper compound: chalcanthon (Zerdoun Bat-Yehouda 1983, 80). Indeed, PIXE studies of ancient Greek papyri from the Louvre collection identified copper in the inks. Without supporting evidence from other analyses, these inks were classified as metal-gall ones (Delange et al. 1990). In contrast to iron, however, copper does not produce a black precipitate upon reaction with gallic acid. The term 'metal-gall' is therefore misleading; only 'iron-gall' should be used.

PIXE and micro-X-Ray Fluorescence (μ-XRF) studies of the Dead Sea Scrolls revealed a number of documents written with inks containing large amounts of copper. In this case, however, the use of infrared reflectography unequivocally proved the soot nature of the inks and helped to avoid erroneous classification (Nir-El – Broshi 1996).

The difficulty and high costs of soot-ink production resulted in various attempts to replace them. We believe that the early appearance of the plant inks can be correlated with such attempts. In some cases, small quantities of soot were added to improve their colour. Some mediaeval Arabic and Jewish recipes for soot inks contain such additives as vitriol and tannins (Schopen 2006).

Even more gradual is the transition from the purely plant (that is tannin) inks to the iron-gall inks since a small addition of vitriol to a tannin ink would produce an imperfect iron-gall ink. Moreover, metals like iron and copper can occasionally be present in the tannin inks due to the water or tools used in the production process. Though a full elucidation of the composition of such inks requires the combination of XRF, Raman and IR reflectography (Rabin et al. 2012), the determination of the main components can be accomplished using their optical properties alone, i.e. their opacity in the spectral range 700–1000 nm.

References

Baraldi et al. 2009; Bartoll et al. 2008; Bicchieri et al. 2008; Bower et al. 2010; Bronk et al. 2001; Brown – Clark 2004; Christens-Barry et al. 2011; Delange et al. 1990; Denker et al. 2006; Fiddyment et al. 2014; Hahn et al. 2004, 2008b; Krekel 1999; Lee et al. 2008; Libby 1946; Lucas 1962; Marengo et al. 2005; Miliani et al. 2007; Nir-El – Broshi 1996; Rabin 2014; Rabin et al. 2012; Salvadó et al. 2005; Schopen 2006; Zerdoun Bat-Yehouda 1983. Web sources: *A2 Technologies* 2011; <http://www.c14dating.com/>.

2.3. Methods in palimpsest research (FA)

Several methods can be applied in order to read faded or erased writing, or different layers of writing on parchment. Once chemicals were used to make ink traces visible, but later damaging effects were noticeable. Nowadays, great success can be achieved with modern imaging techniques.

2.3.1. Chemical reagents

In the nineteenth century, three substances were mainly used: oak-gall tincture, various liver of sulphur tinctures, and Giobert tincture.

(1) *Oak-gall tincture*, an alcohol-based essence of oak apples, brightened the old metallic inks so that the faded writing gained in legibility. It made the unwritten parchment brownish due to tannic acid, which brought about corrosion of the ink, and produced an increasing ink damage (fig. 0.2.5). Oak-gall tincture was used, for example, by Cardinal Angelo Mai (1782–1854), and Barthold Georg Niebuhr (1776–1831).

(2) *Liver of sulphur tinctures*, based on the principle that the metallic traces of the *scriptura inferior*'s ink precipitated through contact with the various sulphide solutions, helped to freshen up the optical effect of the old ink traces. Three types of these tinctures have been employed.

(a) *Liver of sulphur* is a mixture of potassium polysulphide and potassium sulphate, produced from potassium carbonate and sulphur, and was applied as a solution to parchment. It had the effect of precipitating metal ions as sulphides. However, the traces of potassium carbonate left as a rule in this process formed potassium hydrogen carbonate in combination with water. Both salts produced a sediment in the form of a thin film on the surface of the parchment.

(b) *Calcic liver of sulphur* is a mixture of calcium polysulphide and calcium sulphate, produced by a combination of calcium carbonate and sulphur. It possessed the property of precipitating when in contact with sulphides with corresponding metal ions, but at the same time the calcium sulphate crystallized as gypsum in contact with water.

(c) *Volatile liver of sulphur* consisted of ammonium hydrogen sulphide in solution. The ammonium hydrogen sulphide solvent in water was also referred to as sulphurated ammonia or hydrosulphuret of ammonia. The palimpsests treated with volatile liver of sulphur display no damaging changes to the parchment surface that would be worth mentioning.

Liver of sulphur tinctures were used, among others, by Barthold Georg Niebuhr (1776–1831), Wilhelm Grimm (1786–1859), Karl Pertz (1828–1881), Hugo Duensing (1877–1961), and Martin Flashar (1885–1914).

(3) *Giobert tincture*, a weak acid solution of potassium hexacyanoferrate(II), named after the Turin chemist and mineralogist Giovanni Antonio Giobert (1761–1834). It consisted of six parts of water, one part of hydrochloric acid and an eighth part of potassium hexacyanoferrate(II).

The weak acid solution of potassium hexacyanoferrate(II) reacted in contact with the iron(II) sulphate of the ink to produce a deep blue precipitate, so-called Prussian blue. The deep blue, almost black, discolouration of the *scriptura superior* came about through both of the oxidation stages of the iron. The greenish discolouration of the *scriptura inferior* had to do with the precipitates of the iron(II) sulphate in form of hydrous copperas. Partial oxidation from bivalent iron with its blue colour to trivalent iron produced the green colouration. Giobert tincture has caused the greatest damage. The large patches of light-to-dark-blue-greenish-blue discolourations are typical, especially when little care had been exercised (fig. 0.2.5). A striking example of its use is the famous *Codex Ephraemi Syri rescriptus* (Paris, BnF, Grec 2), on which not only Giobert tincture but also oak-gall tincture was employed (Albrecht 2010 and 2012, 165 n. 28).

Giobert tincture was used, among others, by Amedeo Peyron (1785–1870), Ferdinand Florens Fleck (1800–1849), and Constantin Tischendorf (1815–1874).

For more on this topic see Albrecht 2012; Fuchs 2003; Gullath 2003, 83–85; Lo Monaco 1996, 709–717; Gardthausen 1911, 106–109; Posse 1899, 4, n. 1; Wattenbach 1896, 310–315.

2.3.2. Modern imaging techniques

The 'Erste internationale Konferenz zur Erhaltung und Ausbesserung alter Handschriften' in St Gall in 1898 marked a turning-point in palimpsest research: photography was now recommended as the essential tool for scholarly research (Smith 2012). At the beginning, analogue photographs were used, later, digitized analogue photographs. The digital imaging of manuscripts began in the 1970s (cf. Benton et al. 1979).

The use of photography was first tried out in palimpsest research at the Palimpsest Institute of the Abbey of Beuron, founded in 1912. Raphael Kögel (1912) developed a new photographic process that he named 'Kontaktoxydationsmethode'. In the last analysis he also used the inks' reaction to chemical processes. The acidic and metallic inks reacted in combination with an aniline solution, with the aniline salts being precipitated. The First World War interrupted the work at Beuron.

Since then, people have mostly been content to use ultra-violet (UV) light for decipherment purposes. UV-light interacts with the parchment by fluorescence: while the ink traces absorb incident light photons, the parchment reflects them. As a result, the contrast between ink traces and parchment becomes enhanced. The German model 'UV-Handlupe' is commonly used as a standard UV-lamp for library usage (most European libraries feature these old 'Handlupen' with a waveband of 320–380 nm. 2 UV-lamps, each with 4.00 W, i.e. 8.00 W. Cf. also <http://www.carlroth.com>: UV-Handlupe, Art. 1199.1: kurzwellige Leuchtstoffröhre: 254 nm; langwellige Leuchtstoffröhre: 366 nm (320–400 nm)). However, the heat output of these conventional UV-lamps, as well as tungsten halogen or xenon lamps, is enormous; it affects the parchment and causes undulations during longer UV-radiation because it alters the humidity of the parchment.

Therefore, modern LED technology was tried out in research, and is now used in all current projects that deal with the photographic analysis of palimpsests. This lighting method emits very low thermal energy. Furthermore, no additional band-pass filters, which would decrease the optical quality, have to be used since the lighting source itself is monochromatic with narrow wavebands at distinct wavelengths. In this way, sets of images taken at different wavelengths can be compared with each other digitally in order to further improve the discernibility of the underlying scriptures and to reduce the visual prominence of the overlaying texts. For this method, known as 'multispectral imaging' (Gippert 2007), different approaches are available on the market. New systems were developed especially during the 'Rinascimento Virtuale' European research project, which ran from 2002 to 2004. Today, five different multispectral lighting and camera systems are in use, which work in the ultra-violet, visible and infrared (UV-VIS-IR) spectrum of light: 1) the 'MuSIS HS' camera of DySIS, formerly Forth-Photonics; used, among others, for Rinascimento Virtuale, and in the decipherment of the Caucasian Albanian palimpsests of Mount Sinai (Gippert et al. 2007a, 2009; Gippert 2010a); 2) the 'Mondo Nuovo' and 'RE.CO.R.D' system of Photoevolution, formerly Fotoscientifica Record; used for, among others, Rinascimento Virtuale; 3) the 'EurekaVision' system of Equipoise Imaging, LLC/MegaVision, Inc., used for, among others, the Archi-

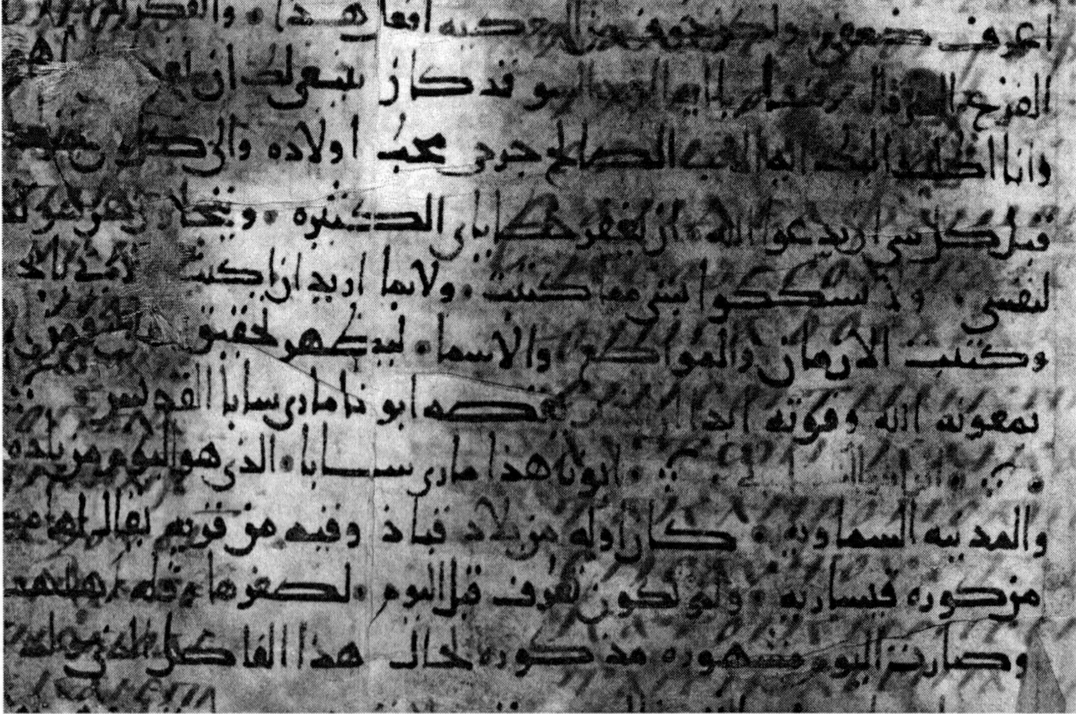

Fig. 0.2.5 Leipzig, UB, Cod. gr. 2, f. 10r (left: Giobert tincture damage, right: oak-gall tincture damage), © FA & Universitätsbibliothek Leipzig.

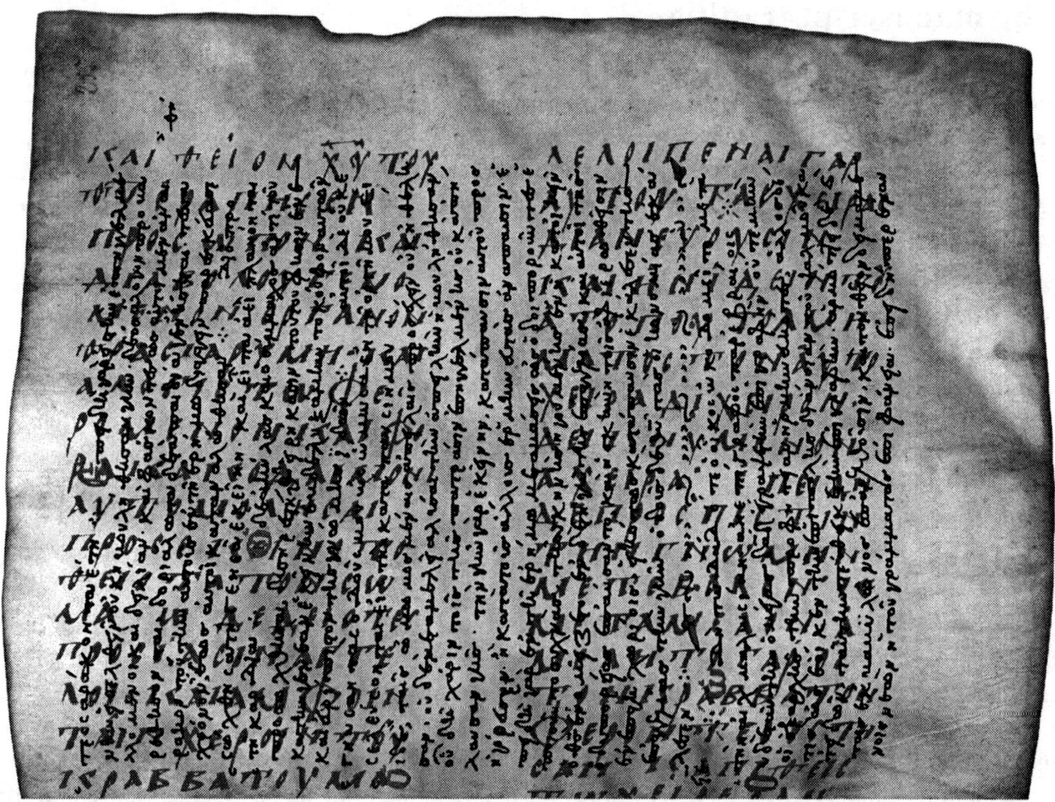

Fig. 0.2.6 Oxford, Bodleian library, MS. Auct. T. 4. 21 (Misc. 259), f. 255r (multispectral image), © FA & Bodleian Library.

medes project; 4) the EMEL 'Next-Generation System', Stokes Imaging Inc., used for, among others, the Mount Sinai palimpsests project; 5) the MSI Revelator of MWA Nova GmbH, used for, among others, the *PALAMEDES* project (Albrecht 2014). For more bibliography see Deckers – Grusková 2010, nn. 1–5 (older literature), Mairinger 1981, 2000, 2004.

All these imaging systems and methods—using the behaviour of light reflection and absorption by ink traces—can be divided into three major categories: 1) cameras with band-pass filters (for example VASARI, CRISATEL, MuSIS HS) plus lamps; 2) lamps with band-pass filters (for example, Rofin Polilight, SPEX CrimeScope, Lumatec Superlite) plus camera; 3) multiple, distinct lamps without filters plus camera (for example EurekaVision system, Next-Generation system, MSI Revelator).

The new systems of category three use distinct monochromatic lighting scenarios without band-pass filters for multi- or full spectral imaging (fig. 0.2.6). The biggest challenge in older approaches was caused by the fact that the overlaying *scriptura superior* hides certain parts of the underlying *scriptura inferior*. However, new techniques are being developed for making the layers of scriptures distinguishable. For instance, X-ray Fluorescence (XRF) imaging has been tried out during the Archimedes project (Bergmann 2011). This method measures the XRF, which is recorded when the parchment is hit by an X-ray beam. The beam penetrates the overlying ink and recovers the underlying writing. However, the contrast of the resulting images is not good enough, and it takes too much time in order to be achieved for more than single leaves (Deckers – Glaser 2011).

References

Albrecht 2010, 2012, 2014; Benton et al. 1979; Bergmann 2011; Deckers – Glaser 2011; Deckers – Grusková 2010; Fuchs 2003; Gippert 2007, 2010a; Gippert et al. 2007a, 2009; Gullath 2003; Lo Monaco 1996; Mairinger 1981, 2000, 2004; Gardthausen 1911; Posse 1899; Smith 2012; Wattenbach 1896.

3. The manuscript traditions

This section introduces in a synthetic way the individual manuscript cultures considered in the handbook, providing the basic geographical, chronological and cultural coordinates. It also prepares for any other subsection dealing with the respective manuscript culture(s) in the subsequent chapters. As in chapters 1, 2, and 4, the language traditions are arranged alphabetically: Arabic (including manuscript cultures using the Arabic script as the main script), Armenian, Avestan, Caucasian Albanian, Christo-Palestinian Aramaic, Coptic, Ethiopic, Georgian, Greek, Hebrew, Slavonic, and Syriac.

3.1. Manuscripts in Arabic script (VSR)

The written heritage in Arabic script and language is the origin of a complex of related manuscript cultures and traditions that share the adoption and use of the same script and salient features. The manuscript in Arabic script cannot be dissociated from the development of writing in some dozens of languages by an indefinite number of ethnic groups and people over twelve centuries. As a matter of fact, Arabic codicology was never a field distinct from Arabic palaeography (see Ch. 2 § 2), and graphical phenomena were mainly evaluated in their relationship with the culture from which they arose—above all the Islamic one—both because of their symbolic and aesthetic value and for their deeply rooted function as a vehicle of textual transmission.

The study of Arabic codicology (understood as the codicology of manuscripts in Arabic script) has so far been mainly stimulated by philological and literary approaches, which have mostly focused on single cases rather than developing systematic studies and quantitative analyses. It must be pointed out that the variety of specific cases cannot be easily standardized, being characterized by a strong specialization of techniques and practices of formats and genres. Production was more often of individual than of serial character, and it was only in the course of time that the manufactured books assumed more uniform features, through the gradual application of craft techniques, and conformed to a regular standard.

Arabic codicology is, therefore, an absolutely virgin field of study, the boundaries of which are hardly outlined. The only exception is represented by the corpus of the ancient Qur'ānic manuscripts produced during the first two centuries of Islam, more deeply investigated through the systematic analysis of scattered fragments and folia, mostly motivated by palaeographical interest, but even by some early codicological phenomena associated to their production (Déroche 1992, 1999, 2009, 2012).

The production of Arabic manuscripts embraces, without interruption, the period from the seventh to the nineteenth century; in some communities in North Africa, western and sub-Saharan Africa (see Ch. 4 § 2.1.1), Bohra in western India, or Yemen it extends until the early twentieth century. From the eighteenth century on manuscripts coexisted with printed books—the latter introduced in the Islamic world in 1730.

Essential historical stages, corresponding to formal and stylistic developments as well as to dynastic characterizations and the succession of local political authorities, may be divided into four periods: the era of the Umayyad, Abbasid and early Shiite Fatimids (seventh to tenth centuries), the era of the late Fatimids and the Seljuk Turks (eleventh to thirteenth centuries), the era of the Ilkhanids, Timurids and Mamluks (thirteenth to fifteenth centuries), the era of the Ottomans, Safavids, Mughals and Qajars (sixteenth to twentieth centuries).

With regard to dating, there is no evidence for dated documents before the ninth century; the most ancient datable witnesses belong to the seventh to ninth centuries, the earliest fragments of Qur'ānic codices being those which have more extensively been studied as representatives of the decisive founding phase. The largest extent of the extant amount of dated or datable manuscripts in Arabic script—from the twelfth/thirteenth to the nineteenth century—has not yet emerged from its obscure anonymity, apart from a few exceptions concerning specific collections or individual books.

Manuscripts in Arabic script surviving to this day cover nearly every aspect of thought and culture. The largest part of these manuscripts belongs to the field of the religious sciences, ranging from Qur'ānic commentaries to manuals of prayer, most of which were exclusively transmitted in manuscript (i.e. non-printed or unpublished) form. The other major categories concern language and literature, philosophy, natural and mathematical sciences, medicine, alchemy, and science of materials and techniques. Here again much is still unedited or not established in a definitive critical form.

The Arabic language attested in all fields of knowledge is also used in non-Islamic areas, either independently or in parallel with other languages. Distant regions, different ethnic groups and languages, from the

Atlantic Ocean to the China Sea, from the strait of Zanzibar to the banks of the Volga, constitute the forge of several million manuscript volumes, whose range and worth are largely underrated or still unknown.

The Christians of the Middle East copied religious texts alongside Arabic in Syriac and Coptic from the eleventh century on, during the eighth/tenth centuries bilingual Greek-Arabic manuscripts are attested, with translations of Christian texts, of biblical and patristic writings, from Greek into Arabic, for the use of Arabophone Christian communities. The Arab-Christian manuscripts show different features from the Arab-Islamic tradition, especially regarding their textual transmission. The Jews transcribed texts in classical or Judaeo-Arabic, next to those in Hebrew, the latter in some cases in Arabic characters.

The contribution of the Persian component in the production of manuscripts from the eleventh century, and more pervasively from the thirteenth century onwards, and that of the Turkish one from the fourteenth or fifteenth century, initially follows the patterns of the Arabic religious tradition in Arabic and then runs an independent route, especially for literary, historical and scientific texts; in the regions ruled by Persian dynasties of Turkish origins, book production expressed the most luxuriant fancy and the most original creative spirit. Persian manuscripts are to be found beyond the borders of Persian-speaking countries, written either in the lands where the people spoke Persian or in Arabic-speaking lands, such as Syria, Iraq, and Egypt, and eventually in the Ottoman Empire. A significant number of Persian manuscripts, with a regional identity, are still kept in those places where they were written, Iran, India and Pakistan, the greatest amount of them still remaining uncatalogued or even unknown.

Turkish manuscripts were written in Arabic script until the second half of the nineteenth century; approximately 60,000 of them survive in Turkey, many of which dating from the end of the Ottoman period have not been either examined or roughly catalogued.

Over one hundred languages coming from different linguistic groups and areas employed Arabic script for writing their texts, eventually developing their own manuscript tradition, each one covering a wide range of content, and spanning several centuries, among others, Berber and its varieties; Swahili and some Niger-Kordofanian languages; Sudanese, Nilo-Saharan; the African Arabic dialect known as *ḥasaniyya*; Malagasy; the Chadic Hausa; Turkish languages such as Azeri, Kazakh, Turkmenian, Kirghiz, Qarluq or Chagatai, Uyghur, Uzbek, Karakalpak, Kumyk, Tatar, Kipchak, Bashkir; numerous Indo-European languages including Albanian and ancient Romance languages (Aljamiado-Arabic script), some Slavonic languages such as Serbo-Croatian, Belorussian, Indo-Iranian languages such as Urdu, Kurdish, Tajik, Punjabi, Kashmiri, Sindhi, Pashto, Baluchi, Saraiki; the Caucasian Lak, Avar, Circassian; Malay, Acehnese and other languages from Indonesia and Malaysia; Javanese, Mongol (few examples); there also exists a Chinese adaptation of the Arabic script (Xiao'erjing; Déroche – Sagaria Rossi 2012, 1–7; Mumin – Versteegh 2014).

The regions where manuscripts were produced are obviously those in which the largest amount of the total manuscript heritage is still kept and preserved, for the matrix of such collections is strongly linked to the territory, to the Islamic substratum grafting onto the pre-existing ones, and to the language—particularly in border areas—as is the case of some countries of Central Asia, former Soviet Republics, Southeast Asia, China, Eastern Europe, sub-Saharan Africa, southern Spain, and the Maghreb. The largest and richest deposits are found of course in those countries where Islam was implanted with unchallenged supremacy for more than thirteen centuries, in mosques, madrasas, libraries, Islamic institutions of any kind and in a wealth of inestimable private collections. Some 800,000 manuscripts at least are kept in Turkey, the country which owns the largest number of codices, Iran, India, Egypt, Iraq and Saudi Arabia; more than 130,000 units survive in the Maghreb; for other African countries no definite figures have yet emerged, but the extant items can be estimated in tens if not hundreds of thousands.

From the sixteenth century onward, Europe acquired a significant portion of manuscripts in Arabic script coming from oriental collections, selected by criteria of genre, content, origin or artistic value. Coming from the most influential and prolific cultural warehouses of Arabic manuscripts, Persian and Turkish included, they offer a limited sample, while marginal productions, as well as those of linguistically and literarily decentralized areas, are less well represented and consequently less studied. In Europe the richest and largest collections are the German, French, English, Bosnian, Dutch, Italian, and Spanish ones; in the Russian Federation there are about 30,000 manuscripts in Arabic script; the Far Eastern countries preserve more than 40,000 items; North American collections keep about 22,000 codices.

Considering the extreme difficulty of assessing the real extent of Arabic manuscript production—seven million units according to a recent estimate—it should be remarked that any census is approximate,

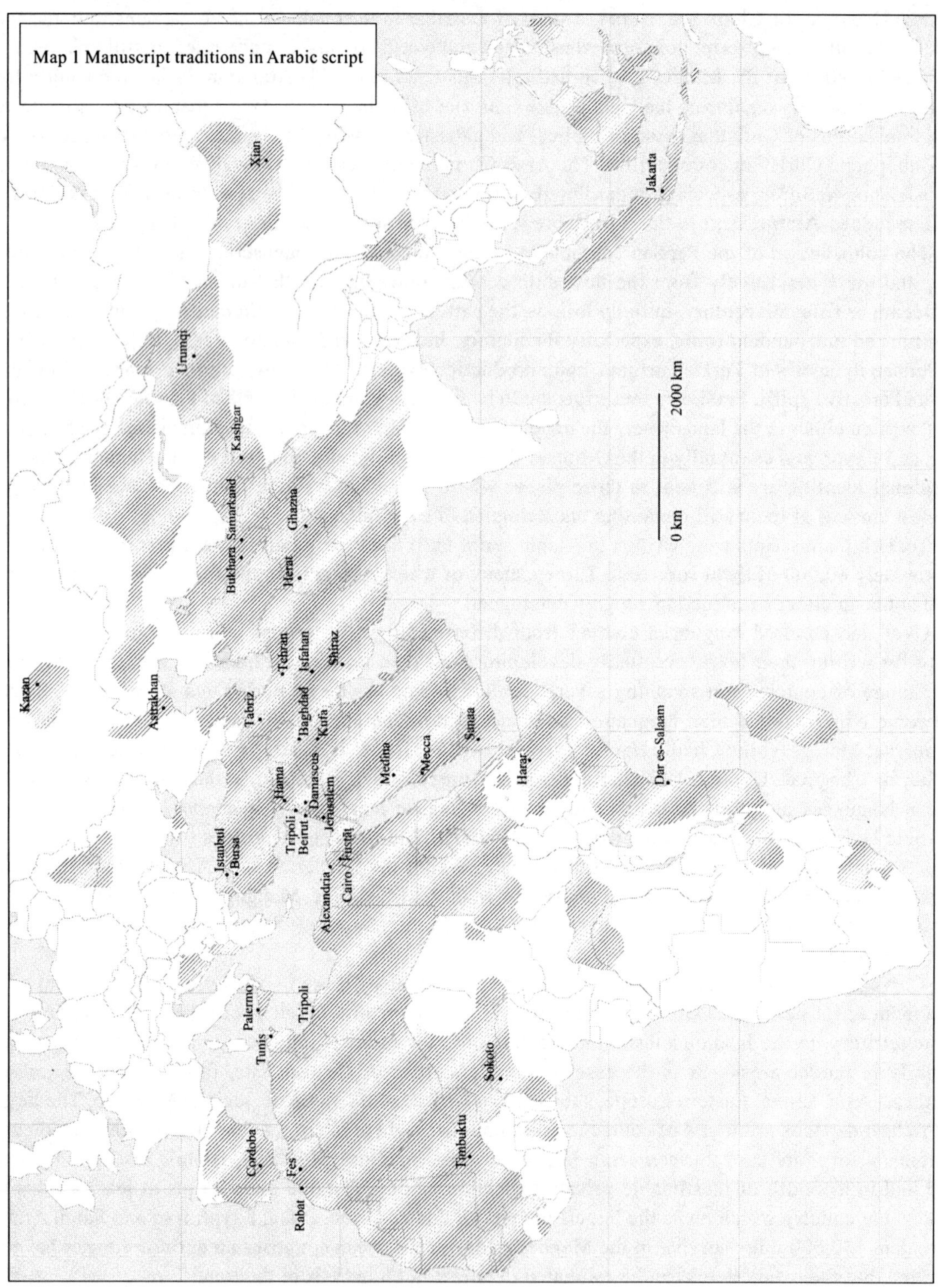

Map 1 Manuscript traditions in Arabic script

mostly based on partial catalogues and local inventories, if not on the preliminary calculation of material not otherwise registered, and estimated—whenever reported—at a glance. Archival documents and manuscript volumes are often counted together without proper distinction.

Arabic codicological literature—developed with an increasing impetus in the past twenty years— is rather discontinuous and fragmentary, because research has been limited to specific aspects and based on narrow and non-homogeneous sampling. Catalogues of manuscripts in Arabic script provide, to a large extent, insufficient codicological information, never detailed enough and conceived neither to support nor to plan research on the material features of manuscript production. They rarely offer detailed codicological descriptions, and do not allow in-depth archaeological investigation. It is therefore necessary to focus directly on the manuscripts, and to compare them with the data provided by the literary sources, mostly in Arabic, Persian, and Turkish (cf. Ch. 4 §§ 2.1 and 2.8).

An increased international effort in the indexing of manuscripts in Arabic script can be observed over the past years, and is witnessed by tools realized with different methods and techniques. A significant example is the *Fichier des manuscrits moyen-orientaux datés* (FiMMOD), a card index of 338 dated manuscripts in Arabic script, published by the École pratique des Hautes Études (ed. Déroche 1993–2000), unfortunately incomplete. Beyond some attempts of digitizing published catalogues, database cataloguing projects have been set up by the Wellcome Library in London, with its online catalogue of the Medical manuscripts of the Haddad Collection (<http://library.wellcome.ac.uk/Haddad/browse_table.asp>). Several other projects for online cataloguing and digitizing can be found in Egypt, Mali, Turkey, Uzbekistan, and Yemen, in addition to the Daiber collection in Tokyo and the geographically distributed database projects such as the West African Manuscripts initiative (<http://www.westafricanmanuscripts.org/index.html>). Similar outstanding efforts can be observed in Iran, with one of the richest collections of Islamic manuscripts in the world (<http://www.islamicmanuscript.org/files/Irani_Akbar_TIMA.pdf>). Organizations dedicated to cataloguing and research on manuscripts are The Islamic Manuscript Organisation (TIMA) and al-Furqān Islamic Heritage Foundation, the latter having promoted a main reference work, that is the *World Survey of Islamic Manuscripts* (Roper 1992–1994), that indexes and describes catalogues and collections all over the world (ed. Brinkmann – Wiesmüller 2009, 21–28).

Instrumental analysis, though applied on a narrow-range of specimens and with different sampling methods, has provided the first reliable results for inks and pigments, mostly in miniatures (Déroche – Sagaria Rossi 2012, 13–25; Roger et al. 2004; Chaplin et al. 2006; Barkeshli 2008; Espejo Arias et al. 2008; Khan – Lewincamp 2008; Sloggett 2008; see also Ch. 1 § 2).

As far as handmade Middle Eastern papers are concerned—whose components are still to be identified—microscopic and spectroscopic analysis may help to detect the structure and morphology of the fibres (Colini 2008 and 2011; Barkeshli 2008; Espejo Arias et al. 2008; Kropf – Baker 2013).

Though quantitative codicology is being increasingly adopted during these latest years, it has been far from being systematically applied to the production of manuscripts in Arabic script, except for some local collections and on a narrow range of specimens. The main attempts in this direction dealt with Middle Eastern papers (Irigoin 1988, 1991, 1993; Loveday 2001; Humbert 2002); although marked by very different methodological approaches, the quantitative investigation on some mediaeval Yemeni papers (D'Ottone 2006) and that on a few Egyptian papers from the fifteenth century (Kropf – Baker 2013) may also be mentioned. Other scientific inquiries on colours (Roger et al. 2004; Espejo Arias et al. 2008) evidenced the need of statistical approaches to gather and compare the results.

Quire numbering systems and catchwords have been described and classified from a number of Arabic manuscripts dated before the fifteenth century (Guesdon 2002).

The attempts at describing and arranging binding typologies (Weisweiler 1962; D'Ottone 2007; Viola 2007; Scheper 2014, forthcoming) and decoration patterns (Vasilyeva 2009) have been mostly carried out with conservation and art historical aims.

The terminology employed for defining and identifying Arabic manuscript books and codicological phenomena reflects the development of Arabic codicological studies. In Arabic, Persian, and Turkish there is over-abundance of words related to book manufacture, but the terms and definitions found in mediaeval and modern sources (often multiple and overlapping) do not always describe clearly the nature of the materials and actions involved in the processes. On the other hand, a classification and selection of native terms is still a premature objective (an Arabic-English glossary ordered according to Arabic roots is given by Gacek 2001 and 2008), since the knowledge of the sources, associated with the recent activity of comparing written texts and the material features of the manuscripts, is in its very beginning (a selected Arabic-Italian glossary, with Arabic and transliterated terms may be found in Déroche – Sagaria Rossi 2012, 293–298).

The lack of terminological uniformity corresponds to the lack of uniformity in the physical description of Arabic manuscripts. Some aspects have been described basing on the example of western manuscripts and applying criteria which are valid for already codified and deeply investigated manuscript traditions and cultures. Material features, such as writing supports and instruments, quires, foliation, pagination, forms and formats, page layouts, ruling, may fall into common categories already standardized in other manuscript studies areas. As to decoration and binding, usually more freely described, it would be suitable to define the proper elements and distinct structural patterns.

References

Barkeshli 2008; Brinkmann – Wiesmüller 2009; Chaplin et al. 2006; Colini 2008, 2011; Déroche 1992, 1999, 2009, 2012; Déroche et al. 2000; Déroche – Sagaria Rossi 2012; D'Ottone 2006, 2007; Espejo Arias et al. 2008; *FiMMOD*; Gacek 2001, 2008; Guesdon 2002; Humbert 2002; Irigoin 1988, 1991, 1993; Khan – Lewincamp 2008; Kropf – Baker 2013; Loveday 2001; Mumin – Versteegh 2014; Roger et al. 2004; Roper 1992–1994; Scheper 2014, forthcoming; Sloggett 2008; Vasilyeva 2009; Viola 2007; Weisweiler 1962; Web sources <http://library.wellcome.ac.uk/Haddad/browse_table.asp>; <http://www.westafrican-manuscripts.org/index.html>; <http://www.islamicmanuscript.org/files/Irani_Akbar_TIMA.pdf>, last access May 2014.

3.2. Armenian manuscripts (DK)

The vast majority of the estimated 31,000 bound Armenian manuscripts, representing some 34,000 discrete items (Kouymjian 2008a, 211; 2011b, 91; 2012a, 19), date from after 1600. More than 80% of the manuscripts have been included in detailed or summary catalogues devoted to the various collections (see Ch. 4 § 2.2). Theoretically, the earliest manuscripts should date from the fifth century CE, when in its first decade the very phonetically comprehensive Armenian alphabet was invented by the monk Mesrop Maštocʿ, but no securely identified or dated manuscripts or fragments have survived from before the ninth century, from which there are two surviving dated manuscripts. Fewer than twenty manuscripts are dated or assignable to before the year 1000. All Armenian manuscripts contained a scribal colophon, written at the moment of copying, and very often other colophons by the painter, patron, or binder. In a short study devoted to the statistical analysis of Armenian manuscripts (Kouymjian 1983), it was determined that just over 59% of all surviving Armenian manuscripts are precisely dated by colophon, and many more can be closely dated through the names mentioned in defective colophons. A more careful counting of the largest collection, at the Matenadaran, the state repository-museum of manuscripts in Yerevan, results in 55% exactly dated manuscripts (Kouymjian 2012a, 20). The discrepancy between the latter figure and the higher one of 59% in the earlier study is probably due to the use of the number of manuscripts rather than the larger number of discrete items in the indexes (*Matenadaran abridged catalogue* = Eganyan et al. 1965–2007, I, manuscripts nos. 1–5,000, rather than the 5,418 items listed in the index). This mass of precise data puts Armenian manuscript studies both at an advantage and a disadvantage in comparison to other traditions in which colophons were less systematically used. The advantage is the relative precision with which we can analyse trends and phenomena related to manuscript studies. The disadvantage is a diminished urgency for developing codicological criteria as tools for dating manuscripts. Consequently, the study of parchment, paper, ruling, quire formations, and related material aspects of manuscripts has lagged behind the study of texts, decorations, and even the bindings.

Armenian manuscripts are preserved in public museums and libraries and monastic collections in Armenia, the Near East, Europe, and the United States. The most important collections are the Matenadaran, the 'Repository of Ancient Manuscripts', in Yerevan (11,000 manuscripts), the Library of the Mekhitarist Brotherhood at San Lazzaro, Venice (4,000), the Armenian Patriarchate in Jerusalem (4,000), the Library of the Mekhitarist Brotherhood in Vienna (1,200), the Armenian Catholic Monastery of Bzummar in Lebanon (1,000), the Armenian Monastery at New Julfa, Isfāhān (1,000), and the Catholicosate of Etchmiadzin (1,000). Important collections of fewer than 1,000 manuscripts are kept at the Oriental Institute, St Petersburg, the Bibliothèque nationale de France, Paris, the Bodleian Library, Oxford, the British Library, London, the Chester Beatty Library, Dublin, Tübingen Universitätsbibliothek, the Catholicosate of Cilicia, Antelias, Lebanon, University of California, Los Angeles, and the Biblioteca Apostolica Vaticana. Hundreds of other libraries have small, but at times artistically very important, collections, for instance the Freer Gallery of Art in Washington, the Pierpont Morgan Library and Museum in New York, the Walters Art Gallery in Baltimore, USA, and the John Rylands Library in Manchester, UK.

From a methodological perspective, the abundant data in carefully prepared catalogues provides a solid mass of evidence to which statistical analyses can be applied. The thoroughness, and thus the usefulness, of these manuscript catalogues is a legacy of a generation of Armenian scholars trained in German universities at the end of the nineteenth and the beginning of the twentieth centuries, and to the majestic first volume of the catalogue of manuscripts of the Armenian Mekhitarist Brotherhood in Vienna, compiled by Fr. Yakob Tašyan (1895). It set a high standard of description, one followed to the present: in addition to a list of the texts, also the date, place, scribe, artist, patron, binder, size, material, script, number of columns and lines, quire structure, and decoration were indicated. However, ruling and pricking were ignored, though in the recent volumes of the *Grand* or *Master catalogue of the Matenadaran* (Eganyan et al. 1984–2013, manuscripts 1–2,700), at least watermarks are noted and photographic samples of the various hands accompany each entry.

Nearly all Armenian manuscripts and collections are listed in Bernard Coulie's *Répertoire des bibliothèques et des catalogues de manuscrits arméniens* (1992, supplements 1995, 2000a, 2004). A master list of catalogued Armenian manuscripts, a project initiated by Michael Stone and Bernard Coulie, waits to be completed. With well over 20,000 manuscripts repertoried with basic information on text, date and place of execution, material, number of folia, and size, serious work on Armenian codicology can move forward.

Codicology is a very new and little explored domain of Armenian studies. No manual exists, not even a substantial general article. Recent research has been confined to two specialized areas, manuscript structure and binding (Merian 1993), and palaeography (*Album* 2002). There have also been studies devoted to pigments (Orna – Mathews 1981; Mérian et al. 1994b; Mathews – Orna 1992–1993) and to a much lesser extent inks. Little or no attention has been paid to writing surfaces, ruling, pricking, quire structure, folding, page layout, or textile linings of bindings (Dournovo 1953; Tarayan 1978). Illuminations and manuscript decorations have fared better, but mostly in the domain of art history rather than codicology (Kouymjian 1996a, 1023–1042). Nevertheless, analyses based on statistics from published manuscript catalogues (Kouymjian 1983), concerning codicological features such as manuscript size (Kouymjian 2007a, 42 Table), material (parchment or paper), script (majuscule or minuscule), or quire type (Kouymjian 2012a, Tables 1–2), can yield very precise information on the chronology of the transition from the dominance of one support to the other, of a change in quire type, shift from one script to another, and so on.

An earlier statistical study surveyed three groups of dated manuscripts covering the years 1200 to 1800 in ten-year periods: the first was based on 6,030 items from the 10,408 manuscripts of the Matenadaran published in the abridged catalogues; the second on 7,973 dated manuscripts from a total of 13,944 in a variety of repositories; the third based on 16,744 manuscripts, which included the manuscripts from the large collection of the Armenian Patriarchate of Jerusalem, but only for the years 1310 to 1620 (Kouymjian 1983, 433, fig. 1). The proportionate number of manuscripts for any period graphically resembles each other very closely, and thus the Matenadaran, perhaps because of its size and diversity, affords an accurate reflection of the whole and can be used to project results valid for all Armenian manuscripts. The manuscript production grew steadily (for example from 69 items in the twelfth to 392 in the thirteenth century, and the true difference must have been much more before the destruction of libraries mentioned in mediaeval sources, see Orbelian 1864, I, 191 as well as the massacres of 1894-1896 and the Genocide of 1915-1923, when tens of thousands of manuscripts perished). The growth slowed down in the fifteenth century, coming nearly to a halt in the first decades of the sixteenth century, because of the enormous unrest caused by the Ottoman–Safavid wars (Kouymjian 1982; Kouymjian 1997, 14–21). The decline was followed by the sudden and dramatic increase in production, already beginning in the second half of the sixteenth century, but continuously accelerating until the late seventeenth century: a nearly 400% increase, from 1,030 to 4,072 manuscripts (Kouymjian 1983, figs. 1–2).

This remarkable growth in manuscript production reveals the rise of the new dynamic mercantile middle class (Aslanian 2011) as early as the late sixteenth and early seventeenth centuries (Kouymjian 1994). The data also very clearly show that the majority of extant Armenian manuscripts date after 1600: 67% from the large, original sampling, 78% from a more recent targeted sampling (Eganyan et al. 2007), and 66% from the 1,800 manuscripts included in the first five volumes of the *Master catalogue* (Eganyan et al. 1984–2013).

The third quarter of the seventeenth century brought about another decline in the copying of Armenian manuscripts. Yet, though there is a roughly 35% decrease in manuscript production in the eighteenth century, the absolute number of surviving eighteenth-century codices is more than the combined quantity from both the fifteenth and sixteenth centuries. Nearly 10% of surviving and catalogued Armenian manuscripts were written or copied in the nineteenth century. In this respect, little thought has been given when conducting statistical analyses to whether all manuscripts kept in a repository should be included.

We can assume that up to 1700 almost all manuscripts were executed by a scribe working from an earlier copy; there are very few autograph copies. On the contrary, a large portion of eighteenth- and

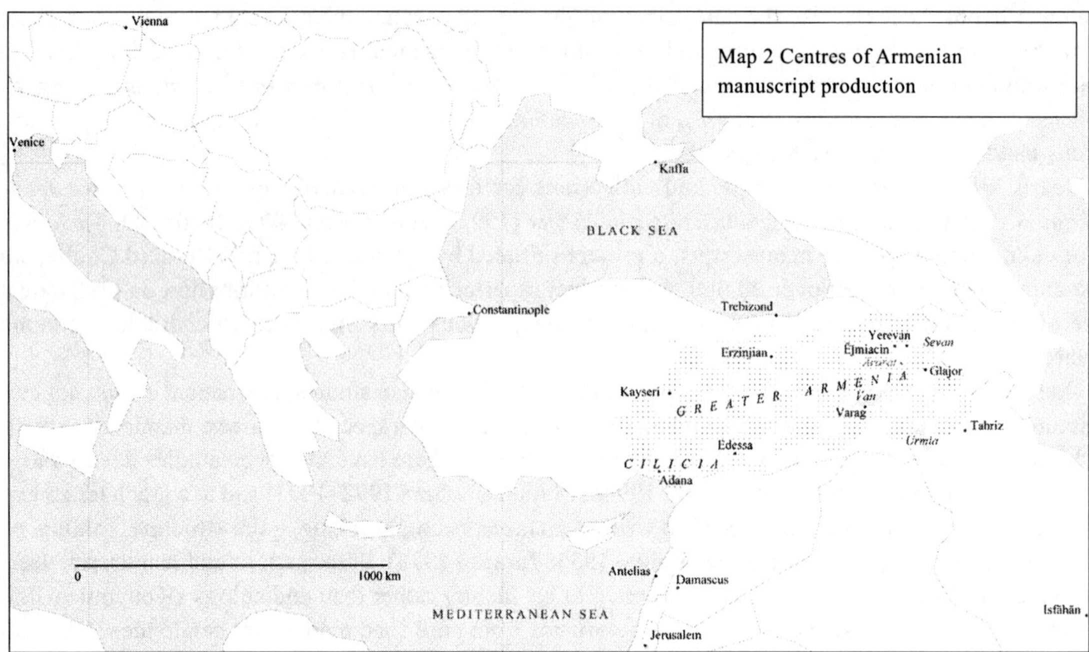

Map 2 Centres of Armenian manuscript production

nineteenth-century Armenian manuscripts contain an original composition by an author (memoir, account book, dictionary, translation), a unique item that perhaps should have a special place in the statistical examination of the history of the last centuries of manuscript production.

Even though the first Armenian printed book dates to 1512, the old technology—copying by hand—continued to grow until 1675 and was much practised until the mid-nineteenth century. For more than three centuries the two technologies, printing and scribal copying of manuscripts, worked in a close, symbiotic relationship (Kouymjian 1983, 2008b). One explanation for the persistence of the manuscript tradition is that the cheap, in some cases free, labour of the monastic scribe was more economical than the purchase of expensive printed volumes. Furthermore, after the mid-nineteenth century, copies were made mostly by scholars who were not scribes, an obsolete profession along with the scriptorium.

Data mined from published manuscript catalogues and other data abundantly available online for the history of early Armenian printing can be used statistically to establish a history of Armenian manuscript production and observe a number of phenomena related to the long transitional period from the handmade book to the mechanically produced one.

References

Album = Stone et al. 2002; Aslanian 2011; Coulie 1992, 1995, 2000a, 2004; Dournovo 1953; Eganyan et al. 1965–2007; Eganyan et al. 1984–2013; Kouymjian 1982, 1983, 1994, 1996a, 1997, 2007a, 2008a, 2008b, 2011b, 2012a; Merian 1993; Mérian et al. 1994b; Mathews – Orna 1992–1993; Orbelian 1864; Orna – Mathews 1981; Tarayan 1978.

3.3. Avestan manuscripts (AC)

The Avestan (Zend, Old Bactrian) language has been used for over two millennia for the Zoroastrian religious cult. It takes its name from the *Avesta*, the collection of the sacred text of Zoroastrianism (see also Ch. 3 § 3.5).

The chant accompanying the Indo-Iranian sacrifice is an oral composition. It took its present form probably in Achaemenid times in Eastern Iran, was then imported into western Iran and from there exported to other areas of the Achaemenid kingdom. For centuries, the ceremony was memorized and recited in different areas so that different ways of reciting the same text emerged. The version of the political centre (the region of Fārs) spread over a wide area and became the standard ceremony which appears in our manuscripts. However, alternative versions existed, as shown by the Sogdian *Aṣ̌əm Vohū*. A Sogdian fragment includes this prayer in a phonetic shape quite different from the standard version, showing notable archaisms and some influences of the Sogdian language (Gershevitch in Sims-Williams 1976).

Thus, in the early centuries CE the need emerged to represent the liturgy correctly in writing. The exact date of the introduction of the Avestan script is disputed, but the sixth century CE is the most widely accepted proposal (Cereti 2008; Panaino 2012, 79–80). It was invented by the Zoroastrian clergy mainly on the basis of the script used in the Zoroastrian Church for Middle Persian (Pahlavi). It was a phonetic script with fifty-four letters created to reproduce the phonetic nuances of the recitation of the Avestan texts in Fārs; thirty of the symbols are variants of the thirteen Pahlavi letters in their cursive form (Hoffmann [K.] – Narten 1989). This was the beginning of the written transmission of Avestan texts. It is unclear, however, which texts were written down at the time of the invention of the Avestan script: the *Great Avesta*, in order to preserve a copy of the collected writings, or the different liturgies, so that the manuscripts served (as was later the case) as tools for learning the ritual.

The two main types of Avestan text are (1) the long liturgy with the complete description of one or several variants of the main Zoroastrian liturgy in honour of Ahura Mazdā (which reached its current form, or at least a similar one, most likely already in Achaemenid times, sixth to fourth centuries BCE); and (2) a collection of minor rituals and other ritual texts not included in the long liturgy (these rituals are quite heterogeneous and no dating for the creation of this type of collection has yet been possible).

The manuscripts can be further classified according to their use. (1) Liturgical manuscripts were used for the ritual instruction of priests. They were not intended to be exact copies of their originals, but rather to adapt perfectly to the current practice. They include complete descriptions of the ceremony, not only the recitative in Avestan, but also instructions in different languages (in Middle and New Persian, in Iran; in Middle Persian in Avestan script—easier to read than the Middle Persian one—and Gujarati, in India) and even indications concerning alternative texts for special days or ceremonies. (2) Exegetical manuscripts contain the text of the basic liturgy as well as a translation and commentary (usually in Pahlavi or Sanskrit). As Avestan fell out of use, it became increasingly difficult to understand; the earliest commentaries go back to pre-Islamic Iran (Sasanian times). These translations and commentaries were initially transmitted orally in liturgical schools, but eventually they were committed to writing. There are some exegetical manuscripts with other variants of the long liturgy, but they only include the sections that needed to be translated. (3) Liturgical and exegetical content could be combined in one manuscript. The oldest testimony to the ceremonies as we find them in extant manuscripts is the colophon in a manuscript copied before 1020 CE, probably near Isfāhān, in western Iran (Cantera – de Vaan 2005), which refers to a manuscript of the combined type (or using a Pahlavi expression, manuscript *pad zand ud nērang*, Cantera 2013b). It was then probably sent to India at the beginning of the sixteenth century, when the Zoroastrian community in the Indian diaspora was seeking advice in Iran about the performance of the long liturgy and the meaning of the Avestan recitative. The oldest extant Avestan manuscripts copied in Iran date from the end of the sixteenth century, corresponding to a certain improvement of the living conditions of the community under the Safavids.

There is a further type of Avestan manuscript, but one that is only very scarcely represented. In Sasanian times there was a collection of works written in the Avestan language and arranged scholastically in three groups of seven books. This collection is described in the Pahlavi literature of the ninth century, but it is lost. Only very few extant manuscripts of the Avesta contain texts that belonged directly to the *Great Avesta* of twenty one books. They are fragments of longer books dealing with liturgical instruction, like the *Hērbadestān* and *Nērangestān*. It was once assumed that the liturgical and exegetical manuscripts go back to this Sasanian collection and that they are only 'surviving fragments'. However, this view has now been definitively abandoned (Kellens 1998, 476–478; Panaino 1999; Cantera 2004, 21–22; Kellens 2012; Panaino 2012, 84–85; Tremblay 2012, 100–101).

In the seventh century, Iran became Islamic, and the Zoroastrian community began to face pressure, in particular after the Abbasids came to power in the second half of the eighth century. Around the ninth century, a part of the community settled in India; Maharashtra and Gujarat have been important centres of Zoroastrianism ever since. It is in India that the oldest extant manuscripts were copied, probably because all earlier Iranian manuscripts are lost. At the beginning of the thirteenth century, a priest came from India to Sīstān and obtained an exegetical manuscript of the *Vidēvdād*, which he brought to India. The colophon of the manuscript Copenhagen, Royal Library, Cod. Iran. 7 (K7) informs us further that an Iranian priest, Rōstam Mihrābān Marzbān Dēnyār, copied in the second half of the thirteenth century a liturgical and an exegetical manuscript of the *Visperad* in Anklesar (India). The original manuscript is lost, but its old copy (K7) is preserved in Copenhagen. In the 1320s, another Iranian priest, Mihrābān Kaixōsrō, came to India and copied in Nawsarī and Kambay two exegetical *Yasna* and two exegetical *Vidēvdād* manuscripts. The oldest extant Avestan manuscripts written in India by an Indian priest (Pešotan Rām Kāmdīn

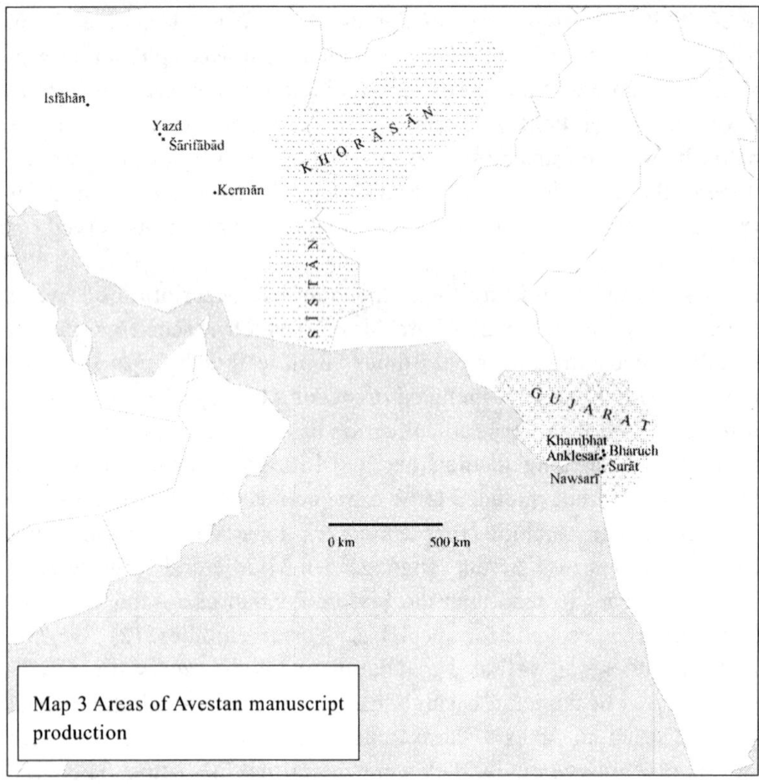

Map 3 Areas of Avestan manuscript production

Šahryār) are an exegetical *Yasna* and an exegetical *Visperad* included in a collective codex together with other Pahlavi works (M6; Munich, Bayerische Staatsbibliothek, Cod.Zend. 51a+b), copied in 1397. The oldest liturgical manuscripts copied in India appear in the second half of the sixteenth century (manuscripts 100 (Bombay, University Library, Geldner's B3) and 2210 (Bombay, Mulla Firuz Library, 8)), and they begin to be frequent only from the seventeenth century onwards. Collections of minor rituals do not appear before the end of the sixteenth century (manuscripts Navsari (Gujarat), Meherjirana Library, F1 and E1) in India.

Beginning at the end of the fifteenth century (and with greater intensity early in the seventeenth century), the Zoroastrian communities of India started to send messengers to the region of Yazd-Kermān (Iran) looking for advice in ritual and religious matters. At that time, it seems that nobody in the Indian communities was able to read Pahlavi, and the right performance of the rituals was not always clear. The answers of the Iranian priests were often accompanied by manuscripts that were then abundantly copied in India. The oldest manuscript sent was probably a manuscript of the *Yasna* combining ritual instructions and the translation into Pahlavi copied by Hōšang Syāwaxš, in Šārifābād, in 1495.

The oldest extant Avestan manuscripts in Iran date from the Safavid period and come from the same area: the region of Yazd and Kermān. The only mention of Avestan manuscripts in western Iran is the old colophon of the *Yasna* manuscript copied by Hōšang Syāwaxš, whose origin is the region of Isfāhān. Further, we can locate in Khorasan an important production of manuscripts around the beginning of the sixteenth century, but we know only copies of these manuscripts, produced in the region of Yazd and Kermān at the end of that century and, mainly, during the seventeenth century. Some of these manuscripts were sent to India during the seventeenth century, but most of them are still in Iran. Contrary to the long-lived assumption that there were no Avestan manuscripts in Iran, recently around fifty new Avestan manuscripts have been found there in private and public libraries, a major discovery (Ǧahānpūr 1997–1998; Mazdāpūr 1999; Cantera 2011, 222 and following; Mazdāpūr 2012).

From the points of view of codicology, palaeography and orthography, Avestan manuscripts from India differ considerably from those from Iran. In India, one must further distinguish between the manuscripts produced before the importation of Avestan manuscripts from Iran in the Safavid time and after it.

The basic source for information for Avestan manuscripts is still the *Prolegomena* to Geldner's edition of the Avestan texts (1896), but it is at many points outdated. For recent descriptions of the typology and history of the Avestan manuscripts, see Cantera 2011 and 2013a. Updated lists of Avestan manuscripts of the long liturgy that have been published in the last years are: Andrés-Toledo – Cantera 2012, Hintze 2012a, and Martínez Porro 2013. The largest collection of published Avestan manuscripts is the *Avestan Digital Archive* (<http://www.avesta-archive.com>).

References

Andrés-Toledo – Cantera 2012; Cantera 2004, 2011, 2013a, 2013b; Cantera – de Vaan 2005; Cereti 2008; Ǧahānpūr 1997–1998; Geldner 1896; Hintze 2012a; Hoffmann [K.] – Narten 1989; Kellens 1998, 2012; Martínez Porro 2013; Mazdāpūr 1999, 2012; Panaino 1999, 2012; Sims-Williams 1976; Tremblay 2012. Web source: *Avestan Digital Archive* <http://www.avesta-archive.com>. See also Ch. 3 § 3.5.

3.4. Caucasian Albanian manuscripts (JG)

The conversion of the southern Caucasus to Christianity by the end of the fourth century brought about the emergence of three manuscript traditions, two of which developed continuously for about 1,500 years, namely those of the Armenians and the Georgians, while the third one, that of the so-called Caucasian Albanians, ended before the turn of the first millennium by consequence of the conquest of the region by the Arabs. The very fact that the eastern neighbours of Armenians and Georgians, styled *albanoi* in Greek sources, developed a Christian literature in their own language and script in the fifth century under the influence of Mesrop Maštocʿ, the inventor of the Armenian script, was known only from historiographical sources until 1937, when a specimen of an Albanian alphabet was detected in an Armenian encyclopaedic manuscript of the thirteenth century (Yerevan Matenadaran, 7117; Abulaʒe 1938; Šaniʒe 1938; Gippert et al. 2009, I, II-1-5); a few epigraphic artefacts that were unearthed in excavations in present-day Azerbaijan in the late 1940s confirmed the use of that alphabet for the first time (Gippert et al. 2009, I, xx–xxi and II-85–91). It took another fifty years for the first (and only) manuscript remnants of Caucasian Albanian to be detected, in the lower text of two Georgian palimpsest codices discovered among the New Finds of the library of St Catherine's Monastery on Mount Sinai. The decipherment of these palimpsests, initiated by Z. Aleksiʒe in 1994 (Aleksiʒe – Mahé 1997; Gippert et al. 2009, I, xx–xxiii) and accomplished in the course of an international cooperation project between 1998 and 2008 (cf. the edition published by Gippert et al. 2009), brought to light that the 242 pages of the manuscripts Sinai, St Catherine, New Finds, georg. N13 and N55 that have an underwriting in the Albanian language and script are fragments deriving from two originally different codices, one a lectionary with lections mostly from the New Testament (Gospels of Matthew, Mark, and Luke; Pauline and Catholic Epistles), and the other about one-half of a manuscript containing the Gospel of John (see Ch. 3 § 3.11). From the remnants of these two parchment codices, both badly damaged by the fire that led to the detection of the New Finds in 1975, it is obvious that the Albanian manuscript tradition shared most of its characteristics (quire structure, page layout, text structure) with Armenian and Georgian codices of the sixth to ninth centuries; as the palimpsests are not dated otherwise, this is the only hint as to the time when the Albanian texts may have been written down.

References

Abulaʒe 1938; Aleksiʒe – Mahé 1997; Gippert et al. 2009; Šaniʒe 1938.

3.5. Christo-Palestinian Aramaic manuscripts (AD)

Documents in Christo-Palestinian Aramaic are little known (Desreumaux – Schmidt 1989). Christo-Palestinian inscriptions do not appear in the *Corpus inscriptionum semiticarum*, nor in any other epigraphic corpus, nor even in the bibliography of Semitic inscriptions (Delavault et al. 2010). The existence of Christo-Palestinian Aramaic texts is not mentioned in the manual by Albert et al. 1993 or in any of the works of Byzantine and Church history.

Even so, the existence of Christo-Palestinian texts has been known for a long time. Texts were published as early as the end of the eighteenth century: starting from Jacob Adler (1780), some real pioneers have discovered, read and edited the Sinai and Cairo manuscripts kept in western European, Russian and private collectors' libraries. The texts were the object of detailed philological and linguistic studies by such researchers as Anton Baumstark, Francis Crawford Burkitt, Matthew Black, and Rubens Duval, who were well aware of the literature and of the enlightening grammar by Friedrich Schulthess (1924). Moshe Bar-Asher (1977) reviewed the manuscripts and offered a number of philological, linguistic and chronological propositions. Alain Desreumaux (1979) proposed a first elementary catalogue of manuscripts and a study of inscriptions. Christa Müller-Kessler (1991) published a modern grammar based on that by Schulthess and on the relevant knowledge of Judaeo-Aramaic, as well as a re-edition of several manuscripts (Müller-Kessler – Sokoloff 1996a, 1996b, 1997, 1999).

Biblical texts in Christo-Palestinian Aramaic have been taken into consideration by New Testament textual critics since the beginning of the twentieth century (for example, in the editions of Augustin Merk, e.g. Merk 1957), yet, as in the presentation of Vaganay (1934), have continued to be designated as one of several Syrian traditions (siglum Syr^{sp})—even though Marie Joseph Lagrange and the Biblical School of Jerusalem (Lagrange 1925) had already detected the autonomy and the historical interest of these versions. In recent decades, these texts have been attracting increasing interest for their linguistic and philological peculiarity;

consider here Bruce Metzger (1977), and the on-going project 'Marc multilingue' (<http://www.safran.be/marcmultilingue/>) directed by Christian Amphoux and Jean-Claude Haelewyck (the Christo-Palestinian versions do not yet appear, pending the integration of the manuscripts from the Sinai New Finds).

The Christo-Palestinian script, written from right to left, was based on the Syriac *ʾesṭrangēlā* script, in the style of biblical Greek uncial.

Judging by the known inscriptions, the distribution area of the Christo-Palestinian Aramaic documents is limited: Egypt, Sinai, Israel, Palestine, Jordan. The archaeological work of the Samra team (Humbert – Desreumaux 1998) and the remarkable historical analysis by Sydney Griffith (1997) brought the communities of Christo-Palestinian Aramaic speakers onto the scene of Late Antiquity in the Byzantine provinces of Palestine and Arabia (today Jordan). The centres of manuscript production were only a few: Jerusalem, Castellion (Hyrcania) in Khirbet Mird (Judaean desert), ʿAbud (Samaria), St Catherine's Monastery on Mount Sinai and probably Antioch (see the map for Syriac below). A palimpsest inscription (under a Coptic painting) was found in the monastery inside the temple at Edfu in Upper Egypt. Manuscripts and inscriptions show that the language was used in common life as a *lingua franca*, in monuments as a public language (churches, monasteries, cemeteries), for liturgical readings as a translation language and as a language of theological works, always within the Chalcedonian communities of the Patriarchs of Jerusalem and Antioch.

References

Adler 1780; Albert et al. 1993; Bar-Asher 1977; Delavault et al. 2010; Desreumaux 1979; Desreumaux – Schmidt 1989; Griffith [S.] 1997; Humbert – Desreumaux 1998; Lagrange 1925; Merk 1957; Metzger 1977; Müller-Kessler – Sokoloff 1996a, 1996b, 1997, 1999; Schulthess 1924; Vaganay 1934. Web sources: <http://www.safran.be/marcmultilingue>, last access May 2014.

3.6. Coptic manuscripts (SE)

The language called 'Coptic' is the latest stage in the long history of the native Egyptian language, which was originally written using the Egyptian hieroglyphs, a large set of signs—partly alphabetic, partly syllabic, partly logographic—that was used also in cursive forms in the Egyptian Hieratic and Demotic writing systems. The writing system of the Coptic period was distinct from the earlier Egyptian systems in that it made use of the Greek alphabet, supplemented from out of the latest indigenous system (Demotic) by a selection of characters representing sounds that were foreign to Greek, there being usually six or seven supplemental characters, depending on dialect (see also Ch. 2 § 4).

What survives of Coptic literature is almost entirely religious in character and predominantly Christian by a wide margin. Along with the Greek alphabet, the Copts also took over the Greek scribal practices as well as the book forms that were typical of Christian Late Antique Egypt, first and foremost the papyrus codex. Almost without exception, Egypt is the provenance of Coptic manuscripts. Unfortunately, 'the extant remains of Coptic literature [are] quite without parallel among the literatures of the Christian east in their fragmentariness and dilapidation' (Crum 1905b, xxi–xxii; see further Emmel 2007). The number of Coptic manuscripts that can be dated with confidence to before the ninth century is not very large, but there are codices of both papyrus and parchment that very likely date from the fourth to sixth centuries, some perhaps from as early as the third century. It is difficult to estimate the precise numbers but we may say that there are at least 4,000 manuscripts and manuscript fragments dating from between the fourth and the eleventh centuries, possibly even a significantly larger number (a complete census remains a desideratum).

The Coptic alphabet developed out of a history of attempts to write the Egyptian language using the Greek alphabet, beginning soon after Alexander the Great's conquest of Egypt toward the end of the fourth century BCE. Thereafter, Egypt became a bilingual country, with Greek becoming the dominant language in politics and educated culture. The hieroglyph-based writing systems fell into disuse during the Roman period (which began with Augustus's conquest of Egypt in 30 BCE), and 'it is fair to say that after about 50 CE there was for most Egyptians only one means of recording things in writing: Greek … For two centuries or so, until the middle of the third century, Egypt witnessed the striking phenomenon of a majority population with no way of recording anything in its own language in writing' (Bagnall 1996, 235–236).

The beginning of the history of 'Coptic literature' is marked by the widespread use of a fully developed and more or less standardized writing system employing the supplemented Greek alphabet for the purpose of writing Egyptian. The term 'Coptic' used for designating the language of this literature is a word that derives from ancient Greek *aigyptios* 'Egyptian', which passed through Coptic itself (as *gyptios*, or *kuptios*) into Egyptian Arabic and from there into the European languages (copto, copte, koptisch etc.). The oldest surviving examples of Coptic writing show clearly that the creators (or standardizers) of the Coptic writing system were thoroughly familiar with the conventions of Greek literary scribal practice, but also appropriately sensitive to features of Coptic that distinguished it sharply from Greek, especially in phonology and syllable structures. By means that are not entirely clear, the Coptic language—especially the literary language—came to borrow a very large number of words from Greek, for the most part adapting the loanwords to Coptic syntax (and sometimes adapting them also orthographically and even morphologically). Thus someone who can read Greek (in the uncial scripts typical of Late Antique literary manuscripts) will be able to 'sound out' a good deal of any Coptic text and will even come across many easily recognizable (Greek) words, without being able to understand even the most basic clauses, for lack of knowledge of Coptic vocabulary and grammar.

Learning to read widely in Coptic literature entails learning multiple dialects, which are distinct from one another not so much in terms of the writing system as such, which remained fairly constant from one dialect region to another, and also through the centuries from Late Antiquity into the Middle Ages, but rather in phonology (especially different vocalizations of identical or closely related words), somewhat less often in morphology, sometimes also in syntax. The greatest number of dialects is attested in manuscripts of the earliest period of Coptic's history, from the fourth (or late third) century up until the time of the Arab Conquest of Egypt in the middle of the seventh century. But even in this early period, one relatively neutral dialect, called 'Sahidic', emerged as a kind of 'standard Coptic' and eventually came to replace the other dialects in the written record of Middle and Upper (southern) Egypt. In Lower (northern) Egypt, two other dialects—'Fayyumic' and 'Bohairic'—became the standard literary dialects, but by this time the Egyptian populace was (for reasons not entirely clear) beginning to give up speaking Coptic in favour of Arabic.

After the fourteenth century, by which time Arabic had replaced Coptic as the medium of spoken communication for nearly all purposes—except in parts of the liturgy of the Coptic Church—Coptic manuscripts were almost always written in the Bohairic dialect, most often with an accompanying Arabic translation. In the present context, 'Coptic manuscripts' are manuscripts that contain, if not exclusively, then at least in large measure, text written in the Coptic language (even if accompanied by texts in Greek or Arabic or any other language). Beginning not long after the turn of the first millennium, Copts had already begun translating selected parts of their ancestral literature into Arabic and composing new theological, pastoral and liturgical texts also in that language. But for the most part, the large number of 'Copto-Arabic' (or 'Egyptian Christian Arabic') manuscripts of the twelfth and later centuries are not treated here, while 'Coptic-Arabic' bilingual manuscripts have been considered as a part of the Coptic manuscript tradition proper.

On the whole, the Coptic-Arabic bilinguals served liturgical or devotional purposes, and so such books continued to be produced even after Coptic had lost almost all chance of ever again being a language of ordinary daily life anywhere. Although printing Coptic with movable type became possible in Europe (specifically in Rome) in 1629, by which time type fonts for Arabic also existed, the Coptic Church in Egypt did not begin printing its bilingual liturgical and devotional books until late in the nineteenth century, at which time the Coptic manuscript tradition proper came to an end.

Surviving Coptic manuscripts from the Middle Ages with a known provenance were mostly preserved in a small number of ancient monasteries, especially those in the Wādī al-Naṭrūn (northwest of Cairo), the Monastery of St Antony on the Red Sea and the Monastery of St Shenoute in Upper Egypt. Not infrequently, the older manuscripts in these repositories survived only as the remains of dismembered books that had long since been discarded and treated as waste paper (or waste parchment). Significant numbers of such manuscripts and fragments were acquired, one way or another, by western missionaries and travelling antiquaries and scholars, beginning in the sixteenth century. Most of the major European national museums and libraries, as well as a number of universities, own at least some Coptic manuscripts. Very large collections outside of Egypt are in Naples (Biblioteca Nazionale), Rome/Vatican (Biblioteca Apostolica Vaticana), Vienna (Österreichische Nationalbibliothek), Paris (Bibliothèque nationale de France), London (British Library) and New York City (Pierpont Morgan Library and Museum); in Egypt, the most salient

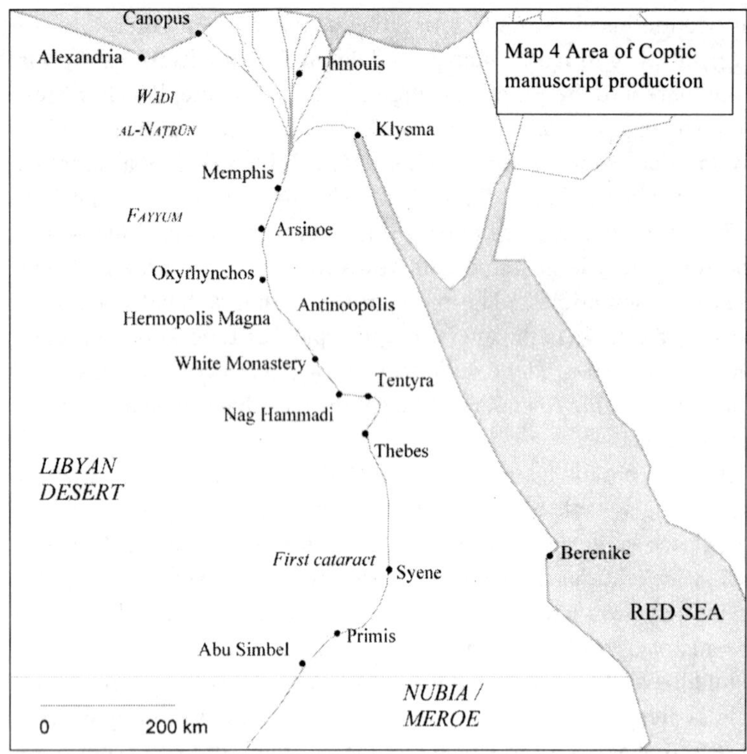

collections are in Cairo (Coptic Museum, Coptic Patriarchate, Institut Français d'Archéologie orientale).

Early mediaeval and also Late Antique Coptic manuscripts, including the earliest surviving papyrus and parchment codices, have been discovered by means of excavation, very often by treasure-hunters rather than by trained archaeologists, for which reason they are often without provenance. Among the large quantities of papyri (sometimes including parchment)—mostly in Greek—that have been excavated from Late Antique and early mediaeval urban sites in Egypt since the beginning of scientific papyrology toward the end of the nineteenth century, there is a relatively small but nonetheless significant amount of Coptic material, some of it literary rather than documentary. Such finds are almost always fragmentary, a description that unfortunately applies in one way or another to the remains of Coptic literature in general. For this reason, much of the study of Coptic manuscripts—whether from the point of view of codicology and palaeography, philology and textual criticism, digitization, cataloguing or preservation—is geared specifically to dealing with fragments, whether they are torn scraps of codex leaves, or leaves deriving from dismembered—and perhaps not otherwise extant—codices, or fragments of some author's otherwise lost work, or a work from an otherwise lost corpus, and so on.

In order for the study of Coptic manuscripts to advance, there is a great need for scholars to organize and to systematize the large quantity of data that has been published during more than two hundred years of scholarship, and to increase the database in a systematic and methodologically informed manner. There is still much basic research to be carried out (in some cases by revising and augmenting work done by previous generations of scholars), both in the form of cataloguing and describing manuscripts—whether in the so often fragmentary condition in which they are now to be found in the many different collections, or as partly notional codices reconstructed from fragments that might now be scattered among any number of those collections—and in the form of publishing the texts. There are Coptic manuscripts that have been in Europe for up to four hundred years and more that have not yet been (properly) published. Editorial practice in connexion with Coptic texts has more or less gone along with the practices of Greek papyrology, which has been both advantageous and disadvantageous for the field of Coptic studies in general. In any case, there is urgent need for clarifying what textually relevant information needs to be drawn from the Coptic manuscripts and how that information should be recorded and presented. The application of digital technology to Coptic texts is partly keeping pace with work in other languages, and there are encouraging signs both of an awareness of the need to coordinate the efforts of widely dispersed Coptologists, and of a willingness to try to do so. Given the amount of basic research and publication that has yet to be accomplished, it should occasion little surprise that methodologically sophisticated textual criticism of Coptic sources, carried out in a systematic and well founded manner, has scarcely begun.

References

Bagnall 1996; Crum 1905b; Emmel 2007; see also Ch. 1 § 5, Ch. 2 § 4.

3.7. Ethiopic manuscripts (ABa)

Writing was adopted by the Semites settled in Ethiopia—meaning the area between the northern highlands of the Horn of Africa and the Red Sea, corresponding to the present-day states of Eritrea and Ethiopia, the northern Tegrāy region of the latter in particular—as early as the first millennium BCE, much earlier than the date of the earliest surviving manuscripts. The existence of an extensive literature going back presumably to the fourth century CE, consisting mostly of Christian biblical and patristic texts translated from Greek, certainly implies the existence and use of manuscripts. Yet there is little positive evidence for the nature of the earliest practices, forms of books or the materials used (see Ch. 1 § 6). Our witnesses for the Aksumite period (first to seventh centuries CE) are mostly inscriptions. While Greek script and language were used for inscriptions and legends on coins, Sabaean script features in some royal inscriptions written in the Ethiopic language as a purely ideological device, neither Greek nor Sabaean are attested in Ethiopian manuscripts. In the second and third centuries CE, inscriptions emerge written in a non-vocalized Ethiopic script. The Ethiopic language (Geʿez) and the vocalized Ethiopic script as they appeared by the fourth century, on the eve of the Christianization of Aksum (mid-fourth century), are, apart from certain specific features, very near to the language and script used later on for centuries as the literary language of the Christian kingdom of Ethiopia. While little or no evidence of interaction with Coptic manuscript culture has been registered so far, there was very strong interaction with the Egyptian Christian Arabic manuscript culture, which played a pivotal role in providing materials and inspiration to the mediaeval and pre-modern Ethiopian literary activity, starting from the thirteenth century at the latest. No interaction is discernible with the coexistent Ethiopian Islamic manuscript culture (see Ch. 4 § 2.1.1.2).

Two parchment codices, the so-called Abbā Garimā Four Gospels manuscripts, recently dated to the sixth century CE at the latest by radiocarbon dating, are believed to be the earliest surviving Ethiopic manuscripts and provide evidence that the codex form was introduced and used early (see Ch. 1 § 6.2.3). They are all the more important since they are also decorated with paintings. In keeping with this evidence, as early as the ninth century CE an Arab tradition connects the word *muṣḥaf*, meaning 'Qurʾān book in codex form', to the Ethiopians, to whom the invention of this book form is attributed. In fact the Arabic term *muṣḥaf* was borrowed from Ethiopic *maṣḥaf*, that is 'book' or 'writing' in all its possible meanings (Sergew Hable Selassie 1981; Bausi 2008a, 521–524).

At present, there is no evidence suggesting any use of scrolls prior to the introduction of the codex in Ethiopia (see also Ch. 1 § 6.2.2), and, consequently, nothing to suggest that there was a passage from one form to the other as it happened, for example, for Greek.

Particularly remarkable in the Ethiopic manuscript culture is the use of manuscripts (particularly Four Gospels manuscripts, so-called 'Golden Gospels') to preserve notes regarding the institution (usually a monastery or a church), the place or the region where the codex was kept. Such notes may be inserted in empty spaces or on blank leaves and/or copied onto separate leaves or quires that were then later bound into the codex (Bausi 2010e; Fiaccadori 2014).

There are only approximate estimates of the number of Ethiopic manuscripts in the Eritrean and Ethiopian regions. The distribution of manuscripts across this vast territory, with a very limited concentration in bigger central institutions and an extremely marked tendency to wide dissemination, is a feature that seems to go back to the time of the establishment of the first monastic settlements in the Late Antique period and that was perpetuated in mediaeval and later periods. This situation means a substantial density of manuscripts also in rural and isolated areas and hinders any attempt to get a precise and comprehensive view of the total number of manuscripts that still exist. The rough estimate of 200,000 extant manuscripts in codex form (that is excluding scrolls; see Sergew Hable Selassie 1981, 35) is based on the assumption that the minimum number of manuscripts necessary for every church for religious services amounts to a few dozen. Given the number of present-day parishes ranging from at least 13,000 to 32,350, the larger average number of manuscripts preserved in the libraries surveyed in the past years, and the persistent use of older as well as new manuscripts along with printed books, this calculation seems probably underestimated. Monastic libraries also have not yet been systematically explored: the figures of approximately 200 manuscripts for Dabra Ḥayq Esṭifānos, around 570 manuscripts for Dabra Bizan, formerly approximately 800 and now approximately 220 manuscripts for Gunda Gundē, around 1,000 in the Patriarchate and several hundred at least for the churches of Dabra Mārqos, Čalaqot, or the cathedral church of Aksum Ṣeyon may provide some hints. The two largest modern Ethiopian libraries of major institutional importance are found in Addis Ababa, the Library of the Institute of Ethiopian Studies and the National Archives and Library of Ethiopia. They have rich manuscript collections, approximately 1,500 and 850 manuscripts, respectively, which are, however, on the same scale as is typical of a very rich monastic library.

Map 5 Centres of Ethiopic manuscript production

By far the majority of Ethiopian manuscripts were produced in the Christian Kingdom of Ethiopia, with the exception of a few small, but not insignificant Ethiopian monastic communities in Egypt (where several Coptic monasteries hosted Ethiopian monks), Palestine (Jerusalem), Cyprus, and Rome. The manuscript production of these communities reflected to some extent their respective environments, and is, for example, marked by a more extensive use of paper instead of parchment, as can be seen from the figures of the older Vatican and Borgian collections, where the ratio of paper manuscripts to parchment manuscripts is much higher than the average value in indigenous collections, which is close to zero (Grébaut – Tisserant 1935, 1936, with 283 described entries and 55 paper manuscripts, with a peak in the sixteenth and seventeenth centuries of 22 paper manuscripts out of 46 manuscripts in total, that is 47.82%).

As appears from approximate estimates, in the absence of any comprehensive and reliable statistics, the large majority of the extant Ethiopic manuscripts does not antedate the seventeenth century. Manuscripts antedating the sixteenth century are rare, and older ones are extremely or even exceptionally rare. Actually it must be emphasized that—excepting the two Abbā Garimā Gospels and less than a handful of possibly twelfth-century examples—only for the period from the thirteenth century to the present do we have a substantial continuum in the evidence. The scarcity of older Ethiopic manuscripts is attributed by Ethiopian tradition, not without reason, mainly to the disruptions caused by the Muslim occupation of historically Christian areas in the mid-sixteenth century. Massive damage also occurred during the Ethiopian-Italian war of 1935–1941, which destroyed approximately 2,000 churches. On the other hand, manuscript books remained the norm of book production until the first half of the twentieth century and the practice of making manuscript books still exists at present. As a consequence, along with codicological, palaeographic, and philological analysis, ethnographic observations may also be taken into consideration (Mellors – Parsons 2002a, 2002b), provided, of course, that one remains aware that practices need not have been the same all across the centuries.

The vast majority of Ethiopic manuscripts that have been investigated and published so far are found outside Ethiopia and Eritrea. The number of manuscripts abroad may amount to several thousand, most of them described in printed catalogues (Beylot – Rodinson 1995, Wion et al. 2006, Bausi 2007; see also Ch. 4 § 4). The four largest collections in Europe are those of the Biblioteca Apostolica Vaticana, the Bibliothèque nationale de France, the British Library and the Staatsbibliothek Preußischer Kulturbesitz, Orientabteilung, in Berlin. The Vatican Library, which was the first collection to be catalogued in printed form, has 1,082 manuscripts, at the least, plus the largest collection of Ethiopian scrolls in the world. The Bibliothèque nationale de France has over 1,000 manuscripts, including scrolls. The British Library has at least 624 manuscripts. The Staatsbibliothek in Berlin preserves 328 manuscripts plus an important microfilm collection of 182 items from the Lake Ṭānā monasteries. Other European and North American institutions hold important collections of Ethiopic manuscripts (Manchester, Oxford, Frankfurt, Munich, St Petersburg, Moscow, Uppsala, Oslo, Florence, Milan, Parma, Rome (besides the Vatican), Athens, Princeton, Baltimore, etc.). Very important are also the collections hosted in Jerusalem, with probably more than 800 manuscripts (569 preserved in the Ethiopian Archbishopric of Jerusalem, 162 in the monasteries of Dabra Gannat and 33 in that of Dayr al-Sulṭān).

As far as microfilms are concerned, the collection of the Ethiopian Manuscript Microfilm Library (EMML), with 9,238 manuscripts, is the most important one. The first 5,000 items have been catalogued in printed form and another volume is forthcoming. The EMML collection is hosted by the Hill Museum and Manuscript Library (HMML), Saint John's University, Collegeville, Minnesota, which has grown in the course of the last four decades into a major centre for the study, recording, digitization, and cataloguing of Ethiopic manuscripts (among others). It has recently digitized several important collections (for example, the monastic library of Gunda Gundē). More digitization efforts have been sponsored by the Arcadia Fund within the framework of the Endangered Archives Programme (EAP) of the British Library. *Mazgaba seelat*, Deeds Project, University of Toronto, stores several thousand images and historical collections of interest to art historians. The *Ethiopian Manuscript Imaging Project* (EMIP), started in 2005 and has located and digitized scattered smaller collections in the possession of university libraries, dealers and private owners, mostly in North America, but also in England, Israel and Kenya. Quite recently, starting from 2009, the European Research Council-sponsored project *Ethio-SPaRe: Cultural Heritage of Christian Ethiopia: Salvation, Preservation, Research*, University of Hamburg, has acquired high quality digital images of more than 2,000 Ethiopic manuscripts from the area of particular historical importance of eastern Tegrāy, in northern Ethiopian highlands (Nosnitsin 2013a, 2013c).

References

Bausi 2007, 2008a, 2010e; Beylot – Rodinson 1995; Fiaccadori 2014; Grébaut – Tisserant 1935, 1936; Mellors – Parsons 2002a, 2002b; Nosnitsin 2013a, 2013c; Sergew Hable Selassie 1981; Uhlig – Bausi 2007; Wion et al. 2006.

3.8. Georgian manuscripts (JG)

Although autochthonous historiography claims that writing was adopted by the Georgians as early as the third century BCE, there is no proof so far that their language was given written form before the conversion to Christianity in the fourth–fifth centuries CE, all written documents of older times being either Greek or Aramaic (or in both languages side by side, as in the famous bilingual inscription of Armazi of the first century CE; Çereteli 1941; Gippert – Tandaschwili 1999). The oldest extant sources written in Georgian are stone inscriptions of the fifth century discovered in the Monastery of the Cross near Jerusalem (inscription of *c.*452; Çereteli 1960; Gippert – Tandaschwili 2002) and in the cathedral of Bolnisi in Lower Kartli (South-East Georgia; inscription of around 493; Musxelišvili 1938, 325–343; Gippert – Tandaschwili 1999–2002; Gippert 2014a); the script used is the fully developed Old Georgian majuscule named *mrglovani*, 'round [script]', which was also the sole script used in the first centuries of the Georgian manuscript tradition up to about the ninth century. A minuscule variant derived from it, named *nusxuri* 'manuscript [script]' or *nusxa-xucuri* 'ecclesiastical [script] of manuscripts', appeared by about the same time, with majuscules continuing to be used as initials, in titles, and the like (*asomtavruli*, lit. 'capital letter[s]'). The combination of *nusxuri* and *asomtavruli* remained in use in religious writings up to the nineteenth century, whereas in secular contexts (but also in colophons), a cursive variant of the minuscule has been used since about the tenth century; this latter script, named *mxedruli* 'knights' [script]', is the one still in use today. With but few exceptions, the Georgian scripts were used only for the Georgian language in manuscripts. Exceptions are, among others, Greek *incipits* of hymns transcribed into Georgian (Gippert 2014b), sporadic cases of a sister language of Georgian, Svan, appearing in secondary notes of a mediaeval Gospel manuscript (Gippert 2013, 101–102), or a seventeenth century Turkish Bible written in *mxedruli* (hitherto unpublished, but see Luffin 2014).

The Georgian manuscript tradition, which developed continuously for about 1,500 years since the invention of the Georgian script and which is attested by about 75,000 manuscript leaves that survive until the present day, has proven to be extremely valuable as a witness of both Christian religious thought and Near Eastern narrative skill; it has preserved a noteworthy amount of early versions of the Gospels and hagiographical, homiletic, and hymnographic texts, mostly translated from Greek. In spite of their importance, Georgian manuscripts have remained under-studied in many respects, especially concerning their history, structure, and composition. Many of the observations assembled in the present handbook must therefore be regarded as preliminary.

The oldest dated Georgian manuscript known so far is the manuscript 32-57-33+N89 of the Georgian collection of St Catherine's Monastery on Mount Sinai, a multiple-text parchment codex (*mravaltavi* 'multi-headed'; Gippert forthcoming) in *mrglovani* script written in St Sabas' Laura near Jerusalem in

863/864 (Šaniʒe 1959). However, there are clear indications of greater age in many other Georgian manuscripts. This is especially true of the so-called *xanmeṭi* and *haemeṭi* periods covering approximately the fifth to eighth centuries, which are characterized by the occurrence of special verbal and nominal affixes consisting of the letters *x* (*kh*) and *h*. Nearly all manuscripts exhibiting these traits have come down to us only in palimpsest form; an exception is the famous 'Sinai Lectionary', which represents an intermediate stage with both *xanmeṭi* and *haemeṭi* forms occurring side by side (Šaniʒe 1944; Imnaišvili 2004, 47–69; Gippert et al. 2007b; Gippert et al. 2007a, xxvi n. 89; see below). Another guide to the (relative) chronology of undated Old Georgian manuscripts is palaeography (Gippert et al. 2007a, xxvi; see Ch. 2 § 6).

Nearly all manuscript codices that have come down to us from the Old Georgian period (up to the thirteenth century) have religious contents, which implies that they were written by clergymen, in churches or monasteries, either in what may be styled the Georgian homeland (south of the Caucasus) or elsewhere in the Christian Near East. The most crucial role in the early centuries was played by Jerusalem, where Georgian monks had settled as early as the fifth century; the Monastery of the Cross, erected there by Georgians in the eleventh century, was dissolved only at the end of the nineteenth century when its library was taken over by the Greek patriarchate. Other centres of the production of Georgian manuscripts abroad were St Catherine's Monastery on Mount Sinai, where Georgians worked continuously between about the ninth and the fourteenth centuries, and the monastery of Iviron ('Iberians', i.e. Georgians' [monastery]') on Mount Athos, which was founded by Georgians in the tenth century. Among the 'autochthonous' centres of Georgian manuscript production, the most outstanding were the provinces of Ṭao-Ḳlarǯeti and Šavšeti in eastern Anatolia, both now belonging to Turkey. There are clear indications that all these centres kept close contacts with each other throughout the Middle Ages.

Manuscript codices with non-religious content came into being by the beginning of the thirteenth century, one of the oldest specimens being a paper codex containing, among other things, the Georgian translation of an Arabic astrological treatise (Ḳaranaʒe et al. 2010, 39). The same century witnessed the Georgians' endeavour to participate in the philosophical dispute about the neo-Platonism of the time, with the schools of Gelati (in West Georgia) and Iq̇alto (in East Georgia) producing relevant manuscript books. While all these books were still written in ecclesiastical *nusxuri*, the secular *mxedruli* was used in codices containing the products of both original and translated poetry and prose literature, among them Shota Rustaveli's epic *Vepxisṭq̇aosani* ('The One [knight] in the Panther's Skin'), the Georgian adaptation of Gurgānī's Persian romance of *Vīs u Rāmīn* (*Visramiani*), and other specimens of courtly literature. Different from the religious (Christian) tradition that visibly linked the Old Georgian production of manuscripts to the Byzantine world, the secular tradition was strongly influenced by Islamic or, more precisely, Persian models, a fact that is evident not only from the textual contents, but also from the layout of the manuscripts, the illustrations they contain, and other features (Gippert – Tandaschwili 2014, 11–12). With the introduction of printing in the middle of the eighteenth century, the production of manuscript books in Georgia started to decrease gradually, and it reached its end during the second half of the nineteenth century.

Only in rare cases have Georgian manuscript books been preserved where they were originally written. This is true, for example, of the major part of the Georgian manuscript collection of St Catherine's Monastery on Mount Sinai, which comprises around 250 catalogued codices (the actual number is considerably smaller due to losses and due to the fact that several items of the so-called New Finds of 1975 actually belong, as fragments, to codices registered earlier). Other collections that have remained in their original locations are those of the Iviron Monastery on Mount Athos (*c.*85 items) and of the Monastery of the Holy Cross in Jerusalem (*c.*160 items, now kept in the Greek patriarchate). On the other hand, most of the manuscripts that were produced in Georgia and eastern Anatolia have been assembled in four collections now hosted in the National Centre of Manuscripts in Tbilisi ('A': the collection of the former Ecclesiastical Museum; 'H': the collection of the former Museum of the Georgian Society for History and Ethnography; 'Q': the collection of the State Museum of Georgia; 'S': the collection of the former Society for the Promotion of Literacy among the Georgian Population; altogether *c.*9,000 codices; <http://www.manuscript.ge/index.php?m=73&ln=eng>, last access 2014). Minor collections within Georgia are those of the Historico-ethnographical Museum in Kutaisi (*c.*700 items), the Museum of Axalcixe (*c.*75 items), the Historico-ethnographical Museum in Gori, and the Historico-ethnographical Museum in Mestia. Three mediaeval manuscript codices (two evangeliaries, one lectionary) are known to have remained in the possession of mountain villages in the highlands of Svanetia (Kurashi, Lakhamula, Lakhushdi), where they are kept in the village churches (Gippert 2013).

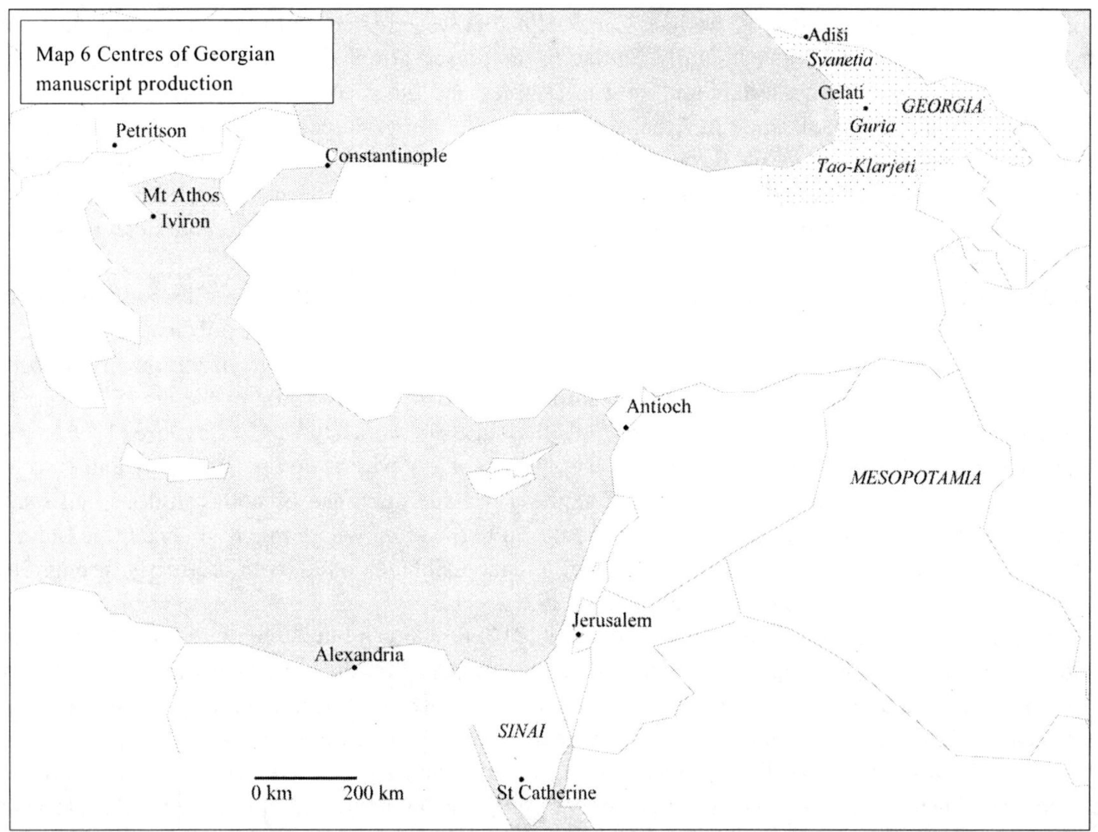

Map 6 Centres of Georgian manuscript production

Apart from the 'authentic' repositories, Georgian manuscripts are found throughout the world, in consequence of their removal mostly from Jerusalem and Mount Sinai. Noteworthy collections are hosted in Graz, Austria, Universitätsbibliothek (including the 'Sinai Lectionary' of about the seventh or eighth century, mentioned already above, MS 2058/1); Vienna, Österreichische Nationalbibliothek (including one of the most remarkable palimpsest codices originating from Jerusalem, Cod.Vind.georg. 2; Gippert et al. 2007a); Paris, Bibliothèque nationale de France; Leipzig, Universitätsbibliothek; Oxford, Bodleian Library; Birmingham, England, Cadbury Research Library, the Mingana Collection; Washington, DC, the Library of Dumbarton Oaks; and St Petersburg, Biblioteka Instituta Vostokovedenija Rossijskoj Akademii Nauk. Fragments of Georgian manuscripts that were reused as flyleaves or the like in non-Georgian codices are found, for example, in the Matenadaran in Yerevan, Armenia (Gippert – Outtier 2009), in the library of the Armenian monastery in New Julfa near Isfāhān, Iran (Outtier 2013) and in the Armenian patriarchate in Jerusalem (Outtier 1986).

References

Çereteli 1941, 1960; Gippert 2013, 2014a, 2014b, forthcoming; Gippert et al. 2007a; Gippert – Outtier 2009; Imnaišvili 2004; Ķaranaʒe et al. 2010; Luffin 2014; Musxelišvili 1938; Outtier 1986, 2013; Šaniʒe 1944, 1959; Web sources: Gippert et al. 2007b; Gippert – Tandaschwili 1999–2002, 2014; Tbilisi, National Centre of Manuscripts, <http://www.manuscript.ge/index.php?m=73&ln=eng>, last access 29 November 2014.

3.9. Greek manuscripts (MMa)

The history of Greek manuscript books extends over a long time span, from classical Greece to at least one and a half centuries beyond the invention of western printing in the mid-fifteenth century. In terms of geography, Greek and Byzantine book making is not confined to Ancient Greece and Constantinople: depending on the time and historical events, it extends to Armenia, Georgia, Syria, islands of the eastern Mediterranean such as Cyprus or Crete, Greece with the monasteries of Mount Athos, the Slavonic nations of the Balkans and Russia, St Catherine's Monastery on Mount Sinai, Egypt, and both southern and northern Italy (see also Ch. 2 § 7).

The existence of books in the Greek language and script may be inferred from written sources, vase paintings and isolated and fragmentary examples (see Ch. 1 § 8 and Ch. 2 § 7) in fifth-century BCE Greece, that is some three centuries after the archaic Greek alphabet was created on the model of the Phoenician alphabet. The use of writing was originally limited to the preservation of mainly religious or administrative texts, recorded on hard materials and kept in temples and other archives; the oldest evidence concerning book-rolls and a book trade in Athens's marketplace and civic centre (*agora*) dates from to the fourth century BCE (Plato, *Apol.* 26). Between the Hellenistic period and Late Antiquity, papyrus (and also parchment) rolls achieved wide diffusion in the Graeco-Roman world: eastern and western *volumina* bear witness to a common ground of manufacturing practices, with some structural differences clearly standing out (Turner 1977).

The long-term transition from roll to codex started at the beginning of the Christian era and was fully accomplished between the fourth and fifth centuries CE: it preceded a period of political, economic and cultural decline, caused by the disintegration of the political and administrative structures of the Roman Empire. The consequences were also felt in Byzantium, from 324 CE the capital of the new Christian empire, where literacy remained quite widespread until the Turkish conquest in 1453, favoured by the extent and pervasiveness of the imperial bureaucracy. Byzantine society was in fact pervaded by a deep-rooted 'bookish mentality' (Cavallo 1982, xi): the existence of a wide audience of both religious and secular readers ensured the transmission of the Classical cultural heritage on which much of Byzantine literature was based; illiterates, to whom books were personally inaccessible, enjoyed them indirectly through liturgical rites, where the Bible was exhibited (Cavallo 2006).

Most scribes were monks (Cutler 1981; Ronconi 2012, 661–663); but Byzantine monastic book production, unlike its Latin counterpart, rarely took on an organized form, the most renowned exception being the metropolitan Monastery of Saint John the Baptist of Stoudios, founded in the mid-fifth century, where reading and writing activities were regulated by the monastic constitution (*typikon*: *PG* 99, 273 B–C; 119, 1740 C–D). More individualistic modes of monastic experience prevailed, such as those practised on Mount Athos, where the monks lived in independent groups or families; only a few large monasteries are known to have housed a significant library with books beyond the everyday liturgical necessities, usually a simple room where books were kept together with other objects.

Byzantine society knew of no strict separation between secular and monastic circles: monks could maintain relations with the outside world and many lay people—even high-ranking ones, including some emperors—might end their life in a monastery. Books were never produced for the exclusive use of religious circles, as was the case with many Latin *scriptoria*: monasteries could receive book commissions from the outside world, as part of a range of secular and monastic scribal performance, which also involved laymen (school teachers, notaries, major and minor scholars…) and occasionally also women. In the Late Byzantine period books might also be written in collaboration by several hands within specific scholarly circles, which has led it to be supposed that manuscript copying was a kind of learned activity, in the form of a collective appropriation of the transcribed texts (Cavallo 2001a, 2004c). Greek scholars of the fourteenth to sixteenth centuries were often active as scribes (Cavallo 1982; Hunger 1989; Reynolds – Wilson 1991; Wilson [N.] 1983, 1992; Waring 2010).

The lack of local writing schools and the interdependence between the secular and monastic worlds are reflected in the highly homogeneous material and scribal features of Byzantine books: at variance with the Latin west, specific artisanal and graphic patterns, styles and trends are more the exception than the rule, and they can only rarely be referred to a given centre or area. Apart from being poorly marked by local peculiarities, Byzantine books exhibit from Late Antiquity until at least the twelfth century (and in some ways even later) a substantial stability in their methods of manufacture, being a mirror of the conservatism that permeated Byzantine civilization. The fact that the scholars acting as book scribes were sometimes the same people who performed public functions may result in a clear osmosis between book and documentary scripts, especially from the eleventh century onwards.

The Greek codices that have come down to us are an essential source for the knowledge of ancient Greek and Byzantine civilization; and yet, as with all other manuscript cultures, we lack reliable estimates of both the quantity of the original Greek manuscript production and of the share of it that survives. The figure of over 65,000 volumes recently calculated in the course of the Diktyon project (<http://www.diktyon.org/en>) is compatible with the estimate of 55,000 volumes suggested by Alphonse Dain (1949, 1975); these and any such figures are most likely to remain merely approximate, given the absence of information on the number of codicological units composing each extant volume. Only twenty-five out of something more than six hundred libraries or collections (*c.*4%) possess more than 400 codices, while

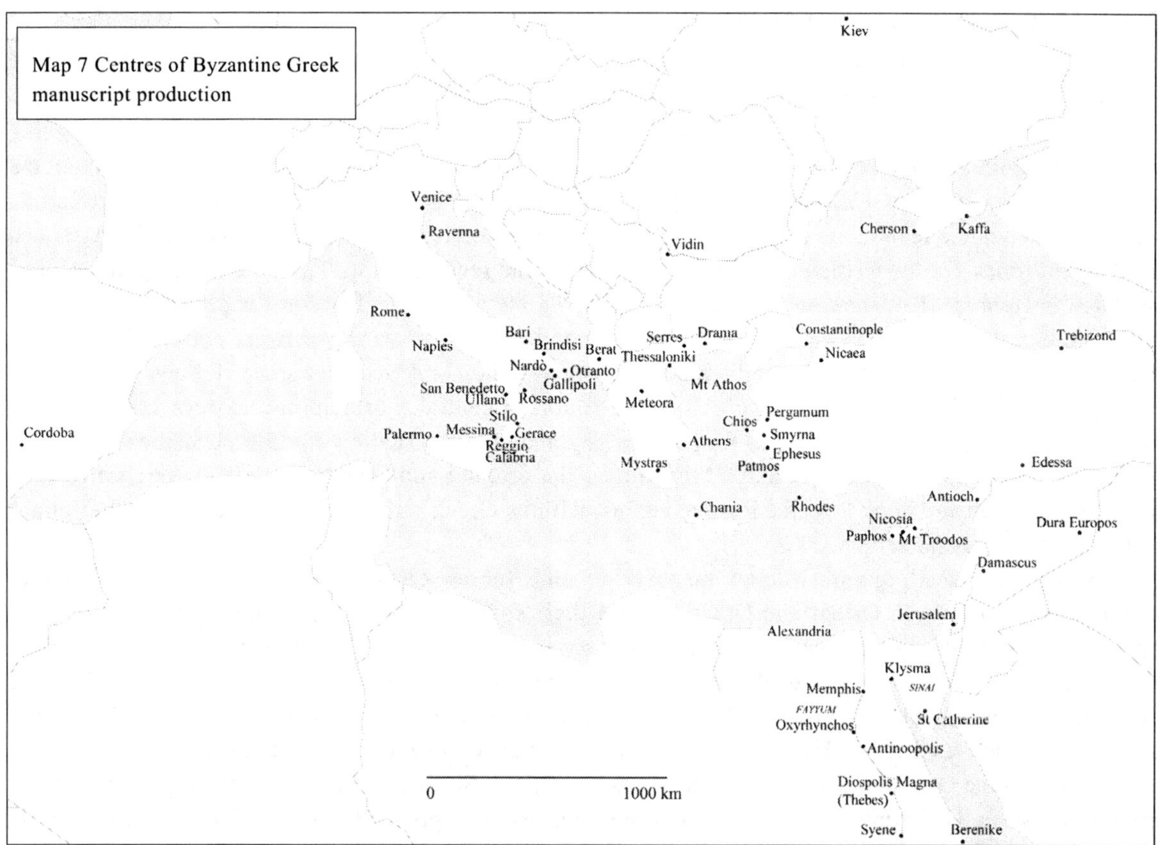

Map 7 Centres of Byzantine Greek manuscript production

about 230 (i.e. more than one third) own only a single codex. In Italy, the number of Greek manuscripts written in or preserved in Europe during the centuries preceding the fall of Constantinople was enriched by those that were brought or produced in the fourteenth and fifteenth centuries by Greek and Latin scholars who were responsible for the creation of the major Italian collections of Greek manuscripts still owned by the most important libraries of the Italian peninsula (among which are the Biblioteca Apostolica Vaticana, the Biblioteca Nazionale Marciana in Venice, and the Biblioteca Medicea Laurenziana in Florence). Similarly, in northern Europe, rich collections of Greek manuscripts began to develop between the sixteenth and seventeenth centuries: in Paris, London, and Oxford, and in Germany and Russia. In the east, large and still largely unexplored collections survived the Turkish conquest in the monasteries of Mount Athos and Meteora, or on various Greek islands. The manuscript collections of Athens, Mount Athos, the Biblioteca Apostolica Vaticana, and the Bibliothèque nationale de France in Paris, in this order, represent the richest collections, ranging from over 5,500 to about 3,600. Normally, though with significant exceptions, the quality of Greek manuscript catalogues (even some of the oldest ones) is acceptable or fairly good as far as the contents are concerned, but very heterogeneous with regard to the material features of the codices (Canart 2010; see Ch. 4 § 6).

Originally, it was sacred literature that was dominant among the contents of Greek codices (and is probably even more dominant among the surviving codices than was the case during much of the history of Greek manuscript book production). As is well known (and confirmed by the results of research centred on the ninth to twelfth centuries), liturgy, homilies and biblical exegesis are the best-represented categories throughout the ages; the Bible (both Old and New Testaments) is also constantly present, and only exceptionally contained in a single volume; more frequently it is divided into various volumes containing more or less standard combinations of books. Secular (Classical and Byzantine, literary and technical) production constitute, in all ages, a minority, probably less than ten per cent of the total quantity of books that were produced.

References

Canart 2010; Cavallo 1982, 2001a, 2004c, 2006; Cutler 1981; Dain 1949, 1975; Hunger 1989; Reynolds – Wilson 1991 (first ed. 1968); Ronconi 2012; Turner 1977; Waring 2010; Wilson [N.] 1983, 1992; <http://www.diktyon.org/en>, last access June 2014; see also Ch. 1 § 8, Ch. 2 § 7 and Ch. 4 § 6.

3.10. Hebrew manuscripts (MBA)

The position of Hebrew manuscripts among oriental traditions or definition is intricate. Hebrew is, of course, a Semitic language and Hebrew codices are written in a Semitic script. The Palaeo-Hebrew alphabet—a local variant of the Phoenician script, for which there is epigraphic evidence in Palestine going back to the tenth century BCE—was replaced by a Jewish variant of the Aramaic script adopted since the third century BCE in Syria, Palestine and Egypt; its most abundant attestation is the Judaean Desert Scrolls and associated documents. Ever since, this Hebrew script continued to be used, into the Middle Ages and until recent times, for the writing of Hebrew manuscripts and records, as well as for other languages when rendered in Hebrew characters, most notably Arabic. Yet due to historical circumstances, Jewish communities were scattered around the Mediterranean basin and farther eastward, westward and northward. The spread of the Hebrew script blurs the distinction between Orient and Occident since Hebrew manuscripts were produced in Yemen and the Maghreb in the south, in central, northern and eastern Europe to the north, eastward in Central Asia and as far west as England, and the Hebrew tradition became surrounded by the book civilizations of Islam and Christianity—the oriental and Occidental Islamic territories with their Arabic script and book lore, the Byzantine East with its Greek script, the Latin west, and other minor oriental languages and scripts.

Consequently, dealing with Hebrew manuscripts and Hebrew codicology inevitably involves manuscripts produced in both Orient and Occident, and their codicological and palaeographical typology is bound to relate to the typologies of the major host zones. Bridged by a shared script, a common culture and literature, as well as certain scribal traditions, Hebrew manuscripts are nonetheless separated by the different environments which affected the codicological practices of their makers. A considerable number of what must be classified as Hebrew manuscripts were written in Judaeo-Arabic using Hebrew characters, mainly in the Orient, but also in North Africa and Spain. Similarly, while Hebrew manuscripts were produced also in the Latin west, some of these western manuscripts in Hebrew characters are written in European vernacular languages, such as Yiddish (Judaeo-German; see also Ch. 4 § 2.7).

Between the rich finds of Hebrew books from Late Antiquity—namely the Dead Sea Scrolls and the fragments from the Qumran caves and the Judaean Desert, dating from the Hellenistic and early Roman

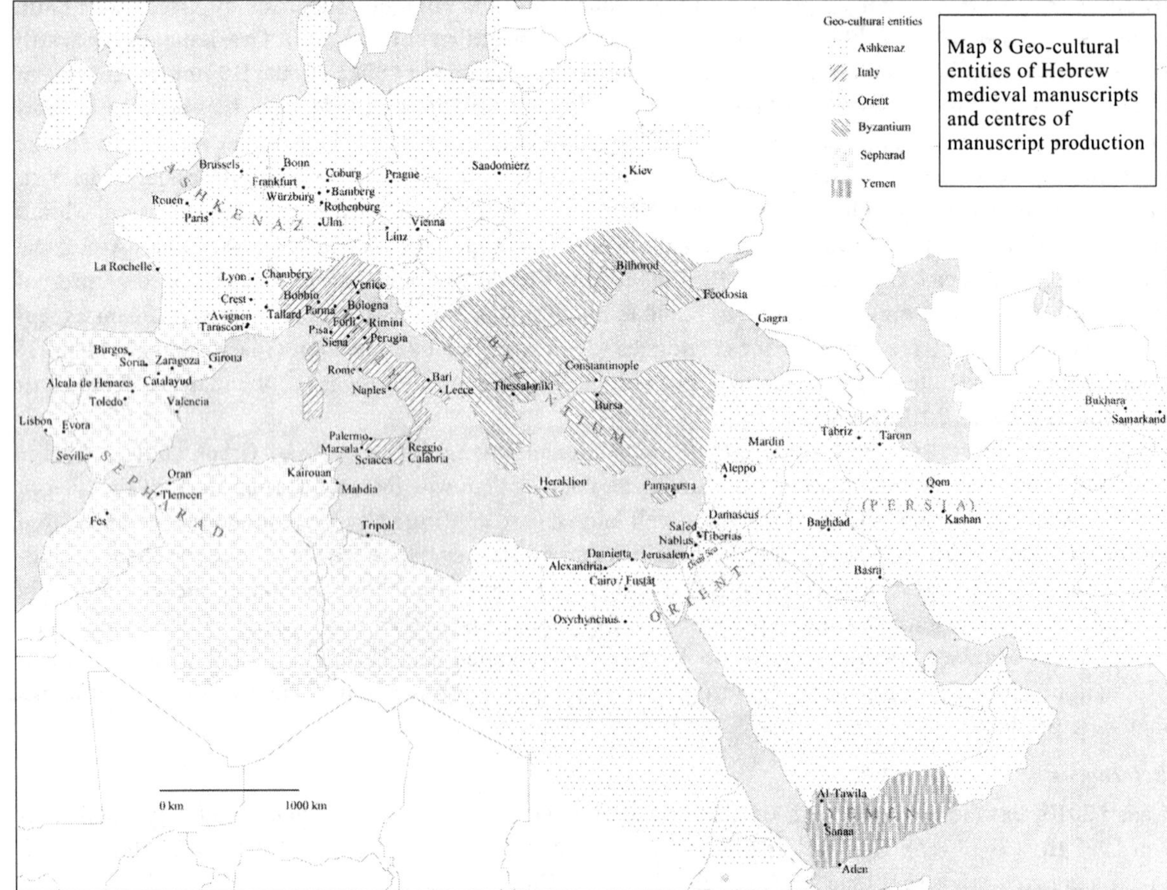

Map 8 Geo-cultural entities of Hebrew medieval manuscripts and centres of manuscript production

periods—and the earliest dated and datable surviving Hebrew codices, there is a salient gap of some eight hundred years with almost no extant evidence of the Hebrew book. Of the few dozen existing literary fragments dating from this gap, mainly papyri of the Byzantine period excavated in Egypt, not one derives from a codex, as post-biblical literature was mainly transmitted orally. The codex was adopted by the Jews in the Orient much later than it had come to be used by the Christians, not before the eighth century, or following the Islamic expansion. The number of the extant Hebrew codices, mostly mediaeval, is about 100,000 (including many composite manuscripts), plus more than 300,000 fragments, kept in some eight hundred collections, mainly in Europe.

Dated codices have survived from the beginning of the tenth century and thereafter, while some undated ones can be assigned to the ninth century. Thus the codicological typology of the mediaeval Hebrew manuscripts, based on the documentation *in situ* of almost all the extant explicitly dated manuscripts—more than 3,000 codicological units documented in 3,400 records, as each hand of a multi-hand manuscript was recorded separately, about half of them with indication of locality—is confined to the central and late Middle Ages.

The following statistics derive from SfarData <http://www.sfardata.nli.org.il>, the codicological database of the Hebrew Palaeography Project sponsored by The Israel Academy of Sciences and Humanities:

Corpus	*palaeographical units*	*codicological units (codices)*
Explicitly dated manuscripts until 1540 studied *in situ*	3142	2777
Unstudied dated manuscripts (partially recorded)	258	249
Unlocated or lost dated manuscripts	179	179
Extant dated manuscripts	3400	3026
Disqualified dated manuscripts	85	85
Studied undated colophoned or named manuscripts	1176	1068
Unstudied undated manuscripts, partially recorded	430	417
Total Hebrew manuscripts documented *in situ*	4318	3845
Selected dated and localized documents	1181	
Dated and localized paper Arabic manuscripts	143	143
Total records	6705	5029

References see Ch. 1 § 9; Ch. 2 § 8.

3.11. Slavonic manuscripts (RMC)

'Formerly', says a ninth-century writer known as the monk Chrabr, 'the Slavs had no writing, being pagan, but used marks and incisions for reckoning and divination; but when they were baptized, they were forced to write Slavonic with Greek and Latin letters, unsystematically (*bez ustroenija*)'. This short sentence indicates both the close connexion between writing and Christianity in the history of the Slavs, and that a genuine native tradition of literacy begins with the introduction of a native alphabet. There are early Slavonic inscriptions written with Greek letters, and the Latin-script manuscript known as the Freising Fragments (Munich, Bayerische Staatsbibliothek, Clm 6426, ff. 78, 158–161), written *c.*1000, probably testifies to a writing tradition that goes back to the activities of Frankish missionaries in Carinthia in the eighth century, but they are indeed unsystematic, as far as rendering the sounds of Slavonic is concerned, and peripheral to the writing cultures to which they belong, in which the normal languages of the written word are Greek and Latin. A distinctively 'Slavonic' tradition of literacy begins only with the invention of a writing system designed specifically for the Slavonic language—attributable beyond reasonable doubt to the work of St Cyril in 863—and it embraces only some of the Slavonic peoples. Those who received Christianity from the Franks received at the same time the tradition of Latin literacy, to which their vernaculars, like those of Western Europe, remained subordinate throughout the period of the manuscript book.

The alphabet devised for the Moravian mission conducted by St Cyril and his brother St Methodius is that which has come to be known as Glagolitic (see Ch. 2 § 9). The basic order of the letters follows that of Greek and Hebrew, but a large proportion of the characters have no equivalent in either of those alphabets. The actual shapes of the letters, however, are original: despite numerous attempts to trace their antecedents, no scholarly consensus has ever been reached. It is generally agreed that nothing survives from the time of SS Cyril and Methodius, and that the earliest extant manuscripts must have been written at the end of the tenth or beginning of the eleventh century.

From the beginning, Glagolitic writing was closely connected with the Slavonic liturgy, and in consequence, when after the death of St Methodius in 885 the Slavonic liturgy was abolished in Moravia, the Glagolitic tradition there came to an end. (It was to be briefly revived in the Czech lands in the eleventh and fourteenth centuries.) It is possible that the Slavonic liturgy had been known in Bulgaria (and in the less politically organized lands between Bulgaria and the Adriatic) even before 885, and it is recorded that the Slavonic clergy expelled from Moravia shortly afterwards found a ready welcome there. Towards the end of the ninth century the Slavonic liturgy was adopted as its normal rite by the Bulgarian Church (which since the official conversion of the country in 864 had used Greek). However, the 'exotic' Glagolitic alphabet was evidently a stumbling block to the educated aristocracy in the Bulgarian capital of Preslav, already thoroughly immersed in Byzantine culture. The result was the development of Cyrillic, with letter shapes very closely based on Greek uncials (see Ch. 2 § 9). The Glagolitic tradition appears to have been maintained in western Bulgaria and Serbia until the middle or latter part of the twelfth century, but with the establishment of the Second Bulgarian Empire and the emergence of a united Serbian state (and later the Serbian national Church under St Sava), Cyrillic became the normal writing system in these areas. Thereafter, Glagolitic was confined to those areas of Croatia (along the Dalmatian littoral and on certain islands in the Adriatic) where a vernacular liturgy of the Western rite was maintained. The last Glagolitic service book was printed at Rome in 1905, and Glagolitic can still occasionally be seen used as a decorative alphabet.

Cyrillic was dominant in eastern Bulgaria from its inception and was also adopted by the Eastern Slavs at their conversion in the late tenth century. The Rumanians also used Cyrillic, having adopted Church Slavonic as their liturgical language and Middle Bulgarian as their chancery language (the earliest documents date from the fourteenth century); Cyrillic continued to be used for writing Rumanian until the nineteenth century.

It is evident that both Glagolitic and Cyrillic writing emerged from the Byzantine tradition—the former the invention of a Greek, and the latter in the cultural penumbra of the Empire. Paradoxically, the older of the two is the more modern in Byzantine terms: the layout and preparation of the oldest Glagolitic manuscripts show distinct affinities with Greek minuscule manuscripts of the ninth and tenth centuries, whereas those written in Cyrillic evidently depend on a more conservative local uncial tradition. The earliest examples of both types of manuscript may be studied in conjunction with the contemporary Byzantine book, with which they share many features in terms of their codicology (see Ch. 1 § 10), writing practice and (for Cyrillic at least) palaeography. Subsequently, however, Glagolitic book culture grew closer to that of Western Europe, to which it was united by religious and political ties, and by the fifteenth century the layout and decoration of Glagolitic codices, and even the ductus of their script, came to resemble those current in Northern Italy.

The Cyrillic book, by contrast, continued to evolve within the same cultural and religious sphere as the Greek book and reflects many of the same developments. This is not to deny the emergence of local traditions, principally Bulgarian, Serbian and East Slavonic ('Russian'), and within the latter the traditions of Novgorod vs. Kiev, or later Muscovy vs. the South-West; but these were never maintained in isolation, to the extent that some fifteenth-century Russian manuscripts are almost impossible to distinguish from their Bulgarian models. The religious pre-eminence of Constantinople, moreover, meant that all were receptive to Greek influence. A partial exception is the somewhat rustic and archaic tradition of Bosnia, which (with some notable exceptions) seems to have been relatively impervious to outside influences.

The Slavs were certainly aware of literacy in the cultures that surrounded them before they undertook to create a writing system for their own language, and this awareness is reflected in the vocabulary surrounding the book. The verb 'to write', *pisati*, means also 'to paint', a polysemy shared with the Greek *graphō*. Greek *grammata* has given Slavic *gramota*, meaning a 'document', 'writing' in general, or facility in it, the same semantic field as Latin *litterae*. The Slavic word for a 'letter', *buky*, is Germanic, and, most remarkably, it is the Chinese 卷, 'scroll' (in modern Mandarin *juàn*, but in earlier periods believed to have been pronounced more like *küen*), borrowed into Turkic and thence, with the Hunno-Bulgarian suffix *-ig-*, into Slavonic as *kŭnigy* (a *plurale tantum* meaning 'anything written') from which the singular

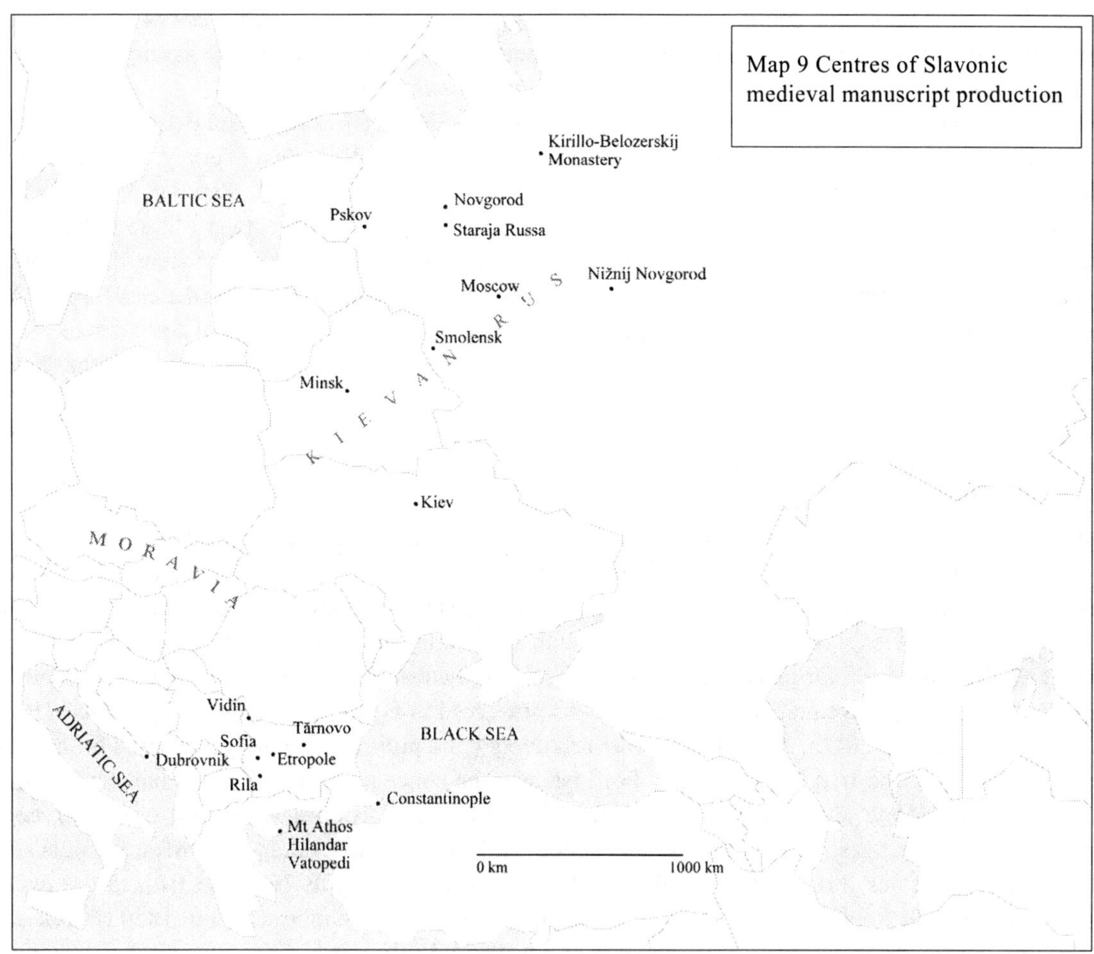

Map 9 Centres of Slavonic medieval manuscript production

kniga/kniha, the word for 'book' in modern Slavonic languages, is derived (Deleva 1997, see also Vasmer 1953–1958). The materials for writing have their native names insofar as they are objects from everyday life otherwise unrelated to the book, such as *pero* ('pen', literally 'feather'). The Greek word *chartēs*, which was borrowed very early into Old Bulgarian, was used to denote a number of writing surfaces; its development among the Balkan Slavs was the same as in Greek, so that *hartija* now means 'paper' (though Serbian also uses *papir*). In Russian *charat'ja,* a word which survived into the twentieth century, meant 'parchment', but this is now universally designated by the Western European borrowing *pergamen(t).* The derivation of Russian *bumaga*, 'paper', is obscure, but certainly connected in some way with Greek *bambax.*

The extant Slavic manuscripts are estimated to number *c.*60,000–80,000, the largest collection being that of St Petersburg; about one third of them have been catalogued (see Ch. 4 § 2.9).

References

Deleva 1997; Vasmer 1953–1958; see also Ch. 1 § 10; Ch. 2 § 9.

3.12. Syriac manuscripts (PGB–FBC)

The history of the production of Syriac manuscripts in the strict sense, that is books in codex form, begins in the early centuries of the Christian era. The oldest dated Syriac manuscript was written in Edessa in 411 CE (London, British Library, Add. 12,150, parchment, 370 × 285 mm, 255 leaves) and contains patristic works of Clement of Rome, Titus of Bosra, Eusebius, and also a martyrology. The production of handwritten books continues to the present day and was still very common in the nineteenth century (in some cases as a result of requests from western scholars and missionaries); recent manuscripts in fact contain several ancient works, and in some cases they are *codices unici.*

The shape of the Syriac manuscript book was set early, and already the oldest manuscripts conform to some kind of formal perfection that later copyists sought to reproduce. Thus there is from the beginning a Syriac kind of manuscript, distinct from the Greek type of manuscript, which was one of the models encountered by Muslim scribes when they developed their own written tradition. The history of the Syriac book is, therefore, an important chapter in the history of the book in the Near East.

The production areas of Syriac manuscripts coincide with the area of origin and dissemination of the culture of Syriac expression. But in addition to the main centres in the Near East (Turkey, in particular the region of Ṭūr ʿAbdīn in the southeast, Syria, Lebanon, Israel, Iraq, Iran, Egypt), there are also peripheral areas: eastward there are southern India (Kerala), Central Asia and China; westward there is Europe, in particular Italy and France. From both the quantitative and the chronological points of view, the peripheral areas are obviously characterized by a relatively limited and recent production; nevertheless, Central Asia preserved some older manuscripts (ninth century), while in Europe the production of Syriac manuscripts dates from the sixteenth century and is primarily a consequence of the contacts between the Roman Church and the Churches of the East.

Worth mentioning from the twentieth century are manuscripts intended to serve as models for printed books, a practice that was abandoned only recently with the adoption of the computer for typesetting Syriac texts. These twentieth-century manuscripts perpetuated the traditional layout, in some cases including the use of rubrics, a practice that necessitated the use of colour in Syriac printed books.

The number of Syriac manuscripts is difficult to assess, but it is estimated that more than 10,000 manuscripts are preserved, about 3,000 of which are dated. The distribution of these dated manuscripts over the centuries varies significantly, in keeping with the history of the Syriac Churches and in relation to material circumstances; for instance, almost all the dated manuscripts earlier than 1000 CE—about 166 in number—and many more undated ones, have been preserved in Egypt, thanks to its dry climate (Brock et al. 2001, 243; Brock 2012a, 25–28) and to the relatively calm political situation compared to the many invasions that Syria and Iraq had to endure. For instance, the concentration of Syriac manuscripts in the Syrian Monastery (Dayr al-Suryān) in the desert of Scetis (Wādī al-Naṭrūn, northwest of Cairo), began already in the Middle Ages, when (in 932 CE) its abbot Mushe of Nisibis brought from Mesopotamia some 250 manuscripts (Brock 2012b). The number of dated Syriac manuscripts from the fifth to the twelfth century is about 229; from the thirteenth to the nineteenth century, the number is about 1850 (Brock et al. 2001, 245: an estimate on the basis of catalogues of western collections).

Collections of Syriac manuscripts are found in monasteries and religious institutions throughout the Near East and as far west as Egypt, as in the above-mentioned Syrian Monastery (Egypt) and St Catherine's Monastery on Mount Sinai. Peculiar to the latter and linked to the presence in the monastery of monks from many different cultural and linguistic communities, is an overlay of languages within single manuscripts, when the parchment was reused for copying new texts (palimpsests); in addition, remains of Melkite Syriac literature have been preserved mainly in St Catherine's Monastery on Mount Sinai. Maronite Syriac manuscripts are kept in the collection of the Maronite Patriarchate, in Bkerké. The Holy Spirit University of Kaslik has established a library and assumed the task of gathering up small collections scattered in different churches and communities. Manuscripts of the Syriac Orthodox tradition are preserved in the region of Ṭūr ʿAbdīn, in southeastern Turkey, in the libraries of the monasteries of Dayr al-Zaʿfarān and Mor Gabriel, and in Mardin; other collections are in Jerusalem, Damascus, Aleppo and Charfet (Lebanon). East Syriac collections are kept in Iraq; as regards the Chaldean Church, the important library of the Patriarchate should be mentioned, as well as that of the monastery of Dora in Baghdad, where many manuscripts of churches and monasteries in northern Iraq had been gathered; since the recent war, the manuscripts have been transferred to Iraqi Kurdistan (the collection of Dora is back in the Monastery of Our Lady of Seeds in Alqosh where part of it originally came from). Finally, mention must be made of the Syriac communities of southern India, from both the Eastern and the Western Syriac traditions—whose many manuscripts are relevant for the history of Syriac book production as a whole—as several others were transferred from northern Mesopotamia to India.

In Europe, the most important collections are those of the Biblioteca Apostolica Vaticana—the oldest one being also particularly varied—and the British Library. In both cases manuscripts acquired in the eighteenth and nineteenth centuries from the Syrian Monastery in Egypt have an important place. They are the core of the British Library's collection, including some of the oldest preserved examples and mostly preserving the tradition of the Syrian Orthodox Church. The beginnings of the Vatican collection go back to the sixteenth century, and as the Church of Rome was involved in relations with all Syriac Churches

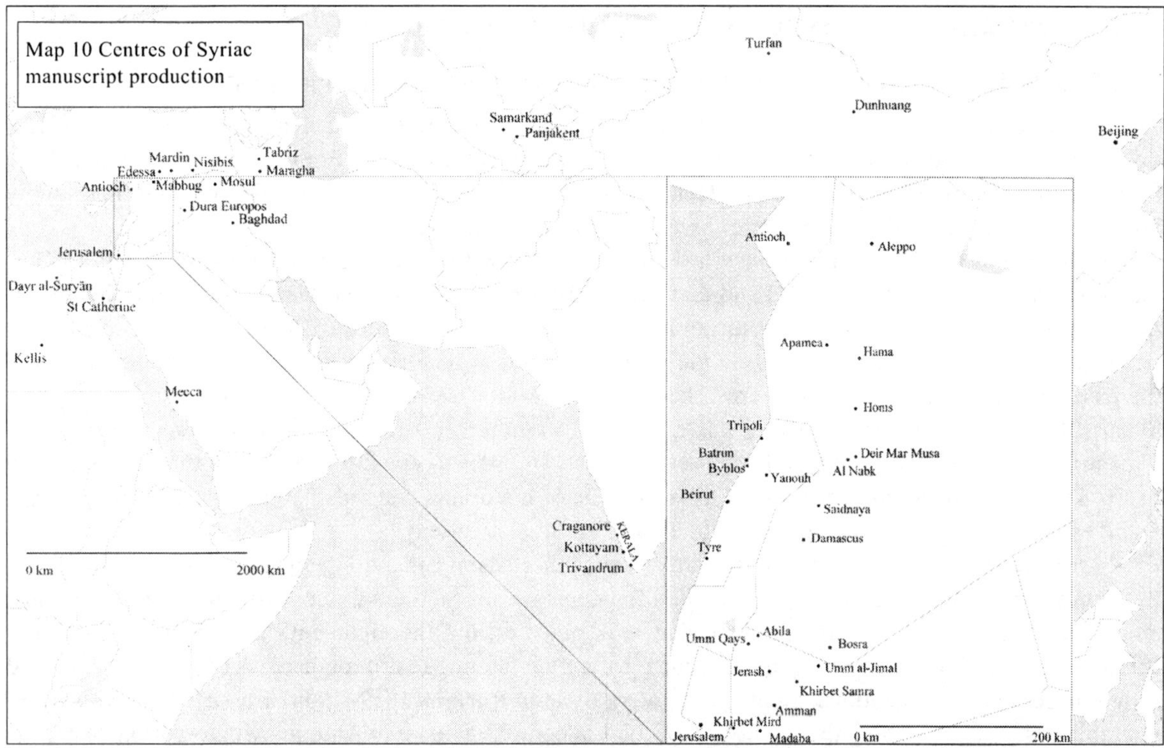

Map 10 Centres of Syriac manuscript production

from that century on, the Vatican collection is also varied in confessional provenance. Smaller collections elsewhere in Italy (Milan, Biblioteca Ambrosiana; Florence, Biblioteca Medicea Laurenziana) are also important, because of certain particularly precious manuscripts. In Great Britain, also the Mingana collection (Birmingham) deserves mention. Other important collections in Europe are found in Berlin (Staatsbibliothek Preussischer Kulturbesitz) and Paris (Bibliothèque nationale de France): in general, their manuscripts are less old than those in the other collections that have been mentioned. The history of these collections in part reflects that of diplomatic relations between the relevant countries and the Near East: for instance, the close relations of France with the Levant certainly explain the large number of Maronite manuscripts in French collections (besides the Bibliothèque nationale in Paris, also for example in Aix-en-Provence, Bibliothèque Méjanes; Lyon, Bibliothèque municipale; Strasbourg, Bibliothèque nationale et universitaire). Conversely, the German diplomatic presence in Iraq and Iran is related to the proportionately greater number of Eastern Syriac manuscripts in German libraries, or in the library of Strasbourg. The role of American missionaries in Urmia in the nineteenth century and the recent emigration of Christians from the Middle East to the United States explain the formation of the majority of North American collections, among them that of Harvard University, Cambridge, MA (for a complete repertoire of places and collections that preserve Syriac manuscripts, see Desreumaux 1991).

References

Brock 2012a, 2012b; Brock et al. 2001; Desreumaux 1991 and Ch. 1 § 11.

4. Ethical and legal aspects of manuscript research

4.1. Ethics in research and conservation of oriental manuscripts (SI)

The professional ethical standards of researchers of manuscripts, persons in charge of manuscript collections, and those responsible for the conservation are not a recent invention. For many years questions have been raised concerning the methods and technical choices allowed in historical research, and these apply also to the treatment of documents in archives, libraries and museums.

At the end of the nineteenth century in France, the *Méthodique* school derived inspiration from German historians (see Bourdeau 1888) and dictated the first rules for the positivistic approach to historiography: August Comte stated that a historian must study all facets of history. The same general principles were applied in the twentieth century by the *Annales* school. A historian must neither judge nor interpret the past, but take witnesses as they are. There must be a total separation between the historian and the historical fact. History exists in and of itself, and we can therefore arrive at a historical fact. The work of a historian is to find and re-assemble the verified facts in order to constitute a history that will organize itself. At the end of the nineteenth century a number of historians were also palaeographers working in archives, and their work influenced the library and archival economy.

In archives and libraries, there has been for years a discussion concerning ethical rules to be respected. In the domain of museums, it suffices to recall the questions of the theoreticians of restoration. The most emblematic case is certainly the polemic that took place during the eighteenth and most of nineteenth centuries surrounding the return of the Laocoon group, the famous sculpture discovered in 1506. Gotthold Ephraim Lessing's publications, and then the work of John Ruskin (1819–1900) who expressed his unfavourable opinion concerning the restitution of the Laocoon by Giovanni Antonio Montorsoli in 1523, are the principal witnesses. In the twentieth century the need was felt to regulate and normalize these aspects at the heart of their respective international professional organizations.

4.1.1. General principles for scientific research

Each country has developed a professional code of ethics used by researchers, but at an international level, this regulation emerges at the heart of the International Council for Science which was founded between the two wars, in 1931, as a non-governmental organization dedicated to the international cooperation for scientific progress. In matters of applied ethics, this organization presents, on its internet site, a chapter dedicated to the freedom and the responsibility of researchers. At a European level, the European Research Council, which depends on the European Union, does not seem to have worked on this aspect of regulation (apart from the Ethics Review that mostly regards natural sciences and sensitive personal data), even though the European Science Foundation (the carrier of the Research Networking Programme COMSt) has put a lot of work into this question.

4.1.2. General principles for archives, libraries and museums

The international professional organizations have not all launched a process for the regulation of ethics. The International Council of Museums (ICOM) adopted its code of ethics for museums in 1986 while the International Federation of Library Association (IFLA) and the International Council of Archives (ICA) do not seem to have adopted, to this day, any similar code.

4.1.3. General principles for restoration

For manuscripts in particular, one must look at the text by the IFLA (*The Principles of Conservation and Restoration of the Collections in the Libraries*, 1979), as first presented at a congress in Copenhagen. A revised version was edited in 2012 in the context of the Preservation and Conservation (PAO) plan. The text of 1979 reminds us already of the importance of necessary measures of preventive conservation. For aspects of restoration, the essential principles were outlined in the 1980s and they remain valid today, even if they are not always easy to apply. The three core principles are repeatedly recalled in Chapter 5: (1) the reversibility of the treatment; (2) the safety of the products and materials used and (3) the honesty of the intervention.

4.1.4. The specific case of oriental manuscripts

Questioning the provenance of manuscripts

Researchers who work on oriental manuscripts, in Europe, Africa, or the Middle East, can be confronted by manuscripts that are in private collections and whose original provenance is uncertain. When approached by a private collector or vendor for an opinion regarding a manuscript of unknown origin, the researcher should question whether the manuscript has not been stolen from a library that has not yet been inventoried or catalogued—as one should also ask whether the document is authentic or a forgery. Otherwise there is a risk to encourage this type of theft—like a possible falsification—merely by providing scientific consultation.

Exhibition and religion

In the case of oriental manuscripts, we deal in most cases with items that are religious or are attached to a living religious practice. This creates additional issues for researchers, collection managers, and conservators. Thus, until recently there existed considerable religious reticence concerning the promotion of manuscripts. For example, a Druze community in Syria that venerates an *al-Ḫitma* manuscript (the complete book of *Rasāʾil al-Ḥikma*, the sacred book of the Druze) refused any exhibition, as for them, this manuscript cannot be seen by non-Druze (according to Eldin 2013). The same limits are also valid for digital copies: a few years ago, a *fatwā* was proclaimed against the digitization of the Qurʾān and its diffusion in digital libraries. Today, mentalities have evolved, and the religious authorities usually accept museum and/or digitization practices, and even encourage them. An awareness has equally evolved that, by recording a manuscript in a database and making the information or a reproduction accessible to the general public, not only do we promote research but also protect the objects from a possible theft: a secure identification is created, and the object, if stolen, cannot be easily sold (Ipert 2005).

Restoration

Restoration is another domain with religious connotations. For example, can one use alcohol to soften the parchment leaves of a Qurʾān? Is it better replace an ancient binding on a Qurʾān to protect it or conserve it following professional rules? On the Sabbath, must one disconnect the electricity of a freezer where flooded Tora scrolls are conserved? After documentation and restoration, must manuscripts from a *geniza* be re-buried? Can a Christian liturgical book continue to be used by a community of monks after having been restored, at the risk of future deterioration? The conservator is often at a loss when confronted with these questions.

Whether for research, enhancing, or restoration of oriental manuscripts, it is sometimes difficult to follow the rules of ethics of the international professional organizations because these rules are most often conceived with a western perspective in mind. The only professional response is to explain well that researchers, museums and libraries cultivate scientific research, and, more specifically, that archives, libraries and museums are cultural institutions where all religions are respected, but that religions should not impose their rules.

References

Eldin 2013; ICOM 2004; ICSU 2013; IFLA 1979; Ipert 2005.

4.2. Legal framework for manuscript protection (MCo)

Strictly speaking, manuscripts are not a legal category. However, a number of legal texts at national, international and European level do refer to manuscripts. The UNESCO Convention of 14 November 1970 defines as cultural property: 'rare manuscripts and incunabula, old books, documents and publications of special interest (historical, artistic, scientific, literary, etc.) singly or in collections', whereas the Hague Convention mentions 'manuscripts, books and other objects of artistic, historical or archaeological interest; as well ... important collections of books or archives or of reproductions of the property defined above'. The UNESCO Memory of the World Programme focuses on the preservation and accessibility of documentary heritage, a broad concept that includes the books, manuscripts and archival collections listed in the Memory of the World Register provided that they are of international interest and universal value. Manuscripts are also covered by the legislation on intellectual property.

We can see that a manuscript is a complex object, a hybrid material valued for its content, for its precious character, singly or in a collection. This multiform reality must be expressed in the law. Firstly, a significant distinction is to be drawn. The physical medium of the manuscript is protected by a number of rules. These rules serve private as well as public interests. They are mostly related to the issue of ownership. Manuscripts are subject to ownership; they can belong to individuals or public entities, institutions, libraries, archives, and so forth. Other rules govern the conditions of use and access to the intellectual content. While in principle there may be a conflict between the legal protection of the physical object and the legal protection of the object's intellectual content, this rarely applies to manuscript studies, as in most cases intellectual rights expire within one or two generations after the death of the author (see below) and thus do not apply to manuscript content. We will discuss the legal status of manuscripts with respect to the great legal challenges they pose: material conservation, circulation, access, dissemination and valorization.

4.2.1. Conservation of manuscripts

This conservation objective is ensured by cultural heritage law, a set of rules at national and international level aiming at preserving the integrity of a number of sites and objects of historical, artistic, or scientific interest.

Protection of manuscripts at international level

There are very few international texts specifically targeting manuscripts or books. Binding legal instruments (that impose obligations on the states signing and ratifying the conventions) concern more widely all the goods that are part of cultural heritage. Nevertheless, some soft law texts are worth mentioning, alongside the programs developed by UNESCO, in particular the Memory of the World Programme.

Within the general framework of cultural heritage preservation, few laws are likely to apply to manuscripts. In 1954, the first international convention to tackle the issue of protecting cultural objects (here, only in cases of armed conflicts) was passed; while providing a more inclusive understanding of cultural property, it expressly mentioned manuscripts. Under Article 4, the *Convention for the Protection of Cultural Property in the Event of Armed Conflict* of 14 May 1954 (Second Protocol, 26 March 1999) states that the parties must respect cultural property situated within their own territory as well as within the territory of other parties by 'refraining from any use of the property and its immediate surroundings or of the appliances in use for its protection for purposes which are likely to expose it to destruction or damage in the event of armed conflict; and by refraining from any act of hostility, directed against such property'. No derogation to this principle of respect for property is possible, unless military necessity imperatively requires it. In addition, the parties 'undertake to prohibit, prevent and, if necessary, put a stop to any form of theft, pillage or misappropriation of, and any acts of vandalism directed against, cultural property…'. In case of occupation, the occupant must 'as far as possible support the competent national authorities of the occupied country in safeguarding and preserving its cultural property'. The convention also provides for refuges to shelter movable cultural property; these refuges are placed under special protection and must be identifiable. Special protection is granted to cultural property by its entry in the 'Inter-national Register of Cultural Property under Special Protection'. The idea of the Convention is to ensure that each belligerent respects cultural property. To this aim, a distinctive and internationally recognizable emblem must be placed on the cultural goods protected by the convention. Apart from this convention, there is no other binding instrument safeguarding movable cultural property as a whole.

There are soft law texts, however, that must be considered. In 2006, the Quebec archival community passed a Declaration on archives. It has been taken up at international level in 2011 when the International Council on Archives adopted the Universal Declaration on Archives which was very influenced by the Quebec declaration. Nevertheless, these declarations carry no legal weight. While recognizing the significance of archives for memory, it is advocated that: 'the management of archives is valued and is carried out fully in civil society, public bodies and businesses; archives are conserved in conditions that ensure their authenticity, integrity and intelligibility; archives are made accessible to everyone, while respecting the rights of individuals, creators, owners and users.'

The Memory of the World programme is based on the principle 'that the world's documentary heritage belongs to all, should be fully preserved and protected for all and, with due recognition of cultural mores and practicalities, should be permanently accessible to all without hindrance' (<http://www.unesco.org/new/en/communication-and-information/flagship-project-activities/memory-of-the-world/about-the-programme/objectives/>, last accessed June 2014). In this view, the two prevailing objectives are preservation and access. As regards the first objective, the program aims at ensuring and facilitating the preservation of the world's documentary heritage by providing subsidies and disseminating advice and information. As regards the second objective, the legal requirements that protect private or public interests (property rights, intellectual property rights, archive rights, and so forth) can sometimes get in the way of access. The programme prescribes that these potential limitations must be recognized. It also recommends that 'indigenous communities' custodianship of their materials, and their guardianship of access' must be honoured.

Protection at national level

Protective measures for documents, manuscripts and archives take multiple forms: some of them focus on the material preservation of the medium, and others set out the conditions governing access to these documents or manuscripts. Generally speaking, there is no specific protection for manuscripts. Just like at international level, it is necessary to invoke either the general rules governing the preservation of tangible heritage, or public property rules.

The heritage protection schemes set up by states often target cultural property as a whole. This allows ensuring the protection of documents and manuscripts. Laws on historical monuments (that generally include immovable as well as movable property), cultural property laws or cultural heritage laws have instituted protective measures that can be very restrictive. They oblige the owner to request an authorization for any activity that may alter the property: restoration work, modification, or any transformation that could impact the character of the property under protection. These measures are intended to protect property of artistic or historic interest, the creations belonging to cultural and intellectual heritage. Manuscripts can be protected on this basis. A certain number of these protective measures apply to isolated items; for example when it is a matter of preserving a given building, manuscript or artwork. But there are different ways of considering a set; for instance, it could arise from the exceptional consistency of a fund or collection from a literary, artistic or historical standpoint. The consequences of such recognition vary according to the country, and it is not always possible to safeguard the whole set.

In a number of states, publicly owned cultural property is relatively well protected. In some countries, cultural property becomes public property because it is thought to serve the public interest, which is why it is considered as inalienable, imprescriptible (it can be claimed without any limit in time) and cannot be seized. The character of inalienability means that the public owner cannot sell or even donate the property for as long as it remains under that special regime, that is to say as long as it serves the public interest. Such property can be found in museum collections, archival funds or libraries. This public nature is frequently used as an argument against restitution claims from other states. However, public property rules are not equally efficient among states.

Customary property laws may also be relevant. Conservation of manuscripts is sometimes ensured by private law instruments such as trusts, foundations, or *waqf* in Muslim law (forms of collective properties), which entail some obligations. For the oriental manuscripts, a very significant amount is privately owned by families; many documents are held in religious institutions such as monasteries, churches, mosques, or synagogues.

4.2.2. Circulation of manuscripts and books

The circulation of manuscripts is another significant theme in cultural heritage law. Such protection has two functions: a preventive one and a repressive one.

Prevention: controls on the movements of artworks

Before studying the domestic principles governing the circulation of cultural property, it is important to consider these rules in a more global context, at international, European and national level. Again, as was the case in terms of protection, international rules come from general instruments concerning movable cultural property as a whole and not specifically manuscripts, books or archives.

On an international level, from the beginning, the General Agreement on Tariffs and Trade (GATT, established in 1947, last updated in 1994) recognized that, to achieve the protection of national treasures, the circulation of cultural property could be subject to restrictions (for exportation or importation) in domestic legislations. Article XX: General Exceptions prescribes that 'Subject to the requirement that such measures are not applied in a manner which would constitute a means of arbitrary or unjustifiable discrimination between countries where the same conditions prevail, or a disguised restriction on international trade, nothing in this Agreement shall be construed to prevent the adoption or enforcement by any contracting party of measures … (*f*) imposed for the protection of national treasures of artistic, historic or archaeological value' (see GATT text at <http://www.wto.org/english/docs_e/legal_e/06-gatt.pdf>, pp. 37–38, last access June 2014). In this view, states are not allowed to act totally freely. A measure not justified or a disguised restriction on international trade can be disputed. As of now, no case has been heard by the World Trade Organization (WTO).

The rules governing the circulation of cultural property at European level are more complex. Insofar as the European Union (EU), like the WTO, promotes trade liberalization, it also needs to reach a compromise between the free movement of goods and heritage protection. Article 36 of the TFEU also allows setting up prohibitions or restrictions on imports, exports or goods in transit justified on grounds of the protection of national treasures possessing artistic, historic or archaeological value. With the creation of the internal market on 1 January 1993, the EU member states' legislations regulating the circulation of cultural property and the prohibition of the most valuable cultural goods have been seriously undermined. To prevent or fight the unlawful removal of cultural property from a member state to another member state or outside the EU, two pieces of legislation have been passed. The first one creates a common control procedure to export towards third countries, whereas the second one regulates the return of the unlawfully removed national treasures that circulate within the Union. Manuscripts are mentioned among the categories listed in the annex to these texts.

Finally, provided that they comply with WTO and EU rules, states establish their own legislations controlling the circulation of cultural property and, in that respect, the cultural objects under protection are not the same ones everywhere, and the techniques and methods for controlling their circulation vary as well.

Some states have developed broad definitions of cultural property, and they control significant cultural objects which are called in different ways (cultural heritage, cultural object, object of cultural significance, national treasure, and the like). Other states choose to list all the objects falling into a given category. Both methods are sometimes combined.

Prevention: the fight against illicit trafficking of cultural property

Several instruments can be used at international, European and national level. Internationally, the two main instruments are the 1970 UNESCO Convention and the 1995 UNIDROIT Convention. Both concern cultural property in general and not specifically manuscripts.

The States Parties to the *Convention of 14 November 1970 on the Means of Prohibiting and Preventing the Illicit Import, Export and Transfer of Ownership of Cultural Property* undertake:

> 'to take the necessary measures, consistent with national legislation, to prevent museums and similar institutions within their territories from acquiring cultural property originating in another State Party which has been illegally exported after entry into force of this Convention, in the States concerned' (Article 7.a);
>
> 'to prohibit the import of cultural property stolen from a museum or a religious or secular public monument or similar institution in another State Party to this Convention after the entry into force of this Convention for the States concerned' (Article 7.b.i);
>
> 'at the request of the State Party of origin, to take appropriate steps to recover and return any such cultural property imported' (7.b.ii); and
>
> 'to admit actions for recovery of lost or stolen items of cultural property brought by or on behalf of the rightful owners' (Article 13.c).

Article 1 defines the term 'cultural property' for the purposes of the Convention, and manuscripts are expressly mentioned in this definition.

Although this Convention is a significant step in the strengthening of the means to fight against illicit trafficking, it is unevenly efficient as only states are concerned. Furthermore, its implementation is limited by the existence of domestic rules which protect the rights of good faith purchasers.

In order to address the aforementioned difficulties, the *UNIDROIT Convention on Stolen or Illegally Exported Cultural Objects of 24 June 1995* was designed to establish 'common, minimal legal rules for the restitution and return of cultural objects between Contracting States, with the objective of improving the preservation and protection of the cultural heritage in the interest of all'.

Stolen cultural objects are subject to restitution, i.e. they must be returned to their rightful owner, whereas illegally exported cultural objects, or more specifically objects 'removed from the territory of a Contracting State contrary to its law regulating the export of cultural objects for the purpose of protecting its cultural heritage' must be returned. The scope of this Convention is the same as the one defined in Article 1 of the 1970 UNESCO Convention, and the list provided for in the annex to the 1970 Convention is repeated in its entirety in the annex to the UNIDROIT Convention. A very similar approach had been adopted with the Council Directive 93/7/EEC on the return of cultural objects, and it can be noted that this instrument shares many common elements with the UNIDROIT Convention. The obligation to return stolen goods is one of the significant innovations in this text, and this constitutes an important exception to the principle of good faith acquisition that prevails in several legal systems. Furthermore, in the UNIDROIT Convention good faith is not presumed; the possessor must establish it. The good faith possessor is entitled to 'payment of fair and reasonable compensation', unless 'the possessor neither knew nor ought reasonably to have known that the object was stolen and can prove that it exercised due diligence when acquiring the object' (article 4.1). As regards illegally exported property, only the objects of significant cultural importance are subject to protection.

4.2.3. Access to public documents and manuscripts

In cultural heritage law, which mainly focuses on conservation, no general principle of access to cultural heritage is really laid down, based on the general interest. Domestic legislations govern this issue, and in most cases they do so by establishing specific rules of access to public archives, which are a set of documents produced or received in the course of a public activity. Some manuscripts, if they are defined as public archives, may be subject to these rules. There is a growing tendency, especially in countries outside Europe and America, to block access to original documents as a rule, and refer researchers to electronic images. Only in exceptional cases limited access to the originals is still granted. This can be understood as a measure to safeguard the originals, but it ignores all research necessities where the originals need to be consulted (if only for reasons of codicological research).

4.2.4. Dissemination and exploitation of manuscripts

The intellectual content of a book may be subject to a number of rights, for example intellectual property rights or rights on the publication, and sometimes those rights are linked to the property rights over the physical object. The aspects of copyright are largely irrelevant for mediaeval and pre-modern manuscripts (see below), as the only legal right a library or archive has is its right of ownership. The general regulations of intellectual property may be valid, however, for manuscripts containing texts composed or translated in the twentieth century, a case not so seldom in the oriental manuscript context.

Intellectual property

Protection of intellectual property rights is ensured at international, European and national level. The *Berne Convention for the Protection of Literary and Artistic Works* of 9 September 1886 was the first major international text in this field, and it was completed by the World Intellectual Property Organization (WIPO) treaties. UNESCO also passed some texts on this issue. One should also mention the *Agreement on Trade-Related Aspects of Intellectual Property Rights* (or TRIPS Agreement, see <http://www.wto.org/english/tratop_e/trips_e/t_agm0_e.htm>) in relation to the WTO as well as the provisions concerning European Union member states. States also develop their own laws.

Whether in application of international law (Berne Convention) or domestic laws (at least most of them), manuscripts can be subject to copyright if they contain intellectual works, i.e. original works which can also be works deriving from another work. A translation is an intellectual work (for obvious reasons, this does not apply to automatic translations). One may wonder whether restorations of cultural objects can be considered as intellectual works. This might be the case if the restorer's work is creative, but this is likely to be contrary to the ethics of the profession.

According to the Berne Convention, authors possess economic and moral rights for forms of exploitation and dissemination of a work (reproduction, performance, translation, adaptation, and so forth, see Article 6 *bis*). The duration of rights is limited to 50 years (extended to 70 years by European law) after the author's death; at the expiry of this term the work falls into the public domain and anyone can use it freely (even prior to that term, as there are exceptions in the European Union law for citations; for reproduction and performance granted to cultural heritage organizations; and for orphan works): this is the case with the overwhelming majority of manuscripts.

The right of reproduction of institutional depositories varies from nation to nation. In some states, the owner of the physical medium of the work may still be entitled to certain rights, even when the work has fallen into the public domain. Consequently, some museums or libraries may require the payment of royalties for using the work, or they may control all reproductions or uses of the work.

Similarly, in some legal systems, publishers are granted neighbouring rights on published works. When for example ancient manuscripts are published, they are not protected by copyright but they can be protected under this publishing right.

Some legislations have a system of legal deposit, following which each published document, each document made publicly available must be deposited with an institution or other public body. The aim of this is to conserve a memory of intellectual heritage. It can also be a means to control publications.

As we have seen, the rules are really dispersed, and very often domestic law, international law and European law must be combined. In addition, in a number of cases it is necessary to take into account the rules provided for either in the regulations of institutional depositaries or in contractual practice.

References

Web sources: World Intellectual Property Organization, *Berne Convention 1886* <http://www.wipo.int/treaties/en/text.jsp?file_id=283698>, last accessed June 2014; World Trade Organization, *General Agreement on Tariffs and Trade* <http://www.wto.org/english/docs_e/legal_e/06-gatt.pdf>, last accessed June 2014; World Trade Organization, *Trade-Related Aspects of Intellectual Property Rights* <http://www.wto.org/english/tratop_e/trips_e/t_agm0_e.htm>, last accessed June 2014; UNESCO Memory of the World Programme <http://www.unesco.org/new/en/communication-and-information/flagship-project-activities/memory-of-the-world/about-the-programme/objectives/>, last accessed June 2014; *UNIDROIT Convention 1995* <http://www.unidroit.org/instruments/cultural-property/1995-convention>, last accessed June 2014.

4.3. Some recommendations on good practice (IL)

In the context of European policies on digitization and access to cultural heritage, we can speak today of a legal recognition of the right of libraries and archives to digitize manuscripts when it serves the purpose of conservation and accessibility of the manuscripts.

However, when approaching manuscripts from the legal point of view one should always regard them from two perspectives: (1) as containers of works that are sources of metadata and scholarly work and are subject to intellectual property rights (see also § 4.2 above) (2) as material objects that are subject to material property rights, and are sources of images that can be produced from manuscripts.

4.3.1. Library cataloguing metadata

Cataloguing of manuscripts (prior to exhibition or digitization) falls within the responsibilities and tasks of the library or archive where they are preserved. The resulting metadata is part of the digital library catalogues. It is recommended—as is already the case in many European countries—that the metadata should be integrated into national or international databases (hypercatalogues) that could be filtered by various parameters, including places of origin and historical periods.

The cataloguing entries themselves may also be subject to intellectual property rights (see also Ch. 4 § 6), especially if they meet the originality criteria and involve scholarly analysis. When, as often happens in basic library catalogues, there is no real originality, the metadata should not be considered independently from the document the description identifies.

Libraries should be advised to specify on their Internet pages the conditions of use regarding these descriptive metadata, indicating that use is free provided the source is fully credited alongside the date of retrieval under an open license.

4.3.2. Manuscript studies

When manuscripts have been the subject of a study that identifies the date and shows their characteristics, such a study (a copyright protected object) may be very useful for those who consult the manuscript and should at least be referenced in the descriptive metadata. While it may be helpful if such studies are available with the manuscripts, they cannot, in principle, be reproduced or distributed without the permission of the authors. However, there are two relevant exceptions in intellectual property rights.

The first is citation, when certain elements of a study have been incorporated into another work. The citation must be appropriately short and justified by the scientific content of the work in which it is incorporated; the name of the author and source must be clearly indicated.

The second is the reproduction and distribution 'for educational purposes or for the purpose of illustration in the context of teaching and research', provided that such use does not give rise to any commercial exploitation.

In addition to studies that have gone out of copyright for time reasons (see § 4.2), so-called orphan works (when we have lost track of the authors) may be reproduced by libraries or archives without permission under European law, provided the institutions can demonstrate that they have tried to locate copyright holders and that the search has been unsuccessful. Orphan works may be made accessible alongside the manuscript metadata provided full bibliographic reference is given.

4.3.3. Reproduction rights

In most European countries, if a manuscript is in a public collection, the institution that keeps it has no rights to the photographic images of this manuscript. However, in some member states of the European Union (e.g. Greece) the reproduction copyright belongs to the state, and therefore prior to any digitization action one should apply for, and receive, authorization. The local legal framework must thus always be clarified before any digitization campaign. If the owner is a private person, an authorization request is always required.

Most museums allow amateur photography of works including manuscripts but the terms are defined by conservation and security demands. For example, the Musée du Louvre in Paris allows photographs without flash and without the use of tripods. Similarly, in France, professional photography can no longer be forbidden in public museums, as such a prohibition would violate the principle of freedom of trade and industry. Still, permission is strictly regulated. These examples show the importance of finding out beforehand what is allowed and under which conditions.

A separate question is whether the person who takes a photograph as an amateur may use it to illustrate a research work. While it may seem logical—since the photography itself is allowed—it is best to make sure, as using an image in a publication can be considered a commercial operation and thus adversely affect the rights of the owners. It is therefore recommended to take precautions and request permission.

Finally, photographers have intellectual property rights on the photographs they have created, and the reproduction or dissemination of manuscript images cannot be done without their permission. The rights, however, may not belong to the photographers themselves but to the person or institution who contracted them if their work has been part of a service or a project. In all cases, the reproduction of a photograph should always be accompanied by the photographer's name.

When libraries create online photo galleries (which meet an important need for researchers), it is essential for each photograph to be accompanied by a statement not only about the subject photographed, but also about the status of the photograph (its author, date, conditions of reproduction, contact person, etc.).

Chapter 1. Codicology

edited by Marilena Maniaci

1. Introduction (MMa)

Among the 'physical' features of the handwritten book, its materials and structure offer, with respect to writing and decoration, greater and more direct opportunities for comparison, thus allowing one to speak of a 'universal grammar' of the manuscript book (and in particular of the codex), aimed at 'identifying the structural elements common to the majority of craft traditions and the profound reasons for their organization in a coherent system' (Maniaci 2002a, 25). Codices written in Latin, Greek, Arabic, Hebrew, Syriac, Coptic, Ethiopic, Armenian, Georgian, Glagolitic, or Cyrillic scripts shared the same materials, similar sizes and proportions, a common structure of quiring normally achieved by folding a certain number of sheets, and the employment of means for ensuring the right sequence of the quires and of the bifolia and leaves within the quires; written and unwritten spaces were most often previously defined and distinguished by means of ruling, and some codices were decorated and illustrated in the margins or within the written area. This common structural setting, which often displays—whether dependently or independently—equivalent technical solutions (for example, concerning quire structure, ruling technique, and layout of the text), was indeed universal and remained remarkably stable, despite its multiple representations over time and space, not only until the beginning of mechanical printing (in many aspects it was inherited and further implemented by the printers), but to a large degree until our own time (Beit-Arié 1993).

The contributions collected in this chapter confirm, in fact—on a more systematic basis than has ever before been established—the existence of a patrimony of knowledge and craft practices shared by a plurality of book traditions, showing significant preferences for certain materials and procedures. These similarities are, however, flanked by just as many more or less relevant and eye-catching differences and peculiarities.

This intricate web of similarities and divergencies involves a multitude of manuscript cultures, divided by religion, political borders, language, social structure, and mentality, distributed over a very wide geographical area, centred on the Middle East and North Africa, but extending—through the Greek and especially the Jewish manuscript tradition—to Italy and transalpine Europe. Three great religious traditions, being also three 'religions of the Book', dominate this spacious setting: some specific technical solutions cluster (although not always in a clear and coherent way) around the two poles represented by Christianity and Islam; the Jewish tradition of book production, embracing as it does all areas of the Jewish Diaspora, occupies a distinct position, resulting in an extraordinary richness and variety of codicological habits.

A multifarious interplay of relations and interactions, still waiting to be fully disclosed, unfolds against this background. In some cases, the direction and weight of the influences appear evident, although they have not yet been adequately detailed (such as the influence of the Byzantine book tradition on the Coptic, Caucasian or Slavonic ones, or the role played by the Arab-Islamic world in the transmission of paper-making technology or in the diffusion of certain ruling methods); in many other regards, the tension between different poles produces less clear outcomes and hybridizations which are far from being sufficiently investigated.

Comparison is further complicated by the existence of significant chronological shifts in the origin and evolution of the various manuscript traditions, some of which basically completed their life cycle by the sixteenth century or earlier, while others remain fully active and vital to this day. In some traditions, the persistence of the handwritten codex (and for specific purposes also the roll) as an object of use and not as a precious relic of the past finds its counterpoint in the late introduction of the printing press, hampered for a variety of historical, technical and economic reasons which would deserve specific analysis.

In this complex scenario, the comparative approach obviously should not and cannot be reduced to an abstract and mechanical juxtaposition of practices, techniques and craft devices: it requires instead an overall reflection on the reasons for the genesis and the development of different book forms—roll and codex above all—as well as for the transition from one to another; on the timing and extent of their diffusion in the different cultural environments; on the influence exerted by cultural, economic, and functional factors upon the definition of their overall aspect as well as their specific features. Comparison points up a need to distinguish between solutions that were inherited from a common substrate or developed independently in response to universal needs; to delineate identities and similarities which may be explained on the basis of clearly documented or indirectly discernible contacts, exchanges and influences; differences with cultural or ideological connotations (as in the case of the opposition between the quiring of Islamic parchment manuscripts, consisting of quinions indifferent as to the alternation of hair and flesh sides, and that of the Christian-Arabic ones, made of quaternions systematically applying Gregory's Rule, that is with matching skin sides facing each other at each opening, see Ch. 1 § 1.3.1); choices with no apparent motivation, whose explanation might be due to correlations that have not yet been identified (such as, for example, the average number of bifolia composing a quire; whether parchment quires begin with a hair or a flesh side; ruling techniques; the position of quire signatures).

The task of drawing a clear and complete picture of differences and similarities and explaining their reasons is still beyond the reach of current research as reflected by COMSt. To date, the understanding of most phenomena is seriously hampered by the significantly disparate quantity of previous scholarship in the various cultural and research traditions. A wide gap remains between our codicological understanding of Byzantine manuscripts and the research on Georgian, Slavonic, Ethiopic, Syriac and Coptic material. Hebrew codicology has benefited greatly from the systematic analysis of a large corpus of dated manuscripts. Important work has been done for the wide and diverse Arabic tradition, although the task still to be accomplished is as vast as the huge number of extant manuscripts.

For most of the oriental traditions which have been taken into consideration in the work of the COMSt project, the state of available knowledge is both quantitatively and qualitatively very heterogeneous, and it is mostly not founded on first-hand research conducted on adequately large and appropriately selected samples of manuscripts (with those that contain explicit indications of their date and provenance representing the core), nor even on the systematic collection of second-hand information offered by catalogues. For most domains, thorough inventories, bibliographies and modern descriptions of collections are still a major desideratum and should be set as a priority for future research (see Ch. 4).

This situation does not allow systematic comparisons or the sketching of a complete overview, which would be premature and is not among the objectives of this introduction. Rather than forcing a variety of disparate pieces of information into a single chapter, with the ambition of outlining a comparative history of the oriental manuscript book, the choice has been made to present separately in the following subchapters the state of knowledge for each individual tradition, without hiding the existence and extent of gaps, problems, and open issues. The adoption of a common arrangement of the topics in each subchapter allows the results presented to stand as a rich puzzle of widely comparable materials, if not as a strictly comparative depiction resulting from their final composition.

The arrangement followed, more or less, by all the subchapters corresponds substantially to the presentation traditionally adopted by modern handbooks, mostly concerning—with the notable exceptions of Arabic and Hebrew (Déroche – Sagaria Rossi 2012; Beit-Arié 2014)—the Graeco-Latin world (Maniaci 2002a, Géhin 2005, Agati 2009, the latter two encompassing also other traditions, Maniaci 2011, on Greek codicology). The presentation proceeds in a logical order from a description of the materials and tools used in the manufacture, writing and decoration of handwritten books, to their formats and techniques of construction—with particular reference to the codex—, the preparation of the page, the strategies adopted by scribes and painters for the exploitation of the available space, and ends with a description of bookbinding.

This logical, analytical arrangement is justified by the requirements of pedagogical clarity, but it must not be forgotten that an overall synthetic project always lies behind the production of any manuscript book and is more or less clearly revealed by the elements that compose its finished state; and that a manuscript's present state is the result of a sequence of events involving readers and owners who have often, and only more or less evidently, influenced the initial state of the book, possibly modifying—or even fully transforming—its original structure and function. Codicology, intended as the application of 'archaeological' methods for historical purposes, allows one to 'read' in manuscript books—beyond the contents transmitted by letters and images—a range of less obvious, but no less significant, information concerning the circumstances according to which they were commissioned, displayed, purchased, traded, variously used, possibly transformed, or more generally perceived and understood as artefacts. For most of the oriental book traditions, a transition from viewing codicology as little more than an auxiliary tool for dating and localizing manuscripts to envisioning it as an 'integral history of the manuscript book'—meant as an intellectual, technological, artistic, and also socio-economic history—still appears not only as a distant goal, but also as a strange and quite unfamiliar one, even to the most experienced scholars. A purely utilitarian interest in codicological data still prevails with regard to their autonomous evaluation, as well as with regard to the capacity to correlate them with the subject matter of the books, their contexts and levels of circulation and use, the categories of users and their needs and expectations, and the constraints exerted by material, cultural, functional, and economic factors. Here, then, is another reason to promote the comparative study of the main oriental book cultures, taking advantage of the methods and data of the scholarly traditions that have progressed the farthest to date.

Not only is the road to the writing of a 'universal grammar' of the oriental manuscript book still long and difficult, but the lack of a 'universal terminology', that is a proper and shared set of technical terms, complicates the task of telling it with the required accuracy. This is true both for individual languages and for English, which is increasingly becoming the common idiom in humanities research. The still unfinished work by J. Peter Gumbert (2010b) has been used, where possible, as a reference tool, but in many cases the wish to use precise and unambiguous terms came into conflict with the still largely undefined state of codicological knowledge or the force of particular traditions. The terminology adopted in the following pages reflects the effort to adopt a homogeneous language, but seeks to avoid a premature standardization.

Despite their shortcomings, we hope that the materials presented in the following pages may constitute a starting point towards the acquisition or consolidation of a common vision of the problems, the development of a clearer awareness of the work to be carried out, and the sharing of methods and research tools. Among these, absolute priority has to be given to the establishment of historical typologies, based on the direct examination of as many manuscripts as possible, focusing on dated ones, and preferably those for which a clear provenance can also be established.

In order to highlight the common ground in which the different manuscript traditions are rooted, and to reduce redundancies in the individual sub-chapters, some main facts concerning oriental book materials and manufacturing techniques are briefly summarized in the following pages. The reader should refer to recent handbooks for further general information and specific bibliography (references in the following pages are limited to an essential minimum) and to the individual sections for an informed and detailed presentation of specific cultural peculiarities. Given the uneven state of research in the different traditions of the oriental manuscript world, most of the technical information in this introductory section derives from work done in Greek, Hebrew and Arabic codicology; generalizations not based on specific investigations can only be proposed, in some cases, as working hypotheses.

1.1. Materials and tools (MMa–SE–IR–OH–RN)

Writing was done on a wide range of materials: rock, metal, wood, bone, clay and plaster, and above all papyrus, parchment and paper.

1.1.1. Papyrus (SE)

The papyrus plant (*Cyperus papyrus*, a long plant stalk composed of cellulose fibres and containing a natural adhesive) grew plentifully along the Nile River throughout Antiquity and was used by the Egyptians for a variety of purposes, among them to manufacture a writing material similar to paper (which word derives ultimately from the ancient Greek word *papyros*).

The writing material made from the papyrus plant was Egypt's most characteristic product and was exported all around the Mediterranean world for many centuries. The vast majority of the surviving papyrus manuscripts has been discovered in the arid parts of Egypt (not in the Delta) and in Nubia, while much smaller quantities have been found in other desert environments such as the Sinai peninsula, around the Dead Sea, and in Palestine and Syria; or else they have survived as a result of special circumstances such as having been carbonized by intense heat (such as the papyrus rolls preserved in Herculaneum by the eruption of Mount Vesuvius), by having been recycled as mummy pasteboard or by having been waterlogged (Ireland's *Faddan More Psalter* cartonnage). A number of papyrus manuscripts also survived into modern times by being preserved in mediaeval European archives.

A sheet of papyrus was manufactured as two layers of thin strips sliced from the stalk of a papyrus plant, with the two layers lying at right angles to one another. After being pressed together and dried (and perhaps also then polished by some means), the cross-hatching layer of fibres and intervening pith provided a quite usable and durable writing surface. The traditional practice was for the manufacturer to paste a number of sheets of papyrus together to create a long strip, being careful always to overlap one sheet and the next in the same way, thus producing a papyrus roll. Normally, the surface intended to support the writing, the inside of the roll, was made to have the fibres running horizontally along it (papyrus fibre direction →). The single manufactured sheet is called a *kollēma* (plural *kollēmata*), and the pasted overlap of two adjacent *kollēmata* is called a *kollēsis* (plural *kollēseis*). In a roll to be used for copying a Greek work (for instance), that is to be written in columns from left to right, the *kollēseis* 'step down' from left to right. The first *kollēma* is called the *prōtokollon* and was typically attached with reversed fibre directions, i.e. with the vertical fibres on the inside of the roll (papyrus fibre direction ↓); the last one is called *eschatokollon*.

Although systematic research is still missing, the dimensions of the *kollēmata* have been witnessed to be not very large. The papyrologist Eric G. Turner (1977, 48–51) observed that *c.*170 mm is a usual width in the Hellenistic and Roman period, the widest *kollēma* that he had ever noted in a roll being approximately 330 mm wide (a number of Coptic codices involve the use of rolls with much longer *kollēmata*). Heights of rolls in Turner's experience ranged between 220 and 410 mm. Much broader *kollēmata* are in fact attested, and the existence of *kollēmata* approaching even as much as 2 m in length suggests that the only natural limit to the size of papyrus sheet that could be made was the length of the usable part of a papyrus plant's stalk (Emmel 1998, 39–42). Some practical limitation might have been imposed by the technology by which the sheet was manufactured, about which we are not well informed; presumably it was easier to make smaller sheets rather than larger ones.

1.1.2. Parchment (MMa)

The history of the use and diffusion of writing supports of animal origin in the manufacture of oriental books differs from one culture to another and is interrelated with the history of the westward spread of paper manufacturing techniques, which were first introduced into the Arab-Islamic world from China and gradually penetrated from the east to the west, except in Ethiopia, where the habit of writing on processed animal skins has remained dominant until modern times. Written information on the manufacture of parchment—a writing material made from animal skin, freed from hair and dried under tension—is scarce in the east, apart from a series of late Armenian recipes (known to most scholars only in Russian and German translations) which have not yet been the object of a detailed study (see Ch. 1 § 3.1.2). This lack of documentation, along with the vagueness of the terminology employed by the sources to designate the use of animal skins as a writing material, makes the distinction between 'parchment' and other kinds of animal-skin support other than leather (such as the lightly tanned skins that were used for most of the Hebrew scrolls found in the Judaean Desert at Qumran and Masada) very difficult to make, as is any exact reconstruction of the procedures by which they were manufactured. The occasional statements derived from sources of various origins and natures converge in documenting the prevalent use of sheep, goat or (less frequently) calf hides, with rarer—and not always trustworthy—mentions of various other domestic animals or wild beasts. Even in the almost total absence of specific visual and instrumental analyses—apart from sporadic surveys based on the microscopic observation of hair implantation on samples of (Latin and) Greek manuscripts—differences based on local availability may reasonably be expected, although in the absence of material evidence (for example DNA analyses, only occasionally applied until now) the possible use of horses, donkeys and camels, antelopes and gazelles, panthers and hyenas, hares or deer cannot be assessed. Different factors (animal species, age and state of an animal's health, more or less careful workmanship) surely influenced the quality of the resulting product; technical differences in the manufacturing process must be also admitted according to places and times, although they are difficult to assess, in the absence of written sources. The essential operation, consisting in stretching a hide on a frame to dry and skiving and smoothing it on both surfaces with an instrument with a curved blade in order to remove residual hair or flesh and fat, could be preceded by chemical and/or enzymatic purification and depilation, by means of one or more lime baths (a method of unknown origin, reported by Latin sources from only as late as the eighth–ninth centuries CE), or through the application of various substances, such as dates, bran, barley flour or pigeon droppings; hair removal could also be done, as in Ethiopia, without the use of any specific agent. The skin was subsequently stretched on a frame—for a time dictated by the speed of drying, the required thickness of the end product, and, of course, the precursor skin—thus forcing the reticular collagen fibres into an arrangement in parallel layers. After being scraped with a blade, the skin might be smoothed with a rough substance (natural pumice or some artificial compound). It would then be subjected to finishing processes (using chalk or a mixture of egg yolk and linseed oil, for example), which were meant to improve the presentation of the surface by making it glossy and smooth, and to enhance the adhesion of ink. A difficult Coptic source (Crum 1905a; see Ch. 1 § 5) seems to transmit recipes for preparing (or improving) the surfaces of parchment pages. Other treatments of uncertain nature could be applied to equalize the two (hair and flesh) sides of the skin, such as scraping in Hebrew Ashkenazi codices produced in the German area from the end of the thirteenth century (see Ch. 1 § 9). Cow hide processed on only one side was used for writing Hebrew Tora scrolls; in the Orient, skins used for Hebrew scrolls could also be superficially tanned, as is attested by halakhic (legal) sources and confirmed by chemical analyses. The assumption that surface tanning, perhaps associated with other treatments, might have made possible, in certain cases, the splitting of the skins into two layers (corresponding to its hair and flesh sides; see Haran 1991) does not appear convincing.

Research on the dimensions, thickness and defects of the skins used, such as has been undertaken recently in Greek and Latin codicology, is unparalleled for the oriental traditions, apart from the data on parchment thickness and dimensions that are available (but not yet fully exploited) for dated Hebrew manuscripts.

In some oriental traditions, the use of purple or indigo-coloured parchment is documented (obtained either by dying or by surface painting, see Ch. 1 § 8.1.2), whereas it is apparently unattested or extremely rare in Armenian, Coptic, Ethiopic, Georgian, and Syriac book manufacture (although documented for Armenian by textual references from the early seventh century; see Ch. 1 § 3). Without the help of scientific analyses, it is impossible to distinguish the expensive murex purple (whose use in western mediaeval manuscripts is often mentioned, but has never been confirmed empirically) from its animal surrogates—the chermes or other insects of the same Coccidae family—or from its vegetable ones—the Mediterranean plant *Chrozofora tinctoria*, or turnsole, and the lichens *Roccella tinctoria* or *Ochrolechia* (the first one having been recently detected, although not with certainty, in a famous Greek purple Psalter; see Crisci et al. 2007). Information from other cultures is a desideratum.

The reuse of already written parchment—due not only to the high cost of writing materials, but apparently also to a widespread 'recycling attitude'—is widely attested in oriental manuscript traditions: such palimpsest manuscripts seem to be rare in the Islamic world, as well as in Ethiopia and in the Coptic and Slavonic regions, but they abound in the Greek, Armenian, Georgian and Syriac traditions, and they are the only surviving witnesses to the Caucasian Albanian written culture prior to the ninth century (see General introduction § 3.4). Palimpsests also document the movement of books between neighbouring cultures: manuscripts with a first, underlying text in one language, written over with a text in a different language, are not infrequent. Given the lack of oriental sources (only a single Latin description of the making of a palimpsest survives, in fact), techniques of erasure and strategies of reuse have to be deduced from a direct analysis of the extant examples.

1.1.3. Paper (MMa)

The use of paper in oriental books (and still earlier in documents) spread from east to west from China via the Arab-Islamic culture to the eastern Mediterranean and from there across North Africa and to Europe. The earliest evidence for paper in the Arab world dates from at least as early as the middle of the second AH/eighth CE century, and the oldest known dated specimen is an Arabic book from 848 (Beit-Arié 1996, 9); an isolated Greek example originating from the Jerusalem area has been assigned to around 800 (see Ch. 1 § 8.1.3). The phase of most rapid diffusion was, for the other cultural traditions, in the tenth and eleventh centuries, with the exceptions of the Slavonic region, where paper (of exclusively western manufacture) arrived much later, and Ethiopia, where it was not employed until the nineteenth century (and to some extent only in the second half of the twentieth century). In the absence of specific studies, the exact timing and routes of acceptance of the new material, as well as the relationship between imported and locally manufactured paper, remain uncertain.

The extraordinary abundance of material available for analysing oriental paper is far from being fully exploited and properly compared to the (not entirely perspicuous) information offered by Arabic sources.

The descriptive classification of the surviving types of paper that has been elaborated by scholars is not supported by detailed data concerning the tools, techniques and manufactured formats, nor by a clear view of the diffusion of each type.

While in East Asia (and perhaps also farther west at the beginning of the Arab manufacture) paper was obtained from plants in their raw state, the major innovation consisting in the use of recycled rags is probably to be attributed to the Arabs (although an eleventh-century Arabic treatise seems still to refer to the use of raw plants). Common to the different kinds of Arab paper is the use of unrefined rag 'pulp', with residues of long fibres whose botanical identification (hemp, linen, or other vegetable fibres) is still uncertain. The close observation of sheets of oriental paper allows one to distinguish various types, based primarily on the different characteristics of the sheet when observed against backlight, which characteristics can be used to formulate conclusions about the configuration of the paper 'mould' (that is the tool used to produce the paper sheet). Although 'one should bear in mind the frequent difficulty in identifying the visible structure of the oriental-Arabic paper even in well-preserved manuscripts, the many cases of ambiguous documentation and the inconsistent or contradicting impressions which blur clear and distinctive description' (Ch. 1 § 9), the main types can be summarized as follows, according to the sheet texture, on which all or part of a grid of perpendicular lines, parallel to the long and the short sides of the sheet—respectively known as 'laid' (or 'wire') lines and 'chain' lines—may be recognized: (1) paper with no visible laid or chain lines (showing, in Yemen, a 'chaotic' pattern); (2) paper with laid lines only; and (3) paper with both laid and chain lines, whether (a) single, or variously clustered in groups of (b) two, (c) three, (d) two/three alternating, or (e) four.

Type 1 can be related to the use of a rudimentary mould, composed of a simple rectangle of cloth stretched over a light wooden frame: such a 'cloth mould', when placed so as to float on water, required the pulp to be spread manually over the cloth in order to obtain a sheet, which consequently would show no grid. Type 3, showing a visible grid of laid and chain lines, was produced with a mould composed of two elements: (1) a wooden frame with a series of wooden or vegetal rods fixed at regular intervals, parallel to the short side of the frame (the pressure of these rods appears impressed on paper as chain lines); and (2) a kind of mat laid on the frame, made of thin flax or hemp threads sewn together, individually or in groups (visible on the paper sheet as laid lines). This 'flexible' form of mould was—as was also later the 'rigid' western one—normally submerged in a suspension of fibres diluted in water. The exact structure of the mould associated with paper with laid lines only (type 2) is still undefined.

In papers showing both laid lines and chain lines, correlations between the size of a sheet and the pattern of its grid led to the (uncertain) distinction of four large groups: (1) eastern Arabic paper (the only type showing unevenly grouped chain lines); (2) western Arabic; (3) Spanish; and (4) primitive Italian (showing single chain lines, regularly—and at the beginning of its manufacture also widely—spaced). The distinction between the types also depends on their typical size, characterized by a variety of equivocally defined standards. Research on Arabic manuscripts has recently questioned the 'traditional' classification into three groups developed by Jean Irigoin, by juxtaposing a different set of criteria (see Ch. 1 § 2.1.4 for a comparative table). More generally, the size of the sheets in use for the various kinds of oriental paper requires further research; with only a few exceptions, the spacing between chain lines and the density of laid lines, as well as the materials employed in the construction of the mould, have not been fully and systematically investigated.

Oriental manuscripts were also manufactured using western watermarked paper, produced first in Italy and later also in other European countries. Watermarking implies the use of a 'rigid' mould, a wooden frame with a great number of thin metal wires fixed parallel to the long side, supported at regular distance by wooden slats parallel to the short side and sewn to each other and to the slats themselves. Even apart from the presence of an image ('watermark') incorporated into the texture of the sheet, western paper is recognizable both by its standardized sizes—four, of which two main ones ('reale' = *c.*615 × 445 mm, and 'reçute' = *c.*450 × 315 mm, as they are called in the text of the Bologna city statute of 1389 and on the so-called 'Bologna stone')—and by the occurrence of a protein-based glue for sizing (obtained by boiling bones, skin or parchment scraps), spread by means of immersion, instead of starch sizing (made from rice, maize or wheat), applied with a brush (both types of sizing material were described by late Byzantine sources: see Schreiner – Oltrogge 2011, 76–79). Western watermarked paper appears in the Byzantine world by the end of the thirteenth century and in other oriental cultures during the fourteenth and fifteenth centuries. Cheap Italian paper produced specially for the Islamic world (with appropriate symbols as watermarks, such as crescents) annihilated most Arab paper making, but the extent of its export, the routes of its diffusion, the ratio of its use in comparison with oriental paper, and the diffusion of specific watermarks remain aspects that require much clarification.

A feature whose origin, manufacture and function are still matters of dispute among scholars is the occasional presence of a 'zigzag' mark, variable in design (a broken line, a series of comb teeth, etc.), visible either under raking light or against backlight. The zigzag mark, first documented in a mid-twelfth-century Andalusian codex, might not be an exclusive feature of Iberian paper production, as has long been believed, and is occasionally found also on watermarked paper.

During the nineteenth and early twentieth centuries, machine-made paper also came to be used in those traditions where manuscript books were still being produced.

1.1.4. Inks (IR)

According to its generic recipe, one of the oldest writing and drawing pigments was produced by mixing soot with a binder dissolved in a small amount of water. Thus, along with soot, binders such as gum arabic (ancient Egypt) or animal glue (China) belong to the main components of soot inks. From Pliny the Elder's detailed account (*Naturalis historia*, XXXV.25), we learn that, despite its seeming simplicity, the production of pure soot of high quality was not an easy task in Antiquity.

Purely organic or tannin inks are solutions of tannins extracted from various plants. The best known among them is the thorn ink, or Theophilus's ink, whose elaborate recipe is recorded in Theophilus's twelfth-century work *De diversis artibus* 49–51.

Iron-gall inks were certainly among the most commonly used writing materials and dominate the black-to-brown palette of many manuscripts. Though the origin of the use of a mixture of iron salts and tannins to produce a blackening fluid can be traced back to Antiquity (Pliny, *Naturalis historia*, XXXIV.43, 48), the earliest evidence of recipes that unambiguously mention a reaction between iron sulphate and tannins does not appear before the twelfth century (Zerdoun Bat-Yehouda 1983, 218–224). Iron-gall inks are produced by mixing natural iron vitriol with gall extracts. Iron(II) sulphate (also known as 'green vitriol' because of its colour and its glassy appearance) is the most frequently named ingredient in ink formulas. In mediaeval writings, however, other names like *atramentum* and *chalcanthum*, derived from ancient sources, are often used. Galls are diseased formations on the leaf buds, leaves, and fruits of various species of oak, caused when parasitic wasps deposit their eggs in them; they contain gallic acid and a number of other tannins, in varying quantities. When iron(II) sulphate and gallic acid are mixed, initially a colourless, soluble complex results; its oxidation through contact with air results in a black, water-insoluble pigment. Historical inks usually contain organic materials such as tannins, as well as a water-soluble binding agent, for example gum arabic. Solvents like water, wine, or vinegar were used to take extracts from the galls. Since the ingredients are mostly naturally occurring raw materials, the inks display a very heterogeneous composition.

In addition to inks of pure types, mixed inks containing components of different types are well known. The study of manuscript inks requires the use of instrumental analyses (on which see also General introduction § 2.2).

1.1.5. Pigments and dyes (OH–RN)

Iron oxide minerals such as red ochre ($Fe_2O_3 \times H_2O$ + clay + silica), haematite (Fe_2O_3) or goethite (FeOOH) belong to the oldest pigments; in Europe they were used since prehistoric times. Due to the variety of colours of iron oxides, there exist many recipes for the preparation of book illumination, whose use has been confirmed in manuscripts from Late Antiquity (Oltrogge – Hahn 1999); their early use has also been proved for Egypt, Mesopotamia and Asia. The pigments were prepared by cleaning, grinding and wet-sifting the minerals; red ochre can also be manufactured synthetically by heating yellow earth at 800°C (Theophrastus, *De lapidibus*).

Cinnabar or vermilion, using either natural (Liu 2005) or synthetic mercury sulphide, was also very commonly used in ancient times. The pigment was prepared artificially by sublimation, heating the pulverized mineral in the air. In the dry-process method, grinding liquid mercury with sulphur results in black mercury sulphide, the compound known in Antiquity as black *Aethiops mineralis*. Heating this compound up to 580°C for one hour in a large-mouthed earthen pot covered with an iron pan leads to formation of red cinnabar on the rim of the pot and on the iron pan cover. In the wet-process method, red mercury sulphide is precipitated from a solution of a salt of mercury by gaseous H_2S under slow heating. Another important red pigment is 'red lead' (Pb_3O_4), a synthetic pigment usually prepared by heating 'white lead' in an oxidizing environment (Pliny the Elder, *Naturalis historia* XXXV).

A yellow pigment known as 'massicot' is obtained by gently roasting white lead, with or without the addition of tin. In addition to yellow ochre (hydrated iron oxide) and massicot, arsenic sulphide-based pigments, natural and artificially produced orpiment (As_4S_6) and realgar (AsS) were also used. Orpiment was manufactured in a dry process by means of sublimation, or by a wet process using arsenic compounds in reaction with hydrogen sulphide. Adulteration of orpiment was usually made by mixing gall of fish, chalk and vinegar. Realgar exhibits a reddish to orange colour.

Copper-based pigments were widely used for green and blue colours since ancient times. The blue mineral azurite ($CuCO_3 \times Cu(OH)_2$) and green malachite ($2CuCO_3 \times Cu(OH)_2$) belong to the copper carbonates. Paratacamite ($(Cu,Zn)_2(OH)_3Cl$) has been detected in wall paintings from the fifth to eighth centuries in East Turkestan (Kühn 1988). One prominent artificial green pigment is verdigris ($Cu(CH_3COO)_2$), a reaction product from copper salts with acetic acid or vinegar. In addition, copper silicate (*chrysocolla*, $CuSiO_3 \times nH_2O$) was used as a painting material in East Turkestan and Egypt (Kühn 1988). Since these pigments are complex weathering products, their main preparation technique consists in cleaning or separating the pigments from other minerals. Green was also produced by mixing blue indigo with yellow pigments. Synthetic blue pigments are 'Egyptian blue' ($CaCuSi_4O_{10}$) and 'China Han blue', a barium copper sulphate ($BaCuSi_2O_6$). Egyptian blue was prepared by heating together a calcium compound with a copper alloy, silica (sand), and soda or potash as a flux at 850–1000°C. The glassy product was then ground and refined for purification (Vitruvius, *De architectura*, VII.11). The mineral lazurite, a sodium alumosilicate ($(Na,Ca)_8[Si,AlO_4]_6(S,SO_4)_2)$), can be extracted from the stone lapis lazuli. It contains additionally calcite, pyrite and other minerals. Deposits in the Hindu Kush mountains in Afghanistan (Oxus River, Amu Darya, near Sar-e Sang/Kokcha Valley in Badakhshan) are the main source. It is mined in open pits by heating rocks and then cooling them with water (Marco Polo, *Il Milione*, 46). It is prepared in order to intensify the colour by heating it several times, cooling it with vinegar, pulverizing it, and sieving it and repeatedly washing it out with water or vinegar as sedimentation. The powder is then kneaded together with resin or gum and linseed oil under cold water. With warm water, pigment particles come out of the wax pellets, which are finally washed and dried again. The early use of lapis lazuli as a pigment is attested in Central Asia (Riederer 1977). French ultramarine is a synthetic pigment that can be produced by heating clay (Ca, Si, Al), sulphur and soda together. In Europe during the Middle Ages, Egyptian blue was replaced by lapis lazuli (Gaetani et al. 2004).

White lead ($2PbCO_3 \times Pb(OH)_2$) is the best known artificial white pigment since Antiquity. The basic lead carbonate was produced by the influence of vinegar present in the atmosphere on metallic lead. White lead, as well as the mineral cerrusite ($PbCO_3$), were also used for the production of 'red lead' by heating. White chalk ($CaCO_3$) and gypsum ($CaSO_4$) were used as pigments not only for painting but also for priming.

The colouring component of 'plant black' or 'bone black' is carbon (see Ch. 1 § 1.1.4).

Not only minerals, but also metals were used for book illumination. Gold is applied as a kind of ink often on a base coat made out of a mineral pigment, for example white cerrusite, or in the form of a gold leaf. Gold powder is prepared with a binder as gold drops for trade. When used as paint, it is ground together with mercury to clean it by amalgamation before mixing it with glue.

However, the historical formulas do not only describe the extraction and production of pigments. Since Antiquity, dyes which were produced from plants and animals were used not only for manufacturing textiles, but also as lakes for the decoration of manuscripts. Historical dyes are less resistant to ageing than pigments are; this is surely the main reason that less is known about their use in Antiquity or in the Middle Ages.

Indigo is surely the most important organic deep blue pigment. The colourless pre-product is present in different plants, particularly in the East Indian *Indigofera tinctoria L.* The extraction of the blue pigment is done by fermentation.

A red dye is obtained from brazilwood and similar types of wood. During the manufacturing process, the deep red colour is extracted from the wood and the bark by using lye, vinegar, alcohol or urine. By extraction with alum, one gets a red violet lake. Depending on the extraction time and medium, one obtains colours between pink, crimson and reddish brown. Brazilwood was imported mainly from Ceylon and India in the Middle Ages. Several red or violet dyes can be produced by fermentation from different lichens (for example, *Rocella*). For the production, crushed lichens were treated with a thinned ammonia or urine and then fermented for some days or months. Other dyes were produced from scaled insects, for example, *Kermes vermilio* PLANCHON, *Porphyrophora hameli* BRANDT or *Kerria lacca* by extraction (Hofenk de Graaff et al. 2004).

1.1.6. Writing instruments (MMa)

Information about writing instruments comes from various kinds of sources: surviving examples (quite rare and mostly antique); texts, both literary and technical; pictures, mainly those appearing in manuscripts themselves; and also—particularly from Ethiopia and sub-Saharan Africa—ethnographic observations (including interviews with local craftsmen). But the available information is very uneven. Written sources (for example, Arabic treatises on penmanship) may contain very detailed instructions, but they do not resolve all doubts concerning the relationship between the use of specific instruments and scripts of different thickness and contrast. As for pictures, miniatures of the evangelists sitting in front of a lectern full of instruments (such as pens, ink pots, knives, scissors) and occasionally copying from a roll to a codex (or vice versa) occur frequently in manuscripts belonging to different Christian book cultures (Greek, Syriac, Georgian, Armenian, Ethiopic, Slavonic), but these conventional portraits, perpetuating ancient traditions and therefore abounding in inconsistencies and anachronisms, seem to be of only limited value; common models and relationships across cultures await specific study. Late Islamic miniatures are more realistic in the depiction of scribes and calligraphers.

Waxed tablets (where attested) were written with a pointed metal or ivory stylus (known from archaeological and literary sources), with one end in the shape of a spatula used to erase previously engraved letters, by smoothing them out of the wax. Flexible supports (mainly papyrus, parchment and paper) required different tools: most often mentioned (and most often described, particularly by Islamic authors) is the 'reed' pen or 'calamus' (Greek *kalamos*, Arabic *qalam*), a hollow plant stem (or also—less frequently—a hollow metal tube?), through which the ink could flow to a tapered point. The cut of the point had a strong influence on the execution and aspect of the written script. 'Quill' pens, made from the moulted flight feather of some large bird, were employed in Ashkenaz according to western practice, but their use is also known in the Orient (an earlier Syriac instance, from 509 CE, is particularly noteworthy (see Ch. 1 § 11.1.7), although its diffusion could perhaps be verified by the analysis of the oriental scripts).

Mentions and representations of other tools connected with writing, or with the preparation of the page (ink pots, knives, scissors, rulers, compasses, burnishers, pieces of furniture, as well as painters' and illuminators' tools) also occur in various sources from the different manuscript traditions.

1.2. Book forms (MMa)

1.2.1. Miscellaneous forms

Writing on a variety of surfaces quite unlike any book of the usual sort—clay tablets and *ostraca* (pottery sherds, limestone chips), bones, seashells, sticks, cloth—was a common practice in most (if not all) oriental book cultures. For books, the 'roll', or 'scroll' (terminology is inconsistent in the different scholarly traditions), both in the horizontal 'multi-column' and in the vertical 'single-column' ('rotulus') arrangement, and especially the 'codex' are the norm in all book cultures, although with salient differences from one to another.

1.2.2. The roll and the rotulus

As already described above (Ch. 1 § 1.1.1), Greek and Coptic rolls were made of a series of papyrus sheets (*kollēmata*) which were glued together (at joins called *kollēseis*) and rolled/unrolled, usually with the help of a wooden or bone stick attached to one or both ends of the roll. Rolls were sometimes made of parchment—or leather—in which case the sheets could be sewn together. The text was arranged, normally only on the inner side (in papyrus rolls, usually along the horizontal fibres), in a series of columns, usually rather narrow, but sometimes broad, whose lines run parallel to the long side of the roll. Height and length of rolls, as well as the number of sheets and the width of the columns, varied according to local conventions (which have been partially investigated only with regard to Greek rolls), with the limits to our knowledge being determined by the fragmentary state of the evidence and its uneven geographical distribution. Although more rarely preserved, parchment rolls might have been more widely used than is usually thought, especially outside Egypt. Talmudic instructions require writing the liturgical Tora scroll on *gevil*, cow hide processed on only one side, and literary halakhic (legal) sources, confirmed by chemical analyses, attest to regional differences in the substances used for the processing of the skins (Beit-Arié 2014). The diffusion of horizontal leather rolls in other traditions is subject to speculation.

Vertical rolls (*rotuli*, also called 'scrolls')—of parchment or paper, exceptionally of papyrus—are attested even in those cultures to which the use of horizontal rolls is unknown (Syriac, Armenian, Georgian, Ethiopic, beside Greek, Coptic and Hebrew; Slavonic liturgical examples seem to be rare imitations of Greek models, while in the Arab-Islamic world the *rotulus* occupies only a very marginal place). Unlike an ancient roll, a *rotulus* was not written horizontally in a sequence of more or less narrow columns, but vertically, in a single long column of lines running parallel to the short side of the roll; Ethiopians scrolls of larger size may be written on two columns. The use of this form for exorcisms, charms, amulets, obituaries, liturgical or magical texts and documents of various sorts is common to the cultures in which it is diffused. Early Greek examples go back to the eighth to ninth centuries, but their wider diffusion starts only with the eleventh century and continues into modern times in oriental monasteries. A comparative typology of the oriental vertical roll (still lacking) could offer interesting insights into their manufacture and use (length and width of the constituent sheets and methods of joining them, writing on one or both sides, decoration, contexts of use, and so on).

1.2.3. The codex

With regard to the use of the codex form of book, two main groups can be easily distinguished among the oriental manuscript cultures, according to the chronology of the earliest witnesses. On the one side are the Greek and Hebrew contexts, the horizontal roll having been the sole carrier of literary texts in the Greek area until Late Antiquity, and the codex having been introduced into the Hebrew book culture only very late, apparently not before the ninth century or a little earlier. On the other side are the cultural areas in which horizontal rolls are completely unknown: the Coptic book culture emerged around the end of the third century CE, at a time when the codex was already the dominant book form in the eastern Mediterranean world, and only very few Coptic horizontal rolls are known; the codex is known as the exclusive form in the Armenian and Georgian book cultures, whose languages were not given written form until the early fifth century; the same is true for the Syriac book culture, whose book production began in the first centuries of the Christian era; the earliest surviving Ethiopic handwritten books (two codices) were probably produced around the fifth and sixth centuries (although the date has been long debated); and also in the Arab-Islamic world the codex is known to the exclusion of the horizontal roll, since the emergence of Islam occurred at a time when the codex (possibly known through the intermediation of Ethiopia) was already dominant.

In Ethiopia, the 'leporello', 'concertina' or 'accordion book', apparently unknown elsewhere in the Near East, has been employed, for devotional purposes, at least since the late fifteenth century (see fig. 1.6.1). A leporello consists of one folded strip of parchment (or several strips folded together), with or without wooden or leather boards to which ties could be attached; the contents could be limited to pictures (one on each fold) or also include text.

Conversely, wooden tablets were widely diffused in oriental cultures. The plain wood could be directly used as a writing surface, or it could be carved out and covered by a thin layer of wax (often darkened with lampblack): this ductile material could easily be engraved with a pointed stylus (which could penetrate the wood beneath the wax, leaving traces of one or more scripts). Tablets were mainly adopted for documentary purposes or for writing ephemeral notes, exercises, drafts of texts to be transferred onto more durable surfaces, and so on. They could be used individually or assembled in groups (as 'diptychs' or 'polyptychs'): these latter have been considered as a direct ancestor of the codex, whose exact genesis—certainly due to a confluence of ideological and practical reasons—is likely to remain unknown. The presence of the wooden 'notebooks' in literary sources (mainly Greek and Latin) and the morphology of the surviving examples have been the object of specific interest.

1.3. The making of the codex (MMa)

1.3.1. The making of the quires

The basic constitutive unit of the codex is the 'quire', or 'gathering', which may be defined as 'a series of bifolia and/or folia [leaves] inserted one into the other' (Andrist et al. 2013, 50; various alternative definitions are offered in the codicological literature). A codex may be made of a single quire of any number of leaves or of a series of individually folded rectangular sheets of some pliable material, but intermediate structures consisting of a limited number of sheets folded together are the norm.

Quires are mostly (but not only) formed by superposed bifolia folded in half, usually along the shorter side; coupling of separate leaves ('coupled leaves' or 'stubbed singletons') which might be glued together to create an 'artificial bifolium' is documented—for instance in parchment Qur'āns, and also in other traditions—but data are wanting on the frequency and diffusion of this practice. 'Tackets', a kind of provisional basting made with threads or thin strips of leather, occasionally found in Latin, Ethiopic, Coptic, Slavonic, and also Greek manuscripts, including the famous Archimedes Palimpsest (Gumbert 2011, n. 16), were particularly useful for ruling or writing on quires containing loose sheets or coupled leaves.

In codices made from papyrus, it is observable that, as a rule, it was the roll that remained the basic material unit. For in the majority of papyrus codices, one almost always finds at least some leaves (and often many leaves) where a *kollēsis* occurs, as one would find at intervals also in a papyrus roll. Such occurrences of *kollēseis* on the leaves of papyrus codices provide clear evidence that the bifolia from which the quires of these codices were made were cut from rolls that had been manufactured in the traditional way by pasting together a series of *kollēmata*. Eric Turner stated as his summary view 'that normally a codex was made by cutting up a roll into lengths of the right size to form the constituent sheets of that codex; that sometimes care was take to cut out the *kollēseis* found in the original roll; and that special reasons ... must be invoked to account for the few exceptions to this norm' (Turner 1977, 50). But specifically in the case of a significant number of Coptic papyrus codices, something unusual has been observed with regard to the characteristics of the rolls from which the bifolia for the quires were cut. In these cases, there is no doubt that the original papyrus rolls had been made of extremely long *kollēmata*, exceeding 1 m and sometimes even approaching 2 m in length, i.e. being on the order of five times as long as what Turner had observed to be the maximum attested length of a *kollēma*. Given that up to now, such very long single sheets of papyrus have been discovered only as constituent parts of papyrus codices, it seems a reasonable hypothesis that the manufacture of such sheets was a technological innovation that was motivated by an increasing preference for the codex form of book over the roll. In the absence of similar evidence for very long *kollēmata* from non-Coptic codices, it is possible that this innovation came about in connexion specifically with Coptic book production, which seems to have begun to increase significantly during the fourth century CE.

In parchment codices, bifolia were obtained by dividing the rectangular surfaces derived from parchment. The recourse to multiple folding that would be used to produce quires in *quarto* and smaller formats (which was often practised in the west from the eleventh century onwards) has recently been questioned for Greek manuscripts on an archaeological basis: surely it cannot be considered as a general rule, and the procedures applied by the craftsmen still await specific analysis, relying on the observation of the skins' natural features (mainly the position of the flanks, still often visible on the surface of the page because of their particular grain). It is interesting to observe that the practice of cutting the skins, sometimes with the aid of templates, is documented in modern Ethiopia (see Ch. 1 § 6).

Skins were assembled either according to Gregory's Rule (see Ch. 1 § 1) or with alternating flesh and hair sides at each opening (except at the centre of a quire): whatever the choice, the arrangement was not usually left to chance. The choice of the parchment side to be shown at the beginning of a quire even varies according to different traditions, but occasionally also in time and place within the same book culture. Consistent information is lacking for most of the oriental traditions: a clear preference for putting the flesh side at the beginning is observed in Greek and Coptic codices (which might be the earlier practice, also documented in ancient Glagolitic codices), while in most of the Hebrew geo-cultural zones, quires usually start with the hair side; both practices are attested in the Arab-Islamic world.

1.3.2. The composition of the quires

'Quire composition' was also subject to a variety of practices. In papyrus codices, 'extreme' structures are documented, i.e. rare codices composed of a series of single bifolia, or more often of a single thick quire. Quaternions and quinions are everywhere the most widely diffused and predominant structures in parchment codices. In those traditions where the codex has an antique history, the two structures appear to have been concurrent initially; at a later stage, a divergence in the quiring of parchment manuscripts occurred, the causes of which have not been adequately explained. Quaternions dominate Greek and part of the European geo-cultural zones of the Hebrew book craft, and this structure prevails with some exceptions also in Armenian, Georgian and Slavonic manufacture; the eastern Islamic world—including Syriac and Hebrew manuscripts—displays a clear preference for quinions, although with the exceptions of Persia and Yemen; the Maghreb shows an unusual propensity for ternions. Greater variety is found in paper codices, where quaternions are also the predominant structure, but they are often replaced by quires of thicker composition, which may have been thought to be more resistant to stress and wear, or possibly they were simply more economical to bind. 'Mixed quires', made of paper bifolia 'protected' by parchment ones, usually placed at the outside, or at both the outside and the inside of a quire, also tend to show thicker structures (septenions or octonions, that is quires of seven or eight bifolia). Much more rarely, mixed quires made of parchment and papyrus are also attested (like the tenth-century Georgian hymnary of Tbilisi, see Ch. 1 § 7.1.1), some of which may have disappeared.

1.3.3. Pricking and ruling

Unlike in papyrus rolls, where writing might be guided by the horizontal fibres, placing content on the empty surface of a codex page requires a preliminary allocation of 'black space' and 'white space', mostly achieved by means of 'ruling' a grid of perpendicular lines drawn on the surface of a page in order to organize the written area (the 'black space') and to facilitate the alignment of text and images. Not all codices show traces of ruling, and in those which are ruled the grid was not always respected by the scribe, with the consequence that the actual written area does not always coincide exactly with the ruled area. When ruling was drawn, it might be preceded by 'pricking' (often removed by subsequent trimming of the margins and therefore not always still fully or even partially visible). Pricking and (even more so) ruling are complex phenomena, still in need of further research for oriental book cultures, with the exception of Greek manuscripts, which have been quite thoroughly investigated.

Pricks for guiding the drawing of the horizontal and vertical bounding lines were most often made with a sharp instrument; although unproven, the use of templates may have been quite common. Specific studies of the shapes and positions of the pricks, and the ways in which they were made are desiderata for all oriental book cultures; exceptionally, the contemporary Ethiopian practice of using two awls and a piece of pierced parchment as a template has been documented (see Ch. 1 § 6). Ink dots or strokes were sometimes used instead of, or occasionally in addition to, pricks, as we find in some Greek papyri, the Judaean Desert Scrolls, and some Coptic parchment codices.

Observations on ruling can be decomposed into several distinct aspects. The main ones are usually called 'technique', generally corresponding to the materials and instruments employed for tracing the lines (using more than one 'method', each implying the recourse to specific tools and gestures); and 'type', that is the grid (or 'grille') of perpendicular lines which is rendered on the page. The notion of 'system' is also required for the description of ruling done with a dry hard point, referring to the orientation and intensity of impressed furrows and ridges within a quire. Current terminology, reflecting the unsatisfactory state of our knowledge, should also be revised.

The two main techniques (or 'classes') of ruling are distinguished by a substantial difference in their visual appearance, depending on whether the grid is (directly or indirectly) impressed on the page (blind ruling) or traced page by page on both sides of each unfolded bifolium with a colouring material (coloured ruling). In both cases, various devices and/or substances may be involved in the operation, still awaiting further research for most oriental book cultures. The simplest tool for impressing lines on parchment (but occasionally also on paper) was a dry hard point, probably used in connexion with a straight edge, widely diffused in the east, allowing the simultaneous ruling of multiple superposed surfaces. A plethora of 'systems' is attested by Greek manuscripts—on single folded or unfolded (mostly parchment) bifolia or on successive leaves or bifolia in one go, on the hair or flesh side, resulting in a variety of sequences of 'direct' and 'indirect' rulings which can be observed on the leaves or bifolia of a single quire. So far, no parallel has been systematically identified in other oriental book cultures, with the exception of Hebrew and of Slavonic manuscripts; nevertheless, 'indirect ruling' is certainly witnessed in Armenian manuscripts and may have been applied also in other traditions.

With the diffusion of paper in the Islamic world, the use of a ruling board (*misṭara* or *masṭara* in Arabic, *kanna* in mediaeval Hebrew sources, *tołašar* in Armenian)—known through Jewish, Arabic and Armenian literary sources as well as being attested by extant mediaeval and modern examples—gradually became a common feature of oriental manuscripts (from whose example it also spread in the west): it is documented from 1131 for Hebrew manuscripts, in late Byzantine and post-Byzantine codices, and in mediaeval Coptic codices (see fig. 1.9.3). The *misṭara* is a frame made of cardboard or occasionally of wood, on which cords of various thicknesses were threaded into grooves and stretched, forming ridges corresponding to the bounding and writing lines, in accordance with the desired layout. The scribe would place each leaf (or bifolium) of the manuscript on the board and rub it with the thumb along the cords, which consequently left their impressions on the surface. Identification of this ruling technique is easy: there is no guiding pricking; the ruled lines are not as deep and narrow as those ruled by hard point, but wide and rather flat, and they are not perfectly straight, but usually slightly curved; in some manuscripts, it is possible to see the impression of the twists in the string; in addition, a uniform layout is observable, and the horizontal lines never exceed the boundary lines. The use of the *misṭara* allowed the creation of complex patterns of ruling in a fast and uniform way.

Some codices were not ruled at all, or were ruled in a crude way, limited to 'bounding lines' ('frame ruling'), and the bifolium could be folded parallel to the four edges in order to have the four lines framing the written area ('justification') indicated. The use of a fingernail for scoring is also mentioned, in Arabic sources.

Blind ruling, however executed, is the only technique used in Georgian, Slavonic and Ethiopic manuscripts as well as (apart from isolated exceptions) in Byzantium and the Arab world. Ruling by 'ink', introduced in the west at least by the end of the eleventh century (and then very common), did not meet great success in the east, despite some very precocious occurrences. Ruling by 'plummet', leaving grey traces, is known from some early Syriac examples already in the sixth and seventh centuries; traces of colour are also sporadically witnessed in a few Greek codices from the ninth and eleventh centuries. Not surprisingly, coloured ruling, overcoming initial religious resistance, spread by the end of the thirteenth century in the Hebrew tradition (see Ch. 1 § 9); Armenians used both metallic hard point ruling and red coloured ruling at least since the late thirteenth and fourteenth centuries and regularly from the seventeenth century (see Ch. 1 § 3). There has been much speculation—without fully convincing results—on the reason(s) for the shift from blind to coloured ruling, which had visual and functional advantages (a greater regularity in presentation and the possibility of adapting the grid to the need of texts with variable layout) and ergonomic disadvantages (given the need for ruling each page).

Whatever the details of execution, ruling produces a more or less elaborate grid of perpendicular lines, traditionally called a 'ruling pattern' or 'ruling type' (although the two expressions are not fully synonymous; Sautel 2012). The abundance of studies, repertoires and encoding proposals concerning Latin and Greek is contrasted by the general lack of such work concerning all the other eastern traditions, the only existing repertoire being one devoted to Hebrew manuscripts (Dukan 1988). No comparable data are available on the richness and variability of the patterns in use in the different traditions, according to dates and places of production and to content types: a higher variety may be admitted for parchment manuscripts, while the introduction of the *misṭara* resulted in a considerable simplification of the types in use.

1.3.4. Ordering systems

Unlike printed books, codices were not always equipped with devices meant to ensure, on the one hand, the correct sequence of quires, bifolia and leaves and, on the other hand, the immediate retrieval of specific passages of the text.

As for the first objective, oriental craftsmen (like western ones) show a remarkable inventiveness both in the development of effective systems and in their customization. The oldest and most widespread device is represented by quire numbering, i.e. the use of 'quire signatures', although with differences in chronology and diffusion in the different traditions; religious prescriptions could function as a deterrent to usage, such as in early Hebrew Bibles or Qurʾāns. Quire signatures may be indicated through an alphabetical or a numerical system (in the latter case, either spelled out or expressed by letters) and may appear on the first recto of each quire, on the last verso, or on both; the practice of 'signing' quires at both beginning and end seems to become more frequent in the course of time, appearing as a possible evolution of the system. The position on the page (upper or lower margin) and within the margin (inner, centred, outer) may also vary. A typology of quire signatures (as well as of other kinds of signatures)—as has been partially attempted for Greek and Arabic manuscripts and extensively for Hebrew ones—should take into account all the elements mentioned, in an effort to evaluate their variations in space and time (or also according to other factors, such as text types). Changes in the style and placement of signatures within the same codex may provide important clues for understanding the historical evolution of a codex and the different phases of its circulation; the co-occurrence of signatures in different languages may also offer clues for the detection of cross-cultural exchanges.

Quire signatures ensure the correct sequence of the quires within the codex, but do not prevent inversions in the sequence of bifolia and leaves within a single quire. As a means to protect the order of the quire (at the time of binding or while copying on loose bifolia and leaves), bifolium signatures could be used in association with quire signatures, specifying the number of the bifolium within its quire. As an additional measure, the opening of the central bifolium of each quire could be marked by special signs of various shapes (as in Hebrew manuscripts from the end of the tenth century, and in Arabic ones). Later in time, and not in all cultures, 'catchwords' appear as an alternative system for ensuring the correct connexion between two quires, with the advantage of making the link immediately visible at each transition. In the most widely diffused form, catchwords consist in writing the first words (or letters) of the following quire on the last page of the preceding one, usually outside the written area (immediately below the text or in the margin): in this last case, the catchwords could be written horizontally, vertically or diagonally (as in Arabic or Hebrew oriental manuscripts) at the lower inner corner, but could also appear at the centre of the bottom margin. It also sometimes happens that the last word of the preceding verso is simply repeated at the beginning of the text on the following recto (a system sometimes called 'counter catchwords', or 'repeated words'). In parallel with bifolium signatures, bifolium and leaf catchwords also sometimes appear. Widely diffused in Arabic, Hebrew and (later on) Greek codices, catchwords seem to appear only very late in other manuscript traditions. Any type of signature or catchword could be enriched by decorative elements. Additional signs such as crosses or asterisks may also appear (usually in the top margin) in order to emphasize the beginning and/or end of each quire.

In contrast to the devices meant to facilitate the work of the scribe and the binder, numbering was rarely employed to enhance the ease and comfort of browsing in the text: after appearing in some early Greek codices, first-hand leaf and/or page numbers are the norm only in Coptic codices, or else only in recent times, for instance in Ethiopia (probably in imitation of printed books).

1.3.5. The codex as a complex object

Unlike contemporary printed books, manuscripts do not always contain a single text, written on a structurally uniform series of quires and bound to remain stable over time. Volumes of miscellaneous contents are frequently found: the texts they contain may be transcribed one after the other without physical 'caesurae' or on independent units, either contemporary or more or less distant in time ('composite manuscripts'). Moreover, the initial appearance of a codex may be preserved until today, or (as often happens) it may have been altered by a series of more or less radical transformations: comments and notes may be inserted in the margins; new quires containing new texts may be added to the original sequence or it may be accidentally or deliberately altered; leaves, bifolia or entire quires may be removed or simply get lost.

Greek and Latin codicologists (Crisci – Pecere 2004; Ronconi 2007; Andrist et al. 2013; Ch. 1 § 8; Ch. 4 § 4) have become increasingly attentive to the 'complexity' of the mediaeval codex and have developed new approaches to analysing the relationship between the structure of the codex and its contents, and to investigating the form a manuscript takes not only in its original state at the time of its manufacture, but also during the various phases of its later life. For other oriental cultures, research is still at the beginning, apart from some pioneering surveys (Maniaci, forthcoming; Ch. 1 § 5).

1.4. The layout of the page (MMa)

The page layout of a codex is conditioned by both the contents and its intended purpose (or destination) and also the natural features of the material used, as well as by the dominant aesthetic canons and the personal preferences of artisans and commissioners. Quantitative codicology, which has focused almost exclusively on Latin and Greek manuscripts, has codified the main parameters to be considered in the analysis of the page layout: absolute and relative dimensions, number of columns and width of the four margins, extent of the written area and 'density' of the writing it contains (Ornato 1997). The absolute dimensions have been often expressed as the sum of height and width, or half the perimeter ('size'), conventionally defining how large a page is; various other indicators and calculation methods are also possible. The ratio of width divided by height is used to characterize a page's more or less slender or stout 'proportion': a page with ratio = 1 is perfectly square, one with ratio = 0.5, or ½, is very slender, one with ratio 0.8, or 4/5, very stout, the central value in the series of possibilities is the so-called 'invariant' ratio of 0.707, which does not change when a rectangle having this proportion is folded parallel to its shorter side (the modern standard paper format 'ISO 216' or 'DIN 476' has a ratio of 0.707). The 'filling rate' is given by the percentage between the written surface and the total surface of the page (of course possibly changing with every rebinding, but in any case always useful as an approximation for statistical purposes), while the 'exploitation rate' approximates the quantity of text contained on a single page, roughly determined by the distance between the ruled writing lines ('ruling unit').

None of these parameters (or others) has been systematically calculated in the study of the layout of oriental codices, even in the case of dated Hebrew manuscripts, for which an impressive quantity of numerical data has been collected, including ratios and proportions which can be classified in relation to other features, such as the number of columns or the text genre. Our knowledge is therefore limited almost entirely to occasional observations and casual statements. Moreover, research has focused (especially in Arabic codicology) on the effort to highlight the aesthetic values of the page (which surely played an important—although not exclusive—role in deciding on a given page's layout, as is shown by the complex organization of many Arabic manuscript pages, often equipped with not just one frame, but multiple frames) or to detect presumed numerical canons believed to be charged with particular elegance and harmony, although the theoretical limits of this approach have been clearly shown by Latin codicologists.

The size of the codices was surely connected, to a certain extent, to genres of text and their functional and social contexts: however, the available data do not allow us to establish chronological and regional typologies, nor to hazard comparisons between one culture and another. For Armenian manuscripts, for instance, it has been observed that Gospels, Bibles, and other liturgical texts were always larger, and parchment manuscripts were usually a bit bigger than paper ones, so that with the increase both of the variety of texts and the use of paper, overall size was reduced (see Ch. 1 § 3): analogous tendencies could also apply to other traditions, but they have not been documented on a tangible basis, except for Byzantine parchment codices.

Oriental (as well as western) books normally show a vertically oriented 'tall format', or occasionally a 'square format': 'oblong' or 'landscape' formats (wider than high) are practically unknown in most oriental book cultures, except for some isolated exceptions, such as ninth- and tenth-century oblong Qur'āns from North Africa or later Persian poetry manuscripts (see Ch. 1 § 2.2). The lack of systematic surveys does not allow us to compare the distribution of the range of sizes and proportions in different traditions, and the correlation with other features of the codex, starting with its contents. Occasional observations hint at some culturally related peculiarities: very big codices—as represented, for instance, by Syriac Gospel books from the sixth to eighth centuries (*c.*360 × 280 mm) or by Armenian Gospels from the ninth and tenth centuries (*c.*330 × 250 mm)—or extreme sizes, such as that of a group of *plano* Qur'āns of the second to third century AH (eighth to ninth centuries CE; *c.*680 × 530 mm) or of an Armenian Homiliary of 1202 (705 × 550 mm), are unknown to Greek and Georgian parchment book production, probably because of the adoption of more economic strategies of skin subdivision. Special shapes, such as that of certain small-format octagonal Qur'āns, are extremely rare.

The same want of data affects our understanding of the proportion of oriental manuscripts, except for the Byzantine production, which shows since Late Antiquity a clear preference for a more or less squarish format (tending to disappear with the introduction of paper). A square or approximately square proportion seem to have been largely, but not exclusively, favoured for eastern parchment books, but this general impression needs to be verified by specific research (for a first attempt concerning Armenian manuscripts, see Ch. 1 § 3).

In fact, with the diffusion of paper, book size and proportion underwent changes associated with the gradual standardization of paper sheet sizes, which for oriental paper still await a more precise definition. The adoption of a more slender proportion, mechanically derived from the in-*folio* folding of paper sheets, seems to be accompanied by a general tendency to size shrinkage.

Research on Greek and Latin codices has shown that the layout of the text in one or two (rarely more) columns, far from being a purely aesthetic choice, is strictly connected to text readability: since the reader's eyes are at ease in anticipating only a limited maximum number of letters, when the lines of text are too long (as might be the case especially in large manuscripts) or too close to each other (as may happen even in smaller manuscripts), it becomes necessary to split them into columns, in order to increase the ease and comfort of reading. In Latin codices—and to a lesser extent also in Greek ones—text layout is therefore more or less strictly correlated to their size (thus explaining the existence of different layouts for the same text, when copied in volumes of different size), and to the density of the text contained in the written area. The choice may also be influenced by other factors, such as the conditions of reading (publicly and aloud, as in the case of liturgical texts, or privately and more or less silently), the weight of local traditions, the influence of specific models, or the practical function of certain types of works (such as glossaries or bilingual texts).

To date, no quantitative study has been attempted—apart from Byzantine codices—to illustrate the relationship between size, content and single- or multi-column layout in oriental books and to define if and how the relationship between layout and readability exerts its effect also in other book cultures, and to what extent the artisan was aware of its implications.

Single-, double- and triple-column layouts appear to be variously represented in oriental book production, with preferences for the one or the other disposition having sometimes been hypothesized. Some correlations are empirically evident, such as the predilection (with some early exceptions) for a double-column layout in Armenian Gospel codices, New Testaments and whole Bibles (rare), while single-column manuscripts were usually reserved for poetry and philosophical or religious treatises; similar remarks have been made only unsystematically for other traditions. Writing lines are usually traced horizontally, but diagonal writing is attested in Arabic manuscripts. Special (sometimes inventive) arrangements were adopted for specific needs, for instance the layout of commentaries associated with a main text, or of images and drawings, whether placed in the margins or within the written area. The available information on these aspects remains mostly at the stage of obvious correlations or impressionistic notations; the same is also true for the general questions regarding exploitation of the page and of the written area.

Both in the design and in the practical implementation of the layout, specific models could be followed (as stressed by contemporary Ethiopian craftsmen), but the existence of layout 'prescriptions' is only sporadically documented, since very few of them have been preserved: these are in fact limited to a late Byzantine set of prescriptions and an Arabic text (apparently corrupt) from the second half of the seventh century AH (thirteenth century CE); a Latin Carolingian text, probably reflecting a Late Antique Graeco-Latin tradition, also deserves mention in this context (Maniaci 2013). Other isolated instructions, such as those concerning the decoration of the Eusebian Canon Tables in Armenian Gospels (see Ch. 1 § 3.5) or some late specifications for the copying of the Qur'ān might also be mentioned here. Given the rarity of explicit prescriptions, the reconstruction of layout rules should rely on the careful examination not of isolated cases, but of adequately large samples of written pages, an undertaking which has not yet been attempted.

1.5. Text structure and readability (MMa)

1.5.1. Writing and decoration

The role of the scribes was not confined to the physical embodiment of the verbal text; it also involved shaping its visual disposition, which in turn affected its verbal perception and reception, and allowed the reader to navigate within it easily. The visual presentation of texts in manuscript books was not an autonomous interpretative or purely artistic act on the part of the scribe and the painter; there were other factors and conventions—material, social, economic, aesthetic, and scholarly—dictating text configuration or at least affecting it.

Headpieces, initial letters or entire words (in the Semitic scripts or in all Armenian texts), titles (and running titles) in display scripts, and the use of colours (among which, various shades of red) may help to organize the text and to guide the reader by establishing dimensional and chromatic hierarchies. At the same time, the insertion of decorative elements adds visibility. Some of them, for example text dividers, break the flow of the text, forcing the scribe to plan his writing carefully and to adopt various graphic resources (abbreviations, changes in the form of the letters or in the width of their spacing, horizontal expansion or compression, and so on), in order to adapt the writing to the available space.

Also by means of spacing, compound punctuation, paragraphing and subdividing, underlining words or passages, pointing out terms, marking citations and lemmata, providing tables of contents and other locating devices and search tools, scribes enhanced the legibility and understanding of the contents.

In making a 'codicological use' of decoration and illustration as a means for structuring the text and shaping the reader's perception, every writing culture develops its own vocabulary and strategies: comparison is therefore limited to some general trends. An eye-catching example is represented by the insertion of an author's or an evangelist's portraits at the opening of a text or its sections, or by the use of single or double opening pages or (rarely) closing pages for religious (mostly liturgical) texts.

1.6. The scribe, the painter and the illuminator at work (MMa)

1.6.1. Colophons

'Subscription' and 'colophon' are generally (and vaguely) employed as synonyms to designate the often formulaic statements with which the scribe ended his work copying a book, usually by stating his or her name and/or dating it, and possibly also contextualizing it by specifying a place, an institution or other details concerning his or (more rarely) her enterprise or person. The genesis of the phenomenon and the reasons why a copyist decided to subscribe his or her work are not entirely clear, and obviously they varied according to time and place, as well as specific circumstances under which a manuscript was copied (from the desire to earn the forgiveness of the copyist's sins, to wanting to declare and advertise his or her own writing skills, to the intention of marking a specific act).

The frequency of the use of colophons varied significantly according to the different writing cultures (available estimates fluctuate from *c.*60% of Armenian manuscripts to less than 10% for Greek or about 7% for Hebrew and Slavonic manuscripts). Also the length and structure of colophon texts, as well as their literary quality, differ considerably from one oriental book culture to another (apparently with a tendency of Hebrew and Armenian scribes to be much more loquacious than all their colleagues) and within each of them.

In general, colophons are composed of variable combinations of the following elements, none of them appearing entirely consistently: the scribe's name, the name of the person on behalf of whom the scribe wrote, and the date of completion of the copy. Other information, such as the place of copying (always declared in Armenian colophons) and other details (reasons for copying, mention of secular or religious authorities; memories of historical facts; painter's or binder's name, exemplar, duration of copying, payments, names of the scribe's parents and so on) may also be found; their frequency changes according to the different traditions. In some cases, the final note may incorporate information relating to the collation and the editorial activity of the copyist (as in Arabic colophons), or a variety of detailed facts (as is often the case in Hebrew or Armenian ones). More or less verbose formulaic sections may be annexed to the colophon and possibly set off visually by some means: any such section should be formally and terminologically distinguished from the colophon itself. Statistics on the frequency of the various elements and their combination, and particularly on the mention of date, place and name of the scribe are missing for all oriental traditions, even when plenty of data are available (as for Greek, Hebrew or Armenian).

Colophons are not always located at the end of the book, but can appear at the end of a text section or of a production unit. Multiple colophons may give information on the 'evolution' of the book, helping us to distinguish its constituent layers. Attention must be paid to the possibility that colophons were copied from a model (particularly, but not only, when they are of particular historical interest) or even deliberately counterfeited or tampered with.

Although colophons are often transcribed in manuscript catalogues, the study of their formal aspects and of their evolution over time is hampered by the general absence of repertoires of formulations subdivided by place and date and accompanied by a detailed description or by an image of their layout. Existence of standard formats, evolution across time, correlations with other aspects (above all the contents of the book) remain to be studied. The same is true for external aspects: the lines containing information on the transcription may be put in a relation of continuity with the text itself or clearly distinguished from it, through the use of dividers of various kinds—lines or frames,— different writing styles or dimensions, colours, and other embellishments particularly related to layout, such as the arrangement of the text in original shapes.

1.6.2. Dating systems

The date of the copy is expressed according to a variety of local systems, whether limited to the year or specifying the month and day, the day of the week, or even the time of day; other elements (such as the solar and/or lunar cycle, cycle of the evangelists, epact, indiction, year of reign of a sovereign) may also appear in addition, or as alternatives to the explicit expression of a date. Details on the methods in use, with reference to bibliography, may be found in relation to the single book cultures.

When more than one dating system is used simultaneously, the consistency of the information they give should always be checked carefully. More generally, it is necessary to verify that the date of a subscription corresponds in fact to the date of the entire manuscript, or of the unit to which it is appended, and has not been copied from its model.

1.6.3. Duration of copying

Colophons as well as various notes in manuscripts and statements by third parties (for instance, contracts stipulated for the transcription of one or more books) provide only sporadic and occasional indications about the duration of the copying and the speed of the scribes. A hypothetical estimate of 2–3 leaves per day has been proposed for Latin mediaeval scribes (Gumbert 1995b; Gullick 1995), while no reliable data are available for any oriental tradition: given the variety of the circumstances and the subjectivity of the scribal experience, any generalization should be carefully avoided, at least until the available evidence has been systematically collected and analysed, which is far from being the case at present.

1.7. Bookbinding (NS–KS)

Although the basic composition and functionality of manuscripts in each cultural tradition appear to be founded on the same model, it is noteworthy that distinctive binding structures were developed. The basic structure consists of folded leaves, assembled in such a way as to form gatherings that were sewn and subsequently covered with a protective binding. The material of which those leaves were made, their number and their format, may differ over regions, historical periods and cultures, but the principle of nesting bifolia in the spine-folds to form gatherings is found in each tradition. However, the manner in which these gatherings were then sewn together differs from culture to culture. As a consequence, recognizing and understanding the differences in structure may be an important step in the process of establishing a manuscript's provenance.

The first difference consists in the use or absence of 'sewing supports'. Sewing systems without supports are link-stitch or kettle-stitch systems, in which the sewing thread links the gatherings directly together. When sewing supports are used, they are found on the spine of the text block where the sewing thread passes around each one, thus forming a structure in which the gatherings are connected to the supports, and also to each other close to head and tail. Sewing supports in general consist of strips of tanned or alum-tawed leather, or parchment, or pieces of cord.

A second characteristic to consider is the method of board attachment, and two main systems can be distinguished. Boards can be attached to the text block after it is sewn, using the binding slips (that is the outer ends) of the sewing supports, or, in the case of unsupported sewing, the extending parts of a spine-lining which is applied after sewing. With the other method, the sewing process starts only after one of the boards is prepared, either with the thread that is also to be used to sew the gatherings, or with the sewing support strips. In the latter case, a difference in the attachment of the two boards will be noticeable. With regard to the material of the boards, in some traditions wood was the predominant material, and in others boards were made of pieces of scrap paper pasted together. When wood was used, specific preferences are noticeable in individual traditions as regards to its grain direction. A final point of attention is the size of the boards relative to the text block. In some cultures, the boards are always flush with the edges of the text block.

Thirdly, small variations in the pattern of the sewing thread can be the clue for distinguishing between certain traditions. The passing of the thread within the fold-line and the positions of exit on the spine-side, linking either with the support or the previous gathering, plus the possible passing of the thread on the spine-side—often underneath the covering material and therefore not always visible—should be noted carefully. Further remarks can be made about thread thickness, the use of a single or a double thread, whether the thread consists of linen or cotton, and the number of sewing stations.

The next step in assessing the structure of a binding is to see whether the text block spine was lined after sewing, and if so, what kind of material was used and what shape and function it has. Generally, binders used parchment, leather or cloth to line the spines of the gatherings. When sewn on supports, the spine-lining often consists of strips made to adhere onto the spine in between the raised supports; with unsupported sewing, the spine-lining material is often full length, covering the text block spine from head to tail. Regardless of the presence or absence of sewing supports, the sides of the spine-lining material in most cases extend beyond the first and last gathering. The protruding sides are then usually pasted onto the inside or outside of the boards in order to strengthen the board attachments. One other aspect of the spine-lining is its function as a supportive material for the 'endband' sewing; often, the endbands will be sewn only after the spine-lining material has been applied.

The endband itself consists of several elements or features, most of which can be indicative for specific traditions. As such, it is important to register whether the endband is sewn on a core, and if so, of what material that core is made. Typically, parchment, tanned or tawed leather, or cord made of hemp or flax was used, but some traditions did not incorporate endband cores in the sewing, and others used double cords or even triple cords. Moreover, the endband core can have the additional function of making up an extra board attachment position, at head and tail of the book. If that is the case, the extending slips of the core are fastened in some way to the boards, otherwise, the endband core is cut at the position of the joint. With regard to the endband sewing, it should be established whether a primary sewing was applied, or if a secondary—usually decorative—endband was added. Furthermore, the gatherings need to be checked for anchoring stations.

Other binding elements of importance for distinguishing the traditions are often not directly related to structure, but concern features that affect the functionality and aesthetics of bindings. Closing systems, for example, diverge widely among the traditions. Sometimes straps, often combined with metal elements, but sometimes with wooden pegs, were used. In other cases, an extension to the backboard in the form of a protective flap was added, instead of an actual closing mechanism, and a combination of these elements is also possible. All measures intended to keep the manuscript closed have primarily the function of protecting the front edge from deformation, but were often included in the decorative scheme as well. The same dual functionality of protection and aesthetics is found with other metal elements fitted on book covers, usually described as 'furniture'. Another characteristic to remark on is the use and appearance of possible reading aids, whether they are flexible tassels or fixed page-markers.

All book traditions display a certain development in techniques and materials used, as is the case for the structure and the functionality of the artefact as a whole. Therefore, to typify any book tradition by its predominant form and construction by definition ignores the interesting, remarkable or even characteristic variant specimen. As a consequence, an introduction into the multiplicity of book structures that can be found in the oriental cultures can only outline the basic characteristics.

It seems that the Coptic codex, with its link-stitch sewing structure, is the basic book form on which the other traditions where modelled. While bulky, one-gathering structures were made in the early centuries of the Coptic tradition, it was the multiple-gathering structure and its unsupported sewing—the boards were attached with the sewing thread—that took root (Szirmai 1999, 7–31). Byzantine manuscripts resemble the Coptic structure but can also be distinguished when the sewing structure is examined carefully: in certain instances, yet not always, instead of sewing the text block from back to front or vice versa, the Byzantine manuscript is sewn in two parts, starting from each board so that the board attachment is similar at front and back; the two halves of the text block are connected by linking their sewing at the middle of the spine. Furthermore, the endbands on Byzantine manuscripts deviate from the Coptic ones. The latter were sewn without an endband core while the Byzantine endband is sewn on cords that extend beyond the joint and are sewn to the boards. The text block is cut flush with the boards at the head, tail and front edge, the spine is rounded in a characteristic manner, and often the bindings are furnished with a fastening system using leather thongs and metal clasps (Szirmai 1999, 62–83).

The Islamic book structure can best be divided into the type that developed in the first centuries of Islam, of which unfortunately little is known due to the scarce material that is left from the period, and the structure that evolved from this initial codex type and became the predominant book structure from the eleventh century onwards. It is generally assumed that the oldest book structure had wooden boards that may or may not have been attached to the text block. Remnants of bindings indicate that the leather covering had protective flaps, or even 'walls' attached to the back cover that covered the edges of the text block. With the later book type, only the flap extending from the front edge of the back board lasted, but developed further with an additional envelope flap. This fore-edge and envelope-flap structure is typical for the Islamic tradition. The Islamic manuscript book is further characterized by a flat spine. Usually the books were sewn with a link-stitch, and the boards are flush with the edges (Di Bella 2011; Scheper 2014, forthcoming).

Syriac and Ethiopic book structures also adopted link-stitch sewing from their predecessor, the Coptic codex. However, seemingly small variations in sewing schemes make it possible to distinguish between the traditions, and both Syriac and Ethiopic bindings display a particular method of board attachment. Furthermore, Ethiopic bookbindings display most often a unique way of sewing the text blocks, using a four-needle sewing in two pairs of sewing holes (Di Bella – Sarris 2012). Syriac bookbindings are further distinguished by a spine-lining of coarse cloth, which outer ends are usually pasted onto the outside of the boards, a feature not often found in other traditions (Checkley-Scott 2008; Szirmai 1999, 45–50).

Armenian bindings developed differently from their direct neighbouring cultures: instead of using link-stitch sewing, the gatherings were sewn on binding supports and the support slips were used for board attachment. The insides of the boards are usually lined with coloured textiles. A further unique binding element is a protective flap precisely the shape and format of the fore-edge, made of leather and attached to the back board. A further closing system is found in the form of leather strips, attached underneath the covering leather on the back board, crossing the fore-edge flap and long enough to be secured on the front board, where usually two wooden pegs are affixed for this purpose (Merian 1993, 2008).

Information on more specific features, concerning binding structures, but also types, materials and decoration of covers, will be found in the sections on the individual traditions.

References

Agati 2009; Andrist et al. 2013; Beit-Arié 1993, 1996, 2014; Checkley-Scott 2008; Crisci et al. 2007; Crisci – Pecere 2004; Crum 1905a; Déroche – Sagaria Rossi 2012; Di Bella 2011; Di Bella – Sarris 2012; Dukan 1988; Emmel 1998; Gaetani et al. 2004; Géhin 2005; Gullick 1995; Gumbert 1995b, 2010b, 2011; Haran 1991; Hofenk de Graaff et al. 2004; Kühn 1988; Liu 2005; Maniaci 2002a, 2013, forthcoming; Merian 1993, 2008; Oltrogge – Hahn 1999; Ornato 1997; Riederer 1977; Ronconi 2007; Schreiner – Oltrogge 2011; Sautel 2012; Scheper 2014, forthcoming; Szirmai 1999; Turner 1977; Zerdoun Bat-Yehouda 1983.

2. Arabic codicology (FD–VSR–AVN)

2.1. Materials and tools (FD–VSR)

2.1.1. Papyrus (FD)

Too few papyrus manuscripts survive to allow any major trends to be extrapolated. Makers continued to prepare papyrus as they had done in ancient times. Papyrus codices were employed very early. For instance, some documentary codices in Egypt have been dated prior to the 'Abbasid period (Gascou 1989, 100–101; see also fig. 2.2.2). The majority of literary papyri subsist in a fragmentary state and provide only an incomplete picture of the use of the material. Nevertheless, a certain number of bifolia in reasonably good condition seem to confirm the conclusion that the codex was indeed the dominant book form.

Papyrus continued in use until around the mid-fourth century AH/tenth century CE, by which time competition from paper became overwhelming, papyrus manufacture practically dying out by the fifth century AH/eleventh century CE (Grohmann 1967, 73).

2.1.2. Parchment (VSR)

Although in the Orient parchment seems to have been well known and used from the beginning of the first millennium BCE (Ryder 1991), collections of Arabic manuscripts include only very few examples written on this support. Though we do not have any manuscripts which we can date with certainty to the period before the third century AH/ninth century CE, there is no doubt that parchment was used in the Islamic world right from the beginning.

The spread of the paper-making technique brought about a progressive disappearance of the production of parchment. Two Qur'āns from the end of the third century AH/ninth century CE, in all probability copied in Persia, show that at this date parchment was still being used in this region in which paper had been widely available for more than a century. In the central area of the Islamic world, where the documentary evidence is more abundant, the use of parchment was still very common in the fourth century AH/tenth century CE (in the following, unless specified otherwise, only CE dates are given).

In the western part of the Muslim world, copyists continued—less and less frequently—to use parchment until the fourteenth century CE, and perhaps even into the fifteenth century CE. A manuscript copied in Syria in 980 AH/1572–1573 CE represents the most recent use of parchment (see also fig. 2.2.6). In India a particular type of very transparent parchment, which could be written only on a single side, was used to copy exemplars or excerpts of the Qur'ān.

Islamic authors refer to sheep (mainly), goat and calf parchment. A treatise by the Sevillian Ibn 'Abdūn (d.1135 CE) strongly suggests that the skin of lean sheep should not be used for the preparation of parchment. Ibn al-Nadīm, the tenth-century author of the famous bio-bibliography *al-Fihrist*, mentions the technique that we know from the Latin west (eighth to ninth centuries CE) of dissolving the fat and facilitating the removal of the hair from the follicles through one or more baths of calcium hydroxide after applying a depilatory paste, *nūra*, composed of quicklime and arsenic, which is inconvenient as it makes the skin dry. The Arabic text spells out the composition of the paste, variously indicated by Arabic, Turkish and Persian dictionaries. Another procedure, in use in Kufa, made it possible to obtain a soft skin thanks to a preparation based on dates, also used in mediaeval eastern Jewish communities. Some authors think that the treatment of the hides in a bath of lime was, if not invented by the Arabs, at least transmitted by them to the Europeans; others hold that this technique spread the other way around. Comparison between manuscript traditions of other Middle Eastern regions may help in integrating the overall picture, which is still rather patchy (Haran 1985, 47–50; Déroche – Sagaria Rossi 2012, 45–50).

Some cities maintained that locally produced parchment was of a superior quality: Kufa or Edessa (al-Ruhā') had a high reputation, yet the reasons for this excellence—technique, geographical location, climate—are not clear. The practice of dying the parchment was well known throughout the Mediterranean area, as is attested by the celebrated tenth-century 'Blue Qur'ān'; other colours, such as saffron, yellow and orange, were also available. Coloured inks were also used on dyed parchment: in a widely read eleventh-century treatise on the production of books by the Zirid sovereign of Ifrīqīya Mu'izz ibn Bādīs, the author provided prescriptions for how to prepare golden and blue inks (Bloom 1989).

The depilation of the hair side of a skin was not always carefully done, as appears in numerous manuscripts from the Maghreb. The parchment might be scratched with a sharp instrument or covered with chalk, as microscopic analysis has shown for the sheets of the *ḥiǧāzī*-style Qur'āns—dated in the end of the seventh and the beginning of the eighth centuries—and others copied in the Maghreb in the thirteenth and fourteenth centuries (Dreibholz 1991).

Regardless of the dimensions of the hides and of the size of the manuscripts, parchment codices are rectangular in shape or, more rarely, square.

2.1.3. Palimpsests (FD)

There survive a few Arabic palimpsests, but only one is clearly from an Islamic context. The Qur'ānic *scriptio inferior* of Sanaa, DAM, inv. 01-27.1, with a leaf in Copenhagen (Davids Samling, inv. 86/2003) was probably transcribed during the last third of the seventh century CE, then erased and covered by another copy of the Qur'ān (Déroche, forthcoming). Other palimpsests exist, however, in which Arabic script masks texts written in other languages (Grohmann 1967, 109 and n. 6). In other cases, the upper text has been added in a Christian context (Lewis – Mingana 1914; George 2011).

2.1.4. Paper (FD–VSR)

Oriental-Arabic paper. History and diffusion (VSR)

Arabic paper can be distinguished within the macrocosm of 'oriental papers', although with some difficulty. Among different types of Middle Eastern paper, the 'Arabic' one is the type produced at the end of the eighth century in the capital of the Abbasid Caliphate, Baghdad, as well as that produced in other regions of the Arab-Islamic world, including the territories of the Iberian Peninsula controlled and governed by Muslims (al-Andalus). The differences between Arabic and Persian paper, with a wide distribution in the Arab countries Yemen and Iraq, are not yet clearly defined (Humbert 2002).

Paper was imported from China well before 751 and spread throughout Central Asia and Persia. Though paper is called *qirṭās* or *waraq*, Persian *kāġad*, Arabic *kāġiḏ* or *kāġaḏ*, Turkish *kâğıt*, is a loanword from the Sogdian language, belonging to the Eastern group of ancient Iranian languages, which passed through Persian into Uyghur and then into Turkish as *kâğıt*. The Sogdians, in contact with Chinese Central Asia, contributed to the spread of paper making techniques, to the point that the first Christian texts on paper might have been written in this ancient Iranian language. Imported paper, already employed by the governors of Khorasan for administrative acts in the seventh century CE and used to copy books in Arabic, was certainly already employed for the Sogdian language. We do not know how long imported Chinese paper was used in those regions after paper manufacture had started in Samarkand, where paper was first produced from rags, and not only from pulped vegetal material (Karabacek 2001; Bloom 2001).

As for the adoption of paper by the Arabs, Karabacek establishes 794/795 CE as the date it arrived in the Abbasid capital Baghdad; in fact a paper mill is attested there in 794 CE, under the government of Hārūn al-Rašīd. Unfortunately, however, no dated book or document written in Arabic on paper from this period and coming from this area has come down to us. Egypt used paper beginning in the ninth century CE, and later a paper mill was set up at Fusṭāṭ. Damascus had a paper industry in the twelfth century CE, but its quality, reputedly better than that of Egypt, quickly declined. The use of paper was imposed by Caliph Hārūn al-Rašid starting in 808 CE.

The expansion of so-called 'Arabic paper' throughout the Mediterranean area occurred relatively rapidly. In the twelfth century CE, Spain had numerous paper mills in the Muslim provinces. In the Maghreb it arrived in the ninth century CE, though it was used along with parchment until the fourteenth to fifteenth century CE. In eleventh-century Sicily, paper was both imported from other Islamic centres and locally produced, using the same techniques. As regards Anatolia and Constantinople, one must note the slowness of the Byzantines in adopting paper, assumed to be imported from Syria. There was a paper mill at Kāğithane, near the estuary of the Golden Horn in 1453, the date Sultan Mehmet II conquered Constantinople, and another at Bursa which was functioning in 1486. Other paper mills only seem to have entered into production starting in the first half of the eighteenth century CE.

Paper trade started rapidly and on a large scale. The presence of mills near some large cities led to styling the different types of paper with adjectives corresponding to the place where it was produced: thus *baġdādī*, *samarqandī* and others. Also the quality of the water used in manufacturing paper was relevant. The paper of Baghdad—hence also the adjective *baġdādī*, referring to a sheet of large dimensions—was appreciated for its quality until the fifteenth century CE. Syrian paper, called *šāmī*, enjoyed particular prestige and set a format in use at the Mamluk chancellery.

If the spread of paper around the Islamic area was fast, the decline was equally rapid, due to a series of factors that occurred starting from the middle of the fourteenth century CE. The inefficient administrations of the Ilkhanate governments (thirteenth to fifteenth century CE) in Persia and Iraq, and of the Mamluks (thirteenth to sixteenth century CE) in Egypt and Syria, together with waves of plague that afflicted Egypt until the early 1500s, resulted in the collapse of local industry. In Egypt, linen production also entered a crisis, and cheaper European wool textiles were preferred over local products, causing a drop in the quantity of rags available for the local production of paper, with a consequent increase in cost (Bloom 2001, 211–212). Conversely, European paper, Italian paper in particular, was much cheaper and therefore competitive. It was the plundering by Tamerlane, in particular of Damascus in 1401 CE, that dealt the death blow to the oriental-Arabic paper industry, above all that of Syria, actually the producer of the best quality paper at the time. Mongol domination introduced Chinese techniques of paper production, above all of paper decoration. The latter consisted in dying, spraying, and painting the paper in gold, and marbling it to the extent that it became an integral part of the cultural baggage of local artisans. These techniques reached their highest level under the Safavid dynasty (1501–1736) and the Mughals and remained in use in the subsequent period also, under the Qajar dynasty (1781–1825) and British colonial rule.

Sources and manufacture (VSR)

Sources on paper manufacture are scarce: they usually report places of production, formats, and quality, but only rarely do they concern the actual fabrication techniques. For example, what we know about the paper made in Samarkand comes from Ibn al-Nadīm, according to whom the Khorasan paper was produced by Chinese artisans following the model used for Chinese paper; Ibn al-Nadīm also provides us with the Arabic denomination for six types of paper, all referring to high-profile functionaries in that territory (Déroche – Sagaria Rossi 2012, 52–53). Thus, one can assume that at least two types of such kinds of paper, which survived their governors, were recognizable by their production techniques, as shown by the recipe for the preparation of *ṭalḥī* paper which has come down to us, known as the 'recipe of Ibn Bādīs', the first real witness to paper manufacturing and moulds in Islamic lands (Humbert 2002, 59–61).

The only authors who provide information on paper production are the geographer al-Muqaddasī (d. after 988 CE), who mentions the production of *kāġiḏ* in Damascus and in Tiberias, and the Syrian biographer and geographer Yāqūt al-Ḥamawī (d.1199) who mentions paper production in a suburb of Baghdad. It has been proved that paper mills existed in various localities of Syria between the ninth and tenth centuries CE, namely in Hama, Tripoli, Manbij and Sanaa in Yemen (Karabacek 2001, 28–33).

The famous Ibn Bādīs recipe is open to a variety of interpretations, as concerns the descriptions and identification of the raw materials, and also their manufacture. Humbert thinks that Ibn Bādīs referred to linen in its natural state. The fibres underwent repeated cycles of submersion into a lime bath and of manual defibration, after which they were left to dry in the sun and then cut and immersed in fresh water for seven days. The pulp, pounded in a mortar, was diluted with water and forcefully beaten with the hand until it turned 'soft as silk', then was poured and evenly spread into moulds of the desired size, like 'baskets opened on the sides' made of reeds, canes or grass, fixed on a vat. After filtering and draining the water, the sheet was removed and laid on a wooden table and pressed against a wall to let it dry (Irigoin 1993, 278–280). The surface was then glazed with flour and starch in equal proportions; this mixture, laced with water, was boiled and then smeared on both sides of the sheet to make the paper able to receive writing. According to Karabacek, the raw materials consisted of hemp rags and ropes, treated with water and milk of lime, then beaten with sticks moved by water mills or, less frequently, by animal labour. Indeed, it seems that rags and old rope were used in Samarkand and in the westernmost regions of China since the first half of the eight century CE (Karabacek 1888, 13–14; Bloom 2001, 44–45).

Irigoin stresses that linen was the prerogative of Egypt, and that by the mid-twelfth century CE the cultivation of cotton had spread from India to eastern Persian, Maghreb and Muslim Spain (Irigoin 1993, 281–282). Although the existence of paper made from cotton fibres has often been denied, the presence of cotton fibres in some papers has been detected by recent diagnostic analysis (Colini 2008, 89–91, 105). The crux of the matter is the meaning of the adjective 'bombycine' from Latin *bombycinus*, itself derived from Greek *bombykinos* 'silken' and *bombyx* 'silk', specifically the 'silk-worm'. The derived Latin words could be applied to any fine fibre, including cotton. It has been suggested that the expression 'bombycine paper' referred not to the material from which the paper was made, but rather to the sheet's texture as being similar to that of silk or cotton (Karabacek 2001, 36–40). It is also possible that the Greek adjective bombykinos referred originally to the city of Hierapolis Bambyke—now Manbij in northern Syria—renowned for its silks, but which could have, by analogy, given its name to the paper it produced. On this theory, an adjective 'bambykinos' referring to the city and designating both the basic origin of some product as 'made in Bambyke', and also the quality of any such product, came to designate a soft-textured paper made in Bambyke by means of a change in the first vowel, from *bambykinos* to *bombykinos*, thus alluding (whether by design or confusion) to the word *bombyx*. If so, then 'bombycine paper' would be just a kind of paper produced in Manbij (Hierapolis Bambyke), about the morphological nature of which nothing can be said. In any case, the analysis of ancient paper pulps (containing both vegetal and rag fibres) is still too limited to offer more precise information on the recycled materials that were used.

Returning to the paper moulds that were in use, the type described by Ibn Bādīs consists basically of a wooden frame on which a flexible linen cloth was stretched. The paper pulp, dissolved in water, was poured onto the cloth and then levelled smooth. This operation was performed while the mould was floating, soaking wet, on the surface of a vat.

The second half of the eighth century CE saw the rise of the dipping mould, similar to the Chinese one, made of an external wooden frame supporting a flexible and removable mesh on which another wooden structure was laid to keep it in the right position and ensure that the sheet would have the right thickness (Déroche – Sagaria Rossi 2012, 56–58, with figures). Also known as *forme souple*, this mould was composed of a mesh made of flexible grass straws or cloth fibres, or of stiffer bamboo canes, laid at regular intervals parallel to the longer side and at broader intervals perpendicularly, bound together by threads or animal hairs. In the majority of cases, such a tool replaced the previous model, allowing the production of multiple sheets from a single mould.

Another Yemeni prescription, dating back to the thirteenth century, is attributed to the Rasulid ruler al-Malik al-Muẓaffar al-Ġassānī (d.1294 CE). It attests a local manufacture developed in a much later phase than the first examples of paper production in Yemen. The suggested raw materials are 'the white internal fibres from the bark of fig trees', a plant in the same family as the mulberry, called *kozo*, whose fibres taken from the inner part of its bark were used to make Chinese paper (Gacek 2002). In his treatise, the practice of piling reams of hundreds of sheets is also described, or of packing them in groups of five, which introduces quiring in quinions, very frequently used in Arabic manuscripts.

Al-Ġassānī may likely refer to the wireless type of paper, with a chaotic pattern in which neither chain lines nor laid lines can be distinguished. Reputed to be the most ancient kind of Arabic paper, it was widely employed in the Middle East from the mid-eleventh century CE until the end of the fourteenth century CE, particularly in the regions of present-day Iraq and Iran, where it is attested even later. A peculiar kind of wireless paper, belonging to the more comprehensive non-watermarked category, was produced exclusively in Yemen, in the fourteenth to the sixteenth centuries: it is thick and opaque, densely filled with fibres in a markedly chaotic pattern (Déroche–Sagaria Rossi 2012, 60–62, and fig. 15; D'Ottone 2006, 16–17).

Sizing was carried out using humid white sorghum; after drying, the sheets were polished with a piece of marble or a burnisher, usually along the long side; a mixture of wheat flour and rice starch is referred to in the Ibn Bādīs prescription.

Typologies and formats (FD)

The identification of the fibres used in the preparation of paper in the Islamic world remains underdeveloped. The relevant information gathered from the very few analyses of the composition (fibre or rag) of paper pulp undertaken to date is not particularly helpful to our investigation. The question arises of the part played, if any, by hemp, linen (sometimes recycled), cotton, or other vegetable fibres (Gacek 2002, 79–93). Finally, a certain amount of paper is said to have been produced from a pulp of silk fabric (*ḥarīrī* paper), but analysis has not substantiated this hypothesis (Déroche 2005, 52).

On the basis of a visual examination of papers, G. Humbert provided a rough typology based on the kind of mould used by the papermakers, focusing mainly on the distribution of the chain lines (Humbert 1998). A first category covers papers with simple, isolated chain lines, with spaces between them ranging mostly from 12 to 25 mm, but sometimes as much as from 30 to 55 mm in some Indian manuscripts of the sixteenth to eighteenth centuries CE (Humbert 1998, 17–18). In papers produced in the western Islamic lands (also in southern Italy), the spacing is in general somewhere between 40 and 50 mm.

In the second category, the chain lines are grouped in twos, threes or fours, lying in uniform arrays over the whole sheet. Groups of double chain lines are attested from at least the twelfth to the fifteenth centuries CE, particularly in Egypt, while chain lines arranged in threes are amply attested from the eleventh to the fifteenth centuries CE in Persia, Syria, Egypt, Asia Minor and even at Mecca. The place of manufacture of this type of paper remains mysterious, but it is known that its use expanded noticeably in the course of the fourteenth and more particularly in the fifteenth century CE (Humbert 1998, 20–22).

Other, less frequent, dispositions of the chain lines are known: in fives (between 1374 and 1420, Baghdad and southern Iran); in regularly alternating groups of two and three (some of them in the thirteenth century in Syria and also in Egypt). Papers where such groups alternate irregularly have been documented from the beginning of the thirteenth to the fifteenth centuries CE in the Middle East, Egypt and Syria, eventually also in Persia. A series of Persian papers of the twelfth and thirteenth centuries CE present simple, double or triple chain lines that alternate more or less regularly (Humbert 1998, 22–25).

In the western part of the Islamic world, papers produced locally sometimes exhibit a specific feature: the 'zigzag'. Often found in the fold or close to it, sometimes also in the upper or lower margin, this mark looks like a succession of tightly joined segments crossing rectilinearly the width or length of the sheet. The occurrence of the zigzag corresponds to a thinner area of paper and can be observed by transparency. The purpose of this device and the way in which it was produced remain unclear (see for instance Estève 2001).

Sheets of paper were seldom used in their original uncut state save in the case of volumes of exceptional size (for example Paris, BnF, Arabe 2324, 760 mm high × 530 mm wide, early fourteenth century CE). As a rule, dimensions rarely exceed 650 × 450 mm. In most fifteenth-century Persian *folio* volumes, the whole sheet measures at least 550 × 350 mm. On this basis, the dimensions of the sheets have been calculated, first by Jean Irigoin on a sample of Byzantine manuscripts (Irigoin 1950), and more recently by Nourane Ben Azzouna, who compiled a corpus of manuscripts produced under the Mongol dynasties (1258–1411; Ben Azzouna, forthcoming).

	According to J. Irigoin	*According to N. Ben Azzouna*
Largest format	660 to 720 × 490 to 560 mm	680 to 820 × 488 to 608 mm
Middle format	490 to 560 × 320 to 380 mm	596 to 668 × 415 to 500 mm
Small format	320 to 380 × 235 to 280 mm	440 to 524 × 305 to 374 mm

Since bifolia were prepared in advance, occasional leaves with lines running in an apparently anomalous direction do appear. In the case of unusual volumes such as the so-called Baysunqur Qur'ān the precise technique that was employed remains unknown; perhaps a fixed mould was used (James 1992b, 104–105; Soudavar 1992, 59–62). Again there exist, especially in the Iranian world, oblong or 'landscape' format volumes (in Persian *safīna*, lit. 'boat'), whose utilization recalls that of the roll. The sheet could be deployed indifferently in either direction the gatherings corresponding to the same formats. Sheets were often trimmed drastically and so off-cuts could be put to use.

After sizing with wheat, rice or maize starch, the sheet of paper was laid on a board to be scraped and smoothed with a tool made of glass, agate or other material designed to reduce roughness. Craftsmen in Iran and the Ottoman Empire seem to have accorded more importance to the preparation and outward appearance of paper than their western Islamic colleagues. A sheet, once scrupulously smoothed, was often brushed down with a primer (glair, or gum tragacanth, also known as dragon gum) or coating, although in many cases the paper was simply painstakingly smoothed. The delamination of leaves is a phenomenon encountered occasionally in manuscripts, due in all probability to the presence of several layers of pulp.

Western and watermarked paper (VSR)

Since the mid-fourteenth century, watermarked papers from Europe were employed in manuscripts produced in the Maghreb and gradually in Middle Eastern countries. From the Ottoman Empire, watermarked paper of the fifteenth century is frequently encountered, coexisting with the other oriental non-watermarked papers, which remained largely predominant; their success is demonstrated by the fact that some watermarks were copied as forgeries. European paper and non-watermarked paper still coexisted in roughly equal proportions during the sixteenth century. After 1550, until the mid-seventeenth century, non-watermarked oriental papers with chain lines grouped in twos or threes are no longer attested, being replaced most frequently by Venetian anchor-watermarked papers. By the seventeenth century in Turkey, Syria and Egypt, as in the Maghreb, the great majority of manuscripts were being transcribed on watermarked papers; by the second half of the eighteenth century three crescents (*tre lune*) watermarked paper competed with French (or Imperial) paper marks (Regourd 2006). In 1744, in Yalova (Sea of Marmara), the production of Ottoman watermarked paper began, following the European models.

From Persia and India, very few manuscripts on European paper are attested before the end of the eighteenth century; starting from 1815, Persia imported Russian, English and Austro-Hungarian paper. The fine-quality paper produced in the Deccan dominated Mughal Indian manufacturing; English papers were occasionally employed in India, but not before the end of the nineteenth century.

Although the Muslim west adopted European paper in the early fourteenth century, non-watermarked paper continued to be produced in the Muslim East down to the beginning of the twentieth century (Déroche – Sagaria Rossi 2012, 67–69).

Industrial papers (FD)

During the nineteenth and early twentieth centuries, papers produced industrially were used in the production of Arabic manuscripts. Very often, in contradistinction to the traditional papers discussed above, they do not show clear traces of the fabrication process. In some cases, however, they have watermarks. As yet, there is little information about these papers.

Decorated papers (FD)

Tinted parchment was a forerunner of a strong tradition of tinted paper used in Islamic manuscripts. Actually, the custom of mixing 'white' and tinted papers within a quire is a proof of the specific way in which quires were prepared in the Islamic tradition. The fifteenth century marked a golden age for coloured and decorated papers in Iran, and it was then that a number of special techniques reached their zenith. Throughout this century, in Timurid and Turkmen states, manuscripts with differently coloured pages were actively sought after, most being collections or anthologies of poetry. Paper was at that time generally dyed on both sides and thus probably made by being plunged into a vat before a finish was applied; it was then often necessary to fix the colours with an acid treatment before rinsing and drying. There even survive sheets of tinted papers that have been deliberately flecked with a different colour. Sheets tinted on one side only are also to be found, though these are rarer; they received their finish prior to being floated on a mixture on the surface of a tank (Déroche 2005, 60–61).

Other paper-decorating techniques were also developed. 'Silhouette' (or 'shadowed') paper was produced by way of two different processes, one practised in fifteenth-century Persia and the other in the Ottoman world at the end of the fifteenth century and in the seventeenth century. 'Gold-speckling' or 'gold-sanding' appeared in Persia around 1460. 'Marbling' was one facet of the sustained effort observed in the Persian and Ottoman worlds to produce paper of varied appearance designed to fulfil specific purposes (Déroche 2005, 61–63).

2.1.5. Inks (VSR)

Recipes for making ink are preserved in a few Arabic sources, dating back to the eleventh to thirteenth centuries CE (Šabbūḥ 1995). As concerns their ingredients, their compositions differed widely (Schopen 2006). Carbon inks, iron-gall inks, and a combination of the two (mixed inks) are the types found in the Middle East, the two former called *midād*, the latter *ḥibr*. Muslim copyists continued to resort to already tested ink-making processes (maceration, drying, pulverization, etc.), though, as might be expected, wine never appears as an ingredient of their ink recipes.

In the carbon inks, the substances and the methods used for carbonization largely varied. Mostly vegetable products were adopted; among them the sources specify wheat flour, gourds, walnuts, and oils from various plants. Several lists of instructions call for raw materials of animal origin: in addition to grease, both horn and wool were used. The transformation of organic or mineral substances into carbon was achieved by burning them, then collecting the residue and reducing it to powder by mechanical action; in order to refine the raw material, often it was sifted; for a better result, lampblack may be collected by vapourizing a substance rich in carbon. Gum arabic is the usual additive for binding the ink, but Ibn Bādīs also records the use of egg white (Levey 1962, 1–17).

Iron-gall ink has been known in the Islamic world since its early period. Iron has been detected in two Arabic manuscripts of the end of the seventh and the mid-eighth centuries CE. The tannin element recommended by the sources derived from the gall of the terebinth or tamarisk tree, though also other plants rich in tannin are mentioned: myrobalans, pomegranate rind, and decoctions of fresh myrtle. The metallic salt was vitriol containing sulphates of iron, copper and other metals (Levey 1962, 16, 20, 21). Iron-gall ink, unstable and alterable over time, has corroded a few Qur'ānic parchment fragments of the eighth century CE. For the early period, the prevalent presence of an iron-gall component has been confirmed by diagnostic analysis of Qur'ānic fragments of the eighth to tenth centuries (Khan – Lewincamp 2008).

The sources—Ibn Bādīs being the major one—enumerate numerous dye components and coloured ink preparations. While modern diagnostic techniques have so far been applied to only a few samples of decorated pages and concentrated on paintings, comparisons between the recent data and the sources suggest good prospects for further research.

From the early period (seventh century CE), red inks or gilding were employed to stress significant features of the text: a word or a group of words, diacritical punctuation or additional signs; the colour blue was also employed. The red Qur'ānic Sūra headings, attested in seventh-century fragments, could be added by copyists as further operations of page layout. The colour red rapidly came to be employed for specific requirements: abbreviations, overlining, single letters. Ninth-century Qur'āns attest the practice of adding the vocalization in red, made more precise by the use also of green and yellow dots in order to distinguish the three Arabic short vowels. In the Maghreb, this refinement became a long-term practice. In the sixteenth century, Persian Qur'āns employed more colours in the body of the text; their functions are far from clear, but in any case they create fancy effects of colour alternation and lining contrast. Coloured symmetrical words were arranged on mirror-image double pages of late Ottoman Qur'āns (eighteenth and nineteenth centuries).

Gold and silver were also used in the Arabic world since ancient times. Apart from highlighted titles or verse counts, certain manuscripts were written entirely in gold or, more rarely, silver inks: the oldest known attestation is a Qur'ānic fragment dating from the early eight century, but the most famous example is the so-called Blue Qur'ān, written in gilded script on blue-tinted parchment (late ninth century). Book artisans employed either gold ink or dusted gold powder. Once the gold was applied, the surface was carefully burnished and then often outlined in black ink (Déroche – Sagaria Rossi 2012, 19–25, 85–95).

2.1.6. Writing instruments (FD–VSR)

The *qalam* was cut from a reed whose selection is the subject of very precise recommendations on the part of many authors. It was recommended first to soak the reed in water until the required appearance was obtained. At this stage, the reed could be trimmed. In the Maghreb, penmen used a *qalam* of a very different form, cut from a reed (*Arundo donax*), the stem being sliced downwards into strips (Houdas 1886, 98; Déroche 2005, 104–106).

The question of how copyists executed the early Qur'ānic scripts (eight–tenth centuries) is a thorny issue. Some scripts are so thick that the use of some special implement may be postulated.

The penknife (*sikkīn, sikkīna*) used to sharpen the reeds, the small board which supported the reed (*miqaṭṭ, miqaṭṭa*), the inkwell (*miḥbara*), the ruler (*siṭār*), and the compass (*birkār*) are the equipment of the copyists. The burnisher—glass, metal or hard stone—is the most widespread type of polishing tool for paper and gilded areas. A special relevance was assigned to the X-shaped book rests (*kursī, mirfa'a*; Gacek 2001, 2008).

2.2. Book forms (FD–LEP)

2.2.1. The roll and the rotulus (FD)

The horizontal roll was not used in the Islamic manuscript tradition, and the vertical roll (or rotulus) occupies only a very marginal place, mainly related to talismanic use, although calligraphic variations on this form are not unknown. In most cases, the surviving rolls are copies of the Qur'ān. A form peculiar to Indonesia is long, narrow strips of palm, along which runs a single line of text (e.g. Jakarta, Perpustakaan Nasional, Vt. 43).

2.2.2. The codex (FD)

The emergence of Islam occurred at a time when the codex was already the dominant form of the book in the eastern Mediterranean basin. It was taken over as such by those who were at the origin of the Islamic book tradition and had to write down the text of the Qur'ān in the form of a book (Déroche, forthcoming). By the end of the seventh century CE, the vertical format was challenged by an oblong format which became dominant during the ninth century CE for the Qur'āns (see fig. 2.2.6). In the end, the Qur'ān itself was again transcribed in vertical codices (see fig. 2.2.7), perhaps in association with the diffusion of paper. From the end of the thirteenth century CE onwards, another kind of oblong codex (*bayāḍ* format or *safīna*) was used, especially in the Persianate world: in this case, the lines are written parallel to the spine (Ben Azzouna, forthcoming).

Codex-like manuscripts are also found. A few *plano* manuscripts were briefly produced at the beginning of the second half of the eighth century CE (Déroche, forthcoming).

2.2.3. Albums (LEP)

Albums are a peculiar kind of Islamic manuscript, made from cut-outs and individual works (paintings, drawings, sketches, calligraphy exercises), usually executed on paper, but occasionally on silk or cotton, mounted on paper sheets, assembled and bound (Parodi 2010). Commonly in codex form, albums may also occur in accordion or 'concertina' form, or in an elongated codex form (*safīna*). A master compiler supervised the selection and preparation of materials—including repairing, resizing, reformatting and decorating with illumination, ruling, the addition of coloured grounds— and their arrangement on the page. Often he would write a preface, providing a historical context and listing the names of practitioners with brief biographical notes strung together according to master-student affiliations (Roxburgh 2001). Prefaces typically survive not inside albums, but as specimens of good prose reproduced in collections of belles-lettres (*inšā'*).

Not unlike Islamic manuscript illustration itself, albums seem to have stemmed from within the Persian-speaking Turko-Mongol milieu that dominated the eastern Islamic world between the eleventh and the eighteenth centuries. They enjoyed popularity in Iran, Central Asia, India and the Ottoman Empire.

The earliest albums to survive almost intact date from the first half of the fifteenth century and originate in the Timurid milieu of Iran and Central Asia (Roxburgh 2005). But the fashion for albums was possibly introduced a century earlier, when the Mongols were ruling over parts of the eastern Islamic world.

While the rationale behind albums has been plausibly traced to collections of *ḥadīṯ*, anthologies and other traditional Islamic compendia (Roxburgh 2005), direct foreign inspiration is likely to have triggered their introduction. The Mongols entertained direct contacts with China, where a fashion for picture albums, prompted by block-printing, was already well established by the twelfth century (Silbergeld 1982). Chinese albums were made up of individual paper sheets folded along the middle, sometimes assembled in concertina form. Further parallels are evident (Parodi 2010), with albums in both traditions seemingly responding to a changing attitude towards the arts, with an appreciation of single, non-narrative painted scenes or even concise sketches, paralleled in poetry by a taste for brief and personal poetic expressions. Both implied an acknowledgment of authorship and encouraged connoisseurship. Calligraphy specimens and, subsequently, graphic or painted works collected in albums increasingly featured (accurate or spurious) attributions to great masters, if not actual signatures. Later albums, whose popularity survived into the modern era and extended outside Islam (as in the Rajput albums of India), assembled works made expressly for them by contemporary masters rather than, or in addition to, masterpieces from the past.

Albums defied book conventions by denying the traditional progression expected of a codex even while adopting its format, presenting a novel theme with each opening. While the role of albums is to some extent comparable to that of picture galleries in Europe, the form was strictly regulated by the conventions of book production, with gathered leaves stitched into a text block and onto a standard Islamic binding with upper and lower covers, elaborate doublures, and an envelope flap to protect the outer edges of the leaves. Albums in codex form, however, were usually larger than illustrated manuscripts: specimens of about 500×300 mm and with more than 150 leaves are not uncommon (Roxburgh 2001). Concertina albums are usually smaller, and *safīna* albums are eminently portable.

Some early albums also mimicked the inner conventions of the codex—frontispiece, illumination, rulings, and markers of progression. But they typically displayed an emphasis on 'facture' (Roxburgh 2005), on the complexity of assembling heterogeneous materials and giving them visual and thematic coherence: juxtaposing works derived from a single prototype, assembling calligraphy from a group of closely connected masters, or focusing on a single subject, such as portraits of courtiers (Wright – Stronge 2008). Thus individual openings became especially important, and were often conceived as visual units. Margins, the single most important element providing coherence, were increasingly ornamented: in seventeenth-century Iran and India, they often featured elaborate figural ornamentation that included calligraphy and almost obscured painted works (Parodi 2011, Wright – Stronge 2008, Welch et al. 1987).

Albums were often refashioned or pillaged for content by successive owners. Many were taken apart by art dealers who sold individual works without caring for the original leaf sequence or subject matter. Unlike Muslim patrons, who understood and valued the form, logic and facture of albums even as they disassembled and reassembled them to suit new purposes, western collectors until recently were often more interested in certain subjects than others and generally valued paintings above calligraphy. The figural pages of some seventeenth-century Mughal albums, whose openings alternated between paintings and calligraphy, were sometimes pasted onto cardboard mounts in the early twentieth century, with irreversible damage to, or loss of, the other side.

Albums pose a great codicological challenge to cataloguers: reconstructing the leaf sequence of a dispersed album is an extremely complex task, although it has emerged as a distinct field of study in the three decades spanning the year 2000 (Welch et al. 1987; Beach 2004; Wright – Stronge 2008, Parodi et al. 2010, Parodi – Wannell 2011).

Digitization has facilitated the virtual reconstruction of albums, as exemplified by the work undertaken by the Staatsbibliothek zu Berlin on the Diez Albums (Berlin, Staatsbibliothek, Diez A fols. 70–74). The albums were assembled from imperial Ottoman specimens when Heinrich Friedrich von Diez (1751–1817) was Prussian ambassador to the Ottoman court and contain materials spanning several centuries from as early as the Mongol period. The individual sketches and paintings were taken apart in Berlin in the twentieth century, but microfilms document the original appearance of the leaves, and lacunae in imperial Ottoman albums in the Topkapı collections (Istanbul, Topkapı, H. 2152, 2153, 2160, 2154) can be matched with individual Diez leaves (Roxburgh 1995). The corpus, made available on the website of the Berlin library in 2013, is leading research in a new direction.

2.3. The making of the codex (FD–VSR)

2.3.1. The making of the quires (FD)

The composition of the quires reveals how sheets of parchment and later paper were used: bifolia were cut to the desired dimensions in advance, then gathered, usually in groups of four or five, and folded in half.

From as early as the thirteenth century, certain *de luxe* manuscripts began to feature tinted papers, so that one pink-tinted bifolium, for example, might be found in a quinion. In the fifteenth and sixteenth century centuries, leaves of white, tinted, marbled, or decorated paper sometimes alternate. This naturally implies the preliminary cutting of sheets and the *ad hoc* assembly of these bifolia by the copyist. These observations can sometimes be confirmed by examining the direction of the laid-lines.

2.3.2. The composition of the quires (FD)

Parchment manuscripts

The oldest surviving Arabic manuscripts are Qur᾽āns, and date from the second half of the seventh century; most of them are fragments written in *ḥiǧāzī*-style script, which provides the basis for the dating, in association with other features like the orthography. Few of these copies contain continuous sequences of leaves, which are essential to understanding how parchment was used to make up quires in those early days. It seems, however, that various kinds of quires were used: quaternions, quinions, even quires with ten bifolia have been mentioned. Hair and flesh sides are not always arranged according to the same sequence. This situation seems to have prevailed until the eighth century CE. The size of the manuscripts also seems to have been evolving. The early material is mainly constituted of small- and medium-sized copies, but big Qur᾽ānic manuscripts appeared at the beginning of the eighth century, perhaps as a result of official patronage by the Umayyads.

Many more manuscripts from the ninth century have survived. Although they are often fragmentary, several contain continuous text sequences over a sufficient number of folia to provide useful information. A good example can be seen in the composition of manuscript Paris, BnF, Smith-Lesouëf 193 (Déroche 2005, 74–75): despite the loss of several leaves here and there, examination shows that the quires contain ten folia arranged in the following manner: HHHHH^FFFFF.

This observation is confirmed by a survey of three large collections of Qur᾽ān manuscripts copied on parchment between the late first and the middle of the fourth century AH (seventh to tenth century CE), namely those at the Bibliothèque nationale de France, the Museum of Turkish and Islamic Art in Istanbul and the Musée des arts islamiques in Raqqada, close to Kairouan (Tunisia). The overwhelming majority of manuscripts in those collections are composed of quinions; the immediate implication of this observation is that such quires cannot be obtained by simple folding, as subsequent analysis confirms. In addition, the very specific format of those copies makes the folding technique quite impractical. The way in which the parchment was used to form each quire shows a consistent approach on the part of those who made the book: the recto of f. 1 (outermost side) is almost always the hair side of the parchment (Déroche 2005, 75). It also appears on the rectos of the following leaves of the quire, that is to say ff. 2, 3, 4, and 5. When the manuscript is opened, a contrast is evident between the two halves of every double page, except at the junction of two quires (where two hair sides face one another) and in the middle of each quire (where, naturally, two flesh sides appear). It sometimes happens that this pattern is accidentally broken within a quire of a manuscript that otherwise strictly follows the normal arrangement. This is due to the fact that the parchment was cut down to the dimensions selected for the manuscript. A single skin could, if necessary, be used for different quires, indeed for different manuscripts. Subsequently, sheets of the same size, usually five in number, were stacked in the same position and folded down the middle to compose a quire.

The way the skins were used is also highly specific: an examination of the quires reveals the fairly regular presence of stubs, beginning at a very early date. The presence of stubs does not always indicate gaps in the text, but sometimes reflects an extremely common practice that involved a 'substitute' for a bifolium in the form of a pair of 'coupled leaves'—two stubbed singletons—inserted symmetrically in relation to the central stitching. Within a quinion, the number of singletons varies from two to eight or even ten. Only a quarter of the quinions were composed of five bifolia proper. In the remaining cases, singletons inserted in symmetrical fashion in the quire replaced the bifolium or bifolia that would normally have been found there (Déroche 2005, 77–78). It would seem that as far as possible the craftsman making the book was careful not to undermine the sturdiness of the quire, and therefore of the manuscript.

Other ways of composing quires of parchment leaves occasionally occur. Quaternions were sometimes used in oblong manuscripts in the third century AH (ninth century CE), which, strangely, had no impact on the arrangement of hair and flesh sides, the first leaf displaying the flesh side outermost in conformity with the description above.

In the western reaches of the Islamic world—the Maghreb—parchment long remained in use, especially for copying the Qur'ān. It was employed alongside paper until the fourteenth century, even as late as the fifteenth. This conservatism did not mean, however, that parchment was used in the ways described above; on the contrary, it is clear that the arrangement of hair and flesh sides generally follows Gregory's Rule, and that there was no marked preference, strictly speaking, for one type of quire or another. Quinions were not unknown—two manuscripts in Paris, BnF, Arabe 6090 (*FiMMOD* 68) and 6499 (*FiMMOD* 65), are composed of quinions—but they were not the only type found. On occasion, gatherings of parchment might be large, for those in Paris, BnF, Arabe 6905 (*FiMMOD* 16) contain as many as fourteen leaves. Copyists also used quaternions. Ternions seem to have been a Maghrebi speciality when it came to parchment manuscripts (Orsatti 1993, 298). In all these manuscripts, from both the Bibliothèque nationale de France and the Biblioteca Apostolica Vaticana, Gregory's Rule is respected. This does not mean, however, that the quires were made by the folding method used in the west, as mentioned above. 'Irregularities' and the heterogeneous nature of the bifolia composing a single quire point into this direction.

Mixed quires combining papyrus and parchment (sometimes only a parchment 'guard') are known, and the introduction of paper resulted in similar associations, combining the sturdiness of parchment where it was most useful with the less expensive paper where the text was least vulnerable. The use of mixed quires is known in Kairouan from the early eleventh century CE (Raqqada, Musée des arts islamiques, Rutbi 247, dated 404 AH/1013 CE; Déroche 2005, 81–83).

Paper manuscripts

The steady growth in the use of paper for manuscripts did not radically change copyists' working methods. As regards manuscripts written in Arabic script, some of the special features already discussed in terms of parchment quires recur in paper gatherings, and the descriptive method explained above can easily be applied to the latter.

The type of quire most commonly encountered in manuscripts made of paper is the quinion: some 70% of manuscripts published up to 2001 in *FiMMOD* are primarily made up of gatherings of ten leaves. However, a variety of other forms were also used. Sometimes different types of quires alternate within the same manuscript. This relatively rare approach has been noted in manuscript Tashkent, IOB, 3106 (*FiMMOD* 253), where quaternions and quinions alternate, and in part of manuscript Liège, BU, 5086 (*FiMMOD* 69), from 696 AH/1297 CE, composed of binions and ternions. Although copyists generally tended to stick with a single type of quire—apart from minor variations dictated by circumstance—there exist manuscripts whose quires seem to eschew all coherence.

Various other types of quire have been noted, although unequal in frequency. Senions are relatively numerous, being characteristic of many manuscripts dating from the twelfth and thirteenth centuries CE (e.g. Paris, BnF, Arabe 1499 (*FiMMOD* 12), Vatican City, BAV, Vat. ar. 1023 (*FiMMOD* 87), Tashkent, IOB, 3102 (*FiMMOD* 247), Tashkent, IOB, 3107 (*FiMMOD* 249)). On occasion, gatherings of a greater number of leaves were used: fourteen (e.g. Genève, Bodmer, MS 527 (*FiMMOD* 174)) as well as sixteen leaves.

Quaternions are relatively common, or at any rate sufficiently numerous to reveal various tendencies. Manuscripts from Iran and the Persian-speaking world, for example, show a preference for this formula. An overview of manuscripts written in Persian (Déroche – Richard 1998)—some of which were copied in Asia Minor, India, or Central Asia—reveals a number of noteworthy trends for the period from the thirteenth to the sixteenth century centuries. In the previous era, quires of eight leaves had been used, as demonstrated by several manuscripts from the eleventh and twelfth centuries (Déroche 2005, 85–88), some of which may have been produced in Iran. They were still dominant in fourteenth-century Persian manuscripts, although by no means exclusively. By comparison, they are comparatively rare among Arabic manuscripts of the same period.

Quaternions still predominated among Persian manuscripts of the fifteenth century (Déroche 2005, 87–88), with some cases of alternation with quinions within a single codex. As for Arabic manuscripts, the sample represented by *FiMMOD* gives the same impression of the rarity of quaternions: only two manuscripts can be cited, one produced in Ṣufi-abad (Paris, BnF, Arabe 6962 (*FiMMOD* 167)), the other perhaps in Mecca (Istanbul, Süleymanie Kütüphanesi, Şehid Ali Paşa 1876, *c.*1406 (*FiMMOD* 138)). In Iran itself, the type of quire generally used during the sixteenth century was the quaternion, or sometimes, in a small number of manuscripts with paintings, the ternion (Déroche 2005, 88). By contrast, in the Ottoman Empire quaternions and quinions co-existed, the former apparently being preferred for manuscripts based on Iranian models. These trends intensified in the following century, with quaternions dominating almost exclusively in the Iranian world and India, where only very rare exceptions can be found, while in the Ottoman Empire quinions won out—only a few eastern outposts of the empire ignored this rule.

Manuscripts from Sub-Saharan Africa

Manuscripts originating from West Africa—where they continued to be produced into the early twentieth century—often take the form of separate single leaves. When quires or bifolia do appear, they bear no trace of stitching. When quires were used, there was a wide variety of formats, ranging from two to twelve leaves per quire, with a relatively high incidence of four and eight leaves. Some manuscripts are composed of bifolia produced by folding a single sheet in four.

2.3.3. Ruling (VSR)

Dry point ruling shows up rather early in a number of Qur'āns written in *ḥiǧāzī* script, dated to the second half of the seventh century or the first half of the eight. Even in cases where we cannot find any rulings on the page, we cannot exclude the use of some other device which in some way regulated the framing and the direction of the writing. The use of a systematic practice was, however, probably not very wide spread.

On paper, the most widely used ruling instrument was the *misṭara*, a panel of cardboard or wood of the same dimensions as the sheet of paper to be written, on which threads of variable thickness were stretched and sewn. Their weft corresponds to the lines of justification and to the rulings. There are rare written and orally reported descriptions of how a *misṭara* was used. According to a practice which had been proven over time, the copyist placed the sheet of paper over the panel and rubbed it, impressing signs visible to the naked eye and perceptible to touch. Sometimes the *misṭara* was placed under a single leaf, in other cases one or more bifolia were ruled at the same time. The differences can be deduced by observing the position of the ridges and furrows on the leaves (Déroche – Sagaria Rossi 2012, 122–126 and fig. 34). The *misṭara* was extremely flexible and allowed one to create very complex ruling schemes, marking dozens of sheets of paper easily and rapidly. There are also examples of mixed rulings accompanied by schemes of simpler *misṭara*. Two, four or six columns can be set up by a *misṭara*, then be filled by verses and bordered in the margins by obliquely placed lines. In the cases in which prose and verse are mixed, the ruling scheme, two columns and a double margin, is respected by the copyist only for the transcription of the verses.

A Qur'ān fragment datable to the end of the seventh century CE is ruled in ink, on both the recto and verso of the sheet of parchment, all through horizontal and vertical ruling. The same technique is observed in a ninth-century Sudanese Qur'ān. Some (rare) mention of the methods and proportions of ruling are made in Persian texts of the fifteenth century dedicated to calligraphy.

2.3.4. Ordering systems (FD–VSR)

Quire signatures (FD)

In Arabic Islamic manuscripts, the quire number is always found on the recto of the first leaf of the quire, in the upper margin, with a few exceptions. At an earlier date, the top, inner corner, near the stitching, seems to have been used, as witnessed in manuscripts dating from between 324 AH/936 CE and 582 AH/1186 CE. In other manuscripts, dated between 528 AH/1134 CE and 695 AH/1295 CE, the quire number occupies various positions in the upper margin. Starting in the eleventh century CE, quires were numbered in the outer corner of the upper margin, a position that became the norm by the second half of the twelfth century CE and was subsequently almost the only one used, despite a few exceptions, from the thirteenth century onwards. Early quire numbers used the *abǧad* system (Arabic letters with numerical values), which was employed until the late twelfth century CE. By the second half of the eleventh century CE, however, numbers were beginning to be spelled out in ordinal form—*al-awwal, al-ṯānī,* etc.—and that soon became the most common method; they are sometimes accompanied by the noun they implicitly qualify *al-kurrās* ('quire'), eventually abbreviated (but *ǧuz'* 'part' in Paris, BnF, Arabe 3841 (*FiMMOD* 147)). Numerals seem to have been used in a purely occasional manner in the eleventh and twelfth centuries CE; they then appear regularly, if not very frequently, in the thirteenth century. It should be noted that the *abǧad* system and the use of numerals appear more frequently in scientific texts than in religious ones. On the other hand, Qur'ān manuscripts apparently never include quire numbers. The numbering of quires seems to have been less common in the Maghreb than elsewhere: only one instance has been published, an undated manuscript produced in the fifteenth century; the numbers are given in *abǧad* form (Orsatti 1993, 310).

The number of the quire usually appears alone, but in several manuscripts produced between 544 AH/1149 CE and 691 AH/1292 CE, it is accompanied by the number of the bifolium within the quire, also placed in the top outer corner of the recto. Sometimes the number of the volume, or the name of the title or author of the work, might also be added (Vatican City, BAV, Vat. ar. 372 (*FiMMOD* 43), Paris, BnF, Arabe 3291 (*FiMMOD* 54), 4088 (*FiMMOD* 226) and 6883 (*FiMMOD* 260)). When quire numbers were spelled out, they might be written horizontally, diagonally downward or, more rarely, diagonally upward, sometimes following a virtual line from the corner of the written text to the corner of the leaf. Numbering thus became an artistic feature of the page. In at least one case (Paris, BnF, Arabe 820, 617 AH/1221 CE (*FiMMOD* 97)), the quire number is written vertically.

Whereas Karaite manuscripts in Arabic seem to follow the same rules as their Islamic counterparts (see for instance London, BL, Or. 2554, transcribed in Ramla in 345 AH/956–57 CE), the manuscripts produced by Coptic copyists sometimes—though not always—display special features from the standpoint of numbering. Some manuscripts have the quire numbers spelled out in Arabic letters, accompanied by foliation in Coptic numerals, both being placed at the top outer corner of the first verso of the quire (Déroche 2005, 93). Occasionally, though much more rarely, a manuscript will have only leaf numbers in Coptic numerals, or only quire numbers in Coptic numerals, or both leaf and quire numbers in Coptic numerals. The practice observed seems often related to the customary uses of the various communities where these manuscripts were produced.

Catchwords (FD)

Catchwords have turned up in two Islamic manuscripts copied in the latter half of the twelfth century (Paris, BnF, Arabe 6042 (*FiMMOD* 57) and Paris, BnF, Arabe 6440 (*FiMMOD* 171)), to which may be added—if it is the case that the catchwords are indeed in the hand of the copyist—a manuscript produced in 536 AH/1142 CE (Berlin, Staatsbibliothek, Sprenger 432 (*FiMMOD* 190)) and another, even older, dating from 404 AH/1014 CE (Leiden, UB, Or. 704 (*FiMMOD* 213)). By the second half of the thirteenth century CE, catchwords were relatively frequent, and in the first quarter of the fourteenth century CE over half the manuscripts employ them. In Maghrebi manuscripts, they appear in the second half of the fourteenth century CE. In the fifteenth century, a catchword on every leaf became the most common system, whereas those affecting only one part of the quire became increasingly rare.

The catchword is usually placed below the bottom line of the text (see fig. 1.2.1 for a Persian example), often written at a diagonal that almost always angles downward. In a few manuscripts from the late fourteenth century CE, the catchwords run diagonally upward. A catchword might also be written horizontally, quite close to the last line of text, itself slightly raised to leave a space for the catchword within the frame of the written area. Horizontal catchwords close to the line of text seem to have been favoured by Maghrebi copyists, at least until the late fifteenth century CE. Catchwords were not usually subjected to special decorative treatment or ornamentation in Arabic manuscripts, except in rare cases in which they were overlined or accompanied by an inverted comma in red ink. In some manuscripts that do not have catchwords, the last word of the preceding verso is repeated on the following recto (a system sometimes called 'repeated words'), as notably found in Maghrebi codices of the fourteenth century CE. A variety of systems was used: catchwords on every verso, on the versos of the first four (in the case of a quinion) and last leaves of a quire, on the last verso.

Fig. 1.2.1 Persian poetry by Abū ʿAbdallāh Mušarraf al-Dīn b. Muṣliḥ al-Dīn, known as Saʿdī (d.1292), paper, seventeenth century, Leipzig, UB, Cod. or. 325, ff. 40v–41r.

Foliation (VSR)

Original foliation in the hand of the copyist rarely appears in the earliest manuscripts; it is attested in *abǧad* in an exemplar of the tenth century CE. The foliation marks are found in the same place as the quire numbers, in the upper left corner of the rectos. That practice did not become widespread until the sixteenth century, although the lack of any systematic study on this matter precludes making such statements with confidence. In Arab-Christian manuscripts, foliation is attested from the fourteenth century CE, throughout by means of the Byzantine *rūmī* or the Western Arabic *ġubār* numerals.

Mid-quire notation (FD)

On opening the central bifolium of certain manuscripts, sometimes one finds notations placed in the top outer corner of the right-hand page, as well as in the bottom outer corner of the left-hand page, but also in the opposite direction: bottom outer corner on the right, top outer corner on the left. Sometimes only one of these notations is found, for instance in Karaite manuscripts in Arabic (for instance London, BL, Or. 2579). They were probably meant to indicate the central fold to the binder.

The *rūmī* numeral 5 appears in the earliest examples of the practice. This form of numeral in fact features regularly in Maghrebi manuscripts. In the Near East, on the other hand, from the fourteenth century onward the notation disappeared from manuscripts. Dashes are also found. Similarly, long bars were also used much later, for example in manuscripts copied or re-bound in India from the late seventeenth to the eighteenth centuries. Other marks have been used, although less frequently (dots, an oriental numeral 2 extended downward, *rūmī* numeral 4 in a Karaite manuscript, the letter *mīm*, groups of three dots, or small circles).

2.4. The layout of the page (VSR)

In Arab-Islamic manuscripts, the ruling pattern is the first and fundamental clue in revealing how the layout was structured. Though ruling is linked to the notion of justification, in Arabic manuscripts the writing does not always correspond exactly to the frame destined to contain the written text. While runover into the left margin is limited (pages are usually perfectly justified except in the case of poetic texts and some

Arab-Christian manuscripts), runover is frequent in the top and bottom margins. At the top of the page, scribes tended to write above or across the top line, so that the written area is generally taller than the ruled area. Text at the bottom of the page also tended to be written below the bottom line, although this phenomenon is less evident than is extension above top line.

Ruling patterns on parchment are rather varied; the progressive introduction of the *misṭara* led to a relative standardization of ruling types. Some copyists used the line as a central guide, that is, the letters were written so that they extend both above and below the line, while others placed the letters entirely above them. Ruled lines do not always occur, for example in the Maghreb, where only the two vertical bounding lines were ruled—and sometimes only one of them.

The absence of methodical studies of the layout of the text area in Arabic manuscripts explains the prevalence of aesthetic and numerological arguments. Empirical remarks related to texts with standardized layout such as Qur'āns, Qur'ān commentaries, collections of religious traditions (*ḥadīṯ*) and bio-bibliographical works of different origins and dates may be the basis for discussing layout variables. The graphic performances of texts in Arabic characters, involving both canonical writing styles and common handwriting, constitute themselves the most essential framework within which any further layout purpose should be investigated.

If the analysis of the ruling allows us to understand the project of the copyist or painter of an Arab-Islamic manuscript, both the frame of a single page and that of an opening may provide an articulated space for complex layouts. Despite the abundance of literature on calligraphy and, to a lesser degree, on the miniaturist's art, only one Arabic text is known that supplies us with some information concerning the architecture of the page. The treatise on inks and colours by the Andalusian vizier and man of letters Abū Bakr Muḥammad ibn Muḥammad al-Qalalūsī (d.1308) is dedicated to the use of the *misṭara* and refers to justification and to the figure of the *šīḥa*, which divides the written area in two equal parts (the same term is used for one of the resulting halves; Déroche – Sagaria Rossi 2012, 125–127).

Since systematic research on the exploitation of the page is missing, local sources are again resources to turn to, as in the case of the calligrapher Sirāğ Šīrāzī, who mentions among the artisan's tools the calamus for drawing the *ğadwal*, which is the frame for the text area, and a *siṭār*, a ruler and a pair of compasses used to trace the *ğadwal*; the principle was that the top margin should be wider than the bottom margin, so that the two margins would appear equal once the text had been written on the ruled lines (Porter [Y.] 2003).

As regards the analysis of the proportions of the written area, a certain number of volumes of different sizes offer similar height-to-width ratios depending on the regions where they were made, the period when they were made, and their support. Discussion of the proportions of the written area in Arabic-Islamic manuscripts has been mostly based on an aesthetic approach, relying on intuition and simplified description. Even the matter of the dimensions of the written area is yet to be investigated, in relation to geographical and chronological distribution, including the relationship of proportions and ratios with reference to specific kinds of texts (Déroche – Sagaria Rossi 2012, 128–136).

There is an evident correlation between the format (*qaṭ'*) of the leaf and the ruling pattern. This quest for harmony can be found above all in *de luxe* volumes, where relatively simple geometric formulae were used for dividing the page. The decorative units and miniatures may also fill spaces defined by further formulae, whereby the role of the copyist in relation to the planning of the layout remains to be clarified.

At first, both the ruled area and the written area showed horizontal lines and nearly square format of page and text layout, such as the most ancient Qur'āns and North African manuscripts. In the Maghreb, in particular, the written surface or the frame for a picture corresponds to a specific rectangle in which the height of the written area represents the side of an equilateral triangle and the width of the written area the triangle's height, so that the height-to-width proportion is between 1.13 and 1.17. This ratio is present in manuscripts copied between the twelfth and fourteenth centuries CE and above all in manuscripts with a square or almost square format. Later it became rarer, but still found in the fifteenth century, during which it was much favoured for the layout of small square prayer books.

Regarding the distribution of the text on the page, the earliest evidence—Qur'āns with *ḥiğāzī* script dated to the second half of the seventh century or the beginning of the eighth century CE—shows that copyists were inclined toward long lines and oblong horizontal justification, while they later switched from an oblong horizontal format to a vertical one (Déroche 2009). The preference for long lines was maintained for non-Qur'ānic manuscripts, as is shown by the first dated copies from the ninth century. During the following period copyists usually remained faithful to this tradition. Attempts to analyse the density of the writing of prose texts have confirmed that the number of lines per page remains relatively constant, although variations and differences must be taken into account.

The lines of writing in prose manuscripts are horizontal. Poetry introduces an exception to the preference for long lines: because of its structure, and in particular because of the presence of rhyme, poetry lends itself to being marked in such a way as to highlight the recurring elements. The verses are often placed in two or more columns (figs. 1.2.2, 1.2.2), and they are readable all along the horizontal lines, that is to say, across the intercolumn(s). The use of a frame (*ǧadwal*) was introduced in Persian manuscripts to delimit the text area and to separate elements of the text (see figs. 1.2.1, 1.2.2); intercolumns and inner margins might be further separated by means of triangles or lozenges, above all in correspondence with the end of the poem (Orsatti 1989, 1997). Sometimes, even in Arab-Christian manuscripts, the text is divided into columns meant to be read vertically.

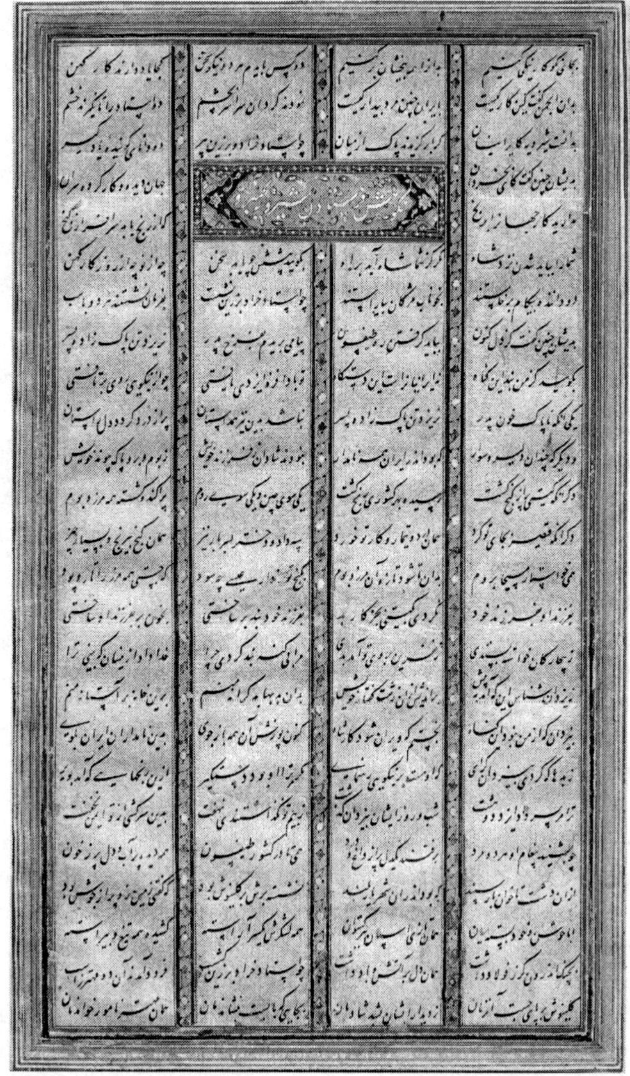

Fig. 1.2.2 Rome, Museo Nazionale di Arte Orientale, inv. 21368/31705r, Firdawsī, *Šāhnāma*, Persia, fifteenth century, four-columns poetical text with a central title panel.

When a second or third text occurs in the margin, it is interesting to see if the layout represents a forced adaptation using the small remaining space or if it is rather the result of a structured and well calibrated plan; the orientation of text written in the margins is generally oblique, regardless of whether or not the *misṭara* was used to create the ruling pattern. The effect created by the doubling of a text is also exploited in frames for Qur'āns (Persia, seventeenth century CE), with text in Arabic in the centre and marginal comments in Persian, assuming the double function of separating texts and languages. During the ninth and the early tenth centuries CE, copyists sought to lighten the justification of small Qur'āns: numerous examples have on a single line, often the one in the middle, only a few letters, with extremely extended connecting strokes. A similar process seems to be the one used at the beginning of the eleventh century CE by copyists of juridical manuscripts that have a part of the line left empty, without any element of text.

Copyists also resorted to graphic solutions for determining the layout for the writing on the line, exploiting the possibility of varying the writing mode and calligraphic style from line to line. This formula does not imply a hierarchy of the components, except in a few cases, where, however, the articulation of the text—titles, divisions—remains easily distinguishable. Another graphic expedient is the technique of *mašq*, the lengthening, more or less accentuated, of the base line that links the letters within a word; one or more lines on a page—the one in the middle, the first, and the last, or a combination of both—can contain a small number of letters, but with numerous and significant lengthenings (see figs. 1.2.2, 2.2.7).

The number of written lines is extremely variable, even when the copyist worked according to a ruling pattern. In one of the earliest ruled examples (Paris, BnF, Arabe 328a), the number of lines varies from 20 to 26 per page. In the course of time, odd numbers were usually preferred. The middle line can also have its role in the *mise en page*. As for the margins, the earliest Qur'āns show very narrow margins (cp. fig. 2.2.5), the reason for which remains obscure.

The layout of pages with tables, geometric drawings and diagrams, in red or other colours, occurring in manuscripts of scientific works of cosmography, geometry, medicine and pharmacopoeia, have not yet been methodically investigated. Analysing the proportions between the text area and the designed portions on the margins or within the ruled frame, the one not always related with the other, may unveil further exploitation of the page by the copyist toward a higher level of autonomy of both the written and the designed parts.

Fig. 1.2.3 Rome, Biblioteca dell'Accademia Nazionale dei Lincei e Corsiniana, Or. 5, Ṣafadī, *al-Wāfī bi-al-wafayāt*, Damascus, mid-fourteenth century, ff. 18v–19r: an Arabic bio-bibliographical dictionary with rubrication for entry titles and names.

The Qur'ān, the sovereign example, is divided into several units of the same dimensions: starting from the classic subdivision in *ǧuz'* (one thirtieth), each in turn divided in *ḥizb* (one sixtieth), the copyists succeeded in defining 15-line pages, for a format close to 180 × 120 mm. With the exception of the first and last pages, the decoration was relatively standardized, from the placing of the text in a frame, to the cartouches with the titles of each Sūra and to the marks of division in the outer margins. Other very popular texts were subjected to analogous layouts. From the beginning of the fourteenth century, above all in Persia, numerous Qur'āns have three lines per page with large writing, between which two pairs of lines of small writing appear, often in black, the bigger letters being in blue or gold. The particular dimensions of the page made it necessary to place the script within a circular or octagonal frame. Effects of mirror-image placement of the text, or of the same words, on two facing pages were sought with particular tenacity and find their most characteristic expression in later Ottoman Qur'āns, in which entire sequences of text were laid out symmetrically. These combinations point out the role of the *mise en page* and the attempts carried out by copyists to rationalize the written area and the non-written area of a page (Déroche – Sagaria Rossi 2012, 132–136).

As for annotations, glosses and later comments added to a text, usually they were placed according to a reader's decision or need, although additions made by the copyist himself cannot always be excluded (fig. 1.2.3).

Subscriptions (colophons) are usually found inscribed in a triangular space at the end of the text. The formulae placed in a rectangle on two or more lines and separated from the text by an empty space or by a decorated divider are quite ancient (twelfth century). Later the colophon mostly took the shape of a circle or a lobed mandorla with rosettes.

2.5. Text structure and readability (VSR–AVN)

2.5.1. Writing (VSR)

The *mise en texte* (text layout), at times adopted for practical rather than aesthetic reasons, may vary according to period, regional customs or text genre. Compact and homogeneous text layout, with continuous word flow, is very common, for example in Arab-Islamic prose from the formative and classical periods (ninth to fourteenth centuries CE), while a more precise and articulate textuality is found in the centuries that follow, when the need to trace and highlight parts of the text (chapters, headings, names, words) stimulated the copyist to elaborate more effective reference systems. Among the most common patterns connected to genre and content are the separation of verses into several columns or, within a prose text, the insertion of schemes and diagrams, in a centred position or indented, into scientific texts, and the highlighting in red of proper names, letters, or key words in historical biographies and in Islamic religious texts (Déroche – Sagaria Rossi 2012, 191–204).

The copies of the same work generally show similar layout, even if examples with fully identical textual patterns are rare. Even incomplete copies reveal the stages in elaboration of the layout and the distribution of the sections of the work or its parts; for example, in Persian manuscripts, the *ǧadwal* frame pre-determins the length of the written lines (see fig. 1.2.1), producing a pattern that is more rigid and less subject to significant variations, as is shown by spaces, lines and columns left blank.

The title page, whether accompanied by the author's name or not, is usually found on the recto of the first page of the text. The title can also appear on the top or bottom margin, on the flap of the binding, on a tag glued to the front cover, or perhaps in the colophon, sometimes together with the name of the commissioner. From an early period, the title of a work might be indicated quite briefly, particularly for works that were frequently copied, but in many classical works the titles are very detailed and elaborate, in large characters, without decoration. In the most routinely produced works, also without decoration, we find a variety of scripts, sizes of characters, and layouts for the title and author's name, the former in a more prominent position than the latter; placing the elements in a sort of upside down pyramid was a rather widespread practice in later periods; the title might also be found above a circle, painted in several colours, where the name of the author was written. It is not always found on the recto, but might occur on the verso of the first page, in a composition that frames and contains the beginning of the text, as in the case of the illuminated title that introduces the text, *ʿunwān*, most frequent in Persian manuscripts. In this frame, sometimes repeated and placed symmetrically on the facing page, the title is inserted either in its complete form or abbreviated, either with or without the author's name, in some cases containing a pious formula, often the *basmala*, which is the introductory verse of each Qurʾānic Sūra and of every text of the Arab-Islamic tradition.

In Qurʾānic manuscripts there is no real title page; a quotation from the holy text or, in the case of multi-volume Qurʾāns, the indication of the number of the volume may appear on the recto of the first page. In the earliest period, the first page did not have decoration on the recto, while the verso of the first and the recto of the second pages constitute a diptych occupied, in the most refined works, by geometrical or floral ornamentation; the text starts on the following page, without any introduction.

In the most refined examples, the decoration of the front page may also include a framed table of contents. In specimens containing Arabic prose texts, generally more sober in the division of the presentation elements, this item takes a more detailed and functional form, though attention is paid to proportions and visual impact.

The canonical beginning of every text, placed generally on the verso of the first page, is the propitiatory *basmala* formula and the doxological *ḥamdala* (praise to God). The temporal adverb *baʿdu* (after) or *ammā baʿdu* (as to, after), generally marks the beginning of the prologue and may be highlighted by thicker strokes or larger-sized letters, in black or red; it may introduce a more or less detailed preface, with justification of the choice of the subject, dedication, abbreviations of authors and cited works, title of the work and, sometimes, a brief list of the contents. Eulogies of various types fill and conclude the preface.

The practice of subdividing the text is very ancient and is already found in the first Qurʾāns, where the main sections of the text were separated by an empty space, originally corresponding to a line. Later this space was occupied by a panel of a basic shape, decorated with vegetal or geometric motifs, presumably inspired by architectonic or textile designs. At the end of the Umayyad epoch headings for Sūra were introduced into this space (fig. 1.2.2).

The terms *kitāb* 'book', *faṣl* 'section', *maqāla* 'treatise', *bāb* 'chapter', *ǧuzʾ* 'part', *qism* 'section', *sifr* 'book', in the manuscripts of the Old Testament, *maṭlab* 'question, inquiry', *maqṣad* 'objective, purpose'—also accompanied by numbers—indicate chapters, paragraphs and internal divisions; often marked in red, they are sometimes highlighted by overlinings in black or red. The size of these sections is variable and does not always interact in a significant way with the structure of the *mise en texte*. Interpolated clauses, explanations and digressions of various types, are often incorporated in the body of the text and, at most, introduced at specific points by terms such as *bayān*, or *tibyān* 'explanation', *taḏkira* 'retrieval', *fāʾida* 'information', *išāra laṭīfa* 'small reference', *mabḥaṯ šarīf* 'noble examination', and others. Chapter headings in prestigious manuscripts are written in a style different from the text, as in the case of the Qur'āns from the eighth and ninth centuries CE with titles of the Sūra in *ṯuluṯ* within illuminated frames.

The poetic sections are centred with reference to the written panel and the two hemistichs set slightly apart; in Persian manuscripts, the column layout makes the poems immediately recognizable (see fig. 1.2.1). Starting from the fourteenth century CE, Persian copyists sometimes placed sayings and verses about their work and the text copied by the calligrapher around, before or after the section dedicated to the colophon.

The end of the text copied cannot be recognized by any particular concluding formulae or graphic artifice; it is simply announced by *tamma al-kitāb* or *intahā al-kitāb* ('the text is finished') or merged into the graphic space dedicated to the colophon, which follows separated by a space in the classical period; in later periods, from the fourteenth and fifteenth centuries onward, it may become part of the elaborate colophon.

Among the aesthetic effects, there is the alternation of passages in different colours, and of styles of writing in numerous Qur'āns. This practice does not correspond to any hierarchy, and its only aim is to enliven the overall presentation of the text. The earliest decorations are found in the outer (but also lower) margins of the Qur'āns, so that they stand out better and carry out their function as highlighting in a more satisfactory way. In the later classical period, decorators and miniaturists used these non-written spaces to give their fancy free rein, as is shown in particular in the technique of framing the page.

2.5.2. Decoration (AVN)

According to Muslim belief, the Qur'ān and works of Islamic science cannot be decorated or illustrated with representations of human beings or animals, and so decorators and painters of religious manuscripts developed aniconic ornamentation (*taḏhīb* in Arabic, *tezhip* in Turkish). It is based on three components: geometry (*tasṭīr*), stylized vegetal motifs with arabesque (*tawrīq*), and epigraphy. Figural decoration was confined to profane manuscripts, which were very limited in the Arabic tradition, more important in the Persian, Turkish and Indian traditions (see fig. 1.2.1).

Since the first century of Islam, painted decoration was added to the Qur'ānic manuscripts. Many illuminated copies were produced at the end of the eighth and during the ninth centuries, but aside from minor stylistic variations according to times and places, the basic ornamental repertory of the Qur'ān became standardized rather quickly. Secular manuscripts also developed complex programmes of decoration, very few in the Arabic copies, flourishing in the Iranian, Turkish and Indian ones.

Some decorative elements are found in the scribal tradition, but the main use of ornamentation, beyond the embellishment of the book, is to indicate to the reader the different parts of the text, for the Qur'ān and also for religious or profane texts. Decorative elements are found at the beginning and at the end of text units and mark divisions within the text (see fig. 1.2.2).

The text is usually written in black ink, and as the Arabic script does not know capitalization, or punctuation, and ignores paragraphing, the copyist uses bold characters and rubrics to highlight the keywords or the articulations of the text, in red or gold and, for the western Islamic tradition, in coloured inks. These practices have served to bring out the signs particularly in order to avoid difficulties in reading. In Abbasid Qur'āns, coloured dots, above and below the letters, were the first way to differentiate short vowels (see fig. 2.2.6). This use of colour for vowels and orthoepic signs has continued in the western tradition in a decorative way for *de luxe* Qur'āns (see fig. 2.2.7). Chrysography and writing in silver has appeared in sumptuous Qur'āns and other luxury copies. Calligraphy can also be considered as a mode of decoration since the copyist used different styles and sizes of writing to differentiate textual parts.

In Qur'ānic manuscripts, the frontispiece is a decorated, often illuminated page or a double page preceding the main text at the beginning of a volume or a section of it. From the late eighth to the tenth centuries, some horizontal-format volumes open with a full-page rectangular decoration of the same dimension as the written area, with vignettes protruding into the margin. Decoration is governed by geometric principles, largely inspired by the practices of the Late Antiquity, and incorporates also vegetal elements. For a short time at the end of the Umayyad period, architectural patterns occur, for example in a manuscript discovered in Sanaa with a frontispiece depicting a mosque (Sanaa, DAM, 20-33.1; cf. von Bothmer 1995). From the eleventh to the sixteenth centuries, the frontispiece is often a double-page carpet, each page being the mirror-image of the other, sometimes followed by other double pages. These pages are generally built as a composition of geometrical figures radiating from a central point and filled with arabesques. After the sixteenth century, the double carpet page often becomes ornamented with two medallions (*šamsa*) facing each other. With or without a decorated frontispiece, the Qur'ānic text necessarily begins at the first opening of the volume and is often arranged within a frame. Frequently, two headings, one above and one below the text, indicate the number of the volume and/or contain quotations from the Qur'ān. The first Sūra is more often on a verso and the second on the facing recto. The text is often written in 'cloudbands', a motif that came from China. The end of the Qur'ān is less decorated than the beginning. Full-page decorations may recall those of the initial pages.

In the earliest Qur'āns, the Sūras are separated by a blank space, sometimes filled by a band with a simple geometric design, sometimes in coloured ink. Afterwards, the Sūra headings are written in gold or enclosed in a framed band with a palmette or medallion in the margin, or still later in a band containing a cartouche. The inscription gives the name of the Sūra, generally the number of verses (*āyā)* and the place of revelation.

Inside the Sūra, rosettes separate the verses; in the text or in the outer margin, groups of five or ten verses are indicated by other decorative elements, circles or medallions with the mention of the verse account written in letters (*ḫams* or *ʿašr*). The letter *hā'* is also used for the groups of five verses. Divisions of the Qur'ān into thirty sections (*ǧuz'*) of equal length, subdivided in halves (*ḥizb*) and quarters for devotional reading, are marked in the outer margin by ornaments shaped as circular medallions. The mention of ritual prostration (*saǧda*) in the margin does not have a standard form.

In non-Qur'ānic manuscripts, the text also usually begins on the verso of the first leaf, the recto being left blank. However, in precious copies, a decorated title page opens the book, on a recto. Taking the shape of rectangular, square or circular ornament, it contains the title of the book, the name(s) of the author(s) and the commissioning patron. It may be followed, in the most elaborate manuscripts, particularly in Persian ones, by several leaves with decorations and/or illuminations occupying the whole page, generally in rectangular form, very similar to those of Qur'āns.

The text often begins with a decorated headpiece preceding the *incipit* in the upper part of the page. Executed in a variety of shapes and sizes, it is designated by the terms *ʿunwān* and *sarlowḥ*, used by different specialists with different meaning. In Ottoman Turkish manuscripts, it takes the shape of an arch (see fig. 1.2.4). Introducing the different sections of the manuscript, illuminated bands appear in the Persian literary classics, Firdawsī's *Šāhnāma* (fig. 1.2.2) or Niẓāmī's *Ḫamsa*, and in poetic anthologies for each book or poem, with smaller-size headings for smaller units. In poetic works, each verse (*bayt*) or hemistich (*miṣraʿ*) is distinguished from prose by verse markers. Verses are written in columns whose layout is ordered by frames (*ǧadwal*). Bands, decorated or plain, separate the text from the margins horizontally, vertically or even diagonally. At the end of the volumes, colophons, which are found in various forms and sizes are sometimes decorated.

Fig. 1.2.4 Leiden, Leiden University Library, Or. 11051, sixteenth century, *Šarḥ-i Dīwān-i Ḥāfiẓ*, the Ottoman Turkish commentary by Muṣliḥ al-Dīn Muṣṭafā b. Šaʿbān 'Surūrī' (d. 969 AH/1562 CE), on the *Dīwān* of Ḥāfiẓ Šīrāzī (d. 792 AH), ff. 1v-2r, photograph by KS.

Other parts of the manuscripts are also decorated. Frames, composed of one or several gilt or coloured fillets, are present in early Qur'āns and secular manuscripts. Rarely, glosses on the outer margins can form various geometrical shapes or vegetal and architectural patterns. Developed in Ottoman Arabic manuscripts in the sixteenth century and more frequent in some later Persian copies, this layout seems to bear a relationship to Hebrew or Byzantine traditions (Vernay-Nouri 2002). In high-quality Persian, Turkish and Mughal manuscripts, margins are ornamented with gold arabesques and animal figures, probably made with stencils. Also in precious copies, additional decorative panels are inserted, after the fifteenth century, in the text area, which harmonize the decorative programme. Coloured and decorated papers (marbled, gold-sprinkled and gold-scattered) are used in part of the manuscript or in its entirety.

The first decorations in Arabic manuscripts are derived from the Greek tradition and deal with science: diagrams, constellation charts, maps, drawings and paintings of medical or technical instruments, pictures of plants or animals, and even sometimes narrative paintings illustrate the text precisely, facilitating a better understanding of it. In the few illustrated literary works, principally al-Ḥarīrī's *Maqāmāt* and *Kalīla wa Dimna*, pictures depict scenes from the narrative.

During the thirteenth and fourteenth centuries, miniatures are rarely framed. They can be as wide as the text area but never as high, placed close to the illustrated passage. The final choice of the place depends on the choice of the scribe and of the painter. The captions are often written in red above the pictures. In some works, like the Dioscorides or the *Maqāmāt*, the manuscript begins with one or several full-page portraits of the author or the commissioning patron, depicted against a coloured background. The background of the other miniatures is blank. Arabic painted manuscripts rarely contain illuminations as well. Written in 1199 CE, the *Book of the Theriac* (*Kitāb al-Diryāq*, Paris, BnF, Arabe 2964) is a rare example of a precious manuscript featuring an elaborate layout with framed paintings, calligraphy and illuminations.

After the fourteenth century, many changes occur in the Persian area. Many poetic works, like those of Firdawsī and Niẓāmī, or historical chronicles are illustrated, often having been produced for a courtly readership. In the *de luxe* manuscripts, miniatures are part of a programme which often includes illuminated elements, calligraphy, ornamented papers or decorated bookbindings. Painted with a coloured background, the pictures are generally inserted in a rectangular frame which may also include portions of text (fig. 1.2.1). In more sophisticated layouts, some pictorial elements cross the frame into the margins. Full-page miniatures do not have a special place in the book, but some princely manuscripts begin with a double dedicatory painting with no relation to the main text.

Unfinished Arabic illustrated manuscripts give us some information about the manufacturing of the miniatures. The scribe first copies the text leaving blanks for the paintings, sometimes with captions. On completion, the painter (or the copyist himself) sketches each image roughly with a red outline. Such outlines—visible under many miniatures or in unfinished ones, such as the *Maqāmāt* (London, BL, Add. 7293)—do not always precisely coincide with the final painting (George 2012). Then the painter applies the gold and adds other colours, completing details such as faces, hands or vegetation. Used for duplicating the decorative patterns or elements of miniatures in Persian and Indian workshops, stencils were already used in the Mamluk period. Decoration and illustrations of Persian and Ottoman *de luxe* manuscripts, which were copied in princely or commercial workshops, implies a significant division of labour between the artists and their assistants and apprentices.

2.6. The scribe, the painter and the illuminator at work (VSR)

2.6.1. Persons, places and methods

Despite the fact that Arabic, Persian and Turkish literature is rich in descriptions of libraries, collectors and personalities linked to books, references to the methods of copying texts are, with the exception of the Qur'āns, desultory, casual and fragmentary (Déroche – Sagaria Rossi 2012, 137–144).

The period spanning the Umayyad and the early Abbasid dynasties saw the growing importance of the role of copyists in culture and society. Tenth-century Baghdad is one of the rare cities for which sources about bookshops and workshops for the manufacture and sale of books abound. The job of the copyist—not an exclusive prerogative of men—underwent fluctuations and changes, from the phase of the establishment of the Arabic script to the late Middle Ages, along with the constant interference of oral transmission, a subsequent move toward writing, and the eventual establishment and fixation of the canons of textual transmission.

Colophons are generally synthetic, and it is not always easy to discover the identity of the copyist, except when the name is given, and the person—an author, a doctor, a scholar—is known from other sources. In the absence of a catalogue of dated manuscripts and of repertoires of names of copyists, the production work is still to be precisely investigated. In the eyes of the copyist, details concerning the antigraph were sometimes relevant and are mentioned in the colophon, though this simple statement was the only guarantee of accuracy.

Certainly most copyists (*nassāḫ*, singular *nāsiḫ*) did not earn a living only from transcribing texts; in fact this was only one of the elements in the transmission of knowledge, as is shown by the certificates authorizing text transmission (*iǧāza*) that are found in manuscripts in many cases. The mastery of the calligraphic art was a common goal of the education of each Muslim endowed with basic culture, and it is possible to encounter both finely written copies, carried out for one's own use or for an acquaintance, or others of mediocre execution. The category of calligraphers is separate from that of copyists and, at the same time, difficult to identify and distinguish. In fact, many colophons of ancient manuscripts contain the names of copyists or calligraphers, who do not define themselves as such. In some cases, instead, they explicitly define themselves as *ḫaṭṭāṭ* 'calligrapher'. Starting at a certain point in the seventeenth or eighteenth century, in the Ottoman world, specialized works about these individuals and the system of teaching, based on that of the religious sciences, introduced the *iǧāza* for calligraphers. Thus it seems suitable to integrate the calligraphers into the vast panorama of the professional copyists (Déroche – Sagaria Rossi 2012, 139–142).

Soon the *warrāq*—from *waraq* 'paper'—came on the scene, a figure to whom it is difficult to assign a precise role. He is defined as an artisan of the book, bookseller and stationer all at the same time, a sort of modern publisher who produced and sold books, and occasionally also worked as a copyist. Thus in the crafts related to the book, the rule seems to be a certain degree of versatility in assuming functions and roles (Pedersen 1984, 43), and it is hard to distinguish between the establishment of textual canons and the application of copying practices, as the two processes, intellectual and physical, overlap (Déroche – Sagaria Rossi 2012, 140–144). It is not clear if the copyists who defined themselves as *nassāḫ* had more specific functions than the *warrāq* or if their products were intended for a more modest kind of customer. Much later, at the beginning of the seventeenth century, we find the *warrāq* in Central Asia carrying on their business in the bazaars.

Colophons and *iǧāza* certificates are also sources of information for other professionals more or less occasionally engaged in the transcription of texts, intended to guarantee the quality of their products.

The *kātib* was a secretary of the chancellery or administration, who might also copy texts, although his tasks in this context are not always clear. *Kuttāb* did not work as regular copyists in important centres, nor were they in contact with princes. Actually, when the chancelleries offered them the possibility of carrying out their work at court, these figures ended by giving up their service as independent professionals, in favour of the administration of the court library. Scholars and students also acted as copyists, both to earn money and to enhance their studies, a combination of interests that made a notable number of texts available to them and was a factor in the process of transmitting knowledge. The final appearance of the manuscripts could vary considerably. A transcription for a third person demanded a certain level of readability, while an entirely different level of care was needed when the copy was only for oneself, and the scribe also worked as a binder. Some exterior criteria, like the layout, may supply relevant information. Amateurs could also become copyists, as happened in the production of Qurʾāns or of works for charity.

Copyists attribute many derogatory adjectives and titles to themselves, intended to indicate their unworthiness. In the Arab-Christian environment, the copyist is called *nāqil* 'he who transports, transcribes', *kātib* 'he who writes', *nāsiḫ* 'he who copies' or *rāqim* 'he who writes, recounts'. In these cases, colophons may bear no reference to the transmission or to the collation with the original. Christian manuscript production, which appears towards the middle of the tenth century CE, descends from three traditions, the Greek used by the Melkites, the Coptic used by the Miaphysite Egyptians, and the Syriac used by the Maronites—these with strongly Arabized literature—and the Jacobite Syrians and the Nestorians, these latter only weakly Arabized.

Our most complete information comes from careful and refined examples, rather than from products made for the mass market. The more important patrons had their own workshops, where artists, with their assistants and apprentices, worked under the supervision of one or more masters. This is how many Ottoman sultans had luxury copies of manuscripts produced, and the documents preserved in the archives of Istanbul supply details of the sums paid and the parties involved. At the height of its splendour, in the sixteenth and seventeenth centuries, the imperial atelier employed numerous specialized artisans in activities such as ruling, the design of the margin, the design of the writing panel, and gilding motifs and arabesques. Workshops were usually rather modest in size and produced works that often reached high levels of execution. The styles of the miniatures produced in Shiraz in the Safavid period, for example, enjoyed wide favour and had an obvious influence on Indian artists and those of other regions. As mentioned already, copyists, including those who copied manuscripts for their own personal use, could also be responsible for less ambitious miniatures.

Painters and decorators did not usually sign their work, and we still know very little about the conditions of their work. Were it not for a few Persian drawings and illustrations of tools and the working environment, it would be hard to imagine any technique related to the profession. They generally worked seated, legs crossed, with the written sheet on their right thigh, the angle between the upper body and the legs varying depending on the region or the epoch. The Persian and Ottoman miniatures show copyists seated in front of rather low pieces of furniture, tables or chests, on which their tools were set up (Baer 1998). It is more difficult to discover how they held the calamus, a piece of information that has been overlooked in the studies, but which is extremely important for understanding the execution of some letters and marks.

The place where scribes and painters worked is rarely mentioned in early manuscripts and written sources. Colophons rarely mention the city, and even more rarely the exact place where the work was carried out.

Certainly real workshops, of differing size, were active in Umayyad Spain, where women may also have been active as scribes; others were created under the direct orders of the bibliophile princes. One famous representative of this category was the Timurid Sultan Baysonqor (d.1433), who gathered at his court in Herat the most illustrious illuminators, painters and calligraphers. In Constantinople, in the area around the royal palace, the artisans of the book were allocated structures which guaranteed their livelihoods. From the middle of the sixteenth century, we find the image of a house transformed into and used as a family workshop, integrated with the domestic functions and highly specialized; probably this activity did not seem to require a specific environment, but a room or cell was sufficient, and it is probable also that in the big cities most of the booksellers dwelt in the same areas where the copyists' activities are attested too.

Libraries and the centres of institutionalized teaching were privileged places for scribal activity. The Bayt al-ḥikma in Baghdad (tenth century), with its one or more copyists, can be taken as emblematic. The library of the Dār al-ḥikma of Cairo, the library of the Fatimids, made its holdings available to those who wanted to transcribe texts. In Rabat in Morocco, the Royal Library of the Alaouites—at present, the National Library—had in the eighteenth century a room reserved for copying and copyists were recruited for the transcription of precious manuscripts. In large Middle Eastern libraries the professionals of the pen, until very recent times, offered their services to the erudite, but the status of this category of professionals and the identity of their patrons still have to be defined. In the eastern part of the Islamic world, the library of the prince (*kitābḫāna*) tended to be associated with an atelier of this type, which functioned in symbiosis with the library itself, and in which luxury manuscripts were produced. From Timurid Persia the model was later exported to Mughal India (sixteenth and seventeenth centuries). The institutions dedicated to the transmission of knowledge appear, instead, well represented in the colophons. Many were the copyists who plied their trade within a *madrasa*. The examples are numerous and extend throughout the Islamized world. Another place which was frequently used was the mosque, but also: *zāwiya*, *mazār*, *ḫānqāh* or more generally *ḥuǧra*. The Rab-i Rašīdī Foundation east of Tabriz, established in 1300 by the Ilkhanid Vizier Rašīd al-Dīn Hamaḏānī, offers a noteworthy example of the organization and planning of the work: a library kept the original manuscripts and the finished copies were exhibited in the mosque within the same academic complex. Other less conventional situations are mentioned in colophons in both earlier and later periods (Déroche – Sagaria Rossi 2012, 144–149).

2.6.2. Colophons

In the Arab-Islamic manuscript tradition, information about the copying (date, place, copyist) was considered to be the seal of a unit of reading that might also coincide with a unit of coherent text, if it was a unitary entity, not separated in *aǧzā'* (plural of *ǧuz'* 'part'). In the absence of repertories of formulations subdivided by place and date, of systematic surveys taken from homogeneous collections and of studies of their content, a preliminary assessment so far has been a sample comparison of evidence representing various centuries, areas and typologies (Şeşen 1997).

In the Qur'āns and in the many other multi-volume works, the choice to proceed by separate units, each corresponding to an autonomous item (*ǧuz'*, or *muǧallada* 'volume'), seems to have been dictated by needs of convenience to facilitate consultation or by the necessity of managing an abundant mass of text. For this reason, it is not an anomaly to find within the same volume sequences of information of the ends of copies, with the function of indicating the end of each *ǧuz'*. At any rate, what is placed in this space is variable in its manifestations and in its contents and does not constitute a constant, above all in Arabic examples, which often do not have this informative area, unlike Persian and Turkish volumes, which usually do have it. This tendency takes on a more disciplined aspect later, in the eighteenth and nineteenth centuries, when we find that colophons containing all the canonical information rapidly become widespread.

Colophons are usually found at the end of the text, or of a certain portion of it, though in some examples they are placed at the beginning. There is also a graphical and textual continuity between this section and the text itself, so that the real end of the text sometimes cannot be perceived. At times there is a line after the last line of the text, separating it from the block of information concerning the copying: in these cases, the lines of the colophon are still justified, yet shorter than those of the text, or they can take peculiar shapes (like a triangle or an inverted trapezoid); rectangular frames of variable width placed in sequence constitute other variants and were chronologically the first to appear. Starting from the fourteenth century, we also find the practice of inscribing colophons within a circle, or in geometric figures with more complex outlines. Decorated subscriptions like those found in some Qur'āns are extremely carefully done in refined frames illuminated in gold.

Not infrequently the copyist adopted a distinctive graphic style, even only for a few lines, as occurs in particular in Qur'ān manuscripts; he might also write a series of letters, the م *mīm*, the abbreviation of *tamma* 'it is terminated', or the ه *hā'*, for *intahā* 'it is finished', often disposed in a triangular shape. In some initial formulae, such as *tamma al-kitāb* 'the book is finished', some of the internal letters can appear elongated. Colophons that are more or less capably counterfeited or modified, whether partially or completely, are not uncommon.

As to the contents of the subscription formulae, date, location and name of the copyist are, when indicated, an integrated communication, within which it is not always easy to establish the demarcation between information related to the exemplar, to the transmission, and to the collation of the copy itself. The introduction of the dating, placed at the end of the manuscript, strengthened the importance of chronology in the Islamic tradition. Generally drawn up in the third person, the wording is often extremely concise and limited to essentials, above all in the eighth and ninth centuries CE, and appears without any regularity. Over the following centuries, a marked propensity for more literary constructions developed, and new elements are found integrated in the stratification of the information relative to the collation and the editorial activity of the copyist. Starting from the thirteenth century, the date of the copy is more regularly expressed, together with the mention of the models and of the list of persons who collaborated on the collation of the text.

Formulations at the end of Persian copies appear in the twelfth century and in Turkish starting from the fourteenth century CE. The name of the copyist does not appear systematically, above all in the case of the lapidary formulations that give only the year of the copy. When, instead, a scribe reveals his name it may only be as an *ism*, the initial segment of the Arabic name, or perhaps the entire genealogical list, with appellatives and nicknames; the same copyist could use more or less complete versions of his name in different manuscripts. This is followed by indications of the means used, the hand or the calamus. It would be wrong to overlook the role of the formulae of benediction and various recurring statements.

The place of the copy is mentioned less often, often in a vague and unspecific way; only rarely is the exact location of the copying revealed.

The patron is often named in the subscription, above all when he is a person of a more modest class, while the name of an important person is generally found at the beginning of the work.

Compared with Arab-Islamic manuscripts, Arab-Christian colophons are composed of fully developed formulae, regular in their recording of dates and methodical in their presentation. The terms used are the same as those found in Arab-Islamic manuscripts. Almost all the examples have a declaration of the end of the copying and the date, accompanied by several elements: the day of the week, the time of day, the day of the month generally expressed in figures, the month according to its Coptic, Syriac or Arabic name, the year indicated according to the Era of the Martyrs, the Era of the World, the Era of Alexander, the Hegira or the Christian Era. The copyist is always declared, but his name is not revealed with the same regularity; beside his self-assumed derogatory attributes—unworthy, servant, humble, sinner and miserable—he also introduces self-denigrating expressions. The collation of the original text is neither a usual practice nor a constructive element of these colophons. The precise place where the copying was done is less often given; it might be a city, a monastery or a church. The person who was to receive the codex is occasionally mentioned. At the end of the colophon we can find two types of request from the copyist to the reader: a supplication that the scribe be pardoned for his sins, so that he could enter the Heavenly Jerusalem, and that the reader correct the errors and lapses that he will encounter while reading the copy (Troupeau 1997). More prolix formulations are intended to obtain the reader's favour: they differ from those found in mediaeval Arab-Islamic manuscripts, which were non-standardized, sober, synthetic and essential.

2.6.3. Dating systems

The date of copying is not mentioned in a significant portion of Arabic manuscripts. There might be the simple mention of the year without any indication of the day or month, indicated according to the Hegira, which started on 1 *Muḥarram,* corresponding to 16 July 622 CE. As the calendar based on the Hegira is lunar in type, it is necessary to convert the dates to the Gregorian calendar. The term *sana* 'year', more rarely *ʿāmm* 'year', precedes the date which is usually expressed in letters, but there are examples in which it is indicated in *abǧad* and in numbers, which, however, is a later practice. It is not unusual to encounter a mention of the lunar month of the Islamic calendar.

The date may be also expressed alphanumerically or as a chronogram, based on the sum of the numeric values of the *abǧad* letters. This consists in a brief enunciation, introduced by *taʾrīḫ* 'date', *sana* or *ʿāmm*, *fī* 'in', and followed by a graphic association of letters, in red or overlined in black or red. This system first appears in prose texts, but above all in poetry, where it can constitute the hemistich of a eulogy in celebration of an event. This way of proceeding is found mainly in Persian and Turkish manuscripts starting in the fifteenth century; it enjoyed considerable favour in the Ottoman area, but it was also used in western areas, in particular in Morocco, where from the sixteenth century it was used to date inscriptions, documents and manuscripts; in later periods, chronograms are also found with a sub-Saharan African provenance. The date is more rarely expressed in fractions, found in Arabic and Turkish manuscripts; though this method is generally attributed to Aḥmad b. Kamāl Pāšā (d.1533), it already existed in the first half of the fourteenth century. The year is divided into two halves, which are then divided into sixths, corresponding to months, divided into three ten-day periods; the dates of either the editing or the copy may be expressed in fractions.

In parallel, other dating systems based on traditional divisions of the solar year could be used in non-Muslim contexts. As the Julian calendar was known, the eastern Melkite community referred to the Era of the World, beginning on 1 September 5509 BCE. The Coptic Christians in Egypt usually referred to the Era of the Martyrs, or Era of Diocletian, which started on 29 August 284. The Era of Alexander, or of the Seleucids, or Greek Era started on 1 October 312 BCE. The Era of Yazdigird was in use in the Iranian world. This was named after the Sassanid king Yazdigird III (reigned 632–642) and began on 16 June 632 CE. It was then adopted by Malikšāh who established the *ǧalālī* or *malikī* era—from the name of the third Seljuk sultan Ǧalāl al-Dawla Malikšāh (reigned 1072–1092)—that started on 15 March 1079. An example of Ptolemy's *Almagest* commented by the astronomer Naṣīr al-Dīn al-Ṭūsī (d.1274) has four parallel dates: according to the Hegira it was 1076, the Era of Alexander 1976, the *ǧalālī* era 587, the Era of Yazdigird 1034, corresponding to 1664 or 1665 CE. However, the concordance among the several dating systems was not always exact. In Mughal India, the *ilāhī* era was established in 1584 by the Emperor Akbar (reigned 1556–1605). It was commonly used to date inventory notes. The practice of dating based on regnal years of sovereigns is encountered above all in manuscripts coming from Persia or India. In al-Andalus, the Spanish Era, *tāʾrīḫ al-ṣufr*, began in 38 BCE (Déroche – Sagaria Rossi 2012, 206–215).

2.6.4. Duration of copying

The rapidity of executing a copy of an Arabic text is information that was recorded quite early in the history of Arabic manuscripts and was used as a criterion for evaluating the quality of the copy: this criterion seems to have enjoyed a certain reputation in the eyes of mediaeval authors, such as the aforementioned Ibn Bādīs, who explains that ancient writings are related to the speed of execution. Sometimes the copyist indicates the time spent in accomplishing the copying of a text, specifying the beginning and the end of his work. In the great majority of cases, the transcription was a solitary exercise, but from the beginning there were cases of manuscripts copied by more than one person, as is the case of some fragments of two very ancient Qur'āns, both attributed to the second half of the seventh century CE, regardless of any homogenization of the styles adopted. Later manuscripts made for ordinary use were also transcribed collectively by several scribes. Nevertheless, a variation in writing, in particular at the end of a work, is not certain evidence that there was a change of copyist (Déroche – Sagaria Rossi 2012, 149–155).

In the case of copying in two or several *ağzā'* ('parts'), the work was carried out in stages requiring a few days, some weeks, or even longer, the one part being executed independently from the other. It was a usual practice to circulate large portions of many multi-volume works (Humbert 1997). Unfortunately, we do not have any systematic study of the length of time required for copying, nor have the works with several intermediary colophons been sufficiently examined.

2.7. Bookbinding (FD)

Leatherworking was widely practised throughout the Islamic world. The commonest skins were goat, though sheep and calf were also employed. The binders prepared the skins carefully, scraping the inner face of the leather in order to reduce its thickness as much as possible.

A number of kinds of book covering were known to the Islamic world. These types can be divided for convenience into three major groups (Types I, II and III).

The largest group of early Islamic bookbindings known today belongs to Type I. They are as a general rule oblong in format with wooden boards. The chief distinguishing feature is a continuous leather protective wall or strip of the same thickness as the text block, glued to three rims of the lower book cover to form a box or case whose spine constitutes the fourth side (Déroche 2005, 286–287). When the book is shut the pages' edges lie snugly within the leather surround. Such a binding-cum-case (or 'box-book') is customarily fitted with some kind of fastening. So far, it has been exclusively associated with Qur'ānic manuscripts.

Type II is by far the most common kind of Islamic binding and is widely known as 'flap binding' (see figs. 1.2.4, 1.2.5). Its most salient feature is the presence of the fore-edge flap and the envelope (or 'tongue') flap, two elements connected by flexible hinges, which extend from the long side of the lower cover. Rectangular in shape, the 'fore-edge flap' is that part of the covering which lies over the fore-edge to protect it when the volume is closed. As broad as the book is thick, the fore-edge flap continues over a second hinge into the pentagonal 'envelope flap', tapering to a point in line with the central axis of the manuscript. In a few early examples of Type II bindings, a strap was attached to the point of the envelope flap in order to keep the book tightly closed. A further characteristic of this type of bookbinding is the absence of a shoulder. Arabic treatises on bookbinding are adamant that any 'swell' at the jointing must be 'knocked out' with a maul or reduced in the press. Finally, the edges of the book covers were flush with the text block.

From a technical point of view, Type II is close to the modern 'pasted down to ends' style in case-binding in which the block is attached directly to the endpapers. Once the gatherings are sewn, the back is lined ('backed') with a strip of cloth (the 'spine lining') wider than the thickness of the volume so that there is enough space to paste the edges down to the boards. Depending on the taste and style of an individual bookbinder, the paste-down consists of the initial (or final) leaf, or else of a genuine doublure whose extremities are stuck to the first or last leaf, thereby ensuring the coherence of the whole. Type III shares the same components as those of Type II, with the exception of the fore-edge and envelope flaps. It represents only a fraction of eastern bindings, notably manuscripts produced in Central Asia—in the broad sense—in later times.

Book boards were made out of wood, particularly for 'bindings-cum-cases' (Type I). However, the most common material employed by bookbinders in forwarding was paper pasteboard. In the Ottoman world and more generally wherever the Ottoman binders' methods predominate, fine bindings occasionally played on differences in layer among the various components of a decoration by creating pronounced relief effects during the preparation of the pasteboard (Sakisian 1927a, 278, n. 5). Lacquer binding boards are traditionally dubbed 'papier mâché': this term in fact disguises the familiar pasteboard made out of layers of sheets of sized paper (Khalili et al. 1996, 10).

Covering the inner surface of a book board fulfilled the purpose not only of enhancing the binding's appearance, but also of strengthening the cohesion between binding and text block; doublures were in fact often set across the 'hinge' that served to reinforce the binding as a whole. It is common to find restoration work in these areas, evidence of the high level of wear to which they were sometimes subjected.

Very fine leathers could be used to line the inner cover, and in this instance the edge overlaps slightly onto the endpaper to which the leather is glued. They were sometimes completely devoid of decoration; however, there was a range of methods at the binder's disposal, including all those techniques employed for the outer boards (Haldane 1983, 145, 148, 158–159), together with leather gauffering (Haldane 1983, 22, 24–5, 26–27; Bosch et al. 1981, 130–135, 141–142, 153, 175–176; Déroche 2005, 271).

The methods by which books were forwarded, and more particularly the importance of the endpapers in ensuring that the final product remained robust, inevitably led to paper being favoured as the lining material for inner covers. Be it the same paper utilized for the gatherings or some special material paper attained a level of popularity that never waned. In the Ottoman world, for example, marbled paper met with enduring success as doublure, while coloured papers with gold decoration also enjoyed a certain vogue. Sometimes, the use of paper was limited to a specific portion of the doublure: a case in point is the filigree decorations executed in paper (see below). Fabric has also been used, for doublures as well as for the coverings.

Oriental headbands were usually built over a fine strip of leather or parchment laid flat along the head of the volume and not connected to the boards, but the Type I bindings may have been somewhat different in this respect. This strip was anchored primarily by threads of the same colour as that serving to sew the gathering, the bookbinder embroidering a chevron design in two colours of thread over a core (*Tranchefiles* 1989, 86–89). This component is not purely decorative, however; the headband also improved the cohesion of the volume.

Stamping is far and away the most common decorative technique in bookbinding (fig. 1.2.5). In the Muslim world, tools utilized for stamping leather left imprints of variable dimensions, from small motifs to large-size panels. In the former case, the binder would use a combination of tools in the decoration, while the latter allowed him to decorate a large surface in one fell swoop, ranging from the central ornament to the whole surface of the board.

Once the use of larger stamps became widespread—by the second half of the fifteenth century—block-stamping was occasionally used in conjunction with preparations designed to improve the end result. Ottoman bookbinders increased the relief effects obtained with panel stamps on boards by recessing the zone destined for the motif (Sakisian 1927a, 278 n. 5; Raby – Tanındı 1993, 216). Another process was to obtain contrast effects by applying to the site of the decoration a thin piece of leather or paper cut to the size and shape of the block, but of a different hue from the rest of the binding. Gilding was frequently applied to eastern bookbindings, sometimes in conjunction with blind-stamping. Later Ottoman bindings from the ninth century are often decorated with gold paint applied directly onto the leather.

Be that as it may, two general tendencies as to composition have been discerned: on the one hand, there are decorations that cover the entire available space, while others rely on a contrast between an element stamped in the centre of the board and a field left plain. In this second category, furthermore, the composition may be completed by other ornaments around the perimeter (pendants, corner-pieces, and edgings of variable thickness); such auxiliaries will not be addressed in the following survey. Max Weisweiler proposed a typology for binding decorations using *petits fers* (Weisweiler 1962; Déroche 2005, 292–299).

Toward the end of the fifteenth century, technical advances were having a profound impact on the art of bookbinding. Irons had grown larger over the course of the preceding decades, particularly those employed for framing covers; all that remained was to increase their size marginally and it would become possible to apply a whole unit, or even an entire decorative scheme, in a single strike. The two major categories described above (central motifs on the one hand, and ornamentation of an entire cover on the other) remain pertinent to these cases. The Ottoman central panels rely on a few patterns covered in part by a typology (Déroche 1985, 17–26; Déroche 2005, 300–309).

Larger panels, which made it possible to lay in decorations covering the whole of the board, have not yet been adequately classified: they usually associate arabesque with geometrical motifs or else, though this is less usual, borrow their decorative stock-in-trade from miniatures (Haldane 1983, 87 and 104); once stamped, the decoration was normally then totally gilded. Thanks to this process, it became feasible to apply in a single operation both figurative and non-figurative decoration to the entire cover of a small-size volume (excluding the frame if desired; Haldane 1983, 160–161). Such tools presupposed a measure of consistency in the formats available.

Fig. 1.2.5 Rome, Biblioteca dell'Accademia Nazionale dei Lincei e Corsiniana, Or. 75, Egypt, fifteenth century, front cover and flap with gilt-stamped brown leather.

Other techniques have also been used: on some early Qur'ānic bindings, designs were applied to the covers by setting (or perhaps pasting) cords on the wooden boards (Marçais – Poinssot 1948, 21, 228–232; Déroche 2005, 283), then stretching a piece of damp leather over the boards. The technique of filigree has long been known. It involves creating a decoration by cutting leather or paper into a pattern; the resulting lattice can be set off against a coloured fabric or paper insert. Filigrees were mainly used for decorating inner covers, these being less exposed to rubbing (Sakisian 1934, 150).

Paper has also been widely used for outer coverings and bookbinders seem to have preferred paper that was already decorated, tinted, or otherwise enhanced. In the Ottoman world, marbled paper began to be used in covers and wrappers during the seventeenth century (see fig. 1.2.4) and frequently appears in quarter-bindings with leather-drawn spines (Bosch et al. 1981, 218–219). In Central Asia and Iran, glossy tinted papers were employed in bookbinding from the seventeenth century; they may even be stamped in the same fashion as leather.

Fabrics too were put to use as a book covering. When cloth is used to wrap the boards, there is normally a thin border strip of leather around the edges in order to protect the textile. The combined use of leather and fabric for decorative purposes is attested in the case of filigree work.

The most common lacquer technique consisted in executing the decoration on boards made of pasteboard. The oldest examples date from the fifteenth century and were made at the court of Ḥusayn Mirza at Herat (ruled 873–911 AH/1469–1506 CE) (Khalili et al. 1996, 16–17). However, earlier examples from the second half of the fourteenth century demonstrate that craftsmen originally applied lacquer decoration to leather-drawn boards (Khalili et al. 1996, 232). In terms of decoration, these bindings are closer to illumination or miniature painting than to bookbinding proper.

References

Baer 1998; Bayani et al. 1999; Beach 2004; Ben Azzouna forthcoming; Bloom 1989, 2001; Bosch et al. 1981; von Bothmer 1995; Colini 2008; Déroche 2005, 2006, 2009, forthcoming; Déroche – Richard 1998; Déroche – Sagaria Rossi 2012; D'Ottone 2006; Dreibholz 1991; Estève 2001; *FiMMOD*; Gacek 2001, 2002, 2008; Gascou 1989; George 2011, 2012; Grohmann 1967; Haldane 1983; Haran 1985; Houdas 1886; Humbert 1998, 2002; Irigoin 1950, 1993; James 1992a, 1992b; Karabacek 1888, 2001; Khalili et al. 1996; Khan – Lewincamp 2008; Levey 1962; Lewis – Mingana 1914; Marçais – Poinssot 1948; Orsatti 1989, 1993, 1997; Parodi 2010, 2011; Parodi et al. 2010; Parodi – Wannell 2011; Pedersen 1984; Porter [Y.] 2003; Raby – Tanındı 1993; Regourd 2006; Roxburgh 1995, 2001, 2005; Ryder 1991; Šabbūḥ 1995; Sakisian 1927a, 1927b, 1934; Schopen 2006; Şeşen 1997; Silbergeld 1982; Soudavar 1992; *Tranchefiles* 1989; Troupeau 1997; Vernay-Nouri 2002; Weisweiler 1962; Welch et al. 1987; Wright – Stronge 2008.

3. Armenian codicology (DK)*

3.1. Materials and tools

The history of the writing supports used for Armenian manuscripts is less complicated than for the Greek or Latin tradition. Though Greek and Syriac writing are textually referred to in the sources, and though there are some pre-seventh century Latin lapidary inscriptions from Greater Armenia, suggesting that Latin during Roman dominion might have also been written, no manuscript example of writing by Armenians has survived from before the invention of the Armenian alphabet between 404–406. The material for writing was parchment from the beginning, with an early introduction of paper in the tenth century and its dominance by the end of the twelfth century

3.1.1. Papyrus

There is a unique papyrus in Greek completely written with Armenian letters, once thought lost but rediscovered (Paris, BnF, Arménien 332, 1512 IV, see fig. 2.3.1) during research for the *Album of Armenian Paleography* (Kouymjian 1996b; 1998a; 2002a). As the only known papyrus with Armenian letters and the only surviving non-book manuscript before the twelfth century, it is an important link between the origin of the alphabet and the earliest codices four hundred years later, thus a key document for the evolution of Armenian writing. It provoked Yakob Tašyan to write his study of Armenian palaeography (1898). Since the text is entirely in Greek, it has been conjectured that the author was either an Armenian merchant (Tašyan 1898, 102) or soldier in the Byzantine army stationed in Egypt trying to perfect his Greek (Leroy [M.] 1938, 514). On historical grounds, it probably dates to the late sixth or early seventh century. Whatever its exact date, it is the oldest example of Armenian manuscript writing and the only early writing in an informal script. The single papyrus sheet (226 × 160 mm) has a twenty-seven-line text on each side. The contents are a run-on list of expressions in everyday Greek, quotations from maxims, for instance of Diogenes, and grammatical exercises (Clackson 2000). Most of the letters have the form of a cursive angular or slanted *erkatʻagir* (majuscule, see details Ch. 2 § 3) with some letters looking more like *bolorgir* (minuscule) and others even like *šłagir* cursive with connected letters (Mouraviev 2010, 152–153).

3.1.2. Parchment

Virtually all Armenian manuscripts up to the mid-twelfth century were of parchment, even though paper was introduced two centuries earlier. During the tenth to the twelfth centuries, a parchment manuscript was always a bit larger than a paper one. The largest Armenian manuscript (Yerevan, Matenadaran, 7729; Venice, Mekhitarist library, 1614/229; *Album* 222–225, nos. 52–53), a collection of homilies of 1202, 705 × 550 mm, is supposedly of calfskin (Matʻevosyan 1969, 138). It is one of the rare Armenian manuscripts laid out in three columns. Originally there were some 660 folia, today only 606, including the two in the Venice Mekhitarist collection, remain; each bifolium, made from calfskin, is made up of two folia sewn together in a sort of chain stitch. For the majority of Armenian manuscripts goat and sheepskin were used, but little has been published on the production of parchment in Armenia compared to the many recipes signalled in catalogues. A discussion of five late Armenian recipes (Yerevan, Matenadaran, 1849 of 1440, 551 of 1650, 7322 of 1694, 6924, eighteenth century, and Jerusalem, Armenian Patriarchate, 1136, undated) can be found in Peter Schreiner's (1983) article on parchment making formulas beginning with Greek and Coptic. The Armenian examples are treated based on an article in Russian by a chemist (Galfajan 1975a). The recipes are short and usually begin with the word 'advice' (*xrat*) or 'concerning' (*vasn*) or even both. They are collected along with longer texts in miscellaneous manuscripts called collection of texts (*žołovacu*), but also in medical treatises (*bžškaran*) and chemistry works (*kʻimiakankʻ*). Some of the texts speak of a treatment of thicker and harder skins with pigeon droppings, following their soaking in one or more hydrated lime (calcium hydroxide) baths; the two more recent texts prescribe bran or barley flour with the same function. Such recipes for parchment, ink, and pigments are found under chemical treatises in the indexes of certain manuscript catalogues. In the catalogue of more than 11,000 manuscripts in Yerevan (*Matenadaran abridged catalogue* = Eganyan et al. 1965, 1970, 2007, see also Ch. 4 § 2.2), there are 122 recipes listed, from which three more on parchment can be added to those treated by Gal-

* Much of this material, originally prepared for the COMSt handbook, has been also used, often without change, in Kouymjian 2014 (DK).

fajan – Schreiner: Yerevan, Matenadaran, 10200, dated 1624–1666; 9303, mid-seventeenth century; 1395, seventeenth/eighteenth century. Among the most important centres of parchment production were the monasteries of Glajor and Tatʿev in the northeast and the Cilician kingdom's scriptoria in the southwest.

A Jerusalem manuscript's text 'This is Advice about (Preparing) Parchment' of some 350 words is published in its entirety (Połarian 1966–1991, IV, 212–213), and Schreiner has translated a large segment of it. It begins, 'First select skins from goats, lambs, doe, deer, wild sheep, hare, and fish from which one can make parchment' (f. 214). Note that cowhide or calfskin is not included. Though there are no Armenian manuscripts on fish skin, there are at least two large fish heads used for writing and especially for very accomplished miniatures from the Life of Christ, one in the Mekhitarist library in Venice and another in a private collection in Paris, both unpublished but probably of the eighteenth century. Though no serious work has yet been done in comparing the various texts or versions of these recipes, one might suppose that the original exemplars must have dated prior to the fourteenth century, after which the use of parchment for codices was dramatically reduced.

Statistical data suggest that by the last quarter of the twelfth century, the number of paper manuscripts surpassed parchment ones; a century later, shortly after 1300, parchment was no longer used as a writing surface except for presentation copies of Gospels or Bibles, and these were very rare (Kouymjian 2013, 27 Table 2). This shift was a matter of economy; it was accompanied by the transition from majuscule to minuscule, thus the smaller sized paper manuscripts still contained as much or a greater amount of text. In the thirteenth century, manuscript production had increased in quantity and dramatically improved in quality; paper had become the dominant medium, and though manuscripts were smaller in size than in the ninth to the eleventh centuries, 280 × 180 mm, they were nearly 15% larger than those of the twelfth century. Nevertheless the trend was moving toward a smaller book. Eventually there was a size standardization from the fourteenth to the nineteenth centuries, roughly 200 × 140 mm, about half that of the earliest manuscripts, which is the size of *quarto* common paper (Italian 'rezute').

Though no coloured Armenian parchment manuscript or fragment has survived, in palaeo-Christian times purple parchment was used as attested in the early seventh-century treatise in defence of images by Vṙtʿanēs Kʿertʿoł, *locum tenens* of the catholicosate of the Armenian Church 604–607. He remarks, 'Car nous voyons le livre des évangiles peint avec de l'or et de l'argent et, de plus, relié avec de l'ivoire et du parchemin pourpre' (Der Nersessian 1973a, I, 385). After the transition to printing, there are several luxury printed books of the seventeenth century, including copies of the 1666 Amsterdam Bible printed on a very fine light blue, paper.

Parchment, an expensive product, was often recycled, most commonly by erasing sheets or at times full manuscripts in order to over-write on them. The palimpsests produced by this procedure preserved old manuscripts or fragments, which with advances in technology are providing a new source of early texts. The Matenadaran, the Repository of Ancient Manuscripts in Yerevan, reports there are about a thousand manuscripts in the collection that are palimpsests or contain fragments of palimpsests (*Rinascimento virtuale* 2002, 91–92). Many of these are guard leaves, since there was a very early tradition that newly copied and bound manuscripts should incorporate protective sheets in the front and back from older parchment manuscripts. Sometimes the underlying strata of palimpsests are Greek or Georgian, while recycled Armenian parchments are found in Arabic (Brock 1965), Georgian (Renhart 2009), and other traditions. A model of methodology in the photographing, transcribing and analysing Armenian palimpsests is offered in Jost Gippert's study of two substantial Armenian biblical fragments reused for a tenth-century Georgian manuscript from Sinai (Gippert 2010a). Thus far, the analysis of such material is firmly in the domain of philology rather than codicology. Nevertheless, it is evident that with the number of documents still to be exploited, information beyond the textual from palimpsests will provide insights not just on textual history and palaeography, but on the construction of the codex: formation of quires, ruling and pricking, signatures, often from a moment prior to the earliest dated manuscripts. By establishing a firm *terminus ante quem*, palimpsests can serve as more powerful tools than palaeography in evaluating the date of some Armenian manuscripts judged to be older than the Mlkʿē Gospel of 862 (Venice, Mekhitarist library, 1144/86; *Album* 2002, nos. 2–3).

3.1.3. Paper

Paper was introduced early into Armenian manuscript production. The oldest example dates to 981, a religious miscellany, entirely of paper (MS Yerevan, Matenadaran, 2679; *Album* 2002, nos. 10–11, 138–141);

it is one of the smallest, 280 × 190 mm, among tenth-century codices. Nevertheless, the precocious date of 981 is followed by a succession of dated paper codices of 1113, 1118, 1137, 1155, 1166, 1167, 1169, with twelve more up to the end of the twelfth century in a random sampling of dated examples from catalogues. Twenty-three are found in the same list from the next fifty years and seventy-seven from 1250–1300. They are from every region of Greater Armenia, from Cilicia to the Georgian border, from Erzinjan to Edessa and Adana. Paper was used to copy Gospel texts from the eleventh century (MS Yerevan, Matenadaran, 6975, dated by style) and specifically 1113 (MS Yerevan, Matenadaran, 6763, Gospels from Drazark in Cilicia), with four more dated examples to 1200. It is generally assumed that parchment was reserved for Gospel manuscripts; in fact, even before paper replaced parchment as the most used support in the late thirteenth century (Kouymjian 2012a, 19 Table 1), paper was commonly employed for Gospels, ten recorded from 1201–1278, but fifteen for the last two decades of the century. The first Bible written on paper, incomplete, was in 1214 (Jerusalem, Armenian Patriarchate, 417); in all there are at least six Bible manuscripts, three complete including the lavishly decorated and illustrated Erzinjan Bible of 1269 (MS Jerusalem, Armenian Patriarchate, 1925), from the thirteenth century, by the last quarter of which, 80% of Armenian codices were of paper. From about 1400 on, paper was the exclusive medium for manuscripts; the rare exceptions were for Gospels or Bibles.

There are a handful of other undated paper manuscripts of the eleventh century and several of mixed parchment and paper. Levon Xažakyan (1984) has reported that paper and ink analysis of the manuscript of 981 and others of the period point to a local production of both the paper and the ink; his conclusion is based on chemical analysis and infrared spectrography. Unfortunately, the colophons of the manuscripts do not mention the exact place of copying. Though this may be the first evidence of paper making in Armenia, it is not the last. Another documented instance is from seventeenth-century Iran, where an abortive attempt to print the Bible in the short-lived press established by the bishop Xačʿatur Kesaracʿi (1636–1650) in New Julfa, the Armenian suburb of Isfāhān founded in 1605, resulted in the issuing of a number of titles (Kévorkian 1986, 114–119) on paper manufactured there as attested by the colophon of the Lives of the Fathers printed in 1641 (Minasyan 1972, 16; Kévorkian 1986, 116; Voskanyan et al. 1988, 24). Though of a mediocre quality, some of this paper was probably used for copying manuscripts, a flourishing art in New Julfa until the eighteenth century.

We have other documented information on paper production at the Holy See of Etchmiadzin (Ējmiacin) initiated by Catholicos Simeon Erevancʿi in 1776 (Abrahamyan 1947). In Armenia, however, already by the last quarter of the twelfth century the majority of manuscripts were made of paper (Kouymjian 2013, Table 2), much of which was supplied from such centres as Baghdad, and later from Damascus and Tabriz as attested by colophons (Abrahamyan 1973, 282, 357; Merian et al. 1994a, 126). Though 'lines' in paper, presumably oriental, are mentioned in some catalogues, there is no specificity about the disposition of laid and chain lines; preliminary research on such a codicological matter needs to be engaged. Watermarked European (*franki, pʿaranki*) paper was also employed, but there seemed to be a preference among scribes for Damascus (Yerevan, Matenadaran, 8689, f. 88, colophon of scribe, 1417); paper types are listed in the *Master catalogue of the Matenadaran* and other collections, but rarely with specificity, though Tašyan in his Vienna catalogue of 1891–1895 already noted consistently whether the paper was polished or not and its colour or tint. The study of the watermarks and the variety of oriental papers waits to be initiated.

3.1.4. Inks

Many early Armenian manuscripts written in majuscule *erkatʿagir* employed iron gall ink that turns rusty brown with time, as compared to the black hue of an Indian or Chinese ink. The same brownish hue is seen in *bolorgir* or minuscule manuscripts of the later twelfth and thirteenth centuries. Yet the majority of manuscripts use ink that remains black, most probably a soot or carbon based type for which at least one eleven line recipe survives: *Vasn mur sineloy* ('On Making Soot-Ink'), Yerevan, Matenadaran, 1261 copied in 1725 in Jerusalem. There are also two recipes entitled 'Advice on Parchment Ink' (Yerevan, Matenadaran, 752, fifteenth/sixteenth century; Yerevan, Matenadaran, 738, seventeenth century). There are a vast number of recipes entitled either 'Advice' or 'On Making or Cooking Ink' dating from the fifteenth to the nineteenth century. In the Yerevan collection alone there are at least thirty-six, including ten with the title *Kerb tʿanakʿ patrasteloy* ('Method for Preparing Ink') from the seventeenth to the early twentieth century. That these are traditional Armenian recipes for ink is perhaps confirmed by a recipe

Franki murakʻap šinel ('[How] to Make Ink of the Franks'), Yerevan, Matenadaran, 737 of 1680-1730. Some work has been done on these texts, but in studies that are hard to access, one in Armenian *The Use of Pigments and Inks in Old Armenian Manuscripts* (Harutʻyunyan 1941), written when the Yerevan collection was half the size, and two in Russian on the preparation of iron-gall ink in mediaeval Armenia and the effect of pigments and ink on paper (Galfajan 1975b, 1975c). An in-depth scientific analysis of the ink that was used on the earliest paper manuscript of 981 (Yerevan, Matenadaran, 2679) with a detailed chemical analysis of all components, including trace elements, has been provided (Xažakyan 1984, 164–165).

3.1.5. Pigments

The most important research on pigment use in Armenia has been by scientists Diane Cabelli and Mary Virginia Orna and art historian Thomas Mathews. In some twenty articles, whose aim was to determine with precision the palette used by painters and illuminators, pigment samples of a large number of Armenian manuscripts were analysed using polarized light microscopy and X-ray diffraction, the methodology outlined in detail (Orna – Mathews 1981; Mathews – Sanjian 1991, 48–51). Three groups of Armenian manuscripts, twenty-four in all, from the tenth to the fourteenth century were analysed and compared with the analyses of Byzantine manuscripts (nine from the tenth to the thirteenth century), and three groups of Persian, Indian, and Turkish manuscripts of the fourteenth century and after (forty-two manuscripts). The detailed list of manuscripts and results of pigment identifications are summarized in a general article on Armenian codicology (Merian et al. 1994b). The results showed that though Armenian artists used some organic pigments, particularly reds, the majority were mineral based, whereas in the Byzantine palette the majority were organic dyes. The main pigments used in the important and brilliant painting tradition of the Cilician kingdom (twelfth to the fourteenth centuries) were white lead, gold, orpiment, red lake, ultramarine, and vermilion (Merian et al. 1994b, 129). Research began on an early fourteenth century Glajor Gospels (Los Angeles, CA, UCLA, Arm. 1) on which five artists worked; the results showed that the source of certain colours was not always the same for each of the painters and offered a codicological way of checking classic stylistic conclusions. It also means that artists, even working in the same monastery, had different paint sets.

The methodology developed is a model for the examination of pigments in a non-destructive way on all oriental manuscripts. It is to be regretted that a further effort was not made to examine and discuss the pigment recipes found in Armenian manuscripts, which are regarded as detached from the actual pigments found in the manuscripts. Nevertheless, already in the early seventh century Vṙtʻanēs Kʻertʻoł had listed a number of colours in his treatise on the defence of images: 'As for those who say that the pigments are vile, they accuse themselves with their own words, because the pigments used for writing are vitriol, gall and gum ... while the materials used for the images are milk, eggs, arsenic, blue, verdigris, lime, and other similar materials' (Der Nersessian 1973a, I, 387). Early in the last century a recipe from a manuscript of 1618, 'Advice for the Painter' (Paris, BnF, Arménien 186, ff. 216v–217v), were published and translated (Macler 1924, 13–23). Among unpublished recipes a fifteenth century treatise, *About Different Colours* (Yerevan, Matenadaran, 573, ff. 238v–242v) offers advice on various colour and gold pigments with thirty-seven recipes for preparing them (*Matenadaran master catalogue* = Eganyan et al. 1984–2013, II, col. 1328). Other recipes are found in later manuscripts on making yellow pigment (Yerevan, Matenadaran, 551 of 1650), on colours (Yerevan, Matenadaran, 8424 of 1744–1748), on preparing colours and using them (Yerevan, Matenadaran, 6285 and 9986, both nineteenth century), but it must be kept in mind that these post mediaeval recipes might have been copied from earlier exemplars. Finally, there is a vast specialized literature and even a research institute in Armenia devoted to the local cochineal red dye, *vordan karmir* known as *kirmiz* in the Near East, from an insect indigenous to the Ararat plain and used for red dyes (perhaps the red lake organic pigment referred to in the scientific analyses above) in brilliant Armenian miniatures as well as Armenian rugs and textiles (Babenko 1988).

3.1.6. Writing instruments

The preferred writing instrument of scribes using papyrus was a split reed from Egypt, the *calamus*, Armenian *kalam*, used in Armenia for codices from the earliest centuries. Use of metal styluses for Armenian manuscripts is unlikely despite the term *erkatʻagir*, iron letters (Kouymjian 2002b, 67–68).

The Armenian instruments have not been the subject of serious studies, therefore, it is not clear if the drawings show the actual tools of the scribe working on the manuscript in which they appear or simply a recopying of earlier tradition. A gateway into this research can be provided by a miniature painting of St Matthew as a scribe in a Gospel manuscript of 1338 from Erzinjan (Yerevan, Matenadaran, 7643, f. 2v) showing fourteen instruments to his right stacked vertically from the top down with nine identifying labels: ruler or straight-edge (*k'anon*), paper polisher (*t'lt'i kokič'*), ink pots (two, *kał[a]mar*), pen (*grič'*), large and small, scissors (*mkrat*), trimmer, rounded and straight-edged (*ǰewič'*), knives (two, *danak*), chest with pots for black and red ink (*sntuk*), cover for the chest (*xup'n*); the miniature of St Luke in the same manuscript shows a marble slab before the scribe-evangelist used like an artist's palette to mix and test colour pigments (Aṙak'elyan 1958, 311, fig. 38; Abrahamian 1973, 283–284). Among innovations was the fabrication of the forerunner of the fountain pen: a small glass reservoir of ink was attached to a goose feather quill allowing ink to run drop by drop without the need constantly to dip into an ink pot (Abrahamian 1973, 357–358).

3.2. Book forms

3.2.1. The roll and the rotulus

In the Armenian tradition there are neither tablets nor *ostraca* or other writing surfaces beside codices and rolls. Armenian vertical rolls or scrolls are most often from after the fifteenth century, but with possible earlier antecedents. They are usually regarded as magic amulets with prophylactic powers. They exist in all major Armenian manuscript collections; there must be close to a thousand that have survived. By the seventeenth century, during the transition from manuscript to print, such scrolls were printed.

Magical talismans, *hmayil* in Armenian, were executed on paper rolls 6 to 10 cm wide and at times more than 20 m long, containing diverse prayers illustrated by miniature paintings. Despite their length, they were portable when rolled up and could be carried easily. Often they were left to hang in the room of a sick person.

Dated examples are known from 1428 to the nineteenth century, most from the seventeenth century and after. Little research has been done on these rolls except a pioneering work *Amulettes de l'Arménie chrétienne* (Feydit 1986); almost nothing has been said about their ultimate origin. In some Armenian Gospels the evangelists depicted as scribes are seen copying from a vertical roll instead of the expected codex. The first surviving Armenian appearance of this anachronism is in the early eleventh-century Trebizond Gospels (MS Venice, Mekhitarist library, 1400; Kouymjian 1977, 1979), which was strongly influenced by Byzantine iconography with both Mark and Luke copying codices from rolls on their lecterns. Yet, this tradition of the roll survives well into the Cilician period and curiously is also found among provincial manuscripts that owe nothing to the Byzantine tradition in either style or iconography (Kouymjian 1992a, nos. 67, 75, 85), including a portrait of 1224 of the four evangelists together each holding a roll rather than the expected codex (Halle University Library, Arm. 1, f. 4v; Kouymjian 2011a, 134, fig. 24, 2011b, 97 ill.). Such relatively late examples could have provided the inspiration for the amulet-scrolls of a century and a half later.

3.2.2. The codex

The early history of the Armenian codex is obscure and may remain so. Our oldest dated manuscripts are the Venice Mlk'ē Gospels of 862 (Mekhitarist library, 1144) and the Lazarian Gospels of 887 in Yerevan (Matenadaran, 6200). Claims that certain not-specifically-dated manuscripts in Yerevan are even earlier are not always convincing on palaeographic grounds (Mouraviev 2010, Annex VI), though some of the collection's 3,000 fragments, mostly recycled as guard leaves, are credibly earlier. Many of these have been studied philologically, but few codicologically. The Armenian case is remarkable because we know with certainty that the first manuscripts were produced between 404–406, but is confounding due to the hiatus of 450 years between the invention of the alphabet and the first surviving dated codices. There are, however, four pages (a bifolium) bearing an equal number of impressive full-page miniatures, but no text, dated by general agreement to shortly after 600, certainly from a Gospel codex bound together with the Etchmiadzin Gospels (Yerevan, Matenadaran, 2374, ff. 221–221v) of 989, but they have not been the subject of detailed codicological analysis (Der Nersessian 1964). We are certain that hundreds of texts were copied and recopied in scores of scriptoria in this 'empty' period simply because those texts have survived to our day through such transmission. It is hard to imagine that the technique of producing books remained static for four and a half centuries. We do not know what the evolutionary processes in the structure of the Armenian codex and the changes in such things as the script form and quire size were.

The philologist Charles Mercier, following a then accepted notion borrowed from Latin palaeography, wondered whether the evolution from an upright *erkat'agir* to a slanted one might be due to the passage from the papyrus roll to the codex (Mercier 1978–1979, 52, 57). Did Mesrop and his disciples first use rolls before codices? If so, none have survived. Nevertheless, it has been conjectured by archaeologists that the thousands of clay seals found in two archives in the excavations of the early capital Artaxata (176 BCE–120 CE) were originally attached to rolls of papyrus or parchment because they resemble seals still attached to rolls (Khachatrian 1996; Manoukian 1996).

The codex triumphed over the roll in the fourth century. Therefore, it is likely as postulated already in the late nineteenth century (Tašyan 1898, 93) that when Maštocʿ devised an alphabet in the fifth century, Armenians used the codex right from the start without a transition from the roll.

3.3. The making of the codex

3.3.1. The making of the quires

No specific studies have been published on the subject, thus all is speculation and assumption, for instance the controversy about whether parchment was folded and refolded to create a four folium group. In a database of 300 dated manuscripts to the year 1600, nearly all Armenian manuscripts to the mid-thirteenth century consisted of quaternions, even though almost all have some inconsistent gatherings of random size from one to seven bifolia. Of the twenty-eight thirteenth-century codices, there are seven gathered in quaternions, two in quinions, fifteen in senions, three in octonions, and one with ten bifolia. By the fourteenth century thirty-two are in senions, one is a septenion, and three are in octonions, while in the sixteenth century there are only eighteen in senions (Kouymjian 2012a, 19, Table 2).

Diagrams illustrating Armenian quire structure are now included in monographs on individual manuscripts (Mathews – Sanjian 1991, 32–42). In the last years of the twelfth and the first of the thirteenth century one encounters ten-folium quires, but these never became popular. In Cilicia starting early in the thirteenth century, the twelve-folium quire took hold and became the standard for Armenian books until the end of the scribal tradition. Nevertheless, from the thirteenth to the sixteenth century, we find occasional manuscripts with gatherings of seven, eight, and even ten bifolia. There has been no study to localize the use of various sized quires, a relatively easy task using published catalogues. The chronology has already been given: the quaternion structure was the most popular at the beginning, but replaced by a larger quire of six bifolia with the shift from parchment to paper and the change in script from majuscule (*erkat'agir*) to minuscule (*bolorgir*) in the late twelfth and thirteenth centuries (Kouymjian 2012a, 19, Tables 1–2).

3.3.2. Pricking and ruling

Pricking was used in the earliest Armenian manuscripts, the holes made either with a fine pointed tool or knifepoint. These holes are found on both the outer and inner margins. Pricking in the gutter can be seen in the Gospels of 986 (Yerevan, Matenadaran, 7735, f. 128, *Album*, no. 12); Adrianople Gospels of 1007 (Venice, Mekhitarist library, 887, f. 75, *Album*, no. 19); Gospels of 1045 (Yerevan, Matenadaran, 3723, f. 59, *Album*, no. 21); Homilies of John Chrysostom of 1046 (Yerevan, Matenadaran, 988, f. 116, *Album*, no. 23); Gospels of 1064 (Jerusalem, Armenian Patriarchate, 1924, f. 64, *Album*, no. 28). Pricking on both sides of the sheet is even visible on very small codices such as a paper miscellany of 1371 for Kaffa, Crimea, 120 × 80 mm (Yerevan, Matenadaran, 5295, f. 20, *Album*, no. 127). There are also examples of double sets of pricking (Yerevan, Matenadaran, 2374, Gospels of 989, f. 225, *Album*, no. 14). Pricking is sometimes found for vertical lines to fix the boundaries of text columns. One also occasionally finds pricking holes in the gutter to mark the place were a notch, usually triangular (*grecquage*), is to be cut as a sewing station (Merian 1993, 23, 36–37). It has been observed that in later centuries pricking was very discrete or replaced by other ruling methods.

Ruling was done with a straight edge using the pricking holes as guides. In Gospels, where the Eusebian concordance numbers are indicated at the bottom of the pages, three or four narrow lines are also ruled there. Otherwise, the ruling is evenly spaced but used variously in different periods. Sometimes letters (usually uncials) stand on the line, other times letters (usually minuscule) hang from the line above. In some earlier manuscripts, an empty ruled space is left between lines, giving the appearance of writing on every other line or double spacing; majuscule letters are tangent to both the upper and lower ruling: the Lazarian Gospels of 887 (Yerevan, Matenadaran, 6200, f. 73, Xalatʿeancʿ 1899; *Album*, no. 4); Gospels of

909 (Yerevan, Matenadaran, 6202, f. 71, I, no. 5); Gospels of 1181 (Yerevan, Matenadaran, 6264, f. 222v, *Album* no. 45); the Homilies of Muš, 1202 (Venice, Mekhitarist library, 1614/229, f. 5v, *Album* no. 52). Ruling also sometimes changed within a manuscript, even one with a standard and single text, for instance the same Gospels of 887. At times regular ruling was executed apparently without the help of pricking, in a free hand manner, with the horizontal ends extending irregularly toward the margin beyond the vertical ruling line (Yerevan, Matenadaran, 6200, f. 111 first folium of quire no. 13). Though most ruling was done with a blunt stylus, already in the late tenth or early eleventh century lines drawn with a lead point or carbon are clearly visible: Roman Breviary of 1381 copied in Bologna (Paris, BnF, Arménien 107, f. 144, *Album* no. 129), both horizontal and vertical. By the thirteenth and fourteenth century we find the occasional use of red ink for vertical ruling: the mixed parchment and paper Glajor Bible of 1332 (Venice, Mekhitarist library, 1007/12, f. 356, *Album*, no. 120; see also fig. 2.3.6 for an example from the seventeenth century). There is no study devoted to ruling and pricking in Armenian manuscripts, just remarks in surveys (Abrahamyan 1973; Merian 1993). Ruling boards were used in later Armenian manuscripts similar to and probably copied from the Arab *misṭara*, called in Armenian *tołašar*, literally 'line arranger' (Abrahamyan 1973, 287; Merian 1993, 27–29 for examples).

3.3.3. Ordering systems

Numbers in Armenian manuscripts or other media are always expressed in letters of the alphabet, each of the thirty-six original letters of the Armenian alphabet has a numerical value. The easiest way to grasp the system is to arrange them in four vertical columns of nine letters each: digits, tens, hundreds, thousands. The first letter in each column starting with the A (*ayb*) represents 1, 10, 100, 1000; the last or thirty-sixth letter K', the bottom of the last column, has a value of 9000. Most quire numbering uses this system, which for convenience is called the alphanumerical system. There are cases, however, in which the value of the thirty-six letters is treated as a continuum of one to thirty-six; this might be called the continuous or alphabetic system. Whereas in the most frequently used method the number eleven would be expressed by two letters, ten plus one (ŽA), in the continuous system eleven would be a single letter, the eleventh (I) of the alphabet, which in the numerical system represents twenty.

Quires of Armenian manuscripts were numbered in the oldest surviving codices. The letter-numbers were most commonly placed at the bottom centre of the recto of the first folium and again at the bottom centre of the verso of the last folium. This is consistently the case from the thirteenth century, even in a single column layout. Among the earliest manuscripts, late ninth to twelfth century, the situation is unstable, though the lower margin was the preferred location. In the Lazarian Gospels of 887 already mentioned, the first signature (no. 2, f. 3) at the beginning of a quire is placed at the bottom in the middle of the first column of this two-column manuscript; the closing signature (f. 10v) is centred to the right below the middle of the second text column. By quire no. 26 (f. 171) all surviving signatures on this badly damaged manuscript are centred at the bottom in between the two columns. Another example affords the same uncertainty, the Gospels of the Catholicos (MS Yerevan, Matenadaran, 10780; Mat'evosyan – Izmaylova 2000, facsimile) of the late tenth or early eleventh century. The initial quaternions of this two column manuscript in majuscule has its first signature (no. 2, f. 6) at the bottom flush with the first letters of the second column, whereas the closing signature (f. 13v) is flush with the last letters of the first column. But the closing signature no. 3 (f. 21v) is centred between the two columns, though the facing no. 4 (f. 22) remains flush with the second column. It is only with the ending signature no. 6 and the initial no. 7 (ff. 45v–46r) that all numbering is centred between the two columns. Other anomalous positionings of numbers are bottom left of centre, one column text (MS Venice, Mekhitarist library, 1268, Gospels, 1001, f. 224, *Album*, no. 16); extreme lower right, again single column, but repeated twice more within red wreaths in the upper right margin and within the text at the third line (MS Dublin, Chester Beatty, 554, 1174 Edessa, f. 11, *Album*, no. 42); upper right corner, two column Gospels of 1007, Adrianople (MS Venice, Mekhitarist library, 887, f. 75. *Album*, nos. 18–19); upper right margin or corner (MS Yerevan, Matenadaran, 2743, Gospels, 1232, f. 39 *Album*, no. 70, MS Yerevan, Matenadaran, 7700, Gospels 1237, Cilicia, f. 45, *Album*, no. 71).

In the Gospels of the Catholicos, quire eleven is marked in the continuous manner with I, the eleventh letter, and not the usual ŽA (11), and continues to the final quire no. 34 (W). This is not an isolated case, since the famous Etchmiadzin Gospels of 989 (MS Yerevan, Matenadaran, 2374; Macler 1920, facsimile) numbers its twenty-eight quires consecutively, each signature placed within a wreath-like coloured roundel in the top margin of the opening folium between and above the text columns; there are no signatures on the final verso folium of the quires. It has been hypothesized (Merian 1993, 184–185; 1995) that this practice of alphabetic numbering began in the Cilician period, twelfth to fourteenth centuries, as a European inspired system during a time when the Crusaders had very close contact with the Cilician Armenian kingdom. This assumption is no longer acceptable because of the Etchmiadzin Gospels and related manuscripts.

One often reads that in Armenian Gospel manuscripts the first gathering with the Eusebian Letter and Canon Tables was not counted, but it is clear from some of the early examples cited above that the first text quire is often numbered two and not one, thus the initial Eusebian apparatus was counted. Caution is necessary, however, until more data is recorded because the opening text quire of the Etchmiadzin Gospels of 989 has one (A) as signature number (Macler 1920, f. 90), thus ignoring the first quire.

Catchwords were almost never used in Armenian manuscripts until after the printing of the first Armenian book in Venice in 1512. Printed books used catchwords not just for quires but eventually for every page. Some manuscripts of the late seventeenth century and after borrowed this habit from Armenian printed books, which was itself borrowed from the west.

It is hard to find Armenian manuscripts with folium numbers that can be dated to the moment of the copying. In almost all cases the numbers were added in modern times. There are, however, isolated exceptions, for instance MS Yerevan, Matenadaran, 7, a prayer book of 1212, has in the right margin almost mid-way down next to the single column text the number fifty-six (*cz*) in the same hand as the scribe, corresponding exactly to the modern numerical foliation found at the top right corner (*Album*, no. 56). Columns were never numbered in Armenian manuscripts, because texts except for a few exceptions were either one or two columns.

3.3.4. The codex as a complex object

There are no studies on multiple text manuscripts combining more than one physical unit. Nevertheless, binding different writings under a single cover, a practice common to all traditions, was common in Armenian scriptoria. When counting the number of discrete items within bound volumes of the largest Armenian manuscript collection, it was clear that there were anywhere from 6% to 9% more items, that is manuscripts or fragments, than the actual number of catalogued codices (Kouymjian 2012a, 19). The components of these multi-manuscript volumes were usually, but not always, on related subjects. A different phenomenon is represented by books containing multiple and often unrelated texts copied in a single sequence by one or more scribes. In Armenian such manuscripts are labelled collections or miscellanies (*žołovacoy*); among the earliest is the paper codex of 981 discussed above (Yerevan, Matenadaran, 2679). These often represent what it is now fashionable to call 'one-volume libraries'. Many are devoted to specific subjects: theology, medicine, advice, and history, while others combine elements at times in a random fashion. Though some are limited to a few texts others contain twenty, forty, and even more works, some long, others less than a *folio* in length. Their number is remarkable: taking the Matenadaran collection, nearly a quarter of the more than 11,000 manuscripts are such *žołovacoy* or collections of sermons.

The most popular text in the Armenian manuscript tradition is the Gospel book. Up to the fourteenth century, 50 to 75% of all extant manuscripts are Gospels; and up to earlier date limits, the percentage was even higher. Their structure and layout are often determined by the required illustrations: Canon Tables, evangelists' portraits and headpieces of the Gospels, and miniatures from the life of Christ.

3.4. The layout of the page

The earliest manuscripts were very large. Those of the ninth and tenth centuries, mostly Gospels, are on average 340 × 270 according to a sampling of 285 dated Armenian codices from various collections (Kouymjian 2007a, 42). Eleventh-century manuscripts remain quite large, 310 × 240, until the last two decades when they drop in size to less than A4. There are also in the eleventh century at least two very small manuscripts, both now in Venice, signalling a future trend: the aforementioned Gospels of 1001, 180 × 140 mm (Venice, Mekhitarist library, 1268, *Album* no. 16), and one of the tiniest books, a Gospel of John dated 1073, measuring 64 × 47 mm, much smaller than a credit card (Venice, Mekhitarist library, 2050); an even smaller codex is preserved in Yerevan (Matenadaran, 7728). Afterward, the size drops dramatically: twelfth-century manuscripts are about 28% smaller, 230 × 160 mm, than eleventh century ones and more than a third smaller than those of the ninth and tenth centuries. In part this is explained by text and writing surface; Gospels, Bibles, and other liturgical texts were always larger, and parchment manuscripts were a bit bigger than paper ones so with the increase of the variety of texts and the use of paper, size was reduced. Furthermore, the twelfth century was difficult for Armenia, kingless and under Seljuk occupation; yet, the next century was the high point in Armenian book culture. Manuscript production had increased in quantity and improved in quality; paper had become the dominant support, and though manuscripts were smaller than in earlier centuries, 280 × 180 mm, they were nearly 20% larger than those of the twelfth century. Nevertheless the trend was moving toward a smaller, more conveniently manipulated book, as was the case in Byzantium and Europe where manuscripts became more portable as a larger public became literate. Eventually there was a size standardization from the fourteenth to the nineteenth centuries, roughly 200 × 140 mm, about half the size of the earliest manuscripts, 45% the size of an A4 sheet.

The general shape of Armenian codices is rectangular, the height always larger than the width. There are no oblong books until late in the printing era. There are unique items, for instance a small (700 × 125 mm) parchment liturgical miscellany copied in 1441 in the northern monastery of Mecopʿ (Yerevan, Matenadaran, 5667, *Album* no.139), which is an oblong volume, but when open it is evident that the text is written in lines parallel to the short side of the volume, that is vertically at right angles to the long axis; instead of turning pages from right to left, one turns the page up to read the text at the top of the verso which follows down to the next recto. Another atypical single paper sheet (406 × 292 mm) of 1653, with apotropaic prayers written in minute minuscule sometimes in red, at other times in black in harmonious alteration within sixteen spaces created by the intersection of large squares and triangles enhanced with three magnificent miniatures in roundels in the centre field of Christ enthroned flanked by Mary and John the Baptist, all with sixteen texts running in six directions (London, BL, Add. 18611, *Album*, no. 168).

The two-column text arrangement for the ease of reading was reserved for Gospels, Bibles, and liturgical texts. Philosophical works, collections, and commentaries were written in a single column, for instance the religious miscellany of 981 (Yerevan, Matenadaran, 2679, *Album* nos. 10–11). There were exceptions to both arrangements, for instance the single-column Venice Gospels of 1001. A later Bible manuscript from New Julfa – Isfāhān of 1648 has its last four quires in three columns (Venice, Mekhitarist library, 623/337, Merian 1993, 29–30).

3.5. Text structure and readability

3.5.1. Decoration

There is a vast literature on Armenian manuscript decoration due to its quantity and remarkable quality. A general introduction to the ornamentation and illumination of Armenian manuscripts including how they were used to structure texts can be found in *The Arts of Armenia* (Kouymjian 1992a, 'Miniature Painting', 27–38 and online), and specifically on their use in the organization of Gospels (Kouymjian 1996a). The Gospel book was by far the most decorated text. Other liturgical manuscripts were also decorated, but in smaller numbers: Bibles (see fig. 1.3.2), lectionaries, menologia and synaxaria, psalters (see fig. 2.3.7 for an ornamental band in a religious miscellany). Almost all surviving manuscripts with ornamentation and miniatures dated before 1300 are Gospels; the exceptions are a codex of the Elegies of Gregory of Narek dated 1173 (Yerevan, Matenadaran, 1568) with four portraits of the author, the Erzinjan Bible of 1269 (Jerusalem, Armenian Patriarchate, 1925), decorated psalters, among the oldest that of Leo II dated 1283 (London, BL, Or. 13804), the Lectionary of Hetʿum II of 1286 (Yerevan, Matenadaran, 979; Drampian 2004), one of the most lavishly ornamented and illustrated Armenian codices, as well as hymnals and ritual books, mostly from the late thirteenth century.

Therefore it is apparent that Armenian manuscript painting is almost entirely devoted to Biblical scenes especially from the life of Christ (see fig. 2.3.3). In the early Gospels miniatures were normally full-page and were grouped at the beginning before the text, after the Canon Tables and portraits of the evangelists. They could also be half or quarter page, sometimes very small placed within one of the two columns of the text. Marginal decorations of all kinds were also common sometimes in red ink and even coloured. Besides the narrative scenes with their figures and landscapes, miniature painters had to be skilled in drawing animal and bird forms, geometric and floral ornaments of great complexity, evangelists' and donor portraits, and very ornate letters composed of bird, animal, and human forms used to decorate chapter headpieces and the opening lines of each Gospel. The illustrating of a Gospel manuscript followed a fixed pattern that some believe had already become traditional in the fourth century: the Eusebian apparatus and the evangelists' portraits. These were in time individually placed on the verso of the folium facing the *incipit* of each Gospel, usually lavishly decorated. In the more important Gospels there was a series of full-page paintings usually placed at the beginning together with and just after the Canon Tables, traditionally in a single quire. Miniatures can be divided into three types: symbolic representations (for example, a cross), portraits (for example, the Virgin), and narrative scenes from Christ's life.

Fig. 1.3.1 Los Angeles, CA, J. Paul Getty Museum, MS 59, Zeyt'un Gospels, 1256, 265 ×190 mm, f. 8r, photograph courtesy of the Paul Getty Museum.

The physical arrangement of Armenian Canon Tables and their evolution serve as important codicological tools for identifying schools and scriptoria (Kouymjian 1996a, 1025–1042). Both the Mlkʻē Gospels of 851–862 (Venice, Mekhitarist library, 1144) and the Etchmiadzin Gospels of 989 (Yerevan, Matenadaran, 2374) have elaborate Canon Tables (Kouymjian 1977; IAA online), the latter closely resembling those of the Ethiopic Gospels of Endā Abbā Garimā (see fig. 1.6.8). As the tradition became conventionalized, the *Letter of Eusebius* was placed on two facing pages followed by the ten Canon Tables laid out on four more pairs, each set with a unique mirror image decoration. In some luxury thirteenth-century Gospels a lavish twin-page dedication highlighted in gold was also added and decorated like the canon arcades (Washington, Freer Gallery of Art, 44.17; Jerusalem, Armenian Patriarchate, 251; Baltimore, Walters Art Gallery, 539; Yerevan, Matenadaran, 10675; Der Nersessian 1993 for details).

Armenian miniature painters preferred to use the hair side of parchment when they had a choice (Merian et al. 1994a, 128). One regularly finds in the most accomplished scriptoria, especially of the Cilician period, that the scribes when laying out the manuscript accommodated the painter by leaving the flesh side of the bifolium blank resulting in an alteration of facing blank pages and decorated pairs in the Eusebian apparatus. This is the case for the manuscripts just cited as well as for the Glajor Gospels (Los Angeles, UCLA, Arm. 1; Mathews – Sanjian 1991). Specialists regard certain Armenian Canon Tables such as those of the Etchmiadzin Gospels (Yerevan, Matenadaran, 2374) as faithful models of Eusebius's prototype of five centuries earlier (Nordenfalk 1938; Kouymjian 1993b, 130). Several mediaeval Armenian recipe-like treatises on the decoration of Canon Tables have survived, but artists were rather casual about following them (Russell 1991; Łazaryan 1995). Nevertheless, such traditions as placing peacocks above the arch of the first page of the Eusebian Letter at the beginning of the series, were carefully maintained.

In the earliest Gospels, the evangelists were portrayed in pairs, either standing (the majority) or seated (Kouymjian 1977–1979, 1996a). Gradually, following the Byzantine tradition, the evangelists were individually painted seated in the posture of a scribe before his lectern. The Mlkʻē Gospels reserve a single full-page portrait for each evangelist two seated and two standing as in the Syriac Rabbula Gospels of 586.

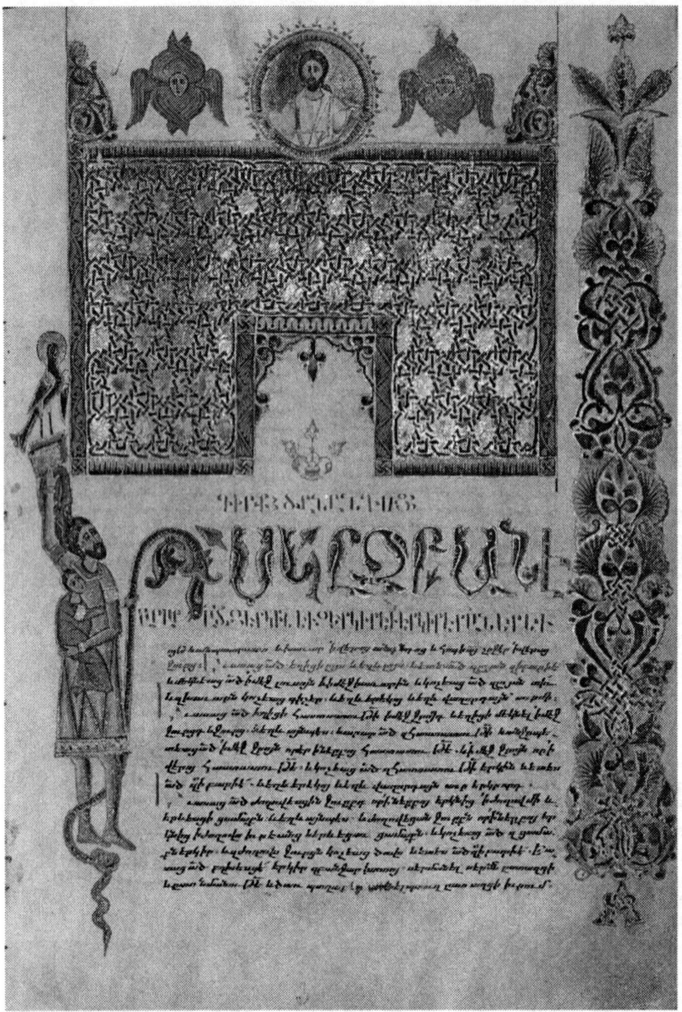

Fig. 1.3.2 Los Angeles, CA, J. Paul Getty Museum, MS Ludwig I 14: Bible, Isfāhān, 1637/1638, 252 × 183 mm, f. 3r, photograph courtesy of the Paul Getty Museum.

In time the portraits were moved into the text opposite the ornamented first page of the evangelist's Gospel.

The Armenians never developed a fixed series of twelve liturgical scenes such as the dodecaorton of Byzantine icons; among eleventh century Gospels there are cycles from seven to fifteen scenes while in the post-Cilician period cycles of sixteen miniatures and more are common. In most Gospels these were grouped together at the beginning before the Gospel texts; however, as early as in the eleventh century, two manuscripts have very extensive cycles of large and small miniatures of major and minor episodes scattered throughout the four Gospels rather than grouped at the beginning. One of these, the exquisite classicizing, but partially mutilated, Gospels of King Gagik of Kars (Jerusalem, Armenian Patriarchate, 2556) originally had over 227 miniatures (Mathews – Sanjian 1991, Table 8): full page, half page, and smaller sizes embedded within one of the two columns of text usually accompanying the corresponding text. The other, the Gospels of the Catholicos (Yerevan, Matenadaran, 10780; Mat'evosyan – Izmaylova 2000) with about seventy subjects, perhaps executed in Arc'ax-Karabagh, is painted in a provincial, indigenous style, far removed from the classical tradition of the other. When, after a hiatus of nearly a century due to the devastation of the Seljuk Turk invasions in the second half of the eleventh century, manuscript production started again in the second half of the twelfth and thirteenth centuries both methods of illustration—grouping narrative miniatures together at the beginning or continuously illustrating the text with an expanded cycle—were practised.

The earliest illustrated secular works date from the late thirteenth century, but they are rare. These include an illustrated History by the fifth-century author Agat'angełos of 1569 (Yerevan, Matenadaran, 1910) and scenes from the Battle of the Avarayr (451) as narrated in Ełišē's *History of Vardan and the Armenian War*, also fifth century (Kouymjian 2007b), but also pictures in hymnals (Yerevan, Matenadaran, 1620 of 1482), medical and scientific texts, illustrated zodiacs and astrology (Kouymjian 2007c), and a book on devs (Venice, BNM, no. 210; Macler 1928, 29–42). By far the most illuminated secular text is the *History of Alexander the Great* by Pseudo-Callisthenes (Kouymjian 1999, 2007d, 2012b), though even that text was given a Christian slant through the addition of *kafas* or moralizing poems by Xač'atur Keč'arec'i (1260–1331). Artistically the most important and beautifully illustrated *Alexander*, the Venice Mekhitarist codex (Venice, Mekhitarist library, 424), is also the oldest illustrated example, *c.*1300–1320 (Traina 2003). Twelve other Armenian *Alexanders* with miniatures are known dating from 1535 to nineteenth century, with equally long cycles averaging some 125 scenes, often different in subject, style, and iconography from that of Venice. Codicologically, these manuscripts are laid out in one column like non-liturgical works often with space left within the frames of the miniatures for the extra-textual commentary of the *kafa*-poems. The *Alexander* manuscripts demonstrate that the layout and arrangement of text and commentary were entirely subjected to the illustration laid out by the scribe prior to the copying; the text with its pictorial representation moved forward in lock step. These largely unstudied Armenian examples offer answers to many codicological questions particularly with the information offered by two examples in which the pictorial component was left incomplete but scribal instructions to the painter preserved (Jerusalem, Armenian Patriarchate, 473 of 1536; Połarian 1966–1991, II, 460–466; Yerevan, Matenadaran, 8003, nineteenth century).

The copying and decorating of manuscripts was exclusively the prerogative of the clergy, usually monks in monasteries both in Armenia and the diaspora; however, a few lay people are noted in colophons and even occasionally a female scribe. Within the scriptorium a team of scribes, artists, and binders usually produced manuscripts. The layout of a manuscript was directed by the principal scribe, especially for illustrated codices like the Gospels or a secular work like the *History of Alexander the Great*. We know this from incomplete manuscripts, which preserve a variety of instructions for the craftsmen. For the Gospels, after the scribe or scribes finished the copying, the book or its quires would be passed onto the artists, who, after illuminating it and decorating the initial quire with the Eusebian Letter and Canon Tables, would pass it back to a scribe, often a different individual specialized in inserting the columns of concordance numbers in the canons. It would then be passed on to an in-house binder. There are innumerable indications of the time needed for copying, from months to years; a specific example from the long and very detailed colophon of a Bible copied in 1332 at the monastery of Glajor (Venice, Mekhitarist library, 1007/12; Sargisyan 1914) gives details of prices paid: it reports that the 471 folia in quinions in two columns of 53 lines were accomplished in eleven months by two scribes, roughly 43 pages a month for each scribe (Sanjian 1969, 10–12).

A particular instance of the working process between the scribe and artist is indicated in red ink in and around picture frames in an *Alexander History* copied by the monk Margarē in 1536 at the Monastery of Varag, high above Lake Van, and illustrated by the Catholicos of Ałtʿamar Grigoris (Jerusalem, Armenian Patriarchate, 473; Połarian 1966–1991, II, 460–466). There are twenty-three preserved miniatures but some one hundred framed empty spaces for the remainder of the miniatures with indications of what is to be painted and small exchanges between the collaborators as the manuscript passed back and forth between the neighbouring monasteries: 'Paint a mounted horse here' f. 16; 'Artist leave some space, oh spiritual brother' f. 47; indication in the empty square, 'Thebans greeting Alexander' f. 50v (Kouymjian forthcoming b).

A pioneering work bringing together an immense corpus of artistic and codicological data from decorated and illustrated Armenian manuscripts was accomplished by Astłik Gēorgyan (general decoration, 1973; portraits, 1978; zoomorphic and anthropomorphic letters, 1996). Her final monograph based on the 11,000 manuscripts in the Matenadaran presents in chronological order the 464 artists identifiable by their colophons (Gēorgyan 1998), and a second volume lists 903 anonymous artists (Gēorgyan 2005). These tomes not only identify all manuscripts in the Matenadaran collection painted by each artist, but provide a complete list of every scene painted, the place of execution, a short biography and bibliography on the artist, and useful for codicology, complete artists' colophons; it is a fundamental resource for the life of artists and how they worked within scriptoria.

3.6. The scribe, the painter and the illuminator at work

3.6.1. Colophons

Thanks to the regular use of colophons by Armenian scribes, illuminators, binders, painters, and patrons, we know much about the making of an Armenian manuscript, with or without paintings, perhaps more than any other book tradition (Sanjian 1969, 1–41; Sirinian 2014). The scribes added one or more such memorials, which in formulaic manner provide date and place of execution, the patron's name, the ruling authority (king, governor, foreign overlord, catholicos), the painter's and even the binder's name (often in separate colophons), and naturally the scribe's, with family details, the circumstances of copying, and frequently political and economic conditions (Sanjian 1969, 8–9; Sirinian 2014, 74–85). The earliest colophon still attached to a complete codex is from 887 (Lazarian Gospels, Yerevan, Matenadaran, 6200). The thousands of dated colophons are a major source on the scribe's work and the organization of scriptoria, as that of a Gospels of 1053, which mentions by name the scribe, painter, binder, the parchment softener, the gold ink preparers, and a general assistant (MS Yerevan, Matenadaran, 3793; Ařakʿelyan 1958, 310). The largest group of Gospel commissioners was Armenian nobility and upper clergy; these were for personal use or as an offering to a religious institution. Merchants and other members of the bourgeoisie were active patrons after the thirteenth century, increasing in number as the nobility began to disappear with the fall of the kingdom of Cilicia in 1375 after which the upper clergy led less privileged lives. In theory, at their inception all Armenian manuscripts had a colophon, but since memorials were usually on the last pages, they were vulnerable to loss.

Colophons were also important for their historical information; as early as the late thirteenth century Step'anos Orbelian used them in his *History of the Province of Siunik'*. Though invaluable sources for codicological questions—organization of scriptoria, division of labour, duration of copying, source and quality of paper, parchment and ink—thus far they have been only rarely and randomly exploited. At times they discuss the price paid for copying and the extremely difficult environment of the copyist as well as relationships between scribes and painters and their superiors and patrons (Sanjian 1969, 9–33). Armenian colophons are usually given in toto in manuscript catalogues. The first collections of Armenian colophons were made in the nineteenth century, but only since the 1950s has their systematic publication been undertaken, now comprising ten large tomes with some 16,000 individual colophons from 8,000 manuscripts. The only translation of collected colophons in a western language is a pioneering work covering a selection from 1300 to 1460 (Sanjian 1969). The late Jos Weitenberg initiated a project to digitize in a searchable database all published Armenian colophons; the Matenadaran and the Academy of Sciences in Yerevan continued the work. The project 'Accessing Armenian Colophons', begun in the 1990s, was focused on lexicography and palaeography. When completed it will provide access to some 7,500 printed pages of colophons. In the period 1995–1997, the project was put online: the complete texts of colophons published by the Matenadaran, including indexes and unpublished corrections and additions (an update on these projects can be found in Sirinian 2014, 71–72).

3.7. Bookbinding

Armenian bookbinding technique was influenced by the Coptic leather bindings, perhaps through the intermediary of Syria and Byzantium. Leather covered boards were the standard for Armenian manuscripts. Like Byzantine examples, the text block and the size of the boards are the same; there is no overlapping or 'squares' as in European bindings. Both traditions used a raised, embroidered headband at the two ends, which required that manuscripts be stored lying flat.

Binding structure has been very well studied by Sylvie Merian (1993; 1994, Merian et al. 1994a, 130–134): the use of *grecquage* (the v-shaped notches for sewing bifolia), the distinctive Armenian headband sewing, the method of attaching the book block to wooden boards, the use of cloth linings to cover the board attachments (but not their artistic analysis as textile fragments). Their decoration has been analysed (Kouymjian 1992b; 1993a; 1998b; 2007e); the characteristics of a particular style, the New Julfa – Isfāhān school of the seventeenth and eighteenth centuries, influenced by westernized decoration has been published (Kouymjian 1995). However, in the same period rural centres far removed from contact with voyagers and merchants, such as the monastery of Tat'ev, held strictly to the traditional motifs. This archaizing tendency coupled with repeated rebinding present problems of dating even when binder colophons exist. Little attention has been paid to these traditional motifs. Fashioned almost exclusively of tooled rope work or braided guilloche bands, they have been classified into three groups, each contained within a guilloche frame: 1) a braided cross on a stepped pedestal, 2) a rectangle filled with braided tooling, and 3) an intricate geometric rosette (Kouymjian 2008a, 2008c).

Yet, among Near Eastern binding traditions, Armenian craftsmen employed a number of different techniques, first pointed out hastily (van Regemorter 1953, modified in 1967), then more thoroughly (Merian 1993; 1996). Armenians used supported stitching to sew quires together, whereas in the Byzantine or other Middle East traditions, quires were sewn to each other without supports. Merian suggests this might have happened through Crusader influence during the Armenian kingdom of Cilicia, but pre-Cilician Armenian bindings seem also to have used supported stitching. Boards of Armenian bindings were usually much thinner (2–5 mm) than Byzantine or Syrian ones; they were also placed with the wood-grain running horizontally, while other east Mediterranean binders placed them running vertically. Furthermore, Armenian leather bindings usually had a flap, precisely the size of the fore-edge, attached to the lower cover forming a box-like container. Armenians always covered the inside boards with a doublure of some distinction (Dournovo 1953; Tarayan 1978). These linings are of cotton, silk, linen, and other fabrics and have both woven and stamped patterns; sometimes they are embroidered. A large number of them were fashioned outside Armenia: Iran, India, Byzantium, and the west. Because they were consistently used, there are thousands of them; only a few dozen have been published.

Armenians decorated the leather with blind tooling, using a variety of stamping irons, though never ones with bird, animal, or heraldic designs. Stamps were usually not applied to the spine, which was normally decorated with thin vertical fillets. Gold stamping was almost never practised. On some volumes binders reinforced the designs of the tooled decoration with rounded metallic studs; these also served to protect the covers of the book (Merian et al. 1994a; Kouymjian 2006, 2008a, 2008c).

The principal decorations on Gospel bindings are a braided cross on a stepped pedestal, sometimes called a Calvary cross, on the upper cover and a vertical rectangle made of dense braids or rope work on the lower. There are some variants of these motifs, which are often made entirely with stamping irons rather than hand-tooled braiding. These designs underline the central theme of the Gospel narrative: Crucifixion and Resurrection. The rectangle on the lower cover represents the empty tomb of the risen Christ (Kouymjian 2008c). The paired motifs seem to be the oldest decoration found on surviving manuscript covers, going back perhaps to the eleventh and twelfth centuries and continuing to the end of the seventeenth. Almost all such bindings are Gospels. Sometimes on bindings other than the Gospels—hymnals, rituals, and secular texts—an elaborate geometric rosette composed of intersecting triangles or squares replaces one or both motifs. Similar designs, ultimately of Coptic origin, but reinforced by Islamic decoration, are found in Mudejar and other traditions.

Though the decoration of Armenian binding continued unchanged until very late, the decor of leather bindings in specific regions underwent a change in the seventeenth century (Kouymjian 1995), when the meaning of the rectangle became obscure. Binders simply replaced it with a visually clearer image of the Resurrection to match what by then had become a very iconic Crucifixion instead of the barren cross; this was especially true of silver bindings of the eighteenth and nineteenth centuries (Kouymjian forthcoming a).

The earliest binder's colophons are from the tenth and eleventh centuries, though the bindings are not preserved: Gevorg, tenth century and Yovannēs, restorer and binder of 1284 (Yerevan, Matenadaran, 5547, ff. 7, 149v); Gevorg, binder-scribe, early eleventh century, Ani (Yerevan, Matenadaran, 988); Grigor, later eleventh century (Yerevan, Matenadaran, 275); Yakob, 1190, Airivank (Yovsēpʿyan 1913, 197); Gevorg, 1194 who mentions his teacher Tʿoros the binder (Yovsēpʿyan 1951); Aṙakel of Hṙomkla, 1260 (Ališan 1901, 489). By this period bookbinding had become a specialized and highly developed art in mediaeval Armenia.

A particular feature of bindings from New Julfa – Isfāhān in the seventeenth and early eighteenth centuries is the presence of stamped inscriptions, usually dated, on the leather covers. More than a hundred are recorded (Kouymjian 1995, 13); they provide precise dates for codicological features of late Armenian manuscripts. Silver bindings (see below) survive from the thirteenth century. There are also silver-enamelled bindings, and at least one of a seventeenth-century Gospel with an icon-like painting executed directly upon the upper leather cover (MS Venice, Mekhitarist library, 1580/183, Sargisyan 1914, no. 183; Kouymjian 2008a, 170 fig. 10). Though leather bindings differ by region and century, they belong to a single recognizable family.

There is a small group of bindings from the eighteenth century decorated with concentric rectangles filled with floral scrolls, the innermost band with a dated inscription: one of 1725 has a western inspired Crucifixion stamp in the centre (Isfāhān, New Julfa, no. 452; Kouymjian 1995, 16 fig. 2). Similar concentric rectangle decorations are known in early Latin bindings (Paris, Bibliothèque Mazarine, no. 142 of *c.* 1200, Coll – Conihout 2003, no. 7). Just how this style was adopted in New Julfa is not clear; perhaps through Amsterdam, where the first printed Bible in Armenian was issued in 1666 (Kévorkian 1986, 51–60). One should also mention a series of late bindings from several localities with simple intersecting diagonal, horizontal, and vertical fillets, much like Byzantine bindings (Federici – Houlis 1988, types 3–8, pl. XIX; van Regemorter 1967, pl. XVI–XVII); these simple patterns have been associated with binders from the Armenian colony in the Crimea (Aṙakʿelyan 1958, 198–200), but they can be found in late bindings from several regions.

Despite these affinities with Byzantine and European decorative systems, the mass of Armenian leather covers demonstrate a clear and immediately recognizable native look, even if motifs are occasionally copied from the European traditions. There was a change in design in the post-Byzantine period, particularly in the colonies of the seventeenth-century Armenian diaspora. The traditional blind tooled braided cross rectangle are abandoned as archaic motifs.

The most characteristic regional style is that of New Julfa – Isfāhān. The leather is lighter in colour; new stamping tools are employed, often western in style and historiated, principally Christ on the cross and the Virgin. An elaborately blind stamped design with a crucifix with radiating tongues of flame like a 'sunburst' is on the upper cover, while on the lower, a stamp of the Virgin within a similar circle with stars replacing the flames for a 'starburst'. The stamped and dated inscriptions serve to date the stamping tools (Kouymjian 1995, 32–35).

In Constantinople, the most important Armenian diaspora community, active in the late eighteenth and nineteenth centuries, western binding techniques replaced conventional Armenian ones, especially printed books, which may have come bound from European centres of printing (Kévorkian 1986, 7).

There were holdouts here and there; occasionally one finds a traditionally bound and decorated Armenian book or manuscript in the early nineteenth century (Tbilisi, National Centre of Manuscripts, Arm. 41 of 1823). Fine binding continued until the twentieth century, however, it was almost always with silver plaques attached to leather covered boards. Liturgical books, considered holy objects, were displayed on the altar with their silver and gilded covers. The tradition continues today; however, silver bindings are purchased from specialized international companies, in most cases Greek Orthodox suppliers, thus, a Greek connexion through bindings continues.

The term silver binding refers to all metal plaques applied to Armenian manuscripts and printed books. Some 95% of these are of silver, the rest in baser metals, often covered with clusters of ex-votos (mostly inscribed crosses and charms). There are rare bindings in solid gold (Etchmiadzin inv. 224 of 1410; Durand – Tarayan 2007), though many of the silver specimens are parcel gilt or have been completely gold washed. A large majority of these double bindings are in the form of individual plaques attached, usually nailed, directly over the tooled leather of the functional binding. Some have silver spines; a small number retain the custom of a fore-edge flap in silver attached to the lower cover. Almost all have, or had, clasps, most commonly two, to hold the covers closed.

Though we use the term silver bindings because of the attached plaques, these crafted rectangles of precious metal added nothing to the solidity of the volume, rather their extra weight contributed to eventual deterioration. They were usually worked in repoussé and were sometimes adorned with gems, gilding, enamelling, filigree work, engraved inscriptions, polishing, chiselling, and other techniques practised by jewellers. Another difference between the making of sliver and leather bindings is the competence and training of the craftsmen involved. Leather bindings were executed by binders, also responsible for the assembling of the manuscript or book: their sewing and consolidation. Silversmiths were only responsible for enhancing the object and not usually involved with the actually binding of the volume.

Through colophons we know there were cases where a scribe would also be the painter and sometimes the binder of the book, but for silver bindings it is hard to find an example of a scribe or miniaturist or even a bookbinder who also fashioned a silver one; silver covers introduced the silversmith or jeweller into the chain of book production. Unlike the rural, monastic production of manuscripts, the crafting of precious metals was in secular hands and an urban activity. We can surmise that the painters of Gospels, Psalters, and other liturgical books understood the rules of how religious scenes were to be constructed, because they were trained within the monastery. How then did the jeweller who might have been very close to the church, but was not formally part of it, learn Christian iconography? There is much less information on these skilled artisans than there is on miniature painters. We might suppose there was an apprenticeship system, which included imitating early objects and copying illustrations from manuscripts or printed books, Armenian and European.

The oldest extant Armenian silver binding was made in the kingdom of Cilicia, now a treasure of the Cilician Catholicosate dating to 1254 on the Barjrberd Gospels of 1248 (Antelias, Catholicosate of Cilicia, no. 1, Agemian 1991; Kouymjian forthcoming a, 'Part II, Silver Bindings', no. 1). The second oldest is also from Cilicia, dated 1255 on a Gospel book of 1249 now in the Matenadaran in Yerevan (Yerevan, Matenadaran, 7690; Durand 2007, 266–267 no.116).

Notable is the school of silversmiths of Caesarea/Kayseri, where by the end of the sixteenth century half of the population was Armenian (Kouymjian 1997, 28–29); there are over forty elegant inscribed bindings produced from the 1650s to the 1740s often with inscriptions mentioning the name of the artist (Kʿurdyan 1948; Merian 1994; Malxasyan 1996; Merian 2013, 170–181 Table 1 lists 47). They eschew the usual Crucifixion-Resurrection motifs for elaborate Biblical scenes often enclosed in frames with busts of the apostles and prophets. The binder-silversmiths' names suggest that they were members of several families of craftsmen who probably immigrated from New Julfa – Isfāhān in the seventeenth century (Malxasyan 1996, 186–190). The rendering of the scenes often follows engravings from Armenian printed books, especially the heavily illustrated Bible 1666 (Merian et al. 1994a; Merian 2013, 182–185, Table 2). Unfortunately, the profiles of other workshops have not yet been established. The Cilician Catholicosal collection has some thirty silver bindings offered by pilgrims or parishioner mostly in the eighteenth and nineteenth centuries, which reveal the outlines of a Cilician school perhaps centred in Adana, for instance the cover of the prized Ritual book of 1765 (Kouymjian forthcoming a, Part II, no. 2).

Who were the silversmiths who fashioned these precious objects? We have little information other than for the Caesarea/Kayseri. Inscriptions mention a large number of towns and cities: Edirne/Adrianople, Constantinople, Kütahya, Karin/Erzurum, Muš, Van, Lim, Arckē, Kars, Ējmiacin, Diyarbakır/Tigranakert, New Julfa, Kishinev/Chişinău, St Petersburg, Moscow, Calcutta, Adana, Sis, Izmir, and smaller localities served by the Cilician Catholicosate. Identifying provenance is doubly difficult because almost all the silver over-bindings are found on printed books published in Amsterdam, Venice, or Constantinople and not on manuscripts in which the expected colophon could have contained the information.

References

Abrahamyan 1947, 1973; Agemyan 1991; *Album* = Stone et al. 2002; Ališan 1901; Aṙakʿelyan 1958; Babenko 1988; Brock 1965; Coll – Conihout 2003; Clackson 2000; Der Nersessian 1964, 1973a, 1993; Dournovo 1953; Drampian 2004; Durand 2007; Durand – Tarayan 2007; Eganyan et al. 1965, 1970, 2007; Federici – Houlis 1988; Galfajan 1975a, 1975b, 1975c; Gēorgyan 1973, 1978, 1996, 1998, 2005; Gippert 2010a; Harutʿyunyan 1941; Kévorkian 1986; Khachatrian 1996; Kouymjian 1992a, 1992b, 1993a, 1993b, 1995, 1996a, 1996b, 1997, 1998a, 1998b, 1999, 2002a, 2002b, 2006, 2007a, 2007b, 2007c, 2007d, 2007e, 2008a, 2011a, 2011b, 2012a, 2012b, 2013, 2014, forthcoming a; Kʿurdyan 1948; Łazaryan 1995; Leroy [M.] 1938; Macler 1920, 1924, 1928; Malxasyan 1996; Manoukian 1996; Matʿevosyan 1969; Matʿevosyan – Izmaylova 2000; Mathews – Sanjian 1991; Mercier 1978–1979; Merian 1993, 1994, 1995, 1996, 2013; Merian et al. 1994a, 1994b; Minasyan 1972; Mouraviev 2010; Nordenfalk 1938; Orna – Mathews 1981; Połarian 1966–1991; van Regemorter 1953, 1967; Renhart 2009; Russell 1991; Sanjian 1969; Sargisyan 1914; Schreiner 1983; Sirinian 2014; Tarayan 1978; Tašyan 1895, 1898; Traina 2003; Voskanyan et al. 1988; Xačʿikyan 1950, 1955, 1958, 1967; Xalatʿeancʿ 1899; Xažakyan 1984; Yovsēpʿyan 1913, 1951. Web sources: Kouymjian 1977, 1979; *Rinascimento virtuale* 2002.

4. Christian Palestinian Aramaic manuscripts (AD)

The relatively few surviving Christian Palestinian Aramaic manuscripts have not previously been the subject of any codicological research. A proper study of the papyrus used, an analysis of the parchment (animal species, technical treatment), of the paper (origins of materials, forms) and an analysis of the ink remain a desideratum, as does a comprehensive overview of layouts (formats, rulings, quiring) and of binding typology. In the following, a first survey based on the available data is presented.

4.1. Materials and tools

4.1.1. Papyrus

In the ancient period (fifth to tenth centuries), Christian Palestinian Aramaic manuscripts are sometimes written on papyrus but mostly on parchment; they are written in uncial-like characters.

Archaeology reveals that parchment and papyrus coexisted during the same period at Kastellion. Papyrus probably came from the shores of the Dead Sea (just some twelve kilometres away); it has been preserved thanks to the climatic conditions of the Judaean desert. The Sinai 'New Finds' brought to light nine more papyrus fragments, all belonging to the same document, *Apophthegmata patrum*, according to the alphabetical tradition (Sinai, St Catherine, New Finds ΣΠ 1-9N). The script is to be assigned almost to the same period as that of the papyrus of the Laura of Marda (Jerusalem, Rockefeller Museum, Mird 1236, 1238, 1239). Written on both sides, these are fragmentary leaves of a codex.

4.1.2. Parchment

The main corpus of Christian Palestinian Aramaic manuscripts is made up of parchment documents. Already in use in the ancient period simultaneously with papyrus, parchment continued to be employed in the mediaeval period (tenth to twelfth centuries). An early eleventh-century lectionary of Sinai, St Catherine, New Finds, CPA Sp 2, is made of parchment. So is Vatican City, BAV, Vat. sir. 19 (lectionary A), which is very similar in terms of script and dates to 1030 CE, and two more lectionaries from Sinai, St Catherine, New Finds, M41N (lectionary E, with the fragments Sp 9, 10 and 11) and M42N (lectionary F).

Although much of what survives is scattered leaves, one can conclude that the majority of the manuscripts were biblical books (both Old and New Testament: Pentateuch, historical books, Prophets, Psalter, Gospels, Acts of the Apostles and Epistles), as well as lectionaries arranged according to the Melkite calendar, and also some patristic texts and hagiographical collections and apocrypha.

The existence of a large number of Christian Palestinian Aramaic palimpsests raises several questions. The fact that many ancient manuscripts were reused for Greek, Syriac, Georgian and Arabic texts suggests that they had fallen out of use around the tenth century. At the same time, this does not explain how it happened that the tradition was revived in the eleventh century, in a cursive script different from the uncial of the earlier manuscripts. Furthermore, a number of not insignificant Christian Palestinian Aramaic parchments were reused for new Aramaic texts during the mediaeval period.

The palimpsests feature superior texts in Christian Palestinian Aramaic (for example, many fragments from Sinai, including the F lectionary and a new version of the *Apophthegmata patrum*), in Greek (for example from Khirbet Mird), in Syriac (for example numerous manuscripts from Sinai, including the famous *Codex Climaci rescriptus*), in Georgian (Sinai), in Arabic (Sinai) and in Hebrew (the Cairo Geniza manuscripts). One can even find double palimpsests such as in the manuscript Sinai, St Catherine, Arab. 588: the Aramaic text of 1 Kings 2 is covered by a Syriac text that has not yet been identified and which is itself covered by an Arabic text of a prophetologion; according to Gwilliam (et al.) 1896, even a triple palimpsest might be found.

In the eleventh century, parchment fragments written in Christian Palestinian Aramaic were often reused for book covers (Sinai, St Catherine, New Finds X17). This practice was not characteristic of Aramaic Melkites.

4.1.3. Paper

The exact date of the introduction of paper is unknown. It remains an open question whether parchment continued to be used for liturgical Aramaic Melkite books beyond the first quarter of the twelfth century and whether paper replaced parchment or the two materials coexisted until the end of manuscript production, at least at Sinai. In any case, it was with paper that the parchment lectionary in the Vatican collection was

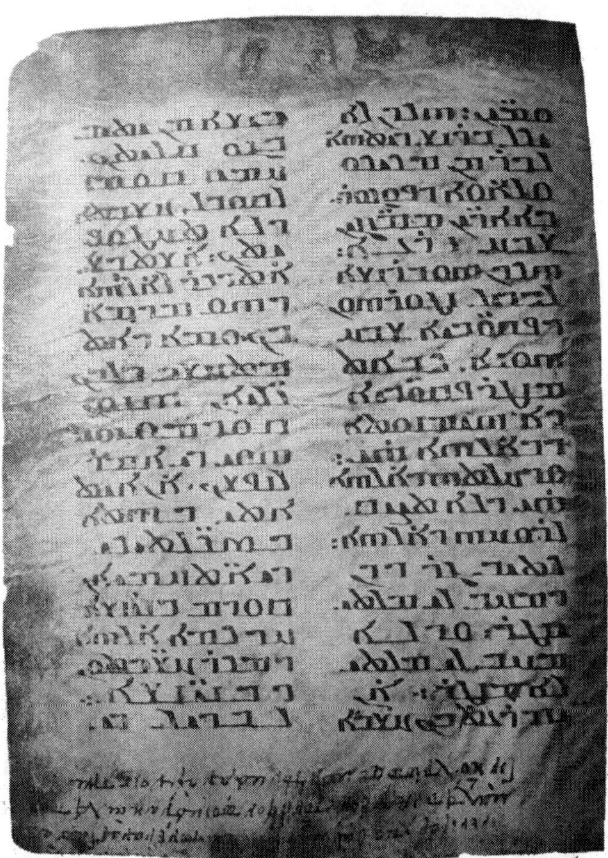

Fig. 1.4.1 St Petersburg, RNB, n.s. 21 (from Kokowzoff 1906, f. 1r): ancient period.

restored. Only five Christian Palestinian manuscripts are made, at least in part, of paper. One is the manuscript Berlin, Staatsbibliothek, Or. oct. 1019 (Black 1954), a horologium written in Jerusalem on 3 October 1187 CE, but found in Cairo (probably originating from Sinai). Two such manuscripts are now in the British Library: London, BL, Add. 14664, f. 34, of the twelfth century, containing three hymns on St John the Baptist, and Or. 4951, a liturgical Melkite book, also of the twelfth century, the writing of which is not very meticulous. The layout corresponds to the ancient parchment manuscript tradition (see also Ch. 1 § 4.3), with well-balanced margins, blind ruling, and the book is sewn tightly with five sewing stations. The quires are mirror-signed. The bifolia of Göttingen, Universitätsbibliothek, Syr. 27, fragments of a Melkite ritual containing a hymn to John the Baptist, a hymn to St Peter and an ordination ritual with Arabic translation, are on thin brown 'eastern paper', possibly of textile origin.

A special case is the aforementioned lectionary A (Vatican City, BAV, Vat. sir. 19): a parchment codex, it has a paper bifolium carefully inserted at the centre of its twenty-fourth gathering, sewn in very skilfully with a thread from the original binding, and with the upper margin aligned with that of the other leaves. The reading that it bears for a fixed celebration (on 20 *Tammuz* = 20 July) attests to a double use with that of Sundays (in the tenth century). Therefore, this addition is evidence for a liturgical update in an age when parchment books were still in use, but paper was already known; possibly a paper bifolium seemed easier to insert, or no parchment was readily available.

4.1.4. Inks

All the manuscripts of the ancient period are written in black ink, but by the tenth century, some leaves also have red ink used for subtitles.

On the majority of parchment leaves, today the ink appears brown: it is possible that the inks used were iron-gall inks that have changed colour from the original black. In some cases, the ink took on an orange hue, probably indicative of the particular metal used in the manufacture of the ink. In rare cases, such as that of the *Apophthegmata patrum* of the Sinai 'New Finds', the ink is deep black.

In the paper manuscripts, three inks were used, black for the text, and both red and green for the (sub)headings, punctuation, liturgical columns and decorations. The black ink remains deep black, and the paper has not corroded, which is a strong indication that it is a carbon ink. The red ink remains a nice red vermilion. All the assumptions concerning the composition of inks still need chemical analysis to be verified.

Luckily, an ink recipe has been found in Christian Palestinian Aramaic, in a small booklet of six parchment leaves, called 'the magical booklet' and discovered at Khirbet Mird in the Judaean desert during the excavations of De Langhe, now preserved at the Université Catholique de Louvain. The editor, Maurice Baillet (1963), dated the booklet to sixth or seventh century. The recipe gives the proportions to be used in making an ink composed of gum arabic, galls and blue vitriol (chalcanthum), which no doubt corresponds to copper sulphate ($CuSO_4$). The recipe goes on to mention the different colours, unfortunately without specifying their compositions: cinnabar, grey green, yellow ochre, marine blue, light green, sky blue, gold, white lead, vermilion, black ink.

4.2. The making of the codex

4.2.1. The composition of the quires

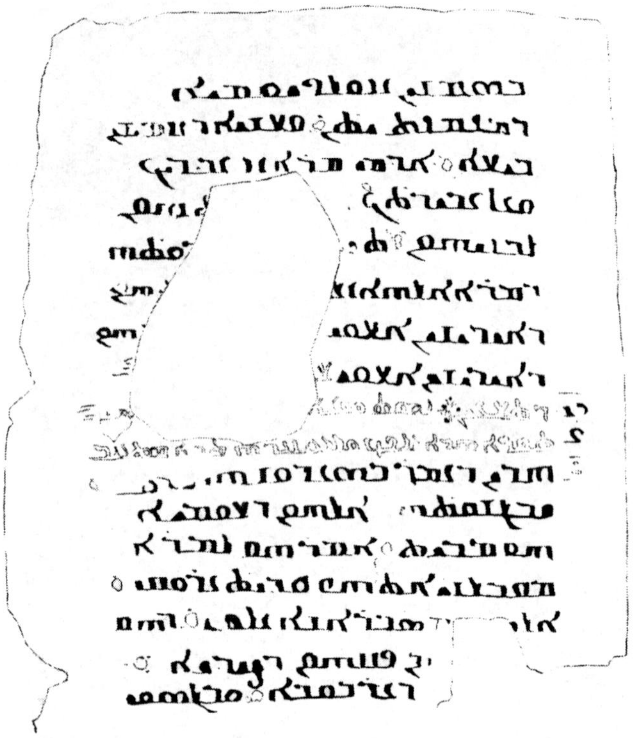

All the manuscripts from the ancient period, or almost all of them, are dismembered and scattered, so that their structure is no longer detectable. The manuscript in Cambridge, Westminster Theological College, known as *The Forty Martyrs of the Sinai Desert, Eulogius the Stone-Cutter and Anastasia* (Lewis 1912 = Müller-Kessler – Sokoloff 1996a), however, is sufficiently well preserved that one can still see how it was made. It is composed of quaternions that follow Gregory's Rule, with the flesh side on the outside. The quires are mirror-signed, a system that seems to be characteristic of Christian Palestinian manuscripts (in any case, this system is not found in Syriac manuscripts): the verso of the last leaf of quire 1 and the recto of the first leaf of quire 2 are signed *alaph*=1; the verso of the last leaf of quire 2 and the recto of the first leaf of quire 3 are signed *beth*=2, and so on, in such a manner that the position of a quire within the codex is known from the verso of the last leaf of the quire, the mirror-signature being there to ensure the correct succession of the quires. Moreover, in certain manuscripts such as the Cambridge lectionary of Westminster College (Lewis 1897), the letters do not really correspond to the Semitic numbering system; indeed, after the initial *kaf* form comes the final *kaf* form, after the initial *nun* form comes the final *nun* form, after *phe* comes *pe inversum*, then after *taw* follows double *alaph*, double *beth* and so on. The remains of the manuscript Sinai, New Finds M58-59N display an identical system.

Fig. 1.4.2 London, BL, Add. 14644, f. 29r (drawing by Land 1875, plate VIII): mediaeval period.

One may conclude that the parchment manuscripts of the ancient period are regularly composed of quaternions (with an exceptional presence of some quinions), and the quires follow Gregory's Rule; only two of the Sinai manuscripts have flesh side on the outside.

The manuscript Sinai, St Catherine, New Finds X17 is a special case. It seems to date from the tenth century, thus between the ancient and the mediaeval periods. It is the only manuscript known to use the 'Syriac' system of quire signatures: the same number is found on the recto of its first leaf and on the verso of its last leaf.

Finally, one should note the presence of signatures on many scattered leaves, thus demonstrating that codices were usually signed. All signatures are placed at the centre of the bottom margin; some are simply decorated with points or dashes around the letters functioning as numerals.

The mediaeval-period manuscripts are much better preserved than those of the ancient period. They are similarly composed of quaternions and mirror-signed. This is the case with lectionary B of Sinai (Palest. syr. 1, dated 1104 CE), lectionary E (M41N, twelfth century), and lectionary F (M42N, twelfth century). The Westminster College Cambridge lectionary (Lewis 1897) consists of twenty-four quaternions and five quinions, all mirror-signed. Lectionary A (Vatican City, BAV, Vat. sir. 19, dated 1030 CE and possibly coming from Antioch), which presents a text similar to lectionaries B and C, is composed of twenty-three quaternions and one quinion. It is singular, however, in using a particular signature system, unique within the Christian Palestinian corpus: quire 2 is signed *alaph*=1 on the recto of its first leaf, quire 3 is signed *beth*=2 on the recto of its first leaf, and so forth, from right to left; in addition, at the same places, it bears a Greek numeration starting from the last quire, so as to enumerate, from left to right, as in a Greek codex. This oddity in the quire signatures may have resulted from a restoration to repair the sewing and the binding.

Thus, the mediaeval parchment manuscripts follow the tradition of the codex structure of the ancient period, except that the leaves, always set flesh against flesh and hair against hair, compose quires with the hair side on the exterior.

As to paper manuscripts, it is difficult to draw a general rule, for there is only a very small number of them, and only two are complete books. The manuscript Berlin, Staatsbibliothek, Or. oct. 1019, dated 1187 CE, is composed of quaternions, except for one ternion and two quinions, mirror-signed. The manuscript London, BL, Or. 4951, of the twelfth century, is composed of seven quinions, mirror-signed. It is possible that these examples indicate a certain technical laxness during the Middle Ages, at the time when paper replaced parchment.

4.3. The layout of the page

One can scarcely reach any definitive general conclusion regarding the dimensions of manuscripts of the ancient period, given the fragmentary state of the documentation and especially the fact that palimpsests were often trimmed to a smaller size. Nevertheless, one can collect information and get an idea of what the dimensions of some manuscripts might have been.

The majority of surviving manuscripts have an average size similar to A4, but generally of greater height (fig. 1.4.1). The *Codex Zosimi rescriptus* Gospels (Oslo, Schøyen, 35 and 36) clearly exceed the A4 dimensions at 315 × 230 mm and the codicological unit containing Cyril of Jerusalem in the same codex reaches 330 × 270 mm. These are obviously books designed for the liturgical service. The *Apophthegmata patrum* codex has a small size, nearly A5, and the Psalter of the Sinai 'New Finds' is even smaller (195 × 125 mm); these are without doubt books designed for individual reading. Between the great A4 and the small A5, a certain number of codices are of average size, like the Gospel of *Codex Climaci rescriptus* (240 × 180 mm). One can also note the sizes according to proportions; one codex with proportion 2/3 (0.67), one with 3/4 (0.75), one with 5/7 (0.71), and six with 4/5 (0.80).

The mediaeval manuscripts are clearly smaller (fig. 1.4.2): only one, a Gospel book of the Sinai 'New Finds' (M41N), is around A4 size; the others are A5 size or a little larger; one is smaller than A5, and a single small manuscript is A6 size (140 × 100 mm). Nevertheless, these are all lectionaries or books with liturgical rituals. This obviously corresponds to the situation of a minor community, progressively moving toward extinction. The proportions remain the same as those of the ancient manuscripts. The stability of these proportions is probably explained by the nature of the materials, but also without doubt by the aesthetics and the ergonomics of reading; this seems to be proved by the constant layout.

A first evaluation of the preparation of the page presented below is based on thirty-two manuscripts of the ancient period and eight mediaeval manuscripts, which is a representative corpus, given the small number of surviving Christian Palestinian manuscripts.

In manuscripts from the ancient period, ruled lines are drawn with a dry point, always on the flesh side. The interline space varies between 8 and 12 mm, usually 8–9 mm. The layout is usually in two columns from 60 to 70 mm wide with an inter-column of *c.*20 mm (but one-column manuscripts exist as well). The most commonly used ruling pattern, represented in fifteen cases, is the one that allows the best regularity: four vertical bounding lines and a horizontal line for each line of writing. Other patterns include: all horizontal lines and three vertical ones: the right margin and two for the inter-column (one example); all writing lines and two bounding lines for the inter-column (two examples); all horizontal lines and one bounding line, for the right column (three examples); all writing lines and no bounding lines (three examples); one horizontal line for two (one example) or three (one example) writing lines and four bounding lines; top and bottom writing line and four bounding lines (one example); one (top) writing line and two vertical lines for the inter-column (one example); only two bounding lines for the inter-column (one example). In some cases, pricking is used instead of or alongside blind ruling. Two manuscripts (Cambridge University Library, Taylor-Schlechter 16325 and *The Forty Martyrs*) have pricks at the ends of all lines, while the writing lines themselves are not visible. Three manuscripts only show pricks, for two columns and at the ends of all written lines; one manuscript shows pricks for text lines and four bounding lines. The desire for harmony in the layout can be appreciated from the fact that at an opening, the bottom margin is equal to the outer margin, and the inner margin is about half the width of the outer margin. Many manuscripts carry running titles, divided between the last page of one quire and the first page of the next.

In the mediaeval period (twelfth and thirteenth century), the signature system and the ruling system stay the same as that of the ancient period, but page preparation is much less meticulous, often lacking justification. Two columns are still employed, with inter-column space reduced to 10 mm. Interlining measures between 7 and 9 mm. For the manuscripts written in two columns, one finds ruling patterns of four vertical and all the writing lines; two vertical and two horizontal lines, top and bottom; four vertical and one horizontal top line; only four vertical lines. For two manuscripts written in one column, the ruling includes two vertical and two horizontal lines forming the outer frame of the text area. The ruling of lectionary A (Vatican City, BAV, Vat. sir. 19) seems to follow no particular logical pattern.

4.4. Bookbinding

Almost all bindings have been lost, but at least three fragmentary examples have been preserved at Sinai. The oldest binding fragment is probably that of Sinai, St Catherine, New Finds M52N (eighth/ninth century) which has kept its spine glued on canvas. The lectionaries B (Palest. syr. 1, 1104 CE) and C (1118 CE) have both preserved the leather covering of the wooden boards.

The other examples are even more fragmentary. Sinai, New Finds, M41N (lectionary E, beginning of the twelfth century) has preserved a part of its headband. Of the binding of manuscript Göttingen, Universitätsbibliothek, Syr. 27 only a wooden board with its strings remains (Byzantine binding type Z1?); it is particularly interesting, for the parchment fragment used as a paste-down carries an ancient Christian Palestinian Aramaic script, datable possibly to the eight century. It is really remarkable that this vestige comes from Mount Athos. The paper bifolia of Göttingen, Universitätsbibliothek, Syr. 27 carry five sewing stations (a central one and two at each side). The sewing of Sinai, St Catherine, New Finds, M41N is three double points (one central point and one point at each side); the quire sewing points are of thick string, the headband sewing points are of thin string.

References

Albert et al. 1993; Baillet 1963; Bar-Asher 1977; Black 1954; Brock 1995a; Delavault et al. 2010; Desreumaux 1979, 1983a, 1983b, 1987a, 1987b, 1989a, 1989b, 1990–1991, 1992, 1996a, 1996b, 1998a, 1998b, 1998c, 1998d, 1999, 1999 [2001], 2002, 2008, 2009; Desreumaux – Schmidt 1989; Griffith [S.] 1997; Gwilliam et al. 1896; Humbert – Desreumaux 1998; Kokowzoff 1906; Lagrange 1925; Land 1875; Lewis 1897, 1912; Merk 1957; Metzger 1977; Milik 1953; Müller-Kessler 1991; Müller-Kessler – Sokoloff 1996a, 1999; Perrot 1963; Rutschowskaya – Desreumaux 1992; Schulthess 1903, 1905, 1924.

5. Coptic codicology (PB–SE)*

5.1. Materials and tools (PB)

5.1.1. Papyrus

In Coptic (which borrowed many words from Greek), papyrus was referred to mostly by the Greek loanword *chartēs* (cf. Latin *charta*), forms of the Greek word *papyros* (itself a loanword from earlier Egyptian) occurring only rarely in Coptic; as elsewhere (cf. English *charter*, French *charte*), the word *chartēs* came in Egypt to mean simply 'document', regardless of material (Crum 1926, 186–187). Papyrus continued to be used in Egypt even after paper became available about two centuries after the Arab Conquest in the middle of the seventh century, but during the tenth century, when the Egyptians began to manufacture paper for themselves, papyrus fell entirely out of use (Grob 2010, 11–14 (her chart 3 is on p. 10, mislabelled 'Chart 2'; her chart 4 is on p. 14, mislabelled 'Chart 3'); Bloom 2001, 27–29). The latest securely dated Coptic papyrus presently known is a tax receipt of 27 December 942 (Till 1958, 10–11 no. 13), but there is also a private letter on which the date 2 April 959 was added secondarily, presumably by a later writer (Crum 1905b, 502 no. 1213); the latest dated Arabic papyri are from 970/971 and 981. Sometime thereafter, even the papyrus plant, the raw material for making papyrus paper, disappeared from the Nile valley, surviving up until modern times only much farther south (Sudan, Ethiopia).

There is no reason to think that the process of manufacturing papyrus in Egypt changed in any fundamental way during the four millennia of its history, nor that the wholesale form in which papyrus was delivered from the factory was ever anything other than rolls, created by pasting together series of papyrus sheets (*kollēmata*), the individual sheets being normally rather narrow, rarely as wide as even half a metre, typically only 150–200 mm wide and 190–330 mm tall, with twenty *kollēmata* per roll being the norm (Johnson 2004, 86–91; Johnson 2009, 257; scribes could paste multiple factory-standard rolls together to create bookrolls of greater length: see Johnson 2004, 143–152). But as the codex form of book came to predominate over the roll, around the fourth century, there occurred a significant innovation in the manufacturing process, in that very long *kollēmata*—well over a metre in length, sometimes approaching two metres—began to be produced and used in rolls whose purpose was, as it seems, specifically to be cut into bifolia for use in codex quires. Papyrologists have discovered such very long *kollēmata* by reconstructing the rolls that were used in the manufacture of certain papyrus codices, especially Coptic ones (Emmel 1998, 38–39; cf. Robinson [J.] 1978, 39–42).

5.1.2. Parchment

Parchment was already in use in Egypt at the beginning of the Coptic period. What is thought to be one of the oldest Coptic codices of all (perhaps from the third century) is a parchment codex containing a translation of the Old Testament book of Proverbs into an otherwise unknown Coptic dialect (Kasser 1960). Parchment remained in use alongside papyrus, and later on alongside paper. Perhaps parchment was always considered to be generally the better material (as papyrus was considered superior to *ostraca* of limestone, and the latter superior to potsherds, at least in the area around Thebes: Crum 1926, 187–190), and the trend over the centuries seems to have been to replace papyrus books with parchment, and the latter eventually with paper. The scant evidence that survives about the costs of blank papyrus and parchment indicates that parchment was the more expensive material, at times perhaps even as much as twice as expensive (Bagnall 2009, 52–58).

To designate parchment, Coptic used the Greek loanword *me(m)branon* (which could be Copticized as *mefrōn*) or the native Egyptian word for 'skin' *šaar*, which could also be used to refer to one or more codex leaves or—in its meaning 'leather'—to a bookbinding (Kotsifou 2011, 221). There survived in Coptic a fragment of a papyrus codex—two leaves, pages 3–6 (present whereabouts unknown), perhaps from the sixth or seventh century—containing a series of instructions for how to improve the writing surface of a parchment leaf (Crum 1905a; Maravela-Solbakk 2008, 32–33). Each instruction relates to a particular condition of the leaf and its surface. Some details of the nine conditions described are obscure, but they include wrinkled, rough, 'corroded', and sticky (?) surfaces, as well as surfaces on which the ink runs. The remedies mostly involve the use of pumice (*kesile* or *kesilei* (?), from Greek *kisēris*), whether 'soft' or 'hard', apparently either as a powder that can be wiped off (or not), or as a stone with which to rub

* The authors would like to thank Ewa Balicka-Witakowska for her valuable comments on § 5.5.2 of this chapter, and Karin Scheper for her help with § 5.7.

Fig. 1.5.1 Turin, Soprintendenza Archeologica del Piemonte e del Museo Antichità Egizie, cod. I, f. 23v, *Vita Eudoxiae*, papyrus, *c.* sixth/seventh century, photograph Archivio fotografico.

the surface, as well as white lead (*psemithei*, from Greek *psimythion*, *psimithion*, etc.) or a mixture of white lead and alum (*obn*), in either case crushed and then shaken through a linen cloth as a powder, either to be worked into the surface or else wiped off; the use of ochre (*okhru*) is also mentioned. Apparent Coptic neologisms based on Greek words are verbs 'to polish' (*leantērie*) and 'to pumice' (*kesile*), the latter apparently meaning to apply powdered pumice.

We do not know of any studies referring to analyses on which firm statements about the manufacture of parchment in Egypt could be based, including statements about skin sizes and manufactured sheet sizes, although one manuscript was said by its editor to be 'mostly or entirely of goat skin,' without giving any reason for this claim (Worrell 1923, xv). In any case, there is no reason to suppose that there were different markets for the production of books in Coptic and for the production of books in Greek (and Latin) and later Arabic. Investigation of the raw materials of Egyptian book manufacture must take into consideration all the surviving products, regardless of language.

With specific regard to Coptic codices, it has been observed that coloured parchment is very rare (Crum 1905b, xiii and 24 no. 112, two bifolia of a Gospel manuscript 'dyed a bright saffron'). Less rare but still rather uncommon are Coptic palimpsests, and those that exist have not been studied systematically as such. See Thompson 1911 for an example of a Coptic parchment codex that was reused early in the tenth century for a Syriac text; Layton 1987, 76 (no. 72) for Greek written over Coptic; Crum 1905b, 14–15 (nos. 48 and 55) and 242 (no. 505) for Coptic over Greek and Latin; Depuydt 1993, 64–65 and 455–456 (nos. 46 and 263) for Coptic over bilingual Coptic-Greek; other examples are Coptic written over Coptic (for example Layton 1987, 215–218, pl. 23.5–6), including magical spells written over erased biblical texts (for example Emmel 1990, 14–22, pl. 1) and over sub- or non-literary texts.

5.1.3. Paper

'Paper had been introduced to Egypt from Syria in the ninth century, and it was manufactured there by the tenth' (Bloom 2001, 74), but 'there is no evidence that the Copts as a distinct social group ever manufactured their own paper, though it is well known that paper was for a time actively produced in Mediaeval Egypt; European copyists' paper seems to have taken over the Egyptian market in the later fourteenth century' (Layton 1987, lx; cf. Babinger 1931). Coptic paper manuscripts were made both from oriental and from European paper but have rarely been described in sufficient detail as to distinguish them and their characteristics. The earliest dated paper manuscripts in Coptic come from deep in southern Egypt, from the end of the tenth century (Boud'hors 1999a, 76). As with papyrus and parchment, further investigation into the material of paper manuscripts from Egypt should proceed without prejudice to language (see, for example, Humbert 1999).

5.1.4. Other writing surfaces

Still other supports employed in Egypt by Coptic writers were leather, wood, potsherds and chips of limestone (together called *ostraca*), bone, ivory, and cloth, not to mention stone inscriptions, carved wooden architectural elements or the like, and various sorts of writing on walls, whether as graffiti or as legends in association with wall paintings, icons, and so forth. These diverse materials were mostly used for documentary and ephemeral—sometimes magical—purposes and so mostly as individual pieces, much as single sheets of papyrus, parchment, or paper were also so used. For a number of Coptic legal documents on leather, see Crum 1905b, 182–217 nos. 389, 396, 435, 447–456. Coptic *ostraca* have been published in large numbers, along with documents on other materials, especially papyrus (consult the online *Checklist of Editions of Greek, Latin, Demotic, and Coptic Papyri, Ostraca and Tablets*: <http://library.duke.edu/rubenstein/scriptorium/papyrus/texts/clist.html>), and sometimes *ostraca* are inscribed with excerpts from literary works; a particularly interesting example is nine lines of text from a known work by the famous Coptic author Shenoute written around some 75% of the circumference of a complete ceramic amphora (discovered broken in an archaeological excavation; see Hasznos 2006–2007).

Wooden tablets were used in two different ways. Either the scribe might write directly on the wood with ink, sometimes after having first coated the surface, for example with some sort of white paint, or a shallow recessed area was whittled out from most of the surface of one or both sides of the tablet in order to hold a thin layer of wax that could be incised and then erased any number of times. A set of tablets could be fastened together along one edge (normally the long edge, parallel to which the writing was often done) to form a diptych or polyptych, i.e. a wooden notebook that formally is the oldest forerunner of the literary codex, although literary texts in the strict sense on wooden tablets are the exception rather than the norm (Van Haelst 1989, 13–15; Sirat 1989; Lalou 1992; Worp 2012). The absolute dimensions of the surviving examples vary considerably, but two main types have been distinguished: (1) tablets that are only somewhat more oblong than square, with proportions of approximately 1.25 to 1.6 (or *c.*0.6 to 0.8), as opposed to (2) those that are markedly oblong, for example with proportions ranging from something more than 2.0 up to 3.0 and even 4.0 (or *c.*0.25 to 0.5). The great majority of surviving examples are Greek, although a few of those tablets include also some Coptic (Worp 2012, 60–61); of the fifty or so purely or largely Coptic wooden tablets known thus far, all but a very few are single pieces inscribed with ink, with no example of a waxed tablet (Worp 2012, 55–60; no. 399 was created to be a waxed tablet, and was perhaps so used originally, but finally it was inscribed directly upon the wood). Particularly noteworthy—for being quite unusual—are two wooden tablets of the fourth century from Dakhleh Oasis with Manichaean Syriac-Coptic glossaries of words and phrases (Franzmann – Gardner 1996, 101–126, pls 17–18*bis*; Gardner 2007, 173).

5.1.5. Inks

The ink on one specimen of Coptic parchment (a handwriting exercise of unknown date) has been thoroughly analysed recently, using several different non-destructive spectroscopic methods (Rabin et al. 2012). Among other results, the ink was found to be iron-gall (but with a difference in the metal salt composition of the inks on the two sides, which might have been written by two different scribes). Although iron-gall ink might have been preferred for use on parchment, of course soot-based ink was also widely used in Egypt throughout its history (Lucas 1922; Lucas 1962, 363–364), and there is no particular reason to think that purely tannin inks were not also in use.

Lucas recorded a method of making soot (carbon) for ink that was reported to him by a Coptic priest: 'Put a quantity of incense on the ground, and round it place three stones or bricks, and resting on these an earthenware dish, bottom upwards, covered with a damp cloth; ignite the incense. Carbon is formed and is deposited inside the dish, from which it is removed and made into ink by mixing with gum arabic and water.' We may also note here that in the list of instructions already mentioned above for how to improve a parchment writing surface (Crum 1905a), the remedy in the case of running ink is to dilute the ink with 'a drop of' some liquid substance, unfortunately not determinable because the word was too badly damaged for the editor to be sure what it was (with hesitation he suggested possibly alum, but some source of tannin is perhaps more likely). A Syriac manuscript from Dayr al-Suryān in Wādī al-Naṭrūn (north-west of Cairo) contains a recipe for the ink that 'the Egyptian Fathers who lived in this desert used for writing', which states: 'If you wish to make ink for parchment, take the parings of the root of a tree which grows in this desert, called *arta*, and pound them whilst fresh, and boil them on the fire in black wine and vinegar made from wine. Then strain, and add a little vitriol and gum arabic' (Evelyn-White 1926, xlv).

5.1.6. Pigments and dyes

Another recent investigation, using only Raman spectroscopy to analyse the pigments black, red, yellow, blue, and green, sampled from a small number of brightly decorated leaves from one Coptic parchment codex (tenth century?) and one Coptic paper codex (mid-sixteenth century), revealed that black was obtained from carbon (soot), red from cinnabar (mercury (II) sulphide, vermilion), yellow from orpiment (arsenic sulphide)—whereby orange was obtained by mixing together the pigments red and yellow—while blue was obtained for the parchment manuscript from lapis lazuli (with an admixture of carbon and some aluminosilicate) but for the paper manuscript from indigotine (indigo carmine), whereas green for the parchment manuscript came from a compound of orpiment and indigotine and for the paper manuscript from some unidentifiable organic substance (Coupry 2007; cf. Coupry 2004). A previous investigation using particle-induced X-ray emission focused on Coptic inks and pigments on a variety of supports thought to be from the sixth to eighth centuries (except for one parchment thought to be of eleventh century) and gave somewhat different results (MacArthur 1995). The red in these samples was either from minium (lead oxide, red lead), or from a mixture of minium and cinnabar, with four different mixtures being detectable without any difference in colour apparent to the eye; alongside orpiment, possibly massicot was used for a pale yellow pigment; and here too the source of green proved rather difficult to determine, but the investigator suggested malachite (copper carbonate) and verdigris (copper acetate) as two possibilities, the evidence suggesting also the possibility of deliberate mixtures of pigments to obtain a range of green colours. With regard to the black inks, a clear distinction was found between the use of carbon ink on pottery *ostraca*, and iron-gall ink on parchment.

5.1.7. Writing instruments

Coptic scribes wrote on the various supports available to them using a pen made from a hollow reed (*Phragmites australis*), which when new might approach 300 mm in length. Sharpening a pen meant trimming its length, whereby it eventually became too short to use, unless the scribe extended its life by sticking a piece of wood into one end. Surviving examples show that the pens were 'pointed and split like old-fashioned quill pens, and ... the taste of different individuals varied from pointed to stub nibs' (Winlock – Crum 1926, I, 93–94, on pens found at the site of the Monastery of Epiphanius in western Thebes). A pen might be sharpened on both ends, presumably either for different styles of lettering, or for using two different inks (black and red) simultaneously. The scribes kept their pens and other tools (which might include a pointed stylus, or several of them, either for use when writing on a waxed tablet, or for marking ruling lines on some surface) in small boxes of wood (*c.*235 × 69 × 36 mm, for example) with sliding covers and several compartments, including a shallow removable metal ink container (Depuydt 1993, 601, pls 465–467; Friedman et al. 1989, 168–169, where in addition to a writing box, a pen, and three styluses, a ceramic inkwell is also shown), or in pouch-like holders made of leather (Bosson – Aufrère 1999, 276–278, 281–282, nos. 96–101; Rutschowscaya et al. 2000, 64–65; for a carved wooden lid showing a monk-scribe carrying such a pouch over his shoulder, see: Rutschowscaya et al. 2000, 110–111; Gabra – Eaton-Krauss 2006, 80–81; Whitfield et al. 2010, 124, and p. 126 for another example of a leather pen case).

5.2. Book forms (SE)

5.2.1. Miscellaneous forms. The roll and the rotulus

Books in Coptic Egypt were almost with no exception codices, made of either papyrus, parchment, or paper. The very few sets of wooden tablets fastened together like codices and written in Coptic have already been mentioned (Worp 2012, nos. 378 and 379 seem to be the only certain examples; Greek and Coptic combined: nos. 132 and 244, no. 102 = Gabra 2014, 88). Coptic rolls and rotuli are also hardly known. Apart from a number of magical and documentary texts in these formats (which remained in use for documentary purposes for many centuries, well into the second millennium; for example Plumley 1975, two very long rotuli from the late fourteenth century, one in Coptic, with a Greek postscript, the other in Arabic, each *c.*4.82 × 0.34 m), we know of only thirteen Coptic manuscripts in either rotulus or roll form. Within the context of Coptic literature as a whole, these thirteen items are oddities, not at all typical for Coptic manuscript culture in general in any period of its history. Just over half of these items—two papyrus rolls, one parchment roll, four parchment rotuli (Robinson [J.] 1990–1991, 34; his items 8 and 9 are rolls in vertical rotulus form)—are only long enough to contain but a single letter (in one case two letters) by the traditional founder of communal monasticism in Egypt, Pachomius, or one of his two of his successors; measuring, for example, only about 300 × 150 mm, or 500 × 100 mm, and in some cases quite irregular in shape (for example, 570 × 90–155 mm (Quecke 1975, 426–427; Robinson [J.] 1990a, photograph no. 14 facing p. 15), or 520 × 94–166 mm (Krause 1981, 220 and 233 n. 4)), some of these manuscripts are more like strips of waste material that were nonetheless put to use. The dimensions of the three rolls are not on record.

The remaining examples known to us of Coptic rotuli and rolls are all made of papyrus: (1) a rotulus written both front and back, 670 × 260 mm but originally somewhat taller (*Psalms* 77–78; Vergote – Parássoglou 1974); (2) the last three columns (of varying dimensions) of a roll, with a final column written on the back, 293 × 443 mm but originally longer (*Didache*, excerpt; Layton 1987, 236); (3) three columns (of varying dimensions) of a roll (later than 413), from which at least one column is missing at the beginning but possibly no more at the end, 280 × 780 mm but originally both taller and longer (Cyril of Alexandria, *Ep. fest.* 1; Till 1931; Camplani 1999); on the back, an unidentified homiletic work was written *transversa charta* (so in rotulus form), starting at the beginning of the roll; (4) the last column of a roll, with a few vestiges of the preceding column, blank on the back, 250 × 208 mm but originally longer (unidentified Psalm-like text; Lefort 1939, 1–7, pl. 1); (5) the first four columns of a roll, with traces of writing (later? earlier?) on the back, 235 × 480 mm but originally longer (*2 Maccabees*, excerpt; Lacau 1911, 68–76, pl. 2); and (6) a roll written in about eighteen columns on the back of a (reused) Greek document of perhaps the third century; the dimensions of this latter roll were not recorded (it was in any case already fragmentary when first seen), and the whereabouts of the manuscript are now unknown, but the only scholar who saw it estimated that originally it was approximately 1.8 m long (*Ascension of Isaiah*; Lacau 1946).

5.2.2. The codex

By contrast, Coptic codices have survived in great numbers, albeit often in a pitiably dismembered, deteriorated, or otherwise fragmentary condition, with the surviving fragments often now dispersed among a number of museums and libraries as a result of the various haphazard ways in which Coptic manuscripts were discovered and sold beginning especially in the eighteenth century. But some of the oldest surviving Coptic codices that are well preserved, in particular several of the thirteen Nag Hammadi codices (NHC), are among the oldest specimens of papyrus books in codex form that survive in any language, dating as they do from around the end of the fourth century. Most of the NHC are single-quire codices, as are a good number of other Coptic papyrus codices, but one is made of three (irregular) quires, and a good number of multi-quire Coptic papyrus codices survive, some of them likely more or less contemporary with the NHC. Thus both types were in use at the same time, as was the case with Greek papyrus codices already in earlier centuries (Turner 1977, 98–99).

By the beginning of the Coptic period, papyrus and parchment were both also in use for manufacturing codices (cf. Turner 1977, 35–42): what is thought to be one of the earliest Coptic manuscripts of all is a parchment codex (*P.Bodmer* VI, Proverbs, perhaps from the late third century, and unlikely—because of its unique dialect—to be much later than the fourth century). Probably papyrus continued to be used for codices down to the end of its use for any purpose at all in the tenth century. Although we cannot say with certainty whether we have any papyrus codices, or fragments of papyrus codices, from as late as the tenth century, we may reasonably identify as such a small group of fragments that were used to make *cartonnage* ('papyrus pasteboard', better termed papyrus laminate) for the bindings of six parchment and four paper codices that were copied at Esna in southern Egypt between 974 and 1005 (Layton 1987, xxx and the relevant entries in his catalogue); thus the dates of the reused papyrus leaves (from at least ten different codices) could be as late as the earlier part of the tenth century, although of course some or all of them could be still earlier (Layton 1987, nos. 19+148 cannot be earlier than the later part of the seventh century, for it bears the remains of an Arabic protocol; on the dates of Arabic protocols, see Grob 2010, 13–14; see Depuydt 1993, l n. 30 for an instance showing that leaves from several mid-ninth-century parchment codices were reused only about half a century later for a paste-down in a new codex).

5.3. The making of the codex (SE–PB)

Coptic codicology is greatly hampered by a dearth of securely dated manuscripts. Dated colophons do not appear in the surviving evidence until the ninth century, the oldest being from 822/823, in a parchment codex (Depuydt 1993, no. 162; cf. pp. lxvi and l–li), but the fragmentary condition of so many of the surviving Coptic manuscripts means that many dated colophons have been lost, or else they survive only as isolated leaves, making it impossible to identify other parts of the codices to which they belong. Thus, for dating Coptic manuscripts, Coptologists have for the most part relied on the uncertain criteria of palaeographical typology (based to a great extent on Greek palaeography) and codicological typology.

Similarly, it is often the case that nothing is known about the geographical origin of the surviving Coptic manuscripts, with the lack of colophons being compounded by the fact that many entered modern collections via the Egyptian antiquities trade, without any reliable information as to provenance.

5.3.1. The making of the quires (SE)

While most known Coptic papyrus codices have been investigated codicologically, more or less thoroughly, there does not yet exist a comprehensive synthesis of the facts (but fundamental now are Robinson [J.] 1978 and 1984, 32–86). As has been stated above, it is the normal expectation regarding papyrus codices that their constituent bifolia were cut from rolls that had been manufactured by pasting together a series of *kollēmata*. The clear evidence of this practice is the occurrence in papyrus codices of the *kollēseis* where two *kollēmata* were joined in the manufacture of the roll that was later used for the manufacture of the codex (for diagrams illustrating this phenomenon, see Turner 1977, 46; Emmel 1984, 24–25); and more often than not, one can also trace the continuity of horizontal papyrus fibres from the edges of one bifolium onto other bifolia in the codex, such as to prove that they are cut-apart sections of what was originally a single roll. The rolls used to make the thirteen NHC, thirty-three of which rolls can be reconstructed to something that is surely close to their original manufactured size, varied in length between 1.44 and 3.15 m, with *c.*2.5 m being the average (Robinson [J.] 1984, 60); although narrow *kollēmata* occur in some of the NHC, most of the rolls that were used comprised *kollēmata* more than half a metre long, the longest being 1.625 m (NHC II, roll 2, *kollēma* 1; Robinson [J.] 1984, 66–70).

The simplest procedure for the maker of a papyrus codex to follow was to begin at one end of a roll and to cut it into sheets (usually from the right-hand end of the roll, working leftward to the beginning), placing each newly cut sheet on top of the growing stack of what would become bifolia for his codex. Assuming that the roll had been laid out for cutting in its usual disposition for reading, the sheets in the resulting stack would have horizontal (→) papyrus fibres facing upward, and any *kollēseis* would 'step down' from left to right. When one roll had been cut up, the manufacturer would continue with a second roll, and so on, until he had a sufficient number of sheets for his purpose. If the final sheet cut from a roll was narrower than half the width of a full-size sheet, then it could not properly be used in the codex; but as long as it was at least a centimetre or so wider than half the width of a full-size sheet, then it could be used in the codex as a leaf with a stub as its conjugate (a stubbed singleton). It is possible that the codex manufacturer sometimes trimmed off one or more *kollēseis* and discarded them, as he might also have done with a *prōtokollon*, i.e. the first *kollēma* of a roll, which was typically attached so that its vertical (↓) fibres faced upward, rather than having → fibres facing upward as in the rest of the roll. It is not always the case that each roll used to make a codex was treated in exactly the same way, there being room here for a number of variations in detail.

Even among just the thirteen NHC and the *Berolinensis Gnosticus* (Berlin, Staatsbibliothek, *P.Berol.* 8502; BG), a codex similar to the NHC, there is variation. NHC XIII was made in such a way that it was the rolls' height that determined the width of the bifolia (*c.*270 mm), rather than the height of the roll determining the height of the codex, as is much more usually the case; this unusual feature is evidenced by the occurrence of a *kollēseis* running horizontally across a bifolium, rather than vertically as one usually expects (Robinson [J.] 1984, 48–49). In several other codices there is evidence that the manufacturer varied his procedure of cutting and stacking the bifolia in other ways (Robinson [J.] 1979, 36–37). Five stubs survive in the NHC and BG, and eight more must be postulated even though they are not extant (Robinson [J.] 1978, 25–26; 1984, 41–44); but the manufacturers of these codices must sometimes have discarded remaining ends of rolls that were not wide enough either to form complete bifolia or to be used as stubbed singletons. The NHC also include several examples of the use of a *prōtokollon* in the making of a quire (Robinson [J.] 1978, 25). In NHC VII, the bottom sheet (which was cut from roll 1) was used not as the outer bifolium of the quire, but as a paste-down covering both left and right boards (but possibly not running continuously across the area where the spine met the cover's back; see Robinson et al. 1972, pl. 3; Robinson [J.] 1984, 42; 1978, 52). The maker of yet another early Coptic papyrus codex (containing *Proverbs* in the Akhmimic dialect) cut his rolls in half horizontally in addition to cutting them into sheets as usual, and in this same codex the bottom four sheets in the original stack were used for the upper layers of the laminate boards in the binding and for the paste-down (Robinson [J.] 1978, 35). For an example of a Coptic papyrus codex in which the bifolia cut from the rolls were made into multiple quires (quinions and senions) in a seemingly random order, see Emmel 2003, 92–95.

The number of leaves in the ten NHC that are certainly single-quire codices and are also well preserved, plus BG, varies between 37 (NHC XI, including one stubbed singleton) and 78 (NHC III, including two stubbed singletons), the average being *c.*50 leaves. NHC I has 72 leaves (36 bifolia), grouped in three quires of 22, 8, and 6 bifolia, respectively; thus it is not a multi-quire codex in the normal sense, but is rather to be described as a single-quire codex of 44 leaves that was extended during writing by the addition of an octonion and senion, both written by the same copyist as wrote most of the first quire (except for seven pages in its middle) and containing the continuation and end of a single work that begins three-fifths of the way into the first quire (Robinson [J.] 1984, 39–40). A much more normal multi-quire codex in Coptic, the 'Manichaean Psalm Book' in the Chester Beatty Library (Dublin), has been said to be the longest surviving papyrus codex in any language, with its 28 senions comprising 672 pages (Richter 1998, 2).

In height, the NHC vary between 237 and 303 mm; in such thick quires as occur in most of the NHC, there can be a considerable difference between the dimensions of the leaves at the outside of the quire and those at the centre, up to as much as 30 mm (Robinson [J.] 1984, 55). Measured at the outsides of the quires, the dimensions of the leaves of the codices vary from 242 × 147 mm (NHC VIII) to 303 × 140 mm (NHC I, quire 1) and from 260 × 122 mm (NHC X) to 292 × 175 mm (NHC VII), with proportions varying between 0.46 and 0.62; BG is both smaller (135 × 108 mm) and more nearly square (proportion 0.8) than any of the NHC. Another early papyrus codex of about the same height is slightly oblong: 147 × 159 mm, proportion 1.08 (Robinson [J.] 1990b, xliii–xliv). One of the largest Coptic papyrus codices on record is 365 × 265 mm (Thompson 1908, v–vi; proportion 0.73). Truly oblong papyrus codices are not known to survive (one Greek papyrus has perhaps a proportion of 1.32; Turner 1977, no. 28).

In contrast to what is known about the manufacture of papyrus codices, we know of no investigations into the precise methods of making quires out of parchment or paper (to our knowledge, quires of mixed materials have not been noticed in Coptic codices). What can be said here is that quires were usually formed by superposed bifolia, although in parchment codices there are examples of coupled leaves (seemingly rare) and also stubbed singletons. The dimensions of parchment quires vary considerably, from very small—for example: 56 × 84 mm, 58 × 90 mm, 64 × 70 mm, 66 × 75 mm (Worrell 1923, xii; if these measurements are height × width, as the descriptions seem to imply, then these small-size codices are all somewhat on the oblong side of square; for exactly square small-size codices, for example 73 × 70 mm and 85 × 84 mm, respectively, see Crum 1905b, 394 no. 947, and Emmel 1990, 24–27, pl. 3)—to very large, for example: 445 × 337 mm (Crum 1905b, 24 no. 112, the abovementioned 'saffron Gospels'). A more normal range of sizes can be seen in a group of forty-seven parchment codices from the ninth and early tenth centuries, for the most part well preserved, part of the liturgical collection of the Monastery of St Michael the Archangel in the Fayyum region, south-west of Cairo (Depuydt 1993, lxiii etc.; cf. Emmel 2005): from 387 × 303 mm down to 280 × 218 mm (Depuydt 1993, nos. 13 and 59), the extreme proportions being 0.67 and 0.89 (338 × 228 mm (no. 166) and 341 × 302 mm (no. 65)), the average dimensions being 343 × 246 mm (proportion 0.72), and the average proportion being 0.78 (which just happens to be also the average of the two extreme proportions, as well as the proportion of the average dimensions of the two extreme sizes). Roughly contemporary parchment codices from Upper (southern) Egypt show a somewhat greater range of sizes (but here we do not yet have anything like a full collection of data upon which to draw), from 389 × 297 mm (Cairo, Institut français d'archéologie orientale, Copte inv. 189 = White Monastery codex XL 260/261; Young 2001, 190, gives the dimensions of a slightly smaller leaf from this codex, 380 × 290 mm) down to 261 × 211 mm (Naples, Biblioteca Nazionale 'Vittorio Emanuele III', Sezione Manoscritti e Rari, IB 11 f. 24 = White Monastery codex XE 63/64; Buzi 2009, 239, gives the dimensions of a smaller leaf from this codex, 250 × 190 mm). The length of parchment codices also varies considerably. For the upper range we may state that the very large White Monastery codex XL was certainly 400 and another codex from the same monastery certainly 552 pages long (Emmel 2004, 116 and 147), while an eminent cataloguer of Coptic manuscripts early in the twentieth century reported having noted 'eight leaves or groups of leaves reaching to a page-number above 400, as many to above 500, three to above 700, one to above 900' (Crum 1905b, xi).

The investigation of Coptic quires made from paper has scarcely begun; but see Zanetti 1986a (especially concerning watermarked paper originating from Venice), and Zanetti 1998 (paper manuscripts in one of Egypt's most prominent monasteries from Late Antiquity to the present), both with reference to Zanetti 1986b (catalogue of manuscripts, all but one being paper, in the Monastery of Makarios in Wādī al-Naṭrūn/Scetis); Layton 1987, esp. pp. lix–lxiii and 424–425 (concerning both European and oriental papers); Boud'hors 1999a (a survey of selected dated paper codices from the tenth to fourteenth centuries).

5.3.2. The composition of the quires (SE)

The result of the simple procedure described above for cutting up a papyrus roll to make a codex would be a stack of sheets that, if folded in half all together, would become the bifolia of a single-quire codex of twice as many leaves as cut sheets (unless there were any stubbed singletons), with one of two possible dispositions, depending on whether the quire was folded with the → fibres on the inside, or with the ↓ fibres on the inside. In the former case, the sequence of papyrus surfaces at each opening, up to the centre of the quire, is →↓, with →→ at the centre of the quire, and then ↓→ through the second half of the quire. In the latter case the openings will be ↓→ at first, ↓↓ at the centre of the quire, and then →↓ to the end of the codex. Of course the maker of the codex might alter this disposition, whether by design or by accident, a purposeful alternative disposition being to have like fibre directions facing like, whether ↓→↓→ and so on, or →↓→↓ and so on (notation is fibre direction of rectos only).

The codex referred to above with its bifolia occurring in a random order in relation to their original order as cut from papyrus rolls is a multi-quire codex in the normal sense, assignable with reasonable confidence to around the middle of the fourth century. The first thirteen quires survive (apart from twenty-nine missing leaves, dispersed among six of the quires), and these are: 2 senions, 1 quinion, 2 senions, 8 quinions (how many quires are lost after quire 13 cannot be determined at present). The disposition of papyrus surfaces in each quire is uniformly →→→ and so on, except that in quire 8 there is a false succession at the second bifolium: →↓→→→ (see further Emmel 2003). Similar irregularities—both divergent quires and false successions—are found elsewhere in Coptic papyrus codices. But at present, it is not yet possible to make generalized statements about the phenomenon. We should add, however, that some Late Antique Coptic papyrus codices survive that seem to show careful and consistent workmanship in their quire structures, such as a collection of seven Coptic Manichaean codices thought to belong to the fourth or fifth century. Despite the poor condition in which they survive, it seems clear that each codex is a multi-quire codex, some consisting either of quaternions or of senions, the disposition of all the quires being like facing like, with ↓ fibres on the outside and on the inside of each quire. In none of these codices has even a single kollesis been observed, which suggests that either the maker of the codices took care to cut the bifolia from rolls in such a way as to avoid using any sections with kollēseis, or else he used papyrus sheets that had never been pasted together into rolls to begin with (Funk 1990, esp. 530–533; Wurst 1996, 5–6).

Normally, Coptic parchment codices consist of quaternions formed according to Gregory's Rule, with the typical disposition of flesh and hair sides being FHFH. But here too there are occasional false successions—for example, FHHH in quire 24 of a small-size codex (*c.*120 × 105 mm) thought to be from the fifth century—as well as divergent quires—for example, after 29 quaternions in the same codex, a final ternion (Schenke 1981, 9); and there are also irregular quires, for example, in a series of nineteen normal Gregorian quaternions in a codex from around the end of the first millennium,

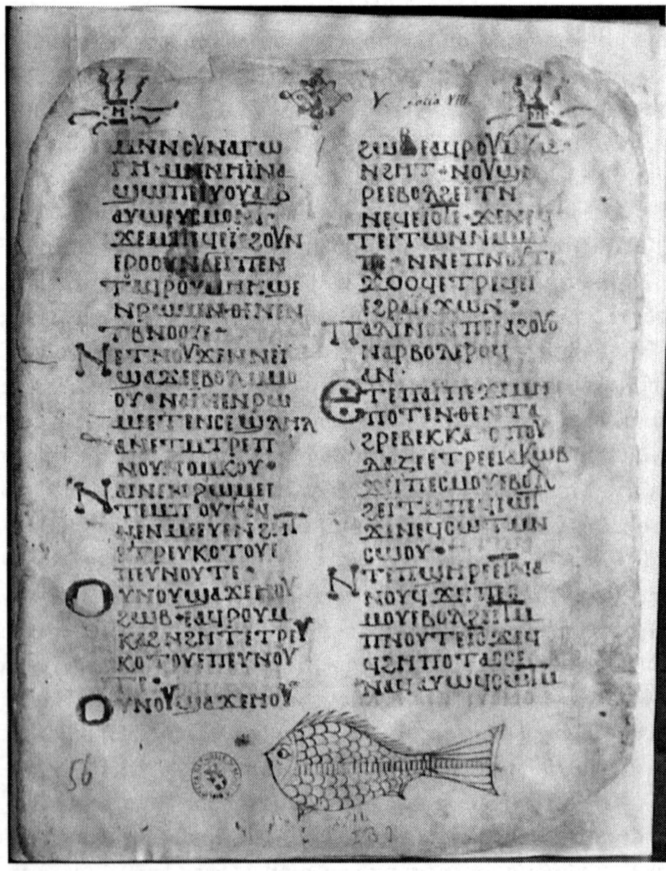

Fig. 1.5.2 Naples, Biblioteca Nazionale Vittorio Emanuele III, IB 3, tenth/eleventh century, f. 56r, Shenoute, *Logos* 5.

quire 16 is an enlarged unit with disposition FH,FHF^HFH,H^FHFH, the result of repairing an omission in the text, not necessarily much later than the original making of the codex: leaves 3–8 are a replacement for original leaf 3, leaves 9^10 are the original central bifolium (originally 4^5), and leaf 11 became a singleton, most likely stubbed (Emmel 2004, 207–208; Boud'hors 2013, 9–12; due to modern trimming and rebinding, it can no longer be determined just how leaves 3–8 were joined surgically to the rest of the quire).

Coptic paper codices divide typologically into two groups. The significantly smaller number of older extant paper codices in the Upper Egyptian ('Sahidic' or southern) dialect of Coptic (fig. 1.5.2) are typically made of quaternions, whereas later codices, the vast majority of which are in the Lower Egyptian ('Bohairic' or northern) dialect, are typically made of quinions. We know of no systematic studies, but for a representative sample see Layton 1987, nos. 120, 160, 161, 163 (Sahidic), and nos. 194–210, 216, 219–221, 226–231, 233–236, 244, 251, 253–255 (Bohairic). Among the four Sahidic codices, there are several divergent senions and quinions. Divergent quires in the Bohairic codices occur, with some exceptions, only at the end of a book (see also Khouzam 1999, 134 and Table 3); for a Sahidic paper codex from the end of the fourteenth century made of quinions, see Hebbelynck 1900–1901.

5.3.3. Pricking and ruling (SE)

Pricking and ruling is found in many Coptic parchment codices. A systematic study of ruling patterns in Coptic manuscripts remains a desideratum, but according to presently available observations, the range of ruling types employed is quite limited. By far the most frequent seem to be Leroy ([Julien] 1976) types 00A2 and V 00A2 (= Muzerelle (1999) types 1-1-11/0/0/A and 1-1-11/0/1-1/0), while for single-column codices (which are on the whole less common than two-column codices) we find types 00A1 and V 00A1 (= 1-1/0/0/A and 1-1/0/1-1/0), with other types occurring relatively rarely; Leroy's X-types X 00A1 (= 1-1/0/0/A-0), X 00A2 (= 1-1-11/0/0/A-0) etc. occur (Layton 1987, 426; Depuydt 1993, *passim*; Emmel 2004, 105–107), as do codices that appear to be without any ruling at all. Pricking for individual horizontal lines occurs typically in the outer margins, but sometimes between the columns (sometimes with variation within a single codex). What we usually find is dry-point blind ruling applied on the flesh side. The fact that such ruling is often faint and difficult to discern might be a symptom of occurrences of transmitted ruling (see fig. 1.5.3 for clear pricking and discernible dry-point ruling). But for the most part, we know next to nothing about the techniques employed. Examples of plummet or coloured ruling do occur (the latter occasionally also on papyrus), as well as the sporadic use of inked points along the left margin (for example, Emmel 2004, 326; also known from some Greek papyrus rolls, see Johnson 1993, and codices, see Emmel 1996, 291–292). Even where a ruling pattern includes text lines, it is not uncommon that the scribe did not pay very close attention to them, thus suggesting that the ruling was done by someone else.

Ruling in Coptic paper codices was typically achieved by means of a ruling board (Layton 1987, lxi). The usual pattern is four bounding lines for one wide column flanked by two narrower columns. This pattern was needed for bilingual Coptic-Arabic codices, wherein the Coptic text occupies the first two columns—covering them both with a single wide column of text—with the narrow third column reserved for the more compact Arabic text.

5.3.4. Ordering systems (SE)

From the beginning, Coptic codices were typically paginated, with foliation becoming typical from the later mediaeval period onward. Both types of numbering normally occur in the top margin (fig. 1.5.2). When pagination occurs, it is either approximately centred, or else it stands at or in the outer margin, the marginal position being more frequent, especially in mediaeval parchment codices. Sometimes pagination starts over again one or more times in a codex, occasionally whenever a new work begins. Quire signatures are attested as early as the fourth century and normally occur at the top inner margin on the first and last pages of each quire (for example, Layton 1987, 4 (the fourth-century papyrus codex already mentioned several times; cf. Emmel 2003); Schenke 1981, 9–10, and Schenke 1991, 17 (two parchment codices, possibly fifth-century)). In addition to decoration of the page numbers and signatures themselves, it is not uncommon to find decorative ornaments centred between the two numbers on the first and last pages of a quire, sometimes accompanied by abbreviated pious phrases such as 'Jesus Christ' or 'Son of

God'; such ornamentation sometimes occurs also on pages within a quire (for example, Depuydt 1993, pls 299, 305, 308, 316, 324, 325, 366, 435; Boud'hors 2004, nos. 19, 28). Especially in mediaeval parchment codices, errors in the pagination are rather frequent, whereas the numbering of the quires tends to be more accurate.

Foliation is typical only of late mediaeval and early modern codices, where leaf numbers are usually found only on the versos (which are recto from the point of view of someone used to reading Arabic books; or perhaps the system was meant to number openings rather than leaves). In such codices, a signature may appear twice on the first page of a quire, or else the leaf number may be written both there and on the verso, either way making the appearance of an opening between quires symmetrical because on the left-hand pages of such openings both the leaf number and the signature occur (cf. Zanetti 1998, 176–179). In the Monastery of Makarios in Wādī al-Naṭrūn around the end of the first millennium, the practice seems to have been to paginate codices (of parchment), but to express the pagination only on the versos and on the first page of each quire; this system is found also in at least one parchment codex from the White Monastery in southern Egypt, but most probably originating in the Fayyum, and dating probably from about the same time as the parchment codices from the Monastery of Makarios (Boud'hors 2011, 107 and 108–110).

Catchwords too are a relatively late phenomenon in Coptic codices. Frequently they occur in bilingual codices, in which case they may be in Coptic or Arabic or both (for example, Layton 1987, nos. 193–199, 227, 234–237); sometimes the catchword is just a single letter (Layton 1987, nos. 228, 235). Running titles are rare but do occur in biblical codices (for example, Depuydt 1993, nos. 14 (Gospels), 34–36 (Pauline Epistles), pls 416–417 (a papyrus codex), etc.; Bosson – Aufrère 1999, 221; Boud'hors 2004, nos. 1, 6, 11).

5.3.5. The codex as a complex object (PB)

As far as one can judge despite the generally fragmentary condition of Coptic manuscripts, many were monomerous homogeneous miscellanies (terminology of Gumbert 2004), i.e. each is a single codicological unit containing multiple texts whose boundaries do not coincide with quire boundaries (except at beginning and end, or else only by chance). In most cases, such codices are either monogenetic or homogenetic and were planned from the outset to be miscellanies. Armando Petrucci, listing the first miscellaneous manuscripts of oriental Christianity, has suggested that it is very likely that the miscellaneous codex was an Egyptian creation (Petrucci 2005), possibly born in the schools (Petrucci 1986a, 179–180); one should note that most of the earliest examples of such codices from Christian Egypt belong to a context of cultural continuity between Greek and Coptic milieux. While uniform codices do occur among what are thought to be the earliest Coptic manuscripts, a number of others are miscellanies: for example, a bilingual papyrus codex assignable to around the turn of the third century that contains the *Acta Pauli* in Greek, the Song of Songs and Lamentations of Jeremiah in Coptic, and Ecclesiastes in both Greek and Coptic (Schmidt [C.] – Schubart 1936; Diebner – Kasser 1989); or another papyrus codex perhaps of about the same age, or somewhat younger, containing (all in Coptic) Melito of Sardis *On the Pascha*, 2 Maccabees 5:27–7:41, 1 Peter, Jonah, and an unidentified homily (Goehring 1990; Pietersma – Comstock 2011); or the fourth-century papyrus codex containing Deuteronomy, Jonah, Acts, and the *Apocalypse of Elijah* (Budge 1912; Emmel 2003); also, most of the Coptic Gnostic codices certainly contain two texts or more, with NHC VI containing eight texts (whereas the Coptic Manichaean codices are for the most part uniform; cf. Richter 2005).

If at the beginning of the Coptic tradition the miscellaneous codex appears to us to be a somewhat haphazard article, by the mediaeval period multi-text parchment codices seem to have become more or less normalized. Probably this change was, at least in part, the result of the Copts systematizing and codifying their literature for liturgical purposes several centuries after the Arab Conquest of Egypt in the mid-seventh century (Orlandi [T.] 1991, 1458–1459). That this was so is suggested by the evidence of the bulk of the surviving mediaeval manuscripts, for example the forty-seven well preserved codices that remain from the library of the Monastery of St Michael, mentioned above. Twenty-four of these codices are non-biblical miscellanies, about half of them with 'contents that are liturgically relevant to a single saint or day', while 'in most other cases, the works ... occur in chronological sequence according to the days on which they were to be read' (Emmel 2005, 65; cf. Depuydt 1993, lxiv); the number of texts in a codex ranges from two to ten (with four being about average). A similar case is a group of eighteen papyrus codices (some quite fragmentary) that have been assigned to about the turn of the eighth century: here too, half of the codices are miscellanies (from two to six works), although in this case the rationales behind the choice of texts remain to be discerned (Orlandi [T.] 1974; for the assigned date, see Orlandi [T.] 1995, 134).

In a sample of 171 reconstructed mediaeval parchment codices from the White Monastery—excluding biblical codices and codices with apocrypha or works of the monastery's most prolific leader, Shenoute—47 are miscellanies containing works belonging to different authors and dedicated to different and apparently unrelated subjects; these volumes contain up to seventeen works, but with four works per codex again being the average (if we were to include codices with works of a single author or pertaining to but a single subject, the number of miscellanies would be even more conspicuous). The White Monastery may have been the only Coptic library that included volumes of florilegia, a special type of miscellany (Buzi 2011a), whose relationship to liturgical lectionaries remains to be explored (cf. Emmel 2004, 116–125, on the 'Florilegium Sinuthianum', and 361–379, on lectionaries containing extracts only, or almost only, from works of Shenoute, see also fig. 1.5.2).

In modern collections of Coptic manuscripts, many items were re-bound in the form of miscellanies combining originally independent codicological units, whether in whole or in part: i.e. they are now composite codices (for example, most of the codices from the Monastery of Makarios now in the Biblioteca Apostolica Vaticana (cf. Funk 2012, 49–50), or the bulk of the leaves and fragments from the White Monastery now in Paris, Bibliothèque nationale de France (cf. Lucchesi 1981, 9–11), etc.). Coptic composite codices from the pre-modern period seem to be rare and in any case have seldom been the subject of specific studies (but see Proverbio 2012a; Nagel 1994 argued that the fourth-century papyrus codex containing Deuteronomy etc. is an ancient composite, but see Emmel 2003 for a counter-argument).

5.4. The layout of the page (PB)

By and large, Coptic codices are laid out in either one or two columns (see figs. 1.5.1, 1.5.2, 1.5.3), with three or more columns occurring only rarely: for example, Boud'hors 2004, no. 25, a Coptic-Greek lectionary; Coptic occupies the third of five columns in the pentaglot Barberini Psalter (Vatican City, BAV, Barb. gr. 372), on which see Proverbio 2012a. In Coptic-Arabic bilinguals, as mentioned above, Coptic occupies a first wide column, Arabic a second narrow column; occasionally two such pairs of columns occur on one page (for example, Boud'hors 2004, no. 3 = Gabra 2014, 104).

5.5. Text structure and readability (PB)

5.5.1. Writing

From the beginning, Coptic scribal practice was modelled on Greek practice, including the repertoires of punctuation marks, abbreviations (Christian *nomina sacra*), devices for adjusting the length of a line, means of paragraphing, and so on. Apart from adding native Egyptian letters to the Greek alphabet, the only innovation was the use of a sign (normally either a horizontal 'superlinear stroke' or a dot (*jinkim* '(way of) movement')) to mark any syllable containing no vowel, a type of syllable that is frequent in Coptic. Punctuation serves to delimit paragraphs, sentences, clauses, phrases and sometimes also words (mostly in the sense of a 'phonological word'), without there necessarily being a clear correlation between the form of a mark and its function. Space is sometimes used for separating units of text, or dividing 'words' (again mostly in the sense of phonological words, or prosodic units). Lines containing a quotation from the Bible may be marked by a sign (typically a *diplē*) to the left of each line. All punctuation occurs for the most part more or less sporadically and inconsistently, presumably depending on the competence of the individual scribes (and their supervisors); while correct punctuation must surely have been a help to reading, clearly it was not regarded as being essential, for there are manuscripts with almost no punctuation at all, as well as manuscripts with a bewildering chaos of marks that seem to have become merely decorative.

Apart from the occasional occurrence of headings and titles (whether superscript or subscript) at boundaries between texts or parts of texts, the main structural feature of a typical Coptic parchment codex page is paragraph division marked by means of a line-initial letter standing in or projecting into the margin, often enlarged and sometimes decorated and/or accompanied by a *paragraphos* or some other free-standing element (figs. 1.5.2, 1.5.3). The real beginning of the paragraph might occur in the middle of the line before the ekthetic line. Especially in mediaeval parchment codices, a single page may display a large number of paragraphs, which do not always divide the text in a way that seems meaningful to us, probably an interest in decorativeness being rather the main motivation. In contrast, the pages of papyrus codices, as well as of early parchment codices, are typically quite plain.

An analysis of the extension and structure of titles in Coptic manuscripts has resulted in the following typology: (1) subject titles; (2) simple structure titles; (3) simple extended structure titles; (4) complex structure titles; and (5) complex extended structure titles (Buzi 2005). Particularly characteristic of Coptic manuscripts, especially in the earlier mediaeval period, are types 3–5, normally placed at the beginning of a work, often framed by decoration and written in a script different from the following text (often right-sloping). Starting from the eighth century through to the end of the ninth, titles become progressively longer, and often their content does not fully correspond to the contents of the work to which they apply. Clearly the function of such extended and complex titles was different from the earlier, shorter types of titles and was not simply to indicate the contents of the following work. The people responsible for these very specific and targeted types of titles were the same ones who undertook to rearrange Coptic literature in new combinations, often collecting them into multi-text codices, for the liturgical purposes of the Coptic Church. Tables of contents sometimes occur, at the end of a codex, but rarely (for example, Emmel 2004, 247–249, 296–297).

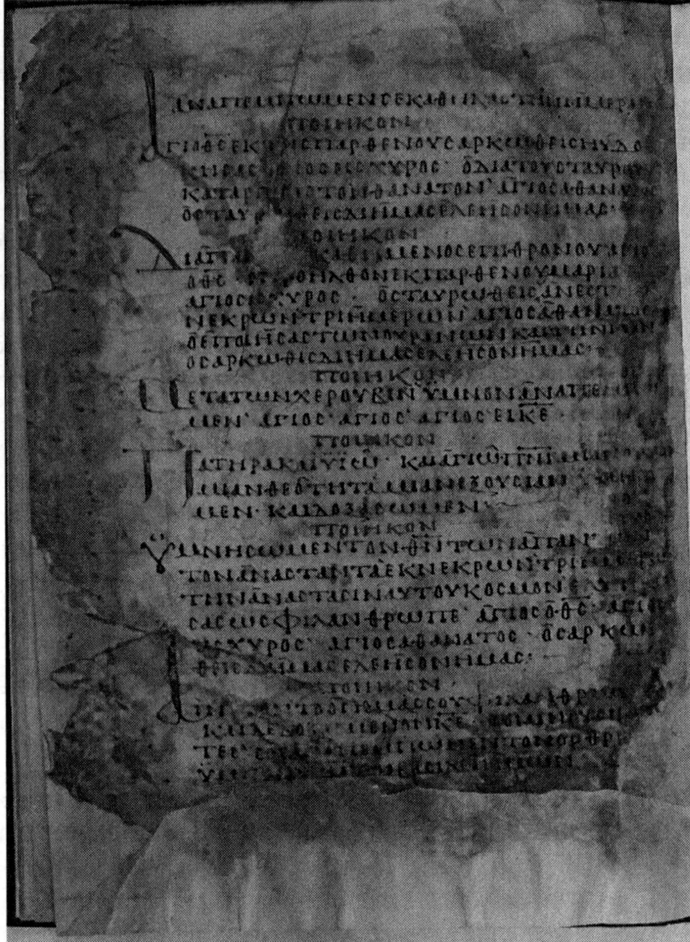

Fig. 1.5.3 Berlin, Staatsbibliothek, MS or. fol. 1609, tenth/eleventh century, f. 6v, *Canon Athanasii*.

5.5.2. Decoration

Decoration in Coptic manuscripts is limited almost entirely to parchment and paper codices, particularly from the mediaeval period and later. Apart from a relatively small number of elaborately illustrated or illuminated manuscripts, the most striking decorative features are frontispieces and miniatures, headpieces (sometimes also tailpieces), decorated initial letters and accompanying ornamented attention marks in the margins, such as *obeloi*, *diplai*, *paragraphoi*, and *coronides*, as well as quire ornaments and decoration added to page numbers and signatures. Within the text, there is sometimes colour (usually red) added to selected letters and punctuation marks, and full stops were eventually turned into small decorative elements on their own (for example Boud'hors 2004, 55; Whitfield et al. 2010, 46–47; Gabra 2014, 157). In liturgical manuscripts, rubricized text and complex layout were used to articulate the contents functionally (for example Gabra 2014, 85). In the top margin of a page at the beginning or end of a quire, the space between the embellished page number and quire signature might be filled with an elaborate ornament—formed as a rectangle, rosette or cross, filled with multi-coloured interlace or some other pattern—flanked by pious phrases (for example, Buzi – Proverbio 2012, 157–160; Boud'hors 2004, 49, 56).

But it was especially in the side and bottom margins and between columns that Coptic decorators often displayed their skills, giving free rein to their fancy. *Obeloi*, *diplai*, and *paragraphoi* might be simply highlighted with red, but they could also be stylized and transformed into intricate ornaments composed of buds, nodes, twigs, rosettes, small birds, etc. (Petersen 1954a). Especially the *coronis* came to be enlarged, extended and decorated to extremes, making the margins of many Coptic books, especially when the ini-

Fig. 1.5.4 Naples, Biblioteca Nazionale Vittorio Emanuele III, IB.16, *c.* tenth century, f. 4v.

tials too are elaborately decorated, a playground of spirals, nodes, curving and curling strokes, overgrown with vegetal, zoomorphic and anthropomorphic elements. In a typical composition, the swirls of stylized leaves extend into the lower margin, where they end with a bird or an animal nibbling at the tip of a final scroll (for example von Falck et al. 1996, 230; Boud'hors 2000, 27; Depuydt 1993, pls. 53, 64, 71, 75, 77, etc.; for some strikingly decorated initials, Boud'hors 2004, 11, 25, 34–38, 45, 49, 54–59; Bosson – Aufrère 1999, 162; Whitfield et al. 2010, 45, 160, 164, 173, 183; Gabra 2014, 157). These fanciful compositions are so various and often so individual that they defy any effort to typologize them.

Figural decoration of this sort was never abandoned by the Copts, whose tradition had much in common with the work of Byzantine book decorators, but they enriched their repertoire of motifs with aniconic and geometrical designs, especially in bilingual Coptic-Arabic manuscripts, partly inspired by exposure to the developing art of Islamic book decoration (a particularly striking example: Gabra 2014, 58–59). This mingling of traditions is observable, for instance, in the various forms of panels, bands, and frames that one finds surrounding or accompanying titles (headpieces): in common with the Byzantine tradition, we find open frames of the *Pi*-type, whether upright or turned sideways (usually open to the right), and the inverted-L- or *Gamma*-type, while in common with the Arabic tradition, we find closed rectangular frames and architectural motifs; all types of panels, bands, and borders were filled with interlaces and other designs, sometimes encompassing small crosses and floral and zoomorphic motifs, all presented in vivid colours (a large set of examples of all types, but reproduced in black and white: Depuydt 1993, pls. 48–198; in colour: Buzi – Proverbio 2012, 64, 70, 103, 105, 160; Whitfield et al. 2010, 157, 165, 173, 182–183; Boud'hors 2004, 39, 42–43, 58, 59; von Falck et al. 1996, 240). The repertoire of ornaments was further enriched by typical Islamic motifs: chained stars, intersecting circles and eight-petalled rosettes. In *de luxe* codices, the headings may also contain a miniature placed at the top of the page, directly above the other decorations, sometimes replacing the patterned rectangle.

The oldest surviving example of a decorated manuscript is the fifth- or sixth-century Codex Glazier (New York, Pierpont Morgan Library and Museum, G67), with a full-page miniature representing an interlaced ankh-cross (*crux ansata*), flanked by two peacocks and surmounted by three smaller birds (doves? sparrows?), on the recto of the penultimate leaf of the book (f. 110r = quire 14 leaf 6r; Bober 1967; Schenke 1991, 23–24, pl. 18; Depuydt 1993, 482, pl. 463); elsewhere in the codex, the only decoration is red ink (now reddish orange) used for *paragraphoi/coronides*, certain punctuation marks, and *diplai*, dashes, and other small signs surrounding page numbers and signatures (Schenke 1991, 24, 41–45, pls. 11, 12, 15; Depuydt 1993, pls. 461–463; for more on the similar Codex Scheide, Schenke 1981, 20–23).

Full-page ornamental crosses became and remained a feature of Coptic manuscript decoration, typically as frontispieces, although not necessarily as the initial frontispiece, but rather on the verso facing the first page of text, which is often highly decorated itself (for example Gabra 2014, 58–59; Buzi – Proverbio 2012, 102; Whitfield et al. 2010, 45; Boud'hors 2004, 33, 43, 47, 58; von Falck et al. 1996, 233; Depuydt 1993, pls. 24–44). Elsewhere we find iconic frontispieces such as representations of *Maria lactans* (von Falck et al. 1996, 250, 252; Depuydt 1993, pls. 10–23). In some extraordinary manuscripts, miniatures were used to illustrate the text. Most famous is a *de luxe* Tetraevangelium copied in Damietta in 1178–1180, now in Paris (BnF, Copte 13; one leaf in Washington, Freer Gallery of Art). It is decorated with full-page, iconic pictures gathered at the beginning of the volume and seventy-four miniatures dispersed throughout. Unframed, the miniatures are inserted tightly in mid-page, occupying the full width of the written area (see Boud'hors 2004, no. 12 and p. 18; Rutschowscaya et al. 2000, 50, 52, 78–79; Leroy [Jules] 1974, 113–148, pls. C, D, 41–74). A richly illustrated bilingual Coptic-Arabic Gospel manuscript from 1249/1250 is also in Paris (Institut catholique, Copte 1), containing eighteen miniatures: four portraits of the evangelists, four heading miniatures, and eleven full-page miniatures containing six scenes each. The portraits and the headings are placed on facing pages and function as double-page frontispieces for the respective Gospels. The six-part compositions also occur at openings, paired with headings and depicting events from the texts that they introduce or divide (cf. von Falck et al. 1996, 237–239). A mixture of indigenous and European-style Gospel illustration (London, BL, Or. 1316) is an early-eighteenth-century manuscript decorated with 130 miniatures, partly copied from the engravings of the *Evangelium arabicum* printed in 1590 (cf. von Falck et al. 1996, 242–245).

For a list of noteworthy illuminated Coptic manuscripts up to the fifteenth century, see Buchthal – Kurz 1942, 28–62 nos. 86–309 (note pp. 5 and 6 n. 2), and for a selection of reproductions (not all in colour) of Coptic manuscript decoration of all kinds, see Cramer 1964a; Leroy [Jules] 1974; Depuydt 1993, pls. 10–330; von Falck et al. 1996, 230–253; Bosson – Aufrère 1999, 161–163; Rutschowscaya et al. 2000, 50–89; Atalla 2000; Boud'hors 2004; Gabra – Eaton-Krauss 2006, 118–133; Whitfield et al. 2010.

5.6. The scribe, the painter and the illuminator at work (SE–PB)

5.6.1. Persons, places and methods (PB)

Hagiographical works often refer to book-copying among the productive activities of monks, and although nothing authorizes us to think that all the monasteries had a scribe, it is reasonable to think that the most important ones had a more or less organized scriptorium. But the existing evidence suggests that Coptic scribes—called *kaliographos* or *syngraphos*, mostly men, but also some women—worked either alone or in small groups, whether within a monastery or in a semi-eremitic community such as the one in western Thebes in the early mediaeval period (see, for example, Kotsifou 2007; Heurtel 2007; Maravela-Solbakk 2008; Boud'hors 2008; Kotsifou 2011; on early mediaeval scribal activity in Tuton, a town in the Fayyum region, see Coquin 1991; Depuydt 1993, cxii–cxvi). A number of documents, both in Greek and in Coptic show clearly that painted decoration (as also bookbinding) was usually done by a specialist and not by the copyist of the manuscript. A kind of 'archaeological' confirmation of this practice are occasional pages on which the outlined design for a decoration, clearly meant to be coloured in (if not necessarily also illuminated), remained bare of any colour: for example, Froschauer – Römer 2008, 153 (on other pages of this mediaeval parchment codex, less elaborate marginal decoration was duly coloured in, cf. Emmel 2004, 129–130).

5.6.2. Colophons (PB)

Dated colophons as usually recognized do not appear in Coptic manuscripts before the early mediaeval period; the (limited) corpus that has been collected systematically and studied has dates from the eighth to eleventh centuries (van Lantschoot 1929). The elements that normally compose a Coptic colophon—inserted in different combinations and sequences—are: (1) name of the donor; (2) recipient of the donation (or name of the possessor); (3) name of the scribe; (4) formulas of blessing and protection (sometimes cryptographic); (5) date of the copying. Some codices have more than one colophon, for example as a result of a change in ownership, while others from the same period have none. When a colophon does occur, normally at the end of the codex (for a colophon at the bottom of a column between two works in the middle of a codex, see Coquin 2001, 4, pl. 1), it may be either in a single column, even when the end of the preceding text is in two columns, or (more rarely) at the end of the second column. Sometimes colophons are subdivided into sections by lines.

5.6.3. Dating systems (SE)

Precisely dated Coptic manuscripts do not appear until early in the ninth century, by which time colophons had come into use (van Lantschoot 1929, I/2, p. 93; cf. Depuydt 1993, l–lii). The most common system for specifying a year was according to the 'Era of the Martyrs' (*anno Martyrum*, AM), which had started out in the fourth century as a continuation of counting by regnal years of the Roman emperor Diocletian (284–305) even after his abdication; sometimes the year was also specified by its 'indiction' number, a recurring cycle of fifteen years counted from 312/313 (or 297/298). When a day is specified, normally it is according to the Egyptian calendar of twelve months of thirty days each, with a 'little month' of five days at the end of the year, plus a sixth, intercalated day every fourth year, which was thus a leap year. The first day of the first Egyptian month, called Thōth, was the same as 29 August in the Julian calendar, or 30 August in an Egyptian leap year (in which case the Julian year beginning four months later will be a leap year). Thus a year AM corresponds to the last four months of one Julian year and the first eight months of the following Julian year (for example AM 532 = 815/816 CE). The Copts have never reformed their calendar, so that the calendrical correspondence changed after the Gregorian reform of the Julian calendar in 1582 and continues to change: the Coptic year 1730 began on 11 September 2013. See above all Bagnall – Worp 2004; concisely but clearly, Cody 1991.

Sometimes the Coptic dating is accompanied, or replaced, by a date according to the Islamic system *anno Hegirae*, which became current in Egypt after the seventh century. More rarely, we find years given according to the Alexandrian 'Era of the World', according to which AM 1 (= 284/285 CE) = year 5777 of the Alexandrian Era of the World.

5.7. Bookbinding (SE)

The earliest surviving Coptic bookbindings, primarily those of most of the NHC from around the end of the fourth century, are well enough preserved for it to be possible to describe them in detail (Robinson [J.] 1975, whence are taken quotations and data; Robinson [J.] 1984, 71–86; instructive drawings in Greenfield 1991, Szirmai 1999, 7–14; for photographs, see: Robinson [J.] 1984, frontispiece; Gabra – Eaton-Krauss 2006, 134–135; Gabra 2014, 94). The covers differ from one another in a number of details (but can be sorted typologically into at least four groups: Robinson [J.] 1984, 80–86). As a general characterization, the spine of each single-quire papyrus codex was attached to the back of a slim leather case (both goat- and sheepskin were used, hair side for the outer surfaces of the binding) by means of two sewing tackets with round leather cord (perhaps flax string in one case). The two ends of each such tacket were knotted either at the centre of the quire, or outside the quire. If the latter, either they were tied at the outside of the cover's back, or at the outside of a strip of leather that was laid against the spine of the quire and then used as a lining along the inside of the cover at its back, thus concealing the knots between this back strip (or: spine strip) and the cover itself. 'At the centre of the quire there are usually two folded oblong pieces of leather ((inner sewing) stays (or: inner sewing guards)) through which the binding thongs pass to prevent them from ripping through the papyrus' sheets of the quire. Most of the covers were cut so as to provide for at least one flap, often more or less triangular in shape, that folded around the codex's fore-edge from left board to right board, with a long leather thong attached for encircling the codex multiple times as a closing slip (or: wrapping band). Typically, additional such closing slips (or: ties) 'emerge from the top and the bottom of the front and back covers at the centre to tie the codex together.' The covers were stiffened with boards that are laminates of sheets of papyrus (often called 'cartonnage' by papyrologists), over which the edges of the cover were turned in and pasted down; where a flap occurs, an edging strip of leather was pasted onto the inner surface of the front cover, later to be turned in over the left board along the length of the flap. Paste-downs were also of papyrus.

Most of the NHC covers were made from a single piece of leather, the largest of which (in terms of area) was at least 362 × 523 mm (to make a cover (with both a head and a fore-edge flap) with closed dimensions *c.*286 × 160 mm), the smallest 320 × 365 mm (closed dimensions *c.*268 × 136 mm); for other covers, several pieces of leather were sewn together. Sometimes the covers were decoratively tooled. For the roughly contemporaneous and typologically similar, but significantly shorter Berlin Gnostic codex (dimensions of the closed cover 145 × 130 mm), the leather binding was cut from either the front or the back cover of an older, decoratively tooled binding, the original dimensions of which have been estimated at 400 × 320 mm (Krutzsch – Poethke 1984).

From the fifth or sixth century there survive two quite well preserved small-size parchment codices with bare wooden boards as covers, which may be taken as typical for parchment codices during the last centuries of Late Antiquity and the early mediaeval period (Codex Glazier: Schenke 1991, 7–15, pls 1–2; Depuydt 1993, 482–483, pls 460–462; Codex Scheide: Schenke 1981, frontispiece, 5–8, 133; for descriptions of these and similar bindings, see Szirmai 1999, 15–31, and for a list, see Petersen 1954b, 52–53 n. 11; for a radiometric dating of Codex Glazier, see Sharpe 1996, 383 n. 13). The binding struc-

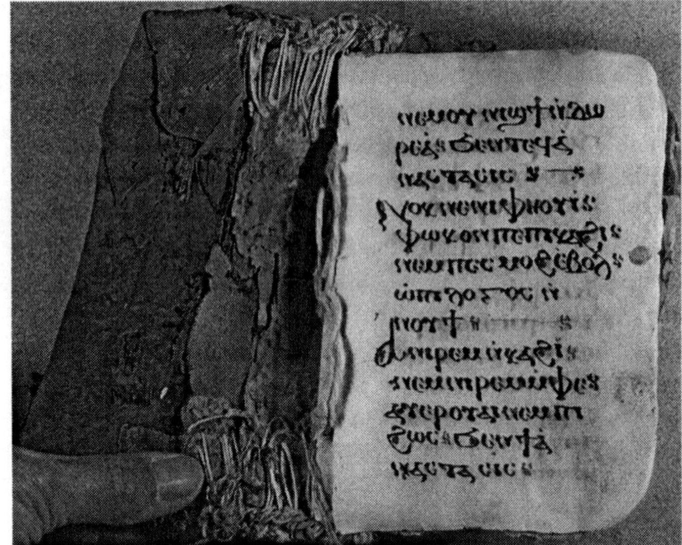

Fig. 1.5.5 New Haven, Yale University, Beinecke Rare Book and Manuscript Library, American Oriental Society Th / F84, *c.* seventeenth century, Coptic paper codex with leather binding, 170 × 125 × 50 mm. Above: left board (damaged), spine, final two quires (incomplete); below: final two quires (incomplete), right board; photograph by SE.

ture entails unsupported link-stitch sewing of the quires, to which the boards were attached both by means of pasting onto the spine a full-length leather back strip that joined the two boards, and also by using the first leaf and the last leaf of the text block as paste-downs. To support and strengthen the board attachment, four (Codex Scheide) or five (Codex Glazier) narrow bands of leather were passed through the back strip for a distance corresponding to the thickness of the text block so that they would lie between the back strip and the book's spine. The ends of each of these hinging slips were then fed through pairs of tunnels drilled obliquely from the outermost corner of the spine edge of each board to the insides of the boards and there pasted down. The extensions of the back strip were then pasted onto the inner faces of the boards, perhaps partly on top of the ends of the hinging slips where they emerge from their tunnels. The paste-downs then covered the extensions of the back strip as well as the ends of the hinging spine slips. Slips attached in the same way to the other edges of the boards (except the fore-edge of the right board) served for tying the book shut. Both codices are *c.*121 × 105 mm in size, while Codex Glazier is *c.*35 mm thick when shut, Codex Scheide *c.*56 mm, the boards being on average *c.*7.5 mm thick.

The larger, mediaeval parchment codices from the Fayyum were bound using papyrus laminates as boards covered in leather, with leaves of older parchment codices re-used as paste-downs or flyleaves. For many details about the binding of these 'late Coptic codices', see Szirmai 1999, 32–44; for concise descriptions of three such bindings, as well as some photographs, see Depuydt 1993, 26, 207, 256, pls 447–459; see also Cockerell 1932, and Hobson 1938, 202–233, who proposed the following classification for the 'extraordinary variety' of the decoration found on Coptic bindings: painted, worked, pierced, tooled, embroidered (Hobson 1938, 209–212; additional illustrations, including several wooden Bible caskets covered with elaborately decorated silver with gilding: Petersen 1954b, 51–64; Rutschowscaya et al. 2000, 66–70; Gabra – Eaton-Krauss 2006, 186–187, 212–213). We do not know that any late mediaeval or early modern Coptic bindings have ever been thoroughly examined and described (but for a description of a partly damaged Coptic binding of relatively late date, see Emmel 1990, 157–160, see fig. 1.5.5).

We may also note the occasional use of a leather tab at or near the middle of the fore-edge of a leaf as a kind of book marker to mark the occurrence of a text boundary, already in early papyrus codices (for example, NHC III, pp. 119/120, and also at the three other text boundaries in the codex, where one can see that a tab has been removed), as well as in somewhat later and mediaeval parchment codices (for example Lamacraft 1940, 218 etc.; Rutschowscaya et al. 2000, 72; Boud'hors 2013, 16–17, 581–582, 691–692,

747–748), occasionally with an ornate pattern cut out from the leather (Amélineau 1907–1914, II, pl. 1; Buzi 2009, 171).

Because Coptic sewing and binding techniques—meaning especially the use of link-stitch sewing to bind together the bifolia of a quire and to bind the quires to one another—as well as techniques of decoration and decorative motifs found on the leather covers of Coptic codices are found later in most other book cultures of the Near East and also in Europe, historians of bookbinding have long accepted that Coptic Egypt was their original common source. Nevertheless, this view might only reflect the fact that nearly all the oldest surviving codices, or parts of codices, come from Egypt.

References

Amélineau 1907–1914; Atalla 2000; Babinger 1931; Bagnall 2009; Bagnall – Worp 2004; Bloom 2001; Bober 1967; Bosson – Aufrère 1999; Boud'hors 1999a, 2000, 2004, 2008, 2011, 2013; Buchthal – Kurz 1942; Budge 1912; Buzi 2005, 2009, 2011a; Buzi – Proverbio 2012; Camplani 1999; Cockerell 1932; Coquin 1991, 2001; Coupry 2004, 2007; Cramer 1964a, 1964c; Crum 1905a, 1905b, 1926; Depuydt 1993; Diebner – Kasser 1989; Emmel 1984, 1990, 1996, 1998, 2003, 2004, 2005, 2007; Evelyn-White 1926; von Falck et al. 1996; Franzmann – Gardner 1996; Friedman et al. 1989; Froschauer – Römer 2008; Funk 1990, 2012; Gabra 2014; Gabra – Eaton-Krauss 2006; Gardner 2007; Goehring 1990; Greenfield 1991; Grob 2010; van Haelst 1989; Hasznos 2006–2007; Hebbelynck 1900–1901; Heurtel 2007; Hobson 1938; Humbert 1999; Johnson 1993, 2004, 2009; Kasser 1960; Khouzam 1999; Kotsifou 2007, 2011; Krause 1981; Krutzsch – Poethke 1984; Lacau 1911, 1946; Lalou 1992; Lamacraft 1940; van Lantschoot 1929; Layton 1987; Leroy [Julien] 1974; Leroy [Jules] 1976; Lucas 1922, 1962; Lucchesi 1981; MacArthur 1995; Maravela-Solbakk 2008; Muzerelle 1999; Nagel 1994; Orlandi [T.] 1974, 1991, 1995; Petersen 1954a, 1954b; Petrucci 1986a, 2005; Pietersma – Comstock 2011; Plumley 1975; Proverbio 2012a; Quecke 1975; Rabin et al. 2012; Richter 1998, 2005; Robinson [J.] 1975, 1978, 1984, 1990a, 1990b, 1990–1991; Robinson [J.] et al. 1972; Rutschowscaya et al. 2000; Schenke 1981, 1991; Schmidt [C.] – Schubart 1936; Sharpe 1996; Sirat 1989; Szirmai 1999; Thompson 1908; Till 1931, 1958; Turner 1977; Vergote – Parássoglou 1974; Whitfield et al. 2010; Winlock – Crum 1926; Worp 2012; Worrell 1923; Wurst 1996; Young 2001; Zanetti 1986a, 1986b, 1998.

6. Ethiopic codicology (EBW–ABa–CBT–DN)

6.1. Materials and tools

6.1.1. Papyrus

Whereas tropical Africa is the probable area of origin of papyrus (*Cyperus papyrus*), which is also found around Lake Ṭānā in Ethiopia (Soldati 2014), we have no evidence for its use as a writing support in Ethiopian manuscripts. Interestingly, however, on the inside of the back cover of one of the three Abbā Garimā Four Gospels books (Abbā Garimā 1, see Ch. 1 § 6.2.3) there are the remains of a deteriorated papyrus board (discovered during a recent restoration: Capon 2008, 7; Mercier – Daniel Seifemichael 2009, 112; Bausi 2011a), a use comparable to that attested by Late Antique Egyptian codices, where papyrus was used to stiffen the leather cover.

6.1.2. Parchment

Positive evidence testifies instead that Ethiopian Christian manuscripts were written on parchment: this is the case of the same Four Gospels books of Abbā Garimā (fig. 1.6.8) and of almost all extant Ethiopian books to the present. Recent archaeological evidence suggests that production of parchment in Ethiopia dates back to the pre-Aksumite period in the first millennium BCE (Phillipson 2013). Yet the Ethiopic term later attested for parchment (*berānnā*—from Latin *membrana*, through Greek *membranē*; Bausi 2008a, 522; Bausi 2014, 42—as literary and documentary texts clearly attest; see also Zaborski 1995, 540 and 542 on a possible connexion between Eth. *ṗarqʷama* 'to write' and Lat. *pergamena*) hints at a probable Late Antique origin. Further evidence might restrict the meaning of *berānnā* to 'parchment leaf' (note on MS Ethio-SPaRe MY-004).

Among animal skins, goatskin is the most widely used, liked for its solidity and thickness, even if sheepskin is lighter in colour and weight. It is maintained by Ethiopian scholars, but not proved, that sometimes large books were written on the skin of cows—or even horses and antelopes, usually considered as unclean—in specific conditions (Assefa Liban 1958, 10; Godet 1980–1982, 203; Sergew Hable-Selassie 1981, 9; Bausi 2008a, 531–532). The most typical book-type of the *Mazmura Dāwit* 'Psalter of David' (hereafter: Psalter), requires twenty to thirty goatskins, a Gospel thirty to fifty. Wild types of animals (like hyena) are reported to be sometimes used for magical scrolls (see Mercier 1979, 15).

Goatskins of young and slim animals are deemed to be the best, because they are possibly without scars or marks of whiplash, the traces of which do not disappear. The skins were usually purchased on the market or were left over after the animal was consumed; there is evidence for skin storage in a suitable tent in royal camps in pre-modern times (Kropp 1988, 53, 79). At the end of the nineteenth century, the scribes of the imperial scriptorium newly established by Menilek II—a case-study that provides useful hints, yet an exception of limited importance for the understanding of the Ethiopian manuscript culture in its historical development—received the number of animals needed for the copy of a given book, sharing the meat with the neighbours who helped them to make the parchment, while after 1919 an imperial decree created a new specialized profession devoted to parchment making (Haile Gabriel Dagne 1989). Present-day ethnographical observation indicates that the scribes themselves prepare the parchment, but this need not always have been so, especially in the case of luxury scribal production: the colophon of the fifteenth-century manuscript Pistoia, Biblioteca Forteguerriana, Martini etiop. 5, f. 195rb, demonstrates that the 'parchment makers' (*sarāḥta berānnā*) were distinct from the copyists (Fiaccadori 1993, 162–163; Bausi 2014, 42–43; Getatchew Haile 2011, II, 14).

The preparation of parchment, a skill that students of traditional church schools might also practice and learn as a part of their education, is not a despised activity like tanning or other crafts (Bausi 2008a, 527). Parchment is prepared when required, but it could also be bought (for example, in exchange for bars of salt, see London, BL, Or. 622, f. 2v; Wright 1877, 41, no. lxii). The main lines of the process for preparing the parchment, as they have been noted by ethnographical observation and described by the scribes themselves in the twentieth century (Assefa Liban 1958, 10; Godet 1980–1982, 230; Sergew Hable-Selassie 1981; Bausi 2008a, 532ff.; Faqāda Śellāsē Tafarrā 2010), are as follows (the fifteenth-century *testimonium* provided in Getatchew Haile 2011, II, 29 also agrees). The skin should be worked as soon as it has been stripped from the animal's carcase, usually after being washed and soaked to make it softer. The skin is stretched over a special wooden frame (*mawaṭṭaryā*/*mawwāṭaryā*, or *qambar*/*qanbar*).

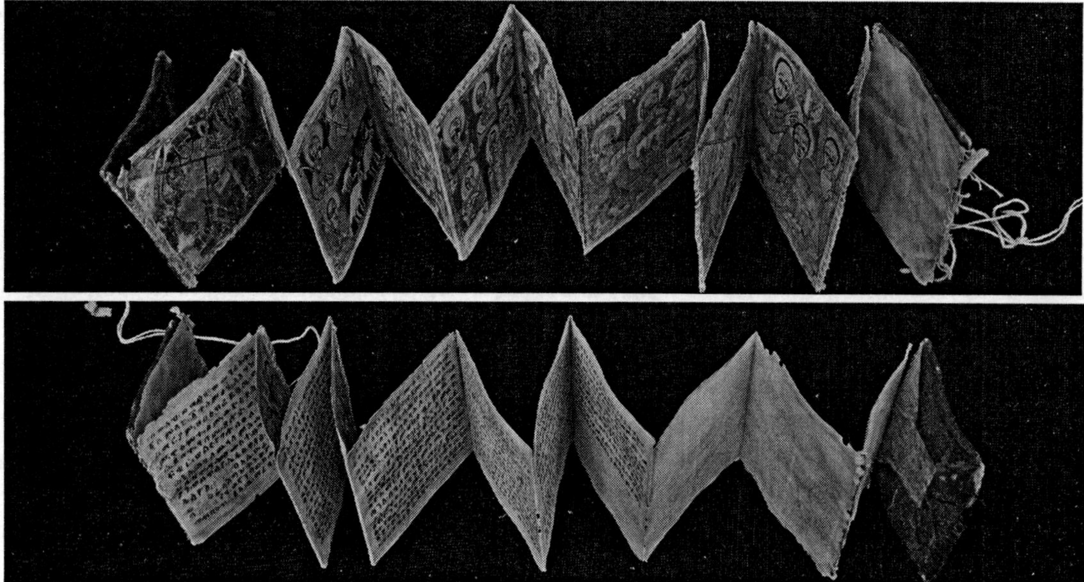

Fig. 1.6.1 Ethiopia, Tegrāy, Dabra Zayt, DZ-005, accordion book, fifteenth/sixteenth century, photograph Ethio-SPaRe.

First the flesh side is worked, alternately with a pumice stone (*marrāmamiyā*) and a large curved knife, to deflesh it and to scrape it clean. When the skin has been dried, the hairs are shaved with a short adze (*mafāqiyā* or *maṭrabiyā*). The skin is then scraped again and washed on both sides. If the parchment develops a hole during the manufacturing process, the strings attaching the skin to the stretching frame are loosened and the hole is sewn together with sinews. The skin is stretched again to give it its final shape, wetted once more and finally dried. It is then squared off according to the size of the intended book, in so far as this can be foreseen without any folding being undertaken. Model sheets can be used too. To be stored, the parchment is folded up, hair side against hair side. Before writing, the scribe pounced it on both sides with a special type of clay (*madmaṣ/madmaṭ*; difficult to find nowadays; at present, pieces of china are used but considered to be inferior) to enable the ink to adhere to the parchment. The skin could also be whitened, following a recipe that differs for each scribe or parchment maker. Ethiopian parchments are always quite thick and light in colour, but rarely white. It should be noted that no chemical treatment was undertaken (for further technical terms related to the production of parchment, see Bausi 2008a, 532–541; Mersha Alehegne 2011).

The quality of parchment for use in making scrolls (henceforth always in the sense of 'vertical scrolls') differs—some pieces are well prepared, thin and whitened but most of them are very coarse, actually a by-product of the production of parchment for codices. The parchment pieces of good quality, sewn together and folded, are used to produce so-called 'accordion-books' (*sensul*, literally 'chained [book]'; fig. 1.6.1).

An analysis of the parchment used for eleven scrolls from the collection of the Musée du quai Branly in Paris, executed with the X-ray fluorescence method (XRF), showed on the surface of the examined pieces significant quantities of calcium (Richardin et al. 2006, 2–3; see also Nosnitsin et al. 2014). The parchment of a scroll belonging to Warsaw University Library, MS 3649, analysed with SEM-EDS (Liszewska 2012), exhibited on both sides a large amount of kaolin. In both cases, the substances discovered confirm recorded observations of the procedure applied during the preparation of the parchment surface for writing and painting.

Palimpsest manuscripts exist, but they are rare. Texts were sometimes washed off or erased in case of either censorship or invalidation of legal acts, and then the cleaned parchment might be re-used (Bausi 2008a, 542–543).

6.1.3. Paper

With the exception of Islamic manuscripts (see Ch. 4 § 2.1.1.2), which are (almost) exclusively on paper (a confirmation of the culturally determined character of manuscript production), this material was not used to any extent in Ethiopia before the twentieth century. The usage of paper is limited to specific contexts, namely in manuscripts produced in Ethiopian communities abroad, especially in Egypt and Rome, or in manuscripts copied by and for European scholars especially in the nineteenth and early twentieth centuries. More recently, it appears that paper is being used in monasteries for school manuscripts (traditional *andemtā*-commentaries are often written in exercise books).

6.1.4. Inks

Inks, particularly the black ones, are still produced according to traditional methods, thus the whole procedure has been followed and recorded several times in ethnographical observations. The most extensive work dealing with the subject was written by Tournerie (1986). It contains testimonia excerpted from the accounts of travellers, recipes collected from Ethiopian scribes and detailed data on the plants and minerals used for the preparations of dyes and pigments. Smaller-scale research was undertaken by Sergew Hable-Selassie (1981) and Godet (1980–82).

For black ink Tournerie collected nineteen recipes and Sergew Hable-Selassie collected six. The composition of vegetal ingredients differs slightly (some fifty plant species can be listed) but the process of production is similar. The basic ingredient is always carbon in the form of powdered charcoal or soot, usually collected from cooking vessels or lamps. The choice of burning material is important and there are different opinions about what gives the best result. The carbonic powder is mixed with a binder, a fermented infusion containing roasted or boiled grains of maize or barley, leaves or bark cut into small pieces or ground to a powder, and insecticidal liquid, usually juice of the fruits of *Solanum* or *Ricinus*. The ingredients are stirred in a pot and left exposed to sunlight. This procedure is repeated everyday for a period of from three to six months. The film which forms on the top of the mixture is skimmed off and dried, formed into cakes or boles, and in this form can be stored for many years. In order to make the material fluid, a small amount of this product is mixed with water and left to stay at least two days for dispersing. The ingredients are not exactly measured and the right balance between them is the secret of the producer. It was thought that there was no evidence for the use of iron-gall inks in Ethiopia (Bausi 2008a, 523–524), but ongoing analyses seem to confirm the use of iron-gall ink along with soot ink in the twelfth and thirteenth centuries (Nosnitsin et al. 2014).

For the production of red ink a mixture based on vegetable ingredients, some roots, bark and petals of red flowers is recorded. The ingredients were pounded and soaked in water for about ten hours, mixed with a binder made of acacia gum or egg yolk and eventually sun dried. One recipe mentions red pepper and volcanic red earth grilled with sugar and the gum of juniper. The full procedure took about three months and often the result was unsatisfactory, mostly because the proportions between the ingredients were wrongly composed (Godet 1980–1982, 216). From the eighteenth and nineteenth centuries onward, scribes gradually started to use imported commercially produced pinkish dyes thickened by a binder.

Detailed recipes for coloured inks that were used only exceptionally are not available, but we do have some general information about the basic ingredients. Yellow ink was made from ground petals of yellow flowers, blue from 'blue earth' mixed with blue flowers and green from the juice of leaves—all mixed with a binder made of acacia gum or egg yolk (Mercier 1979, 16). Although several sources mention manuscripts written or decorated with gold, we may surmise that these are literary commonplaces rather than real descriptions. In fact, among the oldest manuscripts the use of gold ink has been noted only once, in the book of *Ta'āmmera Māryām* 'Miracles of Mary' of Ambā Gešēn, produced for King Dāwit (1382–1411; Spencer 1967, 103; Mercier 2004, 12, 35, 37; the Ethiopian tradition remembers not only the fame of this manuscript, but also the name of its scribe, Marqorēwos; Strelcyn 1976, 89). In the nineteenth and twentieth centuries, imported golden paints mixed with a binder were used as ink.

Rubrication and coloured inks can be used on the one hand to mark specific parts of texts and paratexts (*rubra* for *incipits*, marks for liturgical readings, pericopes, *nomina sacra*, saintly names, figures, and some elements of punctuation marks; Guidi 1901, 404), on the other for a decorative purpose. Sometimes the text of the Eusebian concordance may be written in red, the name of the owner or the book's donor, captions on miniatures and the various numbers (of quires, listed chapters, canons, dates). There is no religious manuscript written entirely with red ink but in some rare cases coloured inks were used throughout the entire text.

In King Dāwit's 'Miracles of Mary', golden characters outlined in red are very sparingly applied to Mary's name in the captions to the miniatures and on the opening pages. The scribe was most probably inspired by the stories recounted in the text but composed outside Ethiopia telling about a scribe who wrote

Mary's name in gold and about a painter who used gold to ornament her portrait (Budge 1923, 10–13; Cerulli 1943, 89–90).

It should be noted that in Ethiopia inks can be used as paints and colours as inks. For lack of appropriate analyses, it is difficult to establish if there is any difference in the components. Possibly the addition of gum in a certain quantity makes the colours more suitable for writing than for painting.

6.1.5. Pigments and dyes

There is no evidence that any particular symbolism was connected to the colours used for decorating codices and their consistent application was ruled only by tradition. Until the beginning of the seventeenth century, only four basic colours appear in all Ethiopian paintings: yellow, dark blue (rarely a pale azure or celurean blue), green and red/brownish red. For white, the colour of the parchment itself had to serve; black, rarely applied on larger surfaces, was prepared in the same way as black inks. The miniatures of the old Four Gospels of Abbā Garimā display a much broader palette of colours (for example, light green, purple, pink, brick red). In the so-called Gunda Gundē school that flourished at the turn of the fifteenth century, the basic range of colours was enriched by a widely used intense light blue, possibly based on ultramarine. Gold has been observed in the nimbi and ornamentation of the clothes of Mary in the royal 'Miracles of Mary' and in the form of grainy powder in the fourteenth century Kebrān Four Gospels (Bosc-Tiessé 2008, 34, 37); in the Paris Psalter, BnF, Éthiopien d'Abbadie 105, produced in the second half of the fifteenth century (Balicka-Witakowska 1983) and in the 'Miracles of Mary' of King Fāsiladās, London, BL, Or. 641, from the middle of the seventeenth century.

In the seventeenth century, white, pink, orange and nuances of red were added to the Ethiopian colour palette. At the end of the nineteenth century, industrial products were introduced to Ethiopia; considered to be superior, they gradually replaced the local paints.

There are no old written recipes concerning the compositions of colours, pigments and their binders. In rare cases we find the enumeration of colours (for example, in a register of materials for a church construction: Bosc-Tiessé 2008, 140), but at present we are not able to relate them precisely to the orally transmitted recipes that have been collected by scholars. In addition to the data gathered by Tournerie (1986), some information about the old techniques was provided by Taye Wolde Medhin (1980–1982), who described methods for obtaining black, red, purple, pink and brown inks, which he learned in a traditional church school, attending the higher level of education (*qenē bēt*).

Raman spectrography, which makes it possible to identify the components of the paints, has been applied twice to Ethiopian paintings. The first analysis (I) was applied to the set of seventeenth- and eighteenth-century miniatures illustrating the 'Miracles of Mary' in MS Paris, BnF, Éthiopien d'Abbadie 114 (Wion 2004), while the second one (II) was carried out on a late fifteenth-century miniature that found its way into a manuscript of the 'Miracles of Mary' that is two hundred years younger, belonging to the Mikā'ēl Māywayni church (Tegrāy; Tomaszewski et al. forthcoming). The two analyses provided partially matching results: for red, cinnabar (I and II) or vermilion (I) was used, also applied (I) to rubricate the names and legends of the miniatures; for yellow, orpiment, natural or artificial (I) versus crocin (II); for blue, indigo (I, in both the seventeenth and eighteenth-century miniatures, and II), and calcium carbonate (II); for green, an organic, vegetable colourant impossible to identify with Raman (I), or indigo and orpiment (II); for black, only carbon (I) or soot and calcium carbonate (II); white was not applied, as the painter used the colour of the parchment as white, while to get pinkish flesh he shaded the natural parchment colour with red (II).

In terms of quality, inks and colours used for writing, drawing and painting magical scrolls are basically the same as for the other types of manuscripts. Since, however, such scrolls are treated as magical and healing remedies, their inks are mixed with several additional substances that are determined in the meeting between the customer and the talisman maker (Griaule 1930). In that context the mixture called 'the seven colours' (*sabāttu qalamāt*) is sometimes mentioned, a concoction containing the juices of medical plants and several other components which are believed to provide therapeutic and supernatural effects (for example, MS EMML no. 790, f. 1r, see Macomber 1978, 105). It is also common that red inks, much more extensively used in scrolls, are enriched with drops of blood from sacrificial animals, the same animals from which the parchment for the scroll is obtained. Scrolls entirely written with red ink, such as Paris, BnF, Éthiopien d'Abbadie 192, are considered to be particularly effective. Generally, however, only introductory formulas are written in red, *nomina sacra* (God, Mary, but also angels, saints etc.), 'powerful' words, sentences providing spells, special blessings, and obligatorily the name of the owner. While in the codices the alternation between black and red in the text is one of the means of decorating a page, in the scrolls it conveys the opposition of good and evil, benediction versus malediction etc. There are also strict prescriptions concerning use of colours in the magic pictures, but they are kept secret as are many other details related to the production of the scrolls—it is generally understood that white symbolizes light, black cursing and enchantment, yet in a positive sense also the water of Baptism; red symbolizes fire, flames, the Sun, the Trinity and also Christ's blood (Mercier 1992, 150).

Eleven scrolls with paintings kept in Paris, Musée du quai Branly, were examined by X-ray fluorescence (Richardin et al. 2006). The findings suggested the use of vermilion (cinnabar), chrome orange, iron-based pigment (haematite) for red, violet and orange; smalt and organic substances for blue; *terre verte*, copper-based pigments and occasionally orpiment and organics for green; organic components and in some cases orpiment, chrome yellow for yellow; haematite and organics for brown. An analysis done with Raman stereoscopy of the scrolls of Warsaw University Library revealed cinnabar for red and a mixture of carbon with iron particles for black (Liszewska 2012, 388–389).

6.1.6. Writing instruments

Ethnographic observations indicate that the scribe worked outside, during daylight. Sitting on the floor or on a stool, he did not use any table but he put the parchment quire or leaf on his knee, possibly using a board or a piece of hard parchment as a support. There is scarce evidence for the use of quills in the past, while he definitely used, and still uses, pens only made out of reeds, such as *maqā*, *šambeqo* and *qastančā* (cf. Faqāda Śellāsē Tafarrā 2010, 168–169). Before writing, he prepared (as appears from ethnographical observation) several pens in advance. He cut them short, no more than a dozen centimetres long, scraped them on only one side and cut the nibs straight or a little bit slanted according to his preferences. He then split the nib and sharpened it again when needed. He used two pens, one for black and one for red ink. Inkhorns are made mainly from goat's horn, but also from those of cows or antelopes. The horns were buried in mud for several days in order to make them softer and easier to cut and shape. They are stuck directly into the ground or into an inkstand made of wood or clay (*ya-qalam qandoč*). The scribe could then begin writing, sometimes putting a cloth on the freshly written parchment on his knee, a place to let his hand rest while reading the text to be copied from the model, in order to prevent ink spotting.

6.2. Book forms

6.2.1. Miscellaneous forms

The accordion-book (traditionally called *sensul* 'chained [book]') is known in Ethiopia at least since the late fifteenth century. It is made of one or several strips of parchment folded together, often—but not always—put between wooden or leather covers. The manuscript typically contains a progressive series of devotional pictures, each fold usually reserved for one figure or scene, in some cases with a related text; accordion books are attested with well over ten pictures. Remarkably, most of the known examples represent high-quality production (for example Barbieri – Fiaccadori 2009, 58–59, 182; Balicka-Witakowska 2010a). Today, however, accordion books of small size (kept in a small leather box and carried on the body) appear to be used predominantly only for certain 'protective' texts, in particular in connexion with burial rituals.

Also a small number of bifolia, folded and held together in whatever way, without boards, as well as single unbound parchment leaves, have been used for transmitting texts. Even today, it is possible to find short texts (hagiographical compositions, hymns, non-literary texts) written in a single small quire being circulated and used in this way, and single large size parchment leaves are still occasionally used for writing texts, for instance a large leaf with a short version of the Vita of Yemreḥanna Krestos and a hymn is attached at the main entrance to the church dedicated to the saint.

6.2.2. The roll (scroll) and the rotulus

There is no evidence in Ethiopia for a passage from roll (scroll) to codex, nor that the scroll existed prior to the codex, the two book forms being used for completely different types of texts. The presence and fairly widespread use of parchment scrolls as protecting and healing amulets (*ketāb, ṭalsam*), containing the appropriate protective and curative texts and pictures, has been attested in Ethiopia for a few centuries (Chernetsov 2007). Two types of 'magical scrolls' exist: a small type, for private and personal use as a portable amulet, only occasionally unrolled, is commonly made of three parchment strips, with an average width of approximately 80 mm, its length depending on how many texts and pictures it contains, and on the height of the owner; the second type is somewhat wider, up to 500 mm wide and *c.*1 m or more long, made for being displayed unrolled on the wall of a house, and thus usually designated as a 'wall-amulet' (Balicka-Witakowska 2006). With very rare exceptions, the scrolls are written and painted on the parchment's flesh side, leaving the hair side empty. The oldest preserved examples of the scrolls can be dated to the eighteenth century but indirect evidence points to their use as early as the fourteenth/fifteenth centuries (Mercier 1979, 10), and the tradition may be much older.

6.2.3. The codex

The oldest surviving Ethiopian handwritten books suggest that the codex was the book form already in use before the eleventh/twelfth centuries. While it might still be maintained that it is impossible today to define the exact time when the codex was first introduced to Ethiopia, the two so-called Abbā Garimā Four Gospels codices, which appear to be the oldest of all surviving Ethiopian manuscripts, despite being somewhat problematic witnesses (cf. Bausi 2011a), have recently been dated by the radiocarbon method to the Late Antique period (around fourth/fifth to sixth/seventh centuries, Mercier 2000; further analyses carried out in 2012 have confirmed this dating). The earliest dated examples from the thirteenth century (Four Gospels book of Lālibalā Madḫanē ʿĀlam church, Four Gospels book from Dabra Ḥayq) provide information warranting the assumption that the codex was in use continuously in Ethiopia since the Christianization of the country in the mid-fourth century. The earliest surviving codices are fully developed, with the usual gatherings of folded parchment bifolia, which were sewn together and bound between two boards. Since Late Antiquity the codex (*maṣḥaf*) has dominated the Ethiopian manuscript culture throughout its history until the present time.

The support for codices has always been parchment. 'Mixed codices' in parchment and paper do exist, but they are extremely rare (there is only one example in the Ethio-SPaRe database).

6.3. The making of the codex

6.3.1. The making of the quires

The required size of a new manuscript is estimated before the parchment is cut into sheets. A model manuscript might serve for that purpose, but templates are also widely used, as present-day observations indicate. The cut sheet is folded in the middle only once, thus making a bifolium (*naṭalā qeṭel*). Any single folia cut from the remaining pieces of parchment are adjusted to the required quire (*ṭerāz*) size. Similar practices are also applied to the extremely rare cases of paper manuscripts.

6.3.2. The composition of the quires

An entire manuscript is seldom composed exclusively of bifolia, this arrangement most often appearing in the *de luxe* codices, as indicated by the examples of the collection of King Tēwodros II (d.1868), better known as the Magdala (Maqdalā) Collection, presently kept in the British Library (Wright 1877; Pankhurst [Rita] 1973, 1990). In most cases, bifolia alternate with singletons joined to form a bifolium ('balanced quire' in the terminology adopted by Delamarter – Demeke Berhane 2007; Getatchew Haile et al. 2009; Tomaszewski – Gervers 2015, 68–72). In order to make a quire stable, the first and last leaves, as well as the central ones, normally belong to a bifolium. Each assembled quire is stabilized by means of tackets (fig. 1.6.2). The leaves are usually arranged according to Gregory's Rule. A preliminary codicological analysis conducted of the codex of the so-called 'Aksumite Collection' (Bausi – Camplani 2013; see Ch. 3 § 3.3.2), probably the most

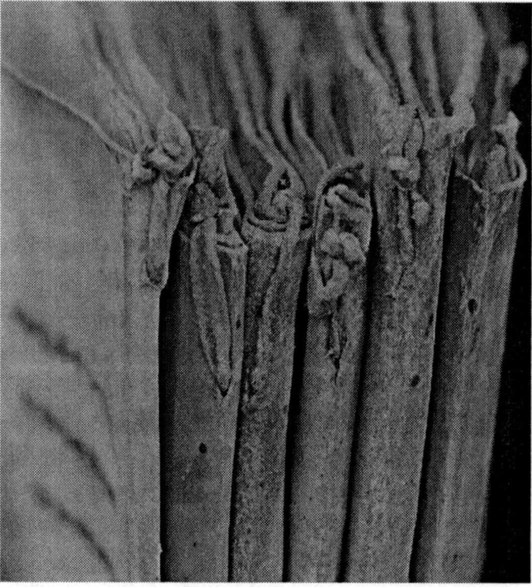

Fig. 1.6.2 Ethiopia, Tegrāy, Alʿāsā Mikāʾēl, AMMG-017, unfinished hymnary manuscript, nineteenth/twentieth century, photograph Ethio-SPaRe.

ancient non-biblical Ethiopian manuscript (*ante* thirteenth century), shows that even in this case Gregory's Rule was followed, not consistently, but in the majority of the quires.

A quire is usually composed of five or four bifolia (or single coupled folia), so as to have ten leaves (a quinion) and/or eight leaves (a quaternion), respectively. The quaternion occurs very often in the older manuscripts, of the thirteenth and fourteenth centuries. Smaller quires, with six leaves, and larger ones with twelve leaves also occur, as well as quires with an irregular number of leaves. The latter are typical of the manuscripts for which the layout seems not to have been carefully planned, and the scribe needed to add some extra leaves at the end of one or more quires, particularly at the end of the book.

A few statistical data are available from catalogues and recent research. In the collection of ninety-one manuscripts from the sixteenth to the twentieth centuries preserved in the Mikā'ēl Māywayni church, 57% codices have divergent quires, and 33% have quires of a single type (British Library Endangered Archives Programme, Project 340). Delamarter – Demeke Berhane (2007), on the basis of 241 quires (out of a total of 277 quires in twenty-three codices), indicate that 104 (43%) are 'balanced' quaternions; 55 (23%) are 'balanced' quinions; 10 (4%) are 'balanced' senions; 12 (5%) are 'balanced' ternions; while 16 are '5/4 adjusted balanced' quires, 5 are 6/5, 4 are 6/4 or 4/3 or 5/3, for a total of 25 'adjusted balanced' quires; 22 quires are 'unbalanced'. Getatchew Haile et al. (2009, xxviii-xxx) state that quinions (49.7%) and quaternions (33%) are by far the most common quire types, and that they are not equally distributed across time, as quaternions seem to prevail in earlier manuscripts. Matching data can be obtained from the analysis of a historical collection of primary importance such as the collection of the Biblioteca Apostolica Vaticana, with manuscripts uniformly distributed from the fourteenth/fifteenth to the nineteenth/twentieth centuries (see Grébaut – Tisserant 1935, 1936), plus data from other Italian libraries (Marrassini 1987–1988; Bozzacchi 2000; Proverbio 2000; Proverbio – Fiaccadori 2004; Lusini 2002, 2006): the prevailing quire type is definitely the quaternion until the sixteenth/seventeenth centuries. Note that the only prevailing quinion type in a very ancient manuscript, namely the famous *Psalterium pentaglottum*, Vatican City, BAV, Barb. or. 2, in Ethiopic, Syriac, Bohairic Coptic, Arabic and Armenian, which also happens to be a paper manuscript, was produced in Egypt (Proverbio 2012a).

Obviously the production plan for each manuscript also took its size into consideration. The most common item, namely the (usually portable) Psalter, consists of *c.* 180–240 leaves gathered in eighteen to twenty-four quires. In the Mikā'ēl Māywayni collection, 63% of the codices have between seven and fifteen quires. Larger or luxury volumes, generally made of fine and thin parchment, may have somewhere between thirty and sixty quires. Text blocks of more than 250 leaves gathered in thirty to thirty-five quires (Four Gospels, collections of the 'Acts of the Martyrs' (*Gadla samā'tāt*) or 'Miracles of Mary' of special types, and some other works) were far from rare, too. The largest manuscript known so far has 601 leaves and over 70 quires; noteworthy also are the monumental manuscripts from Dabra Bizan, Eritrea, with recorded evidence of a codex containing over 570 leaves.

6.3.3. Pricking and ruling

Pricks (*weg*) are clearly visible in most Ethiopian manuscripts (figs. 1.6.3, 1.6.4). Prick holes are mostly round, but other types also occur (note the slits in fig. 1.6.4); the typical tool for pricking is the locally produced awl (*wasfē*).

a) *Primary pricks* (or vertical pricks) are located in the upper and bottom margins of the folia and serve for making the vertical bounding lines which delimit the text columns, two pricks for one column of text. Primary pricks were pierced first.

b) *Text pricks* (or horizontal pricks) serving to guide the horizontal ruling are almost always located in the outer margins of the leaves, only very rarely at mid-page. Usually well preserved and easy to see, the text pricks are normally located at the distance of *c.* ten to thirty mm or more from the edge of the leaf, although in very old codices the worn leaves and crumbled edges make assessment difficult.

Pricking patterns of old manuscripts show some peculiarities. The Abbā Garimā Four Gospels book has the primary pricks located at the top and bottom ruled lines. The manuscript containing the 'Aksumite Collection' (fig. 1.6.4) has the text pricks placed at the outer vertical bounding lines. Even in a microfilm (EMML no. 6907) in which details are not easy to discern, one can see a similar pattern in the Four Gospels book of Lālibalā Madḫanē 'Ālam datable to the thirteenth century: primary pricks located at the top and bottom ruled lines, text pricks located close to the outer vertical bounding line (for example ff. 177v–178r, 187v–188r, 193v–194r).

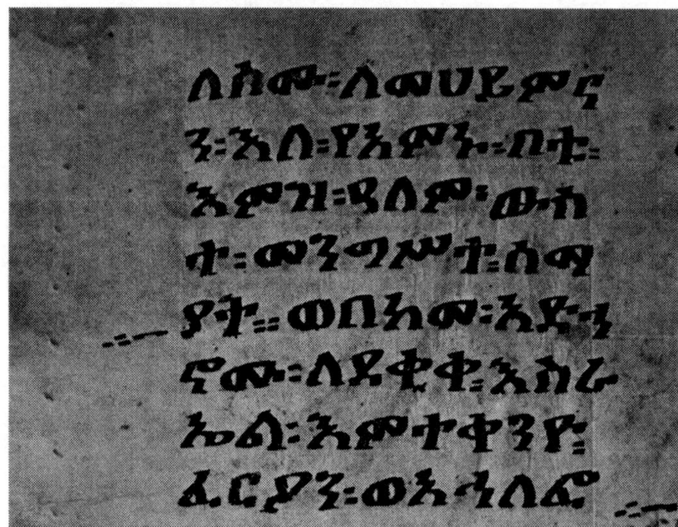

Fig. 1.6.3 Ethiopia, Tegrāy, Dabra Māʿṣo Yoḥannes, MY-002, Homiliary, time of King Dāwit II, *c.*1380–1412, f. 81v, detail, photograph Ethio-SPaRe.

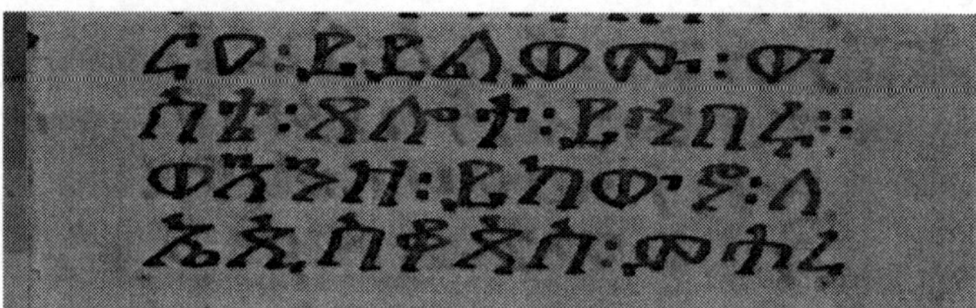

Fig. 1.6.4 Ethiopia, Tegrāy, ʿUrā Qirqos, UM-39, 'Aksumite Collection', twelfth/thirteenth century, f. 76rb, detail, photograph Ethio-SPaRe.

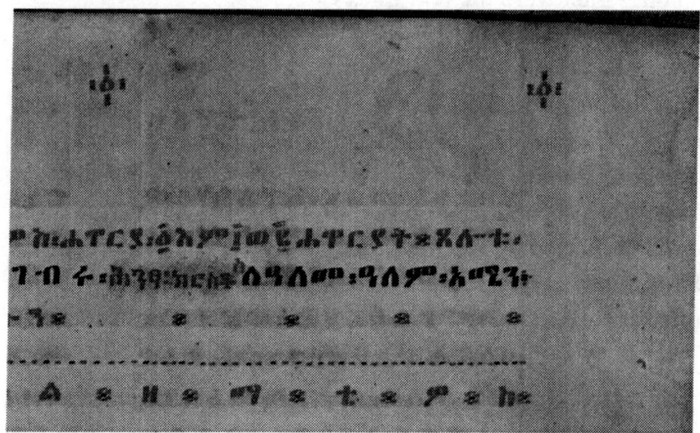

Fig. 1.6.5 Ethiopia, Tegrāy, Muḳāʿ Qeddus Mikāʾēl, BMQM-006, Four Gospels, eighteenth century, f. 15r, detail, photograph Ethio-SPaRe.

In most Ethiopian manuscripts the pricking pattern appears as slightly zigzag vertical lines of small holes. In present-day practice, the use of a ruler to facilitate pricking is self-evident and well documented, and in many recent manuscripts the lines of pricks are nearly straight. Yet traditionally a different, elegant and effective, though time-consuming, method was applied. It has been described (Faqāda Śellāsē Tafarrā 2010, 132–135) and it may be summarized as follows. First the manuscript maker takes a small rectangular piece of parchment and pierces two holes in it, the distance between them being the desired distance between two ruled lines delimiting one line of text. Next he takes a parchment bifolium, fixes the small piece of parchment in the margin on its flesh side with a first awl, and makes a prick through the second hole with the second awl. Then leaving the second awl in the hole that he has just made, he removes the first awl and rotates the piece of parchment 180 degrees. He then pierces another prick through the first hole. This operation is repeated until the desired number of pricks has been reached. The result is a vertical line of pricks, not perfectly straight, but with the distance between the pricks remarkably constant.

The use of two awls and a piece of parchment fixing the distance between the pricks recalls the so-called 'in-and-out' method of 'compass pricking' (Jones 1941, 392).

After one outer margin has been pricked, the bifolium is folded and pricks on the opposite outer margin are pierced through the pricks that have already been made, i.e. one half of the bifolium is used as a guide for pricking the other half, with all slight imperfections repeated. The neatly and carefully pricked bifolium (still unruled) is used as a template (*malakkiyā*). This template is laid upon one or more further bifolia, which then receive pricks all at once through the pricks in the template, usually from the flesh side (Faqāda Śellāsē Tafarrā 2010, 134). At this stage, in order to facilitate the pricking, the bifolia of the quires are tacketed with short threads made of twisted parchment strips (*sir*; fig. 1.6.2). Every experienced scribe is said to have templates prepared for different types of books, and, if necessary, is able easily to produce a new template from a model manuscript.

It is impossible to say how old the pricking method just described might be. Apparently, the Ethiopian manuscript makers (at least in Christian Ethiopia) did not use any sophisticated devices like pricking wheels, rakes or *misṭara*. There are only a few cases in which pricking patterns might have required different techniques: for example, for outlining the decorative bands and frames that are visible in some Gunda Gundē manuscripts. In a few older manuscripts, small black dots can be seen which were possibly used to guide the ruling along with the pricks, for example to outline the Eusebian Canon Tables in the Four Gospels.

Nearly all Ethiopian codices are ruled; also in accordion-books the parts meant to receive text might be both pricked and ruled; in 'magical scrolls', pricking and ruling are very rare but they do appear in carefully designed pieces (see, for example, MS London, BL, Or. 12859, eighteenth century, produced for a nobleman; Strelcyn 1978, 124–127, no. 80). Ethiopian manuscript makers use only a dry-point technique for ruling, using an awl with a dull point. The ruled lines are usually very straight. It is not quite clear which auxiliary means were used in the past to facilitate ruling (Sergew Hable-Selassie 1981, 12, refers to a 'reed ruler'); at least since the late nineteenth century 'modern' industrially produced devices (such as a metal ruler) have been in wide use. Usually, each bifolium is ruled separately (Faqāda Śellāsē Tafarrā 2010, 136). After the bifolia have been pricked, apparently, there are two possibilities (if Gregory's Rule is to be followed): (1) the template and the tackets are removed and each separate bifolium is ruled on the flesh side, after which the bifolia are reassembled in quires and tacketed again (this is what is reported in Faqāda Śellāsē Tafarrā 2010, 136); (2) after the template has been removed, the quire is reassembled and tacketed again, at which point the flesh sides facing each other at every second opening are ruled. The results of both practices seem to be observable in the manuscripts. In the first case, the ruled text lines of the opposite flesh sides do not necessarily coincide at an opening, while they do necessarily coincide in the second case.

The ruled lines are invariably impressed on the flesh side; yet Bozzacchi (2000) noted that in 10.9% of their corpus ruling was done on both sides, a percentage that was represented only by eighteenth- and nineteenth-century manuscripts. The following stages in the process of ruling can be discerned: (1) first, vertical bounding lines are ruled, joining the primary pricks; they can stop before the primary pricks or go beyond them towards the edges of the bifolium; (2) then, the text lines are ruled; they stop exactly at the bounding rules, or occasionally go a bit beyond them toward the text pricks. The inter-column and inner margins are usually ruled. The evidence of the ancient manuscript with the 'Aksumite Collection' (fig. 1.6.4) suggests that in the early practice the pricking and ruling could be done in alternating steps: a frame of horizontal and vertical bounding lines was impressed first; then one proceeded with the text pricks, locating them exactly at the vertical lines, and only then were the text lines ruled.

6.3.4. Ordering systems

In most Ethiopian manuscripts quire signatures appear as a guide-line for binding, but they are not consistently used. Catchwords are used occasionally (for example in the MS Uppsala, University Library, O. Etiop. 41, eighteenth century). The quire signature is usually placed on the first page of each quire, at the top of the inner margin, and sometimes it is written a second time in the middle of the top margin, and again at the top of the outer margin. It can also be repeated on the inner margin of the last page (Grébaut – Tisserant 1935, 778, on MS Vatican City, BAV, Borg. aeth. 2, ante 1441/1442 CE). The quire signatures are frequently decorated, with numbers encircled by black and red dots and strokes, often arranged in the form of a cross (fig. 1.6.5).

6.3.5. The codex as a complex object

In the traditional environment many codices did not remain unchanged, but were modified to accommodate additional texts or images. There is rich philological and codicological evidence that this process was not actually an exceptional one and was a powerful impetus for the development of Ethiopian written culture (in general, Bausi forthcoming a). A significant number of Ethiopian codices show a multi-layer structure. If necessary, the 'core' text block of a codex could easily be enlarged by one or more additional quires, constituting different 'production units', or by single leaves. For example, quires with poetic compositions were sometimes added to the 'Acts' of a saint (fig. 1.6.6); quires with the so-called 'Rule of al-Muʿallaqah' and poetic compositions were frequently added to the 'Miracles of Mary'; as elsewhere in the Christian manuscript cultures, in some Gospel books, the quires with the Canon Tables and/or other prefatory materials and miniatures were produced separately and added to the already manufactured Four Gospels (see Ch. 1 § 6.5.1). In some cases, additions were meant to substitute for a portion of the original text which had been lost.

The additional elements could be newly manufactured, but could also originate from a different codex. This was frequently the case when a quire of the 'core' text block was enriched with a few additional leaves (fig. 1.6.7), or especially when images survived from an older (lost) book.

6.4. The layout of the page

Regularities and changes in size of Ethiopic manuscripts (for both outer dimensions and dimensions of the written area), or relationship between size and types of texts, have not been studied yet. Some tendencies have been highlighted (Uhlig 1988, 86–87, 194–195, 316–317, 442–447, 558–562, 782–783; Uhlig 1989), but mostly in connexion with palaeographic features. We may tentatively assume the existence of three main manuscript sizes: (1) the most common mid-size, with height 170–380 mm; (2) small size, with a height less than 170 mm; and (3) large size, with height around or more than 380 mm (this characteristic can be complemented by layout-types, on which see below). For the moment, trends can be observed only for some texts, and the pre-sixteenth-century period is difficult to assess. For example, the full Octateuch is usually contained in large-size manuscripts. Such a common work as the Synaxarion is mostly found in codices 300–450 mm in height. The manuscripts containing the work *Haymānota abaw* 'Faith of the Fathers' usually range 250–400 mm in height. The Psalters show at least three patterns during the best-attested post-sixteenth-century period. The regular, most common Psalter manuscripts range in height 170–300 mm; smaller Psalters (less than 170 mm in height) might have started circulating from about the eighteenth century. A very few large Psalter manuscripts are also attested (more than 300 mm in height). Out of *c.*620 manuscripts surveyed by the project Ethio-SPaRe (mostly in small, rural collections), *c.*10% are of the small size, while the percentage of the large-size codices is insignificant.

It is possible to follow the evolution of the Four Gospels manuscripts in more detail (around 100 have been evaluated by the Ethio-SPaRe project, to which a number from other collections can be added). In the mid-thirteenth to mid-fifteenth centuries the preferred height of the Four Gospels manuscripts appears to have been *c.*250–350 mm, the width being at least *c.*150/160–250/260 mm, i.e. 90–100 mm less than the height. By the late fifteenth century, the height tends to remain within those limits, and the width increases a little bit, in all cases the gap between them mostly ranging 30–50 mm. In the nineteenth century, the preferred height of the Four Gospels codices remains 290–350 mm and surpasses the upper limit only in rare cases (cf. Uhlig 1989).

Ethiopian manuscripts have a limited variety of layout types. Layouts are not designed for hierarchical organization of the written space (like text/commentary or text/musical notation: for the latter case, in *Deggʷā* and similar manuscripts, the musical notation is simply accommodated in a larger space between the lines, with a smaller script for the text). However, types of layouts are interrelated with the typologies of the texts they have to accommodate. The basic layouts of texts in Ethiopian manuscripts are three: one-column; two-column; and three-column. Four-column layout does exist, but occurs very rarely.

Obviously, the shape of the written area is related also to the formats of the codices, which are mainly three: (1) rectangular (with the width being less than the height of the codex, but with the proportion width/height between 0.5 and 1.0); (2) square (the proportion width/height *c.*1.0); (3) tall (the proportion width/height less than 0.5). At the same time, this relationship is not always direct, since a rectangular codex can have a square written area, and vice versa. For the moment no statistical study on the relationship between size and layout has been carried out and all estimations are very approximate.

Books with one-column layout encompass a sizeable part of the Ethiopian manuscripts, at least 15%. The most frequent book of this category is the Psalter. Irrespective of the size and format of the Psalter codex, the Psalms of David, the Odes of Solomon and the Song of Songs have always been written in one column, each versicle starting at a new line (exceptions to this layout are found in some very rare comprehensive biblical manuscripts containing the entire canon). Two texts that follow the Song of Songs in the Psalter manuscripts (*Anqaṣa berhān*, *Weddāsē Māryām*) are always laid out in two columns.

Besides the Psalter, one-column layout tends to be used in small-size codices, or, less commonly, in mid-size codices. All of these are manuscripts for personal use, study, devotion, or else they are various multiple-text manuscripts of the so-called 'service literature', composed of collections of litanies or daily prayers. An important category, as yet insufficiently surveyed, is represented by older hymnody manuscripts, which sometimes also include portions of liturgy and Daily Office Prayers or poetic compositions. Also codices with 'protective' texts were frequently laid out in one column (in some of them, for example,

Mafteḥē śerāy, the writing is frequently interrupted by numerous talismanic pictures). Also the Gospel of John and the Revelation, if copied separately from the Four Gospels, were frequently laid out in one column.

The trend toward the wider use of one-column layout (in small-size, portable codices) started at least in the eighteenth century, and it became more conspicuous in the nineteenth century. Apparently, it emerged in the area of the Gondarine culture, with increasing number of certain types of (non-liturgical) books intended for private use, which were required by church teachers, high-ranking ecclesiastics, *dabtarā*, healers, monks, and zealous noble believers.

Two-column layout is the most common and dominant type used in mid-size codices, but also occasionally in small- and large-size codices. It is applied to the widest range of texts constituting the bulk of Ethiopic literature. Two-column layout was also used from time to time for most of the texts mentioned above under 'one-column layout'. The most ancient Ethiopic manuscripts have exclusively a two-column layout (Four Gospels of Abbā Garimā, etc.; the manuscript of the 'Aksumite collection' has a few cases of one-column layout for sections with *tituli*, 'tables of contents').

Three-column layout was also regularly used, but applied for a more limited range of texts, mostly those of significant length, copied into mid- or large-size manuscripts. The texts most commonly laid out in three columns include the Synaxarion, the *Gebra ḥemāmāt* 'Lectionary for Holy Week', some theological treatises like *Haymānota abaw*, *Tergʷāmē Ṗāwlos* ('Commentary of John Chrysostom on the Epistles of Paul'), and the like. Especially in the post seventeenth-century period, some texts appear to be laid out predominantly in three columns, such as the Octateuch, Minor Prophets, Proverbs and Kings, sometimes also the Four Gospels, big hymnody collections encompassing more than one of the five main hymnody works, some works of canon law like *Fetḥa nagaśt* ('Law of the Kings'), and others.

Different layout types in the same codex for single sections of the work are regularly applied for the Psalter and the Four Gospels. In general, it appears that the use of three-column layout expanded starting from the sixteenth century, and in particular in the eighteenth to nineteenth centuries, and that it partially replaced the two-column layout (Bausi 2008a, 538). Quite a number of text and manuscript types are attested in more than one layout. But a systematic study of a large number of manuscripts is necessary for defining more exactly when and why the change of layout took place, if there was any link between the history of the text and its use and the layout transformation, and if other factors (readability of the text, economic reasons, pictorial cycles etc.) exerted any influence.

It should be noted that there is clear evidence for the change over the course of time from a two-column to a prevailing three-column layout in the case of long works that are attested from early on (fourteenth century onwards). The biblical Octateuch, laid out in two columns in several pre-seventeenth-century codices of large size, some of them containing more than 230 leaves, was copied only rarely in later centuries, but then always in a three-column layout, with a larger written area than in two-column format and fewer than 200 leaves. Ethiopic Synaxarion manuscripts of the later recensions are written in three columns, practically without exception; but the older version of the Synaxarion attested in a very small number of pre-seventeenth-century manuscripts appears in two columns; the same is true for the big collection of 'Acts of the Martyrs', and for the canon-law collection of the *Sinodos*. Large late-eighteenth- or nineteenth-century copies of the collection of the 'Miracles of Mary', containing some three hundred narratives, are laid out in three columns. Starting from the late eighteenth century, hymnody manuscripts of large size could encompass several or even all five books of the set (*Ṣoma deggʷā* and *Deggʷā*, *Meʿerāf*, *Zemmārē*, *Mawāseʿt*) with a three-column layout, in small script, with musical notation of even smaller size inserted interlinearly.

The most complex change of layout took place over the centuries in the introductory texts to the Four Gospels (*Maqdema wangēl*). Originally characterized by a special layout intended for the richly ornamented Canon Tables and series of miniatures, they were later laid out like the regular text pages of the Four Gospels, although a smaller script was frequently used.

It might be said provisionally that in many older (pre-sixteenth-century?) manuscripts, the first written line of the regular text pages was placed below the uppermost ruled line (fig. 1.6.3) which was sometimes used to guide notes indicating the occasions and appointed readings (or the so-called *tituli* in the Four Gospels); in the post-fifteenth-century manuscripts the first written line was placed invariably above the uppermost ruled line. In the accordion books and in the narrow scrolls the text is always written in one column. In the wall-amulets and particularly elaborate larger scrolls the text may be divided into two or even three columns but the pictures always occupy the full width of the strip.

Fig. 1.6.6 Ethiopia, Tegrāy, ʿAddiqaḥārsi Makāna Ḥeywat Pāraqliṭos, AP-046, *Vita and Miracles of the Martyrs of Pāraqliṭos*, 1523 CE, ff. 10v–11r, photograph Ethio-SPaRe.

It cannot be excluded that layout recipes were used in the past, but today their existence is difficult to ascertain. The contemporary scribes say that in their work they simply follow the layout of model manuscripts, and stress the usage of the templates.

The Ethiopian scribes adapted to what was needed and exercised flexibility in shaping the written area, basing their work on the unsophisticated layouts of the main types. If the scribe envisaged an ornamental headpiece for the *incipit* page, he left a few ruled upper lines blank (fig. 1.6.6 recto). In some texts, the written lines of a heading run across the entire page, exceeding the ruling for columns (hymnody manuscripts, Four Gospels, fig. 1.6.5). Additional texts could be written in the margins, on end-leaves, or on added leaves. Skilled scribes entered glosses and commentaries—usually not subject to written transmission, but written *ad hoc*—in the margins and between the written lines, or wherever there was some spare space. The upper ruled lines were used for accommodating quire signatures, headings, titles, and other elements placed around the written area (fig. 1.6.5).

6.5. Text structure and readability

6.5.1. Writing and decoration

The Ethiopian script does not oppose capital to non-capital letters (it has only one capital-like 'uncial' set), and therefore has no ornamented initials. The ends of the text units are not decorated but only marked by series of repeated diacritical signs or dashes and dots, sometimes drawn with red and black inks. The colophons are rarely presented in decorative frames. In comparison with, for instance, Syriac or Coptic manuscripts, pen-work decoration in Ethiopian books is rather poor (cf. Ch. 1 § 6.1.5; Ch. 2 § 5).

The miniatures are always put within the text frame, and margins are reserved for aniconic ornamentation (typically paragraph marks marking pericopes, *cruces ansatae*, etc.). Three main categories of decoration can be distinguished: (1) the decorative script, in two forms: (a) rubrication and (b) coloured script; (2) aniconic decoration, mostly used in the text headings; and (3) miniatures or drawings.

(1) If applied for the purpose of decoration, rubrication is not meant for hierarchically organizing the written page, but rather for making it aesthetically appealing. Such an effect may be created by lines of text alternately written in red and black, or sometimes even in several colours. The alternation of the colours is sometimes used to create figures, crosses, roundels or stars. The colouristic division is usually applied throughout all text columns, thus creating a horizontal visual entity. Such an arrangement is common in the introductory pages, but is also applied to poetic texts, litanies, repeated expressions or words, various kinds of tables and computational drawings (cf. Ch. 1 § 6.1.5).

(2) The aniconic decoration typically appears, starting from fourteenth-century manuscripts, in the form of bands filled with coloured interlace composed of various motifs. The composition is called in Ethiopic *ḥarag* 'tendril, twig' (Balicka-Witakowska 2005b). Such a decoration is used to mark the headings, primarily the headings of the initial pages, either of a work, or of a chapter, or of a section etc., the importance of which might determine in turn its size and degree of elaboration (the introduction to a large text unit often turning into an ornamental frontispiece). A heading decoration is quite often not kept

within the space reserved for the text, but extends to the margins. Ornamental bands may run along the whole width of the written area or through only one of the columns, or an unbroken border supplied with perpendicular bands may also descend vertically into the inter-columnar space. The vertical ornamental bands may be very short, or as long as the text columns. The heading decoration often extends into the upper margin; the lateral pendants may be short, but sometimes they descend towards the bottom margin. In some cases, the ornamental bands build a frame enclosing the whole written area, or only a part of it (figs. 1.6.6, 1.6.9). Figural elements added to the *ḥarag* compositions (as in the *Gebra ḥemāmāt* MS London, BL, Or. 597, fifteenth century) are exceptional. The colours and composition of *ḥarag* ornamentations often point to a particular epoch and even to a particular scriptorium.

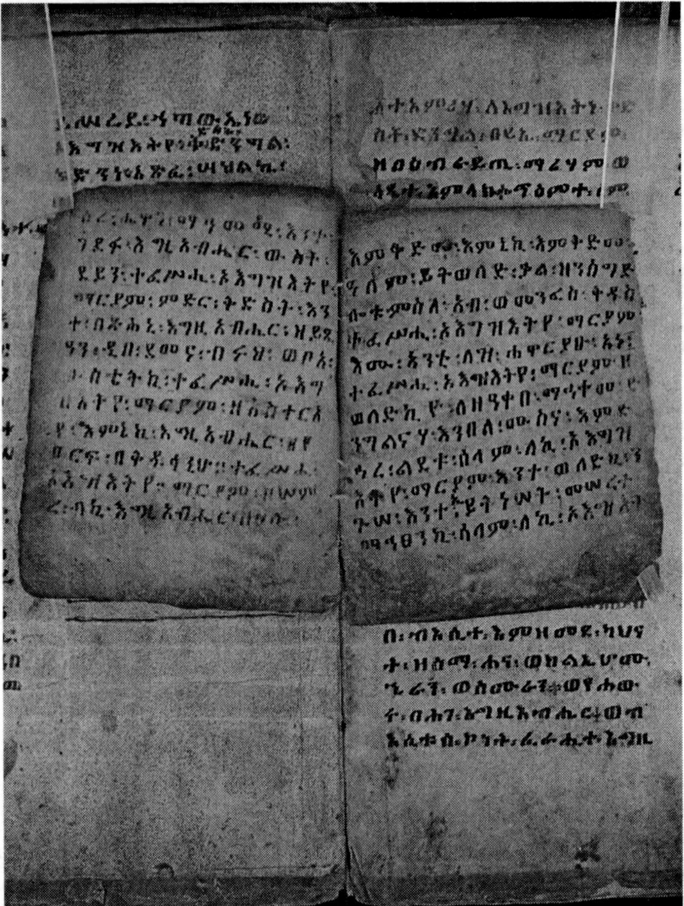

Fig. 1.6.7 Ethiopia, Tegrāy, Mengāś Māryām, MQMA-010, *Miracles of Mary*, nineteenth century, with infixed ff. 9v–10r of an earlier time, seventeenth century?, photograph Ethio-SPaRe.

In the old Four Gospels manuscripts, the Eusebian Canon Tables are laid out and also decorated according to rules developed in Late Antiquity outside Ethiopia (Palestine, and probably Egypt, for the tables at least, but definitely not in Syria; Bausi 2011a). The oldest Abbā Garimā Four Gospels display two distinct typologies, both going back to Byzantine models: three pages of Eusebian prologue plus seven pages of architectural frames with tables (fig. 1.6.8); or two pages of Eusebian prologue plus eight pages of architectural frames with tables (Heldman 2003; Bausi 2004b). In both cases the series is closed by the 'Tempietto' or the 'Fountain of Life'. The later mediaeval Ethiopian Canon Tables tradition can be sufficiently explained on this basis. This ancient system was enriched with the large repertory of aniconic elements created by the Ethiopian pictorial tradition (Leroy [Jules] 1962; Bausi 2004b).

The figural decorations appear as miniatures or drawings, which may or may not be coloured. Their place, size and arrangement within the codex are determined by several factors, the most important being their illustrative or non-illustrative character.

The non-illustrative pictures, also called 'iconic', display the most venerated holy figures, such as St Mary, the archangel Michael, St George, and other important saints. Commonly, they occupy a full page, are portrait-like and seldom narrative. This kind of miniature is to be found from the fourteenth century on. In the more recent manuscripts, they are often not contemporary with the text but either added much later or transferred from older, damaged books. Since the presence of miniatures raises the price of a manuscript on the tourist market, the books presently circulating are supplied with recently added secondary pictures.

The miniatures are almost always presented within simple, rarely decorated frames. Drawings in the old manuscripts are exceptional, mostly sketches for unfinished miniatures. Up to the sixteenth century, the story told by a text was never directly illustrated. The miniatures, even the narrative ones, were either gathered at the beginning of the manuscript or inserted into it as a frontispiece for particular parts of the text. This rule concerns even the narrative texts *par excellence*, for instance the Four Gospels or the Lives of saints. Another general rule was that one subject deserves one full-page miniature, but in the old Four

Gospels, for instance, the Entry into Jerusalem and the Miracle at Cana are customarily displayed on two facing pages, while the Nativity is represented together with the Adoration of the Shepherds.

The illustration of the early Four Gospels books made use of two types, both originating from outside Ethiopia. The older one, called the Palestinian, introduced—directly after the decorated Eusebian Canon Tables—three miniatures illustrating Jesus' passion and resurrection (the Crucifixion, the Holy Women at the Tomb, and the Ascension). The second type, called the Byzantine, introduced at the same place a long Christological cycle, the most developed presently known containing nineteen miniatures (Lepage 1987; Balicka-Witakowska 1997; Lepage – Mercier 2011–2012). In these sets there are miniatures that have two subjects on one page, or one subject extending over two pages (cf. above). In both types, the text of each Gospel is preceded by a portrait of the evangelist (fig. 1.6.9). Placed on a verso, it faces the beginning of the Gospel text on the recto.

A hagiographical text was usually introduced by the full-page portrait of the saint placed on a verso, facing the *incipit* page on the recto. In the collections of the 'Acts of the Martyrs' only selected saints are depicted (the selection criteria are the subject of current research; in MS EMML no. 7602, fourteenth/fifteenth century, almost all saints are portrayed). In such collections, the portrait of the saint is painted on a verso, while the text begins on the facing recto. Sometimes an empty space left at the end of the text is also used for this purpose. In collections from the early fourteenth to fifteenth centuries, narrative miniatures are very rare (for example, the Beheading of John the Baptist in the 'Acts of the Martyrs' from Meslē, Ṭānā, fourteenth/fifteenth century). More common from the sixteenth century onward, they are always limited to one or two episodes.

The old Psalters are decorated with full-page miniatures serving as frontispieces for the sections of the book, representing the figures connected with these sections—a practice which derives from the Greek so-called 'aristocratic Psalters' (Weitzman 1960). Consequently, a miniature of David always appears before the Psalms, Solomon before the Song of Songs, Moses before his canticle and Mary before the 'Prayers of Mary' (Balicka-Witakowska 1983, 1984–1986). From the sixteenth century on, with few exceptions the Psalters keep only the frontispiece representing King David.

The texts listed above are practically the only ones that were decorated with miniatures in the period before the end of the sixteenth century. Exceptions are rare (for example, the fifteenth-century 'Lectionary for Holy Week', kept in the monastery of Marʿāwi Krestos Endā Śellāse, Tegrāy) and concern mainly the first collections of the 'Miracles of Mary' and the books of the Old Testament (for example, Vatican City, BAV, Borg. aeth. 3, or the Old Testament copy from the Bētleḥēm church near Dabra Tābor).

During the sixteenth century and the first half of the seventeenth, major changes occurred in the layout of the decorated and illustrated manuscripts. The painted pages are no longer gathered at the beginning of the codex or placed only as frontispieces before major text sections. Rather, the frontispieces are kept, but the miniatures are distributed all through the book, inserted within the written area in frames. The most ancient manuscript with this new kind of layout is a copy of the 'Miracles of Mary', adorned with pictures drawn with coloured ink in the Italianate style during King Lebna Dengel's reign (1508–1540) kept in the church of Tadbāba Māryām (unfortunately, only partial documentation is available for study); in comparison with the seventeenth-century manuscripts following this tradition, this manuscript is quite innovative and must have been painted by a foreign artist. The collection itself evolved with the addition of new miracles, up to more than three hundred in some codices of the eighteenth century. In the seventeenth century, the texts to be illustrated is fixed at thirty-three miracles, with a set of miniatures (filling an entire page or added separately in a column when there are blank spaces to fill in) placed at the beginning or at the end of the relevant text. In addition, at the beginning or at the end, we find full-page paintings that we can qualify as iconic (for example, a Virgin with Child). None of the manuscripts of the 'Miracles of Mary' from the seventeenth century resemble each other exactly. Even if they depict the same subject, the execution and the layout are always different (Annequin 1972; Balicka-Witakowska 2010a).

In the seventeenth century, the Jesuits must have brought to Ethiopia the *Evangelium arabicum*, an Arabic Gospels book printed in Rome in 1590–1591 for the evangelization missions in the Near East, with engravings by Antonio Tempesta modelled on the Small Passion woodcuts by Albrecht Dürer. Several Ethiopic Four Gospels books were illustrated in the 1660s–1680s, following this model. Each includes more than a hundred miniatures, although the distinct illustrations are actually fewer, as the illustrations to the Gospel of Matthew are repeated in the other Gospels (Leroy [Jules] 1961; Heldman 1993, 240–241; Bosc-Tiessé 2008, 103–105).

Fig. 1.6.8 Ethiopia, Tegrāy, Endā Abbā Garimā, Abbā Garimā 2, Four Gospels, *c*. fourth–sixth century, photograph by EBW.

Further changes occurred from the end of the seventeenth and especially during the first half of the eighteenth century. In general, the number of subjects represented increased, new iconographical cycles were created and the existing ones were expanded. After the Four Gospels and the 'Miracles of Mary', one of the first texts for which an iconographic cycle was invented is the 'Life and Miracles of St George', as evidenced by a manuscript at Lake Ṭānā, Ṭānāsee 17 (= Kebrān Gabreʾēl 17; Hammerschmidt 1973), which contains 55 miniatures. Someone (the scribe and/or the painter, the scholar or the client who ordered the manuscript to be illustrated) must have thought very carefully about the project—selecting the episodes, the mode of representation, location—and acted as an innovative designer. Some episodes are represented twice: the first time at the end of the column where a text ends, and then on the following page with a full-page representation. The insertion of a painting into a column makes it possible to juxtapose immediately image and text and allows for numerous illustrations without the need for overly complex coordination among scribe, painter and binder (Bosc-Tiessé 2008, 145–169). Following the same process, other texts were illustrated, especially the *Dersāna Mikāʾēl* 'Homiliary for the archangel Michael'. The illustrations of the *Ṭabiba ṭabibān* 'Wisest amongst the Wise', a hymnological composition, are laid out in a slightly different way: the paintings usually occupy the entire width of the page, between a few lines at the top and at the bottom of the page, divided into two columns (Heldman 1993; Mercier 2001, 174–177).

Whereas the paintings of the seventeenth century were painted in an unruled frame, in the course of the eighteenth century, later as a rule, they were accommodated within ruling lines, which were also utilized to apply coloured background. Moreover, during the eighteenth century, many new texts were illustrated: the Revelation of St John (McEwan 2006), the *Nagara Māryām* 'Story of Mary' (Balicka-Witakowska 2014), new lives and miracles of saints, and so on (Heldman 1993, 196). In each book, narrative miniatures were multiplied, but became also increasingly repetitive. Generally, the number of images was more concentrated in the initial part of the manuscript. Besides, iconic images depicting saints, the Virgin or the Crucifixion, tend often to be inserted into prayer books.

6.6. The scribe and the painter at work

6.6.1. Persons, places and methods

The scribal profession could be learnt in monastic centres and as an auxiliary ability during the traditional church education. For a good scribe, a certain level of education was necessary, but the scribal work in itself was not an intellectual preoccupation. Hagiographical texts depict monks or priests, praised for their ability in writing, who were also scribes and recognized as saints. In most cases, however, they are writers (authors) at the same time, and their calligraphic work was not distinctly separated from their literary achievements, but only added to their fame. The fact that training took place mostly within the framework of church education, however, does not mean that all scribes were necessarily monks or priests, especially in more recent periods.

During the twentieth century, training to become a scribe or a painter took place after finishing the elementary church school, when students were supposed to have acquired a good knowledge of Geʿez. Yet most of the time they did it after completing another course, for example in church music, at the moment when they needed to copy out a book in order to become a qualified teacher. In this case, they were not necessarily going to become a professional scribe, but sometimes they made writing a second source of income. Some places are well known for the training of scribes, at least for the end of the nineteenth century and in the twentieth century, such as Andabēt in South Bagēmder (Sergew Hable-Selassie 1981, 27–31), where the apprentices learnt calligraphy as well as how to prepare inks, make parchment, paint, bind and decorate leather covers (Mellors – Parsons 2002b).

At the end of the nineteenth century and in the first half of the twentieth, those who managed to join the newly established imperial scriptorium enjoyed benefits and a better social status than others, sometimes becoming a dignitary with the title of *alaqā*, and also with the distinguished title of *qum ṣaḥāfi* ('calligrapher'). Other scribes could perform scribal work for governors or noblemen, receiving similar benefits and privileges (Haile Gabriel Dagne 1989).

The so-called *dabtarā*s, on the other hand, still represent a continuity with past tradition: self-employed, wandering from one church to another, and sometimes also ordained priests, they are copyists-on-demand (especially for 'magical scrolls') and earn a living from their traditional knowledge, selling the manuscripts they manufacture. These scribes are ambiguously regarded by society, as they are believed to be also sorcerers. A text of the sixteenth century that singled out ten social classes put the scribes (*ṣaḥaft*) in the class of the craftsmen (*ṭabibān*), together with very much despised blacksmiths, tailors and carpenters (Guidi 1907, 229–230 (text), 205–206 (translation)).

There is no special term for scriptorium until the end of the nineteenth century, and the questions of where Ethiopic manuscripts were copied, and how the work of copying and production was organized, are open ones. There are few monasteries in Ethiopia for which we can think that a scriptorium as an institutionalized workshop was settled with an administration organizing the work, wherever the work was really done. We have evidence that in these places, not only manufacture and/or copying was carried out, but also translators and authors of original works were active. Among such centres are monasteries and related networks founded in the fourteenth and fifteenth centuries by the followers of the monks Ēwosṭātēwos (for example, Dabra Māryām, in Eritrea, following the old traditions of manuscript painting having their roots in Palaeo-Christian and Byzantine art; Heldman 1989; Lusini 2004) and Esṭifānos (Gunda Gundē, in eastern Tegrāy, characterized by the introduction of several technical and iconographical innovations: an enlarged range of colours, extensive use of *ḥarag*, reduction of the narrative scenes and addition of purely iconic pictures to the decoration programme; Heldman 1989; Balicka-Witakowska 2005a), and also the monastery of Dabra Ḥayq (Bausi 2006a; Heldman 2007; Bosc-Tiessé 2010b).

An analysis of colophons written down in the 1660s–1760s in the Lāstā region, around Lālibalā, reveals the relationships between the different actors. It appears that different authorities, either political or religious, could hire a scribe, ordering manuscripts to be copied for different churches. Scribes worked independently, not being attached to the service of one patron, who in turn could have different scribes working for him. In this context, a scribe was not settled in a particular church (Bosc-Tiessé 2009).

Under the regency of Queen Mentewwāb (1730–1769) and during Menilek II's reign (1889–1913), we have evidence of a more developed hierarchy, with a chief organizing the work of the scribes. During the regency of Mentewwāb, a chief supervised the copyists working for the queen and her son. During the reigns of Menilek II and Ḫayla Śellasē, this function was put under the office of the *ṣaḥāfē teʾezāz*, that is the official chronicler and chancellor of the King (Haile Gabriel Dagne 1989; Bosc-Tiessé 2008; 2010a). Yet already in the fourteenth and the fifteenth centuries, the kings are known to have organized the copying and distribution of manuscripts at home and abroad (Balicka-Witakowska 1997; Derat 2005; Bausi 2013b).

The scribe first writes the main text with black ink, and later adds the rubrics in red after changing the reed; but the rubricator might be another person. The twentieth century pictures of scribes show them working alone. However, there is enough evidence to indicate that the work could be divided among several scribes.

The scribe seems to have been theoretically trained to work also as a painter. In most cases it was the scribe who, if not painted the miniatures, at least sketched the ornamentation (*ḥarag*). The name of the painter does not appear in the colophon, but sometimes the miniatures are signed and thus we can see that in some cases painter and scribe were the same (Bausi 2014, on Fiaccadori 1993, 162–168; Wright 1877,

Fig. 1.6.9 Ethiopia, Tegrāy, Dabra Madhināt, Abuna 'Abiya Egzi', Four Gospels, sixteenth century, ff. 161v–162r: St John and the *incipit* of the Gospel of John, photograph by Michael Gervers.

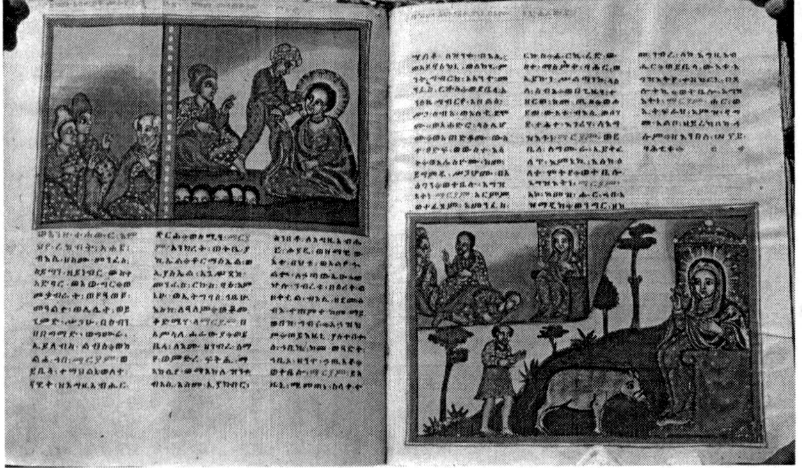

Fig. 1.6.10 Ethiopia, Lālibalā, Bēta Māryām, *Nagara Māryām* (Story of Mary), eighteenth century, ff. 10v–11r, photograph by Michael Gervers.

34, no. lii). Different scenarios might have occurred especially when the amount of work would make a division of labour necessary. For the period up to the fifteenth and early sixteenth centuries, the quires with pictures (with the exception of the frontispieces) and the quires with text were independently produced, while afterwards the painter worked on the same quires as did the copyist, and he had to wait until the scribe had finished before he could start his work.

In several manuscripts of the beginning of the eighteenth century, we have the name of the painter on the preparatory sketch (Pankhurst [Rich.] 1984), yet never in relation to finished paintings, suggesting that the name was intended to disappear under the painted layer and that the manuscript was circulating between different persons working on it. The signature was probably used to remind someone that the work on this specific page was done or had to be continued by a certain person. Painters could have worked to some extent with manuals and iconographic repertories (for some examples, Fiaccadori 2001, 280b–285b, on the manuscript Parma, Biblioteca Palatina, 3853 and further examples).

The scribe who makes the scrolls has to act in a relatively clandestine way because the Orthodox Church formally disapproves of such practices. The scroll-makers claim that their esoteric knowledge is a result of revelation and needs to be protected by deep secrecy. At least a part of this 'hidden wisdom', however, is written down and appears in books of divination and of the medical and/or magical-religious genre, with related pictures (Mercier 1992, 95–121). When ready, the scroll is given to the owner together with a prescription telling him or her how to carry it and when and how to use it in order to make it most effective. The texts in the scrolls mention neither the name of their scribes, nor the dates.

Books have been mostly written at someone's request or on behalf of someone, and they have also been sold and bought (the book market of Aksum has been particularly important). The price is sometimes mentioned in the manuscript.

6.6.2. Colophons

Colophons were definitely an optional element, and there is no colophon, for example, in the most ancient Four Gospels books of Abbā Garimā. The most ancient Ethiopic colophon might be in the MS EMML no. 1832, a Four Gospels manuscript from Dabra Ḥayq Esṭifānos, written down by order of the abbot and saint

Iyasus Moʾa in 1280/1281 CE (f. 24v; Taddesse Tamrat 1970; but cf. also Bosc-Tiessé 2010b). An increasing number of colophons can be noted in the fourteenth and fifteenth centuries (in particular in the age of Zarʾa Yāʿqob, 1434–1468, cf. also Bausi forthcoming b).

A peculiar phenomenon attested mostly for the communities of the followers of Ēwosṭātēwos (Dabra Māryām, Qoḥayn, and Dabra Bizan, Ḥamāsēn, now Eritrea) is the narrative expansion of the colophons, which in some fifteenth-century manuscripts tend to become small chronographical and hagiographical works in and of themselves (Bausi 1994, 1995a, 1997; Lusini 1996).

6.6.3. Dating systems

Chronological indications in colophons refer to the regnal year of the reigning king, but officers in charge and church dignitaries might also be mentioned, whether the book was written for them or not. Dating can also alternatively or additionally be given according to the common calendrical systems in use in written texts, which mostly derive from Christian Egypt, with all its apparatus (cycle of the evangelists, epact, *ṭenteyon*, etc.). Several eras are used: Era of the World (*ʿamata ʿālam* 'year of the world'), also called 'year after the creation' (*ʿāmat emfeṭrat*) beginning in 5493 BCE; Era of Diocletian (*ʿamata samāʿtāt* 'year of martyrs'), beginning 5,776 years after creation, in 284/285 CE; Era of Grace (*ʿamata meḥrat* 'year of mercy'), beginning 5,852 years after the creation, in 359/360 CE; Era of the Incarnation (of Christ) (*ʿamata śeggāwē*), beginning 5,500 years after creation, in 7/8 CE. The Era of Grace and the Era of Diocletian are connected to the five-hundred-thirty-two-year cycle of the eastern computus that combines the nineteen-year lunar cycle with the biblical/Jewish seven-day week (and the four-year leap-year cycle) and often give rise to uncertainties that can be cleared up only by the context and cross-dating (Uhlig 2003).

6.6.4. Duration of copying

Apart from a regulation of the imperial scriptorium issued in June 1919, detailing how much time was needed for copying various books (for example, five months for a Psalter, eight months for the Four Gospels, etc.), only colophons and notes in the manuscripts provide any indications concerning duration of copying, and such indications have not yet been systematically collected. For example, the colophon of a large-size Octateuch manuscript in Pistoia, Biblioteca Forteguerriana, Martini 5, consisting of 195 folia, dating to 1437/1438 CE, indicates that the manuscript was copied by two scribes (one of them also acting as painter) from February to August of a single year, i.e. in the space of six to seven months circa, while the colophon states also that the parchment was produced by specialized craftsmen (Bausi 2014, on Fiaccadori 1993, 162–163).

Antoine d'Abbadie, an erudite individual well placed in the Ethiopian society of the first half of the nineteenth century, had manuscripts copied for him when he could not get possession of the original. In Gondar, capital city of the kingdom at that time, he paid the scribe per page or even per character, counting that an efficient copyist should write around 10,000 characters per day (MS Paris, BnF, Éthiopien d'Abbadie 172, f. 88; Bosc-Tiessé – Wion 2010, 87–88).

6.7. Bookbinding

Ethiopian tradition claims that the main shape of the Ethiopian codex has remained unchanged since many centuries, and the Ethiopian binding method is very old. Some modification, however, did take place, even though there was no complete transformation of the binding structure and techniques.

The main type of binding of the Ethiopian codex, on two boards, is simple (Szirmai 1999, 45–50). The left and right cover boards are commonly made of wood, *Cordia africana* (*wānzā*), *Olea africana* (*wayrā*), or cedar, though other kinds of wood are also used. The boards are cut roughly with an adze; usually they have the same size as the text block, or sometimes they exceed it by just a few mm.

Leather boards made of thick, stiff (ox) leather do occur, but even if cheaper, they are far less usual than the wooden ones. They were normally manufactured for codices of small size. If a codex contains only a small number of leaves (gathered in one quire), one single folded rectangular piece of leather (or even parchment) embracing the text block can be utilized ('limp-binding'). However, some inherent problems (greater vulnerability of the sewing, concave distortion of the spine) rendered leather bindings impractical, and their use remained limited.

Many Ethiopian codices bound on wooden boards are covered with leather. This practice is documented from the fifteenth century at the latest, and is very widespread also today. For this purpose, slightly tanned sheep skin, or better goat skin, is used (just as for a number of household items). Tambēn, a region in Northern Ethiopia, is particularly known for the production of high quality leather (also called *tambēn*). Rarely, also imported Morocco leather (*bāhra ʿarab*) was used. The leather cover is glued onto the outer faces of the boards (at least in some cases, the adhesive was also brought unto the spine-folds of the quires); then protruding edges of the cover are folded as turn-ins and glued onto the inner surface of the boards. The remaining open surface in the middle can be covered with textile inlays; in older codices, it was covered by parchment paste-downs.

While most of the codices commonly have a full leather cover, quite a number have a 'quarter cover', and very few a 'half cover'. A fully leather-covered volume may later receive a leather overback, to strengthen the spine area or to repair damage. For very big codices, the leather cover could be made of two pieces of leather, sewn along the middle of the spine.

In very few cases, the codex could receive a luxurious furnishing made of metal plaques (usually bearing tooled decorations) attached to the boards. The material could be copper or (gilded) silver or gold-like metal. Such an expensive embellishment was usually reserved for the main Four Gospels manuscript of the institution (but some other books decorated in this way do occur, see fig. 1.6.11). Traditionally, the term 'golden gospel' (*wangēla warq*) refers to a Four Gospels manuscript which contains the most significant notes regarding the owning institution (usually a monastery or a church) or the region (Bausi 2010d, see also Balicka-Witakowska forthcoming a), not to a Gospel book with a golden or gilt cover.

The codex is often kept in a special two-part slip case (*māḫdar* and *defāt*), made of crude stiff leather, although high quality examples made of fine leather and furnished with elaborating fastenings also occur. The cases are used to hang the books (in the storage rooms) on a peg inserted in the wall, or from a beam. The big and heavy volumes could be stored on improvized shelves or on a traditional leather thong bed (*algā*), or, in the church, in a special piece of furniture (*manbara tābot*) for the altar tablet (*tābot*). Many codices received a secondary textile cover, or are kept and transported wrapped in textile or brocade. Extremely poor preservation conditions—which started only recently to be slowly improved—have resulted in the great percentage of old bindings being lost or badly damaged. Many manuscripts have been rebound, often unprofessionally.

Fig. 1.6.11 Ethiopia, Amhārā, Saqotā Mikāʾēl Gabreʾēl, *Taʾāmmera Iyasus* (Miracles of Jesus), eighteenth century, front board, photograph by Michael Gervers

Text blocks frequently include end-leaf quires protecting the first and last pages of the text from direct contact with the wooden boards. Such quires usually include a smaller number of leaves (two to six) than usual, which remain unwritten and can be used for additional texts, notes, paintings or drawings of different kinds. The end-leaf quires were an unstable part of the text block and were frequently taken out or modified (Tomaszewski – Gervers 2014, 73–74).

Another important feature which can be observed in older (pre-mid-sixteenth century) codices is the use of the first and the last leaf of, respectively, the left and right end-leaf quires as paste-downs. The leaf was glued to the board surface with an adhesive, and the turn-ins of the leather cover were glued onto it. With time the adhesive (possibly of wheat origin) tends to lose its strength, so that the paste-downs become detached from the wooden surface, and in many cases they were later cut off. However, in a few cases the former function of those leaves can still be surmised thanks to typical discolourations that occur on end-leaves.

Ethiopian manuscript-makers occasionally trimmed text blocks, but only rarely; this practice is attested for a few manuscripts, among others, through the 'cues' for the rubricator in the margins (numbers, titles, instructions), which have partly been cut together with the edges of the leaves.

Threads used for sewing the codex can be of animal or vegetable origin. As to threads of animal origin, they were probably 'sinews', according to recent observations, instead of 'guts', as sometimes reported (cf. Sergew Hable-Selassie 1981, 24; Faqāda Śellāse Tafarrā 2010, 208–209). The vegetable threads are made from different sorts of linen or cotton string or twine. The use of long and narrow twisted strips of parchment has also been observed, although it is a marginal practice. Today, synthetic threads are also widely used.

Depending on the size of the manuscript, the boards receive one, or (most commonly) two, or three pairs of sewing stations (up to six; sewing on three stations has also been attested). For this sewing, channels are made at appropriate places on the boards, where the threads are to be anchored, and they are matched by the holes made in the centrefolds of the quires. The sewing is executed without any sewing supports. Ethiopian chain-stitch sewing has been described in detail (Szirmai 1997, 46–48); it is sometimes referred to as an ancient feature of Ethiopian book production and compared to the Coptic multiple-quire manuscript sewing (for example, Shailor 1988, 55). For each pair of sewing stations, one single thread and two needles are used. The same thread is used for attaching the boards to the text block.

Most of the leather-covered codices have endbands or at least traces of their remains. The core of the endband (*totān*, cf. Faqāda Śellāsē Tafarrā 2010, 222–224) is usually slit-braid (sometimes made of two leather thongs of different colours). Two cores are sewn to the protruding tip of the spine at the top and bottom (making 'headband' and 'tailband', respectively). The threads used for them are led through the centrefolds of the quires, then between the board and text block, and knotted (Szirmai 1999, 49). It appears that in very many cases the holes left by the tackets have been re-utilized for endband sewing (Faqāda Śellāsē Tafarrā 2010, 133–134). The endband structures (especially stitching) are quite fragile and can be observed intact only in a relatively small number of codices.

The accordion book could have a limp binding, or its front and end folds could receive light wooden or leather boards and laces (fig. 1.6.1). Often it is also supplied with a leather case in which the book is carried as an amulet, with a channel for a cord. The scroll is kept rolled in a cylindrical case made in two parts of tinted red leather or of a hollowed piece of bamboo covered with leather. The case has a channel for lacing a cord, to which may be attached shells, beads, dried beneficial plants closed in small cases and additional charms. In rare cases, the case is made of metal, usually silvered alloy, and decorated with filigree and chased (for example, London, BL, Or. 12859).

Leather covering the wooden boards is dyed brown or reddish brown. Different conditions of preservation, exposure to light and humidity produce the whole gamut of these basic colours. Recently executed examples, tinted with industrial products, are pinkish red. Leather is usually blind-tooled with small finishing tools (*deggʷes*), each having a special name recalling its form (Mellors – Parsons 2002a, 17; Mersha Alehegne 2011; Tomaszewski – Gervers 2014, 80–84). Sometimes the decorative pattern is incised or punched. The blind panel design is very simple and repetitive, but it would be difficult to find two identical examples even if they were produced in the same workshop. Usually the ornamentation includes a cross, sometimes flanked by a schematically drawn church building, always framed or encircled by multi-linear borders. The cross appears in innumerable variants. The design of the front cover is repeated on the back cover. The turn-ins, the spine, and the edges of the cover are also sometimes tooled with the same patterns as those on the external covers. The centre of the inside cover is filled with a textile inlay, of varying quality—from cheap Indian chintz to fine silk (Pankhurst [Rich.] 1980, 1981, 1983–1984, 1984, 1985–1986). A leaf with a drawing or even with a miniature may also be pasted in place of the textile. In the centre of some upper boards there is a square cavity which originally housed a piece of locally produced mirror.

The elaborate examples of leather covers may be supplied with metal furnishings. The bosses or studs, usually in the form of rosettes, were executed by means of different techniques, some made of two pieces of solid metal. Quite often a metal appliqué decoration was introduced, arranged into various compositions. The fastening catches and clasps may have ornamented metal parts. For production of all these elements, most often silver or silvered alloy are used, but other metals may occur (Pankhurst [Rich.] 1999); very fine examples are two manuscripts donated by King Nāʾod (1494–1508) to the church of

Marṭula Māryām, Acts of the Apostles and Catholic Epistles, and a two-volume Synaxarion belonging to the church of Māryām Dengelāt, Tegrāy.

Books entirely covered with metal are rare and of recent date, mostly from the eighteenth to early twentieth centuries (a well-known example is MS London, BL, Or. 728, a binding 'in metal covers of copper gilt', Wright 1877, 196, no. 304; also Pankhurst [Rich.] 1983–1984, 249). Made of a cheap silver or alloy, they are fastened by means of metal pegs and usually decorated with engravings representing figural and aniconic motifs. Three among the most ancient Four Gospels books have metal covers dating to a much earlier period: two Four Gospels from Endā Abbā Garimā (with three bronze pieces, plus one fragmentarily preserved, repoussé ornamented, and one possibly gilt), and the Four Gospels book of Dabra Libānos, Ham (now Eritrea), that is also a 'golden gospel'. In the former case, the decorative motifs, the cross encircled by stylized foliage, are similar in all three examples, but not identical (Leroy [Jules] 1960). The latter case from Dabra Libānos (Bausi 1994, 1995a, 1997) has not yet been more closely examined, but the cover has a votive inscription mentioning the name of its commissioner donor (Conti Rossini 1901, 181; Derat 2010, 20; Fiaccadori 2011 [2012]).

Some wooden boards are coated with textile, usually a kind of velvet or thick cotton, providing support for the metal appliqué. The covering textile goes over the boards. Buckram-like textiles, usually cheap ones, are also used to protect the leather covers and the edges of the text block.

Several manuscripts are furnished with bookmarks made of coloured threads or pieces of leather fastened to the outer margin of a leaf some 50 mm from its upper corner. In the *de luxe* manuscripts it is a small, colourful bunch of silk threads. In some manuscripts, the miniatures may be protected by a tipped-in curtain of thin cotton or other textile, but seldom is the whole set protected.

References

Annequin 1972; Assefa Liban 1958; Balicka-Witakowska 1983, 1986, 1997, 2005a, 2005b, 2006, 2010a, 2010b, 2014, forthcoming a; Barbieri – Fiaccadori 2009; Bausi 1994, 1995a, 1997, 2004b, 2006a, 2008a, 2010d, 2011a, 2013b, 2014, forthcoming a, forthcoming b; Bausi – Camplani 2013; Bosc-Tiessé 2008, 2009, 2010a, 2010b; Bosc-Tiessé – Wion 2010; Bozzacchi 2000; Budge 1923; Capon 2008; Cerulli 1943; Chernetsov 2007; Conti Rossini 1901; Delamarter – Demeke Berhane 2007; Derat 2005, 2010; EAE; EMML; Endangered Archives Programme Project 340; Faqāda Śellāsē Tafarrā 2010; Fiaccadori 1993, 2001, 2011 [2012]; Getatchew Haile 2011; Getatchew Haile et al. 2009; Godet 1980–1982; Grébaut – Tisserant 1935, 1936; Griaule 1930; Guidi 1901, 1907; Haile Gabriel Dagne 1989; Hammerschmidt 1973; Heldman 1989, 1993, 2003, 2007; Jones 1941; Kropp 1988; Lepage 1987; Lepage – Mercier 2011–2012; Leroy [Jules] 1961, 1962; Liszewska 2012; Lusini 1996, 2002, 2004, 2006; Macomber 1978; Marrassini 1987–1988; McEwan 2006; Mercier 1979, 1992, 2000, 2001, 2004; Mercier – Daniel Seifemichael 2009; Mellors – Parsons 2002a, 2002b; Mersha Alehegne 2011; Nosnitsin 2012a; Nosnitsin et al. 2014; Pankhurst [Rich.] 1980, 1981, 1983–1984, 1984, 1985–1986, 1999; Pankhurst [Rita] 1973, 1990; Phillipson 2013; Proverbio 2000, 2012a; Proverbio – Fiaccadori 2004; Richardin et al. 2006; Sergew Hable-Selassie 1981; Shailor 1988; Soldati 2014; Spencer 1967; Strelcyn 1976, 1978; Szirmai 1999; Taddesse Tamrat 1970; Taye Wolde Medhin 1980–1982; Tomaszewski et al. forthcoming; Tomaszewski – Gervers 2015; Tournerie 1986; Uhlig 1988, 1989, 2003; Weitzmann 1960; Wion 2004; Wright 1877; Zaborski 1995.

7. Georgian codicology (JG)

7.1. Materials and tools

As in other book traditions of the Christian Near East, Georgian manuscript books (usually styled *çigni* 'book' in Old Georgian, vs. *nusxa* 'manuscript, document'; Modern Georgian *xelnaçeri* 'handwritten') are written on papyrus, parchment or paper. As a matter of fact, the history of the different writing supports used for Georgian manuscripts is poorly understood until today, for lack of extensive investigations into the matter, but also because of the lack of explicit dates in all too many manuscripts, as well as their dispersion over all too many repositories throughout the world. To overcome this problem, it would be desirable to establish a relative chronology based upon palaeography as well as external features (ink types, layout etc.), with manuscripts that contain explicit indications of their date and provenance representing the core. An important prerequisite for this undertaking would be the availability of digitized images, not only from western collections. Another prerequisite would consist in the application of scientific methods of analysis, which has not yet even begun.

7.1.1. Papyrus

Even though there were outstanding centres of Georgian manuscript production in the eastern Mediterranean (Jerusalem, Palestine and Mount Sinai), papyrus (Georgian *çili*) was always exceptional as a writing support for Georgian codices even of Levantine provenance. The most prominent papyrus codex is MS 98 of the (old) Georgian collection of St Catherine's Monastery, parts of a psalter written in *nusxuri* minuscules in about the tenth century. Unfortunately, the codex was badly damaged and has remained practically inaccessible for investigation in the monastery library, so that but little information as to its structure can be given.

Another prominent item to be mentioned here is manuscript 2123 of the H collection of Tbilisi, a hymnary codex of about the tenth century comprising about one half each of parchment and papyrus leaves (the so-called *çil-eṭraṭis iadgari* 'hymnary of papyrus [and] parchment'; Šaniʒe – Marṭirosovi 1977; Ḳaranaʒe et al. 2010, 25 and 139; cf. the coloured reproductions of one papyrus and one parchment page each in Cagareli 1888a between pp. 157 and 158), put together in quinions with three papyrus bifolia between outer and central bifolia of parchment to support them (Šaniʒe – Marṭirosovi 1977, 214–215; Meṭreveli et al. 1978, 229–239). Why, when and by whom the codex was conceived in the given form has remained unknown.

The papyrus used in these two codices originated presumably from Egypt; however, nothing is known about the exact provenance or the manufacture of the bifolia as no colophons survive. From the only photograph available of Sinai, St Catherine, georg. 98 (fig. 1.7.1 showing Ps. 64.11–65.11, photograph kindly provided by the librarian of St Catherine's Monastery, Father Justin, in May 2009; the coloured reproduction of a fragment containing Ps. 118.68–75 printed in Cagareli 1888b between pp. 192 and 193 is not a photograph), it seems that the writing is only across the vertical fibres (recto or verso?), while the other side with horizontal fibres is blank. It was stated in 1888 that the papyrus of H-2123 (then still manuscript 29 of the Georgian monastery of the Holy Cross in Jerusalem) was 'better', 'thinner' and 'smoother' than that of the Sinai Psalter but, at the same time, more 'yellow-brownish' and 'dark coloured' (Cagareli 1888a, 159; my translations); today, the leaves of the Psalter too appear extremely tanned.

7.1.2. Parchment

Parchment was the basic support material of manuscript codices throughout the period of Old Georgian, up to the thirteenth century, and at all the production centres, both in the Caucasus and elsewhere; except for the few papyrus codices from Palestine and Mount Sinai, all manuscript books of that period, including rolls, are made from parchment. The same is true for the small set of noteworthy legal and other documents that have come down to us from that time. During the twelfth and thirteenth centuries, parchment began gradually to be superseded by paper, and its use seems to have ceased by the end of the fourteenth century (if we ignore the reuse of parchment leaves as flyleaves in bindings).

Although the number of Old Georgian parchment manuscripts is very large, little is known so far about the material used, its provenance and its manufacture (a relevant thesis on writing materials, Gogašvili 2004, has remained unpublished, but see Gogašvili 2003 and 2006). Given that the structure of parchment codices is by and large compliant with Greek usage, we may safely assume that the Georgian practices of preparing animals' skin for parchment are derived from Greek practices, most probably those prevalent in Palestine. This assumption is corroborated by the fact that the Georgian word for 'parchment', *eṭraṭi*, likely reflects Greek *tetradion*, 'quaternion', thus indicating that quaternions made of parchment were the normal type of codex units Georgians met with when they commenced the production of manuscripts in their own right.

Fig. 1.7.1 Sinai, St Catherine, georg. 98, page containing Ps. 64.11–65.11, photograph by Father Justin, May 2009.

There has been no investigation yet into the different types of parchment used in Georgian codices and their distribution across chronological or geographical extents (but see Nanobašvili 1973 for popular methods of the treatment of animal hides in Georgia). As a matter of fact, Georgian manuscript books are likely to have been an object of transportation between several centres of production throughout the Middle Ages, and as all too many codices lack any information regarding their origin, we cannot even be sure that they originated from the location where they were first taken notice of. For studying the history of Georgian manuscript production, it would therefore be worthwhile to devise scientific means to distinguish different types of parchment, especially with a view to determining the number of pre-ninth-century manuscripts that were produced in Georgia proper.

Different from other early Christian traditions, Georgians seem not to have used coloured parchment in the production of codices. However, given the quantity of manuscripts that must have been destroyed in the Caucasus during the time of the Mongol invasions and other wars, we cannot be sure that this assumption is not due to a mere gap of preservation.

7.1.3. Parchment palimpsests

Nearly all Georgian manuscripts antedating the ninth century survive only in palimpsest form, overwritten in either (later) Georgian or other languages. Palimpsest codices, such as Vienna, ÖNB, Cod.Vind.georg. 2, often contain parts of more than one original manuscript (in the latter case, fourteen hands extending over approximately six centuries have been distinguished, and another part of one of the originals used has been detected in a palimpsest in Tbilisi, see Kaǯaia 1974, 491; Gippert et al. 2007a, 6-1). On the other hand, Georgian overwriting was also applied to codices of non-Georgian provenance such as, for example, Palestinian Aramaic, Syriac, Armenian, or the only manuscript remnants of the language of the Caucasian Albanians, detected as the first text in two Georgian palimpsests of the 'New Finds' of Mount Sinai (Gippert et al. 2009). Until today, only a few of the relevant palimpsest codices have been studied in much detail (*c.*4,000 palimpsest pages have been counted among the holdings of the National Centre of Manuscripts, Tbilisi; see <http://www.manuscript.ge/index.php?m=73&ln=eng>, last access 29 November 2014); by consequence, questions of (relative) chronology and provenance of the overwritten originals have only partly been investigated.

7.1.4. Paper

Leaving aside a few specimens datable to the tenth and eleventh centuries, evidence for the use of paper as the support material for Georgian manuscript codices begins in the twelfth century, one of the most prominent early codices being the 'Bible with Catenes' (*ḳaṭenebiani biblia*) written in the academy of Gelati in West Georgia (Tbilisi, National Centre of Manuscripts, A-1108). Another remarkably ancient paper codex is the Tbilisi MS A-65 which contains, among other texts, a Georgian translation of an Arabic astrological treatise (with illustrations) and which is datable to 1188–1210 (Ḳaranaʒe et al. 2010, 39). Secular codices proper, i.e. manuscripts containing epics, romances and the like, are all paper codices; this is hardly surprising, as none of those that have come down to us antedates the sixteenth century, due to the fact that many codices of this type were destroyed, if not during the Mongol invasions, by clerical fanatics in the eighteenth century (Ṭimote 1852, 154; Rayfield 2010, 79; Gippert – Tandaschwili 2014, 6–7).

For the majority of Georgian paper codices we may assume that it was oriental paper that was used; but there has been no detailed investigation into this question. The same is true for questions concerning the provenance, the composition, and the manufacture of the paper, and possible differences between paper used in Georgia proper and elsewhere (but cf. P̣aṭariʒe 1965a for the treatment of paper, and P̣aṭariʒe 1968 for the use of Persian paper in Georgia). Western paper is likely to have been introduced only in the eighteenth century, via Russia, where the first Georgian book was printed (the 'Bakar Bible' of 1743); however, there are no detailed studies available for this topic either (but see P̣aṭariʒe 1965b on watermarks in Georgian manuscripts of the fourteenth and fifteenth centuries).

7.1.5. Other writing surfaces

There can be no doubt that wooden tablets (Georgian *picari*) were used as writing supports throughout the time of Georgian literacy, even though we do not have any ancient examples at our disposal; however, there is no indication that they ever bore large amounts of text in the sense of 'books'. The same is true for *ostraca* and other non-flexible writing supports (including stone inscriptions).

7.1.6. Inks

The typology and distribution of the inks used in Georgian manuscripts has not been studied in detail. From multispectral analyses undertaken in connexion with the editing of palimpsests, we may safely state that the main ink used in the early centuries, on parchment, was an iron-gall ink with a brownish (Georgian *q̇avisperi* 'coffee-coloured') to blackish (Georgian *šavi* 'black') colour. The same type of ink was still used in later centuries when the palimpsests were overwritten, and probably also in paper codices as well as the few papyrus manuscripts. Nothing is known so far about the distribution of special types of ink among the different centres of Georgian manuscript production.

There are no original Georgian texts known that describe the production of inks for manuscript use. It is highly probable that 'black' ink was introduced to Georgia from the Greek-speaking world, given that the Georgian term for 'ink', *melani*, is clearly a borrowing from Greek *melan*, 'black'. In contrast to this, the word for 'red ink', *singuri*, cannot be traced to Greek, but must have a different origin (Syriac *siriqōn*?); it is important in this context that *singuri* seems not to be attested before the eleventh century, the plain adjective for 'red', *ç̣iteli*, being used earlier (for example, in manuscripts containing the Euthalian apparatus to the Pauline Epistles; Gippert 2010a, I-1–5).

7.1.7. Pigments and dyes

Rubrics can be proven to have been common everywhere in religious manuscripts since the very beginning of Georgian literacy, with several clear-cut purposes that range from delimitation (in the form of ornamental headpieces and the like separating parts of larger texts) via decoration (such as in crosses added at the end of Gospels) to highlighting (of titles, initials of paragraphs, proper names and the like, as on the title page of the synaxary MS Tbilisi, National Centre of Manuscripts, H-2211, *c.* eleventh century, see fig. 1.7.2, or in the hymnary MS Tbilisi, S-425, written by Mikael Modreḳili in *c.*978-988, which also exhibits neumes in red, see fig. 1.7.3; cf. Gippert 2010b for a preliminary typology). The use of other colours in the same types of codices is rather rare; for example, we find green ink used for liturgical glosses added to the twelfth-century Gospel manuscript Vienna, ÖNB, Cod.Vind.georg. 1, or blue colour used (alongside red and gold) to fill in the initial letters in the tenth-century Gospel codex Tbilisi, National Centre of Manuscripts, S-592, or in the twelfth-century Ǯruč̣i Gospels, MS Tbilisi, H-1667, see fig. 1.7.4. Other types of ornamentation involving extensive use of colours can be found in Gospel (and other) codices which exhibit portal-like frames (headpieces) indicating the beginnings of chapters (Georgian *ḳari* 'gate') as in the Gospel codices from Tbilisi, National Centre of Manuscripts, A-484 (the Alaverdi Gospels, dated 1054), Q-908 (1054, see fig. 1.7.5) or A-1335 (the Vani Gospels, twelfth to thirteenth centuries; see Ch. 2 § 6 fig. 2.6.2), or the codices S-134 (dated 1031) and S-3683 (dated 1708, on paper) containing elements of (ecclesiastical) law.

In the secular codices containing mediaeval epics, romances and the like, rubrics can be found with highlighting functions as in the Tbilisi manuscripts H-84 (dated 1680, containing Shota Rustaveli's *Vepxisṭq̇aosani* 'Knight in the Panther's Skin') or S-1594 (dated 1647, containing a Georgian derivate of the Persian *Šāhnāma* epic); however, red is often replaced by gold in the same types of manuscript as in H-2074 (sixteenth/seventeenth century, another manuscript containing Rustaveli's epic).

A wider range of colours was used throughout the time of Georgian manuscript production in miniatures and illuminations.

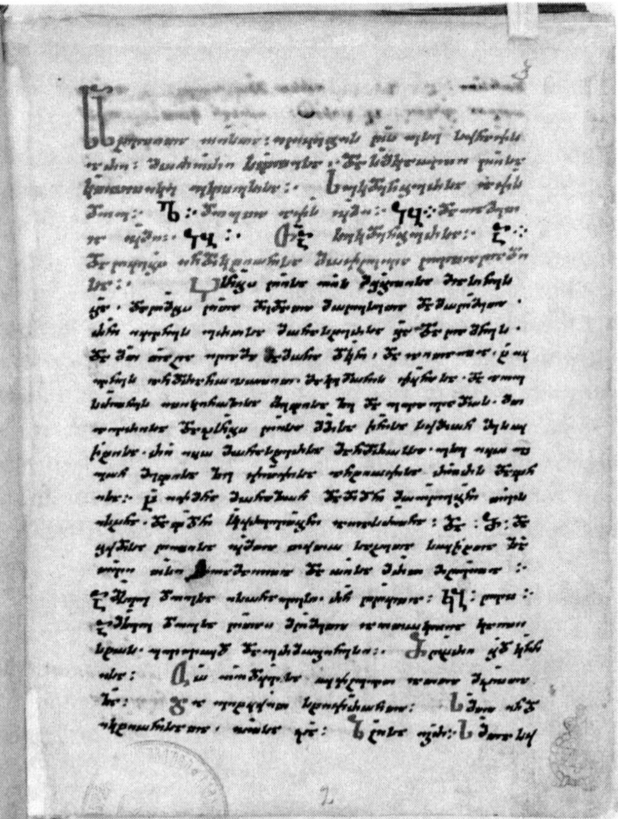

Fig. 1.7.2 Tbilisi, National Centre of Manuscripts, H-2211, *c.* eleventh century, f. 2r; this and the following six photographs courtesy of the National Centre of Manuscripts.

7.1.8. Writing instruments

The main writing instrument used in the production of Georgian manuscripts was the calamus, obviously introduced to Georgia from Greece as its name shows (*ḳalami* < Greek *kalamos*); the word is still used today for any kind of pen. Nothing is known about the source material used in the production of the calamus in the centres of ancient Georgian manuscript tradition; however, it is likely that either quills or reed pens (or both) were used, as in other traditions of the Christian Near East.

7.2. Book forms

The principal form of the Georgian handwritten book was the codex made of quires of parchment (note again the term *eṭraṭi* denoting 'parchment', from Greek *tetradion* 'quaternion') or paper, with but little variation concerning the number of bifolia constituting a quire and other aspects of codex and quire structure. As a concurrent form, parchment rolls appeared during the Middle Ages; they always played a minor role, however, their use being restricted to certain specific purposes.

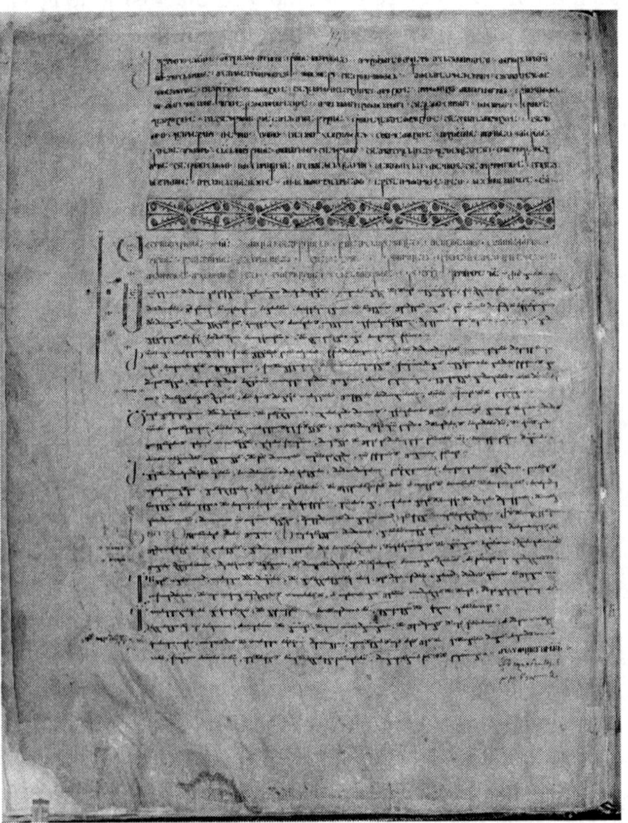

Fig. 1.7.3 Tbilisi, National Centre of Manuscripts, S-425, *c.*978/988, f. 24v.

7.2.2. The roll and the rotulus

Rolls made from parchment sheets have mostly been found at Mount Sinai. As there have been no special investigations devoted to the manufacture and structure of Georgian rolls (*gragnili* 'rolled up'), only a few remarks can be made here. From the specimens mentioned above, it is clear that a roll consists of a series of parchment sheets that were sewn together along the shorter edges and inscribed on both sides parallel to the short edge, which implies that they were unrolled vertically when read and so are to be identified as rotuli. The leaves bound together in rolls usually have a smaller ratio of width to height than those used in codices; cf., for example, MS Tbilisi, National Centre of Manuscripts, A-922 with a ratio of less than 0.3 (Ḳaranaʒe et al. 2010, 80). Typically the Georgian rotuli contain liturgical texts, such as the liturgy of St John Chrysostom, which is contained in MS Graz, UBG, 2058/5 (of Sinaitic provenance; Imnaišvili 2004, 300–313; Gippert – Imnaišvili 2009a). A parchment rotulus containing a king's decree (written in *mxedruli*) is MS 608 of the Kutaisi Historico-ethnographical Museum, from about the eleventh century.

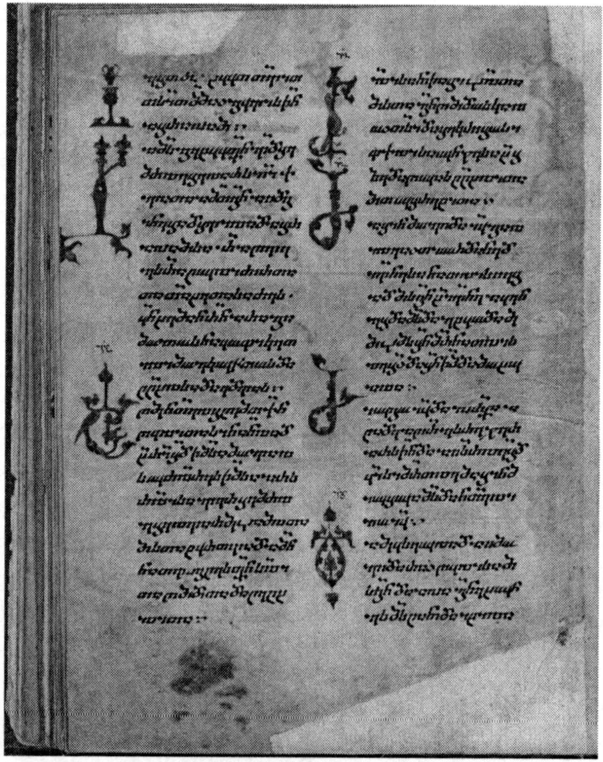

Fig. 1.7.4 Tbilisi, National Centre of Manuscripts, H-1667 (Ʒruč̣i Gospels), twelfth century, f. 14v (Mt. 3.9–16).

7.2.3. The codex

There is no indication whatsoever that the production of rolls antedated that of codices in the Georgian tradition. As a matter of fact, all manuscripts from the early centuries of Georgian literacy (*c.* fifth to ninth centuries) that have come down to us are parchment codices (or fragments thereof), and parchment remained the basic material in the production of codices up to the thirteenth century, when it was superseded by paper. Except for the use of papyrus, which was clearly restricted to the eastern Mediterranean coastlands (Sinai and Palestine), there seems to be no geographical preference discernible in the distribution of codex types. Leaving aside the 'Hymnary of papyrus [and] parchment' from Jerusalem mentioned above (MS Tbilisi, National Centre of Manuscripts, H-2123), mixed codices of parchment and paper all seem to be the result of a later substitution, in paper form, of lost or missing parts of an older parchment codex, as in the case of the 'P̣arxali' Gospel manuscript (MS Tbilisi, National Centre of Manuscripts, A-1453) of 973, twenty-two leaves of which were rewritten on paper in the eighteenth century (cf. Ḳaranaʒe et al. 2010, 33).

Fig. 1.7.5 Tbilisi, National Centre of Manuscripts, Q-908, 1054, f. 88r: the beginning of the Gospel of Mark.

7.3. The making of the codex

There has been no thorough investigation into the manufacture of Georgian codices yet. The following remarks, which are based on the analysis of a small number of parchment manuscripts from Georgia, Jerusalem, and Mount Sinai, are therefore tentative.

7.3.1. The making of the quires

Nothing is known about the making of quires in ancient Georgia as there are no sources describing it. Whether or not the bifolia put together in a quire were derived (by folding and/or cutting) from contiguous pieces of parchment, and whether there was the habit of beginning a quire with the flesh side as in older Greek codices, must still be investigated, as must be possible geographical and chronological divergences in manufacturing practices.

7.3.2. The composition of the quires

If the general Georgian term for parchment was indeed borrowed from the Greek word for 'quaternion' (as already noted above), this can be taken to indicate that quires consisting of four bifolia were the standard quire structure in Georgia, as in Byzantine parchment books of all epochs. Nevertheless, as in Late Antique Greek codices, quaternions co-occurred with other quire structures (quinions, ternions, rarely others; cf. Gippert 2013, 85–90 concerning the quire structure of the Kurashi Gospel manuscript).

When parchment leaves were re-used as palimpsests, new bifolia were normally derived from single leaves of the original codex, the underwriting being rotated 90°; by consequence, the resulting codices were usually smaller than the underlying source manuscripts. Nevertheless, the new quires were again mostly conceived as quaternions (cf. Gippert et al. 2007a, xviii for the quire structure of the palimpsest Vienna, ÖNB, Cod.Vind.georg. 2).

7.3.3. Pricking and ruling

Georgian parchment leaves to be used in codices were prepared for being written upon by applying hints concerning the page layout with both pricking and ruling. Palimpsests preserving the oldest stock of Georgian literacy, such as the *xanmeṭi* Gospel manuscript overwritten in Vienna, ÖNB, Cod.Vind.georg. 2 (*c*. sixth/seventh century), prove that these techniques were used right from the beginning. On the other hand, new ruling could also be done for the overwriting in a palimpsest, as in the case of the Graz Psalter (MS Graz, UBG, 2058/2), a palimpsest with an Armenian undertext (Gippert – Imnaišvili 2009b; Renhart 2009). For lack of more detailed studies, we cannot tell anything about the geographical and chronological distribution of the methods in question, and not very much about the techniques and characteristics; it may be sufficient here to state that pricking was usually positioned in the outer margin of a given leaf and that ruling was more often applied for layouts with columns (but was not necessarily restricted to this layout).

7.3.4. Ordering systems

Leaving aside lection indexes to Gospels and other such textual systems, Georgian codices are rather poor with respect to the reference systems they contain. What we do find generally in parchment codices is numberings placed at the top of the first page of a quire and repeated at the bottom of the last page of the quire (with the first quire sometimes omitted in counting), usually in a centred position (more rarely in the right margin), even when the manuscript is written in columns. The sequence of 'end number' and 'start number' thus achieved guaranteed the correct arrangement of quires in a codex (cf. Gippert forthcoming, § 2.1.2 for the quire signatures proving that the fragmentary Georgian MS Sinai, St Catherine, New Finds, georg. N89, pertains, as part of its quire 11, to the *mravaltavi* codex 32-57-33 of the 'Old Collection'). The tradition can be shown to be quite old, as it is even met with in *xanmeṭi* palimpsests (see, for example, Gippert et al. 2007a, 6-1 on quire signatures of the hagiographical manuscript re-used in MS Vienna, ÖNB, Cod.Vind.georg. 2). It is not always certain, however, that the quire signatures are of the same date as the textual contents of a codex; that quire numberings could be added later (for example, when preparing a new binding) is proven by the co-occurrence of Greek and Georgian signatures in the codex Sinai, St. Catherine, georg. 6 (with the numbering starting to diverge by error with quire 12, f. 201r, bearing Georgian *ḳ̄v̄* = 26 and Greek κ̄ε̄ = 25), or by Georgian signatures being applied to Greek codices as in the Sinai manuscripts graec. 215, 230, 231 (evangeliaries), 566, 582, 622, 632 (menologia), 795, 829 (*oktōēchoi*), 928 (kondakarion), and 1097 (typicon).

Numberings other than quire signatures (foliation, pagination, or even column numberings) seem not to have been wide-spread within the Georgian tradition proper (leaving paginations applied by 'modern' librarians aside). The same is true for catchwords, which seem to occur only late in the Georgian manuscript tradition. They are found, for example, in the Tbilisi paper codex S-3702 from the year 1729 containing the *Visramiani* romance (cf. Ķaranaʒe et al. 2010, 107 showing a page of the manuscript with a two-item catchword, *uqmna laškarni*).

7.3.5. The codex as a complex object

As in many other manuscript traditions, Georgian codices exhibit a strong interrelationship between their contents and their outer appearance, and by far the majority of the oldest specimens we have show that they were prepared for exactly one purpose and for one purpose only. Among the majority of codices we may count evangeliaries and lectionaries, both characterized by considerably enlarged letters arranged in columns for better readability during divine services, while codices containing historiographical or philosophical texts were conceived much less for being read aloud (being of much smaller size and written in one column and in minuscules). This implies that the Georgian tradition does not abound in codices comprising multiple texts that have no inherent thematic linkage; even the so-called *mravaltavi* (lit. 'multi-headed') codices can be proved to be clearly designed according to thematic principles (cf. Gippert forthcoming). Cases of codices that consist of several individual parts without any contentual or productional interrelationship are rare.

7.4. The layout of the page

Georgian parchment codices exhibit quite the same range of sizes and proportions as we find in the Greek tradition, which implies, first of all, that the page is oriented vertically, oblong codices being practically unknown. Books measuring less than 100 mm in height are as rare as books whose height extends beyond 500 mm, which seems to speak in favour of the same preference for *sexto* rather than *quarto* skin division as in the Byzantine book manufacture (see Ch. 1 § 8). As to quire structure, Georgian shows a preference for the quaternion type, in agreement with the fact that the Georgian word for parchment very likely reflects the Greek for 'quaternion'. Similar observations can be made with regard to the ratio of width to height, which proportion usually lies between 0.7 and 0.8; however, little can be said with respect to the early centuries, as nearly all specimens that have come down to us were considerably reshaped when they were prepared for being re-used as palimpsests. A more nearly square proportion (*c.*0.9) is visible in the mixed 'Hymnary of papyrus and parchment' (MS Tbilisi, National Centre of Manuscripts, H-2123; cf. the image in Ķaranaʒe et al. 2010, 25), possibly also in the papyrus Psalter of Mount Sinai (Sin. georg. 98), which, however, has been damaged too badly for it to be possible to establish the original dimensions. With the introduction of paper codices, especially those containing non-religious texts, the proportion tends to decrease down to 0.6 due to a narrowing of the width, while heights remained within the former range.

7.5. Text structure and readability

7.5.1. Writing

For lack of detailed investigations, but also due to the fact that most manuscript codices were reduced in size by trimming (in the process of binding, sometimes repeatedly, or, in the case of palimpsests, through re-use), we cannot give a clear picture of the 'occupancy rate' of written vs. blank portions on a given page; it seems, however, that a ratio of about 1:1 was usual in parchment codices, while paper codices may show a higher ratio. At all times, the ratio may be different when miniatures and ornamentation are present or, as in the case of non-religious codices such as Tbilisi, National Centre of Manuscripts, H-54 and H-2074 (both containing Shota Rustaveli's epic), the text is bordered with decoration (see the images in Ķaranaʒe et al. 2010, 92–95).

For the most part, writing is arranged in two columns in parchment codices written in majuscules, including most of the palimpsests. However, a one-column layout is found as early as in the seventh/eighth-century 'Sinai Lectionary' in Graz (MS Graz, UBG, 2058/1, Gippert et al. 2007b), and it prevails in later times, especially in books of small size, but also in rotuli and in the few extant papyrus codices. In paper manuscripts, a two-column layout remains rather exceptional (an example is the liturgical manuscript Tbilisi, National Centre of Manuscripts, A-30 written in 1681; cf. Ķaranaʒe et al. 2010, 90). In the secular paper manuscripts containing epics and the like, we sometimes find a column-like alignment of the rhyming elements of verses, as in the two codices H-54 and H-2074 already mentioned above.

In the Georgian tradition, no layout prescriptions have been preserved. Nevertheless, it is clear that the decision for a one- or two-column layout often depended, if not merely on the size of the support material, on considerations concerning readability, especially in the case of religious texts. There can be no doubt that a two-column layout was typical for evangeliaries and lectionaries that were meant to be used in religious services, while theological treatises and the like deserved no special attention as to their utility for being read aloud, and therefore they could be written in rather long and narrow lines.

Fig. 1.7.6 Tbilisi, National Centre of Manuscripts, S-391 (the Marṭvili Gospels), 1050, f. 187v, Gospel of John 19.19–24.

Special layouts were required, from the oldest times on, for the purpose of integrating additional information as in the case of the Eusebian apparatus, which was usually placed in a peculiar table-like arrangement at the bottom of a given page in both two- and one-column Gospel manuscripts; it was usually arranged columnwise, as in the so-called Adiši Gospels of 897 (Taq̇aišvili 1916; Gippert et al. 2009, I-32). A peculiar layout was also required, for obvious reasons, for the Eusebian Canon Tables that are found at the beginning of many Gospel manuscripts, as in the Alaverdi (MS Tbilisi, National Centre of Manuscripts, A-484, of 1054) or the Çq̇arostavi Gospels (MS Tbilisi, National Centre of Manuscripts, A-98, tenth century; Ḳaranaʒe et al. 2010, 55 and 35), as well as the Ammonian section numbers that were usually arranged, with more or less decoration, together with ekthetic initials to the left of a given column or line, as in the Gospel manuscript Tbilisi, National Centre of Manuscripts, S-962 of 1054 (Ḳaranaʒe et al. 2010, 42), H-1667 (the Ǯruçi Gospels, twelfth century, see fig. 1.7.4), or S-391 (the Marṭvili Gospels of 1050, see fig. 1.7.6). In Gospel codices, the column containing the last verses of a given Gospel is sometimes shaped tapering off towards the bottom, as in the P̣arxali Gospels of 973 (MS Tbilisi, National Centre of Manuscripts, A-1453; Ḳaranaʒe et al. 2010, 33).

Other special layouts that were required by special contents were, for example, the 'frame-like' arrangement of catenae around the biblical text they refer to, as in the so-called Gelati Bible (MS Tbilisi, National Centre of Manuscripts, A-1108, twelfth century; Ḳaranaʒe et al. 2010, 36–37); a similar arrangement of commentaries to a philosophical text, with an iconographic shaping of individual passages, as in the manuscripts A-110 and A-24 (both of the twelfth century; Doborǯginiʒe 2011, 231–244); or the snake-like shaped 'column' that appears in manuscript H-1669 (twelfth or thirteenth century) containing the Georgian translation of John Climacus (Ḳaranaʒe et al. 2010, 72–73). Tables and other special arrangements are found in scientific codices, for example, the circle-shaped description of the lunar phases in the astrological manuscript A-65 (1188–1210; Ḳaranaʒe et al. 2010, 128).

7.5.2. Decoration

Special layouts are further met with, from relatively early times on, in the case of a mixture of text with ornamentation or miniatures on a given page. Depending on a miniature's size, it may extend over the width of two columns as in the Ǯruçi (MS Tbilisi, National Centre of Manuscripts, H-1667, twelfth century, see fig. 1.7.7), Vani (MS Tbilisi, National Centre of Manuscripts, A-1335, twelfth/thirteenth century), and Alaverdi Gospels (MS Tbilisi, A-484, 1054; Ḳaranaʒe et al. 2010, 43–57), or be inserted into one column as in the Gelati Gospels (MS Tbilisi, Q-908, twelfth century; Ḳaranaʒe et al. 2010, 64–67), or the synaxary MS Tbilisi, A-648, 1030 (see fig. 1.7.8); in other cases, the miniature was sized to fit the column layout as in the case of the Varʒia (MS Tbilisi, Q-899, twelfth/thirteenth century) or Mokvi Gospels (MS Tbilisi, Q-902, 1300; Ḳaranaʒe et al. 2010, 75–79). An insertion of miniatures into the text of a given page is also found in non-religious manuscripts, such as the astrological codex Tbilisi, A-65 (cf. Ḳaranaӡe et al. 2010, 39).

Georgian manuscripts of all times and types exhibit a rich inventory of decorative elements, illuminations and miniatures (examples from religious codices are collected in Burčulaӡe 2012, 191–231; see also fig. 2.6.2), with the exception only of the palimpsests of the early centuries. It is true that the manuscripts that were written on Mount Sinai are poorer than others with respect to the addition of pictorial content, but even here we find typical means such as red-coloured crosses or braids used to demarcate sections of texts (for example, the individual Gospels in evangeliaries) or to divide colophons and other additional materials from the main text (Gippert 2010b, 2–4). Manuscript Sinai, St Catherine, georg. 30 is the only Georgian Gospel manuscript from Mount Sinai that contains miniatures of the evangelists (Matthew, Mark, Luke; John is missing, as the codex is defective), but they are much less elaborate than is usual in other manuscripts, with no colours applied.

Fig. 1.7.7 Tbilisi, National Centre of Manuscripts, H-1667 (J̌ruči Gospels), twelfth century, f. 112r (Mk. 13.35).

The use of red ink is the basic means of decoration to be met with in Georgian manuscripts from the beginning of literacy onwards; even in *xanmeṭi* palimpsests, where the pigments of red ink have vanished totally, there are clear indications that rubrics were used for the titles of individual texts (for example, in a hagiographical collection; Gippert et al. 2007a, 6-1 and 6-89, n. 62). Initial letters of texts or major text sections are usually enlarged and project into the left margin, often in combination with the use of red ink or other colours as well; in minuscule manuscripts, the initials are usually majuscules (see figs. 1.7.2, 1.7.4). Titles, whether at the top of a page or within the running text (as in lectionaries, for example), are usually written in majuscules and also in combination with red ink. In some cases, majuscule rubrics seem to have been used in a way similar to the use of capital letters in modern Latin orthographies to denote proper names (Gippert 2010b, 6).

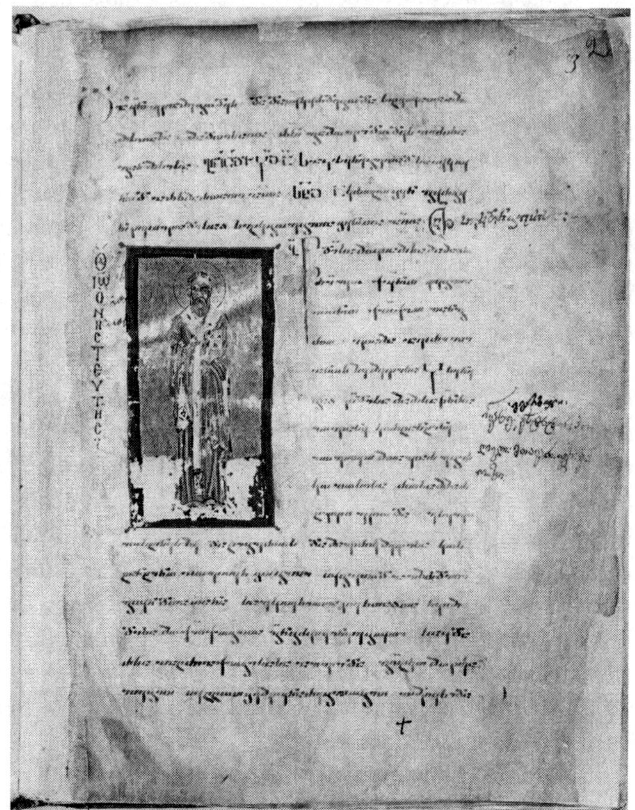

Fig. 1.7.8 Tbilisi, National Centre of Manuscripts, A-648, 1030, f. 2r, with the image of John Nesteutes.

The clear distinction of religious (Christian) and non-religious manuscripts manifests itself in two distinct traditions of decoration and illumination, the one reflecting Greek and the other, Persian models. This is true not only for miniatures such as that of St Matthew in the Alaverdi Gospels (see above), which bears the evangelist's name in Greek (Ḳaranaӡe et al. 2010, 56), or that of

John Nesteutes in MS Tbilisi, National Centre of Manuscripts, A-648, of 1030 (see fig. 1.7.8) but also for 'characteristic' decorations such as the portal-like arrangement of the Eusebian Canon Tables in the Çq̇arostavi Gospels (MS A-98, tenth century; Ḳaranaʒe et al. 2012, 35) or the ekthetic arrangement (mostly in rubrics) of Ammonian section numbers in nearly all evangeliaries (Gippert 2010b, 6–8). A peculiar decoration of codices containing epic texts is the gold-coloured frame designed as a jungle with plants and animals which surrounds the written area in manuscript H-54 (of 1680; Ḳaranaʒe et al. 2010, 92), or the frame with dark green background showing human figures among plants in manuscript H-2074 (sixteenth/seventeenth century; Ḳaranaʒe et al. 2010, 95). A strange cultural crossover is met with in the Psalter A-38 (*c.* tenth/eleventh century) to which was added, below a table on f. 246v, a row containing (from right to left) the Arabic digits from 1 to 9 in red ink (Ḳaranaʒe et al. 2010, 22; the assumption that we might have a 'stylized' part of the 'Albanian alphabet' here is untenable).

7.6. The scribe, the painter and the illuminator at work

7.6.1. Persons, places and methods

As far as we can tell from the limited information we gain from colophons and historiographical sources, nearly all manuscript books of the Old Georgian period were written in monasteries and other places devoted to the Christian religion, either in the Caucasus or in centres abroad. There is no indication of any kind of commercial production; however, in some cases we learn that a manuscript was commissioned by a donor for the sake of his own salvation or the like. This is true, for example, for the oldest dated Georgian manuscript, the Sinai *Mravaltavi* (Sin. georg. 32-57-33+N89) of 863/864 (Šaniʒe 1959), which was, according to its principal colophon, commissioned in the Laura of St Sabas before it was further donated to St Catherine's Monastery (Gippert forthcoming, § 2.2). Among historiographical sources that are relevant here, we may mention the vitae of the founder of the Iviron monastery on Mount Athos, Eptwme, and his son Giorgi (Abulaʒe 1967, 38–207; Latin translation in Peeters 1917–1919, 5–159), which summarize the production of books (mostly texts translated from Greek) in detail, but with no clear indication of methods and means of producing the manuscripts.

7.6.2. Colophons

For lack of a detailed study of Georgian colophons throughout the centuries of manuscript production, only a few characteristics can be outlined here. In general, Georgian codices are much less frequently provided with colophons than are codices of comparable traditions. In many cases, this may be due to damage and loss, especially in codices of the early centuries, most of which have survived only in fragmentary form; as a matter of fact, none of the palimpsest codices that have been analysed so far contains any colophon in its undertext. On the other hand, colophons that have been preserved often indicate that Georgian manuscripts were moved from one place to another, as in the case of the Sinai *Mravaltavi*, which was donated from St Sabas' Laura to St Catherine's Monastery, or in the case of the Adiši Gospels (897), which was removed, together with other codices, from the monastery of Šaṭberdi in Ṭao-Ḳlarǯeti (eastern Anatolia) to Guria in Georgia, as a secondary note tells us (f. 378r; Gippert forthcoming, § 2.3). As in the latter case, much of the knowledge available for the reconstruction of a manuscript's provenance and history can be gained only from information recorded by later hands, rather than a scribe's (or donor's) colophon. A special case is the binder's colophons provided in some codices of the Sinai collection by a certain Ioane Zosime, a Georgian who lived in St Catherine's Monastery in the second half of the tenth century and worked both as a scribe and as a bookbinder (Gippert forthcoming, § 2.2). Another special type of colophon contains the indication of the date of the origin of the individual Gospels appearing in several evangeliaries, with a dating after the Lord's Ascension (for example, Sinai, St. Catherine, georg. 19 f. 199v, for Luke, and f. 262r, for John); this type of 'text colophon' is likely to reflect a tradition going back to Eusebius of Caesarea.

Colophons may be written in the same style as the main text to which they pertain, or differently, for example by employing minuscules instead of majuscules, as in the case of the Gospel manuscripts Sinai, St Catherine, georg. 19 (of 1074) and 30 (of 979), or, rarely, vice versa as in the case of the evangeliary Sinai, St Catherine, georg. 15 (of 978), written by the scribe and bookbinder Ioane Zosime, or the Marṭvili Gospels, MS Tbilisi, National Centre of Manuscripts, S-391 (see fig. 1.7.6). In the Sinai *Mravaltavi* of 863/864, the layout and script of the donor's colophon is exactly the same as that of the main text, whereas the scribe's colophon following it is in minuscules. Colophons typically contain formulae such as *kriste šeiçq̇ale* 'Christ, have mercy' uttered in favour of the writer or donor; detailed information on the persons involved remains rare, however.

7.6.3. Dating systems

The Old Georgian tradition possessed a time-reckoning system (hereafter: AG) based upon calculation from Creation onwards, which differed from the Greek system (the Byzantine Era, BE) by 96 years, the first year of our era (1 CE) falling together with the year 5604/5605, not 5508/5509 as in the BE. Reference to this system is made by counting the total number of years since Creation, or the year within a given lunisolar cycle (Georgian *kronikoni* < Greek *chronikon*) of 532 (19 × 28) years. Whenever Old Georgian codices contain a dating, one or the other of these methods, or both, are applied, as in the colophons of the Sinai *Mravaltavi*, the completion of which is dated to 6468 AG and the year 84 of the (12th) lunar cycle, both corresponding to 863/864 CE (because the year began on 1 September, as in the Greek calendar). In the same way, Ioane Zosime dated his (third) binding of the same codex in the year 6585 AG and in the *kronikon* 201, which is 980/981 CE (Gippert forthcoming, § 2.2.1).

The Georgian system of time-reckoning was continuously used up to the eighteenth century, when it was finally superseded by the Julian calendar (as prevailing in Russia then). Much earlier than this, the Georgians had given up their inherited month names and replaced them with the Latin ones, but the original system can be restored reliably on the basis of attestations mostly in hagiographical manuscripts (see Gippert 1988 for details). More exact datings (mentioning individual days) are extremely rare.

7.6.4. Duration of copying

The time it took a scribe to copy a codex can only rarely be determined on the basis of indications in colophons and secondary notes. The picture we arrive at is similar to that of the Greek tradition. While many scribes have left information about themselves in colophons, practically nothing is known about the artists who added decorations to a codex. The miniature of St Luke in MS Sinai, St Catherine, georg. 30 (f. 122v) is preserved only in the form of a (pencilled?) sketch, which indicates that the illuminator's work was done after the completion of the written text. The same is true for many cases where large initials were sketched for being coloured, but remained unfinished.

7.7. Bookbinding

In the course of an extensive study devoted to the subject, Maia Ḳaranaʒe has drawn up three 'conjectural stages' in the history of Georgian bookbinding (Georgian *q̇da* 'cover'), namely an 'early' stage extending from the tenth to the sixteenth century, a 'transitional' stage in the seventeenth century, and a 'late' stage in the eighteenth and nineteenth centuries (Ḳaranaʒe 2002, 75). This reflects the fact that the oldest bindings of Georgian codices which have come down to us date to the second half of the tenth century, all produced by Ioane Zosime in St Catherine's Monastery on Mount Sinai (Ḳaranaʒe 2002, 75). However, the art of bookbinding must have been known in the Georgian world before this, given that Ioane Zosime himself tells us (in his colophon) that his binding of the Sinai *Mravaltavi* (undertaken in 980/981) was already the third binding of this codex, which had been written 116 years before (in 863/864; Gippert forthcoming, 2.2.1).

Fig. 1.7.9 Sinai, St Catherine, georg. 15, dated 978, back cover of a later binding, photograph by JG.

The specimens of early book binding we have at hand at Mount Sinai clearly show that the basic material of the covers was wooden boards which were bound in leather (Ioane Zosime explicitly mentions *ṭq̇avi zroxisay* 'cow's skin' in his colophon to the *Mravaltavi*) and which were attached to the text block by a thread that was pulled through a series of holes in the boards. Even at Mount Sinai we can observe several types of sewing used in these cases, with a zigzag-like twining (see images in Ḳaranaʒe 2002, I-1, 4d) as in the Gospel manuscripts Sinai, St Catherine, georg. 15 and 16 (codices of 978 and 992, bindings later; fig. 1.7.9), or with a rectangular twining (see images in Ḳaranaʒe 2002, I-4, 15) as in Sinai, St Catherine, georg. 30-38 (of 979) and 29 (*c*. tenth century, bindings later). Another rectangular type (images in Ḳaranaʒe 2002, I-2, 5) is regarded as more typical for the Georgian tradition, which is why it has been styled 'Georgian sewing' (see Ḳaranaʒe et al. 2010, 152–154). The grain of the wooden board is usually horizontal, as in Sinai, St Catherine, georg. 29; however, a vertical orientation of the grain does also appear, as in Sinai, St Catherine, georg. 15 (fig. 1.7.9). On their inner sides, the boards are usually covered by flyleaves, sometimes stemming from other (parchment) codices. For example, the flyleaves of the Sinai *Mravaltavi* were taken from a Christian Palestinian Aramaic Gospel manuscript (Lewis 1894, 118–120). In rare cases, the inner side of the board remained uncovered and could therefore be used for colophon-like additions directly written upon it, as in the case of Sinai, St Catherine, georg. 29.

Fig. 1.7.10 Tbilisi, National Centre of Manuscripts, Q-907 (Çq̇arostavi Gospels), 1195, front cover.

From the earliest times on, leather covers were decorated externally by stamped-in crosses and other ornaments, of either geometrical or other shapes (Ḳaranaʒe 2002 lists, besides crosses, 'rhombic', flower-shaped and band-shaped stamps: II-14, II-4, II-6, II-11). In addition, we find (metal) crosses and other ornaments attached to the cover with rivets or nails, as in the case of Sinai, St Catherine, georg. 19 (of 1074, binding later), or consisting of a decoratively arranged series of nails, as in the Gospel manuscript H-1660 (of 936, binding *c*. sixteenth/seventeenth century; Ḳaranaʒe et al. 2010, 175). In later bindings, we find stylized ornaments stamped into the leather, as in the Gospel manuscript Q-883 (*c*. twelfth or thirteenth century, binding of *c*.1760), where the decoration also has a special (golden) colour (Ḳaranaʒe et al. 2010, 181).

Apart from metal crosses used as decorations, Georgian Gospel codices often bear much more elaborate metal ornamentation, especially in bindings that are later than the fifteenth century. The illustrative material gathered in Ḳaranaʒe et al. 2010, 158–185, shows several specimens of book covers with a total or partial overlay of brasswork illustrating the Crucifixion etc. Additionally, precious stones can be found inlaid into the metalwork, as in the binding of the Çq̇arostavi Gospels (Tbilisi, National Centre of Manuscripts, Q-907, of 1195, fig. 1.7.10; Ḳaranaʒe et al. 2010, 160–161), or in the Alaverdi Gospels (Tbilisi, National Centre of Manuscripts, A-484, of 1054, binding *c*. seventeenth century; Ḳaranaʒe et al. 2010, 177).

In the 'late' phase of Georgian manuscript production, 'European' types of bookbindings and decoration entered the Georgian tradition, including cardboard-based and coloured covers; see Ḳaranaʒe et al. 2010, 182–185 for examples.

References

Abulaʒe 1967; Burčuļaʒe 2012; Cagareli 1886, 1888a, 1888b; Doborǯginiʒe 2011; Gippert 1988, 2010a, 2010b, 2013, forthcoming; Gippert et al. 2007a, 2009; Gippert – Tandaschwili 2014; Gogašvili 2003, 2004, 2006; Imnaišvili 2004; Ḳaranaʒe 2002; Ḳaranaʒe et al. 2010; Kaǯaia 1974; Meṭreveli et al. 1978; Lewis 1894; Nanobašvili 1973; P̣aṭariʒe 1965a, 1965b, 1968; Peeters 1917–1919; Rayfield 2010; Renhart 2009; Šaniʒe 1959; Šaniʒe – Marṭirosovi 1977; Taq̇aišvili 1916; Ṭimote 1852. Web sources: Gippert et al. 2007b; Gippert – Imnaišvili 2009a, 2009b; Tbilisi, National Centre of Manuscripts, <http://www.manuscript.ge/index.php?m=73&ln=eng>, last access 29 November 2014.

8. Greek codicology (MMa)

8.1. Materials and tools

In the course of Antiquity (and well into the Middle Ages) Greek was written on a wide range of hard and soft materials (rock and marble, metals, wood, clay, plaster, or papyrus, parchment, and paper), the soft support reserved for texts intended for transmission and reproduction.

8.1.1. Papyrus

Papyrus was the most widely used writing material in the Graeco-Roman world: it was employed for writing both books and documents at least since the fifth century BCE, first in roll form and later also in codex form. Even after the diffusion of parchment, papyrus continued to be used in Roman and Byzantine Egypt for the manufacture of both books (rolls and codices) and, especially, documents, until the Arab conquest.

The first important modern discovery of Greek papyri was that of Herculaneum, near Naples, where a whole library of carbonized rolls (approximately 1,800 fragments) was found in 1752 in the ruins of a philosopher's house which had been destroyed and buried by the eruption of Mount Vesuvius in 79 CE. After being brought sporadically from Egypt to Europe since the beginning of the nineteenth century, Greek papyri began to emerge in large quantities from archaeological excavations carried out in the Fayyum region toward the end of same century and were later found also in other areas of the Near East: they represent altogether by far the most significant portion of the surviving finds. Despite the efforts made to prevent their illegal traffic, papyri have continued to find their way into the hands of native dealers, and thence into English, Continental, and American collections. Among the most recent finds, worthy of special mention is a partially charred Orphic papyrus of the second half of the fourth century BCE, discovered in 1962 in a tomb near present-day Thessaloniki, which numbers among the most ancient surviving examples of a Greek literary book (see Ch. 1 § 8.2.2 and Ch. 2 § 7).

The overwhelming majority of the extant papyri are documentary (letters, accounts, wills, deeds, contracts, receipts, petitions, notices, invitations, etc.). Literary papyri contain both classical texts and religious (biblical and theological) writings (Turner 1980, 1984; Bagnall 2009).

8.1.2. Parchment

The oldest preserved specimen of Greek parchment (*P.Dura* 15, 225 × 52 mm) is a small portion of a Hellenistic contract dating from the early second century BCE and originating from the colony of Dura Europos in eastern Syria. However, already in the fifth century BCE Greek historians such as Ctesias (Diodorus Siculus, II, 32, 4; *FGrHist* 688 F 5) and Herodotus (V, 58) remind us that Persians and Greeks wrote on leather, while Pliny the Elder (*Naturalis historia* XIII, 21 [70]) attributes the 'invention' of parchment to the scholars of the Hellenistic library of Pergamum, as a reaction to a disruption in the supply of papyrus, which was allegedly ordered by the Ptolemies with an view to fostering the rival library of Alexandria (in fact, the word *pergamēnē*, instead of *diphthera*, appears for the first time, in the form of an adjective, in the Diocletian edict *de pretiis rerum venalium*, 301 CE). During Late Antiquity, parchment gradually prevailed as the preferred writing material for Greek books. For a long time, however, both for sacred and for profane literature the choice between papyrus and parchment was strongly dependent on the books' function, their geographical origin, and the social status of their patrons and owners: according to the Hellenistic-Roman tradition, secular texts (the only exception being Demosthenes) were mainly copied on papyrus at least until the late seventh century (over 50% of the extant witnesses); on the other hand, complete Bibles (among which some prestigious copies in canonical scripts) were the only sacred books clearly associated with parchment, whereas smaller and less ambitious Gospel codices and Psalters were often copied on the cheaper material papyrus, at least until the end of the seventh century. As early as the fourth century CE the manufacturing techniques had reached high levels of professionalism, as is shown by the excellent quality of some surviving examples: among these are some of the most ancient and solemn Late Antique copies of the Bible, such as the *Codex Vaticanus* (Vatican City, BAV, Vat. gr. 1209) and the *Codex Sinaiticus* (London, BL, Add. 43725 plus fragments in Sinai, St Catherine's Monastery, Leipzig, UB, Cod. gr. 1, and St Petersburg, RNB, gr. 2, gr. 259, gr. 843, OLDP.O.156).

Greek codices were usually written on parchment made from goatskin or sheepskin; the use of calfskin, widespread in northwestern Europe (and recently proposed for the *Codex Sinaiticus*), is not documented. Occasional mentions of pony, rabbit, deer, antelope or even snake skins (the latter used for a Ho-meric roll, according to the eleventh-century historian Geōrgios Kedrēnos, *Hist. Comp.* I, p. 616 Bekker), are doubtful and anyway not confirmed by archaeological evidence.

Information concerning places and contexts of manufacture of Greek parchment is very scarce: the monastery of Stoudios had its own *membranarion*, were parchment was prepared by monks, but the profession of parchment-maker does not appear in the commercial manual known as the *Book of the Eparch*. Late Byzantine sources refer to the difficulty of finding parchment of adequate quality, especially in winter.

Almost nothing is known of the methods employed for the manufacture of parchment in the Greek and Byzantine world. A Byzantine origin (unprovable, if not improbable) has been postulated for a series of seven Armenian prescriptive texts (most of which are quite repetitive), attested in manuscripts apparently dating from the fifteenth to the eighteenth century and published in a German version based on a Russian translation (Schreiner 1983; see Ch. 1 § 3). Some of these late sources refer to a treatment of the (bigger and harder) skins with pigeon droppings (rich in fat-degrading enzymes), following (not replacing) their soaking in one or more hydrated lime baths; two texts of more recent date prescribe bran or barley flour for the same purpose. It remains entirely uncertain whether, and in which proportions, Greek craftsmen ever adopted the oriental practice of enzymatic dehairing and degreasing, not *instead of*, but *combined with* the use of chemical depilation. Certain details of the finishing process are comparatively better known. A famous passage from a letter addressed in 1295 by the theologian, grammarian, and rhetorician, but also bibliophile, collector and book restorer, Maximos Planudēs to the monk Melchisedek Akropolitēs offers—among other interesting information—some insights concerning the finishing touches applied to parchment in order to improve its surface qualities and to make it more suitable for writing. Planudēs, who often complains about the poor quality of the writing material he is forced to settle for, strongly condemns the practice of coating its surface with a layer of egg (*mēd'ōō tautas perikechristhai*), which he blamed for causing letters to fall off the page. Egg white, mixed with linseed, appears in two of the previously cited Armenian texts, and its use seems to be confirmed by recent histochemical and microchemical analysis conducted on a small sample of eleventh- to fourteenth-century Byzantine manuscripts (Kireeva 1999); egg yolk was used rather as a binding medium in Byzantine (as well as in western) illuminated codices.

Parchment quality obviously depended on the natural properties of the raw material, but also on the technical details of the process and on the amount of care invested in its execution. The overall impression (based on colour, surface grain and smoothness, presence of hair residues, streaks, holes or other irregularities) may be one criterion for dating and localizing a given piece of parchment: for instance, codices originating in Byzantine southern Italy are often made of poor-quality skins, while the use of parchment with late western features (greyish in colour and evenly smooth on both sides) may help in recognizing the use of a late Byzantine 'archaistic' writing style, based on the imitation of earlier examples, even if perfectly executed, as in the case of MS Vatican City, BAV, Pal. gr. 186 (Irigoin 1981b). Useful but still too sporadic information is offered by the identification of animal species: the only systematic investigation carried out so far shows a clear predominance of sheepskin parchment in 61 eleventh-century Italo-Greek codices (Bianchi et al. 1993). This result agrees with the information provided by the fourteenth-century Latin inventory of the library of Pope Boniface VIII, which includes thirty-three Greek manuscripts (Bischoff 1993); on the contrary, luxury Renaissance manuscripts in Greek may be made of fine kidskin parchment of Latin manufacture. Goat is the only species clearly detected until now by all the experiments with DNA extraction and analysis—the 'new frontier' of species recognition—carried out on Dead Sea Scroll fragments and on (only three) Byzantine parchment manuscripts (Poulakakis et al. 2007; the reliability of the method has been questioned).

Information about the thickness of Greek parchment is also almost completely lacking, with the single exception of Greek books from eleventh-century southern Italy, whose parchment is usually thicker than that of contemporary Latin ones (*c.*23–24μ vs. 20μ): this detail seems to be in accordance with the unsophisticated character of local Greek book manufacture. Greek craftsmen, as well as Latin ones, knew and applied some specific devices to optimize the distribution of parchment thickness within individual codices: for instance, they tended to produce quires of even thickness and to employ the thickest pieces as outside bifolia, or to reserve them for illuminated pages; they also took care to minimize the visual impact of irregularities (holes, tears, *lisières*), by grouping them towards the end of the codex or by hiding them in the middle of the quire (Maniaci 2000a).

Regardless of its qualitative features, parchment was always a very expensive writing support, and not always easy to find (especially in the Late Byzantine period), as is confirmed by the repeated complaints of monks and scholars (among them John Tzetzes, *Scholia in Aristophanem*, for the twelfth century, or the already mentioned Planudēs, for the thirteenth (ep. 95, in which the parchment he has received is so poor that it is compared to donkey's skin; 100; 106)) and by the high costs of parchment book.

Fig. 1.8.1 Athens, National Library of Greece, 223, palimpsest, lower uncial script (*ogivale inclinata*) in two columns, upper script: 28 April 1195 CE, Basil of Caesarea, *Ascetica*; lower script: eight/ninth century, Basil of Caesarea, Homilies in *Hexaemeron*; *Ascetica*, f. 268r, detail.

Reasons of cost and availability most probably played a role in the definition of dimensional standards for Greek parchment manuscripts (see Ch. 1 § 8.4). The high cost of parchment and/or its shortage certainly explain (at least in part) the production of Greek palimpsests (e.g. fig. 1.8.1, Athens, National Library of Greece, 223) although the economic reasons are not enough to justify the frequency of the phenomenon, which is better understood as part of a more general mediaeval tendency to 'recycle'. The high number of extant Greek palimpsests—only partially identified and studied (with the notable exception of the Grottaferrata collection, on which see Crisci 1990)—mostly come from peripheral areas such as the thirteenth to fourteenth century Apulian Terra d'Otranto, but also from other Italian and oriental provincial regions (such as the Syro-Palestinian area) and even from the capital of the declining Empire, after the end of the twelfth century. The 'Archimedes Palimpsest', a unique copy of an otherwise unknown treatise of the great Sicilian mathematician (the *Method of Mechanical Theorems*), but also of other otherwise unattested works, is only one of the most famous examples; in some Greek palimpsests, the parchment was repeatedly rewritten (as in Vatican City, BAV, Vat. gr. 2306 + Vat. gr. 2061A + Grottaferrata, Abbazia Greca di S. Nilo, Crypt. Z.α.43, a copy of Strabo from the fifth century plus a legal collection from the seventh century and various religious texts from the tenth century). There are also volumes in which the upper and lower texts are written in different languages and belong to different book cultures, as in the case of an unknown comedy by Menander transmitted in a large majuscule codex of the fourth century (if not the end of the third), recently found in one of the two lower layers of a ninth-century Syriac manuscript (Vatican City, BAV, Vat. sir. 623: D'Aiuto 2003), an extraordinary but not unique example of a 'complex linguistic, graphic and textual stratigraphy' that is also found in other oriental examples (containing various associations of Arabic, Syriac, Hebrew, Aramaic, Armenian, Latin and Greek leaves). Although a census of Greek palimpsests in European libraries was launched some years ago and the digital techniques for 'restoring' the underlying texts (see General introduction § 2.3) have progressed significantly in the last few years, we are still far from a global understanding of the historical, technical and cultural significance of manuscript erasing and rewriting.

Late Antique Greek scribes knew the use of writing in silver or gold ink on purple- or indigo-coloured parchment (obtained either by dying or by surface painting). This is first attested in a dozen Greek Biblical manuscripts, including three of the most spectacular decorated Greek codices assigned to the sixth century and tentatively associated (mainly on an art-historical basis) with the Palestinian area (alternatively, Asia Minor): the lavishly illuminated Rossano and Sinope Gospels (Rossano Calabro, Museo dell'Arcivescovado and Paris, BnF, Supplément grec 1286) and the Vienna Genesis (Vienna, ÖNB, Cod.theol.gr. 31). Further examples, even though they contain no illumination, belong to the same book type, such as the Gospels *Codex Petropolitanus purpureus* (codex N, today divided between the Russian National Library in St Petersburg (Gr. 537) and various other libraries, such as the Library of the Monastery of St John the Theologian on Patmos, Biblioteca Apostolica Vaticana, British Library in London, Österreichische Nationalbibliothek in Vienna, the Pierpont Morgan Library in New York, the Byzantine Museum in Athens, the Museum of Byzantine Culture in Thessaloniki, and the private collection of Marquis A. Spinola in Lerma) and the *Codex Beratinus* (Tirana, AQSH, 1) or the Zurich Psalter (Zurich, Zentralbibliothek, RP 1), recently attributed to Constantinople (Crisci et al. 2007); other books (such as the Gospels codex St Petersburg, RNB, Gr. 53, ninth/tenth century) contain only a few dyed or surface-coloured bifolia. In the Greek world, the use of highly symbolic purple parchment for display codices of religious content was abandoned in the course of the ninth century, after the end of the iconoclastic controversy (apart from a few isolated exceptions, such as the lectionary Naples, Biblioteca Nazionale Vittorio Emanuele III, Neap. ex Vind. gr. 2, which may have belonged to the emperor Basil I, and the previously mentioned St Petersburg, RNB, Gr. 53); it persisted until the twelfth century for imperial documents and for the emperor's letters to the Latin popes. Without the help of scientific analysis, it is impossible to distinguish the expensive murex purple (whose use in mediaeval manuscripts is often mentioned, but has never been proved) from its animal or vegetable surrogates (the lichens *Roccella tinctoria* or *Ochrolechia* were recently, and only tentatively, detected in the Zurich Psalter).

8.1.3. Paper

The use of paper (probably of Islamic manufacture) in a Greek book is attested early in a collection of theological texts, Vatican City, BAV, Vat. gr. 2200, produced in the Jerusalem region around the year 800 (Perria 1983–1984), i.e. a few decades before the most ancient dated Arabic example (of 848, now in the Regional Library of Alexandria). The paper employed in Vat. gr. 2200 shows a smooth structure (but with visible lumps and vegetable fibres), considerable irregularity in thickness from one sheet to another, the presence of very dense and curved wire lines of variable thickness and a format which does not correspond precisely to any of the known ones, resulting in a very narrow page proportion. Apart from this isolated occurrence, the new material is known to have been used for Byzantine books about two centuries later (the first dated examples are Sinai, St Catherine, Sin. ar. 116, Greek-Arabic Gospel lectionary from 995/996, and two Athos codices, Iviron 258, 1042/1043 and Lavra Θ 70, 1060). Already in the tenth century there is a reference to a tax called *chartiatika* and to paper makers, *chartopoioi*; paper makers may also have been active in Stoudios at the beginning of the ninth century. Paper became widespread in books between the mid-eleventh century and the end of the twelfth (as is shown by the inventory of the monastery founded by Michaēl Attaliatēs in 1077, which lists parchment and paper books separately, and by that of the library of the monastery of St John of Patmos, dated 1201, in which 20% of the codices—57 out of 301—are on paper).

A local manufacture seems not to have existed in the Byzantine Empire: except perhaps in specific areas such as Jerusalem and Mount Sinai, paper was an imported material, initially sourced in the Middle East, and later (but as early as the tenth century) also from North Africa and Spain. The switch from parchment to paper was a gradual process, whose main steps can be roughly traced through the testimony of dated codices (Prato 1984): during the period of the Latin kingdom of Constantinople (1204–1261), in spite of the serious economic difficulties, sacred books continued to be written on expensive parchment, while primitive Italian paper (and perhaps also Catalan paper, as in Vatican City, BAV, Vat. gr. 207: Canart 1982) made its appearance in the (rare) profane codices; after 1261, in the Palaiologan age, paper became virtually the only material used for secular books, appearing in 80% of the dated witnesses, while parchment still prevailed in 70% of the sacred ones (mainly Gospels and lectionaries). From 1340/1341, paper is practically the only material attested in Greek manuscripts, with very few exceptions, such as the volumes made in Constantinople at the monastery Tōn Hodēgōn (which probably produced its own parchment), a few individual books of aristocratic patronage or the luxury Renaissance products.

The paper used in Greek books may thus be watermarked or not. While watermarked paper has been investigated in depth, the characterization and differentiation of papers without watermarks is much more uncertain. The differences concern various elements whose combination may help in establishing provenance: raw materials and features of the pulp; structure of the mould and methods used; size of the sheets; sizing.

Not only are the chronology and diffusion of the different kinds of paper difficult to define, but we still lack systematic studies on the time and ways of their introduction, and the coexistence of or alterna-

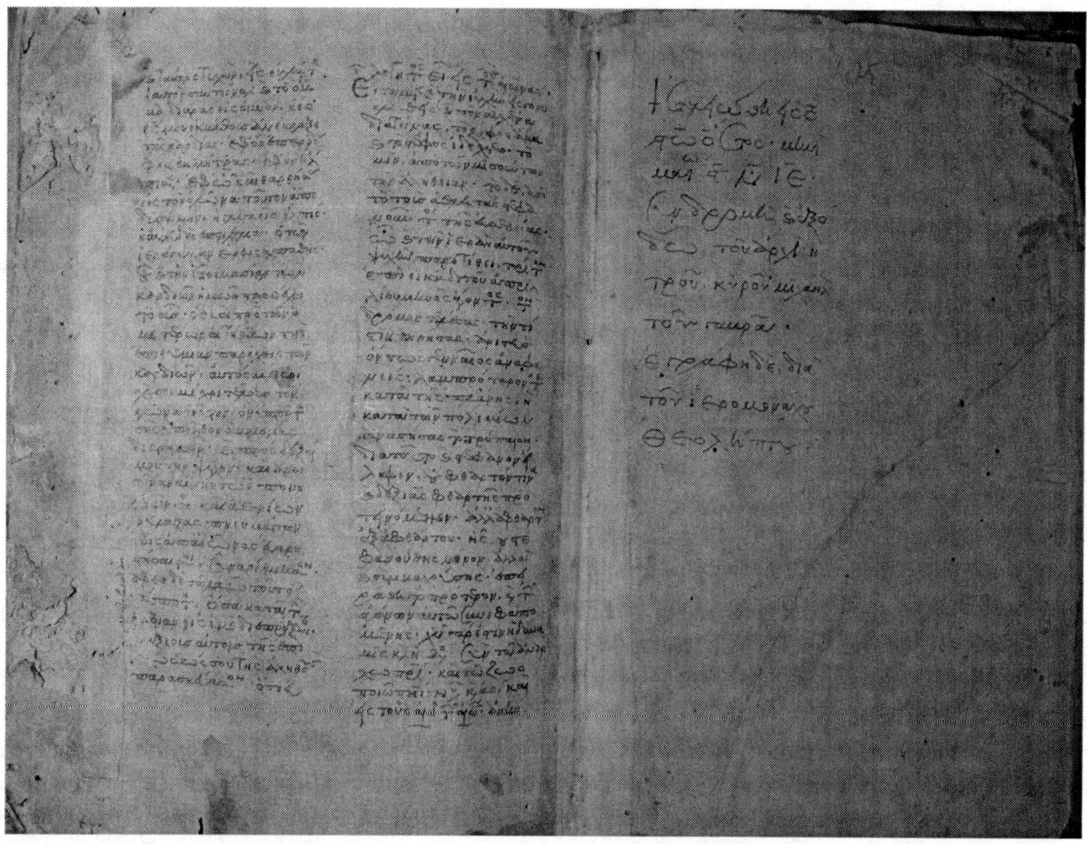

Fig. 1.8.2 Athos, Pantokrator, 84, dated by the colophon 6 May 1362 CE, collection of sermons by various church fathers (*Panegyricon*), ff. 424v–425r.

tion between eastern and western papers: a typology of the use of paper in Greek manuscripts, organized chronologically and by areas of production and book contents, and based on the study of dated—and ideally also provenanced—specimens, is still a desideratum of Greek codicological research. More specific unresolved questions concern the nature and diffusion of paper apparently composed of two splittable layers, and the occasional presence of a zigzag mark that appears with some frequency in Greek manuscripts, but whose function is still unclear, as is the method by which it was created.

Islamic paper was used in southern Italy and Sicily probably as early as in the eleventh century: a bilingual (Greek-Arabic) charter by the Norman Countess Adelaide (today in Palermo, Archivio di Stato di Palermo) dates from 1109; a few Greek codices on Islamic paper (such as Vatican City, BAV, Vat. gr. 469, area of the Strait of Messina) have also survived. The first known Greek codex on non-watermarked Italian paper (produced probably from the 1130s, possibly through the mediation of Genoese and Venetian merchants) is a liturgical book (*oktōēchos*) dating from 1252 (London, BL, Add. 27359), supposed to have originated in Epirus. In Fabriano, paper production probably started by the mid-thirteenth century at the latest, with the introduction of watermarks, which prevailed everywhere (including the Byzantine territories) in the course of the fourteenth and fifteenth centuries. In the fourteenth century, the use of Italian watermarked paper is documented in Crete, Cyprus, Euboea, Mytilene, Lesvos, Rhodes, Macedonia (mainly Thessaloniki) and southern Italy; the oldest example of western watermarked paper in Constantinople dates from 1330/1331; in 1344 it is attested in Asia Minor and subsequently on Mount Athos (see fig. 1.8.2 Athos, Pantokrator, 84: the two-circles western watermark is visible in the centre of f. 424v). In those areas where Byzantine cultural continuity was disrupted before the fall of Constantinople and the Turkish conquest of the last Venetian colonies, the transition from eastern to western paper seems not to have taken place at all: eastern paper was still used in Syria and Palestine in the mid-fifteenth century.

The (somewhat overestimated) contribution of watermarks to the dating of Greek codices explains the early interest shown toward them by historians of western paper. For Greek manuscripts, the general repertoires (Briquet 1907; Piccard 1961–1997 and <http://www.piccard-online.de>, last access October 2014) are complemented by some more specific ones (for example Harlfinger – Harlfinger 1974, 1980;

Sosower 2004), which are most useful for the purpose of dating, although they do not cover all the variety of watermarks attested in Greek manuscripts (not even in dated ones), for which adequate censuses are still lacking.

8.1.4. Inks

Greek manuscript ink (*melan*, *melanion*, *egkauston*) displays a great variety of colours, with shades ranging from pale to bronze brown, dark brown or shiny black. The differences sometimes provide clues to geographical origin (codices from the Palestinian-Cypriot area, for example, often show a very dark, blackish ink); in most cases however colour is not useful for localization purposes. Indeed, naked eye observation does not provide information on the composition of the inks, the knowledge of which developed only recently, through a study of surviving recipes combined with technical examination (Schreiner – Oltrogge 2011).

Ancient and mediaeval recipes concerning the composition of 'soot' ink and 'iron-gall' ink (the use of plant inks has also been detected recently, see Ch. 1 § 1.1.4) are quite numerous, although their frequency grew only from the twelfth century, reaching its climax in the fourteenth/fifteenth century, with the diffusion of real technical literature. Some corpora of Greek technical texts (like the fifteenth-century one due to the learned Cardinal Isidore of Kiev, in Vatican City, BAV, Vat. gr. 914), along with other individual and more or less fragmentary texts, provide a broad overview of the procedures adopted by the scribes (quite similar to those used by their Latin counterparts).

A particularly interesting contribution is offered by four detailed eleventh-century recipes in Milan, Biblioteca Ambrosiana, C 222 inf., which illustrate various combinations of the main ingredients (tannin, metallic sulphate and gum) (Mazzucchi 2005; Schreiner – Oltrogge 2011); another recipe, written by a fourteenth-century hand in an eleventh-century codex, Jerusalem, Church of the Holy Sepulchre, 38 (f. 280r), varies the proportions according to the writing material—parchment or paper. The eighty or so surviving texts, mostly transmitted by a single source (about twenty of which concern the manufacture of iron-gall inks), share a number of features: anonymity, didactic style, lack of information or vagueness about ingredients, quantities, methods of manufacture, and frequent references to other everyday or technical practices and contexts. Most recipes are copied within collections of alchemical or medical texts or are annotations added in originally blank spaces.

The black ink employed for writing was often complemented by a red one, with both an aesthetic and a practical function: to highlight titles and running titles, rubrics, initials, and other 'navigating' devices. The manufacture of cinnabar (mercury sulphide, HgS), also used as background for gilding, is described without significant variations in a number of Greek recipes (including those transmitted by Paris, BnF, Grec 2327; Vatican City, BAV, Pal. gr. 243; Venice, BNM, gr. 299), reflecting the same alchemical processes that are illustrated by various other sources. The colour palette of illuminated manuscripts is much richer, including various shades of blue, green, yellow, pink, purple and white, but Byzantine sources are almost completely silent about their methods of manufacture, with sporadic exceptions.

Texts concerning the manufacture of both gold powder and gold leaf, and of its amalgams (with copper, pyrite or mercury) and surrogates (arsenic sulphide or orpiment), are much more numerous, because of the interest aroused among the alchemists. Other recipes also describe the preparation of binders (gums of various nature, egg white) used to dissolve the gold powder employed for tracing the letters (chrysography), or to increase its brilliance, and of various substances (brazilwood lake, shellac, ochre, vermilion) involved in the preparation of the background. Some texts also refer to hard materials that were used for polishing (quartz, haematite, onyx, along with dog or wolf teeth). Despite the progress that has been made in collecting and analysing the sources, a more accurate classification requires the Greek sources to be compared with those from other book cultures.

8.1.5. Writing instruments

Miniatures of the evangelists sitting in front of a lectern and occasionally copying from a roll into a codex (or vice versa) occur frequently in Byzantine manuscripts. These conventional portraits abound in inconsistencies and anachronisms (cp. General introduction § 1.1.6) and only partially alleviate the shortage of Greek sources concerning the act of writing and the instruments of the scribe. The evangelists are portrayed holding the writing instrument in their hand and are normally surrounded by a variety of other tools, poised on the lectern, on various kinds of shelves or elsewhere: knives of different shapes, used to sharpen the point of the instrument, inkwells or vials containing brown or coloured inks, rulers and squares, punches, compasses, sponges and other items less easy to identify, of which no archaeological evidence survives (see fig. 1.8.3 showing St John depicted on the page facing the *incipit* of the Gospel of John in the manuscript Tirana, Albanian National Archives, 93). It is also very difficult to connect visual testimonies to the terminology found in Byzantine written sources, which is (as usual) very rare.

Fig. 1.8.3 Tirana, Albanian National Archives, 93, first half of the tenth century, Four Gospels, f. 224v: St John the Evangelist, photograph courtesy of the Centre for the Study of New Testament Manuscripts, <http://www.csntm.org>.

Wax tablets were written with a pointed metal or ivory stylus (*stylos*, *grapheion*), while flexible supports (papyrus, parchment, paper) required the use of the reed or calamus (*kalamos*, *schoinos*). Greek handwriting displays little shading or modulation, supporting the opinion that Greek scribes continued to use the calamus up to the Renaissance, long after the diffusion of the split nib quill pen, which occurred during the Latin Middle Ages, producing thick and thin strokes according to the direction of the stroke. The appearance of some Greek majuscules, showing a more or less marked contrast of heavy and light strokes, suggests, however, that the scribes could choose between instruments of different shapes, either with a pointed or a flat nib, depending on the result they wished to obtain. A recent, but still tentative attempt was made to deduce the characteristics of the Byzantine writing instrument and the way it was used from the fluctuations in the colour of the ink trace, in relation to the points where it was detached from the sheet to be dipped into the inkwell (Benedetti 2010).

Compasses, knives of various forms, sharpeners, pumice stone, and various other objects also appear in the Byzantine portraits of the evangelists; they are often hard to identify and to connect to the names given by Greek sources.

8.2. Book forms

8.2.1. Miscellaneous forms

Ancient Greek writing is found on a variety of media: stone or marble slabs bearing engraved display texts (inscriptions); thin metal (usually lead) sheets on which magic formulas were scratched; canvas or linen strips; clay pottery sherds (*ostraca*) for voting procedures, notes, letters and school exercises; wall plaster; wooden tablets, sometimes filled with a compound of melted coloured wax, written individually or assembled in groups of two or more elements.

8.2.2. The roll and the rotulus

Recent archaeological finds from Daphnē (Athens) make it possible to date the earliest surviving examples of Greek books (among which are fragments of tablets and of a literary roll) at least back to the second half of the fifth century BCE (Pöhlmann – West 2012), which is significantly earlier than either the Orphic 'Derveni papyrus' or a papyrus containing Timotheus' *Persians* (*P.Berol.* inv. 9875), both assigned to the second half of the fourth century BCE. The ancient papyrus book roll (*biblos, biblion, chartēs, volumen*), derived from the commercial roll, was normally written only on the inner (front) side, showing the horizontal fibres, although no longer useful documentary rolls were sometimes used to bear literary works on the reverse side (such as Aristotle's *Athenian Constitution*, *P.Lond.* I, 108, written on the back of four rolls containing private agricultural accounts). The opposite case is also well attested, namely, rolls containing literary works on the front side, whose reverse sides were later reused for documents.

In Greek rolls, the sequence of written words is arranged, from left to right, in *scriptio continua* in a series of columns (*selides*) along the roll's length, whose height, width, distance, number and spacing of lines varies from roll to roll, and according to text type. The absence of ruling could result in a gradual leftward shift of the lines as the copyist proceeded towards the bottom of the column ('Maas' law'), although the phenomenon has also been interpreted as a deliberate choice to facilitate the passage of the eye from line to line. Author, title and internal subdivisions were usually mentioned at the end of the roll (but sometimes also at its beginning). Usually, a single sheet (*kollēma*) of unwritten papyrus, sometimes rotated at ninety degrees as compared to the other *kollēmata*, was positioned at each end of the roll (*prōtokollon* and *eschatokollon*). The roll was either wrapped upon itself, or else rolled around a stick made of wood or bone (*omphalos*) that was fixed at the right-hand end of the last *kollēma*; alternatively, two such sticks could be attached, one at each end. The contents of the roll could be written on a small piece of papyrus or parchment (*sillybos*, *pittakion*) which was then fastened to one of the two edges of the roll. Only rarely do such tags survive, but they are mentioned in literary sources and visible in paintings representing book rolls.

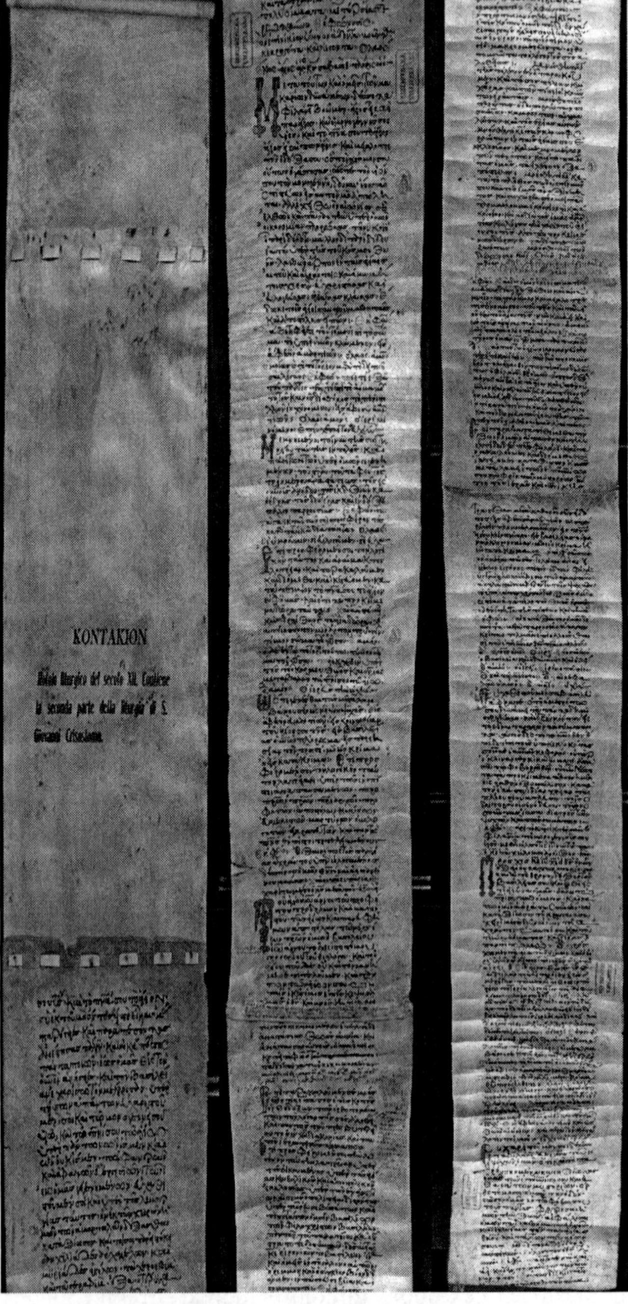

Fig. 1.8.4 Rome, Biblioteca Vallicelliana, G70, end of the twelfth century, the liturgy of St John Chrysostom.

Papyrus book rolls were made either of all or part of a commercially manufactured papyrus roll, or by pasting two or more rolls together. A reconstruction of the conventions relating to their size and contents—probably codified during the Hellenistic period—is severely limited by the fragmentary state of surviving *volumina* and the risk of arbitrarily generalizing the information obtainable from the better-preserved collections of materials, such as those from Oxyrhynchus or Herculaneum. To judge from the surviving evidence, the usual length varied between 3.5 and 11 m, with rare exceptions: a single roll could contain an entire work of limited length (for example a tragedy, a comedy, a speech, a Platonic dialogue) or a section of a larger work that was divided among several rolls. Conversely, texts too short to fill up a roll were transcribed together onto a single roll, to make it fall within the standard range of lengths, for example, series of poems, groups of speeches of one or more orators, or short texts that were part of a single work. Rolls of truly miscellaneous contents have not survived. As regards the height of a roll, the examples from Herculaneum tend to be shorter (between 19 and 24 cm) than those of Egyptian provenance (between 25 and 33 cm). In both cases, the width of the columns does not seem to have been especially large (between approximately 4 and 7 cm for prose, from 8 to 14 cm for poetry): attempts to connect layout and quality of the rolls have not, thus far, produced sufficiently clear results.

Despite the scarcity of surviving evidence, it is certain that leather and parchment rolls existed since ancient times (see fig. 1.8.4); outside Egypt they might have been more common than we tend to think: note, for instance, the parchment roll of the second century CE containing Xenophon's *Symposium* which was found in Antinoopolis (*P.Ant.* I 26) but may have come from outside Egypt.

8.2.3. The codex

The transition from roll to codex, one of the most momentous changes in the history of the book and the transmission of texts, was a slow and gradual process: in fact, it must be understood against the background of the various materials and objects that were used as ancient writing supports. Among these, a particularly important role was played by the (simply wooden or additionally 'waxed') tablets on which Greeks and Romans wrote everyday accounts, various documents, messages, school exercises, and drafts of literary texts: they could be used individually or grouped in sets of two (diptych), three (triptych) or more units (polyptych), much like real wooden books. Already in post-classical Greek civilization, the use of polyptychs for writing literary texts is sporadically attested, primarily for school use: one of the oldest surviving codices of rhetorical content, transmitting three of Isocrates' speeches, is a wooden book of the third/fourth century CE (*P.Kellis* III 95), which emerged in 1988 from the excavation of the ancient Kellis site, in the Egyptian oasis of Dakhleh (Worp – Rijksbaron 1997). On the other hand, frequent allusions by classical Latin authors (maybe Horace, more clearly Martial, Quintilian) state that books in codex form were certainly already in use at the end of the first century CE, a period to which also the most ancient remains of Latin manuscripts refer; a well-known passage in St Paul (II Tim 4:13), in which he asks his disciple Timothy to bring back some books from Troas, including *malista tas membranas* ('especially the parchments'), probably also points in the same direction. Archaeological evidence and literary sources agree in showing that between the first and second centuries CE the codex was already in use (perhaps first in Rome and later in Greek-speaking regions), although the roll still remained the standard form for literary texts.

Calculations made by Colin Roberts and Theodore Skeat (Roberts – Skeat 1983) on the basis of Greek materials of prevailingly Egyptian origin show that the transition from roll to codex was rather slow and was fully accomplished only between the fourth and fifth centuries, probably later than in the Latin context (where the genesis of the parchment codex must probably be placed).

Two kinds of reasons are frequently evoked to explain the rise of the codex: functional reasons (capacity, manoeuvrability, comfort of reading, ease of reference at every step of the text, possibility to combine more than one work in a single volume and to associate a text with an extensive commentary) and sociological ones (preference of the Christians for a more 'popular' book form, symbolically opposed to the 'pagan' roll). Recently, a more nuanced view has been proposed (Crisci 2008), which emphasizes (also on a statistical basis) the long coexistence of the two types of book, the presence of the same texts on rolls and codices, and—from a technical point of view—the parallel evolution of Christian and pagan codices. The relationship between the transition from roll to codex and that from papyrus to parchment has also been the subject of conflicting hypotheses: the origin of the codex seems likely to belong in connexion with the use of parchment, and the papyrus codex should probably be considered a 'by-product' of the roll, most prevalent in the eastern context, where papyrus was a cheap and abundant material.

After the 'triumph' of the codex, parchment rolls (also called 'scrolls' or 'rotuli', when written vertically in a single series of lines) remained in use during the Greek Middle Ages, particularly (though not exclusively) for liturgical contents. Numerous Byzantine examples survive (eastern and western, on parchment or paper), from the eighth and ninth centuries until the introduction of printing, with a maximum frequency in the twelfth to fifteenth centuries; the majority of them contain the liturgies of Basil and Chrysostom, which are the most frequently celebrated liturgies in the Byzantine tradition. A comprehensive history of Byzantine liturgical scrolls has not yet been written: they are usually made up of a long (up to 13 m) and mostly quite narrow (13–25 cm) strip, very soberly laid out (apart from some richly decorated specimens, such as Jerusalem, Monastery of the Holy Cross, 109); writing often appears also on the verso side of the roll, continuing the text on the recto or adding a new (contemporary or later) one (Maniaci – Orofino 2012).

8.3. The making of the codex

8.3.1. The making of the quires

Quires of Greek parchment codices are most frequently quaternions, made by superposing four bifolia obtained by folding a rectangular sheet into two equal parts parallel to its short side; 'coupled leaves' or 'artificial bifolia' could also be used in place of 'natural' bifolia. While assembling bifolia, Greek craftsmen regularly followed 'Gregory's Rule' (already witnessed by *P.Ryl.* I 53, *Odyssey*, third/fourth century CE), requiring the matching of two homogeneous sides at each quire opening. The ancient habit of beginning the quire with a flesh side was maintained in Greek codices until the end of the Middle Ages: the few exceptions (mostly Italo-Greek or Latin-Greek bilingual manuscripts from the tenth to thirteenth centuries) were probably influenced by western practices, although a few eastern examples are also known (among others, the earliest codices copied by Theophanes, an Iviron monk working at the beginning of the eleventh century, or three centuries later those by the Cretan scribe Michaēl Loulloudēs).

Depending on the size of the skins, their quality, and the size of the bifolia the craftsman wanted to obtain, different methods were employed for making the quires, in accordance with the natural desire to get the most out of a single skin. The systematic observation of the thin and porous areas surrounding the animal's leg joints in a sample of Greek manuscripts of the eleventh and twelfth centuries (see fig. 1.8.5) and the use of statistical analysis (Maniaci 1999a and 1999b) has pointed to a specific way of subdividing the skins through a T-cut resulting in three bifolia from each skin, a process not to be seen as a unique alternative to the *folio* and *quarto* folding patterns proposed by Léon Gilissen for western manuscripts. While waiting for new and more extensive archaeological evidence, it can reasonably be assumed that the practices in use among Byzantine craftsmen were motivated by the desire to avoid waste of expensive material—through an intensive exploitation of the available skins, not all of the same size—rather than by the wish to economize gestures and working time. Cutting the skins according to need, and not necessarily in a systematic way, enabled craftsmen to obtain from skins of different sizes a variable number of bifolia, which could coexist in one and the same codex. Additionally, the use of patterns, similar to those still in use in Ethiopic book production (see Ch. 1 § 6), cannot be excluded as a remnant of ancient practice, although undocumented in Greek sources.

As for Greek paper codices, whose manufacture has not been systematically investigated, a wider diffusion of folding for quire composition has to be admitted, given the standardization of paper formats, and the position of chain and wire lines in the resulting quires.

8.3.2. The composition of the quires

Some very ancient and modest Greek papyrus codices are composed by series of single bifolia, separately sewn to one another (such as the Dublin papyrus Chester Beatty I (*P.Beatty* II), Gospels, beginning of the third century, made of fifty-five bifolia). More numerous ones are made of a single quire, obtained by nesting a large number of bifolia (up to fifty or more) one into the other: they could contain a whole comedy or one or more books of the Old or New Testament (such as Martin Bodmer's *Menander* codex, third or early fourth century, a single quire made of sixteen bifolia; *P.Bodmer* XIV–XV, second/third century, containing the Gospels of Luke and John, probably obtained by folding 36 bifolia in a single quire; papyrus Chester Beatty II (*P.Beatty* III), third quarter of the second century, Pauline Epistles, a single-quire codex made of 52 bifolia of slightly decreasing width). These extreme forms, whose chronological relation to each other is unclear, were soon abandoned in favour of the use of quinions and quaternions, which in Late Antiquity coexisted for a while. Quinions were apparently rare (they were used for instance in the Bible manuscript Vatican City, BAV, Vat. gr. 1209, or still two centuries later in the *Codex Marchalianus* of the Prophets, Vatican City, BAV, Vat. gr. 2125); quaternions, more frequently adopted, might alternate with quinions in a single codex, or also in conjunction with other types (they are found for instance in the fourth-century *Codex Sinaiticus* (see Ch. 1 § 8.1.2) and in the fifth-century *Codex Alexandrinus*, London, BL, Royal 1. D. V-VIII), before becoming the standard quire structure for Byzantine parchment books of all epochs. Greater variety is later found in paper codices, where the quaternion is still the predominant typology, but is often replaced by quires of thicker structure (quinions, senions, and more rarely octonions, as in Paris, BnF, Coislin 93), which were probably thought to be more resistant to wear. In the sixteenth century, also thinner quires are attested, including ternions (incorrectly regarded as a clue to Italo-Greek origin and favoured, among others, by the Vatican scriptor Giovanni Onorio da Maglie) and binions, sometimes alternating with quaternions; a regular alternation between quires of different structure (quaternions/senions, as in Vienna, ÖNB, Cod.hist.gr. 39, from the year 1399, or binions/quaternions, as in Vatican City, BAV, Vat. gr. 146, written by the already mentioned Giovanni Onorio) is also found occasionally in later times (no earlier than the fourteenth century). The central (internal and/or external) fold of paper quires is only rarely reinforced by means of a parchment strip (sometimes re-used from an earlier manuscript); Greek 'mixed' quires, obtained by 'wrapping' a regular paper quire in an external and/or internal parchment bifolium are even rarer (fewer than fifty known occurrences, long erroneously connected to Crete or Southern Italy).

The final quires of a codex or of one of its sections may show an irregular structure, thus offering precious clues for understanding the book's genesis and further history.

8.3.3. Pricking and ruling

Unlike papyrus book rolls, in which the writing could be guided by horizontal fibres, the empty surface of the codex page required preparation to accommodate the contents, through the addition of a grid of perpendicular lines designed to demarcate its limits and facilitate its alignment (see also General introduction § 1.3.3).

In most cases, ruling was preceded by pricking, often removed by subsequent trimming(s) and therefore now completely or partially invisible. Pricking already appears in ancient Greek codices, where pricks were usually executed within the written area (in both *Codex Vaticanus* and some sections of *Codex Sinaiticus* they are hidden inside the outer column); later they tended to be located toward the outer bounding line, and then nearer and nearer to the outer margin and the edge of the page (see fig. 1.8.6). The lack of systematic research on the oldest Greek codices and the extreme rarity of dated or datable ones do not allow for more than general observations. The presence of a double row of prickings in both inner and outer margins of the page is rare in Greek codices and deserves special mention: it appears, for instance, in some majuscule codices such as the ninth century Cosmas Indicopleustes manuscript Vatican City, BAV, Vat. gr. 699, of uncertain origin. In the absence of specific archaeological research, it is impossible to say anything well founded about the pricking instruments used, or the way they were applied (on open or folded bifolia, on single or superposed surfaces).

Greater attention has been paid to the study of Greek ruling, which in Late Antiquity and the Byzantine Middle Ages was always executed with a 'dry point' technique. In this case, too, Greek craftsmen showed a conservative attitude and disregarded the coloured rulings widespread in Latin book production by the thirteenth century. Rare (and unexplained) occurrences of coloured ruling found in Greek books before the Renaissance are restricted to well defined areas and functions: in particular, Byzantine manuscripts produced between the eleventh and the twelfth century in the Calabro-Sicilian area around the Strait of Messina may show coloured lines (in fading shades, from grey to brick-red, sometimes associated with a slight scoring) that reinforce existing dry-point grooves; traces of vertical coloured ruling appear sporadically as early as the ninth century, to guide the layout of scholia in Vatican City, BAV, Urb. gr. 35, Aristotle, from the year 914, made for bishop Arethas of Caesarea, or in some ninth-century representatives of the so-called 'philosophical collection'; the practices of Renaissance scribes are yet unexplored. It is worth noting that the analysis of some occurrences of coloured ruling has revealed the use of substances whose composition does not correspond to that of mediaeval Greek inks.

Unlike coloured ruling, which had to be executed individually on the recto and verso of each leaf or bifolium, dry-point ruling could be obtained in a variety of ways. Julien Leroy (1976) drew attention to a diverse range of 'ruling systems'—corresponding to the succession of grooves and reliefs within a quire—and proposed a method for their symbolic notation, which takes into account the difference between primary and secondary grooves and records their alternation within the quire. The data in our possession attest that the different systems (thirteen according to Leroy, and others discovered more recently) are very heterogeneously widespread: Leroy 1, with scored furrows visible on all hair sides, is the most common system from the tenth century in Byzantium and related areas (more than 70% of the cases); some systems which had been mainly or exclusively connected to Italo-Greek manuscripts (especially Leroy 9, the

Fig. 1.8.5 *Codex Sinaiticus*, London, BL, Add. 43725, *c.*360 CE, f. 153r, detail, Wisdom of Solomon 6.10.

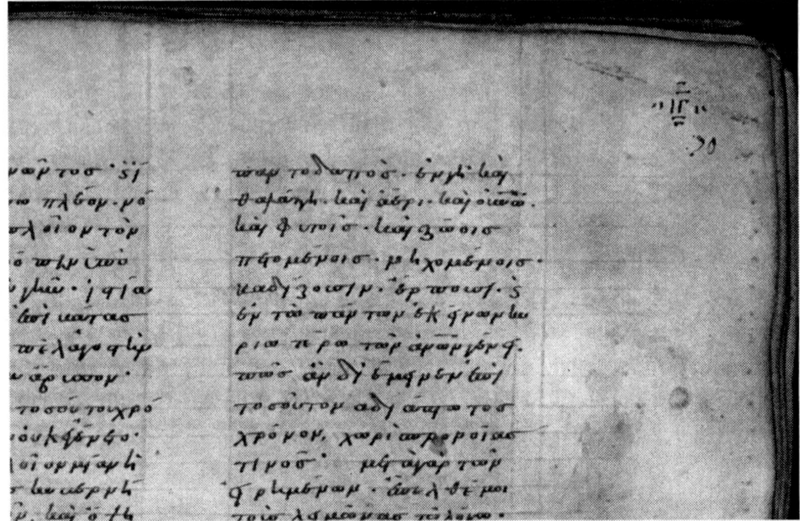

Fig. 1.8.6 Rome, Biblioteca Vallicelliana, B16, early eleventh century, a collection of works by St John Chrysostom, f. 70r, detail showing pricking, ruling for a two-column text layout and a quire signature in the upper right corner.

second in order of frequency after Leroy 1), have been subsequently found in various different areas of the Byzantine Empire; other ones seem to be time-related, such as Leroy 3 and 4, frequently used in old majuscule codices (although this impression has not yet been confirmed by systematic surveys). The parchment is most frequently impressed on the hair side; impressions on the flesh side are particularly common in (but not exclusive to) southern Italy, especially in periods and areas subject to Latin influence. The coexistence of multiple systems in the same codex is quite common, as is the association of two different systems for bounding lines and horizontal ruling within the same quire.

Other possible ways of engraving rulings seem to have spread in Greek codices together with the diffusion of paper, particularly the use of the *misṭara*, which has recently been reported for late and post-Byzantine manuscripts (Agati 2012). On the contrary, there is as yet no evidence of the use of the 'rake', widely employed for ink ruling in late mediaeval Latin books, although the extension of late-mediaeval ruling techniques to late Byzantine codices and those produced in Renaissance Italy is probable, and also the use of sets of ready-made quires, bought from Italian stationers (*cartolai*) cannot be excluded, even before the fifteenth century, as a result of intensified contacts and the increased mobility of scribes between east and west. For paper books of modest quality, the use of 'poor' ruling techniques, limited to the written area (or to the sole vertical justification) and obtained by simple folding, should certainly be considered, although it has never been surveyed; the absence of visible ruling is also occasionally attested.

Whatever the details of execution, ruling produces a more or less elaborate grid of perpendicular lines, traditionally called a 'ruling type'. Besides the essential lines (bounding and writing lines) and others that could serve as a guide for the insertion of running titles, initials, glosses or commentaries, many other—seemingly 'superfluous'—marginal rules often appear in Greek codices in a variety of positions, and seem to be guided by purely qualitative and aesthetic criteria: in fact, the number of 'unnecessary' marginal lines reaches its maximum in Bible manuscripts (Maniaci 2002b), while the complexity of the schemes significantly decreases in paper codices. Lines may be not only more or less numerous, but also of variable extent (for example, horizontal lines may extend all the way across the page, or abut onto the bounding lines) and give rise to a great diversity of types: attempts at classifying them, motivated by the hope of inferring useful hints for dating, suggesting provenance or identifying specific centres, have not given the desired results. The most frequent types are few in number, extend over a large area and are therefore of little use for dating and localization. Of more than 3,000 types (Sautel 1995, based on Leroy [Julien] 1976), only three are represented by more than two hundred codices, and only ten by more than one hundred; more than six hundred types are represented only once. Rarer and/or more elaborate types are peculiar to specific contents (such as associations of texts and commentaries) or depend on individual choices: in the same place, the same codex or even the same quire, multiple types may appear simultaneously, not always attributable to a specific purpose.

8.3.4. Ordering systems

Unlike printed books, mediaeval manuscripts were not always equipped with the devices ensuring, on the one hand, the correct sequence of quires, bifolia and sheets and, on the other hand, the immediate retrieval of specific passages of the text.

In Greek book rolls, column numbering occasionally appears (for instance in PSI XII 1284; *P.Oxy*. III 412; *P.Oxy*. IV 657 = PSI XII 1292). The oldest Greek codices (third and fourth centuries CE) sporadically show page numbers (pagination), unknown in Latin codices, but the figures (written in the upper—central or outer—margin, sometimes only on rectos) are often later than the hand(s) of the scribe(s) (Turner 1977, 75–76). Leaf numbering (foliation) is extremely rare: ancient (but not coeval) traces appear on the versos' upper outer margins in the Bible *Codex Vaticanus* (probably meaning that the opening was numbered, rather than the leaf). Extant foliations were often added much later: sometimes more than one series coexist in the same book, and often they offer useful clues for reconstructing the book's history.

Quire numbering (signature) is found already in ancient Greek codices (one of the oldest examples being *P.Bodmer* II, from the first part of the third century). It is mostly expressed in Greek majuscules, minuscules or mixed characters, used as numerals (with the addition of *stigma* ς = 6, *koppa* ϛ = 90 and *sampi* ϡ = 900) and traced in brown or sometimes red ink, occasionally with decorative elements (horizontal, vertical or oblique strokes, straight or wavy, variously combined, see fig. 1.8.6). A rare curiosity is the use as signatures of groups of letters or entire words to be read one quire after the other, forming a meaningful sentence (as the beginning of Psalm 103 in the tenth-century Venice, BNM, gr. 269).

Signatures are more frequently written on the first page of the quire, preferably in the upper outer (fig. 1.8.6) or lower inner margin, but they are also more rarely displayed only on the last page (lower inner margin), or simultaneously in both positions: all these possibilities are found already in Late Antique codices. The attempt to define geographical and chronological distinctions (Mondrain 1998) so far has not brought about fully convincing results, although some trends do stand out: the placement in the upper, outer or inner, margin seems to prevail in the oldest books; signatures appearing only on the last page of the quire (preferably at the centre of the lower margin) are rarer and could betray a Latin influence; in the (frequent) case of double signatures, at the beginning and end of the quire, the prevailing associations are those between upper-outer and lower-inner margin or between the two lower-inner positions. Double signatures on the first and last page of the quire, both on the lower-central margin, spread in Greek codices from the fourteenth century.

Quire signatures may be inserted by the scribe, or by the coordinator and/or reviewer of a collaborative copy; they can also be due to more than one hand, especially if they are later than the transcription of the text. In some cases, also in codices of miscellaneous contents (but composed of a single 'production unit'), quire signatures may begin anew with each new text (as in Vatican City, BAV, Vat. gr. 204, first half of the ninth century), showing that they were perceived as separate units. Single initial and/or final quires or groups of quires may not bear a quire number, as they contain accessory texts (such as indices, Canon Tables, liturgical calendars) which were—and were perceived as being—distinct from the main work; loose leaves—such as those containing the evangelists' portraits in Gospel books—are usually unnumbered. The presence of several series of quire signatures in a single manuscript or the use of numerals other than Greek (Slavonic, Armenian, Georgian, etc.) may contribute useful information for reconstructing the history of the books in which they appear. Quire numbering may also be associated with other marginal devices, such as one or more small crosses or asterisks (as in *Codex Alexandrinus*), sometimes related to specific copyists or centres: in the absence of any other evidence, risky generalizations must be avoided, as the scribes could change their habits from one codex to another (see for instance the case of the Constantinopolitan tenth-century monk Ephraim, or that of the Stoudite scribes, with their inconsistent ways of affixing crosses in the upper margins of their codices).

From the thirteenth century, under the influence of Latin usage, the appearance of 'quire and leaf signatures' ('segnature a registro', later established in printed books) is sporadically observed in Greek codices: sets of letters, numbers and symbols, combined in various and more or less fanciful ways, appear on the first half of all the bifolia composing each quire, to indicate both the position of the quire within the codex and of the bifolium within the quire (as in Vatican City, BAV, Vat. gr. 1960 or Rome, Biblioteca Angelica, gr. 68, in Greek numerals, or in the tenth unit of Vatican City, BAV, Vat. 1902, in Latin numerals).

Although catchwords are occasionally reported in Greek papyri (West [S.] 1963), their use in Byzantine codices might also be due to Latin influence. The oldest dated Greek example is a copy of the so-called *Suda* lexicon, Vatican City, BAV, Vat. gr. 1296, probably made in southern Italy in 1205; but they were already employed by the scribe Iōannikios and his associates at least half a century earlier (Degni 2008). Catchwords remained sporadic until the fifteenth century, when they became more frequent, under western influence, replacing quire signatures; they are usually placed in the lower inner corner, horizontally or vertically.

8.3.5. The codex as a complex object

Recent research (Gumbert 2004; Andrist et al. 2013) has underlined the centrality of the relationship between the structure of the codex and its contents and the need to investigate the form this relationship takes not only in the original stage of a codex's manufacture, but also during the various phases of its later life.

A high percentage (*c.*50%) of extant Greek codices contain multiple texts, and only some of them are in fact structurally homogeneous books (Maniaci forthcoming): many are the product of assemblage under a single cover of pre-existing units and/or others created ad hoc, which might have occurred at different times, in various ways and for different reasons, according to some principle, or merely out of convenience. Moreover, modularity is not exclusive to multiple-text codices: it may also be a feature of volumes that appear to have homogeneous content ('single-text' codices) but whose structure reflects some commonality among groups of quires and textual sub-units.

The lack of adequate catalogues—sufficiently accurate in listing the contents and particularly in describing the complex structure of the codices—hampers the compilation of an accurate typology of the Greek multiple-text codex, taking into account times and places, contents, cultural contexts, language, functions and uses of the books: the attempts made up to now only provide a rough picture of the spread of multiple-text manuscripts in the Byzantine and Latin Middle Ages. Codices containing a single text show an initial prevalence of religious content in the form of Bibles and commentaries, liturgical texts, homilies, theological treatises and hagiographies, followed from the thirteenth century onward by an increasing presence of literary works of history, poetry, novels and philosophical works, and technical works on grammar, philology, lexicography, astronomy, medicine, mathematics, or law. As already mentioned, the analysis of multiple-text manuscripts is even more limited by their structural diversity: presumably homogeneous books, which are easier to characterize, tend to bring together a limited number of works by different authors (usually two or three of them), and only approximately 15% contain more than ten texts; a significant increase in multiple-text manuscripts occurs only in the late Byzantine period, particularly in the thirteenth and fourteenth centuries, when a main text usually located at the beginning of the book is often followed by a series of short, even very short, texts. With regard to content, Greek multiple-text 'monoblock' books tend to aggregate texts belonging to the same religious or secular genre (which prevails in the late Byzantine period); the first text contained in each manuscript is usually the longest.

The data from ancient and recent catalogues are inadequate for further advances in the knowledge of 'complex' Greek codices, which requires the direct, in-depth analysis of the codices themselves, which need to be considered and described, regardless of the number of texts they contains, as complex objects consisting of one or more elements produced simultaneously or at different times and possibly different places. These elements, or 'production units', may or may not have circulated independently; they may have been joined with other elements and originated new 'circulation units' corresponding to stages in the history of the codex, the last of which coincides with the book in its current form. The archaeological study of the codex therefore requires the reconstruction of a 'genetic' history that investigates the origin of each production unit, and a 'stratigraphic' history that reconstructs the succession of forms taken by the codex as a result of the addition or subtraction of units or changes to the existing ones (see Ch. 4 § 4).

8.4. The layout of the page

The size and layout of Greek manuscripts are favourite themes of Greek manuscript research, especially of the so-called 'quantitative codicology', allowing one to go beyond isolated observations on individual manuscripts and to highlight the existence of some general trends.

Books less than 10 cm tall—although occasionally made for mainly devotional use (Gospels, lectionaries, and especially Psalters: Weyl Carr 1980)—are extremely rare in the Greek-speaking world; at the other end of the scale, volumes whose height is equal to or greater than 60 cm are also very uncommon, probably because of the preference for *sexto* rather than *quarto* skin subdivision in Byzantine book manufacture (making it possible to obtain three bifolia out of a skin, instead of two larger ones). Some manuscripts of astronomical and geographical contents stand out among the isolated exceptions, such as the sumptuous Venice, BNM, gr. 388 (coll. 333), Ptolemy, written for Cardinal Bessarion by the Cretan scribe John Rhosos (Iōannēs Rhōsos), in which each bifolium is the result of the coupling of two skins of about 585 × 435 mm. Aside from extreme cases, the distinction proposed for Latin books by Armando Petrucci (1969a) between large books ('libri da banco'), intended to be read, viewed or simply displayed without displacing them, medium books ('libri da bisaccia'), transportable from one place to another in case of need, and portable books ('libretti da mano') may also be generally applied to Greek codices. This categorization implies the existence of a (sometimes very close) connexion between size and text types, imposed for certain categories of texts by reasons of a technical nature (as in the case of the—necessarily large—codices in which the main text is framed on three open sides by an extensive commentary). Other texts could be accommodated in volumes of very different sizes: this is the case with certain liturgical books, which could be very large or very small, depending on whether they were intended for group worship or personal devotion; the transcription of individual books or groups of books of the Bible is similarly characterized, on the basis of use, by a large range of dimensions.

Apart from the pioneering efforts made by Eric Turner (1977) to typologize the dimensions of papyrus and parchment codices (through the creation of classes based on size and proportion that require a global rethinking), some significant facts emerge from recent research on the construction and layout of Middle Byzantine codices. With regard to proportion (expressed through the ratio of width to height), the squarish shape of ancient Greek parchment codices tends to be perpetuated over time. The oldest examples show a definitely large proportion, averaging about 6/7 (0.86) and rarely narrower than 5/7 (0.71); Middle Byzantine codices evolve toward a slightly slimmer, but still rather large ratio, of approximately 3/4 (0.75). Manuscript books whose proportion is greater than 1.0, i.e. wide rather than tall, are not attested in Greek. As for absolute dimensions, the rarity of exceptionally large Greek codices (semi-perimeter over 700 mm) is balanced by the frequency of medium-sized codices (around 500 mm), favoured even for texts intended for public use (homilies, hagiographic collections, writings of Church Fathers).

With the diffusion of paper, book size and proportion undergo changes associated with the gradual standardization of sheet sizes, which for oriental paper await a more precise definition (see above § 1.1.3). The diffusion of Italian watermarked paper in Greek books involves the generalization of the two formats (*reale* and *reçute*) imposed in the west by Italian paper makers from the mid-thirteenth century.

Only two of the very few known layout canons concern Greek codices, in a more or less direct way. The first one is a Latin (Carolingian) recipe, transmitted by a Parisian codex (Paris, BnF, Latin 11884, f. 2v), which seems indirectly to reflect Late Antique habits, later preserved—with some adjustments—in Byzantine parchment books (Maniaci 1995, 2013). The text provides a series of recommendations aimed at the manufacture of codices of large proportions (4/5, or 0.80), completely incompatible with the standards in vogue in the west, but found in a sample of Greek manuscripts on parchment, with maximum diffusion from the ninth to the twelfth centuries. The second source, recently brought to scholarly attention (Vatican City, BAV, Vat. gr. 604, fourteenth century) proposes a set of detailed instructions in Greek related to the specific layout of Aristotle's *Organon* and its framing commentary, contained in the same volume (Bianconi 2010; see also Maniaci 2013). So far, no other witnesses of the same layout have emerged.

Apart from these isolated and problematic examples, the statistical analysis of dimensional data collected from large samples of manuscripts reveals some general criteria relating to the layout of Byzantine parchment manuscripts (specific studies on paper ones are still lacking). In Middle Byzantine codices (as in Latin ones), the average 'occupancy rate', or 'black' (determined by the ratio of the written rectangle to the total area of the page), remains well below the half of the total available space, i.e. around 43% (whereas it reaches 50% in the oldest Greek codices). Within the written area, writing is arranged over one or two columns (rarely over three, as in Vatican City, BAV, Vat. gr. 1209). After a more or less equal diffusion of the two layouts in the oldest centuries of Greek codex production, two-column layout gradually prevails, reaching its peak in the eleventh century; the following century marks a turnaround, with the return of full-page layout, predominant in late Byzantine manuscripts, both sacred and secular, except for certain text types (such as homiliaries and lectionaries), which remained faithful to older traditions. According to tendencies already well investigated for Latin codices, the two-column arrangement prevails in large codices, for reasons of readability.

Beyond these general trends, the filling, space exploitation and text layout of Greek codices undergo variations related to their chronology and geographical origin, but especially to book contents: research started for the Macedonian and Comnenan ages (Maniaci 2002b) should be extended to later centuries and more systematically related to historical and cultural events. Additionally, the fundamental continuity in book manufacturing techniques and the overall limited amount of typological differentiations generally confirm the judgment of substantial conservatism deserved by other aspects of Byzantine book manufacture. At least between the ninth and twelfth centuries, Greek craftsmen adopted without evident discontinuity the same general criteria: volumes show small or medium sizes, large proportions (3/4 or more) and relatively large margins, respecting a fairly rigid (probably Late Antique) hierarchy.

Nevertheless, Greek craftsmen were also able to construct complex layouts, characterized by the association on the same page of a 'main' text and a 'secondary' one, usually a commentary. Especially when the commentary surrounds the text in the form of a frame, as is most frequent in Greek codices until the thirteenth century, the simultaneous management of two different 'text streams' implies, since the preliminary design of the book, a detailed and complex codicological project, and requires, on the part of the scribe or scribes of the two 'primary' and 'secondary' texts, a delicate coordination, especially if text and commentary are derived from two—or more—different antigraphs. Research based on extensive and detailed surveys has been devoted in recent years to some manuscripts of the *Iliad* and to the layout of biblical *catena* manuscripts, containing a form of commentary made up of excerpts from earlier biblical exegesis (Maniaci 2000b, 2006a, 2006b; Sautel 2000, 2001; Vianès 2000): it has contributed significantly, although still incompletely, to shedding light on the specific strategies used by the scribes to solve the difficult problems they faced in synchronizing text and commentary.

8.5. Text structure and readability

8.5.1. Writing and decoration

The devices adopted by the scribe to highlight the structure of the text and allow the reader to navigate easily within it also belong to the field of page and text layout; the role played by initial letters, running titles and display scripts, however, must be framed in the context of decoration. At least one typical feature of Greek manuscripts is worth mentioning here, namely the way of placing in the margin, as a 'hanging initial', not the first letter of a new paragraph or section, but the first letter of the first full line of that section, with the actual beginning of the paragraph occurring in the preceding line.

Research devoted to a sample of Byzantine minuscule books of the ninth to twelfth centuries showed that Greek scribes were also attentive to 'line management', as is revealed by the tendency to avoid or limit word division at the end of the line, where it was considered an obstacle to reading ease. The control usually became even more attentive at the last line of the page, where the eye trajectory was necessarily longer than from one line to the next on the same page; not surprisingly, fewer divisions are observed between recto and verso (where the reader had to turn the page) than between two facing pages (Maniaci 1997).

Although a detailed discussion of the characteristics and evolution of Greek book decoration pertains to the history of art, it cannot be ignored that decoration also has a codicological significance, particularly underlined by recent research.

Technical sources on Byzantine book decoration are almost totally lacking: knowledge of materials and processes is limited to a few recipes, while the existence of preliminary sketches and the composition of colours and grounds can be detected only through direct observation and scientific analysis.

The variety and richness of Greek book decoration is documented by several manuscripts, and reflected in the art of other cultures influenced by Byzantium (Coptic, Ethiopian, Syrian, Armenian, Georgian, Russian, Bulgarian, Serbian, Sicilian, as well as that of the eastern Latin kingdoms). Narrative miniatures and illustrations, consisting of scenes of various content and size, were restricted to luxury books of specific types (such as the Bible, liturgical and hagiographic collections and secular classics) and to some technical works (military arts, medicine, botany, astronomy, etc.).

Figural miniatures and decorated initials were usually the purview of craftsmen other than the scribes, or executed in specialized workshops. In papyrus rolls, illustrations were freely inserted in the middle of the columns, unframed and without background. With the diffusion of the codex—which allowed for richer and more varied decoration—the layout of the pictures was adapted to the new closed format of the page and to the new text arrangement, acquiring backgrounds and frames and adjusting itself to the width of the page or of the column. Miniatures might be executed on separate leaves which were then inserted into the book (sometimes also at a later date).

The study of early Byzantine miniature painting is based on rare and fragmentary surviving examples. Among sacred texts, there are for instance the remains of two fifth- and mid-sixth-century Genesis manuscripts, both of uncertain provenance: the Cotton Genesis (London, BL, Cott. Otho B.VI) and the Vienna Genesis, written on vellum dyed in purple (Vienna, ÖNB, Cod.theol.gr. 31); two fragmentary sixth-century Gospels are also worth mentioning, also of unconfirmed provenance, the Rossano Gospels (Rossano Calabro, Museo dell'Arcivescovado) and the Sinope Gospels (Paris, BnF, Supplément grec 1286), both on purple parchment. Lay examples include manuscripts such as the fifth/sixth-century *Ilias picta* (Milan, Biblioteca Ambrosiana, F 205 inf.), originally containing more than two hundred miniatures, and the Vienna Dioscorides (Vienna, ÖNB, Cod.med.gr. 1), prepared around 512–513 for the Byzantine princess Juliana Anicia, still containing 383 extant illustrations of plants out of the original 435. These examples represent a range of different types: the pictures can be arranged in the lower half of each page (as in the Vienna Genesis) or in spaces of variable size and extension (as in the Cotton Genesis); they may appear in the form of a series of frontispieces (as in the Rossanensis) or as full-page naturalistic plant depictions, as in the *De materia medica* treatise. In the middle and late Byzantine period the number of decorated manuscripts increased considerably, especially from the mid-eleventh century. The Four Gospels feature Canon Tables and evangelists' portraits painted on the verso page preceding the beginning of each Gospel, followed by a decorated band, a major initial and a distinctive title on next recto often written in gold. The structure of the Four Gospels shows interesting codicological peculiarities: the portraits could be executed on loose (ruled or unruled) leaves, sometimes included in older volumes (as proposed for Mark's portrait in the Rossano Gospels: see Kresten – Prato 1985) or conversely re-employed in later codices; the insertion of the miniatures was facilitated by the correspondence between groups of quires and individual Gospels (frequent until the twelfth century and often marked by one or more unusual or irregular quires). Decorated lectionaries, whose pictures, as well as the text, are distributed according to the liturgical year, are not very frequent but often of high quality. After Gospels, the most frequently decorated biblical books include Psalters, Job with commentary, and Octateuchs; the Major Prophets (Isaiah through Malachi) may also be collected in a single painted volume; Vatican City, BAV, Reg. gr. 1, commissioned in the second quarter of the tenth century by the *sakellarios* Leo, is the exceptional example of an illustrated complete Bible. Some homiliaries (such as Paris, BnF, Grec 510, a codex of John Chrysostom dated 880–883) and liturgical collections arranged according to the calendar (menologia and synaxaria, such as the famous 'Mēnologion of Basil II', Vatican City, BAV, Vat. gr. 1613, written around 1000 CE) have splendid miniatures. An outstanding example of a richly illuminated secular text is the Madrid Skylitzēs (Madrid, Biblioteca Nacional, 5–3 n. 2), most likely produced in Messina before the mid-twelfth century. It features 574 miniatures (having probably lost some one hundred more). Another one is the hunting treatise (*Cynegetica*) by pseudo-Oppian, preserved in a single copy from the eleventh century (Venice, BNM, gr. Z. 479).

'Minor' decoration, often in the scribe's own hand, is represented by lines, ornamental bands, frames (also Π-shaped, *pylai*) enclosing the titles, large 'carpet pages', and also decorated initials (less developed than in western books) and 'distinctive' scripts (see fig. 1.8.7). Abstract ornamentation—widely developed in Byzantine codices from the beginning of the eleventh century, after the conclusion of the iconoclastic controversy—shows a variety of motifs (geometric interlaces, arabesques, vegetal, zoomorphic and anthropomorphic designs), colours and styles. The execution may be monochrome (employing the

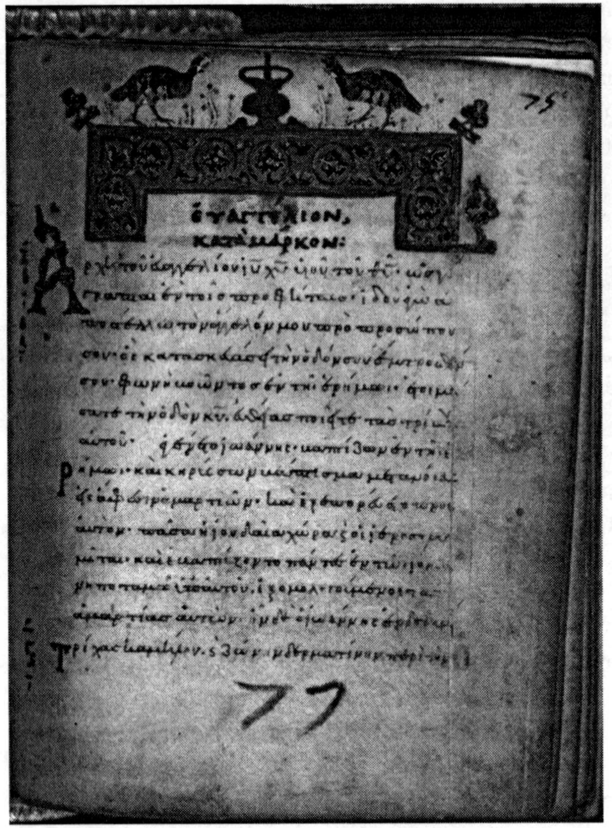

Fig. 1.8.7 Rome, Biblioteca Vallicelliana, B133, mid-eleventh century, Four Gospels, f. 75r: the beginning of the Gospel of Mark.

same ink as the text or more often a minium or carmine red) or polychrome (showing a variety of colours and possibly also the use of gold and silver).

The main (over-simplistic) opposition has been often made between 'Constantinople' styles—such as 'serrated style' (Laubsägestil) or more refined 'flower-petal style' (Blütenblattstil)—and 'peripheral' styles (more contrasted, coarse and spontaneous, marked by the influence of other book traditions; see Džurova 2008). However, recent research suggests that the contrast between 'metropolitan' and 'provincial' book art should not be overestimated, insisting on the mix of patterns and influences within a multi-ethnic empire. In the past years, many suggestions of provenance—often based on this alleged opposition—have been disproved. Although not without uncertainties, the most easily definable province is Byzantine southern Italy, characterized since the tenth century by a marked preference for specific colours (green, orange, yellow, brown), naïve techniques and a contamination with western book crafts (with the exception, in the twelfth century, of the area surrounding the Strait of Messina).

Apart from an aesthetic function, decoration (including display scripts, historiated initials, ornamental bands, the use of red, ranging from orange to brick-red to minium and carmine, or other colours) contributes to the structuring of the text and therefore impacts directly on the fruition of the contents. It introduces precise dimensional and chromatic hierarchies; at the same time, the insertion of decorative elements in certain positions breaks the flow of the text, forcing the scribe (generally coinciding with the rubricator) to plan his transcription carefully and to adopt various graphic devices (abbreviations, changes in the form of the letters or in the width of their spacing, horizontal expansion or compression, and so on), in order to adapt the writing to the available space (Cavallo 1996). The reconstruction of the manufacturing stages of decorated and illuminated manuscripts has similarly been scarcely investigated thus far, particularly with regard to the relationship between the work of the scribe (often also responsible for 'minor' decoration), and the intervention of individual painters or organized teams or workshops for the execution of miniatures. A careful analysis often reveals the hidden presence of guidance letters or signs, intended to serve as a reminder for the execution of titles or decorated letters and mostly added after the transcription of the text: but these sporadic indications do not allow for firm or general conclusions about the working methods and the possible interaction of individuals having different skills.

As for the collaboration between scribes and painters, the few Byzantine examples studied so far point to a wide and elusive range of possibilities, which likely reflect the diversity of ages, places and contexts of production and hint at complex and still largely unexplored ways of interaction. This is particularly evident when the decoration shows different and exotic features as compared to the accompanying writing (as in the eleventh-century Vatican City, BAV, Chis. R.IV.18, John of Damascus, whose decoration echoes that of the ninth/tenth-century Maghrebi Qur'āns) or even when scribes and painters belong to different cultural traditions and the decoration may incorporate a text written in a language other than Greek (as in Athens, National Library, 149, a Psalter produced in eleventh-century Calabria, in which the Pauline Epistles were later supplemented by the portrait of the apostle with a roll showing the *incipit* of the epistle in Slavonic, the language also used for Paul's name; or in Athens, National Library, 127, Gospels with evangelists' portraits in Armenian style, with Mark tracing Armenian letters on the book open on his knees). Apart from single cases, the reconstruction of a sufficiently clear and detailed picture still remains a distant goal.

8.6. The scribe, the painter and the illuminator at work

8.6.1. Persons, places and methods

In the Byzantine 'bibliophile society' (Grünbart 2004), laymen and clerks, scholars, monks, notaries, civil servants, and even, in some cases, emperors and women of high birth could engage in the transcription of books, without distinctions of status and role. Research conducted over thirty years ago (Cutler 1981) on the subscriptions of ninth- to fifteenth-century Byzantine manuscripts (substantially confirmed by recent surveys: see Ronconi 2012) identified the monks, mainly devoted to the transcription of sacred texts, as an absolute majority (53%) of the scribes, against 6% for lay people and 22% for priests. Ecclesiastic scribes wrote mainly, but not exclusively, to gain spiritual merit (but they also made copies for sale); learned laymen often engaged in book transcription as a mean to better understand the text they reproduced (but also as a solution to overcome the high costs of manuscripts). 'Pious' and 'amateur' scribes were flanked by a minority of professional calligraphers, who earned their living by copying manuscripts.

Information on the physiology of the copy, i.e. on the position taken by the Byzantine scribe and the use of any specific furnishings (benches and desks) almost exclusively depends on the ambiguous testimony of miniatures, depicting the evangelist or other author-scribe on a seat in front of a workbench; on the other hand, colophons contain formulaic references to the practice of holding the writing surface on one's knees (*kalamos m'egraphen, dexia cheir kai gony*, 'the reed pen wrote me, the right hand and the knee'). It is unclear whether the scribe wrote on loose bifolia or on already formed quires: the few traces of 'tackets' found until now (see Ch. 1 § 1.3.1) are too uncertain and sporadic to allow one to conclude in favour of the second option, but habits may have changed over time.

References to the duration of the copying process and the speed of the scribes are more explicit, but also quite rare, consisting in occasional notes which would seem to point to the transcription of a medium volume in about forty days (at a rate of about half a quire a day: see Ronconi 2012): a much lower 'productivity rate' as compared to that attested by hagiographic sources, in which saints (usually with divine help) perform the copying of an entire volume within a week or even a few days. The variety of circumstances and the subjectivity of the scribal experience suggest, however, that we should avoid generalizations.

Even though the Byzantines were not used to structured forms of scribal activity similar to those practised in Latin scriptoria, copying was not necessarily solitary work: collaboration between copyists was a frequent phenomenon. The division of labour could be aimed at simultaneous transcription from different and independent models, or from parts of a single model available in the form of loose gatherings (Canart 1998); in other cases, shared copying (also with frequent alternation of a high number of hands) within late Byzantine learned circles could be motivated by intellectual needs (Cavallo 2001a). By highlighting the relationships between textual flow(s), scribe rotation and the physical structure of the books, codicology can help to distinguish different situations, whose reasons, however, cannot always be clearly defined.

8.6.2. Colophons

Colophons are found only exceptionally in older majuscule codices (without mention of date), while their frequency increases significantly in the Byzantine Middle Ages. No figures based on reliable surveys are available to estimate the percentage of subscribed Greek manuscripts; those which are explicitly dated, from the ninth century onward, are rather more numerous than—for instance—Latin ones (from about 8–9% up to the twelfth century to about 50% in the fifteenth century, and 67% in the sixteenth century).

Texts are usually shorter than those found in other oriental book cultures, and they are composed by varying combinations of the following elements: scribe's name, name of the person on behalf of whom he wrote, date of completion of the copy (see fig. 1.8.3, Athos, Pantokrator, 84, f. 425r, with the subscription of the scribe, monk Theoleptos, who wrote the manuscript under the sponsorship of the doctor Michael Gabras, completing it on 6 May 1362 CE); other information, such as the place of copying (toponyms are mostly difficult to identify), and other details (reasons for copying, mention of emperors or other secular or religious authorities; memories of historical facts) are found much more rarely. These main data are integrated by formulaic remarks (refrains or stereotyped phrases of various kinds), containing apologies for copying errors or expressions of satisfaction for the accomplished task; prayers and invocations; speeches to the reader, invectives against theft: they can appear in slightly different formulations, and some of them may have a local connotation, thus offering some hints for localization (but, as for other features of Byzantine books, in most cases making exclusive connexions with specific areas risks being contradicted by further research). Other information—such as price or various remarks of historical interest—appears only occasionally but further contributes to enhancing the value of colophons as historical sources.

Scribes usually mention their name (in late examples, their surname too) and social status or profession. Apart from monks and hieromonks (or priest-monks) there were also priests (*presbyteroi*) with various functions in the ecclesiastical hierarchy, or representatives of professions that involved a high degree of knowledge of writing (for instance notaries or school teachers). The scribe's name is often followed by an epithet expressing humility or unworthiness.

A patron—either an ecclesiastical dignitary or a secular authority—may also be cited, often with flattering titles; if he was an abbot or an emperor, his mention can also serve as a dating criterion (or even a criterion for localization). Patrons appear as *ktētores* ('founders') or are indirectly referred to through words describing their intention (such as *pothos*, *spoudē*, *dōron*).

A systematic structural survey of Byzantine colophons, as well as a typology of their position within the book, lettering and decoration, has not yet been proposed (some preliminary remarks are to be found in Cutler 1981).

8.6.3. Dating systems

The date may be expressed through a mix of various elements (and inconsistencies often occur in their combination). In the most complete form, it consists of the following mentions: year (mainly according to the Byzantine World Era, beginning on 1 September 5508; before the seventh century, according to the Alexandrine World Era, beginning on 25 March 5492; western and Renaissance manuscripts may be dated according to the Christian Era); indiction (a fifteen-year—originally five-year—cycle introduced by Emperor Diocletian for the collection of land taxes, initially starting on 23 September, later on 1 September); month and day of the month; day of the week; sun and moon cycles (twenty-eight and nineteen years, respectively); and (rarely) the hour of the day (often referred to according to the liturgical calendar).

8.7. Bookbinding

Almost all preserved examples of Byzantine original bindings are quite late (fourteenth or fifteenth century); hardly any original bindings survive from the first half of the Byzantine millennium (*c.*500–1000). Byzantine bindings show the following distinctive features (Federici – Houlis 1988):

- Byzantine craftsmen preserved the older oriental tradition of unsupported sewing, using one single thread (or even two in some of the earliest examples). The link stitches were usually accommodated into (three to seven) V-shaped grooves (*grecquage*), cut through the spine-fold, which therefore appears completely flat (not all Greek manuscripts have *grecquage*, which is often omitted in paper manuscripts);
- board attachment occurred: (a) by making the hinging loops on one board and proceeding until the end of the text block; (b) by making the loops on both boards, and proceeding towards the centre of the text block, the two halves being then joined together with figure-of-eight stitches ('biaxial stitch disposition'); or (c) by sewing the text block without the boards, which were attached subsequently by making a series of loops thorough sets of holes along the spine edge of the boards. The connexion could be made with the same sewing thread or with a similar one, by drawing a path from one loop to another, across the inner or outer surface of the boards;
- the (mostly rounded) spine is lined with a cloth, extended onto at least one-fourth of the outer surface of the board, glued with starch or animal glue;
- the wooden boards (poplar, conifer, oak or other species) are given the same dimensions as the leaves, and they do not show the slight protrusion adopted in late Mediaeval Latin bookbindings;
- boards may show grooves (of various form) in the three open edges;
- head and tail endbands, extending far over the board edges, are worked with thread on cord (or leather) cores and then attached to the boards by means of sewing through holes in the boards. They can be

made of natural-coloured thread wound around two overlapping cords or display a colourful chevron-patterned interlace, woven on a single or double support: both types are covered with raised leather caps;

- the fastenings (a single one, or two, or more rarely four), used to keep the volume closed, consist of a metallic peg driven into the edge of the upper cover and a strap (mostly in form of a tripartite slit braid with a final tip) attached through the board at the edge of the lower board.

Coverings are usually made of dark brown or blackish leather, mainly goatskin or sheepskin. The decoration of Byzantine bindings changed considerably throughout the centuries and according to the different geographies. During the early Byzantine centuries (eighth to tenth) geometric designs with blind lines were preferred, and gradually small hand tools appeared with vegetal or animal motifs. During the thirteenth and fourteenth centuries decoration, still accomplished with small tools in blind, became much more elaborate, with new patterns often originating from Europe. The use of centre-pieces and corner-pieces started to appear with some delay in comparison with European binding traditions, but by the end of the seventeenth century most genuinely Byzantine decorative features became extinct and were replaced by Italian or Eastern European type of decoration. Gold tooling was never a preferred technique for the Byzantine binders, with very few exceptions. The leather could be protected by (rarely surviving) metal bosses and corners. The title does not usually appear on the covering, but was usually written in ink on the tail edge. Decoration of the text block edges with rings and interlaces, most often drawn with black and red inks, is another interesting feature of the Byzantine binding.

Sumptuous bindings have been only sporadically preserved, especially those embellished with precious metals, ivories and gems, or covered with silk, velvet or satin damask.

The Byzantine binding tradition survived for several centuries beyond the fall of Constantinople and spread to Armenia, Georgia, and the Slavonic area. It gave rise to Armenian and 'alla greca' bindings, introduced by Byzantine exiles in Renaissance Italy and successfully exported throughout Europe by western craftsmen. These bindings are almost identical to Byzantine ones, except they employ western sewing supports, strong western-style tooled decoration of the leather covers and also hybrid Byzantine–western type of endbands. Thorough examination may reveal evidence of multiple bindings, witnessed by the simultaneous presence of different sets of guards or sewing holes (other than those currently used). More rarely, the comparison between original bindings provides an important clue of provenance and/or for reconstructing ensembles of scattered codices. The description of individual toolings and their groupings opens unexplored research paths, particularly as regards the allocation of groups of bindings related to specific geographical areas (such as Constantinople in the Palaiologan era, the island of Crete, or monasteries such as St John Prodromos of Petra, St John Prodromos at Serres, in Macedonia and St Catherine's Monastery in Sinai) or the reconstruction of specific binding ateliers (and of the scribes' circles connected to them, such as that of the Cretan Michaēl Apostolēs in the second half of the fifteenth century).

Finally, the study of bookbindings may provide valuable evidence for reconstructing the vicissitudes of currently dispersed libraries or collections of codices, or offer clues to the history of the texts, contributing to defining the origin of the volumes to which they belong and to highlighting connexions with specific scholarly circles (as with the aforementioned atelier of Michaēl Apostolēs, which served at the same time as scriptorium, editorial centre and bookbinding workshop).

References

Agati 2012; Andrist et al. 2013; Bagnall 2009; Benedetti 2010; Bianchi et al. 1993; Bianconi 2010; Bischoff 1993; Briquet 1907; Canart 1982, 1998; Cavallo 1996, 2001a; Crisci 1990, 2008; Crisci et al. 2007; Cutler 1981; D'Aiuto 2003; Federici – Houlis 1988; Degni 2008; Džurova 2008; Grünbart 2004; Gumbert 2004; Harlfinger – Harlfinger 1974, 1980; Irigoin 1981b; Kresten – Prato 1985; Kireeva 1999; Leroy [Julien] 1976; Maniaci 1995, 1997, 1999a, 1999b, 2000a, 2000b, 2002a, 2002b, 2006a, 2006b, 2013, forthcoming; Maniaci – Orofino 2012; Mazzucchi 2005; Milne 1927; Mondrain 1998; Perria 1983–1984; Petrucci 1969a; Piccard 1961–1997; Pöhlmann – West 2012; Poulakakis et al. 2007; Prato 1984; Roberts – Skeat 1983; Ronconi 2012; Sautel 1995, 2000, 2001; Schreiner 1983; Schreiner – Oltrogge 2011; Sosower 2004; Turner 1977, 1980, 1984; Vianès 2000; West [S.] 1963; Weyl Carr 1980; Worp – Rijksbaron 1997; Web sources: Wasserzeichensammlung Piccard <http://www.piccard-online.de>, last access October 2014.

9. Hebrew codicology (MBA)

9.1. Materials and tools

9.1.1. The finds from Judaean Desert and the Dead Sea Scrolls

The great majority of the literary works and documents found in the Judaean Desert, mainly at Qumran and Masada, are written on leather, parchment or papyrus. In addition, a large number of pottery sherds (*ostraca*) were used for writing documents. Exceptionally, there is the Copper Scroll from cave 3 in Qumran, and there are also two texts written on wooden tablets. Accelerated Mass Spectrometry (C_{14} analysis) has indicated the time range of the Qumran materials to be between 250 BCE and 70 CE.

In the absence of long literary texts surviving from earlier times, the kind of writing materials used in the Pre-Exilic period is not clear. Scholars interpreting descriptions of scrolls and writing in the Old Testament have reached contradictory conclusions: either papyrus or parchment. Scrolls of parchment are less neatly written than the great majority of leather scrolls. It is possible that papyrus was preferred only for private copies of sectarian literary texts (such as those found at Qumran), for later rabbinic legal literature forbids writing sacred scriptures on papyrus, prescribing instead the use of skins. Thus the few biblical papyrus scrolls among the Judaean Desert finds may have originated in a circle that did not comply with the rabbinic tradition. All the Qumran texts that are written in Palaeo-Hebrew are written on skin-based material (Tov 2004, 31–55).

In later centuries, parchment was the overwhelmingly dominant writing material for Hebrew books, being supplanted by paper in the Orient as early as the middle of the eleventh century, but much more slowly in Europe.

9.1.2. Papyrus

Apart from the few dozen Judaean Desert papyri and small fragments excavated in Egypt together with Greek papyri (Sirat et al. 1985), only one large fragment of a papyrus codex has been found, in the famous Cairo Geniza (a depository of worn-out books and documents in the old Jewish synagogue of Ben Ezra in Old Cairo, al-Fusṭāṭ district; see also Ch. 4 § 2.7; Sirat et al. 1985, 69–80).

9.1.2. Parchment

The use of parchment as standard writing material for Hebrew books started probably at the time of the canonization of the Hebrew Bible (roughly around the beginning of the Common Era) and continued until the end of the first millennium in the Orient, and until the mid-fifteenth century in most parts of Europe. The number of surviving dated Hebrew parchment manuscripts that were produced in the Orient is meagre: twenty-eight codices, mostly fragmentary, constituting 8% of the total corpus of dated oriental Hebrew manuscripts. They were all produced before 1327, all of them containing biblical texts except for two eleventh-century Geniza fragments. All extant codices from the tenth century are parchment biblical manuscripts. However, the Cairo Geniza collection and the Firkovitch collections in the National Library of Russia in St Petersburg contain many undated parchment biblical codices, or remains of them, which can be assigned to the tenth and eleventh centuries. The drastic decrease in the use of parchment in oriental Hebrew book production during this period correlates to the same phenomenon in the production of Arabic codices in the Orient.

The ratio of the parchment manuscripts within the entire corpus of dated manuscripts up to 1500 is 43% (71% in the thirteenth century, 54% in the fourteenth century, 34% in the fifteenth century). In the Sephardic zone it is 36% (84% in the thirteenth century, 46% in the fourteenth century, 22% in the fifteenth century); in Franco-German territories it is 82% (100% in the thirteenth century, 98% in the fourteenth century, 51% in the fifteenth century); in Italy it is 59% (98% in the thirteenth century, 82% in the fourteenth century, 51% in the fifteenth century); in Byzantium it is 14%; and in the Orient it is only 8% (in Yemen 13%).

The selection of the expensive writing material parchment was also dictated by the economic capability and social status of those who commissioned the copies, or who copied books for their own use; it was also genre-bound: Bibles, prayer books and to some extent halakhic (legal) corpora were copied on the more durable and prestigious writing material even after the use of paper had spread. Classification of the writing materials by the destination of the books produced does not show that self-produced copies were made mainly of paper, the cheaper material; however, in all regions (outside the Orient, where parchment was almost entirely abandoned), paper was used twice as much as parchment in user-produced (dated) manuscripts.

Cattle skin of which only one side was processed for writing is called in Hebrew *gevil*. Talmudic instructions require writing the liturgical Tora Scroll on *gevil*, and this dictate persists to this very day. Literary halakhic sources and chemical analyses attest to regional differences in the materials used for the processing of the skins to be made into scrolls, particularly the utilization of tannin in the Orient. No doubt, this kind of analysis can be applied to codices in only a very limited way. Yet it is feasible to grade the kinds of parchment by means of their visual appearance, especially that of the hair sides, which vary from zone to zone (in one specific zone they vary even from period to period). Consequently, these visual differences may serve as a codicological criterion for identifying the provenance of a manuscript (while in Ashkenazic manuscripts they serve for indicating the period as well).

Oriental parchment. Oriental parchment is known from early dated biblical codices and from later Yemenite manuscripts. The method of preparing the parchment makes it difficult to distinguish between the hair and flesh sides, since both sides are glossy and smooth. Nevertheless, it is always possible to identify the sides by their hue, the flesh sides being slightly lighter and brighter than the hair sides. It is obvious that despite the similarity of the two sides, the manuscripts' producers distinguished between them, as the arrangement of the bifolia in a quire and the method of ruling them demonstrate.

Sephardic parchment. The visual features of the parchment used in Christian Spain in the late twelfth century are known from a few dated manuscripts. This parchment is similar to the Italian type (see below), whereas an earlier parchment manuscript (St Petersburg, RNB, Evr. II B 124, the damaged colophon indicates a year dated between 941 and 1039) produced in Kairouan (Tunisia) shows a similarity to the oriental type. The absence of dated parchment manuscripts from Muslim Spain and the Maghreb before the thirteenth century prevents us from establishing whether the oriental-Arabic type had indeed been used there in early times. Later, the appearance of Sephardic parchment changed and it becomes possible to distinguish between the two sides, because in most cases the hair side is not scoured and hair follicles and roots are visible, although in some manuscripts the hair side is scraped and the remains are not visible. The flesh side is very bright and glossy.

Italian parchment. The parchment employed in dated Hebrew manuscripts of Italian origin, from the earliest dated manuscript of 1072/1073 (Vatican City, BAV, Vat. ebr. 31) until the late Middle Ages, typically retains the natural difference between the hair and flesh sides. Their disparity is sharp and easily discernible: hair sides are rough and scraped, yet the follicles and residues of hair roots are visible. Flesh sides are smooth and much lighter than the hair sides. The difference in the appearance of alternate openings in a codex is very conspicuous. Only high-quality manuscripts which were produced during the fifteenth century, more particularly illuminated ones, were written on refined, thin, very light parchment (known from humanistic copies), in which hair roots are not seen, although one can distinguish between its two sides.

Byzantine parchment. The characterization of parchment in Byzantine Hebrew manuscripts is impeded by the small number of dated manuscripts that survive. It seems that this parchment bears a similarity to the Italian type, in that its processing retained the natural differences between the two sides, and thus it allows clear differentiation between them.

Ashkenazic parchment. The appearance of the parchment employed in the German lands and their adjacent territories, and in some variant way in northern France, especially from the last third of the thirteenth century and thereafter, does not resemble parchment types in the other geo-cultural zones; it reflects a shift in the processing technique and in an aesthetic concept of book design. Until this shift, the processing of hides in all areas of Hebrew book production retained substantially or moderately the difference between the two skin sides, and the quire openings were arranged according to Gregory's Rule. Indeed, an appearance like that of the Italian codices is seen in the earliest dated Ashkenazic codices, of the last quarter of the twelfth century, and more distinctly in earlier (but undated) codices. It seems that in Germany, northern France and England, a change in the processing of the parchment had already started to evolve in the late twelfth century, at least as attested by Hebrew manuscripts. The differences between skin sides had gradually been reduced, until they became entirely alike in the last decades of the thirteenth century, most prominently in Germany. It is evident that the parchmenting process aimed at reducing the difference between the two skin sides by the scraping of both, so that the hair and flesh sides would present a very similar or even identical appearance. Nevertheless, it seems that scribes were well aware of which side was which, as they arranged the bifolia according to Gregory's Rule.

Fig. 1.9.1 Vatican City, BAV, Vat. ebr. 468, La Rochelle, 1215; colophon.

Due to the scarcity of Ashkenazic manuscripts with indications of place of origin, classification by the provenance of these manuscripts (either German lands or northern France) has to be established by their contents, mainly the liturgical rite of prayer books. The examination of the parchment in all dated and localizable Ashkenazic manuscripts reveals a difference between the appearance of the parchment of manuscripts produced in the German lands and that of manuscripts produced in northern France. This difference can serve as a basic criterion for distinguishing between 'German' and 'French' manuscripts, which share types of script and other codicological features. In most of the localized and localizable French manuscripts, it is possible to distinguish between the parchment skin sides either easily or with only some small effort. In many of them, starting from the earliest localized manuscript, written in La Rochelle in 1215 (Vatican City, BAV, Vat. ebr. 468, see fig. 1.9.1), up until 1499, remains of hair roots are visible, and there is not one single French parchment manuscript in Hebrew that is written on entirely equalized skin sides. By contrast, most dated manuscripts definitely manufactured in German lands after 1226/1227, and without exception after 1264, were written on 'equalized parchment', that is parchment with equalized sides. Only with great effort can one distinguish the skin sides in a few manuscripts from the late fourteenth and early fifteenth centuries.

9.1.3. Paper

According to the dated Hebrew codices, the replacement of parchment by paper as the main writing material was a rapid process only in the Orient, already complete in the early eleventh century, but progressing more slowly in Byzantium. Elsewhere—in the Iberian Peninsula and Provence, France, the German lands and Italy—the transition was gradual, as was the development of papermaking, and occurred at a much later date. In the Sephardic zone, paper became the main writing material in the second half of the fourteenth century; in Italy and Ashkenaz (central and northern France, the German lands and their adjacent territories), parchment remained the main writing material until the mid-fifteenth century, while in the second half of that century paper was used as often as parchment (*SfarData*; Beit-Arié 1981; Haran 1985, on literary sources).

'Oriental' paper was used in Hebrew codices in the Orient at least since 1005, which is the date of the earliest extant dated paper manuscript (Cambridge, Cambridge University Library, Taylor-Schlechter 8 Ca.1; Beit-Arié et al. 1997, 15; for documents, paper was in use by 933 at the latest). From that time on, oriental-Arabic paper became the standard writing material for oriental Hebrew manuscripts. Only some dozen fifteenth-century oriental Hebrew manuscripts and a similar number from the first four decades of the sixteenth century were written on European watermarked paper, most of them by Sephardic immigrant copyists. The oriental-Arabic paper that was used so predominantly for oriental Hebrew manuscripts displays several different patterns of laid and grouped chain lines that can be distinguished according to regions and periods of time (see below).

The earliest dated paper manuscript in the Byzantine region was written in Gagra (Caucasus) in 1207, on oriental paper (St Petersburg, RNB, Evr. II C 161). However, very few Byzantine Hebrew manuscripts written on oriental paper are dated; almost all the dated manuscripts are written on European paper.

In the Sephardic region (Spain and the Maghreb), the earliest dated paper manuscript in Hebrew was written in Muslim Valencia in 1119 (St Petersburg, RNB, Evr.-Ar. I 2240), on oriental-Arabic paper probably produced in Islamic Spain (that the beginning of papermaking employing an improved oriental technique goes back as far as the mid-eleventh century has been proven by commercial letters in Judaeo-Arabic found in the Cairo Geniza). A fragmentary manuscript (St Petersburg, RNB, Evr.-Ar. I 4587) written in 1125/1126, probably in Mahdia (Tunisia), is made of oriental paper (or rather Maghrebi paper produced by the oriental technique). The rest of the dated Sephardic manuscripts up until 1315 were written on pre-watermarked Spanish paper, some of them showing zigzag marks. Since that time, all the Sephardic paper manuscripts were produced on European watermarked paper.

There was, naturally, no utilization of oriental paper in Italy (earliest dated paper manuscript, produced on watermarked paper, from 1276/1277–1284, St. Petersburg, Oriental Institute, B396), nor in Ashkenaz (earliest dated paper manuscript, 1343/1344, private collection, Australia (formerly Jerusalem)). In both areas, the use of paper had been limited at the beginning and spread only gradually. In fourteenth-century Italy, it is limited to 15% of the surviving dated manuscripts, while in the first half of the fifteenth century it grew to one-third, and in the second half of that century it reached about 50% (likewise in Ashkenaz).

There follows a presentation of morphological types of oriental-Arabic paper based on dated mediaeval manuscripts written in Hebrew characters, with a characterization of their patterns according to chronological and regional distribution. In addition, the corpus includes 140 dated oriental manuscripts kept in the Bodleian Library, Oxford, written on oriental-Arabic paper, all of them in the Near East, mostly in Arabic script, but partly in Persian and a few in Syriac script. Altogether, the typology is based on 620 dated manuscripts (and some additional 110 undated ones, many of which are datable).

One should bear in mind the frequent difficulty in identifying the visible structure of the oriental-Arabic papers even in well-preserved manuscripts, as well as the many cases of ambiguous documentation and the inconsistent or contradictory impressions which blur clear and distinctive description. Only a systematic reproduction of the wire patterns of a large number of leaves (or, when it is feasible, unfolded bifolia), such as is obtainable by means of the beta-radiography technique, might provide us with a clearer typology. Regular small-size beta-radiography reproductions have usually been found to supply insufficient information, because of the irregularities inherent in oriental-Arabic paper.

The earliest paper manuscript that was examined is apparently the earliest known (dated) Arabic paper manuscript, from 848, in the Regional Library of Alexandria (Egypt). The only other pre-1000 manuscript examined is dated 983 (Oxford, Bodleian Library, MS. Huntington 228). The earliest surviving dated Hebrew paper manuscripts are from 1005 (a fragment, Cambridge University Library, Taylor-Schlechter 8 Ca.1) and 1006 (a codex, St Petersburg, RNB, Evr.-Ar. I 4520).

The following seven types, mostly in accordance with those pointed out by Jean Irigoin and his colleagues (Le Léannec-Bavavéas – Humbert 1990), can be discerned, outlined and characterized chronologically and, to certain degree, also regionally.

A. Wireless paper

The occurrence of paper of this type in the earliest dated manuscript (Alexandria, dated 848 CE) may very well indicate that early oriental-Arabic paper was wireless or pattern-less. This type of paper, in which no laid or chain lines are visible, was in constant use from the beginning of the eleventh century until the end of Middle Ages. It has been found in a considerable number of manuscripts, produced everywhere in the Near East, but relatively much more frequently in manuscripts localized in Iraq and in Iran, where it can be found in some 18% of the manuscripts that were recorded.

A particular kind of wireless paper showing some 'chaotic' patterns and conspicuous fibres was extensively and exclusively used in Yemen from the beginning of the fourteenth century until the introduction of Italian watermarked paper around the middle of the sixteenth century. This peculiar type, found in almost 80% of the 110 dated manuscripts produced in Yemen, was most probably manufactured in that region, as it is not to be found in any other oriental manuscript. The only recorded Arabic codex written in Yemen indeed shows a similar type of paper.

B. Laid lines only

An early type, whose first appearance in our corpus is dated 983, was produced continuously and used extensively until 1500. It was the dominant type until 1250, declining thereafter in competition with the emerging and spreading types with clustered chain lines. Yet the 'laid lines only' type still constituted 35%

of the dated paper manuscripts in the second half of the thirteenth century, and about 23% in the following century.

This type was used everywhere, but many of the manuscripts belonging to it were produced in the eastern part of the Near East, namely Iraq, Iran and central Asia, where this kind of paper was the main type from the eleventh century on, constituting an average of about 70% of the dated manuscripts. Thus, lack of chain lines characterizes paper produced in those north-eastern areas. The production of both wireless and particularly 'laid lines only' paper is still attested there in the sixteenth century. The limited use of various types of chain-lined paper in those areas may hint that this kind of oriental-Arabic paper was not produced there, but was imported from neighbouring (western) areas.

C. Laid and chain lines

In many cases, the visible pattern of the chain lines is not clear enough, being seemingly irregular or presenting combinations of more than one type. Two sub-types must be distinguished, the second of which has four sub-sub-types, as follows.

C.1. Single chain lines

Visible chain lines in oriental-Arabic paper are usually clustered in several different groupings. Paper manuscripts showing single chain lines are extremely rare, comprising about 3% of our corpus. This type was found in dated manuscripts from the beginning of the twelfth century (perhaps already in 1048, in a manuscript in which single chain lines seem to be visible, spaced 30–35 mm) until the late fifteenth century. Usually, single chain lines are curved and not evenly spaced. In most clear cases, their distribution is very dense: only 12–25 mm apart. Two cases showing more widely spaced single chain lines (36–40 mm apart) might represent paper produced in North Africa, as might perhaps all the rare occurrences of single chain lines.

C.2. Clustered chain lines

This multi-pattern type emerged clearly at the beginning of the twelfth century, perhaps sometime earlier. Gradually its use increased, equalling the 'laid lines only' paper in the second half of the thirteenth century and becoming the dominant type from the first half of the following century on. This type of paper was hardly found in Iraq, Iran or the Central Asian areas, and never in Yemen after the beginning of the fourteenth century. Everything indicates that it was produced and/or used in the western parts of the Near East—Syria, Palestine and Egypt.

C.2a. Chain lines grouped in twos: This type is the earliest of the 'clustered' kinds of oriental-Arabic papers. Its first clear appearance in our corpus is dated 1119/1120 (Oxford, Bodleian Library, MS. Heb. d. 58). Its peak usage, according to our corpus, seems to have been in the second half of the fourteenth century.

C.2b. Chain lines grouped in threes: This type apparently emerged in the early thirteenth century, although the earliest clear pattern was not found before 1249 (St Petersburg, RNB, Evr.-Ar. I 3911). However, its extensive diffusion came much later: it dominated other types used in the western Orient in the fifteenth and the first half of the sixteenth century (when it remained as the only surviving type of chained paper).

C.2c. Chain lines grouped in twos and threes alternately: This youngest type is attested for the first time in our corpus by an Arabic manuscript dated 1338 (Oxford, Bodleian Library, MS. Arab. d. 223). The late Don Baker, however, noticed it in an earlier Arabic manuscript dating from 1304 (Baker 1991, 31). Only in the second half of the fourteenth century did its spread dominate all other types of paper used in the western regions.

C.2d. Chain lines grouped in fours: This unusual type has so far been noticed, but without certitude, in only two Hebrew manuscripts dating from the fourteenth and the fifteenth century, and clearly only in one Arabic codex, dated 1210 (Oxford, Bodleian Library, MS. Marsh 38). The scarce occurrence may indicate that such a type was produced on a very limited, probably local, scale, or that it has not been properly identified.

Finally, a note concerning the peculiar feature of the splitting of the edges of oriental-Arabic paper sheets. This phenomenon, for which a definite explanation is still lacking, was frequently observed in recently recorded dated manuscripts, both the Arabic ones of the Bodleian Library, and the Hebrew codices of St Petersburg. Among the latter, which were studied more thoroughly, 40% were found to show splitting edges, or rather *splittable* edges. In some cases, the edges, mainly external corners, were split into three layers.

The phenomenon can be seen in manuscripts as early as the eleventh century until the end of the Middle Ages. It seems that it does not characterize wireless paper at all, including the peculiar Yemenite type, which may refute scholarly suggestions (backed by mediaeval literary sources) that such a paper was manufactured by pasting two sheets together. In solving the puzzle of the splitting, or splittable, oriental-Arabic paper, however, one should pay attention to the fact that a similar phenomenon can also be observed in a few Hebrew manuscripts written in early twelfth-century Spain, or thirteenth-century Italy and Byzantium. Thus, this feature should be studied in comparison to the Occidental-Arabic (Spanish) paper and the pre-watermarked Italian paper (Beit-Arié 1999).

9.1.4. Ink

The Dead Sea Scrolls are written with carbon inks. Five scrolls, among them the Genesis Apocryphon scroll, have considerable amount of copper in addition to carbon in accordance with Dioscorides' recipe. No systematic study of inks in the medieval Hebrew manuscripts has been conducted, However, iron-gall inks have been detected in a number of Ashkenazic and oriental manuscripts.

9.1.5. Writing instruments

Hebrew scribes employed two kinds of pens. One was made of reeds, the other was made of birds' quills (or of bones). Reed pens were used in the Orient; they are attested by documentary sources and already mentioned in the Talmudic literature, and they are still employed by religious 'Sephardic' scribes when transcribing Tora scrolls and legal documents. It seems that the reed pen was used also in Byzantium. Quill pens were used in Ashkenaz (in northern France, England and the German lands). The writing instrument used in the Sephardic areas and Italy requires further study. Sephardic scribes seem to have employed reed pens, and so did Italian scribes until they replaced them with quill pens.

9.2. Book forms

9.2.1. The roll/scroll and the rotulus; the codex

The scroll (i.e. the horizontal roll) was the only book form used by the Jews for their scriptures in antiquity and for literary compositions—as in the Judaean Desert finds—in post-biblical times. It became, and remains to this day, the only form for the liturgical Pentateuch (*Sefer Tora*) in its use for reading in synagogues. A Munich palimpsest (Bayerische Staatsbibliothek, Clm 6315, 29022) in which a sheet of a scroll containing a Hebrew prayer book was reused for a Latin text in the Bobbio scriptorium around 800 attests to the late use of the scroll (Beit-Arié 1967–1968). All references to books in the rich Talmudic literature, both of Palestine and of Babylonia, relate to scrolls; only a few isolated passages use, metaphorically, the Greek term *pinax*, apparently meant to designate a concertina-like manuscript, more like a scroll than a codex.

The revolutionary codex form of book, which was adopted and diffused by Christians already in the first centuries CE, was employed by the Jews only much later. Between the abundant finds of Hebrew books (scrolls) from Late Antiquity and the earliest dated and datable surviving Hebrew codices, there is a salient gap of some eight hundred years, for which almost no evidence of the Hebrew book is found, either in roll form or in codex form. The earliest certainly dated extant Hebrew codices were inscribed at the beginning of the tenth century, all of them in the Orient. However, in the structural, figural, and artistic design of the copied texts, in their harmonious scripts and in the mature employment of codicological practices, these earliest manuscripts demonstrate elaborate craftsmanship and regularity, surely attesting to a long-established tradition of codex design and production.

In fact, the earliest reference to the codex form in Jewish literature does not date from before the end of the eighth or the beginning of the ninth century. Moreover, the earliest term designating a codex (*miṣḥaf*) was borrowed from Arabic and persisted in the Orient for quite a long time. Therefore it seems that the Jews in the Orient adopted the codex only after the Arab conquest, very likely not before the ninth century or a little earlier. The long gap with no evidence of a Hebrew codex until the ninth century can be explained by the basically oral transmission of Jewish literature in the Hebrew language and by the belated adoption of the codex. The long rejection of the codex—rejected despite its being the more capacious, durable and usable form of book, easy to carry about, store and refer to—can be explained by assuming that the Jews adhered to the scroll form of book in order to differentiate themselves from the Christians, who first used the codex for disseminating the New Testament and the 'Old Testament' translated into Greek (the Septuagint). Indeed, the *Sefer Tora* and some other biblical books are written to this day on scrolls.

Old rotuli (vertical rolls) were noticed in the Cairo Geniza decades ago, but only recently have their extent, chronology and variety of genres been clarified, by Gideon Bohak (2011) and especially Judith Olszowy-Schlanger, who was the oral source for the information which follows. The production and use of these Hebrew rotuli was rather extensive. So far, hundreds of fragmentary vertical scrolls have been recorded, half of them written on parchment and half on paper. They spread mainly in Egypt in the eleventh century, yet some of them undoubtedly date from the time of the birth of the Hebrew codex. They contain a large variety of texts: about half are liturgical, while the rest include Talmudic treatises, halakhic literature, anthologies of biblical verses, dictionaries, glossaries, medicine and magic. About half of the rotuli were copied on the blank side of re-used documents, some of them in Arabic in Arabic script. The sizes of the pieces that were stitched together to form a rotulus are not uniform; their width is narrow and their length varies. It seems that the rotuli, whose production was cheap and rapid and whose form was conveniently portable, were produced by their users—rabbis, scholars, physicians, and magicians—for personal and professional use.

9.3. The making of the codex

9.3.1. The making of the quires

So far, there is no clear evidence for parchment quires having been constructed by folding. But it should be admitted that no systematic observation of this facet has been carried out in Hebrew codicology. However, the odd number of bifolia (five) in the quires of most of the dated Hebrew codicological units thwarts this possibility. Only a few undated early Hebrew oriental codices, produced probably in Iraq prior to the tenth century, show an arrangement of the parchment sides (HHHHH) that also disproves any hypothesis that imposition might have been used, whereas all the dated manuscripts follow Gregory's Rule. Nevertheless, it seems that most of the Hebrew codices imply that quires were composed by stacking bifolia from a pile of already-cut bifolia, picked up at random.

As for the possible preparation of paper quires by folding oriental paper sheets, in most of the early dated Hebrew paper manuscripts the direction of the laid lines in relation to the width of the folium is horizontal. But it is evident that this characteristic was not conditioned by the format of the book or by the number of times the paper sheet was folded. This fact is demonstrated by a comparison of manuscripts whose bifolia are close in size. While two such manuscripts, nos. 60 and 65 in Beit-Arié et al. 1997, show horizontal laid lines, another, no. 57, shows vertical laid lines. Furthermore, an additional manuscript showing single chain lines and horizontal laid lines, no. 61, actually contradicts the horizontal evidence of nos. 60 and 65, because the size of its bifolia—386 × 294 mm—is twice the size of the more or less identical bifolia of the other manuscripts with single chain lines. Thus, although the dimensions of most of the paper manuscripts attest to considerably standardized production sheet sizes before folding and trimming, it seems that the direction of the wire lines was not uniformly maintained in the making of quires from these sheets. This is demonstrated incontestably by codex no. 51, which was written on two different papers of the same size, one showing vertical laid lines, the other horizontal laid lines. The possibility that there were two manufacturer's sizes of paper sheets, one the double of the other, should be considered and verified, or not, by additional data on the dimensions of the oriental papers.

9.3.2. The composition of the quires

In general, Hebrew parchment quires comprise four to six bifolia (only very rarely ternions, of three bifolia), while paper or mixed quires contain four to fourteen bifolia (but usually not exceeding ten bifolia). The only extant papyrus codex (preserved in the Cairo Geniza) contained at least twenty-four bifolia in a single quire. Only in the Orient did parchment and paper manuscripts share the same standard structure, while some of the Franco-German and Italian paper quires were constructed, to some extent, like the parchment quires from the same regions.

Before presenting the typology of Hebrew quire structures, one must draw a correlation between the quire structure and the disposition of the hair and flesh sides within the quire. As already mentioned, all the dated parchment manuscripts have quires whose skin sides are arranged for matching at the openings (Gregory's Rule). As the earliest dated manuscripts are from the early tenth century, this practice correlates to the Syriac and Arabic shifts to the same arrangement. However, there are two ways of respecting Gregory's Rule—the outer bifolium starts and ends either with the hair side, or with the flesh side. In most of the Hebrew geo-cultural zones, quires start with hair side, but in Italy, beginning from 1280, the practice of starting with the flesh side spread gradually until it was employed in about 60% of the dated manuscripts of the fifteenth century. At that period, almost all the humanistic Latin manuscripts were arranged likewise, according to the extensive corpus studied by Albert Derolez (Derolez 1984). The wide diffusion of this practice since the second decade of the fifteenth century among Hebrew manuscripts ruled in pale ink, unguided by pricking, and the fact that it was common also in manuscripts copied by immigrant scribes (from France, Germany, Spain and Provence) prompt the question whether ready-ruled quires were manufactured and sold by stationers (see below on pricking and ruling). Strangely enough, starting quires with the flesh side is found in only a small part of the Hebrew codices from the Byzantine zone, where this was the common practice for Greek manuscripts.

In most of the mixed parchment and paper quires, both outer and central bifolia are made of parchment; in about 20% only the outer bifolium is parchment (in Byzantium the figures reaches 36%), and in just a few manuscripts is it only the central bifolium that is parchment. Most of the mixed quires start and end with a parchment hair side, including those produced in Italy. Somewhat more than two-thirds of the combined parchment and paper manuscripts in which the central bifolium is parchment display the hair side at the central openings of the quires.

Ternions are very rare amongst the dated Hebrew manuscripts and are found mainly in Spain and North Africa; apparently they were more common in Toledo—a centre of production of accurate copies of the Bible—between the end of the twelfth century and 1300 (a practice possibly inspired by Arabic scribes, particularly in North Africa).

Quaternions were the standard composition of Franco-German (Ashkenazic) parchment manuscripts, found in almost all the dated codices since the earliest, from the last quarter of the twelfth century, until 1540; about half the dated paper manuscripts share this composition. Quaternions were the most common structure of parchment manuscripts in the Sephardic zone (Iberian Peninsula, Provence and Bas Languedoc and the Maghreb). It was very rare in the Orient, except for paper manuscripts from Iran and Uzbekistan, according to localized or localizable manuscripts (the numbers of which are rather limited), where it seems to have been the standard composition. This conclusion is verified by the data on the quiring of Arabic and Persian paper manuscripts from the second half of the thirteenth century. The earliest Persian Hebrew manuscript (Oxford, Bodleian Library, MS. Poc. 96) is dated 1190, but most such manuscripts date to the fourteenth and fifteenth centuries. In Italy, this composition was rather rare, but from the last decade of the fourteenth century it was used in 15% of the parchment manuscripts, most of them produced by Ashkenazic and Sephardic immigrant scribes who settled in Italy in the wake of the expulsion from France and the persecutions in Spain in 1391.

Quinions were the standard composition in the Orient since the earliest dated codices, regardless of the writing material. The same is found in Arabic manuscripts as well as Syriac and Coptic paper manuscripts. This is also the quiring practice found in Italian manuscripts since the earliest dated manuscripts of the eleventh century and later, and in 30% of the dated paper manuscripts of the fifteenth century.

Senions are not common in parchment codices, but are notably employed in paper ones. In the Iberian Peninsula and Provence, senions were a secondary composition in parchment codices since 1275, yet they were used until 1500 in only 15% of them. Senions were used in about 45% of the dated paper manuscripts in the Sephardic zone, and in half of the dated Byzantine manuscripts. They are found in a quarter of the Italian paper manuscripts, but only in very few oriental manuscripts. All these data are from manuscripts whose quire structure is uniform and which survive completely rather than only as fragments.

The compositions of seven to fourteen bifolia were used only in paper quires and in mixed quires of parchment and paper in the Sephardic zone, Italy and the Byzantine zone. All of them were used only occasionally, except for the eight-bifolium quire, which was relatively common in the fourteenth and fifteenth centuries in those areas.

The technique of constructing paper quires by adding protecting outer and central parchment bifolia, as a compromise between the durable but expensive parchment and the more vulnerable but cheaper paper, is not attested at all in the dated oriental Hebrew manuscripts, whether commissioned or self-produced. Notwithstanding the fact that the earliest mixed-quire manuscript, dated 1212 (Frankfurt, Universitätsbibliothek, Heb. 4° 2), was copied in Alexandria, it betrays a Byzantine codicological book craft. Perhaps the speedy replacement of parchment by paper as the main writing material can explain its composition. The practice of using mixed quires was widespread in Byzantine Hebrew codices: one-third of the dated paper manuscripts in the fourteenth century and nearly the same percentage in the fifteenth century have mixed quires. In the Sephardic zone, where the earliest extant sample from Spain is dated 1225 (Jerusalem, NLI, Yah. MS Heb. 1), mixed quires constitute one-third of the dated paper manuscripts in the fourteenth century, and only 10% in the fifteenth century. In Italy, half of the small number of surviving dated paper manuscripts of the fourteenth century show mixed quires, and one-fifth in the fifteenth century. Thus, unlike the situation in Latin manuscripts, the technique was not adopted by Ashkenazic scribes and copyists, who replaced parchment with paper very late.

Finally a remark about a practice witnessed in paper manuscripts, which can be viewed as a reduced and minimal variant of the mixed quires (known also from papyrus codices), namely the placement of a narrow strip of parchment in the central fold of a quire and on its outside fold; usually this strip is pasted onto the paper and sewn in order to reinforce the folds and protect the quire from the sewing thread. The practice is found in Hebrew manuscripts produced in the same areas where mixed quires were used, namely the Byzantine zone, the Sephardic zone and Italy (the earliest manuscript of this kind is a Sephardic codex dated 1282, London, BL, Add. 27113).

9.3.3. Pricking and ruling

The practice of using ruled lines to guide the writing of Hebrew manuscripts is old, predating the birth of the codex. It was employed already in the Judaean Desert scrolls, in dozens of which it has been observed. However, the ruling lines were guided not by pricks, but by dots, or sometimes strokes, written in ink. Pricking for guiding the drawing of the horizontal ruling lines and the vertical bounding lines on the codex page was employed in almost all the parchment Hebrew manuscripts that were ruled in hard point or plummet, in all regions and periods. Only in early oriental paper manuscripts, which were ruled in hard point—like the early parchment manuscripts—, pricking was also employed. This technique of ruling was shared between parchment and paper codices for the most part only during the first century of the Hebrew paper codex, that is during the eleventh century (it reappears again in the late twelfth century). The ruling technique of oriental paper codices was radically and rapidly transformed in the first third of the twelfth century, at the latest, by the use of the ruling board, which did not require any pricking. Outside the Orient, complete sets of pricking were applied only rarely in paper manuscripts.

In most dated manuscripts, pricking was applied to all the folded leaves of each quire concurrently, not only to reduce labour time but no doubt also to ensure ruling uniformity. When the ruling unit comprised an unfolded bifolium—the smallest codicological component—only the outer margin of a folded quire was pricked (fig. 1.9.2), and the horizontal lines were then ruled across the unfolded bifolia. When the ruling unit was a single leaf, or several leaves (or a page), both inner and outer margins had to be pricked, and horizontal lines were ruled across each leaf or page separately.

In the Orient, Byzantium and Italy, the pricking was confined to the outer margins. Manuscripts written by Maghrebi or Spanish scribes in the early period working in the Orient, and some of the manuscripts written in Italy by Ashkenazic and Sephardi immigrant scribes, were pricked in both margins. Since the twelfth century, pricking in both margins was the standard practice in the Sephardic zone and was dictated by the system of ruling the two leaves of a folded bifolium at once. The earliest manuscript to have been pricked in both margins was produced in the Maghreb by a scribe from Libya in 1123 (Cambridge, University Library, Taylor-Schlechter F2(2).60 + London, BL, Or. 5558A f. 17 + Oxford, Bodleian Library, MS. Heb. b 1, ff.10-20), and after that date all the extant Sephardic dated manuscripts until 1279 are pricked also in the inner margins. The earliest Sephardic codex (apart from the Kairouan manuscript) whose pricking is only in the outer margin is dated 1271 (Cincinnati, Hebrew Union College, 563), and after that date single pricking (and the ruling method associated with it) was employed in about one-third of the Sephardic manuscripts, while the old pricking practice (and the ruling) continued to characterize the Sephardic book making.

Pricking both inner and outer margins became the standard practice for most Franco-German manuscripts (unlike Latin manuscripts) from the late thirteenth century. The shift from outer-margin prick-

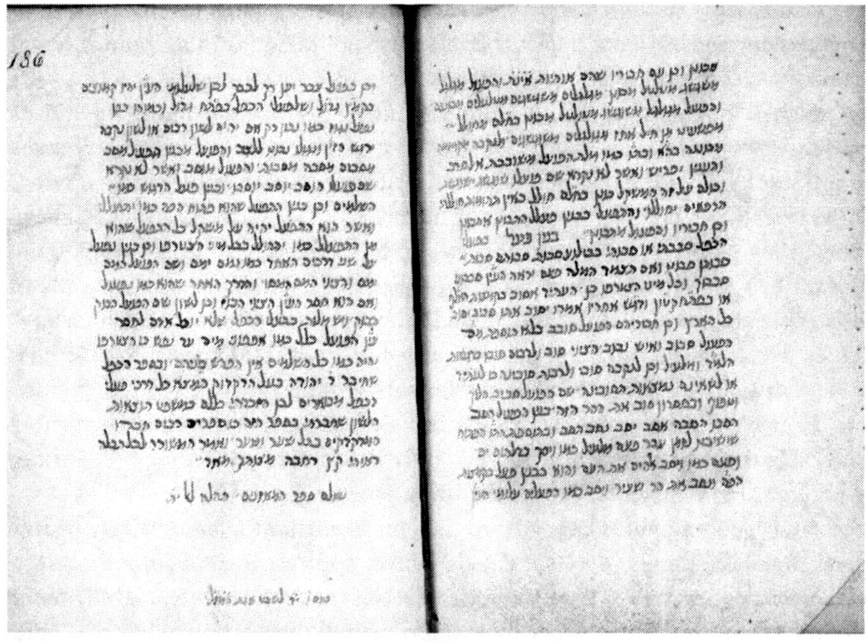

Fig. 1.9.2 Paris, BnF, Hébreu 1221, copied in Italy, 1285–1287, ff. 185v–186r, showing pricking on the outer margins.

ing only, the old standard practice, to outer- and inner-margin pricking, with a concomitant change in the method of ruling, was gradual, and it was associated with the shift in parchment processing (mentioned above), whereby the skin and hair sides became increasingly indistinguishable, or even identical. The additional pricking of the inner margin emerged, at the latest, at the end of the first third of the thirteenth century. The earliest manuscript (private collection of David Sofer, London) which displays a complete pricking of both margins, as well as the new method of ruling and the new appearance of the parchment, is dated 1264. According to the only surviving dated manuscript produced in England before the expulsion of the Jews at the end of the thirteenth century, written in 1189 (London, Valmadonna Trust Library, 1), and a few undated manuscripts, Hebrew manuscripts produced there adopted the English two-margin pricking which became the standard practice after the Norman conquest. Again the shift to pricking both margins was required by a change from blind ruling of unfolded bifolia to coloured ruling of individual pages. However, the one-margin pricking did not disappear, and almost half of the dated Ashkenazic manuscripts in the fourteenth and fifteenth centuries were pricked in the outer margins alone, although they were ruled with plummet.

In some manuscripts, mainly in the Ashkenazic zone, the vertical row of pricks itself has a guiding ruled line to guarantee a straight row. An oriental example of this device can be found in a manuscript copied in Yemen in 1299 (San Francisco, CA, Sutro Library, WPA 106).

A custom that pertains to pricking which is characteristic of Ashkenazic manuscripts is double pricks for special lines—one or two or three lines out of the three upper, three central and three bottom lines. The lines that were pricked by double pricks are ruled as through lines; thus the practice was intended to mark them and remind the scribe while writing. The practice occurs both in manuscripts which were ruled in hard point, and in manuscripts with coloured ruling, particularly in Gothic (Latin) and Hebrew manuscripts, in which the grid structure was emphasized. Almost half the parchment Ashkenazic manuscripts display this practice (46%).

Finally it is worth mentioning the phenomenon which has been recently discovered of marginal single pricks, that are probably related to ruling with ink (see B.3 below).

Ruling already guided the regularity of writing in even and straight lines already in the ancient Near East and on ancient Crete, as is already noticeable on Sumerian, Akkadian and Babylonian clay tablets written in cuneiform script, where the lines are incised, and similarly on clay tablets inscribed in Mycenaean B script, where the lines are in relief. The Judaean Desert scrolls were ruled in hard point, and the Talmudic law requires, according to earlier Tanaitic (post-biblical) sources, that Tora Scrolls should be ruled in blind ruling.

In a considerable number of manuscripts (*c.* 14%), no ruling is visible; or, more frequently, they only have frame ruling that demarcates the written area, or just vertical bounding lines. Most of these manuscripts were written on paper in the Orient in early times; yet some of them were produced later in Europe by copyists transcribing texts for their own use. When the written lines do not correspond one to another on the two sides of a leaf, and their number is not identical, one can infer that indeed no horizontal lines were ruled. Of these 'sloppy' manuscripts in which only the vertical boundary lines (or the frame, or portal) were traced, 3% are parchment and 11% are paper manuscripts (not taking into account oriental Cairo Geniza fragments). It is no wonder that so many paper manuscripts, chiefly those produced for self-consumption, were ruled in a reduced manner. Apparently, ruling required proficiency and time, and its cost in the calculation of the prices of commissioned books constituted a considerable part of the expenses of production, as attested by a unique list of the detailed costs of writing material, ruling and copying, written in Venice in 1393 by the scribe of a commissioned paper manuscript (Moscow, RGB, Guenzburg Collection, MS 666) at the end of his work. According to this evidence, the cost of ruling—which may have not been executed by the scribe—was twice as high as that of the paper. Parchment manuscripts in which the ruling is easily observable show many variations in and modifications of patterns, which suggests that the scribes themselves executed the ruling. If so, then it would seem that specifying the cost of ruling—which was surely simpler to do on paper than on parchment—implies that the job was handed over to be executed elsewhere. However, in some manuscripts there is evidence that they had been ruled beforehand, in a pattern not suited to the copied text, and consequently the scribe had to adjust the ruling, convert one column into two columns, or vice versa, extend the lines, etc.

The wide dispersion of the Jewish communities engendered the employment of a large variety of ruling techniques and systems over the six centuries of extant dated Hebrew codices. In general, they can be classified into two main kinds of techniques: one is the technique of relief (or blind) ruling, and the other is the coloured techniques. Relief ruling was made either by a sharp metallic instrument such as a hard point, a knife or a stylus, or by ruling boards; in the Orient, the boards held cords and were used for ruling paper manuscripts, while in Europe they were allegedly made with strings and were sometimes used for ruling parchment as well as paper manuscripts. The shared feature of the two kinds is the reduced presence of the scaffolding of the grid area and the time saving process by which more than a page or one side of an unfolded bifolium is ruled in one go: namely, either the back of the prime ruling unit, or, in case of hard point ruling, even several leaves or unfolded bifolia at once.

The other techniques used by Hebrew scribes include ruling with metallic plummet, engraving plummet and, only later, in ink.

The various ruling techniques can otherwise be classified from the viewpoint of the ruling guidance method. We can distinguish between rulings which are guided by prickings and those which are guided by ruling boards. The oriental ruling board is mentioned in mediaeval sources, with some specimens surviving. The European boards are attested only in sixteenth-century written sources, but their use can be detected in many paper and some parchment manuscripts which do not show any traces of guiding pricks (particularly in the inner margins, as those in the outer margins were prone to loss through trimming) and yet are ruled by blind ruling leaf by leaf.

In general, Jewish scribes first employed relief ruling, while coloured ruling was employed later on, in the Ashkenazic zone, and still later in Italy.

A. Relief/blind rulings

A.1. Ruling in hard point (dry point)

Relief ruling in hard point was the standard technique in the early Hebrew parchment codices in the Orient, and in early paper codices as well. It was the current technique in parchment codices also in the west, including Byzantium, Italy, Ashkenaz and the Sephardic zone, and in most of these areas it remained so until the late Middle Ages. This technique was always guided by pricking.

A.1a. Ruling in hard point of each unfolded parchment bifolium on the hair side: Such ruling had to be executed before assembling the quire. The ruling was guided by outer-margin pricking, which was made—as far as we can judge by the shapes of the pricking slots and the track patterns of their rows—on all the leaves of each folded quire in one go, while it was arranged according to Gregory's Rule. Thus the pricking process contradicts the ruling process and we must infer that first the quire was assembled according to Gregory's Rule for the pricking, then disassembled for the sake of the ruling, and finally reassembled, again following Gregory's Rule. Each opening displays not only the same parchment skin side on facing pages, but also the same ruled sides, either furrows (on hair sides) or ridges (on flesh sides), alternately. This complex process seems ergometrically strange and uneconomical, but it demonstrates the preference for aesthetic considerations over ergometrical convenience and saving time.

This system was the standard ruling practice in Italy since the earliest manuscripts of the eleventh century; moreover, until the 1380s it had been the only practice. Only in the fifteenth century, following the spread of ink ruling from the 1430s on, the use of hard-point ruling decreased, particularly in the second half of the century. In the Ashkenazic territories, the technique was the only practice that suited parchment with easily distinguishable sides, until the last third of the thirteenth century; then the coloured ruling in plummet and prickings in both margins and the use of equalized parchment started to spread. In the Sephardic zone, this system of hard-point ruling together with pricking was employed in many manuscripts only from 1271 and later, while ruling leaf by leaf in some manuscripts can be observed since 1198. However, as we shall see later, until 1270 (and quite considerably also in later times) the standard system was ruling two consecutive leaves at once.

A.1b. Ruling in hard point on each unfolded bifolium on the flesh side: In the Orient, too, the practice of hard-point ruling on each unfolded parchment bifolium guided by outer-margin prickings was employed, but always on the flesh side, unlike in Europe and the Maghreb. This is a unique codicological practice that enables us to identify the provenance of manuscripts and fragments written in non-localizable script. Ruling on the flesh side characterizes almost all the Latin manuscripts written before the eighth century and produced probably in the Orient.

A.1c. Ruling in hard point on each unfolded paper bifolium: Early oriental paper manuscripts of the eleventh century were pricked and ruled in hard point, apparently like parchment manuscripts. Yet the bifolia within the quire were not arranged by corresponding ruled sides after being ruled; instead, the scribes of the eleventh century arranged the bifolia in such a way that all rectos of the first half of the quire and all versos of the second half display furrows, and furrows face ridges. Only at the end of the twelfth century did one scribe who produced several dated pricked and ruled paper manuscripts in Cairo arrange two manuscripts so that furrows face furrows and ridges face ridges.

A.1.d. Ruling in hard point of successive parchment leaves in one go on the hair side: An economical method of implementing hard point ruling is manifested in many manuscripts produced in the Sephardic areas. Successive leaves, while they are arranged in corresponding sides within the quire, are ruled in one go, the primary page always showing the hair side. The ruled sides in the opening pages do not correspond. The usual number of leaves ruled together is two; the hair-side recto of the first leaf of the pair displays the furrows executed by the direct blind ruling while the flesh-side recto of the second shows the indirect furrows. In a few manuscripts produced in Spain it is possible to discern more than pairs of leaves, even up to an entire quire, as is the case with Latin manuscripts until the Carolingian period. In a few cases ruling was also done on successive bifolia. The ruling of pairs of leaves implied pricking both margins, while the ruling of pairs of bifolia required only outer pricking. The economical Sephardic system characterizes the book production of parchment manuscripts in Spain, Provence and North Africa from the last three decades of the thirteenth century. However, the system was practised about three hundred years earlier as it is attested by a manuscript produced in Jerusalem in 988/989 (St Petersburg, RNB, Evr. II, B 39) and two others produced in Palestine in the third decade of the eleventh century by Maghrebi scribes (St Petersburg, RNB, Evr. II, B 88, dated 1020/1021 and Cairo, Karaite Synagogue, dated 1028). The system was practised in Visigothic Latin manuscripts.

The ergometric advantage of ruling four (or multiples of four) pages at once had also its disadvantage: in many manuscripts we can observe that the secondary, indirect ruling, particularly on the fourth page, is hardly visible, so much so that the scribe had to re-rule it, partially or entirely.

A.1e. Ruling each leaf by means of pricking and hard point: This laborious system is found in a small number of the parchment manuscripts produced in Byzantium and in the Sephardic areas (including manuscripts written by Sephardic immigrants in Italy and Byzantium) from the mid-fourteenth century and later. Many Spanish manuscripts ruled leaf by leaf were pricked in both margins. Some that were not pricked at all must have been ruled by means of a ruling board of some kind. Apparently, ruling each leaf in hard point was the standard system for all the Hebrew paper manuscripts ruled by a relief technique in all geo-cultural areas, apart from the Orient. The fact that none at all of the oriental paper manuscripts was pricked implies that they were ruled with a ruling board or template (method A.2).

A.2. Relief/blind ruling with ruling boards or templates

The other kind of relief (or blind) ruling was not guided by pricking, but was executed by means of ruling boards that ruled leaves mechanically; or possibly the ruling was executed by means of templates

Fig. 1.9.3 A student's model of ruling board (*misṭara*) preserved in the Cairo Geniza, Cambridge, University Library, Taylor-Schlechter K11.54.

that guided the tracing in hard point of some sort. Most oriental Hebrew paper manuscripts were ruled by means of a ruling board, on the verso pages. The nature of the ruling board is known to us through Jewish and Arabic literary sources, as well as by finds of such boards from the mediaeval period and the existence of modern boards. The use of ruling boards in Europe is deduced on the basis of observation and is known from textual evidence in sixteenth-century printed manuals on calligraphy. (To the category of mechanical ruling one can add the technique of coloured ruling executed by means of an instrument whose nature is not clear, ruling in pale ink a group of several lines in one go; see method B below.)

The oriental ruling board—*misṭara* in Arabic, *kanna* in mediaeval Hebrew sources—was made of cardboard or wood; one such board was brought from Yemen at the end of the nineteenth century by German geographers and is now in the Israel Museum. Indeed, in recent generations, Jewish scribes in Yemen were witnessed ruling paper manuscripts with a *misṭara* made of wood (fig. 1.9.3). Cords were threaded into grooves and stretched across the wood, forming ridges in accordance with the ruling needed for the desired *mise-en-page*. The scribe would place each leaf of the manuscript on the board and rub it with the thumb along the cords, which consequently left their impressions in the leaf. Strangely enough, the same kind of ruling board is still used in the western Siberian scriptoria of the Old Believers. Samaritan scribes in Nablus, as well as a single Syriac scribe in a monastery in Jerusalem, use to this very day a similar device, made of cardboard.

That such a device was employed by oriental Jewish scribes in the Middle Ages is clearly proved by a student's model of such a board that was fortunately preserved in the Cairo Geniza and presently is kept in the Cambridge University Library among the Geniza fragments. This model board was made by gluing together used leaves of paper inscribed with Coptic writing. The threads, pulled into two rows of grooves, were glued to the surface of the board. On its other side the board was labelled in Judaeo-Arabic 'a practise *misṭara*', a term mentioned already by Maimonides, in a work that appears in book lists in the Geniza manuscripts. Most oriental Hebrew paper manuscripts were ruled by *misṭara* on the verso pages.

It is easy to recognize this technique of ruling. First, there is no guiding pricking. Second, the ruled lines are not deep and narrow (as are the lines ruled in hard point), but wide and rather flat, and often they are not straight, but tend to be slightly curved. Third, in some manuscripts it is possible to see the impression of the twisted fibres of the cords. Fourth, an identical pattern is repeated page after page. And finally, the horizontal lines never exceed the boundary lines.

The earliest dated manuscript ruled by means of a ruling board dates from 1131 (St Petersburg, RNB, Evr.-Ar. I 1679). Oriental scribes and copyists invented an efficient ruling technique which considerably reduced the time and cost of producing books made of paper, a mechanical device that later on was imitated in Europe.

In fact, it seems that a relief ruling board of some kind that enabled quick, uniform and economical ruling was employed in Europe as well, but unlike in the Orient, it is not attested in written sources earlier than the sixteenth century. Moreover, none of the actual devices is known to have survived. Evidence for the use of a ruling device in European Hebrew manuscripts is the occurrence of a certain kind of ruling in the manuscripts. The conclusion that certain parchment manuscripts were ruled by a ruling device does not stem from the appearance of the traced lines, as it does in the case of oriental paper manuscripts, but from the simple fact that while these manuscripts are ruled leaf by leaf, there is no trace of any guiding pricking in them. Ruling of leaf units without the use of a mechanical device requires pricking in both the outer and the inner margins. While outer margins may have been trimmed over the years, inner margins stayed intact. The absence of prickings in the inner margins of a manuscript indicates that it must have been ruled by the 'mechanical' means of a ruling board, or perhaps a template of some kind. The phenomenon is prominent in the Iberian Peninsula and appears in 87% of the paper manuscripts of the fourteenth and fifteenth centuries. It is found in about two-thirds of the Byzantine paper manuscripts and in almost one-third of the parchment ones, and in about half of the Italian paper manuscripts and some parchment ones.

The ruled lines that result from this method in the European manuscripts are thin and straight, and seem to have been executed with metallic wires or thin strings (rather than thick cords as in the Orient). Indeed, according to a sixteenth-century Spanish calligrapher (citing in 1550 a book printed in 1531), the ruling board was made of wood on which strings for musical instruments were stretched, over which a leaf or bifolium was placed and then rubbed with a cloth.

B. Coloured ruling

The adoption of coloured ruling—executed with plummet or, later on, with ink—was a revolutionary turnabout in the book craft in all the codex civilizations that adopted it, despite its being an ergometrically regressive step. The main change was the shift from the economical technique of the blind ruling system, by which it was possible to rule two sides of one or more leaves or bifolia in one operation, to a technique that required separately ruling each page or each side of a bifolium. However, the coloured-ruling technique enabled flexibility of the ruling pattern and thus of the disposition of the text, while hard-point ruling imposed a uniform layout, at least for the pages that were ruled together.

B.1. Plummet ruling

The use of plummet for tracing lines emerges in Latin manuscripts as early as the late eleventh century. Beginning in the twelfth century, it became a widespread practice everywhere (except in humanistic manuscripts in fifteenth-century Italy). In oriental Christian Syriac manuscripts, the employment of plummet preceded its use in western Christian manuscripts. The vague information on this topic was recently corroborated by Sebastian Brock in his catalogue of the Syriac fragments in St Catherine's Monastery in Sinai (1995a). Brock indicates that plummet was used in many fragments, initially—i.e. from the sixth century—only for vertical lines, then later on for full ruling (first found in an eighth- to ninth-century fragment).

Hebrew scribes in Europe started to employ plummet, gradually and hesitantly, about one hundred years after Christian Latin scribes had adopted it, at first in the Ashkenazic zone, and later, only partially, in Italy and Spain, but never in the Orient and Byzantium. The delay in using the new instrument seems to have stemmed from the halakhic context. The spread of the use of plummet in Latin Europe during the twelfth century raised the question among the rabbinical authorities as to whether it could be used in ruling the ritual Tora Scroll, which had to be ruled—and for about one thousand years had indeed been ruled—by blind ruling and not by coloured ruling. The plummet substitute was rejected by all the Jewish authorities in France, Germany and Provence. It is likely that the rejection of the use of lead plummet in the liturgical scrolls deterred scribes from using it in codices, at first. But the avoidance of plummet ruling subsequently evaporated gradually: initially it was in partial use, in the earliest extant dated codices from France and Germany, since the last quarter of the twelfth century, until it became widespread there in the last third of thirteenth century.

It is possible that the gradual acceptance of the metallic plummet, in spite of everything, was promoted by literary developments and scholarly needs. The adoption of the use of plummet matched the emergence of many glossed works, multi-layer texts and commentated Bibles in the thirteenth century, culminating at the end of the century. These popular copies required a dynamic, changing ruling which the hard-point technique could not provide, whereas plummet ruling did. Perhaps it is no coincidence that the emergence of the twelfth-century Latin glossed Bible coincided with the spread of the use of plummet in Latin manuscripts.

At the beginning, the use of plummet in Hebrew codices was only partial, used mainly for reinforcing invisible lines traced in hard point. Sephardic scribes too employed plummet in the same manner, using it to reinforce vertical bounding lines in manuscripts ruled by hard-point ruling of two leaves at once, where the original ruling was unclear on the fourth or the third page.

In France and in the German lands, complete plummet ruling spread while being associated with the shift in pricking and in the visual appearance of parchment skin sides. In the fourteenth and fifteenth centuries, 94% of parchment manuscripts were ruled by using plummet, either page by page or each bifolium on both sides separately. Apart from the secondary use of plummet for reinforcing the more economical blind ruling practised in Sephardic parchment manuscripts and in other areas (apart from Ashkenaz), plummet ruling was used in some manuscripts in Italy, mostly by immigrant Ashkenazic scribes. Yet, another application of the metallic plummet ruling spread in a limited diffusion, combining the old economical relief ruling with the new coloured ruling, perhaps using a different sort of plummet.

B.2. Ruling by engraving plummet

In certain Ashkenazic and Sephardic parchment manuscripts, and particularly in Italian manuscripts, one notices that the direct ruling is executed by a sharp plummet on one side of each unfolded bifolium or of each leaf, like the Ashkenazic plummet ruling; yet the ruling on the other side of the bifolium or leaf is not coloured at all, but displays the ridges of the direct ruling. In other words, the metallic plummet technique was employed like the system of hard point. Julien Leroy (1976) reported that a few dozen Greek manuscripts from Byzantine Calabria were ruled by plummet used as hard point (or by hard point reinforced by plummet or ink). Such a mixed technique was perhaps created as a compromise between the old technique and the new one, mainly in Italy, where the mixed technique was quite extensively used. The codicological practices employed in Italy were quite conservative, undergoing no transformation until the 1430s, unlike the case with Latin manuscripts. The use of plummet enabled some of the Italian scribes to adhere to the traditional relief technique and at the same time use the new instrument. Indeed, in some Italian manuscripts, part of the quires were ruled by the engraving plummet and some entirely by hard point, which implies that plummet was regarded in Italy as a relief instrument. It seems that there were two kinds of plummet; and indeed several recent scientific analyses have detected in different samples of plummet different chemical elements that had been mixed with lead, which is the main component of the plummet.

The earliest dated manuscript ruled entirely by the engraving plummet was produced in Lisbon in 1278 (Oxford, Bodleian Library, MS. Can. Or. 67). A German manuscript from 1286 (Paris, BnF, Hébreu 1-3) is pricked in both margins in accordance with the new practice, which fits the use of plummet, and was ruled page by page by means of sharp plummet. In Italy, the sharp plummet was first put to use in a manuscript of 1304 (London, BL, Add. 9401-9402); however, like the 1286 manuscript, this one too was ruled on both sides of the bifolia. Soon thereafter, in 1311, in Tarquinia, we find the earliest Italian manuscript (Paris, BnF, Hébreu 81) ruled entirely by the engraving plummet, on the hair sides of the unfolded bifolia, as if the ruling had been done in hard point.

B.3. Ruling with ink

The employment of coloured ink for drawing lines guided by pricking spread in Latin manuscripts during the thirteenth century, about two hundred years after the beginning of the use of plummet. This technique was never used by mediaeval European Hebrew scribes (yet some of the Judaean Desert scrolls are ruled with diluted ink). In Hebrew manuscripts showing ruling executed with ink, it is not the coloured ink characteristic of Latin manuscripts, particularly Gothic ones, but a very light, diluted ink. In these manuscripts, the horizontal ruling was not guided by pricking. This kind of ruling appeared only in Italy, not before the 1420s, and was implemented in parchment and paper manuscripts alike, page by page. Naturally, then, this kind of ruling serves as a useful and reliable codicological criterion for localizing and dating manuscripts in which it is found.

In the first decades of its emergence in Italy, ink ruling was employed only to a limited extent in comparison to the other techniques, especially the hard point ruling that was the standard method until the middle of the fifteenth century. In the twenties and the thirties of that century, only a few manuscripts were ink-ruled; in the forties, the rate was some 22%, in the fifties 16%, in the seventies 50% and then about the same until 1500. In 84% of the ink-ruled manuscripts, only the horizontal lines were traced with ink, while the vertical lines were added with plummet, clearly at a later stage, while copying, as blank ruled pages attest. As mentioned above, ink ruling was not guided by pricking, yet the vertical bounding lines, ruled with plummet, were guided by a single prick in the upper and lower margins, reinforcing the suggestion that the ruling was executed in two stages.

In the beginning of the 1980s, Albert Derolez, while documenting 1,200 humanistic parchment manuscripts, noticed a single prick that does not correspond to any of the horizontal lines that usually occur in the outer margins of ink-ruled manuscripts which do not have pricking. He suggested the existence of an unknown ruling device which guided in a mechanical way the drawing of the horizontal lines. This instrument required minimal pricking to guide its positioning. Derolez further suggested that ink-ruled quires were mass produced and commercially marketed. His assumption was supported by the inventories of Italian Renaissance *cartolai* which listed ruled quires. Meanwhile, more documents have been found to substantiate this evidence. Ten years earlier, Malachi Beit-Arié offered a similar suggestion concerning the marketing and consumption of ruled quires due to the mobility of members of Jewish society. The puzzling fact that more than half of the ink-ruled manuscripts produced in Italy were written by Sephardic and Ashkenazic immigrant scribes from Spain, Provence, France, and the German lands—where ink ruling was not practised at all—led to the assumption that scribes purchased ruled quires or were supplied with them by their patrons, a supposition which might explain the sweeping adoption in Italy of the local practices both in ruling technique and in using quinions.

If these arguments consolidate the assumption of mass production, marketing and consumption of ruled quires, then we see here the precursor of mechanical mass production of an important part of bookmaking before the invention of mechanical printing. Yet, such an assumption, as well as the hypothesis of an obscure and enigmatic ruling instrument, arouses doubts. To begin with, if ruled quires were marketed, we should expect to be able to detect among the many hundreds of documented Hebrew manuscripts some clusters of codices sharing an identical disposition of the ruling, pattern and size. But in fact we find a large variety of patterns, spacing between lines and numbers of lines which do not group even in the same locality, time and genre. Furthermore, ink ruling appears also in multi-layer texts, like commentated works, which require a dynamic and changeable ruling.

No doubt ruled quires were sold by *cartolai*, both wholesale and tailor-made. But it is possible that some scribes used some 'enigmatic instrument' for ruling their own quires. Whether ruling by ink was a scribal initiative or a commercial enterprise, it is still unknown whether it was executed by means of a mechanical device or by means of a template of some kind, which guided the ruling only line by line, as implied by the lack of uniformity in line lengths. If the latter possibility is correct, then we should acknowledge the superiority of the oriental scribal inventiveness, which initiated mechanical ruling long before the European scribes did.

9.3.4. Ordering systems

Hebrew scribes and copyists employed various systems for ensuring the correct order of the codex based on numbering the quires in Hebrew letters, or on the repetition of the last copied words, in two variations, and by marking the central opening of each quire.

Fig. 1.9.4 Signatures at the head of quires, MS Jerusalem, NLI, Heb. 8°2238, (Iran), 1106/1107, ff. 16v–17r.

The dated Hebrew manuscripts of the tenth century do not contain any ordering system, probably due to the fact that all of them are copies of the Bible: the scribes of this early period of the Hebrew codex were no doubt deterred from adding anything to the Masoretic text. (The absence of signatures in the earliest copies of the Qur'ān may be due to similar considerations.) Indeed, a few undated non-biblical codices that probably antedate the tenth century do contain quire catchwords, and traces of sheet signatures were found in a fragmentary scroll from Qumran. However, from the beginning of the eleventh century, both signatures and catchwords appear in oriental Hebrew manuscripts, and in codices produced in all other geo-cultural areas. Moreover, both systems could be used in one and the same book. In Ashkenazic manuscripts, however, signatures are extremely rare.

Quire signatures appear for the first time in dated manuscripts in the earliest extant paper codex, written in Fusṭāṭ (Egypt) in 1006 (St. Petersburg, NRB, Evr.-Ar. I 4520). It is a Karaite codex written in Judaeo-Arabic, which also contains, for the first time, catchwords (Beit-Arié et al. 1997, 16).

The appearance of signatures in a manuscript (containing the Prophets, in Cairo, the Karaite Synagogue, see fig. 1.9.8) written, according to a long colophon, in Tiberias (Palestine) in 894/895 stands at variance against all the biblical codices from the tenth century, thus adding a codicological doubt to philological doubts that have been raised concerning the authenticity of the colophon. Indeed, a C_{14} test conducted at Oxford University yielded a dating range between 990 and 1160 (with a certitude of 95.4%). Since the codex was repaired in 1129/1130, it must have been written before, most probably at the end of the tenth century or early in the eleventh, when biblical manuscripts started to be equipped with means for ensuring the right order of the quires. The same codicological argument relates to another biblical manuscript that apparently has a record of sale dated to the year 847 (St Petersburg, Oriental Institute, D62). The occurrence in it of quire signatures is one of several reasons to doubt the authenticity of the record of sale.

Fig. 1.9.5 Double pricks for special lines (through lines), Vatican City, BAV, Vat. ebr. 438, f. 107v.

Numbering quires was the commonest ordering system in use in the early periods, since the beginning of the eleventh century, but it is absent from the early manuscripts in the Maghreb and Italy. Usually signatures coexist along with quire catchwords. Only a small number of manuscripts, produced in the Orient, the Sephardic zone and Italy, particularly from early periods, employ signatures alone.

The digits in all the numbering systems are expressed almost exclusively by Hebrew letters, which is the normal means of numeration in Hebrew. In the Orient, in almost half (45%) of the manuscripts which contain quire signatures, parallel signatures were added in Arabic, mostly expressed in words, and always in Arabic script (this is witnessed also in a few manuscripts in Yemen and in two manuscripts in Spain). Usually the Arabic equivalent signatures (in numerals) at the beginnings of the quires are written at the outer corner of the upper margin, while the Hebrew signatures (in letters) are placed at the inner corner (in some manuscripts which have double signatures—at the beginning and the end of the quire, or only at the end—the Arabic numbering was added at the end).

This practice of using bilingual signatures can be found already in the eleventh century, and it was employed in the earliest extant complete Bible (St Petersburg, NLB, Evr. B 19a), written in Cairo in 1008 (as in many other manuscripts, the Arabic is written in a different ink; the book also contains Hebrew signatures added by a different hand). No doubt, these Arabic additions were intended for Arabic binders, and probably written by them.

Quire signatures were widespread especially in the Orient, where they were employed in more than half of the dated manuscripts that are not fragmentary up to 1500, particularly in Yemen, where they appear in nearly all the manuscripts (82%), and in Italy, where the device appears in 41% of the manuscripts. The use of partial numbering is found in one of the earliest manuscripts, which most probably was produced in Italy in 1105/1106 (Karlsruhe, BLB, cod. Reuchlin 3); in a regular manner, it appears in a manuscript dated 1246/1247 (Paris, BnF, Hébreu 163). Quire signatures appear in a quarter of the dated manuscripts

Fig. 1.9.6 Marking the openings of the central bifolium of the quires, Oxford, Bodleian Library, MS Huntington 372, ff. 205v–206r.

of the Sephardic zone; however, the use of signatures was very rare until the last quarter of the thirteenth century. Quire signatures in Byzantine manuscripts are also rare, and in Franco-German manuscripts they are exceptions.

In the Sephardic zone and in Italy, there is a conspicuous difference in the use of signatures in parchment manuscripts as against paper manuscripts or manuscripts with mixed quires. The ratio of parchment manuscripts to paper manuscripts in the corpus of manuscripts with quire signatures is, in the Sephardic zone, two to one. In Italy the proportion is close to four to one (78% vs. 22%). This characterization cannot be applied to the Orient, where the majority of surviving manuscripts are made of paper.

The 'placement practice' with regard to quire signatures relates to two positions: the position of signatures within the quire, and their placement on the page on which they are written. The numbering in Hebrew manuscripts may be written at the beginning of each quire, usually in the inner corner of the upper margin; or at the end of the quire, in the inner corner of the lower margin; or both at the beginning and at the end.

In the entire corpus of studied dated manuscripts up to 1500, 56% have double signatures at the beginning and at the end, 30% only at the beginning, and 19% only at the end (the total of 105% is due to those manuscripts in which two systems were employed, and this explains further ratios which exceed 100% in total).

In none of the geo-cultural zones do all the codices conform to one single positioning, but preferences are noticeable. In the Orient, excluding Yemen, 80% of the manuscripts with quire signatures have them at the beginnings of the quires, up until the mid-twelfth century, as attested by all the extant manuscripts. But 32% have double signatures and 7% contain end-of-quire signatures. In Yemen, 63% have double signatures; in the Sephardic zone, 60% have the double system, 23% have end signatures, 19% have beginning signatures; in Italy, 69% have double numbering, 24% end signatures, and 10% beginning signatures. The number of signatures in Byzantine Hebrew manuscripts is meagre.

The earliest partial appearance of the double system is in an oriental manuscript of 1112, and in regular use in a manuscript written in Damascus in 1161/1162 (London, BL, Or. 2595 + St. Petersburg, RNB, Evr.-Ar. II 675). In Spain, the earliest extant parchment manuscript, produced in Girona in 1184, contains double numbering, while in Italy the earliest use is attested in 1246/1247 (Paris, BnF, Hébreu 163).

An exceptional numbering where the number of the next quire is written at the end of the quire preceding it should be termed 'counter-signatures'. The system appears in only a handful of manuscripts and seems to have emerged in Germany and France (where signatures were not used) in the thirteenth century. Outside the Franco-German zone, it appears also in a few manuscripts in Byzantium, Spain, Provence and Italy.

Bifolium signatures appear in only a small number of manuscripts, and it seems that bifolium catchwords or counter catchwords took over their role. In most of these manuscripts, the signatures are not accompanied by quire signatures, except for a few manuscripts written in Judaeo-Arabic (mostly Karaite) between 1146 and late in the fourteenth century, in which the bifolia are numbered mostly in Arabic, but also in Hebrew letters, such as '2 of 3', following the practice of several Arab Middle Eastern manuscripts produced between 1149 and 1292.

Foliation by the scribe is very rare and appears in only 1% of the dated palaeographical units within the codicological units. It was employed sometimes in the Sephardic zone, for the first time in 1272 (Paris, BnF, Hébreu 26), mainly in parchment manuscripts, and in Italy (where the earliest occurrence is from 1286, Vatican City, BAV, Ross. 554, and then in the fifteenth century), but never in the Orient or Byzantium. In Ashkenaz, it appeared in the second half of the fifteenth century.

In some of the oriental manuscripts, and particularly the Yemenite ones, the openings of the central bifolia of the quires are marked by variously shaped signs, but mostly by marks similar to the *ġubār* numeral 5, placed in various corners of the opening, sometimes at the top outer corner of the right-hand page (fig. 1.9.6), as well as in the bottom outer corner of the left-hand page; sometimes only one corner is marked, and occasionally all four corner are marked by short diagonal strokes. Usually these marks are inscribed in an ink different from that of the text. Marking the central opening of a quire follows a practice found in certain Arabic manuscripts in the Orient and the Maghreb, as described by Guesdon (2002). The earliest Hebrew codex with such middle-of-the-quire marks (St Petersburg, RNB, Evr. II, B 39) was written in Jerusalem in 988/989 by a Maghrebi scribe (Beit-Arié et al. 1997, 12), and the next one (St Petersburg, RNB, Evr. II, B 88) was also written by a Maghrebi scribe, in Palestine in 1020/1021 (Beit-Arié et al. 1997, 19). Marks in the central openings are found in a biblical codex written in Kairouan (St Petersburg, RNB, Evr. II B 124); the date is damaged, but it must have been written between 941 and 1039 (Beit-Arié et al. 1997, 29); the marks are usually in both upper corners. Disregarding a few manuscripts from North Africa, most of the marked manuscripts are oriental. The marking was most probably meant for the non-Jewish binder, and very likely was added by the binder himself, as is implied by the use of different inks.

The catchword system is used in two ways. In the commonest one, the first word(s) of a quire or bifolium or leaf is written at the end of the preceding quire/bifolium/leaf, at the bottom of the page, usually placed below the end of the written text, mainly horizontally. Catchwords would sometimes be inscribed in European manuscripts in the middle of the lower margin. Such positioning sometimes occurs also in Byzantium, but not in the Orient. Catchwords would sometimes be placed vertically (mostly quire catchwords, but also a few leaf catchwords), as was favoured by Ashkenazic scribes (in 13% of the dated manuscripts). Since the late eleventh century, the practice of writing catchwords diagonally spread amongst the makers of oriental manuscripts; it appears in about one-third of the manuscripts that contain catchwords of any kind. The tendency to write diagonal catchwords is a part of the line-management practices of many of the oriental Hebrew scribes and copyists who used catchwords, which inevitably exceeded the left bounding line and so required special management (writing catchwords diagonally is a practice that was probably borrowed from Arabic scribes).

Catchwords were usually marked or decorated. In Europe, they were often decorated with complex ornament, and in the Ashkenazic regions they were sometimes decorated by pen drawings, mostly representing animals.

The variant type of catchwords also uses repetition of words from the copied text, but instead of writing the repeated word detached from the written page, it is written within the text. The last word of a quire or bifolium or leaf is doubled at the beginning of the succeeding quire. Following Denis Muzerelle's *Vocabulaire* (1985), this phenomenon can be defined as 'counter-catchwords'.

Quire catchwords are an ordinary device in parchment manuscripts in Europe and the Maghreb, whereas paper (or mixed-quire) manuscripts utilized bifolium or leaf catchwords as well. Quire catchwords were less frequently used in the Orient until the late twelfth century, and at that time scribes preferred quire signatures. In Franco-German areas, quire catchwords were, with few exception, the only system in use for ensuring the order of the quires.

Strangely enough, the practice of writing catchwords on the verso of the first leaf of each bifolium (bifolium catchwords), to ensure the right order of the written bifolia within a quire, emerged later than the practice of writing leaf catchwords, which was more widespread. Despite its earliest use in a mixed quire manuscript from 1225 in Spain (Jerusalem, NLI, Yah. MS Heb. 1), it appeared in all other areas only in the fourteenth century. It was found in about 5% of all the dated manuscripts from all regions. While the writing of a catchword on the last verso of the first half of the quire—i.e. in the central bifolium—was not required, most of the scribes did write it.

Leaf catchwords were the most widespread in the late paper manuscripts in all the zones of Hebrew book production and are found in two-thirds of all the dated Hebrew paper manuscripts of the fourteenth and fifteenth centuries, but only in 10% of the parchment manuscripts. Although the earliest extant dated manuscript (St. Petersburg, RNB, Evr.-Ar. I 1404) that contains leaf catchwords was written on paper in Damietta (Egypt) as early as 1168 (the scribe did not write catchwords in the central openings), the practice started to spread in the oriental paper manuscripts only from the second half of the fourteenth century. In the Sephardic zone, the practice started in correlation with the replacement of parchment by paper in the second half of the century, but its first appearance was in a Provençal parchment manuscript, produced in Tarascon in 1284 (Parma, Biblioteca Palatina, 3239). It became a standard practice for paper manuscripts in the Iberian Peninsula, Provence and the Maghreb in the fifteenth century, and is found in 86% of the dated paper manuscripts (calculated also in consideration of the number of hands in multi-scribe copies). Its first appearance among Byzantine manuscripts is in a parchment codex dated 1298 (Cambridge, University Library, Add. 1733), but it was widely used in paper manuscripts which constitute most of the surviving dated manuscripts. The practice was employed there in two-thirds of the fourteenth-century paper manuscripts, and in the course of the fifteenth century it became almost as widespread as in the Sephardic zone.

The fact that leaf catchwords were mainly used in paper manuscripts implies that the aim of this practice was not only to ensure the right order of the bifolia (which can be achieved by means of bifolium catchwords). Being aware of the vulnerability of the paper and the possibility of detachment of single leaves, it may have been that scribes preferred to secure the position of every leaf in the quire.

Another possibility is related to the catchwords as being instrumental to the copying process on loose bifolia. The recent discoveries of temporary stitching (tacketing) of quires while copying in Latin and Greek manuscripts, at least as early as 800 and then until the twelfth century, and the introduction of bifolium signatures within each quire in thirteenth-century Latin manuscripts, which implies that tacketing was not practised anymore, prompt us to think that the leaf catchwords facilitated the copying sequence on loose bifolia.

Consistent employment of the redundant device of page catchwords is extremely rare. Its earliest example is found in a manuscript (New York, The Jewish Theological Seminary, MS 8225) written in Bursa (Turkey) in 1377 by two scribes, both of whom wrote page catchwords. All other manuscripts are from fifteenth-century Italy, Byzantium, the Orient and Germany (in some of them counter-catchwords occasionally substitute for the page catchwords).

Counter-catchwords (or repeated words) are frequently mixed with regular catchwords. The earliest manuscript containing them is an oriental one of 1112 (Oxford, Bodleian Library, MS. Heb. F.18, ff. 8-41), where the last word of the quire is repeated at the beginning of the next quire. In another oriental manuscript, dated 1282 (St Petersburg, RNB, Evr.-Ar. I 1256), there are leaf counter-catchwords. Counter-catchwords can be observed in many manuscripts in all the geo-cultural areas; however, in a considerable part of them they are not employed regularly, but rather as random substitutes for catchwords. Outside the Orient, counter-catchwords appear in a Spanish parchment manuscript dated 1214 (Vatican City, BAV, Urb. ebr. 54), at the beginning of bifolia (including the recto of the central bifolium of a quire) and at the beginnings of quires; leaf counter-catchwords appear in a mixed-quire codex written in Tripoli in 1293 (Vatican City, BAV, Vat. ebr. 358). Since then, many Sephardic scribes applied the repeated words at the beginning of each leaf. The earliest Byzantine manuscript with regular use of leaf counter-catchwords (St Petersburg, RNB, Evr. I 479) is dated 1319 (mixed quires).

In the fourteenth and fifteenth centuries, counter-catchwords in all their forms are employed, either systematically or mixed with regular catchwords: 21% in Sepharad, 14% in Ashkenaz and Byzantium, 12% in Italy, and 8% in the Orient. One third of these manuscripts are written on parchment.

9.4. The layout of the page

The taxonomy of this aspect of Hebrew codicology is rather meagre. Dukan (1988) classified the ruling patterns prevailing in the dated Hebrew manuscripts of France and Israel (Sirat et al. 1972; Beit-Arié et al. 1979; Sirat – Beit-Arié 1986) without formulating ruling types. Denis Muzerelle, in his online *Analyse des schémas de réglure* (1994, <http://www.palaeographia.org/muzerelle/analyse.htm>), converted those patterns into his formulae. However, one should examine whether Muzerelle's universal formulae indeed suit all oriental non-Christian manuscripts.

As for *SfarData*, in which almost all the dated Hebrew manuscripts are documented, it contains extensive data with regard to the *mise-en-page* and *mise-en-texte*: dimensions and complex proportions of the spatial arrangement, exact measurement of the page, the text area and the margin areas, columns, complex

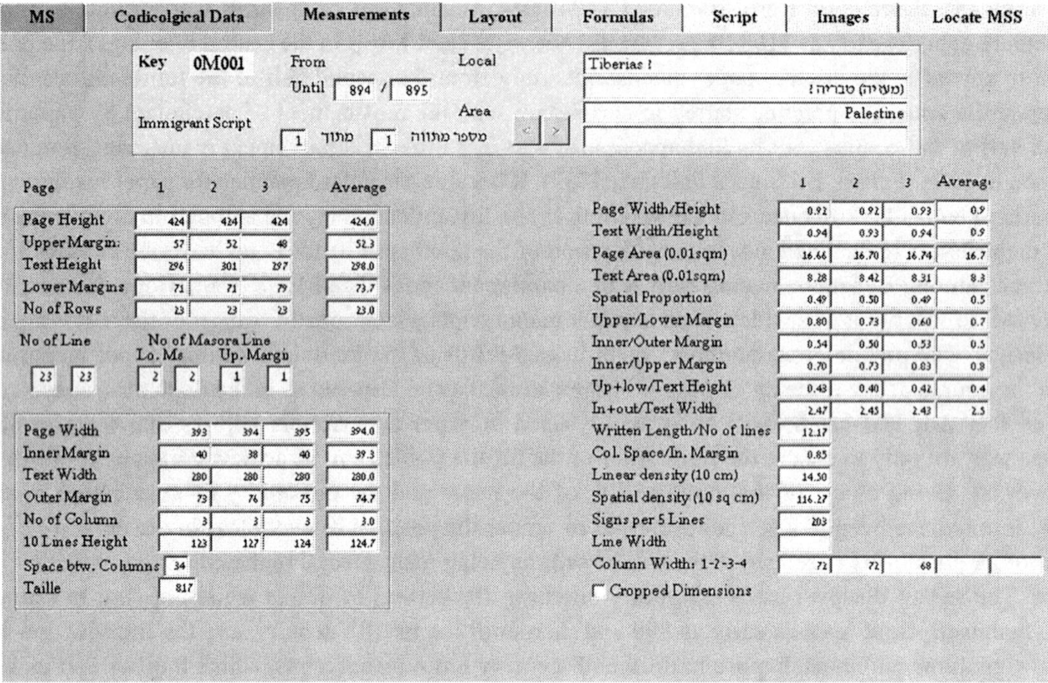

MS | Codicolgical Data | Measurements | Layout | Formulas | Script | Images | Locate MSS

Key 0M001 · From · Until 894 / 895 · Local: Tiberias ? / (מעֿיה) טבריה ? · Area: Palestine

Immigrant Script · 1 מתוך · 1 מספר מתווה

Page	1	2	3	Average
Page Height	424	424	424	424.0
UpperMargin:	57	52	48	52.3
Text Height	296	301	297	298.0
LowerMargins	71	71	79	73.7
No of Rows	23	23	23	23.0

No of Line: 23, 23 · No of Masora Line: Lo. Ms 2, 2; Up. Margin 1, 1

	1	2	3	Average
Page Width	393	394	395	394.0
InnerMargin	40	38	40	39.3
Text Width	280	280	280	280.0
Outer Margin	73	76	75	74.7
No of Column	3	3	3	3.0
10 Lines Height	123	127	124	124.7
Space btw. Columns	34			
Taille	817			

	1	2	3	Average
Page Width/Height	0.92	0.92	0.93	0.9
Text Width/Height	0.94	0.93	0.94	0.9
Page Area (0.01sqm)	16.66	16.70	16.74	16.7
Text Area (0.01sqm)	8.28	8.42	8.31	8.3
Spatial Proportion	0.49	0.50	0.49	0.5
Upper/LowerMargin	0.80	0.73	0.60	0.7
Inner/Outer Margin	0.54	0.50	0.53	0.5
Inner/Upper Margin	0.70	0.73	0.03	0.8
Up+low/Text Height	0.43	0.40	0.42	0.4
In+out/Text Width	2.47	2.45	2.43	2.5
Written Length/No of lines	12.17			
Col. Space/In. Margin	0.85			
Linear density (10 cm)	14.50			
Spatial density (10 sq cm)	116.27			
Signs per 5 Lines	203			
Line Width				
Column Width: 1-2-3-4	72	72	68	

Cropped Dimensions

Fig. 1.9.7 Manuscript measurements in a snapshot from the *SfarData* database.

presentation of the many possibilities of proportion between space and written area, between the various margins, calculation of the surface of the page and the text area and their proportions (fig. 1.9.7).

These measurements and calculations may be retrieved and grouped by search facilities that can expose a chronological and regional typology of the page and text area dimensions, as well as proportions of its height and width, thus enabling the examination of whether they are conditioned by textual genres and their functional and social context, and provide further codicological criteria for dating and localizing undated manuscripts.

A few examples (tables 1.9.1–1.9.6) should illustrate the potentialities of such data retrieval relating to column layout and its relation to text genre and height of page.

9.5. Text structure and readability

The role of Hebrew copyists, like that of scribes using Latin, Greek, Arabic or other scripts, was not confined to the physical embodiment of the verbal text; it also involved the shaping of its visual disposition, which in turn affected its verbal perception and reception. The visual presentation of texts was not an autonomous interpretative act on the part of the scribe; there were other factors, conventions and considerations—material, social, economic, aesthetic and scholarly—dictating text configuration or at least affecting it. And yet Hebrew scribes had played a much greater role in the interpretative forging of the copied text, due to the extraordinarily individualistic mode of book production in Jewish societies, the high rate of user-produced books, and the lack of a guiding authority over the reproduction and dissemination of texts (Beit-Arié 1993, 79–84). These singular circumstances gave Jewish scribes considerable freedom of choice, as well as the opportunity to exercise initiative and inventiveness despite certain restraints, though obviously when copying standard texts many scribes would adhere to inherited traditions. Learned and creative professional scribes and copyist-owners who had the possibility of selecting the physical shape and nature of the text's presentation forged the semiotic representation of various genres of texts and designed different meaningful layouts to fit the different functions of books. Through the interpolation of para-scriptural and peri-textual elements in their copying, they had a significant impact on the legibility, comprehension and reception of texts. By means of spacing, compound punctuation, paragraphing and subdividing, underlining certain words or passages, pointing out terms and foreign words, marking biblical citations and lemmata, scribes enhanced readability and understanding. By adding titles, headings and running heads; by writing initial words in larger characters; by inserting decorations, illuminations, illustrations and diagrams; by selecting the type and size of script, or using different coloured inks; by providing tables of contents and other locating devices—elements that were undoubtedly missing from

Table 1.9.1 Geo-cultural distribution of column layout in dated manuscripts until 1500 (excluding the Orient except for Yemen, since many manuscripts are fragmentary); total numbers and percentage within zone.

Zone	Mss 1 column	Mss 2 columns	Mss 3 columns	**Total**
Sepharad	397 (73%)	117 (22%)	16 (3%)	544
Ashkenaz	158 (48%)	120 (36%)	48 (15%)	330
Italy	637 (80%)	130 (16%)	6 (1%)	798
Byzantium	181 (84%)	22 (10%)	2 (%)	215
Yemen	90 (85%)	13 (12%)	0	106
Total	1462 (73%)	402 (20%)	72 (4%)	**1993**

Table 1.9.2 Geo-cultural distribution of column layout in dated *biblical* manuscripts until 1500.

Zone	Mss 1 column	Mss 2 columns	Mss 3 columns	**Total**
Sepharad	16 (15%)	73 (70%)	13 (12%)	105
Ashkenaz	16 (22%)	27 (37%)	34 (47%)	73
Italy	35 (50%)	28 (40%)	3 (4%)	70
Byzantium	1 (14%)	3 (43%)	2 (29%)	7
Near East	18 (46%)	4 (10%)	18 (46%)	39
Yemen	14 (58%)	10 (42%)	0	24
Uncertain	2 (100%)	0	0	2
Total	102 (32%)	145 (45%)	70 (22%)	**320**

Table 1.9.3 Geo-cultural distribution of column layout in dated *biblical* manuscripts up to 300 mm height.

Zone	Mss 1 column	Mss 2 columns	Mss 3 columns	**Total**
Sepharad	15 (19%)	52 (66%)	9 (11%)	79
Ashkenaz	10 (40%)	11 (44%)	4 (16%)	25
Italy	30 (57%)	19 (36%)	1 (2%)	53
Byzantium	1 (20%)	3 (60%)	0	5
Near East	17 (85%)	1 (5%)	2 (10%)	20
Yemen	12 (86%)	2 (14%)	0	14
Uncertain	2 (100%)	0	0	2
Total	87 (44%)	88 (44%)	16 (8%)	**198**

Table 1.9.4 Geo-cultural distribution of column layout in dated *biblical* manuscripts taller than 350 mm.

Zone	Mss 1 column	Mss 2 columns	Mss 3 columns	**Total**
Sepharad	0	3 (43%)	3 (43%)	7
Ashkenaz	2 (5%)	8 (22%)	29 (78%)	37
Italy	1 (17%)	3 (50%)	2 (33%)	6
Byzantium	0	0	0	5
Near East	0	1 (5%)	13 (87%)	15
Yemen	0	5 (100%)	0	5
Uncertain	0	0	0	0
Total	3 (4%)	22 (31%)	47 (67%)	**70**

Table 1.9.5 Heights of dated manuscripts until 1500 (excluding the Orient).

Zone	≤100 mm high	101-200 mm high	201-300 mm high	301-400 mm high	401-500 mm high	> 500 mm high	**Total**
Sepharad	33 (5%)	108 (17%)	402 (65%)	63 (10%)	7 (1%)	0	619
Ashkenaz	36 (9%)	33 (8%)	173 (44%)	105 (27%)	31 (8%)	12 (3%)	389
Italy	65 (7%)	195 (22%)	526 (59%)	96 (11%)	10 (1%)	0	894
Byzantium	22 (8%)	36 (14%)	190 (71%)	16 (6%)	0	1 (0%)	266
Total	156 (7%)	372 (17%)	1291 (60%)	280 (13%)	48 (2%)	13(1%)	**2168**

Table 1.9.6 Heights of dated *biblical* manuscripts until 1500 (excluding the Orient).

Zone	≤100 mm high	101-200 mm high	201-300 mm high	301-400 mm high	401-500 mm high	> 500 mm high	**Total**
Sepharad	6 (6%)	21 (20%)	51 (49%)	24 (23%)	2 (2%)	0	105
Ashkenaz	3 (4%)	5 (7%)	18 (25%)	21 (29%)	22 (30%)	5 (7%)	73
Italy	4 (6%)	21 (30%)	27 (39%)	14 (20%)	3 (4%)	0	70
Byzantium	2 (29%)	0	3 (43%)	2 (29%)	0	0	7
Total	15 (6%)	47 (18%)	99 (39%)	61 (24%)	27 (11%)	5 (2%)	**255**

most of the original works as they emerged from the hands of their authors or compilers—they interpreted and gave shape to the hierarchical construction of the texts being copied. Consequently, by visually embodying in the texts their structure and hierarchy, those learned and creative professional scribes and owner-copyists made texts more transparent.

This claim is corroborated when manuscripts are examined from this perspective in a chronological sequence. Considered historically, it is obvious that the integration of para-scriptural and peri-textual elements within the copied texts was primarily a creative and interpretative act of scribes and copyists, in view of their gradual emergence and evolutionary nature. Needless to say, para-scriptural and peri-textual elements can hardly be found in Hebrew books of antiquity, but these legibility-aiding elements are found to be underdeveloped even after the belated formative stage of the Hebrew codex, as demonstrated by the earliest codices and fragments of codices which predate the tenth century.

A clear example is the common late mediaeval practice of writing headings and especially initial words at the beginning of textual units—the natural custom of scribes using Semitic scripts—in large square characters (even when the body of the text was written in a semi-cursive script). Writing initial letters, the most common practice in Greek and Latin manuscripts, was practised by only a limited number of Hebrew scribes, mostly Franco-German and not earlier than the early thirteenth century. The practice of writing titles, headings, endings, and mainly initial words in larger letters enabled users of Hebrew manuscripts to search for and locate a specific text more expeditiously. This practice, which later developed into assigning different sizes of letters to initial words according to the hierarchical level of the textual units, effectively assisted readers in perceiving the detailed structure of the text.

In the old oriental codices, prior to the tenth century, a text was configured in dense blocks of uniform script in which the titles, headings and ending phrases of textual units were barely perceptible, being embedded and absorbed in the main body of the text. As a rule, headings in the old codices were not written on separate, independent lines and, furthermore, never in a larger script. In the course of the late tenth century and the eleventh century, there emerged the practice of writing spacious, centred and, frequently, marked headings and endings on separate lines, as well as other visual deployments of the text. Among the dated codices, 'headlines' (i.e. headings occupying a separate line) made their first appearance in the late tenth century; yet they were not highlighted by a larger script—the most distinctive visual means for expressing the organization of the copied work and for increasing the comfort of using it—but by being centred on a separate line. Presenting the text in an unvaried script, thus assimilating the headings to the rest of the text, lasted until the late eleventh century. The practice of giving prominence to titles, headings and initial words by means of a larger script, and frequently also by means of a different style of script, evolved successively in non-biblical manuscripts, from the last decade of the eleventh century and on, in the east as well as in the west. It seems that in the transition period from assimilating titles to emphasizing them, headings and endings were disposed on independent lines and marked by simple signs, but were written in the same style of script and in the same size as the text itself; consequently they were incorporated in the text block and were not easily searchable.

From the end of the eleventh century onward, scribal endeavours to mediate between authors (or redactors) and readers, making texts more readable and usable, started to evolve in all the widespread areas where Hebrew books were produced: in the east, North Africa and the west. Among other interpretative and scholarly initiatives, scribes started to highlight headlines, initial words and endings of textual units, as well as lexical entries and the like within the written lines, by using larger, graded sizes (and styles) of letters and by frequently decorating them simply with a quill or reed pen in ink. By the end of the first third of the thirteenth century, headings and initial words in some European manuscripts were predominantly made noticeable by their decoration and illumination, thus indicating in a more complex and conspicuous manner the hierarchical structure of the text and injecting into it elementary finding aids.

Biblical manuscripts evolved at a slower pace. Initial words, which usually constitute the titles in biblical manuscripts, emerged about a century later than in non-biblical texts. The body of the biblical text in all the copies dated before the late twelfth century is in a uniform script. The scribes did not write initial words at the heads of books or sections in a larger script to facilitate location. This abstention from tampering with the uniformity of the biblical script was undermined only at the end of the twelfth century, when the practice of writing large initial words, and even decorating them, started to spread, mainly in France and the German lands, but also in other areas such as the Iberian Peninsula, Provence, North Af-

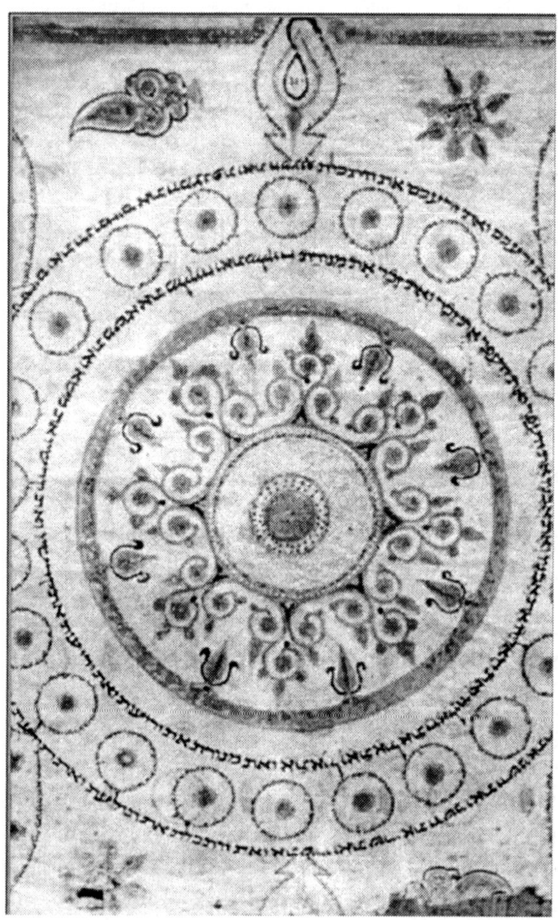

Fig. 1.9.8 Micrographic 'carpet' page of Masoretic notes in a manuscript of The Prophets, the Hebrew codex with the earliest dated colophon, Tiberias (Palestine) 894/895 (copied about a century later). Cairo, Karaite Synagogue, photograph courtesy of MBA.

rica and Italy, but seldom in the Orient. In contrast with their avoidance of graded biblical script, early oriental scribes did not refrain from decorating and illuminating calligraphic copies of the Bible. Such decorations or illuminations were added to Masoretic lists and colophons which were attached to the biblical text or to Masoretic notes at the end of biblical units, as the scribes did not hesitate to arrange the text of the marginal Masora in decorative micrographic shapes (fig. 1.9.8). Moreover, despite the employment of a uniform script size for the biblical texts, one can already notice in the early oriental codices the emerging use of a range of script sizes, which are implemented for the sake of distinguishing the non-biblical strata of biblical codices. This is first and foremost manifested in the conspicuous way in which the Masora—that body of lexical and grammatical notes pertaining to the biblical verses and intended to preserve their precise transmission—is written continuously in a minute script in the margins and between the columns. The use of an entirely different size of script clearly differentiated the two textual layers and reflected their hierarchy.

From the end of the eleventh century and on, in most of the numerous manuscripts copied in semi-cursive scripts that emerged at the beginning of the eleventh century, headlines were rendered not only in a larger script, but also in a different style of script, namely, in square characters.

Ashkenazic scribes expressed their creativity by enhancing the structural and hierarchical transparency of the transmitted texts. Certain literary genres—compound prayer books and multi-layer integrated core texts such as biblical books accompanied by Aramaic translations and various marginal commentaries, as well as annotated, glossed, and commentated halakhic corpora—emerged in the late twelfth century and more so in the thirteenth century as a creative initiative of French and German scribes, probably in response to scholarly needs. These initiatives involved not only sophisticated copying, skilful deployment of alterable layout and the intricate segmenting, fitting and matching of the related and juxtaposed texts; they also required a more composite and transparent visual presentation of the structure and hierarchy of the multiple textual units and their easy location. Hence Ashkenazic scribes in Germany and France, and later in Italy, utilized a range of five graded sizes of square script when copying and shaping large-size prayer books: strikingly large characters for initial words at the head of principal liturgical parts; very large characters for the initial words at the beginning of a division, large characters for initial words of single poems and prayers; uniform characters for the text, and smaller characters, sometimes in a semi-cursive script, for instructions and poetic refrains. In addition, they made extensive use of red ink for entire passages, or any other component deemed to be significant and meriting emphasis. In some of the manuscripts, they further enhanced structural clarity, visibility of hierarchy and ease of usage by themselves decorating initial words, or by assigning major initial words or headings to be decorated by painters.

The other scribal enterprise, that of biblical exegetical corpora, produced first in Ashkenaz and later also in Spain and Italy, had to juxtapose and match different text strata while assigning to each of them a different style or size of script. Thus the central column (or two columns) occupied by the core biblical text was written in larger square characters, its Aramaic translation in parallel columns in smaller characters, and surrounding them, in the margins, commentaries tailored to fit the basic text in a small semi-cursive script. Naturally, initial words in these books were shaped in accordance with the hierarchical level of that part of the text. Differentially scaled initial words were even more meaningful in legal corpora in which various layers of glosses were incorporated, frequently in decorative interwoven designs, in smaller characters, or in a different style of script.

Apart from tables of contents, sophisticated scholarly tools such as those prevailing in Latin manuscripts of the twelfth and thirteenth centuries did not develop in Hebrew manuscripts.

The history of the production of Hebrew manuscripts mirrors a continual linear improvement in their legibility, transparency and serviceability. This progressive process can be confirmed by inspecting the scribal treatment of further peri-textual and para-scriptural elements, such as the signing of citations, marking foreign words and singling out terms, inserting running heads and the revolutionary introduction of paragraph numeration and tables of contents. Hebrew manuscripts unquestionably display an evolutionary process that was radically accelerated in Europe in the thirteenth century.

9.6. The scribe, the painter and the illuminator at work

9.6.1. Persons, places and methods

Whereas the institutional and centralized character of Christian book production and text dissemination—whether carried out in, or initiated by, monasteries, cathedral schools, universities or commercial outlets—enabled supervision and control over the propagation of texts and the standardization of versions, no authoritative guidance or monitoring could have been involved in the private transmission of texts in Hebrew characters.

And yet, within the individualistic mode of reproduction of Hebrew texts, a distinction ought to be made between texts reproduced by professional or hired scribes and texts copied by scholars and learned people for their own use. Such a high rate of self-production, which characterizes the history of the Hebrew book in the west and in the east (excluding Yemen) and surely reflects the extent of literacy in Jewish society, had an immense effect on the nature of the transmission and versions of the texts. Logic dictates that there must have been an essential difference between texts copied by hired scribes and those reproduced by learned persons or scholars copying texts for their own needs. To be sure, neither hired scribes nor copyist-owners could escape the many inevitable snares set by the unconscious mechanics of copying. The complicated psychological and physiological process of copying frustrated the best intentions of both professional scribes and copyist-owners in their efforts to adhere to their model, as the collation of manuscripts successively copied by different scribes demonstrates. Even more telling are those rare cases in which the same hired scribe or learned copyist copied the same text twice from the same model within a short time. Comparisons between such copies betray the astonishing reality that deviation from the exemplar is not, as is usually assumed, rigidly conditioned by certain psychological, linguistic or mental configurations, nor by the copyist's spelling habits and pronunciation; it is a volatile and inconsistent process (Beit-Arié 2000). However, one is probably justified in assuming that the average hired scribe would have been more consciously loyal to his model, repeating its mistakes and refraining from critical or deliberate intervention in the transmission, yet at the same time more vulnerable to the involuntary changes and mistakes conditioned by the mechanics of copying. The scholar-copyist, on the other hand, might intentionally interfere in the transmission, revise his exemplar, emend and restore corrupted passages, and indeed regard copying as critical editing and not merely as duplicating.

If these assumptions are correct, the high rate of user-produced Hebrew manuscripts must have improved the versions of a considerable number of surviving manuscripts by an accumulated process of critical emendation by learned people and scholars who restored texts that had been corrupted by ignorant hired scribes. These assumptions can be substantiated and verified by scribes' and copyists' own statements in their colophons. Reflective colophons of learned copyists who produced books for their own use confirm the assumption with regard to their critical manner of copying. Yet by the same token, those same reflective colophons by scholar-copyists attest to the increasing freedom with which they were interfering in the transmission of the text. They seem to have been confident that they were entitled, even obliged, to improve the copied text by their personal critical judgment.

Copyists of user-produced books testify that their copying involved not only emending and restoring the corrupted model, but also critically revising and editing it. The inclination to editorial intervention in transmission emerged only in the late Middle Ages, from the early fourteenth century onwards, but it is attested primarily in fifteenth-century colophons. One of the main manifestations of the editorial tendency and the critical urge is to be found in colophons of copyists in Italy, Spain, Provence, France and Germany, and later also in Turkey, in which they state that they used two models, sometimes more, blending different sources according to their critical judgment, thus producing totally eclectic versions. These and similar statements by copyists reflect an evolutionary escalation of deliberate interference in the transmission of texts. The individualistic character of Jewish book production and the lack of institutional supervision and authoritative control over the dissemination of texts naturally contributed to this process.

9.6.2. Colophons

Unlike the limited documentary and literary sources on book production and consumption, abundant information can be found within the manuscripts, primarily in colophons. These authentic documents convey information provided by the producer about the copying circumstances. 4,000 colophons of codices written in Hebrew script have survived, some 3,400 of them dated. They constitute about 7% of the estimated 60,000 complete or partial extant mediaeval codices (out of 100,000 Hebrew manuscripts, excluding the many fragments). Half of the colophons include an indication of locality.

A colophon may contain the following details: the scribe's name; the name of the person who commissioned the copying, or an indication that the copyist copied for himself; the title of the copied text; the date of completion of the copy; the locality of the copying; and finally, eulogies and blessings. Sometimes scribes and copyists included valuable information on the circumstances of the copying, on the *Vorlage*, their critical approach and practice, duration of copying, payment and personal and historical data. Not all colophons contain all these components, and some of them are very short, like the earliest undated one, a fourth-century magical papyrus from Oxyrhynchus (London, BL, Or. 9180C), written in Western Aramaic, which contains the scribe's name, definition of the text and an ending formula.

Producer name. The name of the scribe is specified in 85% of the colophons. In addition to scribal colophons, a colophon by the vocalizer might be added in biblical manuscripts, and in rare cases an illuminator added his own colophon. A custom which was common among Hebrew scribes enables us to discover names of anonymous copyists: scribes would often adorn and highlight their own names where these happened to occur in the transcribed text, particularly at the beginning or, less often, at the end of a line, or they might indicate their names in acrostics made from the first letters of a series of lines. This unique practice was common in all areas (but rarely in the Orient) and was implemented in half the extant manuscripts up to 1500, in all literary genres, including biblical manuscripts. It is frequently found even in manuscripts with colophons which include the scribe's name. It appears not only in anonymous colophoned copies, but also in many hundreds of uncolophoned manuscripts and in multi-hand copies in which only the name of the major scribe is indicated. This scribal 'trick' or stratagem provides us with a highly useful tool for analysing multiple-hand copies and assists us in cases of uncertainty as to whether a particular manuscript is homogeneous or a product of several hands, especially if several of the scribes used such a device to disclose their names. The highlighting of the scribes' names also helps in ascertaining the division of the text among different scribes and the distinction of one hand from another (Beit-Arié 2006).

Date. Dates are presented according to five eras. In a considerable number of oriental colophons, two or more parallel eras are used. The commonest is the Jewish Era according to the Creation. The Seleucid Era, which began in 312 BCE, was used only in the Orient, where it was the standard dating practice. There it appears in 61% of the dated colophons (in Yemen, 82%). The calculation according to the destruction of the Second Temple in Jerusalem is the least used era. It appears in 5% of the oriental colophons and in a few dozen Italian ones. Dating by the Islamic Hegira is used only in the eastern Islamic zone (excluding Yemen) and appears in a quarter of the colophons, almost always in manuscripts written in Judaeo-Arabic. The employment of the Christian Era is confined to manuscripts copied by Christian converts. However, since the mid-fourteenth century, a combination of the Jewish calendar and the Christian one is manifested in a considerable number of Italian colophons, where years are rendered according to the Jewish Era of Creation, while days and months are indicated according to the Christian Era.

Locality. Localities are rendered by Hebrew transliteration, reflecting the old mediaeval name, frequently retaining it while disregarding transformations of a political or linguistic nature. Some toponyms are indicated by Hebrew calque translations and some by ascribed biblical names.

9.6.3. Duration of copying

More than 250 colophons provide information on the duration of copying and enable calculation of the speed and output of scribes. There are two ways to retrieve such data, a direct, explicit one, and an indirect one. In a minority of colophons, the scribe specified the duration of their copying explicitly. From the other colophons, duration of copying can be calculated indirectly because either they include either a statement of the dates of beginning and ending the copying, or there are several fully dated colophon at the ends of different textual units of the manuscript, from which the duration of the copying can be inferred. In both kinds of information, we usually lack a specification concerning the daily input, i.e. how many hours per day were spent on copying, and whether the copyist copied continually, day by day (except for Saturdays and feasts). A few multi-colophoned manuscripts containing information of the direct kind show that the scribe was engaged in copying for only part of the time that passed between the completion of one textual unit and the completion of the next. Thus a calculation of the duration of copying based on indirect evidence might be misleading.

The speed of copying is of course conditioned or affected by several factors: the style of script (the square style, which required many more strokes while executing letters, the semi-cursive style and the cursive style); the genre of the text and its social function; the intended aesthetic quality of the copy; and the copy's destination, i.e. whether the manuscript was commissioned and copied uncritically or was user-produced by a learned person who was copying critically. Moreover, any calculation of the speed must take into consideration the dimensions of the surface area, the width of lines and their number per page, and above all, the average number of written signs within a line. Multiplying the average number of written signs per line by the number of lines and by the number of copied pages, then dividing by the number of copying days enables us to calculate the average output per day in terms of written signs, and to compare it to the writing speed of other manuscripts copied using the same style of script, even when they are written in different layouts. For example, the average daily pace of a copyist, who indicates the exact number of copying days in two colophons in each of two different manuscripts (Cambridge University Library, Add. 173, dated 1289, probably in Rome; London, BL, Or. 6712, dated 1287), both written in a semi-cursive script, was 49,550 written signs (about 20 leaves) per day. Three manuscripts in Parma, Biblioteca Palatina, 3118, 3126, 3099, were copied in 1323 by a professional scribe, active in Rome and its vicinity, for his own use. The speed of this scribe, who wrote in a minute, flowing, semi-cursive script, was only 17,685 written signs per day. Calculating a scribe's speed should be based on measurements of the signs written by him, and not on counts of leaves.

References

Baker 1991; Beit-Arié 1967–1968, 1981, 1993, 1999, 2000, 2014; Beit-Arié et al. 1979, 1997, 2006; Bohak 2011; Brock 1995a; Derolez 1984; Dukan 1988; Guesdon 2002; Haran 1985; Le Léannec-Bavavéas – Humbert 1990; Leroy [Julien] 1976; Muzerelle 1985, 1994; Sirat – Beit-Arié 1986; Sirat et al. 1972, 1985; Tov 2004. Web sources: *SfarData* <http://sfardata.nli.org.il/>, last access May 2014.

10. Slavonic codicology (RMC)

10.1. Materials and tools

10.1.1. Parchment

The beginning of native literacy in Slavonic meant the wholesale importation of Byzantine book culture, which in effect meant the parchment codex. No material evidence survives from the Cyrillo-Methodian period (the middle of the ninth century–885). There are no dated 'round Glagolitic' manuscripts, nor are there any dated Cyrillic manuscripts before the middle of the eleventh century ('square Glagolitic' manuscripts do not appear before the fourteenth century). Scholars usually date the earliest extant manuscript material to the beginning of the eleventh century, or, less cautiously, to the end of the tenth. In certain cases, however, external factors allow the date of a manuscript's creation to be estimated with a reasonable degree of probability. The *Codex Suprasliensis* (now divided amongst three libraries: Warsaw, Biblioteka Narodowa, BOZ 201; Ljubljana, National and University Library, Kopitar 2; St Petersburg, RNB, Q.п.I.4; fig. 1.10.1) is a combined reading menaion and panegyricon for March, considered on linguistic grounds to have been written in eastern Bulgaria, of which 285 leaves survive, written in a fine Cyrillic uncial on high-quality parchment in a large format (310 × 230 mm). It was presumably one of a set of twelve volumes covering the entire year. Such a large and expensive commission can hardly have been undertaken except for a major monastery enjoying substantial (probably royal) patronage. The progressive Byzantine conquest of Bulgaria following the death of Tsar Peter in 969 means that no such institution is likely to have remained in existence by the end of the century, suggesting that the manuscript must have been written, if not during Peter's reign, then shortly afterwards.

The extinction of Bulgarian independence in 1018 resulted not only in a loss of patronage and abruption of the tradition of high-quality manuscript production, but also a very considerable loss of manuscripts themselves: the workaday texts succumbed, as ever, to ordinary wear and tear, while the finer books that might otherwise have been specially cared for perished with the institutions that housed them, leaving only chance survivals to witness to the culture that produced them. Under Byzantine rule, it seems that Slavonic book production continued only at the basic level necessary to ensure the continued functioning of the Church. There could be no making and preservation of large, expensive and artistically ambitious manuscripts without patronage of the sort that could be provided only by the sovereign and the greatest of the lords spiritual and temporal under him, which appeared again with the rise of Kievan Rus' at the beginning of the eleventh century, of Serbia from the end of the twelfth, and of a resurgent Bulgaria from 1185. Even from the more fortunate times, though, the number of manuscripts that survives is small in comparison with the Byzantine heritage: from the East Slavonic lands, only about 300 codices written before *c.*1300, or fragments thereof, are known to exist (Franklin 2002, 23; it is difficult to make any reliable estimate for later centuries); from the Balkans the number is even smaller.

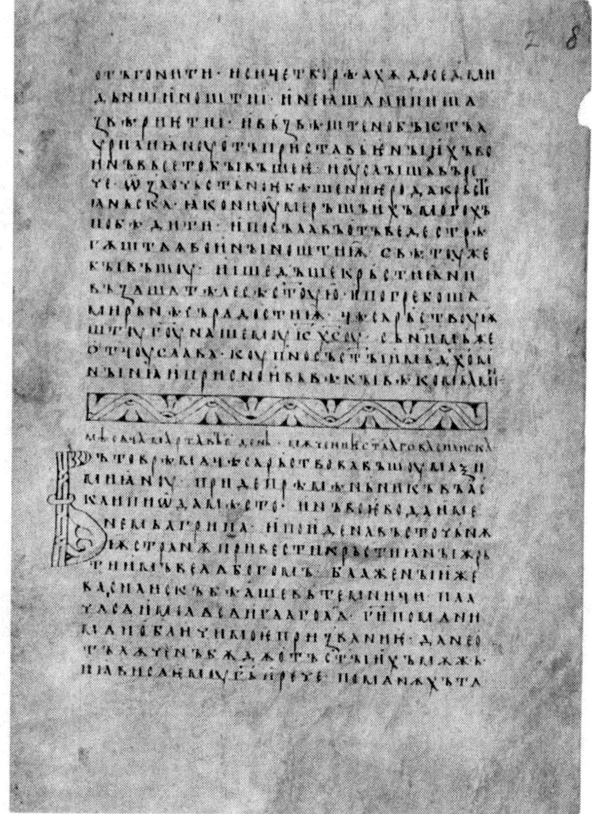

Fig. 1.10.1 *Codex Suprasliensis*, eleventh century, f. 8r, photograph University Library in Ljubljana.

The earliest dated Cyrillic manuscript is the Ostromir Gospels (St Petersburg, RNB, F.п.I.5), written in 1055–1057, a luxury manuscript of exceptionally large format (its pages measure 350 × 300 mm, larger than any other Slavonic manuscript of comparable date; fig. 1.10.2). The place where it was written has long been a matter of debate among scholars: it is certain that it was written for Ostromir, the *posadnik* (governor) of

Novgorod, but art historians in particular have found strong connexions between its decoration and the traditions of Kiev. (The debates do not seem to have taken account of the possibility of craftsmen moving from one place to the other.) Be that as it may, its existence demonstrates that by the middle of the eleventh century the Eastern Slavs were capable of preparing writing materials of the highest quality: although the models for the book and its decoration were Byzantine, the persons involved in its creation were local. This is certainly true of the scribe and the painters, and there is no reason to think otherwise of the craftsmen who prepared their materials. This is, however, to impose a modern distinction on the culture of the period. Though the Slavs of this period were aware of the ethnic and political distinctions between themselves and the Greeks, they saw themselves as sharing a common Christian art, architecture and literature, and the Cyrillic book of this period could even be viewed as a provincial variant of the Byzantine book.

Like the books' contents (intellectual and visual), the technical aspects of their production were imported from Byzantium. For obvious geographical reasons, papyrus was not used among the Slavs, so that in the earlier period the principal support for writing that was not ephemeral in nature was parchment. This was made mostly from the skins of sheep and cattle (that of very young lambs and calves being the most highly prized), though occasionally that of other creatures such as hares, goats and even deer was used (Džurova 1997, 46). Since parchment had been used for centuries at the time of the conversion of the Slavs, it was taken over as part of the 'ready-made' book culture which they adopted together with the Christian religion, and its diffusion amongst them can thus be dated by the conversion of their various nations (though the earliest surviving examples are invariably a century or so later).

The parchment in use among the Slavs rarely matched the highest-quality parchment of Byzantium, and the most luxurious of all, the coloured parchments on which texts were written in gold ink, do not appear to have been used at all. There is a very considerable range in the quality of the parchment used, clearly dependent on the resources available to the people for whom the book was made. It seems that it did not always satisfy the scribes: the priest Dobrejšo has noted at the bottom of f. 3 of the Gospel book that bears his name (Sofia, NBKM 17, a Bulgarian manuscript of the first half of the thirteenth century, see fig. 2.9.2: the inscription is in the lower margin), 'Oh this damned parchment!' (Hristova et al. 2003, 33). Even the best manuscripts may have occasional leaves with holes or other defects, and the parchment used for ordinary work, while by no means substandard, tends to be rather thick and stiff. Almost invariably there is a perceptible difference in colour and texture between the hair side and the flesh side.

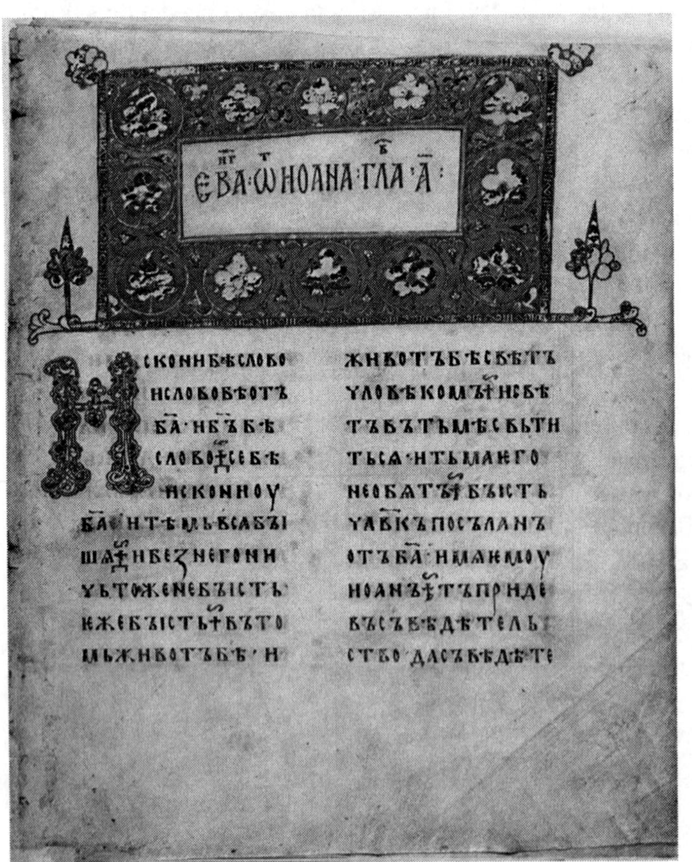

Fig. 1.10.2 Ostromir Gospels, eleventh century, f. 2r, photograph courtesy of the Russian National Library.

The earliest actual records of the manufacture of parchment among the Slavs relate to eighteenth-century Russia (Mefod'eva 2009), but it is clear that it was not a new industry at that time, and it is telling that the extensive Russian foreign trade records relating to the previous century record the import of such items as sealing wax and the raw materials for making ink, but not of parchment (Kireeva 1997, 4). It is reasonable to assume, therefore, that the parchment used for Slavonic books was normally of local manufacture. There is considerable diversity in its thickness, colour and surface texture, which reflects both differences in the raw materials and in the techniques used to prepare it over the centuries, in some cases the result being closer to the type of parchment produced in Byzantium, in others resembling that of Western Europe (Kireeva 1997, 12–15). The Slavs (or at least the Eastern Slavs) do not, however, appear to have followed Byzantine practice in cutting out the parchment bifolia from the hide according to regular patterns (as described by Maniaci 1999a, 1999b), but crossways, lengthways or even diagonally according to the qualities of a particular hide (Petrova – Sadovskaja 2009).

Since parchment was expensive and, except to the greatest patrons, not always readily available, it could also be re-used. Nevertheless, Slavonic palimpsests are few in number, and tend to be relatively early; almost all the known examples are from the Balkans. In some cases, an earlier Slavonic text was overwritten in Greek, perhaps the most famous example being the Vatican Palimpsest (Vatican City, BAV, Vat. gr. 2502), in which a tenth-century Cyrillic Gospel lectionary was overwritten in the thirteenth century with the four Gospels in Greek. The reverse could also occur, as in the Kochno Gospels (Odessa, National Gorky Library, MS 182). Manuscript Vatican City, BAV, Barb. gr. 388 presents a remarkable example of a Greek text written over a Cyrillic text which had itself been written over a Greek text. In the Bojana Palimpsest (Moscow, RGB, ф. 87, № 8), the Cyrillic text is written over an earlier Glagolitic text. One of the quires (a twelfth-century replacement for some missing leaves) of the *Codex Zographensis* (St Petersburg, RNB, Glag. 1) is Glagolitic over Glagolitic. Overall, in about half the known examples the script of the underlying text is different from that of the later text, which is perhaps not surprising, since scribes might be more likely to re-use manuscripts written in a script or language which was not generally understood in the community which they served.

Parchment remained the dominant support in the Balkans until the middle of the fourteenth century, and slightly later in Russia. In Moldavia and Wallachia it retained this position even longer: almost everything written in Moldavia in the first decade of the sixteenth century was still on parchment, though by the end of the century paper accounted for the majority of items here too. This is to some extent connected with the princely patronage that continued in the Danubian Principalities after other Balkan lands had fallen wholly under Ottoman dominion, and indeed the parchment on which some of the manuscripts produced there at this relatively late period are written is of the highest quality of any in the Cyrillic tradition. The use of parchment for particularly luxurious volumes continued into the era of printed books, when individual volumes of works normally printed on paper might be printed on parchment. An example is the copy in Dublin, Chester Beatty Library (W149) of the Festal Menaion published by Božidar Vuković in Venice in 1538: not only is the entire volume (and it is a large book of 432 leaves) printed on parchment, but many of the printed pictures and headpiece decorations have been coloured and gilded by hand. One must assume that it was specially commissioned by an important individual or institution.

10.1.3. Paper

Paper of oriental manufacture is almost unknown amongst the Slavs. The great collector Nikolaj Lichačev (1862–1936), at the end of the nineteenth century, had speculated about its use (Lichačev 1899), but it was not until 1985 that an actual example was discovered by O.A. Knjazevskaja (Morozov 1994). This is a manuscript of the *Scala Paradisi* of St John Climacus in Slavonic translation, written on a mixture of parchment and paper in Galicia or Volhynia (or possibly elsewhere by a native of that region) during the second half of the thirteenth century (Moscow, RGADA, ф. 181, № 452). The paper is of the type manufactured in Samarkand at this period; this example of its use in a Cyrillic manuscript, however, remains unique.

The earliest use of paper in the Cyrillic tradition is represented by two charters issued by the Bulgarian Tsar Ivan Asen II, one to Vatopedi and the other to Dubrovnik (Daskalova – Rajkova 2005, 29–30). They are undated (or rather, the date of the first is imperfectly legible and the second is not dated), but both were evidently written after 1230, and certainly before the Tsar's death in 1241. The paper is believed to be of early Italian manufacture, but since both have been mounted, detailed study of the paper is difficult and does not so far appear to have been attempted. It is most probably the primitive, unwatermarked Italian paper that was beginning to penetrate into the Eastern Mediterranean at this period; this is certainly the material used for the charter issued by Constantine Tih to St George's Monastery at Virgino Bărdo (similarly undated, but the Tsar reigned 1257–1277). Although the authenticity of this document has been disputed (Daskalova – Rajkova 2005, 8–9), the paper makes the position of those who would see it as a fourteenth-century forgery hard to maintain. Similar paper is used for MS Athos, Hilandar, 387, a substantial codex of 366 leaves, written in the Serbian (Raška) redaction of Church Slavonic and dated on palaeographical grounds to the second quarter of the thirteenth century (Bogdanović 1978, I, 152 and II, plate 7).

The first use of Occidental paper in a dated Slavonic codex is in the Tărnovo Gospels of 1273 (Zagreb, HAZU, III a 30), which is a mixed manuscript, consisting of quires of eight leaves, of which the outer and inner bifolia are of parchment and the two in between (i.e. the second, third, sixth and seventh leaves) of paper. The paper is of high quality, but still without any watermark, likewise believed to be of Italian manufacture. Though a rarity at the beginning of the fourteenth century, as the century progresses paper accounts for more and more of the manuscripts produced in Serbia and Bulgaria, especially in its latter half. The first known use of Occidental paper in Russia is in an undated charter of Vasilij Davidovič, prince of Nižnij Novgorod, who died in 1345, and by the end of the century paper was also being used for codices.

Given the early pre-eminence of Italy in the manufacture of paper, it is not surprising that the paper used in these early books and documents is Italian. In the Balkans, where Venice and the Adriatic were the main routes for its importation, Italian paper continued to be used throughout the manuscript period, though from the late fifteenth century paper from Germany and Transylvania is also found here (Mošin – Traljić 1957). In northern Europe Italy soon began to face competition from France and later Flanders. French paper first appeared in Russia and the Ukraine in the middle of the first half of the fifteenth century, and by the middle of the sixteenth century France had more or less displaced Italy as the main source of paper for the Eastern Slavs. Polish paper is found here from the beginning of the sixteenth century, mostly in the western territories, where paper from Transylvania also appears. 'German' or perhaps rather Central European paper begins to be imported shortly afterwards, though German—and English—merchants also imported paper into Russia from France. Dutch paper first appeared in Russia in the second half of the seventeenth century, and soon almost entirely supplanted all other sources (Lichačev 1899, lxi).

Though the first paper mills in Russia were set up in the middle of the sixteenth century, their output was insignificant (Keenan 1971). Native production only began on a serious scale toward the end of the seventeenth century, but it expanded very considerably thereafter, and by the end of the eighteenth century the Russian Empire had become self-sufficient in paper. Those parts of Europe that were under Ottoman control, however, remained reliant on imports.

Since most Slavonic manuscripts are written on imported European paper, they share the watermarks found in manuscripts from elsewhere on the continent, and since the manuscript books themselves are so rarely dated, the watermarks are often the prime means of dating them. Their importance was realized very early in Slavonic manuscript studies. One of the very first studies of watermarks was the book published by Kornelij Tromonin in 1844 with the prolix but eloquent title 'an explanation of the signs visible in writing paper, whereby it is possible to discover when any books, documents, drawings, pictures or other items, ancient or not, on which no year is indicated, were written or printed' (Tromonin – Klepikov 1844). Lichačev, who collected not only manuscripts, but also seals, icons, and much else, published both a monumental three-volume study and album on 'the palaeographical significance of watermarks' (recently republished in a revised and reorganized edition, which reflects its lasting value), and the first major study of the paper production and papermills of the Russian Empire (Lichačev 1891, 1899, 1994).

While Russian scholars continue to contribute to the study of paper, outside Russia, the greatest contribution to the study of watermarks in the Slavonic context was made by Vladimir Mošin and his followers in Belgrade. Like Lichačev, Mošin was a scholar of broad interests, and so it is natural that in Serbia the study of paper has been integrated into the study of the manuscript in all its aspects. It is notable that in this tradition manuscript catalogues usually include albums of the watermarks found in the manuscripts described.

10.1.4. Inks and pigments

As in the rest of Europe, manuscripts were usually written with inks based on iron salts in combination with gallic acid, for which the principal source appears to have been tree bark (oak, alder, etc.) or the cones of various conifers. A number of recipes survive, going back to the fifteenth century; some have been printed by Simoni (1906). The resulting inks vary in quality from a fine black through various shades of brown; occasionally, mostly in the later period, the acid content of the ink has led to corrosion of the paper.

It is relatively uncommon for a manuscript to be written entirely in black (or brown) ink. Most often the titles, sectional initials and (where present) rubrics are written in red, which may also be used for marginalia where they occur (see figs. 1.10.4, 1.10.8). The red pigment is usually cinnabar, to the extent that red ink is invariably referred to in Russian as *kinovar'*, even though other red pigments such as minium are occasionally found. There may be quite abundant red text in manuscripts with long sectional headings or extensive rubrication, and it is also used in combination with black in tables such as paschalia or lectionaries. This reflects a tradition of textual presentation in scriptural and liturgical books which goes back to Byzantium and is continued to this day in the printed service books of the Orthodox Church. To this extent the use of red ink may be said to be an essential, or at least a normal part of book production in the Cyrillic tradition, and not only in religious texts, where it becomes more or less standardized and where tradition acquires the force of obligation; red titles and initials are usual in secular books as well.

The same cannot be said for other colours. In the most luxurious manuscripts gold may be used for the most important titles and in other places (such as headpieces) where red is commonly used, but not so extensively, so that such manuscripts tend to have writing in both red and gold, with the latter occupying a more significant place in the hierarchy of decoration; it may be overlaid on text that had originally been written in red. Occasionally red (and even more occasionally gold) may also be used for punctuation. The use of inks of other colours for text is rare in the extreme, but they are not uncommonly found in purely decorative elements such as headpieces and large initials. On the other hand, there are also some very elegant manuscripts (and some less elegant ones) in which all the decoration is in red.

10.1.5. Writing instruments

The principal writing instrument was the quill. This is clear from occasional scribal notes and *probationes calami*, some as early as the thirteenth century, which refer to it as *pero*, the usual Slavonic word for a feather. Occasional references in text to a reed (*trŭstĭ*) are more likely to be literal translations of the Greek *kalamos* than a reflection of actual local practice. There is little other direct evidence of the tools of the trade until the early modern period, and their use must be more or less inferred from the result: mediaeval depictions of scribes at work (typically the evangelists) probably owe more to Byzantine iconographical tradition than to contemporary observation.

10.2. Book forms

10.2.1. Miscellaneous forms

Since the Slavs inherited from Byzantium a fully-formed tradition in which the codex was the principal form of the book, there is no question of 'the birth of the codex' in their practice. Nevertheless, other formats were known, though they tended to be limited in their use. In particular, in the early period, when parchment was expensive and in limited supply, it was necessary to have some other medium that could be used for ephemeral or unimportant writing. In the north, birch-bark was commonly used for this purpose. A piece of bark was removed from the wood and the text incised on its inner surface using a stylus made of metal or bone. This usually produces a fairly crude uncial, with the angular and irregular lines of equal thickness resulting from such a method of writing. There are occasional references in early sources to the use of birch-bark, but since the letters themselves were always thrown away after use, scholars had no direct knowledge of them until 1951, when the first examples were unearthed during archaeological excavations in Novgorod, where soil conditions proved particularly favourable for their preservation (fig. 1.10.3).

Since that first discovery, more birch-bark letters have been found every year, so that the total now stands at over a thousand, the vast majority from Novgorod, but a few also from other towns such as Pskov, Smolensk and Staraja Russa. Their state of preservation ranges from complete (about a quarter of them) to fragmentary. In most cases their horizontal dimension is between 150 and 400 mm, and their vertical dimension between 20 and 80 mm. The most extensive of them contains only 176 words, and this is exceptional: few of them contain more than fifty, and most of them twenty or less. They are dated mostly by stratigraphy, according to the layer of the excavation from which they were recovered, though in some cases the dating may be confirmed by other means (for example, references in them to known individuals); the oldest come from the second quarter of the eleventh century, and the most recent are four hundred years later. A few contain such varied texts as drafts of official documents, school exercises, love charms, etc., but the vast majority are private correspondence. Many relate to business, but some deal with more personal matters. While it is not always clear that the senders of such letters wrote them in person (though in many cases they did), they provide evidence for the use of the written word in much wider circles than

Fig. 1.10.3 Birch-bark document, fourteenth century, Novgorod, State Historical Museum, gramota 366, photograph courtesy of V.L. Janin, <http://www.gramoty.ru>.

those represented in ink on parchment, including women and peasants. Their informal contents and format are matched by their colloquial language, and it is fair to say that their discovery has revolutionized the study of the history of the Russian language, by providing information unavailable from other sources, particularly about the Novgorod dialect. This reminds us again that 'the book' is by no means the sole repository of language, and that—at least in this tradition—the record it provides is by no means complete.

Another widespread medium for temporary writing was wax. It had long been inferred that written waxed surfaces had been in use among the Slavs, not least from the frequent discoveries of styli with one end pointed for writing and the other flat for smoothing out the wax surface so that it could be used again. Direct evidence, though, was lacking until the sensational discovery in 2000—again in excavations at Novgorod—of a set of three tablets with the wax intact upon them (Franklin 2002, 46–47). These form a triptych, in which the two outer leaves have a wax-filled depression on their inner sides only, and the inner one on both sides. They bear the text of Psalms 75 and 76 and part of Psalm 67. The archaeological stratum beneath which they were found has been dated by dendrochronology to 1036, and thus, in terms of the Slavonic written record, they are very early, and both the text and the letter forms are consistent with such a date.

10.2.2. The roll and the rotulus

As elsewhere in Europe, legal records and accounts might take the form of rolls made of pieces of paper or parchment stuck together with text running parallel to the short edge of the roll: for this particular purpose, this form has the advantages that it is more or less indefinitely extensible, and that it is very hard to remove something from the middle of it without its being noticed. Apart from this, rolls are uncommon. The liturgical rolls prevalent among the Greeks are hardly reflected among the Slavs. Only a few are known, and they are typically found at points of cultural contact, where they are nevertheless heavily outnumbered by codices. There are three on Sinai, all Serbian and written in the middle of the fourteenth century: Sinai slav. 38N, Sinai slav. 39N (another part of which is Vatican City, BAV, Vat. slav. 9), and the fragmentary Sinai slav. 40 / 40N. The first of these has been identified as written by a scribe active in the Middle East, and the second was commissioned by the Cæsar Hrelja Ohmućević (d.1342/1343), who had detached himself from Stefan Dušan's kingdom and allied himself with Constantinople. Both of these may have been open to influence by Byzantine liturgical practice. On Mount Athos there are six rolls at Hilandar Monastery (3/I, 3/II, 3/III, 16/IV, 16/V, 16/VI) and one, associated with the reforming Patriarch Evtimij of Tărnovo, at Zōgraphou Monastery, all of parchment. Equally noteworthy is a very fine parchment roll, written in Russia but according to Bulgarian (Tărnovo) norms, St Petersburg, RNB, F.п.I.33, possibly one of the manuscripts commissioned by Archbishop Evfimij of Novgorod (consecrated 1434, d.1458) in connexion with the introduction of the Jerusalem Typicon at Novgorod. Evidence of a further Novgorod manuscript, now lost, is provided by Moscow, RGB, Uvarov 632 (44/561), a nineteenth-century copy which preserves the colophon of the original with the date 1424. It would appear that these Slavonic liturgical rolls were written in imitation of Greek liturgical practice in the context of liturgical contacts or reforms, but that the tradition never gained a wide currency among the Slavs. The parchment liturgical rolls may be written on both sides and wound around a wooden cylinder; in both these features they differ from the other types of roll. In all types of Slavonic rolls, the text runs in a single column with the lines parallel to the short edge of the roll, so that in this respect the Slavonic rolls resemble the Byzantine, and not the classical tradition in their layout.

In marked contrast to the liturgical rolls is a second group of Slavonic manuscripts that take this form, but have a completely different function and cultural status. These are rolls that typically bear so-called 'apocryphal prayers' (unofficial and sometimes doctrinally suspect Christian invocations) or short narratives describing encounters between Jesus or the saints and the unclean spirits held to be responsible for disease. They are found in both the Glagolitic (Vatican City, BAV, Vat. slav. 11) and Cyrillic traditions. The earliest paper examples date from the end of the fourteenth century, but the practice of using such rolls as amulets evidently goes back to the beginnings of Slavonic literacy. A group of amulets in the form of rolled sheets of lead has been found at various sites in Bulgaria and dated by archaeologists to the tenth or eleventh centuries. These bear incised texts, including some of the same apocryphal prayers and the *Epistola Abgari*. This last (which, although perfectly Orthodox, sometimes appears on the lists of prohibited books precisely because of this superstitious usage) is particularly interesting because of its persistent use as an apotropaic text in the Balkans. It gives its name to the celebrated *Abagar*, famous as the first printed text to contain elements of vernacular Bulgarian, printed in Rome in 1651 by Filip Stanislavov, Roman Catholic Bishop of Nikopolis. This was printed in narrow columns on one side of the paper only, in such a way that the columns of text could be separated and combined into a roll in order, as explicitly stated in the colophon, to be worn on the person 'instead of relics'. It is remarkable both as a move by the Church to adopt elements of folk religion and as the transition of a very specific form of written text from the manuscript to the printed era. Manuscript scroll-amulets continued to be produced in Bulgaria well into the nineteenth century; they may include pictures and other decorative elements.

A third group of manuscripts for which the roll form was preferred is represented by the calligraphic rolls which were produced in Russia from the sixteenth to eighteenth centuries (but most specimens date from the seventeenth; for examples, and illustrations, see Du Feu – Simmons 1970). Although they may incorporate continuous texts of various sorts, their principal purpose is to display the alphabet, each letter usually being represented by a multitude of cursive (*skoropis'*) forms. It is not clear whether they had any purpose beyond the demonstration of the writer's skill. In many cases this was considerable, so that the result may be highly decorative, but not visible unless the manuscript is unrolled.

10.3. The making of the codex

Apart from these very specific categories, 'the book', as far as the Slavs were concerned, meant the codex. By the time they had adopted it, its structure had become largely standardized in Byzantium, and this is reflected equally in the nascent Slavonic traditions.

10.3.1. The making of the quires

Any attempt at a comprehensive study of the Slavonic codex is hindered by the fact that, until quite recently, catalogues of Slavonic manuscripts have tended to omit any codicological description beyond the number of the leaves and the material of which they are made, so that there is much data yet to be collected (cf. Ch. 4 § 2.9). Nevertheless it is clear that from the earliest times the quires (errors and omissions excepted) normally consisted of eight leaves. This is not an absolute rule, any more than it is with Greek manuscripts (if anything, somewhat less), but it is a persistent norm. It continues, moreover, after paper replaces parchment, everywhere except in the Ukraine, where gatherings of ten or twelve leaves become the rule.

The rule of Gregory is by and large observed (though not always and not with total consistency), but—particularly in Cyrillic manuscripts—the quires most frequently begin with the hair side of the parchment. From the Greek point of view this is a 'provincial' practice, and may relate to a local tradition in the Greek uncials of the eighth and ninth centuries on which the earliest Cyrillic manuscripts were modelled. The earliest Glagolitic manuscripts, paradoxically, may follow a more 'modern' practice (for example, the quires of the *Codex Assemanianus*, Vatican City, BAV, Vat. slav. 3, begin with the flesh side; cf. Džurova 1997, 231). It is tempting to see in this the heritage of Constantinople, the city from which the mission of Cyril and Methodius set out.

10.3.2. Pricking and ruling

The Slavs inherited from the Greeks the practice of pricking and ruling the parchment in order to produce a consistency of layout throughout the volume. Pricking was most frequently done with an awl from the flesh side of the leaves; ruling in dry point may be done from the hair side or the flesh side, but most often from the former, at least in those manuscripts in which the flesh side forms the outer surface of the quires. Occasionally the ruling was carried out leaf by leaf, but more often two bifolia at a time. No research on the scale of that done by Leroy for the Greek tradition (Leroy [Julien] 1976) has been carried out for Slavonic manuscripts; however, Džurova and Stančev have provisionally proposed a number of 'Slavonic' ruling types and ruling systems. (Given that Leroy was dealing with manuscripts in which the quires, as a rule, begin with the flesh side, and that in the vast majority of Slavonic manuscripts they begin with the hair side, the direct application of Leroy's categories to Slavonic manuscripts is problematic.) The results are so far somewhat inconclusive, not least because it is not infrequent for different systems to coexist within the same manuscript. However, Džurova has noted that while the earliest Glagolitic manuscripts tend in this respect to reflect contemporary practice at Constantinople, Cyrillic manuscripts are more 'archaic', and their ruling, like the organization of their quires, finds closer parallels in the Syriac, Armenian and Georgian traditions (see the more detailed discussion in Džurova 1997, 47, 92–106, 230–231).

In round Glagolitic manuscripts the text is generally written below the line, as is commonly the case with Greek minuscules after the tenth century; indeed, the alphabet seems to have been intended to be written in this way, as some of the letters, such as Ⱁ, do not reach the base line (cp. fig. 1.10.4). Cyrillic, by contrast, like the Greek uncials from which it is derived, is generally written above the line (cp. fig. 1.10.1), though there are occasional examples of 'hanging Cyrillic', written below the line. These are few in number and almost all very early, including such important manuscripts as the Enina Apostolos (Sofia, NBKM, 1144). They may reflect the practice of scribes accustomed to writing in Glagolitic.

Hardly any research has been done on the ruling systems of paper manuscripts. These can be quite complex, sometimes including guidelines for marginalia, running titles, etc. Double ruling—providing not only a base-line but a head-line—is particularly prevalent in Romanian manuscripts, but rare elsewhere. The use of a ruling board, typically made of wood with cords glued to it to form ridges against which the paper could be pressed down in order to be impressed with the desired ruling pattern, was common from the fifteenth century onwards. This, the equivalent of the Turkish (Arabic) *misṭara* was known as *karamsa* in Russian and *karaksal* in Bulgarian; both words are presumably derived ultimately from Greek *charassō* 'to engrave', though it is not entirely clear by what processes. The use of such a board was evidently very convenient in reducing the labour involved in ruling, to the extent that it might be used even though it did not correspond perfectly to the layout of the book it was intended to produce—two columns instead of one, or *vice versa*, superfluous marginal guidelines, a written area inappropriate for the size of the page. In such cases the scribes were quite capable of using the ruling pattern as only an approximate guide, ignoring unnecessary elements, writing outside the ruled area, etc.

10.3.3. Ordering systems

Quire signatures are often lost when they are placed very close to the edge of a leaf which was subsequently trimmed during binding, so that the fact that they are frequently absent, particularly from the oldest manuscripts, does not mean that they were not originally there, and examples are known from as early as the eleventh century. The signatures are always numerical, and may be on the first recto of each quire, or on the last verso, or on both; the practice of signing quires at both ends becomes more frequent with the passage of time. They are usually placed in the lower margin, either centrally or toward the outer edge (rarely toward the inner edge) of the page (cp. fig. 1.10.8). Signatures in the upper margin are uncommon, but may occasionally be encountered in manuscripts of all periods. Occasionally scribes mark the first leaf of a gathering with a cross placed centrally in the upper margin of the recto; this may be combined with other signing systems and is found mostly in Ukrainian manuscripts. Catchwords and signatures on the inner pages of gatherings are infrequent and appear only toward the end of the manuscript period, evidently under the influence of printed books; the same is true of foliation or pagination, which remain unusual. Running titles, however, are often met with (but not obligatory) in certain types of manuscript such as the Gospels, where the name of the evangelist may appear in abbreviated form at the top of each recto (though there are examples where not every leaf is so marked).

10.4. The layout of the page

The enthusiasm that Byzantinists have shown in recent years for 'quantitative codicology' has not been matched by Slavists, and in the absence of extensive statistical data one can only give a tentative and approximate outline of this aspect of the Slavonic book. An analysis of forty-eight codices in Budapest, carried out for the purposes of this chapter, reveals that the ratio of height to breadth varies from 0.85 to 0.59, with some correlation between this ratio and the overall size of the volumes, the smaller books being 'squarer' (only one book with a vertical dimension over 300 mm has a ratio greater than 0.65). While this may be comparable with Byzantine codices, the proportion of the page occupied by text (the 'black') is not: in fewer than a quarter of the books does it fall below 50%. Those with a very large area occupied by text tend to be late and informal, but even so, in one fourteenth-century Gospel book it reaches 63%. By and large, as one might expect, the higher the quality of the manuscript, the smaller the written area relative to the overall size of the page. However, given the depredations of binders over the years, it is in almost every case impossible to say what the original proportion of text to page was.

Although the above is a very small sample, it is likely to prove typical, at least as far as 'ordinary' manuscripts are concerned. Departures from the norm are more likely in particularly luxurious manuscripts on the one hand, or particularly rustic ones on the other, and not only because of their decoration or lack of it, but even more because of their scribes' attitudes to their materials. In the former case they were able to allow themselves extensive margins to set off the aesthetic qualities of their text, while in the latter considerations of economy seem to have dictated a more intensive use of parchment that was itself not necessarily perfectly regular. Nevertheless, although—as we shall see when we come to look at their decoration—continuing influence and shared development with the Byzantine tradition is easier to trace in manuscripts of the highest quality, it is clear that the major traditions of Cyrillic manuscript production were not only originally derived from Byzantium, but continued to take the Byzantine tradition as their model in later ages.

10.5. Text structure and readability

10.5.1. Writing

The visual arrangement of the text within the manuscript, reflecting its logical structure, essentially continues—or parallels—that of Greek manuscripts, with their headpieces (and more rarely tailpieces), titles and initials. Cyrillic bookhands are derived from uncials, not minuscules, and this does to a certain extent affect the immediate appearance of the page, particularly in the more formal manuscripts (see also Ch. 2 § 9). Nevertheless, the relationship between the majuscule title and the rest of the text is very similar, in usage, proportion, and even the shape of the majuscule characters, to that seen in Greek minuscule manuscripts. The first Cyrillic majuscule titles are very early (in uncial manuscripts such as the *Codex Suprasliensis*, fig. 1.10.1) and the contrast between them and the ordinary bookhand (and, in the more elegant manuscripts, their decorative character) becomes more pronounced with the passage of time. In the later period, and especially in Russia, the use of ligatures in titles may become more and more frequent, until it develops into a style of writing known as *vjaz'*, in which adjacent letters share their vertical strokes, and those without any, such as є, are reduced in size and tucked into the spaces between the others (Ščepkin 1903; cp. fig. 1.10.8); by the seventeenth century this extreme form of ligation, combined with the increasingly elongated proportions of the characters, reaches a point where the titles' decorative function is often achieved at the expense of legibility.

Similarly reminiscent of Greek practice are the large initials which may set off sections of the text which do not merit a separate heading, to the extent that they are known to Cyrillic palaeographers as 'neo-Byzantine'. They normally occur at the beginning of a line, and may protrude into the margin. Typically red, they may be two or more lines in height and may be plain or decorated with nodes and tendrils.

It is not only in their general layout, however, that Cyrillic manuscripts follow their Byzantine prototypes; the resemblance may be even more pronounced in particular books. Thus a page from the Gospels—particularly after the general acceptance of the Jerusalem Typicon in both Byzantine and Slavonic worlds during the fourteenth century—is likely to have exactly the same layout in both Greek and Slavonic traditions: the block of text in black divided by rubrics indicating the pericopes and the occasions for which they are appointed, with, in the margins, pericope numbers in red, chapter numbers in black, and the proems of the pericopes in red.

This is, admittedly, not universal, and some of the finer points of Byzantine textual organization may be lost in Slavonic transmission. One example would be the lists of contents that form part of the Euthalian apparatus preceding each Epistle in continuous texts of the *Apostolos*, in which the sections, numbered in black, may be divided into subsections, numbered in red. The distinction of colour is hardly ever maintained in Slavonic manuscripts, so that the numbering ceases to be comprehensible. Similarly, the *Apostolus Christinopolitanus* (Ľviv, Historical Museum, 39) is unique among Slavonic commentated *Apostoloi* (of which, dating from the twelfth century, it is the earliest example) in having a layout very similar to Byzantine manuscripts of the same type, with the text occupying the centre of the page and the commentary surrounding it. In later manuscripts (even the commentated *Apostolos* of 1220, Moscow, Gosudarstvennyj istoričeskij muzej, Syn. 7) the commentary is brought in from the margin and intercalated with the text, so that the latter is broken up into very short sections (sometimes even single words), within a simple one- or two-column layout. In the better manuscripts, a visual distinction between text and commentary is maintained, but this is not always the case, and confusion does arise. This is a good example of the tendency of Slav scribes to avoid the elaborate layouts that may be found in Byzantine (and still more in Latin) manuscripts, even to the occasional detriment of the structure of the text. Most manuscripts have a single column of text. Two columns may be used in large-format manuscripts where the length of the lines of a single column might be detrimental to legibility, though often very large manuscripts are also written in large script, so that a single column suffices. It is, however, not uncommon for Gospels written in single columns to be followed by lectionaries (consisting largely of calendrical information and rubrics) arranged in double columns; this partly reflects considerations of legibility and scribal convenience, but also the relative status of the two types of text. Subordinate sections of a work, such as prefaces or apparatus, may be written in smaller script than the main text, and in such cases a different layout may be adopted for them. It would, however, be unwise to generalise about particular formats for specific types of text, as practices varied considerably at different periods and in different places.

The early manuscripts are, as a rule, written in *scriptio continua*, though the Kiev Missal (fig. 1.10.4) is a remarkable exception. Word-division—or rather division into prosodic units—establishes itself in the Glagolitic tradition from the thirteenth century (MacRobert 2002, on which this paragraph is largely based). Cyrillic is more resistant to it, though the otherwise conservative and isolated tradition of Bosnia begins to provide examples of di-

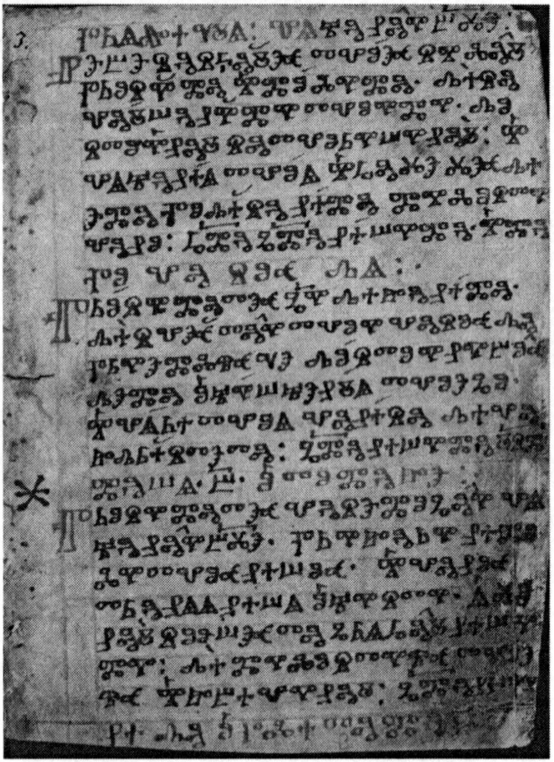

Fig. 1.10.4 Kiev Missal, tenth century, Kiev, Ukrainian National Library, 19264, f. 3r, photograph courtesy of the Ukrainian National Library.

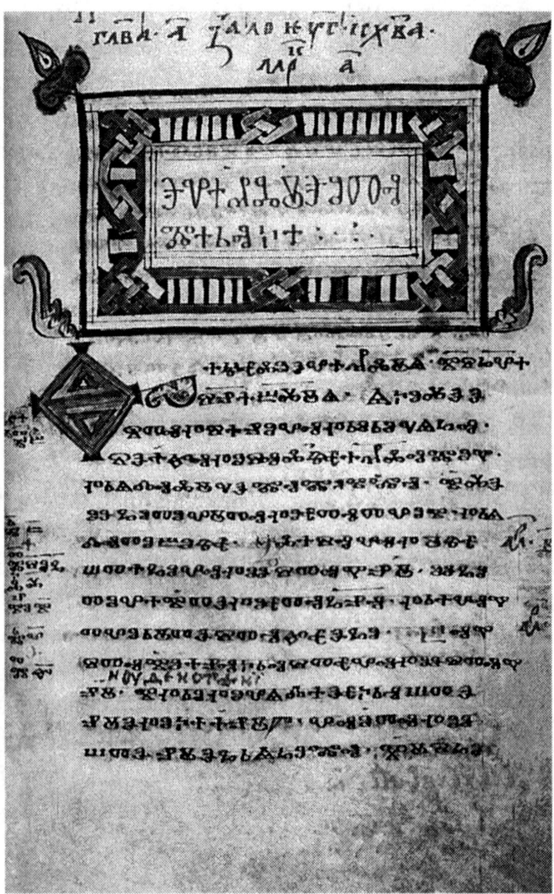

Fig. 1.10.5 *Codex Zographensis*, tenth/eleventh century, St Petersburg, RNB, Glag. 1, f. 1r.

vision on a prosodic basis from about the same period, possibly under Glagolitic influence. Division into prosodic units is observed in the more mainstream Serbian tradition from the beginning of the fourteenth century, though it appears not to have been obligatory and to have been subordinate to other principles governing the disposition of text on the page. By the time of the Second Dragalevci Gospels (Sofia, NBKM, 347, written near Sofia in the 1580s) word-division may be almost modern, with only clitics and non-syllabic words not separated from their neighbours, but in other manuscripts from the same period and even later *scriptio continua* persists: it seems to have been a matter of local or even personal preference. By and large the Balkan Slavs seem to have been more advanced in this respect than those of the east, but it is impossible to lay down hard and fast rules tying the progress of this development to particular times and places. Its general direction is nevertheless clearly from *scriptio continua* toward a progressively more systematic word-division, which was probably assisted by the appearance of printed books, in which prosodic division is used from the beginning.

10.5.2. Decoration and illumination

The illuminators of manuscripts derived their art from the same sources as the scribes, namely the Byzantine codex. The use of decorative elements to reflect the logical structure of the text has already been mentioned, and, just as the practice follows Byzantine models, so does the actual decoration. It is already present in the earliest manuscripts, in which its extent varies considerably. Even in a large and elegantly written manuscript such as the *Codex Suprasliensis* (fig. 1.10.1) the decoration may be confined to simple ribbon-like head- and tailpieces and some outline initials. By contrast, the *Codex Zographensis* (St Petersburg, RNB, Glag.1, a Glagolitic tetraevangelion and one of the major canonical Old Church Slavonic manuscripts, see fig. 1.10.5) has polychrome headpieces, and there is evidence that originally it had miniatures of the evangelists, which do not survive (Zagrebin – Levšina 2009). To some extent, the fact that early Glagolitic decoration is derived from the Byzantine tradition—or even, one might say, represents a provincial strand of the Byzantine tradition—may help to fill in the gaps left by the absence of any possibility of dating round Glagolitic manuscripts by palaeographical criteria. A comparison of the iconography of the historiated initials in the *Codex Assemanianus* (fig. 1.10.6) with Greek manuscripts (which are datable) has shown that the closest parallels are to be found in the eleventh century, which suggests that this is the probable date of the *Codex Assemanianus* itself (Musakova 1996).

The Ostromir Gospels being the earliest dated Slavonic manuscript (1055–1057), its miniatures are also the earliest to which a firm date can be assigned. There are three of them, depicting SS Mark, Luke, and John. (Presumably St Matthew was also originally represented.) They are all of a high quality, and all have evident Byzantine antecedents, which are particularly evident in the treatment of St John's garments. The miniatures of St Mark and St Luke are by a different artist, and while in terms of their iconography and composition they may be compared with miniatures in Greek manuscripts, their technique obviously owes a great deal to Byzantine enamels, the draperies being conveyed by fine gold lines through blocks of colour reminiscent of cloisonné enamel. There had been active artistic contacts between Kiev and Constantinople since the conversion of Rus' at the end of the tenth century (most famously in the decoration of St Sophia in Kiev, but elsewhere as well), so it is not surprising that by the time the Ostromir Gospels manuscript was decorated, local artists had assimilated the styles and techniques of Byzantine painting and were producing masterpieces of their own.

It may thus be said that as early as the middle of the eleventh century, Slavonic book art had acquired a momentum of its own and was capable of an existence without reference to its Byzantine models. It is noteworthy that the miniatures of the Ostromir Gospels were the models for those in the Mstislav Gospels (Moscow, Gosudarstvennyj istoričeskij muzej, Syn. 1203), fifty or sixty years later (in which, incidentally, the miniature of St Matthew survives, providing an idea of its lost original in the Ostromir Gospels). Particularly remarkable is the fact that the Mstislav Gospels are dependent on the Ostromir Gospels for their decoration but not for their text, which represents a different redaction of the Slavonic translation. This shows that its creators did not simply set about reproducing an existing manuscript, but were selective, taking the most admired or most authoritative features from the various sources available to them.

The most luxurious illumination of course depended on generous patronage, which in the eleventh and twelfth centuries meant above all the courts of the Russian princes; from the latter part of the twelfth century, the rulers of Bulgaria and Serbia also began to commission manuscripts, leading up to the golden age in the reign of John Alexander of Bulgaria (1331–1371). Some manuscripts were also produced for members of the higher clergy. It is noteworthy that some of the most outstanding Slavonic manuscripts from an artistic point of view have Greek models. The Kiev Psalter (St Petersburg, RNB, OLDP F 6) is—apart from its Slavonic text—a typical member of the group of so-called 'monastic' illustrated psalters (i.e. with illustrations on the margins), closest in its iconography to the Baltimore Psalter (Baltimore, Walters Art Gallery, W733). It is hardly co-incidental that the prelate who commissioned it, Bishop Michael of Smolensk, had twice visited Constantinople, in the company of two Metropolitans of Kiev (*de facto* of Moscow), Pimen, and (after his death) Cyprian, a Bulgarian who had spent much time in the Imperial City and was an even more important *Kulturträger* for Russia in the context of the liturgical reforms that accompanied the introduction of the Jerusalem Typicon and were to have a very significant effect on book production in Russia. The Psalter was written in Kiev—hence the name by which it is known—in 1397, during which year both Bishop Michael and Metropolitan Cyprian were visiting that city, and the scribe, Spiridon, evidently from Moscow, was part of their entourage.

Fig. 1.10.6 *Codex Assemanianus*, eleventh century, Vatican City, BAV, Vat. slav. 3, f. 81v, from Ivanova-Mavrodinova – Džurova 1981.

The 'aristocratic' illustrated psalter (i.e. with full-page miniatures) is also represented among the Slavs, by the Tomić Psalter (Moscow, Gosudarstvennyj istoričeskij muzej, Muz. 2752) and the Munich Psalter (Bayerische Staatsbibliothek, Cod. slav. 4). The former is believed to have been commissioned by the Bulgarian Tsar John Alexander in the early 1360s, and the latter for Prince Lazar of Serbia (d.1389) or for his son Stefan Lazarević; they show iconographical affinities with each other and with the Byzantine tradition to which they belong. Even more striking is the case of the Gospels of John Alexander (London, BL, Add. 39627), written in 1356, which has been shown to be directly dependent, as far as its illumination is concerned, on an eleventh-century Greek manuscript now in Paris (BnF, Grec 74).

This is partly to do with the prestige that Constantinople and its cultural traditions enjoyed among the Slavs, and also because it provided the model of Empire: John Alexander and his family are depicted in the Gospels in full Byzantine imperial regalia. Equally, however, Slavs and Greeks were working within the same tradition, and probably would not have recognized the dichotomy that modern scholarship has imposed upon them. It was possible, after all, for a Slavonic artist to illuminate a Greek manuscript: such is the case with London, BL, Add. 24376, a fourteenth-century Greek Gospel manuscript with four full-page miniatures which, to judge by their Slavonic inscriptions, are the work of a Slav. To this extent there was a single Orthodox Christian culture which transcended national or ethnic differences. This is not to say that it was uniform—nobody would mistake North Russian teratological ornament for Greek workmanship—but it did possess a certain wholeness which allowed for cultural transference either in particular instances, as in the major commissions just mentioned, or where there was immediate contact, in such cultural centres as the monasteries of Mount Athos. The essential point is that it was not a question of a single borrowing of Byzantine artistic models and techniques at the outset: the local traditions that developed from them developed not in isolation, but within the overarching framework of the Byzantine Commonwealth, and always with the possibility of refreshing their inspiration from the source.

Naturally, it was those books that were most frequently copied that developed the most regular decorative schemes. It is only the more richly decorated books of the four Gospels that have full-page minia-

Fig. 1.10.7 The Anikievo Gospel Book, early fifteenth century, Library of the Russian Academy of Sciences 34.7.3, ff. 92v-93r, miniature showing St Mark and the *incipit* of the Gospel of Mark, photo from Sarab'janov – Smirnova 2007, 457.

tures of the evangelists, each before his gospel, but almost all will begin each gospel with a large headpiece and very large initial, which may incorporate figurative elements (the initial Ꙁ at the beginning of St Mark's Gospel in particular invites the scribe to turn it into a serpent; fig. 1.10.7) or be entirely abstract; lesser components of the book (prefaces, lectionary tables and suchlike) will also have their headpieces, but smaller and less elaborate than those that introduce the gospels themselves. Other widely-used books had their own decorative norms, though the particular prestige attached to the Gospels (particularly those copies intended to be kept on the altar) meant that as a rule they tended to have more care and attention lavished on them than any others, even those which also had a liturgical function.

Conversely, secular books (which in any case constitute a minority of extant Slavonic manuscripts), being less prestigious, are by and large less extensively decorated, or in some cases not decorated at all. Certain works, such as the *Physiologus*, have subject-matter that encourages illustration, though this is by no means always of a high quality. Amongst secular works it was above all histories that attracted illustration of the heroes and events that they dealt with (though it was not an obligatory component and there are historical manuscripts in which the text is not illustrated at all); this is true both of general chronicles and individual works on historical themes such as the *Alexandriad.* Outstanding among these are the historical manuscripts commissioned by rulers, where the resources of high patronage are combined with the prestige generated by the patrons' consciousness of their own position in the flow of world events. Most famous among these are the Chronicle of Konstantinos Manassēs (Vatican City, BAV, Vat. slav. 2), another of John Alexander's manuscripts, and the colossal illustrated chronicle (*Licevoj svod*) written for Ivan the Terrible, which consists of ten very large volumes, now divided amongst three libraries, containing in all over 16,000 miniatures.

10.6. The scribe, the painter and the illuminator at work

10.6.1. Persons, places and methods

Among the Slavs, as among the Greeks, the production of books was not the prerogative of the monastic scriptoria that dominated scribal activity in Western Europe in the earlier Middle Ages. Although archaeologists have identified one building at the ninth-century monastery at Ravna, in eastern Bulgaria, as a 'scriptorium' (Popkonstantinov – Kostova 2010, 120), this is far from certain; and even if books were copied there, there is no basis for assuming the same sort of organization and regular administration that the word 'scriptorium' implies in a Western European context. The very high quality of some of the work, which is to be found wherever there was wealth and patronage, indicates the existence of a body of highly trained scribes who were available for major commissions, but we have no knowledge of who they were or where or how they were employed. The scribe of the Ostromir Gospels identifies himself only as the deacon Gregory, which presumably means that he was a member of the secular clergy, but there is no record of what else he may have done in this capacity, where he served, or of any other books that he wrote, though he was certainly an experienced scribe. Of the illuminators of this book we know even less; all that we can deduce is that they were Eastern Slavs, and that they too were experienced craftsmen. There are other cases where a book can be shown to be the work of a professional team of scribes working in a co-ordinated manner, which, again, implies the existence of scriptoria even as early as the twelfth century (see the analysis of Syn. 262 in the Historical Museum in Moscow by Uchanova 2008), but it is not at present possible to identify them with precise locations. Virtually all the major Slavonic manuscripts of the earlier period are isolated; only occasionally can one identify the same hand in more than one of them. All that one can safely deduce from this is that a large amount of material must have been lost. There is, moreover, other evidence which suggests that by no means all manuscripts were produced in such an organized manner in the early period. A man such as the scribe of the Bitola Triodion (Sofia, BAS, 38, twelfth century) who complains bitterly of the cold, even though he was writing in a monastery, was certainly not working in a room properly appointed for the production of books. He was not the only scribe to complain of his working conditions. It is possible to form only a very incomplete idea of the circumstances in which books were written in the earlier period from such random scraps of information.

It may be in part this absence of material that makes the attribution of manuscripts to particular centres—let alone to particular scriptoria—impossible until very late in the history of the Slavonic manuscript book. For the earlier period, in the absence of any explicit evidence in the books themselves, they can only be attributed regionally—and that on linguistic rather than palaeographic grounds. This is reflected in the traditional practices of manuscript description, which differ from those of Western Europe in that instead of the geographical origin which forms part of the summary data normally provided in a western description, the description of a Slavonic manuscript may specify the recension of Church Slavonic used (in Russia) or the orthographical system (in Serbia and Bulgaria).

However, our inability to identify the place of production of a manuscript with any precision is due not only to the gaps in our information, but also to the apparent absence of 'house styles' at many of the places where manuscripts were written. It is not abnormal to come across a manuscript clearly written at one time and in one place by a team of scribes who made no attempt to standardise their practice. Even individuals could be inconsistent. The manuscript Eton College 40 is a Gospel book in which the actual Gospels and their prefaces are written in Church Slavonic of the Serbian recension, but the lectionaries and other material that follow (which are written by the same scribe and begin on the fourth leaf of a quire) are written in the Bulgarian recension. The scribe had presumably copied the latter from a different antigraph, but what is noteworthy is that he evidently felt no need to impose any linguistic consistency.

It is only toward the end of the Middle Ages, in the sixteenth and seventeenth centuries, that we find centres of book production that are recognisable by their products, such as the Kirillo-Belozerskij Monastery in Russia, or Etropole and (even later) Adžar in Bulgaria. There are several factors operating here. One is, of course, the greater quantity of material that has survived from these later times, but another is the organization of production, where a permanent body of craftsmen—not just scribes, but binders and other persons involved in making books—were engaged in catering not only for the immediate needs of the monastery, but for the wider world as well. Although we do not have sufficient evidence to state positively that such centres had not existed previously, it does appear that a significant proportion of the books that were produced in the earlier period were written ad hoc, to satisfy the requirements of a particular church or monastery, or in response to the commission of a rich donor. This would certainly explain the predominance of the clergy amongst early scribes. (The majority of those who identify themselves give no information beyond their names, but those who do are almost invariably priests or monks.) Although not the only people who could read and write, they were the only ones who actually needed books in their daily lives, and might thus be impelled to write for themselves what they could not obtain by other means. This practice continued well into the eighteenth century, for printing, although by that time established in all the Slavonic countries except Bulgaria, was (depending on circumstances) commercially underdeveloped or a state monopoly, and thus not fully responsive to the laws of supply and demand. There was inadequate provision of certain types of printed book, which continued to be written by hand.

In the early period, people who wrote books usually wrote for the institutions that they served rather than for themselves personally, for the materials were expensive and the ordinary parish clergy are unlikely to have been able to afford them as their personal possessions, while monks have no personal property in principle. Even the great commissions by princes and other prominent individuals were frequently undertaken as donations to major churches and monasteries, although some were for personal use. This means that there was comparatively little trade in books: once a volume was given to the church or monastery, or received by the princely treasury, it was expected to stay there. There is also very little evidence indeed of payment to scribes. In the case of books intended to be used by the writer, the question would not arise, and monks would presumably not expect to be paid for their labours (though their monasteries might, if the books were not for their own use), and in those cases, such as expensive commissions, where it is likely that paid craftsmen were employed, the payment is not recorded in the books.

Fig. 1.10.8 *Codex Rilensis* 4/14, copied by Vladislav Grammaticus in 1456 (*Hexaemeron*), f. 1r, photograph courtesy of the abbot and the monks of the Monastery of St Ivan of Rila, Bulgaria, and the Virtual Library and Digital Archives of the Rila Monastery manuscript collection, Sofia University.

10.6.2. Colophons

Inscriptions regarding the sale and purchase of books become common only in the later period, when a plentiful supply of paper had made books more numerous and affordable. By this time it was common for a book to be purchased, rather than written, for a parish church, so that we find inscriptions such as this: 'This book of the Gospels was bought by the priest Petr Plešovskij and his wife Fenna for the village of Strojne for the remission of our sins and those of our children and of all departed Orthodox Christians. I bought it from Petr Hankuvskij and gave for it a cow and a bull, that was the price of the Gospels. … And I ask for God's sake that whoever shall celebrate using it shall not forget us sinners, and let him serve God in the church to which God shall send it. In the year of Our Lord 1697' (Budapest, OSZK, Fol. Eccl. Slav. 13, ff.5–24). This is informative in several respects. The village of Strojne is in the Subcarpathian oblast' of the Ukraine, which shows that in that region a manuscript written in the middle of the sixteenth century was still a working book 150 years later, for the inscription shows that it was expected to be used in the celebration of the Liturgy. Its price was still substantial, though it seems to have been comparable with prices for large printed books at that time; in 1724 the book was rebound for twelve Hungarian silver pennies (*máriások*). It is unclear (as always in such inscriptions) whether the donor purchased it himself and then presented it to the church, or whether he simply financed its acquisition. Quite exceptional is Father Petr's realism in asking to be commemorated wherever the book was used: usually these inscriptions end with an anathema against anyone who removes the book from the church to which it is given, though this, considering the manuscripts' present locations, was never effective.

Inscriptions such as these, which record events in a manuscript's history, are much more common than those which record its creation. It is customary for cataloguers to record dated manuscripts separately, and a survey of catalogues, despite the variety of the collections that they describe, reveals quite a consistent result: less than an eighth of the manuscripts are dated, and even fewer have anything that could properly be described as a colophon. When scribes' names appear, they are often in brief invocations of God or the saints to have mercy upon them, which say very little about the scribes, or the circumstances in which the book was written.

The formal colophon appears most frequently when the book was commissioned by some dignitary, and as a rule says much more about him than about the scribe. The earliest surviving colophon, that of the

Ostromir Gospels (1055–1057), is typical in this respect. Apart from this, there is no standard format for a colophon. It may mention the place for which the manuscript was written, if it was commissioned by an institution or by a donor for presentation. In an ecclesiastical context, the name of the relevant abbot or bishop may be mentioned, so also secular rulers. It follows that major commissions are more frequently provided with colophons than 'ordinary' manuscripts.

10.6.3. Dating systems

The date in a colophon is given *anno mundi* according to the Byzantine Era (in the seventeenth century sometimes also anno Domini); by and large the indiction is given as well. Occasionally, and particularly in later Serbian manuscripts, quite copious additional calendrical information, such as the lunar and solar cycles, the epact, etc., may be supplied. At the other extreme, the modern researcher may be frustrated by a scribe who gives the day and the month, but omits the year.

Usually only the date of completion of the manuscript is given, but sometimes also the date on which work began. The Ostromir Gospels is such a manuscript, begun on 21 October 6564, and finished on 12 May 6565. Though it is usually dated 1056–1057, this is based on the assumption that the year began in March, which would be most unusual in an ecclesiastical context (Ramazanova 2010). Assuming the normal practice of a September New Year, then this manuscript of 294 leaves, written in a fine uncial, was begun on 21 October 1055, and took eighteen and a half months to write. Since we have no idea of what other calls Gregory had on his time, this tells us very little about the actual time it took him to write the manuscript. However, it is clear that even a less ambitious book was a major labour, though this rarely finds expression in the formal colophon. Occasionally, however, scribes find it possible to address their readers less formally. A seventeenth-century Ukrainian scribe tells us: 'After the beginning comes the end. Glory to the Lord God, who has permitted me, the sinful priest Basil, to complete this book called Šestodnik [a variant of the *oktōēchos*] in the village of Labovo. As the hare rejoices when it has escaped from the stoat and lies safe in its forme licking its paws, so the poor scribe, when he finishes a book, would gladly drink to anyone who could be found to pay him for it' (Budapest, University Library, Cod. slav. 3, f. 271).

10.7. Bookbinding

Like other aspects of book production, the Slavs took over the technique of bookbinding from Byzantium. Like their Greek colleagues, Slavonic binders sewed the quires with the same thread that attached them to the boards, beginning by threading it through grooves on the boards, using a biaxial stitch disposition and finishing by joining the two halves of the book in the middle. The endbands, typically made of a two or more threads wound round a double core of tawed leather, were likewise attached to holes in the boards and sewn into each gathering, providing additional strength very necessary to hold a link-stitched binding together, and giving the book its characteristic appearance, with the length of the spine noticeably greater than that of the fore-edge. Since in such a binding the boards are attached before the text block is fully assembled and the pages can be trimmed, the binding is invariably flush with the pages. The boards would then be covered with leather—in the oldest examples completely undecorated—and might be provided with studs and bosses on the outer surfaces of both boards. Clasps, usually two in number, held the fore-edges together and helped to prevent the parchment from warping (though they continued to form part of the binding long after parchment had been replaced by paper).

In the thirteenth century, Russian binders adopted the sewing frame and began to sew the quires, generally, on tawed thongs, attaching the boards at the end of this process. Initially, however, this had no effect on the outward appearance of the book: bindings continued to be produced flush with the pages and with substantial endbands. It is only in the sixteenth century that we begin to see bindings wider than the text block in Russia, and even later in the Balkans, where binding techniques are consistently more conservative than those farther north. (For a more detailed discussion of Russian bindings, see Mokretsova 1995, and for Serbian, Janc 1974.)

Although the covers of the earliest surviving bindings (which are not numerous) are undecorated, from the fourteenth century blind-tooling becomes the usual technique of decorating the leather. This may take the form of a geometrical division of the surface into various patterns, or the use of small repeating stamps. The patterns created are often very similar to those on contemporary Greek bindings; since the tools used are both durable and portable, the potential for transmission from one place to another is high.

Later, larger tools with figurative depictions come into use, so that by the seventeenth century a typical Gospel book may have an upper cover with a medallion depicting the crucifixion in the middle and the four evangelists in the corners, and some decorative motifs in the intervening space; the lower cover would usually be less elaborately decorated. By this time, gilt tooling is also quite frequently encountered, and the extensive use of larger tools sometimes gives the bindings a somewhat congested appearance.

Although the tooling of the bindings might include images appropriate to the contents of the books they covered, or their actual names, it might also be purely decorative, and this allows a greater cross-cultural influence in the binding than in other aspects of the book. In the Balkans one may find Islamic elements in the bindings of Slavonic books, and very occasionally a binding that is entirely oriental in character, though this is so infrequent that it probably means that the book in question was entrusted to a Turkish binder and does not indicate a wholesale adoption of oriental techniques by Christian craftsmen. Similarly, 'hybrid' bindings combining Russian and Western European practices were sometimes produced in the Grand Duchy of Lithuania.

The usual material used for covering books was leather. The use of metal—usually brass—studs and bosses has already been mentioned, and these may have been both functional, protecting the books when they were stacked horizontally, and decorative. In later bindings these metal fittings may include plates with various designs—again, one most frequently sees a central crucifixion and corner-pieces with the evangelists. These are, of course, intended for the adornment of a book which was held in honour. In the most luxurious bindings, leather may be abandoned altogether, and other materials, usually expensive cloths or precious metals, used instead. Examples are rare: cloth was not durable, and precious metals were not only expensive to begin with, so that they were not often used, but also liable to be despoiled at moments of crisis. The Gospels of John Alexander, for example, originally had a metal binding: the colophon states that the Tsar had it bound with 'golden plates', and this is confirmed by the numerous nail-holes in the boards, which are now covered in red leather. A roughly contemporary binding that does survive is that of the Gospels of Simeon the Proud (Moscow, RGB, ф.304/III, №1), which is dated 1344. It is of silver, with chased decoration of floral and foliar motifs, and has attached to it further silver plates (both chased and niello) depicting the crucifixion, apostles, cherubim, etc. This type of cover also has Byzantine antecedents, and there were definite contacts between Moscow and Constantinople in this area of work: the Altar Gospels of the Cathedral of the Dormition, which is a Russian manuscript, has a gold cover decorated with chased figures, filigree and precious stones made by Greek craftsmen working in Moscow in the first half of the fifteenth century (Sterligova 2013, 150–156). This obviously represents the extreme of luxury in the bookbinder's art; but even so, it exemplifies the close relationship between the Slavonic and the Byzantine book, which manifests itself consistently at all levels of book production.

References

Bogdanović 1978; Daskalova – Rajkova 2005; Du Feu – Simmons 1970; Džurova 1997; Franklin 2002; Hristova et al. 2003–2004; Ivanova-Mavrodinova – Džurova 1981; Janc 1974; Keenan 1971; Kireeva 1997; Leroy [Julien] 1976; Lichačev [N.] 1891, 1899, 1994; MacRobert 2002; Maniaci 1999a, 1999b; Mefod'eva 2009; Mokretsova 1995; Morozov 1994; Mošin – Traljić 1957; Musakova 1996; Petrova – Sadovskaja 2009; Popkonstantinov – Kostova 2010; Ramazanova 2010; Sarab'janov – Smirnova 2007; Ščepkin 1903; Simoni 1903, 1906; Sterligova 2013; Tromonin – Klepikov 1844; Uchanova 2008; Zagrebin – Levšina 2009.

11. Syriac codicology (PGB–FBC–EBW)*

11.1. Materials and tools (PGB–FBC)

11.1.1. Papyrus

Syriac papyri are relatively rare and have come down to us only in a fragmentary condition (on papyri and all other materials, see Briquel-Chatonnet forthcoming). They are kept in various European libraries, in Berlin, Florence, Oslo, Oxford, and Vienna, having been collected from the end of the nineteenth century until the end of the twentieth (for a list, see Brashear 1998, 91 n. 24; updated by Butts 2011). The known surviving fragments—all apparently parts of codices—mostly originate from Egypt (from the monastery of St Catherine on Mount Sinai, and recently from Dayr al-Suryān (Bigoul El-Souriany – Van Rompay 2001), as well as from Kellis in the Dakhleh Oasis), but some were also discovered in Palestine (Khirbet Mird) in 1953; a single fragment kept in Berlin may be of Persian origin. As for the dating, where possible scholars resort to the archaeological context, as in the case of some fragments discovered in Syria, dating back to the second century CE; but in the great majority of cases, dating depends only on palaeographic criteria, according to which most Syriac papyri date from the sixth to the tenth centuries (Sauget 1985). The texts are of religious content, sometimes quoting, or paraphrasing, passages from the Bible. The content of the Kellis papyri is Manichaean (Franzmann – Gardner 1996; Franzmann 1999), and it is not clear if they derive from one codex or from several codices.

11.1.2. Parchment

Several parchment fragments containing private writings and legal documents dating back to the third century CE were found in the 1930s at Dura Europos in eastern Syria. Of particular interest are two fragments studied and published by Teixidor (1990) and subsequently examined by Brock (1991a). The first of them, measuring 200 × 125 mm, bears traces of bending, pricking and seaming at the top, short edge. The content is legal, and the text, written on both the flesh and hair sides, is dated to 552 of the Seleucid Era (239/240 CE). The second fragment, measuring 250 × 150–160 mm and damaged, is an attestation of a sale of land and property. The informal cursive script is extremely difficult to read, but the text is dated to the fifth year of the reign of Emperor Gordian (242).

The oldest extant Syriac manuscript books are written on parchment, such as the oldest dated Syriac manuscript, London, BL, Add. 12150, dated 411. Specific studies on parchment used for Syriac manuscripts do not exist; scholars usually refer to the Coptic and/or Greek use of this material as a suitable and reasonable parallel (see for instance Meščerskaja 1987, 109–110). With the introduction of paper in the tenth century, the use of expensive parchment gradually decreased, being in the end restricted to texts of particular value and sometimes decorated and illustrated, such as Bibles and lectionaries. The most recent dated Syriac manuscript on parchment was written in the Near East (perhaps in Ṭūr ʿAbdīn) in 1567/1568 (Hatch 1946, 6, pl. 94: Berlin, Staatsbibliothek, Cod. Syr. 20 (Sachau 236)) and contains the *Ḥudrā*, hymns for the celebrations of the whole year. Already in the thirteenth century the use of paper had come to predominate. In the collection of dated Syriac manuscripts compiled by Hatch (1946, 6), among sixteen manuscripts written in the twelfth century, eleven are on parchment; but among the twenty-seven of the thirteenth century, only nine are on parchment. Two thirteenth-century parchment manuscripts deserve to be mentioned: both are large-size New Testament lectionaries, related to the monastery of Mor Hnanio (Dayr al-Zaʿfarān) and Mardin, both written by Bishop Theodore Dioscorus (Leroy [Jules] 1964, 371–389, pls 127–140). In more recent times (early seventeenth century), parchment was used in Rome to copy a Syriac manuscript: Florence, BML, Or. 47 (Eusebius of Caesarea's *Letter to Carpian*, the Eusebian Canons, two *Genealogies* of Christ, and the *Doctrina Theophili*); copied by Rabban Adam, an envoy of the Nestorian patriarch, active in Rome from 1610 to 1614.

Palimpsests are numerous in the Syriac tradition (Schmidt [A.] 2009) and are an invaluable source of information because they preserve texts otherwise lost. Among the more important palimpsest manuscripts is the so-called *Codex Sinaiticus Syriacus* (Monastery of St Catherine), which dates back to the fourth century, containing the oldest extant copy of the Syriac Gospels according to the *Vetus Syra* translation, over which lives of saints and martyrs were copied in the eighth century (Bensly et al. 1894). Syriac palimpsests are interesting in a comparative perspective because they are evidence of contacts with other

* The authors are grateful to Margherita Farina for her help in collecting material for the preparation of this chapter.

traditions of eastern Christianity; often the upper and lower layers are both in Syriac, but there are several cases in which the languages of the layers differ and the Syriac text is superimposed over Greek (for example, London, BL, Add. 17210; Add. 17211; Add. 14665; in St. Petersburg, RNB, Gr. no. CXIX, the opposite occurs), over Coptic (London, BL, Add. 14631; Add. 17183; Add. 14665), over Arabic (London, BL, Add. 17138), or over Latin (London, BL, Add. 17212). Recently (in 2003) a Greek fragment of Menander has been identified in palimpsest leaves of a Syriac manuscript in the Vatican Library (Vat. sir. 623, dated 886; van Lantschoot 1965, 151–153).

The oldest dated Syriac palimpsest, in which both texts are in Syriac, is also the oldest dated Syriac biblical manuscript. The upper text, a liturgy for major holidays, is written in western tenth-century *serṭā*, the lower layer being Isaiah in the Peshitta version, in *ʾesṭrangēlā*: the lower text on one of the leaves is dated to 459/460 (London, BL, Add. 14512; Tisserant 1911; Hatch 1946, 5).

Other important palimpsests preserve otherwise lost biblical translations and also secular texts. This is the case with the eleventh-century Melkite liturgical text copied over a Syriac translation from Greek of Galen's *De simplicium medicamentorum temperamentis et facultatibus*, probably by Sergius of Reš ʿayna, dating perhaps from the ninth century.

Also double palimpsests exist, containing three layers of text, sometimes in different languages. Specimens are in London, BL, Add. 17212; Add. 17136; Add. 14665.

11.1.3. Paper

Scholars have not paid particular attention to the paper used for Syriac manuscripts. The only contribution that contains a systematic study in this field is by Nina Pigulevskaja (1960, 154–156; see also Meščerskaja 1987).

The oldest Syriac manuscript on paper is a dated copy of the *Book of the Ḥimyarites* finished in April 932, transcribed in Qaryatēn (published by Moberg 1924).

The Syriac manuscripts produced in the Near East, the Levant, and, to some extent, in the Byzantine area, are written on paper that does not differ from that used for Islamic manuscripts.

From the fifteenth century onwards, watermarked paper produced in Italy begins to be attested in Syriac manuscripts. Comprehensive studies on the watermarks of Syriac manuscripts are nearly absent. Information about watermarks can be found in the catalogues, but in general without illustrations and almost always limited to brief descriptions.

The main reference for watermarks is even now the catalogue by Pigulevskaja (1960). According to her research, mainly on manuscripts preserved in Russia, above all in St Petersburg, watermarks in Syriac manuscripts from the late fifteenth century onwards point for the most part to paper of Italian, in many cases Venetian, production. The most frequently represented watermarks are: (1) an anchor in a circle (possibly topped with a trefoil, as in the case of Venetian paper of the late sixteenth century; in older paper, the anchor is topped by a star and a cross); (2) a crown topped by a star (Italian); (3) a pot with handle (French); (4) crescent moon, in two variants: (4a) three crescents (the so-called *tre lune* paper, produced in Italy for the Levant in the seventeenth and eighteenth centuries; this variously imitated and forged watermark can also be found at the beginning of the nineteenth century); and (4b) a single crescent (western France).

Syriac manuscripts produced in Italy in the late sixteenth and early seventeenth centuries, preserved mainly in Florence and Rome, show a wide sampling of well documented watermarks, including for example: (5) anchor ending in a ring, in a circle surmounted by star; (6) five-pointed crown, possibly topped by a star, a cross or a monogram M; (7) M monogram topped by a star in a coat of arms; (8) monogram F over three hills in a shield.

11.1.4. Other writing supports

Nothing is known about the use of any wax tablets in the Syriac tradition. As for wooden tablets, one single example is attested: Manichaean Syriac-Coptic glossaries are written on two wooden tablets of the fourth century found in Egypt, Dakhleh Oasis (Franzmann – Gardner 1996, 101–126).

Syriac *ostraca* were found in Mesopotamia (Kamil 1957; Hunter 1998) and Central Asia, in the old Sogdian city of Panjakent, now in Tajikistan (Pajkova – Maršak 1976; Pajkova 1979). The *ostraca* from Mesopotamia are dated from the fourth to the seventh centuries; Panjakent's *ostracon* is dated on 'archaeological, historical and palaeographical' grounds to the late seventh or early eighth century. The text reproduces some lines of two Psalms; some features of its spelling allow one to suppose that the piece was written as a school exercise by a Sogdian copyist with imperfect practice with the Syriac script.

11.1.5. Inks

Various recipes (see (Desreumaux forthcoming; Daccache – Desreumaux forthcoming) for the preparation of ink (Syriac *dyawtā* or *ḥebrā*, or *mayyā da-ḥrātā* 'water of vitriol') are handed down in annotations on Syriac manuscripts. The ink is usually a compound of gall nut (*ʿapṣā*) with the addition of vitriol (ferrous sulphate; Arabic/Syriac *zāk*), water and gum arabic (*ṣamgā ʿarabiyyā*) as a thickener (cf. the recipes in Wright 1870–1872, II, 580–581, London, BL, Add. 14632, two recipes in Syriac by two different hands; according to the first, which refers to the way the 'Egyptian fathers, who live in the desert of Scetis' prepare their ink, the bark of a desert plant (Arabic *arṭay*) may be used instead of gall nuts, and wine and vinegar are also employed as an additional tannic element; Wright 1870–1872, III, 1085, London, BL, Add. 14644, a recipe in Arabic and *garšūnī*, probably from the ninth century (Briquel-Chatonnet et al. 2006); Wright 1870–1872, III, 1207, London, BL, Arund. Or. 53; Wright 1870–1872, III, x–xi). Soot (Syriac *samāmā*) was also used (Land 1862, 58; Hatch 1946, 11).

11.1.6. Pigments and dyes

In a Syriac context, Ephrem the Syrian (d.373) seems to evoke the practice of dyeing parchment purple (*Parainesis* 48: *chartokokkina ergazē? Analogisai tous lōrotomous*, 'Do you make coloured parchment? You are like a leather worker'). However, no Syriac parchments of this type are preserved, nor are they mentioned by other sources.

Recipes for silver and golden inks are found in treatises on alchemy/chemistry, in Syriac or Arabic *garšūnī* (Berthelot 1893, 203–205). Chrysography is documented by literary sources and by some splendid manuscripts (e.g. fig. 1.11.1). We know, for instance, of John of Mardin (d.1165), who wrote 'four Gospels in gold and silver' (Assemani 1721, 225), and of the Syriac-Orthodox patriarch Michael (1126–1199), who 'did take care of the copy of a magnificent Gospel book written in gold and silver, and adorned with pictures; its cover was on both sides decorated with silver and gold' (*Anonymi auctoris chronicon ad annum Christi 1234 pertinens*, ed. J.-B. Chabot 1954, 314–315). Specimens of such luxury Gospels dated to the twelfth and thirteenth centuries still exist (see Ch. 1 § 11.5.2); chrysography was adopted for writing certain passages to be read on the most important holidays of the liturgical calendar.

However, a single East Syriac witness to a different use of chrysography, MS Vatican City, BAV, Vat. sir. 622, is a small book (180 × 130 mm) in which the four Gospels are written in golden ink on paper that was dyed blue. According to the colophon, it was finished in March 1298 for 'Sarah ... sister of ... George ... king of the Öngayyē'. This information refers to a Central Asiatic region (today Inner Mongolia), inhabited in the thirteenth and fourteenth centuries by Turkic people called Önggüd. This unique example of Syriac chrysography could thus originate from Mongolia; but the location of the discovery (Diyarbakır), and other clues, does not exclude the possibility that the manuscript was produced in North Mesopotamia (Borbone 2003).

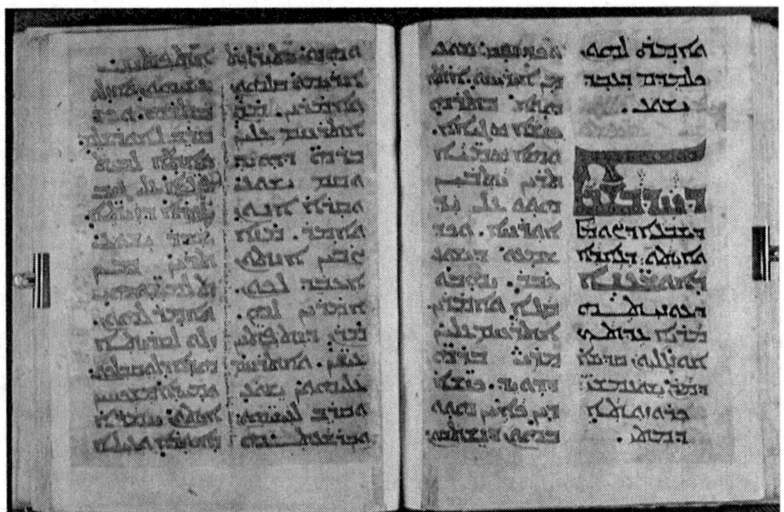

Fig. 1.11.1 London, BL, Rich. 7174, dated 1499, Four Gospels, ff. 94v-95r.

There are no written sources about the use of colours and pigments in the Syriac manuscript tradition. Observations confirm the use of red lead (*siriqōn*) in rubrications and decoration (see below). Yellow, green, purple, pink, black and brown are also widely used, but blue only very seldom.

On the occasion of preservation measures undertaken on a lectionary (London, BL, Add.

7170, paper, about 1220), some archaeometric analyses of the pigments were carried out (Clark – Gibbs 1998). The manuscript contains sixty miniatures, most of them seriously deteriorated. The damage affected in the first place the surfaces covered with white pigment, which turned black (Leroy [Jules] 1964, pl. 82:1, 83:1, 3), but also the ink that was used for a large part of the text had corroded the paper. The analysis revealed the presence of the following pigments: red–vermilion (mercury sulphide), which was also found in red ink; blue–lazurite (extract of lapis lazuli); yellow–orpiment; orange-yellow–realgar and para-realgar (the latter extremely rarely used); white–lead sulphite, in its pure form, and mixed with red, blue, purple and brown (the black compound, causing deterioration of the miniatures, was identified as lead carbonate).

11.1.7. Writing instruments

Information about the writing instruments used by Syrian copyists has been collected on the basis of some notes preserved in Syriac manuscripts (Duval 1881, 2–3; Hatch 1946, 23–24; Wright 1870–1872, III, xxvi; Land 1862, 56–58). The Syrian copyists used both the quill and the reed pen. The earliest mention of the former (*ʾebrā d-pāraḥtā*) is found in a manuscript dated 509 (London, BL, Add. 14542, f. 93v); a reference to the same instrument occurs in a marginal note in London, BL, Add. 17185, f. 61r: *nusāyā d-ḥeṣrā d-gelpānā* 'quill test'. Land and Duval assume that the oldest Syriac manuscripts were written with quill pens. Wright suggests that Syriac references to quill pens are merely repetitions of Greek formulas, because in his opinion the Syriac copyists wrote only with reed pens. According to Land, the reed pen (*qanyā*) was not used before the twelfth century, but Hatch puts the date as early as the tenth or the eleventh century, referring to information in London, BL, Add. 17128, f. 180v. In any case, the reed pen was apparently known in Syria, as written evidence indicates: Isaac of Antioch, in the fifth century, speaks of the 'Spirit's reed' (*qanyā d-ruḥā*), and in the ninth century, Thomas of Marga, the abbot of the monastery of Beth ʿAbe, describes a vision of a reed writing on the wall of his cell. The reed pen was already well known to Jews, Greeks, Copts, and Arabs. Some manuscripts from Central Asia and China could have been written with a brush, as was certainly the case for the Syro-Turkic inscriptions found in Inner Mongolia, Hohhot, in the 'White Pagoda' (Borbone 2013); cf. the bifolium in Dunhuang, Historical Museum, Mogao Ku B 53:14, and the fragment from Qara Qoto no. 123 (Yoshida – Chimeddorji 2008, 9; Muto 2013).

11.2. Book forms (PGB–FBC)

11.2.1. The roll and the rotulus

No horizontal rolls are known in the Syriac book tradition. The vertical roll form (also called 'rotulus') is not attested at the beginning of the Syriac book tradition, but it was adopted for certain uses later on, after the codex was already in general use. Thus there are large liturgical vertical rolls, mainly in the Melkite tradition, and small ones containing magical texts and charms. The oldest Syriac magical rolls date back to sixth or seventh century (Gignoux 1987), but most of them are quite recent (eighteenth and nineteenth centuries) and of East Syriac provenance (as is the case of the rolls kept at Harvard and at Oxford (Goshen-Gottstein 1979; Hunter 1999, 161–172)). For both categories, both parchment and paper were used. Among the liturgical rolls, particular mention deserves to be made of the Liturgy of St John Chrysostom (Moscow, Institut Vostokovedenija, Lichačev S. II, n. 3), and among magical rolls, Yerevan, Matenadaran, Collection of Manuscripts in Foreign Languages, 72 (a, b) (Meščerskaja 1987), and Avignon, Bibliothèque municipale Ceccano, 3858 (Lebanon, sixteenth century (Desreumaux – Gorea 2003), B16-17).

11.2.3. The codex

In Syriac, various terms indicate the codex and its parts. The codex is called *ṣḥāḥā*; the quire *kūrrāsā*; a single leaf *dappā* (the word also means 'board', 'tablet', and then 'wooden altar/mensa'); two opposite pages of a book when it is open *ptāḥā* 'opening' (Wright 1870–1872, III, xxvi; Hatch 1946, 23–24).

11.3. The making of the codex (PGB–FBC)

The structure of the quires in Syriac books is remarkably uniform and stable over time, for all geographical areas in which Syriac manuscripts were produced. They are mainly composed of quinions, both of parchment and of paper (Mundell Mango 1991; Briquel-Chatonnet 1998b). The quires were made by stacking individual bifolia (usually five) and not by folding a sheet twice the size of a bifolium (or larger).

Syriac parchment books do not follow Gregory's Rule. Throughout the entire chronological span of production of Syriac manuscripts, small variations in the composition of the quires are documented: quaternions and senions are found. For example, the first two quires of Paris, BnF, Syriaque 27 (699, parchment) are quaternions; Florence, BML, Or. 230 (1278, paper) is composed of 21 quinions, two senions and two quaternions. Manuscripts produced in Rome from the sixteenth century onwards are still composed of quinions, such as Florence, BML, Or. 2 and 3 (1606, respectively 39 and 27 quires, all quinions), but also of quaternions (for example, Florence, BML, Or. 4, of 1610/1611: 40 quires, 38 of which are quaternions, one a quinion and one a ternion).

A unique example of a Syriac manuscript written in the form of a Chinese book is Manchester, John Rylands Library, Syriac 4 (Peshitta Institute shelfmark: 18-8dt1; Coakley 1993, 120–123): it contains parts of the Old Testament Peshitta, copied not long before 1725 by a Chinese copyist, reproducing the Syriac script 'stroke for stroke so as to produce an exact facsimile' of a much older manuscript. Its leaves are folded, in Chinese fashion, at the fore-edge and are written only on the outer sides. Binding is by a cord through four stab-holes. The copyist reproduced also the quire numbers and their simple decoration, although they are unnecessary in this book form.

11.3.1. Pricking and ruling

Pricking is found applied in parchment manuscripts. Most frequently, the pricking is made at the four corners of the writing area, which may be laid out in two or three columns. Ruling is most frequently used only for the vertical bounding lines, and sometimes also for the top margin, or both top and bottom. Ruling is made by means of a sharply pointed instrument for parchment, with a blunt point or a plummet being used for paper and sometimes also for parchment. The leaves of very few manuscripts were ruled with ink. Only from the twelfth century onwards was ruling used also for the lines. For dated examples of pricking and ruling, see Mundell Mango 1991. The ruling board, called in Arabic *misṭara*, was also used by Syrian copyists; examples date from as far back as the thirteenth century until modern time.

11.3.2. Ordering systems

Quire signatures

Numbering of quires is standard in Syriac books. The numbers are written on the first and the last page of each quire, in the bottom margin. A quire number in the upper margin never occurs, nor do bifolium signatures. Very often, the first quire of a book bears no number at the beginning, because the recto of the first leaf is left blank; in Syriac manuscripts, the text usually begins on the verso of the first leaf. In some of the oldest manuscripts (for example, Paris, BnF, Syriaque 341 (eighth century?)), the quire numbering is a later addition. In some old manuscripts, the quire numbers are placed only at the beginning of a quire, in the bottom inner margin, as in Florence, BML, plut. 1.56 (Rabbula Gospels, 586), where the numbers are Syriac arithmetic numerals (for a list of such figures, see Land 1862, pl. 25, and Duval 1881, xv (pl. 3)), above which Syriac letters with the corresponding numeric values are written. This method is the most ancient device used for numbering quires. Over time, the use of letters with their numerical values completely supersedes the use of Syriac numerals, which are not found after the ninth century (Brock 2010a). At the same time, numbering both the beginning and the end of a quire becomes standard practice, with placement of the number at the centre of the bottom margin. Sometimes Armenian, Greek and Coptic letters are employed as quire numbers (Wright 1870–1872, III, xxvi; see also Hatch 1946, 23). Occasionally the quire numbers were written vertically (for example, Jerusalem, NLI, Or. 63 (tenth century?), f. 42v).

The script used for quire numbers very often changes, by the alternating use of different Syriac scripts, *serṭā* and *'esṭrangēlā*. But exceptions do occur: for instance, London, BL, Add. 14548 (790), f. 33r, beginning of the fourth quire, shows the numeral $d = 4$, in *'esṭrangēlā* script, written twice in the lower margin, once at the centre, and again to the right, the latter numeral being more prominently decorated (Tisserant 1914, xxiv and 28).

Headings, or running titles, are seldom used, but they appear already in the oldest manuscripts, such as the Rabbula Gospels, where they are written in red in the top margin of the verso of the fifth leaf (i.e. at the central opening of a quinion). In other cases, as in Florence, BML, Or. 230 (Bar ʿEbroyo's *'Awṣar rōzē*, 1278), the rubricated headings are written in the top margin of all leaves on the recto. In this case they serve the needs of the reader, and were perhaps added after the copyist finished his work, either by him or by owners/users of the book.

Catchwords

The use of catchwords is not attested in older manuscripts; apparently, it first appears in sixteenth-century manuscripts copied in Europe (for example, Florence, BML, Or. 3, Or. 10, Or. 183, Or. 195 (written in 1585 by Moses of Ṣawro/of Mardin)). The catchwords are placed horizontally or obliquely, upwards or downwards, under the last text line, on the verso in the lower margin on the left side of the page, referring to the first word written on the facing recto (fig. 1.11.2). Some practices should be seen as the idiosyncratic initiative of the copyist, for example Moses of Ṣawro, who writes catchwords vertically (Florence, BML, Or. 185; Vatican City, BAV, Borg. sir. 60; also in Arabic manuscripts copied by Moses: see Vatican City, BAV, Vat. ar. 83). Later on, especially in manuscripts of the East Syriac tradition, the use of catchwords becomes quite frequent (see Vatican City, BAV, Vat. sir. 653 (1820), and Vat. sir. 283 (nineteenth century?)).

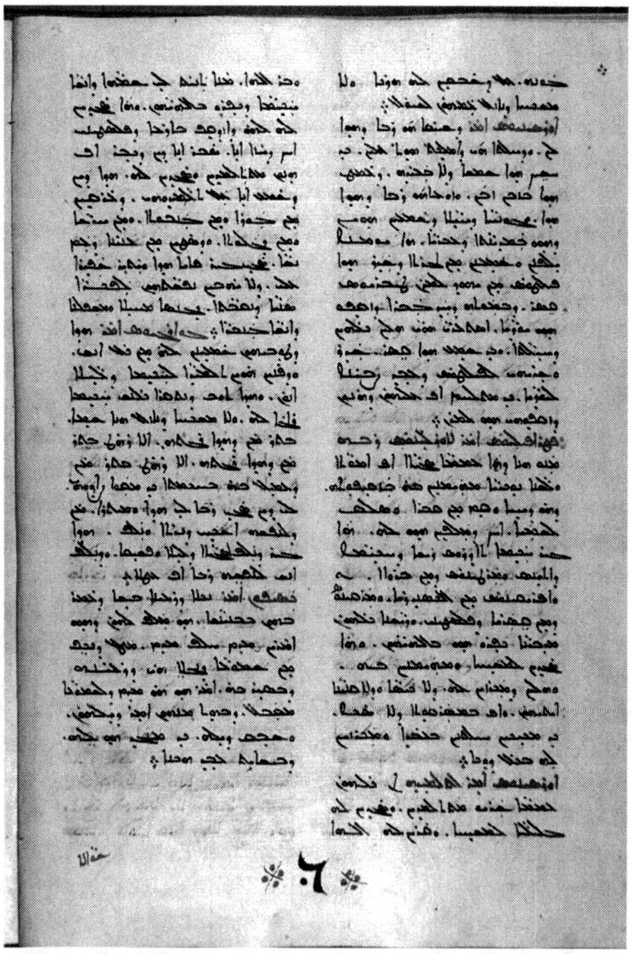

Fig. 1.11.2 Charfet, Bibliothèque patriarchale syro-catholique, Rahmani 79, 1901, f. 40v, courtesy of Bibliothèque patriarcale syro-catholique, Charfet, Lebanon.

Foliation, pagination, column numbering

Foliation began to be used quite late (for example, in the 'Williams Manuscript', written in 1471 in Hasankeyf: Hall 1886; now New York, Utica Public Library, 13501), where leaf numbers in Syriac letters are written in the top margin, perhaps added later), and never developed into pagination, except in very recent manuscripts. Complete foliation is often found in the frequently consulted manuscripts, such as those used in liturgy or in scholarly work, and was added by readers (for example, Florence, BML, Or. 230, finished in 1278, paginated with Arabic numerals in the sixteenth century by its owner, Patriarch Naʿmatallah (d.1587), who also wrote a table of contents on the recto of the first leaf, which had as usual been left blank).

A sign, which we may call the 'quadruple-dots mark', is commonly placed on the verso of each leaf, in the right-hand corner of the top margin, at the level of the first text line (fig. 1.11.2). Its form differs in the West Syriac and East Syriac traditions. Since the colour of the mark usually corresponds to the colour of the first words in the first text line, one may suggest that the mark was written by the copyist when making the copy. In the West Syriac tradition, the mark consists of four dots arranged in a lozenge. In the East Syriac tradition, the three upper dots of the lozenge are separated by a serpentine stroke; this element reveals that the marker is a stylized abbreviation of the divine name, ܝܗ. (*yh*). The marker could also have a practical secondary function, namely the identification of the tops of the bifolia. Such a hypothesis would assume that the copyists wrote on quires that were already made up, but not yet sewn. The 'quadruple-dots mark' does not occur in all the Syriac manuscripts: some bear it only desultorily, in others it is entirely absent. It is found in the eighth century in London, BL, Add. 17170 (774/775), but it is absent in some seventh-century manuscripts (for example, Vatican City, BAV, Vat. sir. 111 (522), 110 and 114 (523), 112 (551), 113, (552); Florence, BML, plut. 1.56 (586)). Later on, this practice becomes widespread, but still there are recent manuscripts that are free of the mark, or nearly so (for example, Vatican City, BAV, Vat. sir. 165 (1663)). The fact that at times the 'quadruple-dot-mark' is written also on the recto, in the same position, and that in some manuscripts written in three columns per page it appears at the beginning of each column (as is the case in portions of Milan, Biblioteca Ambrosiana, B 21 inf., seventh century) could suggest that it marks the beginning of a new work, as a kind of *basmala*.

11.4. The layout of the page (PGB–FBC)

The Syriac written tradition about book production is scant: we are able to mention only one reference to a book format. Patriarch Timothy I (780–823) mentions a 'Nisibene format' (*mšuḥtā nṣībaytā*) when asking for a copy of the Syro-Hexapla (Berti 2009, 293). This format seems related to a book produced for use in the school, like that of Nisibis, or for scholarly use.

The common large format of Syriac parchment manuscripts is *c.*360 × 280 mm, which is the size of the oldest dated manuscript and the standard format for Gospel manuscripts of the sixth to eighth centuries. Only three dated parchment manuscripts copied before the twelfth century survive that are larger than this format: Dublin, Chester Beatty Library, Syr. 701: East Syriac *Ṭeksē* (*d-qaššišā*), a liturgical book dated 719/720, measuring about 430 × 320 mm; Jerusalem, St Mark's Monastery, cod. 25, *c.*440 × 300 mm; London, BL, Add. 12165, dated 1015, 410 × 300 mm (festal and other discourses by various authors). Such very large size parchment books of over 400 × 300 mm reappear later, mostly as Gospel lectionaries measuring *c.*420/450 × 320/350 mm. In these luxury examples made for liturgical use and public display, the easily readable, large and sometimes decorated *ʾesṭrangēlā* script is combined with chrysography (see above). All these books pertain to the Syriac-Orthodox milieu. One lectionary, dated 1227, is still in the region of Ṭūr ʿAbdīn (reproduced in Brock et al. 2001, 184; Leroy [Jules] 1964, 411–413, pls 149, 1–3; and Hunt 2001). The most recent dated Syriac manuscript on parchment, Berlin, Staatsbibliothek, Sachau 236 (1567/1568), is also one of the largest, measuring 440 × 320 mm; it is a liturgical book executed in a Syriac–Orthodox milieu. The use of very large Gospel lectionaries, lavishly decorated and partly chrysographic, was popular also in the Church of the East; some such books are preserved, dating back to the sixteenth to eighteenth centuries. They are often labelled as 'Gospel lectionary for the Sundays and the Holidays according to the ritual of Mosul'. They are written on paper, and their size is in some cases even larger than that of the Syriac-Orthodox lectionaries: Vatican City, BAV, Borg. sir. 169, sixteenth century (Leroy [Jules] 1964, 404–408, pl. 145), is 570 × 385 mm; eleven similar manuscripts are listed by Leroy [Jules] 1964, 406, as preserved in Tell Kef, Alqoš, Rabban Hormizd, Notre-Dame des Semences, Aqra. One of them, in the church of Tell Kef, is described by Foumia 2013, 68.

Among a group of 354 Syriac manuscripts on parchment and paper, dated from the fifth to the sixteenth centuries, the majority (291) measure between about 200 × 130 mm to about 280 × 200 mm. As for the proportions, a 'narrow' format, characterized by a width slightly more than half the height, seems to be typical of the Mosul region (Barṭelli, Bet Ḫudaida (Qaraqosh)) in the thirteenth century (see Florence, BML, Or. 208, 220 × 120 mm; Or. 230, 210 × 120 mm; Dublin, Trinity College, MS 1504, 240 × 160 mm; Cambridge, University Library, Add. 2003, 232 × 122 mm).

Besides the East Syriac Gospel lectionaries already mentioned, and the manuscripts Oxford, Bodleian Library, MS Huntington 1 (about 540 × 350 mm), and Diyarbakır, Meryem Ana Syriac Orthodox Church 1/1 (475 × 305 mm), the largest manuscripts on paper are those written in Europe (Rome) in the sixteenth and seventeenth centuries (for example, Florence, BML, Or. 2 and 3 (1606; Bar Bahluls' *Dictionary*), 420 × 275 mm; Or. 4 (1610/1611, Syriac New Testament with *garšūnī* Arabic translation), 420 × 290 mm). The standard size of the paper accessible in Rome, and the type of text, influenced the choice for these manuscripts of large *in folio* format.

Few dated small-size manuscripts (less than 150 × 110 mm) are preserved, the oldest dating back to 883/884 (London, BL, Add. 18819, 135 × 96 mm). Two others of about the same size, probably from the ninth century, are preserved in Paris, Bibliothèque nationale de France (Briquel-Chatonnet 1997 (manuscripts 389 B 7 and B 3)). In most cases, such small formats do not antedate the eleventh century. The very small (105 × 70 mm) format of a breviary in Florence (BML, Or. 436, written in 1554/1555 in Rome by the Maronite Bishop Šimʿun) suits a type of book meant for private use quite well.

11.5. Text structure and readability (PGB–FBC–EBW)

11.5.1. Writing (PGB–FBC)

The oldest dated Syriac manuscript having the text in a single column was written in Mabbug in 510/511 (Hatch 1946, pl. 8). Previously, layouts in three or two columns were used. The three-column layout fell out of use and after the seventh century is found only very rarely (Vatican City, BAV, Vat. sir. 177, twelfth or thirteenth century; London, BL, Add. 21580, 1478). Some very rare examples of four-column layout exist: Diyarbakır, Meryem Ana Syriac Orthodox Church 1/1 (miscellaneous: Bar ʿEbroyo's scholia, Old

Testament and New Testament, Clement's *Octateuch*, 1496), and Oxford, Bodleian Library, MS Huntington 1 (a collection of works by Bar 'Ebroyo, 1491); these two manuscripts are among the largest Syriac paper books, and it is striking that they were both produced in the 1490s, probably in the same region. The two-column layout is the standard for the large Four Gospels books of the sixth and seventh centuries. In some cases, the number of columns changes in the book, but such examples are quite rare (see Hatch 1946, 14; for example, London, BL, Add. 12151 (804) and Add. 21580 (1478)). The number of columns may change on a single page: in Florence, BML, Or. 298 (*Liber causae causarum*, ff. 105r–139r), in a text plainly copied in two columns, two pages are irregular, f. 105v (half of the page in one column, the rest in two) and f. 107r (a third of the page in one column, the second third in two columns, and the last third again in a single column).

Generally the text begins on the verso of the first leaf, the recto being left blank; at times, f. 1r is now filled with ownership notes, prayers, *probationes calami* and other notes of various kinds. A 'frontispiece' does not occur in Syriac books, where the work's title (and author) is mentioned among customary formulaic *incipits*. The text typology affects the structure and the layout of the page. Bilingual texts are written in two columns (for example, Florence, BML, Or. 86 (1278, Syriac translation by Bar 'Ebroyo of Avicenna's *Kitāb al-išārāt wa 'l-tanbīhāt*), where the Arabic text runs parallel in a column next to the Syriac version). An interesting case is the copy of Bar 'Ebroyo's *Metrical Grammar* in Florence, BML, Or. 298 (1360), where the main poetic text is written in the centre of the page, leaving wide margins for the author's scholia (in later manuscripts, the *Metrical Grammar* is copied in two neat and parallel columns). The antigraph was probably the author's copy, which the copyist decided to reproduce as faithfully as possible also in its layout. Melkisedeq of Hasankeyf had the same aim when he made a copy of a manuscript of the *Divisions of Porphyry's Isagoge* (copied by Moses of Ṣawro in 1585 and preserved in Florence, BML, Or. 209) as an exact facsimile (Florence, BML, Or. 458). One can also mention manuscripts containing chronographies (for example, Elias of Nisibis's) and chronicles, with parallel columns for ecclesiastical history, civil history and other events. A similar layout was applied in the manuscript of the *Chronicle* by Patriarch Michael the Great preserved in Aleppo and faithfully reproduced in Chabot's edition (1899; facsimile edition, Gregorios Y. Ibrahim 2009).

For poetic works, the strophes may be written continuously in a one- or two-column page layout or in a one-column layout where each verse occupies a separate line. In both cases, the beginning and the end of each verse is marked by a red dot, and red and black dots, respectively. Thus a page of poetry in one column may show, in the left margin, a vertical line of red dots, and in the right margin, a vertical line of alternating red and black dots (for example, Vatican City, BAV, Vat. sir. 174 (sixteenth century, some poems by Patriarch Nūḥ the Lebanese, Bar 'Ebroyo and 'Abdišo' of Nisibis)). An example of a continuously written poetic text is represented by Florence, BML, Or. 298 (poems by Bar 'Ebroyo). It should be noted that the one-column layout with alternating red and black dots is used also in regions as far from the centre of Syriac tradition as China: evidence is a bifolium from a Psalter recently found in Dunhuang (Gansu, China; Duan Qing 2000, 2001: Dunhuang, Historical Museum, Mogau Ku B 53:14). The paper and the script of the bifolium testify to a local production; the red dots appear at the end of each verse, and the letters are not elongated.

The persistence of the characteristics of the Syriac manuscript book even in remote areas far from the centres of the Syriac culture is remarkable: a manuscript written in South India (Vatican City, BAV, Vat. sir. 22, copied in Craganore, 1301) does not differ in format and structure from the manuscripts written in Syria. The same is true of manuscripts produced in Central Asia, although since they are fragmentary, the similarities are mostly discernible only in the page layout, rubrics and decoration. One can observe that they conform to the standard established within the East Syriac tradition, but also follow scribal practices of West Syriac scriptoria (such as the above mentioned Mogau Ku B 53:14). In the matter of script, manuscripts written in Central Asia and China display a specific ductus, and particular shapes of some letters (such as *alaph*), that could be a result of the use of a brush instead of a reed pen. In more recent centuries, also in India the East Syriac script took on a specific *ductus*, a phenomenon that seems to be an autonomous development of the peculiarities of this script (Briquel-Chatonnet – Desreumaux 2010).

11.5.2. Decoration (EBW)

The elements embellishing the manuscripts belong to two categories, scribal decoration and painted (or drawn) decoration (Balicka-Witakowska forthcoming b). To the first group belong the elaborate script, punctuation, attention marks, denotations and text dividers. They are highlighted by rubrication or coloured inks (figs. 1.11.1, 1.11.2) and turned into adornments by the addition of dots, dashes and small arabesques. The second group comprises the bands and squares filled with interlace and sometimes figural motifs, as well as the thematic miniatures (or drawings) usually with figural representations. Whether the miniatures are pure decoration or illustrations depends on their placement in the manuscript and relationship to textual content.

The common method for turning the script into ornamentation was to enlarge the normal characters, writing them in coloured inks and refining them by gilding or silvering. In some manuscripts, the letters emerge from a coloured background. Although initials do not exist in the Syriac script, often the beginning letters and their diacritics were stylized and ornamented (Balicka-Witakowska 1998).

Fig. 1.11.3 Kaslik, Ordre Libanais Maronite, 983, dated 1673, lectionary, f. 93r, detail.

Punctuation marks written with black and red inks often function as adornments, the simplest being single or double points, the more elaborate being rosettes. In several manuscripts, a black quadruple-dots-mark, customarily placed in the upper right corner of the recto pages, has evolved into a decoration composed of geometric and vegetal elements. The line-fillers are formed of red-black dots, strokes, small crosses, rosettes and tiny floral arabesques. Such adornments also flank the highlighted titles, elongating them from the inner to the outer margin and rounding out the final columns to the level of previous ones, thus retaining the visual balance of the page.

The common scribal decoration makes ornaments out of small text units, such as notes, comments and corrections. Outlined in a coloured ink, they are often furnished with floral appendages. Another way to enhance the decorativeness of the written text, usually applied for the ending pieces and final notes, is to form a text unit onto a geometrical figure and adorn it with scribal flourishes.

The numeration of text units, such as *incipit*s and *desinit*s, chapters, paragraphs, important verses and pericopes, has usually been converted into decoration. The numerals may be marked by coloured inks or gilding and additionally highlighted in decorative script and embellishments. The quire numbers too were often turned into ornamentation (fig. 1.11.2). The simplest examples combine dots, strokes, vegetal motifs and geometric figures, while more complex examples take the form of interlaced roundels, crosses and stars (for example, Berlin, Staatsbibliothek, Sachau 304, twelfth/thirteenth centuries, fig. 1.11.5). There are also quire-number decorations shaped as birds, fanciful quadrupeds or objects (London, BL, Add. 14601, ninth century; Diyarbakır, Patriarchate Library, now Meryem Ana Syriac Orthodox Church, 00083, written 1540).

The beginnings of text units or headings, written in decorative script, are often preceded by an interlaced band, square or rectangular. From the thirteenth century onwards, the main text sections were usually introduced by the so-called 'gate-ornamentation' shaped like an inverted U or a Greek Π. Very commonly, a miniature might serve as a heading. The text endings were also made clearly visible and aesthetically appealing. The closing sentences or even the whole last columns were highlighted by red ink and supplied by the decorative line- and column-fillers. Quite often, the very end of a longer text unit was written in the form of an inverted pyramid. Closing miniatures are not uncommon. As the heading and ending of the entire book there may be a full-page miniature of a cross or cruciform rosette presented within a frame. Miniatures of

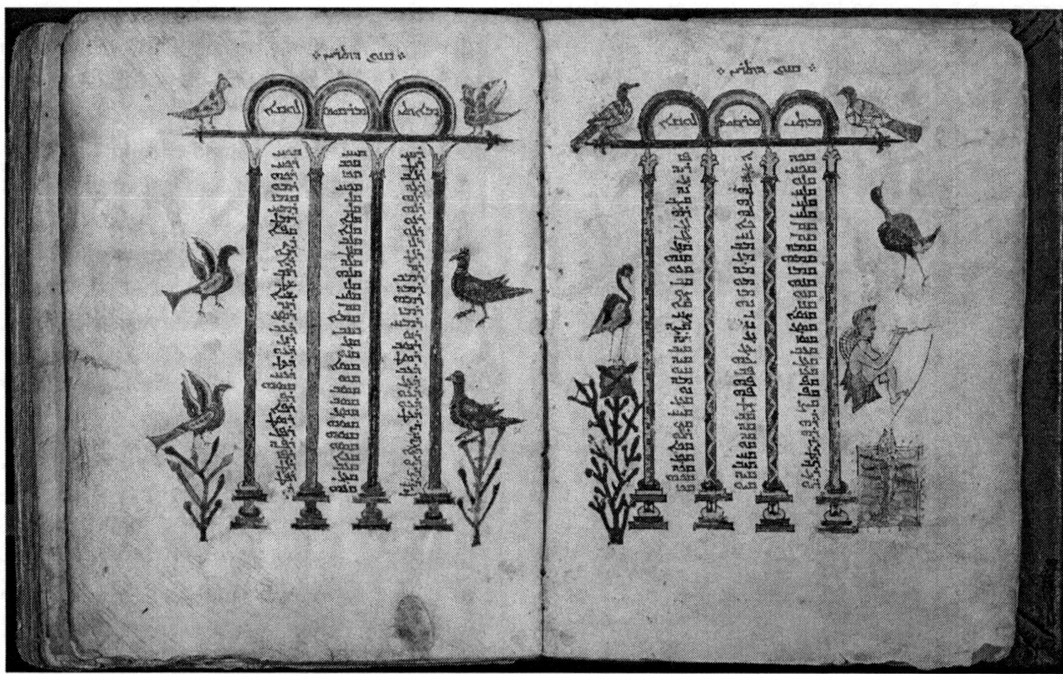

Fig. 1.11.4 Dublin, Chester Beatty, Syr. 3, eleventh century, Four Gospels, ff. 2v–3r.

this kind were mainly used in the twelfth- and thirteenth-century lectionaries, where they also introduce the tables of lections (London, BL, Add. 7169, ff. 1v–2r, 14v–15r, 248r). The cross miniature has a variant called the 'carpet-page', containing a decoratively treated cross emerging from a background entirely covered by ornament (Diyarbakır, Meryem Ana Syriac Orthodox Church, 339, f. 9r, see also fig. 1.11.3).

The 'indexes' of readings from the Old and New Testaments for the liturgical year were customarily presented in ornamented tables and placed at the beginning of a manuscript. This system had developed as early as in the sixth century out of the simple list of readings put in grids and framed by stylized architectural elements (London, BL, Add. 14445). In the twelfth and thirteenth centuries, particularly in the *de luxe* Gospels, it was replaced by sets of joined or interlaced geometrical figures.

According to a custom well documented in the east and west, the Eusebian Canon Tables were traditionally presented in grids drawn inside architectonic decorative frames imitating *aediculae*, flanked by plants, animals and birds. In Syriac manuscripts, the Canon Tables were most often displayed on nineteen pages and never ended with the so-called 'tempietto-miniature' typical for other traditions. This system, adopted for the Peshitta version about 450, was gradually abandoned after the seventh century, the last known examples dating to the eleventh century (Dublin, Chester Beatty, Syr. 3; see fig. 1.11.4). The most sumptuously decorated set, but at the same time exceptional, is preserved in the Rabbula Gospels: *aediculae* are surrounded by vases with flowers, plants, fountains, and several species of birds and quadrupeds. Scenes from the lives of biblical figures and of Christ are depicted in the inner and outer margins, and portraits of the evangelists accompany Canons VII and VIII.

Miniatures in Syriac manuscripts either occupy an entire page or share a page or bifolium with text and/or other miniatures. In the latter cases, the pictures may occupy the spaces within the text units and extend to the margins. The full-page miniatures, irrespective of whether they contain one or more scenes or figures, are presented within a frame that is either very simple or ornamented. Such miniatures were usually placed at the beginning and/or end of the manuscript, functioning as the sumptuous opening and closing of the book. Manuscripts with miniatures distributed throughout the text, situated near the textual episode they illustrate, are rare and relatively late; so, for example, in the thirteenth-century lectionaries: London, BL, Add. 7170 (48 miniatures); Vatican City, BAV, Vat. sir. 559 (54 miniatures; de Jerphanion 1940) (on both see also Leroy [Jules] 1964, 280–320, pls 70–100); Jerusalem, St. Mark's Monastery, cod. 28 (8 miniatures; Hatch 1931, 121–129). Most of the intertextual miniatures are framed, creating clearly visually independent entities which may serve as dividers of the text into sections. Their size was not determined by a disposition of a page or bifolium, but depended on the importance, for instance liturgical, of the illustrated text unit.

Fig. 1.11.5 Berlin, Staatsbibliothek, Sachau 304, thirteenth century, Four Gospels, f. 90v.

The miniatures distributed in the margins decorate a limited group of the manuscripts, primarily the Gospels with embellished Eusebian Canons (fig. 1.11.4). These miniatures, not framed, form instead a kind of frame for the adjoining text. Although related to the text, they do not function as illustrations. Strongly abbreviated, with figures and details kept to a minimum, they serve as pictorial bookmarks assisting the reader to locate particular passages of text (for example, the Gospels, Homs, Patriarchate Library, f. 244r, executed in 1054; Leroy [Jules] 1964, pl. 61.2).

The miniature may or may not be subordinated to the division of the text into columns. Consequently, on a page written in two columns, a miniature may extend from the inner to the outer margin (fig. 1.11.5) or be only as large as one column. There are also examples of miniatures simultaneously arranged horizontally and vertically (in the form of a reversed L), thus occupying unequal parts of two columns. Designed in this way, the pictures create for the beginning of text both a heading and a kind of frame (for example, Berlin, Staatsbibliothek, Sachau 304, f. 90v, thirteenth century; Leroy [Jules] 1964, pls 125.3, 126.3).

In some manuscripts, the miniatures with figural scenes (all or just a selection) do not follow the horizontal direction of reading, which is also the way the manuscript is bound, but are turned 90° (Berlin, Staatsbibliothek, Sachau 220) in some cases even 180° and 270° (London, BL, Or. 6673, written in 1802; Balicka-Witakowska 2008). A similar phenomenon appears in Manichaean manuscripts (Gulácsi 2005, 47). To date, no satisfactory explanation for this practice has been found.

In manuscripts with precisely planned page design, the pictures do not extend beyond the space defined by the text unit. In books made with less care, they may extend into the margins, the space between the columns, and be squeezed between the text sections or lines. All these shortcomings can be partly explained in economic terms: a wish to save valuable parchment and the lack of rich sponsors. The introduction of paper partly changed the situation, and the layout of the manuscripts written on paper, particularly recent ones, is generally better balanced than that of those on parchment (for example, the Gospels, Beth-Zabday, St. Mary, executed in 1851; Hollerweger 1999, 274).

Very little is known about the techniques practised by the painters of the manuscripts. Judging from unfinished pieces, the motifs were first sketched with ink and then covered with colours, often applied in layers (Berlin, Staatsbibliothek, Sachau 220, f. 43r; London, BL, Add. 7154, f. 2r, executed in 1203).

11.6. The scribe, the painter and the illuminator at work (PGB–FBC)

11.6.1. Persons, places and methods

Syriac manuscripts were produced in scriptoria connected to scholarly centres (Edessa, Nisibis), monasteries, towns or villages, usually by professional copyists who in ancient times (the last quotation is dated 817) sometimes called themselves an 'Edessene scribe', regardless of where they were in fact working.

The majority of the Syriac copyists were clergymen: priests, deacons, monks (at times also stylites—in the sense that the copyist *had been* a stylite). Scribal activity was considered to be a spiritual exercise that also provided expiation of sins (for the copyist himself, for his relatives and for the patron). Several bishops devoted their time to copying books (for example, the Syriac Orthodox Patriarchs Michael the Great, d.1199, and Nūḥ, d.1509). In recent times, whole families have been involved in scribal activity, such as the Shikwana, numbering seven generations of copyists, from the late seventeenth to the twentieth century), and the Nasro, both from Alqoš. Few old manuscripts survive that are the work of a single copyist. Exceptions are three Old Testament manuscripts copied by the deacon Saba of Rešʿayna between 724 and 726 (London, BL, Add. 14430 (724), Add. 12135 (726) and Add. 14428 (no date)). Female copyists were also active; for example, in 1701 a learned daughter of a priest copied the Maronite ordination services in a village in northern Lebanon.

In the colophons of manuscripts from the fifth and sixth centuries, the towns of Edessa (seven times), Mabbug (twice) and Amida (once) are named as the places where the manuscripts were written. Nisibis and Tell Dinawar (then in the Sassanian empire) appear in two colophons of the seventh century. Several manuscripts are related to monasteries the locations of which are mostly unknown. Edessa and other towns in Syria were the main places of production of the about 30 extant Syriac manuscripts dated from 650 to 900. In the eighth century, two manuscripts (dating to 760 and 768) were written in Egypt, but the first book copied in Dayr al-Suryān dates to 927. From the tenth century, some originate from the monasteries flourishing in the region of Malatya. It seems that the Monastery of the Syrians became a more important centre of manuscript production in the eleventh century, albeit extant eleventh- and twelfth-century Syriac manuscripts are not numerous. The situation changes for the twelfth and thirteenth centuries, the period called the 'Syriac Renaissance'. Besides the manuscripts copied in the region of 'the mountain of Edessa', Upper Mesopotamia, books were also produced in Iran (Sigistan, Urmia, Maragha). Scribal activity took place also in the villages in the Mosul region (for example, Alqoš and Barṭelli). After a cultural breakdown in the fourteenth century and in the first part of the fifteenth, an increase in production is noticed, mainly in Ṭūr ʿAbdīn. In the following century, several East Syriac monasteries are mentioned as places of book production: Mar Aha and Mar John the Egyptian (Gazarta); Mar Awgen (near Nisibis) and Mar Jacob the Recluse (near Siirt); Rabban Hormizd (near Alqoš); among the West Syriac centres, the monastery of Dayr al-Zaʿfarān flourished, and again the region of Ṭūr ʿAbdīn, which remained most productive in the eighteenth and nineteenth centuries. From the seventeenth century, the scribal activity of Alqoš is particularly extensive. Besides the Near East (to the places already mentioned, also Lebanon and Jerusalem should be added), Syriac manuscripts were produced in every place where the Syriac Churches were established (India, Central Asia, China), or where the presence of Syriac people aroused interest in their culture (for example, Italy and France, from the sixteenth century onwards).

Out of forty illuminated Syriac manuscripts listed by Brock (Brock et al. 2001, 240–241) and dating from 586 (the Rabbula Gospels) to 1851, twenty-nine are Gospels or Gospel lectionaries, two contain the Old and the New Testaments (Paris, BnF, Syriaque 341, and Cambridge, University Library, Oo.1.1.2), one the New Testament alone (Paris, BnF, Syriaque 30), while the remaining eight contain liturgical, homiletic and philological works. Quite another genre of illustration in Syriac manuscripts is represented by the images in small books of charms (Gollancz 1912; Balicka-Witakowska 2008 (London, BL, Or. 6673)).

It is unusual that a colophon mentions the manuscript painter, an exception being the thirteenth-century Gospel lectionary Paris, BnF, Syriaque 356, which contains a prayer for Īšōʿ, 'who painted and wrote'. It seems thus that in some cases the copyist also decorated the book. Another important example is BnF, Syriaque 355, also a thirteenth-century Gospel lectionary, containing a long note (f. 1r) giving the full list of the images and attributing them to the deacon Joseph of Melitene. The note gives information also about the cost of this lavishly decorated book (quoted in French by Leroy [Jules] 1964, 272–273). A third example is Venice, BNM, Or. 60 (Cod. X in Assemani's Catalogue (1787, 8), dated to 1572/1573), written by a copyist who worked in a monastery of Mount Athos: on f. 130v he says: 'The miserable Yohanninos drew (or: painted, *ṣār*)'.

11.6.2. Colophons

Syriac copyists usually wrote a colophon after they had completed copying the text and customarily placed it at the end of the manuscript. Although numerous colophons are preserved (their number corresponding approximately to the number of dated Syriac manuscripts, see above), in the majority of manuscripts they are missing, due to their placement on the final leaves, which like the first leaves of a codex were easily lost. In general, the colophon is clearly separate from the main text: in old manuscripts, besides some simple decorative lines between the text and the colophon, it was also distinguished by use of a different, smaller and/or cursive script, as in London, BL, Add 14542, copied in 509. The same phenomenon is observed in the Rabbula Gospels, from 586, where the large *ʾesṭrangēlā* of the Gospel text is coupled with a cursive script used for the colophon and the notes at the end of each Gospel. Otherwise, when the script of the main text does not differ from that of the colophon, the colophon is framed and/or has a rubricated beginning. At times the colophon is shaped as an inverted triangle, as in Arabic and Persian manuscripts (for example, Vatican City, BAV, Vat. sir. 282; Mundell Mango 1982; Briquel-Chatonnet 1998b).

Some colophons contain plenty of information about the book, the copyist, his milieu, donors, etc.; others state only the copyist's name (for example, Florence, BML, Or. 209, f. 19v: 'Finished. Moses, poor and a sinner, stranger in Rome'), or a date (for example, Paris, BnF, Syriaque 377, indicating only the year, 2166 AG = 1854/1855 CE). The curses sometimes added to the colophons inform us about the perils the books might face: we learn, for instance, that it is forbidden to borrow a book from the library, or when the borrowed book is not returned, the borrower is put under the curse; a curse may also be put on users who rip out sheets, even blank ones. Some colophons mention the collation of the book against its antigraph, which may have been made by the copyist himself just after the transcription was finished, or sometime later by some other person.

The colophon begins with the verb *šlem* 'to finish, complete' ('Ended is [this book]' etc.), often followed by the mention of the help and the strength granted to the copyist by God. Similarly, an invocation may also open a book ('Through the strength of God, we begin to write'). The copyist often includes self-effacing comments about his own person, his unworthiness and lack of talent, and asks forgiveness for his mistakes. There are recurrent formulae adopted by the copyists, such as 'unworthy, priest/monk only by name, but not in deeds', the mechanical use of which at least once produced an interesting inversion, when the copyist Melkisedeq of Hasankeyf called himself 'a priest in deeds, but not by name' (Florence, BML, Or. 49, f. 13r). The copyist may write his name with the so-called 'Bardaisan's alphabet': for example, London, BL, Add. 14431 (the Old Testament Books of Samuel, copied before 545), where the name George, *gywrgy*, appears in the enigmatic form *zṣdšzṣ* as encoded according to the correspondences of 'Bardaisan's alphabet' (see Duval 1881, 13).

A comprehensive collection of Syriac colophons does not exist, but the authors of catalogues of Syriac manuscripts mostly quote them *in extenso*.

A very interesting colophon from a comparative perspective is that of the manuscript Florence, BML, Or. 81 (a Persian *Diatessaron* written by a Jacobite copyist in Hasankeyf, in 1547, for the Armenian catholicos). The codicological features of this book combine Syriac and Armenian characteristics, in particular in the colophon's structure and content (Messina 1951; Piemontese 1989, 104–108). One can also mention the colophons of Paris, BnF, Syriaque 51, and Lyon, Bibliothèque municipale, 1, both copied in Jerusalem in 1138, which give comprehensive information about the situation of the eastern Christians in the Latin Kingdom of Jerusalem, and some important colophons of manuscripts originating from the monastery of Dayr al-Suryān (Van Rompay forthcoming).

11.6.3. Duration of copying

When they exist, notes written between two texts—a sort of 'intermediate colophon'—give information about when the first part of the book was finished and the next part began to be copied, thus indicating the duration of the copying. For example, the first part of Paris, BnF, Syriaque 370 (96 leaves), was finished on 9 July, the second part (ff. 97–173) on 22 July, information which allow us to calculate that approximately six leaves per day were written. In Paris, BnF, Syriaque 398 I, three such notes suggest an average of three or four leaves being written per day (Briquel-Chatonnet 1998a).

11.6.4. Dating systems

The most common dating system in Syriac manuscripts is the Seleucid Era, the beginning of which corresponds to 1 October 312 BCE, mostly designated as 'Greek', 'of the Greeks' (who may at times be qualified as 'blessed', 'crafty' or 'cursed') or 'of Greece', but also as 'Alexander's' or, less frequently, 'of Seleucus'. In fifth- and sixth-century manuscripts, other dating systems occur, for instance, local eras (of Antioch, of Apamea, of Bosra) and the 'indiction', borrowed from the Byzantine tradition (a fifteen-year tax cycle, still used, albeit very rarely, in that Arab period: the most recent example is dated 1177); in two manuscripts written in the Sassanian Empire, the regnal year of the king appears (Khusraw II, 591–628). Occasionally the Era of the Martyrs, the Byzantine World Era (in the late Melkite manuscripts) or, the World Era of Adam are mentioned. In the Arab period, the Hegira Era is used (the era 'of the Arabs/Muslims' (*ṭayyāyē*)), most often accompanied by other dating systems (Brock 2005). The use of the Christian Era (*da-mšīḥā*, *mšīḥāyā* 'of the Messiah', 'messianic' (Kaufhold 2008)) is very late, used especially, but not only, in manuscripts produced in the west or for western patrons. In manuscripts written in Kerala, India, a local era called *kullam* (beginning in 824/825) is also found (for example, the manuscript Kottayam, SEERI, 8).

Dating according to several eras or concordances (sometimes wrong) also occur (Briquel-Chatonnet 1998a). The Rabbula Gospels are dated according to the Seleucid Era (897 AG) and the Indiction (fourth indiction). The manuscript Vatican City, BAV, Vat. sir. 148 (of liturgical content), is dated according to three different eras, the third one being the Turkic calendar of the Cycle of the Twelve Animals. The colophon mentions the dates 30 *Tammuz* 1578 AG (1267 CE, July), *Ḏū 'l-qa'da* 665 AH, and the 'year the hare of the Mongols (Tatars), in the month called *itinč ai* ('seventh month' in Turkic)'. It must be pointed out that the words 'hare' and 'seventh month' are written by another hand, in spaces purposely left blank; perhaps the copyist, unsure about the exotic date, or unable to write the Turkic words correctly, asked for help from somebody.

11.7. Bookbinding (EBW)

The available information on Syriac bindings is scant, practically restricted to two contributions dealing with the Armenian book and using Syriac examples (ninety-six Syriac manuscripts from fourteen different collections) as comparative material (Merian 1993 and 1998), except for a first study on Syriac bookbinding with special reference to the collection of manuscripts of Charfet, Lebanon, Library of the Syro-Catholic Patriarchate (Dergham – Vinourd forthcoming). Information can be found in manuscript catalogues, but in general they do not give detailed descriptions of bindings.

As a rule, no old, original Syriac binding is preserved in western collections, where the manuscripts were mostly bound anew upon their arrival. For instance, in the relatively small collection of the Biblioteca Medicea Laurenziana in Florence (seventy manuscripts), only one manuscript shows an original binding (sixteenth century?), while about ten were bound in the sixteenth century (in the Levant, with 'Islamic' bindings); the rest of the collection received a standard western full-parchment binding in the eighteenth century. About thirty manuscripts with Syriac bindings are found in Paris, Bibliothèque nationale de France: one-third of them date from the sixteenth to eighteenth centuries, for example, Syriaque 438 (see the *e-ktobe* database at <http://www.mss-syriaques.org>). But there are exceptions: portions survive of the original binding of London, BL, Add. 17124 and Or. 8729, dated to 1230 and written in Edessa and probably also bound there.

Several manuscripts preserved in Near Eastern libraries (for example, Baghdad, Library of the Archbishopric of the Church of the East, or Charfet, Lebanon, Library of the Syro-Catholic Patriarchate) and in India (Thrissur) are still in their old bindings.

Fig. 1.11.6 Jerusalem, Biblioteca Generale della Custodia di Terra Santa, Syr. 6, seventeenth century.

In Syriac binding, the wooden boards (of variable thickness, from 4 to 10 mm, and cut with a vertical grain) prepared for sewing were supplied with one drilling for each sewing station, all fully visible on both sides of the boards. The text block was sewn separately, probably with an unsupported link-stitch sewing, then it was securely attached to the wooden boards, using a cord wound into the holes in the boards. After the text block was attached to the boards, the spine was lined with a piece of cloth (either cotton or linen). The spine lining covered one-third to one-half of the wooden boards, onto which it was pasted. Quite frequently, multiple layers of cloth were pasted on (so in the majority of manuscripts examined by Merian). The end bands were raised, with the tie-downs attached to holes drilled into the boards. The book was next covered with leather and might be left plain or blind-tooled (so Paris, BnF, Syriaque 438 (Maronite Missal, eighteenth century)), or the leather cover might be decorated in relief, obtained by inserting moulded cords between the wooden board and the leather (so Thrissur, Syr. 76, with a mixture of relief and blind-tooled decoration). In some cases, instead of the leather cover a cloth cover, multicoloured or monochrome, is used (so Diyarbakır, Meryem Ana Syriac Orthodox Church, 99; 8/19 (1477); 60; 1/28 (1583); Paris, BnF, Syriaque 377 (nineteenth century)). The inside boards were sometimes lined with cloth (so Vatican City, BAV, Vat. sir. 622: red cotton cloth).

Apparently in the nineteenth century, perhaps under the influence of the Armenian communities (see Ch. 1 § 3.7), some manuscripts, mostly highly valued liturgical books that were placed on display for the congregation, were supplied with metal, decorated covers. Such a cover is a revetment of the original binding, added either to an old manuscript or to a newly produced one. In most cases, these covers are silver plaques, fastened to the front and to the back cover by small nails and held together by a metal spine and metal clasps at the front. The plaques were decorated with a variety of motifs (both aniconic and figural) executed by means of different techniques: repoussé reliefs, gilding, chasing, filigree and cloisonné work. Usually they are special donations ordered from silversmiths and occasionally commemorated by inscriptions added to the decoration. Some good examples are to be found in Ṭūr ʿAbdīn, around the Midyat region, which was known for its silversmith craftsmanship (for example, the Gospels of Invardi, Habsus, Hah, Beth Sbirino: Hollerweger 1999, 122, 137, 168, 257). In the same way, two white metal plaques bearing inscriptions were attached to the old binding of Vatican City, BAV, Vat. sir. 622, in 1950, when the book was sent as a gift to Pope Pius XII by the Chaldean Patriarch of Babylon, Joseph VII Ghanima.

References

Assemani 1721, 1787; Balicka-Witakowska 1998, 2008, forthcoming b; Bensly et al. 1894; Berthelot 1893; Berti 2009; Bigoul El-Souriany – Van Rompay 2001; Borbone 2003, 2013; Brashear 1998; Briquel-Chatonnet 1997, 1998, forthcoming; Briquel-Chatonnet – Desreumaux 2010; Briquel-Chatonnet et al. 2006; Brock 1991a, 2001a, 2010a; Butts 2011; Chabot 1899–1910 [2009], 1954; Clark – Gibbs 1998; Coackley 1993; Daccache – Desreumaux forthcoming; Dergham – Vinourd forthcoming; Desreumaux forthcoming; Desreumaux – Gorea 2003; Duan Qing 2000, 2001; Duval 1881; Foumia 2013; Franzmann 1999; Franzmann – Gardner 1996; Gignoux 1987; Gollancz 1912; Goshen – Gottstein 1979; Gregorios Y. Ibrahim 2009; Gulácsi 2005; Hall 1886; Hatch 1931, 1946; Hollerweger 1999; Hunt 2001; Hunter 1998, 1999; Kamil 1957; Kaplan 2013; Land 1862; van Lantschoot 1965; Leroy [Jules] 1964; Merian 1993, 1998; Meščerskaja 1987; Messina 1951; Moberg 1924; Mundell Mango 1991; Muto 2013; Pajkova 1979; Pajkova – Maršak 1976; Piemontese 1989; Pigulevskaja 1960; Sauget 1985; Schmidt [A.] 2009; Teixidor 1990; Tisserant 1911, 1914; Van Rompay forthcoming; Wright 1870–1872; Yoshida – Chimeddorji 2008. Web sources: *e-ktobe* <http://www.mss-syriaques.org>, last access May 2014.

Chapter 2. Palaeography

edited by Paola Buzi and Marilena Maniaci

1. Introduction (DB)

1.1. What is palaeography?

According to the traditional view, which favours the technical and formal aspects of the discipline, the writing material is the first element to delimit the research field of palaeography. Indeed, in a narrower sense palaeography is the science which critically inquires the ancient scripts written on soft writing materials. Only in 'non-monumental documents' (Schiaparelli et al. 1935, 34: 'documenti di carattere non monumentale')—i.e. basically made on papyrus, parchment and paper, where the writing tool can run without any obstacle and the writing can become cursive—it is possible to find out and follow the process of transformation of the individual letter-forms and of the overall graphic system evolving from the cursive developments of writing. The history of the writing is, indeed, a dynamic history of graphic manifestations that the palaeographer above all is called upon to decipher (i.e. to read correctly), to date and to localize, studying and understanding at the same time the material conditions of their production. Only in this perspective we can understand the palaeographic importance of the scripts written in ink on papyrus, parchment and paper: for a long time these have been considered the privileged, if not the unique, topic of palaeography. The cursive execution of the strokes of the letters—possible only on soft materials and made *currenti calamo*, that is without removing the writing tool from the writing surface—and the ligatures between letters—which are present when a letter (or its last stroke) turns, naturally and without interruption, into the next (or into its first stroke)—produce, as a consequence of a not always controlled and sometimes convulsive process, a series of new shapes and graphic variants, which are occasionally able to organize themselves in a new, organic and coherent writing system. The minimum, shared and essential requirement of palaeography is to follow and understand this process of transformation of the individual signs and of the overall graphic system. On this is based the traditional palaeographical method, which is analytical, formal and evidential, and the scientific status of the discipline.

At the same time, writing participates in the historical dimension of human activities, and as such it shares with them—as a specific and autonomous phenomenon—orientations, tensions and all their multifarious conjunctions (Pasquali 1931). This awareness, which emerged in the middle of the twentieth century in the field of Latin palaeography, has forced a redefinition of the subject of study of the discipline: it has been productively extended to 'all kinds of graphical monuments' (Mallon 1952, 11, translation DB), and it now also covers tablets, *ostraca*, engraved or painted inscriptions and graffiti. Therefore, the need of a unitary and integrated analysis, dealing with all graphical monuments, strengthens the historical dimension (in the broader sense) of palaeography. At first, again in the field of Latin palaeography, especially thanks to Armando Petrucci, but then also to other palaeographers, it was tried to link the study of writing—and of reading—to the history of society and culture. This process has been carried on in the awareness, fully and clearly theorized by Petrucci, that palaeography would be able to provide a social interpretation of written documents, instead of being limited to deciphering them and trying to give them a date and a localization: in this way palaeography claims to infer information about the social diffusion of writing and its function in a given environment from the study of the graphic witnesses of a precise geo-cultural context and historical period (see at least Petrucci 1969b and 1973, 1972, 1978, 1986b and 2002). The enlargement, one might almost say the reversal, of the traditional palaeographical method—which at any rate should be conducted, as Petrucci intended, without renouncing the crucial element of formal analysis (Petrucci 1996)—is taken today for granted. However it has raised some resistance, above all from scholars such as Alessandro Pratesi, who perceive a risk of transforming palaeography into something that it is not (Pratesi 1979). The risk would be that palaeography might be replaced by a 'sociology of writing' (Pratesi 1979, 336, translation DB), whose opportunity and importance Pratesi did not deny, but only on the condition that it would not be constituted 'at the expense of a discipline—namely, palaeography—that has a specific and limited subject and keeps in its integrity, albeit with subsequent refinements, a method of investigation of its own' (Pratesi 1979, 336), i.e. the formal and analytical method.

Another characteristic inherent in palaeography is the link with both documentary and literary texts. This connexion has placed the discipline from its beginning in an historical and philological dimension (even if subordinate and subsidiary, compared with other disciplines). If, indeed, Latin palaeography was born in Europe of the Ancien Régime with the aim of providing tools for graphic analysis in order to assess the validity of documents (the foundational book by Jean Mabillon was entitled *De re diplomatica* and was published in 1681 in Paris), Greek palaeography, whose birth corresponds to the publication in 1708 in Paris of the *Palaeographia graeca* by Bernard de Montfaucon, dealt from the beginning with the study of scripts placed in their dynamic history and the cataloguing of manuscripts kept in European libraries. Besides the focus on a total history of writing (as far as the manuscripts, coins and inscriptions, which were available in Montfaucon's day, allowed him to reconstruct), the perspective chosen by Montfaucon was mainly a philological one, which still represents a typical, though not exclusive, aspect of palaeographical surveys: in this way the discipline has finally come to include, not without some confusion, topics which are typical of textual criticism and history of the texts.

Today, some tendencies have been maybe abandoned too early—such as, for example, the application of the models and paradigms of the structural linguistics to the study of the writing (Casamassima – Staraz 1977; Casamassima 1988)—and, on the other hand, other new guidelines are ignored by the most scholars or have yet to show convincing results—such as the so-called *métrologie paléographique*, which suggests the application of the quantitative-statistical method and of informatics with the promise (the mirage?) of giving the discipline a strong scientific status (see among others Rehbein et al. 2009; Fischer [F.] et al. 2010): but we may say that palaeography now lives on the dialectic between writing, texts and society (Cavallo 2012; Bianconi 2014).

1.2. Method and instruments of analysis in palaeography

The fundamental task of a palaeographer, once he has read and interpreted the text transmitted in a given written artefact, is to understand the date and the place of creation of that artefact on the basis of the script employed. It is not an easy task to find an orientation among graphic shapes, which, as products of human activity, do not develop uniformly. In order to date and to localize a manuscript—be it a papyrus fragment or a mediaeval codex—it is necessary to start with what is certain and to compare the manuscript with others which have a definite (or at least probable) date and localization, and so can be taken as terms of comparison (Supino Martini 1995). Some manuscripts, in different proportions depending on the periods and on the places, are dated and localized with certainty, since the scribe himself provides the indication of the year and the place of his activity. Other manuscripts bear a range of objective information, both internal and external, that allows us to ascertain their date and/or localization with a reasonable degree of precision. The documentary manuscripts are very useful for this, and not only because they are generally provided with a date and an indication of the place of writing. A comprehensive understanding of the different ways written culture was produced—and so a real global perception of the graphical phenomenon—may come only if we also study the production of documents, which sometimes interacted with the production of books. Moreover, in some palaeographies, because of the purely philological approach and interests of some scholarly traditions, the linguistic element (i.e. the specific language or its particular dialectal patina) plays a primary role in the possibility of attributing a date and, above all, a localization to a manuscript, often at the expense of the real palaeographical analysis.

The effectiveness of the palaeographical method based on the formal comparison between scripts (*Schriftvergleich*) is favoured by the availability of directories and catalogues of dated and datable manuscripts which can offer a comparison, and by their completeness. They are indispensable working tools, generally organized by textual and writing typology, age of the manuscripts, storage location, and scribes; their number is always increasing and their effectiveness is enhanced by the information technology.

The deeper and more systematic the critical reflection about the elements of graphical evaluation to be examined, the more reliable and objective are the proposals of dates and localizations based on palaeographical analysis. In conclusion, in enquiring writing it is necessary at first to know—and to define scientifically—what to look at, what to dwell on, what to give importance to, without forgetting that the elements of palaeographical analysis themselves change depending on the assumed perspective and they do not always have the same value.

In this regard, it can be useful to distinguish the synchronic from the diachronic analysis. In the synchronic analysis, carried out on a single manuscript or on a group of similar manuscripts, the structure, production and style of the script are the elements which should be considered. Among the structural elements of the script we find the shape of the letters (i.e. their formal/figurative aspect) and the *tratteggio* (i.e. the number, direction, and succession of their strokes), strictly linked to the *ductus* (i.e. the speed of their execution) which, influencing the *tratteggio*, can modify the shape of the letters. Elements related to the production are the writing angle (which measures the variable position of the writing tool relative to the base line), the 'tracing' (sequence of strokes), the form (the absolute or relative size of the signs) and the thickness of the strokes. Finally, aspects of the style are accessory elements of the graphic rendering, such as individual quirks (of an age or of a writer), decorations and even further para- and peri-graphical elements. These characteristics, even if not always together nor altogether, are essential if, for example, one wants to find the date and/or the localization of a manuscript, to follow the development of a writing rule or style, to distinguish contemporary hands, or even to demonstrate the identity of the same writer in different pieces of evidence.

In a diachronic perspective, aimed at the reconstruction of the origin, organization, diffusion, and transformation of different graphic systems, neither models nor universally valid interpretative paradigms exist. The comparison between the cursive and calligraphic levels can be very useful. In cursive writing, the quick execution modifies the basic model of the letters, generating new arrangements that slower scripts, whether or not they form a close and self-referential system, can select, implement and organize, creating new geographical, temporal and functional conjunctions. However, it is necessary to keep in mind that imitations and revisions of more ancient scripts are not rare, nor are scribes with an (at least) dual graphical education, both in cursive and in slow scripts. Such cases must be analysed from two perspectives: at first, with the help of interpretative models based on the dialectic between *tratteggio* and *ductus*, which, as factors of continuity and innovation of the graphic shapes, determine a field of tension between the informal and formal writing; and secondly with a careful expertise able to evaluate all aspects of style and realization, however minimal.

1.3. The description of writing and palaeographical terminology

An integral part of the palaeographic method is the description of scripts (Rück 1999; Cavallo 1999; Petrucci 1999). Although viewed with suspicion, since sometimes considered unnecessarily verbose and virtuosic, especially in the presence of plates and reproductions that could replace it, in fact it is an important cognitive process of conceptual abstraction: as such, reproductions can have a function of support and comparison for it. The description of a script is intended to catch its essential elements, in a clear and scientific way, and with an appropriate terminology, in order to communicate, compare and group them. The description has to be critical and carried out with the method and the terminology proper to the discipline. For example, though the analysis of the *tratteggio* can illuminate the comprehension of the global development of the script, this element will be completely irrelevant in the survey of a rule or a style: to follow their evolution, on the contrary, other factors are essential, such as the writing angle, or the quality of the execution. These last aspects are potentially negligible if one is trying to demonstrate the identity of a hand. In conclusion, the palaeographical description has to be not necessarily detailed, but functional (Cavallo 1999; Petrucci 1979): it must be limited to the essential elements for the selected aims and it must not be extended to all the aspects that can be considered, so becoming unnecessarily redundant or even misleading. This is to give voice to the application—sometimes instinctive and innate—of the palaeographical method, and above all to make it communicable: this is what can transform an art, an individual capacity neither mediated nor rational (the so-called 'palaeographical eye') into an autonomous discipline (Canart 2006; Bianconi 2014).

Moreover, in order fully to achieve this objective, it is necessary to find an appropriate, scientific and—last but not least—shared terminology. The terminological distance between different scholarly traditions is perhaps higher than that in other disciplines and it goes beyond the inevitable linguistic obstacles. Just a few examples: the term 'uncial', used in some languages as a synonym of 'majuscule'—meaning by 'majuscule' a script which can be inscribed within a bilinear system—, may designate a Latin script, which is a mixture of minuscule forms (inscribed in a quadrilinear system) and majuscule forms (so in Italian, retaining the expression *uncialibus... litteris* used by St Jerome: see Cavallo 1967). As for the *ductus*, in the Italian palaeographic tradition it indicates the speed of the execution of a script, but in other languages corresponds rather to the *tratteggio*—a word moreover used only in Italian studies. Such use follows Bernard de Montfaucon, who had not yet reached an understanding of the *tratteggio* separated from its dynamic aspect (i.e. the speed of execution, which influences the number, order and direction of the strokes and determines variations in the original shape of a letter); so the term *ductus* in Montfaucon has rather the meaning of 'tracing', which, with a minimum of approximation, can be considered almost equivalent to 'shape', the final formal and exterior result of the script, since it refers to a route taken by the writing instrument to pen a sign regardless of the distinction of each of the strokes (see Mastruzzo 1995; Bianconi 2012).

References

Bianconi 2012, 2014; Canart 2006; Casamassima 1988; Casamassima – Staraz 1977; Cavallo 1967, 1999, 2012; Fischer [F.] et al. 2010; Mallon 1952; Mastruzzo 1995; Pasquali 1931; Petrucci 1969b, 1972, 1973, 1978, 1979, 1986b, 1996, 1999, 2002; Pratesi 1979; Rehbein et al. 2009; Rück 1999; Schiaparelli et al. 1935; Supino Martini 1995.

2. Arabic palaeography (ADO)

Arabic, like Hebrew or Syriac, is written and read from right to left. It is a phonetic writing system based on syllables rather than a properly alphabetical system (Garbini 1979, 47). The Arabic alphabet (*abǧad*) is the sequence of 28 letters with consonantal value, including the semiconsonants used to denote long vowels. It represents, after the Roman alphabet, 'the second most frequent segmental script in the world' (Gruendler 2006, 148) but the Arabic script never developed an opposition between capital and non-capital forms—despite some failed attempts, dating back to the beginning of the last century, to introduce capital letters. Arabic writing is considered to have been genetically derived from the Nabataean cursive variant of Aramaic, and Syriac influences can be traced in calligraphic and orthographic elements (Gruendler 2006). According to a recent hypothesis which in its attempts to individuate the *milieu* of the origins of the Arabic alphabet not only considers graphic factors but also the social context which led towards its creation, the elaboration of Arabic writing can be dated to the beginning of the sixth century CE due to the impetus, or to the help, given by the ecclesiastic authorities. The Arabic alphabet, according to this theory, answers the need of the Arabs in Syria for political and cultural affirmation (Robin 2006, 327–330). The passage from oral to written Arabic started, according to another theory, because of the interaction between some Arab tribes and the Late Roman Empire 'in the Roman province of Arabia, which, in its original form ... stretched from the southern outskirts of Damascus to the Ḥijāz ...' (Hoyland 2010, 35).

The graffito etched into the plaster of a wall in Jabal Ramm, tentatively dated to the early fourth century CE and considered 'the oldest inscription in Arabic language *and* characters' (Gruendler 1993, 13) is now regarded as written in the Nabataean Aramaic script (Hoyland 2010, 39). Therefore the most ancient inscription in Arabic language and writing known is, at present, a trilingual inscription from Zabad, circa 37.3 miles south of Aleppo. The Arabic part of this trilingual inscription—covering the lintel over the door of a *martyrion* dedicated to St Sergius—can be dated to the year 512 CE by the context provided via the Greek and Syriac texts.

The comparative study of writing materials of different kinds (inscriptions, coins, papyri, codices) seems to be one of the elements which define the field of research of Arabic palaeography which, even though by no means limited to the witness of books and documents, would otherwise concentrate its attention on written specimens executed with a pen (Sijpesteijn 2008, 513). From a different perspective, however, it would be more likely to reaffirm the vast field of Arabic palaeography interested in written material executed with diverse writing tools and on various writing materials which have given rise to a range of specialised disciplines (epigraphy, numismatics, papyrology, codicology). According to this perspective 'la codicologie englobe la paléographie en tant qu'elle s'applique à l'écriture des manuscrits et lui apporte le soutien d'autres savoirs spécialisés que le codicologue met en œuvre' (Déroche 1998, 366).

At any event the wide range and plurality of the Arabic palaeographic material investigated is already reflected in the first contributions which traditionally mark the birth of the discipline (Adler 1780; 1782 and 1792). Therefore, it is no surprise that the word 'palaeography' appears as early as at the beginning of the nineteenth century on the titles of publications that include works which are not only concerned with specimens of books but also with witnesses of an epigraphic and numismatic nature in a broad sense (Marcel 1828).

As far as book production is concerned, Arabic palaeography is not limited to the production of Arabic-Islamic manuscripts but includes Arabic-Christian materials as well. In the Arabic-Christian manuscript production, which already presents its own codicological traits (Orsatti 1994), it is also possible to detect a 'characteristic manuscript hand' (Griffith [S.] 2010, 50). In this sense the case of a *qāf* characterised by the diacritical point placed underneath the letter is meaningful, since it seems peculiar to the southern Palestinian Arabic-Christian production of the end of the eighth to the beginning of the ninth century (Monferrer-Sala 2010). Moreover the production of digraphic and bilingual texts rendered in Greek and Arabic and in Latin and Arabic offers an ideal meeting point for different linguistic and palaeographic competences to which the same level of scientific dignity should be accorded (D'Ottone 2014).

With the exception of Arabic pre-Islamic inscriptions, the Qur'ān may be called the first true Arabic text. Nonetheless, besides the inscriptions and ancient Qur'āns, materials such as papyri and coins are no less important as tools for the study of the development of Arabic writing and of its graphic forms. Inscriptions as well as documentary material—and the research should be extended ideally to include also the vast amount of numismatic material—have, for example, so far constituted the *corpus* for a study dedicated to the presence of and to the selective use of diacritical dots (*i'ǧām*, *naqṭ*) as part of the written production in the Arabic script of the first two centuries of the Hegira (Kaplony 2008).

Apart from the punctuation (*fawāṣil*)—constituted by dots, small lines, circles and rosettes—employed to indicate the division into verses of the oldest Qur'āns, a recent field of research is concerned with the punctuation of Arabic texts (Jaouhari 2009).

Islamic coinage, for the most part of epigraphic character, constitutes an important source of palaeographic information, which so far has not been sufficiently exploited for palaeographic purposes. The roundish shape of the first exemplars of the post-reform *dirham* and *dīnār* (fig. 2.2.1)—the monetary reform of 'Abd al-Malik is dated to 77 AH/696 CE—has been interpreted as a legacy of die-engravers accustomed to Pahlavi writing (Heidemann 2010, 163). These rounded traits of the oldest post-reform coinage in gold and silver were adjusted over the course of the half century after the reform to those more angular shapes of the writing employed on papyri or for inscriptions.

Fig. 2.2.1 *Dīnār* of 'Abd al-Malik, 77 AH/996–697 CE, diameter: 19 mm, weight: 4.25 g; London, British Museum, CM 1874 7–6 1, © Trustees of the British Museum.

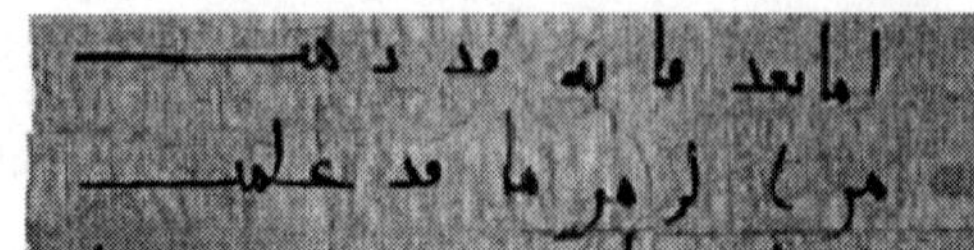

Fig. 2.2.2 Detail of a papyrus from the chancellery of Qurra b. Šarīk, eighth century; Heidelberg, Institut für Papyrologie der Ruprecht-Karls-Universität Heidelberg, *P.Heid. inv.* Arab. 1.

Fig. 2.2.3 Islamic seal, 2 lines of angular script, eighth/ninth century; London, British Museum, no. 1892,0328.94, © Trustees of the British Museum.

Papyri dated or datable to the first century of the Hegira display, in fact, a rather angular writing—a particularly elegant example of angular script can be seen, for example, in the letters issued by the chancery of Qurra b. Šarīk, governor of Egypt from 90 to 96 AH (709–714 CE) (fig. 2.2.2)—which is akin to the writing of contemporaneous inscriptions and graffiti (Rāġib 1990). Despite the existence of some variants, attributable to the form of the letters, to the accuracy of the graphic execution or to the writing material employed, Arabic writing produced during the first century of the Hegira displays a certain fundamental uniformity (Grohmann 1952, 73).

Between the end of the eighth and the beginning of the ninth century the papyri start to offer proof of cursive tendencies. Taking into consideration the presence of structural ligatures between the Arabic letters, Arabic writing is by its very nature cursive and to describe it as such reveals itself to be in essence a case of tautology (Gacek 2009, 241–243).

In a papyrological context we speak therefore of 'cursive tendencies' which can be detected by one or more of the following elements: '1. The transformation of angles into curves; 2. The transformation of curves into straight strokes; 3. The elimination of the necessity to remove the pen from the surface of the papyrus; 4. The reduction of the distance covered by the pen' (Khan 1992, 39–40). Recent studies have been devoted to the identification of dating criteria for undated papyri showing 'cursive tendencies' (Grob 2013). In the context of book production, scholars have preferred to speak about the 'cursive character' of Arabic (Déroche 1998). The concept of cursivity refers to the dynamic aspect of writing and, in particular, to its speed of graphic execution and to the economy of the movement necessary for its creation. The treatment of the ligatures between the letters (roundish rather than angular) as well as the presence of unconventional ligatures which do not conform to the orthographical rules, may be regarded as indicators of the cursivity of Arabic book writing. The *mise en ligne*, i.e. the angle formed by the base of the long letters, or by a sequence of letters, and by the line for writing, real or imagined, would represent, in conjunction with other details which necessitate a contextualization within the written page, a further characteristic element of the cursivity of Arabic script. Another distinction has to be made between *écritures composées*—in which the straight base of the writing line does not preserve, or at least not very clearly, traces of the movement of the hand—and *écritures chirodictiques*—the base of which registers highs and lows and therefore traces of the movement of the writer's hand (Déroche 1998 and 2003).

Even the field of numismatics has experienced these cursive tendencies, the first occurrence of which has been detected in a unique issue of a Fatimid *dīnār* dated 490 AH/1096–1097 CE (Balog 1949). However later exemplars of coins still display the transition from an angular script to a script of more rounded traits which was to become the norm from 571 AH/1175–1176 CE (Heidemann 2010, 167). An analogous process of transformation of graphic shapes, from angular traits to softer shapes, has also been recognised in the context of research into Islamic seals. In this field the terminology which defines the type of writing distinguishes between categories of 'angular scripts' and of 'cursive scripts' (Porter [V.] 2011, 14–16) (figs. 2.2.3–4a/b).

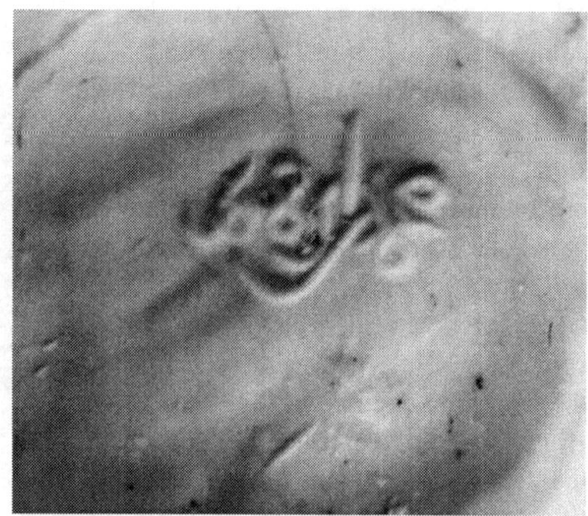

Fig. 2.2.4ab Engraved sapphire and its impression, cursive script, tenth to thirteenth century CE (and later); London, Derek Content collection.

The recent numismatic literature as well as a long tradition of studies dedicated to papyri employ the term *nasḫī* or 'naskh script' in order 'to designate a script with rounded features in contrast to more angular monumental script' and this usage can be accepted for a general classification (Khan 1992, 45–46). Nonetheless, the definition of 'naskh script'—which denotes also what has been described as 'a bookhand, par excellence, of the Islamic East' (Gacek 2009, 162)—gathers together a wide range of categories of graphic expression.

Apart from sharing large categories of script definitions, or at least definitions that can evoke scripts with similar characteristics, it seems that each field (numismatics, epigraphy, papyrology, codicology) has a different chronology for the use of these scripts, as the *caveat* for dating Islamic seals according to epigraphic scripts recalls (Porter [V.] 2011, 22 note 39).

A further distinction, in the field of manuscript production, concerns the so-called 'formal scripts', in which the aesthetic value of the writing is relatively high, and the 'informal scripts' of average accuracy in their graphic design (Déroche 2003).

As far as the graphic competence of the writers is concerned, it had already become clear by the middle of the last century how important it was to understand their social background and level of schooling as well as to study 'specimens of addresses, writing exercises, pen trials (*probationes pennae*), etc.' (Grohmann 1952, 72–73). Nonetheless, research and studies dedicated to graphic education in the Arab world of the early Middle Ages are still rare (Sijpesteijn 2008, 516). Given that the practice of writing requires specific skills, it has been connected in the Arab world until recent times to the existence and the activity of professional copyists (*warrāqūn*). In the Middle Ages reading skills were considered as separate from writing skills and there are numerous cases of established scholars who were unable to write (Hirschler 2012, 16).

As regards the catalogues of manuscripts and the description of Arabic script included, it seems noteworthy to underline that in what might be the oldest known inventory of an Arabic library, i.e. the inventory of the library of the mosque of Qayrawān (Kairouan), the script (*ḫaṭṭ*) is already mentioned and described with a relatively articulate terminology: thirty exemplars are defined as in 'Kufic' script (*bi-ḫaṭṭ kūfī*), others were instead labelled as in 'oriental' script (*šarqī*), or in 'Sicilian' (*ṣiqillī*), *nubārī* (Šabbūḥ Ibrāhīm 1376 AH/1956 CE; Voguet 2003, 536 and 543; Déroche 2007, 149).

The ancient Qur'ānic scripts, without doubt, have been those that have received particular attention since the end of the eighteenth century—i.e. from the very start of Arabic palaeography—and recent catalogues that gather together the fruits of the studies dedicated to the exploration of the scripts of the ancient Qur'ānic witnesses allow us to follow the development of palaeographic studies in this particular field.

For the scripts of Qur'ānic fragments which can be dated to the seventh/eighth century CE the qualification as *ḥiǧāzī* scripts is at present widely accepted: this is a geographical denomination derived from the name of that region in Arabia, *Ḥiǧāz*, where the cities of Mecca and Medina are located. Nonetheless, the expression '*ḥiǧāzī* scripts', at least according to some scholars, is nothing but 'a scholarly artifact' (Whelan (manuscript) n.d.).

Fig. 2.2.5 Qur'ān leaf, vellum, 288 × 203 mm, early eighth century; example of Ḥiǧāzī I script. Sūra X, 102–XI, 3; XI, 4–13; MS Vatican City, BAV, Vat. ar. 1605, f. 1v: Sūra XI, 4–13.

Palaeographical, orthographic and codicological elements help to define the early production of Qur'āns in Ḥiǧāzī I script. For example, one of the few fragments that can be dated to the early eighth century CE (Vatican City, BAV, Vat. ar. 1605, fig. 2.2.5) shows a vertical format—though horizontal fragments are also known—, the absence of vowels and diacritics, the frequent use of *scriptio defectiva* (for example *qala* instead of *qāla*), and a peculiar shape for some letters. In particular, the letter *alif* is characteristic, with a short return at the base and a rather oblique vertical stroke (the oblique tendency occurs also in the strokes of the letters *ṭā'* and *ẓā'*), as well as the letter *kāf*, this latter assuming in final position the so-called 'hairpin' shape (Déroche 1992 and 1999; Levi Della Vida 1947). Some other fragments in *ḥiǧāzī* script (Ḥiǧāzī II, III and IV according to Déroche's system), datable to the end of the eighth and/or early ninth century CE, exhibit the same tendency of the script to be slightly slanted to the

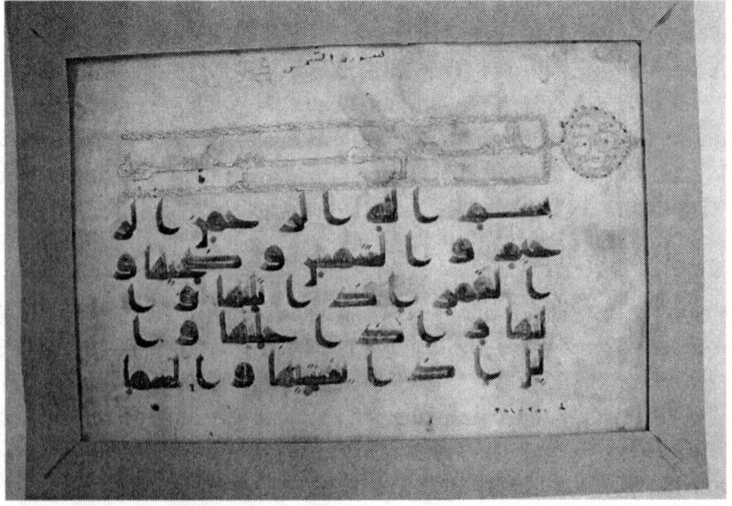

Fig. 2.2.6 Qur'ān leaf, vellum, 155 × 230 mm, ninth/tenth century; example of Group D of the Early Abbasid scripts. Sūra XC, 15–20; XCI, 1–5; MS Damascus, National Museum, Inv. 'ayn 350–351, verso.

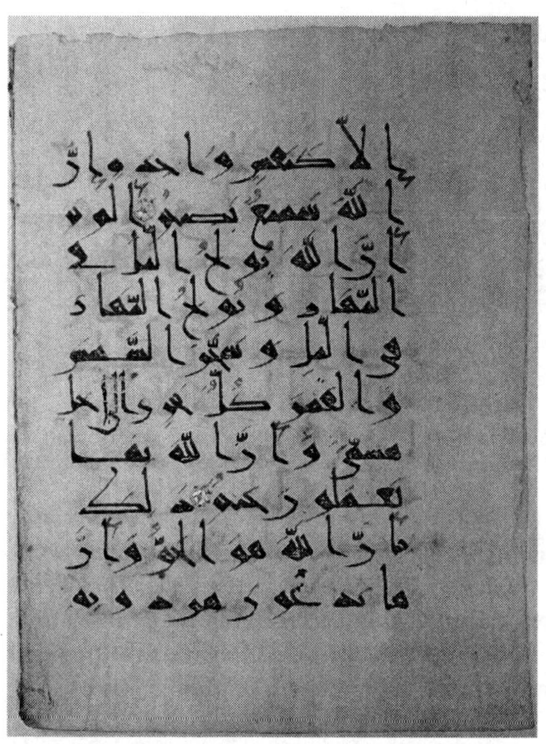

Fig. 2.2.7 Qur'ān fragment, vellum, 100 × 85 mm, eleventh century. Example of New Style (NS) script. Sūra XXX, 50–53; XXXI, 25–30; MS Damascus, National Museum, Inv. 'ayn 344–345, verso.

right, but to a lesser extent than the earlier fragments, and the appearance of diacritical dots, vowels in red ink and simple decorative bands between the *sūras*.

The label of 'Kufic' or the definition of 'Kufic script'—and again this is a name derived from the geographical denomination of the city of Kufa in sourthern Iraq—in order to describe a certain graphic typology of the Arabic script has long stayed in use in manuscript catalogues: already Jacob Georg Christian Adler in his catalogue of the Qur'ānic manuscripts in the Royal Library of Copenhagen entitled a section 'De literis cuficis' (Adler 1780, 27). A new impulse to palaeographic studies came about only when it became necessary to fragment the mass of documents defined by the supergraphonym of 'Kufic' for the creation of more manageable series of manuscripts which can more easily be analysed (Déroche 1980). Such an impulse has been applied in detail for the catalogue of Qur'ānic manuscripts at the Bibliothèque nationale de France (Déroche 1983). The results of the palaeographic research dedicated to the ancient Qur'ānic codices in the catalogue mentioned above, which includes a contribution eloquently titled 'Éléments de paléographie coranique ancienne' (Déroche 1983, 14–53), have been successively illustrated with numerous examples by the publication of material from the Khalili Collection (Déroche 1992).

As far as the labelling of the scripts employed in the Qur'ānic fragments and codices from the second half of the eighth century to the end of the ninth century is concerned, that is for those scripts which are identified as 'Early Abbasid scripts', an alphanumeric classification system is now available (A.I-F.I), which is connected to an indicative chronological grid. According to this classification, the exemplar illustrated here (fig. 2.2.6: Damascus, National Museum, Inv. 'ayn 350–351), can be assigned to group D, which is attested from the third to the fourth century AH (ninth/tenth century CE). Group D comprehends various styles—it has up to five sub-categories (D.I-D.V)—to the first of which, D.I, pertains the fragment under discussion, considering the following distinctive letters: the independent form of *alif*; the form of *mīm* almost triangular and, in final position, with a short tail with bevelled edges; the form of *kāf* with parallels and symmetrical strokes. From a geographical and chronological point of view, it seems useful to point out that this graphic sub-type is attested from Cairo to Sanaa and from Kairouan to Damascus, and that it was elaborated at the beginning of the third century AH (ninth century CE) and continued to be in use, despite showing less elegant forms, until the beginning of the fourth century AH (tenth century CE). Among the codicological characteristics of this fragment it is worthy to note its horizontal format—employed until the fourth century CE/tenth century CE—and the vegetal-inspired motif, connected to the gold frame of the title of the *sūra*, that started to be in use since the second half of the eighth century CE (Bernus-Taylor – Bittar 2001). Following the chronological development of the scripts employed for the copy of the Qur'ān, the so-called 'New Style' should be mentioned. The 'New Style' group (NS) comprehends a number of scripts, traditionally employed for the copying of books or the writing of documents, that, since the beginning of the tenth century CE, started to be used also for copying the Qur'ān and is attested by *muṣḥaf*-s, in parchment and paper, until the twelfth century CE. The parchment fragment Damascus, National Museum, Inv. 'ayn 344–345 (fig. 2.2.7) can be ascribed to the group NS.I and dated to the sixth century AH (twelfth century CE). It shows a vertical, slender and rather angular script and its vertical format reflects the spread of the use of paper as a writing material, marking the return to the vertical format manuscript after two centuries (third to fourth AH/ninth to tenth CE) in which the oblong format was the common one.

Beyond these classifications, for the remaining graphic witnesses the catalogues often employ traditional terminologies which are tied to the names of calligraphic styles (*nasḫī, ṯuluṯ, rayḥānī, muḥaqqaq,*

Fig. 2.2.8 Isḥāq b. Sulaymān al-Isrā'īlī, *Kitāb ma'rifat al-bawl* or *Liber de urinis*; vellum, dated *Rabī'* II 346 AH/2 June–1 July 957 CE; MS Vatican City, BAV, Vat. ar. 310, detail of f. 50v.

riqā', tawqī'), but it seems to be preferable to adopt descriptions referring to a regional character, such as, for example, 'Yemeni script'—in reference to a script with a characteristic system of punctuation of the letters *dāl* and *ṭā'*—or 'Maghrebi script' which is also distinguishable by a characteristic punctuation of the letters *fā'* and *qāf* (Muzerelle et al. 2005, 98). However, an analogous punctuation to the so-called 'Yemeni' variety has also been found in manuscripts of Javanese origin (Regourd 2002, 254), whereas the definition of a Maghrebi script refers to a vast area—since it includes the western Islamic regions (Spain and northern Africa) as well as western Sub-Saharan Africa—and groups together diverse varieties of writing used in the field of book and document production as well as employed for private use; it is ultimately generic and disconnected from any chronological reference (Gacek 2009, 147–150). However it seems useful to remember that the first dated codex in Maghrebi script goes back to the mid-fourth century AH/mid-tenth century CE, its copying having been completed during the month of *Rabī'* II 346 AH/2 June–1 July 957 CE (Vat. ar. 310, fig. 2.2.8). Moreover one of the most ancient examples of this script is a bilingual fragment, in Latin and Arabic, containing part of the Epistle to the Galatians, that Latin palaeographers attribute to the end of the ninth century CE (D'Ottone 2013).

The great necessity for additional studies dedicated to the immense quantity of Arabic evidence, not only Qur'ānic and not only of the first centuries of the Hegira—it is useful to remember that Arabic book production offers a quantity of manuscripts which is 'so immense even from a merely statistical point of view that it cannot be compared to that in any other civilization, either classical or oriental, including the Islamic ones' (Traini 1975, 1, translation ADO) and that exactly the spatial and chronological vastness of Arabic book production is one of the reasons for the 'delay' in palaeographic studies dedicated to this field (Piemontese 1994)—can be understood in the light of disclamatory choices like that of the catalogue of the private library of Zabīd in whose 'Introduction' the inapplicability of meaningful graphonyms is stated. 'Afin de décrire l'écriture, nous avons adopté, faute de mieux, les grandes catégories habituelles qui, à force d'être éreintées, ne signifient plus grand-chose en termes de datation et de localisation de la copie. En cohérence avec cette observation, nous n'avons pas tenté plus de définition' (Regourd 2006, 15). Therefore, the photographic reproductions have been given the task of illustrating the different scripts. However the idea of illustrating the scripts, rather than trying to describe them, is not new: it was employed in the *Fichier des manuscrits moyen-orientaux datés* (*FiMMOD*, 1992–2001), a publication intended to gather together manuscript specimens, explicitly dated earlier than the year 1500 CE, provided with a codicological description and other basic information, for the sake of comparison with other exemplars lacking any date.

The considerable progress made in the field of the study of Qur'ānic scripts provides us with a certain optimism for future research devoted to other fields of the vast Arabic written heritage. A renewed interest, for example, has recently focused on the study of the scripts of the western part of the *Dār al-Islām* (Jaouhari 2013).

References

Adler 1780, 1782, 1792; Balog 1949; Bernus-Taylor – Bittar 2001; Déroche 1980, 1983, 1992, 1998, 1999, 2003, 2007; D'Ottone 2013, 2014; *FiMMOD*; Gacek 2009; Garbini 1979; Griffith [S.] 2010; Grob 2013; Grohmann 1952; Gruendler 1993, 2006; Heidemann 2010; Hirschler 2012; Hoyland 2010; Jaouhari 2009, 2013; Kaplony 2008; Khan 1992; Levi Della Vida 1947; Marcel 1828; Monferrer-Sala 2010; Muzerelle et al. 2005; Orsatti 1994; Piemontese 1994; Porter [V.] 2011; Rāġib 1990; Regourd 2002, 2006; Robin 2006; Šabbūḥ Ibrāhīm 1376 AH/1956 CE; Sijpesteijn 2008; Traini 1975; Voguet 2003; Whelan n.d.

3. Armenian palaeography (DK)

A historical dimension that Armenian writing shares with almost no other ancient language is the secure knowledge of just when and by whom the Armenian alphabet was invented: it was between 404 and 406 CE that Mesrop Maštocʿ, precocious monk with close ties to the catholicos and king of his time, both of whom encouraged him, conceived the letters. Much has been written about the creation of the original thirty-six letters, an invention intimately tied to Christianity and a source of pride to a people who have had a turbulent history (Mahé 2005–2007). This creation *ex nihilo* effectively eliminates any discussion of the evolution of Armenian from earlier proto scripts, a factor that complicates the study of early Greek, Arabic, and Hebrew writing (for a new study on the construction of the alphabet, see Mouraviev 2010). Armenian is not unique in this respect, since Georgian and the virtually vanished language of the Caucasian Albanians (Gippert et al. 2009) were invented shortly after by the same monk Maštocʿ, at least according to contemporary Armenian sources.

The theoretical result is a precise form for the letters of an alphabet conceptualized at a specific time and place by a religious scholar. Maštocʿ made sure to design a letter for every discrete sound in the language, thus eliminating such combination as 'ch', 'sh', 'dj', 'dz', 'kh', 'th', since each is represented by a single sign. Armenian has its own branch in the eastern section of the Indo-European language group. The order of the letters follows closely that of the Greek alphabet with the extra letters sprinkled in. In the mediaeval period two new letters were added at the end, 'ō' and 'f'. The classical written language called *grabar* remained stable in literary texts until the late nineteenth century when a more popular spoken language was admitted as a viable instrument for writing and publishing. Palaeography and codicology are concerned mostly with *grabar* texts.

Methodologically one can hypothesize a process of gradual changes, perhaps an evolution, of the letters over centuries to produce an intelligible profile of the course of Armenian palaeography. Unfortunately, this is not possible in any linear way, at least for the earliest period, simply because no example of fifth-century Armenian manuscript writing has survived. There are undated stone inscriptions from the Holy Land and Armenia from the fifth century, innumerable graffiti from the Sinai of Armenian pilgrims travelling to Jerusalem in the same period, a couple of metal crosses which bear inscriptions of the sixth or seventh century, and the famous fifth- to seventh-century mosaics with Armenian inscriptions from greater Jerusalem. However, when it comes to manuscript writing, the only early example of Armenian is on a unique papyrus from Egypt now in the Bibliothèque nationale de France (Paris, BnF, Arménien 332, fig. 2.3.1), which probably dates from the sixth century, but in any case logically before the Arab invasion of 640 (Kouymjian 1996b and 1998a). The small document is precious but poses many questions, beginning with its text, which is entirely in Greek (Clackson 2000 for a textual analysis), though written with Armenian letters (Kouymjian 2002a). Furthermore, not only is it unique as the only existing Armenian papyrus, but also the form of its script has no parallel.

Scholars, mostly working in Armenia, have dated fragments and at least two manuscripts preserved there to the seventh and eighth centuries, some even to the fifth, but there is no unanimity on this matter, though recent palimpsest studies are providing a more precise way of dating some of these early fragments.

For the palaeographer neat classification and distinct periodization are easier to work with than a confused tradition. Armenian script types are neither neat nor clean-cut. Real standardization only occurs universally after the advent of printing, when the idiosyncrasies of the scribe are abandoned for total consistency in letter forms. The only other moment when there was a quasi uniformity was under the patronage of the aristocracy and the high clergy during the Cilician kingdom (1198–1375), which gave birth to a near print-like minuscule (*bolorgir*) (fig. 2.3.3); one might point out that Yakob Tašyan was correct in remarking that rounded *erkatʿagir* (majuscule) (fig. 2.3.2) also had an extraordinary consistency in Gospel manuscripts of the ninth, tenth, and eleventh centuries irrespective of the region where the manuscript was copied (Tašyan 1898). Yet, even after the start of printing in the sixteenth century making uniform the production of letters in books that reached remote monasteries, scribes continued to mix scripts right up to the nineteenth century. The most recent Armenian manuscript catalogues, those of the Matenadaran in Yerevan, the Catholicosal collection in Antelias, and the Bibliothèque nationale de France, have started the excellent habit of including a small photographic sample of the script of each manuscript, often of each scribe, as well as of older guard leaves.

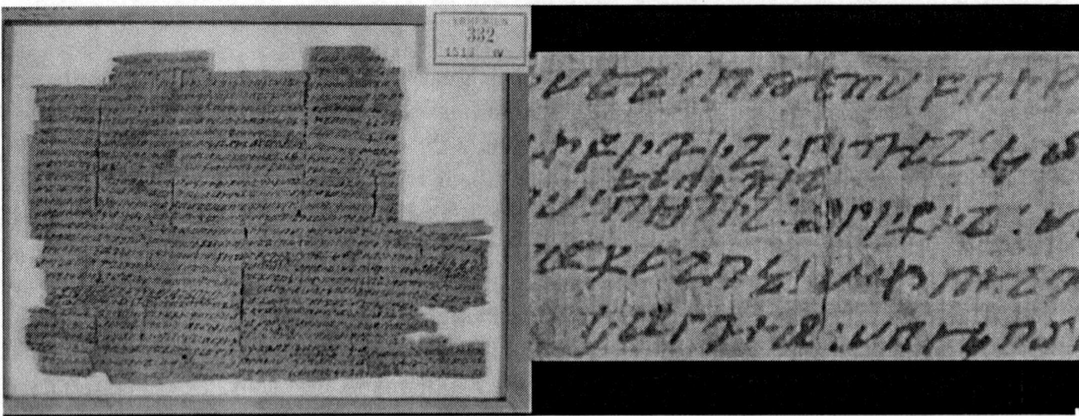

Fig. 2.3.1 Armeno-Greek papyrus, MS Paris, BnF, Arménien 332, pre-640 (Arab conquest of Egypt), recto and detail, photograph courtesy of the Bibliothèque nationale de France.

The first precisely dated manuscripts are two Gospels from the second half of the ninth century after which there is a steady and ever-increasing number of specifically dated codices. The challenge is to try to reconstruct what happened to Armenian writing in the more than four centuries that separate Maštocʿ and his students from the Mlkʿē Gospel (Venice, Mekhitarist library, 1144; fig. 2.3.2) and Lazarian Gospels (Yerevan, Matenadaran, 6200) of 862 and 887. The script of all early dated or datable manuscripts, almost exclusively Gospels, is an upright majuscule called *erkatʿagir*, literally iron letters. These were the ones used in the Jerusalem mosaics (Narkiss – Stone 1979, 21–28) and on a number of lapidary inscriptions preserved or recorded on palaeo-Christian Armenian churches (*Album* 2002, 14–15, figs. III. 2–3, 114–117, nos. 1–4) but they differ greatly from the script of the papyrus or the Sinai graffiti (Stone 1982).

If then we are to approach the history of Armenian palaeography from a theoretical point of view, our first step might be to determine or reconstruct the form of Mesrop's letters and their evolution into the writing we can view today on extant manuscripts. On the other hand if our excursion into palaeography is intended to aid the cataloguer of a disparate collection of manuscripts among which there are one or more Armenian specimens, then an overview of the types of scripts used over time and in different regions would allow for a preliminary classification by a non-specialist. For this perhaps the best approach would be to describe the major scripts found in Armenian manuscripts and comment on problems associated with assigning dates and perhaps even elucidating the text contained in the works.

As in most languages, over time a number of Armenian scripts came into being and were given names. These expressions can be placed into two categories: (1) those that were used by scribes in ancient and mediaeval times, perhaps this can be called the received tradition, and (2) those terms that were created by early modern scholars—palaeographers or proto-palaeographers—writing well after the manuscript tradition had given way to printing. In the first category, only three terms qualify: traditional *erkatʿagir, bolorgir*, and *nōtrgir*. Each term has some textual (manuscript) pedigree. In the second group would be variants of the latter: *mijin* or *ułłagic* (intermediate/semi or angular) *erkatʿagir, pʿokʿr* or *manr* (small) *erkatʿagir, ancʿman gir* (transitional script), and *šłagir* (modern cursive). Even terms like *bun* (original), *boloracev* (rounded), or Mesropian *erkatʿagir* are analytical terms of palaeographers.

This second group represents expressions that clearly describe a script: its size, geometry of the ductus, thinness or slant or relationship to other scripts (i.e. transitional). Confounded by the contradiction between etymological meaning and the appearance of the letters themselves, Tašyan agreed with his eminent contemporary, the linguist Hugo Schuchardt that the terms *erkatʿagir* and *bolorgir* did not conform to the letters as one would expect from their names (Kouymjian 2002a, 25). Ašot Abrahamyan went so far as to say that even certain terms used to describe scripts of other languages fail to invoke the look of the letters, thus reflecting a generalized situation in palaeographic terminology not unique to Armenian. Only the briefest attention has been given to the origin and exact meaning of the labels used to describe the various scripts, some of them going back many centuries (Kouymjian 2002b).

More than two decades ago Michael Stone, Dickran Kouymjian, and Henning Lehmann, set out to produce the *Album of Armenian Paleography* (2002) in order to present an up-to-date study-manual of the discipline. The large *folio* volume with 200 full-colour examples in actual size of an equal number of pre-

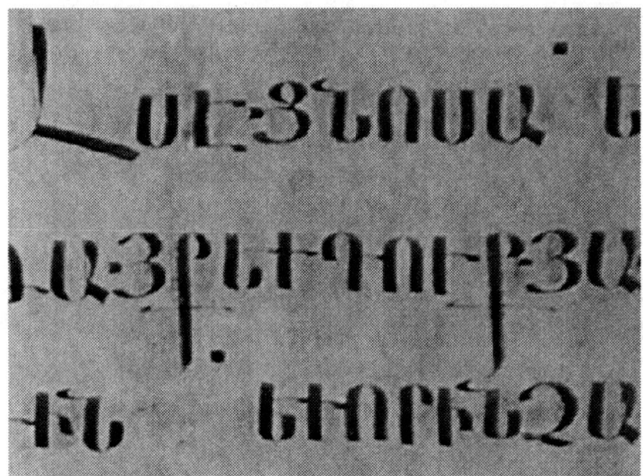

Fig. 2.3.2 Rounded upright or Mesropian *erkat'agir*, Queen Mlk'ē Gospels, 862; MS Venice, Mekhitarist library, 1144, f. 89 detail, photograph by DK.

Fig. 2.3.3 Cilician *bolorgir*, Gospels, Hromkla, 1268, painter T'oros Roslin; MS Yerevan, Matenadaran, 10675, formerly Jerusalem, Patriarchate, 627, f. 137: Entry into Jerusalem, photograph courtesy of Matenadaran.

cisely dated manuscripts from the earliest preserved dated Gospel to the twentieth century contains letter analyses for each sample and exhaustive tables showing the evolution of each letter over time. The authors used what was then new computer technology to extract the individual letters from high-resolution scans rather than reverting to traditional skilful drawings. The Armenian version of 2006 made it accessible to a target audience: researchers in Armenia.

The *Album* presented in elaborate detail almost everything important about the development of Armenian manuscript writing (Kouymjian 2002b), though there are still questions and problems. As an introduction to presenting the major scripts, note that the name of each is designated by *-gir*, 'letter', and preceded by a qualifying descriptive.

Erkat'agir

Erkat'agir, iron letters or writing, has perplexed almost all palaeographers (for a discussion, Kouymjian 2002b, 66–67). In its most majestic form (fig. 2.3.2), it is found in all early Gospels; it is a grand script in capitals similar to the imposing uncials of early Latin manuscripts. It is the form employed in most Armenian lapidary inscriptions through the tenth century. Statistical data (Kouymjian 2012a, 19, plate 1) show it was virtually the only script employed for the parchment codex until the mid-twelfth century, and the exceptions include no Gospel or Biblical texts.

Bolorgir

Bolorgir or minuscule, with compact and very regular shapes (fig. 2.3.3: Yerevan, Matenadaran, 10675) employing ascenders and descenders, dominated scribal hands from the thirteenth to the sixteenth centuries, and continued on into the nineteenth. Ultimately it became the model for lowercase Armenian type fonts just as *erkat'agir* became the prototype for capital letters in printed books. *Bolorgir's* use for short phrases and colophons and even for copying an entire manuscript is clearly attested in the oldest paper manuscript, Yerevan, Matenadaran, 2679, a *Miscellany* of 971 or 981 (*Album* 2002, nos. 10–11), which uses a mixed *erkat'agir-bolorgir* script. It appears even earlier, or at least some of the *bolorgir* letterforms are found in the early or pre-seventh century Armenian papyrus. Like mediaeval Latin and Greek minuscule, *bolorgir* uses majuscule or *erkat'agir* for capitals, resulting in quite different shapes for many upper and lower case letters. Most authorities argue that the spread of *bolorgir* was due to time and economics: it saved valuable parchment because many more words could be copied on a page, and it conserved time because letters could be formed with fewer pen strokes than the three, four, or even five needed for the ductus of *erkat'agir* (Mercier 1978–1979, 53).

A major question concerning Armenian palaeography is: What letters did Mesrop Maštoc' use? Most scholars hold that he conceived and used a large, upright rounded majuscule, similar to that found in early lapidary inscriptions, and thus they called it Mesropian *erkat'agir*. Indeed, Serge Mouraviev's scientific reconstruction of how Maštoc' proceeded systematically from a half a dozen basic forms (including two and their mirror images that produced four of the six) to which were added in a consistent manner descenders and ascenders and lateral strokes to the right and left, would in itself preclude any suggestion of evolution (Mouraviev 2010, 20–45). It has been argued that this script eventually went through vari-

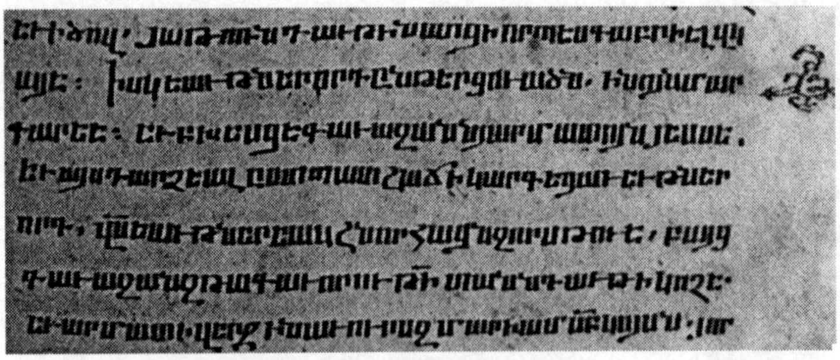

Fig. 2.3.4 Mixed *erkat'agir-bolorgir*, *Miscellany*, 1231–1234, Sanahin; MS Yerevan, Matenadaran, 1204, f. 129, from *Album* 2002.

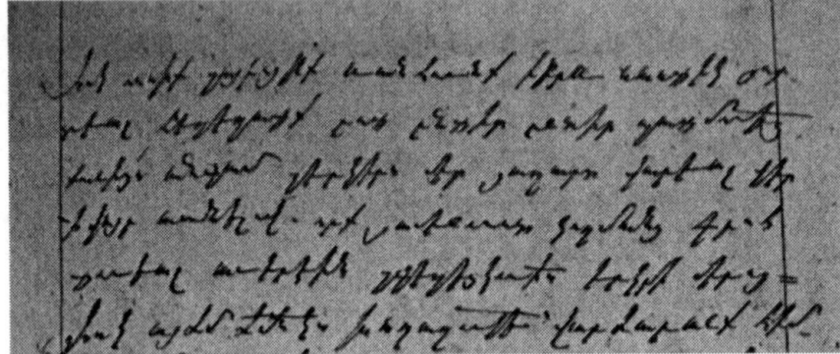

Fig. 2.3.5 *Šlagir*, *Miscellany*, 1853–1854, Tabriz and Salmast; MS Yerevan, Matenadaran, 5138, f. 19, from *Album* 2002.

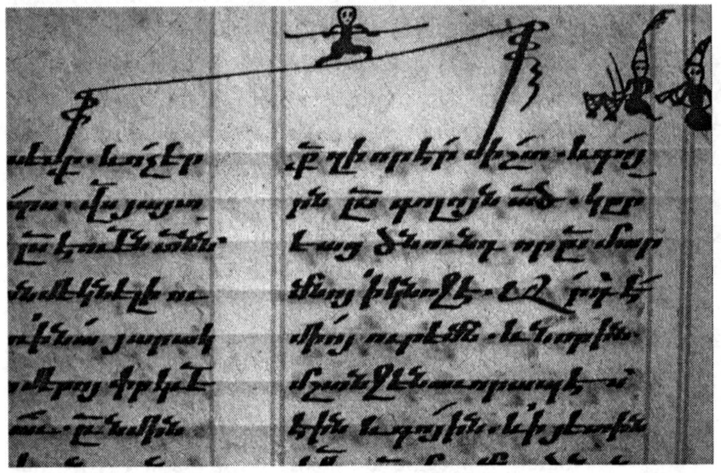

Fig. 2.3.6 Later *bolorgir, Gregory of Nazianzus, Cyril of Alexandria,* 1688, Isfāhān; MS Venice, Mekhitarist library, 1028, f. 95, photograph by DK.

ous changes—slanted, angular, small *erkat'agir*—and eventually evolved into *bolorgir*, and in time into *nōtrgir* and *šlagir*, the post sixteenth-century cursives. Doubt about such a theory started quite early; Yakob Tašyan (1898), the pioneer of the scientific study of Armenian palaeography, hesitated, but Karo Łafadaryan (1939, 71) even maintained that *bolorgir* already existed in the time of Maštocʿ (Kouymjian 2002b, 70–71).

It was also once believed that minuscule gradually developed from earlier formal Latin and Greek majuscule found in inscriptions and the oldest manuscripts. But the late nineteenth-century discovery in Egypt of thousands of Ptolemaic Greek and Roman papyri forced scholars to abandon this notion. Some scholars trace the roots of Greek cursive of the ninth century back to the informal cursive of pre-Christian papyri. Latin minuscule is evident already in third-century papyri (Bischoff 1985, 70). Is it possible that along with majuscule *erkat'agir* some form of an informal cursive script, which later developed into *bolorgir,* was available in the fifth century as surmised by Mercier (1978–1979, 57)?

Uncial was used in the west for more formal writing: Gospels, important religious works, and luxury manuscripts. The data gathered for the *Album* point to a similar pattern. The earliest *bolorgir* manuscripts (tenth century) appear chronologically anomalous until one notes that they are philosophical or non-liturgical texts rather than Gospels.

Examination of pre-Christian Latin papyri shows the origins of Caroline script, which is similar to Armenian *bolorgir*, in earlier cursive minuscule found in them. But the invention of the Armenian alphabet in the early fifth century precludes any pre-Christian antecedents. Greek and Syriac, the languages that most influenced Mesrop Maštocʿ in creating the letters, used both cursive and majuscule in that period. It is difficult to imagine that Mesrop and his pupils, as they translated the Bible, a task that took decades, would have used the laborious original *erkat'agir* for drafts as they went along. The use of the faster-to-write intermediate *erkat'agir* seems more than probable, yet it was not a minuscule script nor cursive. Unfortunately, except for the papyrus, no such informal documents in Armenian have survived before the thirteenth century. The earliest preserved Armenian chancellery documents are from the Cilician court of the thirteenth and early fourteenth century (Kouymjian 2002b, figs. III. 17, 18, 20; Mutafian 2007b, 149–152) and by then minuscule *bolorgir* was already the standard bookhand. Deciding between a theory of evolution to *bolorgir* versus the notion that *erkat'agir* and more cursive scripts co-existed from the fifth century is still an open question.

Mixed erkat'agir-bolorgir script

From the mid-eleventh to the end of the thirteenth century a somewhat bastardized script was used for certain manuscripts (fig. 2.3.4: Yerevan, Matenadaran, 1204), mostly from Greater Armenia to the northeast, employing both uncials and minuscule letters—*erkat'agir* and *bolorgir*—in the same document. It was named 'transitional script' by early palaeographers. However, Michael Stone, during the preparation of the *Album*, proposed it was a separate script (Stone 1998). Kouymjian has not fully accepted his argumentation basing his scepticism on what seems to be a trend showing the use of more *erkat'agir* letters in the earlier mixed script manuscripts, while toward the end, when *erkat'agir* is disappearing as a manuscript hand, the majority of the letters seem to be *bolorgir*, suggesting a transition.

Nōtrgir and šłagir: the cursive scripts.

The secretary working as a scribe (in Latin *notarius*) at the Armenian royal court or the Catholicosate by necessity employed timesaving cursive versions of *bolorgir* and even smaller *nōtrgir* letters (fig. 2.3.7: Yerevan, Matenadaran, 101). The latter term could have entered Armenian from either late Byzantine Greek or Latin. Łafadaryan felt there was no convincing antecedent to the script and, therefore, he assumed that it must have had its origins in the early centuries, even in the time of Maštoc' (Kouymjian 2002b, 74 for discussion). The script when it became formalized in the late sixteenth and seventeenth centuries was composed of small, but thick, unattached letters fashioned of dots and short lines making those without ascenders or descenders hard to distinguish one from the other, though *nōtrgir* is not a cursive script. *Šłagir* (fig. 2.3.5: Yerevan, Matenadaran, 5138), which is modern handwriting with attached letters, usually thin in ductus (it derives from 'fine' and not 'slanted' as some believe), is easy to identify; its beginnings are probably at the end of the eighteenth century (for a longer discussion, Kouymjian 2002b, 73–75).

By the last quarter of the twelfth century minuscule *bolorgir* supplanted majuscule, which was to disappear as a regularly used script about a half-century later. According to the data presented in a sampling of 455 dated manuscripts to 1400, tabulating parchment versus paper and majuscule versus minuscule, this did not coincide exactly with the disappearance of parchment, which followed nearly a century later (Kouymjian 2013, 24 plate 1). By the end of the thirteenth century, one can say fairly safely that the Armenian manuscript was a paper codex made up of senions and written in minuscule *bolorgir*. The only change to be observed in the later period from the seventeenth to the early nineteenth century was the gradual addition of the two cursive scripts, *nōtrgir* (fig. 2.3.7), the so-called notary script, and *šłagir* (fig. 2.3.5), the modern cursive.

A guide for cataloguers

Palaeography has not been used much as a productive tool by cataloguers of Armenian manuscripts, because of the ever-prevalent phenomenon of dated colophons in them. It is used, however, to distinguish between scribes when more than one was involved in the copying. Also, it sometimes served to reinforce the supposition that the person who copied the Canon Tables and the Eusebian Letter in the Gospels (the most copied work) was not the same as the scribe of the text. This would also apply for emendations, whether corrections or marginal additions. Of course, many manuscripts had lost their colophons or that part of the colophon with the date, thus if there was no other evidence, it would be an aid to dating similar to whether parchment or paper was used, or, majuscule or minuscule. At times palaeography could also serve to localize geographically a production centre, even though little work has been done on identifying regional styles of the major scripts.

Fig. 2.3.7 Decorative *nōtrgir*, Religious miscellany, 1740, Constantinople; MS Yerevan, Matenadaran, 101, f. 301, from *Album* 2002.

Below are some basic rules on Armenian manuscripts that can help in supplying rough dating, if the principal colophon is lacking or there is no one who reads Armenian. For a text written on paper, nine chances out of ten the script is not *erkat'agir* and the text dates to after 1200. Guard leaves in parchment are almost always from manuscripts dating before that year, thus written in *erkat'agir* (fig. 2.3.2). Paper manuscripts exist in abundance in three other scripts, *bolorgir*, *nōtrgir*, and *šłagir.* In general the last of these would only be found for modern writing of the nineteenth and twentieth centuries, usually letters or documents rather than texts, but if texts, they would be unique items, diaries, dictionaries, practical manuals, memoirs, novels, poetry, and other modern literature. A manuscript in *bolorgir* (fig. 2.3.6: Venice, Mekhitarist library, 1028) would almost certainly date from the thirteenth to the eighteenth century after which scribal manuscript copying stops; it is hard for the non-specialist to be more precise in dating *bolorgir* with this broad expanse of more than 500 years, without consulting a resource like the *Album of Armenian Paleography*. Finally, a codex in *nōtrgir* would most likely be of the seventeenth or eighteenth (fig. 2.3.7) century. Though these are very approximate guidelines, they would be accurate in more than 85% of cases and could be controlled by comparing an unknown item with the plates or charts in the *Album*, or, if one needs a minimalist guide, four or five good photos, one each of the principal scripts discussed above.

References

Album = Stone et al. 2002; Bischoff 1985; Clackson 2000; Gippert et al. 2009; Kouymjian 1996b, 1998a, 2002a, 2002b, 2007f, 2012a, 2013; Łafadaryan 1939; Mahé 2005–2007; Mercier 1978–1979; Mouraviev 2010; Mutafian 2007b; Narkiss – Stone 1979; Stone 1982, 1998; Tašyan 1898.

4. Coptic palaeography (PB[*])

The Coptic alphabet developed out of a history of attempts to write the Egyptian language using the Greek alphabet, beginning soon after Alexander the Great's conquest of Egypt toward the end of the fourth century BCE. Various selections of characters from the Demotic writing system (which was the last of the native Egyptian writing systems, after the Hieroglyphic and Hieratic systems) were used in addition to the Greek character set in order to represent Egyptian phonemes that were not represented there, and eight of these Demotic characters eventually became a standard part of the Coptic writing system, graphically conformed to the Greek alphabet as written in literary manuscripts around the turn of the third century CE: ϣ [*š*], ϥ [*f*], ϩ [*h*], ⳉ [*x*], ϧ [*x*], ϫ [*č*], ϭ [*ky*], and also ϯ [*ti*] (Kasser 1991b). In addition to the alphabet, the creators (or: standardizers) of the Coptic writing system also borrowed some conventions for line division, abbreviation, punctuation and so on, and they introduced a diacritical sign that was to be written above any consonant or series of consonants that formed a syllable, syllabic consonants being a common phenomenon in Coptic (see also General introduction § 3.6).

To the extent that the Coptic alphabet plus the syllable-marking 'superlinear stroke' was a system for the phonetic transcription of spoken Coptic, it was inevitable that some degree of dialectal variation would be represented in written Coptic, and in fact Coptic manuscripts can be sorted according to phonological features—plus some other criteria—into groups that most likely represent contemporaneous varieties of Coptic from different regions of Egypt (Funk 1988). Broadly speaking, Coptologists distinguish the dialects of northern Egypt, mainly 'Bohairic', of Middle Egypt, mainly 'Fayyumic' and 'Mesokemic', and of southern Egypt, mainly 'Sahidic', among others. In the earliest manuscripts, from around the end of the third century CE until some time after the Arab Conquest of 641, it is rare that we can observe fundamentally distinct styles of script, despite the occurrence of clearly distinct dialect norms in the language as such. But over time, Bohairic (and Fayyumic) came to be written in styles that were quite distinct from the usual appearance of Sahidic. After the fourteenth century, by which time Arabic had replaced Coptic as the medium of spoken communication for nearly all purposes (except in the Church), Coptic manuscripts were almost always written in the Bohairic dialect (often with an accompanying Arabic translation) and in an easily recognizable Bohairic style of script.

Up until the last decades of the eighteenth century, the Coptic manuscripts known in Europe were Bohairic (or bilingual Bohairic-Arabic) codices, with but few exceptions. The first extensive collection of leaves from Sahidic (and a few Fayyumic) codices was assembled towards the end of the eighteenth century by Stefano Borgia at his home in Velletri (Buzi 2009, 15–75). The Danish Egyptologist and Coptologist Georg Zoëga, who catalogued Borgia's Coptic collection, undertook a palaeographical analysis of the fragments and distinguished nine types (*classes*) of script (Zoëga 1810, 169–171 and plates 1–7 after page 663). In order to facilitate further palaeographical study, he included at the end of his catalogue a set of thirty-nine numbered specimens of scripts, grouped according to type (from three to nine specimens per type), which Zoëga himself had prepared by means of laying translucent paper over each selected manuscript page and tracing the letters of a selected passage of text. For each item in his catalogue, Zoëga referred to one or more of his types or specimens: for example, 'characteres ut in specimine n. XI', 'characteres classis VIII', 'characteres classis V ad VI transeuntis'. He was reasonably confident that his class I represented the oldest Coptic manuscripts, for this type of script is very close to that of the oldest Greek codices known at the time, by which Zoëga presumably meant manuscripts thought to be from the fourth and fifth centuries. He was similarly confident that the other extreme of his typology represented the latest Coptic codices, because there he would also place the script of a scholarly Coptic priest, Raphael Tuki, who worked in Rome in the middle of the eighteenth century and some of whose manuscripts were in Borgia's collection. But as for the types between the two extremes, Zoëga explicitly disavowed any knowledge about even their relative chronology. The nine types fall into two distinct groups, which we would now distinguish as 'unimodular' (classes I–IV: 'robustas … et velut quadratas') and 'bimodular' (classes V–IX: 'velut cursivis affines et exiles'), but within these groups Zoëga's distinctions are merely aesthetic, the order of the classes in each group being marked by a perceived decline in quality. There is only one dated manuscript among the Sahidic fragments in the collection catalogued by Zoëga, who used it to illustrate his classes VI (main text, specimen 24) and IX (colophon, specimen 37), giving the date as 519 AM = 802/803 CE, which he found surprisingly early. Later scholars revised the interpretation of the

* I am indebted to Stephen Emmel for his kind suggestions.

Fig. 2.4.1 Unimodular script; MS Berlin, Staatsbibliothek, Or. fol. 1605, f. 5v (detail).

Fig. 2.4.2 Bimodular script; MS Naples, Biblioteca Nazionale Vittorio Emanuele III, IB 3, f. 59v (detail).

date to 719 AM = 1002/1003 CE (Buzi 2009, 119–121).

Zoëga's system of classification was used, although less accurately, also by Agostino Ciasca and Giuseppe Balestri in their edition of Sahidic biblical fragments from the Borgia collection (Ciasca – Balestri 1885–1904, with plates showing entire pages of selected manuscripts), and later by Adolf Hebbelynck and Arnold van Lantschoot in their catalogue of Coptic manuscripts in the Vatican Library, where they applied it mainly to Bohairic and Bohairic-Arabic manuscripts and tried to introduce some more 'technical' terms ('Librarius duplici illa usus est scripturae uncialis specie quam Adolphus Hebbelynck descripsit ..., altera nempe quam vocamus rotunda, in ipso textu biblico, altera quam oblongam appellamus, in titulis, subscriptionibus, emendationibus et notis'; Hebbelynck – van Lantschoot 1937, 4). Zoëga's classes of script remained a point of reference for Coptic palaeography for over a century. For example, Walter Ewing Crum, in landmark catalogues of Coptic manuscripts in two British collections early in the twentieth century, made comparative references either to published plates or else to Zoëga's classes and specimens, for example, '*cf.* Zoëga, cl. iv., no. xix' (Crum 1905b, 67); 'Script of Zoega's 9th class' (Crum 1909, 43); or he made very basic statements such as 'uncial, early type'. But Crum was careful to state clearly that he had intentionally 'scarcely ever made [a suggestion] as to the age of the manuscripts described' (Crum 1905b, xviii) or did so only 'with the utmost diffidence' (Crum 1909, xii), because he was convinced that 'suspended judgment is indeed still imperative on this fundamental question' of the age of the surviving Coptic manuscripts, the vast majority of which are without any recorded date, and his remarks in this connexion still merit consideration even now, a century later (Crum 1905b, xviii–xix).

Henry Hyvernat was the first scholar to publish a Coptic palaeographical album, based largely on Bohairic hagiographical manuscripts that he was editing together with Balestri, without any attempt to define the different typologies encountered (Hyvernat 1888). In this respect, the work undertaken by Viktor Stegemann, who took into consideration both literary and documentary scripts from the beginning of Coptic textual production (third century) to the eleventh century and beyond, represented significant progress (Stegemann 1936). Although Stegemann proposed a chronology of Coptic palaeography largely dependent on the Greek script typologies—an approach which turned out to be, at least in part, misleading—he gave due attention to manuscripts whose dates are known because of the presence of dated colophons. Unfortunately, since then there has been little further progress in the systematic study of Coptic writing, a Coptic palaeography published by Maria Cramer about thirty years after Stegemann representing in this respect a missed opportunity (Cramer 1964b)—being nothing more than a collections of samples of scripts—although increasing attention is now being paid to Coptic documentary scripts (for example, a first classification of Coptic cursive writing has been proposed by Alain Delattre on the basis of the study of the documents from Bawit: see Delattre 2007).

Although Coptic studies have experienced significant improvements in codicology in the last decades (see Ch. 1 § 5)—a manual of Coptic codicology is still a desideratum, but increasing attention has been devoted to the physical description of manuscripts by editors of the texts (see surveys by Emmel 1993;

Emmel 1999; Boud'hors 2006)—up to now, Coptologists cannot depend on a reliable palaeographic classification and on a shared terminology. In 1985, taking as a model what at that time had already been done for Hebrew palaeography, Bentley Layton expressed the need for 'a chronological album of sample photographs of all known dated and datable Coptic manuscripts ... sorted according to date and (so far as possible) locality' (Layton 1985, 155). Such a study—which has been accomplished recently now also for Armenian palaeography—has not yet been realized.

Despite the worthy efforts of individual editors who have not neglected the codicological and palaeographical aspects of an editor's task, as well as increased attention to diacritical signs and the like (for example, Kasser 2001) and some recent systematic attempts at reaching a unified view of some (older) Coptic writings (Gardner – Choat 2004; Orsini 2008a; Orsini 2008b; Orsini forthcoming), 'this science is still far from reaching the maturity needed to satisfy the most demanding among specialized users' (Kasser 1991c, 176; see also Boud'hors 2006, 95). A scarcity of dated manuscripts, or of manuscripts which may be attributed to a sure archaeological context, and the marked taste for the imitation of older scripts—Coptic writings which used the same graphic characteristics as a Greek typology might be much later than their model—represent only two of the several causes of the difficulty in tracing a reliable palaeographic chronology.

It is a well established fact, however, that the scripts of most of the older literary manuscripts (third to eleventh centuries), and also of some official documents, may be described as belonging to only two fundamentally different types, namely the types of Zoëga's classes I–IV and V–IX: (1) the 'Biblical majuscule', according to Guglielmo Cavallo's terminology (Cavallo 1967, 1975)—a round, 'unimodular', bilinear, and slowly written calligraphic style of writing, often exhibiting a marked contrast in thickness between vertical and horizontal or diagonal strokes ('thick-and-thin style')—and (2) the 'Coptic uncial' or 'Alexandrian majuscule'—an upright, bilinear style of writing, executed with a thick pen and characterized by more sinuous glyphs, with a marked contrast between broad letters and narrow letters (especially ⲉ [*e*], ⲑ [*th*], ⲟ [*o*], ⲥ [*s*]), whose extremities could be decorated with round dots and loops (figs. 2.4.1, 2). One of the few certainties in the history of Coptic writing is that between the end of the eighth century and the beginning of the ninth century, a 'bimodular' variant of the Coptic uncial script came progressively to replace the unimodular type, which came more and more to be reserved for specific kinds of literature, such as biblical texts and works from the monastic tradition of Shenoute and Pachomius. There are reasons to suppose that the emergence of this new writing fashion is to be attributed to the monastic centres of the Fayyum oasis.

As a consequence of the situation delineated above, it is not surprising that the palaeographic descriptions included in catalogues of Coptic manuscripts are rarely satisfactory, although since the beginning of Coptic studies, scholars have been aware of the importance of including them.

The first Coptologist to give explicit systematic attention to the problem of palaeography in the context of catalogue descriptions was Bentley Layton, who in the paragraph entitled 'Descriptive Method' in his *Catalogue of Coptic Literary Manuscripts in the British Library Acquired since the Year 1906* explained clearly the criteria that he had applied in describing the 'hand' of a given manuscript that he was cataloguing (Layton 1987, lxiii–lxiv). Avoiding cautiously any categorization and specific terminology, Layton concentrated his attention on the hands rather than on any script typology and noted only 'the minimal number of characteristics needed to identify a given hand in a more or less specific way'. According to this choice, the following palaeographic elements were described: orientation of vertical strokes (upright, left-sloping, right-sloping), types and shapes of some specific and 'revealing' letters (tall, short, wide, narrow, 4-stroke, 3-stroke, etc.), possible presence of superlineation and punctuation, possible use of thick-and-thin style, and the height of ten lines of text together with their ten interlinear spaces. He did not include in his descriptions any explicit statements about the classification of the script as either bimodular or unimodular, but he supplied his catalogue with thirty-two plates containing specimens (consisting in little portions of pages) representing many of the hands described.

The same system was used in the *Catalogue of the Coptic Manuscripts in the Pierpont Morgan Library in New York* by Leo Depuydt, who, however, specified that the 'script most commonly found in the Morgan Coptic literary manuscripts is known to Greek palaeographers as the 'Coptic uncial'' (Depuydt 1993, ci). He listed all the characteristics of this script, including the narrow shape of some letters, although he did not use the term 'bimodular' to describe it. The second volume of Depuydt's catalogue is dedicated wholly to plates (entire pages are reproduced). Several series of plates are dedicated to frontispieces, headpieces and tailpieces, but the main attention is given to the scripts, where again—as in Layton's catalogue—the term is to be meant more as a *specimen* of hands than as a typology. Both scholars clearly considered premature any more detailed and categorized classification.

To conclude, what Rodolphe Kasser declared almost twenty-five years ago is unfortunately for the most part still valid: 'Coptic palaeography is still a new field' (Kasser 1991c, 176). It is a field which is still to be explored, and also by means of that coveted, but until now neglected, systematic and critical collection and analysis of all available dated Coptic manuscripts, which would also benefit philological studies.

Unexpected help might come from the recent attempt to apply radiocarbon dating technique, to Coptic parchments (Schüssler forthcoming).

References

Boud'hors 2006; Buzi 2009; Cavallo 1967, 1975; Ciasca – Balestri 1885–1904; Cramer 1964b; Crum 1905b, 1909; Delattre 2007; Depuydt 1993; Emmel 1993, 1999; Funk 1988; Gardner – Choat 2004; Hebbelynck – van Lantschoot 1937; Hyvernat 1888; Kasser 1991b, 1991c, 2001; Layton 1985, 1987; Orsini 2008a, 2008b, forthcoming; Schüssler forthcoming; Stegemann 1936; Zoëga 1810.

5. Ethiopic palaeography (ABa–DN)

A few inscriptions dating to the second/third centuries CE (cf. the metal object of ʿAddi Galamo, *RIÉ* no. 180, issued by a GDR, king of Aksum, or the inscription on the obelisk at Maṭarā, *RIÉ* no. 223) are the earliest, at least approximately datable evidence of the Ethiopic language (or Geʿez, Geez, Ancient Ethiopic, Classical Ethiopic). These inscriptions already attest the appearance of a clearly defined script, rigorously left-to-right (with a few right-to-left exceptions in the very early period, cf. *RIÉ* no. 181), in purely consonantal form. It included originally twenty four consonants and semivowels, i.e. all those of the subsequent period except *ṗ* and *p* (see below). It mainly consisted of one or more vertical lines, smaller horizontal strokes, circles, and circles and strokes. Enriched and implemented from the fourth century CE at the latest, with an original notation system for seven vowel orders (*a u i ā ē e o*, with the sixth order also used for zero vowel), the resulting syllabary was used for centuries, with very minor changes and additions, for writing Ethiopic and is still used for Amharic, Tigrinya, Tigre, as well as for other vernacular languages of Ethiopia and Eritrea. It is known with the traditional name of *fidal*, of obscure etymology. It is traditionally arranged in the so-called Geʿez sequence (*h*, *l*, *ḥ*, *m*, *ś*, *r*, *s*, etc.) of South Semitic origin, or in the Hebrew- and Arabic-like so-called *abugidā* sequence (ʾ, *b*, *g*, *d*, *h*, *w*, *ḥ*, etc.), following a tradition closer to the Phoenician alphabet and derived ones.

The vocalization system was probably adopted following an Indian syllabic script system and is tangible evidence of South-Asian influences in the area in ancient times. It is the only syllabary used by a Semitic language. The basic form of the first *a*-order are modified in each consonant for the other six orders by the addition of horizontal and vertical short lines, rings and half rings. The earliest vocalized inscriptions were issued by king ʿĒzānā in his pagan period, and are therefore datable to the first half of the fourth century CE (*RIÉ* nos. 187, 188). It can not to be excluded that vocalization was used at earlier times, as legends on coins provide clues in this sense (Schneider 1995). The occasional use and status of *matres lectionis* in inscriptions and coins is controversial (cf. Frantsouzoff 2005).

The Ethiopic script does not mark the beginning of literacy in the area, since a South Arabian script (Sabaean) was used from the eighth/seventh centuries to the fifth/fourth centuries BCE, as attested by a corpus of little less than two hundred inscriptions in Sabaean language. In the Aksumite period (since the first century CE) the use of the Greek alphabet and language is attested, with a series of royal inscriptions datable to the second/third century CE (*RIÉ* nos. 269–286) and legends on coins. The Greek script might be responsible for the left-to-right direction of the Ethiopic script, and Greek capital letters were used since then on to write the numerals (one character each for the numerals from 1 to 9, for the tens from 10 to 90, and for 100). A special revival of the Sabaean script—but not of the language, apart from a few superficial sabaeisms—is attested from the fourth to the sixth centuries CE, when some royal inscriptions were written in Ethiopic language in Sabaean script. The inscriptions were bilingual, in Ethiopic (in Sabaean script) and Greek (*RIÉ* nos. 190 and 271), and pseudo-trilingual, in Ethiopic (in Ethiopic non-vocalized script), Ethiopic (in Sabaean script), and Greek—the latter in two sets for a total of six inscriptions (*RIÉ* nos. 185 I, 185 II, 270 and 185 I bis, 185 II bis, 270 bis).

The Ethiopic script, like the Sabaean, belongs to the South Semitic branch, but its direct relationship and dependence upon the South Arabian script (bustrophedon or right-to-left) was disputed, since non-Sabaean scripts used for pre-Islamic North-Arabian languages attested in Arabia (especially Thamudic) have also been invoked as a possible parallel. The question seems to be probably outdated now, since growing documentation of palm sticks with carved South Arabian cursive writing has emerged, that provides a wide range of possible parallels for the Ethiopian script within the South Arabian scripts (see, for example, Stein 2010). The Ethiopic script uses a smaller set of characters than that used by the Sabaean, since some Semitic phonemes have merged in Ethiopic (*ḏ* > *z*, *ṯ* > *s*, *ẓ* > *ṣ*, *š* > *s*, *ġ* > ʿ). Conversely, an additional set of labiovelars (*k*ʷ, *g*ʷ, *ḫ*ʷ, *q*ʷ, yet only with vowels *a*, *i*, *ā*, *ē*, *e*) and an extended set of labials (*b*, *f* < *p*, *p*, *ṗ*) was developed, bringing the total number of letters to 30 and that of syllabic characters to 202. According to the Geʿez sequence, the letters are the following: *h*, *l*, *ḥ*, *m*, *ś*, *r*, *s*, *q*, *q*ʷ, *b*, *t*, *n*, *ḫ*, *ḫ*ʷ, ʾ, *k*, *k*ʷ, *w*, ʿ, *z*, *y*, *d*, *g*, *g*ʷ, *ṭ*, *ṗ*, *ṣ*, *ḍ*, *f*, *p*.

The forms of the Ethiopic letters are more rounded in comparison to the Sabaean monumental characters and must have been developed while using softer text-carriers—which one, however, is difficult to say, since no positive evidence has emerged so far (but see Ch. 1 § 6.1.1)—as attested also for cursive

South-Arabian palm-sticks inscriptions (cf. Stein 2010). The Ethiopic script has never to this day developed either any opposition between capital and non-capital letter forms, or any extensive use of ligatures: it has always retained the basic, uncial-like appearance attested in the Aksumite inscriptions and each character is written separately, with very few isolated exceptions. Word units were separated by a vertical bar (as in the Sabaean script), that still appears in a late Aksumite inscription (inscription of Ham, *RIÉ* no. 232, variously dated from the ninth to the thirteenth century). Yet horizontal double strokes (=), which turned into the two-dot mark, or 'colon', separating words in manuscripts, were already used in the sixth century inscription of king Kālēb at Mārib (*RIÉ* no. 195, early decades of the sixth century).

Apart from the Aksumite inscriptions, attested not later than the ninth/tenth centuries, the earliest much debated manuscript evidence is that of two Abbā Garimā Four Gospels manuscripts, likely to be dated to around the sixth century CE (see Ch. 1 § 6.2.3). It is actually in these manuscripts that the two additional plosive characters for two labial phonemes *p* and *ṗ* (*p* probably borrowed from the Greek alphabet and developed earlier than *ṗ*, that was easily obtained from the modification of *ṣ*) are attested for the first time. These characters are mainly used to render Greek loanwords (typically, Greek *π*), a need which immediately occurred during the process of translating the Bible and other Christian writings starting from the fourth century CE. For example, the original lengthening of the vertical strokes by the addition of a short line for the formation of the vowel orders by modification of the basic shape turned in the course of time into a symmetric shortening of the opposite vertical stroke(s), with the apparent search for an harmonious, more regular and stable shape of the character. The ancient way of prolonging the legs of the letters under the base-line, however, can still be observed in some ancient manuscripts (cf. Sergew Hable Selassie 1991, for EMML no. 8509; also attested in the Abbā Garimā Four Gospels manuscripts, the manuscript of the 'Aksumite Collection' (for which see Ch. 3 § 3.2), and EMML no. 6907). Generally, this small corpus of very archaic manuscripts attests that many vowel markers appear to be shaped after different principles, dissimilar to those of the apparently 'standard mediaeval Ethiopic'.

Sources not yet fully exploited for palaeographic research are captions on mural inscriptions of mediaeval churches (the best known are those of Gannata Māryām, some of them dating to the thirteenth century at the latest), and the carved inscriptions on wooden altar-tablet chairs (the so-called *manāberta tābot*, the best known are those preserved in the churches of Lālibalā and dated to the twelfth/thirteenth century).

The writing system remained stable in the better known mediaeval manuscript tradition (from the thirteenth century on), notwithstanding the vanishing of Ethiopic as a spoken language. The interference with the vernacular languages had palaeographic consequences which are attested *without exception* in all extant manuscripts, such as the interchangeability in the script of graphic pairs and triplets due to the eventual phonetic merging of phonemes in the spoken language (*s*/*ś*, *ʾ*/*ʿ*, *ṣ*/*ḍ*, *h*/*ḥ*/*ḫ*, and in the vocalism, laryngeals-*a*/laryngeals-*ā*), only partially balanced by the persistence of some traditional spellings (for example *neguś* and not *negus*, etc.). A noteworthy innovation was the introduction of additional characters for the new phonemes of the Amharic (palatals, and later also fricatives in Tigrinya, for loanwords etc.). The palatals are already attested (according to Ullendorff 1951, 209) at the end of the fifteenth century (cf. Oxford, Bodleian Library, MS. E. D. Clarke Or. 39). These additions—namely, of *š*, *č*, *ň*, *ž*, *ǧ*, *č̣*—brought the number of basic letters of the Amharic syllabary to 251, and of Tigrinya—also with *ḵ*, *q̄*—to 265, yet without considering additional further combinations (for example, with the labial appendix frequently occurring in Amharic, *hʷā*, *lʷā*, etc., and others).

Only occasionally attempts were made at correcting the heaviest shortcomings of the Ethiopic script, i.e. the missing mark of gemination (Conti Rossini 1914, 16–17, 161–162 (no. 142), on BnF d'Abbadie 53, where the Arabic *tašdīd* is used for this), and the ambiguity of the sixth order, that indicates either vowel *e* or zero vowel.

The main features of Ethiopic palaeography have been examined by Siegbert Uhlig (1988, 1990; this still remains the only reliable starting point for further research, to be strictly carried out only on the basis of dated manuscripts; see also Uhlig – Bausi 2010). From the early period to approximately the fourteenth century, the context for the development of Ethiopic script can be only described on the basis of a few centres of writing activities that have preserved relevant evidence in the most northern area, namely, Endā Abbā Garimā, Dabra Libānos of Ham and nearby areas, Gerʿāltā, Lāstā and Lālibalā, Dabra Ḥayq Estifānos, and a few others, some of which must have already existed during the Aksumite time. Multiplication of the local scribal traditions must have taken place in the fourteenth century, possibly with local styles influencing each other through migration of books and scribes. For the moment, there is no clear evidence that any political authority—even in the period of King Zarʾa Yāʿqob (1434–1468), who was mostly engaged in manuscript production and dissemination, both as 'author and editor'—tried officially to enforce the use of a specific script and limit the use of others, even though some scripts might have been considered more influential than others. The picture of the subsequent centuries might be defined by coexistence and interference of numerous local styles, some of them represented by single scribes, some by the book production in monastic centres, within a relatively small area of the Christian Kingdom.

The study of Ethiopic palaeography by Uhlig (1988, 1990) established a broad frame for the history of Ethiopic script, with its periods and general features; but it is still not possible to understand how they relate to regional styles and idiosyncrasies of individual scribes. No strictly *palaeographic* regional or scriptorial styles could be clearly identified so far (despite occasional general references to 'the style of Gunda Gundē'; cf. also a first attempt by Nosnitsin 2013a, 2013b). Uhlig 1988 and Uhlig 1990 defined the following stages and respective traits:

1. Monumental script: the earliest manuscripts (including the Abbā Garimā Four Gospels) until the second half of the fourteenth century. The characters resemble much the style of the inscriptions, with very angular shapes. The proportions are tall and slender, with some strictness and rigidity. The distinctive marks of the characters are centred around their upper half, while the strokes placed in the upper half tend to descend to the base line. Punctuation marks seem disproportionately large. The decorative elements are minimal.

In the light of the newly acquired evidence for an earlier dating of the two Abbā Garimā Four Gospels (*c.* fourth–sixth century) and a not very much later dating of the third Abbā Garimā Four Gospels book, as well as a probable twelfth/thirteenth century dating of the 'Aksumite Collection', it appears necessary today to introduce new distinctions. The notion of 'monumental script'—currently used to refer to the very long period of early use and existence of the Ethiopic script, of which only scanty evidence has survived—must be subdivided into at least two typologies of scripts, that show a different degree of 'monumentality': 1a. script with vowel markers shaped according to principles that appear different from those typical for the mediaeval time, including significant deviations in vocalization (fig. 1.6.8); 1b. script which shows mostly the normal shapes of vowel markers. Some distinctive letter forms: *ʿa* of triangular downwards oriented shape, set upon the base line in all orders; *ṭe* with lateral strokes reaching the base line, the central one with articulated kink in the upper part; *se* with the marker of the sixth order composed of two short strokes: the vertical one and a perpendicular horizontal one to the left; *ʾe* has the left leg drawn high up to the headline, kinked vowel marker tending to horizontal position; *lo* has the ring marking the vowel set close to the top of the letter, without a linking line; archaic forms of numerals (see below) (fig. 1.6.4).

2. Second half of the fourteenth to mid-fifteenth century (the definition of 'square script' given by Uhlig 1990, 43, 72 is probably not the most appropriate). The script shows more variability and appears less monumental and somehow irregular in size, slant and space between characters. The basic forms show departure from 'monumentality' and become, to one or another extent, wider and more rounded, the curvatures and crosses go beyond the letter limit, and the distinctive marks of the characters move towards their middle. The number of punctuation marks grows, and the *crux ansata* is also used, probably as a mark to distinguish main sections. Some distinctive letter forms: the triangular body of the *ʿa* letter forms with vowel markers (*ʿā*, *ʿē*, etc.) is raised; the lateral strokes of *ṭe* are also raised, the kink on the central stroke moves to the middle; the left leg of *ʾe* is shorter, the vowel marker is set at it at bigger angle; the vowel marker of *lo* is sometimes set on a link line; the loops of *ma*, with small 'counters' are set tightly together, sometimes one upon another; the horizontal lines of *ne* are short (fig. 1.6.3).

3. Rounded script: mid-fifteenth to mid-sixteenth century. There appears a deliberate tendency for standardization and regularity (for example, in the slant of both the vertical and/or horizontal strokes), with more stable shapes. The letters become rounded and wider. The fifth order loops (half-ring) are open. Some distinctive letter forms: the loops of *ma* are not separated, but are set very closely together; the markers of the vowel *ē* for some letters (*ʿē*, *ʾē*, *mē*, *sē*, *bē*, etc.) as well as the 'counter' of *le* frequently remain open; the vowel marker of *lo* is mostly set on a link line (fig. 1.6.6 recto).

4. Compressed slender script: mid-sixteenth to mid-seventeenth century. The proportions change again, and the letters tend to become smaller and taller, and broadly spaced; however, the lines are even and dense, often drawn with pointed pens. The characters are of uniform height, and the strokes run par-

allel. Some distinctive letter forms: the loops of *ma* in all forms are always separated; vowel markers and 'counters' of more letters remain unclosed; the end of the upper horizontal stroke of *ne* is directed downward.

5. *Gʷelḥ* script: mid-seventeenth to the second half of the eighteenth century. This script is considered the most elegant. The characters are evenly shaped and clear. It is the script typical for the period of the Gondarine Kingdom (1632–1769); it probably originated in Gondar, the capital city (in this sense, it represents a regional script). It is sometimes called 'the script of kings', and is frequently associated with the large luxury manuscript production of that time. Some distinctive letter forms: the bodies or parts of the letters set under the headline (*mā, mi, śā, ṗa, qa, wā*, etc.) are raised high and appear smaller; the vowel marker *-ā* of the letters which is drawn downwards to the left (*tā, qā, yā*, also *wo*, etc.) is strongly articulated; the vowel marker *-ē* and 'counters' of various letters are usually closed; the modern form of *ṗe* appears, to substitute various older forms.

6. *Raqiq* script: mid-seventeenth to mid-nineteenth century. This class runs partly parallel to the previous one. It is characterized by smaller size and less regularity, a lower-quality realization and sometimes also a careless hand. Punctuation marks tend to disappear.

7. Bulky and cursive script: nineteenth and twentieth centuries. The characteristics of different periods gradually disappear; along with irregular (clumsy) handwriting cursive forms with a right slant appear.

The definitions '*raqiq*-script' and 'bulky and cursive script of the nineteenth/twentieth century' currently cover a large variety of local scripts, poorly known and hardly studied.

The general quality of the script depends on the status of the text (the highest reserved, for example, for the Four Gospels), and is clearly inferior in marginal notes. A peculiar palaeographic development is represented by the 'micro-script' of chant manuscripts (not earlier than the sixteenth century), where each line accommodates both the main text line and tiny notation signs above.

The absence of cursive forms, the extreme rarity of monograms (attested on coins, seals and rock inscriptions), abbreviations (rarely on the margins of manuscripts, such as the *qom*-sign, probably from Greek *komma*, cf. Zuurmond 1989, Part I, 34) and tachygraphic forms (essentially limited to the use of the monogram *-gzi-* in *Egziʾabḥēr*, 'Lord', of the graphic form *20ʾēl* for *Esrāʾēl*, 'Israel' (that is '20' *esrā* plus *-ʾēl*), and of the first one or two letters in words such as *qeddus* (*qe*) 'holy, saint', *salām* (*sa*) 'salutation', and proper names, including *nomina sacra*, while a more extensive use is to be found in the *andemtā* commentaries and liturgical literature in dialogic sections) severely limit palaeographic variations that can be observed in Ethiopian manuscripts to very few phenomena. The limits of the periods as described above are not clearly cut, the hands as attested in the manuscripts frequently show the 'progressive' or 'traditionalist' attitudes of the scribes, with both 'new' and 'old features' mixed, the latter still retained in much later times than their respective periods of origin. The palaeographical dating of the manuscripts is in many cases difficult if not assisted by internal and codicological evidence.

Among the most conspicuous features that provide clear and precise evidence of diachronical development, one may mention the archaic forms of numerals 'one' (narrow and slightly downwards-oriented triangular) and 'four' (also triangular, but larger and upwards-oriented); numerals 'six' (compressed and lower, with no ring) and 'seven' (narrow and higher, also with no ring); second and sixth order of *w* (second order with horizontal stroke by the side in the middle, not in the lower end as in later manuscripts; sixth order with stroke at the top, not in the middle). In very archaic manuscripts (such as the Abbā Garimā Four Gospels manuscripts) the real value of these signs can sometimes not be exactly perceived in terms of shape, neither rightly understood but in the context and within an opposition system; the same happens for other signs (*s, t, ḥ*) in first, fourth and sixth orders opposing correlations (cf. Zuurmond 1989, Part I, 303). Numeral 'ten' also occasionally exhibits a peculiar rare archaic form with a ring on the right side of the leg (cf. Dillmann 1907, 33, n. 1; Leroy [Jules] et al. 1961, 20ff., esp. 25; Uhlig 1988, 212).

The study of normal punctuation is also part of Palaeography, yet, in the absence of reliable editions which also take punctuation into consideration, no correlation has been consistently established with manuscript dating (cf. Bausi 2008a, 537, n. 105).

In Ethiopian manuscript studies, palaeography has essentially been applied in its strict sense of establishing correlations between graphic shapes of signs, and dates (see Bausi 2004a, 12–14). As such, it was already employed for dating manuscripts by the authors of the first catalogues of Ethiopian manuscripts (cf. Bausi 2007), when the text itself provided no hint (a colophon, additional notes, etc.) as to the time of writing (for this purpose, facsimiles plates were often included in the catalogues, cf. Wright 1877, Grébaut – Tisserant 1935, 1936, etc.). Cataloguing offered at times an important occasion for palaeographic reflection: such is the case of the catalogue by Carlo Conti Rossini of the d'Abbadie collection in the Bibliothèque nationale de France, where a short treatise of Ethiopic palaeography precedes the description (Conti Rossini 1914, 9–19). Apart from this, one cannot say that there exists any standardized palaeographic terminology or any accepted periodization which is applied in the manuscripts catalogues.

References

Bausi 2004a, 2007, 2008a; Conti Rossini 1914; Dillmann 1907; Frantsouzoff 2005, 2010; Grébaut – Tisserant 1935, 1936; Leroy [Jules] et al. 1961; Nosnitsin 2013a, 2013b; *RIÉ* = Bernard et al. 1991–2000; Schneider 1995; Sergew Hable Selassie 1991; Stein 2010; Uhlig 1988, 1990; Uhlig – Bausi 2010; Ullendorff 1951; Wright 1877; Zuurmond 1989.

6. Georgian palaeography (TP)

The history of Georgian writing: basic considerations

For the study of Georgian manuscripts, palaeography is crucial indeed, given that Georgian codices are much less frequently provided with colophons indicating the date and place of their origin than are codices of comparable traditions. This is especially true for the early period of Georgian literacy (fifth to ninth centuries), the first dated codex being the Sinai *Mravaltavi* of 863–864 CE (Sinai, St Catherine, georg. 32-57-33+N89; see General introduction § 3.8), but the problem persists up to the nineteenth century; for instance, among the fifteen post-fourteenth-century codices used in the edition of the chronicle *Kartlis Cxovreba* ('The Life of Kartli'; Meṭreveli 2008, 23), only seven show an explicit dating (between the seventeenth and nineteenth centuries). Scholars investigating Georgian manuscripts and their history have therefore to rely upon external criteria that enable them to provide at least a relative chronology. For the early period, there is a clear-cut linguistic criterion in the occurrence of the so-called *xanmeṭi* and *haemeṭi* forms, which are characterized by special verbal and nominal affixes consisting of the letters *x* (*kh*) and *h* and which admit of assigning the manuscripts in which they appear (mostly palimpsests) to approximately the fifth to eighth centuries (see General introduction § 3.8) in accordance with contemporaneous epigraphical monuments that show the same features. Linguistic features can also be taken into account for later periods, for example the transition from Old to Middle Georgian by about the eleventh century when, among other changes, the nominative ending, *-i*, started to be omitted after vocalic stems due to the reduction of diphthongs (*-e* + *i* = *-ey* > *-e* etc.), with a concomitant increase of confusion concerning the distribution of the letters *e* and *ē* (= *ey*) and the use of the letter *y* in general (Danelia – Sarǯvelaʒe 1997, 241–246).

In the case of Georgian, the interrelation with epigraphic sources is also crucial for palaeography proper, in the sense of an historical analysis of the elements and the style of writing used in manuscripts. The most prominent phenomenon that has to be dealt with in this context is the internal development and chronological succession of the three script styles known as *mrglovani* (or *asomtavruli*), *nusxuri* (or *nusxa-xucuri*), and *mxedruli*. The first of them, an 'uncial' majuscule, was the sole script attested between the fifth and the eighth centuries. The oldest witnesses available, stone inscriptions of the fifth century discovered in the Monastery of the Cross near Jerusalem and in the cathedral of Bolnisi in Lower Kartli (South-East Georgia, fig. 2.6.1), still exhibit a near-to 'square' layout of the spaces occupied by individual characters (see the images in Gippert – Tandaschwili 1999–2002 and 2002; see also the General introduction § 3.8), while even the most ancient manuscripts we have at hand (palimpsest undertexts with *xanmeṭi* forms) show at least five characters with a long descender (Ⴏ = *ž*, Ⴔ = *p*, Ⴕ = *k*, Ⴗ = *q̇*, Ⴜ = *ç*, probably also Ⴤ = *q*). Another distinctive feature that changed over time in the use of the *mrglovani* majuscules, is the loop to the left in the characters *b* (Ⴁ), *ž* (Ⴏ), *q̇* (Ⴗ), and *w* (Ⴣ), which was closed in the early centuries but tended to be more and more opened at its top in later times (see the table provided in Gippert et al. 2007a, xxvii, for specimens taken from the twelve different *mrglovani* hands underlying the palimpsest Vienna, ÖNB, Cod.Vind.georg. 2). Whether the shorter descenders appearing in the inscriptions represent the initial shape of the letters in question or whether they were the result of vertical compression in adapting the necessities of epigraphical layout, is related to the question of the emergence of the Georgian script in general and cannot be argued with palaeographically for lack of further evidence.

Nusxuri script (fig. 2.6.2), the minuscule deriving of the older *mrglovani* majuscules, is first attested in an inscription of 835 CE found in the *Sioni* church at Aṭeni (on the bank of the river Kura near Gori; Abramišvili 1976); it is also represented in the scribe's colophon of the Sinai *Mravaltavi* (f. 274rb; see image 279 online at <http://www.e-corpus.org/notices/101436/gallery> and Gippert forthcoming for details). Inversely, the colophons of the Gospel manuscript Sin. georg. 15 written by the scribe Ioane Zos-

Fig. 2.6.1 Inscription from the *Sioni* church of Bolnisi, *c.*493–495 CE, from Mačavariani 2008, 34.

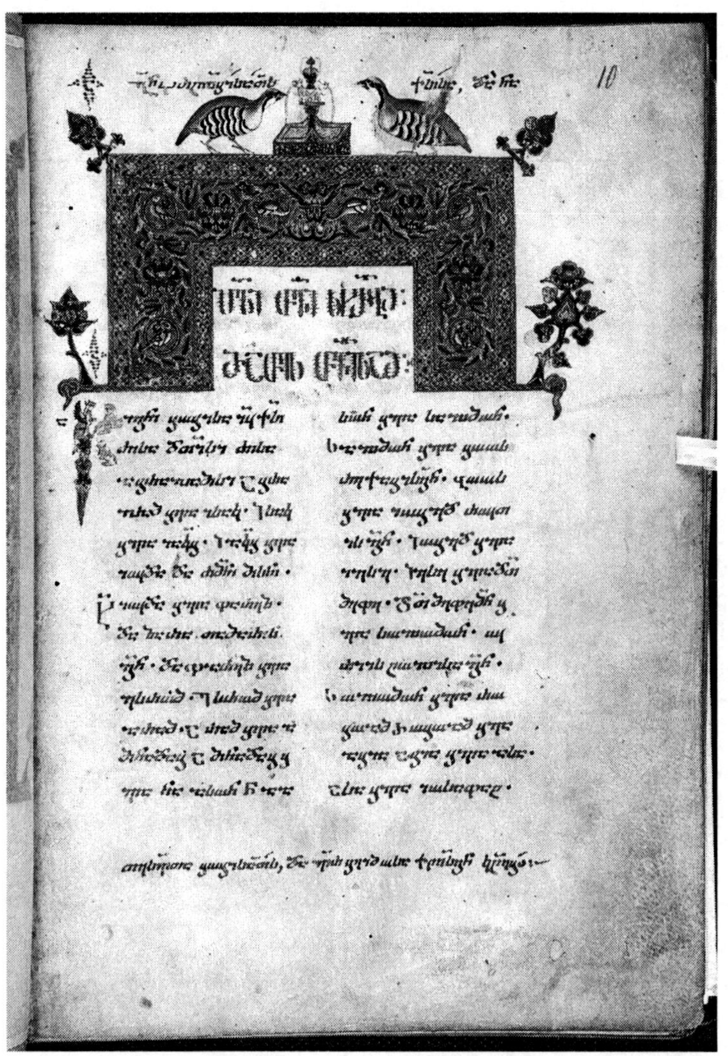

Fig. 2.6.2 Tbilisi, National Centre of Manuscripts, A-1335 (Vani Gospels), twelfth–thirteenth centuries, f. 10r, photo courtesy of the National Centre of Manuscripts.

ime (see Ch. 1 § 7.6.2) in 978 CE are, at least partly, in *mrglovani* script (ff. 84r, 224v), while the main text is in *nusxuri* minuscules (see images 87 and 242 on <http://www.e-corpus.org/notices/98066/gallery>). From the tenth century onward, the number of manuscripts that are written in *nusxuri* script throughout increases notably; we may mention, among others, the Sinai codices georg. 26 (954 CE; <http://www.e-corpus.org/notices/112553/gallery>) and 19 (1074 CE; <http://www.e-corpus.org/notices/98067/gallery>), the *Mravaltavi* of Ḳlarǯeti (Tbilisi, National Centre of Manuscripts, A-144, tenth century), or a manuscript containing the Georgian translation of the *Revelation of John* by the Athonite Eptwme (Tbilisi, National Centre of Manuscripts, H-1346, 978 CE; see Imnaišvili 1961). However, it is important to note that in all *nusxuri* manuscripts, majuscules continue to be used in headers, as initials, and the like, which is why they are also called *asomtavruli* (lit. 'capital letters'). An intermediate stage between 'plain' majuscule and minuscule script styles may be seen in the hand of the so-called 'Hymnary of papyrus and parchment' (*č̣il-eṭraṭis iadgari*) from Jerusalem (Tbilisi, H-2123, tenth century; see Šaniʒe – Marṭirosovi 1977, 216). Whenever codices exhibit contiguous texts in both scripts side by side, they are likely to have been merged from separate original manuscripts; this is true, for example, for the *Mravaltavi* of Svanetia (A-19, tenth century), which, in a total of 242 folia, contains 12 folia written in *nusxuri* (ff. 95–106) obviously substituting the contents of three quires that had been lost (Gorgaʒe 1927, 2 and 19), or the Sinai codex georg. 34 (tenth century), a compilation by Ioane Zosime, the twenty-second quire of which (ff. 196–203) is in majuscules and which also contains four quires on paper (Garitte 1958, 17–18; see images 152 ff. on <http://www.e-corpus.org/notices/112554/gallery>).

An early usage of the third Georgian script, *mxedruli* (fig. 2.6.3), in its turn a cursive variant of the *nusxuri* minuscules, is attested in another inscription of the *Sioni* of Aṭeni, of the late tenth century (982–986 CE; Abramišvili – Aleksiʒe 1978). Among manuscripts, the Sinai Gospel codex georg. 30 of 979 CE is likely to be the first to contain a contemporary scribe's note in *mxedruli* script (f. 75rb; Garitte 1956, 71; see image 78 on <http://www.e-corpus.org/notices/101435/gallery>). The late tenth-century codex S-1141 (the so-called 'Collective codex of Šaṭberdi', *Šaṭberdis ḳrebuli*) contains a note in *mxedruli* script that was added by a hand allegedly of the eleventh century (Gigineišvili – Giunašvili 1979, 22). We may thus conclude that the tenth century marks the beginning of the cohabitation of all three Georgian scripts, which came to an end with the decline of manuscript production in the nineteenth century.

The first publications that focused on the palaeographical development of the Georgian scripts date from the end of the nineteenth century. They comprised lithographic copies of many specimens taken from manuscripts in order to elaborate a first historical overview (Marr 1901; Šaniʒe 1924; Čikobava 1927–1930).

The most systematical effort in this field was undertaken by Ilia Abulaʒe who published a palaeographical album (Abulaʒe 1973) with reproductions of all three types of Georgian scripts as used in epigraphic monuments and, especially, in manuscripts (both dated and undated), arranged in chronological order in tabular form. More exhaustive research into this is the object of an ongoing project of the National Centre of Manuscripts, Tbilisi, which aims at the preparation of a palaeographic album to be published online, based on a larger amount of dated Georgian manuscripts.

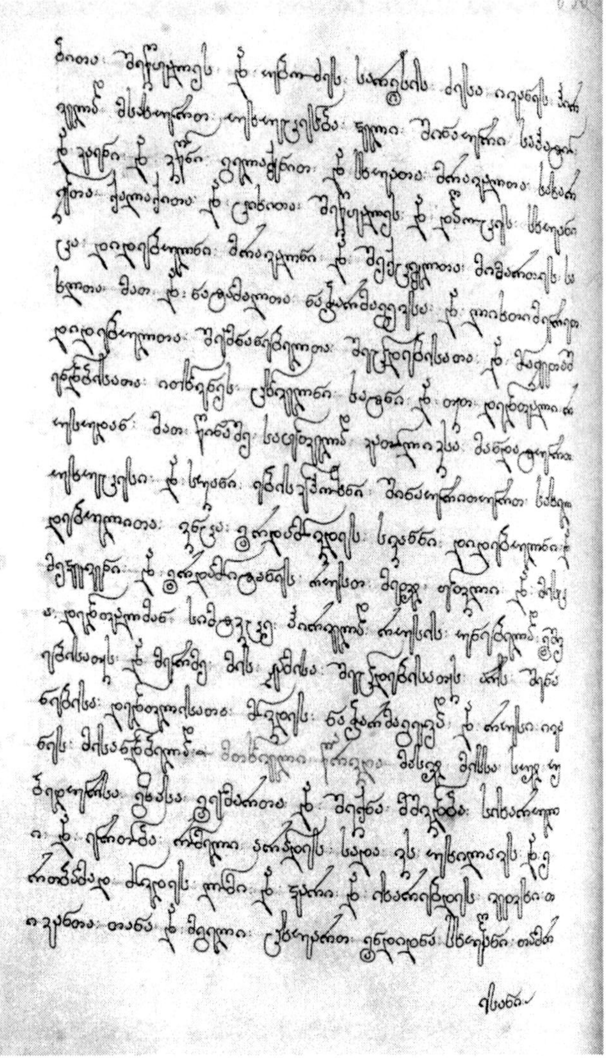

Fig. 2.6.3 'Life of Kartli', Tbilisi, National Centre of Manuscripts, S-30, 1633–1646, f. 470v, from Ḳaranaʒe et al. 2010, 114.

Georgian palaeography as represented in catalogues: scripts and hands

In spite of differences between their styles, the many catalogues that have been produced for the various collections of Georgian manuscripts (see Ch. 4 § 2.5) show quite a homogeneous picture concerning their palaeographical content. Usually these catalogues restrict themselves to naming the type of script (*asomtavruli, nusxuri, mxedruli*) used in a given manuscript, sometimes further characterized according to its visual appearance ('*nusxuri* in small letters': Bregaʒe et al. 1985, 16; 'slightly inclined *nusxuri* of medium size': Axobaʒe et al. 1986, 28; 'beautiful *nusxuri*': Taq̇aišvili 1933, 24). Another detail that may be mentioned in the catalogues is the number of hands. Of course, information on the type of script might be considered as helpful—if only in a very general way—when it comes to the task of determining a manuscript's production date. For example, we would not expect a *mxedruli* manuscript to be older than the tenth century, but on the other hand, it might theoretically have been written between the tenth and the twentieth centuries. What could be useful here is the possibility of identification of the time to which a given hand belongs, as well as the identification of the literary centre from where a given style of writing originates. It should be noted, however, that Georgian palaeography lacks researches characterizing the peculiarities of the individual scriptoria, and no explicit explanations are available about how and on what basis a given hand can be identified as belonging to a concrete epoch or literary centre. Despite this methodological lack, some cataloguers have nevertheless attempted to date manuscripts on the base of the hands at work, but without giving any explicit argumentation for it. For instance, the catalogue of the 'New Finds' of Georgian manuscripts in St Catherine's monastery on Mount Sinai (Aleksiʒe et al. 2005) states that whenever an exact date of a manuscript could not be found, a tentative dating is given (in square brackets) on the basis of palaeographical evidence. The same is true for many other catalogues as well. Only in very rare cases, more developed explanations can be found as in Ekvtime Taq̇aišvili's catalogue of the Georgian manuscripts of the Bibliothèque nationale de France (Taq̇aišvili 1933), which states, for example, that a given manuscript (Paris, BnF, Géorgien 2) must have been copied in the second half of the eighteenth century as proven 'with no doubt' by its hand and orthographical peculiarities (Taq̇aišvili 1933, 23). Taq̇aišvili was especially eager to provide datings on the basis of the comparison of hands because he considered the previous catalogue of the Paris manuscripts (Macler 1908) to be very imprecise in that respect.

Among the catalogues of Georgian manuscripts, those compiled by Robert Pierpont Blake (1932a, 1932b, 1933) prove to be the most exhaustive in terms of palaeographical descriptions. In his catalogue of the Georgian manuscripts in Cambridge, Blake states with respect to the famous Georgian-Hebrew palimpsest (Cambridge, Cambridge University Library, Taylor-Schlechter 12,741; no. 1 in his catalogue): 'The script is large, bold and striking, traced by the hand of a skilled scribe, but I should hardly call it elegant', and he even provides 'a careful tracing of the actual letters in addition to the facsimile reproduction of the leaf' to support the palaeographical analysis (Blake 1932b, 210). Blake was also the first to identify the literary centres where Georgian manuscripts were copied, styling a script a 'small asomt'avruli of Sinai-Palestinian type' (Blake 1932b, 213: Cambridge, Add. 1890,1 / no. 3) or describing manuscripts as being 'written in Sinaitic nusxuri' (Blake 1932b, 214: MS Cambridge, Add. 1890,8 / no. 4), 'en nuskhuri assez grand, incliné, angulaire, d'un type non-athonite' (Blake 1932a, 302: Athos, Iviron, no. 4), 'en nuskhuri grand droit arrondi, du type d'Iskhan' (Blake 1932a, 312: Athos, Iviron, no. 5), etc. The same scholar proposed a more systematical classification of manuscripts on the basis of the different writing styles that were linked to different scriptoria of various epochs; for instance, he identified two distinct layers among the Georgian manuscripts kept in the Iviron monastery on Mount Athos, an older one stemming from Ṭao-Ḳlarǯeti (in eastern Anatolia) and a more recent one representing the properly Athonite production (Blake 1932a, 291–292).

Other palaeographical criteria: punctuation and abbreviations

Of course, there are some other criteria beyond scripts and hands that may prove useful for the dating of Georgian manuscripts. This is true, first of all, for punctuation. Investigations into this topic (Kaǯaia 1963, 1969a, 1969b; Gippert et al. 2007a) have proven that punctuation was a common feature of manuscripts since the fifth century even though it remained absent from epigraphic monuments throughout the early period (fifth to seventh centuries). In the oldest palimpsests, two points were usually deployed to express the end of sentences or paragraphs. The end of a section or longer passage was sometimes denoted by an arrow flying to the right, while a minor break (between clauses or phrases) was noted by a single dot (see Gippert et al. 2007a, xxviii for a survey of the punctuation marks appearing in the palimpsest Vienna, ÖNB, Cod.Vind.georg. 2). Later codices, such as the Sinai *Mravaltavi* of 863/864, the Tetraevangelium of Adiši (897 CE, see Taq̇aišvili 1916), or manuscripts Tbilisi, A-38, S-29 and S-42 (all ninth to tenth centuries) are characterized by less systematic rules, using a single dot or a group of three dots to express the meaning of a minor break, two dots for a major break, or groups of three or four dots for the end of a paragraph (Kaǯaia 1969a; Danelia – Sarǯvelaʒe 1997, 318–323). The scribe Ioane Zosime, who worked in the tenth century first in the Laura of St Sabas and then on Mount Sinai, used one dot for a minor break, two at the end of sentences, and four at the end of a paragraph (Danelia – Sarǯvelaʒe 1997, 322). Eprem Mcire, a famous Georgian translator of the eleventh century, proposed yet another system, using one dot for a minor break, two at the end of sentences, three for major breaks, and six at the end of a paragraph; however, his system was only used by himself and in manuscripts originating from the Black Mountain near Antioch such as, for example, MSS Tbilisi, Q-1158 (eleventh century), A-677 (eleventh or twelfth century), Q-37 (1091 CE), A-162 (eleventh century), A-115 (twelfth century; Danelia – Sarǯvelaʒe 1997, 324). From the twelfth century on, a semicolon-like sign (;) was introduced with the function of an interrogation mark.

It should be noted that marks with the function of separating words or narrow phrases are also known in the Georgian tradition. While the oldest (*xanmeṭi*) palimpsests were still written in plain *scriptio continua* (words were not split), the so-called 'Sinai Lectionary' of the Universitätsbibliothek in Graz (Austria), a codex allegedly of the eighth century mixing *xanmeṭi* and *haemeṭi* forms, exhibits a small apostrophe-like mark (') denoting the end of words (on top of the respective line; see the images and the transcripts provided in Gippert et al. 2007b). The use of a single dot for this function is also known. According to Lamara Kaǯaia, the use of *scriptio continua* first gave way to the use of breaking marks in the seventh century. Spaces between words appeared subsequently, but the process of transition from marks to spaces was not yet accomplished in the tenth century, given that the Sinai *Mravaltavi* of 863/864 CE and other codices such as Tbilisi A-509, Q-209, or Q-211 (all tenth century) still show the non-systematical usage of separating dots. Some manuscripts of the fifteenth to eighteenth centuries still used two or three dots as separation marks (Kaǯaia 1965).

Apart from punctuation marks proper, Georgian manuscripts typically use an abbreviation sign in form of an overbar, which is called *karagma* (from Greek *charagma*). The abbreviations marked by this can be of different types, comprising suspension, contraction, abbreviation by *litera singularis*, and consonantic abbreviation (see Boeder 1987 for a linguistic analysis of the methods involved). An analysis of the most ancient (*xanmeṭi* and post-*xanmeṭi*) manuscripts shows that it was first the *nomina sacra* (Jesus and Christ, God and Lord, Israel and Jerusalem) but also the stem of the relative pronoun (*romel-*) and some conjunctions that were regularly abbreviated. The list was then extended by some postpositions and preverbs (Gippert et al. 2007a, xxix–xxxi where a frequency list of the abbreviated elements in the different undertexts of the Vienna palimpsest is given). The general impression is that in comparison with *xanmeṭi* and *haemeṭi* codices, the number of abbreviated words increased steadily from the eighth century onwards. Good examples for the extended use of abbreviations are the Sinai *Mravaltavi* of 863/864 CE, where almost all frequent words (pronouns, conjunctions, frequent verb forms) are abbreviated, or the 'Hymnary on papyrus and parchment' (tenth century), which goes even beyond this. In general it is assumed that the abundant use of abbreviations was characteristic for manuscripts of private usage as well as liturgical manuscripts whose contents were mostly known by heart (Danelia – Sarǯvelaʒe 1997, 305–318).

References

Abramišvili 1976; Abramišvili – Aleksiʒe 1978; Abulaʒe 1949, 1973; Aleksiʒe et al. 2005; Axobaʒe et al. 1986; Blake 1932a, 1932b, 1933; Boeder 1987; Bregaʒe et al. 1985; Čikobava 1927–1930; Danelia 2009; Danelia – Sarǯvelaʒe 1997; Garitte 1956; Gigineišvili – Giunašvili 1979; Gippert forthcoming; Gippert et al. 2007a; Gorgaʒe 1927; Imnaišvili 1961; Ḳaranaʒe et al. 2010; Kaǯaia 1963, 1965, 1969a, 1969b; Mačavariani 2008; Macler 1908; Marr 1901; Meṭreveli 2008; Šaniʒe 1924; Šaniʒe – Marṭirosovi 1977; Surgulaʒe 1978; Taqaišvili 1916, 1933. Web sources: *e-corpus* <http://www.e-corpus.org>, last access May 2014; Gippert et al. 2007b; Gippert – Tandaschwili 1999–2002 and 2002.

7. Greek palaeography (DB)

Field of study

The objects of study of Greek palaeography are all the handwritten expressions in Greek characters, regardless of their support or their language (in specific areas, indeed, the Greek alphabet has sometimes been used for texts written in other languages, as for example Latin or the dialects of Southern Italy). The discipline covers a wide temporal span. It starts with the first evidences of Greek script, which are inscriptions engraved or painted on different materials—such as the cup of Nestor found in Pithecusa (Ischia) and the Dipylon vase—ascribed to the eighth century BCE, that is a period shortly after the introduction of the alphabet in Greece, a phenomenon of uncertain dating, but that is now believed to refer to the late ninth or the early eighth century BCE. If limiting oneself to the scripts written on soft materials, Greek palaeography covers a period that goes from the fifth century BCE until at least the sixteenth century, when the print, already used for the Greek texts from the last quarter of the previous century, spread more and more (the first incunabulum with a certain date fully written in Greek, the Grammar by Konstantinos Laskaris, was printed in Milan on 30 January 1476 by Dionysius Paravisinus). It is also necessary to consider that Greek handwriting was used for a long time after that date, even in book production, and that, if one looks at correspondence and Modern Greek documents, it seems impossible to identify precisely its end.

The location and extent of the cultural area of reference varies over time and is not easy to circumscribe. For the ancient period, the majority of papyri and parchments comes from Egypt, while a small number comes from Sinai, Palestine and Syria (but it is worth remembering also at least the centres of Dura Europos in Mesopotamia, Petra in Jordan and Herculaneum). For the mediaeval period, the coordinates for manuscripts kept in archives and libraries become those of Byzantium: besides Egypt, Syria and Palestine (at least until the seventh century, but sometimes far beyond the Arab conquest of those regions), this is mainly the rest of the empire, with its centre in Constantinople and its provincial areas in the east (Asia Minor, Crete, Cyprus) and in the west (continental Greece and, above all, South Italy and Sicily), where Greek handwriting continued to be employed also after the end of the political control of Byzantium and its fall in 1453: in this period a production of Greek books is attested also in Italy and in other main European centres.

A short history of Greek writing

The recent publication of the materials from two tombs excavated at Daphnē (Athens) in May 1981—including some fragments of wooden tablets and of a literary roll (now kept in the Piraeus Museum as MΠ 7452–7455 and MΠ 7449, 8517–8523)—allows us to put the beginning of the history of the Greek book as early as in the fifth century BCE (Pöhlmann – West 2012, cp. Ch. 1 § 8.2.2). Indeed all these materials are to be dated to before 430/420 BCE, a date which is proposed for the two tombs on an archaeological basis and, therefore, is a *terminus ante quem* for all the items inside them. But it is above all from the Hellenistic period that it is possible to follow with more precision the written production on papyrus. Indeed, although the surviving documentation continues to be poor and fragmentary, it is possible to refer to the fourth century BCE—no later than the period of Alexander the Great—*P.Derveni* (a comment to an orphic theogony found at Derveni in Macedonia and now kept in the Archaeological Museum of Thessaloniki) and *P.Berol.* inv. 9875 (a fragment of the *Persae* of Timotheus, from Abusir, near the necropolis of Saqqara, in Egypt); the most ancient documents are slightly later, but still datable to the fourth century BCE: UPZ I 1 (*P.Vindob.* G 1), a *defixio* known as the 'curse of Artemisia', SB XIV 11942 (*P.Saqqara* inv. 1972 GP 3), a short order by Peucestas, one of the officers of Alexander (331–323 BCE), and *P.Eleph.* 1 (*P.Berol.* inv. 13500), a marriage contract concluded in 310 BCE and found at the island of Elephantine, which is the most ancient document with a certain date. From what we can infer from such a partial and desultory outline, there are no substantial formal differences between the Greek hands used for documents and those employed for books: they are majuscule scripts, i.e. inscribed in a bilinear system, overall rigid and angular; the strokes are horizontally oriented and the letters are detached and of the same dimensions; only the papyrus from Elephantine shows a contrast between larger and narrower or smaller letters, so anticipating a characteristic which will be typical above all of the third century BCE.

From this century the differentiations between scripts for documents and scripts for books can be more clearly perceived, and they are due in particular to the speed of their execution (*ductus*, in the Italian meaning of the term, see Ch. 2 § 1): hands employed for books are slower and still marked by a

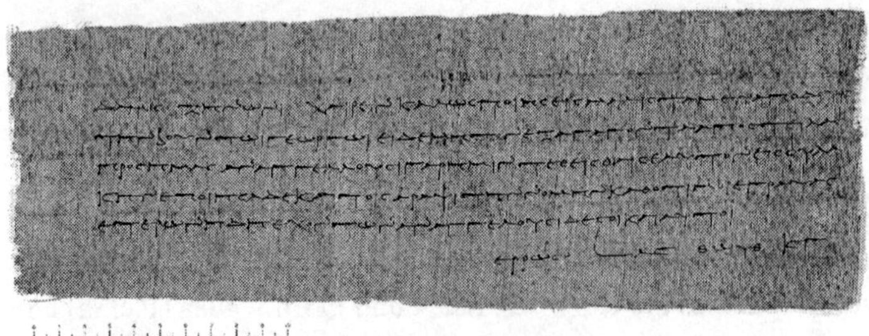

Fig. 2.7.1 Florence, BML, inv. 10720 = PSI IV 367, recto.

Fig. 2.7.2 Florence, BML, inv. 20949 = PSI XI 1213, recto, detail.

Fig. 2.7.3 Florence, BML, PSI XII 1278, recto, detail.

sort of 'archaism', even if they are in part square and unimodular and in part angular and characterized by a contrast in size between broader and narrower letters (as, for example, *P.Petrie* II 50 = Dublin, Trinity College, Pap. F 8 A + Oxford, Bodleian Library, MS. Gr. class. d. 22 (P) and *P.Petrie* I 5–8 = London, BL, Pap. 488, containing respectively the *Laches* and the *Phaedo* by Plato); documentary hands assume a more or less fast tendency, with soft strokes and some incipient joins between consecutive letters and a more or less marked contrast in letter-size. In this context an elegant and fine stylization stands out with deliberately contrived strokes: the so-called 'Alexandrian chancery writing' (e.g. Florence, BML, inv. 10720 = PSI IV 367, fig. 2.7.1), well documented from the Zenon archive. It represents the script *par excellence* of the central offices of the Ptolemaic administration for almost all the third century BCE. The transition from the third to the second century BCE does not mark radical transformations for Greek handwriting. There is always a more pronounced distinction among scripts with a more or less fast *ductus*, semi-cursive or properly cursive (mostly used for documents), and slow scripts, typical of book production but used also to write specific documents (the so-called 'writings of esteem', used above all for requests to high authorities or for important acts).

In second-century BCE book hands two fundamental trends can be identified: accurate but fluid scripts and more elaborate and elegant scripts, enhanced at the ends by decorative *apices*. In both tendencies the contrast in size—which up to that period was a rather frequent characteristic in Greek handwritings—fades or disappears, and is replaced by rounded and unimodular shapes. More radical changes start from the first century BCE and during all the Roman period. On the side of documentary scripts, the development of cursive trends reaches full maturity, with a variety of results—sometimes more rounded and sinuous, sometimes slender and sloping towards the right—and of morphologically new solutions, due to the speed of execution; on the side of book hands, round unimodular scripts have a larger and more systematic diffusion. From the first century BCE to the first century CE, such scripts are sometimes bilinear, and show serifs and contrast in the thickness of strokes, sometimes soft, thin and looped, sometimes fluid and regular; some of them can be fixed in a style, as the so-called 'epsilon-thēta style', from the name of the letters that are its peculiar element, showing the middle stroke reduced, isolated in the centre and with the shape of a point (this style is used, among others, in some papyri of Herculaneum, as the *P.Herc.* 1044 (= Oxford, Bodleian Library, MS. Gr. class. c. 4 0823-0832) which contains the *Life of Philodemus*). But there is also a trend towards rigid, angled scripts with contrast in size, that, even if with a touch of archaism, acquire a new look, more stylistically characterized on the basis of a selection and a revision of different, ancient and new, elements.

During the second and the third centuries CE—a period of widespread literacy—on the side of slow writings, basically used for book production, the two previously identified trends—round and unimodular

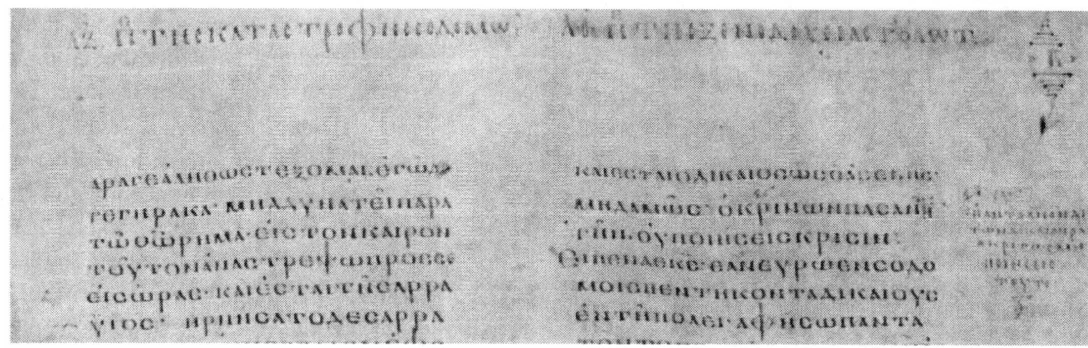

Fig. 2.7.4 Paris, BnF, Coislin 1, f. 15r, detail.

or angular and with contrast in size—are organized in graphical paradigms, that are formally stable and characterized by a strong normative impact. On one hand, we find the 'round majuscule' (Florence, BML, inv. 20949 = PSI XI 1213, fig. 2.7.2; also known as 'Roman uncial': on the limits and the incorrectness of the word 'uncial', see Ch. 2 § 1), one of the peaks of Greek calligraphy, as it is shown by one of the most famous manuscripts written in this script, the Hawara Homer (*P.Haw.* 24–28 = Oxford, Bodleian Library, MS. Gr. class. a 1). The 'round majuscule' was used until the end of the second or beginning of the third century and was intrinsically connected with the secular culture, even if employed in a period of increasing diffusion of Christianity, and mimetically recovered, in the late fifth century, perhaps in the pagan circles of Alexandria, in order to prepare the Ambrosian *Iliad* (Milan, Biblioteca Ambrosiana, F 205 inf.). On the other hand, there is the 'Severe style' (e.g. Florence, BML, PSI XII 1278, fig. 2.7.3) which is very well attested during the second and third centuries. Its manifestations are not always homogeneous: they are sometimes upright, sometimes sloped to the right, but all are marked by a sober and rigorous taste and by the respect of a rigid contrast in size (in particular, *epsilon*, *thēta* and *sigma* are narrow, *omikron* is rather small and suspended above the base line). A famous manuscript showing such handwriting is the Bacchylides *P.Lond.Lit.* 46 (London, BL, Pap. 733) + PSI XII 1278 (Florence, BML, fig. 2.7.3): from this papyrus, the writing is also called 'Bacchylidean uncial'.

Within the slow and calligraphic scripts employed for the production of books, starting from the different graphical tendencies developed in the second and third centuries, in the following period some normative scripts developed: they continued to be used for centuries, structured in frameworks more or less rigidly iterated, until minuscule handwriting started to be used for books, in the eighth and ninth centuries. Among them, there is, at first, the 'Biblical majuscule' (e.g. Paris, BnF, Coislin 1, fig. 2.7.4), a script characterized by an extreme regularity and by an elegant contrast between thinner and thicker strokes: although used also for writing secular manuscripts, this handwriting is linked above all to the sumptuous codices of the Bible of the fourth (the *Codex Vaticanus* and the *Codex Sinaiticus*) and fifth (the *Codex Alexandrinus*) centuries, and continued to be used until the eighth/ninth century in many cases, both on papyrus and on parchment, both secular and, above all, Christian. The 'Alexandrian majuscule' (e.g. Paris, Musée du Louvre, E 10295), employed for the production both of books and documents, has an Egyptian origin; it originates from the graphical experience of the second/third century, characterized by curvilinear and fluent strokes; in the fifth and sixth centuries it presents two typologies: one is unimodular, another shows a contrast between larger and narrower letters (the narrow letters being *epsilon*, *thēta*, *omikron* and *sigma*). This latter prevailed in the Greek world and was used until the eighth century, and, as distinctive writing, even much further. From extant evidence, it seems to have reached its calligraphic perfection inside the patriarchal chancery of Alexandria, perhaps already at the time of Athanasius (328–373), as has been suggested by the recent publication of PSI XVI 1576, containing Festal Letter 9 of Cyril, written in 420/421: here the Alexandrian majuscule is already perfectly realized (Bastianini – Cavallo 2011).

A new rigid and angular script appeared in the fourth and fifth centuries, perhaps a development of the second/third century 'Severe style': the 'pointed majuscule'. It is characterized by a strong contrast in letter-size, angular strokes, and broken curves (hence the name). It presents two styles, upright and sloping. The first one, which at that period was rarely employed, was much more frequent in the Middle Byzantine period, from the ninth to the eleventh century (when the minuscule was already the standard script for book writing) for copying liturgical books, especially the Gospels. The sloping style (e.g. Florence, BML, 10005 = PSI II 126, fig. 2.7.5) was widely diffused from the fourth until the ninth/tenth century. It

Fig. 2.7.5 Florence, BML, inv. 10005 = PSI II 126, recto, detail.

Fig. 2.7.6 Turin, Biblioteca Nazionale, B II 22, f. 199r, detail.

Fig. 2.7.7 Florence, BML, inv. 22015 = PSI XII 1266, recto, detail.

was less compact and monolithic in realization, if compared with other normative scripts, and it was open to local variations, detectable, above all in late periods, from the different inclination of the writing. Beside Constantinopolitan and Italo-Greek styles, we find a characteristic type of it in Sinai and Palestine. The latter area was particularly active in graphical experimentation, as is evident from the elaboration of a 'mixed script'—a sort of sloping pointed majuscule, which is provided with minuscule forms of *alpha* and *mi*—and from some attempts at adapting cursive writings, now minuscule, to book production, resulting in such scripts as the 'Sinaitic minuscule', and, above all, the 'Hagiopolitan minuscule'. The latter can be seen, in its most characteristic shapes, in the manuscript Vatican City, BAV, Vat. gr. 2200 (cp. Ch. 1 § 8.1.3; see Crisci 2012). By contrast, the 'liturgical majuscule' (e.g. Turin, Biblioteca Nazionale, B II 22, fig. 2.7.6) was an expression of the monumentality and of the artificiality typical of later majuscules—especially the biblical and the pointed majuscules—as well as evidence of a decorative taste whose background was more ancient, and not necessarily related to book production. Employed especially in the ninth and tenth centuries, this script exhausted the residual potentialities of majuscules in book production (Orsini 2013).

In the field of informal scripts, of books and above all of documents, a series of changes took place, starting from the third/fourth century. In administration and in law, where since the time of Diocletian Latin entered the oriental regions and imposed itself as the language of the State, the meeting between a Latin script, the 'new cursive' minuscule (i.e. inscribed in a tetralinear system), and Greek bureaucratic writings, still majuscule, led to the birth of the so-called graphic Greek-Latin *koinē*, which provided a series of graphically equivalent but phonetically different signs for Latin and Greek. The *koinē* triggered a quick process of transformation of Greek scripts: between the fifth and the sixth century a new writing appeared, the 'Byzantine cursive', now clearly minuscule and in two different types, one upright (e.g. Florence, BML, 22015 = PSI XII 1266, fig. 2.7.7), the other sloping. Therefore, Greek minuscule was born in the field of documentary writings, and only later, between the eight and the ninth century, was promoted and normalized as book writing. Indeed until this time a certain decline in book production meant that the old normative majuscules—even if clearly separated from ordinary writing and no longer sustained by its vivid contribution—could satisfy the demand for books. But the radical change between the eighth and the ninth century, at first with the iconoclastic controversy and then with the so-called 'Macedonian Renaissance', and the resulting increase of book production imposed, as a necessity, the use of upright Byzantine cursive—minuscule and documentary, and until that period used to write especially acts and notarial or bureaucratic-administrative documents (the adaptation of sloping cursive to book production resulted in the abovementioned 'Hagiopolitan minuscule').

So the minuscule was elevated to the status of book writing in the eighth or ninth century—the most ancient dated codex in minuscule is the Uspenskij Gospel Book, St Petersburg, RNB, Gr. 219, copied in 835 by the monk Nicholas (fig. 2.7.8). During the ninth century, and continuing into the tenth century, minuscule writings show a wide range of articulations, that differ above all in their general appearance,

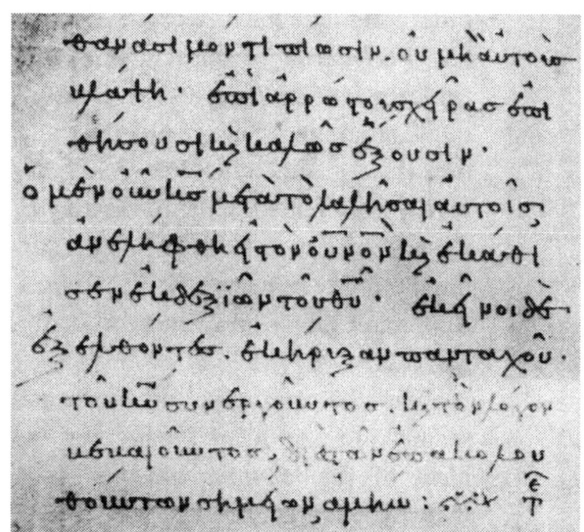

Fig. 2.7.8 St Petersburg, RNB, Gr. 219, f. 158v, detail.

whereas the way letters are executed (*tratteggio*, according to the Italian terminology, see Ch. 2 § 1) is essentially unchanged: we find the 'ancient round minuscule' (or 'Studite minuscule', from the name of the Constantinopolitan monastery of Stoudios, where cursive is thought to have been adopted as book writing, or 'Nicholas type', from the name of the copyist of the Uspenskij Gospel Book); the 'ancient oblong minuscule' (or 'Eustathius type', from the name of the copyist of MS Meteora, Metamorphosis, 591 dated to the year 862/863); the 'square minuscule', upright or inclined; the 'Anastasius type', from the name of the copyist who in 890 copied MS Paris, BnF, Grec 1470 + 1476, a script well attested in Southern Italy although it is not known if it was also born there or if it was widespread there as a more rigid evolution of the 'Eustathius type'; the so-called 'minuscule of the philosophical collection' (e.g. Paris, BnF, Grec 1807, fig. 2.7.9), named after the group of manuscripts, containing philosophical and especially Platonic works, made around the years 850/875; the '*bouletée* minuscule' (e.g. Oxford, Corpus Christi College, 26, fig. 2.7.10), from the thickenings added at the beginning and at the end of the strokes, that represented the most calligraphic writing, almost by definition, of the tenth century. Beside these elegant manifestations, there were many informal, more or less cursive, writings that were used mostly for secular texts, often meant for scholars (cf. Paris, BnF, Grec 1741, fig. 2.7.11).

During the tenth and eleventh centuries, the need to reconcile formal care and speed of execution developed a script conventionally defined as '*Perlschrift*' (e.g. Rome, Biblioteca Angelica, gr. 123, fig. 2.7.12), for its curvilinear appearance and the roundness of the central part of the letters, running on the line like a string of pearls: it soon became the 'normal' writing model for copying parchment, high level books, mostly with religious and sacred texts.

In the provincial areas and above all in Southern Italy peculiar writing styles emerged: the 'ace-of-spades minuscule', named after the typical cursive ligature *epsilon-rho* similar to the ace of spades, used in Calabria and Campania in the tenth and eleventh centuries; the 'minuscule of the Nilian school', widespread in the same period along the route of St Nilus and his brethren from Calabria to Rome; the so-called 'Rossano minuscule', which could represent the evolution of the Nilian script in the eleventh and twelfth centuries; the 'Reggio style', diffused in the area of the Strait of Messina for all the twelfth century and with some forms of persistence until the fourteenth century.

However the passage from the Macedonian age to the Comnenian epoch marked a turning point in the Orient. Beside the '*Perlschrift*', different informal scripts emerged, so that in Greek handwriting a process of substantial and progressive simplification—if compared with the past—was realized. On one side, there was the strand of curvilinear, slow and formal scripts, which were linked to the tradition of the '*Perlschrift*' and were used principally for copying religious books; on the other, there was a strand of informal—more or less cursive and of bureaucratic inspiration—scripts, that were typical of books of secular contents (more and more on paper, from this period) and of (public and private) documents (e.g. Florence, BML, plut. 57.40, fig. 2.7.13).

In the following centuries, until the fall of Byzantium, leaving aside other provincial, more or less ephemeral, stylizations (i.e. the 'epsilon-with-low-pseudo-ligatures style', widespread in the Palestinian-Cypriot area from the twelfth to the thirteenth/fourteenth century, the '*carrée*' and '*bouclée*' Cypriot scripts in the thirteenth and fourteenth centuries, or for Salento the 'rectangular' ('*aplatie*') script in the twelfth century, and the 'baroque' script in the thirteenth and fourteenth century), it is necessary to frame the evolution of Greek minuscule writings considering the perspective of the dialectic opposition of formal scripts linked to the '*Perlschrift*' *versus* informal scripts. Indeed in the formal strand there was a substantial conservation of the curvilinear model of '*Perlschrift*' ancestry and when this, because of changed political-economic and socio-cultural conditions, proved inadequate—as for example during the age of the Palaiologoi (1261–1453)—archaizing attempts were introduced (e.g. Vatican City, BAV, Vat. gr. 1158), in order to imitate the best expressions of the '*Perlschrift*' of the tenth/eleventh centuries and new styles were elaborated, although influenced by the tradition (as e.g. the style '*tōn Hodēgōn*', which was created in the monastery of the same name in Constantinople during the fourteenth century; cp. Oxford, Bodleian Library, MS. Barocci 11, fig. 2.7.14).

On the contrary, the informal scripts are the ideal *humus* for the birth of the '*Fettaugen-Mode*' (e.g. Oxford, Bodleian Library, MS. Barocci 18, fig. 2.7.15), a frantic and messy writing fashion, used above all for copying secular texts in the thirteenth century; in the following century as a sort of reaction we find a recovery of order, regularity and balance by anonymous scribes and prominent scholars (such as Maximos Planudēs and, above all, Dēmētrios Triklinios; e.g. Venice, BNM, gr. 464, fig. 2.7.16). In their individual scripts, they were able to balance the need for speed with aesthetic care (the same need is responsible for the origin and the diffusion, in the thirteenth and the fourteenth centuries, of the '*Metochitesstil*', a script used, often by the same hands, both in the imperial chancellery and for copying books). During the fourteenth and the fifteenth centuries, such scripts, the so-called Triclinian writings—traditionally linked to secular and classical texts—arrived in the west, following the new demand for learning the Greek language: following their model, directly or by the mediation of teachers as Manouēl Chrysolōras (fig. 2.7.17), ranks of western humanists learned to write, the first printed editions were published and, in a certain way, we continue to write even now. On the contrary, in the east, where the link with the classical tradition (and with the scripts which referred to it) had been lost and where the Greek element was shut up in Orthodox monasteries during the Ottoman rule, scripts that repeated the model '*tōn Hodēgōn*' in more and more sclerotic and tired shapes, continued to be used at least until the seventeenth and eighteenth centuries, beside the usual cursive writings.

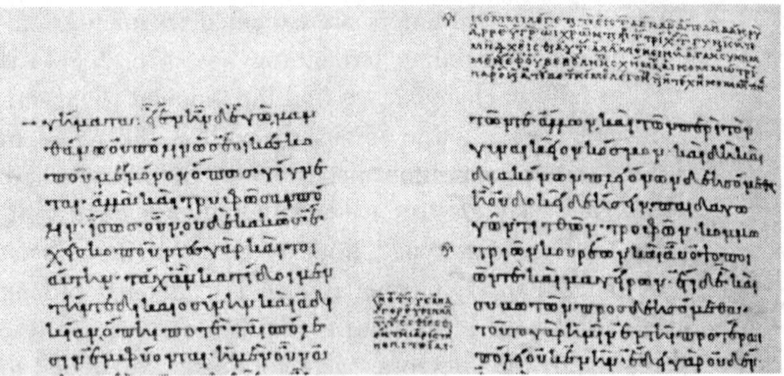

Fig. 2.7.9 Paris, BnF, Grec 1807, f. 20v, detail.

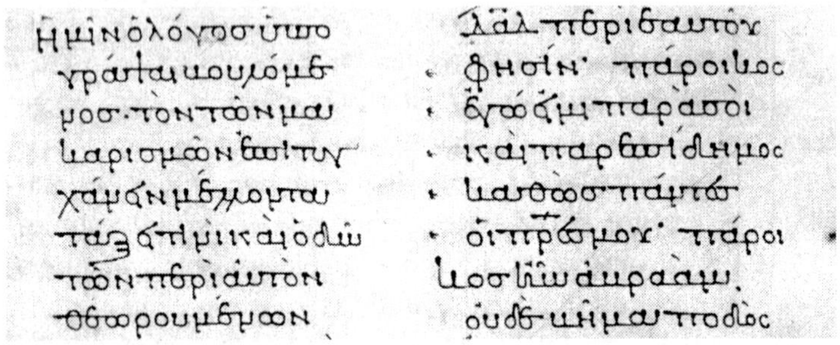

Fig. 2.7.10 Oxford, Corpus Christi College, 26, f. 20r, detail.

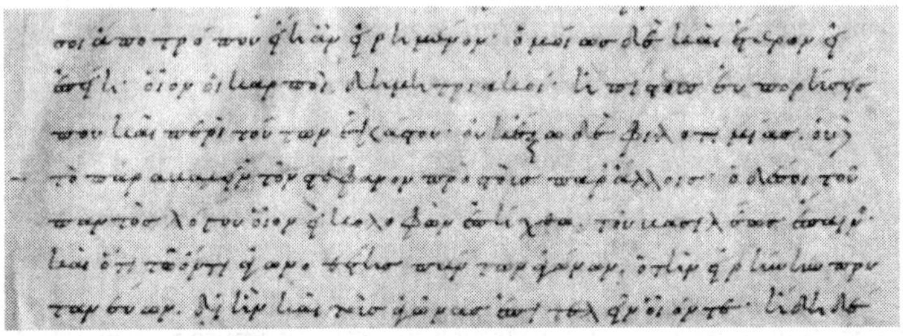

Fig. 2.7.11 Paris, BnF, Grec 1741, f. 2r, detail.

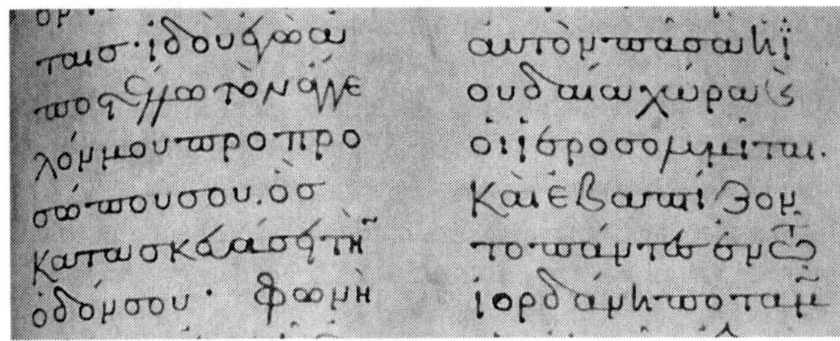

Fig. 2.7.12 Rome, Biblioteca Angelica, gr. 123, f. 5r, detail.

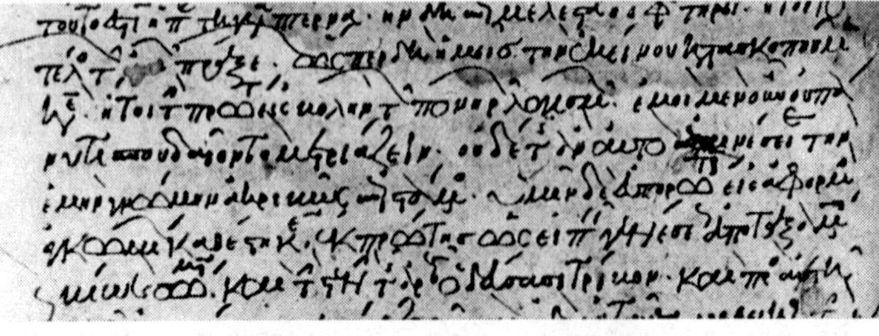

Fig. 2.7.13 Florence, BML, plut. 57.40, f. 19v, detail.

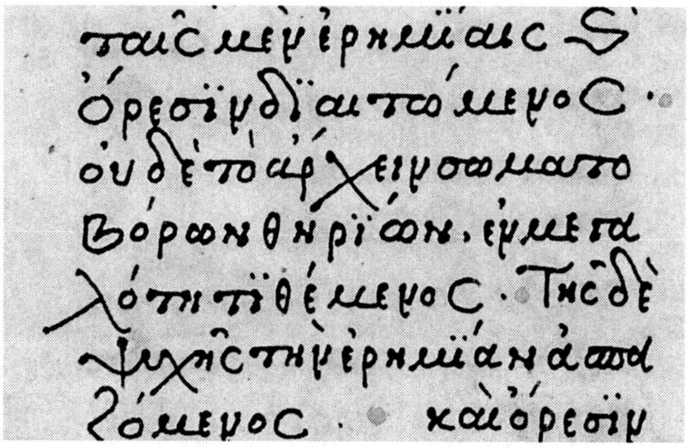

Fig. 2.7.14 Oxford, Bodleian Library, MS. Barocci 11, f. 10v, detail.

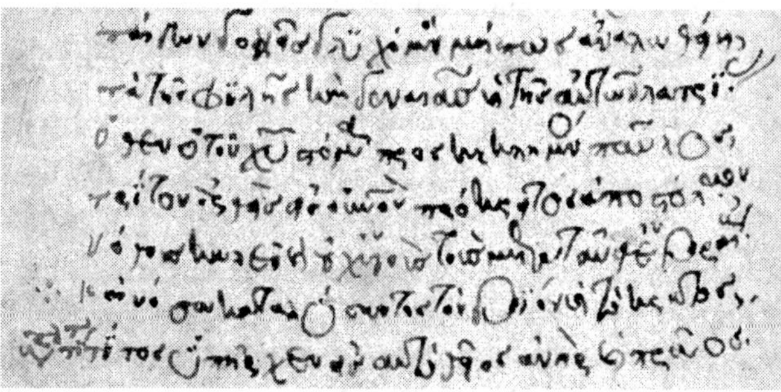

Fig. 2.7.15 Oxford, Bodleian Library, MS. Barocci 18, f. 46b, detail.

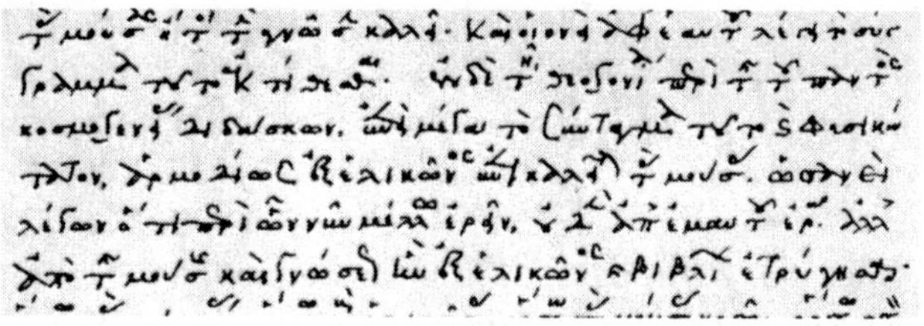

Fig. 2.7.16 Venice, BNM, gr. 464, f. 88r, detail.

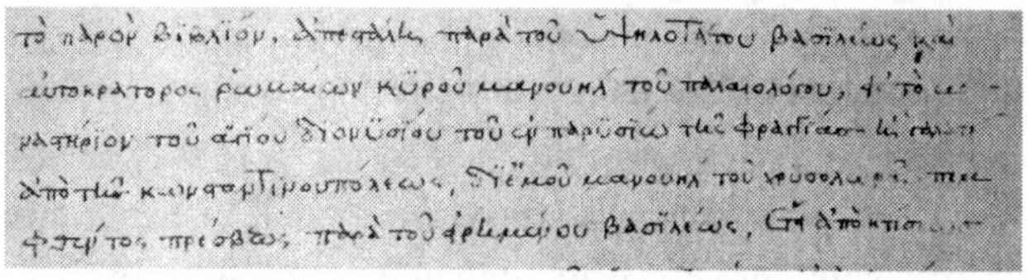

Fig. 2.7.17 Paris, Musée du Louvre, Departement des Objets d'Art, MR 416 (Ivoires A 53; A 100), f. 237v, detail.

For specialized bibliography, the two recent manuals of Greek palaeography, one more detailed (Crisci – Degni 2011), the other more synthetic (Perria 2011), can be recommended, alongside a few studies not quoted there for chronological reasons (Bastianini – Cavallo 2011; Crisci 2012; Orsini 2013; Pöhlmann – West 2012).

Palaeography and Greek manuscripts cataloguing

In order to investigate the contribution of palaeography to Greek manuscripts cataloguing, we should start from the very beginning. Just after publishing, in 1708, his *Palaeographia graeca*—which first introduces the term 'palaeography'—Bernard de Montfaucon turned to cataloguing the Greek manuscripts of the library of Henry-Charles Coislin (see also Ch. 4 § 2.6). Thus, in his *Bibliotheca Coisliniana olim Segueriana* (1715) the Maurist could apply the methodology of the discipline he had just founded, and he could achieve the first practical results. Therefore, while Latin palaeography, as Ludwig Traube wrote, 'was born among quarrels' (Traube 1909, 3)—that is quarrels concerning *chartae*, the documents, and the founding book by Jean Mabillon had the title *De re diplomatica*—Greek palaeography was born with manuscript cataloguing or, at least, it was in manuscript cataloguing that Greek palaeography found its first and most concrete application.

Nevertheless, if we define palaeography as the formal study of a script, we may say that Montfaucon's *Bibliotheca Coisliniana* lacks real palaeographical analysis. Notices on writing, when present, are usually very short and limited to some brief remark of a mostly impressionistic and subjective character (for instance, the John Chrysostom in Paris, BnF, Coislin 79, of the eleventh century, is said '*grandi pulchroque charactere descriptus*'). Sometimes the palaeographical analysis is only apparently more scientific, and in these cases the *Palaeographia graeca* gives the critical and probative basis to the analysis, as for the bilingual, Greek and Latin, Psalter Paris, BnF, Coislin 186, of the seventh century, written '*unciali quadrato & rotundo charactere*'. In conclusion, even if Montfaucon's importance has been recently confirmed (Irigoin 1996 and 1998; Cavallo 2001b; Bianconi 2012; Mondrain 2012a), his palaeography is still a *savoir-faire*, a practical experience useful for dating and, in some cases, localizing manuscripts. Montfaucon does not consider it necessary to describe the script of the manuscript that he is cataloguing. He uses palaeography but, at least when cataloguing the Coislin library, he only offers, so to speak, the finished product of his *expertise* which in substance is a proposal of dating.

As an example, let us take the catalogue of the Greek manuscripts of Corpus Christi College in Oxford (Wilson [N.] 2011). In accordance with the British cataloguing tradition, the format of descriptions is very short and, consequently, writing occupies only a few lines. For example, concerning the manuscript Corpus Christi College 26 (fig. 2.7.10), a very elegant codex of St Basil, dated to the tenth century, the reader has to consult the quoted bibliography in order to find the indication of the script—the beautiful *minuscule bouletée* which was used for copying it, the basis for the dating and, moreover, for the localizing the manuscript in Constantinople. In particular, Agati (1992, 21, 65–69 and 315, with plate 33) attributes the manuscript to 'scribe N', who also copied London, BL, Add. 11300. The descriptions of later manuscripts, forming the bulk of the collection of Corpus Christi College, are also very short. For the manuscript 19, a Psalter of the third quarter of the fifteenth century, the palaeographical analysis is limited to 'Written by Emmanuel of Constantinople, not signed; cf. RGK I, p. 78 (scribe no. 115)' (Wilson [N.] 2011, 3). There is no further word to demonstrate or discuss the identification.

While the dating and identifications in the catalogue are all correct, it does not do justice to the palaeographic method which consists in comparing the uncertain against the certain—the latter being for palaeographers a manuscript provided with a certain (or at least probable) date and hopefully a certain (or at least probable) localization—and cannot be reduced to reproducing the sumptuous plates that are added to the catalogue. Only in this way what seems to be nothing more than an art, an innate and unmediated skill (the so-called 'palaeographical eye') can turn into a real science which aims at reconstructing the history of writing. Within this science, the formal and stylistic comparison has to be followed by the description of the script. Even if sometimes description is—or seems to be—a mere literary exhibition, nevertheless it is a very important heuristic process of conceptual abstraction, where the palaeographer tries to communicate, by using his own terminology and protocols, what he has already guessed. Indeed not only do palaeographers study and describe writing, but so also do teachers, calligraphers, designers, psychologists, and graphologists, each according to his own categories. Thus, a palaeographer has to describe a script, especially in a catalogue, which is, as it were, one of the most natural products for a palaeographer. Certainly, the description does not have to be excessive or redundant; on the contrary, it has to be functional and its function is to understand and make others understand. There must be description. Plates can be a good term of comparison and a useful checking tool, but they can not take the place of the description. A palaeographical description which, if critical and functional, represents a milestone in the process of typological, formal and stylistic comparison, leads on to creating a scientific, common and shared terminology. And such a terminology is still a *desideratum* in Greek palaeography.

The recent catalogue of Greek palimpsests kept in the Österreichische Nationalbibliothek in Vienna (Grusková 2010) pays much greater attention to writing. Because of the complexity of the manuscripts and because of a very different cataloguing tradition, the notices are very rich. Both the upper and the lower scripts are fully described and the reader may judge the analysis and observations by using the beautiful plates which are provided in profusion. Nevertheless, the fact that the section concerning writing is introduced by the lemma *Paläographie und Datierung* reveals that Grusková's attitude towards palaeography, *mutatis mutandis*, is not so far from Wilson's. In short, the palaeographic analysis may occupy a few lines or many pages, but its main goal, *ex silentio* or *apertis verbis*, is to provide a dating.

Palaeography is far more than a dating tool: the script is a feature that deserves to be studied and described, like the parchment, the composition of the quires, and the binding. The two recent catalogues of dated Greek manuscripts of the thirteenth and fourteenth centuries kept in French libraries (Astruc 1989; Géhin et al. 2005) reserve a large space for palaeographical analysis, even if the manuscripts are dated.

The history of the cataloguing and study of Greek manuscripts is marked by many ambiguous cases that only palaeography has been able to solve. Probably the most famous one is represented by the so-called mimetic or archaizing script of the Palaiologan period (thirteenth to fourteenth centuries), that is to say a writing that programmatically imitates a previous one, of the tenth and eleventh centuries, which is taken as a model within a sort of restoration at the same time ideological, political, cultural, and graphical. It is only after a close palaeographical analysis considering both structural elements and stylistic features, that you may recognize the archaizing character of this script which represents a particularly insidious test for palaeographers (Prato 1979).

Sometimes, in order to unravel a particularly tangled skein, palaeographic analysis, even if well informed, may not be enough. In these cases, the palaeographer has to resort to other tools, especially to those of philology and codicology. Thus, in the Byzantine textual transmission of Plato, two manuscripts stand out: Vienna, ÖNB, Cod.Suppl.gr. 7 (W), of the eleventh century, and the *Lobcovicianus* of Prague, Prague University Library, VI.Fa.1 (L), whose dating is uncertain: it has been variously dated from the eleventh to the fourteenth centuries. In Lidia Perria and Paul Canart's opinion, the *Lobcovicianus* should be dated to the eleventh century since it was written by the same scribe as the manuscript in Vienna. However, on the basis of textual evidence, the *Lobcovicianus* must be assigned to the Palaiologan era (see *Studi* 1992). We are faced with another case of graphical mimesis whose aporia only philology was able to solve.

Another example comes from the catalogue of Greek manuscripts of the Biblioteca Medicea Laurenziana by Angelo Maria Bandini (1764, 1768, 1770). On the basis of the paper used as writing support, Bandini divides manuscripts into *papyracei* (or *bombycini*)—manuscripts on paper without watermarks (that is to say by using Arabic paper)— and *chartacei*—manuscripts produced by using paper with watermarks (that is to say Italian paper). In Bandini's catalogue several manuscripts described as *papyracei* (or *bombycini*) are surprisingly dated to the fifteenth century. In Byzantium, however, Italian paper spread from the very beginning of the fourteenth century. Now we know that the *papyracei* manuscripts dated by Bandini to the fourteenth or fifteenth centuries should be rather assigned to the eleventh or twelfth centuries since their writing is typical of the late Macedonian–first Comnenian period. Thus, by combining palaeography and codicology a manuscript may be assigned an earlier date by a couple of centuries and even more. This is also the case with the manuscripts belonging to the so-called 'scriptorium' of Iōannikios—which in spite of previous but erroneous dating are now assigned to the twelfth century (see now Degni 2008)—or with a famous manuscript that transmits Michaēl Psellos (Florence, BML, plut. 57.40, see fig. 2.7.13), previously dated to the fifteenth century and more recently assigned to the eleventh century, just after Psellos' death (Bianconi 2010). The philological implications from such revised datings are obvious.

To summarize: in cataloguing manuscripts we must not forget that a manuscript is a complex entity since it is, at the same time, at least text, material and writing. The palaeographer has to study the script, which is not only a dating tool, but represents a feature, like the text and the material, to be studied and described. Since there are problems, not disciplines, the palaeographer should also be something of a philologist and codicologist. Palaeography, codicology and philology must be, as Jean Irigoin wrote, 'servantes maîtresses en alternance' (Irigoin 2000): when describing a manuscript, we do not have to photograph it—that is to say that we do not give a fixed and iconic image of it—but we have to sketch out the relationship between dialectic tensions (material, textual and graphical ones) and to bring out the genetic dynamics that led a manuscript to be as it is.

It is a hard task, trying to preserve the relationship between (at least) palaeography, codicology and philology, and to connect the book, as a whole of script, material and text, with the social *milieu* and the cultural practices that produced it. Challenging as it is, this is the only way cataloguing could be transformed from an almost technical and instrumental activity into an operation both historical and critical.

References

Agati 1992; Astruc 1989; Bandini 1764, 1768, 1770; Bastianini – Cavallo 2011; Bianconi 2010, 2012; Canart 1992; Cavallo 2001b; Crisci 2012; Crisci – Degni 2011; Degni 2008; Géhin et al. 2005; Grusková 2010; Irigoin 1996, 1998, 2000; Mondrain 2012a; Montfaucon 1715; Orsini 2013; Perria 1992, 2011; Pöhlmann – West 2012; Prato 1979; *Studi* 1992; Traube 1909; Wilson [N.] 2011.

8. (Mediaeval) Hebrew palaeography (EE)

Since its beginnings in the nineteenth century, mediaeval Hebrew palaeography has endeavoured to study the form and evolution of the Hebrew script, examining the major changes that the script has undergone, since its emergence from the Aramaic script up to its manifestation in the late mediaeval and Renaissance period. By analysing both the texture and the individual letters of a written text, it aims to determine the date, provenance and hands by which all kinds of Hebrew texts were written.

Dated Hebrew manuscripts and Geniza documents, as well as inscriptions made on various kinds of materials, are authentic evidence for the state of the mediaeval Hebrew script. Copied by professional scribes, written by scholars, or penned by laymen, these remnants reflect the types, modes, and styles of the script. Inspired by cultural phenomena and by various styles of calligraphy, such as those coming from the surrounding Islamic and Christian cultures, the evolution of mediaeval Hebrew script was intimately connected with Jewish cultural and spiritual life.

Renewed by Malachi Beit-Arié in the latter part of the twentieth century, contemporary Hebrew palaeography classifies the script according to geo-cultural entities and graphical groups, dividing the regional types of writing into two broad branches—the 'Islamic' branch, which includes the oriental, Sephardic, and Yemenite types of script; and the 'Christian' branch, which includes the Italian, Ashkenazic, and Byzantine types.

The *oriental type* was employed in the east: in Palestine, Iraq, Persia, Uzbekistan, Armenia, Egypt, and eastern Turkey. Some of its features can already be found in the Dead Sea Scrolls—evidence that the roots of the oriental script lie in the ancient script that was in use during the first millennium. The oriental script adopted some characteristics of Arabic calligraphy, mainly due to the similar technique of employing a reed calamus as a pen. Writing with a reed contributed to the distinctive texture formed from letters drawn by homogeneous wide strokes, ending always with some tags or heads. Departing from the same characteristics as its oriental ancestor, the *Yemenite type*, employed only in Yemen, became a distinct type only in the thirteenth century. The widespread *Sephardic type*, despite its name, was not limited to the Iberian Peninsula. Imported to the Maghreb by immigrants from the Middle East, it made its way to the Iberian Peninsula, Provence and Languedoc, to the southern parts of Italy, and to Sicily. At the end of the fourteenth century, when Sephardic Jews settled in the northern parts of Italy, the Sephardic script became one of the main scripts in use there. The Sephardic script was transported to western Turkey and the Balkans by Jews expelled from Spain and Portugal. There it served the local scribes in addition to their regular scripts. In the so-called 'Christian' branch of Hebrew script, the *Ashkenazic type* was used in various western European countries, mainly in Germany, northern France, and England. Exported by emigrants from those countries to the northern parts of Italy, it became employed there alongside the Sephardic script. Inspired by Gothic Latin, the Ashkenazic script is characterized by its elegant impression and unique calligraphic texture. The use of a flexible quill contributed to the fine decorations adorning its letters, such as hairlines and shading (the contrast between wide horizontal lines and thin verticals). The *Italian type*, which crystallized as a unique script around the thirteenth century, was mainly in use in central and northern Italy. Its first writing tool was the reed, though the quill gradually came into use as well. A distinctive *Byzantine type* evolved mainly in western Turkey and the Balkan regions. Influenced by the various cultures of the Byzantine Empire, the Byzantine type displays contrasting features that might have served as a bridge between the two broad branches of script—the Islamic and the Christian.

According to graphical criteria, each of the geo-cultural script types is divided into three principal modes: square, semi-cursive, and cursive. When it diverged from the Aramaic script, the 'Jewish' script was also named *merubba*ʿ 'square'. The term 'square' in the Middle Ages referred to letters made in a square pattern, demonstrating features such as erect vertical lines, horizontals that are aligned on the ruled line, and a right-angled connexion between horizontals and verticals. Letters of the *cursive* mode are executed with minimal lifting of the scribe's hand from the writing surface. Letters are reduced to their basic components, rendering a crowded texture with joined-up letters. Beit-Arié revived the Hebrew term *ketaḇ beinoni*, in reference to a middle mode between the square and the cursive. Lacking the squarish pattern, the lines of its letters are more inclined and curved than those of the square.

By analysing the evolutional process of the Hebrew script up to late Middle Ages, it is apparent that due to the dissemination of Hebrew writing throughout Jewish communities all over the mediaeval world, the Hebrew script in all its geographical regions—either that of the Islamic branch or the Christian branch—evolved in a similar manner, pointing to four chronological stages, always retaining the basic character of each type.

The script up to the tenth century

Most of the written texts antedating the tenth century—either calamus writings or stone inscriptions—reflect writing traditions that preceded the square and functioned as a primordial script for all mediaeval geo-cultural types. While they still exhibit some characteristics found already in the Judaean desert scrolls, these writing traditions have an affinity with the oriental square script of the tenth and eleventh centuries, as well. Accordingly, features of the pre-tenth-century letters and lack of the definite square pattern allow its description as a 'proto-square' sub-mode.

Growth and transition: tenth and eleventh centuries

The tenth-eleventh century was the period of origin for many of the oriental script styles. Owing to the new development of the *Masora* in Palestine, the calligraphic square mode emerged as an impressive writing, manifesting a new stage in the oriental script.

The oriental script—in all its modes—carried on the massive waves of Babylonian emigrations to the Maghreb, brought with it a local script that would subsequently be defined as the Sephardic script. Indeed, during the 'growth period' of the tenth to eleventh centuries, all known remnants of Sephardic writings bear many oriental features.

Lack of sufficient dated remnants of the tenth to eleventh centuries from European countries challenges our ability to distinguish their regional script's styles at this period. However, the few which were preserved bear evidence to an anachronistic proto-square style of eleventh-century Italian and Byzantine script. All the same, a tenth-century's square Byzantine mode is discernible in letters written in Jerusalem at the first half of the eleventh century by a Byzantine immigrant in Palestine, indicating an exclusive square Byzantine mode as well.

The crystallization of script styles: twelfth to fourteenth centuries

During the second half of the eleventh century the oriental square script began to vanish, marking a scarcity of square writing in manuscripts written later than the eleventh century. Mainly in Egypt and Palestine, most of the square writings dated to the twelfth century or later exhibit the individual features of the scribe rather than conventional calligraphic square script. Nevertheless, at about the same time, the semi-cursive mode manifested itself in a new formal script. Probably replacing a cursive mode, most semi-cursive writings from the thirteenth century onwards were written in current or careless hands.

The thirteenth century was a period of increasing social and cultural activity within the Sephardic communities. It was at this time, with the fading of the oriental traces in its square script that a unique, fully formed Sephardic script developed. Owing to its oriental origin, some similarity between the oriental square and the Sephardic square still remained. However, a distinction between the two is expressed in the quality of the letters' basic lines and in their additives. While the lines of the oriental letters are mainly characterized by their tags and heads, the thinner lines of the Sephardic letters, in all their modes are usually more stretched, virtually lacking any additional elements.

The earliest appearance of the Ashkenazic script in dated manuscripts is from the end of the twelfth century. A manuscript copied at the end of the twelfth century, and contemporary remnants of tombstones in Germany, display features of a proto-square Ashkenazic script, lagging behind the accelerated development in the east. Only in the thirteenth century did the Ashkenazic script crystallize into a full-fledged square writing. The calligraphy of the Ashkenazic script reached its peak in the final third of the thirteenth century, when Gothic art—in architecture, sculpture, and other arts—flourished in Germany and in France.

At the beginning of the thirteenth century, the development of the Ashkenazic square was marked by a clear distinction between two major styles—French and German—manifested in various modes and styles. Displaying a homogeneous appearance, letters of the German style are strictly made in an elongated squarish pattern, with stretched lines and a large space inside the letter. Letters of the French style exhibit a wavering, unsteady appearance. They have a wider pattern in which most lines are inclined, soft, and undulating. The basic appearance of the thirteenth-century Ashkenazic square is maintained in the fourteenth-century script as well. But, probably due to the expulsions of the Jews from France, the elegant German style remained the sole regional style from the fourteenth century onwards.

The impact of non-Jewish scripts on each of the local mediaeval Hebrew script types is evident, but the most striking resemblance is that between the Ashkenazic script and the Latin Gothic scripts. From as

Table 2.8.1 Hebrew script types and models

	Square	*Semi-cursive*	*Cursive*
Oriental			
Sephardic			
Ashkenazic			
Italian			
Byzantine			
Yemenite			

early as the thirteenth century, the Ashkenazic calligraphic semi-cursive displays some Latin Gothic features and gradually develops a similar texture to that of the Latin. There are several techniques of employing Gothic features in the semi-cursive script, including small internal spaces and a compressed vertical pattern of letters, and heavy shading, all resulting in a general increase in the blackness of the texture. That being said, whereas Gothic features are conspicuous in the semi-cursive, the square still retains its traditional character and features.

More than 200 Jewish families lived in Rome in the thirteenth century, contributing to the accelerated development of Italian script. Most known Italian manuscripts of this period were copied there. Those manuscripts manifest various modes and styles of script, reflecting the highly dynamic development of the Italian script. The primordial styles of the twelfth century gained a new prestige and became formal calligraphic styles in the thirteenth century. The Italian scribes who, until the end of the thirteenth century, used the reed calamus, started to write with a quill, which served to accentuate the decorative elements of letters.

Towards the end of the thirteenth century, also the Yemenite script crystallized into its classic square form. This script continued to be employed alongside some other square styles and variants, as the most widespread Yemenite style.

Decline versus progress: fifteenth and sixteenth centuries

The gradual decline of the calligraphic oriental square script, which had already begun in the twelfth century, was probably an incentive for the emergence of distinct regional modes. Originating as early as the thirteenth century, these reached their peak in the fifteenth century. While most of the oriental non-square styles from the thirteenth century onwards were written in a current or careless semi-cursive, a particular style that commenced in the mid-thirteenth century as a distinctive style in Persia, Iraq, Uzbekistan, Armenia and Afghanistan, ultimately became a prominent script, functioning in the fourteenth and fifteenth centuries as a calligraphic book script. This script developed a close affinity with the square, replacing it as the formal mode of most oriental books.

Both the square and the non-square Sephardic scripts had deteriorated in their calligraphic quality by the end of the fifteenth century. Current writings lacking the accuracy of the calligraphic letters became frequent, introducing new, non-homogeneous, and irregular styles of script at the end of the fifteenth century and into the sixteenth century. Notwithstanding, the increasing number of Sephardic immigrants in fifteenth-century northern Italy contributed to a new Sephardic style of both square and semi-cursive modes that owe their characteristics to the adoption of Italian and Ashkenazic features.

Unlike other regional types of script, the Sephardic script is the only one to have developed a real fluency in its cursive script, probably due to the influence of Arabic calligraphy. The Sephardic cursive script abounds with connexions between letters and demonstrates a high level of simplification of the parts of various letters and the omission of calamus strokes.

While the Ashkenazic semi-cursive script of the fifteenth and sixteenth centuries preserved its calligraphic appearance, the square Ashkenazic script was radically changed. Very few professional Ashkenazic scribes retained the aesthetic quality of the old square script. Most manuscripts of this time reveal a common square script in which letters are built mostly of bare lines, lacking many of the decorative elements.

The end of the fourteenth century witnessed the accelerated progress of cursiveness in the Ashkenazic script, while several letters formed a cursive shape. The increase in the number of those cursive letters came to a climax in the cursive script of the sixteenth century. Due to a new flexibility of the texture and simplification of all letters, the cursive script became a fully-fledged script, combining all the various features of a cursive script.

Inspired by the Latin 'rotunda', an Italian calligraphic semi-cursive mode started its development already in the fourteenth century and reached its calligraphic peak in the fifteenth century. Becoming the formal Hebrew script in northern Italy, this script was used by local scribes as well as by Sephardic or Ashkenazic immigrant scribes. Most likely in response to the vast development of semi-cursive, the Italian square almost completely vanished, giving way to the Ashkenazic and Sephardic square letters in use by immigrant as well as Italian scribes.

Towards the end of the fifteenth century, the tendency to write in a careless style dominated the calligraphic semi-cursive of most script types. An essential part of this process was the conversion of the elegant semi-cursive mode into current and cursive styles of script.

The expulsion from Spain and the accelerated development of print in the sixteenth century may be the main reasons for the decline of the mediaeval Hebrew scripts. Starting at the beginning of the sixteenth century, the spread of the Sephardic script throughout the Ottoman Empire led to the fading of local distinctions between the various mediaeval scripts. Sephardic semi-cursive careless scripts, together with cursive Ashkenazic scripts, overshadowed the distinctive script types of the Middle Ages. Yet, provincial and remote centres such as Yemen and Persia retained their mediaeval character. In the same vein, the eclectic Byzantine script was also preserved. Several variants of the square and semi-cursive Byzantine modes continued to be employed in countries of the Byzantine Empire after the fifteenth century as well.

From all the mediaeval script styles, it is the Ashkenazic cursive script that has continued its development up to the present day. Furthermore, Ashkenazic square letters as well as Sephardic square letters are the source for many fonts in modern Hebrew typography.

References

Beit-Arié 1993; Beit-Arié – Engel 2002; Beit-Arié et al. 1987; Birnbaum 1954–1971; Engel 1999, 2013; Engel – Beit-Arié [2015]; Yardeni 2002.

9. Slavonic palaeography (RMC)

On ne discute pas avec un paléographe; on le laisse parler.
Gérard de Nerval, *Angélique*

It should be stated at the outset that there is no such thing as Slavonic palaeography, since there is no single Slavonic writing system. The Slavs who adopted Latin Christianity (i.e. all the West Slavs, and also the Croats and Slovenes) also adopted the Latin alphabet and tradition of literacy, so that their palaeographic history is part of the wider cultural development of western Christendom as a whole. Amongst those Slavs whose religious orientation was towards Constantinople, two native Slavonic writing systems existed, both dating from the ninth century, Glagolitic and Cyrillic.

The earlier alphabet, known as Glagolitic, was the first writing system invented for a Slavonic language by the Byzantine missionary St Cyril in 863 (see also General introduction § 3.11). While deriving from Greek in its phonetic sequence, Glagolitic features letter forms that appear fully original. Glagolitic exists in two forms, round and square, of which the former is the earlier and the latter is a later development (fig. 2.9.1; see also figs. 1.10.4–6). Square Glagolitic was used in Croatia from the middle of the thirteenth century onward (Vajs 1932, 135–136), that is to say, in a milieu which from a cultural, religious and literary point of view belongs entirely to Western Europe, and thus lies outside the scope of this volume. There is, moreover, not a single dated round Glagolitic manuscript, nor any which can be ascribed with confidence to a particular locale. There can, therefore, be no palaeography of round Glagolitic in the accepted sense: it is possible to trace the differences in the writing of the various manuscripts, but not to assign any chronological or geographical meaning to them, or, therefore, to use them to date or localise manuscripts. This chapter will therefore deal with Cyrillic palaeography.

Cyrillic is dependent on Glagolitic as far as the order and phonetic value of its letters are concerned, but their shapes are (with one or two exceptions) derived not from Glagolitic but from Greek (see General introduction § 3.11; cp. the Greek uncial in Ch. 2 § 7, fig. 2.7.6). The Cyrillic alphabet came into being in eastern Bulgaria at the end of the ninth century, though the earliest surviving examples are a hundred years later. Even amongst the earliest examples there is some variation in the type of hands used, from the extremely formal and monumental to smaller and less carefully formed, but it is generally accepted that with the passage of time, and especially after the middle of the fourteenth century, a much greater range of scripts evolved, and continued in use into the eighteenth century and in certain specific contexts (such as Old Believer communities) even later.

Scholars first began to turn their attention to the hands represented in Cyrillic manuscript books and documents in the first half of the nineteenth century in Russia (compare the brief histories of Cyrillic 'palaeography'—understood as meaning more or less what we would now describe as 'manuscript studies'—in Sreznevskij 1885, 5–41 and Karskij 1928, 66–80), and classified them broadly as *ustav, poluustav* and *skoropis'*, terms which are still in use today and traditionally translated as 'uncial', 'semiuncial'

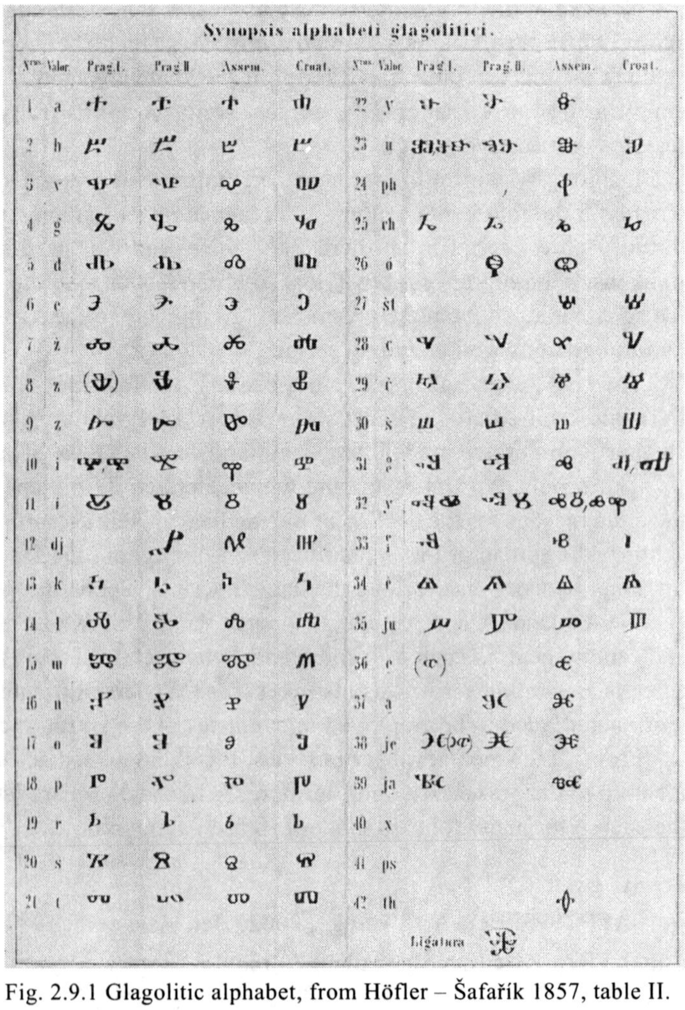

Fig. 2.9.1 Glagolitic alphabet, from Höfler – Šafařík 1857, table II.

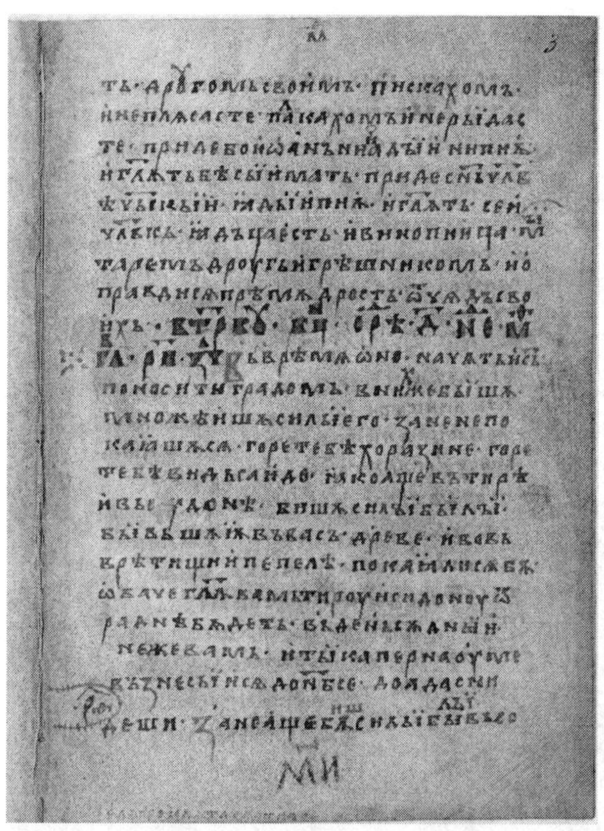

Fig. 2.9.2 Small *ustav*, thirteenth century: Dobrejšo Gospels (MS Sofia, NBKM, 17), f. 3r. By permission of the Bulgarian National Library.

and 'cursive'. It would in fact be more historically accurate to say that it was the latter terms that were so translated into Russian: the earliest Russian palaeographers had some knowledge of the discipline as applied to Latin and Greek writing, and inheriting a terminological triad that goes back to Montfaucon himself, found equivalents for it in the existing vocabulary of the Russian manuscript book.

The consequences of this have not been entirely fortunate, and the foreign scholar must be aware that these three terms, as used in Cyrillic palaeography from the middle of the nineteenth century to the present day, are identical neither with their supposed equivalents as applied to Latin and Greek, nor with their own meanings in earlier usage. The term *ustav*, used to mean a type of handwriting, first appears in the seventeenth century; in this sense it appears to be a back formation from the adjective *ustavnyj*, which means, among other things, 'canonical', so that *ustavnoe pis'mo* is an exact semantic equivalent of such expressions as a *scrittura canonizzata.* The earliest attested use of this phrase may be that quoted by Karskij in a document issued by Vilno city council in 1605 (Karskij 1928, 169; his decidedly unclear footnote has misled later researchers, for example Eckhardt 1955, 131 and Mošin 1965, 155, into dating the document to 1476), provided that *ustavnym* here really does qualify the preceding noun *pismom*, and not the following noun-phrase, which might be a more natural reading. However, when the term *ustav* was used in the seventeenth century, it was used to describe those hands which modern palaeographers call *poluustav;* the latter term first began to be used in the middle of the seventeenth century, at which time it denoted a type of book hand similar in appearance to printed books (Kukuškina 1977, 119–122).

This is not to say that the translation of *ustav* as *uncial* is unjustified. *Unciala* is the term used by Rumanian palaeographers for this type of hand in their own Cyrillic tradition (Bogdan 1978, 196; cf. the analogous use of *semiunciala* and *cursiva*), and scholars writing in Russian or Bulgarian have traditionally called Greek uncials *ustav* (though some more recent writers prefer the Russian term *uncial* for Greek, for example Uchanova 2007, or *majuskul* in Bulgarian). Most importantly, there is no doubt that the earliest Cyrillic letters were derived from Greek uncial hands, and there seems to have been quite a close community of Greek and Slavonic scribal practice at this early period, since several types of Greek uncial current at this time find analogous hands in Cyrillic (Lomagistro 2008a, 156–164; Uchanova 2007), the most immediately obvious to the eye being the existence of both upright and slanting hands. Certainly the application of the term *uncial* to these early Cyrillic hands is entirely unproblematic, since they constitute a relatively formal, regular script largely confined between two lines (cf. figs. 1.10.1–2); nor is there any difficulty in applying the term to many of the much smaller hands used from the eleventh century on (Kukuškina 1977, 122, cf. fig. 2.9.2), since despite the difference in size the proportions of the letters are much the same. However, the term *ustav* is applied to a much wider range of hands than these. In particular—and this is the most significant divergence from Greek or Latin uncials—it is not necessarily a two-line script (Mošin 1965, 152, Eckhardt 1989, 62–64), and the degree of variation in this respect among Cyrillic hands is at least as great as that which in Latin palaeography embraces both uncials and semiuncials. Indeed, it is more or less axiomatic nowadays that all Cyrillic manuscript books up to the middle of the fourteenth century are written in *ustav*, which somewhat limits its usefulness as a descriptive term.

This was not always the case: nineteenth-century catalogues (for example Viktorov 1879) use both *ustav* and *poluustav* to designate twelfth- and thirteenth-century hands. Unfortunately the authors do not define their terms, and have thus failed to provide us either with a basis for a full understanding of their own usage or with criteria which might have been used by later palaeographers. It has indeed been a constant complaint of Cyrillic palaeographers that there is no clear distinction between *ustav* and *poluustav* (for example Ščepkin 1918, 93; Mošin 1965, 155–156); it is generally agreed that *poluustav* is a quadrilinear script, less regular and 'geometrical' than *ustav*, with many more ligatures and superscripts, but there is no unanimity among scholars about precisely where the line should be drawn between the two (for a summary of the various definitions see Eckhardt 1955, 132).

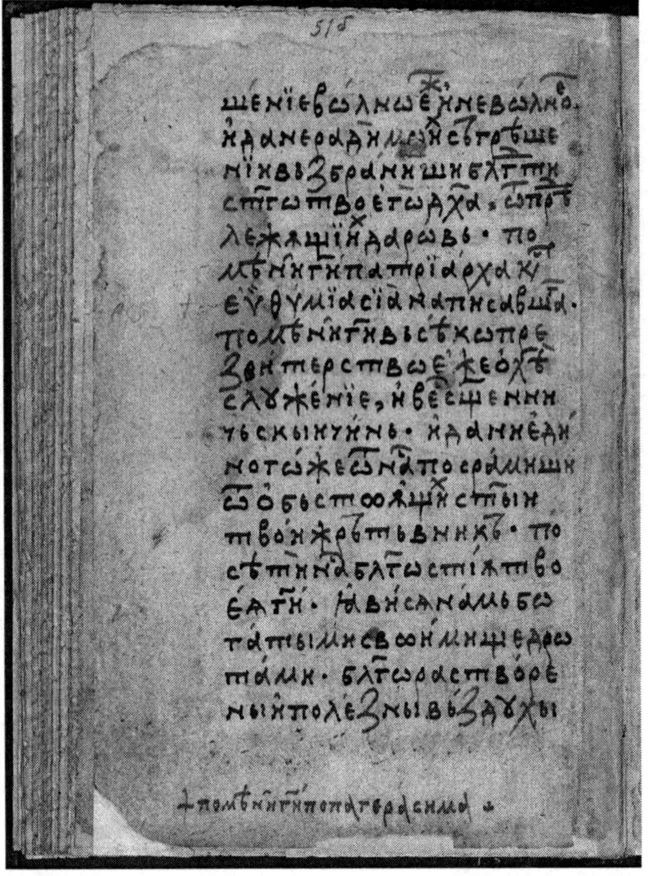

Fig. 2.9.3 Service Book of Patriarch Euthymius (MS Sofia, NBKM, 231), f. 51v, written by the priest Gerasim. By permission of the Bulgarian National Library

According to received opinion, the less formal, more flexible semiuncial (*poluustav*; see figs. 1.10.7, 3.3.20.1) evolved from the older *ustav*, and, after a brief period of co-existence, superseded it. This process is generally placed around the end of the fourteenth century. Russian palaeographers (for example Kostjuchina 1999, 6–10) have tended to connect it with the expansion of book production due to the introduction of paper, which undoubtedly did take place about this time, and the consequent need for a quicker, less labour-intensive style of writing. Historians of Balkan Cyrillic (while admitting that similar processes also took place amongst the South Slavs) are more inclined to see the emergence of *poluustav* as the result of a synthesis between chancery hands and book hands as a result of which the 'minuscule' elements which had established themselves in the former were absorbed into the latter (for example Lomagistro 2008b, 134). Hands of this type evidently evolved more or less simultaneously and more or less independently among the Southern and Eastern Slavs, but it was the Balkan hands that were to have a more important history, as the 'Second South Slavonic Influence' of the fifteenth century saw the Eastern Slavs acquire not only a large number of texts from the Balkans, but also the orthography and style of hand in which they were written. In the Russian context these hands of Balkan origin are known as 'younger *poluustav*', to distinguish them from the native styles which they rapidly superseded.

It is evident from this that there was never any functional differentiation between *ustav* and *poluustav*: the one simply took over from the other within a relatively short space of time. *Ustav* (or 'Cyrillic uncial') is moreover the ancestor of all other types of hand within the tradition (Eckhardt 1955, 141). This must be connected with one of the most striking differences between the Cyrillic tradition and its neighbours, namely the absence of a minuscule book hand. Though Greek minuscule was already well established (at least in Constantinople) by the time Cyrillic was invented, the latter adhered rigorously to letter-forms derived from Greek uncial, so that the Cyrillic manuscript represented, from the Byzantine point of view, an archaic approach to book production. The transition from *ustav* to *poluustav* was a far less radical shift than that from uncial to minuscule in Greek, and there is nothing among Cyrillic book hands equivalent to Greek minuscule. The nearest approach is the so-called *popgerasimovo pismo* (Koceva 1972, see fig. 2.9.3), named after its best-known practitioner, the priest and scribe Gerasim, that was used for a few manuscripts in fourteenth-century Bulgaria; even this, however, is essentially a semi-uncial hand that has adopted the *ductus* of Greek minuscules, and with few exceptions retains the letter-forms of Cyrillic *ustav* and *poluustav*.

With the invention of Cyrillic the Slavs had adopted not only the letter-forms, *typoi grammatōn*, of the Greek uncial manuscript, but its entire *mise en page*, including its titles in larger, typically red, frequently outline majuscule letters. This persisted throughout the whole uncial period, and with the advent of *poluustav* the contrast between title and text became more marked, and the form of the letters of the titles came to resemble even more closely that of the majuscule titles of Greek minuscule manuscripts (see, for example, fig. 1.10.8). This form of Cyrillic, which in manuscripts is hardly ever used except for titles (though one also sees very similar letters in inscriptions on other media, such as silver), has been termed *Majuskel* by Thorvi Eckhardt (Eckhardt 1989, 110–116; she also sees in it the origins of the upper-case letters of early-printed Cyrillic books).

Over the course of time the scribes, especially in Russia, came to exploit the decorative potential of the majuscule titles more and more, and after the end of the fourteenth century—in other words, once *poluustav* had become the norm—the use of ligatures, hitherto only an occasional feature of such writing, became more and more extensively exploited for decorative purposes. These take the form principally of shared vertical strokes in adjacent letters (for which the Cyrillic alphabet offers considerable opportunities), which may become more and more elongated, while their round or curved elements are proportionally reduced. This type of decorative script is known as *vjaz'* (Ščepkin 1903, Eckhardt 1989, 117–122; cp. fig. 1.10.8), and reaches its greatest degree of development in seventeenth-century Russia; Bulgarian and Serbian examples remain relatively restrained.

In all the countries where Cyrillic was used, there was at first no essential difference between the hands used in writing books and those used in documents: both are *ustav*. However, from the thirteenth century—or perhaps even from the end of the twelfth—a distinct diplomatic style begins to develop (Lomagistro 2008b, 124–125). This is broadly characterised in its early stages by a simplified ductus and elongated ascenders and descenders, and is the beginning of the style of hand known in Russian as *skoropis'*, in Serbian as *brzopis* and in Bulgarian as *bărzopis* or *skoropis*, the latter term being preferred by modern writers; all represent loan-translations of *tachygraphia* (though unlike it they never refer to shorthand) and reflect the greater speed with which this more fluent script could be written in comparison with the monumental book hands of the period. The translation of this as 'cursive' is highly problematic, not least because *kursiv* in the languages concerned has a different meaning and denotes the eighteenth- and nineteenth-century hands derived from Western European (Latin) cursive, which do not continue earlier Cyrillic traditions, and equally because by no means all the hands traditionally designated as *brzopis/skoropis* are what one usually thinks of as cursive in a mediaeval context. The hands used in the Serbian and Bulgarian chanceries of the thirteenth century are a case in point: quite distinct, with their flowing ductus and relatively simplified, sloping and elongated letter-forms, from book hands, but not yet a ligated script (Lomagistro 2008a, 166; 2008b, 130). For this reason they have been described as minuscule hands (Čremošnik 1959, 1963), a definition which, while initially meeting some resistance, has more recently found a greater acceptance (Lomagistro 2008b, 111).

Balkan *brzopis/skoropis* continued to evolve throughout the manuscript period, becoming progressively more cursive in character, but Russian *skoropis'*, according to the generally accepted opinion, emerges at the same time as *poluustav*, i.e. at the end of the fourteenth and beginning of the fifteenth centuries (Šul'gina 2000, 16) as a practical hand ('*delovoe pis'mo*', so designated by Čaev – Čerepnin 1946, 89, 145), in which function it continued to develop, in various forms and local variants, into the eighteenth century. There thus arose an opposition between *skoropis'* and *knižnoe pis'mo* ('book hand'), the latter being, in the seventeenth century, another term for *poluustav*; paper could also be described as either *knižnyj*—suitable for books—or *skoropisnyj*—suitable for documents, the latter being cheaper (Kukuškina 1977, 121). This was, however, not an absolute opposition, and it was quite possible for books to be written in *skoropis'*. Thus in contemporary inventories of manuscript books (published, for example, in Zabelin 1915, 595–596) books may be described as *ustavnye, poluustavnye* or *skoropisnye,* and there is no correlation between the type of hand and the form or contents of the books. These terms evidently describe book hands of different degrees of formality, quite possibly all falling within the modern understanding of *poluustav*. Some of the books listed in the old inventories can be identified with extant volumes (see, for example, the lists provided by Kukuškina 1977, 103–117), and it may be possible, with further research, to establish how precisely these terms were used in the seventeenth century, and what types of hands they designated. It may be perfectly correct, therefore, for Šul'gina to call certain fifteenth-century book hands *skoropis'*, even though for other scholars the very same hands are *poluustav* (compare, for example, the treatment of Moscow, Gosudarstvennyj istoričeskij muzej, Syn. 213, or Eparch. 937, to name but two manuscripts, in Šul'gina 2000 and Kostjuchina 1999). The distinction between *poluustav* and *skoropis'*, in the usage of modern palaeographers, is thus just as unclear as that between *ustav* and *poluustav*.

This may well be because this has not, historically, been the sort of problem that the discipline has set itself to solve. In the nineteenth century palaeography was an auxiliary discipline, confined to providing the skills necessary for students of other subjects to cope with their sources; Nerval's *paléographe* was, it seems, not a palaeographer in the modern sense, but simply a scholar who knew how to read old manuscripts. Thus it is that the standard handbooks (for example Sreznevskij 1885, Ščepkin 1918, Karskij 1928, Čaev – Čerepnin 1946, Đorđić 1971) are more concerned with tracing the development of individual letters across the centuries with a view to providing a set of diagnostic features to allow the reader to date a manuscript. An exception is Lavrov's contribution to the *Encyclopaedia of Slavonic Philology* (Lavrov 1914), which is still useful for its breadth of coverage (including all Cyrillic traditions) and wealth of illustration, but it is written in the style of an encyclopaedia, without footnotes, and is mostly devoted to analysis of individual manuscripts as exemplars, and not to the theory or history of writing. It is only recently that the history of Cyrillic writing has emerged as a subject in its own right.

This situation is not a helpful one for the cataloguer who wants to include palaeographic information in his description of a manuscript. In the majority of cases, a catalogue description is intended to define rather than describe the hand of a manuscript, in much the same way that it may define its language or textual tradition. The lack of a precise terminology is therefore a handicap, and has always been so. Early catalogues of Slavonic manuscripts, even those which include very complete descriptions of their contents, give only sparse codicological or palaeographical details; Ljubomir Stojanović's catalogue of the National Library of Serbia, published in 1903, provides no palaeographical information at all. In the course of the twentieth century, manuscript descriptions have come to include more and more physical detail, and some description of the hand is now *de rigueur*, but even today it may be no more than a laconic and uninformative '*ustav*'. It may well be that this reflects the difficulty of conveying comprehensive information in a limited space without a well-defined set of terms, but though palaeographical information in catalogue descriptions is rarely very extensive, most cataloguers nowadays make some attempt to define a manuscript's palaeographical features in a little more detail, even if this is necessarily somewhat impressionistic. The other possible response to this dilemma is not to attempt to define, but to describe, and this is the approach which has been taken in the Serbian tradition in recent decades. In this tradition a catalogue description may include quite an extensive paragraph devoted to palaeography, even to the extent of describing individual letter-forms. This trend has been taken to its furthest extent in the ongoing catalogue of the manuscripts of Matica Srpska (Jerković et al. 1988–2009), in which not only does each catalogue entry include a full palaeographical description, but a volume may also include articles or appendices on palaeographical, codicological, liturgical, linguistic or other subjects relevant to the manuscripts described therein. This amount of detail may change the very concept of a catalogue quite radically: the introduction to the sixth volume is entitled 'A book about one book, again', and the volume includes individual articles on this one book's scribe, contents, palaeography, decoration, etc., but nothing resembling a conventional catalogue entry.

Technical developments in recent years have inevitably been reflected in the cataloguing of Slavonic manuscripts. In particular, the ability to include many more illustrations than was previously possible has meant that catalogues published within the last few years may include at least one image from every manuscript described. This may seem to provide a solution to some of the terminological problems described, to the extent that the reader who is unsure what the cataloguer means can turn to the image and find out. However, this is only a temporary relief, as the advance of technology means that catalogues will increasingly be presented in digital, searchable form, which will increase the need for standardised, unambiguous search terms. This points the direction for one strand of research which will be of great importance in the immediate future, and if it is to produce satisfactory results, it should be undertaken in a spirit of co-operation between the various national traditions, and in awareness of progress being made in other scripts. Immediate results cannot be looked for, given the vast body of material which has not been catalogued, or which has been catalogued inadequately by modern standards; however, it is to be hoped that cataloguers will continue to strive for best practice, and that their endeavours will be informed both by the advance of palaeographical scholarship and by the new technological possibilities that are being opened up.

References

Bogdan 1978; Čaev – Čerepnin 1946; Čremošnik 1959, 1963; Đorđić 1971; Eckhardt 1955, 1989; Höfler – Šafařík 1857; Jerković et al. 1988–2009; Karskij 1928; Koceva 1972; Kostjuchina 1999; Kukuškina 1977; Lavrov 1914; Lomagistro 2008a, 2008b; Mošin 1965; Ščepkin 1918; Sreznevskij 1885; Stojanović 1903; Šul'gina 2000; Uchanova 2007; Vajs 1932; Viktorov 1879; Zabelin 1915.

10. Syriac palaeography (AS)

Syriac belongs to the northwest Semitic scripts with 22 consonant letters. It is a right-to-left script and its writing direction is in a horizontal or occasionally vertical line (Voigt 1997, 61–69). Syriac shares a common origin with the Palmyrene script (Pirenne 1963; Brock et al. 2001, 37), whereas some others suggest that the roots of the Syriac script are further to the east, along the northern reaches of the Tigris in the Parthian region of Adiabene, Hatra and Assur (Aggoula 2005). Originally it was the local type of Aramaic script used in Edessa, the capital of the kingdom of Osrhoene. The script gained more importance when the Aramaic dialect of Edessa slowly emerged as the standard literary language of the Aramaic speaking Christians. Thus Syriac script is sometimes called 'Old Edessenian' or 'Osrhoenian writing' (Aggoula 2005). From Osrhoene it spread eastward of the Euphrates and westward to the region of Antioch, Aleppo and Apamea, where inscriptions in that script have been found dating from the first half of the fifth century CE onwards (Briquel-Chatonnet – Desreumaux 2011).

The earliest witnesses to the old Syriac or Edessenian script are pre-Christian inscriptions from the first three centuries CE on tombs, memorial stones and mosaics, found in the area of Edessa. The oldest extant examples are the inscriptions from Bireçik at the Euphrates (Syr.: Birtha, 60 km south-west of Edessa, an important halt on the Silk Road) from 6 CE (fig. 2.10.1) (Drijvers – Healey 1999, 140–145, plate 40: the year 6 is debated, see the palaeographical analysis by Briquel-Chatonnet 2013a who prefers to read an additional stroke hence dating it to 106 CE; for a profound graphotactic analysis see Kiraz 2012, 234–241, 245–246), and that of Serrin from 73 CE further south of Bireçik. The inscriptions are written in monumental letters of angular shape with numerous straight lines. The letters nevertheless recognize certain variations of shape and in particular in their ductus and ligatures depending on their material support (stones, mosaics). There is even tendency towards cursive forms of letters (Kiraz 2012, 243–244). This Edessenian script of the inscriptions show the earliest features to what is later called *ʾesṭrangēlā* and used in Syriac manuscripts.

The oldest Syriac documents are commercial and juridical; they are written on parchment (for the limited quantity of Syriac papyri, see Brock et al. 2001, 35, and Butts 2011, 320–321) and date from the middle of the third century CE. They are mainly from the regions of Edessa and Dura-Europos; they are written in a Syriac semi-cursive type, a forerunner of the later *serṭā* script (for the characteristics of the cursive employed in Syriac documents from the third to the sixth century CE, see Brock 1991a, 259–267; Healey 2000, 59–63; Briquel-Chatonnet 2000, 84–88; Briquel-Chatonnet 2005, 174–176; Kiraz 2012, 241–244). This less regular cursive writing was used mainly for everyday purposes like business contracts, but it was also associated with the formal monumental script of stone and mosaic inscriptions. These earliest witnesses up to the fourth century had as yet no diacritical mark (a dot over or below the letters) to distinguish the similar letter forms of *daleth* (*d*) and *resh* (*r*) (see fig. 2.10.3).

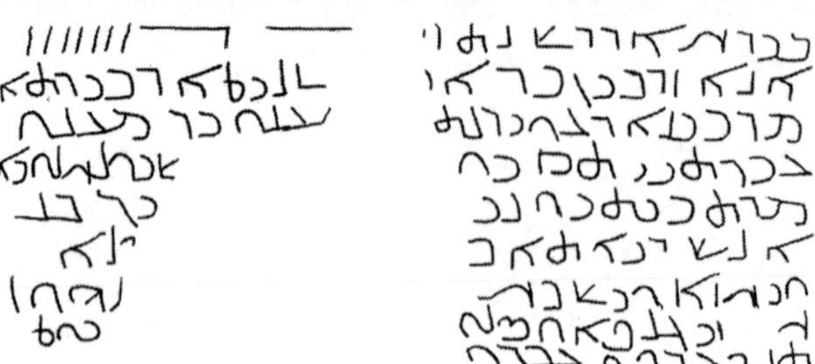

Fig. 2.10.1 Inscription of Bireçik (6 (106) CE), from Drijvers – Healey 1999, pl. 40.

Literary texts in the Syriac language can be dated to the second century CE at the earliest, but the oldest extant parchment codex (London, BL, Add. 12150, see fig. 2.10.2, for a description, see Wright 1870–1872, II, 631–633, no. DCCXXVI; for an analysis see Kaplan 2008, 201–219) is dated 411 CE. The manuscript was written in Edessa. The Syriac writing is a regular and beautiful professional *ʾesṭrangēlā*. The very decorative script shows a high stage of maturity and bears witness to how the script evolved from the third to the fifth century. It is in this shape that *ʾesṭrangēlā* henceforth became

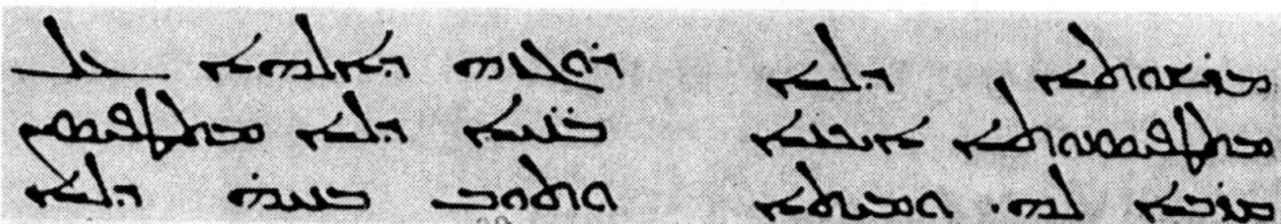

Fig. 2.10.2 *ʾEsṭrangēlā* script. London, BL, Add. 12150 (Edessa, 411 CE), from Hatch 1946, pl. 1.

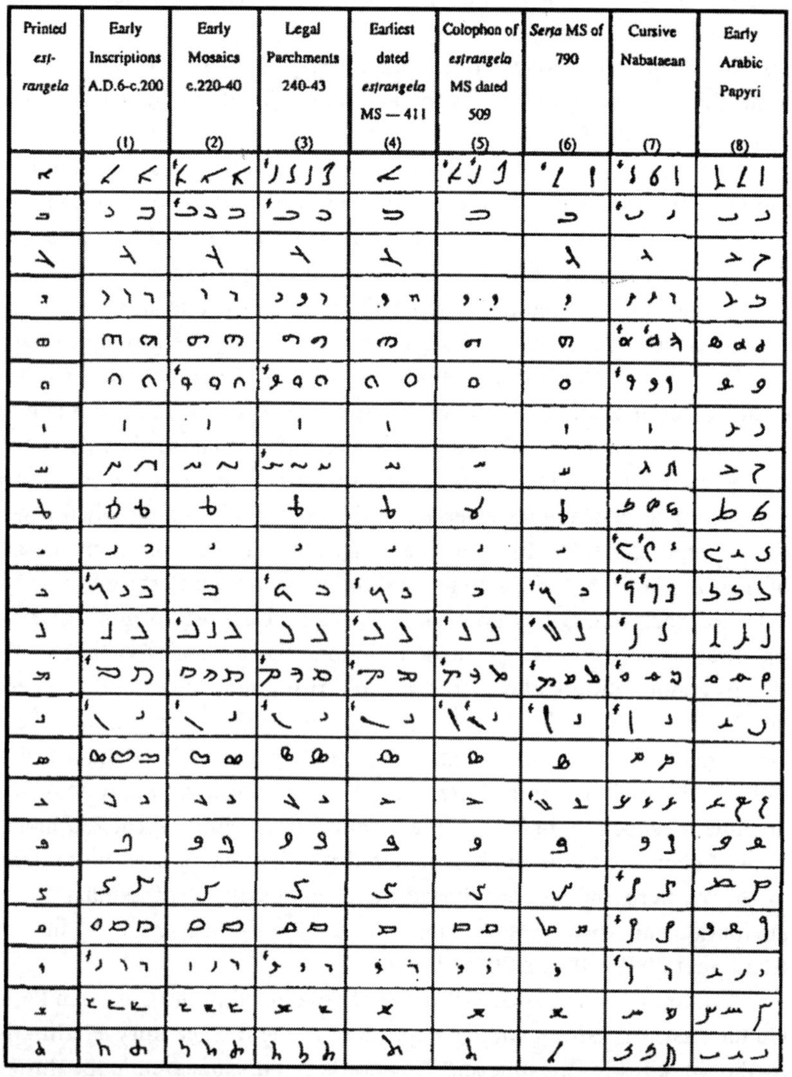

Fig. 2.10.3 Script chart of Syriac letters, first to eighth centuries, from Healey 2000, 62.

Printed *est-rangela*	Early Inscriptions A.D.6-c.200 (1)	Early Mosaics c.220-40 (2)	Legal Parchments 240-43 (3)	Earliest dated *estrangela* MS — 411 (4)	Colophon of *estrangela* MS dated 509 (5)	*Serṭa* MS of 790 (6)	Cursive Nabataean (7)	Early Arabic Papyri (8)
ܐ								
ܒ								
ܓ								
ܕ								
ܗ								
ܘ								
ܙ								
ܚ								
ܛ								
ܝ								
ܟ								
ܠ								
ܡ								
ܢ								
ܣ								
ܥ								
ܦ								
ܨ								
ܩ								
ܪ								
ܫ								
ܬ								

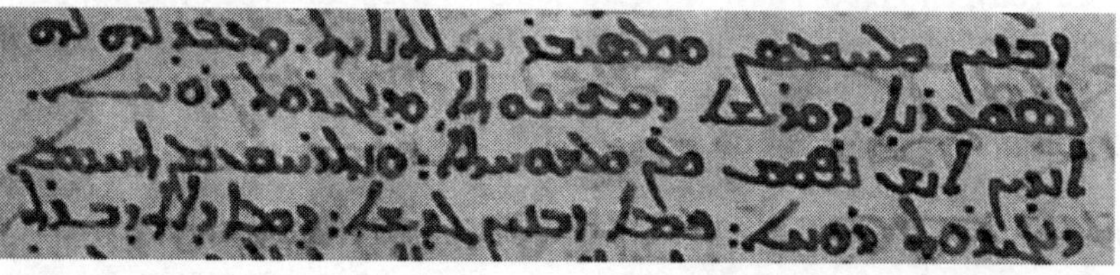

Fig. 2.10.4 *Serṭā* script, London, BL, Add. 14623 (823 CE).

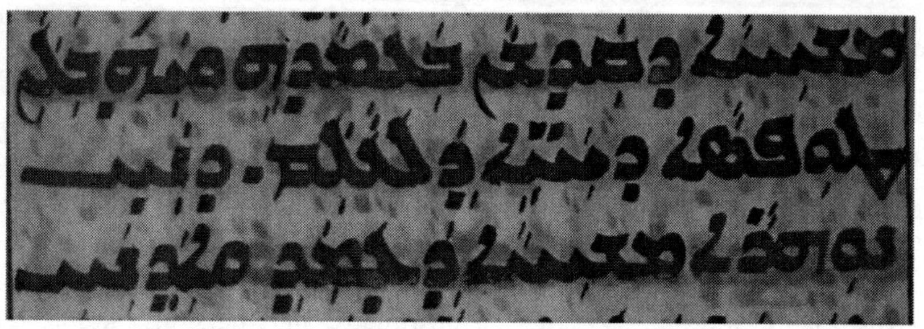

Fig. 2.10.5 Syro-oriental script, Yerevan, Matenadaran, syr. 11/114 (Kirkuk, 1861 CE).

authoritative for the Syrian Christians especially for writing biblical and theological texts. The etymology of the term *ʾesṭrangēlā*, which was certainly coined later, is debated. The most probable meaning is 'Gospel writing' (Brock et al. 2001, 244); others think of a relationship to Greek *strongylos* 'round, spherical [script]'.

At the same time as the formal *ʾesṭrangēlā* a cursive variant was in use. Initially employed for daily practice in ordinary documents (administrative and business texts, or in third-to-sixth-century colophons), cursive writing developed further and was standardized in the course of the eight-ninth century as a distinct script called *serṭā* 'line, scratch' (fig. 2.10.3). Its letters are smaller, rounder and its *ductus* is quite fluent aligning the letters to each other (for its main characteristics see Healey 2000, 64; Briquel-Chatonnet 2000, 88–89 and 2005, 176). Scribes wrote *serṭā* in many individual ways. Studies on its variants and regional particularities are still lacking (See Kiraz 2012 on the variations of cursive letters in the pre-Christian documents of the second and third centuries). During the ninth century, *serṭā* was to replace *ʾesṭrangēlā* especially in the Western Syriac Orthodox and Maronite communities (fig. 2.10.4). However the formal writing of *ʾesṭrangēlā* never went completely out of use. At the turn of the eleventh century in some regions (Ṭūr ʿAbdīn, Melitene) it saw a revival as an alternative to *serṭā* and continued to be employed mostly in sacred and liturgical books as a high representative script for public use.

The ancient 'Nestorian' Church of the East (East Syriac Church of the present-day Assyrian and Chaldean communities in Iraq and Iran) wrote *ʾesṭrangēlā* for a much longer period than the West Syriac churches. On the basis of *ʾesṭrangēlā*, the East Syriac scribes developed their own cursive style during the seventh century. The *Syro-oriental* or East Syriac ('Nestorian') script evolved in several stages; the most distinctive examples emerged in the thirteenth century when it was standardized as a regular script (Brock et al. 2001, 39; Briquel-Chatonnet 2005, 177). The letters are a small angular but fluent variation of *ʾesṭrangēlā* (fig. 2.10.5). In general the Western and Eastern Syriac types of cursive are not very different from each other; they go back to the same Edessene origin; their differences subsist primarily in the ligatures, the open or closed shape of letters, the system of vocalization, and the pronunciation of words.

To denote vowels, the Syro-oriental writing developed in the seventh to eighth centuries a system of dots placed above and below the letters. West Syriac script on the other hand used an adaptation of small Greek majuscules for vowel signs. They first appear in dated manuscripts in the tenth and eleventh centuries (Coakley 2011). Both Eastern and Western vocalization systems can be found employed in the same document especially in West Syriac manuscripts. Fully vocalized manuscripts remain rare in both traditions. According to the modern standard it is now inappropriate to denote the scripts and vowel systems of the Western and Eastern Syriac traditions by the confessional terms 'Jacobite' and 'Nestorian'. The attribution and use of these two main writing traditions is regional in nature and not confessional (Briquel-Chatonnet 2000, 90, and 2005, 177).

Two minor branches of Syriac script developed in the Christian Palestinian and Melkite communities. On the basis of *ʾesṭrangēlā* there appeared in the fifth century a 'Christian- or Syro-Palestinian' type used by the Melkites in Palestine and Transjordan; it disappeared in the thirteenth century (Desreumaux 1987b, 102, 105); and on the basis of *serṭā* another 'Melkite' type of script came into use in the regions of Antioch, Damascus and Sinai in the eleventh to thirteenth centuries (Desreumaux 2004, 561–563, 566–571). These variants of cursive writing were of less importance than the West and East Syriac scripts; the literary documentation is quite limited.

The development of Syriac writing was geographically quite diversified and cannot be explained by a linear palaeographical improvement. Variations of the three main scripts, *ʾesṭrangēlā*, *serṭā*, and Syro-oriental could be used at the same time; they were often mixed by local customs or individual idiosyncrasies of the scribes. A standardization of Syriac writing did not exist before the appearance of printed books; *ʾesṭrangēlā* and *serṭā* are mainly used for typography.

The role of palaeography applied to catalogues

Palaeographic analysis did not receive much attention in Syriac manuscript catalogues. The catalogues from the eighteenth to the second half of the twentieth century reflect the state of knowledge of the time. Cataloguers of manuscript collections classify the script by six main categories: '*ʾesṭrangēlā*' (Assemani 1758–1759 uses 'stronghylis', that is the allegedly Greek etymology for *ʾesṭrangēlā*), '*serṭā*/Jacobite', 'Nestorian/Chaldean', 'Melkite', 'Palestinian', and 'karšūnī' (Arabic texts written in Syriac letters, in general in the *serṭā* script to which are applied special signs; see for this widespread allographic practice among Arabic speaking Syriac churches den Heijer et al. 2014). Other features are given concerning the shape of the letters ('large, small, round, neat, bold, regular, irregular') and about diacritical points and vowels, often supplemented by aesthetical remarks such as: the hand of the scribe is 'good, fine, beautiful, elegant, rough, ugly' etc.: 'stronghylis sive rotundis uncialibus Syrorum literis elegantissime exaratus' (Assemani 1758–1759); 'a good regular, though by no means elegant *ʾesṭrangēlā*', 'an inelegant though tolerably regular current hand' (Wright 1870); 'a clean though somewhat irregular Jacobite serta', 'an inelegant Nestorian hand with occasional points' (Wright 1901); 'a negligent and rather ugly West Syrian hand' (Mingana 1933). It is needless to say that this palaeographic description is the outcome of individual impressions, because a specialized analysis of Syriac handwriting and a scientific terminology were still missing. Up to recent times, palaeographic research in Syriac is in its infancy. Moreover the cataloguer's interest was focused on the texts or on codicological problems of a manuscript. This is for example apparent in the catalogue of Sachau (1899) which takes no notice of the hands of the Syriac collection in Berlin.

To compensate for the lack of palaeographic analysis, plates and images were occasionally added to the catalogues. Wright's monumental catalogue of Syriac manuscripts in the British Library (1870–1872) incorporates twenty colour plates with samples of *ʾesṭrangēlā*, *serṭā*, Syro-oriental, Melkite and Palestinian handwriting from the fifth to the thirteenth centuries; whereas later in his catalogue of Syriac manuscripts in Cambridge (1901), Wright adds no plates. Next to him, Sachau's Berlin catalogue (1899) incorporates nine photos of dated codices in *ʾesṭrangēlā*, *serṭā*, and Syro-oriental from the fifth to the ninth, and the thirteenth to the eighteenth centuries. Some other catalogues follow Sachau's model (see Assfalg 1963b). The recent catalogues of the new Syriac finds in the monastery of St Catherine on Mount Sinai (Philotée 2008) and the catalogue of the Syriac manuscripts and fragments in the library of Dayr al-Suryān in Egypt (Brock – Van Rompay 2014) provide for almost each manuscript a full-page figure. However, the majority of Syriac catalogues, especially those printed in the Orient, do not provide illustrations. The recently established database *e-ktobe* (<http://www.mss-syriaques.org>) intends to cover this lack by offering photos as well as updated descriptions of Syriac manuscripts from a textual, codicological and palaeographic point of view.

In 1946 the *Album of Dated Syriac Manuscripts* by Paine Hatch made an essential contribution to the field of Syriac palaeography. The *Album* contains 200 facsimile-plates of dated Syriac manuscripts from the fifth to the sixteenth centuries. It gives a broad overview of the varieties of the five Syriac types (*ʾesṭrangēlā*, *serṭā*, Syro-oriental, Melkite, Palestinian) and attempts for the first time at a periodization of the history of Syriac writing. The *Album* is still an essential tool for everybody dealing with Syriac manuscripts, and in particular for those confronted with the question of dating undated codices more accurately. However, Hatch's typology of the evolution of the Syriac scripts needs to be redefined on the basis of the larger evidence of manuscripts that have become known to us since the publication of the *Album* (see the introduction by Lucas Van Rompay to the reprint of the *Album*, Hatch 2002, iv).

In present-day research, a broader Syriac script typology as well as a refined methodology is increasingly considered in a systematic way (Briquel-Chatonnet 2000; Healey 2000; Desreumaux 2004; Kaplan 2008; Kiraz 2012). It includes aspects of a methodological character, like joinings, shapes (open, closed…) and measures of letters, their arrangement according to their position in the word as well as towards the baseline of writing, intra-word and inter-word spacing, the degree of curving of strokes, the kerning of final letters, the whole *ductus* of the script etc. (see Kaplan 2008, I, 161–165; Kiraz 2012, 231–234). A comprehensive monograph on Syriac palaeography has yet to be written.

The catalogue of new acquisitions in the Bibliothèque nationale de France pays special attention to these aspects; it distinguishes for each manuscript the system of vocalization and palaeographical variations (Briquel-Chatonnet 1997; see the new term 'half cursive *ʾesṭrangēlā*' for a variant from the eighth century on, Briquel-Chatonnet 1997, 12). The catalogue of the Syriac fragments from the 'New Finds' on Mount Sinai (Brock 1995a) likewise pays much attention to particular palaeographic features and the script in general, and even more so the catalogue of the new finds of Dayr al-Suryān (Brock – Van Rompay 2014). Each fragment is documented through a sample picture of its script. This supplementary photo documentation should become a standard in Syriac cataloguing, although it might be questioned whether an explicit palaeographic description is still necessary in the era of electronic cataloguing and digitized images. Above all, fragments, which are the most difficult to date and identify, should always be accompanied by both a detailed palaeographic analysis and photos. The above mentioned catalogue of the new finds in Dayr al-Suryān (Brock – Van Rompay 2014) is an exemplary model.

References

Aggoula 2005; Assemani 1758–1759; Assfalg 1963b; Briquel-Chatonnet 1997, 2000, 2005, 2013a; Briquel-Chatonnet – Desreumaux 2011; Brock 1991a, 1995a; Brock et al. 2001; Brock – Van Rompay 2014; Coakley 2011; den Heijer et al. 2014; Desreumaux 1987b, 1991, 2004; Drijvers – Healey 1999; Hatch 1946, 2002; Healey 2000; Kaplan 2008; Kiraz 2012; Mingana 1933; Philothée 2008; Pirenne 1963; Sachau 1899; *Syriac Heritage* = Brock et al. 2011; Voigt 1997; Wright 1870–1872, 1901. Web sources: *e-ktobe* <http://www.mss-syriaques.org>, last access October 2014.

Chapter 3. Textual criticism and text editing

*edited by Caroline Macé et alii**

1. Introduction (AM–CM–ABa–JG–LS)

(CM) In this chapter, we would like to offer some insights on textual criticism applied to works preserved in oriental manuscripts, as they have been described in the preceding chapters. In doing so, we wish to offer some guidance not only to those who are planning to produce an edition based on manuscripts, but also to those who are using editions prepared by others.

Much attention has been drawn to the materiality of the manuscript in the preceding chapters, and this material aspect should never be forgotten (see for example Ch. 3 § 3.7). Here the focus will rather be on the contents of the manuscripts.

Scholars are not necessarily editors of texts, and not everyone dealing with manuscripts necessarily publishes texts. Nevertheless, some knowledge about textual criticism is indispensable to anyone dealing with texts, since we read nearly all ancient, mediaeval and early modern texts through an edition of some kind.

The expression 'textual criticism' is here preferred to the more general and polysemic term 'philology'. However, the corresponding adjective 'philological' is sometimes used, referring specifically to textual criticism, especially as opposed to 'codicological' or to 'literary'.

1.1. Textual criticism and oriental languages

Standard manuals of textual criticism exist (see the general bibliography), but they generally do not take into account problems or needs specific to oriental texts. We are not claiming here that textual criticism of oriental texts is of a totally different nature from classical, biblical or mediaeval (i.e. western vernacular) textual scholarships (see Tanselle 1983, 1995; Greetham 1995), but we want to address those issues which are important for scholars dealing with oriental traditions and which may have been neglected or not stressed enough in standard manuals.

(ABa) Modern textual criticism has refined a methodology that has been developing over centuries, culminating in the middle of the nineteenth century in some principles, long connected to the name of Karl Lachmann. They can be very roughly summarized as follows: complete survey of all the direct and indirect witnesses of the work to be edited (manuscripts, printed editions, quotations, allusions, translations, etc.); defining mutual relationships between the witnesses; reconstruction of an archetypal text. Since the critical edition is a scientific hypothesis, it can be disputed and new hypotheses can be proposed or new evidence can be found, which is why some mediaeval texts are edited more than once.

(CM) In recent times, the opponents of the genealogical method of textual criticism and of the reconstructive method of text editing often associated with it are mustered under the flag of 'new philology', a trend in scholarship which came about in the 1990s especially in the United States (see Gleßgen – Lebsanft 1997), following the publication of Cerquiglini (1989), claiming that mediaeval literature being by nature variable, mediaeval works should not be reduced to an edited text, but all mediaeval manuscripts should be considered equally valuable. While this position attracted strong criticism (see for example Ménard 1997), it also seduced some scholars because it may seem more flexible than the stemmatic approach (for an application of some ideas borrowed from 'new philology' in the field of Coptic studies, see Ch. 3 § 3.14). However attractive the 'new philology' approach may be in the field of literary studies, it is nevertheless almost completely irrelevant for the purpose of this chapter, as it does not provide any method to edit texts with a more complex manuscript tradition. In general in this chapter we will adopt a pragmatic view and avoid any theoretically pessimistic approach towards textual criticism (as that put forward by Sirat 1992 for example, see La Spisa 2012 for a response to it). Modern digital approaches to the edition of texts will be taken into account as often as possible (for a synthesis on digital editing, see Sahle 2013).

* This chapter has been edited by: Alessandro Bausi, Johannes den Heijer, Jost Gippert, Paolo La Spisa, Caroline Macé, Alessandro Mengozzi, Sébastien Moureau, and Lara Sels. All contributors to the case studies have reviewed each other. We also thank Francesca Bellino, Pier Giorgio Borbone, Willy Clarysse, Ralph Cleminson, Stephen Emmel, Francesco Stella, and Sever Voicu for their invaluable help, as well as Brian Garcia for proof-reading and revising the English of some of the case studies.

(JG) Of the manuscript cultures addressed by the present handbook, only that of Greek and, to a lesser extent, Hebrew can look back on a tradition of scholarly editions in the modern sense that is as long as that of Latin, which originated by about the fifteenth century. For most of the other 'oriental' cultures, the western approach that was developed by Humanists during the Renaissance was adapted only late, mostly not before the nineteenth century, and only hesitatingly (see General introduction §§ 1.2, 1.3). A comprehensive history of scholarship and text criticism as applied to oriental texts, in the east as well as in the west, has still to be written and falls beyond the scope of the present chapter. Nevertheless, a few preliminary remarks are here necessary in this connexion.

One of the practical problems that scholars faced in editing oriental texts was the necessity to cope in printing with the different scripts that are characteristic for the individual traditions, a problem that was not yet solved by the beginning of the twentieth century when, for example, the bulk of Buddhist, Manichaean, Christian and Zoroastrian texts in Middle Iranian, Turkic, and other languages were discovered in the manuscript finds of Turfan and other sites of East Turkestan. The simple fact that fonts for printing the Sogdian script, the Manichaean script or the variants of the Turkestan Brāhmī used in those manuscripts were not available to any typesetter, was the reason why several ways of transliteration or transcription were developed, among them the representation of Aramaic-based scripts by Hebrew fonts (see Ch. 3 § 3.9). In a similar way, Slavonic texts written in Glagolitic script in the manuscripts have often been transcribed into Cyrillic in the respective editions. *ʾesṭrangēlā* or *serṭā* scripts and East or West Syriac vocalization systems were and are often freely used as almost interchangeable typefaces in printed editions of Syriac texts, disregarding the scripts actually used in the manuscripts (see Ch. 3 §§ 3.17, 3.21).

Moreover the use of Latin-based transcription systems has persisted in western editions to a certain extent until the present day (for instance in editions of Avestan texts; see Ch. 3 § 3.5), not only for lack of appropriate fonts. As a matter of fact, the application of a Latin transcription instead of the original script(s) may claim to have the advantage of making the contents of an edition accessible to a larger scholarly audience, including readers who are not specialists in the given culture or tradition; however, this approach has a clear disadvantage, too, in that the members of the culture in question may feel inhibited from using the edition and taking it into account for their own purposes. The application of a transcriptional rendering in an edition of manuscript contents should therefore rather be avoided; this is all the more true since there are only few scripts left over today (such as that of the Caucasian Albanian, see Ch. 3 § 3.11) that cannot be encoded digitally on the basis of the Unicode standard (see General introduction § 2.1.1).

Another reason why critical editions concerning languages other than Greek or Latin have developed only gradually, is the fact that unlike the 'Classical' languages, which had been taught in schools since antiquity as artificial 'standards' to be followed, many of the varieties of 'oriental' languages that are represented in mediaeval manuscripts are characterized by the absence or scarcity of exhaustive studies concerning their grammar, lexicography and orthography, which renders choices as to the 'correct' wording (including its orthographical representation) much harder to make (see for example Ch. 3 §§ 3.10, 3.13, 3.20). This very fact has sometimes led to different 'standards' being established and applied in 'western' and 'local' editions. For instance, the editions of Georgian religious texts provided in the series *Corpus Scriptorum Christianorum Orientalium* (subseries *Scriptores Iberici*) exhibit typical differences in comparison with editions produced in Georgia in the resolution of abbreviations (for example *raymetu* vs. *rametu* for the conjunction 'that, because' which appears generally abbreviated as *r̃* in the manuscripts) or the treatment of postpositions (for example *tws* 'for' and *gan* 'from' treated as separate words vs. suffixes).

Having different backgrounds and goals, autochthonous traditions and practices in editing texts can indeed turn out to be rather surprising for a western scholar, especially as far as the trend towards drastic normalization is concerned (see Ch. 3 § 3.22 on Persian texts and Ch. 3 § 3.10 on printed editions of Arabic popular texts). Ostrowski (2003) argues that the principles of Russian 'textology' (Lichačev [D.] 2001) developed almost exactly the reverse of western textual criticism. Relatively untouched by Renaissance humanism, Russia did not develop its own tradition of stemmatics and the introduction of the printing press led to the search for a standard of uniformity, largely based on the ideological choices of church clerics, rather than to attention to text history. As a consequence Bédier's anti-stemmatic approach (see General introduction § 1.3) was easily adopted and widely accepted during the Soviet period.

A third feature that distinguishes many of the 'oriental' manuscript traditions from those of Greek and Latin consists in the fact that they are to a much greater extent characterized by fragmentary materials. This is not only true for the extreme case of the manuscript finds of Turkestan (see above) but also, for instance, for the early centuries of the literacy of the Armenians and Georgians (approximately fifth to eighth centuries), the manuscript remains of which are mostly restricted to the underwriting of palimpsests. The special problems resulting from this in the editorial practice are outlined below in the relevant case studies, see Ch. 3 §§ 3.9, 3.11.

(LS) The huge importance of translated texts and texts with multilingual traditions is another typical feature of oriental manuscript studies. Editors are often dealing not with original texts but with translations (often from Greek), which profoundly affects editorial practice and the way in which textual criticism is applied. As far as the source text tradition is known and still extant, it will have to be included in the text critical investigation so as to identify the point where both traditions meet (see for example Ch. 3 § 3.2, §3.20).

1.2. Structure and scope of the chapter

(AM) This chapter is divided in two sections. In the first section (Ch. 3 §§ 2.1–6), we want to provide a synthesis of the set of procedures involved in the editorial process. The second section (Ch. 3 §§ 3.1–23) consists of case studies, illustrating the first section with concrete situations, taken from all languages covered by the handbook and from different literary genres. We do not aim at exhaustiveness, but we find it useful to present a number of traditions and problems, requiring a variety of critical choices and editorial treatments.

Many features of an edition are determined not only by the editor himself and by the material she or he is working on, but also by the series in which this edition will be published (see Ch. 3 § 3.17 and Macé forthcoming). The rules imposed by those series may or may not reflect the state of the art in the field of text-editing. In that respect, as in many others, digital editions pose a different kind of problems: the absence of standardized rules and of recognized circuits of diffusion makes it difficult to guarantee the visibility of editions put on-line.

In what follows, we will try to consider all methodological aspects of the editorial process of oriental texts, in a way which will be as practical as possible. Theoretical questions, such as what is a text, a genre, a corpus, an author, an audience, or for example the way scholarly editing contributes to the shaping of the literary canon, are avoided. Even though they have an influence on the way we edit texts and do show up as major critical issues in several case studies (see for example Ch. 3 §§ 3.4, 3.20), they belong to other disciplines such as semiotics, theory or sociology of literature and literary criticism rather than to the field of textual criticism. Moreover, especially in the case studies, critical editions will be considered and presented as products of practical choices and circumstances rather than from the points of view of methodology and theory in textual criticism. Nevertheless, a number of general assumptions are implicit and will hopefully become clearer as the various cases are presented and discussed:

1) There is no one method or ready-made recipe. Textual criticism shares approximation as an operative limit with all human sciences—the so-called humanities—and probably also most technical and so-called scientific disciplines, even though the latter are probably more reluctant to admit it. In textual criticism, methods vary according to the objective that editors strive to achieve and the objects/products they wish to approximate to. Some aim to reconstruct the original, the authorial text—if such a thing ever existed, for instance in the form of a version authorized by the author or the *Vorlage* of a translation—, others the archetype they posit at the beginning of the transmission chain or chains (on the problems, possibility and desirability of establishing (sub-)archetypes, see Ch. 3 §§ 3.5, 3.7, 3.12, 3.15, and 3.20). In some cases a lost early 'original', supposedly written in a prestigious language (often Greek), may be one of the objectives which motivate the process of textual reconstruction (see Ch. 3 §§ 3.2, 3.4, 3.11, and 3.14). Others are content with restoring one manuscript a little or simply reproducing it 'as faithfully as possible', according to a disclaimer rather commonly found in the edition of oriental texts (see Ch. 3 § 3.17).

2) The variety of methods and the degree of tolerable approximation may depend both on factual circumstances, such as the history of a text and its transmission, and/or on conscious methodological choices of the editor. The quantity of available witnesses matters as well as the more or less complicated structure

of the work to be edited, which may be an original work, a translation or a compilation; the editor may be dealing with a collection (see Ch. 3 §§ 3.12 and 3.19), a single text or fragments of that text (see for example Ch. 3 § 3.6 on literary papyri). The social status and function of texts and copies—private copies (see for example Ch. 3 § 3.3), canonical sacred literature (see Ch. 3 § 3.21), liturgy (see Ch. 3 §§ 3.5, 3.23), support for choral performance or personal reading—, the level of literary production—high classical vs. low popular, often characterized by linguistic variation in the continuum between classical language and mixed or frankly vernacular varieties (see Ch. 3 §§ 3.10 and 3.13)—and, of course, scribal activity are all factors that influence text transmission and therefore editorial choices. There are texts known in only one language, but there are also texts that originated from or were translated into other oriental languages (this occurs in nearly all case studies presented in this chapter).

3) As will be variously exemplified, critical choices and different methodological approaches derive from the academic backgrounds of scholars and the presumed expectations of their readership at least as much as from scientific discussion. The very same text or textual tradition can be regarded from different perspectives, each requiring specific approaches and methodologies (see Ch. 3 §§ 3.2, 3.20). A critical edition is an academic literary genre, developed to bridge the gap between manuscript and book cultures and responds in a variety of forms to the interests of the editors as authors, their readers and to a lesser extent of publishers and universities as stakeholders in cultural production.

1.3. Bibliographical orientation

A. List of standard manuals and handbooks or important collections of methodological articles

For a complete bibliography, see the COMSt website (as of December 2014). We want to provide here a list of the most important work instruments devoted to textual criticism and text editing of oriental works. It must be noted that for several languages and corpora studied in this handbook those instruments are lacking or out-dated.

Arabic: Blachère – Sauvaget 1945; Hārīn 1965; al-Munajjid 1956; Pfeiffer – Kropp 2007; *Qawāʿid taḥqīq* ... 2013; al-Sāmarrāʾī 2013a, 2013b.
Armenian: Calzolari 2014b.
Biblical Studies: Chiesa 1992, 2000–2002; Ehrman – Holmes 2013; Hendel 2010; Kloppenborg – Newman 2012; Wachtel – Holmes 2011.
Ethiopic: Bausi 2008b; Marrassini 2009.
Greek (especially mediaeval): Bernabé – Hernández Muñoz 2010; Harlfinger 1980a; Dummer 1987.
Hebrew: Abrams 2012.

B. List of well-known series of scholarly editions

Äthiopistische Forschungen (Steiner Verlag, Stuttgart), from 1977 until 1993, continued as *Aethiopistische Forschungen* (Harrassowitz Verlag, Wiesbaden)

Besides mostly monographic essays and contributions on various branches of Ethiopian studies, the series also includes important text editions, of biblical (Gospels of Mark and Matthew, Pauline Letter to the Romans), exegetical (traditional commentaries), patristic (the theological treatise *Qērellos*), and historical character (annals and chronicles). Various editorial methods have been applied.

Berliner Turfantexte (Brepols, Turnhout)

Dedicated—but not restricted—to the manuscripts of the Berlin Turfan collection (see Ch. 3 § 3.9), the series represents the most prominent place for publishing editions of the (Buddhist, Christian, and Manichaean) texts in Old Turkic and Middle Iranian languages preserved in those manuscripts. Since 1971, when the series was initiated by the Berlin Academy of Sciences, a total of 31 volumes has seen the light (see <http://www.brepols.net/Pages/BrowseBySeries.aspx?TreeSeries=BTT>).

Bibliotheca geographorum arabicorum (Brill, Leiden)

A series of critical editions of eight works by several Arab geographers; edited by Michael Jan Goeje between 1870–1894, was one of the first attempts to make critical editions of Arabic texts belonging to a specific topic (reprint in <http://www.brill.com/products/series/bibliotheca-geographorum-arabicorum>).

Bibliotheca islamica (Klaus-Schwarz-Verlag, Berlin)

One of the most important series within the framework of Islamic Studies has edited numerous critical editions of Arabic, Persian and Turkish texts since 1927. Topics include history, prosopography, literature, theology of various Islamic schools, and Sufism. The publication of the series is a joint project of the Orient Institute Beirut and the German Oriental Society (DMG) (<http://www.klaus-schwarz-verlag.com/>).

Commentaria in Aristotelem Armeniaca. Davidis Opera (Brill, Leiden)

This series, founded in 2009 and directed by Valentina Calzolari and Jonathan Barnes, aims at publishing a revised critical edition of the Armenian translation of the commentaries on Aristotelian logic which tradition ascribes to David the Invincible (sixth century). Besides the critical text of the Armenian, each volume contains a complete study of the work edited, together with a comparison of the Armenian with the underlying Greek model, and a translation into a modern language.

Corpus Christianorum Corpus Nazianzenum (Brepols, Turnhout)

The *Corpus Nazianzenum* aims at publishing the Greek homilies of Gregory of Nazianzus (only one volume so far), as well as their translations into Arabic, Armenian, Georgian, and Syriac, and some related material in Greek and in translation (mediaeval commentaries). The editorial board is established at the Institut orientaliste of the Université catholique de Louvain (Belgium).

Corpus Christianorum Series Apocryphorum (CCSA) (Brepols, Turnhout)

Founded in 1981, the *Series Apocryphorum* of the *Corpus Christianorum*, directed by the AELAC (Association pour l'Étude de la Littérature Apocryphe Chrétienne), aims at publishing all the pseudepigraphical or anonymous texts of Christian origin attributed to biblical characters or based on events reported or suggested by the Bible. The series' purpose is to enrich the knowledge of apocryphal Christian literature by supplying editions of unedited or difficult to access texts. Besides the critical text, each volume contains a complete study of the apocryphon edited, with commentary and translation into a modern language.

Corpus Christianorum Series Graeca (CCSG) (Brepols, Turnhout)

Founded in 1976, this series of scholarly editions of Greek patristic and Byzantine texts, without translations (some of the volumes have been translated elsewhere, especially in the series 'Corpus Christianorum in translation', started in 2009) is known for the quality of its publications. The editorial board is established at the Katholieke Universiteit Leuven (Belgium). Some volumes contain texts in Syriac or other oriental languages.

Corpus Scriptorum Christianorum Orientalium (CSCO) (Peeters, Leuven)

With the six subseries *Scriptores aethiopici, arabici, armeniaci, coptici, iberici*, and *syri*, the CSCO series (since 1903; see <http://www.peeters-leuven.be/search_serie_book.asp?nr=94>) covers a large amount of Christian traditions in oriental languages. Usually, the 'Scriptores' series contains editions of the original texts with translations (into Latin, English, French, German or Italian) printed in parallel volumes (for the *Scriptores syri*, see Ch. 3 § 3.17). The subseries *Subsidia* (see <http://www.peeters-leuven.be/search_serie_book.asp?nr=244>) provides additional information (lexical materials, concordances, etc.) pertaining to one or several of the individual traditions.

Études médiévales, modernes et arabes (Institut français d'études arabes de Damas).

A number of titles have been digitized since 1996 and are freely available on-line (<http://www.ifporient.org/publications/mediaeval>).

Al-Furqān: Islamic Heritage Foundation (London)

Al-Furqān Foundation supports the edition and publication of a wide selection of manuscripts of particular significance in the Islamic heritage, as well as facsimile editions of well-preserved important manuscripts. The series 'Edited texts' includes a number of important reference works that deal with Arabic history, geography and sciences (<http://www.al-furqan.com/publications/manuscript-centre/editing-texts/>).

Islamkundliche Untersuchungen (Klaus-Schwarz-Verlag, Berlin)

The series 'Islamkundliche Untersuchungen', published by Klaus Schwarz Publishers since 1970, is one of the most important series related to Islamic Studies. It includes a number of important critical editions of texts belonging to various fields and genres (<http://www.klaus-schwarz-verlag.com/>). A number of titles are digitized and freely available on-line (<http://menadoc.bibliothek.uni-halle.de/iud>).

Ismaili Texts and Translation (Institute of Ismaili Studies, London)

Critical editions, introduction and English translation of Ismaili texts in Arabic, Persian and Indic languages (<http://www.iis.ac.uk/view_article.asp?ContentID=104893>). See also the series *Epistles of the Brethren of Purity*, published by Oxford University Press in association with the Institute of Ismaili Studies, a multi-authored critical edition and annotated English translation of the Arabic *Rasā'il Iḫwān al-Ṣafa'* (tenth-century Iraq; <http://www.iis.ac.uk/view_article.asp?ContentID=112055>).

Monumenta Palaeographica Medii Aevi (Brepols, Turnhout)

Albeit focusing mostly upon palaeographical investigations, the series is well suited for (diplomatic) editions of special types of manuscripts such as the Georgian, Armenian, and Caucasian Albanian palimpsests covered by volumes 1 and 2 of the sub-series *Ibero-Caucasica* (see Ch. 3 § 3.11).

Pamjatniki pis'mennosti Vostoka (Nauka, Moscow)

Since 1959, the Russian publishing house Nauka has published the series *Памятники письменности Востока* (*Pamjatniki pis'mennosti Vostoka*, Monuments of the literature of the east; altogether 138 items in 223 volumes by 2013), which covers a great amount of critical editions of original texts in oriental languages (mostly in Persian, Turkish, but also Armenian and others) as well as translations (into Russian). The most famous items include the nine-volume edition of Firdawsī's *Šāhnāma* (edited by Evgenij Ėduardovič Bertel's, volume II.1–9 of the 'major' subseries *Памятники литературы народов Востока—Большая серия* (*Pamjatniki literatury narodov Vostoka—Bol'šaja serija*, 1963–1971), the two-volume edition of 'Omar Ḫayyām's *Rubā'iyyāt* (edited by the same scholar, volume II.1–2 of the 'minor' subseries *Памятники литературы народов Востока—Малая серия* (*Pamjatniki literatury narodov Vostoka—Malaja serija*, 1959), or the critical edition of the Middle Persian *Kārnāmag-ī Ardašīr Pābagān* (*Книга деяний Ардашира, сына Папака / Kniga dejanij Ardašira, syna Papaka*) by Ol'ga Michajlovna Čunakova (volume 78 of the main series, 1987).

Patrologia Orientalis (PO) (Brepols, Turnhout)

Founded in Paris in 1904 in an attempt to extend the 'Patrologiae cursus completus' by Jacques Paul Migne, which aimed to cover the written heritage of Greek and Latin church fathers exhaustively in the two series *Graeca* (161 volumes, 1857–1866) and *Latina* (217 volumes, 1841–1855, plus four volumes of indexes, 1862–1866), the PO series provides a large amount of Christian text materials from nearly all oriental traditions (235 fascicles in 53 volumes up to the present day). Since 1970 (volume 35), the series has been taken over by Brepols Publishers, Turnhout (see <http://www.brepols.net/Pages/BrowseBySeries.aspx?TreeSeries=PO>). The editorial approach is very inconsistent; however, even some of the older volumes have remained valuable sources until today.

Sources Chrétiennes (Cerf, Paris)

This collection has published about 550 volumes of editions of Greek and Latin patristic authors. The quality of the editions is uneven, and sometimes the Greek or Latin text is taken from a previous publication, but the French translation and introduction are always useful. See <http://www.sourceschretiennes.mom.fr/collection/presentation>.

Teksty i razyskanija po armjano-gruzinskoj filologii (Fakul'tet vostočnych jazykov Imperatorskogo Sankt-Peterburgskago Universiteta, St Peterburg)

Twelve volumes were published between 1900 and 1913, mostly *editiones principes* of important Old Georgian texts (by Nikolaj Marr).

Textes arabes et études islamiques (Institut Français d'Archéologie orientale, Cairo)

Studies and text editions, 50 issues, published since 1948 (<http://www.ifao.egnet.net/publications/catalogue/TAEI/>).

Ʒveli kartuli enis ʒeglebi (Tbilisi)

Fifteen volumes, published between 1944 and 1977, comprise critical editions of Old Georgian biblical and theological texts.

References

Cerquiglini 1989; Gleßgen – Lebsanft 1997; Greetham 1995; La Spisa 2012; Lichačev [D.] 2001; Ménard 1997; Ostrowski 2003; Sahle 2013; Sirat 1992; Tanselle 1983, 1995.

2. Steps towards an edition (CM–MCr–TA–JdH–PLS–AGi–SM–LS)

(CM) In this part of the chapter, we attempt to distinguish the different tasks which must be performed during the editorial process. This distinction is somewhat arbitrary and editing a text is a rather iterative process: decisions and choices taken at every stage of the process will have repercussions on the subsequent steps, conversely an editor may need to return to one of the earlier stages of his/her work at the very end of the process. It is often said that every text, or at least each type of text, imposes its own edition method (see Ch. 3 § 2.3), and all editors have gone through the experience of developing an appropriate method during the work process. More often than not, decisions taken in the beginning have to be reconsidered and, in the worst cases, some parts of the work have to be done all over again. Whether or not it is possible to protect the less experienced editor against such situations, this section does aim at presenting the various steps towards an edition in an explicit and instructive way. Digital aspects of the process of editing will be highlighted, but we will insist on procedures and principles rather than on specific tools. In what follows, we intentionally limit the bibliography to a few indispensable references (the choice of which is necessarily subjective, given the extensive literature existing on different aspects of the topic) and instead invite the reader to refer to the case studies for concrete illustrations. We consider only scholarly editions (by opposition to school editions for example, or to what is sometimes called an *editio minor*, that is the reduction of a scholarly edition to what is considered most useful for most readers, that is the text itself, without its scholarly apparatuses), that is editions of different type (diplomatic, genealogical, best-manuscript…) made according to scholarly criteria: following a method which has to be explicated and showing results which can be verified.

2.1. Heuristics of manuscripts and witnesses (MCr)

The first step in any editorial enterprise is to identify and list the witnesses to the work to be edited, and then to gain an adequate familiarity with them. Ideally, all the witnesses should be considered, but in practice the editor may have to limit the heuristics: for instance, to neglect the indirect tradition (see below), or to consider the manuscripts up to a certain period of time after the work was written. Those limitations may be justified for practical reasons, especially if the tradition is abundant, but they are difficult to justify on theoretical grounds: see, for example, the discussion about the principle *recentiores non deteriores* in Timpanaro 1985; and concerning the importance of the indirect tradition, see Ch. 3 § 3.15.

2.1.1. Identifying author and work

It is not a trivial issue in studies on pre-modern texts, especially oriental texts, to be able to classify a given work under one title, let alone under an author's name, and therefore to be able to identify it properly in manuscript catalogues. The phenomenon of manuscript transmission, with its many accidents and variations, often implies that one and the same work can be attributed to various authors and/or transmitted anonymously. Conversely, manuscripts can preserve very different texts, which may or may not be related to one another, under the same name and/or title. It is important to understand and to define how different 'versions' of the same work relate to one another (see Ch. 3 § 2.1.2).

In view of those difficulties, and depending on the amount of details found in the reference tools consulted, the results of this identification should ideally be presented with reference not only to its author and title, but also to its *incipit* (i.e. the beginning of the work), and, possibly, its *desinit* (i.e. its final words), in order to avoid any ambiguity.

The basic instrument in this matter is sometimes called a *Clavis* ('key' in Latin), an index of works, providing pieces of information about their attribution, authenticity, diffusion, previous editions, etc.—for example the *Clavis Patrum Graecorum*, or the *Index apologeticus sive Clavis Iustini martyris operum*. For several oriental traditions, those basic instruments are often old and should be updated (see Ch. 4 on cataloguing).

2.1.2. Direct and indirect tradition

The *testimonia* of a specific work are divided into two types: direct and indirect witnesses. The direct witnesses are the manuscripts and printed editions in which a work is preserved, either in its entirety or in a fragmentary form (for the edition of works preserved only fragmentarily, see Ch. 3 §§ 3.6, 3.9, 3.11). A 'fragment'—which results from a material loss of text in a manuscript—has to be carefully distinguished from an 'excerpt', which is the result of a voluntary selection.

The 'indirect tradition' of a given work may take various forms, and one must keep in mind that the distinction between direct and indirect traditions is often blurred.

(1) The work might be excerpted, and those excerpts then integrated into the work of later authors (for example, they might be used as citations in argumentation, plagiarized, or commented upon), or they are isolated in anthologies (see Ch. 3 § 3.19) or miscellaneous manuscripts (see Ch. 3 § 3.12).

(2) The work as a whole or in part might have been reworked, either by the author himself or by someone else. It is not always easy to determine the status of the reworking and its exact relation to the 'original' work (see Ch. 3 § 3.14, La Spisa 2014). Different terms are used to indicate those re-elaborations of a work, however without a clear terminological precision: recensions, redactions, versions, etc. (see Ch. 3 § 3.20). The reworking can affect several levels: linguistic (the orthography, grammar, or even vocabulary of a work might be adapted to another linguistic context, without crossing the border of one language or one dialect), semantic (the content of the work might be adapted), structural (the length, the order of the text, etc. might be altered). Some specific adaptations may receive specific names, such as, for example, *epitomē* (summary) or *metaphrasis* (stylistic rewriting; see Signes Codoñer 2014). In the case of non-authoritative texts, such as technical treatises, 'popular' literature, or genres which call for adaptation and transformation (hagiography, Apocrypha, etc.), it may prove particularly difficult to gather and order all the required information, and establishing the history of the text(s) will pose several problems (see Ch. 3 § 2.3).

(3) Oriental traditions are often multilingual (nearly every case study in this chapter deals in one way or another with translations). Translations of a work into other languages constitute another type of indirect witness. All imaginable situations are possible and each situation will require a different response: literal translations or rather free adaptations are found, partial translations can be based on an already indirect witness in the original language (in an anthology, for example), double translations, translations of translations, and so on. In cases where the work to be edited is itself a translation, the source text will have to be taken into account as an indispensable indirect witness.

Taking the indirect tradition into account is a time-consuming process, which does not always yield significant results. However, in some cases—above all when the direct tradition is very poor (but not necessarily; see Ch. 3 § 3.15)—resorting to indirect tradition can be very helpful and even compulsory and, in extreme cases, one text might be transmitted only through indirect tradition (see Ch. 3 § 3.18). The degree of confidence which one can put into the indirect tradition will vary case by case: one can choose to resort to a translation, because of its antiquity and faithfulness to the original, and not to an *epitomē*, due to its remoteness from the original form of the work.

2.1.3. Catalogues, bibliography, and databases

To establish the list of all the extant witnesses, direct as well as indirect, of a given work, the editor can rely upon various instruments, such as library catalogues and databases (see Ch. 4), previous editions, and, sometimes, studies on the manuscript tradition of other works preserved together with the work to be edited. It is useful to consult a bibliography as large as possible concerning the work to be edited and related works, as manuscript descriptions may sometimes be hidden in articles or monographs devoted to other topics.

Catalogues, bibliography and databases are very helpful and form the basis of the editor's work. However, the editor must always check their information, which means often that one has to visit the libraries where the manuscripts are allegedly kept. The work is obviously much more difficult when manuscripts have not been catalogued, or when the existing catalogues are very summary, a situation which is unfortunately quite frequent, above all—although not exclusively—dealing with manuscripts located in environments where cataloguing is not a great priority due to political or economic circumstances, or in private collections (see Ch. 4). A recurrent problem is that of locating and designating the manuscripts: much confusion may arise, for example, from the use of ancient or inexact shelfmarks, dismembered or no longer extant libraries, or transferred collections.

A list of witnesses, as complete as possible, and as detailed as possible must be given in the introduction to the edition (see Ch. 3 § 2.6).

2.1.4. Acquiring and reading reproductions of all the manuscripts

In order to make the comparison of manuscripts easier (see Ch. 3 § 2.2), one must obtain a reproduction (microfilm, photos, digital) of all the listed manuscripts. This can be very costly, depending on the number of reproductions to be acquired and on the respective libraries from which they should be bought, and sometimes impossible (some libraries will not answer requests, while others will refuse to sell images of their collections or be unable to provide such a service). Even if manuscripts have been seen in situ (which is advisable, but not always feasible), having a reproduction available is always useful, as the collations may need to be rechecked at some point. Richard rightly argued that photography has transformed philology (Richard [M.] 1980, 11). If today digital reproductions tend to replace microfilms, the microfilm support still remains an unequalled medium for manuscript reproductions (on technical aspects see General introduction § 2.1.4): research centres specializing in manuscripts possess important collections of microfilms or microfiches of manuscripts that are otherwise difficult to access (<http://medium.irht.cnrs.fr/>, the microfilms of Sinai and Jerusalem manuscripts at the Library of Congress and in Louvain-la-Neuve to cite only a few examples), and some libraries are now making digital reproductions on the basis of the microfilms. One should be aware of the shortcomings of many microfilms (and digital reproductions made from them), not to speak of the fact that microfilm readers are often bulky devices, which are becoming rare in libraries and research centres: photographs are almost always black and white, frequently in the form of a negative, the quality of the images is generally quite poor, the microfilm becomes less legible with time, many details, which may be important, such as margins, are not visible. The impression given by the reading of a text from a microfilm may be misleading, the corrections are often invisible (because the difference of ink colours is undetectable in black and white reproductions), the change of handwriting on a page may go unnoticed, etc.

Nowadays, digital images have made things much easier with respect to consultation, but the financial aspect is sometimes still problematic (the acquisition of the digital images of one manuscript can cost several thousand euros), although more and more digital facsimiles are provided online and are freely accessible. Once again, the situation differs widely among specific manuscripts and library collections (for example, with regard to the number of digitized manuscripts, the quality of the reproductions, or the way to browse the images).

Numerous oriental manuscripts are kept in collections located in the Middle East, East Africa, and Asia, and this frequently implies additional obstacles. Whereas some collections are now digitized and accessible, scholars are often compelled to approach keepers of these collections personally and invest considerable time in establishing contacts and building sufficient confidence in order to earn the access that is aspired to. Furthermore, the decision on granting or denying access and reproduction may depend on personal, cultural, ideological, political or economic parameters that cannot always be ignored. Occasionally, texts that are considered heterodox or heretical, or threatening for social or political reasons, can be kept away from researchers. In the same vein, researchers may meet with limited appreciation of the intended project in environments where social and political hardship causes people to define their priorities very differently. Thus, one may have to invest much energy in convincing one's counterparts of the project's intrinsic scientific relevance, for instance when it concerns a text that has already been edited.

In practice, there is almost always at least one or several manuscripts which the editor cannot gain access to, in spite of all attempts. If acquiring such images turns out to be impossible, the editor can try to travel to the library and make an autopsy of the volume, but this may also be very hard and even impossible. For practical purposes, and especially when the available time span and funding for a project are limited, one should not go too far in postponing the next steps until all witnesses have been acquired. In case a specific witness can only be accessed too late to be used for the edition, one can always write an additional study to illustrate its relevance.

2.1.5. Gathering material evidence for a first classification of the manuscripts

The first thing the editor should check is the actual presence or absence of the text she or he wants to edit in the manuscripts listed thanks to the catalogues. If possible, poorly catalogued manuscripts which, for different reasons, seem likely to preserve this text (for example: manuscripts containing similar treatises, or treatises by the same author) should be examined as well.

The editor should also note the other texts preserved in this manuscript and make a precise description of all its contents. As was said above and as we will see again in Ch. 3 § 2.3, the history of other texts contained in the same manuscripts is an important element for the history of the text and of the collection (see Ch. 3 § 3.2).

The importance of giving a more accurate analysis of the manuscripts is a requirement for any modern scholarly edition. A good study of each manuscript as an object can be very helpful to classify it among the other witnesses (see Ch. 3 § 2.3). It must be highlighted that the editor must not limit him/herself to philological analysis, but should complement it by a codicological and historical study (see Ch. 3 § 3.7). This is not always an easy task, since the editor generally has neither the competence nor the time to study the manuscripts from a codicological and historical point of view. However, one should, as far as it is possible, pay attention to the manuscript in itself: it will avoid mistakes in the classification, and will also help to solve some problems for which a strictly philological analysis is not sufficient.

Given the deficiencies of many existing catalogues, the editor of a text will often be compelled to prepare a description of manuscripts that almost meets the requirements of a catalogue or at least of a rather substantial checklist. Such descriptions can reach dimensions that surpass those of an introduction to the edition and might therefore require a separate publication.

2.2. Collation (CM–TA)

(CM) Once one has listed all the manuscripts containing the work to be edited and collected all available reproductions (whether photos, microfilms or images in digital format), the next task is to read them and compare the texts they contain: this process is called 'collation' (Latin *collatio*, from *collatus*, participle of the verb *conferre*, 'bring together').

In order to perform a collation, a good practical knowledge of palaeography is necessary, especially in order to interpret correctly the ligatures, abbreviations and other special features (see Ch. 2). In this first stage, not only all variations, including orthographical ones, but also punctuation, abbreviations (and numbers) should be noted as they stand in the manuscripts (and not resolved). Even though those features will not necessarily be interpreted as differences later on, it might be useful to know whether one word was abbreviated or not in a specific manuscript in order to understand the process of variation. If, for practical reasons (time constraints) and depending on the specific aim pursued, one decides not to record some features, this decision should be carefully weighed and documented, and one must be careful not to infer anything from an absence of record when using the collations at a later stage. As a general rule, one must always be as explicit and clear as possible, as the process of collation may sometimes extend over several years, and it should also be kept in mind that collations may sometimes be used by other people than the person who made them.

Some 'paratextual' elements are also important to be recorded in the collation: changes of folia or pages in the manuscript, possibly changes of columns; if noticed, a change of hand or ink may as well be important to be noted, as are holes or gaps in the manuscripts, lacunae, difficulties in reading something, marginal notes, corrections by the copyist or by someone else, etc.

Already at this stage, it is expedient to use *sigla* to refer to the manuscripts, instead of their full name. The *sigla* should be chosen carefully, as it is advisable to change them as little as possible during the following steps (see Ch. 3 § 2.5 concerning the *sigla* in the apparatuses, and § 2.6 about the *conspectus siglorum*) in order to avoid confusion. Extant manuscripts are usually labelled by one Latin capital letter (A, B, C, etc.), or one capital letter and one minuscule letter (Am, Va, Ve, etc.), or sometimes a letter and a number (A1, B2, etc.), etc. The *sigla* may be chosen totally arbitrarily, or they may be mnemonic of the name of the manuscript (for example V for a manuscript kept at the Vatican library, P for a Parisian manuscript, etc.). If the manuscripts are numerous, more complex systems of identification may have to be found (for example Ch. 3 §§ 3.5, 3.15).

In an ideal world, one should collate the complete text of the work to be edited in all manuscripts. In the real world, this might prove to be unfeasible, because of time constraints (or for some other practical reasons, see Ch. 3 § 2.1), especially if the text is very long and/or the manuscripts very numerous. It may therefore be necessary to do partial collations (for example a few chapters or passages from the work) or even to restrict oneself to samples (namely passages considered to be important in the text). If one decides to perform partial collations, one must be aware of a number of possible pitfalls, especially of the fact that the text in a given manuscript is not necessarily homogeneous (especially, but not only, when there was some contamination in the tradition: see Ch. 3 § 2.3). It is advisable to choose at least three passages from very different places in the work (for example towards the beginning, middle, and end), and to avoid as much as possible passages where some of the witnesses are lacunary. As for the sampling procedure, it requires that a complete collation of some of the most important witnesses (or, those considered as such) is performed first and that a number of variant locations have been identified as significant for the classification of the witnesses (see Ch. 3 § 2.3).

Whether one decides to work by hand or to use a computer-assisted method, while the process is slightly different (see below), the general rules remain the same. In both cases, it is important to note faithfully all features of each witness (even punctuation marks), and not to take any premature editorial decision at this stage. It must be stressed that all differences must be noted, not only those considered 'significant' for the history of the text, since the result of the collation will not only be used to classify the witnesses, but also later on in establishing the critical text and apparatuses (see Ch. 3 § 2.4.1).

2.2.1. Manual collations (CM)

The text of each manuscript is compared with one and the same reference text. As reference text, one may choose either a manuscript or a previous edition. The advantage of a previous edition is that its text may be available in digital form or may be scannable, and that it offers a stable system of reference; one possible disadvantage could be that its text is artificial, containing readings which are not found in any of the extant manuscripts. If there is no previous edition available, one may resort to a manuscript that is chosen for its legibility and completeness. The choice of the reference text may influence the collation—although this influential effect is usually minimal, especially if one is aware of the risk.

Once the reference text has been chosen, collation files must be prepared, containing this text, either in full for a complete collation, or parts of it for a partial collation, arranged either vertically (in columns) or horizontally (in lines). The identification of pages and lines or of chapters and paragraphs of the reference text should be indicated clearly, in order to retrieve each passage easily, as well as the *siglum* of each witness and the changes of folia. Every difference of the manuscripts in comparison with the reference text is then noted. In this way, a large amount of the information is in fact implicit: one notes only the differences, and not the agreements—but this method may be quicker than a full transcription (see Ch. 3 § 2.2.2). The two examples below (figs. 3.2.1, 3.2.2) show a 'vertical' collation: the first column provides the base text, and each manuscript is collated in one column.

The first example shows a manual collation made by different people (fig. 3.2.1). The reference text in this case was a manuscript (C), which was transcribed fully, with its punctuation, titles, etc., and typed. The text was then displayed in one column and printed, with enough space to collate four manuscripts (A, B, T and D) on one page.

In the second case, an Excel spreadsheet was used and the collation was entered directly into the file instead of paper, but the principle is the same (fig. 3.2.2). In this case the reference text was a printed text, and each word contained in it was numbered. The number of columns in an Excel file (or any other comparable software) is not limited by the constraints of the printed page

Abbreviations ('om.', 'add.', 'inv.', 'p. corr.', etc.) and signs ('+', '=', arrows, etc.) are often used to describe what happens in the manuscripts. Such abbreviations might be more personal and less standardized than those used in the critical apparatus (see Ch. 3 § 2.5), but one must keep in mind that they should nonetheless remain comprehensible to other people if one wants the collations to be used by others. One must also find a convenient system to note the uncertainties or doubts which arise when deciphering the manuscripts. It is important to make sure that the system of notation used cannot be misinterpreted (even by the very person who made the collation, when looking back at it sometime later). Transpositions of blocks of text and overlapping variants are especially tricky in that respect, and one should not hesitate to put some explicative notes and cross-references in the collation.

There are cases—especially of abundant manuscript traditions—where the necessity of having full transcripts of each witness (see Ch. 3 § 2.2.2) is not obvious and seems less important than achieving a collation in a limited amount of time. There is, of course, a certain degree of interpretation, and therefore of subjectivity, in any collation, but there is no reason why it should be higher than in the case of a transcription. Ideally every collation should be made twice, by two different people—but in practice this rarely happens, although it is recommended to do it for the most important witnesses, which will be used for establishing the critical text (see Ch. 3 § 2.4.1).

C	A	B	T	D
Διατί	διατὶ	Διὰ τί	[illegible]	
ιθ'				
βασιλεύσαντας		βασιλευσάντων		
ἀπὸ				
Δαυῒδ		.	[illegible]	([illegible])
ἕως	ἕως			
Ἰεχονίου	ἰεχονίου.		,	ἰεχονιου
ὁ				
Εὐαγγελιστής	εὐαγγελιστής			
ιδ'				
ὀνομάζει;	:	;~	;	
Ἐπειδὴ				
οὐ				
διαδοχὰς				
λέγει,		.	·	
ἀλλὰ	ἄλλα			
γενεάς.	.	.		
Ἐπεὶ				
οὖν				
τινὲς				(τινὲς)
αὐτῶν			[illegible]	
ἀπὸ				
εἴκοσι	εἴκοσι		εἰκοσιετοῦς	εικοσιετους
ἔτους	ἔτους	[illegible]		
χρόνου				
ἐπαιδοποίησαν	ἐπαιδοποίησαν.	[illegible]	[illegible]	,
εἰς				
ἀναπλήρωσιν				
τῶν				
γενεῶν				
τῶν				
μακροβιούντων	[illegible]	.		
τούς				

Fig. 3.2.1 Manual collation of *Florilegium Coislinianum*, cf. De Vos et al. 2010.

	A	B	C	D	E	F	G	H	I	J	K	L	M	N	O
1			V	C	A	S	L	F	U	J	M	T	B	D	
70	68	ruses													
71	69	de	des	des	des	des	ok	des	des	des	des	ok	ok	des	
72	70	Sioux													
73	71	du													
74	72	rationaliste	rationnaliste				rationnalis	rationnalis	rationnalis	ok	ok	ok	rationnalis	ok	
75	73	ou													
76	74	la													
77	75	candeur													
78	76	ardente													
79	77	de													
80	78	l'athée.													
81	79	Je													
82	80	n'ose													
83	81	donc													
84	82	jeter													
85	83	la													
86	84	pierre													
87	85	ni													
88	86	à													
89	87	celle		celui	clle*	celui				celui	celui			celui	
90	88	qui													
91	89	croit								croient		p.corr.; crois a.corr., alia manu			
92	90	en	om.	om.	om.	om.	om.	om.	om.	om.	om.	ok	om.	om.	
93	91	des													
94	92	choses													
95	93	qui													
96	94	ne													
97	95	m'inspirent					m'inspire					p.corr.; m'inspire a.corr.; alia manu			
98	96	que													
99	97	le													
100	98	doute,	ok					doute	doute				doute		
101	99	ni													
102	100	à													
103	101	celui													
104	102	qui													

Collat1 / Collat1 (2) / Textes / Collat1 (3) / DescrDta

Fig. 3.2.2 Collation file of an artificial manuscript tradition in French, cf. Baret et al. 2006.

2.2.2. Using digital tools (TA)

For many decades it has been recognized that text collation is a task that is extraordinarily tedious, and requires vast attention to detail— and that such a task would be well-suited for automation (for example Robinson [Pe.] 1989). There currently exist a few tools specifically for scholarly text collation, although the development landscape is changing so rapidly that a textual scholar new to the field would be well-advised to seek a current recommendation for software that might meet his or her needs.

The core principle behind automated text collation is that, rather than choosing a base text (or reference text) against which all subsequent texts should be compared, the scholar refrains from any selection or comparison at all. She or he will instead produce a full transcription of each witness to be collated, in as much diplomatic detail as is feasible, and leave the work of comparison to the software.

At a first glance, the prospect of producing full transcriptions of all textual witnesses can seem at least as daunting as performing a hand collation. In practice, however, diplomatic transcription can often be significantly easier than manual collation (see above), and it confers several advantages:

– A full transcription provides an unambiguous and positive record of the content of the witness, with no need to rely upon arguments from silence in a critical apparatus.

– There is no need to select a base text, in that all the texts will be compared equally with each other.

– There is no need to conform to a regular system of spelling or orthography for the text—collation software should be capable of handling all variations.

– Once transcribed, the witness texts can be subjected to many forms of analysis beyond collation—for example stylistic analysis, author attribution techniques, linguistic analysis.

If the editorial project is a large one, the most reliable way to produce a good transcription of a text is to have it transcribed separately by two readers, compare (i.e. collate) the two transcriptions using a software program, and resolve any differences that arise. In practice, most editorial projects have rather more modest resources. If only one or two editors are available to work on a project, another option for transcription is to begin with a copy of a temporary 'reference' text—for example, a printed edition that has been optically scanned or an existing transcription whose text is suspected to be relatively close to that of the manuscript to be transcribed—and alter it until it matches the manuscript being transcribed. This is not a reference text in the traditional sense, in that it will not be preserved in its original state and has no function but to save the transcriber some typing work. This method carries the risk that the editor will inadvertently preserve a few characteristics of the 'reference' text that do not correspond to the manuscript, but is the best compromise for the efficient production of transcribed texts. While it has been argued above that this 'quick' process of transcription is essentially the same as text collation, the differing purposes of the tasks (to produce a reasonably faithful copy of a single witness, versus a catalogue of divergence between two or more witnesses) would tend to produce different results.

Guidelines for transcription

The rendering of a manuscript text into digital form will necessarily involve a trade-off between the simplicity (and thus ease of analysis) of the transcription and its completeness. The simplest method of transcription is to reproduce the interpreted content of the text into a plain text computer file. This has several disadvantages, however. Such a simple transcription preserves no reference system back to the physical text, making it difficult to search for the original occurrence of a particular word or phrase. The transcriber must choose at the outset whether to expand abbreviations within the text or simply to transcribe the component characters; if she or he encounters symbols that cannot be reproduced alphabetically, the only option will be to interpret them into words that can. In short, all paratextual information will necessarily be lost.

In order to mitigate these problems, the scholar may well wish to adopt his or her own system of vocabulary in order to describe the phenomena of particular texts—the most common example of this will be to insert page and line breaks to represent those in the physical artefact, or use some form of textual emphasis or highlighting to represent, for example, abbreviations or corrections within the text. The resulting transcription is, however, unlikely to be compatible with any existing tools for computational analysis, and so defeats the purpose of using digital methods to a certain extent.

The other, preferable alternative is to transcribe the texts using an existing and well-known system of vocabulary such as that provided by the TEI guidelines (see General introduction § 2.1). At present this presents a technological bar to entry in that it requires the transcriber to learn the basics of XML text markup and to structure the transcription in a hierarchical form suitable for XML encoding. While in theory there is nothing to prevent a scholar from adopting the TEI vocabulary within an entirely different markup system such as those that use range-based annotation, in practice there is currently no consensus and so no generally-available tools for any other sort of transcription apart from XML.

The TEI guidelines provide a means for description of almost all the paratextual information that must be omitted from a simple transcription: page and line information, abbreviations and their expansions as interpreted by the scholar, corrections to the text by the scribe as well as by later hands, uncertainty of interpretation (perhaps due to physical damage to the text), and even page geometry for the indication of non-textual figures within the manuscript. The scholar is free to take advantage of all of this descriptive functionality, or any subset thereof, depending on the volume of texts to be transcribed and the availability of manpower with which to carry out the task.

There is nevertheless a risk incurred by an excessively detailed transcription of a text. The TEI guidelines are very complex and extremely flexible, so that even within their letter and spirit it is possible to produce several forms of transcription. Should the guiding principle be by page (i.e. physical text division) or logical text division? Should abbreviations be recorded with their interpreted expansions as an annotation, or should it be the other way around? The answers to these questions will necessarily depend on how the transcriptions are to be used later, and with which tools. Very few tools comprehend more than a narrow subset of the TEI guidelines, and so the requirements and functionality of the tools to be used for collation, analysis, and presentation must inform the choices made concerning transcription.

Automated collation of transcriptions

When the transcriptions have been completed—i.e. when the text witnesses have been transformed into suitable digital representations—the possibilities of computational tools become clear. The first and most important of these, for most textual scholars, is the collation programme. The principle behind automated collation is that, given a set of texts that resemble each other, the programme will identify and align the matching words and phrases across all text witnesses. Depending upon the collation programme, the scholar might compare all texts to a selected base, or compare each text to every other text without reference to a base. Various tools offer different forms of visualization of the results—side-by-side comparison of two witnesses, a spreadsheet of all witnesses that can be downloaded and used as a more traditional collation table, or even a representation of the text as a graph, with text variants marked as divergent paths. The result can also be used in further analysis, for example in a programme that will compute a hypothesis (partial or full) for the stemma (see Ch. 3 § 2.3).

It is important to bear in mind that, while automated collation identifies the variations existing between witnesses of a given work, it performs no interpretation of the results. It is up to the scholar to identify the meaning and significance of any particular variant. If the collation was performed without reference to a base text, even the concepts of 'addition' and 'omission' of a portion of text are foreign to the programme—it will be noted merely that witness A contains the reading and witness B does not. Whether that is an addition or omission will depend upon the philological judgment of the scholar.

Limitations

At present there exists no automated workflow or software for the collation of texts with their translations into different languages. The scholar working with texts and their translations will probably still need to perform a manual collation, although the other advantages of diplomatic transcription still apply. It is conceivable that scholars working with transliterated texts, on the other hand, may well be able to make use of an automated collation program customized to suit their needs—if both scripts are alphabetic, for example, the transliterated text might be re-converted to the original alphabet through use of an equivalence table, and used with a collation algorithm that allows for imprecise word matching. Any such approach would, however, require a significant investment of software development resources and would need to be well-tested.

	A	B	C	D	E	F	G	H	I	J	K	L	M	N	O	P	Q	R	S	T	U	V	W	X	Y
1	Reference	nr.	Text		Type		Weight				Origin	A	B	C	D			E		F		G	H		K
2			Ref. Text	Variant	type	context	irreversible	irreproducible	length	total						a.c.	s.l.		p.c.		p.c.			p.c.	
11	1.2.1.	8	αὐτόθι	αὐτόθεν	suff.		1	0	0	1	?	0	?	0	0	*	*	1	*	0	*	0	0	*	1
12	1.2.2.	9	ἔχει	ἔχειν	gram.		0	0	0	0	0	0	?	0	0	*	*	0	*	0	*	0	0	*	0
13	1.2.3.	10	γάρ	/	om.		1	0	1	2	?	0	?	0	0	*	*	0	*	1	*	0	1	*	0
14	1.3.1.	11	Ἰουδαῖοι	οἱ Ἰουδαῖοι	add.	article	0	0	1	1	1	0	?	0	1	*	*	0	*	0	*	0	0	*	0
15	1.5.1.	12	οὐδὲ	οὔτε	suff.		1	0	0	1	1	0	?	0	1	*	*	0	*	1	*	0	1	*	1
16	1.6.1.	13	φασί τινὲς	φασί τινες	acc.		0	0	0	0	?	0	?	1	1	*	*	1	*	0	*	0	0	*	1
17	1.8.1.	14	δι᾽ ὧν συγχώρησις γίνεται ἁμαρτημάτων	/	om.		1	1	2	4	?	0	?	0	0	*	*	0	*	0	*	0	0	*	0
18	1.9.1.	15	ἐπειδὴ	ἐπειδὴ γὰρ	add.		1	0	1	2	?	0	?	0	0	*	*	1	*	0	*	0	0	*	1
19	1.11.1.	16	μετανοήσῃ	μετανοήσει	gram.	phonetic	0	0	0	0	0	1	?	0	0	*	*	0	*	0	*	0	0	*	0
20	1.13-14.1.	17	ὡς εἴρηται	/	om.		1	0	2	3	?	0	?	0	1	*	*	1	*	1	*	0	1	*	1
21	1.14.1.	18	ἐνταῦθα	/	om.		1	0	1	2	?	0	?	0	0	*	*	0	*	0	*	0	0	*	0
22	1.14-15.1.	19	ἐνταῦθα ἁμαρτήσας καὶ πάλιν ἀδιαφόρως	/	om.		1	1	2	4	0	0	?	0	0	*	*	0	*	0	*	0	0	*	0
23	1.14-15.2.	20	ἁμαρτήσας καὶ πάλιν ἀδιαφόρως ἀγαθοεργήσας	ἀγαθοεργήσας καὶ πάλιν ἀδιαφόρως ἁμαρτήσας	inv.		1	1	2	4	0	0	?	0	0	*	*	0	*	0	*	0	0	*	0
24	1.17.1.	21	ἔχομεν	ἔχωμεν (1)	gram.	phonetic	0	0	0	0	0	1	?	0	1	*	*	2	*	1	0	0	0	*	2
25				ἐχόμενα (2)	gram.		1	0	0	1	0														
26	1.20.1.	22	τις	/	om.		1	0	1	2	0	0	?	0	0	*	*	0	*	1	*	0	0	*	0
27	1.21.1.	23	κρίνετε	κρίνεται	gram.	phonetic	0	0	0	0	0	1	?	0	1	*	*	0	*	0	*	0	1	0	0

Fig. 3.2.3 Table of collations of *Florilegium Coislinianum*, cf. Macé et al. 2012.

2.2.3. Processing variants (CM)

As we already said above (see Ch. 3 § 2.2.1), the results of the collation (whether made manually or using digital tools) may be used for different purposes. Some of them will be described further on: the classification of the textual states represented in the manuscripts (see Ch. 3 § 2.3), the establishment of the edited text (see Ch. 3 § 2.4) and the composition of the critical apparatus (see Ch. 3 § 2.5). The results of the collation can also be recorded in a database and used for palaeographic or linguistic analysis (see Ch. 3 § 3.5). Fig. 3.2.3 shows a table of analysis of the collation, which can be used for statistical purposes.

2.3. Witness classification and history of the text (CM)

The very necessity of understanding the relationships between different witnesses to the same work and the method of achieving it have been brought into question by some scholars, past and present. Without dismissing the constructive contributions and the justified warnings (see Witkam 2013) of the detractors of the stemmatic approach (see Ch. 3 § 2.3.1), the view held here is that it is always necessary and useful to try to determine the relationships amongst the witnesses (if there is more than one) to the same work, using all pieces of evidence in a methodical way. However uncertain or disappointing the results might sometimes seem, no solid conclusion about the text could ever be drawn without such an inquiry, and therefore no serious edition can be made without it. Several practical factors may be a hindrance to this research (see below), but this may never be an excuse to reject it. To take only one example, Peacock's conclusion about 'the futility of attempting to establish stemmata in the case of many Islamic traditions', because of their high degree of horizontal transmission (or contamination) (Peacock 2007, 103) is based on a careful examination of the witnesses and of their relationships and could never have been drawn without such an examination; furthermore it may be valid for the specific tradition Peacock has been working on, but should not be taken for granted in other cases. Besides, it must be said that applying the stemmatic method does not by itself determine the type of edition one will produce, if any (see Ch. 3 § 2.4.1). The stemmatic method, as will be shown below, is one of the tools scholars may use in order to reconstruct the history of a text, which, in its turn, may be the basis for an edition. Traditionally, this part of textual criticism is called recensio (recension; Reynolds – Wilson 1991, 207).

It is difficult, however, to give much practical advice in this matter, as the method followed and the results obtained very much depend on the material and textual evidence on which the research is based, and this in turn depends on several factors: the type of work (genre, language, translated or not, etc.), the type of tradition transmitting it (*codex unicus*, fragmentary transmission, over-abundant tradition, etc.), and the unpredictable and random way in which history works. This last point must always be kept in mind: the evidence we have now (no matter how huge it may seem) is only a very small part of what existed once, and our histories of texts resemble archaeological reconstructions, that show what is left, but also what has been lost. This is why the following subchapter cannot give ready-made recipes that can be applied in all cases (the variety of the solutions adopted in the case studies will amply illustrate this point), and will therefore confine itself to the explanation of some important concepts and practices.

2.3.1. The stemmatic approach

The stemmatic method has been associated with the name of Karl Lachmann (1793–1851; see Timpanaro 2005, Reeve 1998), whereas its opponents often claim the patronage of Joseph Bédier (1864–1938; on Bédier's method, see Trovato 2013). It is beyond the scope of this chapter to deal with this question in all bibliographical and historical details, but it is necessary to mention it, because it is still at the core of recent debates in textual scholarship. To make a long story short, the method of Lachmann, or 'common errors' method, as theorized by Paul Maas (Maas 1957), came about in the historicist/positivist context of the nineteenth century, as a way of analysing the textual variation in manuscripts in genealogical/hierarchical terms: mistakes produced in the course of the copying process are transmitted in the subsequent copies, which add their own mistakes etc.; this genealogy of mistakes contained in manuscripts provides us with an objective tool to reconstruct the pedigree of the manuscripts themselves, which is called the stemma (see a good synthetic presentation of the method in West [M.] 1973, 31–37). Finally, it must be said that this more scientific approach to the texts came from 'the rejection of the vulgate text as the basis for discussion and with it the illogical conservatism which regarded the use of manuscripts as a departure from a tradition rather than a return to it. In this … the first impulse came from New Testament studies, where the problem was more obvious: the wealth of manuscript evidence left little scope for conjectural emendation and the task of choosing the truth from the variant readings was hampered by the almost divine sanction which was attributed to the *textus receptus*' (Reynolds – Wilson 1991, 209).

The stemmatic representation of the descent of manuscripts may be considered too simplistic (in reality, the process of 'descent with variation' is complicated by several phenomena, which will be briefly mentioned hereafter), too mechanical, or even unrealistic; however, as a methodological tool, it remains the most powerful device scholars may use in trying to determine the relationships between witnesses to a text, and it has been improved on two sides: (a) technically, thanks to the implementation of formal calculation methods (Quentin 1926, Greg 1927) and, later, computerized methods (Dearing 1968, Froger 1968, Griffith [J.] 1968, Zarri 1971 are pioneering studies—see Andrews – Macé 2013, and the bibliography cited there; for an application of statistical approach in oriental studies, see Weitzman 1985 and 1987, and Walter 2001); (b) conceptually, by the bringing-in of 'material philology' (Pasquali 1934, [2]1952), linguistic studies, biology, etc., to form a new synthesis sometimes called 'neo-Lachmannism' (see the very rich and thought-provoking collections of *Studies in Stemmatology* edited by van Reenen – van Mulken in 1996 and van Reenen et al. 2004, including contributions on oriental languages, such as Arabic, Greek and Slavonic).

As said above, for practical guidance about stemmatics, the reader may recur to Maas 1957, West [M.] 1973, Reynolds – Wilson 1991 (pp. 207–241), and Trovato 2014, and there is no need to give a full exposition of the method here. Several statistical methods and computerized tools have been applied or developed in the context of stemmatics: see the bibliographical appendix in Macé et al. 2001; several contributions in Andrews – Macé 2014 are devoted to stemmatics. Only a few problematic concepts will be discussed here, hoping that this might help those confronted to similar questions. See also Haugen 2014 for the terminology and Reeve 2011 for useful and always sharp insights into difficult questions.

2.3.2. Building a stemma on the basis of textual variation

A stemma is a synthetic representation, in the form of a graph, of an explanatory model, based both on an empirical analysis of a historical reality and on a theory about the way texts are transmitted. This model can be refuted or validated, both on empirical and theoretical grounds.

Depending on the type of information that has been used to build the stemma and on the method applied, it may represent various things. A philogenetic tree of variants may be described as the best statistical hypothesis about relationships between states of text, it is based on the textual variants alone, and does not imply any a-priori decisions about errors (see Ch. 3 § 3.1). As for automated methods in stemmatics, a set of useful tools is provided on the website created and maintained by Tara Andrews (<http://stemmaweb.net/>). A logical stemma would also be based on the variations, but implies decisions about errors, as only errors (innovations) are kinship-revealing (see below about variants). Then, historical data about the manuscripts as objects (date and place of copy, places where the manuscript was kept, notes by possessors etc.) must be added in order to draw a *stemma codicum* in the fullest sense, a historical stemma (see Ch. 3 § 3.7).

In the example shown in fig. 3.2.4, eleven Greek manuscripts are considered, represented by the Latin majuscule letters A, B, C, D, E, F, G, H, K, L and T. It is often easier to start with the witnesses which have a significant number of clear individual mistakes, because (except if all those mistakes can be easily corrected) they cannot be the ancestor of any of the other extant witnesses. In this case it was clear that L must be a copy of K, because it had all the mistakes of K (and shared the same peculiar contents), plus a number of individual mistakes; in addition, L is younger than K. D, E, G and K share common mistakes, which are not to be found in other witnesses, they must therefore form a family. In addition, E, G and K have common mistakes which are not in D and each of them has individual mistakes; this fact forces us to postulate a lost intermediary between E, G and K on the one hand, and D on the other hand; this intermediary is the lost ancestor of E, G and K. In fig. 3.2.4, the postulated lost intermediaries are represented by asterisks (and not by Greek letters, as is sometimes the case), and they are all hypothetical. The probable date of copying of those manuscripts (based on palaeographic evidence, with an approximation of half a century) is given in the left margin, and the length of the branches represents the time span between the extant manuscripts.

In other types of treelike representations, such as phylogenetic trees (statistical analysis based on phylogenetic algorithms), the branch lengths may represent the 'distance' (for example the number of additional individual variants) between witnesses. In fig. 3.2.5 for instance, more or less the same manuscripts as in fig. 3.2.4 can be seen (L is not present there, and a new manuscript, P, has been added). The readings of the manuscripts have been statistically analysed, using a phylogenetic method (a method used in biology for the classification of character states). A comparable distribution of the manuscripts can be observed (with some differences which can be explained by the method used: see Macé et al. 2012), but, here, a longer branch means that the manuscript is farther away from the ones next to it: manuscript B appears on a very small branch, because it is indeed the direct ancestor of manuscript P (manuscript P has many peculiar readings on its own).

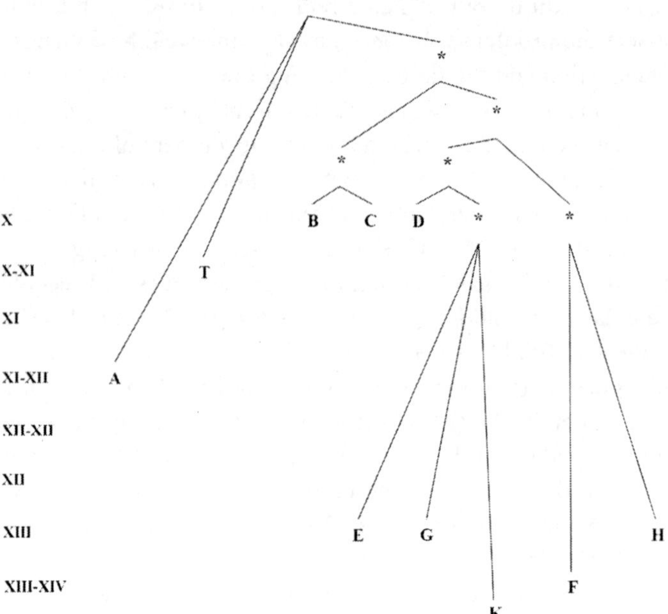

Fig. 3.2.4 Stemma codicum of *Florilegium Coislinianum*, cf. De Vos et al. 2010.

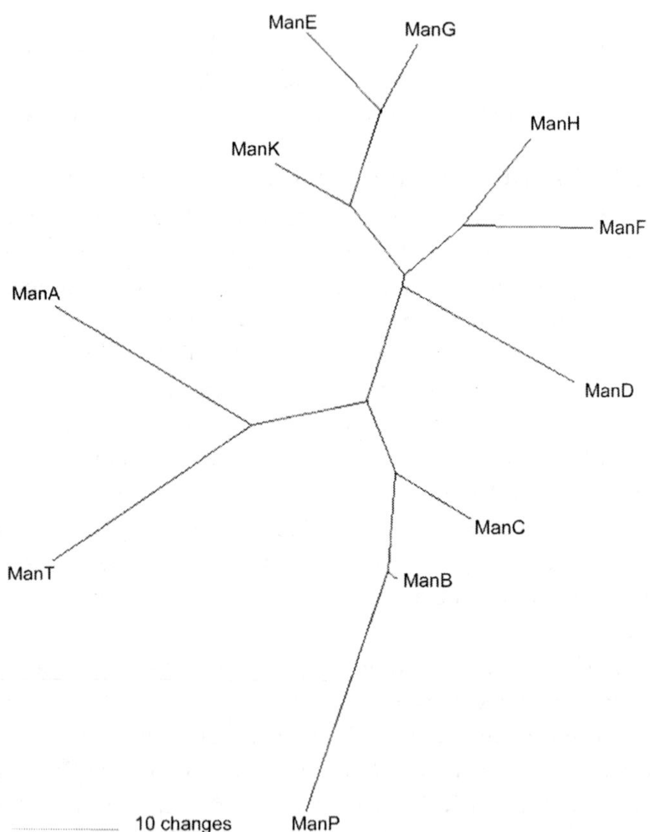

Fig. 3.2.5 Phylogenetic tree (parsimony, unrooted) of *Florilegium Coislinianum*, cf. Macé et al. 2012.

The term *archetype* is used with several meanings, and is sometimes considered controversial (see Trovato 2005). Here again, we will adopt a pragmatic view: the 'archetype' is the extant or postulated manuscript at the top of a stemma (partial or complete), from which the other manuscripts in that stemma ultimately derive. Almost everything is possible: a tradition may have several archetypes, or it may prove impossible, because of lack of evidence, to postulate any archetype (in that case, the stemma is left topless). In fact, cases when it is really possible to identify the archetype of a tradition are rare, and even if it is possible, it must be kept in mind that the archetype is generally not the 'original' text, that is the text as written by its author(s), except in case of autographs. Moreover, even if it is possible to postulate an archetype through reasoning, in many cases this postulated archetype is not what will be edited (see Ch. 3 § 2.4.1). In fig. 3.2.4, for example, none of the extant manuscripts is the archetype, and the manuscript tradition is clearly divided into three branches: A, T and the other manuscripts (those three branches are confirmed by other pieces of evidence than the variant readings–see below). In this case, the text of the three branches was sufficiently similar to postulate that there was only one archetype, which can be reconstructed with enough certainty by using the three branches. Terms such as 'subarchetype' or 'hyparchetype' are also used, to indicate extant or lost ancestors of a subset of manuscripts within a tradition.

A recurrent debate in stemmatological studies is the issue of the surprisingly high number of bipartite stemmata (that is with two branches arising from one node) amongst stemmata drawn by scholars since the nineteenth century (see Timpanaro 2005, Grier 1988, Reeve 1998, amongst many others). Leaving aside the question whether those bipartite (or mainly bipartite) stemmata reflect reality and can be explained by the high number of manuscripts which must have disappeared in the course of time (Guidi – Trovato 2004), one can also suspect that a number of those bipartite stemmata were actually wrong and the result of a misconception of the method, which is unfortunately not uncommon, namely the overlooking of the fact that only errors can be used to ascertain branches, and not all the variants. Let's take a simple example, before explaining further what is exactly meant here by 'error'. At one place in a text, where not all witnesses agree on the text, there are usually two variants, sometimes but less frequently three or more. For example in fig. 3.2.2, at word 72, some manuscripts read 'rationnaliste' instead of 'rationaliste'—the first word is a common spelling mistake, whereas the second one is correctly spelled. Notwithstanding the fact that such a trivial mistake, which can easily be done by anyone independently at any time, will normally not be used in the classification of witnesses (see below), those two variants do not point to two families / branches, because one cannot say anything about the manuscripts that share the correct reading, only transmission of a 'deviation' or of an 'innovation' is relevant to determine families of manuscripts. More often than not, however, some people may wrongly consider that every time there are two variants at one place in a text, they prove the existence of two branches; in this way, all the trees they will build will necessarily always be—wrongly—bipartite.

2.3.3. Evaluating variants

The concept of 'error', which is so central in the Lachmannian method, has been used several times, but not yet defined so far. The term 'error' can be misleading and it has been rejected by many scholars, not without reason, but no other term is as conveniently short (except perhaps 'innovation'). It would be more accurate to speak about 'secondary' reading versus 'primary' reading, because a secondary reading can for example be a correction, and a correction can hardly be called a mistake. In addition, 'secondary' is a relative term: a variant B can be secondary vis-à-vis a variant A and primary vis-à-vis a variant C (A > B > C). The decision about what is primary and what is secondary has often been accused of being subjective. In addition, the variants used for the classification are often reduced to a small number of secondary variants considered 'significant' or 'kinship revealing', i.e. variants which cannot be made by two scribes independently nor easily corrected without recurring to another model. This reduction of the evidence used has also sometimes been criticized. There might be some truth in those criticisms, but, again, they do not hold if the method is correctly applied, that is if the amount of variants used is sufficiently large, and if the arguments to decide what is secondary and what is significant are sound and clearly exposed (see Love 1984).

What might those arguments be? Several scholars have tried to provide typologies of variants valid for manuscript traditions in several languages: for example Gacek 2007 for Arabic, or Havet 1911 for Latin (by far the most encompassing survey). Those typologies are usually based both on an external description of the variants and on an attempt at defining the (voluntary or involuntary) cause of the variation: addition (dittography, interpolation, ...), omission (haplography, *homoioteleuton*, ...), grammatical variant, lexicographical substitution, inversion, etc. A *homoioteleuton* (or *saut du même au même*, that is jump from one element to another—identical or similar—further down in the text), for example, is due to the fact that the copyist usually reads a few words in his model, memorizes them for a short time, writes them down, and then his eyes go back to the model not necessarily exactly at the same place. It is typically a mistake that can happen more than once independently, but which is very difficult to correct once it has happened, especially if this omission does not disturb the meaning of the text (in a repetitive context for example). This type of secondary reading can therefore be used to separate a manuscript or group of manuscripts from the rest of the tradition, because a manuscript which has this error cannot be the ancestor of a manuscript which does not have it (*Trennfehler* or separative error), but it is not as good to join manuscripts together (*Bindefehler* or conjunctive error), because it may happen independently.

In evaluating the variants, one must use all possible criteria: grammatical correctness, lexicographical evidence, sources used by the author, metric, stylistics, possible repetitions of the same ideas or sentences in the same text or in several texts by the same author, historical evidence, traces of a material accident (for example one page lost or misplaced), and so on. One might object that the argumentation is ultimately based on the assumption that the archetype is 'faultless' and that the author made no mistake. The first criticism is simply not true, for in some cases one has to admit that the archetype was faulty (if all extant witnesses share what is obviously a mistake—this is best proven by comparison with the indirect tradition, see Ch. 3 § 2.3.5)—if sufficiently argued for, the existence of mistakes in the archetype is in fact the best proof that there is only one archetype of the extant tradition. As for the second criticism, the idea that an ancient or mediaeval author wrote nonsense or bad grammar on purpose is less probable than the opposite view.

2.3.4. Limits of the method

As it has been said earlier, the application of the method knows some limitations. An essential distinction was made by Pasquali between a 'closed recension' and an 'open recension' (Pasquali ^{2}1952, 126; see also Alberti 1979, 1–18): in the second case the evidence we have is such that it does not allow us to draw a reliable stemma. Again, we must insist that this conclusion can only be drawn after a close examination of the tradition, never *a priori*. Moreover, the ways a manuscript tradition evolved and was preserved may not be homogeneous: some parts may be obscure and difficult to reconstruct, whereas others may be more straightforward—in this case, partial stemma(ta) may be proposed. The causes for a recension (or part of a recension) to be open may be diverse. Some are intrinsic (depending on how the text was transmitted from the beginning), others are extrinsic (depending on the hazardous way in which any tradition survives). A tradition may be more or less 'authorial' and 'controlled', and several factors may play a role in this. Certain types of texts call for adaptation: *some* technical treatises, *some* hagiographical accounts, *some* rather popular literary genres, *some* genres with an allegedly oral root (popular poetry, sermons noted by tachygraphs, etc.; see Ch. 3 §§ 3.4, 3.13, 3.16). In each case the restriction 'some' is important, because the literary genre to which a work belongs does not tell by itself whether or not this precise work will in reality be felt by copyists as freely adaptable. On the other hand, no law can predict how a manuscript tradition will evolve in the course of time: works which have been banned and censored may survive by chance (for example 'heretical' texts), celebrated texts may nearly disappear by accident (for example several pieces of the Latin and Greek classical literary canon). The state in which the work has been preserved, as accidental as it may be, has indeed a major impact on how accurately and reliably we can reconstruct the history of its transmission.

Another phenomenon which can render the classification difficult or impossible is the so-called contamination (when one witness was obviously copied using more than one source—note that a contamination must be proven, and this can only be by detecting mistakes from at least two different families in one witness). In fact, several very different phenomena lie hidden behind this term:

- use of several exemplars to copy a text: this implies that several exemplars were present at the same place at the same time, or that the manuscript copied on one exemplar was later annotated or corrected using another model; in this latter case, the corrections, which are visible in the corrected manuscript (if it still exists), will possibly be undetectable in its copy;
- several copies made at the same time on few dismantled exemplars: this implies that there was a high demand for copies of the same text and an organized workshop to deal with this demand;
- corrections and scholarly interventions by the copyist or a reader of the manuscript;
- influence of a text which the copyist might know by heart: this is typically the case for quotations of a very well known text, such as the Bible, the Qur'ān or a literary monument, inside another text.

A careful examination of the variants may help in dealing with such complicated cases (see Love 1984), because some variants will be less likely to be transmitted by contamination than others (less 'significant' variants for example will generally not be 'contaminated'), and, at any event, it may be possible to classify at least a part of the tradition (see La Spisa 2014).

2.3.5. Use of indirect witnesses

When any piece of indirect evidence exists and it is possible to use it, this is an invaluable help in understanding the tradition of a text, because it may give some insights about lost parts of this tradition, and it may shed light on essential events in the evolution of the tradition that we cannot know of through the direct witnesses.

The indirect tradition proper (see 2.1), especially if it is older than the extant direct witnesses is extremely precious in this respect: it comprises (1) citations of the work in later works, (2) other recensions of the work, (3) ancient translations of the work in other languages. All those types of indirect witnesses can be especially helpful when deciding about the primary / secondary character of the variants, because they provide information about and earlier stage of the text (see Macé 2011).

One can also consider as indirect tradition, traces of the text kept on a different medium than codices, those media generally having a totally different path of transmission from the codices: epigraphic evidence (famous examples are verses from Shota Rustaveli's twelfth-century Georgian national epic *Vepxisṭq̇aosani* 'Knight in the Panther's Skin' inscribed on stone in the fifteenth or sixteenth century, see Cisḳarišvili 1954, whereas most manuscripts of this work date from the seventeenth and eighteenth centuries; or amulets from the sixth to seventh centuries BCE in ancient Hebrew script preserving three verses of Numbers Ch. 6), papyri (cf. Ch. 3 § 3.6), or even traces of an oral transmission, for example through a collection of proverbs borrowed from the work in question.

Another type of 'indirect' evidence is any element which is not the text itself nor the material evidence provided by the manuscripts (see Ch. 3 § 2.3.6), that is evidence related to the history of another text inside the tradition under consideration, either (1) kept in the text itself (citation, interpolation...) or (2) in multi-text manuscripts (history of textual tradition of other works preserved in the same manuscripts). These elements are contemporary with the history of the text, and not older as the indirect tradition proper often is, but they are nevertheless potentially interesting, because they have a parallel history, outside the direct tradition, which can be confronted with it. These elements must be treated with caution though, because arguments in this matter can often be used both ways. About the second case (multi-text manuscripts), see Ch. 3 § 3.2.

When editing a translation or an anthology, the source-text of this translation (see Ch. 3 § 3.20) or of the excerpts gathered in the anthology (see Ch. 3 § 3.19) must also be considered as an indirect witness to the history of the text to be edited. As Bausi has pointed out (see Ch. 3 § 3.2), the philology of translated texts must go backwards and forwards (see also Ch. 3 § 3.8).

2.3.6. Use of material evidence

All pieces of evidence about the manuscripts as historical objects (cf. Ch. 3 § 2.1) are relevant for the classification and must be used to validate or falsify the reality of the textual relationships observed between witnesses (cf. Ch. 3 § 3.7). In extremely fortunate cases, the manuscripts contain colophons that sometimes say from which model they were copied (see Ch. 3 § 3.1). But normally one must use less direct evidence, such as the approximate date of the manuscripts or traces of the places where the manuscripts were copied or kept.

The contents of the manuscripts are also an important piece of evidence: manuscripts with the same or similar contents in the same or similar order are likely to be related. The layout and other codicological features (for example marginalia, scholia etc.) may be an additional element to bring manuscripts together.

It must also be kept in mind that a manuscript is not a static object, it evolves with time: the parchment or the paper can deteriorate with time, the book can be damaged more or less heavily due to natural or human factors, leaves can be lost or misplaced, especially in the process of rebinding, and readers may add their own comments, or make their own corrections. One single manuscript can therefore have several 'states' in the course of time, and it can be copied several times at different stages of its evolution (see Irigoin 1954).

2.3.7. Towards a history of the text

Taken all together, those pieces of evidence about the textual relationships between the manuscripts, about their evolution as material objects, and all that we can learn from the indirect tradition, all that forms a puzzle which is the history of the text, and sometimes its prehistory (that is the period of existence of a text for which we do not have any direct sources of information). The history of a text is itself part of the intellectual, social and cultural history of the civilization from which this text originated. It is also the basis for any study about this text, and for a possible edition of the text.

2.4. Establishing and presenting a scholarly text edition (CM–AGi–PLS–TA–SM–LS)

The huge amount of work that was presented above (Ch. 3 §§ 2.1, 2.2, 2.3) is indeed 'preliminary' to the edition; once all this is done, the editorial work proper begins. To go from the history of a text to its edition is never an automatic step: in each case the editor will need to find which is the best way of presenting a readable text, which is also reflecting the historicity of the manuscript tradition. No edition is perfect, but it is important to give it all possible care, because it will become the way other people will access the text, and preparing an edition is such a time-consuming work that it cannot normally be redone several times for the same text.

2.4.1. Types of scholarly editions and editorial decisions and choices (CM)

As was said above, different types of text are transmitted by different types of manuscript traditions, and the edition needs to be adapted to the specificities of the text and needs to deal with the incompleteness of the manuscript evidence. It also has to accommodate the needs and requirements of its future readership. The edition of a poetical text will be different from the edition of a hagiographical account, for example, and the edition of a text preserved in a *codex unicus* will pose other problems than that of a text of which the tradition is 'over-abundant'. In all cases, the editor will have to explain his/her choices and principles in the introduction (cf. Ch. 3 § 2.6.1). The case studies (Ch. 3 § 3.1–23) offer a large range of possible solutions to different issues.

1. An essential distinction needs to be made between editing a text or a work and editing a document (see Ch. 3 § 3.20). In some cases, the unique character of a document preserving a text may prompt scholars to edit this document for its own sake. Such is the case of papyri (see Ch. 3 § 3.6), palimpsests (see Ch. 3 § 3.11), or fragments (see Ch. 3 § 3.9) being the only witnesses of some texts: a *diplomatic* edition (see Ch. 3 § 3.11 for a presentation of the method), sometimes called a *documentary* edition is the best option.

2. If one wants to edit a work from multiple documents, the possibilities are more numerous, depending on the conclusions about the history of the text. In some cases, it will be possible to prove (or at least to convincingly argue) that there was only one archetype. If this archetypal manuscript is preserved, it should serve as the base text for the edition, sometimes complemented by other witnesses, if the *base manuscript* is lacunary for example, or if some other manuscripts have a special intellectual or historical value. As a rule the editor will follow his/her base manuscript to establish the text.

3. If the archetype is not preserved, but it is possible to reconstruct it with enough confidence from the manuscript tradition, the edition will be based on several witnesses. That type of edition may be called a *genealogical edition*. The editor will first need to choose the manuscripts on which the edition will be based, as they are usually not all taken into account to establish the text, depending on their position in the *stemma codicum*. Normally, the editor will not consider the manuscripts which are obviously copies of extant manuscripts (*eliminatio codicum descriptorum*; see Timpanaro 1985, but note that Timpanaro has strongly criticized the way Maas dealt with the *eliminatio*). In fig. 3.2.4 for example, manuscript L, clearly being a copy of K, will not be considered. Other criteria may be used to select manuscripts, especially if they are numerous. There is theoretically no limit to the number of manuscripts which may be used for an edition and referred to in an *apparatus criticus* (see Ch. 3 § 2.5.1), and some editions (of the biblical texts for example) indeed display a large number of manuscripts (see also Ch. 3 § 3.15), but it might also be advisable to consider only the manuscripts which are 'useful' for the edition, in order to save some work and to keep the apparatus readable. According to the stemma in fig. 3.2.4, all manuscripts except for L should be kept for the edition. However, D, E, F, G, H and K, although they cannot be eliminated on stemmatic grounds (and were indeed kept for the edition, cf. De Vos et al. 2010), are clearly a derived family (corroborated by material evidence) compared with B and C, and could be left aside without changing anything in the edition. The choice of the variants, then, must also be based on the stemma, although not mechanically (it must always be validated by philological judgment). Again, the stemma of fig. 3.2.4 clearly has three branches: A, T and B-C (+ the other manuscripts); therefore an agreement of two branches against the third one must logically point to the reading to be kept in the edited text.

An *eclectic edition* is also based on several witnesses, but the selection of the manuscripts and of the variants is not justified by the history of the text, and is therefore arbitrary. Many editions made in the past were eclectic rather than truly genealogical.

4. A *synoptic edition* or a *multiple-version edition* may be the best solution if the work is preserved in several recensions, each recension being then genealogically edited on its own. It is the editor's choice to edit all texts separately or to choose the ones which are older, more important etc. (see Ch. 3 § 3.4).

5. Other types of editions, for different purposes, may be envisaged, but the types listed above are the most common.

Whatever type of edition one chooses, there will be almost inevitably some conjectures or emendations by the editor, as no historical transmission of a text can deliver a text which is absolutely uncorrupted. Editor's conjectures should be limited to correct what is an obvious mistake in the tradition (against the rhyme, for example, or the versification ...) and refrain from hyper-corrections. Any intervention of the editor in the text should be clearly marked (see Ch. 3 § 2.4.2). The editor should have a clear idea of what one wants to edit, and be careful not to go beyond the goal. In editing a translation, for example, it might sometimes be tempting to correct the edited text using the source-text, but this would be a mistake, because one has to edit the translation as it was: errors of translation should therefore be kept in the edited text (they could be highlighted as such in the apparatus), whereas errors in the manuscript tradition of the translation should be corrected.

2.4.2. Presenting the critical text (PLS–CM–SM–LS)

Script

In most cases, the editor will use the script in which the text is written in the manuscripts (although usually transliterating the majuscule script, if this is the script of the main text, into minuscule). Some particular cases, however, such as very rare scripts or allographic systems, may raise special difficulties (see General introduction § 2.1.1 about the encoding of oriental scripts). Avestan manuscripts, for example, will generally be transliterated (see Ch. 3 § 3.5), as well as the multilingual fragments of the Turfan collection (see Ch. 3 § 3.9). In the case of allography (using an alphabet normally used for a different language), it may be advisable to use the script as it is in the manuscript for the critical edition, and to provide next to it a transliteration into the 'normal' script of the language in question, as a help to the reader (see the contributions in den Heijer et al. 2014).

Word-splitting, accentuation, diacritics, majuscules, etc.

In many mediaeval manuscript traditions, *scriptio continua* was used. Except in the case of a very faithful diplomatic transcription (see Ch. 3 § 3.11), words should be split, otherwise the text may be totally incomprehensible. Similarly, the choice is left to the editor to add diacritical signs which may be indispensable to the reader, and whether to capitalize proper names or not.

Abbreviations, numbers, etc.

Abbreviations are usually resolved in the edited text, without any mention in the apparatus criticus (see Ch. 3 § 2.5.1), unless there are some variants in the manuscripts (in the apparatus abbreviations should not be resolved: cf. Ch. 3 § 2.5.1).

As for numbers, there is no rule: the editor may decide to write them numerically (using numbers or letters depending on the system developed in the language under consideration), even if they are written in full in the manuscripts, except if this may have an incidence on the understanding of the edited text or of the variants.

In cases where a (semi-)diplomatic transcription of a manuscript text is used as a basis for the edition of a particular work—which is common in palaeoslavistic editorial practice, for example—the boundaries between a diplomatic and a critical edition of texts are often blurred. Insurmountable problems of normalization of most mediaeval languages (the later stages of Church Slavonic, for example) have favoured the use of manuscript texts as a basis for critical editions (namely best-manuscript editions where the text of one manuscript is rendered more or less faithfully and variations from other witnesses are only recorded in the apparatus, or copy-text editions with better readings introduced in the manuscript text). The editor will need to decide on the question of how to deal with abbreviated words such as, for example, *nomina sacra*, frequently used words, or common endings. One option is to resolve the abbreviations, which can be done by reconstructing the omitted part of the word in between brackets (see for example Sels 2009, 105). However, orthography is a notable problem: the use of standard orthography for the expanded abbreviations goes against the grain of the use of a manuscript text, while a reconstruction of the abbreviated word according to the orthographical particularity of the manuscript is often problematical as well, especially in the case of words that are rarely written out in full (mostly *nomina sacra*). This is one of the reasons why some editors prefer to preserve the abbreviations as they occur in the manuscript. The latter choice is most likely made by editors with a reluctance to interfere with the manuscript text in other respects as well (i.e. a reluctance to introduce modern punctuation, capitalization, text division etc.). Some editors have taken an intermediate position and have elaborated fine-grained systems for dealing with various sorts of abbreviations (see Kakridis 2004, 186–188).

Punctuation

The punctuation of the edited text is another point which scholars working on mediaeval texts have become gradually aware of (cf. Careri 1998, Parkes 1998). In older editions, the punctuation was normally given by the editor, without any reference to the manuscript. The rationale behind it was that punctuation is mainly aiming at making the text easier to read, and that the system of punctuation in each language has often changed over time, the mediaeval system is therefore often incomprehensible to modern readers and must be adapted. On that point, the practice of modern editors is usually pragmatic: rather than introducing signs which are closer to the manuscripts but will not be understood by modern readers, they generally 'translate' the mediaeval signs into modern punctuation. In some cases though, special signs can be adopted, especially in diplomatic editions (see Ch. 3 § 3.11).

There are no prescriptions in this matter, but one should be aware that (1) punctuation matters, it has to do with the syntax of a text and to its semantic divisions, it is part of the text as much as any other feature, (2) even if it is not possible to adopt the punctuation system of the manuscripts (and in a reconstructed text it is, indeed, hardly possible, because almost every manuscript is different), one must at least look at the punctuation marks in the manuscripts (and therefore collate them: see Ch. 3 § 2.2), and try not to overload the edited text with a personal punctuation, often influenced by the editor's mother tongue. The choice of using a majuscule or not after a strong punctuation mark is generally left to the editor (or to the series in which the edition will be published).

Critical signs and marking

In order to allow the reader to have a direct and clear perception of important editorial interventions in the text, editors usually use critical signs to indicate where they make substantial changes. They usually note the additions and suppressions between various types of brackets, the meaning of which varies from one edition or one series to the other. The significance of the signs should be indicated in the introduction and/or in the *conspectus siglorum* (see Ch. 3 § 2.6.2). In addition, there must be an entry in the critical apparatus (see Ch. 3 § 2.5.1) to explain the interventions of the editor. For instance, in many classical editions, editor's additions will be surrounded by parentheses ( ), and suppressions of text which is found in all or most of the manuscripts will be enclosed in square brackets [ ], but other signs may be used, depending on the field and the school of practice (they are even sometimes the opposite as, for example, in papyrology), as well as the publisher. The citations and quotations should be typographically marked in the body of the edition in order to be easily recognized. Editors usually identify these citations in the appropriate apparatus (cf. Ch. 3 § 2.5.2 and fig. 3.2.8).

2.4.3. Division of the text, titles, layout, reference system (PLS–SM–LS)

When choosing the way of dividing the parts of the edited text, the editor should try to follow the original division of the text, if there is one, or the division which is supposed to be closer to the original when the witnesses present various divisions. However, some practical reasons may interfere. The layout of the text sometimes imposes a different way of distinguishing the different sections of the text. In addition to this, publishers sometimes impose a specific way of division, especially in collections. Readability also occasionally causes problems: some texts have no division at all, which makes the text difficult to access for the modern reader. A possible way of solving this difficulty is to elaborate a clearer division of the text in the accompanying translation, if there is one, so that the original division can be kept in the edition.

Sometimes, however, the editor may feel the need to superimpose another, more practical, division, and to divide the text or chapters into smaller paragraphs, which are then numbered and/or titled. In the latter case one must specify whether the titles are a choice of the editor or if they were already present in the manuscript tradition. In the former case, such devices as square brackets, boldface or specific fonts can be recommended for headings added by the editor. The division of the text into paragraphs has several functions: (1) to help the reader to identify the structure and logic of the text (see Samir 1982, 80–85), (2) to facilitate quotations of the critical text by users and scholars, (3) to give the possibility of creating synoptic editions with parallel texts, quotations, identification of indirect sources, and so on.

The division of an edited text is based either on a division present in the extant manuscript tradition or on the editor's understanding of the structure of the text. However, in the case of an edition of a translation—whether represented in parallel with a source text or not—editors often choose to bring the division of the translated text into agreement with that of the (assumed) source text. Although this approach has the advantage of clarity of (cross-)reference, it holds the risk of imposing on the text a structure that is alien to it, and it often fails to do justice to the particular nature of the translated text (which usually functioned independently of its sources).

If a previous edition already exists, it may be useful to note the references of the previous edition in the new edition, to allow an easy cross-referencing between the two editions. The editor may indicate the pagination (or any other reference system) of the older edition in the margin of the new one, or directly in the text, depending on the layout. Another option (for example in case of important discrepancies between the two editions) is to provide a concordance between the two (or more) editions as an appendix or in the introduction.

It is also advisable, when editing a text on the basis of one (main) manuscript, to give the references to the manuscript in question (page or folium, recto/verso, if possible columns), for example in the margins of the edition, to enable the reader to check the text more easily against the manuscript.

The page layout is a very important question, which cannot be treated here in sufficient detail. Mediaeval scribes usually cared very much about page layout: colours, capital letters, margins, letter size and the like were extensively used to make the book more user-friendly and sometimes simply more beautiful (see Ch. 1). In a modern printed edition, the page layout must be as clear (must immediately show what the text is: a poem, a dialogue, a treatise...) and as reader-friendly as possible: titles, headers, running titles, margins should be used to help the reader navigate in the text.

2.4.4. Orthography and linguistic features (PLS–CM)

Orthography and linguistic variations were mostly neglected in handbooks of editorial technique, and in the editions of classical and biblical texts, where normalization towards a classical ideal was usual (not only for a priori reasons, but also because of the huge and unbridgeable time gap between the conception of the text and the first extant witnesses, or because of the large number of manuscripts presenting irreconcilable orthographical features). It is one of the great merits of mediaeval scholarship to have made scholars and readers aware of the importance of taking into account orthographic and linguistic features of mediaeval manuscripts (Giannouli 2014).

The issue is far from simple and the two following elements always need to be considered: (1) the time span between the composition of the work and the extant witnesses, (2) the difficulty of assessing what corresponds to a standard or at least to a widespread trend, and what is idiosyncratic and specific to a scribe.

In the case of a diplomatic edition based on a single, unique witness (see Ch. 3 §§ 3.6 and 3.11), all orthographic and linguistic features of the manuscript will be reproduced in the edition, even though they pertain to the period of the copy of the manuscript, which may be different from the time of composition of the work—it must always be kept in mind, that, in the edition of ancient and mediaeval texts, except in rare cases of autographs or copies contemporary with the author, there is always a superimposition of two (or more) different periods of time within the edited text (cf. Ch. 3 § 3.20).

For editions based on multiple witnesses, the problem is more complicated, because the edited text will often be based on several manuscripts, as far as the variants are concerned—but on what will the 'form' of the text rely? There is no ideal solution to this problem, and most editions will be a more or less unsatisfactory compromise between two extreme positions: (1) a complete normalization of the spelling and grammar, based on assumptions about the language of the work or according to modern criteria, (2) the choice of one witness, considered the most conservative and reliable as far as the orthography is concerned, to be used as a guide to establish the form of the edited text. Here as well the editor will need to find a balance between two contradictory goals: readability for modern users of the edition, and faithfulness towards the mediaeval tradition. Furthermore, it must be noted that no mediaeval scribe is entirely 'consistent' in his copy—it is also a choice of the editor to keep those inconsistencies, at the risk of presenting a text which will sometimes appear odd or mistaken, or to iron them out for the convenience of the reader (but this must be traced in the apparatus—see Ch. 3 § 2.5.1). Whatever the editor chooses to do, it must be stated and explained in the philological introduction (see Ch. 3 § 2.6.1).

If the text of one or more witnesses is so different from the rest of the tradition that one can consider it another redaction of the work, the editor may decide to edit it separately, either synoptically or as an appendix, or indeed, in a separate edition (see Ch. 3 § 2.4.1).

This question of the 'form' of the edited text is related to, though different from the question of the representation of the form of each witness within the edition. A digital edition offers the possibility of displaying a full transcript of each witness (see Ch. 3 § 3.1); a database of variants is another way of digitally presenting that kind of variation (see Ch. 3 § 3.5). Obviously, a printed edition does not allow the editor to give all this information, and one is forced drastically to reduce it to what s/he considers most relevant, and to place it in an apparatus (either the critical apparatus or a special linguistic apparatus: see Ch. 3 §§ 2.5.1 and 2.5.3) and/or in the philological introduction, where a chapter or a paragraph should be devoted to the orthography and linguistic peculiarities of the manuscripts (see Ch. 3 § 2.6.1).

We may exemplify this point with the help of editions of pre-modern Arabic texts. In the past, most editions of texts in Arabic preferred a complete normalization of the text according to modern spelling in order to make it accessible to modern readers (cf. Blachère – Sauvaget 1945; Samir 1982, § 210 p. 77). This practice, however, does not correspond to modern views on textual scholarship: the form of the edited text as such must be faithful to the manuscript tradition and should not be anachronistic. As we have said before, for an edition to be critical, the editor must provide the reader with exact information about the source of what he is reading: this applies equally to the form of the text. There are other means to give easier access to the text: translations, commentaries, and similar (see Ch. 3 § 2.6), but the edited text itself must remain free of modern interventions as much as possible. In Arabic (as in other languages), the question is complicated by the fact that several varieties of what is called 'Middle Arabic' by scholars coexist. As defined recently, Middle Arabic is 'an intermediate, multiform variety, product of the interference of the two polar varieties on the continuum they bound, a variety that, for this very reason, has its own distinctive characteristics' (Lentin 2008, 216). The Arabic language in all its aspects (orthographic, phonetic, morphological, syntactic and lexical) has indeed evolved over time, and manuscripts often bear linguistic phenomena of crucial importance for the history of the Arabic language. For the critical edition of written Middle Arabic texts, the methodological distinction that is still nowadays applied in Romance philology between 'criticism of forms' and 'criticism of variants' (cf. Ch. 3 § 3.13), is a possible solution to overcome the apparent impasse between a blind fidelity to a chosen witness and changing both forms and variants by creating an eclectic text. With 'criticism of forms' we mean here the distinction of all the linguistic phenomena within a manuscript tradition; the linguistic form of the critical text, however, should be chosen among the witnesses which are closest to the author (if there is one) from a geographical and chronological point of view.

2.4.5. Desiderata for digital editions (TA)

In addition to a printed book—or even in place of a printed book entirely—the editor may wish to make his or her edition available in an electronic form (whether with online access or not). There are several different ways of accomplishing this, with increasing levels of functionality and sophistication. The simplest, and least functional, option is to reproduce the book in a static electronic form such as PDF; the text can now be made available electronically but otherwise has very little advantage over a printed book, except for searchability. Such an edition might more correctly be called a 'digitized edition' rather than a 'digital edition'.

While in the past a number of digital editions were produced on electronic media such as CD-ROM or DVD, almost all digital editions produced today are made available directly online, meant to be accessed through a Web browser on a computer or other networked device. The primary defining characteristic of digital publication, in comparison to print or publication of an electronic book, is that, for better or for worse, the page is no longer a meaningful boundary or limitation. The editor is free to make available as much text, analysis, commentary, and raw manuscript transcription as she or he sees fit—even high-quality manuscript images can be included if the rights can be obtained. This in itself poses an interesting problem of presentation. When the size of the book is no longer a limiting factor, and the page is no longer a natural means to guide the layout of information, how is the editor to present citations, references, text variants, quotations, and many of the other pieces of information discussed here?

One of the greatest difficulties surrounding the publication of a digital edition is that, despite roughly two decades of their existence, no detailed set of 'best practice' for digital editions has been developed that compares, either in form or function, to the practices for printed edition outlined above. To some extent this is a necessary effect of the rapid pace of technological change—no particular standard or practice, beyond the very simple approach of putting a text online in some form such as plain text or TEI XML, has survived a descent into obsolescence. Functionality and user interfaces that would have been considered sophisticated and cutting-edge in 2001 were seen as anything but by 2011; conversely, the possibilities presented by newer web technologies have continually disrupted the process by which scholarly editors would ordinarily settle on a common practice or standard for publication. Already, a decade after their appearance, the question was being asked: do digital editions have a future? (Robinson [Pe.] 2004) Nevertheless, the determination of several editors, including Robinson himself, to go on making digital editions has ensured that the field remains very much alive and, slowly, is beginning to flourish. One recent and helpful contribution to the problem of 'best practices' surrounding digital publication has been offered by Rosselli Del Turco (2007), who discusses the requirements and desiderata for a graphical user interface to a scholarly edition.

The second difficulty of digital publications is the lack of any user-friendly tool for their creation. Unless the editor can find a professional academic publisher willing to create the edition in digital form, or can afford the money necessary to hire expertise in computer programming and website development, his or her only option is to invest the time and energy necessary to learn about all aspects of online publication: image processing and text encoding, including the technical issues surrounding the representation of right-to-left script or even bidirectional texts, markup languages such as XML for TEI-based transcription and HTML for publication of the text (see General introduction § 2.1.2), technologies such as CSS for layout and presentation within the browser or Javascript for more dynamic functionality, and of course the fundamentals for using and perhaps maintaining a web server for the purpose, either through commercial computing cloud services such as Amazon or personal server software such as Apache. The editor must also put some thought into the problem of survival of the edition—what happens to the work if its creator changes institutions, dies, or simply fails to keep software up to date? In short, the editor of a digital publication is, at present, forced to exercise all the expertise and specialist knowledge for which the editor of a print publication can safely rely on a commercial or academic publisher.

For all this, however, the 'sky is the limit' nature of digital publication continues to hold immense promise and advantage for textual scholarship. The nature of the enterprise remains the same as for print publication. The editor must present a text—whether a constructed critical text, a diplomatic reproduction of a single manuscript, or a text derived from some other principle—and must present the evidence upon which it is based. Since there is little practical limit to the amount of information that can be presented, the digital editor will usually be expected to err on the side of completeness: to provide as faithful as possible a record of each manuscript that went into the edition, and as complete as possible a rationale for each editorial decision that was made. Here the principle of scientific transparency can shine a light on our field as never before. With digital publication, the editor's critical text can coexist peacefully with the transmitted versions of the text in all their variation; the reader can explore the text in all its variation from semantic to linguistic to orthographic. The prospect is too tantalizing, and the technology too rich, for the publication of digital editions to be abandoned in the foreseeable future.

2.5. Apparatuses (CM–SM–AGi)

As we have seen before (2.4.1), the edited text reflects the state of preservation of the manuscript tradition, a certain view on its history, and the decisions taken by the editor in order to provide modern readers with a mediaeval text in the most adequate form. In itself the edited text cannot contain all the information that scholars can extract from the manuscript tradition (readings of other manuscripts than the one used for the *constitutio textus*, sources of the text, etc.). In order not to overload the text and to allow it to stand on its own, 'apparatuses' (often placed at the bottom of each page in a book) are used to store any information that supports the edited text or is considered relevant for the reader to understand it.

An edition must often provide several apparatuses, each of them containing a different type of information. There are various possibilities of displaying them and the layout of an edition with apparatuses is generally a complicated matter, even though some software, such as Classical Text Editor, LaTeX, TUSTEP, etc. make it possible nowadays to deal more easily with a complex *mise-en-page*. It must be noted, however, that the series where the edition will be published often imposes a certain layout as well as the way to produce it (see Macé forthcoming).

A digital edition offers different possibilities of displaying that kind of information (see Ch. 3 § 2.4.5), but, as no standards exist yet (see Fischer [F.] 2013, 88), each editor must more or less construct his/her own system for this. The next pages are therefore focused on paper editions.

2.5.1. The *apparatus criticus* (SM)

The critical apparatus contains the information which is relevant to understand the editor's choices concerning the edited text. The decision about what is relevant or not is not always easy (see Ch. 3 § 2.3.3 about evaluating variants) but often necessary: it is impossible to keep all the information from the collations in the apparatus, which would become unreadable and therefore useless.

Various options and formats of the critical apparatus (and indeed of other apparatuses) in printed editions are presented here. The four main options when formatting an apparatus criticus are the language, the layout, the format of the data, and the syntax. To choose the best format for each concrete case, it is advisable to look at as many examples as possible of existing editions, in order to decide what are the possible answers to the needs of the edition one wants to make.

As a rule, the script used to indicate the readings of the manuscripts in the apparatus is the same as the script used for the edited text (see Ch. 3 § 2.4.2). It may happen, however, that the editor has to mention manuscript readings written in another language or script than the main text (when referring to an ancient translation, for example (see Ch. 3 § 2.3.5), or when using a witness written in an allographic system, see Ch. 3 § 2.4.2). If possible (that is if allowed by the rules of the series and if there is enough space), the best option is to keep those variants in their original language or script and to provide next to them a translation (into the language of the edited text, or, perhaps more conveniently, into a modern language) or, in the case of allography, a transliteration into the script of the edited text.

Readings are usually written exactly as they are found in the manuscripts, that is without any homogenizing or formal polishing as the editor must do in the edited text (see Ch. 3 § 2.4.2): rare or ambiguous abbreviations are not resolved, spelling is kept exactly as it is in the manuscript, and so on.

The critical apparatus of readings may be positive, that is mention all the witnesses in each note, or negative, that is mention only the witnesses disagreeing with the chosen reading. If these two different ways of constructing the critical apparatus do not fundamentally change the format of the apparatus, they nevertheless infer some changes, as explained below.

1. Editor's language in the apparatus

The language of the editor in the apparatus is the first thing to choose when beginning a critical apparatus. The traditional language is Latin, but nowadays, many scholars use other, mostly vernacular, languages (English, French, Italian, etc.). Arabic is also often used in editions of Arabic texts. The choice of the language influences directly the direction of the apparatus, as an Arabic apparatus will go from right to left, and a Latin apparatus will go from left to right.

Abbreviated forms of often repeated words are usually used in the apparatus, to make it shorter: for example *add.* for *addidit*, marking an addition. A list of abbreviations used can often be found together with the *conspectus siglorum* (see Ch. 3 § 2.6.2) or with the introduction. For a fairly complete list of such abbreviations see Bernabé – Hernández Muñoz 2010, 155–163, Apéndice I.

Some modern scholars also use a system of symbols to avoid the use of one specific language and save space. For example, the sign + may be used to point to an addition (see fig. 3.2.6).

2. Layout

Two characteristics affect the layout of the apparatus: the kind of notes and their place. Notes can be (a) numbered through or (b) referred to by line numbers with respective lemmata. These notes may be placed at the bottom of the pages, or at the end of the edition. Each system has its advantages and disadvantages. But the choice is not always up to the editor, as one of the key factors in the layout of the apparatus is the publisher. In addition to these common layouts, some scholars have proposed to put the *apparatus criticus* in the margins (as in the mediaeval system of *marginalia*).

(a) Numbered notes

The numbered notes system is made in the same way as contextual footnotes or endnotes in books and articles. The editor puts a number (typically in superscript) in the text, and the critical information in a note at the bottom of the page or at the end of the document, after the same number. Unfortunately, most editions of this kind put each numbered note on a single line, often due to software limitations.

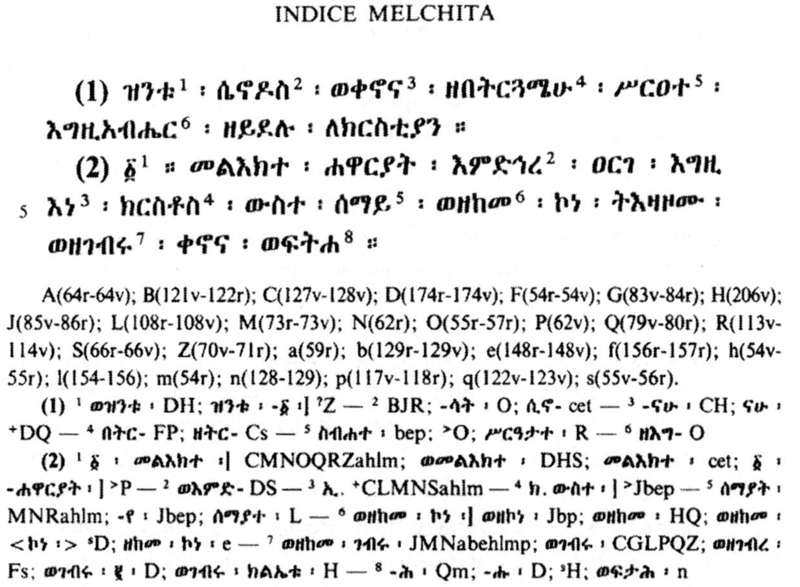

INDICE MELCHITA

(1) ዝንቱ[1] ፡ ሲኖዶስ[2] ፡ ወቀኖና[3] ፡ ዘበትርጓሜሁ[4] ፡ ሥርዐተ[5] ፡ እግዚአብሔር[6] ፡ ዘይደሉ ፡ ለክርስቲያን ።

(2) ፩[1] ። መልእክተ ፡ ሐዋርያት ፡ እምድኅረ[2] ፡ ዐርገ ፡ እግዚእነ[3] ፡ ክርስቶስ[4] ፡ ውስተ ፡ ሰማይ[5] ፡ ወዘከመ[6] ፡ ኮነ ፡ ትእዛዞሙ ፡ ወዘገብሩ[7] ፡ ቀኖና ፡ ወፍትሐ[8] ።

A(64r-64v); B(121v-122r); C(127v-128v); D(174r-174v); F(54r-54v); G(83v-84r); H(206v); J(85v-86r); L(108r-108v); M(73r-73v); N(62r); O(55r-57r); P(62v); Q(79v-80r); R(113v-114v); S(66r-66v); Z(70v-71r); a(59r); b(129r-129v); e(148r-148v); f(156r-157r); h(54v-55r); l(154-156); m(54r); n(128-129); p(117v-118r); q(122v-123v); s(55v-56r).

(1) [1] ወዝንቱ ፡ DH; ዝንቱ ፡ -፩ ፡| [s]Z — [2] BJR; -ሳት ፡ O; ሲኖ- cet — [3] -ናሁ ፡ CH; ናሁ ፡ ⁺DQ — [4] በትር- FP; ዘትር- Cs — [5] ስብሐተ ፡ bep; >O; ሥርዓታተ ፡ R — [6] ዘእግ- O

(2) [1] ፩ ፡ መልእክተ ፡| CMNOQRZahlm; ወመልእክተ ፡ DHS; መልእክተ ፡ cet; ፩ ፡ -ሐዋርያት ፡] >P — [2] ወእምድ- DS — [3] እ. ⁺CLMNSahlm — [4] ክ. ውስተ ፡] >Jbep — [5] ሰማያት ፡ MNRahlm; -የ ፡ Jbep; ሰማያተ ፡ L — [6] ወዘከመ ፡ ኮነ ፡| ወዘኮነ ፡ Jbp; ወዘከመ ፡ HQ; ወዘከመ ፡ <ኮነ ፡> [s]D; ዘከመ ፡ ኮነ ፡ e — [7] ወዘከመ ፡ ገብሩ ፡ JMNabehlmp; ወገብሩ ፡ CGLPQZ; ወዘገብረ ፡ Fs; ወገብሩ ፡ ፪ ፡ D; ወገብሩ ፡ ከልኤቱ ፡ H — [8] -ሕ ፡ Qm; -ሑ ፡ D; [s]H; ወፍታሕ ፡ n

Fig. 3.2.6 *Apparatus criticus* in the edition of the Ethiopic *Sinodos*, ed. Bausi 1995b, 1.

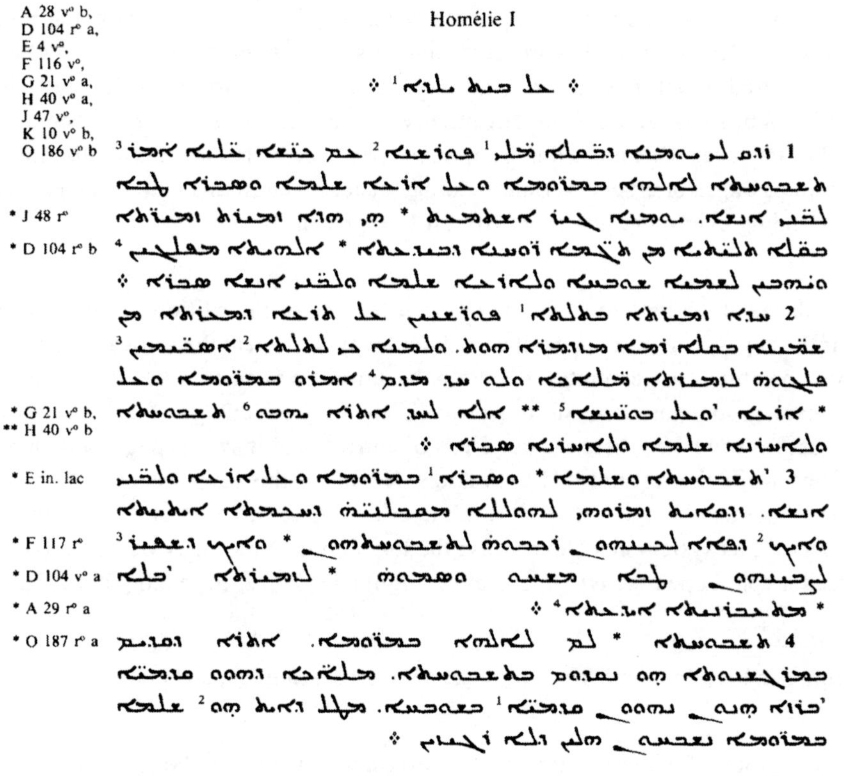

A 28 v° b,
D 104 r° a,
E 4 v°,
F 116 v°,
G 21 v° a,
H 40 v° a,
J 47 v°,
K 10 v° b,
O 186 v° b

Homélie I

✣ ܥܠ ܒܝܬ ܝܠܕܐ[1] ✣

1 [illegible]
ܬܫܒܘܚܬܐ ܠܐܠܗܐ ܒܡܪ̈ܘܡܐ ܘܥܠ ܐܪܥܐ ܫܠܡܐ ܘܣܒܪܐ ܛܒܐ
* J 48 r° [illegible]
* D 104 r° b [illegible]
[illegible] ✣
2 [illegible]
[illegible]
[illegible]
* G 21 v° b, ** H 40 v° b [illegible]
[illegible] ✣
* E in. lac 3 [illegible]
[illegible]
* F 117 r° [illegible]
* D 104 v° a [illegible]
* A 29 r° a [illegible] ✣
* O 187 r° a 4 [illegible]
[illegible]
[illegible]
[illegible] ✣

Lemme: [1] cf. introduction p. 8-ss.

1 [1] GJK [illegible] — [2] A sey. — [3] J [illegible] — [4] O [illegible].

2 [1] JK sey. — [2] DEJKO [illegible] — [3] DEO [illegible] — [4] K om. — [5]' DEFGHJKO [illegible] — [6] DEFGJKO om.

3 [1]' DFGHJKO om. — [2] GHK [illegible] — [3] FKO [illegible], GH [illegible] — [4]' DFGH [illegible].

4 [1] HO om. - [2] K [illegible].

Fig. 3.2.7 Apparatus in an edition of a *Homily* by Jacob of Serugh, ed. Rilliet 1986, 26.

The advantages of this layout are not substantial. The main benefit is that the passages for which critical information is relevant are highlighted and immediately evident, and the attention of the reader is directly captured (for an example, see fig. 3.2.7). In addition to this, this layout is easy to make, even with programs like MS Word and OpenOffice. The second interest is that the proofreading is very easy: each reading has a number. However, this layout implies many disadvantages. It often takes too much space, as each note will usually occupy one line. The text may become illegible if there are many entries, as the edition will contain a long series of note references. The last inconvenience, but not the least, is the great risk of confusion when more than one word requires attention in the edition, insofar as the number in the text is placed after or before only one single word. In order to avoid this risk, it is necessary always to note the lemma at the beginning of the entry. This inconvenience is in some editions avoided by double-marking the passage, either with a marker at the beginning in addition to a footnote number, or with two numbers, still at the beginning and at the end of the relevant passage. It is certainly better to use numbered footnotes only when there are few variant readings (see fig. 3.2.7).

(b) Line (or other) referred footnotes with lemma

In classical studies, the most commonly used system is that of line referred footnotes with lemma, but, unfortunately, it is quite rare in oriental studies. The text of the edition shows line numbers in the margin (usually counted by five), and the apparatus presents, for each line containing variant readings or editorial information, the line number and the lemma followed by the editorial information. The line numbers may be counted by page, but also according to other divisions of the text: many editors employ the practice of referring to the chapter lines instead of page lines. Besides the line references, one may use references based upon the divisions of the text (for example paragraphs), which usually influences the reference system.

The advantages of this method are numerous. There are no obtrusive numbers in the text so that it is easy to read, even when there are notes to many places. This layout saves much more space than the numbered footnotes. However, it also presents some disadvantages. This layout is actually quite difficult to construct with traditional text editors, and requires the use of special software, which is sometimes not accepted by publishers. Another inconvenience is that proofreading can become a nightmare if the publisher makes mistakes. One more important inconvenience is that it is definitely not immediately clear where uncertain passages or crucial variant readings occur; even in this kind of apparatus the overlapping of variants extending over more words is difficult to represent.

Place of notes

Notes can be placed at the bottom of the pages or at the end of the edition. In most cases, they are put at the bottom of the pages, which is the most convenient way to present the critical information to the reader. Older editions sometimes use endnotes, generally because it was easier to do using the old editorial tools, but it is even used in some modern editions as well. The only advantage of using endnotes is the fact that the text is readable even when there are hundreds of entries, and it avoids pages which might contain only five lines of text while the rest is filled with notes. However, this layout is actually almost unusable: the disadvantages of the text being separated from the critical notes are obvious. Nevertheless, some modern editions have used this system in a clever way: the text and the notes may be put in two distinct volumes, so that the reader could open the two books at the right pages (see, for example, Mahdi 1984).

3. Format of data

We may distinguish between three kinds of data: witnesses, readings, and additional editorial information.

Witnesses

The witnesses or group of witnesses are usually designated by sigla in the apparatus (on this, see also Ch. 3 § 2.2). These sigla may be abbreviations (usually capital letters), but also names, and/or symbols. If one manuscript contains various versions, or some additions (corrections, glosses, etc.), it is preferable to mark the siglum (for instance, two hands in the manuscript A can be noted A^1 and A^2). What is important is to choose logical sigla, and pay attention in order to avoid confusion. The editor usually tries to highlight the manuscripts in his apparatus (for example by using italics), which allows the reader quickly to distinguish them. But some editors sometimes even choose to put brackets around their manuscripts' sigla to call the reader's attention to them. The sigla are explained in the *conspectus siglorum*, at the end of the introduction (cf. Ch. 3 § 2.6).

Readings

The lemmas and the readings are usually noted with the same font and format as the edition, however using a smaller size such as that of notes. It is important to keep the same letter case as the word(s) in the text for the lemma. The lemma may be abridged if it contains too many words. When using line referred notes, if we find more than one occurrence of the lemma in the same line, the editor usually puts a number (whether in superscript, between brackets, or something similar) after the lemma in order to avoid confusion. Longer passages can be indicated by referring to chapters, verses, and whatever internal subdivision has been used in the text.

Additional editorial information

The content of the additional editorial information might vary considerably: from information about the readings (such as 'written in the margin' or similar), to more specific and precise explanations (such as 'I correct this reading because of this or that'). This additional information should always be distinguished from the manuscripts and the readings. Classical studies use italics to specify such information, which is very handy. As for Arabic studies, this additional information is unfortunately almost never distinguished from the rest, which is uncomfortable for the reader. Another crucial rule about the additional editorial information in the apparatus is to note every change made by the editor. The reader must be able to understand what the editor has done in each case.

4. Syntax

The syntax of the apparatus is also a varying feature in editorial techniques. The main characteristic is a general order: the entry always contains the number of the footnote or the number of the line (or paragraph), then the lemma, and the editorial information.

In classical studies, editors have the habit of writing in the first place the lemma (that is the editor's choice), then possible commentaries (explanation of a correction and the like), and separate it from the readings of the other witnesses by a colon in a positive apparatus and a square bracket in the negative apparatus (see below). The colon and square bracket are used only to separate the lemma from the other readings; if the note only contains editorial information, there is no need to write it. The various readings of the witnesses are often separated by commas or semicolons. However, these features can vary, and different schools of practice exist (see fig. 3.2.7); but the editor must always keep in mind that the apparatus must be legible, and avoid any ambiguity. The order of the witnesses is usually philological (that is families of witnesses and similar), but some editors chose another order, as, for instance, the proximity between the variant readings and the chosen reading, etc. (see Example box).

Example

For pedagogical purposes, we have made up a fake example, in Latin, that we will use throughout this section. The text consists of the first four verses of Virgil's Aeneid. The witnesses (A, B, C, D) and the variants are imaginary.

Arma uirumque cano Troiae qui primus ab oris
Italiam fato profugus Lauiniaque uenit
litora multum ille et terris iactatus et alto
ui superum saeuae memorem Iunonis ob iram

1 cano A] canis B ; canam CD	= *cano* in A (chosen by the editor), *canis* in B, *canam* in CD
2 profugus *correxi*] praefugus ABCD	= editor's correction
2 uenit *in margine* B	= *uenit* is written in the margin in B (here, the bracket is superfluous as no variant reading is mentioned)
4 saeuae BCD] *omisit* A	= A omitted *saeuae*

When pointing to more than one word:

1 cano… ab *omisit* B	= B omitted the words from *cano* to *ab* in the first line.
1 cano… 3 ille *omisit* B	= B omitted the words from *cano* in the first line to *ille* in the third line.

5. Positive apparatus, negative apparatus, and apparatus of available witnesses

The apparatus of readings is itself divided into two kinds: the positive apparatus, and the negative apparatus. The apparatus of available witnesses will appear in the description about the negative apparatus, as it is a support for it.

Positive apparatus

The principle of the positive apparatus is simple: the editor notes all the witnesses in each entry. This means that all the available witnesses must be present in each entry.

If we take again the example of the Example box, when ABCD are the four only witnesses:
3 litora CD : littora AB
4 superum A : superus BCD

This kind of apparatus has the advantage of avoiding any confusion, as each witness is quoted. In addition to this, it is easy to read, at least when there are few witnesses. As for the disadvantages, the obvious problem is that this kind of apparatus is usually much longer than the negative apparatus. This implies that the publisher might not want to accept it. However, the most disturbing disadvantage is that this kind of apparatus works when we have few witnesses, but becomes illegible when we have many witnesses.

If ABCDEFGHIJKL are the witnesses, we might have:
2 fato ABDEFGHIJKL : lato C
3 litora CDHIJL : littora ABEFGK

Negative apparatus

In order to avoid the inconvenience of the positive apparatus when we have many witnesses, editors employ a negative apparatus. This kind of apparatus consists of noting only the witnesses which give a variant reading. So all the witnesses which contain the same reading as the reading chosen by the editor are not mentioned in the entry.

If ABCD are the witnesses:
2 fato] lato C = ABD have *fato*
4 superum] superus BC ; superorum D = A has *superum*

The advantages of this solution are numerous. First, it is much shorter than the positive apparatus, and publishers appreciate it. Secondly, it is easy to read, whenever there are many or few witnesses. Finally, this apparatus allows a very fast reading. And even with many manuscripts the apparatus is not unclear.

If ABDCEFGHIJ are the witnesses:
2 fato] lato CEF = ABDGHIJ have fato

However, this kind of apparatus implies an important inconvenience, which is the risk of confusion, as the reader must perform a subtraction in order to know which witness contains the edited reading. In order to avoid such confusion, it is important to add one specific rule and one new tool.

The additional rule is that the apparatus must become positive when there is a risk of confusion, and, if there is a base manuscript, when this base manuscript is not followed.

If ABCD are the witnesses and A is the base manuscript:
1 cano… 2 uenit *omisit* D
~~2 fato] lato C~~ => there is a risk of confusion about D, because it omits this passage, the apparatus must therefore become positive in this omission :
2 fato AB] lato C
3 litora CD] littora AB => the base manuscript is not chosen, so it is easier to write it in a positive way

Apparatus of available witnesses

In order for a negative apparatus to be comprehensible, a list of the available witnesses (also called *traditio textus*) must be provided for each page or each section of the text. This list may be displayed as the first line of the critical apparatus (see fig. 3.2.8), in a special apparatus (see fig. 3.2.6), or even in the margin of the text (see fig. 3.2.7). In figs. 3.2.6 and 3.2.8 the siglum of the manuscript is followed by the folia where the text can be read. Here below we offer another example of how to display the *traditio textus*.

If the witnesses are ABCD for a page, a line ABCD will be written above or under the apparatus of readings. In addition to this, it is also possible to write in the apparatus of available witnesses the lacunas, beginning and ends of manuscripts.
ABCD = ABCD are available at the top of the page
2 profugus D] = D lacuna begins at profugus
3 alto [D = D lacuna ends at alto
4 memorem *explicit* C = end of the witness C
=> in the next page, the apparatus of available sources will begin with ABD

In general, however, the purported rigid, unavoidable alternative between positive and negative apparatus should not be stressed too much. On the one hand using notations such as *ceteri* (all the other witnesses) or *reliqui* (the only remaining witnesses) may help reduce the size of a positive apparatus; on the other hand, a mixed apparatus—that is negative in principle, and positive only in some particularly intricate cases—might also be used.

2.5.2. Apparatuses of sources (AGi–CM)

As was said before (see Ch. 3 § 2.3.5), it is important to identify the sources of the texts quoted in the work to be edited, as well as possible parallel passages (i.e. similar expressions, stemming from the same context and the same sources), because the confrontation of a quoted passage with its source may constitute a relevant piece of information to evaluate possible variants and establish the text. Besides, this is also an important element in the appreciation of the composition technique and literary impact of the edited text. The place where the information about the sources and parallel passages is stored is a special apparatus, which is usually placed above the critical apparatus. Editors may wish to distinguish between different types of sources, as in the example in fig. 3.2.8, where three apparatuses precede the critical apparatus: an apparatus of sources ('Fontes'), an apparatus of Biblical quotations ('Script.'), and an apparatus of parallel passages within the same work ('Parall.') (see Ch. 3 § 2.5.3); this indication may help the reader but is not compulsory (see fig. 3.2.13).

Χριστοῦ καταγώγιον, τὴν τῶν ἁγίων κλάδων ῥίζαν, τὴν ὡς
ἀληθῶς *μητέρα τέκνων εὐφραινομένην* τε καὶ εὐφραινομένων.
Οἶδα τοῦτο καὶ πέπεισμαι ἐν Κυρίῳ καὶ διὰ τοῦτο λέγω
θαρρῶν **ὅτι** οὐ μὴ ἀποσβεσθῇ ὁ λύχνος τοῦ Ἰσραήλ, κἂν ταῖς
αὔραις τοῦ πονηροῦ ῥιπίζηται. Τίς δὲ μείζων ἑορτὴ τοῦ
τοιούτοις συνεορτάζειν; Ταῦτα **δὲ** τὰ **ἡμέτερα** καλλωπίσματα,
ᾧ μόνῳ δυνατὸν ἡμῖν τοὺς εὐεργέτας ἀμείβεσθαι. **Ἀλλὰ** | μὴ 6v
διὰ γραμμάτων ὄκνει παραμυθεῖσθαι ἡμᾶς, **δέσποινά μου**,
σφόδρα τῷ χωρισμῷ κάμνοντας. **Καὶ** σὺ μὲν οὖν ποθεῖς τὴν
ἡμετέραν συντυχίαν, ὡς γράφεις, καὶ καλῶς ποιεῖς· ἔδει γὰρ
οὖσάν σε ὅπερ εἶ μὴ περιφρονεῖν τοὺς φίλους. Ἄλλος μὲν
ἄλλο τι τῶν σῶν ἐπαινείτω, πάντως δὲ ἀρκέσεις γλώσσαις
πολλαῖς μεριζομένη. Μὴ ἀμέλει τῶν φίλων **τοῦ γράφειν**, κατὰ τοὺς Ὁμηρικοὺς νεανίας ἐν μέσῳ πολέμων τὰ φιλικὰ
σπουδάζοντας, ἐπειδὴ καὶ τούτῳ ποικίλλει τὴν ποίησιν ὁ
σὸς Ὅμηρος. Πολλὰς ἐλπίδας ἔχω **καὶ** τῇ τοῦ Θεοῦ φι-
λανθρωπίᾳ θαρρῶ, | ὅτι πάντα κατὰ νοῦν ὑμῖν ἐκβήσεται 7r

Fontes

54/55 Τίς - συνεορτάζειν Greg. Naz., Ep. 100.4 (I, 118.18-19) **55** Ταῦτα - καλλωπίσματα Greg. Naz., Ep. 233.1 (II, 124.4-5) **56** ᾧ - ἀμείβεσθαι Greg. Naz., Ep. 181.3 (II, 71.5-6) **56/58** μὴ διὰ - κάμνοντας Greg. Naz., Ep. 133.2 (II, 22.12-13) **58/60** σὺ μὲν - φίλους Greg. Naz., Ep. 70.2 (I, 89.13-90.1) **60/62** Ἄλλος - μεριζομένη Greg. Naz., Ep. 71.1 (I, 90.13-14) **62/65** Μὴ ἀμέλει - Ὅμηρος Greg. Naz., Ep. 71.5 (I, 91.10-12) **65/66** Πολλὰς - ἐκβήσεται Greg. Naz., Ep. 74.1 (I, 92.7-9)

Script.

51 Ps. 112.9 **52** Rom. 14.14 **53** οὐ μὴ - Ἰσραήλ cf. II Reg. 21.17

Parall.

55 Ταῦτα - καλλωπίσματα = 40.31

App. Crit.

P

54 μείζων *nos*: μεῖζον *P* **60** οὖσάν *nos*: ὄντα *P fontem secutus*

Coll.

54 δὲ *e tr.*: δὴ *ed.* **59** ἡμετέραν συντυχίαν *e tr.*: συντυχίαν τὴν ἡμετέραν *ed.* **62** Μὴ ἀμέλει τῶν φίλων *e tr.*: Τῶν φίλων μὴ ἀμέλει *ed.* **63** πολέμων *e tr.*: πολέμῳ *ed.*

Fig. 3.2.8 Example of apparatuses in *Iacobi monachi Epistulae*, Jeffreys – Jeffreys 2009, 8.

The beginning and end of the quotation must be identified with exactitude, and one must also indicate to the reader whether this is a more or less exact quotation or rather an allusion (allusions are often indicated by using the sign 'cf.' before the reference). As explained in Ch. 3 § 2.4.2, the citation is often marked in the edited text itself, like in the example of fig. 3.2.8, where the words taken from the patristic text are in roman characters (not bold) and the biblical quotations are in italics (and not bold in this case, because it is a biblical quotation within a patristic quotation). When the quotation is clearly marked in the text and there is no ambiguity, it is not necessary to indicate its first and last word(s) in the apparatus (as it is the case in the example for the biblical quotations at lines 51 and 52, which cannot be mistaken). When the borders of the quotations are not so clear, or when it is an allusion (normally not marked in the text because the words used can be different), the beginning and end of the quotation or allusion must be indicated in the apparatus, as in the example for the quotations from Gregory of Nazianzus which follow one another at lines 54–55, and for the biblical allusion at line 53. The references to the quoted text are often abbreviated, according to some standard list (which should be indicated in the introduction, see Ch. 3 § 2.6.1), and the abbreviations must be resolved and explained, usually in the index or indexes of sources (see Ch. 3 § 2.6.5) and/or in the introduction. It is important to use always the best available critical editions of the texts quoted in the *apparatus fontium*, if they exist, or, in their absence, the standard edition. The editions used must also be mentioned in the *index fontium* and/or in the introduction.

2.5.3. Other apparatuses (CM)

Some editors may wish to display other types of information in separate apparatuses. The purpose is generally to provide pieces of information which may be useful for the reader, but which do not really belong to the two types of apparatuses considered above (Ch. 3 §§ 2.5.1 and 2.5.2), and might blur their legibility (there might be some overlapping between apparatuses—for example, information which, by its nature, does not belong to the critical apparatus may be necessary to understand a critical decision of the editor: in such a case, it is perhaps better to repeat this information at two different places). These kind of apparatuses do not have canonical names and not all series will accommodate them. Their purpose and contents should be explained in the philological introduction (see Ch. 3 § 2.6.1). They are usually situated below the critical apparatus. If the number and variety of apparatuses on the same page seem confusing, the content of each apparatus may be indicated in the margin on every page (as in fig. 3.2.8).

1. Codicological apparatus

If the text is edited on the basis of one (main) manuscript and if some material features of this manuscript may be of importance for the establishment of the text, it may be useful to add an extra apparatus. For example, if the main manuscript is heavily damaged, it may be useful to indicate with some precision which words are legible and to what extent, but that kind of information would clutter up the critical apparatus (see fig. 3.2.9, where the second apparatus gives all information about the state of legibility of manuscript G, the main witness to the edited text, which was damaged due to mice).

2. Orthographical / linguistic apparatus

The status of orthographical variants is very much debated, and there are many cases where an orthographical variant could also be considered morphological. Editors (and series editors) may have divergent opinions about what to do with orthographical variants: (1) discard them all together, (2) register them all (for all witnesses, or more likely for one or two witnesses, typically the oldest ones, or the most divergent geographically or dialectologically), (3) select the most 'important' ones (especially those concerning proper names, or reflecting a dialectal difference, etc.). Those orthographical variants can be kept in the critical apparatus, but this may make the critical apparatus difficult to read, by mixing truly critical variants with others, or registered in a special section of the introduction (see Ch. 3 § 2.6.1), or in an appendix (see Ch. 3 § 2.6.6 and fig. 3.2.15), or in a special apparatus (see fig. 3.2.10, and Ch. 3 § 3.5).

3. Apparatus concerning the indirect tradition

A separate apparatus may contain information concerning the indirect tradition of the edited text (see Ch. 3 §§ 2.1.2 and 2.3.3). Citations of the text in later works may provide some interesting information about the history of the text, especially when they are older than the direct witnesses, as it is the case in fig. 3.2.11, where the third apparatus contains the reference to a citation of the edited text in a collection of Questions-and-Answers dated from the ninth century, i.e. five centuries earlier than the unique manuscript preserved of the edited text.

Similarly the same kind of apparatus can serve to store references to parallel passages, if one does not want to mix them with the real sources (see Ch. 3 § 2.5.2), as can be seen in fig. 3.2.13, where the last apparatus contains references to similar anthologies, related to the *Florilegium Coislinianum*, but for which it is impossible to ascertain the exact relationship between those anthologies. See also the examples in Ch. 3 § 3.19.

Fig. 3.2.9 Example of apparatuses (not final state) in *Christophori Mitylenaii Versuum variorum collectio cryptensis*, ed. De Groote 2012.

1. *GV inde ab v. 1*

Tit. Εἰς τὴν ἑορτὴν] *suppl. Ro* *ante* δόντος *lacunam statuimus (illeg. G)* α′] *supplevi* **1** θαύματος] καὶ *praem. V, illeg. G* **2** σὴ] γὰρ *V* **4** πτερωτὴν *V* **5** ἦν] *coni. Ku, illeg. G,* ἣν *V* **6** ἐμβόλων] *sine accentu G, om. V* **8** τὰς] τῆς *G* **9** τραυματισθέντων σφόδρα] *coni. Ku, illeg. G, spat. vac. V* **10** *versus abest V* **12** ὁ δὲ τρέχων] ὁ δ᾽ ἕτερος *V* **13** ἦν ἄλλος] ἄλλος δὲ *V* **16** λαμπάδος *V* **21** τῷ] *coni. Ku,* τοῦ *GV*

G

1 Ὢ θα- *tantum legi potest* **3** δίχα *tantum legi potest* **5** τὸ πρ- *tantum legi potest* **7** πάντων *tantum legi potest* **9** πληγαῖς τ- *tantum legi potest* **11** τούτων ὁ μὲν *tantum legi potest* **13** ἦν ἄλλος ἡμίφ- *tantum legi potest* **15** ἄλλων κατεφλέχθ- *tantum legi potest* **17** τυφθεὶς βαρείαις χερσιν ο- *tantum legi potest* **19** -σφόρει *legi nequit* **21** -κ ἔχω· *legi nequit*

Fig. 3.2.10 Example of apparatuses in *I trattati teologici di Sulaymān Ibn Ḥasan Al-Ġazzī*, ed. La Spisa 2013, 49.

[T4] وله ايضا رحمه الله

Ed 41 رساله * رد على المخالفين للامانه المستقيمه الارثوذكسيه

S 166r * عبد عبيد يسوع المسيح واصغر اولاد بيعته يرد على من قال كمقاله § 1
اريوس، الفاصل الاهوت الى ثلثه مغتربه، الحاصر اللاهوت للاب وحده،

Testes: S 165v, W 69v, H 95v, Y 64v, M 103r, Q 53r, Ed 40

1,2 اريوس...3 موسسا.] *cf.* Dīwān 1, 25

T4,1 وله...الله] من هذا البارقليط القدس والروح الوسيط والابن البسيط الاب بسم
بسم الاب والابن والروح ;H سليمان2 *del.* قول سليمان بن سليمان حسن الغزي
M; بسم الله الواحد الابدي الازلي السرمدي وبه نستعين;Y القدس الاله الواحد امين
وايضًا نكتب شيٍّ من برهان الامانه ممّا;Q بسم الاب والابن والروح القدس الهٌ واحد
رتبوّه المجامع المقدسه والآباء الثلثمايه وثمانيه عشر والابآ القديسين مسايل واجوبه من
M *add.* ديوان الغزي وكان اسمه سليمان وكان مطران غزه رضي الله تعالي عنه
Y الكتاب الثاني من قول سليمان ابن حسن الغـــزي ;H *om.* [رســـاله **2**
المجمع الاول الثلثمايه وثمانية عشر اجتمع على اريوس الكافر [رساله...الارثوذكسيه
M الذي قال ان الابن مخلوق وذلك المجمع كان على ايام قسطنطين ابن هلانه الكبيره
HY *om.* [عبد...يرد **1,1** HY *om.* [الارثوذكسيه | HY الامانه [للامانه |
M فاصل [الفاصل **2** M مقالة [كمقاله | M *om.* [من قال | M *om.* [يسوع
[الحاصر | M متعرّيه [مغتربه | M *add.* متفرقه [ثلثه | HY *om.* [الى...وحده
Ed بالاب ;M الاب [للاب | M *a. corr.* وللاهت [اللاهوت | M *add.* للسمآء

T4,2 الارثوذكسيه] الارثدكسيه W **1,1** على] وعلى HY **2** اريوس] اريوسً H
الاهوت] اللاهوت YM

Fig. 3.2.11 Example of apparatuses (not final state) in *De Beneficentia*, ed. Holman et al. 2012.

33–34 cf. Matth. 5.43 etc. **35–36** = I Ioh. 3.18 **46** cf. I Reg. 1.28 **57–59** = Luc. 16.9

33 τίς P 36 δὲ^{2}] deleuimus 40 ἀποδώσει] correximus, ἀποδοῦναι P 41 Χριστὸς] P$^{ut\ vid.}$ | οὐκ] P$^{p.c., ut\ vid.}$, legi nequit P$^{a.c.}$ 42 πολλαπλασίωνι P 53 σωτηρίαν] P$^{p.c.}$, legi nequit P$^{a.c.}$ 58 φίλους] P$^{p.c.}$, legi nequit P$^{a.c.}$ 59 ἐκλίπητε] scripsimus, ἐκλείπ*ται P

50–59 δυνατὸς – σκηνὰς = Ps. Anastasius Sinaita, Quaest. 14, PG 89, col. 465 A 12 - B 7 (τοῦ ἁγίου Βασιλείου ἐκ τῶν Ἀσκητικῶν)

As was said above (see Ch. 3 § 2.4.1), other recensions/redactions and ancient translations of a work may sometimes be edited synoptically or in parallel, and the same is true when the edited text is itself a translation, for the source text (see Ch. 3 § 2.6.3). Alternatively, the contents of those indirect witnesses or of the source text may be summarized in an apparatus, as is the case in fig. 3.2.12: the first apparatus is in fact the apparatus of available witnesses (see Ch. 3 § 2.5.1) to the edited text, followed by the critical apparatus, then the last apparatus gives the version of the work contained in two divergent witnesses, P and Z.

It may also happen that an author uses the same sentence or set of sentences several times in his writing, it may be useful to indicate this, also because it may have some influence on critical decisions: see, for example, the third apparatus ('Parall.') in fig. 3.2.8, referring to passages within the same work where the author is using exactly the same quotations.

M V S Ph L

---

18 εἰδοποιεῖ] εἰδ᾽ ὁποιεῖ *M,* ὁδοποιεῖ *V* **20** γενήσωνται] γενήσονται *Ph,* γενήσεται *S,* γεννήσωνται *V*[p.c.] **20–21** τῶν ἐνύλων] τῶν ὅλων *V* **21** ἑκάστῳ] *legi nequit M,* ἑκάστου *V* | ἀλλ᾽] τϊνὸς *M*[a.c.] | οὐχ – ἐστίν] οὐ τῇ ὕλῃ *V* **56,1** καδδινάλιοι] *legi nequit S* **2** ταῖς ὑδρορρόαις] τὰς ὑδρορόας *V* **3** αὐτοὺς] αὐτοῖς *V*[a.c.] **7** δὲ] *post* ἐκ *transp. V* **57,1** βασιλεύς] *legi nequit S* | ὑμῶν] ἡμῶν *V*[a.c.] **4** ἐνέργεια] ἐνέργει *V* **6** ἔκφανσιν] ἔκφασιν *M,* ἔκφαος *V* **7** ἀτελής] ἐντελὴς *V* | ἔτι] ἐπί *V* | ἐνοικουροῦσα] ἐνοικαροῦσα *V* **9** ὑπέρακμον] ὑπέρανμον *V* **12** τῆς^2] ἐπὶ *V* **58,1** καδδινάλιοι] *legi nequit S* **2** ἀντειπεῖν] ἀντιπεῖν *V*[a.c.] **59,1** βασιλεύς] βασιλεῦ *M, legi nequit S* | οὖν] *om. PhSV*

P Z

---

15 πρὸς ὑπόδειγμα] προυπόδειγμα Z **16** τὸ] *om. P* **17** ἑαυτὸ] ἑαυτὸν *P* **18** τι] *om. Z* **19** οἷόν τε] οἴονται Z **20** γενήσωνται] γενήσεται *P,* γενήσονται Z **22** αὐτὸ – ἑαυτοῦ] ἐξ ἑαυτοῦ αὐτὸ Z **56,1** καδδινάλιοι] *om. P,* ὁ λατίνος Z **1–3** δένδρον – προσήκοντι] *om. PZ* **4** ἀλλ᾽ – ὑποδείγματος] ἄλλου ὑποδείγματος ἄκουσον *PZ* τῆς^2] *om.* Z **7** γεγέννηται] γεγένηται *PZ* **57,1** βασιλεύς] *om. P,* ὁ γραικός Z **1–2** κλίνατε – κατευθύνοντες] *om. PZ* **2** γὰρ] *om. PZ* **3** ἐπὶ] ἐκ *P* **4** τί] *om.* Z **5** γὰρ] *om.* Z **6** ἔκφανσιν] ἔκφασιν *P* **7** τῷ βάθει] τὰ βάθη Z **8** τοὐμφανὲς] τὸ ἐμφανὲς *PZ* **10** τυγχάνειν^2] *om. PZ* **11** ἐκ τοῦ] *om.* Z **12** δοκεῖ μοι] δοκίμως Z | κἀπὶ] καὶ ἐπί Z | τῆς^2] ἐπί *praem.* Z | τὸ] *om.* Z **13** τῇ] *om.* Z | θεωρουμένων] *om. P* | παρείληπται] παρείλειπται *P*[a.c.] **58,1–2** καδδινάλιοι – οἰόμεθα] *hanc cardinalium partem om. PZ* **59,1** βασιλεύς – πρόβλημα] *hanc imperatoris partem om. PZ*

Fig. 3.2.12 Example of apparatuses (not final state) in *Andronici Camateri Sacrum Armamentarium*, ed. Bucossi 2014.

Γ′ περὶ βλασφημίας

4 Ἰώβ

Τί ἐτόλμησας ἐν τῇ καρδίᾳ σου, ὅτι θυμὸν ἔρρηξας ἐναντίον τοῦ θεοῦ, φιλάνθρωπον πνεῦμα σοφία, καὶ οὐκ ἀθωώσει βλάσφημον ἀπὸ χειλέων αὐτοῦ.

5 τοῦ Χρυσοστόμου

Τοὺς ἐν τῇ πόλει βλασφημοῦντας, σωφρόνιζε. Κἂν ἀκούσῃς τινὸς ἐν ἀμφόδῳ, ἢ ἐν ἀγορᾷ βλασφημοῦντος τὸν Θεόν, πρόσελθε, ἐπιτίμησον, κἂν πληγὰς ἐπιθεῖναι δέῃ, μὴ παραιτήσῃ· ῥάπισον αὐτοῦ τὴν ὄψιν, σύντριψον αὐτοῦ τὸ στόμα, ἁγίασόν σου τὴν χεῖρα διὰ τῆς πληγῆς, κἂν ἐγκαλῶσι τινές, κἂν εἰς δικαστήριον ἕλκωσιν, ἀκολούθησον.

---

4 A BCPS **5** A BCPS

4.1–2 = Iob 15.12-13 **2–3** = Sap. 1.6 **5.1–8** = Io. Chrys., Ad populum Antiochenum, PG 49, col. 32.44-51

Γ′] κεφάλαιον μδ′ BCPS

5.2 ἀμφόδῳ] ἢ ἐν ὁδῶ add. BPS **4** παραιτήσῃ] παρεστήσῃ

4.1 Τί… σου] τί ἐτόλμησεν ἡ καρδία σου LXX **2** ἐναντίον… θεοῦ] ἔναντι κυρίου LXX | φιλάνθρωπον] γὰρ add. LXX **5.2** ἀγορᾷ] μέσῃ add. Chrys. **5** αὐτοῦ^2] om. Chrys.

Fig. 3.2.13 *Florilegium Coislinianum*, β 4–5, ed. De Vos et al. 2010.

4. Comparative apparatus

The editor always needs to compare, at least for him/herself, the edited text with its sources, indirect tradition and parallel texts. In some cases it may be useful to show the results of this comparison in a special apparatus. In fig. 3.2.8, the last apparatus ('Coll.') displays the results of the comparison between the edited text and the edition of its sources. In fig. 3.2.13, the same has been done in the penultimate apparatus. This may help the reader to visualize immediately the differences between the two texts, and it is especially useful in the case of *florilegia* or patchwork texts, sometimes called *centones* in poetry (NB: Iacobus' text, as shown in fig. 3.2.8, may rightly be considered a patchwork, as almost no word is original).

5. Titles, marginalia, scholia etc.

Finally, information concerning para-textual elements may also be displayed in an apparatus, if one does not want to mix it with critical information properly concerning the text, as those para-textual features may have a less authorial status. In fig. 3.2.13, the variants concerning the subtitles and identifications of authors have been put in a special apparatus (i.e. third apparatus), above the critical apparatus, which is the fourth apparatus.

2.6. Philological introduction, translation, commentary, indexes and appendices (JdH–CM)

This section briefly addresses various aspects of an editorial project that are not strictly speaking part of the critical text itself but constitute indispensable elements of an edition. In what follows, the description of those elements will be oriented towards the production of a printed book. However, most of them also pertain to digital editions, even though in a different form. The digital environment will allow different features, especially of the possibility of linking to other web resources (online dictionaries and grammars, digital images of manuscripts, and so on; see Fischer [F.] 2013, esp. 88–89).

2.6.1. Philological introduction

The introduction should enable any user to understand how editorial choices were made and what kind of practice has been adopted. In concrete terms, this means that all elements of the process described above in this chapter (Ch. 3 §§ 2.1–2.5) must be summarized and explained in the introduction to the edition.

First of all, the text to be edited and its author, if such an author exists, must be identified and possibly distinguished from related texts with which it may be confused (on the difficulties inherent to this task, see Ch. 3 § 2.1.1). Sometimes a short account about the author and his time, about the genre, context and audience of the text may be useful, especially when this is not so well known.

Then one must provide a list of witnesses, both direct and indirect, with a succinct description (see Ch. 3 § 2.1). Here it is important to aim at exhaustiveness, and to mention all known witnesses, including those that were not used for the edition and even those that could not be consulted (and to explain why they could not be consulted). For each manuscript, the following elements must be noted (on the basis of the catalogues and bibliography, critically used, but also of personal examination)—such descriptions sometimes are more elaborate, particularly when existing catalogues provide insufficient or incorrect data:

— general elements of description: city, library, collection, shelfmark, dating (at least a century) (and the source for the dating: colophon, catalogue…), material, dimensions, total number of folia. Any type of information about the copyist and/or the date, place of origin, sponsor, possessors, etc., should also be written down.

— concerning the text to be edited: folia or pages of beginning and end, title. It is essential to establish whether the text is complete or only composed of excerpts or fragments. In the event that some parts of the text are missing, the lacunas must be carefully noted and one must determine if it was originally the case in the manuscript or if this is the result of a material accident: for this, the analysis of the quire composition is fundamental (see Ch. 1).

Subsequently, the conclusions of the research about the history of the text should be given, and a stemma, when possible (see Ch. 3 § 2.3). If no stemma could be obtained, the introduction should explain what considerations have led to such a negative conclusion.

On the basis of those conclusions, a method of edition should be chosen (see Ch. 3 § 2.4.1). The principles followed to establish the text are explained in a section of the introduction sometimes called *ratio edendi*. The editorial choices must be soundly argued there: choice of the witnesses, form of the text, orthographical features, presentation of the apparatuses, and the like.

2.6.2. *Conspectus siglorum*

The list of sigla mentioned above, traditionally called *Conspectus siglorum*, is necessary for a good understanding of the apparatus. In order to allow for convenient reading, it is best placed immediately before the beginning of the edited text or on a separate page. It contains the *legenda* of all sigla, symbols and abbreviations that are used in the apparatuses (see fig. 3.2.14). One should be careful, however, to avoid excessively lengthy lists that are more likely to confuse readers than to facilitate their reading experience.

CONSPECTUS SIGLORUM

Traditio directa

A — *Athous, Batopediou* 320, *saec.* XIV, ff. 311-320^{v}
B — *Berolinensis, Phill.* 1439, *saec.* XI, ff. 148^{v}-159
G — *Athous, Lauras* Ω 59, *saec.* XIV, ff. 12-14^{v}
I — *Athous, Ibērōn* 49, *saec.* XI, 66^{v}-75
K — *Oxoniensis, Bodleianus, Holkham* 41, *saec.* X-XI, ff. 307^{v}-322
N — *Genuensis, Biblioteca Franzoniana, Urb.* 11, *saec.* X, ff. 323-335^{v}
P — *Athous, Pantokratoros* 1, *saec.* XI, ff. 128^{v}-138^{v}
R — *Parisinus gr.* 818, *saec.* XII, ff. 80-86^{v}
T — *Taurinensis* B. I. 11, *saec.* X-XI, ff. 207-213^{v}, 215
U — *Venetus, Marcianus gr.* 111, *saec.* XI in., ff. 249^{v}-254^{v}
Z — *Vaticanus gr.* 551, *saec.* X-XI, ff. 267^{v}-272^{v}
a — *Parisinus gr.* 1019, *saec.* XII, ff. 42^{v}-59^{v}
c — *Oxoniensis, Christ Church* 4, *saec.* X-XI, ff. 61^{v}-71^{v}
h — *Monacensis gr.* 6, *saec.* XI, ff. 315-320^{v}
r — *Parisinus gr.* 765, *saec.* XII, ff. 159^{v}-174
u — *Lesbiacus, Leimonos* 32, *saec.* X-XI, ff. 1-13^{v}
v — *Vaticanus gr.* 1920, *saec.* X, ff. 9-19

Codices passim laudati

S_{4a} — *Oxoniensis, Bodleianus, Auct.* E. 3. 15 (*Savilii Liber* Q), *saec.* XVII, pp. 1-9^{v}
S_{4b} — *Oxoniensis, Bodleianus, Auct.* E. 3. 15 (*Savilii Liber* Q), *saec.* XVII, pp. 106-112^{v}

Editiones

Sav. — Τοῦ ἐν ἁγίοις πατρὸς ἡμῶν Ἰωάννου... τοῦ Χρυσοστόμου τῶν εὑρισκομένων... Δι' ἐπιμελείας καὶ ἀναλωμάτων Ἐρρίκου τοῦ Σαβιλίου..., Etonae 1612, t. VIII, pp. 9-17
Front. — Joannis Chrysostomi *Opera omnia*... *cura* Frontonis Ducaei, Parisiis 1621, t. II, pp. 1008-1022
Montf. — Joannis Chrysostomi *Opera omnia quae extant*... *opera et studio* D. Bernardi de Montfaucon, Parisiis 1718-1738, t. IV, pp. 747-759
Patr. — *PG* 54, 675, 46 - 686, 61
edd. — *consensus Sav. Front. Montf. Patr.*

Traditio indirecta

ecl^{17} — *Ecloga* 17: *De invidia*, *PG* 63, 677-682
ecl^{29} — *Ecloga* 29: *De mansuetudine et malorum patientia et iniuriarum memoria*, *PG* 63, 777-788

Fig. 3.2.14 *Conspectus siglorum* in *Iohannis Chrysostomi De Davide et Saule homiliae tres*, ed. Barone 2009.

2.6.3. Parallel texts

Ancient translations

In many of the oriental traditions covered here, texts were not only transmitted in their own language but often also translated into other languages, sometimes quite soon after they had been written. On the other hand, many oriental texts were themselves translations from other texts in other languages. As mentioned above (Ch. 3 § 2.5), the readings of the ancient translations may appear in the apparatus, but it may also be appropriate in some cases to publish them together with the source text (which may not correspond

ἀγνοίᾳ τοῦ πρέποντος γίνεσθαι τοὺς ἐν μέθῃ καρηβαρήσαντας.

2. Προστιθέασι δὲ καί τινας φυσικωτέρας αἰτίας τῆς τοιαύτης περὶ τὸ ἡγεμονικὸν ὑπονοίας ἑκάτερος τῶν ταύταις ταῖς δόξαις παρισταμένων. Ὁ μὲν γὰρ πρὸς τὸ πυρῶδες συγγενῶς ἔχειν τὴν ἐκ τῆς διανοίας κίνησιν λέγει, διὰ τὸ ἀεικίνητον εἶναι καὶ τὸ πῦρ καὶ τὴν διάνοιαν· καὶ ἐπειδὴ πηγάζειν ἐν τῷ μορίῳ τῆς καρδίας ἡ θερμότης ὁμολογεῖται, διὰ τοῦτο τῷ εὐκινήτῳ τῆς θερμότητος τὴν τοῦ νοῦ κίνησιν ἀνακεκρᾶσθαι λέγων, δοχεῖον τῆς νοερᾶς φύσεως τὴν καρδίαν εἶναί φησιν, ἐν ᾗ τὸ θερμὸν περιείληπται. Ὁ δὲ ἕτερος πᾶσι τοῖς αἰσθητηρίοις οἷον ὑποβάθραν τινὰ καὶ ῥίζαν εἶναι λέγει τὴν μήνιγγα (οὕτω γὰρ ὀνομάζουσι τὸν περιεκτικὸν τοῦ ἐγκεφάλου ὑμένα) καὶ τούτῳ πιστοῦται τὸν ἴδιον λόγον· ὡς οὐχ ἑτέρωθι τῆς νοητικῆς ἐνεργείας καθιδρυμένης, εἰ μὴ κατ᾽ ἐκεῖνο τὸ μέρος, ᾧ καὶ τὸ οὖς ἐφηρμοσμένον τὰς ἐμπιπτούσας αὐτῷ φωνὰς προσαράσσει· καὶ ἡ ὄψις κατὰ τὸν πυθμένα τῆς τῶν ὀφθαλμῶν ἕδρας συμπεφυκυῖα, διὰ [vii] τῶν ἐμπιπτόντων ταῖς
162 κόραις εἰδώλων πρὸς τὸ ἔσω ποιεῖται [viii] τὴν τύπωσιν· καὶ τῶν ἀτμῶν αἱ ποιότητες διὰ τῆς τῶν ὀσφρήσεων ὁλκῆς ἐν αὐτῷ

[vii] διαπέμπει pro διὰ habent ABCIKMNQT
[viii] ποιεῖται om. ABCIKMNQT

невѣдѣни под(о)бнаго бывати иже вь пїан'ствѣ главою ѻтеготѣвшимь.

2. Приложише же и нѣкыє єс(ть)ст'вьнѣише [5] вины таковаго ѹмышленїа ѻ вл(а)д(ы)чьственомь кыждо ѡт(ь) их'же таковаа ѹмышленїа [6] прѣд(ь)-ставлꙗющим(ь). Ѡвь ѹбо кь ѡгн'номѹ сьроднѣ имать єже ѡт(ь) сьмысла движенїє гл(агол)еть, ꙁа єже пр(и)сно-движень быти и ѡг'нь и прѣбывати и сьмысль, и понєже истекати вь ѹдеси ср(ь)дьчномь топлота исповѣдѹетсе, сего рад(и) ѹдобьдвижимѣи топлотѣ ѹмномѹ двиꙁанию растваратисе гл(агол)е, приєтилище ѹмномѹ єс(ть)ствѹ ср(ь)д(ь)цоу быти рече, вь нєм'же топлотное ѻбь-ємлетсе. Дроугыи же вьсѣмь *чювьст-вителницамь* [7] ꙗкоже ѡснованїє нѣкое и корень быти гл(агол)еть ꙁатильк (сице бо именѹють сьборнѹю ꙁатилка тьнчаишѹю кожѹ), и семѹ ѹвѣраеть свое слово: ꙗко не инде ѹмномѹ дѣиствѹ вьдроуженѹ, развѣ вь ѻнои чести, идеже и [8] ѹхо оустроено быс(ть), вьпад(а)ющих(ь) томѹ гласовь раꙁдѣлꙗє, и лице, по дьноу ѳчесных(ь) сѣдалища сьприбывше, по-силаеть AGR вьпад(а)ющих(ь) вь ꙁеницѣ сѣневных(ь) под(о)бїи кь вьнѹтрьним AGR вьѻбражени, и вьспаренїωмь качьствїа ѡбонꙗнїи крѣпостию вь нємь

[5] єс(ть)ст'вьнѣише et sim. CH,N,R,Z: єс(ть)ствѣнѣє B
[6] ѻ вл(а)д(ы)чьственомь ad ѹмышленїа om. B
[7] чюв'ствителницамь et sim. N,R,Z,B : чювьстителницамь CH
[8] и om. R,Z,B

§2. (1-10) app. crit. [6] ms B: *saut du même au même* // (5-10) ѡт(ь) их'же ... прѣд(ь)ставлꙗющим(ь): contamination of dat. and gen. // сьроднѣ имать, that is {συγγενῶς ἔχει} for συγγενῶς ἔχειν // the addition и прѣбывати seems to be an inserted supralinear gloss, cf. Prol. p. 80 // (15-20) underdifferentiation: τὴν μήνιγγα - τοῦ ἐγκεφάλου: ꙁатильк - ꙁатилка // (20-26) προσαράσσει, 'dash against, slam in, shatter' (L&S), Sl. раꙁдѣлꙗє, 'divide, discern' // ѳчесных сѣдалища for τῆς τῶν ὀφθαλμῶν ἕδρας: one would expect {ѳчесна} in agreement with сѣдалища, or gen. dual. {ѳчию}; here probably nominal ѳчесьноє as a counterpart for ὀφθαλμός // посилаеть кь вьнѹтрьним вьѻбражени: вьнѹтрьним dat. pl. instead of sing.; вьѻбражени for acc. sing. вьѻбражениє? // крѣпостию < крѣпость 'Kraft, Stärke; ἰσχύς, κραταίωμα' (SLOVN.), for διὰ τῆς … ὁλκῆς, here 'drawing in (of breath)' (LA)

Fig. 3.2.15 Gregory of Nyssa, *De hominis opificio. O obrazě člověka*, ed. Sels 2009, 163.

exactly to the edited text; on the problematic relationship between translations and source text see Ch. 3 § 3.20). This edition in parallel proves to be especially relevant when the source text is lacunary (such is the case in *Corpus Christianorum Series Graeca* 82 for instance, where the Greek original and its Syriac translation are edited facing each other, the Syriac occasionally standing alone).

Conversely, it may be useful as well to publish the source text (often taken from a previous edition) together with the edition of its translation, and the reference system of the source text may be adopted for the translation as well (see fig. 3.2.15).

Modern translations

A distinct issue is that of a modern translation, to be produced as part of an edition project. The decision on whether or not to add such a translation often depends on the policy of a series editor and is related to the readership one has in mind.

A translation is intended as an additional key to an in-depth understanding of the edited text. It is especially important in the context of multilingualism characteristic of oriental traditions, to allow scholars working on related texts in one language and not familiar with some of the other languages, to be able to understand the text. Accordingly, in the *Patrologia Orientalis* (PO) and *Corpus Scriptorum Christianorum Orientalium* (CSCO, see Ch. 3 § 1.3B for a bibliographical orientation), editions are often accompanied by a translation.

In the past and at least up to the 1960s, oriental texts were sometimes translated into Latin—see for example Blake – Brière 1961–1963 (PO, 29,2–5/30,3), where the Georgian edition is facing a Latin translation (in four fascicles of PO 29), and the apparatus (also translated into Latin) is published as a separate volume (fig. 3.2.16)— but in general the use of Latin is not advisable anymore.

The translation must follow the original text closely. Even if the translation is not published together with the edited text, it is always advisable that the editor makes the effort of translating the text form him/herself, as this is a great way of controlling his/her edition.

While a digital environment may allow for a variety of formats, edited texts with translations in printed ones may be provided synoptically, that is on the same page, either in two parallel columns or in the format of an edited text on top and the translation below. In other publications, the text and the translation are given separately at the beginning and the end of one and the same volume (which is not practical for the reader) or indeed in two separate volumes that can be read simultaneously. Translations are often accompanied by footnotes, providing explanatory observations on matters of content, context and interpretation. More rarely, the footnotes to a translation even correspond to the critical apparatus of the edition itself and thus inform even the less specialized reader about aspects of the text tradition and about the editorial choices made.

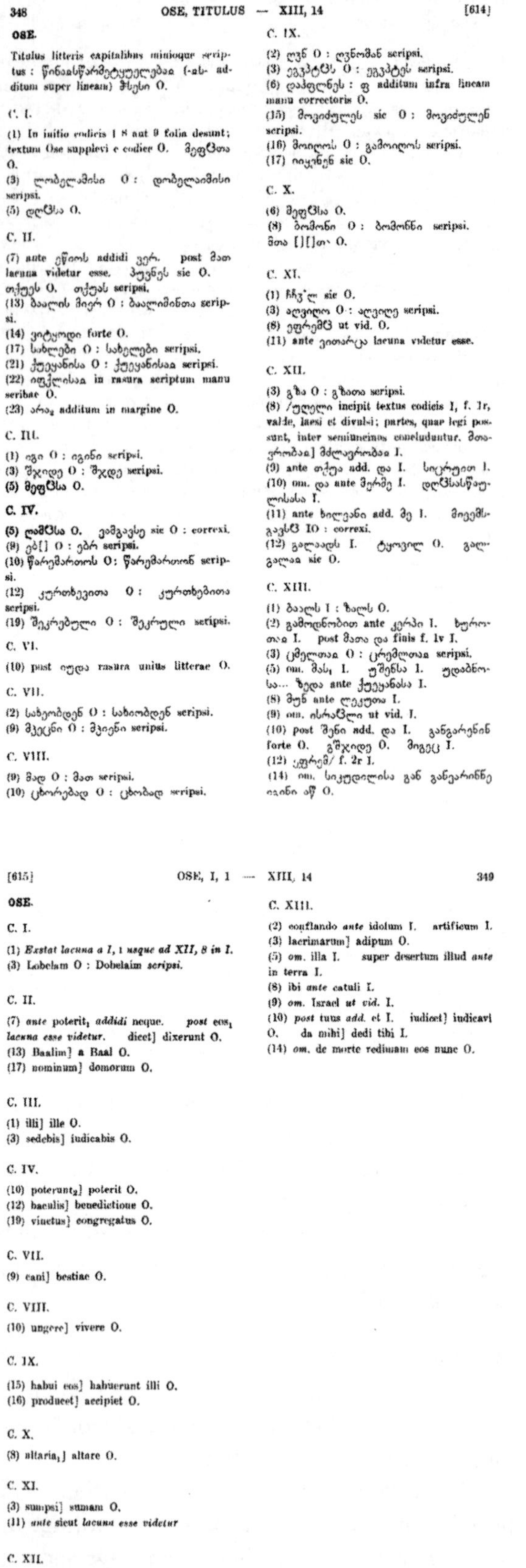

[615] OSE, I, 1 — XIII, 14 349

OSE.

C. I.

(1) *Exstat lacuna a I, 1 usque ad XII, 8 in I.*
(3) Lobelam O : Dobelaim *scripsi.*

C. II.

(7) *ante* poterit$_1$ *addidi* neque. *post* eos$_1$ *lacuna esse videtur.* dicet] dixerunt O.
(13) Baalim] a Baal O.
(17) nominum] domorum O.

C. III.

(1) illi] ille O.
(3) sedebis] iudicabis O.

C. IV.

(10) poterunt$_2$] poterit O.
(12) baculis] benedictione O.
(19) vinctus] congregatus O.

C. VII.

(9) cani] bestiae O.

C. VIII.

(10) ungere] vivere O.

C. IX.

(15) habui eos] habuerunt illi O.
(16) producet] accipiet O.

C. X.

(8) altaria$_1$] altare O.

C. XI.

(3) sumpsi] sumam O.
(11) *ante* sicut *lacuna esse videtur*

C. XII.

(8) / iugum *incipit textus codicis* I. principatum] tyrannidem I.
(9) *ante* dixit *add.* et I.
(10) *ante* iterum *om.* et I.
(11) *ante* visiones *add.* ego I.
(12) Galaad] in Galaad I.

C. XIII.

(2) conflando *ante* idolum I. artificum I.
(3) lacrimarum] adipum O.
(5) *om.* illa I. super desertum illud *ante* in terra I.
(8) ibi *ante* catuli I.
(9) *om.* Israel *ut vid.* I.
(10) *post* tuus *add.* et I. iudicet] iudicavi O. da mihi] dedi tibi I.
(14) *om.* de morte rediman eos nunc O.

Fig. 3.2.16 Apparatus to *The old Georgian version of the Prophets*, ed. Blake – Brière 1963, 348–349.

2.6.4. Annotations and commentary

Further types of annotations and commentary may concern either matters of content or text historical information for which the apparatuses are not the most suitable outlet. Specially in editions without translation, it may be useful to look for different ways to discuss problems of interpretation of contents, but here the focus is on issues that concern the text itself, its transmission and possibly, more background information and explicit justification of the editorial choices. Such annotations can be given as footnotes under the text if desired or allowed by the series editor, in the introduction or after the text at the end of the volume, or indeed in a separate publication.

2.6.5. Indexes

Several types of indexes may facilitate the use of a printed edition; digital editions normally do not require these because they are searchable in other ways. Some of the most commonly used categories of information covered by indexes are:

— proper names (*index nominum*), with, for instance in editions of historiographical texts, often a separate index for names of ethnic groups, tribes, and religiously defined communities, index of place names, etc.;
— concepts, phenomena, themes, etc. (thematic index);
— all words that occur in the text (*index verborum*),

which may be given in the original language(s), in translation or both—printing a full index of words will probably be too costly and space consuming and it will probably be more useful in a digital form;
— sources and parallel texts (*index fontium et parallelorum*) sometimes divided into several sub-indexes (Old Testament, New Testament, Patristics, Qurʾān verses, etc.).

For some languages, the concept of an index of all words has lost much of its practical value due to the availability of large digital text repositories and on-line thesauri (although these do not usually cover variant readings). For most oriental traditions covered here, however, such databases do not yet exist or do not meet the requirements of textual scholarship, so that indexing and automated lemmatizing remains an important and useful task (see the General introduction § 2.1.2).

2.6.6. Appendices

All kinds of further material can be provided in the form of an appendix to the edition, such as marginalia or additional lists of variants (see fig. 3.2.17), other texts that are somehow related to the one edited but cannot be systematically compared to it, and tables and graphs.

Appendix I : Orthographica, Elisiones, Iotacismi

617.13-14 τέλεον AFR : τέλειον GW
617.14 δὲ AFR : δ᾽ GW
617.22 ἐνθεῖναί A : ἐνθῆναί Σ
618.19 τελέως Σ : τελείως A
619.9 διδασκαλείου A : διδασκαλίου Σ
621.2 γοῦν Σ : οὖν A
623.19 τέτταρας Σ : τέσσαρας A
623.31 διδασκαλείου A : διδασκαλίου Σ

Appendix II : Variantes lectiones codicum recentiorum qui a Σ pendent (ubi A textum incorruptum praebet)

617.23 τὴν A : τ. GR τὸ FW
624.7 φανερὰν AW : -ρὰ FGR
624.31 αὐτὸς AG^{mg}RW : αὐτοῖς FG
626.15 τῆς AW : τοὺς FGR
627.11 ψυχαῖς AFW : ψυχῇ GR
629.4 δαῖτά AW : διαῖτά FGR
631.8 ἰδόντες AR^{c}: ἰδόντε FGW
633.11 κατακωχὴν AF : κατ()κωχὴν R κακωχὴν GW

Appendix III : Menda codicis A et emendationes librariorum posteriorum

622.30 ὑπόθεσιν M^{c}Σ : ὑπέρθεσιν A
636.13 βάθος Σ : βάθους AM
638.20 τῇ MΣ : τοῦ A
670.5 καὶ τὸ Σ : l. dub. A om. M
671.7 ἐκείνων MΣ : εἰκόνων A^{2}
675.42 καὶ AMΣ : τῆς A^{2}
678.20 φύσεις MΣ : γνώσεις A^{2}

Appendix IV : Appendix lectionum interpretationis Latinae Guillelmi de Moerbeka quae a textu recepto discrepant

618.23 καὶ om. **g**
621.3 πού om. **g**
622.2 ταῦτα : *eadem* **g** (ταὐτὰ ?)
622.6 θαύματος : *mirabiliter* **g** (θαυμαστῶς ?)
622.32 λέγων : *est* **g**

Fig. 3.2.17 Proclus, *In Parmenidem*, ed. Steel et al. 2007. Appendices (samples).

In some cases, it may be useful to add a glossary of technical terms or specialized vocabulary that occurs in the edited text (for example Sedacer, ed. Barthélémy 2002, I, 203–232), or, in the case of translated texts, a lexicon of the terminology of the text in the two relevant languages (see fig. 3.2.18).

A special kind of appendix is that of photographic reproductions of the manuscripts used. Except in the case of short texts, printed editions will contain only samples of such photographs. In the case of short or fragmentary texts, such as the Turfan fragments (see Ch. 3 § 3.9) or papyri (see Ch. 3 § 3.6) the accepted norm is to reproduce the entire text photographically (even if it is relatively lengthy). Finally, palimpsests

APPENDICE II

LEXIQUE ARABE-GREC

Les mots ou expressions sont classés par racine et suivis du mot grec auquel se trouve la référence dans le lexique grec-arabe. Les entrées grecques suivies du signe ** désignent des mots traduits de façon erronée par le traducteur. Les hendiadys sont signalés par le sigle □.

Racine	Arabe	Grec
أثر	المشتهين الموثرين	ἐφίημι (ἐφιεμένων) □
أخر	(الاسباب) الاخر	ἀολλής **
	الاخريات	ἑτερότης (αἱ ἑτερότητες)
أدى	تكون موديه	χειραγωγέω (χειραγωγοῦσα)
أرض	ارض	γῆ
ألف	ذو الفه	ἑνωτικός
	التاليفات والالفات	ἕνωσις (αἱ πρὸς ἑαυτὰς ἑνώσεις)
	بتاليف	ἑνιαίως
	مولفه\امولفات	ἐφαρμογή / ἁρμονία / ἕνωσις
	مولفه \ مولفات	ἑνόω (ἑνοῦσα, ἥνωται, ἡνωμένας)
أله	الاله	θεός
	الله	θεός
	الهى	θεῖος
	الذات الالهيه الاولى	θεαρχικός (ἡ θεαρχικὴ ὕπαρξις)
	القول الالهى (ذات علامه واماره)	θεολογία (ἡ Συμβολικὴ θεολογία)
	الكلمات الالهيه	θεολόγος (θεολόγοι) **
	مسميات بالالهيات	θεωνυμία (θεωνυμίαι)
أمر	ذو علامه واماره	συμβολικός (ἡ Συμβολικὴ θεολογία) □
	مامورات	ἐφίημι (ἐφιέμεναι)
أول	اولا	πρῶτον
	الذات الالهيه الاولى	θεαρχικός (ἡ θεαρχικὴ ὕπαρξις)

Fig. 3.2.18 Appendix in *Corpus Dionysiacum Arabicum*, ed. Bonmariage – Moureau 2007, 214.

also often require special images (see Ch. 3 § 3.11). Here, as in other cases, the digital medium is more suitable than the printed one for a variety of practical considerations (see the General introduction § 2.3).

References

Alberti 1979; Andrews 2009; Andrews – Macé 2013, 2014; Baret et al. 2006; Barthélémy 2002; Bausi 1995b; Bernabé – Hernández Muñoz 2010; Blachère – Sauvaget 1945; Blake – Brière 1961–1963; Bonmariage – Moureau 2011; Bucossi 2014; Careri 1998; Cisķarišvili 1954; De Groote 2012; De Vos et al. 2010; Dearing 1968; den Heijer et al. 2014; Finney 1999; Fischer [F.] 2013; Froger 1968; Gacek 2007; Giannouli 2014; Greg 1927; Grier 1988; Griffith [J.] 1968; Guidi – Trovato 2004; Haentjens Dekker – Middell 2011; Haugen 2014; Havet 1911; Holman et al. 2012; Irigoin 1954, 1979, 1981a; Jeffreys – Jeffreys 2009; Kakridis 2004; La Spisa 2012, 2013, 2014; Lentin 2008; Love 1984; Maas 1957; Macé 2011, forthcoming; Macé et al. 2001, 2012; Mahdi 1984; Parkes 1998; Pasquali 1934, [2]1952; Peacock 2007; Pierazzo 2011; Quentin 1926; Reeve 1998; Reynolds – Wilson 1991; Richard [M.] 1980; Rilliet 1986; Robinson [Pe.] 1989, 1994, 2004; Roman – Poirier 2013; Rosselli Del Turco 2007; Samir 1982; Schmidt [D.] 2010; Schmidt [D.] – Colomb 2009; Sels 2009; Signes Codoñer 2014; Steel et al. 2007; Timpanaro 1985, 2005; Trovato 2005, 2013; van Reenen – van Mulken 1996; van Reenen et al. 2004; Walter 2001; Weitzman 1985, 1987; West [M.] 1973; Whittaker 1991; Witkam 2013; Zarri 1971. Web sources: <http://medium.irht.cnrs.fr/>, last access May 2014; Stemmaweb <http://stemmaweb.net>, last access May 2014.

3. Case studies

Many problematic issues and practical problems in publishing and dealing with critical editions have been systematically presented in Ch. 3 §§ 2.1–2.6. In the following part, twenty three case studies have been collected to cover most of the languages under consideration in COMSt and to give COMSt scholars the opportunity to focus on aspects specific to their literary, textual and scholarly traditions. Unfortunately, Turkish is missing, and Arabic is represented by cases such as the Qur'ān, Middle Arabic and popular epic that leave the bulk of Classical Arabic literature untouched.

Each author is responsible for his/her case study, and the point of view is often rather personal. Similarly, the terminology may be quite different or even slightly discordant in each case study, since differences may reflect different scholarly traditions and the variety of theoretical and practical approaches is precisely what we intended to survey in this part of the chapter.

1. Tara Andrews (TA), The *Chronicle* of Matthew of Edessa. Digital critical edition of an Armenian historiographical text
2. Alessandro Bausi (ABa), The *Aksumite Collection*. Ethiopic multiple text manuscripts
3. Malachi Beit-Arie (MBA), Private production of mediaeval Hebrew manuscripts
4. Valentina Calzolari (VC), Christian Apocrypha in Armenian
5. Alberto Cantera (AC), The Zoroastrian long liturgy. The transmission of the *Avesta*
6. Laurent Capron (LCa), Greek literary papyri
7. Marie Cronier (MCr), A Byzantine recension of Dioscorides. Historical analysis of manuscripts and text editing
8. Lorenzo Cuppi (LCu), The Septuagint, its *Vorlage* and its translations
9. Desmond Durkin-Meisterernst (DDM), The Turfan fragments
10. Zuzana Gažáková (ZG), Arabic epics
11. Jost Gippert (JG), Palimpsests of Caucasian provenance. Reflections on diplomatic editing
12. Gregory Kessel (GK), Syriac monastic miscellanies
13. Paolo La Spisa (PLS), Middle Arabic texts. How to account for linguistic features
14. Hugo Lundhaug (HL), The Nag Hammadi codices. Textual fluidity in Coptic
15. Caroline Macé (CM), Gregory of Nazianzus' *Homilies*. An over-abundant manuscript tradition in Greek and in translation
16. Michael Marx (MMx), Manuscript London, BL, Or. 2165 and the transmission of the Qur'ān
17. Alessandro Mengozzi (AM), Past and present trends in the edition of Classical Syriac texts
18. Sébastien Moureau (SM), Pseudo-Avicenna's *De anima*. The Latin translation of a lost Arabic original
19. Denis Searby (DSe), Greek collections of wise and witty sayings
20. Lara Sels (LS), The *Vidin Miscellany*. Translated hagiography in Slavonic
21. Wido van Peursen (WvP), Sacred texts in Hebrew and related languages. Dealing with linguistic features
22. Jan Just Witkam (JJW), The *History* of Bayhaqī. Editorial practices for Early New-Persian texts
23. Ugo Zanetti (UZ) and Sever J. Voicu (SV), Christian liturgical manuscripts

3.1. The *Chronicle* of Matthew of Edessa. Digital critical edition of an Armenian historiographical text (TA)

The *Chronicle* of Matt'ēos Uṙhayec'i (Matthew of Edessa) was written in the first half of the twelfth century, probably in stages between the years 1102 and 1131. Uṙhayec'i was an Armenian priest resident in, and probably native to, Edessa (nowadays Urfa in Turkey); he wrote in the vernacular form of Armenian with which he was familiar. His Chronicle covers the history of the Armenian principalities as well as Byzantium and the emirates of the Near East between the years 952 and 1129. The text was extended by a priest who identifies himself only as Grigor, a resident of the nearby town of Kesun, to cover the year 1136 to 1162.

Although the *Chronicle* was known to have been read by others within a century after it was written—Smbat, the brother of king Het'um of Cilicia in the thirteenth century, relied almost entirely upon Uṙhayec'i's text for the relevant portion of his own history (Smbat Sparapet 1980)—the 35 surviving manuscripts that appear in published catalogues all date from 1590 or later, and the two oldest of these (Venice, Mekhitarist library, 887 and Vienna, Mekhitarist library, 574) represent two distinct recensions. The manuscripts are held in libraries throughout Europe and the Near East; roughly half of them can be dated to the seventeenth century. This was the period of 'rescue' of Armenian literature—a concerted effort to copy and preserve the texts that had survived the ravages of war and invasion between the fourteenth and sixteenth centuries. The manuscript (Yerevan, Matenadaran, 1896) usually regarded as 'best', due partially to the claims of its provenance made in the colophon and partially to the presence of two passages of text that are missing in all other versions, was copied only in 1689, well after many others, and has a marked textual affinity with another, less complete, manuscript (Yerevan, Matenadaran, 1767) copied in 1623 that is missing not only the passages in question, but also a substantial chunk of text at the beginning.

The text has been published in two editions; the first, printed in Jerusalem in 1869 (Matthew of Edessa 1869), used two manuscripts held in the library there that both probably derive from the manuscript of 1590 (Venice, Mekhitarist library, 887). The second edition, published in Vałaršapat (Armenia) in 1898 (Matthew of Edessa 1898), used Matenadaran MS 1896 as a base text and included a limited set of variants taken from five other manuscripts in the same library, namely the collection of the Armenian Apostolic patriarchate in Etchmiadzin (Ējmiacin), removed to Moscow at the outbreak of the First World War and later moved to Yerevan; today they reside in the Mesrop Maštoc' Institute of Ancient Manuscripts (Matenadaran). Although the edition of 1898 drew upon a much wider selection of texts than that of 1869, neither edition was truly critical and each was based on a small subset of manuscripts without reference to any held in western Europe, and particularly without reference to those held by the Mekhitarists of Venice and Vienna.

In this case it is very difficult to apply the usual principles of classical philology in order to reconstruct an archetypal text, or even to establish a reliable *stemma codicum*; almost none of them are helpful or applicable to the *Chronicle*. Although the relationship between the age of a manuscript and the authority of its text is very often problematic, in the case of the *Chronicle* we have not even that familiar dilemma to face: there is no manuscript whose age merits special consideration. There is no poetic metre to provide guidance, to hint at what might be a 'true' reading as opposed to an 'error' in the Lachmannian sense. Likewise, the use of the Armenian vernacular makes it impossible to rely on grammatical principles to distinguish the text that Uṙhayec'i himself is likely to have written, both because we have in modern times only a hesitant understanding of the specifics of twelfth-century Edessene Armenian, and because we have little assurance that Uṙhayec'i would have abided by all of these rules even if we possessed them. Moreover, the text is relatively long and segmented according to year, which gives immediate rise to a suspicion that copyists may not have been concerned with which exemplar they used for any particular individual record. The possibility of witness conflation could therefore not be ignored. Given the situation, there was a clear need for a full evaluation of all manuscripts, without recourse to the existing editions. Here we describe the process used by a single scholar with training in computer programming to produce a full critical edition of four key excerpts from the *Chronicle* (roughly 5,000 words; Andrews 2009).

Digital workflow for edition

In order to cope with the large volume of text, and to get to grips with the problem of recovering the history of its transmission, the editor chose to embrace digital methods from a very early stage; the decision was facilitated by the editor's prior expertise in computer programming. While some of the methods used are today more easily available to scholars without a computational background, not all of them are, and the philologist who chooses to use digital methods is still best advised to have some computational expertise (whether of his or her own, or hired into the team).

The first requirement was to transcribe as many witnesses as possible into a digital format, as efficiently as could be managed. This was accomplished through the use of OCR (optical character recognition) to digitize the printed edition of 1898, and successive modification of copies of the digitized text to produce full transcriptions of all witnesses. The resulting transcriptions were converted through an automatic process into a digital format suitable for interchange, based on the TEI guidelines for XML encoding of scholarly texts (see General introduction § 2.1). This was by far the most time-consuming stage of the project, although the total time taken was still less than would have been required for the digitization and correction of a base text of the *Chronicle*, and a sufficiently detailed, accurate, and unambiguous non-normalized collation of all witnesses against that text. Although the transcription process described was designed specifically for the edition project, the common scholarly need for a good system for manuscript transcription has more recently borne fruit. Options include the eLaborate system maintained by Huygens ING in the Netherlands (<https://www.elaborate.huygens.knaw.nl/>), the T-Pen system maintained by the Center for Digital Theology at St Louis University (<http://t-pen.org/TPEN/>), and the transcription environment for New Testament texts maintained by the Institut für Neutestamentliche Textforschung in Münster (<http://ntvmr.uni-muenster.de>).

The next step was to collate the transcriptions of the witnesses. The aim of the exercise was to compare all witnesses against each other without assigning any single witness greater significance than the others, and so the traditional form of collation against a base text was rejected. Instead the editor submitted the transcribed excerpts to an automatic collation program, in which a 'baseless' comparison method was used to produce a collated text. The result was available both in spreadsheet format and in a form of TEI XML known as 'parallel segmentation'. The editor was then able to review and, where necessary, correct the collation proposed by the software. The total time needed to produce a detailed collation (i.e. a collation that included minor variation as well as major) of the text to be edited, from the initial invocation of the program to the final correction of results, was approximately an hour and a half. The collation program used in this case was developed in 2008, specifically for this project; its source code is available online (<https://github.com/tla/ncritic/>). Since then other collation programs have emerged for general use, among which CollateX (<http://collatex.net/>) best fits the requirements for baseless collation of an arbitrarily large number of witness texts. For collation against a single base text, the best tool currently available is probably Juxta (<http://www.juxtasoftware.org/>).

With the collation stored in a machine-readable format, it was the work of a few hours to produce a script to transform the data into a format appropriate for use in programs for the construction of stemma hypotheses, such as statistical packages for cladistics and other phylogenetic analysis. Although these packages do not produce stemmata per se, they give a very useful preliminary indication of how the manuscripts are related to each other. With that knowledge, and with information about the provenance of the manuscripts and information contained in colophons, derivation of a reasonable stemma became possible. The scripts necessary for stemmatic analysis were also developed within the context of the edition project. A better option today would be to use the tools available on the Stemmaweb site (<http://stemmaweb.net/>); alternatively, scholars using the Classical Text Editor software have an option for generation of an appropriate data file for direct use in the statistical packages. Some of these are also online, for example the parsimony tools provided by the Institut Pasteur (<http://mobyle.pasteur.fr/>).

Another advantage conferred by a machine-readable collation is the ability to work through the text systematically and efficiently for editorial consideration and selection of a lemma text. For this purpose another script was written to step through each of the instances of variation and accept input from the user/editor; this was used in the first instance to classify the variation (for example, to categorize certain parallel readings as variations in spelling of the same word) so that the information could be taken into account for generation of stemmatic hypotheses. The use of the tool ensured that these classification decisions were applied uniformly throughout the text.

Once a stemma hypothesis was created, the editor used the same script to step through the variants again and choose a lemma reading, taking into account the stemma and the surrounding context and recording an emendation or editorial note wherever necessary. (This script, developed in the context of the edition project, has not yet been reproduced in a form more accessible to textual scholars, although the ability to classify variants prior to stemmatic analysis exists within the Stemmaweb system.) The choices of lemma, emendations, and annotations were saved into the collation file itself.

Publication of the digitally-edited text

In recent years, primarily driven by the European COST action 'Interedition' which ran from 2008 until 2012, there has developed an ever more robust tool-chain for the creation of digital editions, from transcription and linking of text to manuscript images, through automated collation, to stemmatic and stylistic analysis. Nevertheless, the scholar who wishes to publish a completed critical edition in digital form faces the difficulty that there is essentially no standard and well-supported way to do it.

In the case of the excerpts of the *Chronicle*, the immediate requirement was for a printed version of the text to be published as part of a Ph.D. thesis. This was relatively straightforward to accomplish: since the edited text was stored in a machine-readable format, the editor was able to prepare the edition for print by converting it programmatically into a format suitable for use with the LaTeX publishing package (<http://www.latex-project.org>).

The process of digital publication has been more complex, due to the lack of a standard framework, layout, or interface for digital critical editions. A satisfactory online critical edition should include all witness transcriptions (with facsimiles, if copyright restrictions allow), the edited text with all relevant annotations, and a suitable display of the degree and location of variation within the text. In the case of the *Chronicle*, the fact that the text edition, its annotations, and the full witness transcriptions already existed in digital form meant that they needed only to be transformed to a form suitable for viewing through a browser. This has nevertheless required quite a bit of custom Web development that, at present, would need to be repeated and tailored to any subsequent text edition. Every text has its own unique character; every editor must make decisions about what features of the text are important to convey and how these might be visualized in the digital medium. A vast amount of work remains ahead of us to explore the possibilities.

References

Andrews 2009; Matthew of Edessa 1869, 1898; Smbat Sparapet 1980; Web sources: <https://www.elaborate.huygens.knaw.nl/>, last access October 2014; <https://github.com/tla/ncritic/>, last access October 2014; <http://www.juxtasoftware.org/>, last access October 2014; <http://www.latex-project.org>, last access October 2014; <http://mobyle.pasteur.fr/>, last access October 2014; <http://ntvmr.uni-muenster.de>, last access October 2014; <http://www.tei-c.org/>, last access October 2014; <http://t-pen.org/TPEN/>, last access October 2014.

3.2. The *Aksumite Collection*. Ethiopic multiple text manuscripts (ABa)

An Aksumite collection

This case-study is concerned with the texts transmitted in a multiple-text manuscript of 162 folia that is preserved in a small church in an isolated area at the border of Ethiopia and Eritrea, an area which was once the cradle of Christian civilization in the northern highlands of the Horn of Africa. The manuscript has no colophon and is not dated, but it contains a series of palaeographic and linguistic features which put it into relation with the Abbā Garimā Four Gospels books, as well as to other ancient biblical manuscripts, that probably make it the oldest non-biblical Ethiopic manuscript.

The example of the 'Aksumite Collection' is useful to highlight some specific features of Ethiopian philology that have not been sufficiently considered in the past years, with the exception of the field of biblical (New and Old Testament) philology (for a general presentation of the state of the art, current practices and innovative proposals in classical Ethiopian Philology, cf. Marrassini 1987, 1996, 2008a, 2008b, 272–273, 2009; Lusini 2005; Bausi 2006a, 2008b, 2010a). The case study of the 'Aksumite Collection' appears to be particularly interesting and fruitful for questions of *textual history*—that is, history of textual transmission and history of reception. It can also be used—though to a lesser extent—to show *how to deal* with editorial questions, since it has a very recent and still only partially accomplished editorial history.

The manuscript has probably remained in the same location for several centuries, thus escaping the attention of the metropolitan Ethiopian clergy and foreign visitors. It was discovered, digitized, and finally also restored only a few years ago. It has been affected by some losses that do not seem to prevent a reliable estimation of its original content, since only a small part of it seems to be lost. It contains approximately thirty-six main pieces of patristic, liturgical, and canonical literature, as well as a historical text that is a *unicum*. (They can be reckoned in different ways, depending on whether the sections and possible subsections are identified as independent texts.) A few of the texts in this recension are transmitted in other Ethiopic manuscripts as well; some were known in other recensions only, and a few were not known at all (see Bausi 1998, 2002a, 2003a, 2005a, 2006b, 2006c, 2012, 2013a; Dolbeau 2012). I have called it the 'Aksumite Collection', since it was apparently translated from Greek into Ethiopic in the Late Antique Aksumite period, probably also in an arrangement to some extent reflecting the present one in the *codex unicus* preserved to us (Ethiopia, Tegrāy, ʿUrā Qirqos, Ethio-SPaRe UM-39).

Albeit quite different in terms of precise content, the collection as a whole closely resembles and parallels the so-called *Sinodos*, 'Synod', an authoritative canonical work translated from Arabic in the thirteenth/fourteenth century, and widely circulated since then (far more than a hundred manuscripts of the *Sinodos* probably exist, the most ancient ones coming from the fourteenth/fifteenth centuries; see Bausi 1995b, 2010b). The *Sinodos* was believed on sound evidence to be derived from mediaeval Arabic textual recensions, but a few liturgical texts, although problematically mixed with later Arabic-based ones, were supposed to be more ancient and Greek-based. Among these texts transmitted in the *Sinodos*, particularly important is the Ethiopic version of the *Traditio apostolica* 'Apostolic Tradition', which is unanimously believed to transmit for some passages ancient materials going back to the most ancient phase of the textual tradition, corroborated by the fact that it matches the most ancient Latin version, which is presumed to transmit the earliest phase of the text, against the younger Coptic and Arabic versions (Bausi 2009, 2010c, 2011b).

Dynamics of the textual tradition of Ethiopic texts: Aksumite and Post-Aksumite

The evidence found in the manuscript of the 'Aksumite Collection' sheds new light on the enigmatic question of the coexistence in the *Sinodos* of texts with different *Vorlagen*, i.e. Greek- and Arabic-based versions. But let us have a brief look at the background.

The linguistic evidence (for example loanwords, misreadings, phonetic rendering, syntactic calques) has for a long time demonstrated that non-original Ethiopic texts were *directly* translated in different periods from two languages only: Greek, in the Aksumite period (from the fourth until probably not later than the seventh centuries, or even earlier) and Arabic (starting from the twelfth/thirteenth century on, at the earliest, and continuing for some centuries) in the Post-Aksumite period and throughout pre-modern times. Very isolated cases of translations from other languages, such as Latin, exist in modern times, but they have no relevance here. Purported translations from Aramaic and also Syriac in the Aksumite period have been hypothesized concerning biblical and apocryphal texts (New and Old Testament, New

Testament in the 'Diatessaron' recension, 'Book of Enoch'), but they have been ruled out by all detailed analysis of the evidence carried out so far. That Greek and Arabic are the languages from which Ethiopic texts were translated is nothing else but what is to be expected from the institutional dependence of the Ethiopian Church upon the Egyptian Church and the Patriarchate of Alexandria. It was the Church that practised, and to a large extent also controlled, together with the monarchy, every aspect of literary activity throughout the history of pre-modern Ethiopia. The Egyptian Church first used Greek, later Coptic, and then from the tenth century on, Arabic as the main literary language. The missing evidence for *direct* Ethiopic versions of Coptic-based texts has been variously and even convincingly explained by the asynchronous development of the Egyptian and Ethiopian Churches (Bausi – Camplani 2013, 207–210).

The 'Aksumite Collection' preserves an Ethiopic version of the *Traditio apostolica* that is, on the one hand, a translation independent from the Ethiopic version in the *Sinodos* (save for some passages; see below), and on the other hand, much more strictly parallel to the Latin than any other known versions and witnesses. Moreover, it also appears that the few passages in the *Sinodos* recension matching the Latin version belong to the same recension as that in the 'Aksumite Collection', which demonstrates that these passages descend from one and the same version going back to a common archetype. It should be noted that the 'Apostolic Tradition' is lost in its Greek original, and the series of reworkings in different languages and times it has undergone have made it appear as a piece of 'living literature' (Bradshaw et al. 2002, 13–14). The debated question of the existence of such an original might be considered outdated now, due to the existence itself of the Ethiopic version in the 'Aksumite Collection' that strictly matches the Latin version (preserved within the 'Veronese Collection' of the manuscript Verona, Biblioteca Capitolare, Codex LV [53]): this matching certainly presupposes a relatively precise and unitary recensional phase, to be identified with the Greek original. This evidence is strengthened by the presence of a considerable amount of common features in distant lateral areas (Latin domain, Egypt and Horn of Africa).

Points of view: backward and forward connexions

As stated before, the manuscript also contains in eight leaves a historical text that is an absolute unicum in the Ethiopic tradition. This text is somehow prefixed to the collection, since it immediately follows the opening text (a pseudo-apostolic section, so-called 'Statutes of the Apostles', known in the original Greek as well as in several oriental versions). It is a 'History of the Episcopate of Alexandria' from Mark the Apostle to Saint Peter bishop of Alexandria (the 'last of the martyrs'), which is exceptional in consideration of two aspects.

First, no literary text dating from the Aksumite period and of historiographical genre has been transmitted in Ethiopic manuscripts thus far (Baumeister 2006, 41–42; the inscriptions written at the initiative of the kings of Aksum are obviously not texts transmitted by manuscripts, cf. Lusini 2001; Witakowski 2012). Second, the historical text may be identified as belonging to a lost Greek 'History of the Alexandrian Episcopate' (not to be confused with the later Copto-Arabic 'History of the Patriarchs of Alexandria'). This text has been traced in collections (one Latin excerpt consisting of two letters and a narrative portion in between, in the manuscript Verona, Biblioteca Capitolare, Codex LX [58]) as well as works (Sozomen's *Ecclesiastical History*, also hagiographies in Latin versions; see Camplani 2003a, 41–42, 51, 2003b, 38–39, 2006, 2007, 2008, 2009, 2011a, 2011b; Bausi – Camplani 2013). Yet the 'Aksumite Collection' is for most of the passages the unique witness of the 'History', it preserves the *incipit* and *desinit* (at least for this recension), and therefore provides by far the most important evidence for reconstructing the original text.

This situation is further complicated by the relationship this historiographical text entertains with, on the one hand, (and looking backwards) its sources, of which the 'History' is a witness, and on the other hand, (looking forwards) its later reworkings, which are textual witnesses of the 'History'. We can establish that the anonymous author of this 'History' also consulted and at times inserted materials drawn from the Alexandrian archives, as it was customary in Church historiography, also incorporating documents into the narrative text (in this case: biographical notes, lists of bishops appointed by Maximus (264–282), Theonas (282–300?), and Peter (300–311), and official correspondence). But we can also determine that quotations from this 'History' survive in a few Ethiopic texts from much later. One of them, an Ethiopian arrangement of the 'Acts of St Peter' attested in at least two fourteenth-century manuscripts, retains older materials and explicitly quotes passages of the 'Aksumite Collection', styling it the 'Synodicon of the

Law', which is probably the name the collection was to some extent still known by in the Ethiopian literary tradition at the time.

As it appears, the case of the 'Aksumite Collection' is extremely useful and seminal in that it highlights textual phenomena that were thus far hypothesized in Ethiopic only for the Bible, since the Ethiopic Bible was translated from the Greek in Aksumite times and subsequently revised in the Post-Aksumite period on the basis of Arabic texts, in turn also based upon Syriac. The collection positively documents the existence of double parallel independent translations, as is the case of the 'Apostolic Tradition' (there are several other texts not considered here; Bausi 2006b), also with older texts occasionally re-used within younger versions, and a redactional process that is very difficult to suppose in the absence of positive evidence. It also opens new perspectives for research. The 'Aksumite Collection' could not be an isolated case (only the preservation of the *codex unicus* that transmits it is, for the moment at least). On the contrary, one might think that the old Aksumite translations from the Greek were replaced with new translations from the Arabic. Peculiar cultural and linguistic features (obscure mirror-type translations which in the course of time became unintelligible, theologically outdated texts) might also have played a role (Bausi 2005b).

Editorial perspectives

Such a complex textual tradition can be viewed from several different perspectives, which might also require specific approaches and methodologies (see Ch. 3 § 2.1.2). I will try to elaborate briefly about a few of these:

(1) The first remark is that the case of the 'Ethiopic Collection' is a typical case-study of the philology of translated texts. The manuscript of the 'Aksumite Collection' is actually a witness to the Ethiopic translations of some Greek texts (i.e. the earlier versions, since some texts were later re-translated from a different *Vorlage*); because these translations took place in the early phase of Ethiopic literature, there are some factors to be considered that are not obvious, such as the possibility of linguistic variations, and the consequent question of defining standards—these are not easy to discern since the archaic palaeography of the manuscript witness also poses problems.

(2) The texts (in themselves also an innovation) shared by the 'Aksumite Collection' and partially or not by other Ethiopic manuscripts (such as in the *Sinodos* collection, *for some passages*), show that the 'Aksumite Collection' (apart from other palaeographic considerations) is not the archetype of these translations. The Ethiopic text of the earliest version must be reconstructed by taking into account all the extant Ethiopic witnesses: there are good readings (that can and must be checked against the extra-Ethiopic evidence) that must be preferred to the readings of the 'Aksumite Collection'. It must also be considered, however, that these supplementary witnesses do represent a different recension, as arranged in the *Sinodos*. This recension is also marked by shared innovations and conjunctive errors of its own, which points to a further textual stage, depending upon a subarchetype: the reconstruction of this subarchetype should be first undertaken before using it as a witness to the earliest Ethiopic version. This is a typical case of the twofold character of texts *subject to recensional reworking* placed along a chain of textual transmission (typically, translations are also such a case): they are potentially at the same time witnesses to the previous textual stage, and a subject of editorial reconstruction in themselves; looking forwards, this definitely concerns the 'Apostolic Tradition', reworked for some passages within a new, later and independent translation, and the 'History of the Episcopate of Alexandria', reworked for some passages in the 'Acts of Peter' of Alexandria, in this case possibly by additionally using other Aksumite materials.

(3) In keeping with what has been said on the twofold character of texts *subject to recensional reworking*, the earliest Ethiopic versions to be reconstructed starting from the manuscript of the 'Aksumite Collection' shall be edited, taking into account all parallel textual witnesses that might contribute evidence (for example, the oriental versions for the 'Apostolic Tradition', but above all the Latin version, and the same applies to the 'History of the Episcopate of Alexandria', which also requires the consideration of Latin excerpts). Obviously, since the Ethiopic version also represents to some extent a recension of its own in comparison with the others, every attempt at retrieving the earliest Ethiopic text shall consider that reconstructive hypotheses and conjectures are only reasonable if supported by, or compatible with, the available Ethiopic evidence; to define the extent of this process of analysis would be crucial, but it is extremely difficult: it is exactly the philological and text-critical domain where all possible competencies and evidence should be combined and contribute (historical, cultural, linguistic, stylistic, palaeographic pieces of evidence).

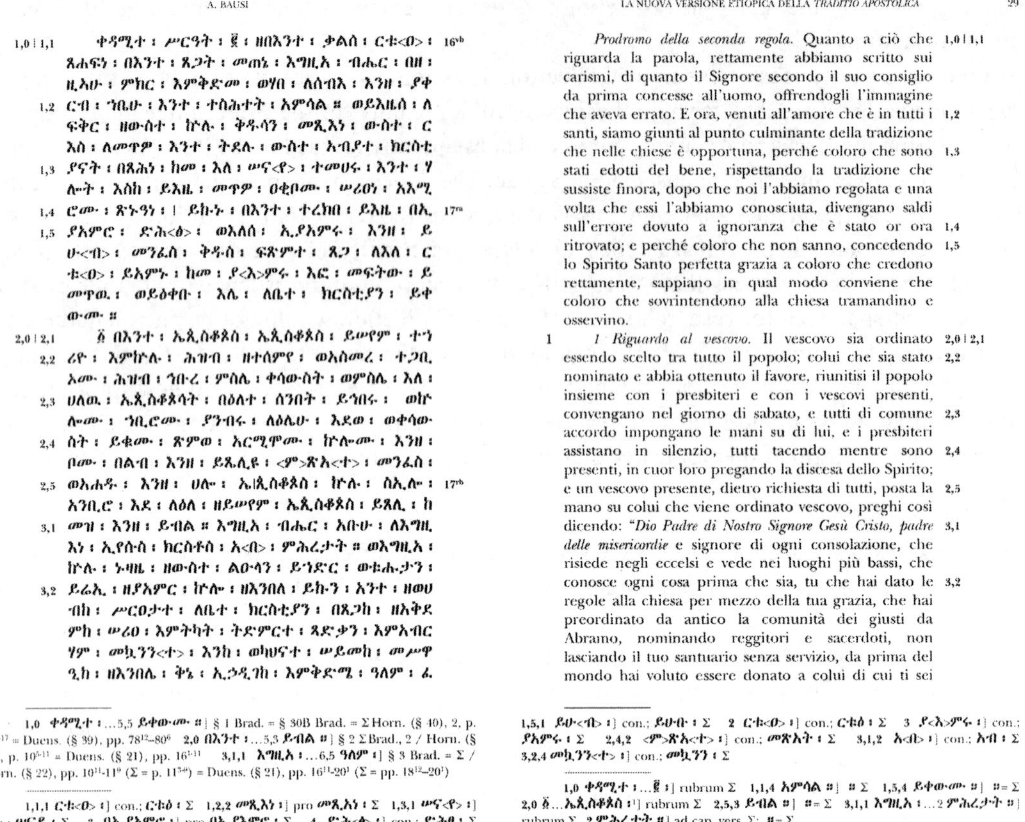

28 A. BAUSI

LA NUOVA VERSIONE ETIOPICA DELLA *TRADITIO APOSTOLICA* 29

Prodromo della seconda regola. Quanto a ciò che 1,0 | 1,1
riguarda la parola, rettamente abbiamo scritto sui
carismi, di quanto il Signore secondo il suo consiglio
da prima concesse all'uomo, offrendogli l'immagine
che aveva errato. E ora, venuti all'amore che è in tutti i 1,2
santi, siamo giunti al punto culminante della tradizione
che nelle chiese è opportuna, perché coloro che sono 1,3
stati edotti del bene, rispettando la tradizione che
sussiste finora, dopo che noi l'abbiamo regolata e una
volta che essi l'abbiamo conosciuta, divengano saldi
sull'errore dovuto a ignoranza che è stato or ora 1,4
ritrovato; e perché coloro che non sanno, concedendo 1,5
lo Spirito Santo perfetta grazia a coloro che credono
rettamente, sappiano in qual modo conviene che
coloro che sovrintendono alla chiesa tramandino e
osservino.

1 *1 Riguardo al vescovo.* Il vescovo sia ordinato 2,0 | 2,1
essendo scelto tra tutto il popolo; colui che sia stato 2,2
nominato e abbia ottenuto il favore, riunitisi il popolo
insieme con i presbiteri e con i vescovi presenti,
convengano nel giorno di sabato, e tutti di comune 2,3
accordo impongano le mani su di lui, e i presbiteri
assistano in silenzio, tutti tacendo mentre sono 2,4
presenti, in cuor loro pregando la discesa dello Spirito;
e un vescovo presente, dietro richiesta di tutti, posta la 2,5
mano su colui che viene ordinato vescovo, preghi così
dicendo: "*Dio Padre di Nostro Signore Gesù Cristo, padre* 3,1
delle misericordie e signore di ogni consolazione, che
risiede negli eccelsi e vede nei luoghi più bassi, che
conosce ogni cosa prima che sia, tu che hai dato le 3,2
regole alla chiesa per mezzo della tua grazia, che hai
preordinato da antico la comunità dei giusti da
Abramo, nominando reggitori e sacerdoti, non
lasciando il tuo santuario senza servizio, da prima del
mondo hai voluto essere donato a colui di cui ti sei

Fig. 3.3.2.1 Bausi 2011b, 28–29.

(4) Looking backwards still, a further step is the attempt at reconstructing the common phase of a heavily reworked and varied text: this is typically the case of the 'Apostolic Tradition'. Whereas in this specific case there is little chance of reconstructing a consistent unitary text from textual witnesses that have varied and evolved under the pressure of practical needs in the course of time (the 'Aksumite Collection' is not exactly a practical liturgical text, however it behaves and can be considered as such to some extent), the reconstruction of common phases cannot be excluded: this is actually the case for the common Ethiopic-Latin stage and layer.

(5) The manuscript represented in this case-study, of course, can also be the object of a 'new philology' investigation, with reference to the specific role *this precise manuscript* of the 'Aksumite Collection' has played within its context of production and fruition, of which, at the moment at least, we can say very little. Yet it also definitely challenges the *exclusive* character of 'living literature' attributed to the 'Apostolic Tradition', that is one of its most important texts, since the precise convergence of two distant manuscript traditions (Latin and Ethiopic) points to a very low degree of fluidity and variation in the tradition (the same occurs for the 'History of the Alexandrian Episcopate') and leaves open the way to a possible reconstruction of common ancestors.

References

Baumeister 2006; Bausi 1995b, 1998, 2002a, 2003a, 2005a, 2005b, 2006a, 2006b, 2006c, 2008b, 2009, 2010a, 2010b, 2010c, 2011b, 2012, 2013a; Bausi – Camplani 2013; Bradshaw et al. 2002; Camplani 2003a, 2003b, 2006, 2007, 2008, 2009, 2011a, 2011b; Dolbeau 2012; Lusini 2001, 2005; Marrassini 1987, 1996, 2008a, 2008b, 2009; Witakowski 2012.

3.3. Private production of mediaeval Hebrew manuscripts (MBA)

The singular individual circumstances of mediaeval book production and transmission of Jewish texts in Hebrew script require a different approach to textual criticism and editorial methodology than most of the current critical approaches and practices. The production of Hebrew codices was never initiated by the intellectual establishments. Manuscripts were never fabricated in clerical, academic, or commercial copying centres. All the mediaeval Hebrew manuscripts were produced as a private enterprise, and they were likewise privately kept and consumed. They were either privately commissioned from independent hired scribes or were owner-produced books copied for the copyist's own use. The individual circumstances of Hebrew book production are firmly attested by approximately four thousand, mostly dated, mediaeval colophons. Less than half of them were copied by professional or semi-professional or even casual scribes commissioned by private people to produce books for them; the rest were prepared by learned users of books or scholars, for their own personal use. The phenomenon of manuscripts being copied by their owners prevailed in all the vast territories where Jews lived and reproduced literary texts in the high Middle Ages in the west and in the east (except for Yemen). Such a high rate of non-professional, personal copying reflects the extent of Jewish literacy and education, but it must also have affected the transmission of written texts and their versions. Whereas institutional and centralized book production and text dissemination enabled supervision and control over the propagation of texts and the standardization of versions, no authoritative guidance or monitoring could have been involved in the private transmission of texts in Hebrew characters.

Within the individual mode of Hebrew text reproduction there is a fundamental difference between texts reproduced by professional or hired scribes, and owner-produced texts. One is entitled to assume that the average hired scribe would have been consciously more loyal to his model, probably would have avoided critical and deliberate intervention in the transmission, yet would have been more fallible and vulnerable to the involuntary changes and mistakes conditioned by the mechanics of copying, while the scholar-copyist might intentionally interfere in the transmission, revise his exemplar, emend and reconstruct the text, add to it and modify it according to his knowledge, memory, conjecture or other exemplars, and indeed regard copying as a critical editing and not merely as duplicating. Moreover, logic suggests that scribes would tend to repeat mistakes in their models, while scholars-copyists would correct corrupted text. The individual mode of Jewish book production and the lack of institutional supervision and authoritative control over the dissemination of texts naturally contributed to this process. Indeed, these assumptions can be substantiated and verified by scholars-copyists' own statements in their colophons.

Reflexive colophons of learned copyists who produced books for their own use confirm the assumption with regard to their critical manner of copying and attest to the freedom with which they were interfering in the transmission of the text. They seem to have been confident that they were entitled, even obliged, to improve the copied text by their personal critical judgment. Copyists of user-produced books testify that their copying involved not only amending and restoring the corrupted model but also critically revising and editing it, sometimes while using several models and creating eclectic versions. The inclination to editorial intervention in transmission emerged only in the late Middle Ages, from the early fourteenth century.

While applying the genetic approach, stemmatical classification, Lachmannian editorial principles or intentional methodology to mediaeval manuscripts which were produced by professional scribes can be justified, at least for restoration of corrupted texts caused by the copying mechanisms, they are not valid at all in handling self-produced copies which constitute at least half of the extant manuscripts. Contrary to what one might expect, the high ratio of user-produced manuscripts and the critical reproduction of texts did not necessarily improve the transmission of literary works by eliminating their scribal mistakes and restoring their authentic versions, but often engendered scholarly modifications, revisions and re-creations of the copied text that may very well have distorted and transformed the original work. Although the copies of hired scribes may have been corrupted by accumulated scribal errors, there is a fairly good chance that modern editors and textual critics would be able to detect a significant part of them by applying philological methods of conventional textual criticism. The versions created by learned copyists on the basis of several exemplars or by scholarly conjecture, on the other hand, mixed inextricably disparate channels of transmission or conflated different authorial stages of the text and were dominated by personal choices and judgments. Such versions present artificial and contaminated texts that mislead modern critical editors in their attempt to classify and integrate them within the chain of transmission. In this respect, the damage inflicted on the text by the consecutive reproductions of professional scribes, vulnerable as they were in the traps of the copying mechanism, can be much more easily discerned and the authentic text reconstructed than is the case with damage caused by the scholarly improvement of user-produced books, which is often irreversible.

The role of the modern editor of Hebrew texts inevitably has to be reduced. Stemmatic analysis is usually thwarted and any reconstruction of archetypes in various editorial methods does not fit the singular ways in which Hebrew texts were transmitted and should be avoided. Synoptic editing seems to be the safest way and should be recommended, particularly when it is considerably facilitated in our digital age. Yet even when presenting a diplomatic edition of a single manuscript refraining from critical intervention in the text itself there is still sometimes a justification to integrate genealogical criticism. When the number of the manuscripts is too large for a synoptic presentation, or when they represent distant versions, it is justified to combine diplomatic and synoptic methods by grouping versions, while each is represented by one base manuscript accompanied by an *apparatus criticus* of its group. In the latter case, when several versions are separated in parallel columns, one is entitled sometimes to consider deviation from the rigid Bédier method and be assisted by genealogical or eclectic criticism *within each version group* when necessary. Limiting critical reconstruction while not entirely eliminating the critical aspiration of the genealogical theory, may be justified in these cases.

References

Beit-Arié 2000, 2014; Milikowsky 1988; Schäfer 1986, 1989; Schäfer – Milikowsky 2010.

3.4. Christian Apocrypha in Armenian (VC)

Closing of the canon and Christian apocryphal literature

The notion of Apocrypha is closely related to the constitution of the canon of the New Testament books, which was the result of a long process of selection that each eastern and western Christian community elaborated in its own way. By the fourth century there seems to be a consensus about the contours of the New Testament collection in most Christian communities, with the exception of some texts which remain of uncertain status, such as the *Revelation of John* and certain Epistles. The closing of the canon, issued from this selection and consensus, caused very old texts, which until then were regarded with authority, to take second place or, in certain cases, to be rejected. As soon as the works of the canonical collection imposed their authority as the only authentic accounts of the words of Christ and early Christianity, the works excluded from such a canon, considered as 'apocryphal', started to be progressively disregarded, being considered either forgeries, questionable, or even heretical products (for a definition of 'Apocryphal literature', see Junod 1992). This hostile attitude toward apocryphal literature had consequences for the textual transmission of these works. Without being fixed by ecclesiastical usage that could guarantee these texts some form of stability, certain Apocrypha simply disappeared, or survived only in a fragmentary form. Furthermore, other texts became subject to the opprobrium of censorship, thus being corrected to such an extent that it is now difficult to recover their primitive content. This programme of 'purging' these texts did not take place in a homogeneous way among the different communities. The ancient oriental versions, including the Armenian ones, sometimes preserve a state of the text that is closer to the original than that preserved in the manuscripts written in the original language (often Greek). Thus, the ancient translations constitute important witnesses for the reconstruction of the primitive text.

In some cases, the lack of institutional supervision—a supervision that was conversely sometimes applied to canonical texts, concerning which not even a jot could be changed—had a different consequence and allowed extremely unstable transmission of western and oriental apocryphal texts, as well as their continuous rewriting and amplification. In this regard, it is important to stress that even after the fourth century and the closing of the canon, the different western and eastern Christian communities continued to write, and rewrite, apocryphal texts. Often, apocryphal writings have developed multiple textual forms through processes of abridgement, expansion, paraphrase and other editorial rewritings. Confronted with the 'movable' nature of this literature, an editor of texts should not ignore the recent results of the 'Nouvelle critique littéraire' and of the New Criticism, and especially its new approaches to such concepts as 'text', 'author', 'authority', and 'authorship' (for an introduction to the question, see Compagnon 1998, 2000; see also, in France, the classical essays by Barthes 1984 and Foucault 1994).

The Christian Apocrypha in Armenian

The Christian Apocrypha in Armenian are a rich corpus still largely unexplored. After the invention of the Armenian alphabet, at the beginning of the fifth century, Armenians took a keen interest in literature that was later regarded as apocryphal, translating from Greek and Syriac, and creating their own versions. Armenians manifested much interest in the apostolic traditions (Leloir 1986–1992). Almost all the most ancient apocryphal Acts related to the different apostles (second or third century) were known and translated, at least partially. The text that has often been preferred is the final section of such *Acts*, i.e. the *Martyrdom* (or the *Dormition*, in the case of the *Acts of John*), as it was easy to use for liturgical purposes because of its limited length. This was certainly well suited to be read on the day of the commemoration of each apostle. Among the Apocrypha related to Jesus, the Armenian tradition preserves the works that deal with Jesus' birth and infancy, and the Passion cycle. The Marian cycle includes, among others, the *Dormition*, the *Epistle of pseudo-Dionysius the Areopagite to Titus*, the *Apocalypse of Mary,* as well as other Panegyrics and Homilies. In addition to the *Apocalypse of Mary*, the apocalyptic genre includes the *Apocalypse of Paul*, and an apocryphal *Apocalypse of John*. Among the epistles, undoubtedly the most important are those that form the *Correspondence between Paul and the Corinthians*, which, for a certain period of time, must have been canonical in Armenian, under the influence of the Syriac canon.

As in other eastern and western traditions, apocryphal Armenian Christian texts also lent themselves to many possibilities of transformation and new regeneration. Manuscripts that remain often contain traces of several alterations, which may include single words, phrases or entire sections. Predisposition to a continual rewriting is undoubtedly one of the key dimensions of this literature. The complexity of the transmission of apocryphal texts often pushes the method of textual criticism to its limits and forces scholars to ask themselves the following questions. How to deal with variations and changes, sometimes very abundant, which characterize the manuscripts preserving the Apocrypha? What were the editorial practices followed in the past and what can we suggest for further investigations?

The editorial methods and practices adopted by the Mekhitarist Fathers and by Paul Vetter

The first and in most cases the only editions of Christian apocryphal texts in Armenian language are due to the Mekhitarist Fathers of Venice, starting from the end of the nineteenth century. It was in 1898 that a work entirely dedicated to Christian Apocrypha appeared with the title of *Ankanon girkʿ nor ktakaranacʿ* (Uncanonical Books of the New Testament, ed. Tayecʿi). This work was the second volume of the series *Tʿangaran haykakan hin ew nor dprutʿeancʿ* (Museum of Ancient and New Armenian Literature), which was preceded by the publication of the *Ankanon girkʿ hin ktakaranacʿ* (Uncanonical Books of the Old Testament, ed. Yovsepʿeancʿ), in 1896. In 1904 a third volume dedicated to the apostolic legends was published, the *Ankanon girkʿ aṙakʿelakankʿ* (Uncanonical Books on the Apostles, ed. Čʿrakʿean). The editorial methods and practices adopted by the Mekhitarist Fathers are based on principles that are very easy to sum up: the choice of a base manuscript, called the *bnagir*, and the conservative editing of a single manuscript text (best manuscript method); the preparation of a very succinct apparatus offering imprecise indications of readings of auxiliary manuscripts (*ōrinak mə* 'an exemplar', *miws ōrinak* 'another exemplar'); and a study almost exclusively of the manuscripts of the easily accessible Venice collections.

Towards the end of the nineteenth century the German scholar Paul Vetter had also begun a project of edition of apocryphal texts, basing his editions essentially on manuscripts of the Bibliothèque nationale de France. Unlike the *Ankanon girkʿ* collections, Vetter's volumes were enriched with translations and, sometimes, a Greek retroversion. But, as explicitly stated in the 1906 edition of the *Acts of Peter and Paul*, Vetter considered it useless to continue his editorial work, having heard about the parallel enterprise begun by the Mekhitarists.

New perspectives

Even though the enterprise of the Mekhitarist Fathers does not meet the rigorous requirements of modern textual criticism, their pioneering work was immense and saved a whole corpus of Armenian literature from oblivion. Nonetheless, today these texts should be re-edited using modern principles of text edition. A study of the textual traditions that characterize Christian apocryphal texts shows the difficulties that editors often have to face. Sometimes such difficulties can be compared to those faced by editors of Mediaeval texts and stem from the conditions of transmission that are typical of apocryphal texts (Cerquiglini 1989). It is essential to appreciate their textual fluidity, for which the fixity of the printed page is a poor representation.

Which attitude should be embraced when confronting such reworking and multiple textual forms? How should such texts be edited? At least two approaches are possible. 1) We can aspire to identify and edit only the most primitive version of the text. However, if we choose not to edit later reworkings, we deprive ourselves of important witnesses to the transmission history and the reception of the text, as well as of their implications for our understanding of the history of Christianity. 2) On the other hand, we can regard each recension as an interesting witness and decide to edit as many stages of the text as is feasible. In the second case, how to proceed when the number of recensions and their textual variants are so abundant that their inclusion in an apparatus is impractical? Should we edit each recension independently? This is the option sometimes adopted by the Mekhitarists. In the case of the *Martyrdom of Philip* (Calzolari 2013) and the *Gospel of Nicodemus* (Outtier 2010), two recensions were published on the same page, one above the other. The Mekhitarist Fathers sometimes chose to publish different recensions of a given text one after the other: for example the *Apocalypse of Paul* (four recensions), the *Protevangelium of James* (three recensions), and the *Infancy Gospel* (two recensions; ed. Tayecʿi 1898; see also Calzolari 2011; Dorfmann – Lazarev 2010; Terian 2008). In itself, a separate edition could be a diplomatic-interpretative one, and on this topic it is worth recalling the *caveat* of Cerquiglini about what he called the 'tentation fac-similaire' (Cerquiglini 1989, 43); the editor should avoid to step away from interpretation and choice, which should be the foundations of an edition. In the case of the *Anaphora Pilati*, the Mekhitarists adopted the principle of synoptic columns.

Martyrium Pauli (*MartP*)

(Final section, preserved in the Armenian MSS Pb Pc U F)[1]

Pb Pc	*U*	*F*
(Paraphrasis of *MartP* § 5, first section)		**(*MartP* § 5)**
1. *Եւ Ներոնն զայրացեալ ի վերայ արանցն այնոցիկ տայ ի ձեռս Պարթէնոսի եւ Փարոսի, զի տարցեն ի տեղի սպանմանն եւ փաղփաղակի հատցեն զգլուխն Պաւղոսի սրով:*	1. *Եւ Ներոնն զայրացեալ ի վերայ արանցն այնոցիկ տայ ի ձեռս Պարթէնոսի եւ Փարոսի, զի տարցեն ի տեղի սպանմանն եւ փաղփաղակի հատցեն զգլուխն Պաւղոսի սրով:*	1. Եւ մինչդեռ նոքա զայս խաւսէին, առաքեաց Ներոնն զՊարթենիոս եւ զՓերէս՝ տեսանել թէ զգլխատեա՞լ իցէ Պաւղոս:
2. Եւ մինչդեռ տանէին արքն զՊաւղոս ի տեղի սպանման խաւսէր վասն փրկութեան նոցա եւ հաւատոցն որ ի Քրիստոս եւ հանդերձեալ դատաստանին եւ յարութեան մեռելոց:		2. Եւ իբրեւ եկին, գտին զնա կենդանի: Եւ Պաւղոսի կոչեցեալ զնոսա առ ինքն ասէ. « Հաւատացէ՛ք ի կենդանին Աստուած, որ եւ զիս եւ զհաւատացեալս իւր յարուցանէ ի մեռելոց »:
Եւ նոքա ասեն. « Այժմ հրաման կայսեր կատարեսցի եւ յորժամ յարուցեալ երեւեսցիս որպէս ասացերն, յայնժամ հաւատասցուք յԱստուածն քո »:		Եւ նոքա ասեն. « Երթամք այժմ առ Ներոն: Եւ յորժամ մեռանիցիս դու եւ յարիցես, յայնժամ հաւատասցուք յաստուածն քո »:
Իսկ Ղոնկոս եւ Կեստոս աղաչէին զՊաւղոս վասն փրկութեան իւրեանց: Ասէ ցնոսա. « Ընդ արշալուսն առաւաւտուն, եկեալ ձեր ի գերեզման իմ՝ տեսանիցէք արս երկուս որ յաղաւթս կան՝ Ղուկաս եւ Տիտոս. նոքա լուսաւորեսցեն զձեզ »:		Եւ Ղունկոս եւ Կէստէս աղաչեցին զնա վասն փրկութեան իւրեանց: Ասաց Պաւղոս. « Ընդ աշալուսն եկեալ ձեր փաղփաղակի ի գերեզման իմ՝ գտանիցէք արս երկուս որ յաղաւթս կայցեն, Տիտոս եւ Ղուկաս. նոքա տացեն ձեզ զկնիքն Տեառն »: *Եւ կացեալ Պաւղոս յառաջոյ անտի յարեւելս կոյս՝ յաղաւթս եկաց յերկար, եւ կատարեալ զաղաւթսն եւ խաւսեալ եբրայեցերէն ընդ հարսն՝ ձգեալ զպարանոցն եւ այլ ոչ եւս խաւսեցաւ:*
	(*APeP*[2] 80a-c ; Č'[3] 24, 9-25)	**(*APeP* 80a-c ; Č' 24, 9-25)**
	3. (a) Եւ մինչդեռ տանէին զՊաւղոս զգլխատել հեռագոյն ի քաղաքէն,	**3. (a)** Եւ մինչդեռ տանէին զ<Պ>աւղոս ի զգլխատել՝ հեռագոյն ի քաղաքէն

[1] F = Yerevan, Matenadaran, arm 993 (a. 1456); Pb = Paris, Bibliothèque nationale de France, arm 110 (a. 1194); Pc = Paris, Bibliothèque nationale de France, arm 118 (a. 1307); U = Yerevan, Matenadaran, arm 994 (a. 1409).

[2] *APeP* = *Acta Petri et Pauli* (BHG[3] 1490-1491, CANT 193): M. Bonnet & R.A. Lipsius, *Acta Apostolorum Apocrypha*, vol. 1, Leipzig 1891 (Darmstadt 1959).

[3] Č' = K'. Č'rak'ean, *Ankanon girk' aṙak'elakank'*, Venice 1904.

Fig. 3.3.4.1 Calzolari, forthcoming.

This is the principle we adopted in our edition of the Armenian text of the *Acta Pauli* (Calzolari, forthcoming in the *Corpus Christianorum Series Apocryphorum*, Calzolari 2004) for the final section of the *Martyrdom of Paul*, which is known in multiple families of manuscripts in different, interpolated forms (Calzolari 2007). In particular, the *codex optimus* of the text—Yerevan, Matenadaran, 993—contains several interpolations from the final section of the Armenian translation of the *Acts of Peter and Paul*, a work which became more popular than the *Acts of Paul* since the third century, after the introduction of a common celebration of the two apostles in the liturgy, in the western and in the eastern Churches. The manuscript Matenadaran 993 is an interesting witness of the influence of this liturgical evolution on the transmission of the text. Some other interpolations or rewritings are contained in two other manuscripts (Paris, BnF, Arménien 110 and Yerevan, Matenadaran, 994). A synoptic presentation makes it possible to clearly show the differences between the three rewritten forms.

The case of the *Martyrdom of Paul* is easy to treat; more difficult is the case of the *Martyrdom of Philip* (new critical edition in progress by Emilio Bonfiglio) or the *Apocalypse of Paul*, which were transmitted in several recensions and in a great number of manuscripts. A century later, in order to solve such editorial issues, are we better equipped than the scholars who lived between the end of nineteenth and beginning of the twentieth century? As a general remark, we can stress that, of course, the philological criticism has its history now in Armenian studies also, especially in the field of Patristic literature, and we can learn from the experience of these modern editions. In addition, concerning the particular case of fluid transmission and multiple texts, we should pay more attention to the possibilities offered by computer tools, which with their memory and resources might be more capable of reproducing the variability of apocryphal works. Employing simultaneous screens, exploiting zoom effects, immediate approaches, moves in the text(s), as well as consulting data belonging to different groups in a collective action by means of windows, all this would be another way to visualize the different textual forms of a given text. All these actions are able to show the dynamic nature of a continuously evolving process of writing (Calzolari 2014a).

References

Barthes 1984; Calzolari 2004, 2007, 2011, 2013, 2014a, forthcoming; Cerquiglini 1989; Compagnon 1998, 2000; Č‘rak‘ean 1904; Dorfmann – Lazarev 2010; Foucault 1994; Junod 1992; Leloir 1986–1992; Outtier 2010; Tayec‘i 1898; Terian 2008; Vetter 1906; Yovsep‘eanc‘ 1896.

3.5. The Zoroastrian long liturgy. The transmission of the *Avesta* (AC)

The problems involved in the edition of Avestan texts have been discussed recently by West (2008), Hintze (2012b), and Cantera (2012b). The present case study concentrates upon the edition of the so-called 'long liturgy' (for an overview of the Avestan tradition see General introduction § 3.3).

The Zoroastrian 'long liturgy' in reverence of the god Ahura Mazdā has been celebrated in the form in which it appears in the manuscripts (or in a similar form) since Achaemenid times (*c*.550–330 BCE) and continues to be celebrated today among the Parsis, the Zoroastrians in India. Throughout the centuries this liturgy has been one of the most characteristic features of the Zoroastrian community.

The liturgy of the ceremony in question was composed at different stages in eastern Iran, before the Achaemenid times. The liturgy was exported to western Iran, the centre of the Achaemenid power, probably during the Achaemenid reign. The version of the liturgy that appears in the manuscripts represents the western Iranian transmission, where Avestan, the language in which the recitative was composed, was not the performers' native language. Centuries of transmission in western Iran, preceding the beginning of the written transmission, have obviously left some traces in the linguistic form of the recitative.

There are different variants of the ceremony. The most basic one is the daily ceremony, known as the *Yasna*. For more solemn celebrations, an extended form (the *Yašt ī Vispered*) is used, which includes some additional ritual actions and texts as well as variants of some parts of the *Yasna* ceremony. The *Yasna* is the basis for a series of liturgies ('intercalation ceremonies'), in which other texts are intercalated between the central texts (the *Gāthās* and the *Yasna Haptaŋhāiti*). The central texts are composed in Old Avestan, an older layer of the Avestan language.

The Great Avesta, the hyparchetypes and the Ritual Avesta

In Sassanian times there were two different collections of Avestan texts: (1) the *Great Avesta*, a scholastic collection of all known Avestan texts at Achaemenid times and (2) a series of recitatives of some rituals still celebrated in the Avestan language. This distinction has only recently been given serious consideration (Kellens 1998). However, it has enormous consequences for the editorial practice of the Avestan texts, and especially for the edition of the long liturgy. Another important distinction to draw is that between manuscripts produced for liturgical and for exegetical purposes (see also General introduction § 3.3).

The editorial practice of the Avestan textual heritage has always assumed that there was continuity between a Sassanian 'archetype' written down at the time of the invention of the Avestan script (see General introduction § 3.3) and the extant manuscripts. The obvious discrepancies between the contents of the assumed archetype of the *Great Avesta* and the texts contained in the manuscripts have been explained recurring to the hypothesis of a series of shorter hyparchetypes, to be dated around the tenth century, which were regarded as being nothing but fragments saved from the *Great Avesta*. Karl Hoffmann believed that he had provided a decisive philological argument for the hypothesis of the hyparchetypes (Hoffmann 1969). In *Yasna* 12.3, the manuscripts of the different classes show variant readings that allow us to reconstruct a common reading *ziiåiienīm* for all of them. This, however, is likely to be a corruption of *ziienīm*: an early scribe mistakenly wrote *ziiå*, noticed his error, marked *iiå* with deletion dots and continued writing the rest of the word (*iienīm*). Later copyists failed to note the deletion dots and hence wrote *ziiåiienīm*. Since this corrupted form appears in the *Yasna* manuscripts as well as in the other witnesses of the long liturgy, and in liturgical as well as in exegetical manuscripts, this seems to imply that all manuscripts of the long liturgy (of every type and origin) go back to a single hyparchetype. Similar arguments were brought forward by Humbach (1973) for the collection of short liturgies as well as for the *Vidēvdād*, a collection of prescriptions for keeping the demons away. Thus the linearity of the transmission seemed to be granted.

The first direct consequence this view of the transmission has for the editorial praxis is the preference for the exegetical manuscripts above the liturgical ones. Since the descriptions of the *Great Avesta* in the Pahlavi literature are based upon the Pahlavi translation, it has been assumed that the codices of the *Great Avesta* contained the Avestan text along with its Pahlavi translation. Accordingly, the exegetical manuscripts were considered to go back more or less directly to the Sassanian archetype, and were taken to be the source of the liturgical manuscripts. The liturgical usage of these texts was believed to have been secondary, and accordingly, the liturgical manuscripts were deemed secondary as well. Therefore, the editions were based mainly upon the exegetical manuscripts.

The liturgical manuscripts attest to different variants of the long liturgy, compiled for different purposes and dates. Actually, only the daily ceremony is included in complete form in the exegetical manuscripts. Other variants of the long liturgy that exist include only the sections that do not appear in the daily ceremony and therefore needed a translation. Thus, the exegetical manuscripts of the solemn ceremony (*Visperad*) include only a selection of fragments of the complete liturgy, which do not form a coherent text. Nevertheless, our editions of this ceremony are based on the exegetical manuscripts, and therefore contain just the fragments included in them, without indication that they are fragments disseminated in different sections of the ceremony. By consequence, some modern translations render these fragments as if they together formed a coherent text, and not as different alternatives or extensions of some sections of the *Yasna*.

A further consequence of the dependence of the available editions from the Pahlavi manuscripts is that the ritual instructions have been discarded in the editions. The liturgical manuscripts include—together with the recitative in Avestan language—ritual instructions in Pahlavi, Persian, or Gujarati which are essential for understanding the course of the liturgy. Cf. figs. 3.3.5.1–2 which contrast a section of the beginning of the long liturgy as it appears in Karl Geldner's 1885–1896 edition and in an edition based upon the liturgical manuscripts.

A new edition of the long liturgy must therefore be based primarily upon the liturgical manuscripts. It must reproduce the ritual variety, including the different variants pertaining to different types of ceremonies, different days and celebrations, and indicate the different options for the mobile sections that alternated in every performance (Cantera 2010). Accordingly, numerous sections of the text must be represented in several variants. Each variant must have a special numeration and be edited in such a way that the correspondence with the sections in other variants of the liturgy is recognizable. I have published on-line provisional versions of each variant of the liturgy (<http://ada.usal.es/pages/completeceremonies>) and created a synoptic table of the correspondences (<http://ada.usal.es/pages/table>). Former editions (as well as the recent revised editions of Geldner's text) provide only the standard version of the daily ceremony without any other variant, mainly due to their dependence on the exegetical manuscripts that include only the standard daily ceremony.

The ritual character of the manuscripts challenges their supposed dependence on a single archetype as well. For centuries, these ceremonies had been orally performed and transmitted. The priests knew them by heart, since the use of manuscripts was not allowed during the performance. The invention of the Avestan script provided a new, complementary tool for learning the recitatives and ritual instructions. Our manuscripts are thus guides for learning the right performance of the liturgy. Based on their own liturgical knowledge, many priests created new manuscripts at different historical stages. In fact, as late as the sixteenth century, new manuscripts were copied not only from older written sources, but as well directly from the ritual practice and knowledge of the scribe. For instance, the non-dated manuscript 231 (Pune, Bhandarkar Oriental Research Institute, Bh5) shows clear traces of having been recorded directly from the actual recitation, as we can see from the differences that exist in an Iranian manuscript originating from a written source (Y1.3):

100 (Library of the Bombay University, Geldner's B3)

asnaiie.biiō. aši. rataobaiiō. hāuuane. aṣ̌aone. ašahe. raθaβi. niuuae: šāuuṇŋhē.

vīšiiāica. aṣ̌aonae. ašhe. raθaβe. nauue: maiθarahe. vōuro.gōiiaōitōiš. hazṇŋ́hari.ɤošhe.

bēuuaracašmanō. aoxtō.nāmanō. yazatahe. rāmanō. x́āštarae.

Many features of manuscript 231 reveal a clear influence of the recitation such as for example the use of ē̆ for *aē* (*nauue*^{a} for *niuuaēδaiiemi*; *bēuuaracašmanō* for *baēuuarə.casmanō*); of ō̆ for *ao* (*vōuro.gōiiaōitōiš* for *vōuru.gaōiiaōtōiš*, *hazṇŋ́hari.ɤošhe* for *hazaŋra.gaōšahe*), of *-ae* for *-ahe* (*x́āštarae* for *xvāstrahe*) and the total confusión between *s*, *š* and *ṣ̌* (*šāuuṇŋhē* for *sāuuaŋhəe*, *vīšiiāica* for *vīsiiāica*, *x́āštarae* for *xvāstrahe*), etc.

It is the ritual uniformity—and not a continuous process of more or less careful copying from one single original—that is responsible for the homogeneity of the manuscripts, as well as for some mistakes common to all of them. Efforts have been made indeed at different times and with different methods to keep the celebration of the long liturgy homogeneous throughout a vast territory (at least in Iran and Gujarat). Manuscripts were one tool for this; others include a carefully maintained oral tradition, travelling priests, and frequent contacts and consultations between the two communities (especially from the Indian Parsi community to their Iranian co-religionists). We have been able to determine how in modern times

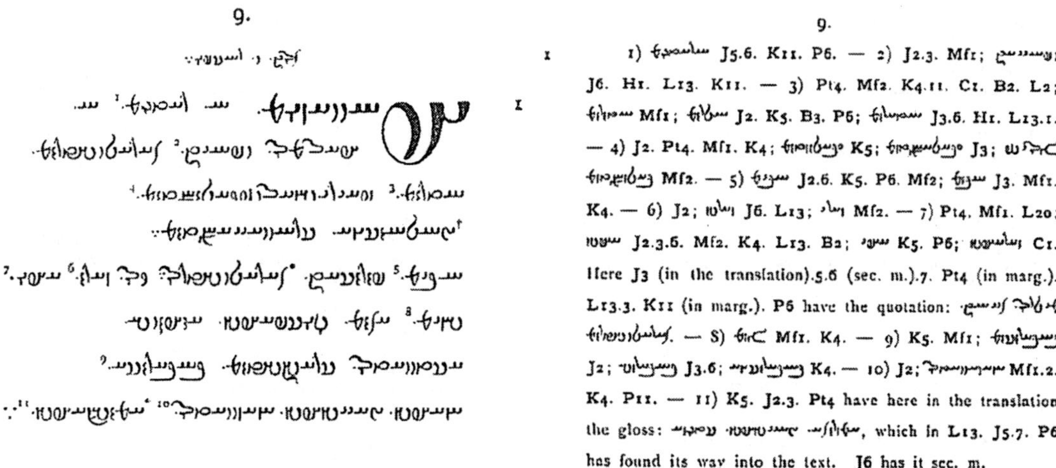

Fig. 3.3.5.1 Geldner's 1885–1896 edition of Y. 9.1 (details of pp. 38 and 39 combined).

certain readings became fashionable and spread from manuscripts of different types to other types over thousands of kilometres (Cantera 2012a, 304 and following). Similar processes can be assumed for older times and could be responsible for wrong readings shared by all manuscripts, like *ziiāiienīm* in *Yasna* 12.3, an error that was first produced in the written transmission, then entered the ritual practice and is indeed the form recited today (for another obvious example cf. Cantera 2012a).

There was thus a reciprocal influence between the written transmission and the ritual practice. Since the text copied from a manuscript (often drawn up in its turn by the scribe's own quill) had previously been acquired and learnt by heart, either completely or at least partially, and recited daily over years by the scribes, unconscious influences were unavoidable. Furthermore, the aim, when copying a manuscript, was not to produce a faithful copy of a given original, but a trustworthy guide to the performance of the ritual. In this way, manuscripts were consciously adapted to the current liturgical practice. This adaptation concerns small changes in the recitative and in the ritual, as well as in the phonetics of the recitation.

The infinite variant readings

The direct influence of the ritual performance on the manuscripts is at the root of the most noteworthy particularity of the Avestan transmission: it does show a great homogeneity regarding the wording (the text of each variant of the liturgy is almost identical in all manuscripts, with only minor differences between the Indian and the Iranian manuscripts), but every single word of the text appears in an almost infinite number of variant readings. Even within the same manuscript, every word will very often be spelt differently in different attestations (see fig. 3.3.5.3).

The choice of the right variant and, generally, the handling of this huge amount of readings of every single word is one of the main difficulties awaiting any editor of an Avestan text. Traditionally, editors have been very selective about the number of readings to quote. The undisputed superiority of Geldner's edition is hence to be attributed to the fact that his apparatus is much more complete than the one provided by former editors such as Niels Ludvig Westergaard. Nevertheless, Geldner's apparatus is chaotic, far from being exhaustive, and it does not enable readers to know the exact form they will find in the quoted manuscripts (since he unifies the variants in groups of manuscripts containing similar but not necessarily identical readings).

Most of these variants are minimal and do not change the understanding of the text. Nevertheless, they are important for a linguistic analysis. Therefore, simply to dispense with quoting all these minor variants cannot be the right solution. The most convenient method seems to be setting up a typological classification of the variants that allows us to accumulate them in different apparatuses. There are indeed some types of variants that can be put together in apparatuses to be printed separately (at the end of the edition or in a separate volume), namely palaeographic, orthographic, and phonetic variant readings.

Indian and Iranian manuscripts do exhibit both palaeographic (for example, the use of a different letter for *ą* or for initial *y*, etc.) and orthographic divergences (such as the different spelling of the diphthongs *ao*, *ae*, etc.). These kinds of variants should be included in the apparatus, since the distribution is not constant in all the manuscripts. The majority of readings are phonetic variations. Apart from a certain

hwmst' bwn
Y9.1
hāuuanīm. ā. ratūm. ā.
haōmō. upāit̰. zaraϑuštrəm.
ātrəm. pairi.yaōždaϑəṇtəm.
gāϑåsca. srāuuaiiaṇtəm.
ādim. pərəsat̰. zaraϑuštrō.
kō. narə. ahi. yim. azəm.
vīspahe. aŋhəuš. astuuatō.
sraēštəm. dādarəsa.

Y9.1,7 kō…10 aməṣ̌ahe] cf. H2.10 **8 vīspahe…astuuatō]** cf. Yt1.2. 1.4. Yt8.54. Yt13.152. Yt19.79. V18.30. 31. P27 (28). Vyt36

1 hwmst bwn] 20. 2010. 2030. 2102. 2104. 2106. 4000. 4010. 4025. 4040. 4050. 4055. 4060. 4140 **Y9.1,2** 20. 40. 60. 83. 100. 110. 120. 230. 234. 235. 400. 409. 410. 415. 420. 450. 500. 510. 530. 613. 677. 682. 2010. 2040. 2101. 2200. 4000. 4010. 4020. 4025. 4031. 4040. 4045. 4050. 4055. 4060. 4100. 4140. 4200. 4210. 4220. 4230. 4240. 4250. 4400. 4410. 4420. 4510. 4515. 5020. 231. 681. 15. 82. 84. 408. 602. 605. 683. 2030. 2104. 2106. 2230. 4065. 4070. 4080. 4320. 4340. 4360. 4440. 4450. 4500. 4503. 4504. 4506. 4507. 5102. 418 | ā[1]] 2200. 4230. 2230] **3 zaraϑuštrəm]** 40. 2200. 4230. 2230] **5 gāϑåsca]** 4050]

1 hwmst] 2010. 2030. hwmstwn 20. hwm st' 2104. 4010. 4025. 4040. 4050. 4055. 4060. hwm yšt 2106. | **hwmst bwn]** *hwmst bn krdn* 2102. *hwmst bn fh yzd u k m b'd* 4140 **Y9.1,2 ratūm]** ərətūm: 4065 | **ā[2]]** hā: 2040. 2104. om. 4360. 4500. 4506 **3 upāit̰]** upāiiat̰ 110. 120. 234. 235. 409. 415. 4200. 4210. 4220. 4240. 4400. 4410. 4420. 4510. 4515. 231. 681. 408. 418. 602. 683. 4440. 4450. 4500. 4503. 4507. upāiit̰ 4250. pāiiat̰: 420. upāat̰: 15 | **zaraϑuštrəm]** zltwhštym: 681 **4 ātrəm]** om. 4050 (ātrəm s.l.) **6 ādim]** 110. 120. 234. 400. 409. 410. 420. 450. 500. 510. 530. 613. 4000. 4020. 4515. 605. 4450. 4504. ā.dəm: 83. 2010. 4055. 4060. 4200. 4420. 4065. 4320. 4500. ā.dim: 2030. ā.dəm: 83. 2010. 4055. 4060. 4200. 4420. 4065. 4320. 4500. āat̰: 4400. **7 narə]** nara: 409. 4031. 231. 4340. 4504 | **ahi]** om. 110. 235. 231. add. miθrō.ziiāt̰ zaraθuštrəm 110 (vl. miθrō.ziiat̰ zaraθuštrəm ahe). 235 (vl. məθrō.°. zaraθuštarəm). 409 (vl. zaiiat̰). 415. 420 (vl. zaiiat̰). 677. 682. 4400 (vl. zaraθuštarəm). 4410 (vl. zaraθuštarəm). 4420. 4510 (vl. məθrō.). 4515. 231 (vl. maiθarō. ziāt̰:). 681 (vl. zaiiat̰). 408 (vl. zaiiat̰). 418. 602 (v.l. zaraθustrəm). 683 (vl. ciiāē). 4320. 4340 (vl. zaraθuštarəm). 4360 (vl. zarθuštrəm). 4440. 4450. 4503 (vl. jaiiāt̰). 4504 (zarθuštarəm). 4506. 4507 **8 vīspahe]** vīspe: 409. 420. 682. 4210. 4220. 4240. 4250. 4410. 4420. 4510. 408. 4340. vīspō: 4515. 4360. 4504. vīspa: 415. 418. 602. vīspə: 231. vīspi: 4440 **9 dādarəsa]** dādarəš: 110. 234. 682. 681. 418. 683. 2106. 4500. dāδarəš: 120. 235. 415. 4220. 4400. 4515. 602. dādarəsca: 2010. 2040. 4055. 5020. dāδarəsca: 4240. 2104. dadərasca: 82. dādirašca: 230. dāturašca: 100. dādarəsəm: 500. dādarəse: 420

Fig. 3.3.5.2 Cantera's provisional edition of Y. 9.1.

Y9.1,2 hāuuanīm] hāuuanūm 60. 4010. 4025. 4055. hāuuanəm 4210. 4510. 231. 418 | **ā ratūm]** āratūm 120. 235. 4200. 4240 | **ratūm]** . ratīm *20, 60, 83, 2010, 2040, 2101, 4000, 4031, 4040, 4045, 4050, 4060, 4100, 4140, 5020, 15. 82, 84, 2030, 2104, 2106. 4070. 4080, 5102*. ratī: 4020. **ā haōmō]** āhaomō 100. 120. āhaōmō 4240 **3 haōmō]** 15. 60.82.83.84.100.234.2010.2030.2040.2101.2102.2104.2106.4000.4010.4020.4025.4040.4050.4055.4060.4065.4070.4080.4090.4100.4140.4150.4160,4210.4220.4240.4260.4280.4491.5020.5102. haomō: 110. 120. 230. 235. 400. 409. 410. 415. 420. 450. 500. 510. 530. 613. 677. 682. 4200. 4250. 4410. 4420. 4510. 4515. 681. 408. 418. 602. 605. 683. 4320. 4340. 4360. 4440. 4450. 4503. 4504. 4506. 4507. humō: 4400. 4370. 231. hāomō: 4500. hōmō: 20 | **upāit̰]** upāit̰ 83. 100. upait̰: 2104 | **zaraϑuštrəm]** zarϑuštrəm 120. zaraθuštarəm: 235. 420. 4400. 4410. 418. 4340. 4507. zltwhštym: 681 **4 ātrəm]** ātarəm: 120. 235. 409. 415. 420. 450. 677. 682. 4200. 4240. 4250. 4400. 4410. 4510. 4515. 231. 408. 418. 602. 683. 4340. 4360. 4440. 4450. 4504. 4507. āθrəm: 100. 230. 500. 510. 530. 2040. 4100. 4140. 15. 82. 2104. ātərəm: 20. 83. 2010. 2101. 84. 2106. 4080. 5102 | **pairiyaōždaϑəṇtəm]** pairi.ẏaoždaθəṇtəm: 400. 410. 415. 500. 613. 4400. 4510. 4515. 408. 602. 605. 4340. 4450. 4503. 4504. 4506. pairi.yaōždaθəṇtəm: 60. 2010. 2040. 2101. 4010. 4025. 4040. 4050. 4060. 4140. 84. 2030. 2106. 4065. 4080. 5102. pairi.yōždaθəṇtəm: 20. 4000. 5020. 4070. pairi.ẏaoždaθəntəm: 4200. 4250. 4420. pairi.yaōždaθəṇtəm: 15. 82. pairi.ẏaoždaθəntəm: 510. 530. pairi.yaoždaθəm.təm: 4220. 4240. pairi.ẏaoždaθəm.təm: 4440. 4507. pairi.ẏaoždaθən.təm: 100. 230. pairi.ẏaoždaθaintəm: 4500. pairi.yōiždaθəṇtəm: 4020. pairi.yaōdaθəṇtəm: 4055. pairi.yaōždətəṇtəm: 4100. pairi.ẏoždaθəntəm: 4320. pairi.yaōžōaθəṇtəm: 2104. pairi.ẏaoždaiθaṇtəm: 4410. pairi.yaōždaθəm.təm: 4210. pərə.ẏoždaθəṇtəm: 4360. pairi.ẏaoždaθaṇtəm: 677. pərə.yōžavaθinatəm: 231. pairi.ẏaōždaθəm.təm: 234. pairiiyždaθəm.təm: 120. pairiiẏō.žda.θəm.təm: 110. pairi.yaōždaθəntəm: 83. pairi.ẏaozdaθəm.təm: 235. parai.ẏaoždaθəṇtəm: 409. pairi.ẏaoždaθantəm: 681. pairi.ẏaoždaθəṇtīm: 682. pairi.ẏaoždaθə̄ṇtəm: 450. pairi.ẏaoždaṇtəm: 420. pərəi.ẏaoždaθətəm: 418. pairi.ẏuaoždaθantəm: 683 **5 gāϑåsca]** gāϑāsca: 20. 4020. 4100. 4070. gāθā.sca: 4210. 4240. gāϑā-šca: 100. 230. gāθāscā: 4140. γāθāsca: 231. gāθāṇsca: 4065 | **srāuuaiiaṇtəm]** srāuuiiaṇtəm: 20. 4515. 4507. sarāuuaiiaṇtəm: 4410. 4420. srāuuaṇtəm: 100. 230. srāuuaiiṇtəm: 420. 231. srā.iiṇtəm: 4400. srā.iiṇtəm: 4400. srāuuiiaṇṇtəm: 4360. srāuuaiiaṇtəm: 4500. asarāuuaiiṇtəm: 4440. srāuuaiiaṇəm: 4055. srāuuantəm: 683. θrāuuiiṇtəm: 4000. srauuaiiaṇtəm: 4070. srāuaiiaṇtəm: 4320 **6 ādim]** ādəm: 20. 60. 235. 415. 677. 2040. 2101. 4010. 4025. 4031. 4040. 4045. 4100. 4140. 4210. 4220. 4240. 4250. 4510. 5020. 681. 15. 82. 84. 408. 418. 602. 683. 2106. 4080. 4360. 4503. 4506. 5102. āδəm:

A (-60) α (-110. 234) a Δ (-4030. 4041. 4051. 4110) δ (-4201. 4220. 4260) 231 400 415 420 500 530 613 681 2010 2040 2101 2200. 4065. 4015. 5300. 570

Fig. 3.3.5.3 *Phonetica et orthographica* of the first verses of Y. 9.1.

instability or insecurity concerning the pronunciation of complex consonant clusters, it is obvious that the language spoken by the performers of the liturgy influenced the recitation and, consequently, also its representation in the manuscripts. Thus manuscripts from Yazd and Kermān typically show a confusion of *ī* and *ū* from the middle of the seventeenth century on—a dialectal feature of the Yazdī dialect. It is important to observe that manuscripts whose colophons declare them to be copies from other ones which distinguish the sounds still perfectly may show just this confusion (such as manuscript 4050 = Tehran, Ketābḫāne-ye Mağles, 16626, which is declared to be a copy from manuscript 4010 = Yazd, private collection of Vahid Zolfeghari, or another manuscript of the same scribe). Another confusion which can be similarly explained is the occasional use of *u* for *ā* in the Iranian manuscripts (*Yasna* 9.8 *dahukəm* instead of *dahākəm*: manuscripts 20 = Tehran, Ketābḫāne-ye Mağles, 15284; 4000a = Tehran University, no shelfmark; 4100 = Tehran, Ketābḫāne-ye Mağles, 15283; 4090 = Tehran, Yegānegi Library, no shelfmark). These variant readings provide lots of information about the evolution of the recitation of the liturgy in different areas during the last five hundred years. Nevertheless, if we confine *phonetica et orthographica* to separate apparatuses, the edition will be more convenient. Compare figs. 3.3.5.1–3 showing *Yasna* 9.1 in the edition of Geldner and in a provisional edition with separate apparatuses.

The choice between readings and the geographical and chronological scope of the edition

All editors have noticed that the text of the recitatives was influenced by the ritual performance (known as Vulgata recitation), but these influences were considered to be occasional and never systematic. Nevertheless, the ubiquitous confusion of *ī/ū* in Iranian manuscripts proves that such influences can be systematic indeed. I have recently revealed other instances of an independent, regular phonetic evolution in Indian and Iranian manuscripts (Cantera forthcoming). This concerns disyllabic words ending in *°oiium*, which always appears as *°ōīm* (*ōīm* acc.sg. of *aēuua-* 'one', *hōīm* acc.sg. of *haoiia-* 'left', but *vīdōiiūm, harōiiūm*, etc.) in India, whereas in Iran they appear as *ōiium, hōiium*.

Although the invention of the Avestan script has slowed down the phonetic evolution of the Avestan recitative of the long liturgy, it has never completely stopped it, and the changes that continued to take place are reflected in the manuscripts, especially in the liturgical but also (although to a minor degree) in the exegetical ones. Thus the Iranian manuscripts show a different text from the Indian ones. Geldner's edition was based mainly on the Indian manuscripts, but he often used readings from Iranian manuscripts as well. The texts of the old editions and those of the modern ones are frequently a *totum revolutum* of Iranian and Indian readings.

The Iranian manuscripts usually prove to be more conservative. For instance, the distribution between *ṣ̌* and *š* (but not *ś̌*) is still maintained in the Iranian manuscripts of the seventeenth century but already lost in Mihrābān's manuscripts from the fourteenth century (500 (J2 = Oxford, Bodleian Library, MS. Zend d.2), 510 (K5 = Copenhagen, Royal Library, Cod. Iran. 5), 4600 (L4 = London, British Library, Avesta 4), 4610 (K1 = Copenhagen, Royal Library, Cod. Iran. 1)). But their text can by no means taken to be identical with the recitation in Sassanian times. There is no doubt that phonetic, textual, and ritual changes modified the liturgies from Sassanian times to the date of the first Iranian manuscripts (end of the sixteenth century). The differences are not enormous, but undeniable.

Consequently, any editor must determine the geographical and chronological scope of his edition. The editors of the nineteenth century took a different stance on this question, albeit only theoretically: Westergaard wanted to edit the Sassanian *Avesta*; Geldner, the hyparchetypes of our manuscripts produced some centuries after the end of the Sassanian empire. In fact, both editors assembled almost the same text, mainly based upon the readings of Mihrābān's manuscripts, but interspersed with readings of other manuscripts whenever they considered it convenient for philological or linguistic reasons. The number of inconsistencies thus achieved is enormous. Karl Hoffmann tried to rationalize the choice of readings and to avoid inconsistencies. In his view, after a philological and linguistic analysis the editor has to decide which was the original reading in the Sassanian archetype, and to edit accordingly, independently of the testimony of the manuscripts.

Today, Hoffmann's methodology has been widely accepted because of some obvious advantages. However, it is not without its own difficulties, because the choice of reconstructing a Sassanian archetype free of inconsistencies poses certain problems: (1) the existence of such an archetype is extremely dubious, as was demonstrated above; (2) even if it had existed, it is very unlikely to have been consistent, since it was the result of a long oral tradition (which has survived until modern times); and (3) the exact reconstruction of the Sassanian shape of the Avestan recitation archetype is extremely difficult, if not impossible. We can only trace the history of our manuscripts back to the tenth century. Therefore, the textual-critical analysis cannot provide us with any information about changes that took place between Sassanian times and the tenth century. The dead letters (letters that are still used in the manuscript but not in their original use) are fortunate exceptions that allow us to know some features of older witnesses, but they do not yield the exact shape of the complete recitation. Linguistic analysis can help us only to a limited extent, since we are unable to determine the exact shape of a text at a given time and in a specific place. Therefore, it is more realistic to edit the liturgy as it was celebrated at a time which we can reconstruct through both textual criticism and linguistic analysis. In my opinion, the oldest version of the liturgy we are able to edit is its celebration in Iran between the tenth and the sixteenth century. The data of the apparatuses will then allow us to follow up the ceremony's history in India and Iran until the nineteenth century.

References

Andrés-Toledo – Cantera 2012; Cantera 2010, 2011, 2012a, 2012b, 2013, forthcoming; Geldner 1886–1896, 1896; Hintze 2012a, 2012b; Hoffmann 1969, 1971, 1986; Humbach 1973; Kellens 1998; Martínez Porro 2013; Sims-Williams 1976; de Vaan 2003; West 2008; Westergaard 1852–1854. Web sources: *Avestan Digital Archive*, <http://ada.usal.es> or <http://www.avesta-archive.com/>, last access December 2014

3.6. Greek literary papyri (LCa)

Literary papyri present many aspects that are not usually found in other kinds of manuscripts. First of all, a papyrus is a peculiar witness to a text: it is sometimes even the only one, or in most cases, one of the oldest. The text contained in a papyrus is therefore edited on its own, even if the edition may requires the help of one or several other witnesses (if they exist and are known). Physical data about the papyrus must be studied with special attention: a papyrus is usually a fragment, or a group of fragments, which conveys an incomplete text; the reconstruction of the original layout, as well as palaeographical peculiarities, can provide information on the context of writing and can help to determine the size of possible lacunae.

Description of the papyrus

It is recommended to start the edition with a precise description of the papyrus or of the fragments. Such a description will include: the number of fragments and their size; the orientation of fibres and whether or not the papyrus is written on both sides, on recto and/or verso (recto is the inside of the roll, verso the outside—NB: the recto is normally written first; if a text is written on the verso, it normally indicates a secondary use of the papyrus, which gives a *terminus ante quem* for the date of the text on the recto); the presence of margins and intercolumns, as well as their sizes, the presence of *kollēseis*, and, if several are visible, the distance between them.

After the physical description, the codicological part will follow. This will include: the number of lines of the column, or of the page; the approximate number of letters per line, if this is possible to determine; the size of a line (height of the letters and of the spacing, and length of the line); in the case of a page, the size of the written surface.

For the typology of ancient books, one can refer to Turner, who proposes a classification of codices according to their layout specificities (Turner 1977); otherwise, Johnson proposes a close analysis of formal and conventional features for over four hundred bookrolls from Oxyrhynchus (Johnson 2004).

Lastly, a palaeographical description is provided. This will include: the form and possibly *ductus* (in the sense of *tratteggio*, cf. Ch. 2 § 1.2–1.3) of the letters; identification of the scribe (see for example Johnson 2004, 17–32, for the scribes in Oxyrhynchus; Cavallo 1983, 28–46, for the scribes in Herculaneum); marginal annotations (*paragraphos*, *korōnis*, stichometric annotations, etc.) and *vacat*s in the text; punctuation and accentuation; presence of a second hand, of corrections, etc.

Other elements are useful to determine the structure of the text. For example, in the case of a theatre piece, the change of character can be noted with a *paragraphos* under the first letter of the line. In Herculaneum papyri, the end of a sentence is normally indicated by a one-letter-size *vacat* and a *paragraphos* under the first letter of the line; the presence of a *korōnis* indicates the beginning of a new chapter.

The letters can be compared with other published papyri in order to establish the date of the fragment. Nowadays, many editions offer excellent plates of papyri, and more than 2,800 photographs of Greek literary papyri are accessible on the Internet (their URL can be found via the *Leuven Database of Ancient Books*, <http://www.trismegistos.org/ldab/>). One can first refer to the palaeographical studies in Turner 1971, in Cavallo – Maehler 1987 and Cavallo – Maehler 2008. The *Leuven Database of Ancient Books* provides a research field for the script type: even though this field is not systematically filled, and the terminology employed is not clearly indicated, it can be used as a tool to find photographs of similar scripts. If the script is easy to define (for example biblical majuscule, Alexandrian majuscule, uncial, etc.), one can easily consult specialized books about this script.

Edition of the text

In most cases, the papyrus is partly or severely broken, and fragmentary. It is thus necessary to indicate clearly what remains. Papyrologists commonly use a set of diacritical signs as editorial convention (this list can be found in Schubert 2009, 203). It is important to follow these conventions as they warn the reader about the real state of preservation of the papyrus, and the level of certainty of the reading.

Regarding well-known texts, a diplomatic edition can be sufficient; but in many other cases, it is preferable to present both a diplomatic transcript of the papyrus and a normalized edition, one facing the other. The transcript should respect the exact presentation of the papyrus, including *vacat*s, abbreviations, *nomina sacra*, corrections, accentuation, annotations, punctuation, iotacisms, and scribal errors. Since there are many uncertain readings, corrections, abbreviations, and unusual forms, it is preferable to use a font and/or software that allows for the easy typing of all required signs (underdotted letters, simple and double square brackets, abbreviations, etc.). The edition, on the other hand, will give a normalized text, with a standardized accentuation and punctuation, indicating where the text has been corrected. Where it is possible to complete the missing text, these supplements should appear clearly in the edition, so that it is evident for the reader that the text is supplied by the editor and does not appear in the papyrus. If the restitution of the text is uncertain, however, it is preferable to give hypotheses in a commentary rather than in the text itself.

Apparatus and commentary

An apparatus will depend on the state of the papyrus: it may be necessary to give a palaeographical apparatus when readings are really difficult and doubtful. If the text is already known, the palaeographical details may be better studied in the commentary, and the apparatus used for comparison with the mediaeval and papyrological tradition.

The commentary is the freest part of the edition: it can contain proposals for supplements, explanation of interesting passages, comparison with other known texts that can help to understand the content of the papyrus. However, it should always be as brief as possible so that the edition remains a valuable resource for a long time, whereas the commentary can always be improved via further analyses. In an unidentified text, it is quite useless to give all the parallels of a given word, or to provide all the words fitting with the remaining letters of a broken word. The *P.Oxy* series provides a good overview of the diversity of texts found on papyri and, as a result, of the possibilities of apparatus accompanied by a commentary, and of what is expected from a papyrological edition. Nevertheless, other corpora of literary papyri (for example Porter – Porter 2008, containing only New Testament Greek papyri; *P.Gen.*, containing a variety of literary texts; etc.), or isolated editions may be a precious help, depending on the kind of papyrus one has to edit.

Photographs

Last, but not least, no edition is complete without access to good quality photographs of the papyrus. It is necessary for readers to be able to check the readings of the editor and, eventually, to improve them. Further, reproductions provide an image of the papyrus, which itself can always get damaged or lost. It also contributes to the greater knowledge of literary palaeography, and offers the possibility of discovering connexions between fragments dispersed in different collections. However, in order to be really useful, photographs have to be made in a high resolution (600 dpi is a good standard), and with a focus that gives a good view, not only of the text, but also of the fibres and of the texture of the papyrus. At such a high resolution, it is possible to tell that separate fragments were formerly parts of the same manuscript, while the connexions remain doubtful if the fibres are not precisely visible. Nowadays, more and more institutions propose to make the catalogues of their published papyri available online, which is a great help for scholars. In such cases it is possible simply to share the URL of the photograph.

References

Cavallo – Maehler 1987, 2008; Cavallo 1983; Johnson 2004; *P.Gen.* = Gaffino Moeri 2010 and Schubert 1996; *P.Oxy.* = *The Oxyrhynchus Papyri* 1898–2012; Porter – Porter 2008; Schubert 2009; Turner 1971, 1977. Web source: LDAB: *Leuven Database of Ancient Books*, <http://www.trismegistos.org/ldab>, last access November 2014.

3.7. A Byzantine recension of Dioscorides. Historical analysis of manuscripts and text editing (MCr)*

The present contribution deals with a special textual form of Dioscorides' pharmacological encyclopaedia known as *De materia medica* ('On medical materials'), written in Greek during the second half of the first century CE. It describes about 800 'simples'—that is, basic products (mostly vegetable, but also animal, mineral, etc.) that one can use for the preparation of medicines. This provides a good example of how scientific or technical texts are often re-elaborated, in order to make them fit for practical uses, and of how palaeography and codicology can be useful for classifying the various witnesses to such texts.

About a third of the Greek witnesses of *De materia medica* (eighteen manuscripts out of more than 60) preserve this treatise in a longer version than what is considered to be its original form (see fig. 3.3.7.1 for a partial stemma of the manuscripts of *De materia medica*). Indeed, although as a whole this version follows the original division of the work (into five books, where chapters are grouped according to their subject: for example, animals, minerals, wines, oils, trees, cereals, vegetables, plants, and so on), it contains some more chapters and, within the authentic chapters, more information (for example, synonyms for names of plants in Greek and other languages). It also often presents variant readings, some of which are not necessarily erroneous. The last editor of Dioscorides, Max Wellmann, called this longer recension *Di*, for *Dioscorides interpolatus* (Wellmann 1906–1914, II, xii–xiii): he demonstrated that almost all the additions it contains are not authentic, but he could not determine the time when this reworking happened, nor its precise place. Consequently, he gave it a considerable importance in his *apparatus criticus* although he generally does not choose *Di*'s variant if it is not supported by any other witness.

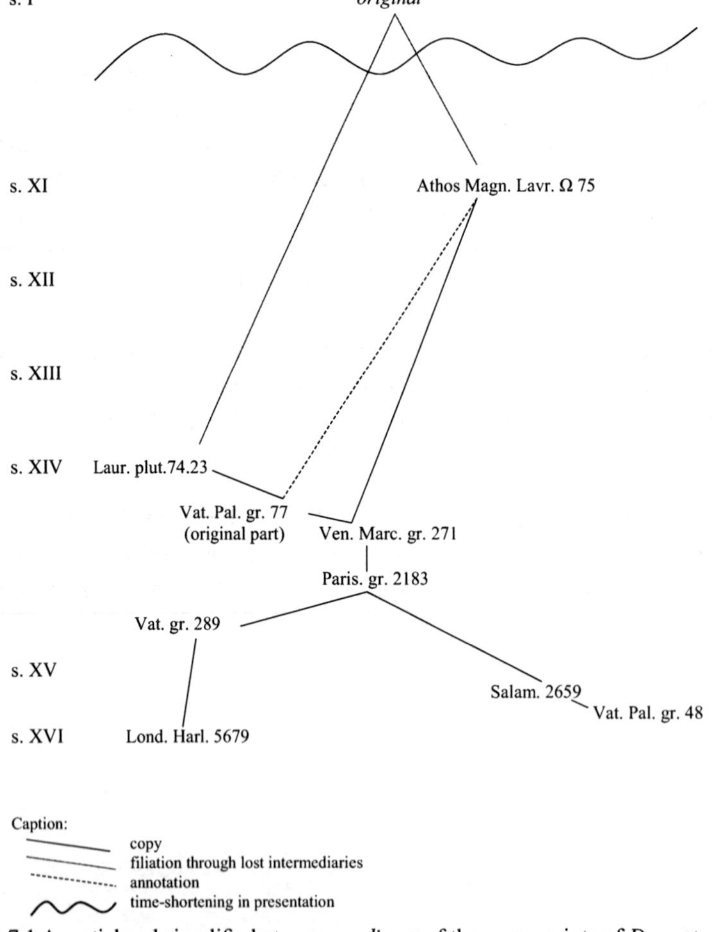

Fig. 3.3.7.1 A partial and simplified *stemma codicum* of the manuscripts of *De materia medica*.

* This contribution is the result of the studies I dedicated to the manuscript tradition of Dioscorides' *De materia medica* in my (unpublished) PhD thesis (Paris, École pratique des Hautes Études, 2007). For a more detailed demonstration on this subject and complementary information, see Cronier – Mondrain forthcoming.

This textual form had a large diffusion not only through manuscripts but also in printed editions, since it was the basis of the first Aldine edition of Dioscorides (Venice, 1499) which, although its text was somehow reviewed in the second Aldine edition (1518) thanks to another manuscript, was the basis of all subsequent printed editions and translations into modern languages until Wellmann's edition at the beginning of the twentieth century (Wellmann 1906–1914). It is therefore under this interpolated form that Dioscorides' text was read in modern times.

I would now like to show how one can behave when faced with such textual variations, so as to determine whether or not they are authentic and whether the editor should take them into account for the *constitutio textus*.

A first observation is that all the manuscripts preserving this textual form are made of paper with watermarks, and most of them (according to watermarks, but also to palaeography) go back to the fifteenth century and none is prior to the beginning of the fourteenth century.

A few relevant variant readings and some external elements allow a rough classification of these manuscripts. For example, manuscript Paris, BnF, Grec 2183 (middle of the fourteenth century) contains, in its wide margins, some excerpts of Galen's *De simplicibus medicamentis*, added by a second hand (but contemporary with the main scribe). Thus, one can presume that all the manuscripts bearing such excerpts most probably descend (directly or indirectly) from the Paris manuscript. Such are, for example: London, BL, Harley 5679 (end of the fifteenth century or very beginning of the sixteenth); Salamanca, Biblioteca General Universitaria de Salamanca, 2659 (second half of the fifteenth century); Vatican City, BAV, Pal. gr. 48 (end of the fifteenth century) and Vat. gr. 289 (third quarter of the fourteenth century).

The philological analysis (which does not demand a complete collation) leads one to establish that all manuscripts of the *Di* form descend from Venice, BNM, gr. 271 (collocazione 727) (first half of the fourteenth century). Alain Touwaide reached the same conclusion in his 2006 study. In particular, he convincingly established that Paris, BnF, Grec 2183 descends from Venice, BNM, gr. 271, contrary to Wellmann's assertion that both were copies of a common lost ancestor (Touwaide 2006, 205). As a consequence, we can consider Venice, BNM, gr. 271 as the archetype of this branch and, therefore, as the only witness to consider in the philological analysis of the *Di* form.

We now have to determine its philological value for the *constitutio textus* of *De materia medica*. As Wellmann established, *Di* is a sort of mix between two different textual versions: its basis is an exemplar of the original form but it bears numerous and deep additions and emendations coming from a distinct source, hence its designation by Wellmann as *Dioscorides interpolatus*. Wellmann rightly identified the manuscript of the original form that was the source of this work: Florence, BML, plut. 74.23 (end of the thirteenth century or beginning of the fourteenth; see fig. 3.3.7.2). As for the additions and variant readings, however, he could establish that they came from what we now call the 'alphabetical five books recension' of *De materia medica* but, since he did not have access to the main witnesses of this family, he could not arrive at further results. I have established that the original exemplar of the 'alphabetical five-books recension' is New York, The Pierpont Morgan Library and Museum, M. 652 (beginning of the tenth century; on this manuscript and the 'alphabetical five-books recension', see Cronier 2012): during Wellmann's time it was kept in a private library (that of Sir Thomas Phillipps in Cheltenham). This last manuscript was the model of Mount Athos, Monē Megistēs Lauras, Ω 75 (end of the tenth century or beginning of the eleventh), whose scribe also resorted to a second model, now lost (Cronier 2006).

Actually, many peculiarities of *Di* have no equivalent in New York, The Pierpont Morgan Library and Museum, M. 652 but go back to Athos, Monē Megistēs Lauras, Ω 75, which we can thus consider as a source of *Di*. Apart from minor variant readings, some of them consist of personal commentaries on Dioscorides' text, criticizing or confirming such and such an assertion by Dioscorides. They reveal a good knowledge of the therapeutic properties of some plants and, as such, probably constitute personal remarks of a medical practitioner. John M. Riddle offers an interesting account of these additions thanks to his examination of several witnesses (Riddle 1984); however, he focuses on their pharmacological interest and he does not in any way attempt to determine their origin, which is nevertheless easy to find (the Athos manuscript). More recently, Touwaide (2006, 205) underlined the importance of the Athos manuscript in the constitution of *Di*'s text but he did not clearly explain the modalities of this work of comparison between Athos, Monē Megistēs Lauras, Ω 75 and Florence, BML, plut. 74.23. However, one can firmly establish this by an examination of the manuscripts.

Let us go back to codex Venice, BNM, gr. 271 and make a material analysis of it. Its watermarks situate the making of its original part (ff. 14–145) in the second quarter of the fourteenth century, whereas ff. 1–13 and 146–153 are a restoration of the first half of the fifteenth century. The single scribe (apart from the restoration) has not signed his work but, as Alain Touwaide rightly suggested, he is also the copyist of another Dioscorides manuscript: Vatican City, BAV, Pal. gr. 77. Contrary to what Wellmann thought (and this led him to a philological aporia), this last one is not homogeneous but it also consists of an original part (ff. 32–39, 50–55, 57–114) going back to the second quarter of the fourteenth century according to its watermarks—this is the part due to our scribe—a restoration of the first half of the fifteenth century (ff. 9–31, 40–49, 56) and a supplementary quire of the end of the fourteenth century (ff. 1–8).

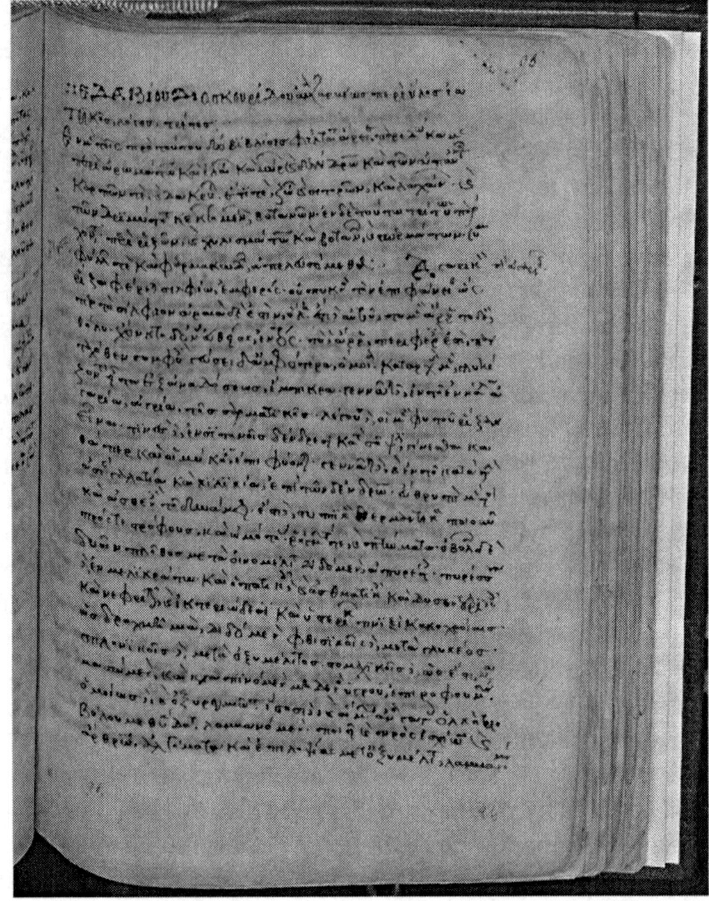

Fig. 3.3.7.2 Florence, BML, plut. 74.23, end of the thirteenth or beginning of the fourteenth century, f. 96v (*De materia medica*, beginning of book III). The first model of Vatican City, BAV, Pal. gr. 77.

An interesting phenomenon appears when examining the original part of Vatican City, BAV, Pal. gr. 77: the main text is obviously a copy of Florence, BML, plut. 74.23, as Alain Touwaide rightly demonstrated (Touwaide 2006, 205): since Vatican City, BAV, Pal. gr. 77 contains all the erroneous readings of Florence, BML, plut. 74.23 and never offers a good reading against it, there is no necessity to postulate, as Wellmann did, the existence of a lost common ancestor. But what autopsy indeed reveals (and not microfilm reading, which is unclear) is that the same scribe, after having copied the Florence manuscript, reviewed its text by comparison with another manuscript—i.e. Athos, Monē Megistēs Lauras, Ω 75. Consequently, in Vatican City, BAV, Pal. gr. 77 there are numerous interlinear variant readings coming from the Athonite manuscript and, in the margins, several longer additions from the same source. However, the influence of the Athonite codex is much less important in Vatican City, BAV, Pal. gr. 77 than in Venice, BNM, gr. 271.

From a philological point of view, the relations between these last two manuscripts are very hard to establish, because of the complexity of the emendations in the Vatican manuscript: in some places, one can hardly distinguish the original reading from what are corrections. However, one can find a very satisfying solution by considering the manuscripts themselves and wondering about the reasons why they were made. While Vatican City, BAV, Pal. gr. 77 looks like a sort of draft, Venice, BNM, gr. 271 bears all the aspects of a fair copy: one must keep in mind that both are due to the same scribe, even for the emendations and annotations. Evidently, a Byzantine man in the first half of the fourteenth century—i.e. our scribe—considering that Dioscorides' text was transmitted under very different forms (the original one and the alphabetical five books recension), decided to establish a new edition of this treatise by comparing two manuscripts (Florence, BML, plut. 74.23 and Athos, Monē Megistēs Lauras, Ω 75). After having completed a copy of the first (the original state of Vatican City, BAV, Pal. gr. 77), he annotated it according to the second one: in this way, he established a draft of his new edition. Then he made a fair copy of it (that is: Venice, BNM, gr. 271), which would be the official exemplar of this new edition. There was probably a large demand for Dioscorides' text in the milieu where this scribe was working: this explain why it was quickly reproduced in several copies during the next decades.

This explanation becomes even more convincing when palaeography allows us to identify the scribe responsible for this work: as Brigitte Mondrain recently stated (Mondrain 2012b, 632), it is a man known as Geōrgios Chrysokokkēs, who was a physician in Constantinople in the middle of the fourteenth century and copied several manuscripts, not only of medical content, but also dealing with astronomy and classical literature (on this man, see Gamillscheg et al. 1997, 64, no 126). As a physician, he was very likely to be interested in possessing a book of *De materia medica* bearing a text as accurate and exhaustive as possible.

This historical explanation allows us to consider codex Venice, BNM, greco 271 as the first exemplar of what we can consider an edition of Dioscorides' treatise, and Vatican City, BAV, Pal. gr. 77 as its draft. As the two ancestors of these manuscripts have survived (Athos, Monē Megistēs Lauras, Ω 75 and Florence, BML, plut. 74.23), the editor should not give any more weight to *Di*'s readings in the *constitutio textus* of the original treatise by Dioscorides (even if the *Di*-version could be edited and studied on its own; in this case, Venice, BNM, gr. 271 would be the only base-manuscript for such edition).

Obviously, this assertion, establishing the relationships between these four manuscripts, is not valuable in itself but demands philological confirmation, and actually a philological analysis leads us to the same results but, as we have seen, less easily. It should be stressed that both types of analysis are complementary. Indeed, when classifying manuscripts the editor should try, as much as possible, to resort to as many clues as possible.

References

Cronier 2006, 2012; Cronier – Mondrain forthcoming; Gamillscheg et al. 1997; Mondrain 2012b; Riddle 1984; Touwaide 2006; Wellmann 1906–1914.

3.8. The Septuagint, its *Vorlage* and its translations (LCu)*

The Greek translation of the Book of Proverbs, preserved in the corpus known as the Septuagint (LXX), has long been well known to biblical scholars (see Thackeray 1909, 13–16, where the author classifies the translation of Proverbs among the 'Paraphrases and free renderings. Literary' (13) together with 1 Esdras, LXX Daniel, Esther and Job all of them from the *Kethubim*) for both its peculiar literary Greek, and for its *ad sensum* renderings, which often make it difficult to recognise which is the Hebrew text underneath. A note may be useful here: the semantic field of the word *literal* being strongly disputed, I prefer here to employ the terminology used already in the ancient time among the others by Jerome (Epistle 57, esp. 6) when dealing with translation theories and methods. In particular, the expression 'translation *ad verbum*' would apply to the trend found in Greek biblical translations up to the one by Aquila of Sinope, whereas 'translation *ad sensum*' would apply mostly, according to Jerome, to translations from non-sacred texts.

Being a translation from the Hebrew language, the LXX of the Book of Proverbs was nonetheless in its turn translated by Christians, before the Muslim expansion, into several ancient languages and dialects: Latin (second century CE), Sahidic (third century), Akhmimic (fourth century), Coptic dialect of *P. Bodmer* VI (fourth century), Armenian (fifth century), Palestinian Aramaic (fifth century), Ethiopic (fifth to seventh cent.), Syriac (*c.*617), in approximate chronological order. All these versions are completely or fragmentarily preserved.

After the text critical work of Origen, the destruction of the sacred books under emperor Diocletian's persecution, and the refining of the codex making technique, which allowed the whole Bible to be copied out in only one manuscript, a standard textual type began to emerge and some readings were completely lost in the Greek tradition.

As for other books of the Old Testament, also in the book of Proverbs the Pre-Nicene translations in particular, namely the Latin (usually the *Vetus Afra*) and the Coptic (especially the Sahidic), prove sometimes to preserve readings which are not preserved by the Post-Nicene Greek manuscripts. These readings may occasionally represent a different, if not better, Hebrew *Vorlage* in comparison with the Masoretic Text (MT).

This complex situation may be elucidated by the case found in Prov. 8.31. Here, the MT reads as follows:

məśaḥèqèt bətébél 'arṣŵ, wəša'ăšu'ay 'èt-bnéy 'ådåm

'[I was] rejoicing in the habitable part of his earth; and my delights were with the sons of men' (KJV).

The LXX renders as follows:

hote euphraineto tēn oikoumenēn syntelesas
kai eneuphraineto en huiois anthrōpōn

'When he rejoiced while completing the world
and rejoiced among the sons of men'.

As it can be seen, the MT and the LXX present different texts, but one may easily infer that the first Greek stich corresponds to the first Hebrew clause, while the second Greek line renders the second Hebrew clause.

Still some problems are left open: the feminine participle piel מְשַׂחֶקֶת *məśaḥèqèt* is rendered by *hote euphraineto* as if the translator had read בְּשַׂחֵקוֹ *bəśaḥéqŵ* (infinitive construct piel) and referred it to the Lord. While תֵּבֵל *tébél* is probably translated by *tēn oikoumenēn* there is no precise counterpart for אַרְצוֹ *'arṣŵ*, furthermore *syntelesas* looks like an addition, unless it is a double translation of בְּתֵבֵל *bətébél* read as בְּכַלֹּת *bəkalot* (infinitive construct piel from כלה *klh*) with the common exchange of the consonant order and the equally common confusion between ב *bet* and כ *kaph*. The interpretation of the second line is easier; however וְשַׁעֲשֻׁעַי *wəša'ăšu'ay* (noun plural construct) has been read וַיְשַׁעֲשַׁע *wayəša'ăša'* (*wayyiqtol pilpal*) and translated *kai eneuphraineto*.

Be that as it may, the picture is further complicated by the witness of the Latin and Coptic translations which both add a third stich. The Latin reads as follows:

* This case study was read in a revised form at the International Congress of the International Organization for Septuagint and Cognate Studies held in Munich, on 1–3 August 2013.

thesauri autem eius faciunt homines gaudibundos
'And his treasures make the men joyful'.

This reading is confirmed by the Sahidic:

šare nefahōr de tre ənrōme raše
'And his treasures are making the men rejoice'.

The reading *thesauri eius/nefahōr* must depend on the Hebrew reading אֹצָרוֹ *'oṣårŵ* ('his treasure') instead of the Masoretic אַרְצוֹ *'arṣŵ* ('his earth') with a position exchange of the consonants ר *resh* and צ *ṣade*. This solution originates from the difficulty posed by the juxtaposition in the construct state of the nearly synonyms תֵּבֵל *tébél* and אֶרֶץ *'èrèṣ*.

Since it is attested by both the Latin and Coptic, which independently from each other witness to a Hebrew variant, this reading must have been present in the Greek *Vorlage* of both translations.

In fact, an attempt at recovering the original Greek text has been made by R. Geoffrey Jenkins (1987, esp. 71–72, 75 n. 25) who, after identifying a new fragment containing the letters]θη[(*thē*), proposed to read in the relevant passage of the Antinoopolis papyrus 8+210 (Rahlfs 928) *hoi de thēsauroi*. I believe the proposal from Jenkins is rather likely. Unfortunately no fragments which would correspond to *eius faciunt homines gaudibundos* have been identified until now.

Furthermore, a number of problems are raised by these facts and need to be dealt with. First it is to be inquired which was the original Greek text. The third stich indeed represents a doublet of the second one: both lines aim at rendering the second Hebrew clause which was read in two different ways. The Hebrew *Vorlage* of the second line may have been as follows:

wayəša'ăša' 'èt-bnéy 'ådåm
'and he took delight in the sons of man'.

Whereas the *Vorlage* of the third line may have been as follows:

wə'oṣårŵ yəša'ăša' 'èt-bnéy 'ådåm
'and his treasure will delight the sons of man'.

In this reconstruction the י yod of ושׁעשׁעי *wš'š'y* would have moved from the end to the beginning of the word, and the ו waw would have passed to the previous word by allowing a different division of the verse (the group ארצו/אצרו *'rṣw/'ṣrw* is moved to the second clause). A rendering with the plural (*thesauri*) for the singular (אֹצָרוֹ *'oṣårŵ*) is normal in the translation of the book of Proverbs, as is the use of the present for the *yiqtol*.

In my yet unpublished doctoral thesis I have argued that in most of the cases the long doublets depend entirely on the first translator. In the present case the third line can be easily considered original because of the use of the particle *de* (Latin *autem* / Sahidic *de*), a typical feature of the original translator, nearly absent in the later versions by the *kaíge* group and Aquila, and more in general because the text is further away from the MT. Also, the third line offers a rendering for אַרְצוֹ *'arṣŵ* (even if read אֹצָרוֹ *'oṣårŵ*) which is otherwise left completely untranslated. However, since the second line also does not match the MT but fits well with the context offered by the Greek first line—in both lines the verb is in the third person so that the Lord, and not Wisdom, is the subject—it may be tentatively ascribed to the first translator.

Another problem arises because of the loss of the Greek witness: even if the presence of the third line in the original text is virtually certain, what shall we put in the edition of the Greek text? In most of our critical editions, any text, even if original, which is lacking in the Greek manuscripts, is relegated to the first apparatus. However, here the third line is not only original, but also partially preserved by the Antinoopolis papyrus. If the text preserved by the papyrus has full rights to be edited in the main text, how should one complete the line? We may agree with Jenkins who filled the lacuna after the letters *thē* with the remaining part of the word [*sauroi*]. But what to do about the rest of the verse? Is a retroversion to be attempted? Moreover, if *autou* for *eius/nef-* is virtually certain, and *poiousin* for *faciunt/šare ... tre* is extremely likely, what to do about *homines/ənrōme*? The original translator of Proverbs renders the locution בְּנֵי אָדָם *bnéy 'ådåm* with the phrase *huioi anthrōpōn* in 8.4 (and also in the second line of the present verse, if it is not a later interpolation), and with the simple *hoi anthrōpoi* in 15.11. Since the translations consistently uses *filii hominum/ənšēre ənənrōme* in 8.4, 31b, and *homines/ənrōme* in 15.11, *anthrōpous* may well be their Greek *Vorlage*. The presence or absence of the article *tous* cannot be decided on the basis of our translations.

What is more difficult is to retrotranslate *gaudibundos/raše*. First the Latin attests an adjective, whereas the Sahidic shows a verb. The participle *euphrainomenos* might be represented by this twofold witness. However, one would be struck by the use of the same root for the fourth time in a row. If the translator wanted to adopt some variation he could have chosen, as in 2.14, the participle *chairontes* to alternate the root *euphrainomai*. This is even more likely if we consider that the *Vetus Afra* in 8.30 translates *prosechairen* with *adgaudebat*, in 2.14 renders *chairontes* with *qui ... ga[u]detis*, and in 24.19 translates *mē chaire* with *noli gaudere*. In other words the *Vetus Afra* consistently uses (*ad*)*gaudeo* for (*pros*)*chairō*. Similarly the Sahidic has the root *raše* for (*pros*)*chairō* in 6.16, 8.30, 17.19, 23.25, 24.19. Finally it can be observed that the Greek translator had already rendered the root שעשע *š'š'* with *proschairō* in 8.30.

Hence the Greek original translation may have looked like this:

hote euphraineto tēn oikoumenēn syntelesas
kai eneuphraineto en huiois anthrōpōn
hoi de thē[*sauroi autou poiousin anthrōpous chairontas*]

The present author is aware of the conjectural character of any retroversion. However, in putting forward his reconstruction, he thinks that it may be of some help at least in identifying the remaining unidentified fragments of the papyrus. Moreover, in the major Göttingen editions the fragments from the Syro-Hexapla are usually retrotranslated into Greek, as it was usually done by Frederick Field in his monumental edition of the Hexaplaric fragments.

A further observation can be of some interest: the third stich, although nearly certainly original, died out almost completely from the received tradition: the Greek fragments we now possess were uncovered under the sands of Egypt so as the Coptic manuscripts. The Latin witness, which originally belonged to the so-called *Vetus Afra*, the first translation of the Bible into Latin later superseded by the Vulgate, has come down to us, out of its literary context, as a marginal note in an incunabulum of the Vulgate. Hence, should we relegate to the apparatus a very probable original reading which was by no means rejected in the Greek, Latin and Coptic traditions but was, nonetheless, read by ancient Jewish and Christian readers? Indeed there are cases in which what is received and what is original do not coincide.

Moreover, some observations can be made as far as the Hebrew text is concerned. We have seen that the Greek text of Prov. 8.31 implies a few readings which diverge from the MT. This is a very well-known fact for the Book of Proverbs and for the LXX as a whole which has been often used as a mere mine of variant readings. What is of main interest here is how the Latin and Coptic translations of the LXX increase our knowledge of the Hebrew text. As I have mentioned, it appears that the Greek translator or his *Vorlage* were puzzled by the tautological phrase בְּתֵבֵל אַרְצוֹ *bətébél 'arṣŵ*. Hence they preferred to read אֹצָרוֹ *'oṣårŵ* while connecting it to the second clause of the verse (this implied the movement of the conjunction וְ *wə*). As for שַׁעֲשֻׁעַי *ša'ăšu'ay* this appears to have been known to the *Vorlage* of both the second and third line as יְשַׁעֲשַׁע *yəša'ăša'*.

A full appreciation of these variants cannot be achieved without examining the *Vorlage* of the whole verse as indicated by the first and third Greek lines:

bəśaḥéqŵ bətébél wə'oṣårŵ yəša'ăša' 'èt-bnéy 'ådåm

'When he rejoiced in the inhabited world and his treasure was delighting the sons of man'.

Although a confusion between the letters מ mem and ב beth seems to be possible in the Hasmonean hand, the variant בְּשַׂחֵקוֹ *bəśaḥéqŵ* for מְשַׂחֶקֶת *məśaḥèqèt* seems to stem from syntactic and literary reasons. In vv. 27–29, six temporal clauses are found at the infinitive construct governed by the preposition ב *b-* all referred to the Lord. It is thus likely that under the influence of the masculine pronoun ו *-ŵ* in ארצו/אצרו *'rṣw/'ṣrw* the female participle מְשַׂחֶקֶת *məśaḥèqèt* has been referred to the Lord and read בְּשַׂחֵקוֹ *bəśaḥéqŵ*. This implies a variation with the מְשַׂחֶקֶת *məśaḥèqèt* found in the previous line (v. 30) and referred to Wisdom. In this way both Wisdom and the Lord are subject of the rejoicing (שׂחק *śḥq*) and are in some way more strictly connected. It is equally produced a further allusion to Gen. 2 and 3—the other one being *syntelesas* (cf. Gen. 2.1, 2)—where the Lord is openly mentioned to be present with the first human beings. There might be, thus, in the Greek translation and probably in its *Vorlage* not only a literary allusion but also a peculiar theological stress towards the role of the Lord among human beings.

A final evaluation must be made on the quality of the variant readings with which we have dealt here. As I have already suggested, it seems likely that these alternative readings developed for theological reasons (exclusive monotheism) or because the tautological phrase בְּתֵבֵל אַרְצוֹ *bətébél 'arṣŵ* may have seemed awkward to some early scribe. In any case, it seems that in this passage the Hebrew text, as preserved by the Masoretic tradition, because of its difficulties, might have generated the variants which we have studied. It has also to be stressed that from a merely literary point of view the variant loses the formal balance of the two members in the Hebrew verse. Hence, also from this point of view, the more likely original text is the one preserved by the Masoretic tradition.

Some words must be added concerning the problem of the mentioning of these kind of variants in the apparatuses. As for the editions of the Hebrew text, one may wonder, for instance, if at least the variant אֹצָרוֹ *ʾoṣårŵ* for אַרְצוֹ *ʾarṣŵ* should have been mentioned in the apparatuses of the *Biblia Hebraica Stuttgartensia* or the *Biblia Hebraica Quinta* on the authority of the Old Latin and Sahidic witnesses. In fact, although the variant seems to be secondary, it could be still worth mentioning because of its antiquity. The present author, while studying the book of Proverbs, has often found the choices of the editors either incomplete or not fully consequential.

Finally, concerning the edition of the Greek text, we can recall the difficult status of the passage discussed here which is likely to be original, but has been lost almost completely in its Greek wording, and must be partially reconstructed. Should it be relegated in the apparatus, maybe only in its Latin or Sahidic form, or has it the right to be reinserted where it was originally?

References

Essential bibliography on the Septuagint: Rahlfs – Hanhart 2006; Pietersma – Wright 2007. Reference works: Brock et al. 1973; Dogniez 1995; Dorival et al. 1988; Fernández Marcos 1998; Jellicoe 1968; Jenkins 1987; Jobes – Silva 2000; Law 2013; Swete 1914; Tov 1981.

3.9. The Turfan fragments (DDM)*

The Berlin Turfan Collection of *c.*40,000 items consists of some complete or almost complete texts, for example on scrolls or in Indian loose-page books as well as some individual pages, such as letters, contracts or exercise pages from writing school, but also of a large number of fragments of destroyed books (codex, scroll or Indian-style). A rare example of a codex book with a partly intact binding is the Syriac liturgical book (Berlin, Museum für Asiatische Kunst, MIK III 45) with 61 bifolia.

The Manichaean material in particular is badly damaged. The pattern of tears on some fragments demonstrates the deliberate destruction of these codices from which individual pages, even sequences of pages but often enough just fragments of a page have survived. The destruction, which happened at an unknown time and for unknown reasons (the possibility ranges from religious reasons to simple vandalism), was accompanied by a dispersion or removal of the main body of the torn fragments so that the fragments collected by various expeditions and now chiefly in Berlin, St Petersburg and Kyoto cannot be joined together to reconstruct whole books. Rather the fragments derive from a whole range of books and texts that will always remain incomplete.

The edition work on the Turfan fragments consists of preparing a diplomatic edition which aims to recover the text and also to indicate the structure of the text and its presentation on the page. The edition in book form in the series *Berliner Turfantexte* also contains a translation, a commentary and a glossary. Digital colour images of all the fragments in the Berlin Turfan Collection are freely available online in the Digitales Turfanarchiv of the Turfanforschung (<http://www.bbaw.de/forschung/ turfanforschung/dta/index.html>) and on the site of the International Dunhuang Project (<http://idp.bbaw.de/>).

The main task of the editor is to join fragments where possible, recognize texts or textual units that, if short, may be contained on one page, or, if large, may be distributed across a number of pages or be present in a number of duplicates. In some cases, the original of the text in another language or a subsequent translation into a third language can play a major role in the reconstruction of the text on the basis of surviving fragments. Old Turkic and Sogdian Buddhist texts translated or adopted from Chinese originals are regularly approached in this way. Tibetan and Tocharian originals of Old Turkic Buddhist texts also exist. Other examples include using the later Chinese version of a Manichaean text to aid the reconstruction of the Parthian fragments or interpreting Christian Sogdian texts on the basis of the Syriac originals.

Features of the diplomatic edition

Transcription vs. transliteration

Already in 1904 Friedrich Wilhelm Karl Müller in Berlin recognized in some of the fragments from Turfan remnants of original Manichaean literature. He was able to read the script because it was very close to Syriac *ʾesṭrangēlā* but, rather than using a corresponding font or a one-to-one Latin transliteration, he chose to attempt to transcribe the texts in a semi-interpretative way that was neither graphemic nor phonological, retaining the initial *alef* (ʾ) and *ayn* (ʿ) and some other features of Manichaean script (*ḥ* and *ṭ*) and introducing a circumflex to indicate that a consonantal sign was being used to indicate a vowel, for example in the following Parthian passage (M4a/I/V/13–15/ in Müller [F.] 1904, 51–52):

ʾô ʿišmâ yazdân padvaḥâm ḥarvîn bagân ḥêrzêdû ʾô man ʾastâr pad ʾamûždêfṭ
I entreat you gods: All the gods, forgive my sins out of mercy!

Here the circumflex indicates that the vowels read by him are written with the signs ʾ (*â*), *y* (*ê* and *î*) or *w* (*ô* and *û*) whereas the short vowel in *man* or *pad* is not written explicitly. But, though consistent, Müller's system is confusing because the circumflex suggested vowel length without any certainty that this was in fact the case. His *ḥêrzêdû* is actually *hirzēd* with the letter *y* used to write a short vowel in the first syllable. The spelling includes a final *w* which can only be a mistake or an attempt to combine the spelling of this word with that of the following *ō* (Müller's ʾô).

The same passage in present-day transliteration and transcription:
ʾw ʿšmʾ yzdʾn pdwhʾm hrwyn bgʾn hyrzydw ʾw mn ʾstʾr pd ʾmwjdyfṯ °°
/ō išmā yazdān padwahām harwīn bayān hirzēd{w} ō man āstār pad āmuždīft/

Modern transliterations comprise the following conventions concerning brackets:

* I would like to heartily thank Caroline Macé and Jost Gippert for advice and help.

() indicates that a letter is visible and identifiable though not complete.
[] indicates that a letter is no longer visible on the page.
<> indicates that a letter has been supplied that was never written on this page.
{} indicates that a letter is incorrect; also indicates a comment about a gap, colour of ink, language etc.

Carl Salemann (1908) reacted to Müller (1904) by reprinting the fragmentary texts in a transliteration in Hebrew script, essentially providing the same information as the present transliteration in Latin script. Salemann's version is an accurate reflection of the original fragments as Müller read them and does indeed testify to the convertibility of Müller's transcription. Salemann's use of Hebrew script had two reasons: Firstly, for Salemann's description of Pahlavi (Sassanian or Zoroastrian Middle Persian) in the *Grundriß der iranischen Philologie* (Salemann 1901) the printers in Strasbourg chose a Hebrew font because they did not have access to a Pahlavi one. Secondly, Salemann was acquainted with Judaeo-Persian manuscripts available to him in St Petersburg and recognized their value as a source of archaic early Modern Persian. He adopted some of the conventions used there to reproduce the diacritic dots used in Manichaean script.

Unfortunately, Hebrew script, despite its common Aramaic origin with Manichaean script, is not particularly suited to represent its Manichaean counterpart. It introduces ambiguities that are unique to it rather than to Manichaean script, for example the Hebrew letters ו <w>, י <y> and ר <r> can be easily confused whereas Manichaean script distinguishes them clearly.

The main point of Salemann's treatment of the texts was not the use of Hebrew script but his rejection of Müller's idiosyncratic transcription in favour of a convertible and non-interpreting transliteration. For some years from 1911 on, a Manichaean font was used in publications of the Academy in Berlin. Salemann's Hebrew transliteration was adopted by Friedrich Carl Andreas and his students and quickly became the standard. The prohibition on using Hebrew type in Nazi-Germany from 1933 on meant that Henning moved from Hebrew to a Latin font in the last of the three publications from Andreas' papers in Andreas – Henning 1934 and provided a new transliteration table that has remained standard since then, though with minor changes (some scholars use *w*: rather than *u* to represent the abbreviation *w* with two dots of the normal spelling *'wd* for /ud/ 'and'). These developments contrast with the more complicated history of the transliteration of Zoroastrian Middle Persian.

Müller 1904 also transcribed rather than transliterated Sogdian (for example Müller [F.] 1904, 97–98), a practice soon abandoned by himself and which, because of the difficulties represented by Sogdian, has generally never been continued by other scholars.

In a different development, Old Turkic texts, whether written in Manichaean or Uyghur script, have generally been published in transcription. This is possible due to explicit spelling conventions used in the original scripts particularly to designate vowels but also to the predictability of Old Turkic phonology and features such as vowel harmony.

In the transliteration of the Manichaean and Christian Sogdian scripts, both of which are derived from Aramaic, the conventions used by Iranian scholars are based on the desire to avoid supplementary diacritics. Therefore, in Manichaean script, Müller's *ḥ* (see above) was soon abandoned in favour of *h* and the emphatic *ṭ* is often rendered as *ṯ* because the letter no longer designates an emphatic phoneme. However, in the transliteration of Christian Sogdian this has resulted in a discrepancy between the transliteration of Christian Sogdian and Syriac even on the same page. The letter ʿ (*ayn*) with the value /ʿ/ in Syriac is assigned the value <γ> in the Sogdian transliteration, again introducing features of a transcription into the transliteration, for example Sogdian *γwbtyʾ* /γuβtya/ 'praise' in a genuine Sogdian word but Sogdian *yšwγ* beside Syriac *yšwʿ* 'Jesus'. Likewise, the letter ṭ which represents an emphatic /ṭ/ in Syriac is assigned the value <t> in the Sogdian transliteration and the letter t is assigned the value <θ>.

Line-numbers and reference systems used in editions

It is important that the edition indicates the gaps on the fragments, shows if a heading is present, if the top and bottom lines can be determined, and properly indicates columns, though on some fragments this is impossible to do with certainty.

The editor identifies and numbers the lines of the fragment as in the example from M4579 (fig. 3.3.9.1). Werner Sundermann (1981, 70) edited the text of this fragment which is written in two columns but for which only five lines of the column on the right (column i) are visible, whereas the column on the left (column ii) clearly has six lines; on the verso traces of six lines are preserved in both columns. By

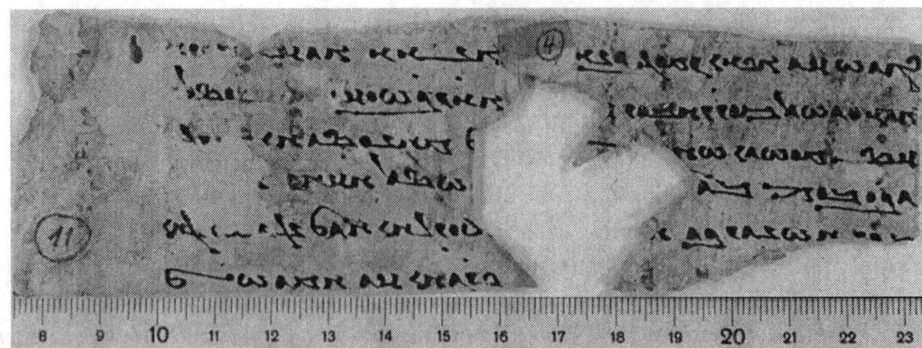

Fig. 3.3.9.1 M4579 recto, © Berlin, Staatsbibliothek Preussischer Kulturbesitz, Reprography department.

consequence, column i of the recto will also have had six lines. The following updated edition indicates not only the loss of lines both before and after the preserved text but also includes an indication that after line 5 of column i one further line is missing. This allows the reader to form a more complete picture of the shape and condition of the fragment:

aM4579/ {MKG 4a.12: M4579} {Parthian}
cR/

ei/	{lines missing}	eii/	{lines missing}
l(975)/1/	'wš hw 'pdn zmyg knd	l(980)/1/	'nd(r) 'wh(rmyzd)
l(976)/2/	'wd ywšt qyrd'byd (c)[y]	l(981)/2/	'rdxšyh(r šhr)yst['n]
l(977)/3/	hs myšwn š'(ẖ)	l(982)/3/	[p](ṯ) m'nyst'n (qdg)
l(978)/4/	wxybyẖ bw(ṯ)[•••]	l(983)/4/	['gw]št{?} 'h'z (.)[•••]
l(979)/5/	(byd) 'šnwd kw (')[•••]	l(984)/5/	[w]jydg'n 'wṯ ng(wš')g'n
	{1 line missing}	l(985)/6/	prw'n hw 'mwšṯ
	{lines missing}		{lines missing}

Sundermann did not only number the lines of each fragment, he also included a sequential number for all the fragments edited by him in his book (Sundermann 1981 = MKG); texts are quoted with the abbreviation and the sequential number, for example line 1 of this fragment is MKG(975). This number is simply used for referencing and does not indicate that the fragments edited in the book, despite having related contents, form a continuous text. Similarly, the numbering system can make no attempt to include estimates for the size of the gaps between preserved pieces of text.

The attempt adequately to record the damage to a fragment leads to lines of a two-column text at the same height on the page being given different numbers, for example in the joined Parthian fragment M275a+/ where the top of the page and two lines in column i but four lines in column ii are missing. Therefore, the first preserved traces in column (1) have the line-number 1 whereas line 1 of column (2) is in fact two lines farther down and on the same level as line 3 in column (1):

cR/	{}		
	{top of page missing}		
ei/	{}	eii/	{}
	{2 lines missing}		{4 lines missing}
l1/	[•••• ••• •](.g)[•• ••••]		
l2/	[ṯwm{?}](x)[w](d)'yy{?} 'yy [••••]		
l3/	[••• ••• w](y)g'ng'n · my(š)	l1/	[••](..) ••• ••• •••]
l4/	[•••• •••• •••](g) 'št:m	l2/	pd z(m)[•• ••• •••]
l5/	[•••• •••• ••••] ṯwm ·	l3/	y'd m' •••• [•••]
l6/	[•••• •• •• ••••]'ẖ	l4/	'yy 'd ws'n 'wt

A problem is sometimes incurred by a short-cut in the way the headlines are presented, for example Andreas – Henning 1934, 25 with the headline meaning 'hymn(s) to the Living Soul':

Heading	V	grywjywndgyg
	R	b'š'ẖ

Headlines often form a textual unit in the open book, i.e. from the verso of one page to the recto of the next. The presentation chosen here assumes that the heading on the preserved recto R was preceded on the lost verso of the foregoing page by the same words as actually occur on the verso V of this fragment. This is very likely to be the case. But the following presentation is more faithful to the verifiable facts:

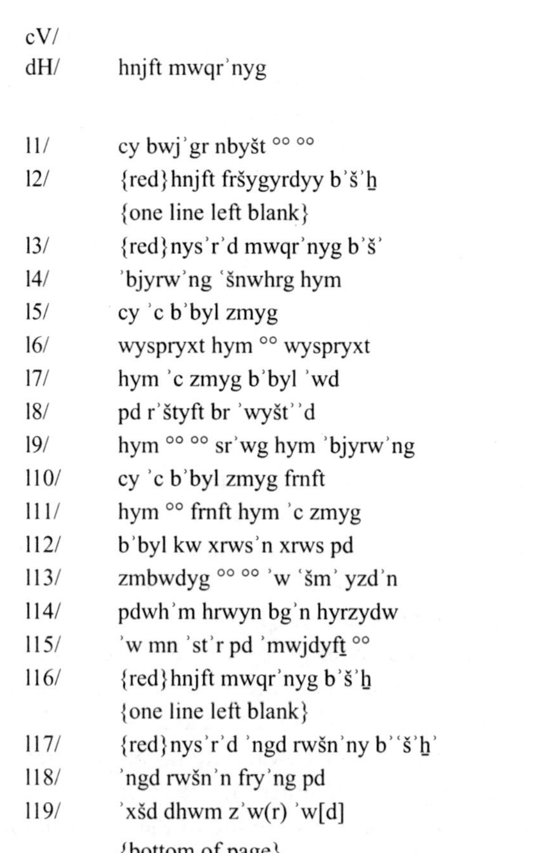

cV/
dH/ hnjft mwqr'nyg

l1/ cy bwj'gr nbyšt °° °°
l2/ {red}hnjft fršygyrdyy b'š'h̲
{one line left blank}
l3/ {red}nys'r'd mwqr'nyg b'š'
l4/ 'bjyrw'ng 'šnwhrg hym
l5/ cy 'c b'byl zmyg
l6/ wyspryxt hym °° wyspryxt
l7/ hym 'c zmyg b'byl 'wd
l8/ pd r'štyft br 'wyšt''d
l9/ hym °° °° sr'wg hym 'bjyrw'ng
l10/ cy 'c b'byl zmyg frnft
l11/ hym °° frnft hym 'c zmyg
l12/ b'byl kw xrws'n xrws pd
l13/ zmbwdyg °° °° 'w 'šm' yzd'n
l14/ pdwh'm hrwyn bg'n hyrzydw
l15/ 'w mn 'st'r pd 'mwjdyft̲ °°
l16/ {red}hnjft mwqr'nyg b'š'h̲
{one line left blank}
l17/ {red}nys'r'd 'ngd rwšn'ny b''š'h̲'
l18/ 'ngd rwšn'n fry'ng pd
l19/ 'xšd dhwm z'w(r) 'w[d]
{bottom of page}

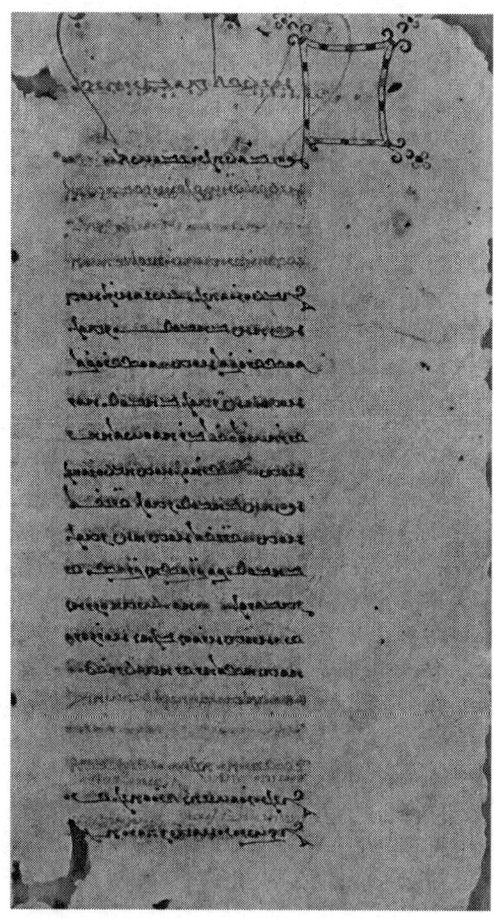

Fig. 3.3.9.2 M4a/V/: transcription and manuscript image, photo <http://www.bbaw.de/forschung/turfanforschung/dta/m/images/m0004a_seite2_detail2.jpg>.

Heading	*V-1	{lost}	R	b'š'h̲
	V	grywjywndgyg	*R2	{lost}.

Despite appearances, the headings might have been different, if the previous page contained hymns other than those addressed to the Living Soul. Note that some of the early German publications use the German word 'Vorderseite' for recto and 'Rückseite' for verso, yielding potentially confusing abbreviations 'V' and 'R' with the opposite distribution to that used here.

Demarcation of texts

Some texts are so short that they fit easily on a page, for example a short Manichaean Parthian text on M4a/V/ which is marked off by blank lines after lines 2 and 16 and by an opening caption in line 3 and a closing caption in line 16, both in red ink (see fig. 3.3.9.2).

The text consists of two strophes of equal length, the end of each of which is marked by '°° °°', followed by a third, shorter, strophe (for an edition and commentary, see Durkin-Meisterernst 2004). Preceding and following this text are lines of other texts, similarly marked by a closing caption in line 2 and an opening caption in line 17.

The following is an example for a text that began before the part that survives on the page. In this case, the subject of the first preserved sentence can be assumed to be Mani, and this is supplied in angle brackets, because these words were never actually written on this page:

aM3/ {Middle Persian}
cR/
<*m'ny ...>
l1/ 'md kš 'n nwhz'dg
l2/ 'yg trkwm'n 'wd kwštyh̲
l3/ d(h.)rh̲ 'wd 'bzxy' 'y p'rsyg
l4/ '[mwšt] bwd hym ° 'wd š'h̲
etc.

Dealing with duplicates

A particular feature of the Manichaean texts in the Berlin Turfan Collection is the existence of (fragmentary) duplicates. For example, Sundermann 1992 reconstructed extensive parts of a Parthian sermon from partly overlapping fragmentary duplicates. He presented the critical text, formed by a synopsis of duplicates (here 's', 'p' and 't') in the following manner (Sundermann 1992, 51):

Section 41a:	s	°° (ʾw)[d] /7/ hrdyg rwc wxd ʾst s(xw)[n](t)n(b)[ʾr]
	p	ʾwd hrdyg rwc] /6/ wxd (ʾst)[sxwn tnbʾr
	t	(ʾ)wd hrdyg rw(c)[wxd]

etc.

He established the following 'compiled' text on the basis of the duplicates (Sundermann 1992, 68):

Section 41a:	(ʾ)wd hrdyg rwc wxd ʾst s(xw](n](t)n(b)[ʾr]
Section 41b:	rt(y) [ʾštyk] my-δ x(w)ty xcy ZK (wʾ)[xšy] tnpʾr

etc.

Sundermann assigned section numbers to the text and used the accompanying letters 'a' and 'b' to designate the Parthian and Sogdian versions of the same text. The status of the compiled text is indicated in a way that is specific to each language, i.e. the word *hrdyg* 'third' is attested in an entirely undamaged manner for the Parthian version but this information is not used to do anything more than indicate that the corresponding word * *ʾštyk* in the Sogdian version is expected but entirely unattested.

Here the section numbers only undertake to supply a limited amount of information about the text. They indicate a section of the text which may contain a sentence or part of a sentence but also a number of sentences. The section numbers do not in themselves point to the structure of the text and, despite the fact that a Chinese and an Old Turkic version of the text sometimes provides this information, Sundermann has resisted the temptation to use the section numbers to perform any function other than to reference attested passages. There is a case though for providing some information about the structure of the text, even if it is restricted to indicating the putative sizes of the gaps between the surviving portions of the text.

Variants?

Are parallel/double attestations duplicates or do they point to different redactions of the text? The evaluation of variants in the text is not always easy, because, for example, it is hard to be sure in an incompletely preserved text containing recurring phrases if the apparent duplicates with a variation have not been perhaps wrongly identified. In the case of parts of texts attested more than once the editor is normally more anxious to make use of whatever is available, and will want to reconstruct the main structure of the text rather than worrying about minor variants. In fact, the duration of Manichaean scribal activity in Turfan was no longer than *c.*250 years and the quality of duplicates is very good, so that hardly any significant variation can be observed. The longer duration of Buddhist Uyghur scribal activity makes it much more likely that more significant variation, pointing to redactions of the text, will be found in the Old Turkic Buddhist tradition.

References

Andreas – Henning 1934; Durkin-Meisterernst 2004; Müller [F.] 1904; Salemann 1901, 1908; Sundermann 1981, 1992.

3.10. Arabic epics (ZG)*

Introduction

The Arabic popular epic can be regarded as a genre of Arabic literature which originated and developed within a flourishing tradition of oral story-telling. It should be understood as part of an exceedingly large corpus of traditions that include pseudo-historical accounts of military campaigns and conquests (*maġāzī* 'raids'), legends on the Qur'ānic prophets (*qiṣaṣ al-anbiyā'* 'stories of the Prophets'), accounts of miracles and numerous genres of popular poetry, as well as tales of wonder and fantasy, the best known being *The Thousand and One Nights*.

These works of battle and romance, primarily concerned with depicting the personal prowess and military exploits of their heroes, are often referred to in Arabic with the somewhat polysemic term *sīra* (plural *siyar*) which may cover such concepts as 'course of life', 'biography', 'chivalrous romance', 'epos', 'saga', 'folk epic', and 'popular epic'.

Arabic literature has produced a rich harvest of these heroic cycles that taken together cover almost the whole of recorded pre-Islamic and Islamic history, with most heroes based on actual historical figures. For a long period of time, they were transmitted orally and constantly innovated by popular narrators and simultaneously by scribes or editors of written versions in a complex and dynamic interplay. References to written exemplars appear only in the twelfth century, while the earliest preserved manuscripts date back to the fifteenth century (cf. Heath 2004). They were generally composed in rhymed prose (*saǧ'*) frequently interspersed with poetry (although, for example, the *Sīrat al-Ẓāhir Baybars* is cast mainly in unadorned prose). Only the *Sīrat Banī Hilāl* has been fully preserved in verses.

In the oral-generated form, the Arabic popular epic is performed by an illiterate narrator (*rāwī*), often to the accompaniment of a one-stringed violin (*rabāb*) held upright on the knee. In the semi-literate form, it is read aloud from written versions by an urban storyteller (*ḥākī, ḥakawātī*) in coffee-houses or other public places either with or without musical accompaniment. Even in its purely written form, the Arabic popular epic has always enjoyed great popularity, as it is proved by the huge numbers of manuscripts as well as printed editions (Ott 2003b, 443).

Manuscripts of the Arabic popular epic

The manuscripts represent the most authentic sources of the Arabic popular epic accessible to us nowadays as the number of recordings is very low and all unfortunately bear witness to the diminished status of the oral narrative tradition in the twentieth century. In this regard, it must be kept in mind that the texts in question are generally very long: some manuscripts of the *Sīrat Ḏāt al-Himma* have almost 12,000 folia (Ott 2003a, 51). According to some testimonies, reading or reciting such a long *sīra* would take a year and three months; *al-'Antarīya* would take about a year (Reynolds 2006, 302–303). Naturally, they are only rarely preserved in complete copies written by one hand, and the overall picture is one of numerous manuscripts that contain fragments of the texts or individual volumes. They were quite frequently bound together into one work and the history of such compound manuscripts can cover several centuries (e.g. the manuscript of the *Sīrat al-Muǧāhidīn* Paris, BnF, Arabe 3859–3892 contains a fragment from the year 1430 and the latest contribution from the year 1808). They remain scattered over various collections housed in public and university libraries. The most notable is probably the Wetzstein collection in Berlin, which was so excellently described by Wilhelm Ahlwardt (Ahlwardt 1887–1899, VIII). He lists 173 copies of *Banū Hilāl*; according to Abderrahman Ayoub, today the Staatsbibliothek has 189 manuscripts of this popular epic that date from 1785 to 1854 (Ayoub 1978, 348).

The process of textualizing an oral epic, however, must have been considerably more complex than the simple act of writing down the sequences of spoken words. Its circumstances varied and had a profound influence on the final shape of the whole text. It was, for example, important whether a scribe fixed the text immediately after its recitation or wrote down the narration which was recited sometime beforehand, whether he reconstructed the text on the basis of more 'hearings' or several written source materials, and whether he was faithful to the one source or let his imagination run wild. The economic background of the process should also not be neglected. Copyists were probably faithful to an original text because copying without making profound changes or taking a dictation was, quite simply, the fastest way to produce a new product that could be sold. However, when the creative urge struck, or when it was more lucrative to produce a new product, they had no qualms about reorganizing texts and substituting parts with more

* I thank Francesca Bellino and Jan-Just Witkam for their comments on an earlier version of this paper.

entertaining material, or updating vocabulary in passages that had become hard to understand over the passage of time (Reynolds 2006, 269).

All these (and probably also other) conditions had a distinctive impact on the quality and character of each handwritten document. Moreover, the overwhelming majority of such texts bears witness to a deliberate effort to develop them and shows that this was done predominantly out of a desire to innovate them not only from the point of view of the content, aiming at re-telling the story (or its parts) in what appeared to a particular redactor or scribe to be the most appealing way, but possibly also from the point of view of the language endowing the text with a more literary character or liberating it from the classical style when it seemed necessary. In this context, the imposing of elements of *inšā'* style and other rhetorical devices of Classical Arabic (for example the rhymed prose *saǧ'*) should also be mentioned as they adorned popular narrations and upgraded them, being closer to *adab*. As a result each redactor or scribe in effect made his own contribution to the story-telling tradition. However, as the comparative study of manuscripts of popular *siyar* is very complicated (only a few of the existing manuscripts of the *sīra* are the work of one hand; the great majority are compilations copied by different scribes at different dates, sometimes as separate volumes of different sizes) it is difficult to determine textual contributions of a particular anonymous scribe or narrator.

Apart from these quite general reflections, we know almost nothing about the genesis and the earliest developments of these texts. Most of the complete *sīra* manuscripts at our disposal are relatively late versions. Only fragmentary remnants of the older layers have survived. Therefore, in order to establish the time, place and social context of the genesis of such a text we have to rely on the indirect evidence provided by the text itself, such as specific references to the social or political points of view of its creators. Such an analysis gives us an insight into the different functions that the *sīra* acquired in the course of its development (Herzog 2003, 137–138).

Recent research has also yielded a deeper understanding of the 'oral connexion' of the most famous (but probably also the most complex) work in Arabic popular literature, *The Arabian Nights*. This connexion and the relationship to Arab folklore and *siyar ša'bīya* can also be demonstrated by the fact that some popular *siyar* were included in the *Nights* editions. For example, a shortened version of *Sīrat Sayf ibn Ḏī Yazan* appears in a specific version in the Reinhardt manuscript of the *Nights*, which carries the title *Sīrat Alf Layla wa Layla* (cf. Chraïbi 1996). The foremost example, however, is the *sīra* about King 'Umar an-Nu'mān and his sons whose character and position in the *Nights* were thoroughly explored by Rudi Paret with a partial facsimile of Arabic texts (Tübingen, Universitätsbibliothek, Ma VI 32, cf. Paret 1927, 1981).

The manuscripts of the Arabic popular epic were generally transmitted without punctuation; and if some does appear, it is too sporadic to be considered significant. Moreover, they contain sections or passages that may be regarded as literary with respect to language, style and rhetoric, as well as parts that are written down in varying degrees of colloquializing or 'vulgar' language. Although there are no absolutely reliable criteria for a neat classification of these texts, it is nevertheless possible, in terms of the prevalent linguistic and stylistic registers in each of them, cautiously to distinguish two types of manuscripts here (cf. Gavillet Matar 2003, 377).

The first category comprises manuscripts that were primarily written to be read, because popular *siyar* were not only publicly performed, they were also read privately. People would frequently borrow a written version from a scribe or manuscript lender (*warrāq*) either to read the *sīra* on their own or read it out aloud in a circle of family or friends (Herzog 2012, 642). These texts were rather consciously moulded by a scribe or redactor to somehow mimic the prevailing style of oral storytellers. On the one hand, such scribes would consciously aim to imitate an oral narrative style, but on the other hand intentionally classicize the language register. Colloquialisms are allowed for, but only to a limited degree. An example of this is Galland's fifteenth-century manuscript of the *Nights* (Paris, BnF, Arabe 3609-3611). Muhsin Mahdi dated this manuscript to the fourteenth century, but on the basis of the numismatic evidence Heinz Grotzfeld (Grotzfeld 2006, 105) showed that it can not have been composed before 1450.

The second group of manuscripts is represented by the so called *maḫṭūṭāt ḥakawātiyya* 'storytellers' manuscripts', that were used and written down specifically for public performances. They helped the storyteller perform his narrations, often departing from the text to improvise by following his spontaneous inspiration. In these texts many features of colloquial language are apparent (it is hardly possible to find passages of several lines that contain no noteworthy Middle Arabic phenomena) despite the fact that the majority of the vocalization details are concealed by the Arabic script. Moreover, when assessing their linguistic structure it is necessary to count not only the features of modern Arabic dialects, the forms that correspond to Classical Arabic and so called pseudo-corrections, but also to distinguish when the influence of the Middle Arabic texts became so strong that authors attempted to imitate them rather than Classical Arabic. In these cases we may justly speak about Middle Arabic literary standards (cf. Blau 1986). It goes without saying that the orthography of such a text is open to different interpretations. However, the Arabic writing system can be used to convey the sounds and grammar of various colloquial forms of Arabic only with a certain amount of difficulty, particularly for the reader. One can read a text written in a dialect correctly only if one already knows how that particular dialect is pronounced, which is a rarely acknowledged but serious problem in the case of older dialects (den Heijer 2012a, 67–68).

'Storytellers' manuscripts' represent a primary source of the Arabic popular epic to the extent that their text is the least altered, because the scribe was aware of the fact that it was addressed to an audience (or, in certain cases, possibly a readership) who did not expect pure Classical Arabic. In this respect, some passages, especially dialogues, were difficult to represent orthographically according to classical norms, so that scribes would not hesitate to record them spontaneously and freely. Therefore these texts can also be identified as dictated texts with a distinct phonetic orthography (Herzog 2012, 642).

Manuscripts of the Arabic popular epic are of utmost interest for several reasons. First of all they reflect the narrator's (or the scribe's) personal vision of the narration. Furthermore, they are the only available hard evidence of an oral tradition that lasted for centuries because the tradition of oral composition diminished significantly in the twentieth century. There is only one Arab folk epic which has survived fully as an oral tradition and only secondarily in written form: the *Sīrat Banī Hilāl* (al-Abnūdī 1988, 18), which has been rightfully acknowledged by UNESCO as a 'masterpiece of the intangible heritage'. Manuscripts were in circulation until the second half of the nineteenth century, after which time their place was taken by printed editions (mainly *kutub ṣafrā'* editions).

Popular editions

The first most accessible and well-known printed editions of popular *siyar* were the so-called *kutub ṣafrā'* or 'yellow books', that is very inexpensive books, or in many cases, booklets, printed on low-quality paper whose colour quickly darkened. This format is often used, in the Arab countries but elsewhere in the Muslim world as well, for the diffusion of all kinds of knowledge, religious or otherwise, on a particularly large scale. Such *kutub ṣafrā'* represent the final phase of a manuscript tradition now produced by other technical means.

The motivation of editors to produce such works was both literary and social. Folk narrations were very popular and as the chapbooks were cheap, it was expected they would sell well. Due to the low price and large-scale distribution (in comparison to very expensive manuscripts) such publications massively contributed to the sustained circulation of popular narrations in Arabic-speaking communities until quite recently. However, not all popular *siyar* that exist in manuscript form were published in such folk editions. For example, the *Sīrat Iskandar Ḏū 'l-Qarnayn* and *Sīrat al-Ḥākim bi-Amrillāh* were never printed, and this is probably the reason why they are somewhat less known than other popular *siyar*.

The *kutub ṣafrā'* editions also offered the first visual representations of the Arabic popular epic, as the first illustrations (albeit sparingly) started to be included no matter how simple and unsophisticated they seemed to be. They represented simple oriental ornaments or depicted the main heroes (and heroines) and animals (for example lions). Over the course of time they became more elaborate and accomplished.

These editions were always done anonymously and even the most basic information on the identities of the persons behind their production is quite impossible to obtain. Generally speaking, such anonymous editors systematically obscured the traces of the oral recitation of their source manuscripts and generally tried to give their editions a more formal, classical and literary mode of presentation. They published the texts from source manuscripts with more significant editorial amendments on such issues as style and language aimed at 'decolloquializing' the text.

Nevertheless, in such publications one can still identify evident deviations from Classical Arabic grammar, as well as numerous devices and formulas that bear witness to its underlying oral composition and recitation. Also the general layout of these publications still highly resembles that of manuscripts: there is no or only sporadic punctuation and only an occasional division of the text into paragraphs.

Editors, for example, had to cope with the frequent repetitions of story patterns, which they usually chose to reduce, and with the numerous formulaic descriptions which they tended to eliminate as redundant or confusing. The reason was that the original manuscripts of popular literature which they meant to edit contained a lot of contradictory story patterns without a further mutual relationship. Part of this discrepancy can be explained by the fact that scribes often created a new version from several loosely related manuscripts or according to a particular oral performance. Because of the fact that the narrations were lengthy, lively and rich in action, the storytellers' audiences were not really likely to worry much about the logical coherence of the events and most probably did not even notice such irregularities. On the other hand, such discrepancies would surely disturb readers of written versions. Against the background of writing, such over-abundant repetitions of story patterns were considered to be a serious aesthetic drawback of pre-modern Arabic popular literature.

The scholarly editions of Arabic popular literature

There are only a few editions of Arabic popular literature that can be considered scholarly, although research in this field has increased rapidly in the last decade and some very detailed studies were dedicated to the Arabic popular epic (for example Ott 2003a, Herzog 2006, Doufikar-Aerts 2010 and others). Among the significant instances of text editions and manuscript studies produced at the earlier stages of oriental studies it is essential to mention Duncan B. Macdonald's edition of manuscript Oxford, Bodleian Library, MS. Orient. 633 which contains the well-known story of ʿAlī Bābā and the Forty Thieves. This story was not originally part of *The Arabian Nights* (it was included into the ninth and tenth volume of the *Nights* by Antoine Galland and it was allegedly based on a living source of the *Nights*—a Maronite Christian from Aleppo, cf. Mahdi 1984–1994, III, 33), but shares many typological features with the Arabic popular epic.

There are also numerous other manuscripts containing single stories that appear in recensions of the *Nights* and that were consequently classified as the *Nights* texts (for instance the *Ebony Horse* and the *City of Brass*). The stories in these single manuscripts do not have the 'night breaks' characteristic for the narrative structure of the corpus nor is there any evidence that such breaks were either intended or eliminated (Grotzfeld 2006, 57).

In his edition, Macdonald describes the language as pseudogrammatical Arabic with mistakes and appearances of colloquial words on the one hand and patches of rhetoric more befitting the sophisticated *maqāma* genre on the other, suggesting that fine writing was evidently an aim (Macdonald 1913, 329). In editing he did not insert into the text any punctuation, claiming that he followed the manuscript as closely as possible and endeavoured only to clear away evident surface errors because, as he explained, it was not his business to make the Arab redactor to write good Arabic. Finally, when Macdonald stated that no one who had not worked on the manuscripts of the *Nights* could have any idea of the corruptness of their style (Macdonald 1913, 49), we can now read this assessment as a reference to the abundance of Middle Arabic elements in these text witnesses.

Another edition of Arabic popular literature worth mentioning is Hans Wehr's edition of the entertaining tales of various genres entitled *Kitāb al-ḥikāyāt al-ʿağība wa ʾl-aḫbār al-ġarība* (Wehr 1956). This collection has long been recognized as closely related to the *Nights*. In the introduction, the editor discussed the position of this text and its literary affiliations, and he qualified it as a mixture of Classical Arabic and the spoken language of the narrators (*Umgangssprache*), which he associated with the Christian-Arabic literature, the manuscripts of the *Nights* and memoirs of Usāma b. Munqiḏ (p. xv). He also produced a detailed survey of characteristics of grammatical and orthographic 'deviations' (especially from the norms of Classical Arabic), some of which he 'in the narrower sense marked as mistakes' (p. xiv). He sought to maintain them as such in his edition 'otherwise he had to correct the syntactic and stylistic imperfections as well', although he accounted for them and partly suggested their corrections in a rather rudimentary critical apparatus. In contrast to Macdonald, Wehr decided to introduce into the text some very light but clearly present punctuation. Hans Wehr's edition was thoroughly reviewed and commented on by Anton Spitaler (Spitaler 1994).

Among more recent achievements, Muhsin Mahdi's edition of the *Nights* (Mahdi 1984–1994) stands out as an indispensable example for future *Arabian Nights* studies. In this monumental work the editor provided us with the invaluable service of editing Galland's manuscript (originally intended by Macdonald) with an entirely text-critical approach. The critical edition as such is to be found in the first two volumes. The third volume is fully devoted to the textual history and the composition of the Nights, which is rather intricate, and the major problems of its origin and authenticity still remain a subject of lively discussion. In the foreword Mahdi introduces his method of critical edition, claiming that the only proper approach is to choose the oldest and the most reliable manuscript, then consult other manuscripts in general and those close to the chosen one in particular, and ultimately to include in the critical apparatus only those amendments of the stories that are relevant to the historical evolution of the text (Mahdi 1984–1994, II, 16). The edition was divided into chapters (each chapter covers a night), and, similarly to Wehr's edition some light but systematic punctuation was introduced. Despite the fact that Mahdi's aim was clearly to maintain language peculiarities in his edition, he did not produce a text preserving all of them; he corrected them sometimes according to other manuscripts and sometimes according to his personal judgment (Halflants 2012, 120). The forthcoming reprint of Muhsin Mahdi's edition should contain a new introduction by Aboubakr Chraïbi and errata by Ibrahim Akel (cf. Mahdi 2014).

More recently, Bruno Halflants remained more systematically faithful to such linguistic characteristics (Halflants 2007). His objective was to contribute to the description and analysis of Middle Arabic grammar by selecting one long tale from Galland's manuscript. The text he provides is distinct enough from Mahdi's critical edition because it was edited with a different purpose. One of the main differences is that Halflants did not insert into his edition any punctuation, maintaining even the original length of the lines. In order to make the text easier to follow, he graphically separated individual manuscript folia, dividing the text into 'nights'.

Scientific editions of recited manuscripts (*maḫṭūṭāt ḥakawātiyya*) were attempted only at the turn of the twenty-first century. Recently, Marguerite Gavillet Matar has presented the critical edition of the *Sīrat al-Zīr Sālim* (Gavillet Matar 2005), which she accompanied with a French translation. She prefaces her work with an important study on the reconstruction of the entire manuscript tradition of the *sīra* as well as on the style and linguistic differences among various manuscripts mainly from three different regions: Yemen, Syria, and Egypt. She also includes many important philological notes and illustrations on the language and on the poetry it contains, making full concordances among the three different traditions. Particularly interesting are her comments on *Les Manuscrits de la Tradition des Conteurs—makhṭūṭāt ḥakawātiyya* (Gavillet Matar 2005, 56–59). Thanks to inserted punctuation, paragraphing and subchapters, the edition is easy to follow even for readers without expert knowledge of the Arabic popular epic.

The language and style presented in the edition of the *Sīrat Baybars* worked out by George Bohas, Katia Zakharīya and Salam Diab (Bohas et al. 2000–2011) is an analogue to the edition of Gavillet Matar. Here the aim of the editors to make the *Sīrat Baybars* accessible not only to scholars but also to the wider intellectual public is very apparent. In order to meet the requirements of researchers, they decided to preserve the complete and uncorrected text of the relatively new manuscript (1949) from Damascus without the elimination of morally improper parts or words. On the other hand, in order to make the text reader-friendly the editors added some new chapter divisions to the already existing ones, divided the text into meaningful paragraphs and inserted logical punctuation. With the intention of preventing ambiguous readings, they quite frequently vocalized archaic, colloquial or foreign phrases and expressions (French, Turkish and even Hebrew) and explained their meaning.

Conclusions and recommendations

Several comparative studies of narratives that belong to Arabic popular literature (for example the Arab popular *siyar* and the *Arabian Nights*) have persuasively shown that it is quite futile to aim at establishing a definitive text for such popular narrations. It is simply unthinkable that successive generations of storytellers over the centuries would have transmitted their stories literally, in stable and static versions. Research on oral literatures worldwide has yielded the insight that most traditional storytellers used techniques of remembering only a sort of frame of each story with a large stock of fixed sequences yet plenty of room for improvisation, which would be moulded into a unique version during each single performance. This is why some manuscript versions are longer and some shorter, some are older and some are newer, with larger or smaller numbers of Middle Arabic phenomena or oral storytelling patterns.

Popular storytellers or scribes could easily enlarge any seemingly insignificant episode from the hero's life by means of such techniques of oral and written composition. Every performance or manuscript version has its own taste of originality because neither the storyteller nor the scribe was bound by a precise and stabilized text which had to be consistently interpreted. Some narrators or scribes lingered upon detailed descriptions of battle scenes, dangerous adventures or witty dialogues. Others focused on the explanation of religious elements, not hesitating to insert into their tales Qur'ānic quotations or extracts for their audience's edification. Therefore the understanding of Arabic popular literature through any one manifestation, whether an oral performance, a manuscript fragment or a printed edition, needs to be based on the recognition that this is a mediated and fragmentary access to what is a larger and more flexible fluid entity, which also received a certain literary shape by being written down.

The critical edition of this kind of textual material comes with huge methodological challenges due to its characteristic features: the typically formulaic structure of the rhymed prose in which much of it is composed, the continuous repetition of a limited number of narrative patterns and motifs, the lack of punctuation, the distinctive oral character of the language and its enormous proportions, to the extent that most of these texts cover several thousand pages or manuscript folia. The most important methodological questions which must be answered are related to the choice of the source manuscript(s), the insertion of punctuation and whether or not an editor ought to be scrupulously faithful to the orthography and grammatical features of the available manuscripts. In this context it must be taken into consideration that what has been pointed out referring to the editing of Middle Arabic texts in general is valid also for the originally Arab fluid oral traditions that concern us here: the quest for a scholarly sound approach to editing texts of such a hybrid nature is still far from fulfilled and a consensus among scholars will probably remain beyond reach for some time to come (den Heijer 2012b, 19).

Nevertheless, it would be a good idea to start the editorial process with the selection of one manuscript or an interesting fragment, because of the enormous length of epic narrations as the basis for an edition. As demonstrated above, this could be the oldest reliable witness (cf. Mahdi 1984-1994), which reflects the oldest accessible version of the particular epic tradition, or a late version (cf. Bohas et al. 2000–2011), which documents the richness of later developments taking into account the fact that many manuscripts of the Arabic popular epic are not securely datable. As Kātyā Zaḫariyya proposes (Zakharia 2010, 12), the manuscript should be treated as an *unicum* despite the fact in the information age a researcher could be tempted by the idea of a hypertext which would combine various manuscript witnesses of the same tradition. This could, however, once again lead us to the idea of the reconstruction of the original, which contradicts the stress on fluidity. On the other hand, this does not reduce the importance of the systematic comparison of various manuscript witnesses, which might give a clearer impression of the process of the *sīra*'s composition, evolution and transmission in different cultural environments.

The insertion of punctuation is entirely related to the goals of the edition. If editors intend to reproduce the original as faithfully as possible from a scholarly point of view (cf. Halflants 2007), it is expected that the text would be only minimally altered. On the other hand, if the editors hope that the edition will be enjoyed also by common readers who are not knowledgeable in the Arabic popular epic, the insertion of logical paragraphing and punctuation is justifiable (cf. Gavillet Matar 2005 or Bohas et al. 2000–2011).

Already Goldziher (1850–1921), who was not a linguist in a narrow sense of the word, came to grips with the problem of editing the texts of mixed character (he had Judaeo-Arabic texts in mind) and described it as an inner conflict (*Gewissenskampf*) that had to be confronted by editors who must decide time and again whether or not to 'correct' grammatical 'errors' (Blau 1999, 222). As shown above, attempts to normalize Middle Arabic elements and oral storytelling features at least partly according to Standard Arabic usage, were common practice for centuries. The motivation to do so was related to the importance of Classical Arabic as the language of the Qur'ān or similar standards, or simply to the fact that the manuscript redactors were the heirs and recipients of a venerable storytelling lineage. Some of these trends or their remnants can also be found in modern editions. However, such interventions can have catastrophic results for our knowledge of Middle Arabic and of the authentic features of oral story-telling.

Jérôme Lentin, one of the most experienced authorities in the field of Arabic historical dialectology today, insists that Middle Arabic displays its very nature through its orthography, and that this should not be disguised in the edition. For that reason it is important for editors of Middle Arabic texts to preserve all linguistic and orthographic particularities found in the manuscripts, regardless of how insignificant or incomprehensible they might seem (Lentin 2012a, 209; den Heijer 2012b, 18–20). Put another way, while some words may seem to have a very peculiar and even erratic or illogical spelling which makes the scholar inclined to correct them, it could very well be that they are not simple mistakes and that the underlying systems for such spellings have escaped the editor's attention.

References

Al-Abnūdī 1988; Ahlwardt 1887–1899; Ayoub 1978; Blau 1986, 1999; Bohas et al. 2000–2011; Chraïbi 1996; den Heijer 2012a, 2012b; Doufikar-Aerts 2010; Gavillet Matar 2003, 2005; Grotzfeld 2006; Halflants 2007, 2012; Heath 2004; Herzog 2006, 2012; Lentin 2012a; Macdonald 1910, 1913; Mahdi 1984–1994, 2014; Marzolph 1999, 2004; Ott 2003a, 2003b; Paret 1927, 1981; Reynolds 2006; Spitaler 1994; Wehr 1956; Yaqṭīn 1994; Zakharia 2010.

3.11. Palimpsests of Caucasian provenance. Reflections on diplomatic editing (JG)

Palimpsests of Caucasian provenance

Of the three manuscript traditions that emerged with the conversion of the Southern Caucasus to Christianity by the end of the fourth century CE, that of the so-called Caucasian Albanians (cf. General introduction § 3.4) remained an outsider, given that it came to an end before the end of the first millennium while both Armenian and Georgian literacy have subsisted until the present day. There can be no doubt that the production of manuscripts developed very fast in the early centuries of literacy in all three languages; however, even for Armenian and Georgian, it is only the ninth century CE that provides us with the first dated codices. All older manuscript materials, with but very few exceptions (for example, the famous Georgian 'Sinai lectionary' codex, now Graz, UBG, 2058/1, which is likely to date from the seventh or eighth century, see General introduction § 3.8), are only preserved in fragmentary form, as flyleaves used in the binding of later codices (not necessarily of the same tradition), or overwritten (not necessarily in the same language) as palimpsests.

Since 2003, two international projects funded by the Volkswagen Foundation (Hanover) have focussed on palimpsests of Caucasian provenance, that is reinscribed codices whose underwriting was either Georgian, Armenian, or Caucasian Albanian, with a view to deciphering and editing the contents of the undertext and to establishing the basis for a palaeography of the 'early centuries' for the languages and scripts in question. The results of the work have been published in four volumes of the series *Monumenta Palaeographica Medii Aevi* (Sub-series *Ibero-Caucasica*) at Brepols Publishers, Turnhout, between 2007 and 2010 (Gippert et al. 2007a; Gippert et al. 2009; Gippert 2010a). In the case of the Caucasian-Albanian palimpsests, which were discovered in the underwriting of two Georgian codices from the 'New Finds' of St Catherine's Monastery on Mount Sinai, the edition provides the only manuscript material of the language in question that has come down to us at all, and the fact that neither the language itself nor the script used in writing it was known well enough before the palimpsests were investigated rendered the decipherment extremely difficult; had the texts not been identifiable as biblical, it would surely have failed. In the following pages, the peculiar tasks and methods applicable in editing palimpsest content will be outlined on the basis of the results of these projects.

General characteristics of palimpsests

The re-use of parchment leaves containing 'older' or 'outdated' content in the production of 'new' codices was by no means restricted to the Caucasian world but a characteristic feature of nearly all traditions that used parchment for manuscripts in Antiquity and the Middle Ages. It is decisive in this context that the 'undertext', i.e. the first written content of the leaves in question, played no role whatsoever for the person re-using the leaves, which is why more or less sophisticated methods were applied to erase the older text (by scraping and/or washing it off), and there are many cases where the language of the 'underwriting' is different from that of the upper layer. This is exactly what we find in the case of the Armenian and Caucasian-Albanian palimpsests of Mount Sinai (of approximately the seventh to ninth centuries CE), which were overwritten in Georgian (script and language) by a Georgian monk in about the eleventh century CE.

In general, it is not only the fact that the underwriting has been erased which makes the decipherment of palimpsests a tedious task, but also the fact that the leaves were often clipped in order to match the page layout of the 'new' codex to be produced, with notable amounts of the original text being lost; the underwriting may thus abound in gaps that must be restored in re-establishing the content. Depending on the method applied in erasing the undertext, rubrics of the original manuscript (for example, lection titles in red colour) may have disappeared totally, thus bringing about further 'seeming' gaps in the text flow. In the case of the Sinai palimpsests, additional gaps have emerged from damage to the parchment leaves that was caused by the fire which led to their detection (among the 'New Finds') in 1975 (Gippert et al. 2009, I-1–2 as to details on the circumstances of the discovery of the 'New Finds'). Frequently, the original leaves were turned 90° in being re-used as palimpsests; this may be advantageous for the decipherment as only parts of the letters were overwritten in this case, but it usually led to greater losses of text, especially in the margins. Lastly, palimpsest parchment leaves were often chosen 'at random' in the process of re-use, with the effect that the original sequence of folia was not maintained and leaves from different original codices were intermingled in the establishment of 'new' ones. As a matter of fact, palimpsests mostly contain but fragmentary pieces of the underlying codices and no 'complete' ones; for example, the

Georgian palimpsest codex of Vienna (ÖNB, Cod.Vind.georg. 2, see Gippert et al. 2007a, xviii–xix as to details) comprises fragments from at least fourteen different manuscripts of different ages (*c.* the sixth to tenth centuries CE).

Aims and methods of editing the underwritings of palimpsests

As was stated above, nearly all manuscript materials available for the 'early' centuries of literacy in the Caucasus (*c.* fifth to eighth centuries CE) are only preserved in palimpsest form, which makes the underwritings in question especially valuable for the history not only of the languages in question but also of the textual tradition of Christianity in general. As a matter of fact, the Caucasian traditions have proven to be highly conservative in the sense that they have preserved many otherwise lost 'early' texts or text versions. The decipherment, restoration and edition of the underwritings of Caucasian palimpsests is therefore a task of major importance. On the other hand, the very fact that the texts contained in the lower layer of palimpsests may be unique (this is especially true for the Caucasian-Albanian materials) made it necessary to conceive a combination of special editing techniques that reflect the different degrees of certainty achievable in the decipherment.

1. The 'diplomatic' approach

The scholarly traditions of both Armenians and Georgians have developed similar standards in the editing of ancient texts that have been preserved in manuscript form. Editions like those of the *Vita of Mesrop Maštocʿ* by the fifth-century historiographer Koriwn (Abełyan 1941) or of the Old Georgian Chronicle *Kartlis Cxovreba* (Qauxčišvili 1955–1959) establish a common text by assuming 'leading' manuscripts, deciding between variant readings, resolving abbreviations (suspensions and contractions) and alphabetic notations of numbers and hyphenations, emending scribal errors, storing more specific information on individual witnesses in apparatuses, adding chapter or paragraph numberings, and printing the texts in 'normal' text-flow with modern punctuation in modern scripts (sometimes even in an orthography adapted to modern usage as in the case of the vowel *u* of Georgian which in the majuscule script was written as a digraph <ow> but has been replaced by <u> in most modern editions). As far as the latter features are concerned, this practice is also met with in editions of individual manuscripts as in the case of the ninth-century Sinai *Mravaltavi* (Sinai, St Catherine, georg. 32-57-33+N89), which is the oldest dated Georgian manuscript (Šaniʒe 1959; see General introduction § 3.8 and Gippert forthcoming for details of the codex in question), or the late tenth century codex of Šaṭberdi (Tbilisi, National Centre of Manuscripts, S-1141; Gigineišvili – Giunašvili 1979). Unlike this, the edition of the undertexts of palimpsests requires a more 'diplomatic' approach, which has been adapted throughout in the editions discussed here. This approach has the following characteristics:

a) the undertext is represented in a facsimile-like manner facing the images of the respective manuscript page; this implies that

b) it is arranged line by line (and, where applicable, column by column) as found in the original, with marginal and interlinear glosses, indentations, superscriptions, subscriptions and the like retained and with line numbering added at the side of both the image and the edited text;

c) it is printed in the original script(s) used in the manuscript (majuscules and/or minuscules), in matching character sizes (retaining enlargements for initials and the like);

d) word spacing is represented as it occurs in the manuscripts—given that all Caucasian traditions used *scriptio continua* in the early centuries of their literacy, there are usually no spaces visible at all, at least in majuscule manuscripts;

e) abbreviations (suspensions and contractions) and alphabetic notations of numbers are retained as such, with the respective marks (usually bars above the elements in question) applied;

f) hyphenations, whether with or without specific marks, are retained;

g) punctuation marks are retained as such; and

h) struck-out letters and words are represented as they were first conceived, but with a special markup (outlining or light red colouring) to indicate their being struck out.

In order to distinguish different levels of readability (and, at the same time, certainty of the decipherment), a given passage, word, or letter is printed in different degrees of blackness, ranging from black (on a white background) for perfectly preserved items down to light grey (on a dark grey background) for hardly discernible ones. Passages or elements that have not been preserved (due to clipping or dam-

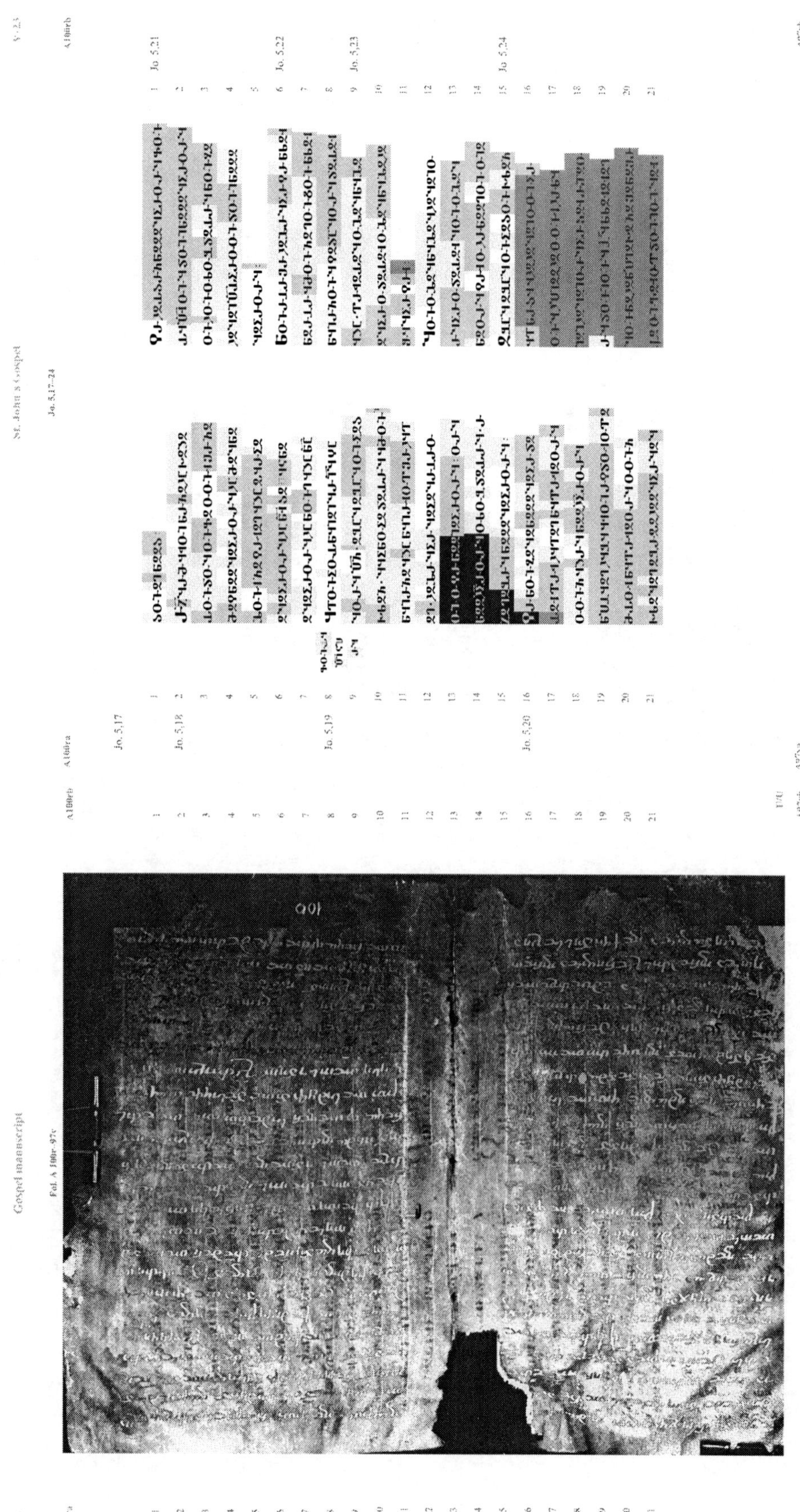

Fig. 3.3.11.1 Edition of John 5.17–24, from Gippert et al. 2009, V-22–23.

A100ra		O	E	A	K	P	G	R	U	S
Jo. 5,17			But Jesus answered them, My Father worketh hitherto,	Եւ յ̄ս պատասխանի ետ նոցա· Հայր իմ մինչեւ ցայժմ գործէ.	მიუგო მათ იესუ: მამაჲ ჩემი მოაქამომდე იქმს	ხოლო იესუ მიუგო და ჰრქუა მათ: მამაჲ ჩემი მოაქამდე იქმს,	ὁ δὲ Ἰησοῦς ἀπεκρίνατο αὐτοῖς, Ὁ πατήρ μου ἕως ἄρτι ἐργάζεται,	Иисус же говорил им: Отец Мой доныне делает, и	Isusenal pine šotġo: bez baban isanalcirik̦ benesa, va'	ܗܘ ܕܝܢ ܝܫܘܥ ܐܡܪ ܠܗܘܢ ܐܒܝ ܥܕܡܐ ܠܗܫܐ ܦܠܚ ܐܦ ܐܢܐ
	1	(z)ow-(a)[l] (ba)[a-z :]	and I work.	Եւ ես գործեմ։	და მეცა ვიქმ.	და მეცა ვიქმ.	κἀγὼ ἐργάζομαι.	Я делаю.	zual bezsa.	ܦܠܚ ܐܢܐ.
Jo. 5,18	2	(E)[˜ṭ'](neš ix)oy (be)[s](a-hē Vača)\[r](owġon)	Therefore the Jews sought the more	Վասն այնորիկ առաւել խնդրէին Հրեայքն	ამისთჳს უფროჲს ეძიებდეს მას ჰურიანი იგი	ამისთჳს უფროჲს ეძიებდეს ჰურიანი იგი	διὰ τοῦτο οὖν μᾶλλον ἐζήτουν αὐτὸν οἱ Ἰουδαῖοι	И еще более искали	va' sayal abuzq̇un furuexai šoṭux	ܡܛܠ ܗܕܐ ܝܬܝܪܐܝܬ ܒܥܝܢ ܗܘܘ ܝܗܘܕܝܐ
	3	[owṗ]a oow[x̣ te sa aṭ˜n]	to kill him, because he not only	սպանանել զնա· զի ոչ միայն	მოკლვად, რამეთუ არა ხოლო	მოკლვად იესუს, რამეთუ არა ხოლო	ἀποκτεῖναι, ὅτι οὐ μόνον	убить Его Иудеи за то, что Он не	besbesan ǯuhuṭġon, šeṭabaxṭinte, šeṭin sa	ܠܡܩܛܠܗ ܠܐ ܒܠܚܘܕ
	4	[ša](d-b)a-a(n)a(k̦e)-o(e)n-[hē] (š)a(nba)\[ṭ]ow[x	had broken the sabbath,	լուծանէր զշաբաթս,	შაფათთა დაჴსნისათჳს,	შაბათსა დაჰჴსნიდა,	ἔλυεν τὸ σάββατον	только нарушал субботу,	šamaṭ ġenax tene xa'xa'exa,	ܕܫܪܐ ܗܘܐ ܫܒܬܐ
	5	sa dex̣-al ičē çi-e](k̦)a-	but said also that	այլ եւ Հայր իւր կոչէր	არამედ რამეთუ მამად თჳსა იჩემებდა	არამედ ღმერთსაცა მამად თჳსა იტყოდა	ἀλλὰ καὶ πατέρα ἴδιον ἔλεγεν	но и Отцем Своим называл	amma ič babane k̦allexa	ܐܠܐ ܐܦ ܕܥܠ
	6	-(a)[n](a)[k̦e-oen-hē b˜](x̣) [z]a[∗ig]-(b)a-	God was his Father, making	զա̄ծ· եւ հաւասար առնէր	ღმერთსა და	და სწორ-ჰყოფდა	τὸν θεόν, ἴσον	Бога, делая Себя равным	bixoġox, ičux barabarbi	ܐܠܗܐ ܕܐܒܘܗܝ, ܐܡܪ ܗܘܐ, ܘܡܫܘܐ ܗܘܐ
	7	-a(nak̦)e-oe(n-hē) b[ow]l (ičē) b[˜](ē)	himself equal with God.	զանձն ա̄յ։	თავსა თჳსსა ასწორებდა ღმერთსა.	თავსა თჳსსა ღმრთისა.	ἑαυτὸν ποιῶν τῷ θεῷ.	Богу.	bixoġoxol.	ܢܦܫܗ ܥܡ ܐܠܗܐ.
Jo. 5,19	G	po(wri\å˜)v gä\(e)n[10]	For the dead							
	8	Il'ow-(k̦)or-biyay-ne Y˜n p(ē)-	Then answered Jesus and said unto	Պատասխանի ետ յ̄ս եւ ասէ ցնոսա·	მიუგო იესუ და ჰრქუა მათ:	მიუგო იესუ და ჰრქუა მათ:	Ἀπεκρίνατο οὖν ὁ Ἰησοῦς καὶ ἔλεγεν	На это Иисус сказал:	meṭa laxo Isusen pine:	ܥܢܐ ܕܝܢ ܝܫܘܥ ܘܐܡܪ ܠܗܘܢ
	9	-(n)-[o](en å˜s) [.amēn] (a)[mēn owk̦](a-z)	them, Verily, verily, I say	ամէն ամէն ասեմ	მართლიად მართალსა გეტყჳ	ამენ, ამენ გეტყჳ	αὐτοῖς, Ἀμὴν ἀμὴν λέγω	истинно, истинно говорю	doġridan, doġridan exzu	ܐܡܝܢ ܐܡܝܢ ܐܡܪ ܐܢܐ
	10	[vˤ](as . ni-k̦bo-k̦a ġaren i)[š](ow)[´y`]	unto you, The Son can	ձեզ· ոչ կարէ որդի մարդոյ	თქუენ: ვერ ჴელ-ეწიფების ძესა კაცისასა	თქუენ: არა ჴელ-ეწიფების ძესა კაცისასა	ὑμῖν, οὐ δύναται ὁ υἱὸς	вам: Сын ничего не может	efa': ġara ek̦al bes teṭubako	ܠܟܘܢ ܕܠܐ ܡܫܟܚ ܒܪܐ
	11	(biyesa i)[č](ē biye)[x̣oc te h](il')-	do nothing of himself,	առնել յանձնէ եւ ոչ ինչ.	საქმედ თავით თჳსით არარაჲ,	საქმედ არცა ერთ რას თავით თჳსით,	ποιεῖν ἀφ' ἑαυτοῦ οὐδὲν	творить Сам от Себя,	ičen ičxol,	ܠܡܥܒܕ ܡܕܡ ܡܢ ܨܒܝܢ ܢܦܫܗ
	12	-(a)[l .] (h)a(ṭe)n(k̦e) n-ak̦a-n-en'e-o\<ow	but what he seeth	եթէ ոչ տեսանիցէ	არა თუ იხილოს,	უკუეთუ არა იხილოს	ἐὰν μή τι βλέπῃ	если не увидит	ägänä naiṭu ak̦o	ܐܠܐ ܡܕܡ ܕܚܙܐ
	13	o de baa>-[yak̦e-oen :] (oen)	the Father do: for what things soever he	զՀայրն զի առնէ. զի զոր նայն	რასა მამაჲ იქმნ, რამეთუ რასაც იგი	რაჲმე მამისაგან საქმჱ, რამეთუ რავდენსა-იგი მამაჲ	τὸν πατέρα ποιοῦντα· ἃ γὰρ ἂν ἐκεῖνος	Отца творящего: ибо, что	babax bal: šeṭabaxṭinte ek̦k̦a	ܠܐܒܐ ܕܥܒܕ ܐܝܠܝܢ ܓܝܪ ܕܐܒܐ
	14	<baa-h˜k̦e-oen> (oˤ)o(m) ġa(ren .) e\<ṭ'a	doeth, these also doeth the Son	առնէ, զնոյն եւ որդի նմին	იქმს, მისა	იქმს, მას ძჱ ეგრევე	ποιῇ, ταῦτα καὶ ὁ υἱὸς	творит Он, то и Сын творит	yaratmišnebesa šeṭin, ṭetäral va' yaratmišnebesa	ܥܒܕ ܗܠܝܢ ܐܦ ܒܪܐ
	15	la>[men ba](a)-anak̦e-o(en :)	likewise.	նման գործէ։	მსგავსადცა ძჱ იქმს.	მსგავსად იქმს.	ὁμοίως ποιεῖ.	также.	ġaren.	ܐܟܘܬܗ ܥܒܕ.
Jo. 5,20	16	<D>[e] (b)o(w)q̇a(n)a-[ba](a-an)[ak̦e ġa]\{r}[ax̣	For the Father loveth the Son,	Զի Հայր սիրէ զորդի.	რამეთუ მამასა უყუარს ძე	რამეთუ მამასა უყუარს ძჱ	ὁ γὰρ πατὴρ φιλεῖ τὸν υἱὸν	Ибо Отец любит Сына	šeṭabaxṭinte baba buṭuq̇sa ġarax	ܐܒܐ ܓܝܪ ܪܚܡ ܠܒܪܗ
	17	cex] (hi)l'-a(l) [b](i)[cex](a-oe)[n]	and sheweth	եւ զամենայն ինչ ցուցանէ	და ყოველსავე უჩუენებს	და ყოველსავე უჩუენებს	καὶ πάντα δείκνυσιν	и показывает Ему все,	va' ak̦esnesṭa šoṭu bütün,	ܘܟܠܡܕܡ ܕܥܒܕ ܡܚܘܐ
	18	(oows i)[č]e(n) [baa]-(h)[˜k̦e]-(o)[en]	him all things that himself doeth:	նմա զոր ինքն առնէ։	მას, რასაცა იგი იქმს,	მას, რაოდენსაცა-იგი იქმს,	αὐτῷ ἃ αὐτὸς ποιεῖ,	что творит Сам;	ek̦k̦ate yaratmišnebesa ičen;	ܠܗ
	19	[bån'i-al himi ixoy edġox̣](oc) [a\šrox̣	and he will shew him	եւ մեծամեծս եւս քան զսոյնս	და უდიდეს-ღა ამისსა	და უფროჲსიღა ამისა	καὶ μείζονα τούτων	и покажет Ему	va' ak̦esnesṭa šoṭu	ܘܕܝܬܝܪܢ ܡܢ ܗܠܝܢ
	20	bicexa-o](en) oow(s)	greater works than	ցուցանէ նմա	უჩუენნეს მას საქმენი,	უჩუენოს მას საქმჱ,	δείξει αὐτῷ ἔργα,	дела больше сих,	aš moṭġoxo abuz,	ܥܒܕܐ ܡܚܘܐ ܠܗ
	21	[vˤ](a)[n]-(a)[l ameç-aha-ank̦](e-na)[n]	these, that ye may marvel.	զգործս. ընդ որ դուք զարմանայք։	რაჲთა თქუენ გიკჳრდეს.	რაჲთა თქუენ გიკჳრდეს.	ἵνα ὑμεῖς θαυμάζητε.	так что вы удивитесь.	ṭetärte va'n aq̇naneġo.	ܕܐܢܬܘܢ ܬܬܕܡܪܘܢ.
A97ra		O	E	A	K	P	G	R	U	S

Fig. 3.3.11.2 Synoptical arrangement of versions of John 5.17–20, Gippert et al. 2009, V-22.

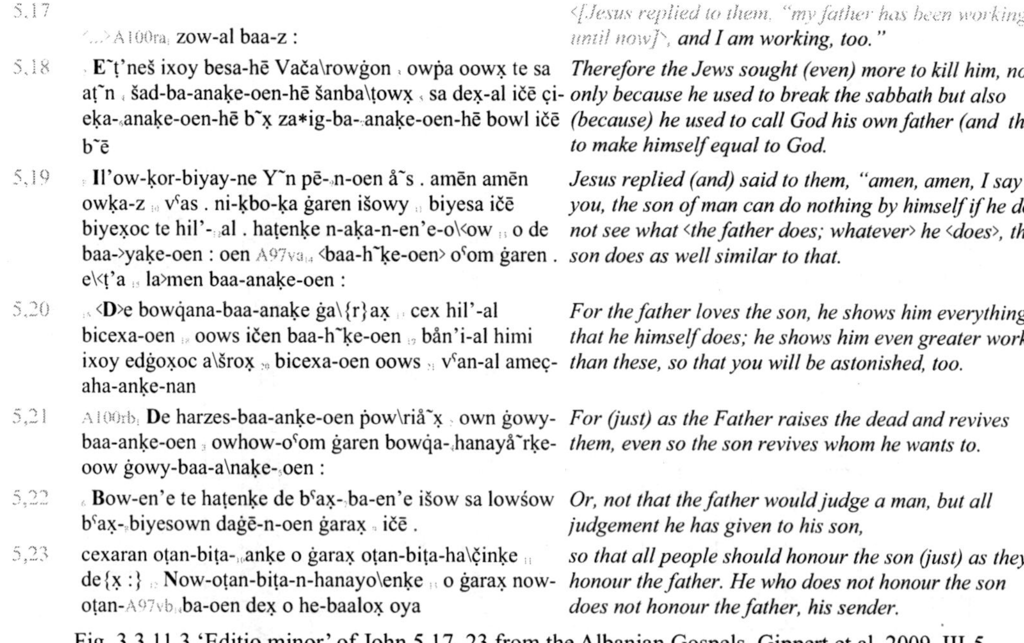

5.17	<...>A100ra zow-al baa-z :	*<[Jesus replied to them, "my father has been working until now]>, and I am working, too."*
5.18	**E**˜ṭ'neš ixoy besa-hē Vača\rowġon owṗa oowx̣ te sa aṭ˜n šad-ba-anaḳe-oen-hē šanba\ṭowx̣ sa dex̣-al ičē çi-eḳa-anaḳe-oen-hē b˜x̣ za*ig-ba-anaḳe-oen-hē bowl ičē b˜ē	*Therefore the Jews sought (even) more to kill him, not only because he used to break the sabbath but also (because) he used to call God his own father (and thus) to make himself equal to God.*
5.19	**I**l'ow-ḳor-biyay-ne Y˜n pē-n-oen å˜s . amēn amēn owḳa-z vˤas . ni-ḳbo-ḳa ġaren išowy biyesa ičē biyex̣oc te hil'-al . haṭenḳe n-aḳa-n-en'e-o\<ow o de baa->yaḳe-oen : oen A97va <baa-h˜ḳe-oen> oˤom ġaren . e\<ṭ'a la>men baa-anaḳe-oen :	*Jesus replied (and) said to them, "amen, amen, I say to you, the son of man can do nothing by himself if he does not see what <the father does; whatever> he <does>, the son does as well similar to that.*
5.20	<**D**>e bowq̇ana-baa-anaḳe ġa\{r}ax̣ cex hil'-al bicexa-oen oows ičen baa-h˜ḳe-oen bån'i-al himi ixoy edġox̣oc a\šrox̣ bicexa-oen oows vˤan-al ameç-aha-anḳe-nan	*For the father loves the son, he shows him everything that he himself does; he shows him even greater works than these, so that you will be astonished, too.*
5,21	A100rb **D**e harzes-baa-anḳe-oen ṗow\riå˜x̣ own ġowy-baa-anḳe-oen owhow-oˤom ġaren bowq̇a-hanayå˜rḳe-oow ġowy-baa-a\naḳe-oen :	*For (just) as the Father raises the dead and revives them, even so the son revives whom he wants to.*
5,22	**B**ow-en'e te haṭenḳe de bˤax̣-ba-en'e išow sa lowśow bˤax̣-biyesown daġē-n-oen ġarax̣ ičē .	*Or, not that the father would judge a man, but all judgement he has given to his son,*
5,23	cexaran oṭan-biṭa-anḳe o ġarax̣ oṭan-biṭa-ha\ç̣inḳe de{x̣ :} **N**ow-oṭan-biṭa-n-hanayo\enḳe o ġarax̣ now-oṭan-A97vb ba-oen dex̣ o he-baalox̣ oya	*so that all people should honour the son (just) as they honour the father. He who does not honour the son does not honour the father, his sender.*

Fig. 3.3.11.3 'Editio minor' of John 5.17–23 from the Albanian Gospels, Gippert et al. 2009, III-5.

age) but can be restored with a certain probability are printed in white on a black background (with non-restorable characters being replaced by a rectangle-shaped placeholder, ⬚).

The manuscript pages themselves are represented by monochrome images stemming from ultraviolet photographs or from the 'spectral cubes' (sets of multispectral images) assembled during the project, electronically enhanced so that the prominence of the overtext is reduced and the contrast between the undertext and the parchment is reinforced (see Gippert et al. 2007a, xxxii–xxxiv and Albrecht in General introduction § 2.3, as to the technical background of the procedures involved). The interplay of these rules is illustrated in fig. 3.3.11.1 showing a sample double page from the edition of the Albanian palimpsests containing John 5.17–23 (Gippert et al. 2009, V-22–23).

2. The 'semi-diplomatic' approach

In order to enable readers with less knowledge of the original scripts to perceive and comprehend the information gathered in the diplomatic rendering, the contents of every single page (or column) is represented a second time in a 'semi-diplomatic' way. This implies the following characteristics:

a) the text is transcribed into the modern scripts (in the case of Armenian and Georgian) or Romanized (in the case of Albanian);

b) it is again arranged line by line, but with no distinction of letter sizes; instead, capital letters (where applicable) are used to represent enlarged initials;

c) marginal and interlinear glosses are marked in special ways (using italics or cursive variants);

d) spaces and hyphens are inserted according to present-day usage;

e) abbreviations are resolved whenever possible (in the case of Caucasian Albanian, the restoration of abbreviations was not possible for many words in question, the unabbreviated variant having remained unknown) but with the restored elements put in (round or curly) brackets;

f) the different degrees of readability and restorations of lost text elements are marked by other types of brackets; however,

g) digraphs and punctuation marks of the original script are still transcribed as such.

To facilitate the verification of the decipherment, the 'semi-diplomatic' rendering is contrasted in tabular form (line by line) with other relevant witnesses of the same text. In the case of the Albanian Gospel texts, these are Old Armenian, Old Georgian, Greek, Syriac, Russian, and Udi versions, the Udi language of the East Caucasus representing the modern successor of Caucasian Albanian (see Bežanov – Bežanov 1902 for the translation of the Gospels into Udi, which was based upon the Russian text); additionally, the English text of the King James Bible was collated. Fig. 3.3.11.2 illustrates this arrangement with the table showing John 5.17–20 (Gippert et al. 2009, V-22).

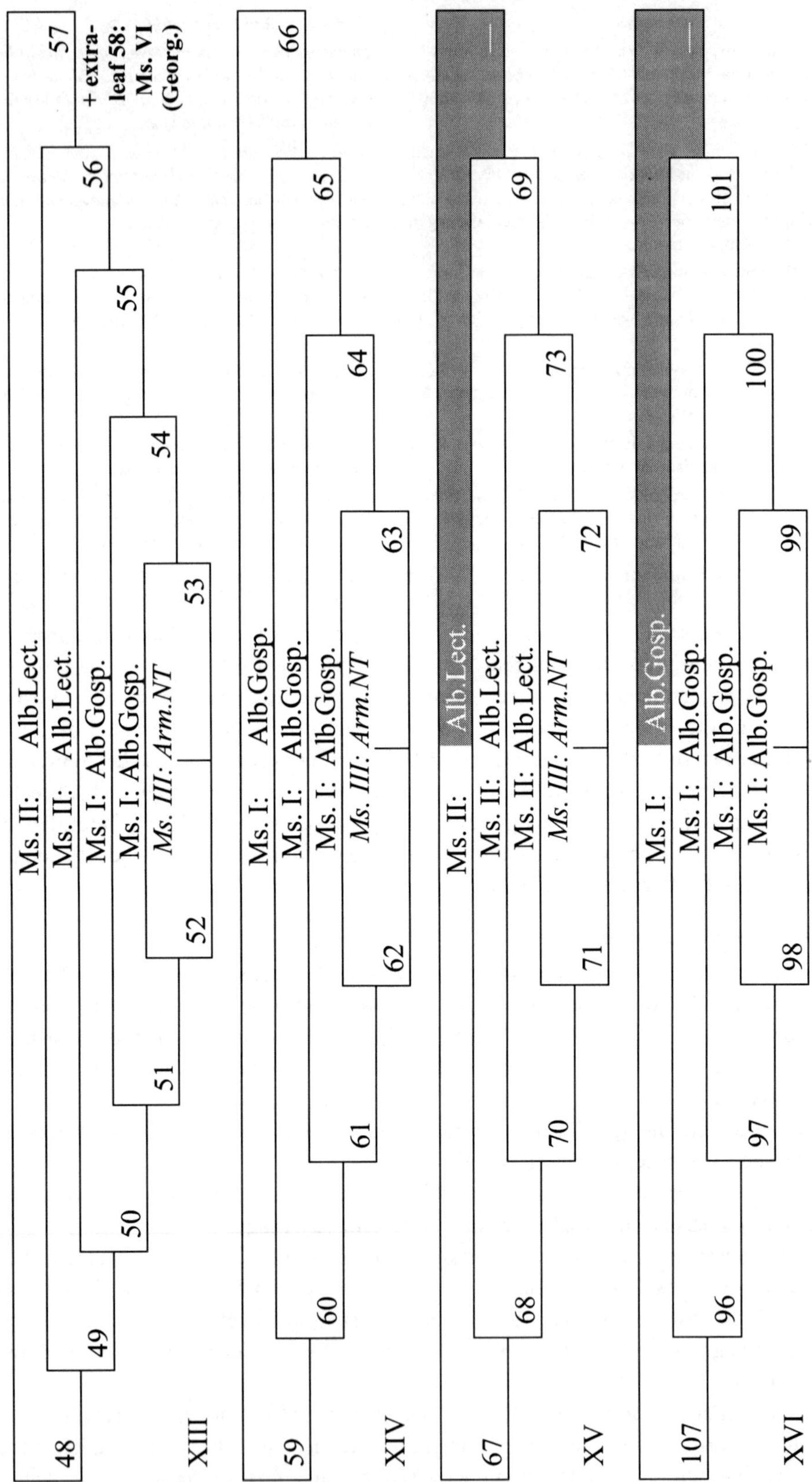

Fig. 3.3.11.4 Manuscript structure of the palimpsest codex Sinai, St Catherine, New Finds, georg. N13 (excerpt).

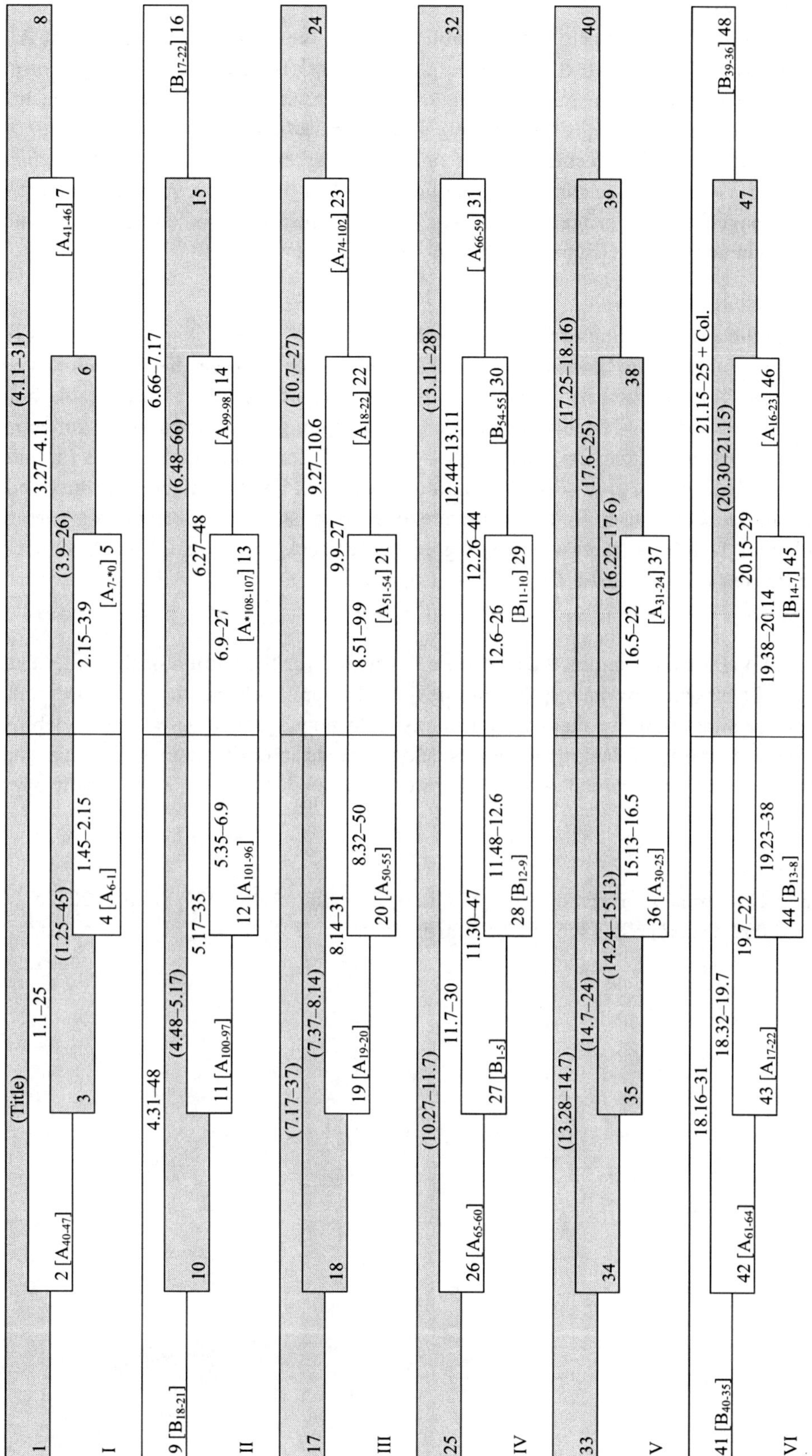

Fig. 3.3.11.5 Quire structure of the Gospel codex underlying MS Sinai, St Catherine, New Finds, georg. N13/N55.

3. Editiones minores

To further facilitate the reading of the re-established texts, the editions of the Caucasian Albanian palimpsests and the Armenian undertext of the Georgian manuscripts Sinai, St Catherine, georg. N13 and N55 were further reassembled in a simplified version, together with an English translation. In this rendering, there is no indication of the degree of certainty of a given reading; however, amendments of unreadable or lost passages are marked with curled braces and angle brackets, respectively, in the Albanian and Armenian texts and with angle brackets throughout in the English translation. Passages that are restored in toto (on missing pages etc.) are printed in grey. Fig. 3.3.11.3 illustrates this 'editio minor' with John 5.17–23 from the Albanian Gospels (Gippert et al. 2009, III-5).

4. Codicological information

To facilitate the understanding of the complex distribution of original manuscript leaves (usually bifolia) over the quires of the 'new' codex, a special illustration technique has been developed as shown in fig. 3.3.11.4. Here, Roman numbers (XII–XV) indicate quires of the new codex, Arabic numbers (48–99), pages of the new codex (as established during the cataloguing, in some cases not reflecting the intended order represented in the diagram), and 'Mss I–VI', the different original codices the palimpsest leaves derive from. Fields with a grey-shaded background represent leaves that have not survived. In the case of the Albanian Gospel manuscript, it was possible to re-establish the quire structure of the original codex in toto, including the bifolia (represented by a grey-shaded background again) that have not been preserved in the palimpsest (Gippert 2012, 62; fig. 3.3.11.5).

Outlook

Even though the methods outlined above were developed for the edition of the undertexts of a few palimpsests of Caucasian provenance, they are likely to be applicable to other palimpsests, too, and several edition projects that will use them are underway right now. Depending on the readability of the given objects, the availability of flanking witnesses, and the needs and expectations of editors and readers, some of the methods may be regarded as superfluous or overstated. However, a diplomatic approach seems to be justified in any case.

References

Abełyan 1941; Bežanov – Bežanov 1902; Gigineišvili – Giunašvili 1979; Gippert 2010a, 2012; Gippert et al. 2007a, 2009; Q̣auxčišvili 1955–1959; Šaniʒe 1959.

3.12. Syriac monastic miscellanies (GK)

This case study aims at presenting a distinctive type of Syriac manuscripts containing monastic literature. For anybody willing to make use of this type of witness, it is of vital importance to be aware of a specific character of textual transmission within such miscellanies. Since that type of manuscript has not been studied properly, the following presentation is based on the research carried out by the author, while taking into account available publications.

Introduction

Manuscript miscellanies (or multiple-text manuscripts) constitute a special phenomenon in the history of the book. Conventionally, it is accepted that miscellanies appeared in the Late Antique period in Christian communities of Egypt and immediately spread all over the Mediterranean region (fourth to seventh centuries), eventually becoming the predominant type of manuscript (Petrucci 1986a). Without consideration of specific language and cultural affiliation, miscellanies usually reveal common traits, among which two deserve to be singled out: individual content and instability. One of the greatest hindrances to the study of the relevant manuscripts is the imperfection of the manuscript catalogues. Furthermore, there is no agreement with respect to the relevant terminology; codicological approaches differ as well (Thorndike 1946, Robinson [Pa.] 1980, Shailor 1996, Gumbert 2004, Maniaci 2004, Bausi 2010e).

As far as the state of the art is concerned, the study of the miscellanies is very young and disproportionate: whereas Greek, Latin and later European vernacular miscellaneous manuscripts have been studied quite deeply (Foehr-Janssens – Collet 2010; Ronconi 2007; Van Hemelryck – Marzano 2010), the miscellanies that were produced in the Christian oriental traditions have not yet become the object of elaborate research (Birnbaum 2003; Buzi 2011a; Miltenova 2013). In order to determine whether the phenomenon of the miscellanies has a universal nature, or whether there are some regional or cultural peculiarities, it would be necessary to pursue a comprehensive study of miscellaneous manuscripts in the Christian oriental traditions; this is, however, not feasible at present due to the unequal development of the respective fields.

Within the context of Syriac philology, which is itself a relatively young field, a study of the peculiarities of the manuscript transmission of all the varieties of texts has never been undertaken. The only exception is offered by the biblical texts, the character of the transmission of which is now known quite well. Generally speaking, the Syriac Bible (Peshitta) demonstrates very minor variation. Compared with the biblical text, all other literary genres show a significantly higher degree of instability.

The overwhelming part of the Syriac monastic literature (texts that were produced from approximately the fourth until the fifteenth century, Brock 1986) as well as translations of monastic texts from Greek are preserved in monastic miscellanies—for a considerable number of texts miscellanies constitute the only available type of witness. Without miscellanies, one would know much less about Syriac Christianity and Syriac literature than we do today and some Greek texts would have continued to be considered lost (for example some of the works of Evagrius Ponticus). On the other hand, the fragments of otherwise unknown texts can give us a hint as to how much of the Syriac literature has gone into oblivion.

Potential difficulties

A study of a text preserved within a miscellany may pose serious difficulties of different kinds. To name just the most salient ones:

First of all, the study of the Syriac monastic literature is particularly young and began at the end of the nineteenth century when Paul Bedjan and Ernest A. W. Budge published a number of ascetic and mystical texts (Bedjan 1897, 1898, 1902, 1909; Budge 1894, 1904). While many Syriac monastic texts (including translations from Greek) were published during the twentieth century, a lot still remains to be done (for a bibliography, see Kessel – Pinggéra 2011). A census of all extant monastic texts in Syriac is an urgent desideratum. Moreover, the study of Syriac monastic literature has been heavily dominated by research into doctrine with a gross neglect of the textual transmission of the texts. As an outcome, many of the texts have been represented in an inaccurate and inauthentic form.

Second, although many miscellanies were used for editions of singular texts, they have never been studied per se, as collections that existed according to specific principles. Usually, the fact that a text is preserved in a miscellany does not affect its study in any way: a miscellany is assumed to be a copy that is not different from other types of witness. Besides a few facsimile reproductions (Mingana 1934b; Strothmann 1978; Çiçek 1985), there are some studies that contain descriptions of a particular miscellany (Baethgen 1890; Brock 1998; Vosté 1929; Colless 1966; Teule 1997; Vööbus 1978). Only three articles are to be noted as exceptional since they are not purely descriptive in character, but rather approach some of the issues from a methodological perspective as well (Brock 2004; Teule 1998, 2008).

Third, a body of already published material is not available in searchable format similar to the *Thesaurus Linguae Graecae*, although some attempts have been made recently in that direction (a Syriac Corpus project under the auspices of Brigham Young University).

Fourth, the problem of editing extant texts is closely related to another issue that every prospective editor will have to deal with—namely, the search for the extant manuscripts and the procurement of copies. Thus, if European and North American collections have been catalogued (with varying degrees of detail) the Middle Eastern collections (especially in such countries as Turkey, Syria, and Iraq) still remain generally unknown and inaccessible. The instability in the region threatens the survival of those collections. The on-going imaging projects of the Hill Museum and Manuscript Library (Collegeville, MN) may change the situation radically.

Core information about the miscellanies

Preliminary study of miscellanies demonstrates that they were produced and circulated in three ecclesiastical communities of the Syriac tradition: Chalcedonian (known also as 'Melkites'), Syrian Orthodox ('Jacobites'), and East Syriac ('Nestorians'). However, the largest number of monastic miscellanies that survive comes from the Syrian Orthodox tradition. Some one hundred and thirty miscellanies have been found up until today; they were produced over a period of fifteen centuries that roughly corresponds to the entire history of Syriac monasticism.

In the earliest manuscripts one can already detect some features that remain a constant characteristic of the miscellanies during the entire period of their history: (a) each miscellany is a unique collection of various monastic texts: whereas some texts and groups of texts may appear also in other miscellanies, the contents as a whole always have an individual profile; (b) the introduction of a large number of texts translated from Greek; (c) the transfer of texts from one ecclesiastical tradition to another. It should also be noted that miscellanies contain not only complete texts, but fragments (for example chapters, excerpts) as well. Though perhaps over-simplifying the actual situation, we may say that apparently the compilers were not satisfied with simply copying available miscellanies, but intended to create a new collection answering to the demands of their time. However the actual reasons that entailed the unrepeatable character of a given miscellany require special and individual research.

Beginning from the earliest miscellanies we find special titles that were applied to them by the scribes. An extended version would sound like: 'Book of collections (*kunnāšē*) from [the texts by] the holy fathers and monks'. This very fact signifies that for the Syrians themselves the miscellanies represented a special genre of literary production.

Miscellanies quite often have rich scribal notes that allow one to locate their place of production. The extant miscellanies come from the main area of the presence of the Syriac Christians during the pre-modern period: Northern Mesopotamia, including south-eastern Turkey and the famous Ṭūr ʿAbdīn region, northern Iraq, and also Egypt, including Sinai. There seems to have been no single centre where the miscellanies may have been conceived as a new genre; neither it is plausible that there existed special centres for the production of miscellanies. Rather, the available evidence suggests that basically any scribe was in a position to compile a miscellany. Nevertheless, it is worth noting that the oldest miscellanies were produced in Edessa and this very association with the cradle of Syriac Christianity may have contributed to their success and popularity.

Not surprisingly, the majority of texts included in the monastic miscellanies are of Greek origin. Authors such as Evagrius Ponticus and Macarius the Great provided the foundation for the nascent Syriac monastic traditions, and their works did not cease to be copied and appreciated over time. Besides the profound influence of the Greek monastic tradition, Syriac monasticism managed to engender its own rich tradition that is represented by such authors as John the Solitary, Philoxenus of Mabbug, Isaac of Nineveh, and John of Dalyatha, whose works gained an authoritative position not only in their own ecclesiastical tradition but also managed to cross confessional borders and were used by Syrians of other traditions as well (and later by other Christian traditions—Coptic or Ethiopic—that had access to them in translation).

Almost every Syriac monastic miscellany has its own content that is not mirrored in any other miscellany. An acquaintance with the works included in the miscellanies demonstrates a varying frequency of presence of particular texts. That the works of Evagrius Ponticus are consistently present is easily comprehensible, whereas the texts of Pseudo-Dionysius the Areopagite appear more rarely than one might expect considering their impact on the development of Byzantine mysticism.

Greek authors dominate in the earliest miscellanies, whereas by the turn of the second millennium one finds collections that include only Syriac authors. A comparison between the oldest extant miscellany and one from the fifteenth century can help to illustrate that:

London, BL, Add. 12175 (534 CE)	*Mardin, Church of the Forty Martyrs, Orth. 417 (1473 CE)*
Evagrius Ponticus (d.399) The Life of Evagrius Mark the Monk (fifth century) Macarius the Great (fourth/fifth century) Basil the Great (d.379)	John of Dalyatha (eighth century) Joseph Ḥazzaya (eighth century) Isaac of Nineveh (seventh century) Athanasius Abu Ghalib (twelfth century) Evagrius Ponticus (not authentic) Jacob of Serugh (d.521) Abraham of Nathpar (sixth/seventh century)

It is remarkable that the majority of texts included in the fifteenth-century Syrian Orthodox miscellany are of East Syriac provenance. This situation is very common in such late miscellanies as this.

Handling of texts

Unfortunately, very little attention has been paid in earlier scholarship to the actual manuscripts that preserve the monastic literature. Scholars, while looking for the texts they were dealing with, generally neglected the manuscripts they used. And in the case of monastic literature it is most often miscellanies that contain Syriac texts. Editors, while relying on the evidence provided by miscellanies, tend to disregard the context in which the text had been circulating, and fail to scrutinize how the text was understood and transmitted. This kind of approach may lead to imperfect editions, as the editors, not paying attention to the specific character of the manuscripts that preserve the text, do not realize that the text transmitted within miscellanies was subject to certain (quite often substantial ones) editorial interventions.

The study of texts that are found in miscellanies reveals that they quite often have a different form when compared with the same texts as preserved in other types of manuscripts. Now it is clear that the very fact that a text was selected to be included in a miscellany, as well as its transmission, entailed its being handled in a process of scribal revision. The scribes themselves felt free enough to introduce changes both into the content of the miscellanies in general and into any text in particular. On the one hand, such an attitude led to a great variety in the content of miscellanies, but on the other hand, it had dramatic repercussions upon the individual texts. In some cases it is even no longer possible to determine how the text had looked like before it was introduced into the miscellany.

Thus, the main problem in dealing with a text preserved in miscellanies will be to trace all of the possible editorial interventions. A number of typical changes have been detected (but not sufficiently studied): changes of the authorship, abridgements (whether slight or more substantial), interpolations, excerptions, and the introduction of chapter divisions and rubrics.

Failing to recognize such possible alterations inevitably results in a misrepresentation of the text, which is especially dangerous if a particular text is known to exist only in miscellanies, and thus its form cannot be controlled by means of other types of witness. A proper critical study of any such text requires considering all possible changes that might have occurred to it from the moment it was for the first time introduced into one or more miscellanies and in the process of manuscript transmission.

Examples

Fifteen manuscripts that were written in the period from the thirteenth to the beginning of the twentieth century contain a brief text attributed to the otherwise unknown Thomas the Monk (based on Kessel 2009). The considerable number of copies indicates that the text enjoyed a steady popularity among the Syrian Orthodox monks and scribes. A quest for information on the author does not reveal more than a vivid account by Michael the Great (d.1199) concerning the life of a certain monk Thomas, who may be identified as the author of the *Letter*. No direct data concerning the time and place of its composition can be found within the text. However, external evidence makes this identification plausible.

The *Letter* is a brief text and is ordinary in its ascetic contents. Nevertheless, it exemplifies the possible history of transmission of a treatise in the Syriac monastic miscellanies. The fifteen witnesses can be grouped in three recensions, of which only one (Recension I) provides a complete text. The archetypal text underwent a process of partition which resulted in the irregular order of two parts of the text (Recension III). Partition and the subsequent incorrect reestablishment of the order triggered the interpolation of an inauthentic passage (Recension II). Witnesses of Recension II demonstrate that a treatise may have been abridged more than once. Finally, a text can lose its original attribution (one manuscript belonging to Recension II) and be taken over in another ecclesiastical tradition (an East Syriac manuscript that represents Recension I).

The second example will show how dramatically a text may change while being circulated within miscellanies (based on Draguet 1973; Graffin 1963). The transformations could have been in fact so profound that in some cases it is no longer possible to put the extant witnesses into coordination and therefore the task of preparing a critical edition with an attempt to draw near the archetype appears to be highly problematic.

In 1963, the renowned Syriac scholar, François Graffin, published a brief text that is attributed in the manuscripts to the famous Egyptian author, Abba Isaiah. Apparently, Graffin simply relied upon the attribution provided by the miscellany he used, because in all the extant manuscripts the text is indeed explicitly attributed to Abba Isaiah. Graffin does not go into discussion on the authenticity of the text, although, as he correctly notes, the text cannot be identified with any known Greek text attributed to Abba Isaiah.

Since its publication and up to the present day the text and its publication by Graffin continues to be mentioned among the authentic works of Abba Isaiah, or even as a witness to his *Asceticon* (for example it was allocated a special number in *Clavis Patrum Graecorum* (5556)). This, however, is not correct, for already in 1973 another renowned Syriac scholar, René Draguet, was able to clarify the provenance of the text. One ought not forget that René Draguet was one of the best experts on the *Asceticon* by Abba Isaiah and its commentary tradition. Thus, he not only thoroughly studied and published all extant redactions of the Syriac version of the *Asceticon*, but also published an extensive commentary on the *Asceticon* written by the East Syrian Dadisho' Qaṭraya (seventh century). Draguet was able to ascertain that the text piece edited by Graffin in fact comes from an original Syriac commentary on the *Asceticon* that survives in fragmentary form in eight Syriac monastic miscellanies. The results of the study of Draguet can be summarized as follows. A total of eight manuscripts contain fragments from an *Anonymous commentary on the Asceticon of Abba Isaiah*. The commentary can be safely considered to be written originally in Syriac because its author relies profoundly on a commentary on the *Asceticon* by another Syriac author, Dadisho'. Although an original contribution by an anonymous author who might have lived in the eighth century is rather limited, the text of a new commentary provides important evidence for the commentary of Dadisho' that is not preserved in a complete form. The anonymous commentary had a long transmission history. An extant manuscript tradition presents the text in a confused form where the lemmata of Abba Isaiah are no longer separated from the commentary. The text of the commentary is preserved only in a fragmentary form, and the extent of the fragments varies from one manuscript to another. Comparison with the sources used by the anonymous author reveals that the text had undergone considerable alterations. The manuscript transmission must have been so extensive that none of the eight extant witnesses can reliably be put into a relationship with any other. Consequently, as argued by Draguet, the task of producing a stemma appears to be absolutely impossible in this case.

References

Baethgen 1890; Bausi 2010e; Bedjan 1897, 1898, 1902, 1909; Birnbaum 2003; Brock 1998, 2004; Budge 1894, 1904; Buzi 2011a; Çiçek 1985; Colless 1966; Draguet 1973; Foehr-Janssens – Collet 2010; Graffin 1963; Gumbert 2004; Kessel 2009; Kessel – Pinggéra 2011; Maniaci 2004; Miltenova 2013; Mingana 1934b; Petrucci 1986a; Robinson [Pa.] 1980; Ronconi 2007; Shailor 1996; Strothmann 1978; Teule 1997, 1998, 2008; Thorndike 1946; Van Hemelryck – Marzano 2010; Vööbus 1978; Vosté 1929.

3.13. Middle Arabic texts. How to account for linguistic features (PLS)

When we face the issue of preparing a critical edition of a given text belonging to any cultural tradition whose language remains alive, or at least was still alive at the time of the copy—as it is the case, for example, of Romance and Arabic traditions—two types of criticism should be considered: the criticism of forms and the criticism of variants, that is the linguistic form of the edited text and the criticism of the textual variants respectively. Gaston Paris, a French philologist who lived in the second half of the nineteenth century, was the first to introduce this distinction within the field of textual criticism (Paris – Pannier 1872). However, both types are intimately linked to each other. Accordingly, the choice of the proper linguistic form to be given to the edited text is closely related to the method adopted by the editor in order to choose among different variants of the tradition. It must be admitted, however, that editors of pre-modern Arabic texts, generally speaking, have all but totally ignored this distinction, as much as they have often remained quite unaware of much of the western philological tradition as developed mostly in Europe in the nineteenth and twentieth centuries.

A case in point is the famous *al-Fihrist* of Ibn al-Nadīm (438 AH/1047 CE), a basic historical source which presents the lives and works of the most prominent cultural, political and scientific personalities of the early Abbasid period. Despite its generally acknowledged authority, this text was only recently made available in a critical edition that takes into account all obtainable manuscript witnesses (Sayyid 2009). In contrast, such an edition as the one produced by Yūsuf ʿAlī Ṭawīl, printed by the Dār al-Kutub al-ʿIlmiyya ('The House of Scholarly Books') in Cairo in 2002, is a telling example of the ways in which the classics of Arabic literature are commonly edited. In his introduction, the editor informs us that two editions of this text already existed prior to his project: that of Tehran published in 1971 and that of Beirut, published by Dār al-Maʿrifa ('The House of Knowledge') in 1978. However, while failing to account for other sources he consulted, Ṭawīl actually chose to note the variants that he had found in those existing editions: in doing so, he sometimes granted preference to the variants of the Tehran edition and in other cases to those of the Beirut edition. Such a method leads us to the rhetorical question as to whether one should collate editions rather than the text witnesses found in the manuscripts themselves.

With respect to another well-known Arabic literary work, such methods were denounced earlier on by Jan Just Witkam, who noticed that several editions of the *Ṭawq al-ḥamāma* by Ibn Ḥazm (456 AH/1064 CE) contained exactly the same error at the very beginning of the text, which is preserved in a unique manuscript (Leiden, Leiden University Library, Or. 927). This error actually turned out to be nothing but a mistake by the first editor, which sadly persisted in the subsequent editions. Hence, one can only come to the somewhat embarrassing conclusion that none of the editors of this classic of Arabic literature had actually bothered to scrutinize the sole extant manuscript. Instead, all these editors had confined themselves to scrupulously reproducing the first edition, so that it would be actually more appropriate to speak of successive reprints rather than of new editions.

In line with Witkam's critical remarks, these two examples can be generalized to the extent that the poor methodological state of affairs described in them applies to the bulk of the monuments of Arabic literature (Witkam 1988).

Nevertheless, some editors of Arabic texts have indeed tried to formulate methods for producing critical editions. Among the most explicitly articulated approaches, we can distinguish at least two opposing schools or trends:

(1) The first approach, considered out of date by many but still practised by others, is that of selecting a manuscript supposed to be 'good', or which for various reasons should be considered the 'base manuscript', and whose variant readings and linguistic form are to be reproduced in the main text body, even in the case of obvious scribal errors.

(2) The second trend is represented by those who are in favour of further action in the edited text, both in the form—always correcting the text according to the rules of the classical language—and the choice of readings, often adopting subjective criteria.

The first method was followed, for Arabic texts as well as for those published in other relevant languages, in some editions published in the *Corpus Scriptorum Christianorum Orientalium* series in the period in which it was directed by René Draguet (Platti 1981, 1987). In his manifesto of what one may consider an utterly conservative point of view on editing Syriac texts in a radically diplomatic kind of way (Draguet 1977), Draguet basically rejected the legitimacy of any degree of intervention by the editor in the text body itself.

Although primarily concerned with Syriac texts, this publication is relevant for Arabic as well, or at least for Christian Arabic texts, because it is precisely as a response to it that the most prominent and outspoken plea for the second trend was voiced by Samir Khalil in several articles as well as introductions to his editions.

After having dismissed the editions of autographs, which are rare in the literature of the pre-modern era, Samir (1982, 74) argues that the purpose of editing is 'on the one hand to give a readable and correct text, on the other hand to edit a clear and structured text in which the structure of the author's thought appears' (translation PLS). Hence for Samir, and with him for most editors of Arabic texts, the criterion of the readability of old texts by modern readers is a priority issue (Blachère – Sauvaget 1945; al-Munajjid 1956). Samir summarized the methods used by editors of Arabic texts in order to choose among variant readings in a tradition with multiple witnesses. Two possibilities are considered:

(1) The editor selects a copy that qualifies as the 'best witness' and collates it with the others;

(2) The editor chooses, from the multitude of available manuscripts, a text or portion of a text that appears to him (*yuḫayyalu ilayhi*) to be closest to the original. Such a conclusion will of course have to be based on perusal of other (published) works by the same author (Samir 1980).

According to Samir, the first option makes sense when there is a witness that has genuine readings as compared with other witnesses. However, one has the feeling that Samir comes with the risky tendency to equate the 'good' reading, that is to say the original one, with the antiquity of the manuscript. As a result, the most ancient manuscript will always be considered to be the best manuscript, against the principle *recentiores non deteriores*, at least *non semper*.

The second possibility is to be considered where various witnesses have the same importance or value, that is to say when there is no known manuscript closer to the original or no particularly old copy. Many examples of this latter approach can be found in the *Patrimoine Arabe Chrétien* collection which was founded by Samir himself. In many instances, the result seems to be an eclectic edition without significant attempt to examine the genealogical relationships between witnesses (Edelby 1986). It seems appropriate here to point out that outside Arabic studies, this type of eclectic method has met with methodological objections such as the one by Dominique Poirel (2006, 163) who states that it 'reduces the examined witnesses to reservoirs of variants and offers to the editor a complete freedom to draw from them with his grammatical, stylistic, doctrinal or historical preferences as the only rule' (translation PLS).

The two methods described above are intended, in their own way, to provide a solution to two fundamental requirements for any critical edition: the principle of loyalty (to the author, the witnesses, the archetype) on the one hand, and the legibility of the edited text on the other. In the first case the editor usually opts for an almost fetishist fidelity to the witness, while in the second he takes the freedom to intervene both in textual substance and in linguistic form, in order to make the text more readable and accessible to modern readers and so to disseminate it as much as possible. In other words, the editor who chooses to maintain fidelity to one witness conserves linguistic forms of the manuscript in the edition as well, renouncing even a minimal effort at critical reconstruction, while the other school provides us with texts deprived of both the textual and the linguistic dimension found in the manuscript sources. As we shall see, criticism of variants and criticism of linguistic forms are closely linked to each other, that is to say, the one affects the other.

Is a diplomatic edition the only way to preserve the ancient language? Does any attempt to reconstruct an archetype entail levelling the language to conform to Modern Standard Arabic rules? To these questions, we can add another regarding the originality of the standardized language. Is it reasonable to assume *a priori* that the authors, as cultivated scholars and writers, always wrote in Classical Arabic? Indeed, the attempt of an editor to standardize the language always presumes that the author has always chosen to write in the high register of the language and any deviation from that register is interpreted as an error. Is Middle Arabic nothing but a peculiar form of Arabic, which had been altered and corrupted by inexperienced and insufficiently educated copyists? Fischer ([W.] 1991), for one, tried to answer these questions by demonstrating that many authors of Arabic literature often freely chose a more 'relaxed' register of language for stylistic and rhetorical issues. Since the study of Middle Arabic was established as a true sub-discipline within Arabic studies (see den Heijer 2012a with further references), specialists have further developed this more balanced understanding of the reality of the Arabic language in its social and historical settings, but outside these circles, the outdated questions just dealt with can still be heard quite frequently.

However, as Lentin remarked, 'One cannot but observe that many writers have left us works both in faultless or even sophisticated Classical Arabic and works written in Middle Arabic. For those writers at least, one has to abandon the idea of their inadequacies in Classical Arabic. Moreover, it can be supposed that their choice to write some of their works in Middle Arabic was not arbitrary and was probably dictated, among other considerations, by the kind of audience they were writing for' (Lentin 2008, 216–217 and 2012b, 44–46). Actually it is well known by scholars that in pre-modern Arabic literature, numerous works are known to have been produced in Middle Arabic by authors who elsewhere demonstrated their perfect mastery of the literary language, as in the cases of Usāma Ibn al-Munqiḏ (1095–1131), Yāqūt al-Rūmī (1179–1229), al-Tanūḫī (941–994), Abū Farağ al-Iṣfahānī (897–967) and others.

Criticism of variants and criticism of forms

Whereas criticism of variants has the aim of retrieving the archetype of a given tradition, the aim of criticism of forms is to retrieve as far as possible the original linguistic features of the text. However, as we have already mentioned, the most common method adopted among editors of Arabic text, is to correct the linguistic features found in the manuscript witnesses, considering them as an altered form of the classical language. As a matter of fact it is often overlooked that a fair amount of pre-modern (as well as modern) Arabic texts are written in the mixed variety of the language that is often called Middle Arabic (or simply mixed Arabic) and that somehow oscillates between Classical Arabic (also known as Standard Arabic) and colloquial Arabic (for recent assessments of the study of this field, see Lentin 2008, 2012b; den Heijer 2012a; La Spisa 2012). And in many other cases, texts are written according to Classical Arabic grammar but with spelling conventions that today are considered closer to the colloquial register and do not correspond to current Standard usage.

As pointed out earlier, many editors of Arabic texts follow the method of correcting the linguistic or orthographical particularities of such texts, since they consider these to reflect an altered or even corrupted form of the classical norms. This kind of linguistic features are usually attributed to copyists who are supposed not to have mastered the rules of the Arabic language. Consequently, many editors correct their texts (*tanqīḥ al-naṣṣ*) by following a 'synchronic' or anti-historical approach to the language that is bound to obscure its linguistic reality, in terms of phonetic, morphological, lexical and syntactic data. According to a method that is duly informed by historical linguistics, sociolinguistics and dialectology, however, such data are also of historical relevance, and they ought to be examined in the context of their diachronic evolution. As Joshua Blau, the pioneer of Middle Arabic studies, contends, much is to be learnt from Romance philology, which addresses the old European dialects and their continuous rejuvenation throughout their written tradition (Blau 2003). Therefore the Romance philological experience may be of great interest for editors of mediaeval Arabic texts seeking a solution to the paradox pointed at here. Thanks to the above mentioned forerunner Gaston Paris, Romance philologists still today fruitfully distinguish between the two kinds of criticism advocated by him (Balduino 1979; Brambilla Ageno 1984; Contini 1992; Stussi 2002, 2006). Thus, it may be appropriate to quote Paris's own words on which the criticism of forms is based:

> One of the criteria that has but a subordinate role for choosing the readings, is of primary importance here: the closer a manuscript is to the author's times, in other words the older it is, the worthier of consideration it is. However, this is only one of the aspects of the problem: with the issue of time there is also that of place (Paris – Pannier 1872, 14; translation PLS).

In general, however, after Paris's endeavours to retrieve the language of the author by using available copies and historical grammars, or those of Michele Barbi who tended to normalize the old spellings (Barbi 1938), Romance philologists today prefer to respect the language and the spelling of a single manuscript witness which they choose on the basis of chronological and geographical criteria, taking in consideration the place and time of the author (Contini 1992; Stussi 2004, 183).

Criticism of forms and Middle Arabic

Within the larger framework of Arabic text editions, the issue of criticism of forms is of particular relevance for the numerous pre-modern texts that were written or transmitted in Middle or mixed Arabic. In this mixed language, classical, dialectical and hybrid forms of Arabic mix, alternate and coexist quite frequently in the same manuscript and sometimes even in the same folium (Blau 1966–1967, 2002; Lentin 1997, 2008, 2012b). Therefore variation is an intrinsic feature of the nature of Middle Arabic. From the analysis of the documents it is clear that authors and copyists have had at their disposal a wide range of linguistic forms from which they drew as they wished according to their stylistic and literary requirements. Moreover we must not forget that manuscripts are copies and so they still represent a kind of compromise between the language of their model and the language of the copyist himself who, consciously or not, adapts the language of the text read to his own linguistic system (Segre 1976, 285 and 1979, 53–70; Orlandi [T.] 2010, 109–115).

As we already noted, Arabic is a language that has evolved throughout its history. This evolution is evident when one compares, for instance, the Qurʾān with a text written in Modern Standard Arabic. Such a comparison was made possible thanks to the sacredness of the Qurʾān that gives us archaic forms as in a sort of fossilized amber; otherwise such forms would have disappeared. Certain orthographic forms of the Qurʾān are also attested in some Christian Arabic manuscripts. We illustrate now a few examples taken from the theological treatises by Sulaymān al-Ġazzī, a Christian Arab author of the late tenth and early eleventh centuries (La Spisa 2013). Two manuscripts of this text, referred to here with the sigla S and Q, are distinguished by the use of a typical Qurʾānic script as in the words *al-ḥayāt* (life) and *al-ṣalāt* (prayer) that are written with *wāw* (reflecting the vowel *-ū-* or possibly *-ō-*) instead of *alif* (reflecting the vowel *-ā-*) (Wright 1896, 12A).

f. 163r line 13) S)	الصلوه والصوم والاتضاع
f. 58r line 17) Q)	ليظهر الحيوة الدهرية
f. 67r lines 10-11) Q)	بهِ كانت الحيوة، والحيوة كانت نور العالم

Since this very spelling is also attested in Arabic manuscripts of Palestinian origin, one could argue that this is a phonetic spelling that derives from Aramaic (Syriac *ḥayūtō*). It is true that as late as the eighteenth century Aramaic was still living in the Palestinian countryside (Spitaler 1960), but this is just one of the assumptions made by specialists, and in fact the origin of this phenomenon has been explained differently by scholars (Fleisch 1990, Blau 1988, Robin 2001). Ultimately, this spelling may reflect a specific level of Middle Arabic that Palestinian authors of the tenth and eleventh centuries might have utilized for the redaction of their works.

Another central question that has already been mentioned is that there is a close connexion and mutual conditioning between the process of establishing the text and the linguistic information contained in it, in other words between the criticism of variants and criticism of forms. The following example is a case in point. In this passage from the treatise *On the Uniqueness of the Creator* by Sulaymān al-Ġazzī (La Spisa 2013, 32), a linguistic variant (namely the exchange between a plosive emphatic sound and an interdental fricative emphatic sound) can become a reading variant:

SWM	عالم الامور قبل كونها والسراير قبل اضمارها
BHA	, , , اظمارها ,
Y	, , , اظهارها ,

The word *iḍmār*, which means here 'the hiding of a secret', via *iẓmār* (a graphic variant), becomes *iẓhār* i.e. the 'revelation of the secret'; that is to say the exact opposite of the original.

References

Balduino 1979; Barbi 1938; Battista – Bagatti 1979; Bausi 1998, 2002b, 2003b, 2004b; Bausi – Gori 2006; Bettini – La Spisa 2012; Blachère – Sauvaget 1945; Blau 1965, 1966–1967, 1988, 2002, 2003; Brambilla Ageno 1984; Cerquiglini 1989; Contini 1992; den Heijer 2012a; Déroche 2005; Déroche et al. 2000; Draguet 1977; Edelby 1986; Fischer [W.] 1982, 1991; Fleisch 1990; Gacek 2009; Géhin 2005; Gibson 1901; Graf 1944; Hamzaoui 1965; Heyworth 1981; Khafaji 2001; La Spisa 2013; Lentin 1997, 2004, 2008, 2012a, 2012b, 2012c; Lentin – Grand'Henry 2008; Marrassini 1992, 1993, 2003; Müller [R.] 1964; al-Munajjid 1956; Orlandi [G.] 2008; Orlandi [T.] 2010; Paris – Pannier 1872; Pétrof 1914; Platti 1981, 1987; Poirel 2006; Rafti 1988; Rezaei 2008; Robin 2001; Samir 1980, 1982; Sayyid 2009; Schen 1972, 1973; Segre 1976, 1979; Spitaler 1960; Stussi 2002, 2004, 2006; Timpanaro 2003; Witkam 1988; Wright 1896; Yūsuf ʿAlī Ṭawīl 2002; Zack – Schippers 2012.

3.14. The Nag Hammadi Codices. Textual fluidity in Coptic (HL)

This case study discusses the problems of editing and interpreting fluid, or 'living,' texts in cases where there are very few, or even unique, textual witnesses. The case in point is the texts preserved in Coptic in the much studied Nag Hammadi Codices (NHC).

The chimera of the hypothetical original

While those who work on, for instance, mediaeval textual traditions often have to deal with a profusion of exemplars and are confronted directly by an abundance of variants (cf. for example Driscoll 2010), in the case of Coptic manuscripts we are more often than not faced with works that are preserved in one, or very few, witnesses. Especially in those cases where we have only a single copy preserved, it is easy to think that we are looking at a stable text. This impression would not have been problematic had it not been so closely connected to certain other key presuppositions of Nag Hammadi research, namely the assumption that all the texts are translations from Greek, and the almost exclusive scholarly focus on the hypothetical Greek originals and their original contexts of composition. Importantly, the assumption of textual stability has led to overconfidence regarding the possibility of gaining access to the original texts, and in using the preserved texts as evidence of a period of time long before the production of the extant manuscripts.

The combination of these factors is very common in Nag Hammadi scholarship. It can for instance be seen in the work of one of the most distinguished scholars of Coptic, Bentley Layton. Although Layton, in a clearly formulated article on philological method, noted with regard to the Nag Hammadi manuscripts that 'it is crucially important to observe that the original language (Greek) is precisely what we do not have' (Layton 1981, 97), the methodological implications he drew from this observation were diametrically opposed to those drawn by the proponents of the so-called 'new philology' or 'material philology' on the basis of their work on highly fluid mediaeval textual traditions (see for example Nichols 1990; Driscoll 2010). Having great confidence in the modern scholar's ability to get back to the hypothetical original, he argued that 'if we cannot reconstruct that lost Greek original on paper, still we can hope to approximate the ancient author's own culture and thought through a recovery of its meaning in a sympathetic English translation keyed to a commentary oriented above all towards Greek usage' (Layton 1981, 97). Layton consequently suggested that 'conceivably the ancient Coptic version might be substituted for the English translation: but since ancientness in itself is no virtue, and since Coptic diction is notoriously non-philosophical, modern 'classicist's English' (provided that it is accurate) will probably be in closer touch with the ancient author's Hellenistic thought than ancient Coptic, whose nuances of diction, philosophical or otherwise, are largely lost upon us and in any case are certainly not Greek' (Layton 1981, 97; implemented most clearly in Layton 1979). Similarly Frederik Wisse (1997, 141–142) has argued that the ideal is for the English translation 'to bypass the Coptic translations to get as close as possible to the common Greek text behind them'. While very few scholars have followed Layton's suggestion that one should translate the hypothetical Greek rather than the preserved Coptic texts (cf., for example, the opposite position as argued by Wilson [R.] 1975, 38), most have shared his presuppositions, including the low esteem in which the Coptic texts have often been held in relation to their hypothetical originals. There are, however, several reasons why such an approach is problematic, not least the above mentioned issues relating to textual fluidity and living literature.

Indeed, with regard to the study of the Nag Hammadi Codices it is a much overlooked problem that these texts, which are attested either in a single copy or in very few copies, might in fact have been significantly and intentionally changed in transmission. There has indeed been a tendency to regard these texts as representatives of fundamentally stable textual traditions, and variants have generally been regarded as errors of transmission rather than as evidence of intentional rewriting (notable exceptions include Painchaud 1995; Painchaud – Janz 1997; Barc – Painchaud 1999; Emmel 1997; Emmel 2008; Lundhaug 2010). As John Bryant (2007, 18) has rightly pointed out, 'most readers are initially inclined to assume that textual fluidity is merely textual corruption'. Although the illusion of textual stability may be easily upheld with regard to the singularly attested Nag Hammadi texts, such as the *Apocryphon of James*, the *Apocalypse of Peter*, the *Gospel of Philip*, or the *Paraphrase of Shem*, to mention but a few, the fluid nature of the texts witnessed in the Nag Hammadi Codices becomes clear once we take a closer look at those tractates that are preserved in multiple copies. We will now take a closer look at two such examples.

Example 1: The Gospel of Truth

The *Gospel of Truth* is attested in two manuscripts, both of them from the Nag Hammadi discovery. Only one of these, the third tractate of NHC I, preserves a complete text, comprising twenty-eight manuscript pages (see Attridge – MacRae 1985). The other witness, in NHC XII, is only fragmentarily preserved in three significantly damaged leaves (six pages; see Wisse 1990). There are a number of differences between the two preserved versions, and although the latter version is only partly preserved, the differences between the two are still suggestive of the fluidity of the textual transmission of this work.

First of all, the two versions of the *Gospel of Truth* are written in different dialects of Coptic, the NHC I version in Lycopolitan and the NHC XII version in Sahidic. Secondly, the difference in scribal quality is quite apparent, the untidy and rather ugly scribal hand of the NHC I version exhibiting a number of mistakes, while the rather more tidy and skilled hand of NHC XII appears, from the few fragments preserved, to be quite accurate. Finally, and most importantly, there are substantial and significant textual differences between the two versions that go beyond those that are easily explainable by different dialects and errors of transmission. What conclusions can be drawn on the basis of these differences? In fact, most scholars working on the *Gospel of Truth*, or who have used the *Gospel of Truth* in their reconstructions of early Christianity or 'Gnosticism', have been content with working on the NHC I version and have either explicitly or implicitly dismissed the version contained fragmentarily in NHC XII (for example, Thomassen 2006, 147). Indeed, the impression given by most studies of the *Gospel of Truth* is that there is no significant variation between the two versions. However, on the basis of a detailed comparison between the NHC XII fragments and the NHC I version, it is quite clear that there is in fact significant variation between the two. As Wisse noted (1990, 330), 'the differences between the two versions of the *Gospel of Truth* go far beyond those expected for independent translations into different dialects'. Not only does the NHC XII version represent 'a somewhat shorter text' that often differs in substance from NHC I, but 'the many serious problems of syntax in [NHC] I,*3* are not evident in [NHC] XII,*2*'. To account for this, he suggests that either the Coptic translator of the NHC XII text 'produced a version that was a simplification of the Greek', or 'the Coptic of Codex I is awkward and at times corrupt' (Wisse 1990, 330). The NHC I version may thus be 'an inferior Coptic translation of a corrupted Greek text' (Wisse 1990, 331). From the same evidence, other scholars have come to the opposite conclusion, such as Thomassen (2006, 147), who states that 'the text transmitted in Codex XII was significantly inferior to that of Codex I'. Moreover, while Thomassen admits that 'the text of Codex I may have been reworked in places', he nevertheless claims that 'in substance' we are 'justified in treating NHC I,3 as representing a Valentinian document dating from before the time of Irenaeus' work of the 180s' (2006, 147–148).

Such judgments are, however, subjective, and other options are available. In an addendum to an important article by Raoul Mortley (1992), Michel Tardieu noted the major differences between the two codices, and argued that the Sahidic version of NHC XII 'provides evidence of a non-glossed [Gospel of Truth], i.e. the writing of Valentinus himself' (Tardieu in Mortley 1992, 250). The NHC I version, on the other hand, should then be seen as a text that 'belongs to a later stage of development of a school which calls itself Valentinian, but whose theological interests were very different from those of its founder'. In Tardieu's opinion, the NHC I version seems to be a commentary on a shorter Greek text of which the NHC XII version is a translation. Mortley (1992) himself argued on the basis of theological parallels that the *Gospel of Truth*, as preserved in Codex I, presupposes the Arian debate, and consequently dated it to the fourth century, close to the time of the production of the codex itself.

Still, a majority of scholars researching 'Valentinianism' or 'Gnosticism' have continued to regard the NHC I version as essentially identical to an 'original' second-century composition, simply, it seems, because this is the only completely preserved copy (for example Williams [J.] 1988; Schenke 2001; Thomassen 2006; some even claim it was written by the famous heretic Valentinus himself, for example Standaert 1976; Williams [J.] 1988, 4–5). We may observe that even those scholars who recognize the substantial differences between the versions in NHC I and XII are still wedded to the notion of a stable textual tradition where variants are explained away as errors of transmission rather than as an endemic quality of the textual tradition. Instead, we may say that these two codices provide us with 'snapshots' of a longer, more complex textual tradition. Trying to get back to the 'original' text or even its essential qualities or its original context on the basis of these very different exemplars must be regarded as a highly speculative venture. As David Parker has argued on the basis of the plethora of variants in Greek New Testament manuscripts, 'the attempt to produce an original form of a living text is worse than trying to shoot a moving target, it is turning a movie into a single snapshot, it is taking a single part of a complex entity and claiming it to be the whole' (Parker 2007, 586). What is needed with regard to studies of a text like the *Gospel of Truth* is for scholars to acknowledge the fact that our surviving textual witnesses constitute exactly such snapshots, and that these snapshots are not necessarily representative of the entire movie.

Example 2: The Apocryphon of John

Another example is provided by the *Apocryphon of John*. In this case we are fortunate enough to have no less than four textual witnesses, three in the Nag Hammadi Codices (NHC II,1; III,1; IV,1) and one in the codex Berlin, Staatsbibliothek, *P.Berol.* 8502, all in Coptic. Here too, the implications of the textual fluidity evidenced by the differences between the copies have largely been ignored in favour of the notion of a hypothetical Greek original (sometimes identified with Irenaeus' source for *Adversus Haereses* I.29 in the late second century).

On the basis of the major differences between the surviving Coptic witnesses, the editors of the excellent English-language critical edition (Waldstein – Wisse 1995) gave up the attempt to establish a single critical text, and opted for a synoptic presentation of all four witnesses in parallel columns (Wisse 1997, 141–142). However, even when opting for this solution they also reconstructed much, at times arguably too much, text in each version on the basis of the others (on their emendation policy, see Wisse 1997, 139–141). They argue that the four copies represent two independent Coptic translations from the original Greek of a shorter version of the *Apocryphon of John*, and two copies of a Coptic translation of a longer version of 'the same tractate' (1995, 1). They hold the Greek *Urtext* of the *Apocryphon of John* to have been written in the early third century, and they speculate that this work then 'underwent a major redaction, represented by the longer version' also in the third century. Sometime in the late third or early fourth century these two versions were then both independently translated into Coptic, the shorter version at least twice. They believe that these versions were then copied in Coptic and eventually ended up in our four extant Coptic codices. The remaining differences between the versions that are not readily explained as results of different translations of different Greek versions they then account for by errors of transmission in Coptic. Interestingly, the differences between the two copies of the shorter recension (NHC III,1 and *P.Berol.* 8502,2) are explained by Waldstein and Wisse as the result of different translations of the same Greek work, while the two versions of the longer text (NHC II,1 and IV,1), which they regard as copies of the same translation of the longer Greek text, still contain differences that lead them to the conclusion that these two copies 'do not appear to stand in a 'sister' or 'mother-daughter' relationship' (1995, 1).

Yet there is reason to suspect that even this complicated picture is too neat. Waldstein and Wisse's reasoning relies upon the premise that the variants are primarily to be explained by differences of translation and errors of transmission (see, for example, Waldstein – Wisse 1995, 7; Wisse 1997, 145–46), and although they briefly discuss the question of redaction with regard to the differences between the short and long version, they do not take intentional rewriting fully into consideration when considering the full breadth of variance among all four witnesses. Access to the hypothetical Greek original, pure and uncontaminated by the errors brought in by later transmission, remains the ultimate, although unreachable, goal, and the primary focus for most scholars working on the *Apocryphon of John*. The hypothetical Greek original and its historical and sociocultural context, sometimes imagined as 'an urban school setting, probably in Alexandria' (King 2006, 9–13, 244), has generally been privileged in interpretations, a context far from that of the preserved Coptic manuscripts, even though we may reasonably suspect that the latter context has significantly influenced the text in the versions that are in fact available to us (on the perils of over-emphasizing the hypothetical original, see the insightful comments of King 1997, esp. 130–137).

If we change perspective, however, and instead think in terms of living literature (Bradshaw 1993; Bradshaw 2002, 5)—or textual fluidity (Bryant 2002, 2007)—and regard our four Coptic witnesses as snapshots of a fluid textual tradition, without privileging the original text, it becomes necessary to reconsider how we treat the *Apocryphon of John* and use it as a historical source, as each witness becomes important in itself as evidence of the text's reception and use in different contexts.

Texts in their manuscript contexts

The *Gospel of Truth* and the *Apocryphon of John* are just two examples. The situation is similar in the case of other Nag Hammadi texts with multiple witnesses (sometimes in various languages, including Coptic,

Greek, Latin, and Arabic), such as the *Gospel of Thomas*, *On the Origin of the World*, the *Gospel of the Egyptians*, *Eugnostos the Blessed*, the *Wisdom of Jesus Christ*, *Zostrianos*, the *Letter of Peter to Philip*, (the *First Apocalypse of*) *James*, the *Teachings of Silvanus*, the *Sentences of Sextus*, Plato's *Republic* 588b-589b, the *Prayer of Thanksgiving*, *Asclepius* 21–29. Of course the extent of attestation and the degree of both absolute and observable fluidity varies from case to case, but in all of them the differences are significant enough to warrant paying closer attention to the preserved texts as they appear in their various manuscript contexts.

In addition to the variance attested by the above mentioned cases, there is also a need to take seriously the implications of textual fluidity for the other Nag Hammadi texts. There is no reason to believe that those texts that are attested only by single copies are characterized by greater stability than those texts for which we have multiple attestation. On the contrary, there is good reason to treat them as single frames (to stay within the cinematic metaphor) of fluid textual traditions. If the implications of this perspective are taken fully into consideration with regard to the Nag Hammadi collection as a whole, the way in which the texts are used as sources for the history of early Christianity may have to be radically reconsidered, as they can no longer be used uncritically as sources for the second and third centuries. As Stephen Emmel has noted, 'there is one obvious task that has not yet been carried out thoroughly and consistently' with regard to the Nag Hammadi Codices, namely to read them 'as a part of Coptic literature' (Emmel 1997, 42). Such a task involves reading 'the texts exactly as we have them in the Nag Hammadi Codices in an effort to reconstruct the reading experience of whoever owned each of the Codices'.

Michael Williams (1997, 209) has highlighted a tendency among scholars of the Nag Hammadi tractates 'to equate rather too facilely or thoughtlessly the 'text' of a given writing only with what is after all our own modern text-critical 'guess-timate' about the 'original', skipping past on our way perfectly real, physical copies of that writing that someone did use'. Similarly, Emmel (1997, 40–41) has noted the tendency among scholars to 'move back and forth between the Coptic text we have and the original we would like to have', on the basis of the often unstated assumption 'that the Nag Hammadi tractates bear some more or less close relationship to a hypothetical original composition'. As Emmel (1997, 41) has rightly pointed out, this practice is tantamount to traversing a minefield, for 'the Coptic phases of transmission pose nearly insurmountable barriers to recovering the translators' *Vorlagen*', not to mention the hypothetical original Greek. Even the common assumption of the existence of Greek originals needs to be questioned in each individual case. Firstly, we need to remain open to the possibility that at least some of the Nag Hammadi texts were originally composed in Coptic, and secondly, when we take textual fluidity fully into account, it is not always clear what consequences we should draw from the assessment that a document's original language was Greek (Lundhaug 2010, 357–358). With the Nag Hammadi Codices there has, for instance, been a tendency by editors and interpreters to disregard wordplays that make sense only in Coptic, based on a presumption that the original language was Greek. One such case can be seen in an important passage in the *Gospel of Philip* (58.14–17), where editors have emended the Coptic word for 'door' (*ro*) to 'king' (*rro*), thus ruining the Coptic wordplay, which indicates that one needs to see the door in order to enter in to the king. Not only does the emendation dissolve the wordplay, however, but it also removes a biblical allusion to the Gospel of John (10.9) that is necessary for a proper understanding of the passage (see Lundhaug 2010, 281–284). In fact, such editorial and interpretive practices, which clearly show some of the consequences of a focus on a hypothetical Greek original, can be described as yet further examples of textual fluidity, as modern editors and translators change the texts to comply with their own presuppositions and expectations, just like their counterparts in Late Antiquity.

An issue that also needs to be addressed when discussing the Nag Hammadi Codices in relation to textual fluidity is the underlying attitudes, by authors, readers, and scribes, toward textual variation. Bernard Cerquiglini (1989, 1999) has argued that the people of the Middle Ages embraced textual variation. Against this view, however, it has been argued that 'the awareness of the very fertile variability of mediaeval and modern texts does not by any means imply unbridled enthusiasm for variability as such' (Varvaro 1999, 57; Busby 1993). Alberto Varvaro (1999, 57) asserts that 'mediaeval variability (variance) is never the simultaneous presence of variants, but rather of the instability of a text in different locations, environments, and times'. This is a useful distinction, but it does not quite work for the Nag Hammadi Codices, where we have different versions of the same works preserved side by side in what appear to be contemporaneous codices from the same milieu, for example the *Gospel of Truth* and the *Apocryphon of*

John discussed above. In these cases we do indeed seem to witness 'the simultaneous presence of variants'. The implications of this fact for our picture of the textual culture of the producers and users of these codices remain to be explored. What, for example, was the *Apocryphon of John* for those who may have read the text in NHC II, III, and IV together?

While an increased emphasis on studying the preserved Coptic texts in their manuscript contexts may in many ways heighten the complexity of our work and lead to different conclusions, analyses from such a perspective should potentially be less speculative and lead to more secure results (Emmel 1997, 42–43).

References

Attridge – MacRae 1985; Barc – Painchaud 1999; Bradshaw 1993, 2002; Bryant 2002, 2007; Busby 1993; Cerquiglini 1989, 1999; Driscoll 2010; Emmel 1997, 2008; King 1997, 2006; Layton 1979, 1981; Lundhaug 2010; Mortley 1992; Nichols 1990; Painchaud 1995; Painchaud – Janz 1997; Parker 2007; Schenke 2001; Standaert 1976; Thomassen 2006; Varvaro 1999; Waldstein – Wisse 1995; Williams [J.] 1988; Williams [M.] 1997; Wilson [R.] 1975; Wisse 1990, 1997.

3.15. Gregory of Nazianzus' *Homilies*. An over-abundant manuscript tradition in Greek and in translation (CM)

Editing Greek Patristics

Kurt Treu summarizes the task of an editor of Patristics as follows: 'Die meisten Editionsprobleme erwachsen dem Patristiker nicht daraus, daß ihm die Materialien fehlten, sondern daß sie ihn überschwemmen. Man kann etwa folgende Punkte nennen: 1. Es gibt zu viele Handschriften. 2. Es gibt zu viele Übersetzungen. 3. Es gibt zu viele Testimonien. 4. Es gibt zu viele Variationen' (Treu 1980, 618–619). Emmanuel Amand de Mendieta (1987) therefore states that one may not require that an editor of Patristic texts complies with the theoretical ideals of textual criticism: i.e. exhaustive heuristics (direct and indirect tradition), complete collation of all witnesses, classification of the manuscripts synthesized in the form of a stemma codicum, etc.

In theory, there is no reason why an abundance of witnesses would make the classification of the witnesses, and therefore the stemma, 'une entreprise irréalisable et même fallacieuse', as Amand de Mendieta puts it (1987, 41). On the contrary, one could argue that the stemmatological analysis is more appropriate to a large tradition, than to a tradition where too few manuscripts have been preserved. In practice, however, the task is indeed extremely costly in terms of time and monetary expenses, and the results may often appear disappointing in the end. Amand de Mendieta claims that, in the event of an over-abundance of witnesses, the editor must limit him/herself in two ways: (1) to the manuscripts earlier than the sixteenth century, and (2) to the direct tradition, including, however, the ancient translations (Amand de Mendieta 1987, 35–38). Those two limitations are indeed justified, again for practical reasons, although they are difficult to be argued for in theory, since the high number of preserved manuscripts does not guarantee in itself the quality of the preserved text.

Specificities concerning the tradition of Gregory of Nazianzus

Compared with other Greek Church fathers, Gregory of Nazianzus' tradition shows a few features that can be considered rather peculiar. The writings by Gregory of Nazianzus (*c.*330–*c.*390) that have come down to us consist of 44 sermons, approximately 18,000 verses, and 243 letters. All together they form a coherent corpus, probably authorized as a conscious selection of 'opera omnia', to which hardly any ancient *spuria* were added. In the case of the homilies, it is quite clear that those 44 were selected as exemplary (the normal production of a bishop would comprise much more than 44 sermons), and that they circulated in collections, and not individually. This last point can hardly be proven, yet there are many elements pointing in that direction, and above all the fact that all the ancient translations preserve only those 44 homilies.

For an overview of a different, and very complicated case, see Voicu (2013) about John Chrysostom.

Previous scholarship

Scholarship devoted to Gregory of Nazianzus' homilies has a long history. The first modern edition was produced by the Maurists and published between 1778 and 1840, and is on the whole of high quality, even though the manuscript basis of their edition is not easy to trace back, and of course not explicitly mentioned in the notes. This edition was reproduced in Migne's *Patrologia Graeca* (hereafter PG) (volumes 35–37). At the beginning of the twentieth century, a Polish scholar, Tadeusz Sinko, published a remarkable study on the history of the text (Sinko 1917), in which he examined several manuscripts containing a complete collection of the homilies, as well as some of the ancient translations into Latin and oriental languages. Sinko concluded that the manuscript tradition of Gregory's complete collections of *Discourses* should be divided into two branches, which he called M and N, according to the number of pieces contained in the manuscripts (either 47 or 52—those numbers are written in Greek as MZ′ and NB′, respectively). Sinko's theory served as a basis for the editions of the homilies in the collection *Sources Chrétiennes*, which used ten manuscripts (and sometimes more) amongst the oldest known members of the two families defined by Sinko, as well as the Latin translation (this last witness, however, was not used in a systematic way). Homilies 1–12 and 20–43 were edited between 1974 and 1995 in the collection *Sources Chrétiennes*, on the basis of Sinko's hypothesis. The quality of the editions very much depends on their individual editors (see Somers 1997, 17–41).

Between 1981 and 1998, Justin Mossay completed his census of (all) manuscripts containing one or more homilies of Gregory; the results of his research filled six volumes, describing about 1,500 Greek manuscripts prior to 1550. The Université catholique de Louvain (Louvain-la-Neuve) acquired about 1,000 microfilms of Greek manuscripts containing the homilies. In 1997, V. Somers published a doctoral dissertation (Somers 1997, see also Somers 2001), in which she challenged Sinko's theory, on the basis of her examination of all manuscripts containing a complete collection, and in the light of her discovery that many manuscripts contain a complete collection in another order than the order prevalent in M or N manuscripts. In the ten years following this publication, the Université catholique de Louvain (Louvain-la-Neuve) hosted a large project of critical editions and studies of the ancient translations in oriental languages—namely, Armenian, Syriac, Georgian, Arabic (see Coulie 2000b).

This inventory of the witnesses must indeed be done before the editorial work proper can even commence. This shows that the edition of texts preserved in an over-abundant tradition can only be undertaken by a team and with long-term funding—something which has become very problematic in the present academic environment. This should also remind us that socio-economic constraints are important elements in any editorial enterprise.

History of the text of Homily 27—an incomplete story

My own research (1997–2001) focused on one specific homily, and my task was to collate all the Greek manuscripts containing it, to classify them, and then to retrace the history of the text, using all direct and indirect witnesses. Homily 27 was selected because it does not belong to the sixteen so-called liturgical homilies, which are kept in special collections, represented in hundreds of copies (see Somers 2002). In addition, it is preserved in all the oldest translations: Latin (*c.*400, by Rufinus of Aquileia, who translated only nine homilies: 2, 38, 39, 41, 26, 17, 6, 16, 27), Armenian (*c.*500), and Syriac (last revision *c.*675 by Jacob of Edessa). For a list of 139 Greek manuscripts containing homily 27, see: <http://pot-pourri.fltr.ucl.ac.be/manuscrits/GRECS/DEFAULT.HTM> (search 'par discours', select 'Or.27').

It must be noted that the oldest Greek manuscripts do not antedate the ninth century. The age of a manuscript is no guarantee of the quality of the text it preserves—and in this case we can verify this assumption by concrete facts. The few palimpsest manuscripts preserved do not contribute anything to the history of the text, as Véronique Somers showed (Somers 2009, 69). The two complete collections in uncial, X.11 and N.23, survived because of their illustrations, but they are both late uncial manuscripts, luxury products, and the text they preserve is often faulty, and, as neither of the manuscripts seems to have even been copied, they can be considered dead-ends of the tradition.

As I have stated before, Sinko's division of the tradition into two branches according to the content and order of the homilies in the collection has been challenged by Somers (1997), but has not been wholly replaced. Still, Somers (1997) has put the validity of external criteria of classification into doubt, and any further research should therefore start with textual elements alone.

The first task was therefore to collate all the Greek manuscripts, which I did, at that time on paper, using the edition in PG as reference text. Homily 27 being a relatively short text, it was possible to collate it entirely, and the collation was as careful and as complete as possible. It took me several months to complete this stage, and I am aware that it may often be impossible to devote so much time to collations. At that time (1997–1998), a manual collation, on paper, seemed the only possibility—collating tools existed then (like Peter Robinson's *Collate*), but they did not seem usable for my purpose: producing full transcriptions of each of the 139 manuscripts seemed a waste of time. Because of the over-abundant manuscript tradition, however, it proved necessary to encode the variants, excluding punctuation and trivial purely phonetic mistakes, in a database (Dubuisson – Macé 2006) that is not usable anymore, because it used pre-Unicode fonts and an outdated version of MS Access. One of the possible outputs of this encoding was a matrix (fig. 3.3.15.1).

In abscissa are the variant locations and in ordinate the manuscripts. A variant location is a word or group of words for which there exists at least one variant reading, differing from the reference text. I have defined 556 variant locations (homily 27 counts 2,105 forms) and have noted a total of 691 variants. As can be seen in fig. 3.3.15.1, the matrix is not binary, for in one variant location, more than one variant may occur: 0 means that the manuscript bears the same reading as in the reference text, 1 is the first variant which appeared during the collation, 2 is the second one, etc. The question mark is used to indicate a lacuna, which should not be treated as 0, for it is not the same as the reference text.

This kind of matrix allows for the application of statistical methods. We first tried multidimensional scaling (Macé et al. 2001) and then software used in phylogenetics (PAUP, PHYLIP) (Macé et al. 2004).

```
                     111111111122222222223333333333444444444455555555556666666
Taxon/Node  123456789012345678901234567890123456789012345678901234567890123456
------------------------------------------------------------------------------
EA          000000000000000000000000000000000000000000000000000000000000000000
L 010       000000000000000000000000000000000000000000000100000100000000030200 00
L 017       000000000000100000000000000000000000000000000000000100000000000020 00
L 024       000000000000000000000000000000000000000000000000000100000600000000
L 026       000000000000100000000000000000000200000000000000000100000000000022 00
L 028       000000000002000000000300000000000000000000000000000100000000001300 0
L 079       000000000000000000000000000001000000000000000000000100000000000020 00
L 090       000000000000000000000000000000000000000000000000000100000600000000
L 093       000000000000000000000000000000000000000000000000000100000000000000
L 104       000000000000001000000000100000000000000000000000000100000000000000
L 105       001000000000100000000000000000000000000000000000000100000000000000
L 123       000000000000000001000000000000000000000000000100000100000000000000
L 125       000000000002000000000000000000000000000000000000000100000000000020 00
L 140       000000000000000000000000000000000000000000000100000100000000000000
L 143       000000000000000000000000000000000000000000000100000100000000000000
L 172       000000000000000100000000000000000000000000000000000100000000000020 00
L 179       000000000000000000000000000000000000000000000000000100000000000000
L 194       000000000000000000000000000000000000000000000100000100000000000000
L 261       000000000000000000000000000000000000000000000000000100000000000000
L 283       000000000000000000000000000000000000000000000000000100000000000000
L 295       000000000000100000000000000000000000000000000000000100000000000020 10
L 300       100000000002000000000100000000000000000200000000000100000000000000
L 305       000000000000000000000000000200000000000000000000000120000000000000
L 318       000000000000000000000000000000000000000000000000000100000600000000
L 379       000000000000000000000000000000000000000000000000000100000000000000
L 414       000000000000000000010000000200000000000000000100000100000000000000
M 01        000000001002000100000000000000000010100000001001000100000002002010
M 02        000000000000000000000000000000000000000000000000000100000000000000
M 06        000000001002000100000000000000000010000000000001000100000000000010
M 07        000000000002000100000300000000000000000000000000000100000001000000
M 09        000000000000000000000000000000000000000000000000000100000000002200
M 10        000000001000000100000000000000000010000000000001000100000000002010
M 11a       000000001002000100000000000000001010100000001001000100000000002010
M 12        000000000002000100100000000000000010100000001001000100000000002010
M 14        000000000000000000002000000000000010000000000001000100000010002010
M 15        000000000000100100000000000000000000000000000001010100000000000010
M 16        000000000002000100000000000000000000010000000001000100000000002010
M 17        000000000000100100000000000000000010000000001001010100000000000010
M 19        ????00?????????????????????0???????????????0100100010000000000000010
M 20        000000001002000100000000000000000010000000001001000100000000002010
M 21a       000000001002000100000000000000000010100000001001000100000000002010
M 22        000000001002000100002000000020000010000000001000000100000000002010
M 23        000000001002000100000000000000000010000000001001000100000000022010
M 24        000000000000000000002000000000000010000000001001000100000000002010
N 05        000000000000000000000000000000000000000000000000000100000000000000
N 06        000000000000000000000200000000000000000000000100000100000000000000
N 07a       000000000000000000000000000000000000000000000000000100000000000000
N 08        000000000000000000000000000000000000000000000000000100000000002000
N 10        000000000000000000000200000000000000000000000100000100000000000000
N 13        000000000002000000000000000000000000000000000000000100000000000000
N 14        000000000000000000002000000000000000000000000000000100000600000200
N 15        000?0000000??00?000000000000000000000000000000000000?0000000002000
```

Fig. 3.3.15.1 Matrix–Manuscripts / Variant locations–not binary.

Fig. 3.3.15.2 shows one of the trees we were able to produce on the basis of variants alone, not employing any other type of information. It should also be noted that this tree is unrooted and unoriented: 0 does not necessarily indicate the original reading, although, since the PG edition is actually a good one, in fact it often does. The reader will easily observe that almost all M manuscripts are on two branches on the right side of the tree, whereas N manuscripts, which have a rather standardized text, without much variation, are on several branches at the left and bottom side of the tree (these directions are relative).

This tree is by no means a stemma: it is not rooted, the variant locations have not been polarized (primary reading => secondary reading), there is no timeline, no codicological information, etc.

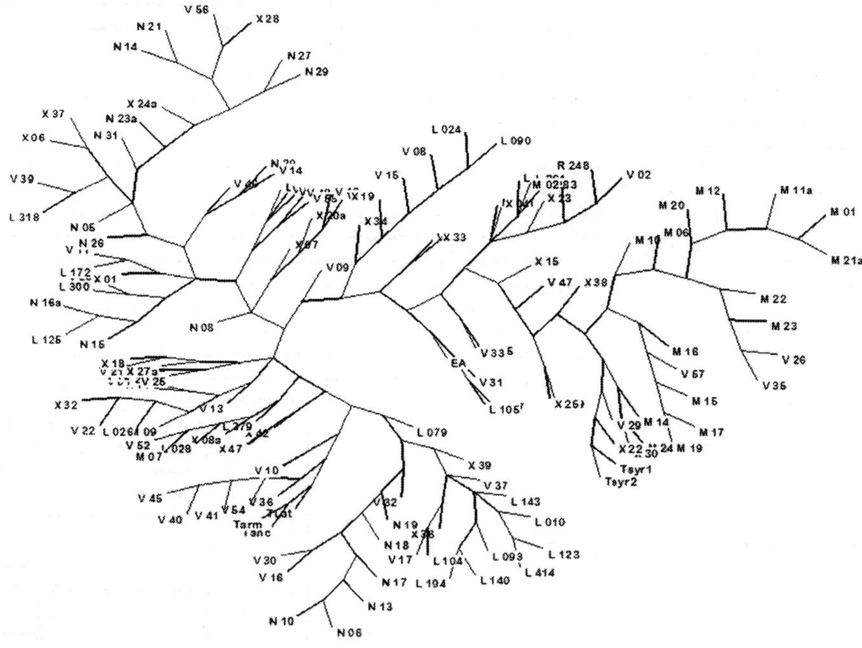

Fig. 3.3.15.2 Parsimony, unrooted tree. Homily 27, all manuscripts and ancient translations.

In order to go further than this statistical grouping, I have examined more closely the ancient translations, which one can find on the tree already, because they have been coded as lacunary witnesses (it is indeed impossible to reconstruct with certainty their Greek *Vorlage* on each variant location; this is why only the variant locations for which this reconstruction is certain have been coded). I was able to demonstrate that the Latin and Armenian translations share a number of variants which are absent from all known Greek manuscripts, and in some cases those variants in the translations are better than the transmitted Greek text (Dubuisson – Macé 2003, Macé 2011). Simonet (2010) tried to confirm our discovery, but this article is very confusing, and its methodology is flawed on several points: it relies on the edition in *Sources Chrétiennes* for the Greek text, but this edition gives only a very partial view of the Greek tradition; it is not based on a critical edition of the Armenian text; the variants are put in odd categories and their quality as kinship-revealing is never evaluated. Nevertheless, our demonstration (Dubuisson – Macé 2003) is sufficient to claim that all Greek manuscripts depend upon one subarchetype, and that the agreement between the Latin and Armenian translations may be used to orientate the tree (see fig. 3.3.15.3).

As can be seen, the Syriac translations (S1 and S2) belong to the same group of manuscripts as the M collections, and indeed I have shown in an article about homily 38 that a sub-group of M (anchored in Southern Italy) and the Syriac translations must be related (Macé 2004).

Is a new edition desirable / possible and under which form?

I have prepared, though have not published, a new edition of homily 27 (see fig. 3.3.15.4). Even if the history of the text is relatively clear now, we are still a long way from a new critical edition of Gregory's homilies. Justin Mossay did try to produce an edition of homilies 10 and 12 (Mossay 2006), but he was not very successful. The reviews of his edition were quite reserved (Bady 2008) or even negative (Macé 2008). Whereas his unconvincing introduction occupies about one hundred pages, the edition of the two homilies covers seven pages and is unusable: the apparatus is unreliable and the editorial choices are based on wrong assumptions.

Nevertheless, a new edition of the homilies is indeed desirable and possible. It does not make sense, however, to keep all the manuscripts in the apparatus, as Mossay did. The editor must make a selection amongst them, which cannot be completely justified on scholarly grounds, but is necessary on practical grounds. It will probably be necessary to edit the text as it is in the Greek manuscripts, that is the text of the Greek sub-archetype, which can be dated somewhat earlier than the second Syriac translation, that is before 675. Even though the Latin and Armenian translations would allow the opportunity to go back

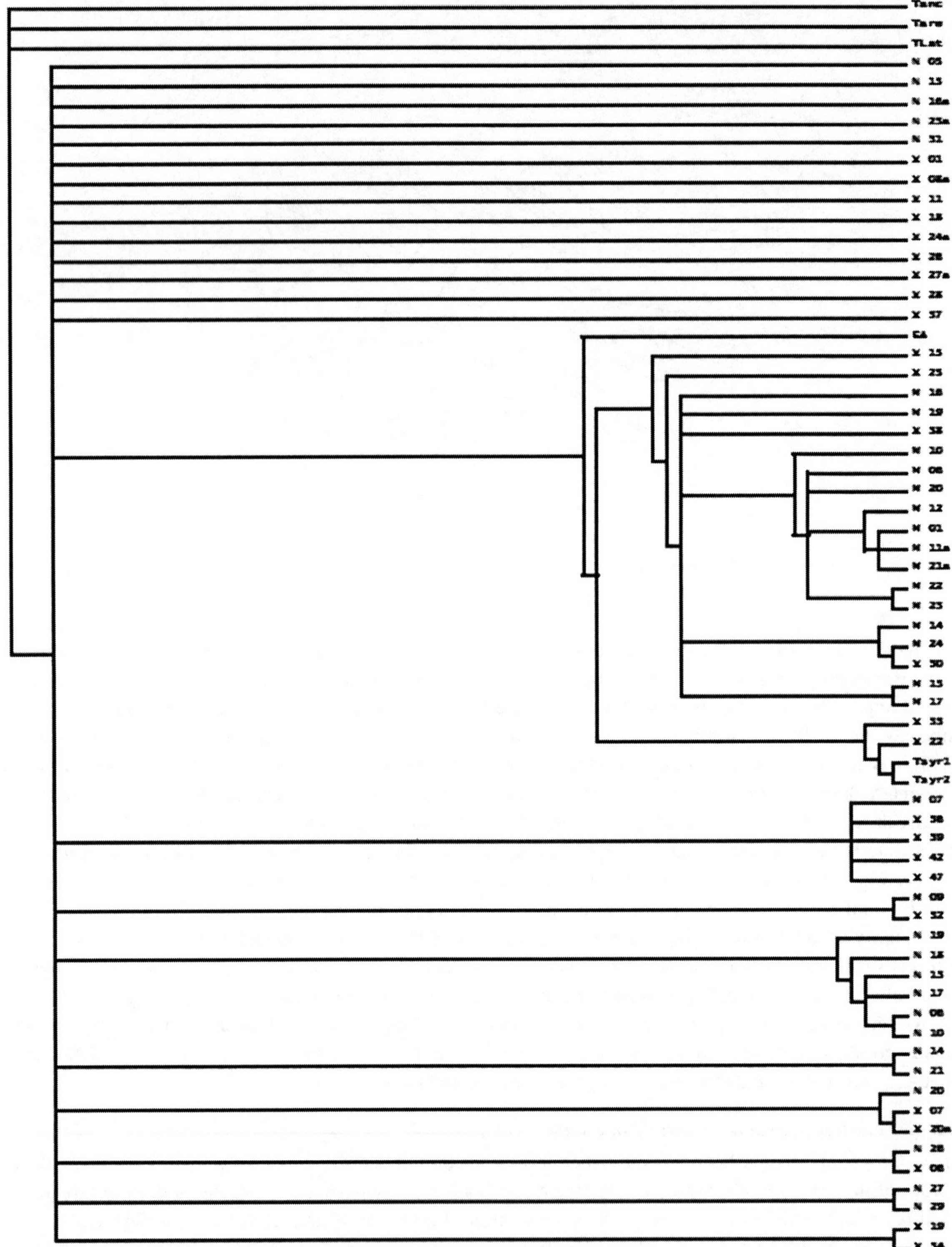

Fig. 3.3.15.3 Parsimony, consensus tree. Homily 27, complete collections, rooted on the Latin and Armenian translations.

Πρὸς Εὐνομιανοὺς προδιάλεξις,
ἢ ὅτι οὐ παντὸς τὸ περὶ θεοῦ διαλέγεσθαι ἢ πάντοτε

1. [12A] Πρὸς τοὺς ἐν λόγῳ κομψοὺς ὁ λόγος. Καὶ ἵνα ἀπὸ τῆς γραφῆς ἄρξωμαι· «Ἰδοὺ ἐγὼ ἐπὶ σὲ τὴν ὑβρίστριαν». Εἰσὶ γὰρ *εἰσί* τινες οἱ τὴν ἀκοὴν προσκνώμενοι καὶ τὴν γλῶσσαν, ἤδη δὲ ὡς ὁρῶ καὶ τὴν χεῖρα ταῖς βεβήλοις κενοφωνίαις καὶ ἀντιθέσεσι τῆς ψευδωνύμου γνώσεως καὶ ταῖς εἰς οὐδὲν χρήσιμον φερούσαις λογομαχίαις· οὕτω γὰρ ὁ Παῦλος καλεῖ πᾶν τὸ ἐν λόγῳ περιττὸν καὶ περίεργον· ὁ τοῦ συντετμημένου λόγου κῆρυξ καὶ βεβαιωτής· ὁ τῶν ἁλιέων μαθητὴς καὶ διδάσκαλος. Οὗτοι δὲ περὶ ὧν ὁ λόγος, [12B] εἴθε μὲν ὥσπερ τὴν γλῶσσαν εὔστροφον ἔχουσι καὶ δεινήν, *ἐ*πετίθεντο** λόγοις εὐγενεστέροις τε καὶ δοκιμωτέροις, οὕτω τι καὶ περὶ τὰς πράξεις ἠσχολοῦντο *μικρόν γ' οὖν*. Καὶ ἴσως

***Cap.* 1**

2 Ἰδοὺ — ὑβρίστριαν: *Ier.* 27, 31 **2/3** τὴν ἀκοὴν προσκνώμενοι: *II Tim.* 4, 3 (κνηθόμενοι τὴν ἀκοήν) **3/4** ταῖς — γνώσεως: *I Tim.* 6, 20 **4/5** ταῖς — λογομαχίαις: *II Tim.* 2, 14 (τοῦ θεοῦ μὴ λογομαχεῖν, ἐπ' οὐδὲν χρήσιμον) **6** τοῦ συντετμημένου λόγου: *cf. Rom.* 9, 28 (*refertur Is.* 10, 23: ὅτι λόγον συντετμημένον ποιήσει ὁ θεὸς ἐν τῇ οἰκουμένῃ ὅλῃ) ‖ ἁλιέων: *cf. Matth.* 4, 19 (καὶ ποιήσω ὑμᾶς ἁλιεῖς ἀνθρώπων) //

Titulus

ἢ (1)] *om. V.25*, καὶ *X.06 X.19 L.105a.c. L.414 V.15 V.17*, ἤτοι *L.079* ‖ τὸ] *om. N.06 N.10 N.13 N.16 N.17 N.19 X.06 L.093 L.140 L.194 V.10 V.17 V.41*, *iter. V.15* ‖ ἢ πάντοτε] *om. L.104 V.56* ‖ ἢ ὅτι οὐ παντὸς τὸ περὶ θεοῦ διαλέγεσθαι ἢ πάντοτε] ... παντὸς ἀνθρώπου τὸ περὶ θεοῦ διαλέγεσθαι ... πάντοτε *N.26 (legi nequit)* ‖ Πρὸς Εὐνομιανοὺς προδιάλεξις ἢ ὅτι οὐ παντὸς τὸ περὶ θεοῦ διαλέγεσθαι ἢ πάντοτε] De Arrianis quod non licet semper et publice de Deo contendere *Ruf.*, Πρὸς Εὐνομιανοὺς καὶ περὶ θεολογίας προδιάλεξις *M.01 M.06 M.10 M.11a.c. M.12 M.14 M.15 M.17 M.19 M.21a.c. M.22 M.23 M.24 N.05 X.08a.c. X.30 L.028 L.172 L.305 V.11 V.26 V.33 V.35 V.46 V.47 V.49 V.55 V.57*, Πρὸς Εὐνομιανοὺς καὶ περὶ θεολογίας προδιάλεξις ἐρρέθη ἐν Κωνσταντινουπόλει *M.07*, Πρὸς Εὐνομιανοὺς καὶ περὶ θεολογίας M.16, Πρὸς Εὐνομιανοὺς προδιάλεξις *S1 N.14 X.11 X.33 X.38 L.010 L.017 V.29 V.30 V.31 V.38 V.59 Gallay*, Πρὸς εὐνομιανοὺς προδιάλεξις δευτέρα *V.20*, Πρὸς Εὐνομιανοὺς *Arm. S2 M.09 M.20 X.22 X.32 L.026 V.22*, Πρὸς Εὐνομιανοὺς καὶ περὶ θεολογίας προδιάλεξις ἢ ὅτι οὐ παντὸς τὸ περὶ θεοῦ διαλέγεσθαι πάντοτε *X.15*, Πρὸς Εὐνομιανοὺς καὶ περὶ θεολογίας προδιάλεξις ὅτι οὐ παντὸς περὶ θεοῦ διαλέγεσθαι ἢ πάντοτε *X.25*, Κατὰ Εὐνομιανῶν προσδιάλεξις *Ald.*, θεολογικὸς πρῶτος Κατὰ Εὐνομιανῶν προδιάλεξις Maur., θεολογικὸς πρῶτος Πρὸς Εὐνομιανοὺς προδιάλεξις *Mason*

Titulus ἐκ τοῦ σχεδιασθέντος πρὸς Εὐνομιανοὺς λόγου (Maximus Confessor, *Ambigua ad Iohannem*, 13, col. 1208 C 12-13); ἐκ τοῦ κατὰ Εὐνομιανῶν (Pamphilus, *Capitulorum*, 16, 92 [n° 128]); ἐν τῷ κατ' Εὐνομιανῶν περὶ θεολογίας λόγῳ (*A.C.O.*, Ser. II, II, 2, p. 905, 2)

***Cap.* 1**

1 *post* κομψοὺς] *add.* νῦν *X.33 V.26* **2** ὑβρίστριαν *Ruf. Arm.*] ὑβρίστριαν καὶ παίδευσιν καὶ ἀκοὴν καὶ διάνοιαν *M N.16 X.22 X.33. L.093 Maur. Gallay*, ὑβρίστριαν καὶ παίδευσιν καὶ διάνοιαν *S1 S2 X.01 X.19 X.32 X.34 L.024 L.026 L.090 L.379 V.08 V.15 V.20 V.22 V.36 V.40 V.41 V.45 V.54 M.12p.c. L.105p.c. L.318p.c. V.03p.c. V.17p.c. V.38p.c. V.55p.c. M.09mg N.20mg N.23mg N.29mg X.18mg X.26mg X.27mg X.28mg* ‖ εἰσί (2) *S1 S2*] *om. Ruf. Arm.* **3** προσκνώμενοι] πεπυκνώμενοι *V.03* ‖ καὶ τὴν χεῖρα] *om. L.026* ‖ χεῖρα *Ruf. Arm.*] χεῖρα τοῖς ἡμετέροις λόγοις καὶ χαίροντες *M X.22 X.32 X.33 V.22 V.36 M.09mg N.20mg N.23mg N.29mg X.07mg X.18mg X.20mg Maur. Mason Gallay*, χεῖρα τοῖς ἡμετέροις λόγοις καὶ χαίροντας *X.26mg X.27mg X.28mg V.38mg* ‖ ταῖς] τοῖς *V.57* **4** κενοφωνίαις] καινοτομίαις *X.32* ‖ ψευδωνύμου] ψευδωμένης *V.21* ‖ ταῖς] τῆς *M.22* **4/5** χρήσιμον φερούσαις] φερούσαις χρήσιμον *X.36 L.104 L.123 L.140 L.194 V.17* **5** φερούσαις λογομαχίαις] λογομαχίαις φερούσαις *L.143a.c.* ‖ ἐν] *om. L.140* ‖ λόγῳ] λόγοις *V.24 V.29* **6** συντετμημένου] ὀρθοῦ καὶ τετμημένου *V.21*, συντετριμμένου *V.46* ‖ λόγου] *om. M.24a.c. V.03 V.10* ‖ καί] *om. V.14* ‖ βεβαιωτής] βεβαιωτέραν V.46 ‖ μαθητὴς] νομομαθὴς *V.08mg* **7** *ante* διδάσκαλος] *add.* ἡμῶν *X.20 X.07mg* ‖ ὁ] *om. V.10, V.47* ‖ λόγος] *om. V.32* **8** ἐπετίθεντο *Ruf. Arm.*] ἐπιθέσθαι *S1 S2 codd. edd.* ‖ *ante* λόγοις] *add.* τοῖς *V.17a.c.* **9** οὕτω τι καὶ περὶ τὰς πράξεις ἠσχολοῦντο μικρόν γ' οὖν *S1 S2*] οὕτω τι μικρόν γ' οὖν καὶ περὶ τὰς πράξεις ἠσχολοῦντο *Ruf. Arm. ut uid.* ‖ τι] τε *X.22*, *om. L.305 L.414*

Fig. 3.3.15.4 Beginning of Homily 27 (§ 1), new edition of the Greek text, with all known witnesses.

earlier than that, they would not allow it systematically: it is therefore safer to limit the edition to what is certain—i.e. the Greek subarchetype.

References

Amand de Mendieta 1987; Bady 2008; Coulie 2000b; Dubuisson – Macé 2003, 2006; Macé 2004, 2008, 2011; Macé et al. 2001, 2004; Mossay 2006; Mossay et al. 1981–1998; Simonet 2010; Sinko 1917; Somers 1997, 2001, 2002, 2009; Treu 1980; Uthemann 1996; Voicu 2013.

3.16. Manuscript London, BL, Or. 2165 and the transmission of the Qur'ān (MMx)

Manuscript London, BL, Or. 2165, containing 121 folia, and two smaller fragments from Paris (BnF, Arabe 328e: six folia) and Kuwait (Dār al-Āṯār al-Islāmiyya LNS 19CA[ab]: two folia) form a remarkable document of a *c*.60%-complete codex of the Qur'ān. Generally speaking, manuscripts of the Qur'ān have not been sufficiently studied, although the last two decades registered significant progress in this field (Rezvan 2004; Altıkulaç 2007, 2009, 2011). This may seem surprising as the study of the Qur'ān has played a central role in Muslim scholarship since its very beginnings. The Qur'ān can indeed be considered the first Arabic book, of which copies on parchment are datable to the second half of the seventh century: a small number of early Qur'ānic parchments have been dated by C_{14} analysis, and a systematic analysis of a larger number of early fragments is currently being undertaken within the framework of the German-French research project 'Coranica', by Tobias J. Jocham, Eva Yousef-Grob, and myself (see <http://coranica.de> and Jocham – Marx forthcoming).

Since early times, the Qur'ān played a central role in Muslim life where, for example, the obligatory daily prayers require the recitation of its very short first Sūra, *al-Fātiḥa*, and another Qur'ānic passage to be chosen freely. Besides early witnesses on parchments, passages of the text are attested in Arabic papyri (Grohmann 1958), coins, graffiti and inscriptions of the seventh century (for early rock inscriptions containing Qur'ānic text, Imbert 2013) that show that the Qur'ānic text had swiftly become a significant marker in art and architecture. A famous example is the mosaic inscription in the Dome of the Rock, built by caliph 'Abd al-Malik in 691 CE, one of earliest calligraphic expressions of the Qur'ānic text, containing a selection of Qur'ānic verses focussing thematically on the theological positions of Jesus and Muḥammad (Grabar [O.] 2006). In collective prayer, such as the Friday communal gathering in a mosque, the Qur'ān was apparently always (and still is) recited and never read from a codex. Indeed, the Arabic term *muṣḥaf* (a loanword from Ethiopic not appearing in the text of the Qur'ān) refers to a Qur'ān manuscript or, in modern times, to a printed version as well, and thus underscores a widespread awareness of the quintessential distinction between the Qur'ān as a text in the abstract sense and its physical materialization in the shape of a book. Looking at its liturgical function from the perspective of the medium involved, the Qur'ān is a text of hybrid nature: physically present in the shape of written books, the 'first nature' of the text, at least seen from within Muslim religious tradition, the first medium nevertheless seems to be the human voice (Marx 2012). Apart from the technique of reciting the text (*taǧwīd*) (Kellermann 1995), to the extent that a chain of oral transmission from the lifetime of the Prophet until the present day grants authority to the recited text. Due to this type of transmission, different versions of the text, slightly differing from each other in word morphology (case, number, mode, etc.) and textual segmentation (verse numbering and regulation of pauses) exist until today and are all permitted for prayer and other religious purposes: these are the well-known 'seven canonical readings' (*al-qirā'āt al-sab'*), variants of the texts permitted in prayer (for more details see Marx 2012).

This dogma of an oral transmission by a chain that reaches back to the first recitation of the text by the Prophet Muḥammad himself neither can be proved easily nor should be dismissed out of hand. Suffice it to stress that it strongly reflects the attitude of Muslim scholarship towards written transmission. Perhaps the experiences of different textual versions of the holy text of neighbouring religious communities, of which early Muslims were well aware, lead to focussing on oral (non-written) transmission. On the other hand, Muslim sources tell us that already the first caliphs Abū Bakr and 'Uṯmān b. 'Affān took measures to restrain growing variant readings among the first Muslims. We do not know if 'Uṯmān had actually sent reference copies of one specific Medinan codex to the most important cities Basra, Kufa, Damascus and Mecca—and, according to another version of the account, also to Bahrain and to Sanaa—, but apparently things were not that simple with a 'liquid oral tradition' of the holy book.

The aforementioned reading systems are all compatible with a written standard that by the ninth century is identified with the reference copies sent by the caliph 'Uṯmān. Whatever one may think of the traditional Muslim narratives on these issues, the material evidence of extant copies attests to a relatively large number of written witnesses for the first two centuries, even before other Arabic texts took their written shape. This very first layer of textual transmission may be linked with the manuscript highlighted here, London, BL, Or. 2165. It has a striking resemblance with manuscript Paris, BnF, Arabe 328e, which is part of a *Sammelhandschrift*, a 'heterogenous manuscript' Arabe 328, consisting of five originally different manuscripts and merged by Michele Amari (1806–1889) from Qur'ānic codices acquired in Cairo in the first half of the nineteenth century. The reason for the merging of six different fragments is not known. Arabe 328a and 328b belong to the same codex (*Codex Parisino-petropolitanus*, together with manuscripts St Petersburg, RNB, Marcel 18 + Vatican City, BAV, Vat. ar. 1605/1 (see fig. 2.2.5) + London, Khalili Collection, KFQ 60; see Déroche 2009); 328c may be together with MS Birmingham, Cadbury Library, 1572; 328d and 328f do not belong to any known manuscript. Just like London, BL, Or. 2165, Arabe 328e has no vowel signs, and consonants are often distinguished from each other by dashes. Six dots grouped in two vertical lines denote a verse separator, a red circle indicates every tenth verse separator. The style of writing and the size of (1) London, BL, Or. 2165, (2) six folia of Paris, BnF, Arabe 328 labelled as 328e and (3) a parchment bifolium that was sold in 1979 at an auction at Sotheby's in London and is preserved now in the Kuwaiti Dār al-Āṯār al-Islāmiyya (ed. Jenkins 1983, 18) indicate that they are fragments of a single codex of the Qur'ān that could be dated according to palaeographical evidence to the early eighth century (in the typology of Qur'ānic scripts, London, BL, Or. 2165 is classified as *ḥiǧāzī*-II, according to Déroche 1992; see Table 3.3.16.1).

This sketch on the textual transmission of the Qur'ān is too brief to include evidence from more than twenty larger Qur'ānic manuscripts or fragments dated to the first two hundred years of the Islamic era. As the diagram on important manuscripts and their numbers of folia illustrates (Table 3.3.16.2), material evidence for the early history of the Qur'ān can be considered substantial in terms of quantity—especially if we were to compare it with material evidence for the New Testament where the important larger codices with the exception of fragments on papyri are usually dated to the centuries after the year 200.

Against this background, London, BL, Or. 2165 allows us to get insight into the textual history of the Qur'ān at least in six relevant fields: codicology; ornaments and illustrations; palaeography; text segmentation; spelling; and variant readings. For all these six levels of evidence, preliminary remarks on the manuscripts, partly referring to earlier studies, can be made, but here only the last three categories will be discussed.

In terms of the first three aspects, all that can be said here is that, codicologically, manuscript London, BL, Or. 2165, together with its two fragments, contains 129 folia, covers *c.*60% of the canonical text of the Qur'ān; just like the reconstructed *Codex Parisino-petropolitanus*, it is an example of Qur'ānic codices that are in line with the book culture of the Late Antique Middle East; the scarce use of metatextual

Table 3.3.16.1 Comparison of MSS Paris, BnF, Arabe 328e, Kuwait, LNS, 19CA[ab], and London, BL, Or. 2165

Parchment; *c.*315 mm × 215 mm; 24 lines per page; script: Arabic: *ḥiǧāzī*-II; early eighth century; probably of Syrian provenance

Paris, BnF, Arabe 328e	*Kuwait, LNS, 19CA[ab]*	*London, BL, Or. 2165*
6 ff.	2 ff.	121 ff.
5:7–65 (ff. 90–92) 6:39–6:112 (ff. 93–95)	5:89–6:12 (2 ff.)	7:42–9:95 (ff. 1–14) 10:9–39:47 (ff. 15–113) 40:61–43:71 (ff. 114–21)
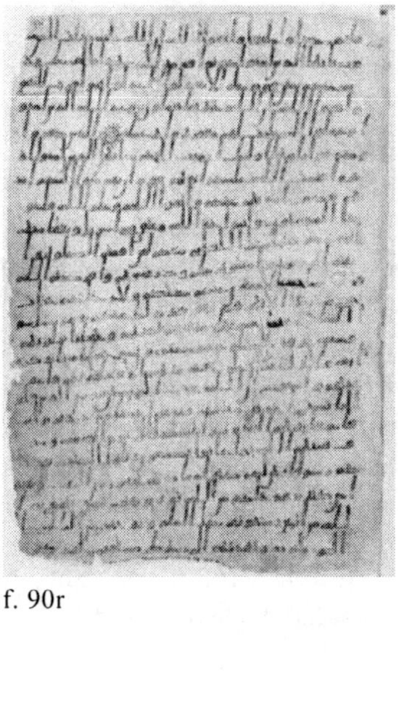	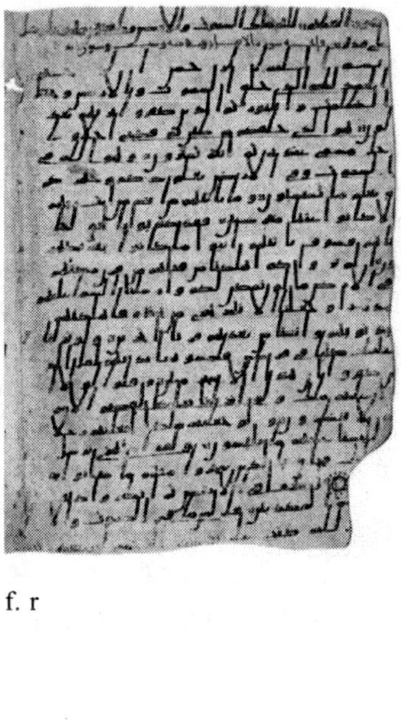	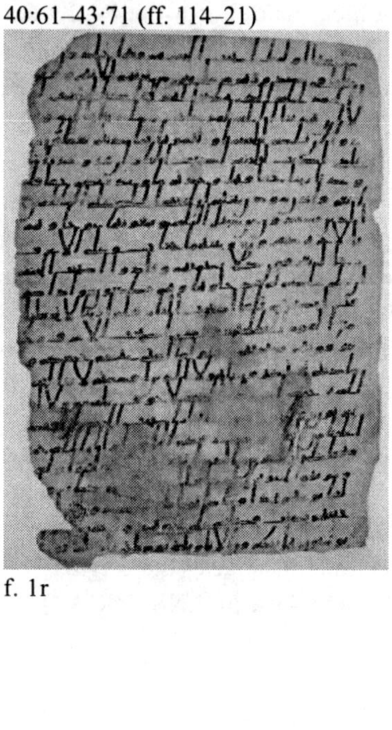
f. 90r	f. r	f. 1r

signs and ornaments reflects the earliest writing conventions of the sacred text (Rieu 1894, 37–38). In terms of palaeography, it is written in the style dubbed *ḥiǧāzī*-II (on which see Déroche 1992, 27–29), which points to a dating of the manuscript in the first half of the eighth century.

Text segmentation

Starting with the oldest extant manuscripts of the Qur'ān, such as the palimpsest Sanaa, DAM, 01-27.1, the use of verse separating signs can be observed. By using colour to mark every tenth verse, as in the London codex, numbering is implicitly given. In Kufic manuscripts, Arabic letters were inserted to explicitly state (by the numerical value of the letters) the number of decades. Thus, the segmentation of verses belongs to the very beginnings of Qur'ānic manuscript culture, a system probably aiming at structuring and controlling the written text. The verse numbering system may serve as an indicator for the origin of Qur'ānic manuscripts, as there are specific regional features.

In manuscript Paris, BnF, Arabe 328e, f. 92r, line 10, a red-ink separator marks the end of verse 50, corresponding to verse 48 in the Kufic verse numbering system used today. Anton Spitaler (1935) compiled a list of regionally established verse numbering systems (presented in practical tables) described in Islamic sources of the eighth and ninth centuries for the cities of Basra, Damascus, Homs, Kufa, Medina and Mecca. This regional vs. Kufic numbering difference of the two verses is mentioned in early Islamic sources (Spitaler 1935, 36). Intisar Rabb (2006, 84–127) has shown that MS London, BL, Or. 2165 follows in general the verse numbering system attributed to the Syrian city of Homs. The origin can find further attestation by the identification of variant readings that are also linked to regional systems, as the study of Yasin Dutton (2004) on ff. 1–61 of the London codex has shown.

Orthography

MS London, BL, Or. 2165 spells the long vowel /ā/ in medial position without the letter *alif*. Since the writing of Arabic had not yet been harmonized, the usual phonological value of the *alif* in the seventh century is the glottal stop (*hamza*). During the eighth century, the *alif* was increasingly used to mark the long vowel /ā/, an additional common use that lead to ambiguities in spelling and reading. Thus, the missing *alif* is a feature of Arabic in old manuscripts.

This feature can be highlighted by comparing London, BL, Or. 2165 to the Cairo printed edition of the Qur'ān of 1924—the reference text used today in the Muslim world and in western scholarship. The orthography of the Cairo edition looks archaic to us; according to the postface it follows the principles described by the Andalusian scholar (Abū 'Amr) al-Dānī (d.1052) and Ibn Naǧāḥ (d.1103). In MS London, BL, Or. 2165, on f. 92r alone there are sixteen instances where *alif* is missing in comparison with the Cairo edition. Thus, the earliest known codices of the Qur'ān seem to go beyond the 'normative line' of al-Dānī.

Variant readings

Since MS London, BL, Or. 2165 is not vocalized, just like Paris, BnF, Arabe 328, there are some words that display differences in comparison with the received Qur'ānic text of our times as well as with the seven canonical readings of the tenth century. Yasin Dutton closely compared the first part of the London codex (ff. 1–61) with the 'standard' reading of Ḥafṣ (d.795; also used in the Egyptian print of 1924) and suggested that the reading of the London codex was that of Ibn 'Āmir of Damascus (d.736), proclaimed one of the canonical Seven Readers by Ibn Muǧāhid (d.936; see Dutton 2004, 43–71). Just to illustrate: where in Sūra 5, verse 50 the majority reading attested by exegetical literature has *tabġūna*, London, BL, Or. 2165 (f. 92r, line 15) has *yabġūna*, corresponding to the reading of Ibn 'Āmir (cf., for instance, Aḥmad Muḫtār 'Umar – 'Abd al-'Āl Sālim Makram 1982–1988, II, 216). The Ḥafṣ reading of Sūra 5, verse 54 has *yartadda* where London, BL, Or. 2165 (f. 92r, line 25) has *yartadid*, a *qirā'a* known in the literature for the readers Nāfi', Ibn 'Āmir and Abū Ǧa'far ('Abd al-'Āl Sālim Makram – Aḥmad Muḫtār 'Umar 1988, II, 218). The difference is more than just a diacritical mark (*yā'* instead of *tā'*) or a missing *alif*. Even if there are some cases in London, BL, Or. 2165 that are not in line with the reading of Ibn 'Āmir (for instance, on f. 48r we find *li-yahaba*, written with the letter *yā'*, instead of *li-'ahaba* written with the letter *alif*), the reading of the manuscript is for the most part in line with the reading system that was later ascribed to Ibn 'Āmir.

Conclusion

The London codex (the *Ḥiǧāzī*-II-Syrian-codex consisting of London, BL, Or. 2165, Paris, BnF, Arabe 328e, and Kuwait, LNS, 19CA[ab]) covers 60% of the Qur'ān and can be considered one of its oldest witness-

Table 3.3.16.2 Fragments of the Qur'ān on parchment before 750 CE

Collection	*Manuscript*	*Folia*
Bahrain, Bayt al-Qur'ān	1611-mkh235	1
Berlin, Staatsbibliothek	or. fol. 4313	7
Berlin, Staatsbibliothek	We. II 1913	210
Birmingham. Cadbury Research Library	1572	9
Cairo, National Library of Egypt	Qāf 47	31
Cambridge University Library	Add. 1125	2
Cambridge University Library	Or. 1287: Palimps	*c.*32
Chicago, Oriental Institute	A 6959	1
Chicago, Oriental Institute	A 6978	1
Chicago, Oriental Institute	A 6988	1
Chicago, Oriental Institute	A 6990	1
Chicago, Oriental Institute	A 6991	1
Chicago, Oriental Institute	A 7000	1
Dublin, Chester Beatty Library	1615 I	32
Dublin, Chester Beatty Library	1615 II	4
Istanbul, Türk ve İslam Eserleri Müzesi	ŞE Signatures	*c.*500
Istanbul, Topkapı Sarayı Müzesi	'Medina 1 a'	308
Raqqada, Musée national d'art islamique	R 119	86
Kuwait, Dār al-Aṯār al-Islāmiyya	LNS 19 CA ab	2
Kuwait, Tareq Rajab Museum	QUR-1-TSR	1
Leiden, University Library	Or. 14.545 a	4
Leiden, University Library	Or. 14.545 b	1
Leiden, University Library	Or. 14.545 c	1
London, BL	Or. 2165	121
London, Nasser D. al-Khalili Collection	KFQ 34	1
London, Nasser D. al-Khalili Collection	KFQ 60	1
Paris, BnF	Arabe 326a	6
Paris, BnF	Arabe 328a	56
Paris, BnF	Arabe 328b	14
Paris, BnF	Arabe 328c	17
Paris, BnF	Arabe 328d	3
Paris, BnF	Arabe 328e	6
Paris, BnF	Arabe 328f	4
Paris, BnF	Arabe 330a	2
Paris, BnF	Arabe 330g	20
Paris, BnF	Arabe 331	56
Paris, BnF	Arabe 334c	25
Paris, BnF	Arabe 6140a	4
Paris, BnF	Arabe 7191	1
Paris, BnF	Arabe 7192	1
Paris, BnF	Arabe 7193	1
Paris, BnF	Arabe 7194	1
Paris, BnF	Arabe 7195	1
Paris, BnF	Arabe 7196	1
Paris, BnF	Arabe 7197	1
Paris, BnF	Arabe 7201	1
Paris, BnF	Arabe 7202	1
Paris, BnF	Arabe 7203	1
Philadelphia, PA, Paul J. Gutman Library	E. 16269 D	1
Doha, Qatar, Museum of Islamic Art	*unknown sign.*	*c.*50
Doha, Qatar, Museum of Islamic Art	MS 68, 69, 70, 699	13
Doha, Qatar, Museum of Islamic Art	MS 67	3
Vatican City, BAV	Vat. arab. 1605	1
St. Petersburg, RNB	Marcel 3	26
St. Petersburg, RNB	Marcel 9	32
St. Petersburg, RNB	Marcel 16	12
St. Petersburg, RNB	Marcel 17	18
St. Petersburg, RNB	Marcel 18	26
St. Petersburg, RNB	Marcel 19	13
St. Petersburg, Inst. of Or. St. + fragments	E-20	97
Sanaa, DAM	01.25-1	30
Sanaa, DAM	01.27-1: Pal.	*c.* 38
Sanaa, DAM	01.29-1	31
Tübingen, Universitätsbibliothek	Ma VI 165	77
Princeton University Library	14G a	1
Vienna, ÖNB	A Perg. 2	1
Vienna, ÖNB	A Perg. 213	1
TOTAL		***c.*2054**

es. The manuscript shares several features in format, style, and textual variants with the *Codex Parisino-petropolitanus*. Both manuscripts seem to be written according to the Syrian reading that is later referred to in the literature as the reading of Ibn ʿĀmir. The verse numbering system of both manuscripts is in close relationship with that used in the cities of Damascus and Homs.

The London codex was produced, as it seems, in a way similar to Greek and Syriac codices of Late Antiquity. The victory of the parchment codex over the scroll by the fourth century is reflected in the early Islamic period; and the similarity to Syriac codices is perhaps related to the fact that the emerging religious culture of Muslims was still dependent on the already existing cultural techniques. The London codex can be dated palaeographically to the first half of the eighth century. Both its verse numbering system as well as the variant readings hint to a Syrian context.

The evidence contained in the London codex appears to be to a very high degree (though not perfectly) in line with data obtained from Islamic sources on variant readings and verse numbering system for the early Islamic period.

The manuscript is written in a rather uncalligraphic style. The almost complete absence of ornaments may be an indication of the scope of the manuscript, created in order to record the text rather than exhibit a beautiful copy. The codex seems to have been written by at least two different professional hands (Rabb 2006, 99), using 24 lines per page, meaning that, assuming it originally contained the complete text, it must have had approximately 220 folia, probably arranged in twenty-two quinions—an example of a fairly developed, professional, and also costly way of handling the Qur'ānic text.

The study of the London codex has been somewhat limited, as most of the analysis carried out so far was based on the first 61 folia of London, BL, Or. 2165. An extensive study on the complete manuscript is still a desideratum. Moreover, similar in-depth studies on other extant old manuscripts or fragments of the pre-Umayyad period written in *ḥiǧāzī* script would be needed in order to pave the way for a comprehensive history of the Qur'ānic text.

References

Aḥmad Muḫtār ʿUmar – ʿAbd al-ʿĀl Sālim Makram 1982–1988; Altıkulaç 2007, 2009, 2011; Déroche 1992, 2009; Dutton 2004; Grabar [O.] 2006; Grohmann 1958; Imbert 2013; Jenkins 1983; Jocham – Marx forthcoming; Kellermann 1995; Marx 2012; Rabb 2006; Rezvan 2004; Rieu 1894; Spitaler 1935.

3.17. Past and present trends in the edition of Classical Syriac texts (AM)

CSCO, Scriptores Syri: A 'base manuscript', defects included

In a recent survey of electronic resources for Syriac studies, Kristian Heal (2012, 74, n. 17) tells of oral tradition concerning the scientific and emotional value of the *Corpus Scriptorum Christianorum Orientalium* (CSCO) for eastern Christian scholars: 'Sebastian Brock once observed in casual conversation that, 'The corpus is our life', referring to the CSCO'. Together with the *Patrologia Orientalis*, the CSCO and a few other editorial projects do indeed represent the life of Syriac philology and the solid skeleton for its growth in the twentieth century. So it is perhaps appropriate to start the present survey of text-critical choices in the edition of Classical Syriac texts from the sub-series *Scriptores Syri* of the CSCO. We can distinguish three main periods in its history: The Latin Period, from 1906 to 1949; Draguet's CSCO, from 1950 to 1995; and what we could label as 'new direction(s)' from 1995 onwards.

In the first period, all introductions and translations are written in Latin, the classical language of philology—and Roman Catholic liturgy—which virtually disappeared from the CSCO after 1950, when it was replaced by European national languages. To this period usually belong historiographical texts edited between 1903 and 1949, under the direction of Chabot. Their stocks were lost in 1940, when, during the second German invasion of Leuven, the building of the University Library was largely burnt down. Draguet directed their reprint in the years 1952–1955.

The Latin period includes various kinds of editions: diplomatic editions by Guidi and Vaschalde, eclectic texts by Labourt and Connolly, emended texts by Chabot, who clearly expresses the goal and limits of his editorial pride in the introduction of *Scriptores Syri* 36 (Chabot 1920): 'Editoris autem munus non est novam recensionem, etiam meliorem, constituere'.

Most of the Syriac texts published in the CSCO are in fact diplomatic editions, thanks to or because of the method elaborated, used and recommended by René Draguet, (re-)founder and director of the series for many years (1948–1995). Former professor of theology, in 1948 he took over the direction of CSCO and devoted most of his life to a monumental enterprise that required his total commitment (Ponthot 1981). Draguet (1977) exposes and summarizes his method in an article published in a miscellaneous volume in honour of Arthur Vööbus. It is clear that he is not discussing theoretical and methodological questions, but proposing a method in the sense of practical instructions or even directions for editors of Syriac texts. Following classical philological standards, he makes a detailed *recensio* of the manuscript witnesses a first requirement. Their evaluation should be in terms of closeness to 'the original', but the rather unclear expression 'textual profile which seems best to approximate the original' might in fact be the equivalent of Lachmann's concept of the archetype.

As we will see, the first recommendation made by Draguet to choose one manuscript as a base text and reproduce it as it is, with all its faults, is taken very seriously by all editors of CSCO in Draguet's period, preferred to any form of hybrid text, arbitrary contamination or conjectural reconstruction. The idea of reproducing the manuscript as it is, is much more fictional than it sounds. Besides concessions to the tacit normalization of the punctuation system (second recommendation), the subdivision of sentences, paragraphs and sections—procedures that profoundly alter the *mise en page* of the manuscript and its value as a historical witness of the punctuation system and the history of the language in a given moment—Draguet fails to mention another major change introduced in the reproduction of the manuscript in printed form, that is the substitution of all kinds of Syriac script with the *ʾesṭrangēlā* available to *la typographie orientaliste* and probably most appreciated by Syriac students the world over.

The adverb 'tacitly' in the description of editorial methods should rouse especial alarm. Draguet is certainly right when he stresses that the works of scribes and editors ('objective data and subjective editorial judgment') must remain clearly distinguishable throughout the edition. Throughout text, apparatus—and to a certain extent also in the translation—one should be able to recognize what manuscripts and other primary sources actually attest and what has been legitimately altered, changed or omitted by the editor. Editors, however, should be allowed to propose a readable corrected text, close to the archetype or even to the original—if they think such a thing exists and can be reconstructed—and must be visible even in their intervention in choice of characters, vocalization, punctuation and page layout.

Draguet's opposition to any correction and reconstruction is surprising when we consider the rich and detailed introduction that he wrote for his own text editions within CSCO. They are impressive and regularly contain an accurate codicological description of the witnesses, a discussion on their interrelationships and sub-grouping, and a *stemma codicum* (on Draguet's achievement as a Syriac scholar see Brock et al. 2011, 131–132). There are at least three explanatory hypotheses that do not necessarily exclude each other to understand Draguet's strenuous defence of mistakes and defects of the manuscript chosen as the base text. 1) A practical explanation is suggested by Draguet when he says that 'this method most conveniently allows for modifications when new textual evidence is found'. Although it is not clear why a reconstructed or emended text would exclude the recording of new evidence in the apparatus, Draguet may have come to this conclusion for practical typographical reasons—as Alessandro Bausi suggested to me informally: in the pre-digital world, reprinting the apparatus only, with minor up-dating, would be easier than the whole text. 2) A psychological explanation was envisaged by Bausi (2004a, 17, n 45; 2006a, 542; 2008b, 29), when he wittily pointed out that the base-manuscript method reflects the almost fetishistic attitude towards the manuscript, that Luciano Canfora observed among Hellenistic and Late Antique scholars. 3) From a historical point of view, Draguet's 'method' can be easily understood in the academic context in which he was trained and worked. It is clearly in line with Bédier's theory of the *bon manuscrit*. Draguet is even more radical than Bédier, who accepted correction at least of the most obvious mistakes of the base manuscript (Bausi 2004a, 16). On the other hand, Draguet—no doubt like most authors and readers of the CSCO—had a theological background and/or theological interests and was therefore familiar with the text history of the Hebrew Bible and Biblical philology. As is well known, what is generally intended as a critical edition of the Hebrew Old Testament is in fact the transcription of one manuscript, with all its mistakes and idiosyncrasies. Better readings or editorial corrections laid down in the apparatus as a *lege*—as required by Draguet—resemble very much the Masoretic practice of the *qere*. In this connexion, it is remarkable that the only 'bibliographical reference' given by Draguet (1977) is Origen's work on the pre-Masoretic Hebrew biblical text, as if no-one ever discussed textual criticism after Origen or there were no philology but ancient and mediaeval Bible philology.

In the CSCO and in general in Syriac philology, the editions are regularly and laudably accompanied by translations, which—especially in the case of diplomatic editions—represent the truly critical texts and are offered to a wider readership than Semitists and Syriac scholars only: students of the Bible, eastern Christianity, Late Antique and Byzantine history, Christian and pagan literatures written in Greek and Latin, Judaism, Islam, etc.

Faithfulness to the manuscript chosen as a base text is expressed in monumental sub-series of CSCO *Scriptores Syri* such as the editions of Ishodad of Merw, published between 1950 and 1981 by Ceslas Van den Eynde, OP, and Ephrem, published between 1955 and 1979 by Edmund Beck (see Brock and Van Rompay in Brock et al. 2011, 65 and 423). 'L'édition reproduit le texte de A tel qu'il est, fautes comprises' becomes a mantra-like refrain, declined in a variety of forms and translated in the various languages even after Draguet's departure from this earth in 1980. Indeed, Draguet managed to posthumously direct and influence the CSCO for 15 years at least after his death: from 1980 to 1995, the second page of the cover gives his name, followed by a crux, as the director of CSCO.

When the CSCO was Draguet's CSCO, there was at least one editor who opted for corrections in the critical text. Curiously he is the same Arthur Vööbus (see Buck in Brock et al. 2011, 433–435) to whom Draguet dedicated his notorious article of 1977.

Finally, in 1995, Bernard Coulie and Andrea Schmidt were chosen as members of the scientific board of the CSCO instead of Draguet, fifteen years after the latter's death. New methodological choices were made. It may be a coincidence, but the first text published under their direction 'is not a diplomatic edition'. The same Robert W. Thomson, who thirty years before had faithfully reproduced the manuscripts chosen as bases for the various texts, with all of their errors and accepting inconsistencies in the vocalization from item to item (CSCO *Scriptores Syri* 114, Thomson [R.] 1965), is now proud to announce that he has 'corrected the Syriac where it is clearly wrong' (CSCO *Scriptores Syri* 222, Thomson [R.] 1995). Other editors preferred to continue the tradition of diplomatic editions or to present eclectic texts.

Brock's work on dialogue poems: 'A readable text'

CSCO volumes usually represent points of arrival of many years of research on the same author or textual tradition—sometimes published in several volumes over years and decennia—and thus presuppose middle- or long-term projects compatible with the 4–5 years of a doctoral fellowship or rhythm of life and teaching tasks in a Benedictine school or a Dominican seminary

Sebastian Brock, lecturer at Oxford University and universally recognized as the leading scholar of Syriac Studies today, opted for other strategies for the publication of Syriac dialogue poems. Text editions, with translation and ample philological, literary and theological commentaries, are disseminated in more than twenty different periodicals and miscellaneous volumes, published in various countries, from India to Canada, from Lebanon to the United States. A coherent and ambitious project is clearly there and it becomes evident when reading Brock's programmatic survey (1983, 1984, 1987b) or lists such as Brock (1991b, up-dated in 2010b), where the researcher takes stock of progress and announces further publications as forthcoming.

From the literary point of view, dispute and dialogue poems are treated as a more or less unitary corpus, as the Christian continuation of a very old Mesopotamian tradition (Brock 1983, 1989, 2001), and representative of a characteristically Syriac genre, fascinating for its exegetical and theological content and influential in the emergence and development of Greek hymnography (Brock 1985a, 1987b, 2008) and, indirectly, in the diffusion of the dispute—and perhaps the religious drama, too—as popular poetic genres in the Arab and Persian East and in mediaeval Europe. As a matter of fact, the rather homogeneous literary corpus does not exist in the manuscript tradition and has been created by the editor. Brock compiled a list or inventory of dispute and dialogue poems, selecting them from liturgical manuscripts of various ages and origins and printed books, on the basis of the genre to which they belong or the textual structure (dialogue or dispute) they present.

Brock published the critical editions of texts in single papers and contributions, a choice which fits the 'publish or perish' policy of contemporary universities better and allows the scholar to make progress in his knowledge of the genre as a whole and to deal in depth with the literary richness of a single text, the often long and complicated history of its transmission, its fortune and web of intertextual references. One cannot find texts and translations of the dialogue poems by picking a couple of volumes from the same library shelf, as Draguet's grandiose project has made possible for various Syriac authors and corpora, but in doing so Brock certainly succeeded in reaching a wide and varied readership. In this connexion, he clearly intends not only to serve the needs of qualified readers of universities and specialized libraries—the target market of a publishing house like Peeters, which prints and distributes the CSCO—but he also makes this Syriac genre more widely known to scholars who do not read the language, and easily accessible to non professional readers—probably many Syrians among them—whose interests range from the search of inspiring devotional readings to the enhancement of a cultural and national heritage. This purpose is evident in the texts published exclusively in English translation (for example Brock 1987a; 1992, 2010b) and in the most complete collection of Syriac dialogue poems available in the original language, that Brock (1982) published in cooperation with first-class scribe, scholar and publisher: twenty-six poems—some in more than one version—were prepared for publication by Brock and copied by the elegant West Syriac hand of the late Mor Julios Yeshu Çiçek, Syrian Orthodox Archbishop of Central Europe and founder of the publishing house hosted in the St Ephrem Monastery of Glane (the Netherlands). It is one of those publications in which print and manuscript cultures seem to fade into each other.

Literary remarks on the poems and philological notes on the manuscripts used for these printed handwritten texts are discussed in an article of *marginalia* published in English in *Le Muséon*. Although Brock declares there (1984, 39–40) that his aim was 'to select those dialogue *soghyatha* that might be of interest to a modern Syrian Orthodox readership (hence the absence of any pieces known only from East Syrian tradition)', he nevertheless included the exclusively eastern *Dispute of Gold and Wheat*. He then presents the collection as 'no more than an *editio minor*' and hopes 'one day to provide fuller editions, with critical apparatus, translations and commentaries of these intriguing and often delightful poems'. However, philologists should always keep in mind commented translations, minor editions and any form of popularization as complementary objectives of their editorial work, especially in times when philology—traditionally perceived as a discipline ancillary to literary, linguistic, historical or religious studies—is more and more marginalized in the university study programs and desperately needs to gain appeal among students and across disciplines.

Most dialogue and dispute poems are anonymous compositions, as is typical of liturgical poetry, and not authorial works like the vast majority of the CSCO texts. Being liturgical texts, they are intended for vocal performance—probably most often by choirs in the case of the stanzaic *sugitā* meter—and their use in the liturgy left marks in the history of their transmission in a number of ways. Some poems, evidently intended for alternating choirs, have been preserved only partially or fragmentarily due to the—eleventh century and later—habit of separating the alternate verses in two manuscripts, each to be used by one choir. We are thus left with the verses and the arguments of only one of the two characters engaged in the dialogue or in the dispute. The half, apocopated text of some dialogue poems have been reproduced even in the printed editions of the West Syriac collection called *fanqiṯo* (Mosul 1886–1896 and Pampakuda 1962–1963; see Brock 1984, 38–39).

It is difficult to date anonymous texts and Syriac dialogue poems are no exception. Brock suggests that the texts preserved in both the West and East Syriac traditions may antedate or be contemporary with the Christological disputes of the fifth century that eventually led to the formation of two separate Churches and liturgies. In certain cases, a relative antiquity of the texts (fifth and sixth centuries) is suggested by the way they handle themes derived from early authors such as Ephrem (d.373; Brock et al. 2011, 145–147) or echoed by later ones such as Jacob of Serugh (*c.*451–521; Brock et al. 2011, 433–435). Dating texts on the basis of the content is however rather risky and it seems unwise to exclude contacts and reciprocal influences between the two churches, especially in a field like hymnography with its obvious links with sacred music. The two Syriac traditions do differ in the transmission of dialogue poems in that we have western manuscript witnesses from the ninth century onwards, whereas eastern collections are—sometimes considerably—later than the thirteenth century. Moreover some poems have been preserved in two distinct versions, the Eastern one being generally shorter and adapted to late literary forms and taste: end rhyme is introduced on the model of Arabo-Persian poetry and style and formalism reflect the poetic production of the so-called Syriac Renaissance (tenth to thirteenth centuries, but especially thirteenth century as far as East Syriac poetry is concerned).

Rather than following a hypothetical chronological order or arranging the texts according to the position they occupy in the liturgical calendar, Brock groups the poems according to the characters involved and orders them according to the biblical narrative: Old Testament, New Testament and others (personifications, saints and martyrs). Whenever possible, he publishes the two versions of a dialogue together, and in these cases the focus of the thematic and intertextual analysis is generally on the oldest—which usually means the West Syriac—version. Thus we get a comparative glance at two different texts, often separated by a considerable lapse of time and reflecting distant contexts of use and transmission, rather than a whole picture of the dialogue poems as preserved and used in a given period and within a certain—western or eastern—liturgical tradition. Interest in the contents would seem to prevail on philological concerns, but the history of tradition—in Pasquali's terms—of each text could have not be emphasized more efficaciously.

At least in one case—the *Dispute of the Months* in Brock (1985b)—the comparison is extended to 'related texts', such as a Jewish *Dispute of the Months* added as an interpolation to Exodus 12:2 in the so-called *Fragment Targum* and the *Dispute of Gold and Wheat*, preserved only in the East Syriac milieu, in the classical language and in Modern Aramaic. The earliest and longest West Syriac version of the *Dispute of the Months* turns out not to be as reliable as one might expect. A fragment included as a quotation in the *Book of Rhetoric* by Antony of Tagrit (probably ninth century; see Watt in Brock et al. 2011, 23) shares a number of good readings with the East Syriac shorter version of the *Dispute*, attested in manuscripts of the nineteenth century. *Recentiores, non deteriores*.

The anthology of dialogue poems explicitly planned for Syrian Orthodox readers (Brock 1982) is in fully vocalized West Syriac script (*serṭā*), even for texts preserved in old *ʾesṭrangēlā* or late East Syriac manuscripts. Elsewhere, Brock usually transliterates the Syriac text of both West and East Syriac versions in *ʾesṭrangēlā* script, as in the CSCO, but he excludes vowel signs. This produces a neat readable text for western scholars primarily interested in the content of the poems and significantly reduces the number of spelling forms and readings to be recorded in apparatus—however, a brief discussion of the spelling is generally to be found in the introductions—as well as the number of corrections and interventions the editor needs to make. Nevertheless, the choice of suppressing the vocalization is questionable from at least two points of view: dialogue poems are liturgical texts and are preserved in liturgical manuscripts that often have vowels, being conceived and copied as supports for public performances; the vocalization may therefore be contemporary with the copy, it reproduces the pronunciation of a given time and is a potentially precious source of information about metric and the history of the Syriac language.

As far as philological methods are concerned, Brock is much more open to emendation and reconstruction than most CSCO editors. It is perhaps not a coincidence that he published his edition of Isaac of

Nineveh (*Scriptores Syri* 224 and 225; Brock 1995b) in the third period of the history of the *Corpus* as we have outlined it above. In a passage that is worth quoting in extenso, he would seem to distance himself from Draguet's method as applied by 'many' Syriac scholars:

> Since no manuscript ever presents a text free from corruption (often obvious), the modern editor is compelled to produce an eclectic text, if his edition is to appear in a readable form (something many editors of Syriac texts choose to overlook).

The factual premises of classical philology—ubiquitous and explainable corruption of the copies—and the necessary conscious intervention of the editor, especially in cases of omissions and fragmentarily or partially transmitted texts, are clearly recognized. However, he stresses that the aim of the philological work is not so much the approximation to an archetype—as all (post-)Lachmannian theories and approaches in textual criticism entails—but the publication of a readable text.

In the metrical form of the *suġiṯā*, in which most dialogue poems are written, verses or pairs of verses are very often connected by means of an alphabetic acrostic—each verse or pair beginning with one of the letters of the Syriac alphabet—which clearly has a mnemotechnic function in oral performances. The mnemonic device is also integrated in the scribal technique, since the first letters are normally rubricated in the manuscripts. This has prevented omissions in the copying process, showed them up when they did occur and leads the editor in the reconstruction process, which is moreover enhanced by the relatively stable textual transmission and uniformity of Classical Syriac through the centuries. To exemplify the necessity of an eclectic text, Brock mentions the West Syriac version of *The Sinful Woman and Satan*, that he reconstructs using no less than five manuscripts (Brock 1988).

References

Bausi 2004a, 2006a, 2008b; Beck 1955, 1957, 1960, 1979; Brock 1982, 1983, 1984, 1985a, 1985b, 1987a, 1987b, 1988, 1989, 1991b, 1992, 1995b, 2001, 2008, 2010b; Brock et al. 2011; Canfora 1974; Chabot 1920; Draguet 1977; Heal 2012; Pasquali 1934; Ponthot 1981; Thomson [R.] 1965, 1995; Van den Eynde 1955, 1958, 1963, 1969, 1972, 1981; Van den Eynde – Vosté 1950.

3.18. Pseudo-Avicenna's *De anima*. The Latin translation of a lost Arabic original (SM)

When editing and translating texts, scholars sometimes encounter texts written in a given language A, however with features of another given language B and/or linguistic peculiarities typical of translations; or, they encounter texts that have been written in language A, however are attributed to authors who are known to have written in language B. In these cases, one of the main questions is to determine whether the text represents a translation from language B into language A, or whether it was originally written in language A. Indeed, the way in which to edit a text varies precisely according to this fact (whether or not it is a translation), especially when the original is no longer extant.

Typical examples can be observed in the alchemical texts wrongly attributed to Avicenna, especially the alchemical *De anima* (Moureau 2010a, 2010b, 2013a, 2013b, forthcoming). This treatise is the compilation and Latin translation of three lost Arabic treatises, composed between the mid-eleventh and the mid-thirteenth centuries in Andalusia, and erroneously ascribed to Avicenna. It may have been translated around 1226 or 1235, according to a colophon in three witnesses. This translation is to be situated within the impetus of translations from Arabic into Latin that arose at the end of the eleventh century and flourished during the twelfth and thirteenth centuries in Italy (especially Sicily) and Spain. During this period, an important transfer of Arabic knowledge enriched the Latin west and brought new elements to most fields of knowledge; among these, many Greek texts which were translated into Arabic, often through Syriac intermediaries, from the sixth century onwards, and mainly during the ninth and tenth centuries.

Identifying a Latin translation of a lost Arabic treatise

When a Latin text is suspected to be a translation from Arabic, the first step to be taken in order to corroborate or invalidate this hypothesis is bibliographical research. If no Arabic original can be found, the researcher must look for indirect traces of the text in Arabic literature, searching for one of the following: (1) its title, conjecturing possible titles in Arabic by back translation—however, titles often change; (2) the author's name—however, attributions often change, and the text can be attributed to an author of another language tradition or even to the translator (for example, the case of the *Pantegni*, the Latin translation made by Constantine the African of the *Kāmil al-ṣināʿa al-ṭibbiyya* of ʿAlī ibn al-ʿAbbās al-Mağūsī, which is not presented as a translation but as a Latin composition, Burnett – Jacquart 1994); or, (3) typical content. As far as the *De anima* is concerned, no mention of it can be traced in Avicenna's genuine work or in other Arabic treatises: the text seems to have been unknown to Arabic scholars. It is, however, often referred to in Latin texts. This lack of Arabic traces is important for the history of the text, but this argument *a silentio* alone does not prove that *De anima* is a later forgery.

Philological research is a more accurate way to identify a translation. Mediaeval translations from Arabic into Latin were made according to two different translation methods that correspond, to some extent, to two stages. The first method implies a greater distance between the translation and the original text: translators do not hesitate to rewrite the whole work, and sometimes even attribute it to themselves, and they tend to use a more 'classical' Latin. They also often write a prologue in which they explain their work. The second method is concerned to provide a Latin version that is as close as possible to the Arabic text, which has been called by translators *de verbo ad verbum* or *verbum de verbo*, i.e. 'word by word'.

Here I am summarizing and simplifying this question for the sake of clarity; in reality the periods are not so clear-cut, nor are the methods. The first method is generally said to be more commonly used in the early translations from Arabic, namely around the first half of the twelfth century, whereas the second is usually attributed to the later period, namely from the second half of the twelfth to the end of the thirteenth century. However, both methods were used in both periods, with only the number of translators who were using one or the other method varying. Moreover, some translators combined both approaches (Burnett 1997; Mandosio 2010).

It may be difficult or even impossible to identify a translation made according to the first method, i.e. if it is not clearly described as a translation in its prologue. The content may provide a clue, especially if the author—real or fake—is known, but this is clearly not significant since, indeed, the text could be an apocryphon written in Arabic or in Latin. For example, the fact that the genuine Avicenna denied the possibility of transmutation of species, and therefore alchemical transmutation, is not sufficient to claim that the *De anima* is not a translation (*Kitāb al-maʿādin wa ʾl-āṯār al-ʿulwiyya* (Book of metals and celestial phenomena), the fifth part of the *ṭabīʿiyyāt* (physics) of the *Kitāb al-Šifāʾ* (Book of healing), translated under the title *De mineralibus*, but better known by historians under the title *De congelatione et conglutinatione lapidum*, Mandosio – Di Martino 2006). A more trustworthy indicator is the presence of Latin transcriptions of Arabic words. However, these are not sufficient either: some transcriptions were used in compositions originally written in Latin, even for proper names and place names. The Arabic word alembic, for instance, is found even in later Latin texts. We can also mention the special case of the Latin translation of Avicenna's *Kitāb al-maʿādin wa ʾl-āṯār al-ʿulwiyya*, in which the translator, Alfred of Sareshel, attempted to erase all Arabic traces and inserted fake Greek ones (Mandosio – Di Martino 2006, 414–416). However, a large number of transcriptions, as well as transcriptions of rare words (*hapax legomena* or words with few occurrences), can indicate a translation. But a frequent occurrence of transcriptions is rare when a translator employs the first method. As a consequence, we can only hypothesize concerning this kind of translation and it remains impossible to make firm assertions if we do not have an extant original. When the text is a translation made according to the second method, the problem is less difficult to solve. As in the case of translations made with the first method, the content may provide the addition of some information. But it is the language itself—the transcriptions, the morphology, the syntax, and the style—that bears evidence to the fact that we are dealing with a translation. As already mentioned, transcriptions, which are usually more frequent in literal translations, can betray an Arabic origin. In the *De anima*, common words are found such as *alcofol* for *al-kuḥl* (the kohl) (*De anima*, 154 (= DA, quoted according to the pagination in Celsi 1572)) as well as more rare terms such as *azer* for the Arabic *al-zīr* (the highest-pitched string of the Arabic lute) or *acercon* for *al-zarqūn* (minium) (DA, 118–119). The word 'in' is sometimes used in the sense of 'about', corresponding to the Arabic *fī*. We also encounter Spanish words such as *plata* for *argentum* (silver) (DA, 45, 47, 99), or *raton* for *mus* (mouse) (DA, 50), and even a specifically Andalusian word, *morabetini* for *al-murābiṭūn*, the Almoravid, which in this case designates a coin (the *maravedis*) (it occurs thirty-four times in the treatise and as a consequence it does not appear to be a later interpolation), but this does not further aid the identification, as will be made clear. The morphology can bear traces that point towards a translation as well: in the *De anima* we come across many infinitives ending in *-ar* instead of the Latin *-are*, which is a Spanish feature. Syntax is also a good indication: in the *De anima* the presence of many concessive formulas is a trace of Arabic syntax; the text abounds in *nisi*, much more than a typical Latin text. The specific construction of the Arabic word *bayna*, which means 'between', is notable as well: the phrase *inter laminam et laminam* ('between the slices') sounds like an Arabic construction; Latin would normally prefer *inter laminas*. The style of a text is sometimes interesting to observe, however it is never conclusive: the tendency to use supposed objections, such as 'if somebody asks us… we will answer…', is characteristic of Arabic style. However, these results need to be interpreted: in the *De anima* the presence of Spanish words does not simply indicate that the treatise was translated from Spanish into Latin, so far as other elements need to be taken into account: the Spanish characteristics are not as numerous as the Arabic features, and the historical background—i.e. the context of the translation from Arabic into Latin—leaves us with the impression that the *De anima* is a translation from Arabic (specifically, Andalusian Arabic) made in Spain. Moreover, we must pay attention to interpolations: the *De anima*, for example, contains an Italian word, *scorza* (which means 'the bark') (DA, 295), but this sole term is not sufficient to assume an Italian origin; its presence in the *De anima* is likely due to a later gloss.

Even if these observations help to put forward hypotheses, they cannot be considered indisputable proofs. The best indication that a text really is a translation is the presence of translation errors. In the *De anima*, the translator uses the Latin word *porta*, which means 'door', to designate a chapter (the word is used nine times in this sense), which seems to be due, at first glance, to a confusion: in Arabic, the word *bāb* means 'door' but also 'chapter', so the translator could have made a mistake. However, this error could also be intentional, following from the *verbum de verbo* method; the word *porta* also occurs in the treatise with the meaning 'door', so the translator may have used the same word *porta* to translate all the occurrences of *bāb*. Some passages of the *De anima* are so obscure that the only possible explanation seems to be a lack of understanding on the part of the translator. However, one indisputable error is found in two passages of the *De anima* (DA, 78, 116, the mistake is the same in both): speaking about the human sperm, which is used in pseudo-Avicenna's alchemy, the texts read, 'tempta inter digitos si se peccat aut non', literally 'test with your fingers if it makes a mistake or not' which does not make sense. The word *se peccat* is actually a bad reading of an Arabic word: the translator read *ġaliṭa*, which means 'to make a mistake', 'to be wrong', and translated it into *se peccat*, instead of *ġaluẓa*, which signifies 'to be thick' (I thank Charles Burnett for helping me to find this translation error). This last proof is the only conclusive one.

If we find only indications that a text is a translation but no indisputable evidence, the text may have been written directly in Latin but with Arabic features or/and with an Arabic attribution. This question is much more difficult to solve than the previous one.

The first step is, once more, bibliographical research. In searching for an original, references to the text, fragments, or other translations may be found, i.e. evidence that the text is a translation, and not a text written directly in Latin. But one must pay attention to the fact that proving that a Latin text attributed to an Arabic author is not authentic produces an argument, but no evidence (it could be an apocryphon written in Arabic). Concerning the philological research, we can observe the same traces, in the content and in the language, as explained above. First, if some of the linguistic elements described above are found, i.e. indications of Arabic origin in vocabulary, morphology, syntax, or style, three hypotheses can be put forward. (1) The text may be a translation, as mentioned before. (2) The text could also be a revision of a translation, joined to other revisions of texts that are also translations, or Latin texts, or even to original compositions of the compiler. For example, the *Declaratio lapidis physici Avicennae filio suo Aboali*, another alchemical treatise attributed to Avicenna, is clearly a pseudepigraphical treatise directly written in Latin but it contains some Arabic linguistic features (Ruska 1934, 45–48). This can be explained by the fact that the *Declaratio lapidis* is actually a compilation of two texts: the beginning is a rewriting of quotations from the *De anima*, the second part is composed of quotations from the *Turba Philosophorum*, another Latin translation of an Arabic alchemical treatise. In this case, the *verbum de verbo* method brings with it ambiguity: differences stemming from the Arabic are also found in the Latin translation, which makes it difficult to say whether the compilation was made in Arabic or in Latin. (3) The text may also be a Latin treatise written in the style of a translation; for example, the *Summa perfectionis*, wrongly attributed to the Arabic author Ǧābir ibn Ḥayyān, is actually a Latin composition written as a translation (Newman [William] 1991). Second, if we do not find any (or enough) Arabic elements in the language, two hypotheses can be put forward: either (1) the text is a translation made according to the first method, i.e. a translation in classical Latin, or (2) it is a text written directly in Latin.

With regard to texts written directly in Latin, we may not find evidence that the text is a pseudepigraph, but only that it *could be* a pseudepigraph. There are only hypotheses. If a text shows no evidence of Arabic origin, although it is attributed to an Arabic author, we can never assert that it has been written directly in Latin without further external evidence (even if the content is not compatible with the doctrine of the Arabic author to whom the text is attributed, the pseudepigraph could have been written in Arabic and then translated), such as another translation of the same treatise, or quotations from a Latin treatise posterior to the composition/translation: the *Tractatulus Avicennae*, for example, is an apocryphal alchemical Latin treatise attributed to Avicenna, in which we find quotations from a commentary on the *Tabula Smaragdina* by Hortulanus, which was written in Latin around the middle of the fourteenth century (Ruska 1934, 48–50). However, even this kind of quotation can be dubious because of possible later interpolations.

Edition of a Latin translation of a lost Arabic treatise

A critical edition of a translation differs from an edition of an original text, and, in the case of a translation of a lost original, the differences are even more significant. The principles of this kind of edition are closer to those used to edit a *textus receptus* (i.e. the text representing the most diffused version of the text in a certain period) than to those used for a reconstructive edition intending to represent an archetype, even if the edition of the translation is reconstructive. Indeed, the editor must keep in mind that he should correct the text as little as possible, as any mistake could be a translation error: he is editing the translation and not the lost original. For example, some passages in the *De anima* are completely unintelligible, however, it is nonetheless important not to correct them so as to try to give them a meaning which was maybe not understood by the translator and was therefore not present in the translation. The same must be said about glosses: many Latin translators of Arabic texts used glosses to explain transcriptions or complex sentences, which means that they belong to the text and should not be deleted by the editor.

References

Burnett 1994, 1997; Celsi 1572; Mandosio 2010; Mandosio – Di Martino 2006; Moureau 2010a, 2010b, 2013a, 2013b, forthcoming; Newman [William] 1991; Ruska 1934.

3.19. Greek collections of wise and witty sayings (DSe)

The following case study is based on my own 2007 edition of the so-called *Corpus Parisinum* (*CP*), a Greek 'gnomological' compilation (Searby 2007; for an edition of the ethical sentences attributed to Democritus, see Gerlach 2008a). That edition may be justly faulted on a number of points, and if I were doing it again today, I would make a lot of changes in editorial approach (for criticisms, see Martinelli Tempesta 2010 and Gerlach 2008b; for a more positive assessment see Dorandi 2007). However, this study will focus on one important feature that I would retain and refine in a new edition, one that may be useful to scholars considering editions of similar compilations in Greek or other languages.

Introduction

Let me begin by distinguishing between an anthology and a gnomology or gnomologium. I here use the term 'anthology' to denote collections of quotations in verse or prose (or both) from one or more authors. Hence, the essential feature of an anthology is that it contains excerpts of choice quotations from written works of other authors. The anthologist's or compiler's creative role is limited to the choice and arrangement of the selections along with such intertextual items as titles and headings and, frequently though not necessarily, a preface (Searby 2011). For all practical purposes, I consider 'florilegium' to be equivalent to 'anthology', even though the former is more often associated with 'sacred' texts (as in dogmatic and spiritual florilegia), the latter with 'profane' or 'secular' texts (as in the Greek Anthology; for a concise overview of terminology, see Searby 2007, 1–8).

The word 'gnomologium' or 'gnomology' is used here to denote a collection consisting primarily of maxims or of apophthegms relating to one or more authors. Such collections are usually arranged either alphabetically or thematically or by author. The distinction between maxim and apophthegm is made advisedly: it follows ancient Greek rhetorical practice. The material in the extant Greek gnomologies can be easily classified into categories of sayings identified by ancient rhetoricians (for example Quintilian, Hermogenes, Aphthonius). Primarily these are, on the one hand *gnōmai* (Gr., *sententiae* in Latin) of the kind Aristotle dealt with already in *Rhetorica* 2.21—a typical gnome would be: 'One who spares the wicked injures the good' (*adikei tous agathous o pheidomenos tōn kakōn*, *CP* 3.1)—and, on the other hand, *chreiai* (Lat. *dicta*) as defined by later rhetoricians. In the manuscripts these *chreiai* are called *apophthegmata*; Diogenes Laertius, though he knows the term *chreia* well, also usually refers to the same kind of sayings as apophthegms. (Although apophthegm is not used as a technical term in rhetoric, for the purposes of this case-study, the terms 'apophthegm' and 'chreia' are used to describe the same kind of saying, a very brief narrative the purpose of which is to convey the words or actions of some well-known personage. A very typical form would be, 'When told or asked that, so-and-so answered this'. Aphthonius divides *chreiai* into three categories—verbal, conveying someone's words; practical, describing an action of someone; and mixed, conveying both words and actions.) A *gnōmē* is a maxim, while an apophthegm is a brief narrative or anecdote, normally with its own embedded saying or statement (including gnomic ones). One function of *gnōmai* and *chreiai* is argumentative in providing illustrative examples and moral propositions. (Note that, when 'anecdote' is used here it is without the implication that it ever was considered a special stylistic category in ancient authors. In current usage, anecdotes are often understood to be illustrative examples of the point a speaker wants to make. Overwien 2005 attempts a more precise discussion of the issue. Russo 1997, 50 calls the anecdote 'an elusive but documentable oral genre most often characterized by dialogic content and memorable concluding utterance').

The practice of compiling collections of sayings by Greek wise men and philosophers and other notables, from courtesans to kings, began already in Classical Antiquity and continued throughout the centuries into mediaeval times and beyond (see the overview by D. Gutas in the preface to Searby 2007). The practice was not confined to Greek, but also flourished in other language cultures under Greek influence such as Latin, Syriac, and Arabic. Greek gnomologies were translated or more often heavily adapted into Arabic, and these adaptations were in their turn translated into Spanish—as in the mediaeval *Bocados de Oro*—and from there into other western European languages as in Earl Rivers' early modern English translation *Dicts and Sayings of the Philosophers* (1477).

Those interested in exploring the Syriac and Arabic material can begin with the *Corpus der arabischen und syrischen Gnomologien* <http://casg.orientphil.uni-halle.de/?lang=en>, in which the role played by the Syriac tradition in adaptation of Greek gnomologia is a focus. A basic work on the Arabic tradition is

Gutas 1975; some of the Arabic collections dealt with are currently available on the site of the EU (HERA) project Sharing Ancient Wisdoms (SAWS) <http://www.ancientwisdoms.ac.uk/library/arabicphilos/>. On Greek to Arabic to Spanish, see Rodríguez Adrados 2009.

The problem of textual fluidity

In general we are dealing here with very open textual traditions for which it is not possible to establish an archetype that all later witnesses derive from or even to place the extant witnesses in a clear-cut stemmatic relationship to each other. In his well-known work on editorial technique, Martin L. West remarks: 'Some kinds of text were always subject to alteration. Commentaries, lexica and other works of a grammatical nature were rightly regarded as collections of material to be pruned, adapted or added to, rather than as sacrosanct literary entities. When the rewriting becomes more than superficial, or when rearrangement is involved, one must speak of a new recension of the work, if not of a new work altogether' (West [M.] 1973, 16). To the categories that West mentions here we must add gnomologies.

A scribe copying a gnomology may rearrange the contents in various ways, for example going from a thematic to an alphabetic arrangement or an arrangement by author (there are examples of this kind of rearrangement in *CP*). He may add sayings from other traditions or from his own memory or subtract them. He may attribute a saying to a different speaker, deliberately or by mistake. A practice prevalent in the Greek tradition, especially in gnomologies organized by author, is to indicate the main speaker by name only in the first in a series of sayings and afterwards to indicate the main speaker with the simple formula *o autos* ('the same man'). The practice of using *o autos* instead of repeating the full name greatly increases the risk of confusion in attributing the various sayings to specific persons—a risk which would still be significant even if all the scribes carefully repeated the full names of persons to whom the sayings are attributed. Moreover, a scribe may deliberately vary the vocabulary and word-order of the sayings he is copying. We must recall that this is a textual tradition which was often intentionally manipulated for instructional purposes in the schools. Even apart from immediate school settings, it was a textual tradition which it was acceptable to manipulate in other contexts as well (letter-writing, other forms of literary composition).

This much bruited fluidity of the tradition is, however, a truth requiring some modification. While it is true that a scribe may copy a gnomology and intentionally manipulate the contents in various ways, thus creating 'a new work altogether', there are also a number of examples of gnomologies which were evidently meant to be at least more or less exact copies of an archetype. In fact, *CP* itself is an example of this: the two main manuscripts are evidently intended to be exact copies of their common source. Thus, one can not merely assume that variance in copying is always the rule in the gnomological tradition. Each case must be studied on its own. However, it remains a fact that even if a scribe's intention in copying out an anthology or gnomology is to reproduce his source faithfully, there is a greater risk of error and confusion in copying such texts than in more straightforward and continuous texts. This arises from, among other causes, the patchwork quality of an anthology or gnomology as well as, in the case of gnomologies of relatively brief sayings, the greater proximity to oral traditions.

The particular example of the Corpus Parisinum

CP is primarily represented in two relatively late manuscripts: Paris, BnF, Grec 1168 and Oxford, Bodleian Library, MS. Digby 6 (P and D); for the purposes of this case study, I ignore other, partial text witnesses. P and D are evidently meant to be exact copies of their source (a hyparchetype of the earliest state of *CP*). P contains no more than the corpus itself but D has a few other unrelated texts at the end. Two fundamental facts to understand are that *CP* is a collection of gnomological collections, and that it was the main source of pagan selections in the large and widely distributed florilegium known as the *Loci Communes* of pseudo-Maximus Confessor. The oldest manuscript of this florilegium is from the late tenth century, so *CP* must have existed in some form already earlier in the tenth or more probably in the ninth century. P and D share the following collections in the same order and arrangement:

CP 1 (568 selections), the single largest part of the collection, consisting of quotations taken from the Christian Fathers, the wisdom literature of the Old Testament and, in a few cases, from the New Testament, as well as from the Jewish philosopher Philo. It is an anthology arranged by author's name (or title of biblical book), although in no apparent order. The major source for *CP* 1 is the large, thematically arranged anthology known as *Sacra Parallela* attributed to John of Damascus (the only available edition of which is in PG 95 and badly needs redoing).

CP 2 (14 selections), a series of theosophic oracles foretelling Christian dogmas but attributed to pagan Greeks; a good, brief summary of the tradition of oracles may be found in van den Broek 1978.

CP 3 (556 selections), the second largest section of *CP*. It contains gnomes, apophthegms and a number of brief quotations (for example from Greek novels of Late Antiquity) associated with eighty names, all but two of them pagan. It can be characterized as a gnomology arranged by author, although, again, in no immediately apparent order. Within each authorial section, there is a fairly systematic attempt to keep maxims (gnomes) and apophthegms separate. This is the section for which *CP* is most famous. Among other things, it contains a long series of ethical sayings attributed to Democritus.

CP 4 (214 selections), extracts from the large, thematically arranged anthology of Stobaeus. Unlike the preceding section, these excerpts are arranged thematically with approximately the same headings as in the chapters of Stobaeus from which they mostly are taken. Hense made use of Anton Elter's transcription of P for his edition of Stobaeus (for a summary of the manuscript and editorial situation of Stobaeus, see Searby 2011, 31–32).

CP 5 (97 selections), an abbreviated version of a collection of maxims from the relatively brief, thematically arranged gnomology variously called Democritus, Epictetus and Isocrates (DEI or DIE) also known as *Gnomologium Byzantinum* as first published by Curt Wachsmuth (1882). Like the other extant versions of the same gnomology, *CP* 5 arranges these maxims in short thematic chapters.

CP 4 B (16 selections), a brief series of maxims and apophthegms arranged thematically as in the two preceding sections. All of these selections derive from Stobaeus and ended up here due to a displacement in the course of transmission, really belonging to *CP* 4. For reasons I need not go into here, I left them in my edition in the position in which they occur in P and D.

CP 6 (228 selections), a substantial collection of apophthegms arranged by author and related somehow to the fairly well known *Gnomologium Vaticanum* (GV; Vatican City, BAV, gr. 743) edited by Leo Sternbach, a gnomology arranged alphabetically by author. Thus, CP 6, too, is alphabetically arranged primarily by author, although a number of anonymous gnomic sayings are added in alphabetical sequence according to initial letter. These sayings stem from another source belonging to a gnomology designated as *Ariston kai prōton mathēma* (ΑΠΜ) after the first words of the first saying. (In addition to the parts I label *CP* 1–6, there is a section which I label *CP* 7, found in both P and D, that offers 304 alphabetically arranged selections of the monostichoi attributed to Menander. *CP* 7 was not part of the original *CP* tradition (as we can see from pseudo-Maximus), so I leave it aside here.)

The compiler(s) behind the *CP* did not simply bring together representative collections from each separate tradition. The third section above, *CP* 3, draws from the traditions represented in *CP* 4, 5 and 6, i.e. from Stobaeus (and perhaps Diogenes Laertius), DEI, ΑΠΜ and other sources. The compiler of *CP* seems not merely to have intended to create a series of gnomological collections copied directly from various sources but a unified, selective collation of collections which avoided unnecessarily repeating identical sayings in the various collections. The compiler seems to have gone through his sources, making selections to copy into *CP* 3. This resulted in a gradual 'thinning out' of his sources, for the compiler was only interested in adding new, previously unincluded sayings as he went along. For whatever reason, the compiler(s) of *CP* 3 did not complete an integrated edition of all the source collections. Instead we find an attempt at an integrated edition of gnomological sources arranged by author in *CP* 3, with leftover materials left in the original arrangement of the source collections in *CP* 4, 5 and 6.

This brief survey of *CP* shows how complicated the gnomological tradition can be for the editor to deal with. Within this corpus we find many extracts, of course, although not from original literary works but from anthologies, primarily the *Sacra Parallela* and Stobaeus. So we have the relationship of *CP* to the source anthology. However, this in turn entails the following chain of relationships: *CP* to source anthology, source anthology (perhaps through other intermediaries) to original work. Furthermore, *CP* contains selections of maxims or apophthegms taken from gnomologies. These sayings can sometimes be traced to a specific source (such as Stobaeus which not only has quotations but also sayings material), but very often not—in principle they derive from oral traditions. However, we are often able to identify a number of parallels. These parallels may be found in other gnomological collections (the exact date of which is often very difficult or impossible to determine) or in continuous prose texts of particular, earlier authors (for example Plutarch or Diogenes Laertius who themselves may have taken them from some Hellenistic gnomology). Then, of course, there may be parallels in later sources—other anthologies (such as pseudo-Maximus) making use of *CP* or even in later authors (for example many of the sayings in *CP* are

CP 3

103 {S112} Μὴ ἔλαττον ἡγοῦ τοῦ ἐπαινεῖσθαι τὸ νουθετεῖσθαι.

104 {S113} Ἡ πενία πολλῶν ἐστιν ἐνδεής, ἡ δὲ ἀπληστία πάντων.

105 Χρήματα ποιεῖσθαι μᾶλλον τῶν φίλων ἕνεκα προσήκει ἢ τοὺς φίλους τῶν χρημάτων.

106 {S114, V78} Ὁ πολλοῖς φοβερὸς ὢν πολλοὺς φοβεῖται.

107 {V79} Οὐ πόρρω τοῦ ἀναμαρτήτου καθίστησιν ἑαυτὸν ὁ τὸ ἁμαρτηθὲν ἐπιεικῶς ὁμολογήσας.

108 {V80} Ἐκ τοῦ βίου κράτιστόν ἐστιν ὑπεξελθεῖν ὡς ἐκ συμποσίου, μήτε διψῶντα μήτε μεθύοντα.

109 {S115, V81} Ὁ ἐν νόσῳ διαθήκας γράφων παραπλήσια πάσχει τοῖς ἐν χειμῶνι θαλαττίῳ εὐτρεπίζειν ἀρχομένοις τὰ τῆς νεὼς ὅπλα.

110 Ὥσπερ ὁ καπνὸς ἐπιδάκνων τὰς ὄψεις οὐκ ἐᾷ προβλέπειν τὸ κείμενον ἐν τοῖς ποσίν, οὕτως ὁ θυμὸς ἐπαιρόμενος τῷ λογισμῷ ἐπισκοτεῖ καὶ τὸ συμβησόμενον ἐξ αὐτοῦ ἄτοπον οὐκ ἀφίησι τῇ διανοίᾳ προβλέπειν.

111 Δεῖ τοὺς νοῦν ἔχοντας τῶν δυναστευόντων μὴ διὰ τὰς ἀρχὰς ἀλλὰ διὰ τὰς ἀρετὰς θαυμάζεσθαι, ἵνα τῆς τύχης μεταπεσούσης τῶν αὐτῶν ἐγκωμίων ἀξιῶνται.

A 7 ἐπιεικῶς ὁμολογήσας] ὁμολογήσας ἐπιεικῶς V 8 ὡς] ὥσπερ V | μήτε διψῶντα om. D 11 θαλαττίῳ] θαλαττίοις S | νεὼς] νηός MaxI MaxII (C) 12 ὁ om. Max | προβλέπειν] βλέπειν Stob 13 ἐπαιρόμενος] ἐπερχόμενος Max | λογισμῷ] γισμῶ D 14 ἀφίησι hab. codd., in ἐφίησι emend. Meineke, quod rec. Hense 15 Δεῖ] δεῖ γὰρ Aristot. *Ep.* apud Hercher 17 ἀξιῶνται] ἐξιῶνται D

B **103** Max 16.17./21 || **104** Max 12.51./56 || **105** Max 6.57./91 || **106** Max 9.48./51 || **107** Max 26.38./32 || **108** Max 65.16./36.15 || **109** Max 65.17/36.16 || **110** Max 19.24./35 || **111** Max 9.49./52

C **110** Stob 3.20.55, Ἀριστοτέλους || **111** Stob 4.4.18, Ἀριστοτέλους

D **111** Aristot. *Ep. ad Phil.* 1 Hercher

Fig. 3.3.19.1 Searby 2007, 226. A = Apparatus criticus; B = Parallels in florilegia closely dependent on *CP* as a source; C = Parallels in collections of sayings that may have served or probably did serve as a source for *CP*; D = Parallels in earlier literary works (probable or possible original sources).

used in the life of St Cyril Phileōtēs by Nikolaos Kataskepēnos, though he was evidently using pseudo-Maximus and not *CP* directly). It is a thorny situation, indeed.

Dealing with levels of relationship in the apparatuses

Given such a situation, the editor must distinguish between various levels of relationships. The first level consists in the extant witnesses to the particular tradition being edited. In my case I took into account not only the manuscripts but also the witness of the pseudo-Maximus tradition which I could prove beyond doubt used *CP* as a source. Variants from these sources can be put in the *apparatus criticus*. I would put references to the dependent traditions (i.e. pseudo-Maximus and other dependent florilegia in this case) in their own apparatus.

Given the fact that the *CP* can be regarded in its parts as both gnomology and anthology, the editor must also confront the relationship to original sources. For example, in *CP* 1, we have quotations from the Church fathers and even from the sapiential books of the Old Testament. *CP* almost always borrows these quotations from another anthology—the *Sacra Parallela* (unfortunately still poorly edited)—which in turn took them (probably) directly from some copy of the original source. References to source anthologies such as *Sacra Parallela* or *Stobaeus* (including references to specific manuscript copies) were placed in a separate apparatus. When literary works (conventionally understood) could be identified as an indirect source (i.e. sources for the anthologies used as sources for *CP*), references to these along with any significant variants were placed in yet another apparatus.

Many times it was not possible to indicate a direct source for a given saying or section in *CP*, whereas it was usually possible to indicate parallels for the sayings. In this context, however, one must be strict about what one means by 'parallels'. Sometimes editions of gnomologies are full of a lot of what I call 'clutter'. An instance of clutter in editions of gnomological texts is Sternbach's edition of *Gnomologium Vaticanum* (Sternbach 1887, 1888, 1889). After each excerpt he adds a great deal of information in an unsystematic way, blithely mixing parallels of thought with genuinely related textual parallels and unsorted variant attributions. This kind of thing is, however, not limited to Sternbach alone but is present in varying degrees in quite a number of editions. One frequent example is the listing of so-called fragments for a given author without indicating whether they derive from a different source or in fact from the very text being edited. In my opinion, it is necessary to sort through the often large number of parallels for a given text in order to discover which of them come from clearly related (dependent or source) collections and which belong to a more independent tradition. The latter are not immediately relevant to actual editorial work and have no business being present in the same apparatus as the former. In order to allow for the inclusion of the not strictly relevant testimony, I included a commentary in my edition of *CP* the primary purpose of which was to provide space for these other references not immediately relevant for the textual history.

Editions of gnomological material are worthwhile because the gnomological tradition was a widespread genre, and the material itself has a cultural, historical and even literary interest. Cross-cultural studies may be facilitated by good editions allowing the comparison of Greek gnomologies with their adaptations in Arabic and other languages. However, it is a complicated tradition, and the would-be editor must from the start make clear-cut distinctions between the different levels of textual relationships and decide upon an adequate display without too much clutter in a critical edition.

References

van den Broek 1978; Dorandi 2007; Gerlach 2008a, 2008b; Gutas 1975; Martinelli Tempesta 2010; Overwien 2005; Rodríguez Adrados 2009; Russo 1997; Searby 2007, 2011; Sternbach 1887, 1888, 1889; Wachsmuth 1882; West [M.] 1973. Web sources: *Corpus der arabischen und syrischen Gnomologien*, <http://casg.orientphil.uni-halle.de/?lang=en>, last access May 2014; *Sharing Ancient Wisdoms*, <http://www.ancientwisdoms.ac.uk/library/arabicphilos>, last access May 2014.

3.20. The *Vidin Miscellany*: translated hagiography in Slavonic (LS)

An intricate complex of circumstances influences the shape that an edition of a mediaeval text will take. However, of all formative factors *tradition* is probably the most important. Obviously, the state of the particular *textual tradition* dealt with will determine both the editorial process and the nature of the edition, but the *scholarly tradition* within which an editor works—or against which s/he chooses to react—is a significant determinant as well. The case of palaeoslavistics is interesting in this respect. The majority of (Old) Church Slavonic texts handed down to us consists of translations of Byzantine-Greek religious writings. Perhaps contrary to expectations, this situation has not resulted in heightened attention to genealogical approaches to text editing that take the Greek tradition into account. Ever since the early days of the discipline Slavists have shown more interest in manuscripts than in texts (as remarked for example by Panzer 1991 and Grünberg 1996, 6–8). The amount of documentary (facsimile or diplomatic) editions of single manuscripts or manuscript texts far outnumbers that of critical editions based on all available text witnesses, and the relation to the Greek source text material has often been left unexplored. Manuscripts have often been approached more as witnesses to a particular linguistic system or to a particular culture of writing than as text witnesses and the distinction between manuscript and text—both termed *pamjatnik* or 'monument'—has not always been sharply felt (Veder 1999, 5–13). Today, no scholar would deny the importance of the study of extant texts as linguistic structures and of manuscripts as socially embedded artefacts; it is not so much the habit of publishing documentary editions that is to be regretted as the fact that the critical research into the genesis, the transmission and the transformation of texts—both within and across linguistic and cultural boundaries—has often been neglected. With few notable exceptions (for example Veder 1999, 5–60 and Ostrowski 2003, xvii–lxxiii, both introductions to critical editions) there is little explicit theorizing and methodological reflection in the field, which lacks firmly established or broadly accepted standards for text editing. (It needs to be stressed, however, that in pre-revolutionary Russia high standard text critical work was done in the field of Biblical studies. Unfortunately, the revolution prematurely halted the development of Slavonic Biblical philology, which obviously affected the direction taken by textual scholarship in general; cf. the survey of early Slavonic Bible Studies in Thomson [F.] 1998, 607–631.)

Editing the Vidin Miscellany

In the early 1970s two editions appeared of the so-called *Vidin Miscellany*, a codex kept in the Ghent University Library (Belgium) as *Codex gandavensis slavicus* 408. The manuscript contains sixteen translated vitae—interestingly all of female saints—together with a short topography of Jerusalem (see Sels – Stern 2012, 355–361); the text collection has been examined in considerable detail in the (hitherto unpublished) PhD thesis by the Bulgarian scholar Maya Petrova (2003). Although the colophon states that the book was commissioned by Anna, tsaritsa of the Bulgarian principality of Vidin in the year 6868 (1359/1360), recent palaeographical and codicological research has shown that the manuscript is not Anna's book, but a fifteenth-century copy (Petrova 2001). However, early research into the *Vidin Miscellany* was based mostly on an interest in the codex, perceived as the result of a royal commission and the product of a fourteenth-century scriptorium. Typically, the editions—a facsimile published in the *Variorum Reprints* series (*Bdinski zbornik* 1972) and an annotated transcription by Scharpé and Vyncke (*Bdinski zbornik* 1973)—represented the *Vidin Miscellany* more as a document than as a text. It is clear, however, that the 1973 editors aspired to do more than that, as they added a critical-interpretive layer to their transcription, on the one hand by introducing critical notes and occasional emendations to the text, and on the other by enhancing it with modern punctuation, capital letters, expanded abbreviations, paragraphs etc. However, by doing so they blurred the lines between the documentary and the interpretive level. The diplomatic rendering refers to the *Vidin Miscellany* as a material text, whereas emendations on the basis of Greek source text material refer to the editors' understanding of the undocumented moment of translation. The erroneous idea that the *Vidin Miscellany* vitae were translated, compiled and copied within the same time frame—namely around 1360, for Anna of Vidin—has contributed to the use of 'Vidin Miscellany' as an umbrella term in which the codex coincides without complication with the text collection, and the text collection with the sum of the individual vitae.

Many challenges remain to be met by future editors of the Ghent codex and its texts (Sels 2013) and it is to be recommended that they (1) distinguish more sharply between *the document and the text*; (2) make a clear distinction between the *collection as a text* and the *collection as a collection of texts*; (3) give full weight to the critical research into the origins and the transmission of the individual entries, taking into account their specific nature as translated, non-authorial texts that are part of complex multilingual traditions, to arrive at a better understanding of the *Vidin Miscellany* as a whole.

The Vidin Miscellany *as a document*

A text has a textual tradition, a document does not (although, as an object and a material text, it has a history). A document has materiality, a text as an abstraction extrapolated from its various attestations does not. The label 'Vidin Miscellany' refers to a document to the extent that it applies to the codex kept in Ghent, which, as a whole of lexical and bibliographic codes, is a meaning-bearing object. It is a text in its material embodiment, written in a dark-brown ink on fourteenth/fifteenth-century paper, bound in 31 *octavo* quires of 13 × 20 cm; it has particular palaeographic and iconic properties, such as its sloppy, slightly angular late South-Slavonic semiuncial script or its decorative system of neo-Byzantine initials (Petrova 2001, 117–120). Any edition of the *Vidin Miscellany* as a document would be as much about the reconstruction of a mediaeval reading environment as about the establishment of a text, hence the precedence of formal-physical aspects such as rubrics, lines and folia over divisions of intellectual content such as sentences, paragraphs or chapters.

The Vidin Miscellany *as a text*

The title 'Vidin Miscellany' also refers to a hagiographic collection compiled at the request of Anna of Vidin. As a text in its own right, the collection has a textual tradition, even if it is limited and largely undocumented: We know that the Ghent manuscript is a copy of Anna's book, but no other manuscripts are known to contain the same set of vitae.

An edition of the *Vidin Miscellany* as a text, based on the *Vidin Miscellany* as a text witness, would start from exactly the same material evidence but the approach would be markedly different: The editor would want to focus on those aspects of the text that can be transmitted from one copy to another, to arrive at an understanding of the collection as it was conceived around 1360, with its particular linguistic, semantic and literary features. This could imply a decision to substitute the *syntagmata* of the manuscript with sentences and a foliated view with running text divided into paragraphs. However, as the Ghent codex is a *codex unicus* from the point of view of the collection as a whole, the editor would have little other option but to publish the text as it stands, with preservation of its orthography, correcting only obvious scribal errors.

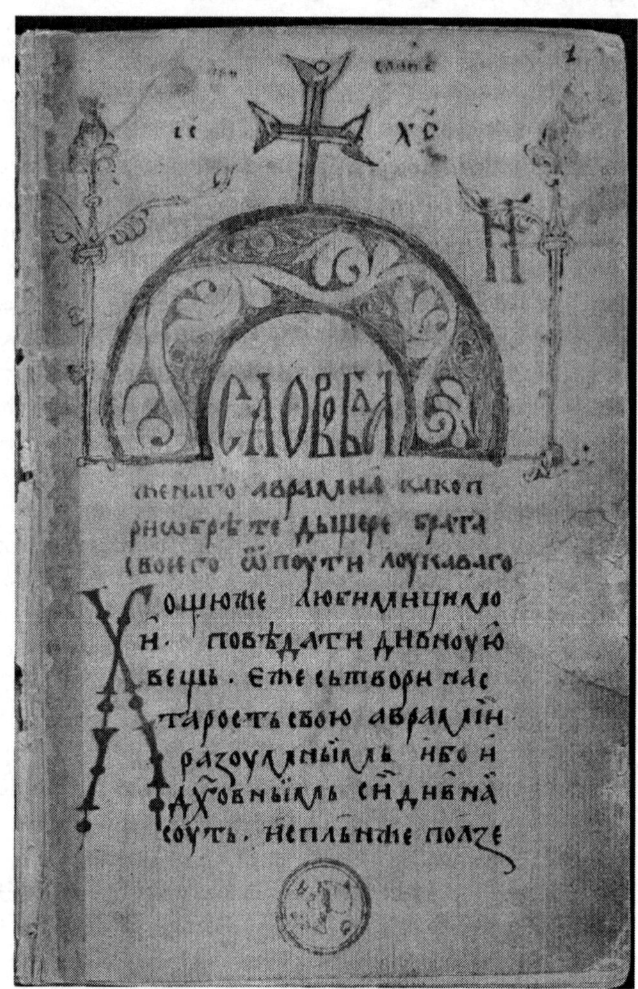

Fig. 3.3.20.1 Ghent University Library, slav. 408, fifteenth century, f. 1r: beginning of the *Life of Abraham of Qidun and his niece Mary*.

Contrary to what the 1973 editors believed, the Vidin collection was not translated directly from a Greek collection. Its compiler selected existing Slavonic vitae of a particular type of female sanctity and arranged them according to a purposefully chosen organizing principle, adapting some of the vitae to meet the requirements of the collection (as, for example, the *Story of Mary, the niece of Abraham* (ff. 1r–17v), where the narrative of a female ascetic's lapse into sin and her return to the straight path was isolated from the vita of her pious uncle). Helmut Keipert was certainly right to criticize the 1973 edition for its neglect of the textual tradition of the individual vitae and to advocate a collation of the variant texts, the establishment of 'eine Art Normalversion' for each vita and a comparison with the Greek source texts (Keipert 1975, 283–284). However, an important distinction must be made: Whereas, indeed, insight into the origins and the transmission of each vita would enable a better understanding of the texts and of the principles underlying their selection and adaptation, it would be methodologically flawed to use this material—the individual variant texts or their Greek source texts—for the *constitutio textus* of the Vidin collection. This would imply reaching back too far and blurring the distinction between the collection as a text and the texts attested to in the collection—which the 1973 editors frequently did.

The Vidin Miscellany *as a collection of texts*

The *Vidin Miscellany* can also be approached *as a collection of texts*, namely of individual hagiographies with their own, typically complex multilingual traditions. From that point of view, the Ghent codex is a text witness—one of many—for each of its entries.

The already mentioned *Story of Mary*, for instance, is exemplary for both the wealth of these hagiographic traditions and for the intricacies involved in the search for their origins and textual dynamics. Mary's story is actually the second part of the *Life of Abraham of Qidun* (BHO 16–17; BHG 5–7), a text originally written in Syriac, probably in the fifth century, and erroneously ascribed to Ephrem the Syrian (Capron 2013, 53–123). The *Life* was translated into Latin and Greek around the sixth century and it appeared in Slavonic as part of an anthology of Ephrem's works as early as the tenth century, some four centuries before a truncated version would be included in the *Vidin Miscellany*. The Slavonic translation of the *Life of Abraham* has been shown to be much closer to the Syriac and to Greek papyrus fragments kept in the Louvre than to the other Greek witnesses of the *Life* (Hemmerdinger-Iliadou 1965, 302), and, indeed, the printed versions (i.e. the text published in the *Acta Sanctorum* for March and that in Assemani's edition of Ephrem's works) are markedly different. A comparison of the Slavonic text with the Louvre Papyrus (ed. Capron 2013, 70–105; 64, note 99) confirms that the Slavonic depends on an archaic, no longer fully attested layer within the Greek tradition. A critical edition that takes both traditions into account is called for. Some forty text witnesses of the Slavonic *Life of Abraham* have been identified so far and the tradition has begun to be studied in some detail (Stern 2013). As is often the case, the broad distribution of the text throughout *Slavia orthodoxa* has brought linguistic proliferation and the co-existence, within one tradition, of an Eastern Slavonic (Russian) and a Southern Slavonic (Bulgarian and Serbian) branch. As can be seen from the example below—which is a normalized, interlinear collation of eighteen text witnesses, the upper part Southern Slavonic, the lower part Eastern Slavonic—the two branches develop along the lines of their own internal dynamics, departing from a point where they still coincided. That point is embodied by the witnesses that represent the earliest documented stage of the text, that is manuscript Athos, Hilandar, 397 (*Codex Chilandaricus* 397) for the Southern and the *Uspenskij sbornik* (Moscow, Gosudarstvennyj istoričeskij muzej, Syn. 1063/4) for the Eastern branch. The clear and easily identifiable directionality of textual change as seen in the example might be surprising as hagiographical traditions are notoriously open and fluid. However, only part of the tradition is represented in the illustration, which does not show the contaminated witnesses that blur the picture of the *Life*'s textual transmission. The text included in the *Vidin Miscellany*, for instance, is of a mixed nature, as orthographically speaking it belongs to the Southern group, while its content combines features of both, although in most of its readings it is closer to the eastern group.

For many hagiographic texts researchers disagree on the number of independent translations reflected in the attested material and indeed, there is nothing exceptional in hagiography about rewritings and retranslations that do or do not integrate material from older versions, which is why, in editorial practice, recourse is often had to parallel editions or hagiographic dossiers (cf., for example, Hinterberger 2014). However, some caution is warranted as an isolated comparison of two extant texts may give rise to the idea that they represent two independent translations, while a closer look into the broader tradition might reveal immediately that they occupy extreme positions in the stemma but ultimately go back to one translation. Some of the questions concerning independent translations or redactions will only be solved in the course of the historical-critical investigation of the sources and the corpus of material to be used for an edition may well be redefined in the course of that process.

The fact that a textual tradition allows for the reconstruction of the archetype, as in the case of the *Life of Abraham*, does not automatically mean that that is how the edition should be shaped. An editor oriented more towards the dynamics of the tradition may still consider a synoptic or an interlinear presentation of various extant text versions. A reconstructed, eclectic non-manuscript text, however, necessarily implies orthographical normalization. Because the Abraham text was translated in the early period of Old Church Slavonic, a reconstruction of the 'earliest retrievable text' can be rendered in 'standard OCS', i.e. according to the standard laid out by the Slovník of Prague (Kurz – Hauptová 1958–1997). However, normalization remains a huge stumbling block for any editor of later Church Slavonic writings, as there are no standards against which to normalise these texts. The presence of various linguistic recensions within textual traditions further complicates matters, especially when it is unclear which recension has more ancestral rights. The want of a norm for orthographical normalization is one of the reasons why editions of Church Slavonic texts keep being made on the basis of manuscript texts (for example Sels 2009, 104–105).

The Vidin Miscellany *as a collection of translated texts*

As already shown, the *Vidin Miscellany* should not itself be approached as a translation but as a collection of translated texts. If a mediaeval translation's quality as translation is to be given its full weight, an editor will need to go into the source text tradition in some depth. However, the question is how far one can go in exploring the multilingual tangle of these hagiographies. The feasibility of an integral approach strongly depends on the availability of scholarly editions and specialized studies on the source text tradition under scrutiny. In the case of the *Life of Abraham of Qidun*, no critical edition is available, although the work of the French scholar Laurent Capron has recently shed light on the Greek tradition (Capron 2013, 53–123). Too often, editors of Slavonic texts have juxtaposed their transcriptions to readily available print versions of Greek texts in the *Patrologia Graeca* or the *Acta Sanctorum*, or to self-made patchwork versions made up out of bits and pieces of particular Greek witnesses to perfectly match the Slavonic (as was done for the text on St Thais in Voordeckers 1964). While, on the ideal level there is a source text and its translation, on the level of the material evidence there is only a number of extant texts, Greek and Slavonic, that cannot be meaningfully related without insight into the nature of the translation model and the particulars of the original translation. To gain that insight is a process that oddly works in two directions, i.e. from a general idea of the Greek source text to that of a particular (but mostly non-extant) source text version that marks the point in the Greek tradition from where the Slavonic tradition took off, and from the extant Slavonic text witnesses to a general idea of what the original translation might have looked like. This is typically done by comparing the Slavonic translation (which we only know through its extant copies) to the Greek variant readings to learn about the nature of the source text, and by comparing that Greek source text to the Slavonic variant readings to come to a better understanding of the original translation. Clearly, some circularity cannot be avoided. However, what theoretically looks like aporia is in actual practice feasible as a process of repeated comparison in two directions.

The nature of the translation relationship is of consequence as well. Extremely literal translations, such as those typical of the fourteenth century (Sels 2009, 52–55), will facilitate not only the identification of relevant Greek variants but also of secondary readings in the Slavonic tradition, while a free translation may leave the editor in doubt with regard to the nature of the Greek exemplar and the place of the translation within the Greek stemma. It should be kept in mind, however, that a reliable assessment of the translation relationship can be made only through the philological work described above; misguided judgments have arisen as the result of comparing a Slavonic translation with a wrong version of the Greek source text or comparing a Greek source text with a Slavonic manuscript text that has evolved away from the text as it was originally translated (cf., for example, the juxtaposition of the *Vidin Miscellany*'s *Story of Mary* and the Greek Abraham text as published in the *Acta Sanctorum* by De Beul et al. (1965), with countless brackets to indicate non-correspondence). It is the editor's responsibility to link the Greek source text material meaningfully to the Slavonic text as it is established in the edition, which is ideally done by means of a special section in the introduction and a Greek-Slavonic parallel presentation of the text itself. If a critical edition of the Greek is available the critical text of the Greek can be juxtaposed to the Slavonic with indication of the particular Greek variants that have shaped the Slavonic tradition, for instance in a special apparatus (as in Sels 2009). In the absence of a critical edition of the Greek the editor

Greek	καὶ	πατάξας	αὐτοὺς	ἐπέστρεψεν	Λῶτ		τὸν ἀνεψιὸν	αὐτοῦ.	
Alpha	и	попьравъ	ѩ	възврати	Лота		сынови	своѥго.	
Ch397	и	попьравъ	ѩ	възврати	лота		сынови	своѥго	
Ch384	и	побѣдивъ	ѩ	възврати	лота			своѥго	сынови
Nbkm298	и	побѣдивъ	ѩ	възврати	лота			своѥго	сыновьца
Berlin	и	побѣдивъ	ѩ	възврати	лота			своѥго	сыновьца
Rila	и	побѣдивъ	ихъ	възврати	лота		сына брата	своѥго	
Ch648	и	побѣдивъ	ихъ	възврати	лота		сына брата	своѥго	
Nbkm299	и	побѣдивъ	ихъ	възврати	лота		сына брата	своѥго	
Kop	и	побѣдивъ	ихъ	възврати	лота		сына брата	своѥго	
Usp	и	попьравъ	ѩ	възврати	лота		сынове	своѥго	
BOZ99	и	попьравъ	ѩ	възвративъ	лота		сынови	своѥго	
VMC	и	попьравъ	ѩ	възврати	лота		сыновьца	своѥго	
MGU	и	попьравъ	ѩ	възврати	лота		сыновьца	своѥго	
TrS	и	попьравъ	ѩ	възврати	люди		сыновьца	своѥго	
V1199	и	попьравъ	ѩ	възврати	люди		сыновьца	своѥго	
Sar60	и	попьравъ	ѩ	възврати	люди	и	сыновьца	своѥго	
Sar61	и	попьравъ	ѩ	възврати	люди	и	сыновьца	своѥго	
GIM332	и	попьравъ	ѩ	възврати	люди	и	сыновьца	своѥго	
Sar1115	и	попьравъ	ѩ	възврати	люди	и	сыновьца	своѥго	

Fig. 3.3.20.2 Normalized interlinear collation of eighteen text witnesses to the Slavonic *Life of Abraham of Qidun and his niece Mary* (screenshot from a collation demo developed by David Birnbaum and Lara Sels).

may want to consider representing the Greek source text on the basis of the manuscript text(s) that best parallels the Slavonic translation, with indication of instances where other Greek witnesses offer a better match.

An editor needs to make clear statements about the nature of the text s/he is about to edit, even if the reality of the text is not always as clear-cut as presented here. Everyone agrees that palaeography belongs to the document and literariness to the text, but language is already much harder to pinpoint (on the idea of the extant text as a linguistic compromise between the scribe's own linguistic usage and the language of his model, see Segre 1976, 283–285). A colophon usually belongs to a document, but the one in the Ghent codex does not properly belong to it—it was copied and thus acquired a tradition. Once the boundaries are clearly drawn an editor can safely let information gained from one perspective spill over in research that takes another point of view, i.e. to have the document explain part of the history of the text and to have the history of the text explain some of the particulars of the document. Even if it is true that a document is self-sufficient and used independently from its sources, an awareness of the textual and linguistic layers that make up the fabric of its text remains of pivotal importance. Retracing the origins and the life of a text through textual criticism is not necessarily about textual idealism or essentialism; it is about understanding extant texts. In the case of hagiographical texts, editors should not be discouraged by the *a priori* assumption of textual fluidity from exploring the textual traditions as fully as possible, even if the establishment of an archetypal text is not always possible and not always desirable. No single way of publishing and presenting a text is incompatible with critical research into its textual history, both within and beyond linguistic boundaries.

NB For the use of the terms 'recension' and 'redaction', see Schenker (1995, 200): 'Texts sharing features introduced spontaneously and unconsciously (for instance, dialectal characteristics) represent a particular recension (Russian *izvod*). Texts sharing features introduced intentionally and consciously (for instance, ideological tendencies) constitute a redaction (Russian *redakcija*). In other words, a recension refers specifically to the linguistic properties of a text, while a redaction is defined primarily by its cultural context'.

References

Bdinski zbornik 1972; *Bdinski zbornik* 1973 = Scharpé – Vyncke 1973; Capron 2013; De Beul et al. 1965; Grünberg 1996; Hemmerdinger-Iliadou 1965; Hinterberger 2014; Keipert 1975; Kurz – Hauptová 1958–1997; Ostrowski 2003; Panzer 1991; Petrova 2001, 2003; Schenker 1995; Segre 1976; Sels 2009, 2013; Sels – Stern 2012; Stern 2013; Thomson [F.] 1998; Veder 1999; Voordeckers 1964.

3.21. Sacred texts in Hebrew and related languages. Dealing with linguistic features (WvP)

Sacred texts

Sacred texts, authoritative texts, and normative collections

The question as to how to define 'sacred texts' is open to debate. As working definition we use: 'texts that are accepted as authoritative by a religious community and are regarded as formative for its identity'. However, the use of 'authoritative' in this definition (also used by Emanuel Tov in relation to the textual criticism of the Hebrew Bible, see Tov 2001, 177; Jenner et al. 2006, 14, n. 5) can be challenged, because not all 'authoritative' texts are also 'sacred'. In the Christian tradition some Classical authors were held in high esteem, but that did not mean their writings were considered 'sacred'. Yet, their authority had an effect on the textual transmission: Whether or not a scribe allowed himself to emend and change the text did not primarily depend on whether or not the text belonged to the Scriptures, but rather on whether it was attributed to a named author—regardless of whether this author was Matthew or Cicero—or not. It was especially in the transmission of the anonymous literature, including many Apocryphal stories such as the *Life of Adam and Eve*, that the scribes allowed themselves much freedom to alter the text considerably (for example Tromp 2005).

Related to concepts of sacredness and authority of texts, is the concept of 'normative collections'. It should be recalled that such collections were not only formed of those books that have become the 'canons' of present day's world religions, but that in Antiquity all kinds of normative collections were established. In the ancient Greek literature we can think of collections such as the *Sibylline Oracles* or the Alexandrian *Canon of the Ten Orators* (Norelli 2004).

Different degrees of authority

The complexity of the relationship between 'authoritative' and 'sacred' texts is not only due to the fact that texts such as juridical canons or esteemed classical authors could have authority without necessarily being sacred, but also because within religious traditions, when we are dealing with the foundational texts of religious communities, 'authoritative' and 'sacred' cannot simply be equated. In Sunnite Islam, for example, the *sunna* is authoritative, but not 'sacred' as the Qur'ān is.

One could attempt to refine the notion of sacred texts by taking into account different degrees of authority that may exist in a religious community. In the Jewish tradition, for example, the Mishna and the Talmud have a certain kind of authority, but they are not treated on the same level as the Tanakh. To find a conceptualization of 'sacred texts' that does justice to the status of these Rabbinic sources within Judaism without taking the Tanakh, the Mishna and the Talmuds together as if they were three equal parts of the Jewish canon, the notion of gradual authority may be helpful.

Regarding the Syriac tradition it is worth observing that the so-called *Masora* were added not only to the biblical text (of both the Old Testament and the New Testament), but also to some Church Fathers. Does this demonstrate that they had an authoritative status? (Loopstra 2009) And if so, how does this status compare to that of the Bible? This requires further research.

'Sacred' texts and the divine

If we want to take into account in our research not only the contents of the 'sacred texts', but also the way in which these texts were written down, treated and preserved, it should be recalled that sometimes 'secular' texts received in certain respects a special treatment similar to that of sacred texts. In the Jewish tradition, for example, there were rules how to treat manuscripts that contained the Tetragrammaton, the name of God, regardless of the contents of the text and thus including, for example, contracts or personal letters containing an invocation of God. As a consequence, the very fact that a document contained an inscription of the divine name could have a great impact on its fortunes (on the question what books one was obliged to store in a *geniza*, see Stemberger 2004, 124–125). In such a context it may be preferable to define 'sacred' in terms of its supposed relationship to God or the divine rather than in terms of an authoritative or canonical collection of writings.

Derived authority

The authority of a sacred text may generate other claims of 'derived authority'. This is especially clear with the genre of the commentary, which, by its claim of being the correct interpretation of the sacred text, may claim authority for the interpretation as well (Gumbrecht 2003). This may motivate, for example, the description of natural phenomena and other encyclopedic information in the form of a *Hexaemeron*, a commentary on the Six Days of Creation.

Also translations of sacred texts could receive an authoritative status derived from the sacred status of their source texts. Sometimes such translations figured side by side with their source texts (the role of the Aramaic Targums side by side with the Hebrew Bible in the Jewish tradition); sometimes they eventually replaced their source texts (the role that the Septuagint played in early Christianity).

Consequences of the 'sacred status'

Starting from the working definition of 'sacred texts' given above, we can ask what consequences the sacred status of a text may have. This may apply to all material, formal and functional aspects of texts.

The material carriers of the text, how they are produced, and how they are treated

In Rabbinic literature we find all kinds of instructions and rules related to the proper production of biblical manuscripts. These instructions reflect not only a concern for a correct rendering of 'the text' as the sequence of characters, but also for material aspects, such as writing materials, the sewing and repairing of parchment, and the preservation of scrolls that had become unfit for use. The tractate *Massekhet Soferim* (eighth century?) is an extensive collection of such instructions, but in earlier literature, such as the Mishna, the same concerns are reflected. (It should be noted, however, that these instructions applied only to the Tora scrolls, not to study codices.)

The idea that the material carriers of the text are sacred objects also enhanced concerns related to purity, reflected in terminology such as 'books that defile the hands' and in debates about the question whether or not a menstruating woman is allowed to touch a Tora scroll (but note, again, that these discussions concerned Tora scrolls, not study codices; hence they do not relate to material carriers of the sacred texts in general, but to those material carriers that had specific liturgical functions). The sacred status of the scrolls is also reflected in the treatment they receive in the synagogue and in liturgy.

I have taken a few examples from Judaism, but in other traditions parallels can be found as well. Similar questions regarding material aspects and about purity play a role in Islam, although the answers given sometimes differ from those given in Judaism. Thus the custom of storing worn-out scrolls in a special storage place, a *geniza*, which was widespread in Judaism, may have been adopted in early Islam (compare the large collection of manuscripts found at the Great Mosque of Sanaa in Yemen), but alternative treatments of those worn-out scrolls, such as burning them, also received acceptance (Dr. Umar Ryad's personal communication).

The sacred status of a text may also effect the size and form of manuscripts. It is now generally accepted that the codex cannot be considered a Christian invention and that it is an oversimplification to consider the opposition between scrolls and codices as running exactly parallel to that between Jews and Christians. Still, the obligation to write the Tora on scrolls rather than codices, means that the sacred status of the text had an effect on the material aspects of its carrier. Likewise, in the Christian tradition there is a certain interaction between the use of the codex as a means to collect a large amount of texts in one volume and the idea of the canon consisting of a collection of books (Hurtado 2006 and various publications by Robert A. Kraft). However, as we have argued elsewhere, the evidence is complicated because sometimes biblical and non-biblical books occur in one and the same codex, and even the most famous complete manuscript of the Syriac Bible, the *Codex Ambrosianus Syrus*, contains some texts that probably did not belong to the canon of the Bible in the Syriac tradition (see van Peursen 2008a).

For the study of oriental manuscripts, it is of the utmost importance to be aware that not only 'the text' in its abstract sense as it is used in scholarly textual criticism or in literary studies, but also the text carriers were considered 'sacred'. For this reason we should welcome the shift in textual scholarship that has taken place over the last few years from an interest in 'the text' as an abstract scholarly construct to an interest in texts as artefacts. The formation of the COMSt network can be seen as one of the results of this shift (van Peursen 2010, 6). This shift will hopefully make us more sensitive to the way in which the documents we are dealing with were produced and treated, not only as 'content' but also as objects.

Scripts

If we consider a text as a sequence of graphemes, as is done in modern philological or literary studies, the question as to how these graphemes are realized, the actual graphs, is arbitrary. Thus text editions of ancient Hebrew inscriptions often use the Hebrew square script, rather than the palaeo-Hebrew script, to render the text of the inscriptions. Likewise, in Syriac text editions, the choice as to which script is used is often made on the basis of practical or technical considerations, regardless of the scripts used in the manuscripts. In scholarly literature from, say, a century ago, we find even Syriac words printed in Hebrew characters. These practices reflect the idea that the choice of scripts is arbitrary. From a linguistic viewpoint this may be true, but in religious communities this is often not the case, since the script often functions as an identity marker of a community or as a means to set a sacred text apart from other texts. The role of scripts as identity markers at times motivated allography: the writing of a language in the script of another, which we see, for example, in the use of the Hebrew script for Ladino or Judaeo-Arabic, the use of the Syriac script for the Arabic language (*garšūnī*), and the use of the Arabic script for many Turkic and Indo-European languages (den Heijer – Schmidt 2014).

The most common Hebrew script, the square characters (which receives its name from the square forms of the characters), is in fact a development of the Aramaic script. Before this script came into use for writing Hebrew, Hebrew texts were written in the palaeo-Hebrew script, which is attested in ancient inscriptions, and from which also the Samaritan script developed. Among the Dead Sea Scrolls (third century BCE–first century CE), most texts are written in the square script, but there are some fragments written in the palaeo-Hebrew script. There are also a number of scrolls written in the square script in which the divine name is written in the palaeo-Hebrew script (for further details about the scripts used in the Dead Sea Scrolls, see for example Tov 2001, 217–220). This latter custom may reflect a certain sacred status that the ancient script still had. In later periods, however, we find also texts that assign a higher status to the square script. In some forms of Jewish exegesis, value was attributed even to the form of the letters (as in the explanation why the Tora begins with a Beth), so that the forms of the letters—in the square script—could not be considered as something arbitrary, nor as a secondary development, a borrowing from a foreign people. The fact that the 'heretic' Samaritans used a later development of the palaeo-Hebrew script also fed its rejection by Rabbinic Judaism. As a consequence, in addition to traditions that considered the palaeo-Hebrew script more venerable (probably reflected in some Qumran scribal practices), other traditions evolved that, on the one hand, reflected a historical awareness of the Hebrew square script being a later development, but, on the other hand, assigned it a status that was superior to the palaeo-Hebrew script. According to a well-known tradition, the square script was the proper, original script of the Tora, given to Moses on Mount Sinai, but when the people of Israel sinned with the Golden Calf they had to continue with the palaeo-Hebrew script, until in the post-exilic period, Ezra 'rediscovered' the square script. We do not need to go into all details of these Midrashim, but the point I want to make is that the script that is used may play a role as religious identity marker and be considered as an inherent part of the 'Scriptures'.

Much innovative research has been dedicated over the last years to the various forms of the Syriac scripts. This led, among others, to a revision of the traditional view of how the scripts are historically related (van Peursen 2008a, 206, with reference to publications by John Healey and Françoise Briquel-Chatonnet). These new insights may provide a basis for further study of the relationship between these scripts and the various religious communities. Apart from the question as to whether certain scripts were assigned a superior or even 'sacred' status, we can observe a tendency that the script for the 'sacred' books is in general clearer and sometimes also bigger.

There are some interesting parallels from other traditions. In his valedictory lecture entitled *Religion and Alphabet*, H. W. Obbink (1968) discusses various ways in which certain alphabets function as identity markers in religious communities. Obbink describes a situation on the Balkan where the Eastern Orthodox use the Cyrillic script, the Roman Catholics the Latin script, the Lutherans the Fraktur script, and a small group of Catholic Croats at the Dalmatian coast (who, unlike the other Catholics, keep the Old Slavonic liturgy) the Glagolitic script.

Textual aspects

In addition to the formal aspects such as the writing materials used or the form of the letters, there are the textual aspects. We can distinguish between elements of the text itself, such as linguistic or stylistic phenomena that are typical for religious texts, which will be discussed below, and additional textual elements, such as rubrics, indications of sections used in liturgy, or devices to secure a correct transcription of the text, such as the *Masora* in Hebrew Bible manuscripts.

The concern for the correct transmission of the sacred text led not only to additions to the text, such as the *Masora*, but also to other scribal activities, including the collation of manuscripts. In the case of the Greek New Testament this resulted in a conflation that prevents us from building any *stemma* of the existing manuscripts. In the case of the Old Testament, Origen's *Hexapla* can be regarded as a masterpiece of text comparison in Antiquity and its influence extended, for example, to the form of the Bible text that was used in liturgy. Origen's fifth column, the text of the Septuagint together with text-critical symbols to mark the differences with the Hebrew text, was translated into Syriac. This translation, the Syro-Hexapla was for some time rather influential (on the appearance of Syro-Hexaplaric readings in lectionaries see van Peursen 2011, 156–159). The fact that for some books the Hexaplaric recension, including the text-critical symbols, did not result from a Hebrew-Greek comparison, but rather from a comparison of various Greek manuscripts, further shows how the production of this version was embedded in the ancient philological tradition (on the Hexaplaric version of Ben Sira see van Peursen 2011, 153–159 (= section 5.3)). The origin of the Syro-Hexapla was probably related to the needs of Syriac scholars who translated many Greek commentaries into Syriac and discovered that the text that the exegetes were writing about was not identical to their own Syriac Bible (see ter Haar Romeny 2006, 297), and its reception to the prestige of the Greek language and literature. Both the origin and the reception can be approached from various socio-linguistic and religious-historical perspectives.

Textual scholarship in Antiquity deserves our attention not only because we can regard it as the predecessor of our own philological work and because some philological principles that are still applied nowadays have their roots in Antiquity (Dahlström 2010, 81, 93, on the role of the Alexandrian and the Pergamenian editorial ideals in modern digitization practices), but also because it has shaped the sacred texts themselves, which are the object of our own philological research. Some signs of it are immediately visible, such as the *asterisk* and the *obelos* in witnesses to the Hexapla or the Masoretic notes in the margins of a Hebrew manuscript. In other cases it influenced the text itself, for example when a scribe used various manuscripts which resulted in conflated manuscripts. The point that I want to make here is that in our study of sacred texts we should be aware that the textual witnesses that we have are themselves the product of scribal and scholarly activities and that hence we cannot separate texts from their transmission and interpretation over the centuries.

Though in some cases we see a correlation between the sacred status of a text and the accuracy with which it was transmitted, the level of accuracy that was aimed for shows variation.

In the Hebrew Masoretic tradition we see a great concern about an accuracy of the textual transmission up to the letter, even in cases of spelling variation that from a linguistic viewpoint is arbitrary, such as the alternation between defective and plene spelling. However, this fixation of the text followed a period in which there was much more fluctuation and variation. In the Dead Sea Scrolls we see much more spelling variation as well as the existence of various text forms side-by-side. This should not be taken as an indication that, for example, the book of Isaiah was not considered a 'sacred text' by the scribes of the Dead Sea Scrolls, but rather that different scribal practices were applied to the same text and that the existence of various versions of this text side by side was not conceived of as opposing its sacred status.

In the transmission of the Greek New Testament the situation is comparable to that of Hebrew Bible before its textual fixation. In the first centuries CE, up to the fourth century, the transmission seems to be free and the manuscripts reflect abundant variation of all sorts.

Syriac Bible manuscripts reflect a remarkable uniformity and if we compare the critical apparatus of the Leiden Peshitta Old Testament edition with that of the Nestle-Aland New Testament, the range of variation in the former is extremely small. Our view is restricted, however, by the materials that we have. In the case of the Old Testament Peshitta, for example, we can postulate on the basis of linguistic observations that the text of the Bible had undergone considerable revision between its origin in the second or early third century and the oldest preserved manuscripts, which date from the fifth century onwards (van Peursen 2008b).

Also the liturgical use of texts had an impact on their transmission. The concern for a proper recitation of the Hebrew Bible led to the development of vocalization and accentuation systems, which, in turn, can be seen as the first step in the native Hebrew linguistic tradition. Other linguistic traditions, such as that of the native Arabic grammarians or the development of the native Sanskrit linguistics are also rooted in the needs of religious communities who wanted a correct interpretation of the sacred text (as in the case of Arabic) or to have their rituals performed properly (as in the case of Sanskrit). In other contexts, liturgical practices may have influenced the form of the text as it is in the manuscript (see, for example, Gutman – van Peursen 2011, 77, 203). More generally we can say that for those texts that had a place in religious practices, there was an interaction between the text that found its way in the manuscripts and the use of the text in liturgical or ritual contexts.

Linguistic aspects

If we deal with the language of sacred texts, two sets of questions are at stake. The first set concerns socio-linguistic questions: Why is a certain language used? What status did that language have? How did users of the text respond to changes in their linguistic environment, be it language development (for example, do we see signs of linguistic updating of the text?) or a complete change of language (for example, Jews using Hebrew scriptures or Christians using Syriac scriptures in an Arabic environment). Was the language retained? Was the sacred text translated? This set of questions is very broad and includes, for example, the various ways in which the Hebrew Bible and/or its translation were recited in public in the Jewish tradition (Smelik 2007) and the debate about the *Hebraica veritas* versus the Septuagint in the Christian tradition. These questions are relevant for philological research because they may affect the text itself (for example corrections in the text of the Septuagint towards the Hebrew text), as well as the ways they are presented (for example in multilingual biblical manuscripts).

The other set of questions concerns the linguistic and stylistic characteristics of the text, and relates, for example, to conservative elements in written language, and especially in religious and liturgical language and texts. That in the study of ancient manuscripts we are dealing with written texts has in itself an impact on their linguistic features. Among linguists opinions differ whether this is a disadvantage (Bloomfield considered written language a poor representation of 'real' language, that is spoken language) or an advantage (because of linguistic features that are unique to written language, such as layout and interpunction). For us, however, there is no other choice than to take the corpora that we have as the basis of our linguistic and stylistic analysis.

When we speak about the linguistic analysis of ancient corpora, it should be recalled that there is a fundamental difference between a 'corpus' as it is usually understood in corpus linguistics, and a corpus of religious texts such as the Hebrew Bible. The first is a purposely selected representative samples of texts; the latter is a collection that is not selected on the basis of linguistic criteria, but rather on the basis of religious criteria. It is nowadays generally acknowledged that the Old Testament is only a part of the literature of ancient Israel, which has undergone processes of redaction and selection by a particular group of Judaean scribes. Although the scope of the Hebrew Bible is broad, including laws, proverbs, poems, stories, and both more secular and more religious texts, it remains a fact that the formation of the Hebrew Bible is completely different from the formation of linguistic corpora.

The conservative tendency that can be observed in written languages appears to be even stronger in the case of religious and liturgical language use. Archaic elements may be preserved in religious texts whereas they have become obsolete in daily language. (A phenomenon that could certainly also be illustrated by modern examples as various studies on religious language show.) Sacred texts often represent a literary, standardized form of the language (Jenner et al. 2006). It deserves further study to see to what extent this may explain the linguistic homogeneity of sacred texts that have been composed over a long period of time, such as the Hebrew Bible. Although the homogeneity may also be the result of updating, rather than retention, the commonly accepted view that in the Second Temple Period the Hebrew vernaculars differed from the standardized written language suggests that the language of the foundational religious texts did not develop at the same pace as the spoken varieties of the language, In the case of the Syriac Bible we see also a standardized form of the language (van Peursen 2008b).

The conservative tendencies may in the end result in various types of multilingualism or 'multidialectalism' in which the classical language is used for the sacred text whereas another dialect or language, genetically related to the classical language, is used as vernacular. There are various examples in which a sacred text figures in a community the vernacular of which is a language that in some way or another is related to the language of the sacred text (for example: a cognate language; a later stage of that language). Compare Classical Syriac versus Modern Aramaic dialects (but note that the Modern Aramaic dialects are not direct 'descendants' of Classical Syriac); Biblical Hebrew as against Israeli Hebrew (in this case the situation is complicated by the recourse taken to the classical phases of the language in the revival of Hebrew as an everyday language) or Latin as against the Romance languages.

In other cases the language used in liturgy and other religious contexts and the everyday language are completely different languages. This applies, for example, to the use of Hebrew or Syriac in Arabic contexts. Apart from the sociolinguistic issues mentioned above, this is relevant because such a language situation may have an effect on processes of language representation (for example the invention of vowel systems if knowledge of the proper pronunciation is no longer self-evident).

References

Dahlström 2010; den Heijer – Schmidt 2014; Gumbrecht 2003; Gutman – van Peursen 2011; Hurtado 2006; Jenner et al. 2006; Loopstra 2009; Norelli 2004; Obbink 1968; Smelik 2007; Stemberger 2004; ter Haar Romeny 2006; Tov 2001; Tromp 2005; van Peursen 2008a, 2008b, 2010, 2011.

3.22. The *History* of Bayhaqī: editorial practices for Early New Persian texts (JJW)*

Abū al-Faḍl Muḥammad b. Ḥusayn Bayhaqī (385–470 AH/995–1077 CE) was a high chancery official under the Ghaznavid Sultans Maḥmūd (reigned 389–421 AH/999–1030 CE) and Mas'ūd (reigned 421–433 AH/1030–1041 CE). Ghazna then was certainly not the provincial Afghan backwater that the Ghazni of today has become. It was a place with a thriving culture, where a few decades earlier Firdawsī had come to offer Sultan Maḥmūd his *Šāhnāma*. Manuscript Leiden, Leiden University Library, Or. 437, one of the oldest preserved illuminated Arabic manuscripts, was written in Ghazna and dates from Bayhaqī's lifetime. It shows the outstanding quality of book production the copyists of Ghazna were capable of. During the reign of Sultan Maḥmūd's son 'Abd al-Rašīd (440–443 AH/1049–1051 CE) he was appointed head of the chancery, but he fell from favour and was imprisoned. After his release in or after 451 AH/1059 CE he did not try to be reinstated at the court. Instead he worked on his huge history of the Ghaznavid dynasty, of which, according to later authors, only volumes 5–10 out of a total of thirty volumes have been preserved. These remnants have, in course of time, acquired the collective title of *Tārīḫ-i Bayhaqi*, 'the History of Bayhaqī'. The title 'Annals of Bayhaqī' would be more appropriate. Sa'īd Nafīsī (1940–1953) has preferred the title *Tārīḫ-i Mas'ūdī*, the 'History of Mas'ūd' as the preserved parts of the *Tārīḫ-i Bayhaqī* only contain episodes from the history of Sultan Mas'ūd. Gilbert Lazard (1963) mentions the *Tārīḫ-i Bayhaqī* as the most important historical text in Persian of the fifth century AH/eleventh century CE. Ehsan Yarshater, in his foreword to Bosworth's translation (Yarshater 2011), goes even further: 'arguably the best known and most liked of all Persian histories'. Storey (1927) mentions sixteen manuscripts extant, Lazard (1963) mentions some twenty, and the count by Yāḥaqqī and Sayyidī (2009) has exceeded the number of fifty manuscripts, none of them very old, though. It shows the progress of bibliography.

The language of the 'History' is a relatively old form of Persian, which in the mid-fifth century had only recently been emancipated from Arabic as a literary language. Old forms of Persian are the subject of Lazard's monograph of 1963, and Bayhaqī's 'History' takes an important place among the 72 texts that Lazard selected for his research. The importance of the 'History' lies in the fact that we have precise knowledge about the person of the author, who is exactly dated and located. Another reason for the fact of the relatively ample attention that the 'History' has received in the past century and a half is its outstanding narrative quality. The only drawback in all this is that there do not seem to exist old manuscripts of the text. Storey gives an enumeration of the manuscripts known at his time and indicates which were used for the early editions of the 'History'.

The 'History' has enjoyed the attention of a large number of editors. W.H. Morley first published the text in Calcutta in 1862, on the basis of three manuscripts dating from the sixteenth and seventeenth centuries (Morley 1862). The critical apparatus is almost non-existent in his edition, nor is it the ambition of the series *Bibliotheca Indica* in which it was published to go deep into textual history. It does not give more than a few variant readings of proper names. There is no editor's introduction (the edition was published by Nassau Lees after Morley's death), nor any index. It is the plain text, just that.

Then there is the lithograph edition from Tehran of 1307 AH/1889–1890 CE brought out by Aḥmad Adīb Pīšāwarī, which cannot be called critical either. The lithograph editions that were for a while very popular in the Middle East and beyond are not much more than manuscripts in printed form and they usually represent a late, and not seldom defective, unreliable and contaminated, stage in the transmission of a text. The lithograph edition of the 'History' is no exception to this: it is probably based on manuscript Tehran, Ketābḫāne-ye Mağles, 229, which is dated 1265 AH /1848–1849 CE, or on a textual witness closely related to the Mağles manuscript. Apart from the text, it contains linguistic and historical commentary and some variant readings and remarks on moral and philosophical issues. Some editorial work has evidently been done on the text in the lithograph edition, with the result that it is more readable than Morley's edition, but that does not automatically make the lithograph more authentic. In fact, in problematic passages it frequently leaves the reader in the lurch (Lazard 1963, 77). Smoothing the text is a feature in some of the later editions as well. Lazard convincingly establishes the date of publication of the lithograph as 1307 AH/1889–1890 CE, rejecting the 1305 AH/1887–1888 CE that some bibliographies have (Lazard 1963, 76). The former is the year of publication, the latter the year in which the model manuscript after which the lithograph was printed was completed.

* I gratefully acknowledge the valuable advice for choosing Bayhaqī's 'History' as the subject of the present survey, given to me by Prof. J.T.P. de Bruijn of Leiden, my first teacher of Persian, way back in 1964.

Next is the three-volume edition by Saʿīd Nafīsī (Tehran 1319–1332 š./1940–1953 CE). It is based on the two earlier editions and on a number of manuscripts in private collections, which are not of great value (Lazard 1963, 77). As if to compensate for the lack of quality of his textual witnesses, Nafīsī provides a very detailed critical apparatus and provides a wealth of notes. A few years later (Tehran 1342–1343 š./1963–1964 CE), Nafīsī brought out a companion publication in two volumes containing an edition of fragments quoted by later authors from the parts of Bayhaqī's *Annals* which are now lost, *Dar pīrāmūn-i Tārīḫ-i Bayhaqī*, 'Around the *History* of Bayhaqī'. Nafīsī's edition remained the best documented survey of variant readings of the text till the edition by Muḥammad Ǧaʿfar Yāḥaqqī and Mahdī Sayyidī of 1388 š./2009 CE.

The edition by Qāsim Ġanī and ʿAlī Akbar Fayyāḍ was published in Tehran in 1324 š./1945 CE. It contains the entire extant text of the *Tārīḫ-i Bayhaqī* with an introduction, notes, and indexes. It is based on all earlier editions, on the Mağles manuscript plus on a manuscript in Mashhad (now known as Āstāna Quds, 14105) which is dated by provenance to before 1075 AH/1664–1665 CE. It provides a rather heavily reworked version, 'less rich and less adventurous' than Nafīsī's edition as Lazard has it, and it was destined for a general readership. Lazard primarily based his linguistic analysis of the *Tārīḫ-i Bayhaqī* on the edition by Nafīsī, because of its rich critical apparatus, with additional references to the edition by Ġanī and Fayyāḍ (1945). The latter brought out another edition of the text (Mashhad 1350 š./1971 CE), which saw a second edition published in Mashhad in 1355 š./1976 CE. It contains an introduction and incomplete notes (Yusofi 1988), and the second edition in addition contains a long glossary by Yāḥaqqī, who, in 2009, brought out what seems, at least for the time being, the definitive edition of the 'History' (Yāḥaqqī – Sayyidī 2009).

An edition of selections of the 'History', *Guzīda-yi Tārīḫ-i Bayhaqī*, was published by Muḥammad Dabīr Siyāqī in Tehran in 1348 š./1969 CE. The edition, *Tārīḫ-i Bayhaqī*, by ʿAlī Iḥsānī (Tehran 1358 š./1979 CE) seems to be based on the editions by Fayyāḍ, but I could not ascertain this, neither edition being at my disposal.

The edition by Ḫalīl Ḫaṭīb Rahbar (*Tārīḫ-i Bayhaqī*, 3rd edition, Tehran 1373 š./1994 CE, I–III) is almost entirely silent on the editorial method applied and the textual witnesses employed. Rahbar's introduction almost exclusively focuses on the content of the *Tārīḫ-i Bayhaqī*. Only on pages xxxvi-xxxvii of his introduction Rahbar gives a list of the previous editions of the text (Calcutta, the Tehran lithograph, the Nafīsī edition, the edition by Ġanī and Fayyāḍ, with its two later versions). It is a contribution to bibliography without any ambition in textual criticism. At the end of the third volume the edition does have a glossary and indexes. The textual foundations of this edition remain unmentioned, which in the Middle East, and maybe elsewhere as well, means that they were probably one or more of the earlier printed editions.

The latest edition of the *Tārīḫ-i Bayhaqī* is the one that was brought out by Muḥammad Ǧaʿfar Yāḥaqqī and Mahdī Sayyidī (Tehran 1388 š./2009 CE). It contains, apart from the text, a long introduction, and notes and indexes. The introduction does not go very deep into the textual criticism of the two editors, but it provides a useful survey, with many illustrations, of the twenty-four manuscripts used (pp. cxi–cxxx). These manuscripts are 1. the lithograph edition of Pīšāwarī; 2. the Calcutta edition by Morley; 3. the Mashhad manuscript that was first used by Ġanī and Fayyāḍ; 4. the Mağles manuscript that was already used in several earlier editions; 5. by implication an 'unimportant manuscript' that Fayyāḍ had had at his disposal; 6. manuscript London, BL, Or. 1928, without date; 7. manuscript Paris, BnF, Arabe 3224; 8. microfilm 8734 in the Central Library of Tehran University, dated 1288 š. (1871–1872 CE); 9. by implication yet another manuscript that had been used by Fayyāḍ; 10. the edition by Nafīsī; 11. manuscript Tehran University, Central Library, 5933, a copy the lithograph edition by Pīšāwarī; 12. manuscript Tehran University, Central Library, 6569, dated 1169 š. (1755–1756 CE), which had already figured under other references in the editions of Nafīsī and Fayyāḍ; 13. by implication yet another, unspecified, manuscript from among those used by Fayyāḍ; 14. manuscript Tehran, Ketābḫāne-ye Mağles, 61334; 15. manuscript Tehran, Mağles, 3139, dated 1296 AH (1879 CE); 16. manuscript Tehran, Mağles, 40762, dated 1208 š. (1793–1794 CE); 17. manuscript Tehran, Mağles 61937, dated 1209 š. (1794–1795 CE); 18. manuscript London, BL, Or. 455 and Or. 456; 19. manuscript London, India Office, 3736, dated 1907 CE; 20. manuscript London, BL, Or. 1925, not dated; 21. manuscript London, BL, Or. 1927, not dated; 22. manuscript Tehran University, Central Library, 2983; 23. manuscript London, BL, Or. 1926; 24. manuscript Kabul, National Museum, 3417 (21/14). The editors provide some general characteristics about their textual witnesses, and in their extensive critical apparatus they note down numerous variant readings. They have hardly made any effort at textual criticism. Any Lachmannian scholar would immediately have eliminated the earlier printed editions, and also, to name but one example, no. 11 of the list, a copy of the lithograph edition. There is no attempt to stemmatology. Yāḥaqqī and Sayyidī give as their main reason (p. cxxxv) for bringing out their edition their wish to clean away the numerous mistakes and alterations that in course of time had become attached to the text. Whether this is at all possible when one has only recent copies, mostly of the nineteenth century, at one's disposal, remains to be seen. It is evident from the wealth of variants that Yāḥaqqī and Sayyidī had the ambition to replace Nafīsī's edition of 1940–1953.

Of all editions of the 'History' should be said that they show the four extra letters that Persian phonology adds to the twenty-eight letters of the Arabic alphabet. They also normalize the *ḏāl* into a *dāl* whenever modern orthography makes that necessary. This entirely unhistorical procedure is not limited to the *Tārīḫ-i Bayhaqī*, however. It is common practice among Persianists, both in Iran and abroad. The casual observer that I am in these matters remains amazed by this.

The most recent work done on the entire text of the *Tārīḫ-i Bayhaqī*, is the annotated translation into English *Abu'l-Fażl Beyhaqi, The History of Beyhaqi* (*The History of Sultan Mas'ud of Ghazna, 1030–1041*), by C.E. Bosworth, in the revision by Mohsen Ashtiany, and published in three volumes in Boston and Washington, DC in 2011. This work is not primarily concerned anymore with the textual criticism of the Persian text. Its ambition is to enlarge the readership of the 'History' to those who have no command of the Persian language. The lengthy introduction in the first volume places the content of the 'History' in a historical context. The third volume entirely consists of explanatory notes, which only in an indirect way are useful for textual criticism.

References

Bertotti 1991; Bosworth 2011; Ġanī – Fayyāḍ 1945, 1971=²1976; Iḥsānī 1979; Lazard 1963 (esp. 76–78), 1974; Meisami 1999 (esp. 79–108); Morley 1862; Nafīsī 1940–1953, 1957, 1963–1964; Pīšāwarī 1889–1890; Rahbar 1994; Siyāqī 1969; Stern 1969; Storey 1927; Waldman 1980; Yāḥaqqī – Sayyidī 2009; Yarshater 2011; Yusofi 1988.

3.23. Christian liturgical manuscripts (UZ–SV)

Introductory remarks

There are many different Christian Churches in the east, which took shape along both confessional and linguistic lines mostly in Late Antiquity and the early Middle Ages. Their liturgies have evolved continuously, so much so that it is difficult even to recognize the common origin of their rites, which mostly derived from Antioch or Alexandria. Occasional influences, more often than not reciprocal, and also from Jerusalem and the west, have compounded the situation. This process of differentiation has continued even beyond the age of printing (admittedly late in some areas). Therefore a wide variety of books, contents, and terminologies has developed in the Christian East.

Liturgical books are, strictly speaking, those actually used for performing a church service, as lectionaries, missals (for the priest and/or the deacon), breviaries (*hōrologia*), psalters (which may contain more material than the Psalms themselves), service books (*ritual* and *pontifical*), prayer books for various rites (*euchologia*), hymnaries, etc. Liturgiologists (scholars studying the historical development of liturgies) would also include in the same definition books which are subservient to the proper performance of services, as manuals (*typika* in Greek) and calendars. Other types of books, such as collections of private prayers, would be *rather* called 'para-liturgical' (for the terminology see for example Kaufhold 2007, 297–315 on 'Liturgische Bücher').

Additional historical and textual information may be gathered particularly from liturgical commentaries, which explain systematically the symbolism of the rites (see Bornert 1966), but also from other sources which have a rather remote connexion with liturgy, as patristic and historical writings and Bibles with marginal annotations about readings.

All this makes the publication and interpretation of Eastern Christian liturgical manuscripts a rather complex venture.

Liturgical vs. literary manuscripts

Typically, liturgical manuscripts share some unique features, which are less prominent among literary manuscripts: (1) Liturgical books were devised for practical purposes, as guidelines for the performance of a rite. Therefore they were consulted more often than other kinds of manuscripts, became worn by use, and were liable to be replaced more often. (2) For a variety of reasons—among them, the influence of an important see, contamination between monastic and cathedral practices, theological issues and literary concerns, but also simply the natural tendency of liturgy to expand filling the calendar with saints and devising services covering the whole day and rites for important social events—liturgical rites were subject to change, and manuscripts prior to important innovations became obsolete and usually were destroyed. (3) The transcription of liturgical books was also subject to continuous interference from the oral tradition, since often scribes were clerics and therefore familiar with the texts and the gestures. (4) Along history, there has been a growing tendency to make more comprehensive manuscripts, fully transcribing the texts and describing the gestures. As a consequence, more complete (and recent) manuscripts tended to replace more concise (and earlier) manuscripts. The thrust towards completeness is quite visible in musical manuscripts: melodies were first learned by heart; later, perhaps from the sixth century onwards, they were transcribed according to simple notational systems which, in turn, were replaced by more precise transcriptions.

All these factors explain why comparatively few ancient liturgical manuscripts survive and why, on the whole, they lack an 'original', in a proper philological sense.

Since manuscripts were expensive, budget problems were also involved in their production: (a) they were normally 'specialized', providing only the portion of the service assigned to the priest or deacon, or the cantors. Thus, a manuscript rarely offers a full service for the whole liturgical year; (b) except for some luxurious products (for the royal chapel, the main cathedral, etc.), liturgical manuscripts were modest, often made for 'private' use, and economical, trying to save space by different means (using abbreviations, avoiding repetitions, etc.).

Authorship vs. anonymity issues

Liturgical texts may be either anonymous or explicitly attributed to an author, who, in turn, may be true or—very often—fictitious. Some types of liturgical pieces, such as poetical texts, are more likely to be authentic works of an author: for instance, the *madrase* and the *memre* attributed to Ephrem or Jacob of Serugh used in the Syriac liturgy, or also the Byzantine *kontakia* (a genre imitated perhaps from the Syriac tradition) and the liturgical 'canons', which often have been transmitted under an author's name.

However, an author's name does not imply that a text is wholly original, and has not been reworked or has not incorporated earlier sources. On the other hand, it does not prevent further alterations to the text. Such phenomena are clearly visible in the case of literary texts, such as the anaphora (the central part of the Eucharist). An interesting, if questionable, attempt to determine the authorship of the anaphora attributed to John Chrysostom can be seen in Taft 1990.

At least once, an author's second edition has been preserved. The Coptic liturgiologist Abū ʾl-Barakāt ibn Kabar (d.1324 CE) wrote in Arabic an encyclopaedia called *Miṣbāḥ al-ẓulma fī īḍāḥ al-ḫidma* 'The Lamp of the Darkness to illuminate the [church] Service', which has been transmitted in two main manuscripts (along some others of lesser importance), Paris, BnF, Arabe 203 and Uppsala, Univ., O. Vet. 12, both from the fourteenth century; the first one is a direct copy of the author's 'first edition', while the second preserves corrections made by the author himself in view of a 'second edition' (see Zanetti 1985, 247 n. 124).

Publishing liturgical manuscripts

For liturgiologists any liturgical text that was actually in use is in itself interesting, whatever its relation to the rest of the corpus, even when it can be proved that its contents stem from some kind of factual 'error'. For example, St Benedict died on 21 March, and his feast was kept on the same day in the Latin Church (even if it was hampered by the observance of Lent); in the Byzantine Church, however, his feast-day is celebrated on 14 March, due to a misplacement in the old calendars. The scholar must take notice of this discrepancy, and try to understand how it appeared, but should not 'correct' it. See also the case of the printed Coptic annual lectionary below. See Budde 2004, 48–63 (and the criticisms levelled by Winkler 2005a and 2005b, 30–37).

The editor of liturgical texts usually has to face a complicated task (see Polidori 2013). Some unique manuscripts may be worth a diplomatic edition, which makes the editor's work much simpler (although this solution is not fully satisfactory, it has been chosen for western sacramentaries). However, a comprehensive coverage of the rites of a given region or Church would require the inclusion of as many manuscripts as possible, in order to account for the evolution—both historical and local—of the rites.

In fact, the liturgical tradition of an important see (typically a 'patriarchate') has often replaced local peculiarities and/or rites, sometimes by compulsory means (like the imposition of the Latin liturgy among the Malabarese in the sixteenth century), but also by imitation (various rites spread from Jerusalem, for example the mystagogical system). However, total control rarely obtains and usually does not prevent the retention of local peculiarities or the appearance of new ones. For example, the Italo-Greek liturgy, despite its radically Byzantine structure, retained archaisms, imported features from the Palestinian area (see Jacob 1976), and introduced new rites for local saints (Arranz 1969).

Given the evolutionary nature of liturgical rites, each branch of their tradition, indeed each individual witness, has to be assessed on its own merits, since the influence of the various factors mentioned above may vary very much. For example, the Armenian Lectionary of Jerusalem is transmitted by three strands of tradition. The two older types, even if they are conveyed by late codices (the Jerusalem and Paris manuscripts, respectively), are only slightly adapted to the Armenian context and may function almost as Greek witnesses. The third variety, the *čašocʿ*, shows various degrees of adaptation to the local situation in Armenia (see Renoux 2003). Another example is the Georgian Lectionary of Jerusalem, which also conveys mainly translations from Greek, but on occasion retains older features within a more recent context (for a recent *status quaestionis* about the influence of Jerusalem, see Janeras 2005).

Standard models

Today, liturgical books are standardized in most Christian traditions (despite possible minor variants) and are printed. But the situation is rather different in the manuscripts, where, even within the same (branch of a) liturgical tradition, complete uniformity was comparatively rare.

Therefore, the publication and/or description of a typology, that is a standard model for each type of liturgical book within a given tradition, might prove useful, since it may help to single out variants with regard to this model. Describing the manuscripts according to this typology allows, on one hand, to give a clear general survey, and, on the other, to reveal deviations, which are liable to be witnesses of past practices. For examples of typologies, see Zanetti 1987; Zanetti 1995, 88, for the Coptic 'annual psalmody'.

Lectionaries

Describing or editing liturgical manuscripts may be exemplified by lectionaries, namely the books containing the readings, biblical or other, to be used during the services for a given occasion (first Sunday after Easter, or Christmas day, etc.) or a specific service (for example a Baptism, or a Marriage); usually they have also rubrics explaining what should be done.

One-volume handwritten lectionaries, which would supply the readings for the whole liturgical year and all the services, perhaps never existed, because of their sheer size and price. Two methods (or some combination thereof) were adopted to make lectionaries manageable and affordable, and both produced multi-volume sets: 1) following the sequence of the liturgical seasons: Lent, Eastertide, from Pentecost to Advent, etc.; 2) splitting the contents of the lectionary among the various liturgical actors: gospel for the deacon, 'Apostolos' for the reader, Psalms for the cantors, etc.; some lectionaries will have readings only for some weekdays (typically, Sundays, Saturdays, together with major feasts).

Since each church was supposed to need a complete set, lectionaries were numerous, and in some traditions hundreds of them have survived. However, complete sets are rarely preserved, since individual volumes may have been lost in the course of time. Also different traditions might have been merged together. For an interesting case, see Zanetti 1985, 50–52: for the very last days of the liturgical year, the official printed annual lectionaries of the Coptic Orthodox Church provide services belonging to a different 'style' than the rest of the year. The reason for this is that, when the first yearly lectionary was printed, the editor took as his model a (good) manuscript which lacked the last folia, and completed the missing pages with those from another manuscript, which happened to belong to a different 'style'.

Such problems are not uncommon. They exist even in the western tradition, where usually only Latin was at stake (see Kunze 1947). In the oriental tradition, several languages and various influences can be involved (such as Greek, Arabic, Syriac, Coptic, and so on), each of them bringing in its own possible deformations in the text, in the rubrics, and in the reference-system. Samples and explanations for the

Fig. 3.3.23.1 Monastery of St Macarius, Lit. 157 (= catalogue Zanetti no. 201), eighteenth century (?), Collection of 'Fraction prayers' of the Coptic Missal, ff. 34v–35r: prayer for the Commemoration of the Dead of the Liturgy of St Gregory, preceding the Fraction prayer.

present Coptic liturgical tradition (i.e. the Lower Egyptian tradition) are accessible in Zanetti 1985 (for possible sources of errors, see 55–60 and 69–72). Intricate problems compound the study of the (now lost) Upper Egyptian tradition, where nearly no complete manuscript has been preserved; see Zanetti 2007, Brakmann 2004, and Zanetti forthcoming.

What follows is a list of some aspects which deserve primary attention when researching lectionaries.

A) Readings. A typology with the *incipit* and *desinit* is a good tool to identify each pericope precisely. The readings which follow the model may be considered identical to it, and only variant readings will require further discussion. However, in some cases precise identification might be elusive, since, particularly during the Holy Week, there are also readings made up from discontinuous sections taken from one or more Biblical books (Byzantine rite). The text itself, which is properly speaking within the scope of Biblical scholars, may supply additional information about the origin of a given reading, since the lectionary might have been expanded by accretion, and the Bible (or at least parts thereof) was translated more than once into some languages (Syriac, Arabic, Armenian, Georgian). But this is an exceptional situation, which requires specific tools and competence.

B) The Psalms often offer a complicated picture, because of 'combined verses' made from bits taken from several parts of the same Psalm, from different Psalms, or even from other books. Also, the division of the Psalms is not uniform: for several oriental traditions, the Septuagint numbering should be used primarily, with the addition of its Hebrew equivalent. The Septuagint numbering is paramount since it is continuously used in the manuscripts for cross-referencing; the Hebrew allows a wider use of the research.

C) The saints of the day. Liturgical services being often related to the feast days of saints, the study of lectionaries (and calendars) implies the identification of the saints commemorated, which is not always straightforward. Not all the saints are well-known: when a saint is an obscure one, the name could be local and/or forgotten, surviving only in a few manuscripts; it could be also a simple mistake or have been borrowed from another tradition. In the east, an additional problem may be caused by the script, since names have been transliterated even more than once, for example, from Greek into Coptic, then into Arabic, then into Ethiopic, or from Greek into Syriac, then into Armenian, then into Georgian (see Nau 1912a, 1912b; Tisserant 1912).

D) The rubrics. They should be paid careful attention, because of their utmost importance in the development of liturgical services. However, interpreting them requires true familiarity with the given liturgical tradition and liturgical architecture, since in many cases they are not self-explanatory.

The actual publication of such a vast amount of material is difficult: it would be hardly usable if only the reference of each reading were provided, while it would take an enormous amount of space to print entirely each pericope; a full publication on paper would be too expensive; in addition, it would also require several indexes to meet the needs of all readers. A digital edition, with its almost infinite possibilities of displaying and linking, seems to be a better choice, provided a uniform and flexible method of presentation is agreed upon. This is certainly one of the fields where modern tools are liable to improve scholarly research significantly.

A starting point for bibliography on Christian oriental liturgies remains Sauget 1962 (and for the Coptic tradition, Malak 1964); a precious source of information about liturgy is Brakmann 2011. The *Societas Orientalium Liturgiarum* (founded recently in 2005) brings specialists together every other year, and has started to publish selected papers from its International Congresses.

References

Arranz 1969; Bornert 1966; Brakmann 2004, 2011; Budde 2004; Jacob 1976; Janeras 2005; Kaufhold 2007; Kunze 1947; Malak 1964; Nau 1912a, 1912b; Polidori 2013; Renoux 2003; Sauget 1962; Taft 1990; Tisserant 1912; Winkler 2005a, 2005b; Zanetti 1985, 1987, 1995, 2007, forthcoming.

Chapter 4. Cataloguing

edited by Paola Buzi and Witold Witakowski

1. What a catalogue is and the emergence of scientific cataloguing (PB)*

The history of catalogues is strongly interwoven with that of book collections. A book collection without a catalogue would be just a repository, while a catalogue without a book collection would be a *contradictio in adjecto*. This statement is even more valid in the case of manuscript collections, since a manuscript, unlike a printed book, represents an *unicum* and only a detailed and precise description may tell its complete history.

Outlining the long history of catalogues in a few pages, even if limited to catalogues of manuscript books, is not an easy task. Descriptive models have undergone profound changes over the centuries, both because of the different cultural contexts in which they have been conceived and because of the diverse organization and function of the book collections over the ages. Moreover, it is undeniable that the dimensions of a collection have a strong influence on the applied descriptive models: large collections, accessible to the public, require longer and more detailed descriptions compared with small, private collections.

Despite these necessary preliminary remarks, it is possible to state that three main aims have more or less always characterized cataloguing praxis: 1) identification of a book within the collection in which it is preserved; 2) economic evaluation of a book as a precious object; 3) identification of a book for administrative purposes.

The first of these aims, in particular, involves the double nature—physical and intellectual—of the 'accessibility' of a book, the first being guaranteed by the description of the most evident external features (such as the bookbinding or the dimensions, but also the mention of the most important work contained in the book). The intellectual 'accessibility', on the other hand, is clearly related to the interests and the purposes of the person who makes use of the collection and consults its catalogue(s). Since traditionally these interests have been almost exclusively limited to the texts (and sometime extended to the decorations) contained in a manuscript, for a long time catalogues have been mainly conceived as the answer to the questions of philologists, and sometimes of art historians. Dealing with a text, a scholar might need to discover how many manuscripts were involved in its transmission; being aware of the existence of a specific manuscript (or of its shelfmark) he might want to know which texts it contained; knowing that a manuscript contained a specific work, he could be interested in finding out if the text was complete and in comparing it with that transmitted by other manuscripts; or, more simply, he could be interested in defining, at least approximately, the date of the manuscript or its history (its owners, its passages from one library to another, etc.).

In brief, texts (including music) and decorations are the main elements which for centuries have conditioned the preservation and the use of manuscripts, and therefore also the structure of catalogues. Consequently, it is not surprising that the 'modern' catalogues of western and oriental manuscripts compiled by learned scholars who visited European libraries during Renaissance, were merely inventories which only mentioned the texts. On the other hand, the material aspects of books have been neglected for a long time, to the point that the first 'scientific' catalogues (eighteenth century) limited the physical description to the writing support and the date. Only from the nineteenth century have other features been slowly taken into consideration systematically: dimension of the leaves, layout (mainly in one, two or more columns), decoration, bookbinding, provenance, and later, number of lines.

Only very recently have catalogues tried to satisfy other kinds of interests, providing information about the physical and material characteristics of manuscript books, about their manufacture and their nature of complex objects, in order to endeavour to answer the questions of other categories of scholars, such as codicologists and historians of manuscript books.

Remaining in the geo-chronological limits of this volume (cf. General introduction § 1) and therefore excluding archives and libraries of more ancient cultures—such as those found in Ebla (Syria), in Tell el-Amarna (Egypt) or in Mesopotamia—, which would require a separate analysis, we will try to summarize here—without any claim of being exhaustive—some of the main steps in cataloguing history.

* I would like to express my sincere thanks to Patrick Andrist and Marilena Maniaci for their valuable suggestions.

It can be asserted that the necessity of cataloguing books dates back to the end of the fifth or the beginning of the fourth century BCE, a period that marked a crucial moment in the history of culture, which has been appropriately defined as the passage from the 'civilization of the oral word' to the 'civilization of the written word' (Cavallo 1988, 29–67).

At that time, oral tradition was no longer perceived as a satisfactory means of preserving the contents of a literary product, and extensive efforts were made to fix the 'official version' of it, often under the supervision of its own author or of the cultural milieu related to him. At the beginning, it was judged sufficient to preserve only one copy of a work—sometimes authenticated by means of a seal or a sign—normally depositing it in the main town temple or within the 'school' of its author. At that time the few structures where books were kept (temple storerooms, private buildings or philosophical schools) were intended mainly as places for conservation and not for consultation.

The situation changed completely with Hellenism and the creation of the first libraries (in Rome they would appear only at the end of the Republic), many of which were founded in lands of conquest (Alexandria, Pergamum, Antioch, etc.). The book, from a mere mnemonic aid and guarantee of the official character of the text, then became a tool for conservation of knowledge and, slowly, also of cultural circulation. At the same time the nature of the places where manuscripts were preserved changed radically from archives to scriptoria and reading places, although only accessible to a select group of people (Cavallo 2004a, 2004b; Andrisano 2007).

The next logical and indispensable step was that of controlling the book patrimony of a library, which was in continuous growth and therefore in need of a classification. It is the birth of the catalogue.

The first example of such a new tool about which we have enough information is represented by the *Pinakes*, attributed to Callimachus of Cyrene (fourth–third century BCE), first librarian of the library of Alexandria. Composed of 130 books, later enlarged by Aristophanes of Byzantium, Callimachus' work not only registered the volumes contained in the library, systematically describing the physical aspect of each manuscript, but also provided a brief profile of the authors, who, subdivided according to the literary genre—tragic poets, historians, philosophers, rhetoricians, etc.—were listed in alphabetical order, mentioning all the works attributed to them. The title of the works—probably introduced systematically specifically in this period—was followed by the literary genre, the dialect, the number of books the work was composed of, the incipit, the number of lines, and a brief summary (this last only for tragic poems). It is extremely interesting to notice the presence of a systematic mention of the *incipit*, which has represented for a long time—and in a way it continues to do so—the most trustworthy means of identifying a work transmitted by a manuscript, especially in the case of works with the same title or in that of more recensions of the same work (cf. Ch. 3 § 2.1).

From that moment on, the description and quantification of the book heritage of a library—no matter if private or public, big or small—became a necessity, and, although we do not have many other examples of ancient catalogues as articulated and detailed as the *Pinakes* (and very likely the library of Alexandria itself was also provided with more concise inventories), Ptolemaic-Roman Period and Late Antiquity produced a long list of catalogues and indexes of different nature. Book lists and inventories of monastic communities, private collections and 'state libraries'—on *ostraca*, papyri, parchments, wall paintings (White Monastery of Shenoute, Egypt) and inscriptions (Basilica of Rhodes, harbour of Piraeus)—have been found during several excavations carried out in Egypt, Greece and Rome. Literary sources are no less generous. Athenaeus of Naucratis (VIII, 336e) and Dionysius of Halicarnassus (*Dein.*, 1,2; 11, 18), for instance, confirm that the library of Pergamum also had its own *Pinakes*. In Rome, Quintilian (*Inst. or.* X, 1, 57) stresses the importance, even for a private library, of being equipped with an index, while Seneca (*De tranq. an.* 9, 4) laughs at those who collect hundreds of books but during their lifetime do not even find the time to read the catalogue. Thematic catalogues are also well attested, such as those which list works of the same literary genre or of the same author. This is the case of the *index philosophorum* that Seneca recommends Lucilius to consult (*Ep. ad Luc.* 39,2) or of the so-called 'Lamprias catalogue' (third–fifth centuries?) mentioning Plutarch's works thematically.

The catalographic praxis of the Middle Ages, both western and oriental, until at least the end of the fifteenth century, normally consists of very concise lists characterized by rather brief descriptions—limited to the title and the author's name—often intended to assess the value of the book collection for probate purposes (cf. for instance the six mediaeval inventories preserved in the Capitulary and Episcopal archives in Pistoia, Italy; Fiesoli – Somigli 2009, 243–257).

These inventories are mostly lists of *auctoritates* (Bible, Early Church Fathers, etc.) and do not follow any 'model'—even in the same document, books may be described in different ways—although, as is obvious, the features which are more often taken into consideration are the most evident ones (format, bookbinding, writing, etc.). On the other hand, more accurate descriptions, which required a longer preparatory work, are not absent, above all in the case of large libraries.

Sometimes, book inventories of private collections are compiled in order to be included in a will. Representing an important part of the property of an individual, it is not rare for a description of a private library also to include the economic value of a book, a datum which does not appear in the inventories of monastic libraries, their books being less subject to be sold, exchanged or dispersed.

Slowly, however, the physical description of books was integrated with information about their use (prayer, meditation, exercise of a profession, etc.) or about the place where specific manuscripts were preserved, combining the traditional necessity to identify a book as a precious object with the cultural interest it represents (Nebbiai-Dalla Guardia 1992; Petrucci 2001).

Among examples of mediaeval oriental catalogues there are several inventories found in Egypt, mainly on *ostraca* and mostly to be attributed to monastic communities (seventh to eleventh centuries), which list nothing more than the contents of the works, the language (Greek or Coptic) and sometimes the writing support (papyrus or parchment).

It is worth mentioning also the existence of numerous book lists found in the Cairo Geniza (see Ch. 1 § 9.1.2), which represent the earliest surviving catalogues of Hebrew manuscripts (eleventh to thirteenth centuries), recording the contents of private libraries, booksellers' collections, synagogue libraries, etc., where the books are listed by subject, author, or shelf on which they are preserved in the library. They do not describe anything more than texts and, sometimes, bookbinding (cf. Ch. 4 § 2.7).

More accurate, on the other hand, is the inventory of the library of the monastery of St John the Theologian on Patmos (*c.* 1200), written on an oriental paper roll, where information about the contents, the material (parchment or paper), and sometimes the date and the dimensions of manuscripts are provided (Diehl 1905; Astruc 1981; Bompaire 1979; see also Ch. 4 § 2.6).

The necessity of describing manuscript books in a way which was detailed enough to enable their identification and their use by the owner of the library or other users is a later achievement, which took place during the age of the Renaissance and, above all, during the age of the Enlightenment in Western Europe, but had a strong influence also on the cataloguing of oriental manuscripts.

Good examples of this progress are represented by the 'old' catalogues of the Burgerbibliothek in Bern and in particular by that compiled by Samuel Hortin (1634). Almost six hundred Greek, Arabic and Hebrew manuscripts—plus more than three thousand printed books—are subdivided in thematic classes and described both under the textual and the material aspect; an index of the authors is also provided (Andrist 2007a, 36–43).

Several elements contributed to such decisive progress in cataloguing in general and in the cataloguing of oriental manuscripts in particular: the formation of more and more private and public libraries, the systematic acquisition of manuscripts from the Near and Middle East, the interest in the witnesses of the spread of ancient Christianity in exotic lands, the foundation of oriental studies all over Europe, the increasing activities and travels of philologists, often operating under the protection of owners of libraries (this is the case, for instance of Stefano Borgia or Giacomo Nani who both had important collections of manuscripts, in Rome and Venice, respectively), most of whom were specialists in oriental languages, and the consequent edition of unknown texts, to mention but a few of them.

Slowly but progressively the catalogue stopped being a mere list of books, and began to fulfil the task of scientifically describing a manuscript, answering all the possible questions of users—although, at the beginning, mainly those of philologists (we should not forget that accurate cataloguing is the necessary premise for any serious study of a text, see Ch. 3 § 2.1.3), and of art historians, and only much later those of other scholars, such as codicologists, palaeographers, historians of books, etc.

Unlike a printed book, a manuscript represents an *unicum* and only a detailed and precise description can tell its complete history. In brief, a catalogue of manuscripts, whatever the catalographic choice behind it—analytical or summary catalogue (see Ch. 4 § 3)—and the cultural and linguistic area to which it is applied (see Ch. 4 § 2), is a scholarly tool, produced by someone other than the authors of the manuscripts themselves, which should provide, in a clear and consistent form, all the information that a scholar would expect to find and which allows him to work on a manuscript for his own research even before an inspection *de visu* or, at least, prior to obtaining photographic or digital reproductions of it.

This chapter outlines the history of cataloguing of the main oriental manuscript traditions (Arabic, Armenian, Coptic, Ethiopic, Georgian, Greek, Hebrew, Persian, Slavonic, Syriac, Turkish), describing how the 'philosophy' of description has changed over the centuries, from the first scientific catalogues, normally dating back to the age of Enlightenment, to the most recent projects of digital catalogues (see Ch. 4 § 2). Two brief sections dedicated to describing the different types of catalogues in use—checklists or inventories, summary catalogues, analytical catalogues—and the catalogues of decorated manuscripts follow (see Ch. 4 § 3). The analysis of new trends in codicology and study of the history of books, which look at the ancient manuscript as a complex object, and the consequent 'stratigraphic' organization of the codicological descriptions in some recent cataloguing projects is the topic of Ch. 4 § 4. This section aims to suggest the best practice of cataloguing when time and economic conditions permit an accurate approach. The elements that cannot in any case be omitted from the description of a manuscript are the subject of the fifth subchapter (see Ch. 4 § 5). Lastly, the closing section is dedicated to the cataloguing of oriental manuscripts in the digital age, to the description of ongoing projects and to the different descriptive and methodological choices which are behind them (see Ch. 4 § 6).

References

Andrisano 2007; Andrist 2007a; Astruc 1981; Bompaire 1979; Cavallo 1988, 2004a, 2004b; Diehl 1905; Fiesoli – Somigli 2009; Hortin 1634; Nebbiai-Dalla Guardia 1992; Petrucci 2001.

2. A summary history of cataloguing

2.1. Catalogues of Arabic manuscripts (IP)

Arabic manuscripts were written during a period of fourteen centuries starting in the seventh century CE and extending to the first half of the twentieth century. The estimates of Arabic manuscripts that have survived and are held in various libraries and private collections vary. *The World Survey of Islamic Manuscripts* edited by Geoffrey Roper and published in 1992–1994 provides information on numbers of Arabic manuscripts in various holdings world wide. Although the information given is not complete, a total estimate of seven million provided recently seems probable. Approximately one third of the existing manuscripts have been presented in published catalogues. A further third is recorded in unpublished catalogues or hand lists in various collections. The final third lies uncatalogued in cupboards, on open shelves, in sacks, and in wooden or cardboard boxes in private and public libraries in the Middle East, Asia and Africa.

The World Survey of Islamic Manuscripts, mentioned above, provides titles and occasionally even short descriptive comments on catalogues published up to early 1990s. The survey is complemented by the more recent 'Catalogues of catalogues' and 'Catalogues and lists of rare manuscripts' in Adam Gacek's *The Arabic Manuscript Tradition* (Gacek 2001) with further updates in the *Supplement* (Gacek 2008). These bibliographies replace older surveys such as Vajda – Durantet 1949, Huisman 1967, Pearson 1971, and the lists of catalogues given in volumes VI and VIII of Fuat Sezgin's *Geschichte des Arabischen Schrifttums* (Sezgin 1967–2010). A good list of on-line manuscript catalogues can be found in the Islamic Manuscript Studies section of *Research & Technology Guides* provided by University of Michigan Library <http://guides.lib.umich.edu/islamicmsstudies/onlinecatalogues>.

The earliest catalogue containing Arabic manuscripts was *Bibliotheca Orientalis Clementino-Vaticana* by Assemani, printed in Rome 1719–1728. Assemani wrote the catalogue in Latin but added the titles in original languages. The catalogue focused on the content of the texts but codicological details were also given, yet not in a systematic order (Heinen 1994, 631). Further early catalogues were Casiri 1760–1770 on manuscripts in the Escorial Library and Uri 1787 on manuscripts in the Bodleian Library, Oxford. In these catalogues the manuscripts were arranged first thematically and then according to size (*folio*, *quarto*, *octavo*). The titles and the names of authors were given in Arabic and the short descriptions are in Latin. The same method continued to be observed in many of the catalogues published up to the middle of the nineteenth century, among them William Cureton's catalogue of the Arabic manuscripts in the British Museum, printed in London in 1846. The focus of these early catalogues was in establishing the identity of the text and in defining its content and subject matter. The description of the physical details of the manuscript was restricted to the absolute minimum, listing support material (paper, parchment), approximate size (*folio*, *quarto*, *octavo*) and number of folia. Any major damage was mentioned. The calligraphic style was only rarely specified and sometimes a comment on the quality of the calligraphy is added (*nitide exaratus, elegantissime, manu rudi*) and, when relevant, the decoration was briefly described. The binding was never described and only sparse information on provenance was given.

In the latter part of the nineteenth century, Latin gradually lost its position as the western scholarly language. This is reflected in the manuscript catalogues, as well, and the national languages began to dominate: German libraries published their catalogues in German and French libraries in French but though changing the cataloguing language, the cataloguers followed the classical standard established by the early cataloguers such as Casiri, Uri and Cureton. The cataloguers saw as their main goal reliably to identify the author and title of each manuscript and briefly to describe their content. One of the best examples of the classical standard is Wilhelm Ahlwardt's catalogue from 1887–1899 describing the holdings of the Royal Library in Berlin. Compared with the above mentioned early catalogues, Ahlwardt's entries are longer and more detailed. He usually lists the table of contents stating the folia where the chapters begin. In addition, he gives 1–2 lines both from the beginning and the end of the texts. Ahlwardt's major work of reference is Ḥaǧǧī Ḫalīfa's (1609–1657 CE) bibliographic lexicon *Kašf al-ẓunūn* edited and published in 1835–1858.

Although the main focus in Ahlwardt's catalogue remains on identifying the texts and describing their contents, his description of the physical aspects of the manuscripts is somewhat more detailed than in the above mentioned Latin catalogues. He describes in few words not only the support material and its condition but also the binding. In addition, he gives the number of lines on each page and adds the dimensions of both the folia and text area in centimetres. A major improvement on the earlier catalogues is Ahlwardt's detailed indexing (volume 10 of the catalogue). Not only are the titles and authors indexed but also scribes, calligraphic types and copy dates. The fact that Ahlwardt prepared an index of calligraphic types is a first indication that scholarly interest was no longer solely focused on the texts themselves but was beginning to include palaeography.

Ahlwardt's meticulous descriptions made his catalogue a valuable reference work for later cataloguers trying to identify manuscripts. The other major reference works favoured and routinely quoted by cataloguers in western libraries are the above mentioned *Kašf al-ẓunūn* and Carl Brockelmann's *Geschichte der Arabischen Litteratur* I–II, originally published in 1898–1902. Brockelmann's work contains biographical information on authors and lists their works, giving references to the manuscript holdings of various libraries. Brockelmann's work excludes Christian Arabic religious literature and is in this respect complemented by Georg Graf's *Geschichte der christlichen arabischen Literatur* I–V (1944–1953).

There are a few catalogues specifically devoted to Christian Arabic manuscripts. One of them is Georg Graf's catalogue of Cairo manuscripts published in the Vatican in 1934. Graf compiled the catalogue while working on his history of Christian Arabic religious literature mentioned above. The Mount Sinai collection in the Monastery of St Catherine is the largest collection of Christian Arabic manuscripts and it also contains many of the oldest existing manuscripts. The first 300 manuscripts are described in the first volume of the *Catalogue raisonné* by Aziz S. Atiya and Joseph N. Youssef, published in Alexandria in 1970. Among the very best catalogues of Christian manuscripts is the two-volume work by Gérard Troupeau published in Paris in 1972–1974. Apart from identifying the various texts, Troupeau gives a succinct physical description of the manuscripts keeping to the tradition exemplified by Ahlwardt. Another feature resembling Ahlwardt's catalogue is the inclusion of extensive indexes. For further remarks, cf. Bausi 1993.

In the early decades of the twentieth century appear the first catalogues describing collections in Algeria (Ben Cheneb 1909), Morocco (Lévi-Provençal 1921), Egypt (Abū ʿAlī 1926–1929), and India (Ivanow – Hosein 1939). The description followed the standards set by the late nineteenth century European cataloguers. In Europe, the major collections had been recorded and the interest focused partly on updating the existing catalogues (for example Blochet 1925) and partly on cataloguing smaller collections. A good example of the latter type is Alphonse Mingana's catalogue of the Arabic manuscripts in the John Rylands Library in Manchester (Mingana 1934a). In addition to textual comments, Mingana paid attention to the number of hands involved in the copy and he also commented on the marginal notes. Further, if the manuscript displayed seal stamps, he deciphered the names engraved in them.

Mingana's comments on hands, marginal notes and seal stamps attest a continuation of the gradual understanding of the manuscript not only as a repository of text but also as an artefact of its own right. This change of attitude culminated in Jan Just Witkam's catalogue of Arabic manuscripts in the Netherlands printed in Leiden 1983–1986. Witkam did not only pay attention to the number of scribes who had been involved in creating the manuscript but was, more importantly, the first cataloguer to describe the composition of quires.

Among recent large cataloguing projects in Europe, is the on-going German series *Verzeichnis der orientalischen Handschriften in Deutschland* (VOHD). Within this project, ten volumes of catalogues of Arabic manuscripts have been published in the period 1976–2010 (Wagner 1976–2010). These catalogues follow the classical system exemplified by Ahlwardt's catalogue. They focus on identifying the texts and authors with references to both Ahlwardt and Brockelmann. The palaeographic and codicological information follows the example set by Ahlwardt and remains rather sparse. A new feature in these catalogues when compared with Ahlwardt's is the inclusion of owners' marks among the description parameters, which speaks of a growing interest in the ownership history of the individual manuscripts. This interest is also reflected in the recent catalogue of the Arabic manuscripts in the Royal Library, Copenhagen (Perho 2007) where an effort has been made to establish the provenance of the manuscripts.

The classical cataloguing method developed in western libraries continues to be observed by cataloguers working in the Arab countries and Iran. Among the best examples of recent catalogues are Yūsuf Zaydān's catalogue of the Arabic manuscripts in the Rifāʿat Rāfiʿ al-Ṭahṭāwī Library in Sūhāg, Egypt (Zaydān 1996–1997) and the catalogue of the manuscripts in the library of Āyatollāh al-ʿOzmā Naǧafī Marʿašī in Qom, Iran, by Sayyed Aḥmad Ḥosaynī (Ḥosaynī 1975–2010).

The classical catalogues restricted themselves to describing the manuscripts in words and did not contain any photographs of the manuscripts. In recent decades this has changed and some catalogues include black and white or colour photographs. For example, the above mentioned Iranian catalogue contains some photos placed as an appendix to each volume. Richly illustrated catalogues of Arabic manuscripts have been produced in The Royal Library, Copenhagen. The catalogues Alhussein Alhaidary – Rasmussen 1995, Perho 2003 and Perho 2007 contain good quality photographs of the beginning and end of each manuscript. The latter two catalogues have in addition some colour reproductions. Otherwise, these catalogues follow the classical standard in that the main focus is on the texts and codicology receives less attention.

All the above mentioned catalogues are traditional printed catalogues but in recent years some libraries have included their Arabic manuscripts in electronic catalogues available on the internet. Some of these catalogues are very basic, like the *Indian National Mission for Manuscripts* (<http://www.namami.org/pdatabase.aspx>), giving only the minimum of information in each entry whereas others give more detailed descriptions. A fine example of a more detailed approach is *Wellcome Arabic Manuscripts Online* that is a partnership between the Bibliotheca Alexandrina, Wellcome Library and King's College London (<http://wamcp.bibalex.org/home>). Another good example of this new focus is the on-going catalogue project of the *Islamic Manuscript Collection* at the University of Michigan, Ann Arbor (<http://www.lib.umich.edu/islamic/>).

In both the Wellcome and Michigan catalogues, the entries contain extensive description of the manuscripts as physical objects giving details of collation, layout, script, decoration, support and binding. They respond to the growing scholarly interest in the codicology of Arabic manuscripts by including information on production detail. While the classical catalogues mainly benefited the philologists and other text based scholars, new catalogues such as the Wellcome and the Michigan have begun to give relevant information to codicologists and art historians, as well. An added bonus of the two electronic catalogues is that each entry connects with complete digitized versions of the manuscript and enables the user to leaf through the manuscript in a virtual form.

The cataloguing of Arabic manuscripts has supported the interests and trends within research. In the eighteenth and nineteenth centuries, the catalogues helped to establish the history of the various genres of Arabic literature; later research interest and, correspondingly, the cataloguers' interest gradually expanded to consider the manuscript not only as a carrier of a text variant but also as an artefact that documents the history of manuscript culture. As only about one third of existing manuscripts are described in published catalogues, a vast task remains to prepare complete catalogues of partly or inadequately described manuscripts and, especially, to locate, record and secure the survival of the large numbers of completely uncatalogued material.

References

Abū ʿAlī 1926–1929; Ahlwardt 1887–1899; Alhussein Alhaidary – Rasmussen 1995; Assemani 1719–1728; Atiya – Youssef 1970; Bausi 1993; Ben Cheneb 1909; Blochet 1925; Brockelmann 1899–1902 = 1943–1949; Casiri 1760–1770; Cureton 1846; Gacek 2001, 2008; Graf 1934, 1944–1953; Ḥağğī Ḫalīfa 1835–1858; Heinen 1994; Ḥosaynī 1975–2010; Huisman 1967; Ivanow – Hosein 1939; Lévi-Provençal 1921; Mingana 1934a; Pearson 1971; Perho 2003, 2007; Roper 1992–1994; Sezgin 1967–2010; Troupeau 1972–1974; Uri 1787; Vajda – Durantet 1949; Wagner 1976–2010; Witkam 1983–1986; Zaydān 1996–1997. Web sources: *Indian National Mission for Manuscripts* <http://www.namami.org/pdatabase.aspx> accessed August 2013; *Islamic Manuscript Collection* at the University of Michigan, Ann Arbor <http://www.lib.umich.edu/islamic/> accessed August 2013; *Wellcome Arabic Manuscripts Online* <http://wamcp.bibalex.org/home> accessed August 2013.

2.1.1. Catalogues of Arabic manuscripts from Africa (MN–AGo)

Another area of Arabic manuscript production is the African continent, as testified by the *Arabic Literature of Africa* coordinated by John O. Hunwick and Rex S. O'Fahey (ALA). Although not a catalogue, this multi-volume work is an indispensable research tool comparable to the above mentioned *Geschichte der Arabischen Litteratur* for the African context—and especially as sub-Saharan Africa is almost completely neglected by Brockelmann.

2.1.1.1 West Africa (MN)

As for West Africa, the first pioneering work on Arabic collections dates back to the early twentieth century, when Louis Massignon presented an index of selected manuscripts from the inventory compiled by the French colonial administrator Henry Gaden of the *Šayḫ* Sīdiyya Bābā (1862–1924) family library, one of the most important in Mauritania (Massignon 1909). However, it is from the late colonial period to the early post-colonial period, that the first attempts to describe West African manuscript collections systematically started, with the publication of a number of checklists of manuscripts kept in different collections from Ghana, Nigeria and Senegal (Kensdale 1955–1958; Arif – Abu Hakima 1965; Boyo et al. 1962; Diallo et al. 1966).

The first description of a collection of West African manuscripts in Europe is the inventory of the Fonds Archinard kept in the Bibliothèque nationale de France published in 1985 (Ghali et al. 1985). The same model of manuscript description was followed by Ulrich Rebstock who accomplished the amazing task of microfilming 2,239 manuscripts from Mauritanian libraries and completed an inventory of these materials that was published (Rebstock 1989). A more detailed catalogue of another important European collection of West African manuscripts, the Fonds de Gironcourt, has recently been published by Nobili (2013) within the *Series Catalogorum*, a series devoted to cataloguing collections of Arabic manuscripts.

However, the main contribution in the field of cataloguing and manuscript studies comes from the al-Furqān Islamic Heritage Foundation, which has launched an important project of analysis of manuscript collections from sub-Saharan Africa. With more than ten publications, the al-Furqān endeavour consists of works of very a different nature, ranging from checklists of manuscripts, like the inventory of the manuscripts of the Institut des Hautes Etudes et de Recherches Islamiques Ahmed Baba in Timbuktu, Mali—formerly Centre de Documentation et de Recherches Ahmed Baba (Sīdī ʻUmar et al. 1995–1998) or that of the libraries of *Šayḫ* S.M. Cisse *al-Ḥāǧǧ* Malick Sy and Ibrāhīm Niasse (Ñass) in Senegal (ʻUṯmān Kan 1997), to catalogues, such as the ones of the Mamma Haidara library of Timbuktu (ʻAbd al-Qādir Mammā Ḥaydara – Ayman Fuʾād Sayyid 2000–2003) or the Institut de Recherche en Science Humaines of Niamey, Niger (Ḥasan Mawlāy – Ayman Fuʾād Sayyid 2004).

A number of online catalogues have also been developed in the last decade, such as the one of the West African collections of manuscripts of the Herskovits Library of African Studies at Northwestern University (<http://digital.library.northwestern.edu/arbmss/index.html>), and the new, updated version of the Bibliothèque nationale de France (<http://archivesetmanuscrits.bnf.fr/cdc.html>, section 'Manuscrits d'Afrique sub-saharienne'). A database, including complete images of 2,600 Mauritanian manuscripts (most of them described in Rebstock 1989), along with a scanty description, is the Oriental Manuscript Resource (OMAR), developed by the University of Tübingen, which includes full reproductions of the manuscripts described (<http://omar.ub.uni-freiburg.de>). Finally, worthy of mention under the category of electronic catalogues is the West African Arabic Manuscripts Database, a bilingual (Arabic and English) union catalogue that includes a search engine developed by Charles C. Stewart (<http://www.westafricanmanuscripts.org>). In its 3.0 version, the database contains descriptions of more than 20,000 manuscripts included in eleven different collections. (For a more complete overview, see Nobili 2011, 2012 = 2012/2013.)

While all these contributions represent a crucial step towards the appreciation of the West African manuscript heritage, it is possible to extend the observation that Graziano Krätli makes on some of them, when he states that 'they were conceived and implemented to serve literary interests and purposes. Therefore, they meet the expectations and the needs of literary scholars, but inevitably disappoint codicologists and other students of the book as a material and technological object' (Krätli 2011, 329).

2.1.1.2 Northeast and East Africa (AGo)

Unlike West Africa, the Horn of Africa has been long neglected by scholars of Arabic and Islamic manuscripts. The lack of attention and interest is clearly mirrored in the very limited number of known manuscript collections and in the astonishingly scanty amount of available catalogues which, moreover, contain only vague palaeographical and codicological descriptions of the items (for a general assessment of the situation see Gori 2007).

The Institute of Ethiopian Studies at Addis Ababa University hosts the biggest well structured collection of Arabic-Islamic manuscripts in Ethiopia. The collection was summarily described by Jomier 1967 and Hussein Ahmed 1994. A first descriptive handlist of three hundred and three Islamic manuscripts (mainly in Arabic but also in local languages written in Arabic script, *ʻaǧamī*) has now appeared within the framework of the Ethiopian Manuscript Imaging Project (Gori 2014). Far from being a full-fledged catalogue, the handlist basically aims at the identification of the main texts preserved in the manuscripts; it also contains some pioneering remarks by Anne Regourd on bindings and watermarks.

In Pavia a small collection of twelve Ethiopian Islamic manuscripts is kept at the Civic Library 'Carlo Bonetta'. The items were acquired in the Muslim town of Harar (East Ethiopia) in 1888–1889 by the Italian engineer and adventurer Luigi Robecchi Bricchetti. Renato Traini in 1973 catalogued the collection which represents a valuable example of the manuscript culture in Harar and gives a clear idea of the Muslim religious literature circulating in the town (see also Vicini 1987 and Gori 2009).

The Biblioteca Apostolica Vaticana has fourteen Islamic manuscripts from the Horn of Africa (five from Somalia; nine from Ethiopia) which were all but one acquired by Enrico Cerulli during his stays in the area. Despite their small number, they were placed in two different collections. Ten manuscripts were included in the general Arabic Islamic collection and were catalogued by Giorgio Levi Della Vida (1965, xx, 146–159). The remaining were considered part of the 'Cerulli Etiopici' collection and were described by Osvaldo Raineri (Cerulli 2004, 232–239).

Ewald Wagner (1997) has produced the only so far existent catalogue programmatically and exclusively devoted to Islamic manuscripts from Ethiopia. The items described in the volume are basically of three kinds: 1) photocopies of manuscripts kept at the Staatsbibliothek in Berlin the originals of which are scattered in different locations in Ethiopia and Europe; 2) manuscripts of the private collection of Ewald Wagner now preserved at the Staatsbibliothek in Berlin; 3) manuscripts of the Nachlaß Hans Martin Schlobies kept at the Archiv der Berlin-Brandenburgischen Akademie der Wissenschaften. The structure of the catalogue and the description of the items strictly follow the model of Wilhelm Ahlwardt's *Verzeichnis der arabischen Handschriften der Königlichen Bibliothek zu Berlin* (see above) and differ from the standardized format of the VOHD series to which it belongs (for the review of the catalogue see Gori 1999).

The Library of the Institute of Oriental Manuscripts of the Russian Academy of Sciences in St Petersburg preserves the manuscripts acquired by the Russian poet and adventurer in Ethiopia, Nikolay Gumilev. No catalogue of the collection is available: only a brief description of the items has been provided by Dobronravin 2006.

A few more Islamic manuscripts coming from Ethiopia can be found scattered in several different libraries in Europe (for example the Bibliothèque nationale de France and the British Library). They are normally described in the general Arabic-Islamic catalogues of the institutions that house them.

Thirty-one Islamic manuscripts from Somalia are kept at the Library of the London School of Economics. The collection is made up of copies of manuscripts which Ioan M. Lewis had made during his field work in Somaliland between 1955 and 1957 and was described in a handlist first published by Andrzejewski – Lewis 1994 (reprint 1998). No other collection of Somali Arabic Islamic manuscripts is so far known (see for a general assessment O'Fahey 1994). The same can be said for Eritrea and Djibouti.

Moving towards East Africa, the situation described above shows some little but significant improvement. Not as forsaken as in the Horn of Africa, Islamic Arabic and Swahili manuscripts from Kenya and Tanzania have managed to draw the attention of some scholars, in particular of those specializing in Islamic studies and in Swahili traditional poetry. A few collections of manuscripts have come to light, especially in the main urban centres. For some of these collections handlists and general catalogues are available. Yet the study of the palaeography and the codicology of the East African Islamic manuscript is practically non-existent.

Several different collections of Islamic manuscripts are listed in the survey made in Kenya by Ahmad Shaykh Nabhani, Yahya Ali Omar and David Colton Sperling (Nabhani et al. 1993). None of these collections has so far been duly catalogued. However, the collection of the Riyadh Mosque in Lamu which hosts one hundred and thirty manuscripts and is considered the largest known in the country was fully digitized in 2011–2012 within the framework of a project financed by the Endangered Archive Programme of the British Library and Arcadia Fund and conducted by Anne Bang of the Christian Michelsen Institute in Bergen and the University of Cape Town; for seventy-nine of them brief descriptions have been provided online (EAP466: *The manuscripts of the Riyadh Mosque of Lamu, Kenya*, <http://eap.bl.uk/database/overview_project.a4d?projID=EAP466;r=13064>).

In Tanzania, Hamad Omar and Tigiti S.Y. Sengo (1994) list a few collections of manuscripts located in Dar Es Salaam and in Zanzibar (no data are available on other places). In the capital of the country, the

University Library hosts one hundred and two Islamic manuscripts (twenty-two Arabic; eighty Swahili), including photocopies and recently made copies of originals kept elsewhere (also in neighbouring Kenya and on the Comoros Islands). The items were catalogued by Allen 1970. The now apparently closed Eastern African Centre for Research on Oral Traditions and African National Languages (EACROTANAL) in Zanzibar had a collection of one hundred and twenty two old manuscripts from the island: twenty-five of them were catalogued by Mkelle in 1981 and the remaining ninety-seven were described in the anonymous three-volume *Bibliographie annotée* 1986–1988. Finally, the Zanzibar National Archives keeps a collection of Arabic and Swahili manuscripts: a checklist of the Arabic items is in Declich 2006.

As for the Comoro Islands, Ahmad Shaykh Nabhani and David Colton Sperling (1994) mention a few very small collections of manuscripts mostly in private hands. According to this source, the Centre national de documentation et recherche scientifique in the capital town of Moroni keeps twenty seven manuscripts in Arabic, Swahili and in the local Comorian language (Ngazija or Kingazija) but no catalogue is available.

Collections of manuscripts originating from Kenya and Tanzania and containing texts in several different dialects of Swahili written in Arabic script are also hosted in some European libraries. Those kept in Germany were catalogued by Dammann 1993 for the VOHD while those preserved at the School of Oriental and African Studies in London are catalogued in the on-line database <http://www.swahilimanuscripts.soas.ac.uk>.

References

‘Abd al-Qādir Mammā Ḥaydara – Ayman Fu’ād Sayyid 2000–2003; Allen 1970; Andrzejewski – Lewis 1994, 1998; Arif – Abu Hakima 1965; *Bibliographie annotée* 1986–1988; Boyo et al. 1962; Cerulli 2004; Dammann 1993; Declich 2006; Diallo et al. 1966; Dobronravin 2006; Ghali et al. 1985; Gori 1999, 2007, 2009, 2014; Ḥasan Mawlāy – Ayman Fu’ād Sayyid 2004; Hunwick – O’Fahey 1995–; Hussein Ahmed 1994; Jomier 1967; Kensdale 1955–1958; Krätli 2011; Levi Della Vida 1965; Massignon 1909; Mkelle 1981; Nabhani et al. 1993; Nabhani – Sperling 1994; Nobili 2011, 2012 (= 2012/2013), 2013; O’Fahey 1994; Omar – Sengo 1994; Rebstock 1989; Sīdī ‘Umar et al. 1995–1998; Traini 1973; ‘Uṯmān Kan 1997; Vicini 1987; Wagner 1997. Web sources: Bibliothèque nationale de France <http://archivesetmanuscrits.bnf.fr/cdc.html>; EAP466: The manuscripts of the Riyadh Mosque of Lamu, Kenya, <http://eap.bl.uk/database/overview_project.a4d?projID=EAP466;r=13064>; Herskovits Library of African Studies at Northwestern University <http://digital.library.northwestern.edu/arbmss/index.html>; Oriental Manuscript Resource <http://omar.ub.uni-freiburg.de>; Swahili manuscripts at SOAS <http://www.swahilimanuscripts.soas.ac.uk>; West African Arabic Manuscripts Database <http://www.westafricanmanuscripts.org>.

2.2. Catalogues of Armenian manuscripts (AS)

About 31,000 Armenian parchment and paper manuscripts are known to be extant worldwide (Coulie 2014, 23; Kouymjian 2012a, 19; up to 34,000 if we count separate flyleaves and fragments). Of them, ninety percent or more have been identified and recorded (Kouymjian 1983, 425–437), making Armenian manuscript research quite advanced comparing to the other Christian oriental languages (Syriac, Ethiopic, and Coptic). The progress has been possible due to the fact that most Armenian manuscripts are not scattered in different ecclesiastic or private libraries but have been transferred to relatively few major collections. The most important repositories are in Yerevan (Matenadaran), Jerusalem (Armenian Patriarchate), Venice and Vienna (monasteries of the Mekhitarists), Isfāhān (Armenian diocese of New Julfa), and Bzummar in Libanon (Armenian Catholic monastery). Smaller collections are found in libraries in the United States, Russia, England, France, Germany, Italy and other parts of Europe (see also General introduction § 3.2).

Catalogue of Armenian catalogues

For Armenian cataloguing, researchers are in a quite comfortable situation having a ‘Catalogue of Catalogues’ at their disposal, which covers Armenian manuscript collections in public and private libraries and their status of cataloguing (Coulie 1992, with supplements 1995, 2000a, 2004, and 2014, 25). The *Répertoire* is arranged in alphabetical order according to the places of manuscript collections. An updated version by Coulie is in preparation at the Université catholique de Louvain, Belgium. It also lists collections that have now disappeared or identifies manuscripts displaced from those former collections.

CATALOGUE
DES MANUSCRITS ARMENIENS DE LA BIBLIOTHEQUE DU ROY,

Dreſſé en 1735.

I.

Volumes qui ſe ſont trouvés à la Bibliotheque ſous le Regne de Louis le Grand.

A.

1. TRaduction Armenienne du Miſſel Romain faite en 1381. par un Franciſcain appellé Frere Boſius. Ce manuſcrit a été copié ſous le Pontificat d'Urbain VIII. dans le dix-ſeptiéme ſiecle, *in-folio.*

B.

2. Recueil de pieces concernant la Religion, contenant quinze petits ouvrages dont 6. ſont fabuleux, *tranſcrit en* 1554. *in*-4°.

C.

3. Verſion Armenienne des Epîtres de S. Paul parmi leſquelles, après la II. aux Corinthiens, ſe trouve une pretenduë Lettre de l'Egliſe de Corinthe à S. Paul, & une reponſe de ce S. Apôtre. Cette réponſe a pour titre, III. Epitre de S. Paul aux Corinthiens, *tranſc. vers le* 15. *ſiecle*, *in*-8°.

D.

4. Machetots, c'eſt-à-dire Rituel d'Armenie ainſi appellé de Machetots, 48. Patriarche de cette nation, qui eſt l'Auteur de ce Livre, & qui occupa le ſiege Patriarchal pendant le cours de l'année 899. *tranſc. en* 1574. *in*-8°.

E.

5. Charaknots, ou Recueil des Cantiques qui ſe chantent à l'Office Divin dans toutes les Egliſes d'Armenie, *tranſc. en* 1554. *in*-12.

F.

6. Ordre des prieres publiques qui ſont en *Tom. II.*

B uſage dans les Egliſes d'Armenie, *tranſc. en* 1608. *in*-16.

II.

Voulumes trouvés parmi les Manuſcrits de M. Colbert dont le Roy Louis XV. a fait l'acquiſition.

A.

7. Aïſmavourq, c'eſt-à-dire, Menologe Armenien dans lequel ſe trouve la Vie des Saints, non-ſeulement de l'Egliſe d'Armenie, mais de toutes les autres Egliſes, *tranſc.*
C *en* 1689. *in-fol.*

B.

8. Explication de pluſieurs paſſages du Nouveau Teſtament. Le reſte de ce volume contient des pieces de controverſe, compoſées par differens Auteurs, *tranſc. en* 1276. *in*-4°.

III.

Manuſcrits choiſis par les ſoins de Monſieur l'Abbé Sevin, de l'Academie Royale des Inſcriptions & des Medailles, qui, par ordre du Roi, s'eſt tranſporté juſqu'à Conſtantinople en 1728.
D *pour y faire l'acquiſition de quantité de Manuſcrits Grecs auſquels il a réuni les volumes Armeniens qui ſuivent. Il a eu pour adjoint, dans ſon voyage, Monſieur Fourmont le jeune, Profeſſeur en Langue Syriaque au College Royal.*

MANUSCRITS RELIEZ.

A.

9. D-Jarrintir, c'eſt-à-dire, Recueil d'Ho-
E melies pour les Fêtes des Myſteres de la Croix & de la Sainte Vierge. Ce Livre comprend auſſi les actes des Martyrs les plus celebres de l'Egliſe, & l'on y trouve pluſieurs traités concernant les mœurs & la diſcipline.

4 I

Fig. 4.2.2.1 Villefroy in Montfaucon 1739, 1017, fragment.

History of Armenian cataloguing

Prior to the nineteenth century, researchers, monks or travellers had described individual (or a few selected) manuscripts, just because these were easily accessible, or due to specific interests. The first outstanding conscious effort of cataloguing was undertaken in Europe by the French orientalist Guillaume de Villefroy (1735; an abbreviated version was published in Bernard de Montfaucon's *Bibliotheca bibliothecarum* in 1739, fig. 4.2.2.1). In 1735 he edited a catalogue of 113 Armenian manuscripts and old books in the French Royal collection in Paris (Kévorkian et al. 1998, xvi; Outtier 1999–2000, 47) which had been deposited there since the middle of the sixteenth century. Villefroy's account was the very beginning of Armenian cataloguing. Even if unordered or random, he made notes of codicological features of Armenian manuscripts like writing types, abbreviations, ink, binding, measures and the material of the codices. He tried to ascertain the author, work, place and date of the texts (see Villefroy's preface to his catalogue, cf. Outtier 1999–2000, 50–53), exchanging letters, among others, with the Armenian monks of the Mekhitarist order in Venice. Villefroy's catalogue with its sometimes long commentaries or paraphrases about the contents of the manuscripts set at the same time the basics of knowledge in Armenian prosopography, history and literature at the early commencement of Armenian studies in Europe.

Systematic cataloguing by Armenian and western scholars started in the nineteenth century and reached an important level of scholarly experience at the end of the nineteenth/beginning of the twentieth

ОБЩІЙ КАТАЛОГЪ

книгамъ и манускриптамъ Эчміадзинской вивліотеки.

ПЕРВОЕ ОТДѢЛЕНІЕ.

АРМЯНСКІЯ КНИГИ И РУКОПИСИ.

I. Священное писаніе и толкованіе онаго.

1. Библій, на пергаментѣ.
2. Тоже печат.
3. Евангелій, на пергаментѣ.
4. Священная Исторія — разныхъ авторовъ.
5. Дѣяній апостоловъ и писаній Новаго Завѣта. П.
6. Толкованіе Священнаго Писанія — неизвѣстнаго.
7. Толкованіе 5-ти книгъ Моисея — архимандрита Вардана Бардзирберди, XIII вѣка
8. Толкованіе тѣхъ же книгъ — Св. Корнилія.
9. Толкованіе Царствъ, Іисуса Навина и Судей — Св. Егише епископа армянскаго, V вѣка.
10. Толкованіе военныхъ предметовъ Священнаго Писанія — архимандрита Григорія, сына Аббаса.
11. Толкованіе книги пророка Іова — архимандрита Іоаннеса Ванакана, XIII вѣка
12. Толкованіе той же кники — Григорія Татевскаго, XIV вѣка.
13. Толкованіе той же книги и Св. Литургіи — неизвѣстнаго.
14. Толкованіе Псалтыря — Св. епископа Нерсеса Ламбронскаго, XII в.
15. Толкованіе той же книги — Данiила.

CATALOGUE

de la bibliothèque du couvent d'Edchmiadzin.

SECTION PREMIÈRE.

LIVRES ARMÉNIENS MANUSCRITS ET IMPRIMÉS.

I. Sainte-Ecriture et ses commentaires.

1. Bibles manuscrites, sur parchemin.
2. id. imprimées.
3. Evangiles manuscrits, sur parchemin.
4. L'histoire sainte, par divers auteurs.
5. Actes des apôtres et épîtres du N. T. I.
6. Explication de la Se.-Ecriture, par un anonyme.
7. id. des cinq livres de Moyse, par l'archimandrite Vardan de Bardzrherd, auteur du XIIIe siècle.
8. Le même, par S. Corneille.
9. Explication des livres des Rois, de Josué et des Juges, par S. Eghiché évêque, au Ve siècle.
10. id. des sujets militaires de la Sainte-Ecriture, par l'archimandrite Grigor, fils d'Abbas.
11. id. du livre du prophète Job, par l'archimandrite Ioannès Vanacan, XIIIe siècle.
12. Le même ouvrage, par Grigor Tathévatsi, XIVe siècle.
13. Explication du même livre et de la sainte liturgie, par un anonyme.
14. id. du Psautier, par l'évêque S. Nersès de Lampron, XIIe siècle.
15. id. par Daniil.

Fig. 4.2.2.2 Brosset 1840, 62–63.

century. The French-Russian scholar Marie-Félicité Brosset (1802–1880) in St Petersburg set up in 1840 a systematic catalogue of 481 manuscripts and old books in the possession of the Catholicate in Etchmiadzin (the catalogue is based on a general thematic inventory prepared by an Armenian monk in 1828; for the later augmented collection, now housed in the Matenadaran, Yerevan, see the references in Coulie 1992, 66–71). However, the catalogue is merely a bilingual Russian-French handlist (fig. 4.2.2.2). It arranges the manuscripts and books into eleven thematic fields—1. 'Sainte-Ecriture et ses Commentaires', 2. 'Théologie', 3. 'Poésie', 4. 'Livres d'Église (Liturgie, Exégèse, Commentaires, etc.)', 5. 'Histoire et géographie', 6. 'Livres classiques (philosophie, rhétorique, grammaires, astronomie etc.)', 7. 'Discours instructifs et Sermons', 8. 'Livres divers ecclésiastiques et autres', 9. 'Lois religieuses et règlements ecclésiastiques', 10. 'Livres dogmatiques', 11. 'Livres de prières')—giving for each a short title, the author and its time.

The cataloguing of Armenian libraries developed considerably at the end of the nineteenth century. Several catalogues of monastic and ecclesiastical libraries were published. In his Russian-language catalogue of 110 manuscripts in the monastery of Sevan, Nikolaj Marr (1892) specifies, after the shelfmark, the size and material of codex and binding, the number of folia and columns, the type of script, the author, the date and a general title of the work (in Armenian); however, there are no details on the contents. The same year a much better catalogue of 13 manuscripts in the Vatican library was published in Armenian by Yakob Misk'č'ean (Jacob Misktjean; see Misk'č'ean 1892). The author groups the manuscripts according to literary genres. After the shelfmark and date, a concise block of main codicological entries follows: number of folia and lines, dimensions and condition of the manuscript, material, script and ink, date, provenance and the name of the scribe, as well as information on any missing folia. This block is followed by the description of the content; the *incipit* and *explicit* of the texts are quoted with folium references, and so are the colophons. This much more elaborate method (codex number and date—technical block of codicological data—content) served as the basic model when the awareness among Armenian and non-Armenian scholars for the need of detailed manuscript recording increased.

The Armenian Catholic order of the Mekhitarists in Vienna and Venice were the most prominent centres for manuscript preservation and research. They contributed much to the cataloguing of Armenian manuscripts during the late nineteenth and the first half of the twentieth century. Between 1891 and 1971,

Fig. 4.2.2.3 Tašyan 1895, 1.

the Vienna branch of the congregation published fifteen catalogues in Armenian with German summary (they are published in the special series *Haupt-Catalog der armenischen Handschriften*; besides their own collections, the Mekhitarists published in this series also the catalogues of Armenian manuscripts in Turkey, Iran, Poland and Germany). Yakob Tašyan (Jacob Dashian) and G. Galēmkʿerean (G. Kalemkiar) became pioneers with their catalogues of Armenian manuscripts in Vienna and Munich (Tašyan 1891–1895; Galēmkʿerean 1892; fig. 4.2.2.3). They laid the foundation for the modern method of cataloguing Armenian manuscripts: the editors of the new catalogue of the Matenadaran collection (Eganyan 1984, xlii) just like the cataloguers of the Paris collection (Kévorkian et al. 1998, xvii) refer to the system established by Tašyan as their model. Well trained in modern western scientific research and inspired by the advanced experience for Latin and Greek manuscript cataloguing, Tašyan had a very systematic approach. He first groups the manuscripts into thematic fields and then in chronological order, which makes his catalogues particularly user-friendly. For each manuscript, he includes a header with basic information (catalogue number, former shelfmark, title, date), followed by a concise block of codicological data (besides the usual entries such as dimensions, writing style, material, provenance, date, scribe etc., he also pays attention to fly- and guard leaves, miniatures, ornaments and initial letters, names of binders and former owners). The description of the contents includes the *incipit* and *explicit* as well as supplementary references to scientific editions and studies. Colophons are quoted in full. Innovations include the indexes of names and places as well as the plates of ornaments and miniatures at the end of the catalogues (Tašyan 1895, plates I–VIII, 1051–1163). He paid also attention to the book history of a manuscript or to the history of the collection itself (former owners and libraries). Another prominent scholar of the Vienna congregation was Nerses Akinian, who followed this method in several catalogues of Armenian collections in Russia, Armenia, Near East and Eastern Europe, published between 1920 and 1946 (Krikorian 1997, 173f.).

Barseł Sargisyan, from the Venice branch of the Mekhitarists, followed the same model in cataloguing the ample Armenian collection in the monastery of San Lazzaro (Sargisyan 1914, 1924, 1966; the cataloguing was continued with five further volumes by Sahak Čemčemean in 1993–1998; the cataloguing of the Venice collection is not yet finished). The tripartite system of cataloguing established by the Mekhitarists (header, codicological data, and contents with bibliographical references) was likewise adopted in Armenia. As an early kind of example can be pointed out the catalogue of the Vaspurakan manuscripts by Ervand Lalayean (Lalayan 1915).

Up to the second half of the twentieth century, the Armenian-Catholic Mekhitarist Fathers dominated by quality and quantity the cataloguing of Armenian manuscripts; their model has been in use until today. Their example inspired European scholars of the first half of the twentieth century, in particular the catalogues of the Armenian collections in Berlin, Tübingen and London (Karamianz 1888; Finck – Gjandschezian 1907; Conybeare 1913).

Modern catalogues

The progress in research on Armenian literature, history and arts, and improved techniques in conservation and digitization have changed nothing in the basic principle established the century before; modern catalogues supplement the same key data. As for Armenian catalogues in Europe, fine examples are the catalogue of Armenian manuscripts at the Bibliothèque nationale de France in Paris (Kévorkian et al. 1998) and in Italian libraries (Uluhogian 2010). More precision can be now given to watermarks, stamps, quire composition, and hands of scribes, miniatures, initials and marginal decoration, binding, book cover and specially the historical 'career' of a codex. Instead of a subjective palaeographical assessment, one can accompany descriptions by photographs of the specific handwriting. The bibliography with references to similar manuscripts, editions and studies is quite comprehensive. The colophons are fully appreciated as very important sources for Armenian history (an important number of colophons from the fifth to seventeenth centuries are published in chronological order in separate editions; they are an important tool for Armenian studies; for their historical significance see Sanjian 1968, 181–195; Stone 1995, 463–471; Dédéyan 1998, 89–110; Sirinian 2014). Not only the scribal colophon but all those present—of the commissioner, painter, binder, owner, restorer, etc.—are reproduced in full.

As for modern catalogues in Armenian, Norayr Połarian (Bogharian) did an extraordinary work between 1953 and 1991 for the important manuscript collection in the Armenian patriarchate of Jerusalem (in eleven volumes; see also Coulie 1992, 96). Unlike in the Mekhitarists' system, the codices are catalogued according to their shelfmark and not to their literary genre or chronology; this makes the catalogues less user-friendly. The fly- and guard leaves are fully taken into account; the later volumes include photographs of painted decoration and handwritings.

The National Institute of Manuscripts (Matenadaran) in Yerevan is the largest collection of Armenian manuscripts, with about 14,000 documents. The cataloguing started in 1959, and the first two catalogues listed *c.*10,400 manuscripts (Eganyan 1965, 1970). Together with the third volume (Eganyan 2007), nos 1–11,077 are now covered (cf. Coulie 2014, 26). Due to the immense size of the collection, the descriptions were done very quickly; the data which derived from former catalogues were summarized or even shortened into very brief entries (Mahé 1986–1987, 583). Since the 1970s the work on more detailed catalogues has been going on. Seven catalogues in Armenian have been so far published, with the description of 2,400 manuscripts altogether (Eganyan et al. 1984, 2004, 2007, 2008, 2009, 2012, 2013). At this rate, at the end of the process the series might grow to up to forty volumes. These revised catalogues of the Matenadaran collection are prepared by a team of specialists, and no more by a single person as before. The team profits fully from the cataloguing experience of the past two centuries: besides the standard codicological entries, the general condition of the manuscript is mentioned, attention is paid to different types of binding, inks, pigments, watermarks, and the chemical analysis of paper. Fly- and guardleaves, palimpsests and other elements are investigated; photographs of various handwritings are added to each manuscript description. The contents are quoted with *incipit* and *explicit*, and even the titles of every single chapter are indicated with their folia numbers. All colophons, even minor ones, are given in full. Just like the Jerusalem catalogue, the new Matenadaran catalogues sort entries according to the catalogue number, without grouping manuscripts according to the genre or date. Thus it is indispensable to make full use of the inventories added to each catalogue. Besides names, places and topics, the indexes include lists of dated manuscripts, fragments, stamps, watermarks, types of binding, Armenian terms and other data.

Specialized catalogues, digitizing

The second half of the twentieth century showed a growing progress in cataloguing Armenian manuscripts. The recent catalogues of Paris, Jerusalem and Yerevan take into account as far as possible the latest studies about the physical, artistic and textual elements of an Armenian codex (for example, in the fields of bookbinding, palaeography and pigment analysis, see Merian 1993; Kouymjian 1998b; Stone et al. 2002; Merian et al. 1994b; Galfajan 1975a, 1975b; further study is required on the organization of writing surfaces, ruling, pricking, quire composition, folding, page layout, textiles used in binding; Kouymjian 2012a, 18–23). For their historical significance, colophons are edited in the catalogues in full and are often even translated into a European language.

Another trend can be observed due to the wealth of data assembled in the catalogues of the previous centuries in combination with the new results of specialized research. More and more thematic manuscript catalogues have been recently published which synthesize the already available facts and add specialized information. There are for example catalogues of specific literary genres such as biblical, medical or legal manuscripts, catalogues on a specific region or period like the Cilician Kingdom, or catalogues of particular artistic schools and scriptoria like those from Cilicia, Vaspurakan, Crimea or Artsakh (see the bibliography in Coulie 2014, 33–37).

Digitizing Armenian manuscripts has been a tendency in all European libraries and in some Armenian libraries like the Matenadaran and the Armenian Catholicate of Antelias. However, the important monastic libraries in Vienna, Venice and Jerusalem are not yet engaged in any digitization project, and access to their manuscripts is quite difficult. The Hill Museum and Manuscript Library (<http://www.hmml.org>) in Collegeville has digitized 1,800 Armenian manuscripts, among them the complete collections of the Armenian Catholic monastery in Bzummar, the Armenian catholicate in Antelias, the Armenian diocese in Aleppo, and the Armenian patriarchate of Istanbul. Smaller digitized collections or single Armenian manuscripts from western libraries are also available online, for example the Armenian manuscripts from the Goodspeed collection in Chicago (<http://goodspeed.lib.uchicago.edu/search/index.php?search%5B0%5D=armenian>) or the collection in Tübingen (<http://idb.ub.uni-tuebingen.de/digitue/tue/Ma_orientalische_Handschriften?liste=1>). The digitization of printed catalogues is in its initial stage; a few can be found online.

References

Brosset 1840; Conybeare 1913; Coulie 1992, 1995, 2000a, 2004, 2014; Dédéyan 1998; Eganyan et al. 1965, 1970, 2007; Eganyan et al. 1984, 2004, 2007, 2008, 2009, 2012, 2013; Finck – Gjandschezian 1907; Galēmkʻerean 1892; Galfajan 1975a, 1975b; Karamianz 1888; Kévorkian et al. 1998; Kouymjian 1983, 1998b, 2012a; Krikorian 1997; Lalayan 1915; Mahé 1986–1987; Marr 1892; Merian 1993; Merian et al. 1994b; Miskʻčʻean 1892; Outtier 1999–2000; Połarian 1966–1991; Sanjian 1968; Sargisyan – Čemčemean 1914, 1924, 1966, 1993–1998; Sirinian 2014; Stone 1995; Stone et al. 2002; Tašyan 1891–1895; Uluhogian 2010; Villefroy 1735=1739. Web sources: Hill Museum and Manuscript Library <http://www.hmml.org>, last access May 2014; Goodspeed collection, Chicago <http://goodspeed.lib.uchicago.edu/search/index.php?search%5B0%5D=armenian>, last access May 2014; Orientalische Handschriften Tübingen <http://idb.ub.uni-tuebingen.de/digitue/tue/Ma_orientalische_Handschriften?liste=1>, last access May 2014.

2.3. Catalogues of Coptic manuscripts (PB)

As in the case of other Christian oriental languages, it was at the end of the eighteenth century that European and extra-European countries began to show interest in the documents related to the first stage of the spread of Christianity into Egypt. Because of the extraordinary climatic conditions of the deserts and the Nile Valley, Egypt preserved an impressive amount of manuscript material, often dating back to the very beginnings of the new faith.

Unfortunately, however, when the local people, including the monks, realized the keen interest of the Europeans in the first documents pertaining to Christianity, they did not hesitate to dismember Coptic codices in order to sell single leaves of them to the highest bidder. This aspect bears a strong influence even now on the study of Coptic manuscript material and Coptic cataloguing, because leaves, originally belonging to the same codex, are often preserved today in several European and non-European collections.

It is not easy to quantify the exact number of these leaves, but according to the database of the Corpus dei manoscritti copti letterari (CMCL) it is possible to state that about 4,000 call numbers correspond to Akhmimic, Fayyumic, Sahidic and Bohairic groups of fragments (less frequently, entire codices) dating between the fourth and the eleventh century. It is more difficult to calculate the number of later Bohairic and Bohairic-Arabic manuscripts mainly preserved in small collections, especially in Egypt. The most famous cases of dismembered codices are those of the so-called White Monastery of Atripe in Upper Egypt (in Sahidic dialect) and those from the monastery of Abū Maqar in Wādī al-Naṭrūn (in Bohairic dialect), to give but a few examples (see also General introduction § 3.6).

At the end of the eighteenth century, fragments of dismembered Sahidic codices had already reached two important Italian collections, namely that originally belonging to Giacomo Nani and now preserved in the Biblioteca Nazionale Marciana, in Venice, and that belonging to Cardinal Stefano Borgia, a part of which today is to be found in the Biblioteca Nazionale Vittorio Emanuele III of Naples (Buzi 2009), while the other part is to be found in the Biblioteca Apostolica Vaticana (Hebbelynck – van Lantschoot 1937).

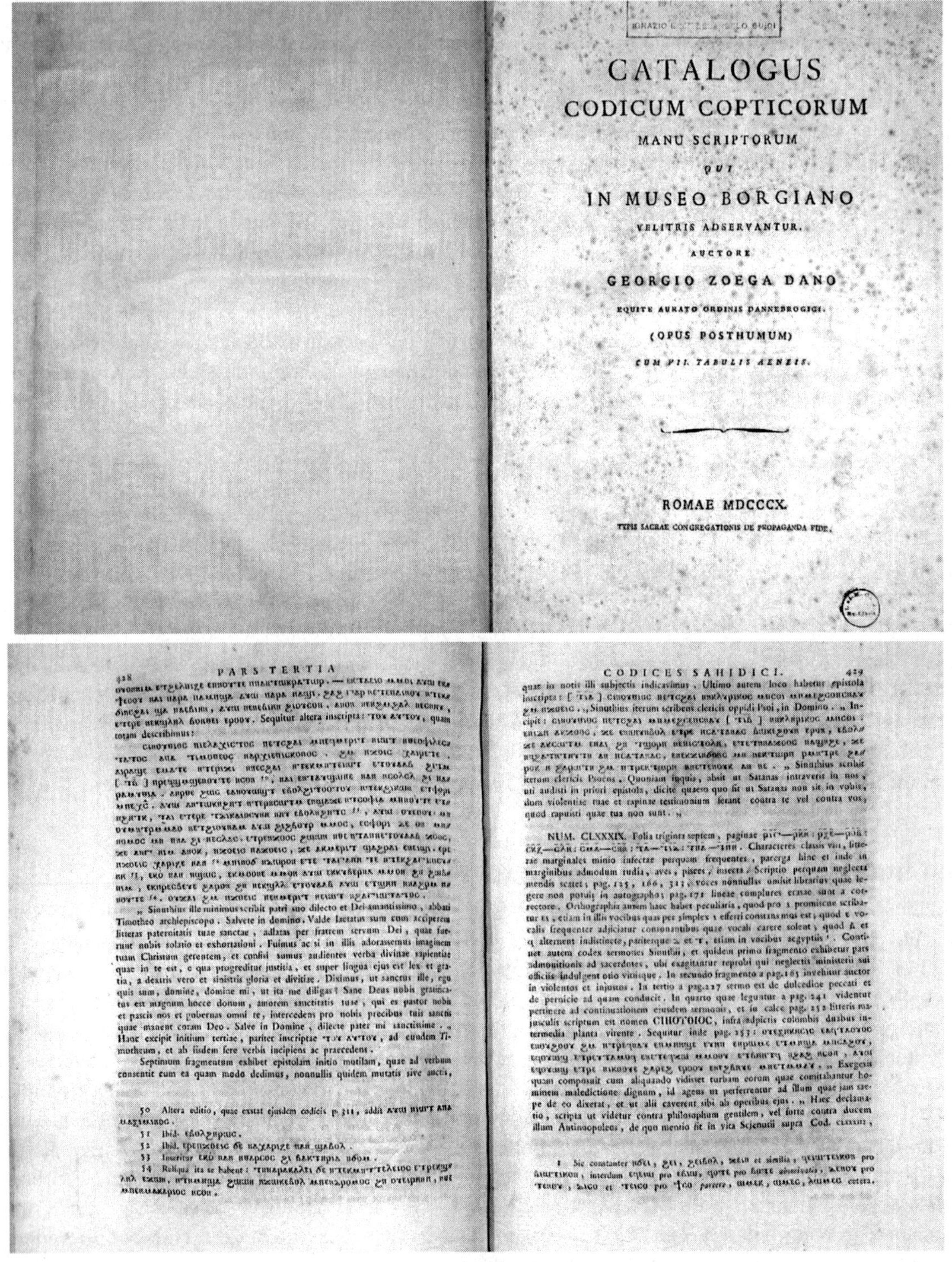

CATALOGUS
CODICUM COPTICORUM
MANU SCRIPTORUM
QUI
IN MUSEO BORGIANO
VELITRIS ADSERVANTUR.
AUCTORE
GEORGIO ZOEGA DANO
EQUITE AURATO ORDINIS DANNEBROGICI.
(OPUS POSTHUMUM)
CUM VII. TABULIS AENEIS.

ROMAE MDCCCX.
TYPIS SACRAE CONGREGATIONIS DE PROPAGANDA FIDE.

428 PARS TERTIA

CODICES SAHIDICI. 429

Fig. 4.2.3.1 Zoëga 1810, frontispiece and pp. 428–429.

The well-known classicist Giovanni Luigi Mingarelli was made responsible by Giacomo Nani for the cataloguing of the Coptic collection preserved in Venice (Mingarelli 1785), while Stefano Borgia entrusted the same task to the Danish scholar Georg Zoëga (Zoëga 1810; fig. 4.2.3.1).

It is not surprising that the authors of the respective catalogues—which still fill us with admiration and surprise for the monumental work they represent—included long textual passages of the leaves they were cataloguing: they were both very aware that this was a necessary step for the comprehension and reconstruction of Coptic literature. What is much more surprising, on the other hand, is the fact that they had perfectly understood—perhaps Mingarelli more than Zoëga—the urgency of finding the related fragments of the leaves they were cataloguing. In 1787, for instance, Mingarelli wrote to Cardinal Borgia to find out if the first four pages of a codex, of which the remaining part was preserved in the Nani collection and contained a work of Rufus of Shotep, were to be found in the Cardinal's collection (Buzi 2011b). More modern Coptologists would not show the same sensitivity towards this aspect of cataloguing.

In short, to serious scholars like Mingarelli and Zoëga it was immediately clear that the main difficulty in cataloguing Coptic manuscripts—with few exceptions, such as manuscripts coming from modern excavations conducted with advanced methodology, very late codices, etc.—was that Coptologists do not deal with complete or quasi-complete codices but rather with a virtual reconstruction of their original codicological unit(s), based on the identification of leaves belonging to the same codex but preserved in different collections.

If the beginnings of Coptic cataloguing appeared so promising, however, in the following decades no further important steps were made (Tattam 1853; Delaporte 1909, 1910, 1911, 1912, 1913), except for the catalogues prepared by Walter Ewing Crum for the Bodleian Library, the British Library and the John Rylands Collection, respectively (Crum 1893, 1905b, 1909; Crum et al. 1922). In all the catalogues by Crum, the descriptions are in fact rather brief, nevertheless the reader can always get all the essential data (shelfmark, material, dimensions, layout description, contents, information about superlineation and punctuation, possible provenance). Manuscripts are subdivided according to the dialect (Sahidic, Akhmimic, Fayyumic, Bohairic, etc.) and within this first classification, as in the case of the catalogues of Mingarelli and Zoëga, catalogued by literary genre (Bible, Liturgical works, Canons, Biographical works, Hagiography, etc.). Particular attention moreover was dedicated by Crum to the identification of the related fragments, which was based on his very extensive knowledge of the Coptic manuscripts collections scattered all over Europe.

Unfortunately most of the other catalogues which were published during the eighteenth century appear as bare and often unsatisfactory checklists, the most meaningful examples in this respect being those realized by Beltz (1978, 1980, see also Hebbelynck – van Lantschoot 1937 and Till 1940).

The first 'modern' catalogue of Coptic manuscripts, which was conceptually inspired by the descriptive standards of the Greek and Latin ones, was realized by Bentley Layton in 1987, in order to describe the Coptic manuscripts purchased by the British Library after 1906. Layton was the first Coptologist to elaborate a systematic 'descriptive method', where all the elements of a manuscript description were eventually taken into consideration. In particular, the space reserved for the physical description of a codex (layout, ruling, quires, binding, etc.) imposed a revolutionary breakthrough, while the praxis of mentioning the known related fragments catalogued elsewhere has become standard since. Moreover, the catalogue contained accurate and systematic identification of the texts (including titles and colophons) and of the writing material. In particular, for the first time, the paper in use in Egypt was carefully described. Due to the lack of specific studies in Coptology, as far as the codicological aspects are concerned, Layton made wide use of a terminology borrowed from the Greek tradition, while for palaeography he attempted to re-elaborate the terminology applied by Guglielmo Cavallo (Layton 1987).

The 'model' for cataloguing elaborated by Layton was re-proposed, without any significant change, by Leo Depuydt, who described the Coptic manuscripts preserved in the Pierpont Morgan Library in New York. It must be stressed, however, that, unlike the London manuscripts, those of New York are in most cases complete or quasi-complete codices (Depuydt 1993). An alternative but equally valid 'model' was used by Anne Boud'hors (Boud'hors 1987, 1998) for describing the Coptic biblical fragments preserved in Paris and in Strasbourg.

More recently, Layton's catalogue has also been used as a base for cataloguing the Coptic manuscripts once belonging to Cardinal Borgia. As mentioned above, the entire Borgia Coptic collection was catalogued and described by Zoëga. Although Zoëga's work is still a necessary point of reference for anybody intending to deal with the Borgia collection, it is undeniably obvious that nowadays it appears out of date, and there was urgent need of revising the information of the catalogue and of adding the data the Danish scholar could not obtain, if only because the catalogue was written before the cardinal's collection was divided. The new catalogue of the Borgia manuscripts preserved in Naples is more schematic than Layton's and Depuydt's, above all as far the description of the punctuation and the decorative elements are concerned, but gives much space not only to all the different call-numbers which have been in use over the ages to identify a leaf (or a group of leaves)—which is an aspect of cataloguing often under-estimated—but, even more important, also to the list of related fragments and to the reconstruction of the original codicological unit(s) the catalogued leaves belonged to (Buzi 2009).

Other recent catalogues, such as those produced so far within the *Verzeichnis der orientalischen Handschriften in Deutschland* (VOHD) series (Burmester 1975; Störk 1995, 1996, 2002) unfortunately cannot be considered satisfactory, because of the reduced space dedicated to the codicological description of the manuscripts and to the bibliography. In part, this may be explained by the fact that they deal mostly with liturgical texts, which still represent a problematic category of Coptic literature, but it does not alter the fact that they cannot be considered valid 'models'.

To summarize, the critical aspects of Coptic cataloguing are the search for the related fragments, the elaboration of a descriptive method which faithfully respects the 'stratigraphy' of the codex, and the identification and adoption of a satisfactory palaeographic description. If the first two aspects largely depend on the scrupulousness and the initiative of the cataloguer, as far as the second is concerned—in the absence of a long-awaited complete and convincing palaeographic study, which is still missing—the best solution seems to be to provide, in addition to a textual description, a photographic *specimen* of the script typology of the described leaf (or group of leaves). As for the remaining aspects, every cataloguer describing the Coptic manuscripts should apply the valid rules of common sense, i.e. clarity, consistency of description and completeness.

Lastly, it is important to stress that Coptic studies did not pay great attention to the opportunities offered by the so-called 'electronic revolution' until now. If we except some very useful databases, such as the Corpus dei manoscritti copti letterari (CMCL) founded by Tito Orlandi (<http://cmcl.aai.uni-hamburg.de>), or *Brussels Coptic Database* elaborated and managed by Alain Delattre—which however is dedicated only to Coptic documents (<http://dev.ulb.ac.be/philo/bad/copte/baseuk.php?page=accueiluk.php>)—and the Coptic section of the *Leuven Database of Ancient Books* (<http://www.trismegistos.org/ldab/>), electronic catalogues of Coptic manuscripts are still a *desideratum*.

References

Beltz 1978, 1980; Boud'hors 1987, 1998, 1999b; Burmester 1975; Buzi 2009, 2011b; Crum 1893, 1905b, 1909; Crum et al. 1922; Delaporte 1909, 1910, 1911, 1912, 1913; Depuydt 1993; Hebbelynck – van Lantschoot 1937; Layton 1987; Mingarelli 1785; Störk 1995, 1996, 2002; Tattam 1853; Till 1940; Zoëga 1810. Web sources: Brussels Coptic Database <http://dev.ulb.ac.be/philo/bad/copte/baseuk.php?page=accueiluk.php>, last access May 2014; Leuven Database of Ancient Books <http://www.trismegistos.org/ldab/>, last access May 2014.

2.4. Catalogues of Ethiopic manuscripts (WW)

The expression 'Ethiopic manuscripts' is to be understood as the manuscripts written in the classical Ethiopic language, properly known as Geʿez, and sometimes referred to as the 'Latin of Ethiopia'. This language, dead since the end of the first millennium CE, was nevertheless used until the nineteenth century as the literary language of Christian Ethiopia, and is still being used in the liturgy of the churches of both Ethiopia and Eritrea. The Muslim manuscripts originating in what is today Ethiopia belong to other scriptorial and book producing traditions (see Ch. 4 § 2.1.1.2 on East Africa, including Ethiopia and Eritrea). On the other hand catalogues and collections of Ethiopic manuscripts may also include, much less numerous, manuscripts written in Amharic (today, the most widely spoken language of the country, and an important medium of traditional Christian education).

The exact number of Ethiopic manuscripts is unknown, but estimates range from *c.*200,000 (Uhlig – Bausi 2007, 738b), excluding scrolls, to some 750,000 (see General introduction § 3.7). Most of the manuscripts originate in the northwestern part of modern Ethiopia and in Eritrea, namely the areas in which the classical Christian Ethiopian civilization developed. Ethiopian manuscripts in western collections, *c.*15,000 (estimate augmented by a probable increase, particularly in the US, since the 1995 data of Beylot – Rodinson; Bausi 2007, 93) original items or microfilms, are growing in number, but represent a tiny fraction of the estimated total (respectively, 7.5 to 2.0 per cent). In practice, only the manuscripts in the western collections have been properly catalogued due to their greater accessibility to scholars. The largest leading libraries, the British Library, the Bibliothèque nationale de France, the Staatsbibliothek Preussischer Kulturbesitz Berlin, the Bodleian Library, etc., had in most cases catered for the needs of scholars and financed the production of catalogues as early as the nineteenth century. Other large collections, including Cambridge, Uppsala, several Italian collections (including the Biblioteca Apostolica Vaticana), and many others, followed suit in the twentieth century. The largest microfilm collection of Ethiopic manuscripts in the west—Ethiopian Manuscript Microfilm Library (EMML)—is kept at the Hill Museum and Manuscript Library, Collegeville, Minnesota (HMML); copies of all EMML microfilms are deposited with the library of the Ethiopian Ministry of Culture, and partly the library of the Institute of Ethiopian Studies, Addis Ababa. Since 1975, the HMML has been producing a catalogue of the microfilms, ten volumes of which have been published in printed form to date, covering 5,000 items.

It seems likely that practically all public, and many private, western collections will in due course be catalogued, provided funds, and the necessary specialists can be mustered. Small collections are also being catalogued, often in publications that cover several such collections in the possession of public institutions, college or university libraries in a particular country (Germany, USA) or even private persons. In cases where collections grow through various acquisitions, cataloguing is a slow but continuous project. The situation to 1995 (with a few omissions) is given in Beylot – Rodinson (1995).

Cataloguing, or rather the listing of manuscripts was first practised in Ethiopia itself. The lists of manuscripts held by certain churches or monasteries, written as additional notes in manuscripts, testify to this practice (see for example Kolmodin 1916). Today, almost all churches and monasteries have registers of their possessions, including manuscripts. Scholarly cataloguing in the west seems to have begun with the catalogue of the collection in Tübingen compiled by Heinrich von Ewald in the 1840s (Ewald 1844, 1847). While Thomas Pell Platt had provided an example of a special catalogue of Ethiopic biblical manuscripts from the then Royal Library of Paris and the Library of the British and Foreign Bible Society as early as 1823, his can hardly be considered a cataloguing attempt. These pioneering works were followed by catalogues in established series, such as the catalogue of the Ethiopic manuscripts in the possession of the British Museum and the Bodleian Library by August Dillmann (1847, 1848), a disciple of Ewald. In 1859 Antoine d'Abbadie published the first catalogue of a French collection, namely that which he himself had brought back from Ethiopia. Uniquely, this important collection was catalogued three times (d'Abbadie 1859; Chaîne 1912; Conti Rossini 1914), thus reflecting the progress and different approaches in Ethiopian studies, with the two later scholars identifying more items and providing corrected information.

These early catalogues predated the firm establishment of Ethiopian philology as an academic field within Semitic studies. However, with the appearance of Dillmann's grammar of Ethiopic in 1857, and his dictionary in 1865, an epoch of 'classical' catalogues of major collections followed. Dillmann himself produced one for the Berlin Royal Library (1878). The British Museum, substantially enriched in 1860s by the royal Ethiopian collection of Maqdalā brought to England by Lord Napier's expedition, entrusted its cataloguing to William Wright (1877: in accordance with the title, the catalogue does not repeat the descriptions of the items catalogued by Dillmann; however, these are included in Wright's index). In the same year, Hermann Zotenberg's catalogue of Ethiopic manuscripts in the Bibliothèque nationale de France of Paris appeared.

The main objective of these cataloguers was, of course, identification of the main text, or texts copied in a given manuscript, accompanied by quotations of *incipits*. Codicological information was marginal, and so was that concerning decoration. On the other hand, in many cases, cataloguers provided long extracts of then unknown texts they regarded as particularly interesting. For instance, Wright's entry on the *Maṣḥafa Ḥawi* is twenty pages long (Wright 1877, 235–254), and on John of Nikiou's 'Chronicle', nine pages (Wright 1877, 300–309); Zotenberg's account of the same chronicle goes over nineteen pages (Zotenberg 1877, 223–241). One must bear in mind that these catalogues were compiled when publications of Ethiopic literature had barely begun and the catalogues actually served as anthologies of previously unknown texts.

A major cataloguing project was launched in the late 1930s to deal with the material gathered in Ethiopia and brought to France by the so-called Dakar-Djibouti Expedition (1931–1933), led by ethnographer

Marcel Griaule. The catalogue of this collection, in four volumes, was initiated by Sylvain Grébaut and finished by Stefan Strelcyn (Grébaut 1938, 1941, 1944; Strelcyn 1954).

Dillmann's, Wright's and Zotenberg's catalogues established a standard that persisted over the next century and developed only gradually to cater to new and different expectations. A few examples of recent cataloguing projects are presented below.

The first is the catalogue of the Ethiopian acquisitions of the British Library since the appearance of Wright's work, compiled by Stefan Strelcyn (1978). The material in his catalogue is grouped into sections covering items of similar content, at least as far as the main text is concerned. The sections (which resemble those found in Wright) are biblical manuscripts, apocrypha and pseudepigrapha; service books including prayers and hymns; theology *sensu strictiore*, hagiography; vocabularies and grammars (*sawāsew*), chronography; followed by magical, divinatory and medical writings (which in Ethiopic literature belong very much together), and miscellanea, such as letters and loose leaves. Strelcyn also provided indexes (as also Wright, Zotenberg, and others did). There is first a general index, and then a separate index of the names of the owners and scribes of the manuscripts, another that lists the collection by the date or estimated age of the manuscripts, and yet another for Amharic items. Strelcyn privileged the criterion of contents, that favours readers interested in specific genres, to the disadvantage of the shelfmark criterion—an unfortunate legacy of Wright and a general feature of many catalogues—which caused him to use his own numbering and to add a concordance of Strelcyn's own numbers and the shelfmarks of the library.

The description includes the following information: writing support, size, number of leaves, columns and lines, and age (as in Wright's work: all in all a few lines). The physical description of the item is somewhat fuller than that provided by his predecessor, particularly if the item is a scroll. In such cases the reader is informed about the accessories it has, such as shells, glass beads, etc., as well as whether the scroll is preserved in a cylindrical leather case (the collection catalogued by Wright did not include scrolls). For codices, sometimes the number of quires is provided, but not invariably or frequently. The palaeographical description is quite advanced: it includes what Wright provided (whether in a good hand or not, number of columns, lines per page), but also the type of script where known (i.e. whether *g*^{w}*elḥ* or *raqiq*; but see Ch. 2 § 5). The latter refinement, of course, reflects the progress in our knowledge of the history of Ethiopic script (Strelcyn's catalogue appeared before Siegbert Uhlig's study of palaeography of 1988). In addition, Strelcyn provides more information on the decoration, sometimes even identifying the subjects of miniatures and drawings where inscriptions are present.

Another difference from Wright's work, is Strelcyn's inclusion in his catalogue of references to manuscripts in other collections and bibliographical data for published texts. Self-evidently, the compilers of the classical catalogues simply did not have antecedent works to refer to for comparative purposes. Although there are quite meticulous analyses of some of the texts in Strelcyn's catalogue (for example, London, BL, Or. 2083, a 'Lectionary for the Passion Week', covering 15 pages; Strelcyn 1978, 57–71), there are no long quotations from the texts. Thus all catalogue descriptions are of equal balance and depth.

Another example of a modern catalogue is volume X of the Collegeville EMML catalogue prepared by Getatchew Haile in 1993. It covers items 4,001 to 5,000, in a total collection of 9,238 recorded items (Bausi 2007, 89). Many of the peculiarities of this catalogue arise from the character of the collection itself, for instance the lack, or irregularity, of physical descriptions, a natural consequence of the 'virtual' character of the collection, which consists of microfilms.

The description of the contents is often sketchy, but sufficiently informative. One notices that some manuscripts are described in more detail than others. This is, however, a consequence of the expansion of the collection: instead of providing a breakdown into sections of relatively well-known material (such as psalters or liturgy books), there are references to other manuscripts in the same collection, catalogued in detail in previous EMML volumes. But this is also a consequence of the choice of the cataloguer, Getatchew Haile, who allocates more or less space, more or less detailed descriptions, according to his opinion on the importance of the item.

There is no grouping of the manuscripts into biblical, liturgical manuscripts and so on, the ruling principle is *numerus currens* instead, as is expected in dealing with such a huge collection. Indexes list manuscripts according to subject matters (such as Bible, canon and civil law, etc.) for readers interested in specific matters.

The next example of cataloguing in the last century is the catalogue of the collection in the Biblioteca Medicea Laurenziana in Florence compiled by Paolo Marrassini (1987–1988). This is an impressive work.

All the metadata are collected at the beginning of the catalogue entry, not split by being put before and after the description of the contents, as in the above mentioned catalogues. The codicological information is fuller, including, for instance, data on quires and the palaeographical description which includes the characteristics of the hands of the scribes (for example, 'mano meno esperta', etc.). The description of the contents is equally excellent, with relatively long *incipits*, and lists of pertinent literature, including Russian. However, it seems that a catalogue when prepared by a passionate scholar can be 'overdone'. For instance, the entry devoted to the *Dersāna Mikā'ēl* 'Homiliary in honour of Archangel Michael' (Marrassini 1987, 77–87) grew into a small study on the various redactions of the 'Homiliary'. This is, of course, a valuable piece of scholarship, but a catalogue is not a proper place for publishing it.

Another great cataloguing achievement in the last decades of the twentieth century is the series of catalogues of German collections published in the series of the *Verzeichnis der orientalischen Handschriften in Deutschland*, and compiled by Ernst Hammerschmidt and Veronika Six (Hammerschmidt 1973, 1977a; Hammerschmidt – Six 1983; Six 1989, 1994, 1999; for a characterization of these catalogues, see Bausi 2007, 97–99).

One further example shows how the appeal of codicology has been felt in Ethiopian cataloguing too. This is the catalogue of new acquisitions by several British libraries, prepared by Steve Delamarter and Demeke Berhane (2007). Unfortunately, this work cannot be regarded as successful, because a catalogue of manuscripts cannot be provided by a codicologist lacking the necessary competence in the language and literature of the manuscripts he is cataloguing. Delamarter was clearly preoccupied with codicological analysis only, leaving the textual analysis of the contents to his collaborator, whose competence was not adequate to the task. (By contrast, all the catalogues named above were prepared by the best specialists in Ethiopian philology.) The titles of the main texts are provided but seldom a breakdown of their content. Information on decoration is misleading. There are no references to parallel manuscripts in other collections and neither editions nor literature are provided. On the other hand, the 'quire maps' were prepared meticulously (cf. also Bausi 2007, 104–106).

However, for his next cataloguing endeavour (Getatchew Haile et al. 2009), Delamarter cooperated with competent scholars and the result is much better. Perhaps this last catalogue demonstrates that in order to achieve a satisfactory description of a collection of manuscripts collaboration between textual scholars and codicologists, and, where necessary, art historians and conservators, is desirable.

Such collaboration will also be the case in preparing online catalogues. Several institutions and scholars are currently working on this type of catalogue, including the HMML at Collegeville and the Ethio-SPaRe project led by Denis Nosnitsin, Hamburg (Nosnitsin 2013a; see also Ch. 4 § 6.1). As this type of cataloguing allows for the addition of new information, and correction of earlier entries, one may expect that collaboration between cataloguer and specialists with other areas of competence will become more common.

References

d'Abbadie 1859; Bausi 2007; Beylot – Rodinson 1995; Chaîne 1912; Conti Rossini 1914; Delamarter – Demeke Berhane 2007; Dillmann 1847, 1848, 1857, 1865, 1878; Ewald 1844, 1847; Getatchew Haile 1993; Getatchew Haile et al. 2009; Grébaut 1938, 1941, 1944; Hammerschmidt 1973, 1977a; Hammerschmidt – Six 1983; Kolmodin 1916; Marrassini 1987–1988; Nosnitsin 2013a; Platt 1823; Six 1989, 1994, 1999; Strelcyn 1954, 1978; Uhlig 1988; Uhlig – Bausi 2007; Wright 1877; Zotenberg 1877.

2.5. Catalogues of Georgian manuscripts (JG–BO)

Academic research into Georgian manuscripts—about 75,000 manuscript leaves (see General introduction § 3.8)—began rather late, in the first half of the nineteenth century. The first investigations were not quite what we could characterize as catalogues, but simply notices about manuscripts sent from St Petersburg to the French Société asiatique by the Georgian prince Teimouraz; they contain nothing but an enumeration of the general content of the four manuscripts in question (Brosset 1833). Remarkably enough, in the course of the nineteenth century, all descriptions of collections of Georgian manuscripts are about manuscripts kept abroad.

In May, 1845, N. Čubinov (Čubinašvili) undertook the first examination of Georgian manuscripts preserved in the Monastery of the Holy Cross in Jerusalem. His account, which addresses but a minor number of manuscripts, is confined to transcripts of colophons and a few superficial observations; it was only published 50 years after Čubinov's sojourn in Jerusalem (Čubinašvili 1894).

In his *Anecdota sacra et profana* of 1855 (slightly revised in 1861), Constantin Tischendorf provided the first descriptions of Georgian manuscripts, including palimpsests, that were taken by him 'itinere orientali' to Leipzig. It is noteworthy that for five Greek palimpsests (his nos. VIII, IX, XII, XIII, XV, 8–13), the overwriting is still declared to be Armenian in his descriptions, a mistake corrected by Tischendorf himself in the table of content of his work ('Index Libri', xi–xii: 'rescripta sunt Georgice, non ut in textu dictum est Armeniace'). His description of Georgian manuscripts proper (Codd. Tisch. XXXIX–XLIII of the Leipzig collection; 74–75) is confined to an indication of the size and format of the manuscripts, with a short indication of their contents and their age (for example, 'satis vestustus').

In 1886 and 1888, Aleksandre Cagareli (Tsagareli) provided the first detailed descriptions of Georgian manuscripts kept on Mount Athos (Iviron), in Jerusalem and on Mount Sinai. He indicates the content, the measures, the number of leaves, the material, the date and the type of script, sometimes adding indications on a particular text (*incipits*) or scribe (part of colophons). Cagareli's work meant great progress in Georgian manuscript studies indeed, but his descriptions were still rather imprecise so that Gérard Garitte was not able to identify with Cagareli's account eighteen of the ninety-six manuscripts he saw during his re-investigation of the Georgian manuscripts of St Catherine's Monastery on Mount Sinai in 1950 (Cagareli 1886, 1888a, 1888b; Garitte 1956, see below).

The Georgian manuscripts of Jerusalem and Mount Sinai were re-investigated by Nikolaj Marr and Ivane Ǯavaxišvili (Javakhishvili) in 1902. The catalogues provided by them were published considerably later (Marr 1940, 1955; Ǯavaxišvili 1947); they give much more detailed descriptions of both the format and the contents of the manuscripts dealt with, including transcripts of larger text passages (sometimes complete texts) and colophons. It is clear from Marr's survey of the Jerusalem manuscripts that some of the items described by Cagareli were no longer present in the collection of the Monastery of the Holy Cross after this had been removed to the Greek patriarchate by the end of the nineteenth century; some of these items later re-appeared in other collections (Vienna, Österreichische Nationalbibliothek; Washington, Dumbarton Oaks: Peradze 1940, Gippert et al. 2007a). The same is true for some of the Sinai manuscripts, which are now kept in Graz, Universitätsbibliothek, or, for parts, at other places (Šaniʒe 1929; Outtier 1972; Imnaišvili 2004).

The investigation of Georgian manuscripts preserved within Georgia was initiated by the beginning of the twentieth century when Tevdore Žordania, Mose Ǯanašvili (Džanašvili, Janashvili), Ekvtime Taq̇aišvili (Takajšvili) and David Ḳaričašvili published the first catalogues of the collections of the former 'Ecclesiastical Museum' (now the 'A' collection of the National Centre for Manuscripts, Tbilisi; Žordania – Ǯanašvili 1902–1908) and the 'Society for the Promotion of Literacy among the Georgian Population' (now the 'S' collection of the National Centre for Manuscripts, Tbilisi; Taq̇aišvili 1902–1912 and Ḳaričašvili 1905). These descriptions remained rather superficial and unbalanced even though they added valuable types of information such as, for example, the identification of water-marks of paper manuscripts, and sometimes even full collations of the texts contained; for example, Taq̇aišvili provides a full account of the 'History of Kartli' in his description of manuscript no. 74, including ninety pages concerning textual variants (Taq̇aišvili 1902, 1908 and 1912).

In his catalogues of the Georgian manuscripts of Jerusalem and Mount Athos, Robert Pierpont Blake was the first to pay real attention to a codicological description of the manuscripts, including information as to their binding, quires, dimensions of the written area, ink, and punctuation. He very briefly indicates the content of the colophons but does not give their text in full. For each text, he provides an *incipit*, indicates the presumptive model if the text is a translation, and bibliographical information if the text has been published (Blake 1922–1923, 1924, 1925–1926, 1932a, 1932b, 1933).

Full codicological descriptions can be found in the catalogue of the 'literary' Georgian manuscripts of Mount Sinai worked out by Garitte in 1950. Garitte adds indications about ruling and ornamentation and provides the full text of the copyists' notes and colophons as well as a bibliography of each manuscript; for the texts, he gives titles, *incipits* and *desinits*. He also adds a very detailed index. In order not to duplicate the work undertaken by Marr and Ǯavaxišvili, he confined himself with the description of non-strictly liturgical manuscripts as these were dealt with in detail by his predecessors (Garitte 1956).

Even in the twentieth century, we still find catalogues with more simple descriptions, especially for minor collections in Europe. This is true, for example, for Frédéric Macler's and Ekvtime Taq̇aišvili's descriptions of the Georgian manuscripts in the Bibliothèque nationale de France (Macler 1908; Taq̇aišvili

1933), Paul Peeters' and David Barrett's accounts of the Georgian manuscripts in Oxford (Peeters 1912; Barrett 1973, 305–354), Jan Braun's account of the Georgian manuscripts in Poland (Braun 1958), or Gregor Peradze's catalogue of the Georgian manuscripts in Austria (1940). More detailed investigations have been provided for the Leningrad / St Petersburg collection (Orbeli 1956; Cerаʒe – Xoperia 2009; Ceraʒe forthcoming), the Georgian manuscripts in Germany (Assfalg 1963a), or the Georgian manuscripts in the Mingana collection at Birmingham (Garitte 1960).

In 1946, the Georgian Academy of Sciences initiated the project of a comprehensive cataloguing (in Georgian) of the Georgian manuscripts kept in Georgia and abroad. So far, a total of twenty two volumes describing the four major collections of the former K. Kekelidze Institute of Manuscripts (now styled the National Centre of Manuscripts) at Tbilisi have been published ('H' collection: six volumes, Kutatelaʒe – Ḳasraʒe 1946; Kutatelaʒe 1951; Šarašiʒe 1948; Meparišvili 1949; Meṭreveli 1950; Ḳasraʒe et al. 1953; 'Q' collection: two volumes, Meṭreveli et al. 1957–1958; Bregaʒe et al. 1958; 'S' collection: seven volumes, Bregaʒe et al. 1959; Bakraʒe et al. 1961; Enukiʒe et al. 1963; Bregaʒe et al. 1965, 1967, 1969, 1973a; 'A' collection: six volumes, Bregaʒe et al. 1973b, 1976, 1980, 1985, 1986, 2004). These catalogues provide precise codicological descriptions throughout, including detailed indexes, but no reproductions. The same is true for the catalogues of the Historical Archive at Tbilisi (two volumes, Ḳaḳabaʒe – Gagošiʒe 1949–1950), the Marx Library at Tbilisi (Čiḳvašvili 1964), the Historico-Ethnographical Museum at Kutaisi (two volumes, Niḳolaʒe 1953–1964), the Axalcixe Museum (Abulaʒe et al. 1987), and the Museum of Gori (Bregaʒe – Ḳaxabrišvili 2002), but also for the catalogues of foreign collections that were published in Georgia (Mount Sinai: three volumes, Meṭreveli et al. 1978; Ç̣anḳievi – J̌ġamaia 1979; Gvaramia et al. 1987; Mount Athos: Axobaʒe et al. 1986). The catalogue of the Georgian manuscripts discovered among the 'New Finds' of St Catherine's Monastery on Mount Sinai (Aleksiʒe et al. 2005; published in three languages: English, Greek, and Georgian) has been the first to add sample images of each manuscript described.

Some collections still want detailed descriptions. This is true, for example, for the collections of the museum of Mestia in Svanetia (but cf. Silogava 1986, 41–60). Among foreign collections, we are still missing a thorough account of the Georgian manuscripts kept in the Matenadaran in Yerevan, Armenia, or in the Armenian patriarchate in Jerusalem (but cf. Outtier 1986).

References

Abulaʒe et al. 1987; Aleksiʒe et al. 2005; Assfalg 1963a; Assfalg – Molitor 1962; Axobaʒe et al. 1986; Bakraʒe et al. 1961; Barrett 1973; Blake 1922–1923, 1924, 1925–1926, 1932ab, 1933; Braun 1958; Bregaʒe – Ḳaxabrišvili 2002; Bregaʒe et al. 1958, 1959, 1965, 1967, 1969, 1973a, 1973b, 1976, 1980, 1985, 1986, 2004; Brosset 1833; Cagareli 1886, 1888a, 1888b, 1889; Ç̣anḳievi – J̌ġamaia 1979; Ceraʒe – Xoperia 2009; Ceraʒe forthcoming; Čiḳvašvili 1964; Čubinašvili 1894; Enukiʒe et al. 1963; Garitte 1956, 1960; Gippert et al. 2007a; Gvaramia et al. 1987; Imnaišvili 2004; Ḳaḳabaʒe – Gagošiʒe 1949–1950; Ḳaričašvili 1905; Ḳasraʒe et al. 1953; Kavtaria 2002; Kutatelaʒe 1951; Kutatelaʒe – Ḳasraʒe 1946; Macler 1908; Marr 1940, 1955; Meparišvili 1949; Meṭreveli 1950; Meṭreveli et al. 1957–1958, 1978; Meṭreveli et al. 1978; Niḳolaʒe 1953–1964; Orbeli 1956; Outtier 1972, 1986; Peeters 1912; Peradze 1940; Šaniʒe 1929; Šarašiʒe 1948; Silogava 1986; Taqaišvili 1902–1912, 1933; Tischendorf 1855, 1861; J̌avaxišvili 1947; Žordania – J̌anašvili 1902–1908.

2.6. Catalogues of Greek manuscripts (ABi)

The *Répertoire des bibliothèques et des catalogues de manuscrits grecs* published in 1995 by Jean-Marie Olivier listed some 2,500 catalogues covering the description of over 65,000 Greek manuscripts surviving in the libraries around the world (see also General introduction § 3.9). These figures concern only parchment and paper manuscripts, as Greek papyrus codices and scrolls (and fragments of parchment codices) are generally preserved in separate collections described by papyrologists (for a description of a papyrus see, e.g., Ch. 3 § 3.6).

Amongst the oldest 'catalogues' of Greek manuscripts is the very famous mediaeval inventory of the treasury and the library of the monastery of St John the Theologian of Patmos made in the year 1200 (Astruc 1981; Bompaire 1979; cf. Ch. 4 § 1). Although this document is hardly more than a list of manuscripts that was primarily established to register the movable property of the monastery, it already presents some of the general features that are to be found in modern catalogues: general content of the volume, material (parchment or paper), and in some cases, details on the age and the size of the manuscript or on a precious binding. During the Renaissance, after the arrival of Greek manuscripts in the west and the consequent organization of the great European libraries, systematic inventories of Greek manuscripts in these libraries were established; a good example of this type of library inventory was compiled in 1544 by Angelos Vergikios and Konstantinos Palaiokappas for the Greek manuscripts of the Royal Library installed by François I at Fontainebleau near Paris (Omont 1889). Today, such inventories have mainly a documentary value and serve for reconstructing the history of collections and libraries.

The first modern catalogues appeared in the late seventeenth century with the catalogue of the Imperial Library in Vienna by Peter Lambeck, and most notably in the early eighteenth century with the undertaking of the Maurist Bernard de Montfaucon who laid the foundations of modern Greek catalography with his *Bibliotheca Coisliniana olim Segueriana* published in 1715. It indeed provides a much more minute description of the content of the manuscripts. Authors and texts are identified, with their Greek title, *incipit*, and beginning folium; comments on the physical state of the text or on the version present in the manuscript are sometimes added; significant portions of unknown texts are even edited in some cases. Montfaucon's main innovation, however, as the founder of Greek palaeography with the publication of his *Palaeographia graeca* in 1708, lies in a special attention to the dating of manuscripts and the transcription of their colophons (Irigoin 1998; see also Ch. 2 § 7). Material description, however, is limited to the distinction between paper and parchment. Between the eighteenth century catalogues of the Biblioteca Medicea Laurenziana in Florence by Angelo Maria Bandini or that of the Royal Library in Madrid by Juan de Iriarte and the late nineteenth-century catalogues of Mount Athos by Spyridōn Lampros or of Mount Sinai by Viktor Gardthausen, the basic data found in Greek catalogues remained the same, although the formal presentation could change from one catalogue to the other. All these catalogues served fundamentally the same bibliographical purpose: making accessible to scholars the sources they needed, and helping them find the texts they were looking for in manuscripts and libraries.

With the first catalogue of the collection of *Vaticani graeci* manuscripts in the Vatican Library published in 1923, Greek cataloguing enters a new phase. As a preface to the book, one can find a short text entitled *Leges quas procuratores Bybliothecae Vaticanae in codicibus graecis recensendis sibi constituerunt* which has had a lasting influence on Greek cataloguers (Mercati – Franchi de' Cavalieri 1923, xi–xv. The *Leges* are reprinted at the beginning of the subsequent volumes of the *Codices Vaticani graeci* collection. They are also reproduced and commented on in Devreesse 1954, 278–285). This set of rules gives the general features of a tripartite description of the manuscript: 1. Summary description of the external features of a manuscript; 2. Inventory of authors and texts; 3. Exposition of the material aspects of the book and of its history, which are for the first time fully taken into account. These rules have been systematized and redeveloped by others (Richard [M.] 1954; Canart 1980), and with minor modifications, and more or less analytical versions depending on the idiosyncrasies of each cataloguer, this model has been adopted by most enterprises of Greek cataloguing since the early twentieth century, for example for the new catalogue of the Österreichische Nationalbibliothek in Vienna made between 1961–1994 by Herbert Hunger and his team.

Since the publication of the first edition of the *Répertoire des bibliothèques et des catalogues de manuscrits grecs* by Marcel Richard in 1948 (Richard [M.] 1948 [1958[2]]), which listed only 529 catalogues, the cataloguing of Greek manuscripts has undergone an exponential proliferation over the last decades. Most collections in the east and the west have already been inventoried and the actual effort is concentrated on producing new and more detailed catalogues of formerly described collections. This is possible thanks to all the reference works that have been developed over the last century for the identification of texts and authors, but also repertories of copyists (Gamillscheg et al. 1981, 1989, 1997), rulings (Sautel 1995), watermarks (for example Harlfinger – Harlfinger 1974, 1980), etc., that allow a more accurate description of the manuscript as a physical object. These repertories are not specific to Greek catalography, although some of these repertories, like Harlfinger – Harlfinger 1974, 1980, have been made by using specifically Greek manuscripts.

At the same time, specialized catalogues are being produced that are dedicated to manuscripts according to content (for example the enterprise of cataloguing Byzantine musical manuscripts by the Institute of Byzantine Musicology in Athens has produced, since 1975, seven volumes entitled *Τὰ Χειρόγραφα*

Βυζαντινῆς Μουσικῆς (Stathis 1975, 1976, 1993, 2006; Chaldaiaki 2004; Balageorgos – Crete 2008; Giannopoulos 2008), which cover the collections of different monasteries on Mount Athos, Meteora, Sinai, England and the island of Hydra; the project on Byzantine law manuscripts by the Max Planck-Institut für Europäische Rechtsgeschichte in Frankfurt-am-Main has produced two volumes entitled *Repertorium der Handschriften des byzantinischen Rechts* (RHBR) since 1995), place of origin (for example Kotzampasē 2004, on manuscripts from Asia Minor), date (for example on the dated manuscripts of the thirteenth and fourteenth centuries four different series of catalogues have been produced on the manuscripts of Vatican, Italy, England (Turyn) and France (Astruc, Géhin, Förstel)), palaeography (for example Orsini 2005 on biblical uncial manuscripts both on papyrus and parchment), codicological features (for example Crisci 1990 on palimpsest manuscripts; catalogues of decorated and illuminated manuscripts are also very common, see also Ch. 4 § 3.2), or just a specific author whose works are transmitted by manuscripts (for example, on John Chrysostom, the most prolific author in Greek manuscripts, see the *Codices Chrysostomici graeci*, with seven volumes published by the Institut de recherche et d'histoire des textes in Paris since 1968). Another example for classical Greek is the *Aristoteles Graecus* project; a first volume was published by Moraux 1976, and the project is currently pursued online (<http://beta.teuchos.uni-hamburg.de/projekt>). All these catalogues of a particular type offer different gateways to the collections of manuscripts, but also different angles of view on the manuscripts according to the field of specialization. A catalogue of dated manuscripts will analyse in detail the manuscript as a material and historical object accurately describing the colophon and the script, and more generally all the physical and historical aspects, as each dated manuscript is meant to serve on a reference scale for dating other manuscripts, and every physical detail can be relevant; conversely a catalogue on a specific author will put the emphasis on the state of the text in each particular manuscript, as the catalogue is to serve as a reference tool for the text editor.

New issues in Greek catalography

In 2007, Patrick Andrist published a new catalogue of the collection of Greek manuscripts in the Burgerbibliothek in Bern (Andrist 2007a). This 'experimental' catalogue of a new type, as the author himself describes it, comes with a booklet of some fifty pages named *Règles de catalogage*, where Andrist exposes his approach to cataloguing (Andrist 2003; see also Ch. 4 § 4). The size of the collection (only forty manuscripts) offered indeed the ideal opportunity to experiment a practical application of the theoretical principles that had been developed a few years earlier by Peter Gumbert around the concept of codicological unit (Gumbert 2004). The main innovation of this catalogue lies in the fact that each description is structured, not around the codex as a whole, but around the codicological unit, which becomes the heart of the description. In itself the understanding of the structure and stratigraphy of the manuscript, i.e. the different phases of production of the manuscript and of its use and circulation, is not new and many modern catalogues had already in some way or another tried to account for it. This catalogue does however offer a complete reversal of the viewpoint giving priority to the archaeological reconstruction of the physical object through its codicological features over a more traditional description of the codex that begins by its textual contents. To what extent this experiment can be applied more generally to cataloguing manuscripts remains an open question, but it has generated some challenging reflections on the process of cataloguing, and is an incentive to account more accurately for the structure of the codex and its history.

Another question in the spotlight in recent years, which goes far beyond the field of Greek manuscripts, is the impact of the numeric revolution on cataloguing. The issues at hand can be grasped by browsing some recent publications on the subject (Fabian – Wagner 2007; Crisci – Maniaci 2010; Rehbein et al. 2009; Fischer [F.] et al. 2010). It is still too early to draw up a general policy regarding online cataloguing of Greek manuscripts. The project of a new catalogue of the Greek manuscripts in the Bayerische Staatsbibliothek in Munich started in 2002 offers an interesting example of some general trends. While the manuscripts are digitized and the images put online in a digital library, the descriptions of the manuscripts are concurrently available in two versions, a printed version and an electronic version on *Manuscripta mediaevalia*, the German web portal for manuscripts (*Katalog der griechischen Handschriften der Bayerischen Staatsbibliothek München*, Wiesbaden, five volumes published since 2002; Hajdú 2002, 2003, 2012; Tiftixoglu 2004; Molin Pradel 2013; <http://www.manuscripta-mediaevalia.de/>). The two descriptions have the same content but differ in style: the printed catalogue follows the traditional presentation, while the descriptions in the electronic version are structured according to codicological units. Electronic cataloguing has also opened the possibility to larger scale collaborative enterprises and other projects have been launched on a national level, like the *Manoscritti Greci d'Italia* project for Italy (<http://www.nuovabibliotecamanoscritta.it/MaGI/index.html>), *e-codices* for Switzerland (<http://www.e-codices.unifr.ch/>), or the *Greek Manuscripts in Sweden project* (<http://www.manuscripta.se/>). As a result the researcher around the world has access at the same time to the virtual object and its description. However this general effort is fragmented and the different enterprises are not always compatible; so the issues at hand concern more generally the way to structure all this web input and make it readily available and searchable by scholars. A collective reflexion has started in this field, among other initiatives around the database *Pinakes*: textes et manuscrits grecs (<http://pinakes.irht.cnrs.fr/>), which aims originally at referencing the texts that are contained in all Greek manuscripts around the world; the aim of this reflection is not to unify the description of manuscripts in existing databases but to interrelate databases by cross-referencing their electronic data.

References

Andrist 2003, 2007a; Astruc 1981; Balageorgos – Crete 2008; Bompaire 1979; Canart 1980; Chaldaiaki 2004; Crisci 1990; Crisci – Maniaci 2010; Devreesse 1954; Fabian – Wagner 2007; Fischer [F.] et al. 2010; Gamillscheg et al. 1981–1997; Giannopoulos 2008; Gumbert 2004; Hajdú 2002, 2003, 2012; Harlfinger – Harlfinger 1974–1980; Hunger 1961; Hunger – Kresten 1969, 1976; Hunger – Lackner 1992; Hunger et al. 1984; Irigoin 1998; Kotzampasē 2004; Mercati – Franchi de' Cavalieri 1923; Molin Pradel 2013; Montfaucon 1708, 1715; Moraux 1976; Olivier 1995; Omont 1889; Orsini 2005; Rehbein et al. 2009; Richard [M.] 1948 [1958[2]], 1954; Sautel 1995; Stathis 1975, 1976, 1993, 2006; Tiftixoglu 2004. Web sources: *Aristoteles Graecus* at TEUCHOS <http://beta.teuchos.uni-hamburg.de/projekt>, last access May 2014; *e-codices* <http://www.e-codices.unifr.ch/>, last access May 2014; *Greek Manuscripts in Sweden* <http://www.manuscripta.se/>, last access May 2014; *Manuscripta mediaevalia* <http://www.manuscripta-mediaevalia.de>, last access May 2014; *Manoscritti Greci d'Italia* <http://www.nuovabibliotecamanoscritta.it/MaGI/index.html>, last access May 2014; *Pinakes* <http://pinakes.irht.cnrs.fr/>, last access May 2014.

2.7. Catalogues of manuscripts in Hebrew characters (DSk)

Throughout the centuries, Jews used Hebrew characters to write down a variety of languages. Primary, of course, was Hebrew. There are, however, Hebrew-character manuscripts containing texts in the dialect of Middle High German known as Yiddish, Castilian (often referred to as Judezmo or Ladino), Aramaic, Arabic, Persian, Greek, Old French, Italian, Tatar, and others. These languages are thus called 'Judaeo-' languages, such as Judaeo-Arabic, Judaeo-Persian, Judaeo-Italian, and so on. The cataloguer of a large collection of Hebrew manuscripts must therefore be prepared to deal with range of different languages. For example, the Christian Hebraist Giovanni Bernardo De Rossi (1742–1831) put together one of the most important collections of Hebrew manuscripts, now found in the Biblioteca Palatina in Parma. De Rossi published a catalogue of his own collection, at the end of which he describes manuscripts in Hebrew characters, but containing texts in Italian, Spanish, German and Polish (De Rossi 1803–1804). It should also be pointed out that the Hebrew script itself can also be an issue for cataloguers. The ancient Hebrew script used in the period of the First Temple in Jerusalem fell out of use soon after the return from the Babylonian Exile, during the fifth century BCE. The script which replaced it was actually an Aramaic script, variations of which we still use today. A variant of the ancient Hebrew script, though, is still used by the Samaritans (even in their newsletter) and is found in mediaeval manuscripts, sometimes even as marginalia in Judaeo-Arabic texts.

Hebrew-character manuscripts were produced over a long chronological period of time and in quite diverse geographical areas (the earliest surviving Hebrew-character manuscripts appear to be the Aramaic papyri from Elephantine in southern Egypt, dating from the fifth century BCE. Hebrew manuscripts continued to be produced up through the twentieth century). This resulted in a large variety of manuscript production techniques and codicological and palaeographical characteristics to which the cataloguer must pay attention. Hebrew-character manuscripts were copied throughout the Middle East, in the areas now known as Iran, Iraq, Azerbaijan, Syria, Israel, Lebanon, Turkey, and Yemen; and in North Africa, in Egypt, Libya, Tunisia and Morocco. (The furthest east that such manuscripts were produced was in Kaifeng, China, in the sixteenth and seventeenth centuries. But these perhaps can be set aside as a curiosity. Nevertheless, early Judaeo-Persian manuscripts from the eighth century found in China's western desert indicate that such manuscripts did find their way quite far to the east. As a matter of curiosity, it should also be mentioned that there exist a number of early mediaeval Jewish texts in Arabic characters, including transliterations of Hebrew texts, mostly biblical, into Arabic script. These manuscripts indicate the high degree of cultural assimilation found among some groups of Jews at the time.) Hebrew-character manuscripts were, of course, also produced throughout Europe, in Spain, France, Italy, England, Germany, Austria, the Netherlands, the Balkans, Poland, Russia, and the Crimea. With this in mind, it is possible to raise the question as to whether or not a manuscript produced in ninth-century Italy, where the Jewish community goes back to the time of the Roman Empire, or sixteenth-century Prague should be considered an oriental manuscript, particularly if the language is, let us say, German/Yiddish, even if it is in Hebrew characters. This question, however, belongs perhaps more to a discussion of the boundaries of European identity than to a handbook on manuscript cataloguing.

The earliest surviving catalogues of Hebrew-character manuscripts are book lists found in the Cairo Geniza. (Almost all of the Geniza book lists were published in Allony 2006. On the Cairo Geniza, see Ch. 1 § 9.1.2 and below.) More than a hundred such lists have survived, most of them having been written in the eleventh to thirteenth centuries. These lists record the contents of private libraries, booksellers' collections, synagogue libraries, estate collections, and so on. The books listed may be organized by subject, author, or even by the shelf on which they are to be found in the library. Some book lists record whether or not the book is bound and what sort of binding it has (many books in this period were left unbound with the signed quires lying in a pile on the shelf).

As with a number of oriental manuscript traditions, systematic cataloguing of Hebrew-character manuscripts in Europe began in the late seventeenth and eighteenth centuries when Hebrew manuscripts were catalogued together with other languages such as Arabic or Syriac which made up a library's oriental collection. It appears that the first collection to be catalogued was that of the Rijksuniversiteit in Leiden which had received the manuscript collections of Josephus Scaliger and Levinus Warner. Catalogues of this collection were published in 1674 (Spanheim 1674) and again in 1716 (Senguerdius et al. 1716). This collection was catalogued again a number of times afterwards by Moritz Steinschneider in 1858 and by Albert van der Heide in 1977. An inventory of the collection was published by Jan Just Witkam in 2007 (most of the Hebrew manuscripts are listed in volume I). Such recataloguing over the years is typical of a number of the larger collections of Hebrew manuscripts. Also to be mentioned is the catalogue of the oriental manuscripts held by the Bibliothèque nationale de France in Paris, published in 1739 (Melot 1739). The basis for the Hebrew section was the work done in 1689 by a converted Jew, Louis de Compiegne, and then revised by Abbé Eusèbe Renaudot. In 1752, a catalogue of the oriental manuscripts held in the Biblioteca Medicea Laurenziana in Florence was published by Antonio Biscioni (1752). The Maronite cleric Giuseppe Assemani and his nephew Stefano published in 1758 and 1759 a catalogue of the Syriac and Hebrew manuscripts held by the Biblioteca Apostolica Vaticana, most of which Giuseppe Assemani himself had acquired for the library (Assemani – Assemani 1758–1759). The descriptions of the Hebrew manuscripts were actually prepared by the *scriptor hebraicus* Giovanni Costanzi. This printed catalogue was preceded by handwritten lists of Hebrew manuscripts compiled in the seventeenth century by Carlo Federigo Borromeo, Giovanni Battista Jonah and Giulio Morosini. In 1693, the Bodleian Library at Oxford acquired the Pococke and Huntington collections of oriental manuscripts, which included manuscripts in Hebrew and Judaeo-Arabic. A catalogue of these collections was published by Johannes Uri in 1787 (Uri 1787).

These early catalogues were prepared by individuals who were not great scholars of Hebrew literature, to say the least, and the cataloguing descriptions are often of limited value. For example, the Assemani catalogue of the Vatican manuscripts was seen by contemporary readers 'to include a considerable number of errors of transcription, identification and interpretation, and even forgeries' (Proverbio 2008). An exception to this would be De Rossi's catalogue (De Rossi 1803–1804). Nevertheless, these catalogues were of considerable historical importance, for through their descriptions and transcriptions of sample texts, they exposed European scholars to Hebrew texts for which they had few sources of information.

By the middle of the nineteenth century, however, this situation changed, as Jewish scholars who were part of the movement known as *Wissenschaft des Judentums* began to take part in cataloguing manuscript collections. These individuals often combined a rabbinic education with university training. As opposed to the earlier catalogues, the catalogues produced by these scholars focused mainly on Hebrew-character manuscripts, although sometimes including Arabic-character manuscripts of Jewish texts. Moritz Steinschneider, the father of modern Jewish bibliography, among his many publications also published a series of Hebrew manuscript catalogues. These include catalogues of the Hebrew manuscript collections held by the libraries in Leiden, Munich, Hamburg and Berlin (Steinschneider 1858, 1875, 1878, 1897). His catalogue of the printed Hebrew books in the Bodleian Library also contains some cataloguing comments on some manuscripts at the end (Steinschneider 1852–1860). In this period, catalogues were made for some of the largest collections of Hebrew manuscripts at the time, those of the Bibliothèque nationale de France in Paris, the Bodleian Library in Oxford and the library of the British Museum. Work on a new catalogue of Hebrew manuscripts held by the Bibliothèque nationale de France was begun by Salomon Munk in 1838. When his eyesight failed in 1850, the effort was continued by Joseph Derenbourg and then completed in 1865 by Hermann Zotenberg who described the Samaritan manuscripts (Zotenberg 1866). Adolf Neubauer began re-cataloguing the Hebrew manuscripts of the Bodleian Library in 1868 and the first volume of the catalogue appeared in 1886 (Neubauer 1886; a supplement to this catalogue was also published, Beit-Arié – May 1994). A second volume, completed by Arthur Cowley, appeared in 1906 (Neubauer – Cowley 1906). The collection of the British Museum (now the British Library) was described by George Margoliouth in three volumes published from 1899–1915. A fourth volume of the catalogue prepared by Jacob Leveen appeared in 1935. Even though the title of his catalogue indicates that it includes the Samaritan manuscripts, they were actually not catalogued until Alan D. Crown's catalogue was published in 1998.

These catalogues are characterized by accurate, sometimes quite lengthy descriptions of the manuscripts' contents. Colophons and owners' marks are quoted and information on obscure authors or individuals is provided when available. Codicological information is generally limited to number of folia, a general description of quiring, the material of the manuscript and size. One problem in these catalogues is a lack of uniformity in palaeographic terminology. Some catalogues were also organized by subject and so re-numbered the manuscripts in their collections. While this is a convenience for users who are interested in a particular field, it has created a significant amount of confusion over the years. In addition to the collections mentioned, many other collections, often smaller ones, have been catalogued. Information concerning collections of Hebrew-character manuscripts and their catalogues can be found in Richler 1994.

Recent years have seen some important developments in the methods of cataloguing Hebrew-character manuscripts. Among these is the increased use of teamwork in cataloguing large manuscript collections. Hebrew-character manuscripts contain texts from an extremely large variety of subjects and genres, in numerous languages. One individual cannot be expected to acquire the knowledge required in order to provide accurate and in-depth cataloguing. Furthermore, a team of cataloguers/researchers can deal with a large collection in a much shorter period of time than the many decades required when cataloguing was done by an individual or two. Two collections recently catalogued in this way are the Biblioteca Apostolica Vaticana (Richler et al. 2008) and the Biblioteca Palatina in Parma (Richler – Beit-Arié 2001). Both catalogues were edited by Benjamin Richler, who served for many years as the director of the Institute for Microfilms of Hebrew Manuscripts (IMHM, see below) located in the National Library of Israel in Jerusalem. The IMHM has a team of such specialists who contributed to these catalogues. The teamwork, however, went further. The expert codicological and palaeographical descriptions were provided by Malachi Beit-Arie, who has served many years as the director of the Hebrew Paleography Project.

It is relevant at this point to mention that there are still no published detailed, systematic catalogues for some of the largest collections of Hebrew-character manuscripts. These include the collections of the Jewish Theological Seminary in New York, the Firkovitch collections held by the Russian National Library in St Petersburg, the Russian State Library in Moscow (which among other collections holds the very important Guenzburg collection), the Vernadsky Library in Kiev, and the National Library of Israel (for some of these collections there do exist handlists, partial type-written descriptions, or partial descriptions in Internet databases).

The second development in recent and on-going cataloguing efforts is the use of digitized databases accessible on the Internet. The first and perhaps most important digital database I would like to describe is that of the IMHM mentioned above. The IMHM was founded in 1950 for the purpose of gathering microfilms of manuscripts in Hebrew characters from all manuscript collections around the world, a sort of literary ingathering of the exiles. In 1963, the Institute became part of the National Library in Jerusalem. Sitting in the Institute, one can easily move around the world, going from library to library, bringing together manuscripts in a way which would be quite difficult if one had physically to visit the libraries holding them. In addition to searching out Hebrew-character manuscripts and making microfilms, the IMHM also began to catalogue the manuscripts based on the microfilm images it had received. For many years, the cataloguing information was kept in a card catalogue. When the National Library began to digitize its card catalogues a number of years ago, the Institute also began to convert its cataloguing information to digital format and to add all new cataloguing data directly into a digital database called ALEPH, much in the form of free text fields. The result of this effort is that today there is a digital record for nearly every Hebrew-character manuscript in the world. The cataloguing records are not all uniform. There were years when the IMHM took in thousands of microfilms and the records were necessarily done in a cursory fashion. Many records are stubs, labelled as temporary records, and may only contain author or title information, or a brief description of the manuscript. On the other hand, there are many manuscripts which have quite full cataloguing information. This database is now accessible on the Internet by way of the National Library of Israel's website (<http://www.nli.org.il>). The IMHM can also thus provide us with some rough statistics. According to their microfilm collection, there are more than 86,000 Hebrew-character manuscripts (not including *geniza* fragments), which are held by more than 700 public libraries and private manuscript collections.

The second Internet database to be described is concerned with the manuscripts found in the Cairo Geniza (on the 'Cairo Geniza' see Ch. 1 § 9.1.2, on the Jewish *geniza* tradition see also Ch. 3 § 3.21). The Ben Ezra Synagogue was first built in the middle of the tenth century and, after various re-buildings and renovations, still stands today. The manuscript fragments placed in its *geniza* were not buried for the most part and were preserved by the dry Egyptian climate and the continuous use of the synagogue. The congregation's reverence for the written word was not limited to sacred texts. They threw into the *geniza* bits and pieces of almost anything that was written. The Cairo Geniza thus contained fragments of a very wide variety of texts in a diversity of languages and scripts, reflecting the dynamic religious and intellectual world of the mediaeval Jewish community in Egypt. It also had a very large amount of documentary material from which the daily life, politics and business activity of the community can be reconstructed. Pieces of autograph manuscripts by famous individuals such as Maimonides are to be found together with someone else's (eleventh-century) shopping list. (There has been a recent spate of publications concerning the Cairo Geniza. For an overall description, one may consult Reif 2000; Hoffman – Cole 2011.)

This Geniza was emptied out by various individuals at the end of the nineteenth century, most notably by Solomon Schechter of Cambridge University, and the manuscript fragments have been spread around the world, with the largest collections to be found in the Cambridge University Library, the Jewish Theological Seminary in New York, Oxford, the British Library and dozens of other public and private collections. There are approximately 250,000 fragments, most consisting of one to ten folia, although there are some having dozens, even over a hundred folia. Cataloguing of the various Geniza collections has been rather sporadic, although a few libraries, such as Oxford or Cambridge (for parts of its collection), do have detailed printed catalogues.

Albert Friedberg of Toronto established the Friedberg Genizah Project in 1999 with the aim of encouraging and organizing research in the field. Out of this has come a very sophisticated website on which are being placed high-quality digital images of almost all of the Cairo Geniza fragments together with cataloguing and bibliographical information, transcriptions and translations (access through the portal <http://www.jewishmanuscripts.org>). The cataloguing program developed for the project entails digital encoding of a large number of details, including many elements of the physical description of a fragment, its content, and palaeographical and codicological elements. This allows for complex searches of the database. Furthermore, the website is designed to encourage communication and cooperation among scholars of Cairo Geniza manuscripts with a number of ways for users to add information to the site, including a forum for discussion, making the database a shared project of scholars.

There was a second important *geniza* in Old Cairo, that of the Karaite Synagogue. This synagogue had a library and the *geniza* seems to have been used mostly to store its worn-out books. This *geniza* thus for the most part contained literary manuscripts, with a significant percentage of them being large manuscripts (up to 1,005 folia). Most of these manuscripts were removed in 1863 by Abraham Firkovitch, a Crimean

Karaite born in Lutsk. The manuscripts were subsequently sold by Firkovitch's family to the Imperial Public Library in St Petersburg (now the Russian National Library). Abraham Firkovitch actually acquired manuscripts from a number of sources during his trip to the Middle East, but the vast bulk of what became to be known as the Second Firkovitch Collection apparently came from the *geniza* of the Karaite Synagogue in Old Cairo. Firkovitch collected the manuscripts of his first collection (also sold to the Imperial Library) during an earlier trip through the Caucasus and Crimea (on the formation of Firkovitch's collections, see Elkin – Shapira 2003). The Firkovitch Collections have been divided by the Russian National Library into several sections (a brief description of the divisions of the collection may be found in Sklare 2003, 895, 905-908). The largest part of the collection is that of the sections containing Judaeo-Arabic and Arabic materials, having nearly 10,000 shelfmarks. This is by far the largest gathering of Judaeo-Arabic materials, mostly from the tenth to fifteenth centuries. This collection is extremely important as most of the works contained in its manuscripts are unknown (or nearly unknown) to scholarship. A considerable number are *unica*. From the Stalin period until glasnost, these collections were virtually *terra incognita*, closed to western scholars, until they, too, were microfilmed and made available in Jerusalem. The daunting but essential task of cataloguing this collection was taken up by a team of researchers of the Center for the Study of Judaeo-Arabic Culture and Literature, a unit of the Ben-Zvi Institute for the Study of Jewish Communities in the East in Jerusalem. The cataloguing records of this team are entered into both the ALEPH database of the IMHM and the Friedberg Genizah Project database. Up to the present, approximately 3,500 manuscripts have been catalogued.

The final digital cataloguing project to be described is concerned with what has been called the 'European Genizah'. In the mediaeval period and the renaissance, folia taken from early European Hebrew manuscripts were used for binding notarial files and were also glued together to make a kind of 'cardboard' used in book bindings. Projects have been set up in a number of countries to recover these fragments. And indeed, thousands of such manuscripts have been identified in various libraries and collections in Austria, England, France, Germany, Hungary, Italy, Poland, Slovakia, Spain, Switzerland and the Czech Republic. For many years, the national projects worked more or less independently of one another, some establishing their own databases or inventories, while others are in a less advanced stage. A network called 'Books within Books' (<http://www.hebrewmanuscript.com>) was established in 2007 in order to bring together all of the separate initiatives concerned with the 'European Genizah'. Among its activities, this network is setting up an online database which will be accessible to registered users. The network is coordinated by Judith Olszowy-Schlanger of the École Pratique des Hautes Études, Sorbonne.

We have thus gone from the beginnings of the cataloguing of Hebrew-character manuscripts in the eleventh century to the new possibilities of cataloguing made available to us in the twenty-first century. And all of this is but an aid to help us understand the remnants left to us of the cultural world of people writing in Hebrew characters in the tenth, or perhaps fifteenth, centuries.

References

Allony 2006; Assemani – Assemani 1758–1759; Beit-Arié – May 1994; Biscioni 1752; Crown 1998; De Rossi 1803–1804; Elkin – Shapira 2003; Heide 1977; Hoffman – Cole 2011; Leveen 1935; Margoliouth 1899–1915; Melot 1739; Neubauer 1886; Neubauer – Cowley 1906; Proverbio 2008; Reif 2000; Richler 1994; Richler et al. 2008; Richler – Beit-Arié 2001; Senguerdius et al. 1716; Sklare 2003; Spanheim 1674; Steinschneider 1852–1860, 1858, 1875, 1878, 1897; Uri 1787; Van der Heide 1977; Witkam 2007; Zotenberg 1866. Web sources: *Books within Books* <http://www.hebrewmanuscript.com>, last access October 2014; National Library of Israel <http://www.nli.org.il>, last access October 2014; The Friedberg Jewish Manuscript Society <http://www.jewishmanuscripts.org/>, last access October 2014.

2.7.1 Types of catalogues of Hebrew manuscripts (JdB–MTO)

It is well known that it was in the early 1950s that the foundations of modern codicology were laid and the range of the discipline defined. Alphonse Dain (1896–1964), who first coined the term 'codicology' in 1944, intended it to include the history of manuscripts and manuscript collections, research on their current locations, problems of cataloguing, the coverage of catalogues, the trading of manuscripts and their use, but not the study of the material production of the book, which together with analysis of the script belonged more properly, in his view, to the field of palaeography. Reaction to this position was expressed by the Belgian François Masai (1909–1979), founder in 1946 of the journal *Scriptorium*, who in two articles in that same journal (Masai 1950, 1956) called for a separation between 'paléographie' and 'codicologie', saying that the former should concern itself with the study of script on any writing surface, and independently of it, whereas the latter should focus on analysis of the material production of the manuscript, establishing a sort of archaeological study of the book (Masai 1950, 293). This perception led to the establishment of two views on the range of codicological work: one which understands the discipline in its most restrictive sense, as limited to archaeological study of the book in order to describe the techniques of production of the book as an artefact, and another broader view which does not content itself with such description but also gives itself the mission of interpreting the data both on the production and use of the object and on the copying and transmission of the text (Muzerelle 1991, 350 refers to these two views as 'codicologie *stricto sensu*' and 'codicologie au sens large.').

In the studies which applied the broader view of codicology, the establishment of a chronology and a typology in the production of the mediaeval book became fundamental. This led to the emergence of several projects designed to catalogue dated manuscripts, since they ensure the dating of physical features of the codex and make it possible to establish the chronology of the evolution of production techniques of the mediaeval book, which is essential to the dating of codices lacking a colophon. As early as 1953, the *Comité international de paléographie* oversaw a project to catalogue all the Latin manuscripts in the world, providing information on the date, place and/or scribe. Following this model of the study of dated manuscripts, two figures emerged within the field of mediaeval Jewish history who were to influence the development of Hebrew codicology and palaeography until the present day: Colette Sirat and Malachi Beit-Arié. 1965 saw the creation of the *Comité de paléographie hébraïque*—מפעל הפאליאוגראפיה העברית, with the participation of the Institut de recherche et d'histoire des textes of the CNRS, the Israel Academy of Sciences and Humanities, and the Jewish National and University Library (today the National Library of Israel). The first volume of *Manuscrits médiévaux en caractères hébraïques portant des indications de date jusqu'à 1540*—אוצר כתבי־יד עבריים מימי־הביניים בציוני תאריך עד שנת ה'ש' (Sirat et al. 1972; Beit-Arié et al. 1979; Sirat – Beit-Arié 1986), appeared in 1972, and the idea was that each entry would occupy one or several loose-leaved sheets, so that the reader could organize the descriptions in accordance with her or his needs, following either a chronological criterion (the first volume covered the period from 1207 to 1528), or a geographical or thematic one. Despite these possibilities, the final intention of the authors was to present the manuscripts in the chronological order in which they had been copied, for it is the only criterion by which to establish the development of the typologies of production of the manuscript Hebrew book throughout the Middle Ages. The numbering of the entries reveals the chronological criterion behind the concept of the catalogue of dated manuscripts. The description of the oldest manuscript in the first volume (Paris, BnF, Hébreu 82; copied in 1207) is given the number I,1, the Roman numeral standing for the number of the catalogue volume. The most recent (Jerusalem, Schocken Institute, 13869) is number I, 179.

The publication of the third volume of *Manuscrits médiévaux en caractères hébraïques* in 1986 coincided with a period in which so-called quantitative codicology had already taken its first steps. This was a new methodological approach nourished indirectly by post-structuralist theories of the text which benefited from the new computer tools developed in the early 1980s. The publication in 1980 of *Pour une histoire du livre manuscrit au Moyen Âge. Trois essais de codicologie quantitative* (Bozzolo – Ornato 1980) represented a sort of manifesto of the new approach, not only because it was the first time that the word 'quantitative' had appeared in association with codicology, but because of the methodological approaches it proposed, which were opposed to an understanding of the mediaeval book as an object of cultural analysis. According to these new approaches, the aim was not to analyze an object and understand its function in relation to its material, intellectual and cultural context. The key was to define the material elements which could be unequivocally described in order to study them in large groups or entire 'populations' of manuscripts from a particular period and area, and be able to understand their use, application and evolution (Derolez 1988, 5, explains: 'Which aspects can a catalogue deal with? Since *the aim is to compare many manuscripts*, only those facts which lend themselves to a rapid and unequivocal description' (our translation and italics)).

Within the framework of the research carried out by the Comité de paléographie hébraïque and before the third volume of *Manuscrits médiévaux en caractères hébraïques* even came out, Beit-Arié published the first manual ever to be entirely devoted to Hebrew codicology (Beit-Arié 1977). The book had a clearly quantitative methodology aimed at tracing the most important tendencies in the production of mediaeval Hebrew manuscripts, following geo-cultural criteria and, as far as possible, using a chronological perspective (Beit-Arié 1977, 12–13 mentions even at this early date that the working process includes the recording of information on computer tapes for its subsequent analysis). Commenting on the quantitative approach, Colette Sirat, who has admirably analysed and interpreted Hebrew manuscript culture in the Middle Ages (Sirat 2002), has highlighted just how little attention has been paid by quantitative codicology to the text and the individuality of manuscripts. She defends the idea of the specificity of each manuscript as an historical artefact subject to cultural analysis. In her opinion, the 'population' of manuscripts examined by quantitative codicology has to be representative of total production, and her view is that this does not occur in the domain of Hebrew manuscripts since the vast majority of surviving codices were written between the thirteenth and fifteenth centuries, with very few examples from before 1200. She also stresses the fact that quantitative codicology occasionally forgets that the manuscript is fundamentally a bearer of text. For Sirat, textual production and transmission cannot be separated from the production and transmission of the physical book, and we cannot therefore omit to highlight and value all the features relating to these processes in each manuscript individually.

This is best exemplified in the ongoing cataloguing project of the Hebrew manuscripts in the Bibliothèque nationale de France, coordinated by Sirat (the volumes of this catalogue are appearing in the series published by Brepols entitled *Manuscrits en caractères hébreux conservés dans les bibliothèques de France: Catalogues*, as a joint initiative carried out by the Bibliothèque nationale de France and the Institut de recherche et d'histoire des texts, CNRS). The importance of the material characteristics of the individual manuscript lies at the heart of this catalogue. Each of the entries in the catalogue is made up of three parts which reflect the three areas of description of interest in an approach in which the manuscript is analysed as a cultural artefact: first, a physical description of the codex, based on the composition and structure of the quires; second, a description of the content, with a mention of any added material or later interventions; and third, a section dedicated to the history of the codex containing a reconstruction of the use and transmission of the object (and, therefore, of the text which it transmits) based on the colophon and any later annotations, as well as signs of use and ordering to be found within the manuscript (five volumes came out so far: Bobichon 2008, Di Donato 2011, Del Barco 2011, Bobichon 2014, Ciucu 2014).

Extensive codicological descriptions, with the identification of the production area and the type of script, differentiation of hands and of the codicological strata in relation to the texts, in addition to dating based on the documentation of the dated manuscripts, are provided by the recent catalogues of Oxford (Beit-Arié – May 1994), the Biblioteca Palatina in Parma (Richler – Beit-Arié 2001), and the Biblioteca Apostolica Vaticana (Richler et al. 2008).

The manuscripts catalogued in the previous examples belong to a single library. However, various cataloguing projects since the beginnings of codicology as a discipline in the 1950s have been guided by different selection criteria. These 'special' catalogues follow one or several criteria such as the type of manuscript (catalogues of decorated and illuminated manuscripts), thematic criteria (catalogues of biblical codices), special situations (auction catalogues), geographical criteria (by region or country of production or by location) and chronological criteria. As far as the chronological criterion is concerned, in addition to the development of various tools focusing on a particular aspect of production (for instance, ruling or watermarks, cf. Dukan 1988 and Zerdoun Bat-Yehouda 1997) a new catalogue of dated Hebrew manuscripts has seen the light, entitled *Codices hebraicis litteris exarati quo tempore scripti fuerint exhibentes*—אוצר המצחפים העבריים כתבי יד בכתב עברי מימי הביניים בציוני תאריך (Beit-Arié et al. 1997; Glatzer et al. 1997; Sirat et al. 2002; Beit-Arié et al. 2006). This work complements the one published between 1972 and 1986 and focuses on the immediately previous period, from the start of the Middle Ages until 1280. The need to produce this new catalogue arose when foreign researchers gained access to the Russian collections of Hebrew manuscripts after the fall of the Soviet regime, a development which had a truly revolutionary effect on the study of mediaeval Hebrew manuscript culture. Indeed, most of the earliest codices which appear in the first three volumes of this work are from the collection of the Russian National Library in St Petersburg. The first volume was published in 1997, and the four which have so far appeared cover all the extant dated Hebrew manuscripts until 1200.

Concerning the geographical criteria, Javier del Barco's catalogue of the Hebrew manuscripts in the Region of Madrid is an example of a catalogue gathering different collections in one particular region (Del Barco 2003–2006). Judith Olszowy-Schlanger's pioneering work *Les manuscrits hébreux dans l'Angleterre médiévale: étude historique et paléographique* (Olszowy-Schlanger 2003) focuses on the production of Hebrew manuscripts in one specific geographical region, and admirably combines the presentation of manuscript descriptions in an appendix with the study and interpretation of the data which constitute the work's main contribution. Indeed, the geographical distribution of manuscript production is a key aspect to bear in mind when seeking to understand Hebrew manuscripts. Jews played an active role in all the processes of cultural contact and exchange in different areas across Europe and around the Mediterranean, and the objects they produced, especially manuscripts, are hybrid products which participated in the artistic and technical trends in these areas. Therefore, a comparative view of Hebrew manuscripts in relation with Latin (and Romance), Greek and Arabic manuscript production has increasingly been adopted since the mid-1970s, and has offered very promising results, both in the field of codicology and in that of palaeography. In the latter, Beit-Arié has shown that cursive and semi-cursive Hebrew scripts were developed in the different cultural areas by reference to the script used by the surrounding host culture (Beit-Arié 1993). The use of the comparative method in Hebrew manuscript culture has led codicologists working on western codices to compare production techniques of Latin, Greek, Arabic and Hebrew manuscripts in order to explore which elements might constitute a 'universal grammar of the codex', and to identify the structural elements common to most artisanal traditions (Maniaci 2002a, 25).

References

Beit-Arié 1977, 1993; Beit-Arié et al. 1979, 1997, 2006; Beit-Arié – May 1994; Bobichon 2008, 2014; Bozzolo – Ornato 1980; Ciucu 2014; Del Barco 2003–2006, 2011; Derolez 1988; Di Donato 2011; Dukan 1988; Glatzer et al. 1997; Maniaci 2002a; Masai 1950, 1956; Muzerelle 1991; Olszowy-Schlanger 2003; Richler et al. 2008; Richler – Beit-Arié 2001; Sirat 2002; Sirat – Beit-Arié 1986; Sirat et al. 1972, 2002; Zerdoun Bat-Yehouda 1997.

2.8. Catalogues of Persian manuscripts (IP)

Persian manuscripts were produced from the tenth century to the early twentieth century. The number of surviving manuscripts is not known. According to Mahmoud Omidsalar, there are one million Persian manuscripts in various private and public collections in the Middle East and India (Omidsalar 2004). The *World Survey of Islamic Manuscripts* published in 1992–1994 provides information on numbers of Persian manuscripts in various libraries and private collections worldwide. The information provided is not exact and serves only as an indication, but it does suggest that Omidsalar's one million is somewhat too generous a figure; *c.*500,000–600,000 might be closer to the mark.

The cataloguing of Persian manuscripts in European libraries began in the middle of the nineteenth century. Among the major holdings to be catalogued were the Persian manuscripts in the British Museum. The collection consisted of 2,536 manuscripts that were described by Charles Rieu in a three-volume catalogue printed in 1879–1883. About a decade later (1895), Rieu published a supplement volume describing a further 425 Persian manuscripts acquired by the British Museum since 1883. Rieu's catalogue is a good example of the classical standard of Persian catalogues providing detailed information on the contents of the manuscripts. The codicological information is sparse, consisting of the number of folia, size of the codex, number of lines to page, the size of text area, the name of the calligraphic style used by the scribe, and, finally, the copy date. Details of the paper and the binding are not given but decorations are briefly mentioned.

The focus of the catalogue is clearly on the correct identification of the texts and the description of their content. In addition, Rieu exerted himself to give detailed information on the authors, and, according to Rieu himself, the aim of the catalogue was not only to function as a guide to the collection but also to serve as 'a useful book of reference to the student of Persian literature' (Rieu 1879–1883, III, xxvii). Bibliographical reference works on Persian literature were not yet available in Rieu's time and it was not before the early twentieth century that Charles Ambrose Storey (1888–1968) began to work on his lifework *Persian Literature, A Bio-bibliographical Survey* (Storey 1927–1958, 1971–1977). Storey's model was Carl Brockelmann's *Geschichte der Arabischen Litteratur* that had been published in 1899–1902 but where Brockelmann had an edited version of Ḥaǧǧī Ḫalīfa's (1609–1657 CE) bibliographic lexicon *Kašf al-ẓunūn* at his disposal as a major source, Storey had to glean the required information from published manuscript and book catalogues of uneven quality. Storey did not complete his arduous task, and even though the continuation of his work commenced by François de Blois in the early 1990s resulted in the publication of volume 5, the whole work still remains incomplete (Bregel 2005).

As a comprehensive survey of Persian literature is still waiting to be written, the best catalogues—old and new—remain important sources for both cataloguers and scholars. Among other bibliographical sources is Āqā Bozorg Ṭehrānī's (1876–1970 CE; 3rd ed. 1983) *al-Ḏarīʿa ilā taṣānīf al-šīʿa*, a survey of all classes of literature written by Shīʿa authors. Āqā Bozorg Ṭehrānī's survey is written in Arabic but contains entries on Persian works, as well. For the purposes of identifying texts and authors, a good recent catalogue is *Fehrest* by Sayyed Aḥmad Ḥosaynī describing the vast holdings of manuscripts in the library of Āyatollāh al-ʿOẓmā Naǧafī Marʿašī in Qom (Ḥosaynī 1975–2010). For identifying anonymous verses of poetry, a good internet based resource is <http://ganjoor.net/> containing a searchable database of the verses of, until now, 49 Persian poets.

The above mentioned 38-volume catalogue of the library of Āyatollāh al-ʿOẓmā Naǧafī Marʿašī follows the classical standard by focusing on the texts and providing only very little codicological information. It provides ample quotations of the beginnings and endings of the texts, short summaries of the content and occasionally tables of content. In addition the catalogue has three separate index volumes listing authors, titles, subjects and places. Each catalogue volume contains an appendix with black and white photos of some of the manuscripts.

One of the recent trends in cataloguing Persian manuscripts is to move from printed catalogues to electronic ones. Some libraries have included manuscripts in their electronic catalogues. These library catalogues give only the minimum of information on each manuscript (title, author, language, shelfmark) as is the case with the British *Fihrist—Islamic Manuscripts Catalogue Online* (<http://www.fihrist.org.uk/>). Others attempt to give similar information as in the classical printed catalogues, for example Emilie Savage-Smith's electronic catalogue *Islamic Medical Manuscripts at the National Library of Medicine*, Bethesda, Maryland (<http://www.nlm.nih.gov/hmd/arabic/welcome.html>). An additional feature of this particular catalogue is that it uses a hypertext feature to give additional bio-bibliographical information and explanations of textual and codicological terminology.

The best electronic catalogues take the presentations beyond the classical standard to include more profound codicological details and to provide digitized images for browsing. Until now, the best of the more ambitious electronic catalogues is the *Islamic Manuscript Collection* at the University of Michigan, Ann Arbor (<http://www.lib.umich.edu/islamic/>) that contains complete digital images allowing the user to browse the pages and zoom into details. The catalogue entries contain extensive description of the manuscripts as physical objects and give details of collation, layout, script, decoration, support and binding. Thus, the catalogue caters for a larger variety of interest than the classical catalogues that mainly benefited the philologists and other text based scholars. The University of Michigan catalogue gives relevant information to codicologists and art historians, as well.

References

Āqā Bozorg Ṭehrānī 1983; de Blois 1992–1997; Bregel 2005; Brockelmann 1899–1902 = 1943–1949; Ḥaǧǧī Ḫalīfa 1835–1858; Ḥosaynī 1975–2010; Omidsalar 2004; Rieu 1879–1883; Storey 1927–1958, 1971–1977. Web sources: *Fihrist–Islamic Manuscripts Catalogue Online* <http://www.fihrist.org.uk/>, last access May 2014; *Islamic Manuscript Collection* at the University of Michigan, Ann Arbor <http://www.lib.umich.edu/islamic/>, last access May 2014; *Islamic Medical Manuscripts at the National Library of Medicine,* Bethesda MD <http://www.nlm.nih.gov/hmd/arabic/welcome.html>, last access May 2014; Poetry resource <http://ganjoor.net/>, last access May 2014.

2.9. Catalogues of Slavonic manuscripts (PAm)

At least since the mid-nineteenth century the cataloguing and description of Slavic mediaeval manuscripts has constituted an important field within Slavic studies. Most catalogues have been focused on individual collections that are located in a particular place or in a particular repository (for a still useful example see Gorskij – Nevostruev 1855–1869), but also union catalogues with different scopes have been published (cf., for example, *Svodnyj katalog* ed. Šmidt et al. 1984, which describes Slavic manuscripts written in the eleventh to thirteenth centuries located in more than twenty repositories in the then Soviet Union).

The total number of Slavonic manuscripts is unknown, but an estimate of 60,000–80,000 may perhaps be not too far from the actual number. Out of these, the Russian National Library in St Petersburg seems (according to the statement on its website) to hold *c.*30,000, but there are impressive collections also in

Moscow, Kiev, Sofia, Belgrade, Skopje, Mount Athos, etc. The extant catalogues of various collections cover perhaps one third of the estimated total.

In most Slavic countries, the descriptions of their respective collections have also served a goal of establishing national scholarship: thus, collections located in Russia have as a rule been described by Russian scholars in Russian, collections located in Bulgaria by Bulgarian scholars in Bulgarian, etc. Thus, paradoxically, manuscripts written in Church Slavonic, the supranational ecclesiastical language common to the Slavic Christian Orthodox culture (albeit with local varieties and subvarieties), are even today usually described in the language of the country where they are located (for recent examples cf. Naumow – Kaszlej 2004; Holovata – Kol'buh 2007). However, collections located in non-Slavic countries have more often been described in more widely used languages such as French, German, or English (cf., for example, Roubetz 1919; Matejic 1983; Steensland 2005), or in Russian, which in some non-Slavic countries such as, for example, Sweden, sometimes has functioned as the 'default' Slavic language for the publishing of Slavic scholarship (cf., for example, Davidsson 1975a, with a parallel version in Swedish, Davidsson 1975b; Glubokovskij 1918, with a separate translation into French, Glubokovskij 1919). Bilingual catalogues of Slavic manuscripts were also published in some of the non-Russian republics of the Soviet Union (cf., for example, the Russian-Moldavian catalogue by Ovčinnikova-Pelin 1989).

The introduction and rapid spread of digital technologies from the 1990s and later has fundamentally influenced not only the production and dissemination of catalogues and descriptions of Slavic manuscripts, but also, and perhaps even more significantly, the accessibility of the described objects themselves (both through 'facsimile' editions and text editions: for the latter the discussion has focused on the distinction between the concepts *character* and *glyph* and their relation to encoding models such as Unicode, cf. Birnbaum 1996, as well as the discussion at the Fourteenth International Congress of Slavists in Ohrid, Macedonia, in 2008, see Birnbaum et al. 2008; Miklas et al. 2008). Of course, various types of editions cannot replace the actual manuscript objects for all types of research, but many tasks that would earlier have necessitated extensive travel, obtaining of permits, etc. can now be solved much more easily provided the researcher has access to a computer with an Internet connexion. During the last decade a considerable number of collections of Slavic manuscripts have become accessible through the World Wide Web, see, for example, the presentation of some of the most important manuscript collections at the Russian State Library in Moscow (*Dom živonačal'noj Troicy. Slavjanskie rukopisi* <http://www.stsl.ru/manuscripts/index.php>) of the Kopitar collection at the National and University Library in Ljubljana (*Kopitarjeva zbirka slovanskih kodeksov*; <http://www.nuk.uni-lj.si/kopitarjevazbirka/>), and of the collections of Mediaeval Slavic manuscripts in the Former Yugoslav Republic of Macedonia (*Srednovekovni slovenski rakopisi vo Makedonija*; <http://staroslovenski.nubsk.edu.mk/>). There are also sites focusing on particular, well-known manuscripts such as, for example, the excellent site on the tenth-century Glagolitic Kiev Folia at the *Biblioteka Frontistesa* (<http://ksana-k.narod.ru/kodex/11_kiev.html>); and the Russian National Library site dedicated to the Ostromir Gospel (*Ostromirovo evangelie (1056–1057) i rukopisnaja tradicija novozavetnych tekstov*; <http://www.nlr.ru/exib/Gospel/ostr/>). In addition, the TITUS project (*Thesaurus Indogermanischer Text- und Sprachmaterialien*; for Old Church Slavonic see <http://titus.uni-frankfurt.de/indexe.htm?/texte/texte2.htm#aksl>) includes both pictures and text transcriptions of some Old Russian and Old Church Slavonic texts.

Dissemination of cataloguing data has also been revolutionized by the possibilities of the Internet: many nineteenth- and twentieth-century printed catalogues and descriptions of Slavic manuscripts are now available through, for example, the *Biblioteka Frontistesa* (<http://ksana-k.narod.ru/>), *Ėlektronnaja biblioteka po paleoslavistike* (<http://byzantinorossica.org.ru/paleoslavistics.html>) and other websites, and the catalogue records of the Hilandar Research Library microfilm collections can be accessed through the Ohio State University Library on-line catalogue.

However, many catalogues are still published as traditional printed books (cf., for example, Naumow – Kaszlej 2004, Holovata – Kol'buh 2007, etc.), even if they sometimes have been produced with the help of computer description methodology (cf. Cleminson et al. 2007). At the moment, the possibilities of applying the principles of Text Encoding Initiative (TEI; <http://www.tei-c.org/>) seem to promise most for the future, but much work is still needed before the potential of this approach will be fully realized. Some of the relevant discussion is conducted within the Commission on Computer-Supported Processing of Mediæval Slavonic Manuscripts and Early Printed Books to the International Committee of Slavists, set up in 1998 (see *Obshtezhitie*), and since 2003 the journal *Scripta & e-Scripta* has been publishing articles and materials within this field. Among ongoing cataloguing projects that try to address these problems can be mentioned the Russian *Manuskript"* (<http://manuscripts.ru/>), the Bulgarian *Slovo* (<http://slovo-aso.cl.bas.bg>), and the Swedish *Digitalised Descriptions* (cf. Ambrosiani – Granberg 2010).

To conclude: presently, the most important task seems to be the development of stable methods that can combine the best of the scholarly tradition with the new technical possibilities, not only by producing new catalogues and descriptions of Slavic manuscripts, but also by integrating both earlier and more recent scholarship and making it widely available to both the multinational Slavic research community and international research outside the Slavic field.

References

Ambrosiani – Granberg 2010; Birnbaum 1996; Birnbaum et al. 2008; Cleminson et al. 2007; Davidsson 1975a, 1975b; Glubokovskij 1918, 1919; Gorskij – Nevostruev 1855–1869; Holovata – Kol'buh 2007; Matejic 1983; Miklas et al. 2008; Naumow – Kaszlej 2004; Ovčinnikova-Pelin 1989; Roubetz [1919]; Šmidt 1984; Steensland 2005. Web sources: *Biblioteka Frontistesa* <http://ksana-k.narod.ru>, last access May 2014; *Dom živonačal'noj Troicy. Slavjanskie rukopisi* <http://www.stsl.ru/manuscripts/index.php>, last access May 2014; *Ėlektronnaja biblioteka po paleoslavistike* <http://byzantinorossica.org.ru/paleoslavistics.html>, last access May 2014; *Kopitarjeva zbirka slovanskih kodeksov* <http://www.nuk.uni-lj.si/kopitarjevazbirka>, last access May 2014; *Manuskript"* <http://manuscripts.ru>, last access May 2014; *Obshtezhitie* <http://www.obshtezhitie.net/>, last access May 2014; *Slovo* <http://slovo-aso.cl.bas.bg>, last access May 2014; *Srednovekovni slovenski rakopisi vo Makedonija* <http://staroslovenski.nubsk.edu.mk>, last access May 2014; TITUS <http://titus.uni-frankfurt.de/indexe.htm>, last access May 2014.

2.10. Catalogues of Syriac manuscripts (ABi)

Syriac manuscripts must be understood here as a generic term including all manuscripts in Syriac script, which served naturally to write Syriac, but also other languages used by Syriac Christian communities: mainly Arabic (generally called *garšūnī*), and occasionally Malayalam, Sogdian, Turkish, Kurdish and Persian. Indeed in the libraries of Europe, Middle East and India, all manuscripts in Syriac script are put together and described in the same catalogues, regardless of their language, considering the manuscripts themselves often mix several languages. Syriac manuscript collections also include manuscripts in Christian Palestinian Aramaic, which has its own specific script very closely related to the Syriac script.

The exact number of Syriac manuscripts is not known but the general estimate is somewhere under 10,000 (see also General introduction § 3.12). Alain Desreumaux's *Répertoire des Bibliothèques et des catalogues de manuscrits syriaques*, published some twenty years ago, listed 858 titles, including both full-scale catalogues and articles on particular manuscripts (Desreumaux 1991; a new updated version is currently under preparation). By then, most of the major collections of Syriac manuscripts in western libraries (London, Vatican, Paris, Berlin, Oxford, Cambridge, all of these collections possessing between two hundred and one thousand Syriac manuscripts) had long since been catalogued. Many of the more ancient catalogues which were made between the eighteenth and the late nineteenth century are still widely used today. The pioneer work of Giuseppe and Stefano Assemani who catalogued the Syriac manuscripts in the Biblioteca Apostolica Vaticana, presents in many cases an extremely detailed description of texts; one can only regret that their transcription of notes and colophons are sometimes inaccurate (Assemani – Assemani 1758–1759). The monumental catalogue of the Syriac manuscripts in the British Library in London by William Wright, the largest collection in Europe, still remains a reference in the field of Syriac studies, providing us with an inexhaustible source of information concerning both the texts contained in the manuscripts and their history; indeed Wright made the painstaking effort of copying extensively notes and colophons both in Syriac and in Arabic, and his dating of manuscripts on palaeographic examination is usually sound (Wright 1870–1872). One particular feature of this catalogue, which does not reappear in the catalogue of Syriac manuscripts of Cambridge published some years later by Wright, is that the descriptions are not organized by shelfmarks but thematically (biblical, service books, theology, etc.). Each description concerns not the manuscript as a whole, but a specific codicological unit. As a result, the same manuscript can be described in up to twenty different places in the catalogue (see for example

MS London, BL, Add. 14667), and the reader has some difficulty in reconstructing mentally the codex as a whole in its modern form.

Since the publication of Desreumaux's repertory, cataloguing projects have extended to more eastern regions and started filling in the gaps in our knowledge of monastic and episcopal or patriarchal libraries in the Middle East and India, where manuscripts are still kept by the Syriac communities they were produced by and meant for. The libraries of the East Syriac Church in Iraq were thus catalogued by clergymen of the Chaldaean community (Ḥaddād – Isḥāq 1998; Isḥāq 2005); the same is true for the libraries of the Syrian Catholic Church in Lebanon, Syria and Iraq (Sony 1993, 1997, 2005), or the Maronites in Lebanon (Baissari 1999, 2001). At the same time were also published detailed handwritten catalogues of the collections of the Syriac Orthodox monasteries and churches in Syria and Turkey that had been made earlier this century by Mar Filoksinos Yoḥanna Dolabani, future metropolitan of Mardin (compiled between 1920 and 1960; Dolabani 1994a, 1994b, 1994c; Dolabani et al. 1994), and Mar Ignatios Afrem I Barṣawm, future patriarch of the Syrian Orthodox Church (compiled in the 1910–1920s; Barṣawm 2008). However, if all of this amounts to considerable new material, many of these catalogues are mere inventories, which list the main texts with minimal information on the manuscripts themselves, and they only rarely meet the standards of cataloguing as far as identification of texts, codicology and palaeography are concerned. It must be said, nevertheless that some recent catalogues are much more detailed (for example Río Sánchez 2011; Harrak 2011; Río Sánchez – Zomeño 2012). In the field of digital cataloguing, the Hill Museum and Manuscript Library in Collegeville (<http://www.hmml.org/research2010/catalog/search_home.asp>) offers descriptions of a large amount of uncatalogued manuscripts in eastern libraries, not only Syriac for that matter, but pretends to be no more than a first inventory of their very large digital library.

Some recent catalogues stand out in this general picture and appear to draw new trends in Syriac cataloguing. The catalogue of the Syriac fragments from the 'New Finds' made in 1975 in the St Catherine Monastery on Mount Sinai (see Ch. 1 § 9.3.3) by Sebastian Brock (1995a) is of a very particular type, which offers some similarities with catalogues of papyri. It concerns very fragmentary manuscripts, sometimes mere confetti that were found in the '*geniza*' of the monastery. It gives an accurate codicological description and textual identification of the fragments. Each manuscript is fully documented through photographical reproductions, in order to allow the reconstitution of the complete codices with other existing fragments in the library of Saint Catherine or in western libraries. In this respect, the catalogue by Mother Philothea of the more complete manuscripts found in Sinai in 1975 that was published recently and should have offered much more substantial material is a real disappointment (Philothée du Sinaï 2008). Different articles by Paul Géhin and Sebastian Brock have nonetheless allowed the reconstitution of these Sinai manuscripts (for example Géhin 2009). Another cataloguing project of the same type which concerns the Syriac manuscripts that still remain, most very fragmentary, in Dayr al-Suryān in Egypt has just been published by Sebastian Brock and Lucas Van Rompay (Brock – Van Rompay 2014).

The originality of Françoise Briquel-Chatonnet's catalogue of recent acquisitions in the Bibliothèque nationale de France in Paris published in 1997 lies in the attention paid to the history of the manuscript, as it takes into account the material aspects of the manuscripts, both palaeographical and codicological (Briquel-Chatonnet 1997). Compared to Greek or Latin, palaeographical studies in Syriac are still in their infancy and the very broad typology of handwritings elaborated by William Hatch in 1946 in his palaeographical album of dated manuscripts (Hatch 1946) definitely needs redefinition and refinement in order to be able to date more accurately handwritings and narrow down the age bracket of each manuscript. As for codicology, even such basic information as the quire collation had been almost completely ignored by Syriacists until Briquel-Chatonnet's catalogue, albeit with some exceptions (Coakley 1993). Mention should also be made here of the catalogue of decorated manuscripts by Jules Leroy (1964; see also Ch. 4 § 3.2).

The breach made into Syriac catalography on the ground of codicology and palaeography is bound to widen in the next few years with the completion of several catalogues, for example the projects for new cataloguing of the manuscripts in the Syriac Catholic monastery of Charfet in Lebanon (Briquel-Chatonnet et alii), in the Biblioteca Medicea Laurenziana in Florence (Pier Giorgio Borbone), in Tbilisi and Yerevan (E. Reinhardt and Andrea Schmidt) (for a presentation of some current cataloguing projects: Briquel-Chatonnet – Debié forthcoming), but also with such projects as the developing database *e-ktobe: manuscrits syriaques*, which offers updated descriptions of manuscripts, both from textual and codicological point of view (<http://mss-syriaques.org/>).

References

Assemani – Assemani 1758–1759; Baissari 1999, 2001; Barṣawm 2008; Briquel-Chatonnet 1997; Briquel-Chatonnet – Debié forthcoming; Brock 1995a; Brock – Van Rompay 2014; Coakley 1993; Desreumaux 1991; Dolabani 1994a, 1994b, 1994c; Dolabani – Lavenant – Brock 1994; Géhin 2009; Ḥaddād – Isḥāq 1998; Harrak 2011; Hatch 1946; Isḥāq 2005; Leroy [Jules] 1964; Philothée du Sinaï 2008; Rio Sánchez 2011; Rio Sánchez – Zomeño 2012; Sony 1993, 1997, 2005; Wright 1870–1872. Web sources HMML <http://www.hmml.org/research2010/catalog/search_home.asp>, last access May 2014; *e-ktobe: manuscrits syriaques* <http://mss-syriaques.org>, last access May 2014.

2.11. Catalogues of Turkish manuscripts (DVP)

The cataloguing of Turkish (Anatolian / Ottoman) and Turkic (particularly Central Asian / Chagatay) manuscript sources has known a comparatively long history.

As early as 1702, Michael Talman published the *Elenchus librorum orientalium manuscriptorum, videlicet Græcorum, Arabicorum, Persicorum, Turcicorum ... a domino comite Aloysio Ferdinando Marsigli ... collectorum* in Vienna (Kut 1972, 210, no. 147). The sixth and last chapter of the catalogue dealt, in some detail, with a first bulk of Turkish manuscripts collected by Luigi Ferdinando Marsili (1658–1730) (Gullino – Preti 2007) during his sojourns in Constantinople starting from the year 1679. Marsili's Ottoman collection (now preserved in the University Library of Bologna) is still to be considered the most momentous in Italy—by the way, also still in need of a 'modern' catalogue. A few decades later, Stefano Evodio Assemani (1711–1782; regarding this Maronite prelate, see at least Tisserant 1932; Levi Della Vida 1962), the brilliant nephew of Giuseppe Assemani (1687–1768)—in his turn an active collector of *Turcica* (Proverbio 2010, 28 and following)—'edited' the *Bibliothecae Mediceae Laurentianae et Palatinae codicum mms. Orientalium catalogus*. The volume, published in Florence in 1742, was an outstanding achievement that has not been superseded. Sadly enough, the invaluable Medicean treasure of Ottoman books is also still in need of an analytic, up-to-date catalogue.

A general and well-documented (if not completely exhaustive) bibliographic glimpse into the field of Turkish cataloguing, from the earliest modern records up to the present time, is provided by Kut 1972. His itemized list extends also to Afghanistan, India, Iraq, Iran, Cyprus, Lebanon, Egypt, Syria, and obviously to Turkey (Kut 1972, 220–228).

Just a decade later, Eleazar Birnbaum completed his world survey of cataloguing accomplishments (Birnbaum 1983a-c, 1984a-b; İhsanoğlu 1984, a special catalogue which actually serves as an index of the gigantic four volumes *Osmanlı Tıbbi Bilimler Literatürü Tarihi*, edited by İhsanoğlu and Şeşen in 2008, is not included in Birnbaum 1984b), an authentic watershed in the broader domain of Turcology. Incidentally, we may recall that, at the very beginning of his career, Birnbaum had set a pivotal benchmark in treating the preliminary question of transliteration (Birnbaum 1967; see now Proverbio 2012b).

Very recently, Türkmen (2010) reviewed and thoroughly analysed the twentieth-century 'autochthonous' cataloguing production (it had been preceded by Bayraktar – Lugal 1995)—from the dawn of republican Turkish history up to 2006—which culminated with the long-lasting TÜYATOK project (i.e. the *Türkiye Yazmaları Toplu Kataloğu*, The Union Catalogue of Manuscripts in Turkey; cf. also Flemming 1986). Besides a detailed bibliography (Türkmen 2010, 215–226), the monograph provides useful statistics, along with a provisional evaluation of the total number of Turkish manuscripts preserved in Turkish libraries and collections—though the real number is certainly higher than the 214,272 items mentioned.

A main question, already raised by Birnbaum 1983a and Kut 1988—whether scholars ought to attend primarily to the compilation of extensive checklists that would cast new light on undetected collections, or rather perform in-depth analyses of a relatively small amount of manuscripts—now deserves a clear focus. Even if one cannot agree entirely with Birnbaum regarding the comparatively low quality of contemporary catalogues (see Birnbaum 1983a, 414*a*: 'Almost none of the twentieth-century catalogues are comparable [to previous ones]. Many reasons have been adduced, among these a shortage of well trained scholars and the lack of money for printing and publishing. Such specialized works have, after all, a very limited commercial market. The fact is that recent catalogues are much more skimpy in their descriptions and evaluations, and compare unfavourably in other ways too with their counterparts of the nineteenth century'), it is true that, in many respects, their average level lies far below that of some special catalogues, such as Maue 1996—which, by the way, does not fall within the range of the present paper. Obviously, Maue

1996 may be regarded only as an atypical model (all the items included in this catalogue, if not previously published, are transcribed *in extenso*).

Though an even cursory survey of the last decade's cataloguing issues is here impossible, one may observe that each of the following entries, which concerns only a few major western libraries (Schmidt [J.] 2000, 2002, 2006; Kut 2003, Balić 2006; Duda 2008; not to mention the now unavoidable <http://www.yazmalar.gov.tr/>, the present-day version of TÜYATOK) reflects a different cataloguing tradition. On one side, Duda 2008 represents the German-language area. But its tight, extremely rich structure is more due to its being a special catalogue, dealing exclusively with illuminated manuscripts, than to its adhering to the *Richtlinien* (Deutsche Forschungsgemeinschaft 1992). On the opposite side there are Kut 2003 (2010^{2}) and Balić 2006. In spite of the fact that this latter is written in German, the only salient difference between the two catalogues is to be found in the external description, which is more meagre in Kut 2003. Otherwise the structure (quite skeletal) is identical: shelfmark, (external description), author and transcribed title, a (very) short *incipit*, reference to other (few) witnesses, chronological data and *marginalia*. No significant effort to retrieve any additional information, especially in case of anonymous texts, is detectable.

The reliability of such a 'short-title catalogue' is quite low. These are only a few examples, among many more, of such unreliability. In July 1929 the young Herbert W. Duda (1900–1975), who was finalizing his research dealing with the 'Forty Vezirs' text, sojourned in Venice, attending to a thorough inquiry into the Ottoman collection held by the Biblioteca Nazionale Marciana. But, notwithstanding the fact that the Marciana Library holds at least two manuscripts which bear this text (Venice, BNM, Or. 182 (= 35) and Or. 132 (= 108); see Proverbio 2010, 72), he failed to find either. The reason lies in a severe ambiguity in the old manuscript checklist by Pietro Bettio and Giovanni Veludo (1877), which, echoing the *Catalogo* published in Padua in 1792, reads: 'Historia Sansonis et moralia aliqua'.

Hindrances of past times? More than seventy years later, a manuscript special list, as exhaustive as that which is encompassed in Hazai – Tietze 2006, remains inevitably incomplete. One of the missing items is manuscript Manchester, John Rylands Library, Turkish 82. The reason is indirectly revealed by the recently published Schmidt [J.] 2011 (see p. 153 and following), which fails to identify the manuscript's content. A second missing item is manuscript Ankara, Milli Kütüphane, A 2868, classified as an *Arabian Nights* witness in the on-line catalogue of the National Library of Turkey (<http://www.yazmalar.gov.tr/detay_goster.php?k=136863>).

Nevertheless, although 'many [catalogues] cannot claim to be more than finding lists, furnished with author or title indexes ... we have learned to be grateful for almost any listing that is published, however inadequate it may be, because in most cases no other access is available' (Birnbaum 1983a, 414*a*).

When approaching a manuscript, a number of preliminary questions arise in order to describe it, including the question of how to distinguish between the date of the manuscript and that of the text. Oddly enough, if the former is not explicitly stated somewhere, the usual (and increasingly well-established) palaeographic and codicological tools are to be implemented. For the latter, the Turkologist, with few other options at his disposal, can rely on the instrument of the 'linguistische Datierung', not unknown in other fields of research, but for which a sound theoretical base, unavailable elsewhere, is provided by Doerfer 1993. His methodical classification of linguistic data, along with his chronology of linguistic changes (see Doerfer 1993, 26–64), is a paradigm to be implemented into other branches of Turkish tradition.

References

Assemani 1742; Balić 2006; Bayraktar – Lugal 1995; Birnbaum 1967, 1983a, 1983b, 1983c, 1984a, 1984b; Deutsche Forschungsgemeinschaft 1992; Doerfer 1993; Duda 2008; Flemming 1986; Gullino – Preti 2007; Hazai – Tietze 2006; İhsanoğlu 1984; İhsanoğlu – Şeşen 2008; Kut 1972, 1988, 2003 (^{2}2010); Levi Della Vida 1962; Maue 1996; Proverbio 2010, 2012b; Schmidt [J.] 2000, 2002, 2006, 2011; Talman 1702; Tisserant 1932; Türkmen 2010. Web sources *Türkiye Yazmaları* <http://www.yazmalar.gov.tr/>, last access May 2014.

3. Types and kinds of catalogues

3.1. Types of catalogues: checklists, summary catalogues, analytical catalogues, 'special catalogues' (PB)

The history of modern cataloguing, the beginnings of which may be attributed to the end of the seventeenth century (Petrucci 2011[6], 19–56), has seen three different catalographic models alternate and often exist side by side: the inventory or checklist, the summary catalogue and the analytical or full scale catalogue (according to the usual classification of western 'cataloguing science').

The first model, that is the checklist, which has venerable mediaeval precursors, consisting of an extremely concise description—author and contents of the work, writing material, number of leaves (sporadically), and some other information—not surprisingly represented the dawn of cataloguing, without ever having been completely abandoned, to the point that until recently it has been used to catalogue important collections, such as that of the Coptic manuscripts preserved in the Staatliche Museen of Berlin (Beltz 1978, 1980). However, an inventory based on a defined classification—alphabetical order of authors, subject, or similar—should be considered already a real catalogue (Derolez 1979).

Moreover, despite its limits, the checklist still represents a reasonable option when contingent factors—mainly the lack of time and economic resources—do not permit more detailed cataloguing. However, being not much more than a bare list, the checklist does not represent a satisfactory solution for the necessity of evaluation of a manuscript collection, nor does it offer full knowledge of the collection itself. It is not surprising, therefore, that the summary catalogue and the analytical catalogue, over time, imposed themselves as the only two valid options for a scientific cataloguing.

While the analytical or full scale catalogue is quite easy to define—consisting of a description, as accurate and exhaustive as possible, of all the physical and textual elements composing a manuscript (or a fragment)—the definition of the summary catalogue is more complex, since it 'appears definable only in terms of subtraction when compared to the analytical catalogue and in terms of addition when compared to the bare inventory, and not for what it is in itself' (Petrucci 2001, 105). In brief, a summary catalogue consists of presenting the maximum amount of data compatible with the maximum conciseness.

Analytical catalogues and summary catalogues have had mixed fortunes over time. Since the Second World War, the first model has seen, among its most valuable applications, that of the Union Catalogue of Oriental Manuscripts in German Collections (*Verzeichnis der orientalischen Handschriften in Deutschland*) and that of the cataloguing of the Vatican Greek manuscripts. It is interesting to point out, however, that not all the catalogues which are presented as 'analytical' maintain their promise (see for instance the case of Keshavarz 1986). On the other hand, the summary catalogue had great success in several other catalographic experiences, having been used for the manuscripts of Madrid National Library (*Inventario general* 1953–1995), for those of the Bodleian Library (Madan et al. 1895–1953) or for some Italian collections, such as the Rossi collection of the Biblioteca Corsiniana in Rome (Petrucci 1977), to mention but a few examples. In all these cases indexes play a very important role.

Compilers of summary catalogues—and not only they—have not hesitated to express at times their dissent or their doubts towards the use of analytical catalogues, underlining their irrepressible defects, such as very long times of completion and extremely high costs.

In the same way, however, compilers of analytical catalogues have often defended their own choice, discarding any form of description which is not totally exhaustive (Casamassima 1963, 181–195), although the most recent guidelines tend to lighten and simplify the description, without invalidating the completeness of cataloguing (Deutsche Forschungsgemeinschaft 1973; Derolez 1974a; Institut de recherche et d'histoire des textes 1977; Jemolo – Morelli 1990).

It is worth stressing, however, that almost all the works mentioned above take into consideration only complete or semi-complete codices and that much less attention has been dedicated to fragments until now, although they represent a large part of oriental—and to some extent also of western—manuscript heritage.

It is evident that such an approach depends on the fact that theoretical reflection, rules, guidelines and handbooks on cataloguing so far have been produced mainly by specialists in Greek and Latin manuscripts, with particular attention to mediaeval and Renaissance codices. On the other hand, in 1963, Casamassima clearly declared: 'The notes that we have collected refer exclusively to the manuscripts of western culture, mainly in Latin, and to Greek manuscripts. Manuscripts of other cultures (above all the oriental ones) are in fact objects belonging to other sciences, of different traditions of studies which, despite some affinities, make use of a different methodology' (Casamassima 1963, 182).

Such an observation has strongly influenced the following studies. Only recently different oriental manuscript cultures have tried to fill this gap and, although without homogeneous results, have set out a systematic catalographic and codicological reflection, which of course cannot leave out the experience of the cataloguing of Greek and Latin manuscripts, but it adds to this a series of specific problems.

Whatever the catalographic choice (analytical or summary catalogue) and the cultural and linguistic area to which it is applied, however, a good catalogue should have some features which cannot be disregarded: a concise and formular style and a homogeneous and consistent description, which always follows the same expositive scheme and makes use of a clear and shared terminology.

Besides the already described typologies, there are other kinds of catalogues. If the compilation of a union world catalogue, which has been proposed several times without ever being effected, turned out not to be an achievable enterprise (Richardson 1933–1937; Pelzer 1936, 621–630; Casamassima 1963, 187), other 'special' or 'thematic' catalogues have been more successful. Among these, catalogues of copyists, of owners, of collections, and also catalogues of catalogues, although they are much less established in oriental manuscript cataloguing than in Greek, Latin, and western catalogues in general.

The limited competence of scholars involved in cataloguing in art history, however, makes the category of catalogues of decorated manuscripts particularly notable, above all in the field of oriental manuscripts where the ornamentation and miniatures often have a central role. The following pages are therefore dedicated to this specific category.

References

Beltz 1978, 1980; Casamassima 1963; Derolez 1974a, 1979; Deutsche Forschungsgemeinschaft 1973; Institut de recherche et d'histoire des textes 1977; *Inventario general* 1953–1995; Jemolo – Morelli 1990; Keshavarz 1986; Madan et al. 1895–1953; Pelzer 1936; Petrucci 1977, 2001, 2002 (2011[6]); Richardson 1933–1937.

3.2. Catalogues of decorated manuscripts (EBW)

The first catalogues were written for users who were interested primarily in texts, and at best in codicological matters. In a standard entry, data on painted decoration were omitted or signalled in general terms like 'illustrations', 'illuminations' or 'miniatures', sometimes completed with the number. The binding decoration was likewise only mentioned and seldom described. These short observations were occasionally developed to more comprehensive notices in the case of the texts having decoration as standard (the Gospels, the Qurʾān, etc.) or if that aspect for some reason caught the attention of the cataloguer. However, they were seldom systematically provided. Exceptions are catalogues of the manuscripts belonging to the cultures giving equal importance to text and its illustration. There, a distinction between the decorated and undecorated book seems artificial, and in the titles of catalogues words such as 'decorated', 'illuminated' or 'illustrated' are often omitted (Der Nersessian 1958, 1973b; Richard [F.] 1989; Schmitz 1997; Nersessian 2002).

As manuscript decoration and illustration became an important sub-discipline of art history, the need for pertinent tools for this kind of study inclined the cataloguers to provide more substantial information about this matter. This concerned in the first place Latin manuscripts being the best known and of the greatest interest to European scholars. An early example of this approach is the catalogue of the Pierpont Morgan collection in New York (James 1906), a paradigmatic work which after more than hundred years still satisfies large groups of researchers, art historians included. The author applied the following description categories: title referring to the main text; book's shelfmark; writing material; size; number of folia, lines per page or per column; date; type of script; binding with reference to material and type; marks of ownership; collation, i.e. structure of the text block given in a numeric formula; textual content; ornamentation; list and description of the miniatures; characteristics of painting styles.

While the descriptions of the decoration in general catalogues gradually improved, art historians still found it important to write catalogues devoted exclusively to decorated manuscripts, applying description criteria which better responded to the interests of this group of scholars (Der Nersessian 1936–1937; Robinson [B.] 1958; Hutter 1977–1997). In part of these catalogues, textual contents, even of the greatest interest, are only listed, and the description of codicological characteristics is limited to a minimum or omitted (Macler 1924; Marava-Chatzinicolaou – Toufexi-Paschou 1978–1997). In some cases such an approach was justified because the manuscripts concerned had been codicologically and philologically described on other occasions (for example Sargisyan 1914 and Der Nersessian 1936–1937; Blochet 1900 and 1926; Hammerschmidt – Jäger 1968 and Hammerschmidt 1977b). Some catalogues of decorated manuscripts provided very technical and purely codicological data, for instance the ruling schemes and the details of binding construction (Džurova 2006). Since the current tendency is to see the manuscript as a whole, catalogues that focus exclusively on manuscript decoration, extracting it from its environment, are an exception.

As one can expect, the best balanced level of information concerning decorated manuscripts is achieved in works written in cooperation between a philologist and an art historian or involving a whole group of specialists (Mackeprang et al. 1921; Luzatto – Mortara-Ottolenghi 1972; Pelikanidis et al. 1974–1991; Robinson [B.] – Skelton 1978; Korxmazyan et al. 1984). However, catalogues of this kind are rare, usually being planned for important collections belonging to rich institutional or private owners or included in long-term national projects. Published in several volumes over a period of years if not decades, they follow the same description scheme and the same design (Dublin, Chester Beatty: Der Nersessian 1958; Minorski 1958; Arberry et al. 1959–1962; Vienna, Österreichische Nationalbibliothek: Buberl 1937; Duda 1983, 1992, 2008; Athens, National Library of Greece: Marava-Chatzinicolaou – Toufexi-Paschou 1978–1997; *Verzeichnis der Orientalischen Handschriften in Deutschland*: Hammerschmidt – Jäger 1968; Stchoukine et al. 1971).

Since decorated manuscripts are a minority when compared with all handwritten books, the number of dedicated catalogues is also smaller. Among them, not surprisingly, works that deal with manuscript cultures distinguished by extensive practice in book decoration and/or written in scholarly centres known for their long-lasting tradition in manuscript studies predominate.

The type of catalogue, quantity of data provided and proportions between the descriptive sections are determined by several factors, such as the character of the manuscripts, the accumulated knowledge about them, their cultural background, the number of surviving examples, the type of collection, its size, accessibility, and, last but not least, the needs of the target audience. Here, catalogues of decorated manuscripts do not differ significantly from general catalogues. For instance, it would be unfeasible to produce a reasonably complete catalogue of Ethiopic illuminated manuscripts, their number being even impossible to estimate, but such catalogues exist for Syriac and Coptic.

Among the catalogues of decorated manuscripts one can distinguish the following main types (some of them may overlap):

- manuscripts written in one language and gathered in one country (Lichačeva 1977; Narkiss 1982; Sed-Rajna 1994), institution/library (Adamova 1996, 2012; Furlan 1978–1997; Simpson 1980), collection (Welch 1972–1978; Lowry – Nemazee 1988; Eleuteri 1993; Marava-Chatzinicolaou – Toufexi-Paschou 1978–1997);
- manuscripts written in one language but dispersed across countries (Leroy [Jules] 1964, 1974);
- manuscripts written in different languages but gathered in one country/city (Hatch 1931; Lameï 2000, 2002, 2005, 2013), institution (Gengaro et al. 1959; Pächt – Alexander 1966, 1970, 1973; Schmitz 1997) or collection (Plummer 1968; Pelikanidis et al. 1974–1991);
- manuscripts written in one language, executed during a particular period, kept in one or several places (Omont 1929; Popova 1975; Spatharakis 1981; Weitzmann – Galavaris 1990);
- manuscripts containing a particular text (Grabar [O.] 1984; Feydit 1986; Nersessian 1987);
- manuscripts selected for an exhibition (whether exclusively of manuscripts or not) (Greene et al. 1934; Vikan 1973; Evans – Wixom 1997; Werner [P.] 2002);
- manuscripts or collections sold by the auction houses (Sotheby's 1977; Fogg 1991);
- manuscripts executed in a single scriptorium, artistic school or workshop, kept in one or several places (Sed-Rajna 1970; Grabar [A.] 1972; Agemian 1991; Mostafa 1960).

Like general catalogues, many catalogues of decorated manuscripts are preceded by overviews of matters raised by the manuscripts collected in the publication, thus supplementing the individual catalogue entries. Consequently, instead of the codicological or palaeographical issues, the authors may present the cultural ambiances/relations, histories of the styles of miniatures, schools of painting, and studies on specific iconographic problems (Der Nersessian 1958; Minorski 1958, Weitzmann – Galavaris 1990).

Beside these catalogues *sensu stricto* there are publications complementing data gathered by the cataloguer. Here belong the albums of miniatures (Maçavariani 1970; Weitzmann 1977; Popova 1984; Atalla 2000), the publications accompanying the manuscript exhibitions (Jäger 1957; Nersessian 1987; Tahom 2007), and monographic studies of particular types of manuscripts or groups of manuscripts (Galavaris 1969; Ševčenko 1990; Narkiss – Sed-Rajna 1976, 1981, 1983, 1990, 1994). Several of them are written, at least partly, in the form of catalogue entries.

Also as a particular category of catalogues one can regard the lists of manuscript collections, divided according to the languages and specifying the repository place of the books and the number of codices (Buchthal – Kurz 1942; Arberry 1967), the iconographical indexes accompanied by the lists of the manuscripts containing the specific subjects (Davis – Norgren 1969; Titley 1977, 1981), and the facsimile editions complemented by the publications containing the collection of studies (*Ilias Ambrosiana* in Calderini et al. 1953 and Bianchi Bandinelli 1955; *Rabbula Gospel* in Cecchelli – Furlani 1959; *Maqamat Al-Hariri* 2003).

Almost all catalogues of decorated manuscripts and similar publications are supplied with illustrations, often as plates at the end of the book or in an accompanying volume (Werner [J.] 1920; Der Nersessian 1958; Depuydt 1993; Duda 1983, 1992, 2008). In the early catalogues, drawings, photogravures or collotypes were used; later on, black and white photographs and microfiche. In the catalogues published before the 1960s, the number of colour illustrations was very limited, an inconvenience that was sometimes compensated for by descriptions of the colours.

The number of illustrations included and the decision as to which part of the decoration is reproduced depend on the character of the catalogue, but generally priority is given to the miniatures and the ornamentation that is most important from the stylistic and iconographic point of view, the best preserved ones and those that have not been published previously. Generally the extent of the manuscript description is determined by how much information the reader can extract from the accompanying illustrations. The most ambitious publications comply with the principle of total registration of the decorated pages and with providing most of them, if not all, in colour (Der Nersessian 1973b has 502 illustrations; Buschhausen et al. 1976, 250 illustrations all in colour; Marava-Chatzinicolaou – Toufexi-Paschou 1978–1997, 1,600 illustrations most in colour). Illustrations of particularly good quality are often featured in catalogues by auction houses (Fogg 1991). The importance of illustrations was also recognized by some authors of general catalogues, who, while unable to provide data on art historical matters, compensated for this disadvantage by long series of colour reproductions of miniatures and ornamentation from the manuscripts described (Löfgren – Traini 1975, 1981; Depuydt 1993; Traini 2011).

The outlines of the manuscript descriptions used in our catalogues differ, but some categories constantly appear and may be regarded as standard. Basic information about the text(s), the manuscript's provenance and date are always specified, being important for all readers. The number and type of miniatures are provided, an indication of other ornamentation, a note on binding, and frequently also information on the condition of the manuscript. Subsequently, catalogues focus on decoration. The miniatures and historiated initials are listed by title or subject in the order of the folia, sometimes also described and commented on from the stylistic point of view. The same type of presentation may be applied to ornamentation (decoration of Canon Tables and calendars, initials, marginal decoration, head and tail-pieces, frames and backgrounds, the latter important for Islamic manuscripts), but usually they are grouped in categories, thematic or other, and treated collectively. This approach is useful for richly decorated manuscripts and those adorned with small ornamental units (initials, headpieces etc.), which are often repetitive. The colours are specified when the reproductions are in black-and-white or omitted. Decoration of undated manuscripts is analysed from stylistic and iconographical point of view in order to estimate the date of book production, an approach that requires considerable space for developing the relevant discussion. Notes about the identified scribes/painters are provided, followed by the lists of their other works. While manuscripts are often grouped by categories according to the contents and arranged chronologically within each group, the presentation of decoration follows the chronological order regardless of the textual content, in order to give an idea about the artistic evolution within the corpus described.

Particularly detailed catalogues add to the codicological section information on the size of the miniatures, the place of the ornamentation on the page, the range of pigments and colours of inks used with the results of chemical analysis (Uchova 1960; Mathews – Wieck 1994). They give precise descriptions of the covers and the materials used for their decoration. The account of the provenance of the manuscript and the circumstances of its production is usually elaborate. The list of miniatures may be completed with transliteration and translation of the accompanying captions or, on occasion, longer texts (Der Nersessian 1973b; Hammerschmidt – Jäger 1968). Sometimes even a synopsis of the story illustrated appears (Appleyard 1993). The iconographic peculiarities are examined in a broader context. Comments concerning stylistic matters may include comparative material and develop into small monographs on the painting schools and artists (Der Nersessian 1958; Korxamazyan 1984). In the bibliography, citations from the basic catalogues may be found, alongside with references to the more important recent books and articles concerning the decoration of the manuscript described. Iconographical indexes and concordances are common.

Recently, several libraries have placed catalogues of decorated manuscripts on line, in connexion with the digitization of their collections. These online catalogues contain images, descriptions and search tools. Not infrequently, the selected material is presented in virtual exhibitions. Most of these catalogues are regularly updated. The most advanced digital cataloguing still concerns western illuminated books (cf. for instance the material presented by the British Library, <http://www.bl.uk/catalogues/illuminatedmanuscripts/welcome.htm>, last access June 2014).

References

Adamova 1996, 2012; Agemian 1991; Appleyard 1993; Arberry 1967; Arberry et al. 1959–1962; Atalla 2000; Bianchi Bandinelli 1955; Blochet 1900, 1926; Buberl 1937; Buchthal – Kurz 1942; Buschhausen et al. 1976; Calderini et al. 1953; Cecchelli – Furlani 1959; Davis – Norgren 1969; Depuydt 1993; Der Nersessian 1936–1937, 1958, 1973b; Duda 1983, 1992, 2008; Džurova 2006; Evans – Wixom 1997; Feydit 1986; Fogg 1991; Furlan 1978–1997; Galavaris 1969; Gengaro et al. 1959; Grabar [A.] 1972; Grabar [O.] 1984; Greene et al. 1934; Hammerschmidt 1977b; Hammerschmidt – Jäger 1968; Hatch 1931; Hutter 1977–1997; Jäger 1957; James [M.] 1906–1907; Korxmazyan et al. 1984; Lameï 2000, 2002, 2005, 2013; Leroy [Jules] 1964, 1974; Lichačeva 1977; Löfgren – Traini 1975, 1981; Luzatto – Mortara-Ottolenghi 1972; Maçavariani 1970; Mackeprang et al. 1921; Macler 1924; *Maqamat Al-Hariri* 2003; Marava-Chatzinicolaou – Toufexi-Paschou 1978–1997; Mathews – Wieck 1994; Minorski 1958; Mostafa 1960; Narkiss 1982; Narkiss – Sed-Rajna 1976, 1981, 1983, 1990, 1994; Nersessian 1987, 2002; Omont 1929; Pächt – Alexander 1966, 1970, 1973; Pelikanidis et al. 1974–1991; Plummer 1968; Popova 1975, 1984; Richard [F.] 1989; Robinson [B.] 1958; Robinson [B.] – Skelton 1978; Sargisyan 1914; Schmitz 1997; Sed-Rajna 1970, 1994; Ševčenko 1990; Simpson 1980; Sotheby's 1977; Spatharakis 1981; Stchoukine et al. 1971; Tahom 2007; Titley 1977, 1981; Traini 2011; Uchova 1960; Vikan 1973; Weitzmann 1977; Weitzmann – Galavaris 1990; Welch 1972–1978; Werner [J.] 1920; Werner [P.] 2002.

4. Syntactical description of manuscripts (PAn)*

> 'Finding the breaks in a volume is the most directly relevant task of codicology, especially for those who are interested in texts... But the catalogue—made by a person who did see and handle the manuscript—should at least help the reader to be at least aware of at least the more important breaks. And very many catalogues are deficient in this respect.' J.P. Gumbert (1995a, 62)

Built on the development of codicology and book historical studies, a new awareness of the ancient manuscript as a complex object gradually developed in scholarly circles in the second half of the past century (for a history of the study of the complexity of the codex, see Andrist et al. 2013, 11–44; see also Ch. 1 § 1.3.5). Scholars noticed that the way data were presented in standard scholarly catalogues often did not make it easy for the readers to understand the historical structure of the object, and sometimes even gave food to the suspicion that this complexity had escaped the attention of the cataloguers themselves (see Gumbert 1995a, 2010a; Andrist 2008). This led to the development of an important new paradigm in organizing the descriptions, which has been spreading in some recent cataloguing projects, a paradigm that needs explanation.

4.1. Most manuscript books are complex objects

Has any reader ever found a full manuscript, containing one text, written in one shot by one scribe in a very regular script, showing no writer's, reader's or owner's notes or marks whatsoever, and still preserved in its original integral and unaltered binding? Maybe such an object, made in recent times, exists. But most of the manuscript books oriental scholars work with are from older times. For example, codices from the Middle Ages that are kept in today's libraries always betray some—and usually quite many—changes to their original state.

Of course, the level of complexity varies a lot from one book to another. In some cases, it is limited to a few notes and a new binding, or to some restorations and a label with a shelfmark. But in many cases, books bear the scars of an adventurous life. For example, an original unit from the ninth century could be heavily annotated by several enthusiastic readers, then accidentally mutilated in the eleventh century, and immediately but poorly restored. In the twelfth century, a new owner maybe bound it in a larger volume together with similar texts, copied at various times by various scribes, putting his name on the first page. Another fifty years later, his grandson started a new text on the last two leaves, which were empty, and added a small quire in order to finish his copy, etc. There is almost no limit to the types and amount of changes ancient manuscript books may have lived through.

As a result, an ancient manuscript book can be compared to an archaeological site: the original leaves and each set of changes are strata testifying to the progressive making of the object as it is today. If a reader wants to understand the history of this book, he or she has to be able to recognize the various strata and their specific content, as an archaeologist needs to know which layer any object or stone found belongs to (for a similar usage of this metaphor, see Derolez 1974b, 31). In many cases these strata are easily identifiable by the direct users of the book, because they were copied by different hands using various scripts, with a different layout and sometimes even a different material support; older folium numbers or quire signatures often confirm the diagnosis, or even give a clue to the amount of what has been lost. In other cases, the strata are more difficult to identify, for example when a regular scribe, or two scribes with very similar hands, produced two different books in different points in time, which were only later—sometimes much later—gathered together. On the other hand, two scribes or two artists working together on the same project could have produced their respective parts on different quires, with a different ruling and layout, or different techniques: this is also a type of complexity, but it informs the analysts about the working methods of these people, rather than about discrete strata of the book.

As one sees, complexity is also a complex concept. There are several types of strata, and the four most common ones, which allow for describing almost every situation provided enough information is available, can easily be defined. The cases presented in this sub-chapter only aim at explaining the relevance of structured descriptions, and the vocabulary used here serves this purpose only (technical vocabulary and deeper, more thorough analysis are found in the various descriptive systems; for an introduction to them see Andrist et al. 2013, 11–44).

* This sub-chapter has benefited considerably from discussions with and remarks by J. Peter Gumbert, Marilena Maniaci and Paola Buzi, whom the author thanks warmly.

Some strata are 'paratactic' constitutive parts of the book. They were produced independently from one another and could fairly easily be taken away without damaging their physical integrity or their content because they begin and end at boundaries between quires and, in normal cases, their content is also self-standing. For example, when two independent books were bound together, there are two strata, but both strata were produced independently of one another; they correspond to two different writing projects. Let us call them 'primary strata'.

In other cases, like most of the restorations or added supplements on new folia, a new stratum on its own writing support is produced to supplement an already existing one. Both strata could be physically separated, but often with difficulty and damage. One can distinguish two situations:

a) first, when both strata remain autonomous as far as their content is concerned; this occurs for example when the owner of a volume, let us say an old Gospel book in good shape, has some extra texts entirely copied on new quires, for example more New Testament books, and has them then bound with the first book. As far as the projects are concerned, this 'secondary stratum' was never meant to stand alone, even though it can be withdrawn without damaging any of the contents. This situation is sometimes difficult to distinguish from two primary strata (or two phases of the same production), but it is important to differentiate between them, because, in a codex, a secondary stratum joined to a primary one implies the circulation of two books, while the presence of two primary strata implies the circulation of three books (see Andrist et al. 2013, 63, 66);

b) second, when one or both content(s) would be damaged if the strata are separated. For example, in the case of an ancient restoration of the first leaves of a codex containing the beginning of a text, on a new writing support, the leaves can theoretically be taken out again or unbound, and each of the two resulting parts is coherent as far as their production is concerned (providing there were no other modifications) but neither of the two resulting parts contains a full text. In the case of an added table of contents into an already existing book, for example, this new stratum can be cut off without damaging the main text; but the cut off leaves make little sense alone. In any case, the leaves of the original book clearly belong to the primary stratum. The new leaves, however, which were never meant to stand alone and are not textually autonomous, can be called a 'tertiary stratum'.

Added written elements, small drawings in the margins or full texts copied on empty leaves are new contents on already used folia. Even though they can be very important, they are not materially independent production and cannot be physically separated from their host folia without damaging them. These are 'quaternary strata'.

In some cases, the choice between the strata is not immediately obvious. For example, when a scribe starts a new content in an empty part of an existing book, then uses new folia in order to continue his work, one could think of a mix of a quaternary and tertiary strata. However, this is not the case, because both parts of the new content belong to the same new project and production, which must be clearly distinguished from the already existing production. Since this new production cannot be taken away without damaging the first stratum, it is considered a quaternary one. Another difficult case is that of the lower content of palimpsests. It may seem a special type of quaternary stratum because it is a peripheral production when compared with the main strata of the existing book. However, unlike quaternary strata, the lower production of a palimpsest is older than the main strata including the upper production. Besides, and even more importantly, the lower production implies the existence of another book that it used to belong to. As a result, palimpsests must be considered a special type of primary stratum.

In the past thirty years, codicologists have explored the stratigraphy of the codex from a methodological point of view, searching for new concepts and a new vocabulary to describe it (for example Munk Olsen 1998). This culminated in the first systematic proposal by J. Peter Gumbert in 2003, published one year later, who offered a complete set of concepts and a corresponding terminology, as a result of a long evolution testified by a series of publications (Gumbert 2004; for a survey of Gumbert's evolution, see Andrist et al. 2013, 14–15, 17–18, 23–26). It is centred on the now popular notion of the 'codicological unit', defined in the first instance as 'a discrete number of quires, worked in a single operation, containing a complete text or set of texts' (Gumbert 2004, 25); a manuscript containing more than one codicological unit is called a 'composite' manuscript. Gumbert also coins a complex vocabulary to designate codicological units which underwent transformations. Even though this system is fully operative and represents a major step forward, it sometimes results in complex expressions or subtle distinctions, which are not fully convincing (see Andrist et al. 2013, 41–44). Besides, the expressions 'codicological units' and 'composite manuscripts' are sometimes misused in publications by people who do not precisely understand them, creating regrettable ambiguities. New research was thus triggered, notably around the concept of the 'production unit', which can be applied indiscriminately to any stratum of the codex, no matter if it is delimited by a quire or a text boundary. In this new system, 'production units' are clearly distinguished from 'circulation units', which describe the full state of a codex at a certain point in time. The history of the codex can then be easily modelled as a continuum of circulation units which evolved according to added, removed or shifted production units or pieces thereof (Andrist et al. 2013, 59–81).

Once it is admitted that most manuscript books are complex objects, a few questions, discussed in the following paragraphs, remain. What does this complexity means to the user of the manuscript? How does it affect the cataloguers and their readers? Is it important, after all, that this complexity be totally or partially made visible in their catalogues? And if it is, what are the best ways to achieve it?

4.2. The importance of the awareness of the strata of the manuscripts

Any historical research on ancient manuscripts relies to a greater or lesser degree on the dating of what is studied. Most of the time, scholars need to know more or less precisely when—and where—what they study was produced. For example, for a philologist working on the critical edition of a text, it does make a difference if a crucial passage was written at the same time as the bulk of the other sheets, or if it is on a leaf restored some years later; in the latter case it could depend on another branch of the textual family and its variant readings should be evaluated differently. If he or she is studying the transmission of a series of small pieces, it is crucial to know if the series was copied together within the same project, or if it was gradually built up through centuries, and if it was partially damaged through time. For art historians, it is potentially very significant if two paintings from different artists are on two pages of the same bifolium, or if both were produced on two independent leaves, later than the date of the copy of the main text. A book historian working on the history of paper cannot escape the question of whether the sheets with undated watermarks were used simultaneously with the ones with dated watermarks, or at a much later time. Any study on the reception of an author or the transmission of an iconographic model is bound, of course, to a reasonable dating of the leaves concerned (see also Andrist 2014).

Dated colophons or notes can only be securely used when it is clear to which stratum they belong: were they written by the main scribe, or added by a restorer a few centuries later? As a result, if a place and time are mentioned, do they apply to the whole codex or only to part of it, no matter if it is written by one or several hands?

The codex is a complex object, and therefore it is, as a whole, an undated object. Any given or deducible date applies only to its own stratum; every stratum has its own date. What matters to most users is the date of the production of the text copy or the picture they are interested in, that is the date of the stratum to which the features they are working with belong.

From a traditional catalogue description, it is often difficult to visualize a codex and its strata, especially if no standard or electronic facsimiles are available. Cataloguers, on the other hand, are working directly on the book, so they are often immediately and intuitively aware of its main strata and, in case of doubt, they can easily check the object directly. It is thus one of the most important basic tasks of a cataloguer to give the reader precise indications about the main strata of the object in question, and their time and place of origin (at least approximately). Ideally everyone using a description in a catalogue should have a way easily to know how many strata the book is made of, their respective extent and the date and place they were produced. In reality, there are many complicated cases, and often there is not enough time for a complete analysis to be made within the scope of the cataloguing project. In this case, the reader ought to find at least correct information on the primary and secondary strata and a brief note explaining the situation.

4.3. Recognizing the major historical strata: the physical language of the codex

As mentioned above, some strata are easily recognizable at first sight; others are more difficult to identify. For obvious reasons, the gradual making of manuscript books leaves scars or marks in them, particularly at the boundary of two strata. Anyone who can 'read' and 'interpret' these discontinuities in a codex is also in a good position to identify its strata correctly and reconstruct its constitutive history. This is why the physical complexity of the codex can be compared to a language, with its own syntactical rules. One can thus also speak of the syntactical structure of the codex, and also name the strata 'syntactical elements'.

Fundamentally, any discontinuity can be significant; but places where there are concomitant discontinuities, i.e. wherever several features of the codex change at the same point, are even more significant. As far as primary, secondary, and tertiary strata are concerned, the descriptive features that can reasonably be observed while preparing a catalogue are the following (more details and special cases are discussed in Andrist et al. 2013, 83–110):

The quires. Every primary stratum of a codex was originally delimited either by the beginning or the end of the codex, or by a quire boundary. Most are made up of a series of quires and consequently, if they are bound with another book, the 'border' between them is necessarily delimited by a quire boundary.

The quire types. Often, books are made of a series of quires with the same number of leaves, while the last quire may be shorter or longer, in order to fit the remaining content to be copied. A discrepancy in the quire type may point to a mutilation, or to the end of a constitutive part of the manuscript; but it could also be an original irregularity in the quire composition. Of course, the real cause must be further investigated.

Ancient 'sequence marks'. Scribes, binders or owners used to indicate the order of the folia or the quires by 'sequence marks', for example folium numbers, quire signatures, catchwords, religious symbols. Any discontinuities (such as systemic change or apparent errors) in the system could be at the border between two strata.

The writing support. Changes either between major categories (paper, parchment, papyrus) or, within a category, for example between different types of paper or different qualities of parchment, can be significant. Manuscripts using mixed materials, for example quires made of bifolia of paper embedded in a bifolium of parchment must naturally be dealt with at the level of the recurring sequence and not at every discontinuity of material support (two per quire).

The ruling technique. For example, if a part of the codex is blind ruled and another is ink ruled.

The layout, understood as both the resulting grid from ruling (the ruling pattern), and the way it is used. The ruling type can change, but also, for example, the number of written lines, or the way vertical lines in the margins are used.

Scribes, hands, and writing systems. For example if all the titles are written in a special characters and red ink, then suddenly they are written in normal characters and ink.

The decoration principles and characteristics, if any.

The content. Most importantly, where the content changes, and where fully or partially blank leaves are located.

Concomitant discontinuities are more significant. The most important components are definitely quires: a new text at the beginning of a new quire should immediately suggest that there could be two originally autonomous parts; also, a new scribe at the beginning of a new quire should raise the question if both persons were working together on the same project, or if one of them restored a mutilated codex many years later. Blank leaves at the end of a quire within the codex also call for an explanation. Some other concomitant discontinuities are not so important. For example, a change of ruling type almost always occurs at the beginning of a new quire, and a change of hand often means also a change in writing system, but neither is necessarily significant.

The list is just an indication; some features are not applicable in some cases, while other discontinuities could be meaningful (the ink; the presence and estimated frequency of glosses, if any; the style of the miniatures, if any; and so on).

Quaternary strata are usually distinguished by their special position, script and/or content, which represent also discontinuities against their surrounding context. But this is not the place to analyse them more deeply.

Several factors play a role in identifying the strata. Among them, the nature of the considered features: for example, a major change in layout is hard to hide, while a change of ruling system is often hidden and difficult to see. Another factor is the ability and knowledge of the cataloguers. For example, if a cataloguer is also a good palaeographer and has some experience in dating writings, he/she will more easily see the changes in scripts and hands from different centuries. It takes also some skill and practice to see significant changes in ruling types; this is also why it is advisable that cataloguers work in a network of specialists with complementary skills (it is also important they stay in touch with the progress of research in the various areas they need for their cataloguing work, and, from time to time, as possible, try to describe a particular codex as profoundly as possible, in order to improve their skills). Naturally, the state of the art in related studies plays a significant role. Even if one has good skills as far as recognizing script is concerned, these will be of little use if there are no palaeographic studies in one's field.

Finally, there is the time factor. In a catalogue project the available time often does not allow for checking every aspect of every feature. For example, fully identifying all the watermarks of a codex takes several days.

This is why it is important that cataloguers plan ahead which aspects they are going to check systematically, and which they will apply only to specific objects, depending on circumstances and experience, giving the most attention to the potentially more significant discontinuities (see Ch. 4 § 5.2). In the introduction of the catalogue, the readers should be informed of the choices made.

4.4. Rendering the complexity of the described codex: syntactical types of descriptions

There are various ways to structure a catalogue description of a codex, but not every way makes it possible to inform the readers efficiently about its strata. In the following pages the traditional scholarly structure of a description is first considered, then four alternative types of description, whose overall structure allows a clearer representation of the physical complexity of the codex, are presented.

4.4.1 Traditional structure of a codex description

The traditional scholarly catalogues from the second half of the twentieth century represented major progress towards giving the readers a way to perceive, at least partially, the primary strata of the codex. One major reason for this progress was the systematic analysis of the quires (collation), since these are very important for determining the structural parts of a codex, as explained above. Provided the cataloguer worked precisely and the reader carefully compares the quire boundaries against other discontinuities in the description, the latter can often get a good idea of the primary and secondary strata of the codex; but it is work that the reader has to do himself, on his own initiative. (In the best catalogues of this type, most of the tertiary and quaternary strata, like restorations or marginal notes, are also mentioned in specific paragraphs or side comments. But this is by no means always the case, and when it is, it is not always done systematically).

The structure of this type of description can be summarized through the representation in Skeleton 1. Technically, there are many formal variants of this structure, depending on whether the content is described before (as here) or after the physical features, and how paragraphs and small capitals are used, etc. There are also many ways to apply it (see for example Deutsche Forschungsgemeinschaft 1992; Jemolo – Morelli 1990). But the general principles stay the same.

Since the various categories of information are presented for the whole codex at once, concomitant changes are not obvious, sometimes even difficult to identify. And the conclusion that there are several strata remains fragile because it is a deduction based on the catalogue only and it is not confirmed by someone who has seen the codex (unless there is a clear statement somewhere in the description, of course).

Besides, experience show that descriptions often are not precise enough, including too many errors in the quire analysis; or a 'main hand' and a 'secondary hand' are mentioned, without specification of the folium extent of each; or information about layout is given for one page only, whereas the codex is composed of three main strata. The situation can be dramatic when this type of situation occurs in a catalogue of dated manuscripts, where the given dates should provide landmarks for further historical research, for example history of the scripts, the material supports, the transmission of a text and so on; there are cases where the date written by the hand responsible for a small later addition is presented in the catalogue as the date of the manuscript.

Codex N
Heading
Content
Physical feature a
Physical feature b
etc.
Bibliography

Skeleton 1: basic structure of a traditional scholarly description.

Even if these kinds of situation are not the most frequent ones, they disturb the research and demand new catalographical solutions. The question about how to represent the main syntactical elements of a manuscript book correctly and usefully in a catalogue description has occupied a number of people since the last decades of the twentieth century. Several systems have been suggested and experimented with, and each of them definitely, though not equally, allows the user to understand the syntactical structure of the codex better.

4.4.2 Syntactical description type A (type 2a in Andrist 2014)

The clearest and easiest way to convey the structure of a codex in a description is to describe each main stratum fully, one after the other, within a more global description of the codex. The resulting basic structure of the description is represented in Skeleton 2.

Codex N
Heading
Stratum 1
  Content
  Physical features
Stratum 2
  Content
  Physical features
etc.
Common features (Binding, History…)
Bibliography

Skeleton 2: basic structure of the syntactical description type A.

As far as manuscripts in Greek scripts are concerned, this structure was already used by Paul Canart for the description of collections of fragments (Canart 1970; see for example his description of Vat. gr. 1892, 528–540). Since then, this method has been used more broadly, for example in the catalogues of the Bibliothèque nationale de France (see its first mention in the *Catalogue général des manuscrits latins*, see Bibliothèque nationale 1975, 3; for example codex Paris, BnF, Latin 3548B, 46–52. For COMSt-related manuscripts, see for example the description of Paris, BnF, Syriaque 434 in the catalogue of Syriac manuscripts, Briquel-Chatonnet 1997, 178–183).

After a series of pioneering theoretical studies (see the cataloguing rules version 2.0 in Andrist 2003 and the study in Andrist 2006), the catalogue of the Greek manuscripts in Bern applied this structure type systematically, using primary, secondary, and some tertiary strata as description units (Andrist 2007a; for a detailed explanation, see the cataloguing rules 3.0 in Andrist 2007b; for further theoretical developments, see Andrist et al. 2013, 135–169).

Since then, this method has been taken up by various paper and online catalogues or descriptions. One can mention for example the catalogue of the French and Occitan manuscripts in the Staatsbibliothek zu Berlin (Stutzmann – Tylus 2007; see for example the description of MS 338, 50–61), where the same structure is also found quite extensively but, unfortunately, not systematically; or the beautiful series *Manuscrits en caractères hébreux conservés dans les bibliothèques de France* (see for example the description of codex Paris, BnF, Hébreu 673 in Bobichon 2008, 54–63), including colour plates *ad locum*, and the relevant bibliography after each descriptive section.

One also occasionally finds online descriptions based on the same principles (see for example the description of codex Paris, BnF, Grec 1823 in the database 'Archives et manuscrits' of the Bibliothèque nationale de France where, after the general features, the description breaks down into four 'Sous-unités de description' (<http://archivesetmanuscrits.bnf.fr/cdc.html>); partially reproduced in Andrist 2014, where other examples in European online catalogues are also mentioned); the new version of the database *Pinakes* fully allows for this structure. However, as far as we know, no electronic catalogue has been entirely organized on these principles, so far (see Andrist 2014).

In this description type, the structure of the description matches the main structural articulations of the codex very well, and thus allows visualizing it. Related elements are described side by side and it is very difficult to mix information which is not contextually relevant. By presenting all the historically related elements of the various features at once, it almost mechanically reveals part of the most important internal history of the codex. This descriptive principle could also allow for a new generation of catalogue databases, where, providing it is strictly implemented, electronic searches including a date would retrieve all the relevant available data, and only those.

However, in such descriptions 'per stratum' there is a risk of losing the general vision of the codex, especially in case of long 'full size' descriptions. This is why, in some of the catalogues based on these principles, the initial headings have been expanded into an overview of both the codex and the description (such is the case of the catalogues of the Greek manuscripts in Bern and the Hebrew manuscripts in Paris, in both of which this expanded heading is called a 'chapeau'; see Andrist 2007a and Bobichon 2008).

4.4.3 Syntactical description type B (type 1d in Andrist 2014)

A more radical way to use the main strata as the basis for the description is to dedicate a full description to each primary stratum, independently from the other ones, as if it were an independent book, including all the usual descriptive features.

Gumbert is the first theoretician of this type of description. Since the early eighties, he both developed a precise definition of the parts of the codex around the concept of 'codicological units' (see above) and published the first practical method, called IIMM (presented below), of using these parts as the primary units for compact descriptions of every type of codex.

The same structural principles are also sometimes used for online descriptions, for example in the database of Syriac manuscripts *e-ktobe*, about some manuscripts made of several primary strata, but, unfortunately, not yet systematically (<http://www.mss-syriaques.org>; see for example the description of Paris, BnF, Syriaque 434 in five units).

This structure (see Skeleton 3) is very easy to implement but, as a result, the one-to-one relationship between the number of the descriptions and the number of volumes being described is lost. In online databases, it is more difficult for the user to get an overview of the manuscript, particularly when the online description is obtained as a result of a search; database designers must always provide a way to set internal links to the related descriptions of the same codex within each description, as is for example convincingly done in the relevant e-*ktobe* descriptions (in the printed IIMM catalogues, this function is done through marginal arrows).

Codex N (first part)
Content
Physical features

Codex N (second part)
Content
Physical features
etc.

Information about the grouping
Bibliography

Skeleton 3: basic structure of the syntactical description type B.

4.4.4 Syntactical description type C (type 1c in Andrist 2014)

An acceptable compromise between the traditional structure and the syntactical description types A and B consists in numbering each stratum to be described (for example in the heading) and then systematically dividing each usual descriptive feature into as many strata as there are, explicitly using their stratum number.

The use of this structure (Skeleton 4) was suggested by Pamela Robinson as early as 1980, as she was working on Insular mediaeval manuscripts and developing her theory of the 'booklets' (Robinson [Pa.] 1980; about this publication and further studies of Pamela Robinson, and their impact, see Andrist et al. 2013, 12–14, 33, 42).

More recently, it was convincingly applied in various catalogues, for example in the catalogue of the Panagia of Chalkē (Kouroupou – Géhin 2008; see for example the description of cod. 90, 259–260) or the catalogue of the Greek manuscripts in Munich (Hajdú 2003; see for example the description of Bayerische Staatsbibliothek, Cod. graec. 113, 43–48).

The advantage of type C is the possibility for the readers to know quickly all the relevant data in a manuscript for any feature they are interested in. Since catalogues are mostly used by specialists in a particular field, they are thus able to find more quickly all the primary data they need: philologists see all

Codex N
Heading
Content
  1. … of stratum 1
  2. … of stratum 2
  etc.
Physical feature (a)
  1. … of stratum 1
  2. … of stratum 2
  etc.
Physical feature (b)
  1. … of stratum 1
  2. … of stratum 2
  etc.
Common features (Binding, History…)
Bibliography

Skeleton 4: basic structure of the syntactical description type C.

the content at once; art historians immediately find the miniatures and the decorative elements. There is, however, a major risk that they overlook the other features of the same unit, or lose sight of the chronological and contextual discrepancies, and make undue links between the elements they work on. Besides, anyone interested in visualizing each historical unit of the codex as a whole must, for each one of them, browse through all the features of the description.

Syntactical description type D (= type 2b in Andrist 2014)

Type D (illustrated by Skeleton 5) is one type of hybrid solution out of several existing ones. It has been sometimes advocated and used firstly by people interested in text history. It consists in presenting the textual content according to type C, and some or all other features according to type A, in order to get a quick overall access to the contents of the codex. In fact, any feature could be handled so, depending on the cataloguer's interests.

Codex N
Heading
Content
  1. content of stratum 1
  2. content of stratum 2
  etc.
Stratum 1
  Physical features
Stratum 2
  Physical features
etc.
Common features (Binding, History…)
Bibliography

Skeleton 5: basic structure of the syntactical description type D.

This type is acceptable, providing the strata are also clearly distinguished in the Content section (or any special section). Some rare examples of this type are found in the catalogue Cleminson et al. 2007 (see for example the descriptions of Budapest, OSZK, Quart. Eccl. Slav. 17), where the features Layout, Hand, and Ink are sometimes described per stratum, contrary to the features Content or Paper, described globally, but structured per stratum.

4.4.5 Choosing a syntactical model

The first beneficiaries of any of the syntactical models presented above are the cataloguers themselves, because the structure of the description immediately pinpoints any omission. Besides, it helps them see the main discontinuities in the codex and thus suggests some aspects of its history. As a result, syntactical descriptions clearly contribute to a higher quality in a catalogue, and provide its users with a more accurate and legible presentation of the codex.

But choosing a syntactical model implies also some thinking about which type(s) of strata should be used as the basic description units. All the primary and secondary strata only? Some of the tertiary strata as well, such as restoration leaves? Or should these be always described together with the strata they are now linked to? In any case, an acceptable descriptive solution must be found for the tertiary and quaternary strata, such as added slips or long notes; they must be either integrated with the relevant main description units, or grouped in some extra common feature unit.

In order to ensure some coherence throughout the catalogue, it is advisable to write up these decisions at the beginning of the project, then stick to them through the cataloguing process and finally inform the users in the introductory pages of the printed or online catalogue.

4.5. *Illustrated Inventory of Medieval Manuscripts* (IIMM)

As mentioned above, in the last thirty years Gumbert has developed, published and used the first method for making small size descriptions based on the structural parts of the codex (see Gumbert 1984, 2009a and 2009b including the description *Rules*). According to this method, called IIMM and meant to produce enriched inventories rather than regular catalogues, each primary and secondary layer is described autonomously, in four paragraphs, each of them taking up one to four lines (most often one line) with, on the opposite page, a full-size black and white picture of a small part of the manuscript.

A look at pages 44 and 45 of his last published IIMM catalogue (Gumbert 2009b) confirms the interest of his method: on these two pages, seven manuscripts, amounting to ten codex layers are described. For example:

BPL 78 is a one-layer manuscript:

Paragraph 1 (one line) gives the shelf-number, the origin and the date.

Paragraph 2 (one line) gives the content.

Paragraph 3 (two lines) gives the physical description, using many abbreviations.

Paragraph 4 (one line) gives the bibliography to the manuscript.

Besides, a 4 × 7 cm full-size reproduction of an extract from f. 2r is given on p. 45.

BPL 76C is also a one-layer manuscript, but the information in the first paragraph uses four lines.

BPL 81 is a three-layer manuscript. The description of the whole codex includes:

Three independent descriptions, one for each layer, but limited to the three first paragraphs of a normal description. Each description is marked in the left margin by an arrow pointing down.

At the end of the series, an extra bloc gives general information about the codex. It is marked in the left margin by an arrow pointing up:

Paragraph 1 (one line) gives the date when the layers were grouped.

Paragraph 2 (one line) gives the bibliography to the whole manuscript.

Three sample pictures, one for each layer, are given on page 45.

By doing so, Gumbert prevents the reader from dating the Hymns of SS Peter and Paul (in part 3, dating from the eleventh century) to the tenth century like part 1, or imagining that the copy of the *Regula canonicorum* (in part 2) was once on the bookshelf of Airvault of Poitiers (part 1).

Even though Gumbert inventories 'Latin' manuscripts, IIMM can be used, as it is or with very slight adjustments, for any kind of oriental codex. As a result, IIMM provides an unconventional way to do very compact, systematic and clear 'syntactical' descriptions of any codex.

4.6. Misconceptions about syntactical descriptions

Before concluding, it is worth addressing some recurring questions and misconceptions about syntactical descriptions.

1. Contrary to a widespread idea, a syntactical description is not necessarily a long one. IIMM is a good counter-example. For any given 'depth' of description, a syntactical description does not result in many more lines than an equivalent traditionally structured description, even when applied to codices of more than average complexity. And it does not necessarily take much more time, as soon as the cataloguer's eyes are accustomed to reading the language of the codex.

2. As we have already seen, syntactical descriptions are not restricted to printed catalogues of 'text manuscripts', but can be used for any kind of description, including for decorated manuscripts, and any kind of cataloguing project, including thematic catalogues or on-line ones. It is foremost a matter for the cataloguer to get into the habit of seeing and representing the codex syntactically. Where electronic catalogues are concerned, none of the above solutions is linked to any particular software or language

or database type, even though some software can make it easier to implement them. In many respects, electronic descriptions are not another world, because they address the same objects, with the same needs for exactness, even though electronics provides more opportunity for retrieving data or making links to images or electronic resources.

3. Syntactical descriptions do not compensate for the shortcomings of the cataloguing team, even when implemented online. The quality of the catalogue, its adequacy to the objects described and the relevance and systematics of its data always depend ultimately on the qualities of the people writing the descriptions.

4.7. Conclusion

Syntactical descriptions were born from the need to understand the strata of the codex better, and to make them better visible. After a few years, they have proved to be a new and improved way to understand and 'communicate' ancient Greek and Hebrew manuscripts. There is no reason why Syriac, Armenian, Arabic, and other catalogue readers should not also benefit from it.

As we have seen, the codex is like a language with its own rules, made of small significant details, recurring elements and more or less important discontinuities. When understood properly, this language informs the readers about the stratigraphy of the codex and, ultimately, its history. As Gumbert wrote in a recent email, 'the stratigraphy of an excavation is not the same as the history of the site, but it is a diagram which provides the facts that are the basis of that history. And the history cannot be drawn in a diagram, but has to be told. But it cannot be told if the basic facts have not first been clearly set out. Similarly, the stratigraphy of a codex is not the same as its history... but it provides the basic facts; and the history of a book cannot be given in a schematic model, but can only be told'. The syntactical description types presented above are privileged ways to express this diagram unambiguously, tell this history in a closing section of the description, and share them with people who usually do not have access to the 'excavated codex'.

References

Andrist 2003, 2006, 2007a, 2007b, 2008, 2014; Andrist et al. 2013; Bobichon 2008; Briquel-Chatonnet 1997; Canart 1970; Cleminson et al. 2007; Derolez 1974b; Gumbert 1984, 1995a, 2004, 2009a, 2009b, 2010a; Hajdú 2003; Kouroupou – Géhin 2008; Munk Olsen 1998; Robinson [Pa.] 1980; Stutzmann – Tylus 2007. Web sources: Bibliothèque nationale de France, *Archives et manuscrits*, <http://archivesetmanuscrits.bnf.fr/cdc.html>, last access May 2014; *e-ktobe: manuscrits syriaques* <http://mss-syriaques.org>, last access May 2014; *Pinakes* <http://pinakes.irht.cnrs.fr/>, last access May 2014.

5. The physical description (PAn)*

From a practical point of view, even at different levels of investigation, both analytical and summary descriptions are expected to include a description of the main features of the 'objects' to be catalogued. Even though there is no accepted definition of what exactly those main features are, they can be grouped in four categories, as a pragmatic way to overview them: 1) the manufacture of the manuscript and its physical features; 2) the contents; 3) the history of the manuscript after its making; 4) the bibliography related to these three categories. Mainly because of national traditions and field habits, there are no standard ways of organizing these categories or the features within each of them. For example, where should the miniatures and ornamentation in a codex be dealt with? Some would bring them up alongside the textual content; others would consider them at the same level as the writing; other would rather put them in a fifth category.

As a general tendency in the past thirty years, the physical description of the codex has received more attention than before, probably due to the spread of a codicological awareness and wider interest in the objects as such and their conservation. Consequently, the space dedicated to the physical features in each description has grown considerably; while the relevant information was traditionally condensed to a few points in a few lines, it is often now either a large paragraph containing all the features addressed—where the information is not always easy to find—or a series of paragraphs, one per feature, each with its own heading.

No matter how skilful the cataloguers or how big the cataloguing team can be, the heads of the cataloguing project are always faced with the need to make a series of choices, for example: (1) Which features are to be described, and which ones are not? (2) How deeply is each feature to be described? Which aspects thereof must be addressed? In reality, it is scarcely possible to give all the information specialists in the related fields need or would like to have. It is however possible to draw their attention to objects which can be potentially interesting to their work, allowing them thus to study them later according to their standards; (3) According to which formal rules are they to be presented? Usually, there are many possible solutions, which are not always fully satisfactory, as a few examples below will illustrate.

However, because of these many preliminary and sometimes unconscious choices, there is no such thing as 'an objective description' of any manuscript. Every description is necessarily a subjective interpretation of the object; but within the frame of these initial decisions, the cataloguers can strive to discriminate between what they observe and the conclusions they draw from it, criticize themselves, and systematically, clearly and usefully bring the data to their future readers. There are various ways of taking the many initial decisions, for example, again, according to the surrounding habits, or haphazardly according to one's personal interest. But the description of a codex can also be seen as the place where a global historical assessment of the object can be made by a person who can actually see and study it—and in many cases this is the only chance in a long period of time for this assessment to be made. An awareness of this opportunity and potential, and a readiness to exploit them will help in making appropriate decisions, as the description of the physical features of the object is an important part of this assessment.

This short sub-chapter is only a brief and incomplete survey and discussion of some of the main physical features of the codex, as one finds them in catalogues. They roughly match the main features expounded in Ch. 4 § 4, because they also play a role in understanding the internal structure and constitutive history of the codex, but this is not the place to discuss them in depth.

One is struck by the excessive level of heterogeneity in the descriptive solutions regarding the physical features of the manuscripts, especially since the features described are essentially the same in the various cultural areas, and the solutions used are not all equally convincing. By sharing remarks and illustrating a few solutions among many possible options, the author's double goal is to help cataloguers reflect on the meaning of a physical description before they start their work, and encourage them to define their own practice better, explain it clearly to their readers, use it systematically, and, as a result, more efficiently communicate the fascinating dimension of the physical features of ancient handwritten books. He also hopes to contribute to bringing some harmonization to the way the most basic and universal features of the book as a physical object are described. More theoretical discussions and some examples of the potential scholarly use of this information can be found in specialized codicological studies (see Ch. 1 § 1). Some practical information can also be found in some general publications (for example, Géhin 2005; Clemens – Graham 2007, 129–133; Petrucci 2001); or in sometimes outdated cataloguing rules for

* The author warmly thanks Marilena Maniaci for her comments as he was preparing this subchapter.

national projects (for example in Germany, Deutsche Forschungsgemeinschaft 1992, as well as Riecke 2009; in Italy, Jemolo – Morelli 1990, De Robertis et al. 2007); or in introductions or 'companions' to more local cataloguing initiatives (for example, Del Barco 2011, vii–xvii; Layton 1987, liv–lxvi; Andrist 2007b). Peter Gumbert's method of quickly and efficiently compiling an inventory of larger collections in a sound way could easily be adapted to the needs of oriental manuscript collections and deserves a special mention (see Gumbert 2009a, 2009b; see also Ch. 4 § 4.5).

As catalogue descriptions can be structured in different ways, for example according to the whole codex, or the codicological or production units (see Ch. 4 § 4), the neutral expression 'description unit' designates here whatever part of the codex is being described.

5.1. Page / folium numbers

Before presenting some of the main features of the physical description of a codex, some recurring situations about the way manuscripts' pages are sometimes numbered must be briefly mentioned.

The two usual ways to number pages in a codex are by folium (plus the indication recto or verso) or page numbers, starting at the beginning of the codex and ending at the end thereof. But it happens that these two methods are mixed within the same codex; and the numbers sometimes start afresh at the beginning of the production units or even of each text. No matter what the situation, the readers need to know about it immediately, since it is a key to understanding the description and, for the future users of the codex, to finding whatever they need in it. Whenever the codex to be described is neither thoroughly paginated nor foliated, it is strongly recommended to ask the responsible librarian to foliate it before beginning the description, in order to avoid mistakes and facilitate the location of the features described.

Cataloguers are often faced with special situations, including unnumbered folia (gaps), numbers used more than once (doublets) or unused numbers (jumps). Should then the codex be renumbered starting with the first problematic page or folium? Even though it could make sense to do so (as some libraries do), it brings new difficulties in cases where the codex has already been referenced in some publications. Modifying the numbering could result in making previous literature, including scholarly publications, hard or impossible to use correctly. However, if the codex has received no attention (or very little) in publications, renumbering it is harmless; as a preventive working method, the old numbers should never be erased, but just crossed out. If the problematic numbering is not modified, there are still several ways to create an unambiguous system where no two folia or pages have the same number, for example by adding one or two stars (or adding 'bis' or 'ter', or 'a', 'b'... etc.) to the repeated numbers, and adding numbers (with stars, or 'bis', 'ter' etc., maybe even in square parentheses to stress their late inscription) to unnumbered pages or folia.

Another problem sometimes occurs with a codex bearing two or more numbering systems; there are even situations in western libraries where Hebrew or Arabic manuscripts have received a modern foliation according to the Latin order of the pages against an original foliation in the natural order of the content. Again, the cataloguers must make their readers aware of the situation at the beginning of the description and clearly tell them which system is being used in the catalogue.

The numbering system used in the catalogue, which must of course match the main or best visible system in the codex, can be expressed in different ways, for example through a small formula like 'p. 1–16, f. 17–104, 104bis, 105–110, 121–216'.

5.2. Number of folia

There seems to be a consensus among catalogue writers that each description should include the number of folia at the beginning of it. Indeed, there is an obvious interest for the readers or the owners of a codex to know how many leaves there are in a manuscript, as it allows one to visualize 'how thick' the volume is and also possibly determine whether a leaf has been lost since the catalogue was published.

However, there are various ways and sometimes a certain amount of confusion on how to communicate this very basic information. Some include all the folia in their figures without differentiating the end-leaves, even though these belong to the binding of the codex (see below); as result, it is not possible easily to find out how many folia are from the more ancient time(s). Others exclude the end-leaves or even any empty leaf before the first text page and after the last one, so that the total number of folia remains a mystery.

In a modern catalogue, the readers can expect to distinguish clearly how many folia are used as end-leaves and in the main body of the book. Among several good ways of giving this information, one can mention short formulas with the structure 'el body el', which have been widely adopted albeit with many formal variations. For example, a simple codex made of 3 end-leaves, then 240 folia, then 3 end-leaves could easily be represented as 'III, 240, III'. Using a similar convention, a more complex codex made of 2 end-leaves of the current binding, then 1 end-leaf of an older binding, then 160 folia of a first production unit, then 50 folia of another production unit, then 3 end-leaves of the current binding could be represented as '210 f. = (2; 1) 160; 50 (3)'. Some catalogues mention numeration problems in this overview, rather than separately (see above), for example: '210 f. = (2; 1) 160 [p. 1–200; 200bis–ter, 201–319]; 50 (3)'. In case of recurring problems, the resulting formula can be hard to read, no matter how correct it is.

5.3. Writing support *(for a theoretical discussion, see Ch. 1 § 1.1.1–3)*

In catalogues, this important feature is always dealt with, but the depth of details varies a lot according to the type of support, the time available and the peculiarities of the codex.

Parchment: not much extra information is generally given about parchment in catalogues. In particular, it is not usual to identify the animal. One sometimes finds information about the quality of the original material, for example, if it was a fine or a coarse sheet; if it was irregularly scraped when it was manufactured; or if there are holes or stains. If visible, it is also interesting to note if the parchment was treated with special products including colourings, and the exact extent of it in the codex. Remarks of this kind can be very subjective, and they should be used very cautiously.

Paper without watermarks: there are different types of paper without watermarks (besides the reference publications mentioned above, see also Irigoin 1993, Humbert 1998 and an abundant useful sometimes annotated bibliography in Le Léannec-Bavavéas 1998, see also Ch. 1 §§ 1.1.3 and 2.1.4). When dealing with such material, it is expected that cataloguers will give all the information clearly to identify the type(s) found in the codex and, if applicable, the section(s) of the codex where each one of them is used. Paper historians have stressed the following aspects: (a) *the texture*: if it is regular or not; if the surface is smooth or coarse; (b) *chain lines*: if they are visible; if yes, if they are grouped or isolated; if the distance between two chain lines is roughly constant; if yes, roughly how many millimetres; (c) *laid lines*: if they are visible; if yes, if they are straight or curved; if they are regularly spaced; how many millimetres 20 lines take; (d) *format*: projected dimensions of the original sheet, if determinable; (e) *zigzags*: in Arabic paper, a sign called a *zigzag* can very occasionally be found.

Paper with watermarks: watermark analysis, consisting of comparing watermarks in a codex against dated watermarks in albums, is usually rewarding as far as dating the corresponding production unit is concerned, even though doing it properly is often a time-consuming activity. However, a careless analysis often results into a too optimistically precise dating. The various methods of drawing watermarks and their correct interpretation have been described several times (La Chapelle – Le Prat 1996; including theoretical considerations, Irigoin 1968 and Harlfinger 1980b; see also Rückert et al. 2009, 67–73, and the introduction in Sosower 2004; a huge amount of bibliography as well as a watermarks database are available on the website of the Bernstein consortium, <http://www.memoryofpaper.eu>).

Combined writing supports: the presence of combined writing supports is of major interest, and all the types (generally two) must be described. The way they alternate is significant for understanding the making of the book and should also be explained, for example 'quires made of four bifolia of paper embedded in a bifolium of parchment'; or 'two quires of parchment followed by four quires of paper'. One finds also embedded quires made of papyrus and parchment bifolia, or two types of paper bifolia of various paper thicknesses.

See also Agati 2009, 57–121; Déroche – Sagaria Rossi 2012, 43–50.

5.4. Quire structure *(for a theoretical discussion, see Ch. 1, § 1.3.1–2)*

Many catalogues of oriental manuscripts do not pay a lot of attention to the quire structure of the codex, even though it is a crucial information to perceive its internal organization, identify potential losses of folia and the clue to recognizing most of its production units (and, definitely, all the main ones). A precise collation is thus always needed. There are several ways to achieve this goal, again according to local or field traditions.

Using plain words is the easiest way and allows for any situation, but it takes much time and space, and the discontinuities in the quire structure do not usually appear very clearly. This is particularly true when only irregular quires are mentioned: for example, if a quire structure is described as 'all quaternions, except the second, the twelfth and the twentieth quires in seven folia, besides the fifth and sixth quires in six folia, and the thirteenth quire with an added leaf', who can easily tell if the text starting for example at the top of folium 104r is also at the beginning of a quire? Specialists have also designed specific formulas, two of which are frequently used in catalogues. Their principles and main advantages were described by Frank Bischoff in 1992 (see also Agati 2009, 166–172), but they have since been sometimes adapted to better suit the needs of the cataloguers (for example Layton 1987, lvii–lix; Andrist 2007b, 28).

For example, in the case of a codex whose body is made of four quaternions, then a quaternion whose eighth leaf has been cut off, then three quinions, then a quinion to which two leaves have been added,

– the so-called 'English formula' would be

$1\text{–}4^{8}$(f. 32) + 5^{7}(f. 39) + $6\text{–}8^{10}$(f. 69) + 9^{12}(f. 81).

Each bloc of the formula has three elements: the position of the quire in the sequence; then in superscript the number of leaves in these quires; then in parenthesis the number of the last folium in the bloc;

– the so-called 'German formula' or 'Chroust formula' would be

$4\ \mathrm{IV}^{\mathrm{f.\,32}} + (\mathrm{IV}\text{-}1)^{\mathrm{f.\,39}} + 3\ \mathrm{V}^{\mathrm{f.\,69}} + (\mathrm{V}+2)^{\mathrm{f.\,81}}$.

Each bloc of the formula has three elements again: the number of quires in a row that shows the same basic quire structure; then the related quire structure (roman numerals designate the quire type; generally corresponding to the number of bifolia), to which the number of added or cut-off leaves is specified within parenthesis; then in superscript the folium number of the last folium in the bloc;

– an 'improved German formula' is preferred by the author because, like the English formula, it gives the position of the quires, and like the German formula, it puts the quires in the middle of the string and allows for a precise description of each quire, whenever its composition is known:

${}_{1\text{–}4}4.\mathrm{IV}^{\mathrm{f.32}} + {}_{5}(\mathrm{IV\text{-}pos.8})^{\mathrm{f.39}} + {}_{6\text{–}8}3.\mathrm{V}^{\mathrm{f.69}} + {}_{9}(\mathrm{V}+2^{\mathrm{f.80\text{–}81}})^{\mathrm{f.81}}$.

Compared to the previous formula, the position of the quire in the sequence is now added in subscript as the first element of each bloc. Besides, the position of added leaves is specified according to their number, while the position of cut off leaves is specified according to their position in the quire.

– an improved 'English formula' is being currently developed for the project MaGI: *Manoscritti Greci d'Italia*.

Nota bene: within the two main systems, there are slight formal variations according to the cataloguers or special situations; for example, '+' signs are sometimes replaced by commas; sometimes, in the case of an irregular numbering system in the codex (see above), the starting folium of each bloc is also specified.

In the above examples, the ending folium numbers are always specified, even though many catalogues omit them. However, specifying them clarifies the formula and also allows cataloguers easily to check there is no inconsistency in their descriptions, since it is self-consistent: the ending folium number of each bloc must be equivalent to the number of folia in the bloc added to the ending folium number of the previous bloc (0 for the first one).

For parchment manuscripts in cultural areas where Gregory's Rule is usually respected, it is useful to note whether the hair and flesh sides of the folia respect it, and indicate which side is the first one, because discrepancies could point to losses of folia. For watermarked paper manuscripts, the position of the watermarks is a clue to the type of folding used to make up the bifolia (or even the quires). A change of watermark position could be significant in the production history of the book.

See also Agati 2009, 149–174; Déroche – Sagaria Rossi 2012, 98–108.

5.5. Ordering systems *(for a theoretical discussion, see Ch. 1 § 1.3.4)*

As described above, the correct order of the folia or the quires was sometimes secured by various types of 'sequence marks' in ancient times. Even if these signs were often cut off during the binding or rebinding processes, describing them (or whatever is left of them) often allows for a better understanding of the work of the scribes as well as for checking the unity and completeness of the volume. This is why it is worth noting all the extant quire marks of the codex described, as well as any change of practice and discontinuities in sequences. For example, in the case of quire signatures, it is useful to indicate where in the quires and on the page the marks are found, in which language, which numeric system (for example, ordinal or cardinal numbers; in full words...) and, if discernible, if they were written by the scribe or another maybe later hand. This last information is important for evaluating such situations where two otherwise autonomous parts are united by a single quire mark system. The author generally gives also the value of the first and last fully readable numbers and the place where they can be found, in order to allow the readers to do any cross-checking they wish.

There is again no standard on how to convey this information, even though it is usually given in full directly after the description of the quires. Some cataloguers have developed specific formulas which could help save space and time (Layton 1987, lvii–lix; more generically, Andrist 2004).

See also Agati 2009, 279–285; Déroche – Sagaria Rossi 2012, 108–120.

5.6. Ruling (and pricking) *(for a theoretical discussion, see Ch. 1 § 1.3.3)*

It is often difficult for cataloguers to decide what to describe as far as ruling is concerned, especially since recent research has confirmed that some of ruling aspects can vary a lot even within the same production unit (for example Sautel 2012). As a result, ruling is too often neglected in catalogues or even entirely omitted.

Pricking: information about the presence of holes made to guide the ruling of the pages is sometimes found in catalogues. However, if their position and some precise information on the ruling type is not also given, this information is not significant.

Ruling technique: this is the most frequently mentioned aspect of ruling (even though the instrument used in this process is not frequently mentioned), and is usually and usefully done in a few words. Since variations or clear-cut changes in ruling technique within the description unit are potentially important for understanding the making of the codex, it is worth mentioning them, including where changes occur.

Ruling type / ruling pattern: some catalogues give information on what the ruling grids look like, but the way they convey it varies a lot. Some simply refer to a published ruling type diagram (as in Dukan 1988 or Lake – Lake 1934–1945, XI), while cataloguers of Greek manuscripts have for decades been in the habit of using ruling type formulas, following the pioneer work of Julien Leroy (1976), whose description method triggered other ones (for a discussion of the various methods, see Albiero 2011). Today Leroy's more compact formula is the most used one, while Denis Muzerelle's more analytical one is gaining momentum, because, unlike the first one, it is open and allows the reader mentally to visualize the grid easily and directly.

For example, let us consider the diagram shown in fig. 4.5.1. Leroy's formula describes it as '22C1a' (Sautel 1995). '22' means there are 2 extra vertical lines (outside the 2 necessary ones) and 2 horizontal lines in the margin; 'C' means the lines used for writing start at the left end of the page and usually stop at the right vertical lines; '1' means there is 1 text column; 'a' means the 2 extra horizontal lines are in the top margin. There is no extra letter about the two supplementary vertical lines, because they are equally positioned on either side of the text column.

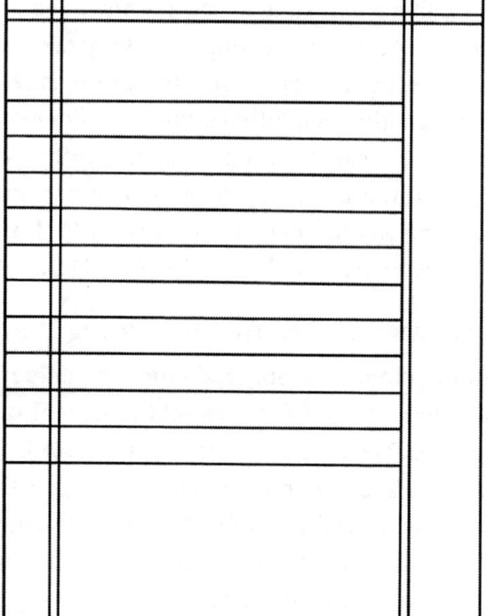

Fig. 4.5.1 Ruling diagram for type 22C1a (Leroy), 2-2/2-0/0/C (Muzerelle).

Muzerelle's formula describes it as '2-2/2-0/0/C' (see Muzerelle 1994, 1999). '2-2' describes the 2 vertical lines on either side of the text column; '2-0' describes the 2 vertical lines in the top margin and the lack of lines in the bottom one; '0' means that the first and last lines used for writing are normal; 'C' conventionally means the lines used for writing start at the left end of the page and usually stop at the right vertical lines.

Ruling pattern: should the effective ruling grid of the selected pages be also fully described, including the number and position of the lines, the space between them and the possible pricking holes? Ideally, yes. However, since the pattern generally varies through the manuscript, it is less characteristic than the ruling type, and therefore should not be 'preferred' to it. For the same reason, it is better to follow the recommendation of the codicologists and give the information for one specific page rather than artificially reconstructing a 'standard' ruling pattern out of supposed average values, as explained below.

Ruling system: it is generally not described in catalogues, but codicologists have repeatedly expressed the wish that it should be.

See also Agati 2009, 175–215; Déroche – Sagaria Rossi 2012, 121–126; Andrist et al. 2013, 51–57; Gumbert 2008; Sautel 2012.

5.7. Layout (besides ruling) *(for a theoretical discussion, see Ch. 1 § 1.4)*

Layout, dealing with the design of individual pages, is distinguished here from *mise en texte* dealing with the way a specific text is overall organized in the book (see Andrist et al. 2013, 95–100; Gumbert [2010b], no. 331.1; Déroche – Sagaria Rossi 2012, 191–226), for example how the main title and the chapter titles are distinguished from one another, if there is a conscious effort to begin the main chapters at the top of a page, or how the end of the chapters and the text are dealt with. In catalogues, the *mise en texte* is mostly not described, even if some elements thereof appear in the description of the decoration (see below). Basic aspects of the layout, including the number of columns and written lines per normal column are always explicitly given in catalogues, generally at the beginning; they allow the readers to visualize the pages and quickly compare the description units. More complete information about the writing space is generally also given, but often in an unsatisfactory manner. According to specialists, (1) giving the dimensions of the writing space is more useful if the dimensions of the margins are also given, so that it is possible to locate the 'black' and the 'white' areas on the page; (2) it is more useful to provide the description of a typical sample page, including the number of lines, rather than information about 'average' or 'extreme' situations; (3) for two-columns manuscripts, the dimension of the empty central space is also relevant; (4) the writing space should not be confused with the justification square, based on the ruling pattern; as a result, the justification space and the corresponding margins should be measured against the real written area, and not the ruled one; the right-end of the writing area(s) should then be measured on a typical line. Special situations can also be explained. Very few catalogues clearly distinguish them and give both pieces of information.

The way the ruling has been interpreted by the scribe is always an interesting piece of information, even though it is scarcely found in the catalogues: how many horizontal text ruling lines there are; how they effectively relate to the writing lines, for example if the text stands or hangs on the lines, if the first line and last lines are used, etc. Practical information about how to describe the layout is given below (see *Sample page*).

Other interesting aspects of the page layout include non-rectangular pages, pages with marginal commentaries, or with strongly varying written lines. The same overall principles apply in all these cases, where a higher quality of information is reached if one or several real sample page(s) are described rather than generic unqualified situations. For example, what can a reader deduce from a description telling there are 4–30 written lines per page? On the one hand, incompletely used pages, for example at the end of a text, should not be taken into account; on the other hand, in case of conflicting information within the description unit, one can always write, for example, '25–30 written lines, generally 28 or 29'.

See also Agati 2009, 219–240; Déroche – Sagaria Rossi 2012, 126–136.

5.8. Sample page *(for the ruling pattern and the layout)*

As mentioned before, codicologists agree that the description of the effective ruling pattern and the effective layout, if done, should represent one (or a few) carefully selected typical page(s), rather than an 'average' or reconstructed 'normal' grid or text area. There are various ways to describe a page layout and a ruling pattern. One can again give all the figures one after the other with an explanation, but there are also several possible methods allowing for a more or less easy to visualize representation of it, like Muzerelle's method to describe the ruling pattern of a specific page, which can also be adapted to describe its layout, as sketched now.

Describing the ruling pattern: according to Muzerelle's method all the horizontal then vertical distances between the lines are given, together with a series of signs both symbolizing the lines and indicating their position relative to the text area (see Muzerelle 1999, 155–156). For example, in the above example (fig. 4.5.1), assuming it is the recto side of a page, the measure could be

‘10 < *5 ≤ 119 ≥ 5 > 15[×] 8 ; 5 ; 15 ≤ 160 ≥ 28[’.

It means there are 10 mm from the left edge of the page to the first vertical line, and 5 mm to the second line; these 5 mm are used to accommodate initials (sign *) and this second line actually limits the writing space (≤), which is 119 mm wide; the right vertical lines are also 5 mm distant from one another, and the right margin, which has been significantly trimmed ([), is 15 mm broad. After the sign ‘x’, the distance between the horizontal lines is described on the same principles. However, the author always provides vertical information before horizontal one.

Describing the page layout: the method used by the author is inspired by Muzerelle’s method for ruling patterns. The following example describes the written space for a two column page; both vertical and horizontal dimensions are taken in the middle of the page:

‘(p. X) m columns, n lines –
total height of the page × total width of the page –
(size of the top margin) vertical writing area (bottom margin) ×
(size of left margin) left column (central empty space) right col. (right margin)’.

In practical terms, this could take the shape

‘(f. 36r) 1 col., 22 l. – 167 × 109 mm – (21) 116 (30) × (17) 28 (5) 28 (31) mm’.

The cataloguer can then take advantage of the fact that this method is self-controlled: adding all the vertical information should result with the same value as the total height; the same is true with the horizontal figures.

In practice, both pieces of information can easily and meaningfully be combined, for example in Andrist et al. 2013, 162:

‘*Pages*: (f. 102r) 1 col., 29 l. – 264 × 218 mm =
traits: 18<12<13≤160≥13>24>24 × 18<8≤114≥6>10>29>7>26 mm;
text: (43) 162 (59) × (26) 107ca (85ca) mm.’

5.9. Script *(for a theoretical discussion, see Ch. 2 § 1).*

Script is usually mentioned in the catalogue descriptions. However, there is no common practice in the catalogues, nor, on the theoretical level, any widely admitted objective way of describing it or even a widely accepted terminology. Some would like to have a full description in words, while others deem it too much linked to specific scholarly traditions and would just date the script (if possible) and publish a picture of it. In-between, there is a long continuum of different possibilities. Let us share some subjective considerations on this very subjective and sensitive topic from a cataloguing point of view. (a) For sure, no matter which solution is preferred, a picture of the script will definitely make more sense to most of the readers than whatever is written, especially if the script on the picture is legible. In fact, many palaeographers prefer to get a 100% sized small part of a written page, or a good sized picture on the internet, than a strongly reduced full page in print. As a result, no matter what the basic description options are, it is a good idea, if possible, to publish also a sample of each script. (b) Most of the oriental traditions have some words to designate broad types of scripts (see Ch. 2) and it would not make sense not to use them in catalogues. For those cultural traditions where the story of script is advanced enough, it also makes sense to suggest a copying date and/or place according to the script, and compare it to the other dating elements. If one does not feel confident enough in dating scripts, it is not wrong to ask a specialized colleague. (c) Writing in a codex is often based on a system of several scripts used in different textual situations, often combined with a change of ink or size (see Andrist et al. 2013, 95–100); for example, there could be one script for the main body of the text and some others for the various levels of titles, the first words of the text or the chapters, the marginal commentaries, the colophon, etc. (d) Before cataloguers choose to give a full description and/or use a technical terminology, it is worth asking themselves how clear the resulting paragraph will be to most of the readers, at least to people working on the same cultural world. As terminology also evolves, including new meanings for old words, it is in any case necessary to provide some bibliographical references in the introduction, which will give much later readers a chance to understand the description correctly. (e) Describing a script, or a script system, is not the same as describing the way it is executed or its quality (see Ch. 2 § 1). Information on both these things is interesting and may contribute to a subjective evaluation of the quality of the production unit. Nor is it the same thing as identifying a scribe; as a result, information on the script is expected even if the scribe is named in a colophon or was recognized by the cataloguer or another specialist. (f) As far as assessing the codex is concerned, it makes sense to distinguish how many script systems as well as how many different hands there are, and where (or according to which 'rules') they change. If a secure result cannot be reached, because of the peculiarities of the scripts and the hands, the available time and/or the competence of the cataloguers, it is best not to give this type of information.

5.10. Decoration *(see also Ch. 1 § 1.5.1 and Ch. 4 § 3.2)*

The state of the description of decoration in catalogues is much like the script:

- usually catalogues give some information about it, especially when it has to do with miniatures or the use of coloured ink;
- there is however no common practice among cataloguers;
- neither is there any widely accepted objective way of describing decoration in words nor any standard general terminology (at least not in all the cultural areas, even when art historians are involved). Admittedly, the decoration of some codices is a complex achievement and its description cannot be fully done in a standard catalogue (but see Ch. 4 § 3.2 on specialized catalogues). As a result, there are various scholarly traditions, generally using their own terminology;
- pictures generally communicate it much better than any verbal description;
- evaluating the decoration in a reasonably subjective way in a catalogue is usually accepted, since it helps visualise the quality level of the description unit;
- a technical analysis is potentially useful for dating and locating the description unit;
- decoration often also works as a system adding sense or legibility to the main content and 'usability' of the book, as it often underlines the structure of the content and the hierarchy within each text copied (see also Ch. 1 § 1.5.1 and other tradition-specific relevant paragraphs in Ch. 1). For example, as far as the non-illustrative decoration is concerned, the title and beginning of a text is often particularly enhanced by decorative elements, while chapters and smaller text units can begin with various levels of coloured and decorated initials, which help the readers both better to understand the text and more quickly to find particular parts of it. Thus, describing the major aspects of the decoration also allows the readers better to understand the strategies of the people producing this unit as far as the *mise en texte* is concerned.

There are several reasons why the interest in the decoration is traditionally greater than in the script: because of its visual impact; or the implied monetary value, both at the time of production and now; or the greater fragility of the codex; sometimes also because of its significance for the history of art.

The author's current way to avoid too subjective a description and present usable information is inspired by Canart 2005, and follows the following principles: (1) firstly, miniatures are singled out and described with the help of an art historian, or very briefly on the basis of existing publications; (2) secondly, the main elements of ornamentation are classified (in the typology of the relevant cultural area); (3) each major element is described individually, giving its location in the codex, position on the page, measurements, used motifs and colours; (4) other and more common elements (common initials, rubrication, ornamental patterns, etc.) are described en bloc.

For an example of a specialized catalogue, see Hutter 1977–1997; her cataloguing practice is explained at the beginning of each text volume.

5.11. Bindings *(for theoretical considerations, see Ch. 1 § 1.7)*

In the cataloguing habits of the oriental cultural areas, there is a fairy widespread tradition of mentioning the binding of the codex. However, it is usually limited to the most visible external aspects thereof, while specialists, mostly restorers, have developed very complex protocols for the technical description of all the analysable elements of binding (see for example Grosdidier de Matons – Vinourd 2010; see also <http://www.studite.org>). It is of course not expected that standard catalogues should provide such descriptions, but, depending on the available time, a systematic description of the following not-too-difficult to observe elements (or at least a relevant subsection thereof as far as the cataloguing project is concerned) should be considered, since they are useful to describe the codex, and usually interesting to book or art historians dealing with bindings as well as people in charge of the long-time preservation of the codex.

General technique and type: plain information if the binding is a modern or an ancient one, a western or an oriental one. Giving the type, if known ('half binding', 'Limp vellum binding' etc.), helps to visualize the codex.

Outer dimensions: the three basic measurements. Ideally, the information distinguishes the width of the board and the width of the object, including the thickness of the spine.

Sewing: number of sewing stations; sewing supports; materials used.

Endbands (if any): the material; the colours and patterns of the threads, if any.

Boards (if any): the material (wood, cardboard); if visible, the technique how the thread(s) or supports are fixed.

Spine: its shape (rounded, straight...); how many raised bands, if any.

Covering and decoration: the material, colour and extent of the covering (the outside and the inside of the boards); the decoration (embossed ornamentation, gilding, etc.). Specialists are always interested in a full-size reproduction of the tooling.

Clasps (if any): the position, material and working system of the clasps; state of preservation.

End-leaves and paste-downs: the number of front and back end-leaves (if not already given), and a description as of any writing support. In the case of paper, an analysis of the watermarks, if present, can result in a good dating of the binding; however, one must make sure the sheets were not reused from an older binding or added during a later restoration.

Edges: if the edges are angular or rounded; if they were decorated (coloured, gauffered...).

Remains of previous bindings: traces of previous bindings, if any, including unused holes in the gutter, reused end-leaves, traces of clasps, etc. Other elements in the codex can indirectly also point to previous bindings, such as trimmed marginal notes, ancient quire signatures or similar.

Inscriptions: possible notes or ancient shelfmarks on the spine or the end-leaves and paste-downs often preserve important information for tracing the history of the book. Presenting them all at the same place in the description, rather than together with the description of every element, helps see them and evaluate a possible relationship between them.

Date of the current binding: based on the previous elements, an assessment of the date of the current binding is often possible. Since the current binding is necessary younger than the latest standard main copying, dating the binding provides a *terminus ante quem* for the latest scribe's work. Inversely, dating the copying provides a *terminus post quem* for the binding. However, there is *a priori* no other direct chronological relation between both aspects, because, ever since the Middle Ages, manuscripts were often rebound. Unless it can be shown that the quires were bound shortly after being copied and the current binding is the original one, dating the scripts and the binding must be based on two independent analyses. Besides, since decorative elements are sometimes added by new owners in a later time (including the Middle Ages), one must be very careful when using visual elements (stamps, coats of arms, etc.) to date the binding.

As far as describing the binding is concerned, seeking the help of conservators could save the cataloguers a lot of time and guarantee the correct use of standard terminology. Since the general terminology varies among 'schools' and is subject to evolution, it is useful, in the introduction to the catalogue, to inform the readers about the system used and give some bibliography. See also Agati 2009, 347–381; Déroche – Sagaria Rossi 2012, 247–280; Szirmai 1999; Mouren 2013.

5.12. State of preservation

Many catalogues give an evaluation of the state of preservation of the manuscripts, but there is no rule as far as the place where the information is to be found. Some catalogues combine it with every relevant feature (writing support, binding, etc.), while others make it in an independent paragraph. The depth of the information varies also according to the scope of the cataloguing project.

5.13. Conclusion

A good physical description should be reliable and consistent. Reliability is important because both the ethics and the needs of manuscript studies require that one should give and receive information that reflects reality as closely as possible, even though, ultimately, studying the codex itself is the only way to get closer to the full reality of it. Consistency, both in the choice of the features to be described and the way to do it, is central because it allows the reader to go through all the main features of the codex, and compare the manuscripts on a sound ground. However, systematic consistency is not a goal in itself but a means to understand and communicate better the physical reality of the codex and allow further research. There are exceptional objects and situations, where one needs exceptionally to convey 'extra-systemic' information. However, the cataloguer should never intentionally neglect any of the features that are included in the cataloguing project.

The physical make-up of the codex is definitely a language that is worth learning and using. Describing it systematically makes the cataloguer notice details and gather information that can help to assess and 'communicate' the codex better.

References

Agati 2009; Albiero 2011; Andrist 2004, 2007b; Andrist et al. 2010; Bischoff 1992; Canart 2005; Clemens – Graham 2007; De Robertis et al. 2007; Del Barco 2011; Déroche – Sagaria Rossi 2012; Deutsche Forschungsgemeinschaft 1992; Dukan 1988; Fingernagel 2007; Géhin 2005; Grosdidier de Matons – Vinourd 2010; Gumbert 2008, 2009a, 2009b, [2010b]; Harlfinger 1980b; Humbert 1998; Hutter 1977–1997; Irigoin 1968, 1993; Jemolo – Morelli 1990; La Chapelle – Le Prat 1996; Lake – Lake 1934–1945; Layton 1987; Le Léannec-Bavavéas 1998; Leroy [Julien] 1976; Mouren 2013; Muzerelle 1994, 1999; Petrucci 2001; Riecke 2009; Rückert et al. 2009; Sautel 1995, 2012; Sosower 2004; Szirmai 1999. Web sources: Bernstein consortium <http://www.memoryofpaper.eu>, last access 24 September 2013; *e-corpus* <http://www.studite.org>, last access 24 November 2014.

6. Catalogues and cataloguing of oriental manuscripts in the digital age (JG)

With the introduction of electronic means and methods into the cataloguing of manuscripts since the late 1980s, both the production of catalogues and their dissemination have begun to change considerably. As a matter of fact, the number of cataloguing projects concerning oriental manuscripts that are not digitally-based is steadily decreasing these days. A major difference in this context concerns the question whether the catalogues to be produced are still meant to be published in the 'traditional' way, that is in printed form, with digital means remaining restricted to preparatory functions, or whether the envisaged output is planned to be digital itself, that is online or via an electronic storage medium such as a DVD. If we leave the case of mere electronic typesetting (as a preliminary stage of printing) aside, both these aims usually build upon similar grounds in that they presuppose the conceptualization of database structures, but with different requirements concerning the scope, the granularity, and the retrievability of the data to be compiled, and with different prospects concerning their later usage. In the following sections, we will discuss the basics of database schemes and structures that are applicable to the cataloguing of manuscripts, the formats of electronic catalogues and their potential, and the challenges electronic cataloguing brings about.

6.1. Database schemes and structures

No matter whether a cataloguing project aims to result in book form or as an online website, databases that are meant to cover the information to be disseminated will have to address the basic issues of manuscript cataloguing as outlined in Ch. 4 § 1, namely (1) the manufacture of the manuscript and its physical aspects; (2) the contents of the manuscript; (3) the history of the manuscript after its making; and (4) bibliographical data related to both the physical and textual aspects of the manuscript. To what extent these data are compiled mostly depends on how detailed the catalogue is meant to be—anything between a mere 'inventory list' and a fully-fledged 'analytical' catalogue can be covered by the database structures of today, and as a matter of fact, database-like structures have even been underlying, explicitly or implicitly, many cataloguing projects that were initiated before the digital age. Thus, for example, the giant project of a 'Union Catalogue of Oriental Manuscripts in German Collections' of the Göttingen Academy of Sciences (*Katalogisierung der orientalischen Handschriften in Deutschland*, with the series *Verzeichnis* etc.) has been designed since its foundation in 1958 to follow a description pattern which comprises 26 sub-items, including shelf number, cover, material, state of preservation, page number, format, number of lines, writing style, decoration, scribe, date, origin, author, title of the work, quotations of the first and the last lines of the text as well as of colophons, further remarks and a number of registers (or concordances); and it should well be possible to continue the work 'by using the format of the newly developed database framework which was set up on the basis of the MyIHS system developed by Leipzig University in 2006 according to the conditions of GNU (General Public License)' as envisaged now (Raschmann 2012). The very fact that older catalogues usually possess an inherent database-like structure has been the reason why many digital cataloguing projects of today started by transforming the information stored in printed works or file cards into electronic data fitting into a database scheme, and 'digitally-born' cataloguing projects are not necessarily richer right from the beginning with respect to the data fields they contain, for example, the DOMLib / Ethio-SPaRe Manuscript Cataloguing Database project comprised a 'minimal data model' in its application phase (2009), consisting of 'Signature; Short title; Material; Measurements; Number of folia; Dating; Scribe; Author; Donor; Location original; Location current; Short contents; *Incipit*; Illuminations; *Additiones*; Further details; Bibliography' (the set has since been extended; see Nosnitsin 2012b).

However, database schemes developed for the cataloguing of manuscripts are anything but identical even today, and there are still some major differences in the database structures proper. First of all, it may be crucial for the database in question whether (1) the main concern of the compilers is the manuscript as an object of codicology (for example in establishing a catalogue of manuscripts of the same provenance); whether (2) they are rather interested, as philologists, in the texts contained in the manuscripts they intend to describe (for example in cataloguing all manuscripts containing the works of a given author, which may result in individual manuscripts being described only partially—an example of this is the online catalogue of the 'Handschriftencensus' project, <http://www.handschriftencensus.de/>, which aims at surveying the manuscript transmission of German texts of the Middle Ages and which does not always mention texts in other languages present in the codices under consideration); or whether (3) they are primarily engaged in providing additional information ('metadata') concerning digitized images of the manuscripts they intend to make available. Differences may further be due to the scope of a given catalogue, depending, for example, on whether the object of cataloguing is the complete manuscript collection of a given country or repository, a special collection of a country or a repository determined by language, script, writing support, or age of the manuscripts, or manuscripts across different collections that share certain features. Noteworthy differences between databases may also arise from the level of consistency they require, especially with a view to how many fields must effectively be filled in, and, more importantly, how they have to be filled in; the existence of 'descriptive standards' (a good example—though in a poor design—for a descriptive standard usable for manuscript cataloguing is the Swiss 'Verbundkatalog Handschriften – Archive – Nachlässe (HAN)', <http://aleph.unibas.ch/F?con_lng=GER&func=file&local_base=DSV05&file_name=verbund-han>) may be crucial for later interoperability of the database (in the sense of data linkage and integration into portals and hypercatalogues, cf. below).

The most crucial question determining the structure of a database from the codicological point of view is to what extent and how it is able to reflect the different 'production units' that may be present in a given manuscript codex (cf. Ch. 4 § 4). To give but one example (kindly provided by P. Andrist): let us assume that part 1 of a given manuscript contains a text of Plato copied in the twelfth century, while part 2 of the same manuscript contains a text of Aristotle copied in the sixteenth century. It must be guaranteed in this case that the manuscript will not be 'hit' when executing a query for codices containing twelfth century copies of Aristotle's texts. The problem may even be more crucial if we take into account smaller production units such as reader and owner notes, as well as restoration and bindings, each with their own dating, and for the time being, no database (or search engine) seems to guarantee the contiguity of individual production units with the chronological information pertaining to them. This is due to the fact that relational database structures that were developed in the beginning of the digital age were mostly not flexible enough to adequately cover the structure of 'mixed' manuscripts consisting of several parts of different age, provenance, and/or content; but future generations, be they based upon SQL ('Structured Query Language', a widespread programming language to be used with relational databases) or XML ('eXtensible Markup Language', a more freely adaptable encoding system, cf. General introduction § 2.1) are likely to be able to overcome the problem. This is especially true for tree-like database structures using the XML-based 'MS Description' recommendation of the Text Encoding Initiative (TEI P5). However, it should be clear that this is not primarily a question of technology (relational databases vs. XML schemes) but of methodology, i.e. it depends on the overall design of the database.

6.2. Electronic catalogues and their potentials

With the establishment of digital databases containing the data to be catalogued, and especially with the development of the World Wide Web offering online access to them, it has become more and more tempting to disseminate the catalogued information on manuscripts electronically instead of or alongside a printed form, and the number of 'electronic catalogues' that are accessible online is steadily increasing today. Among the main advantages of this type of catalogues, we may mention, (a) that the data they contain can be retrieved dynamically via interactive search entry forms or the like, instead of static indexes (we may neglect here the mere electronic reproduction of a printed catalogue, for example, in PDF form, as this does not imply peculiar retrieval facilities other than sequential searches in the text); (b) that they can be linked to any other kind of electronic content in the web such as, for example, other catalogues, image repositories, or bibliographical materials; (c) that they can be steadily corrected, updated, extended and expanded. A few examples may suffice to illustrate these advantages.

(a) Search facilities and human interfaces

To access and retrieve the information contained in databases, it is necessary to provide human interfaces that allow for interactive communication between the user and the database in terms of search queries. Depending on the complexity of the database structure, search interfaces can be more or less sophisticated; in the maximum case, the search form may offer as many fields for the entry of query items as the database structure contains. This is true, for example, for the query forms offered by *SfarData*, the codicological database of the Hebrew Paleography Project run by the Israel Academy of Sciences and Humanities, which provides, among others, seven check boxes to choose a given subset of data (styled 'corpus': for example, 'documented dated', 'documented undated with identified scribe'); nine select boxes to choose a 'major area', 'specific region', 'country', 'city', etc.; several input boxes to enter search terms like 'catalog no.', 'microfilm at IMHM', or 'words in colophon'; and a large set of additional entry points for searching the names of scribes, illustrators, and others (note that the site <http://sfardata.nli.org.il> is still under construction as of October 2014).

In accordance with recent practice developed for the retrieval from electronic catalogues of libraries, there is a strong tendency today to facilitate the entry of queries by enabling 'full text' searches, i.e. searches across many or even all the fields of the database without having to specify the fields in question. This has been implemented, for example, by *e-codices*, the Virtual Manuscript Library of Switzerland, which offers a facility to 'search in manuscript descriptions' right on its start page, thus allowing the user, for example, immediately to find 164 catalogue entries containing the word *parchment* among the 981 manuscripts catalogued in the database (<http://www.e-codices.unifr.ch/>). Even with this comfortable 'Google-like' search facility, users will have to be aware of possible differences in the interpretation of their queries; this is true, for example, for the entry of query strings consisting of more than one word: a search for *parchment codex* may be taken by the search engine to represent the two words *parchment* and *codex* individually, delivering all instances of descriptions that contain at least one of them (*parchment* 'or' *codex*), or it may expect that both words must both be present in a given description (*parchment* 'and' *codex*; this is the assumption of the *e-codices* search engine, which delivers 68 occurrences for the 'collocation' of the two words). In order to search for *parchment codex* as a two-word unit, it may be necessary to enter the string in quotation marks, again in accordance with 'Google-like' practices (this is true for *e-codices*, which delivers 6 occurrences of 'parchment codex' in its database).

b) Data linkage, portals and hypercatalogues

The possibility of linking data up with materials residing elsewhere in electronic form is with no doubt a major advantage of the digital age. In the case of electronic catalogues of manuscripts, this opens a wide range of hitherto unavailable functions that may be styled revolutionary indeed. For example, while printed catalogues normally contain but a few sample images of the manuscripts they describe or even no images at all, online catalogues may offer links to digital images of every single page of a given codex, provided they are accessible via an internet address (URL = Uniform resource locator). In the same way, the content description of a given manuscript can be linked up with a full representation of the text(s) it contains within an online edition or an electronic corpus, and bibliographical data in a catalogue can be linked up with digital representations of the works in question (for example, a first account of a manuscript in a traveller's report, a former catalogue, or a scientific treatise concerning the codex). It goes without saying that all these links can be established in both directions, thus opening wide perspectives of cooperation for cataloguers with philologists and other people dealing with manuscripts.

Another great advantage of the linkability of online data consists in the possibility to put the information contained in various catalogues together, for example with respect to manuscripts of the same provenance that are stored in different repositories or even countries, or codices with similar textual content spread over the world. In this connexion, we can distinguish two different approaches which may be covered by the terms 'portal' and 'hypercatalogue', albeit the two terms are not always sharply differentiated. Portals in the proper sense are web sites that offer more or less structured access to a set of related web sites. Different from simple link-lists which contain nothing but a collection of links to internet addresses (cf. <http://titus.fkidg1.uni-frankfurt.de/curric/comst/links.htm> for the COMSt-internal link-list as of February 2010, last accessed June 2014; another example concerning manuscripts is <http://palaeography_training.bangor.ac.uk/paleo.php>, last accessed June 2014), portals may be able to combine the search facilities of the sites they are linked to, either by collecting their data via 'data harvesting' and storing them locally, i.e. on the portal site itself, or without doing so; this can be achieved via so-called protocols which allow for inter-machine communication, distributing a query across the sites involved and gathering the query results 'on the fly'; an example of a portal working with both methods is the portal of the *Consortium of European Research Libraries* (CERL; <http://www.cerl.org/web/en/resources/cerl_portal/organization>; the CERL portal operates with the OAI-PMH protocol for data harvesting

('Open Archives Initiative' Protocol for Metadata Harvesting) and the Z39.50 protocol for data access 'on the fly'), which is mostly dedicated to manuscripts and early printed material of western provenance and which assembles the data from twelve online catalogues (or, to be more correct, the databases underlying them) to date. Unlike the 'portal' approach of this type, a 'hypercatalogue' would be more restricted thematically, bringing together the contents of different individual catalogues that have common objects such as, for example, a certain language, a script, a country, a time-span, or the like; one example of this is the *Pinakes* database hosted at the Institut de recherche et d'histoire des textes in Paris, which aims at providing a 'census of all Greek texts from the beginning up to the end of the sixteenth century which are contained in manuscripts described in printed catalogues, with the exception of papyri' ('*Pinakes* a pour objet principal le recensement de tous les textes grecs, des origines à la fin du XVIe siècle, contenus dans les manuscrits décrits dans les catalogues imprimés de bibliothèques à l'exception des papyrus', cf. <http://pinakes.irht.cnrs.fr/>; the project was initiated as early as 1971 at the Pontifical Institute of Mediaeval Studies in Toronto and moved to Paris in 1993). In contrast to this project, which is explicitly based upon printed information digitized manually, hypercatalogues that are based upon electronic catalogues presuppose the ability of intercommunication between servers and databases, with at least a small common set of metadata elements distinguishing, for example, fields containing information on textual content, authors, scribes, provenance, or the like; for this purpose, database developers may refer to several international standards that have mostly been designed for library catalogues: cf. the so-called 'Dublin Core' metadata set, which consists of 15 elements (Title, Creator, Subject, Description, Publisher, Contributor, Date, Type, Format, Identifier, Source, Language, Relation, Coverage, Rights; cf. <http://dublincore.org/documents/dcmi-terms/>, last accessed June 2014). More recently accepted standards are METS (Metadata Encoding and Transmission Standard), an XML schema for encoding descriptive, administrative, and structural metadata regarding objects within a digital library, and MODS (Metadata Object Description Schema), a schema for a bibliographic element set that may be used for a variety of purposes.

c) Dynamic data

Unlike printed catalogues, electronic catalogues can be steadily corrected, updated, extended and expanded, provided they are built upon a database. As a matter of fact, many cataloguing projects of today make their data accessible long before they are completed, not only for better visibility but also in order to enable users to provide feedback. For portals and hypercatalogues, the resulting flexibility of the data they rely upon has a strong impact in that it forces them continuously to keep track of changes. This strongly speaks in favour of accessing the data 'on the fly' instead of data harvesting, because the latter method yields a snap-shot of a given moment that may then be perpetuated longer on the harvesting server than in its source.

6.3. Challenges and problems of electronic catalogues

The problem of the 'dynamicity' of digital data as outlined above is not the only challenge that compilers and users of electronic catalogues have to cope with. A few other problems that may be crucial will be treated below; they are related to the reliability of query results, to questions of authorship, and to the maintenance of data.

a) Reliability of query results

As was stated above, one advantage of electronic catalogues consists in the fact that the data constituting them are accessible from various perspectives via more or less sophisticated search engines. However, it may be questionable whether or not the data retrieved in this way are reliable, especially in the case of hypercatalogues and portals. The reason is that the more complex a database structure is, the more it has to be consistent in the data it contains, and the more its developers have to take care for users not to be misled. To give but two examples: a) as was shown above, the *e-codices* project offers easy access to the information contained in the manuscript descriptions it has stored, via a 'Google-like' full-text search. However, the user should be aware that the manuscript descriptions that are accessible in this way are written in several languages (German, French, English) so that a search for *parchment* will yield different results (164 hits) from a search for *Pergament* (452 hits) or *parchemin* (129 hits), and even the abbreviated form *Parch.* gives 60 hits. To find the information that the *e-codices* database comprises a total of 791 manuscripts whose support is parchment (including 2 mixed codices with papyrus, and 6 with paper), the user has to move to the main search page instead (<http://www.e-codices.unifr.ch/en/search/all>); b) under the title of *e-corpus*, the Centre de Conservation du Livre (CCL) in Arles is establishing, together with several partners, 'a collective digital library that catalogs and disseminates numerous documents: manuscripts, archives, books, journals, prints, audio recordings, video, etc.' (<http://www.e-corpus.org/>). Structured in the form of a portal, it provides access to several 'virtual collections', among them the complete collection of digitized microfilms of the Georgian manuscripts from Mount Sinai hosted at the university library of Louvain-la-Neuve in Belgium, an invaluable tool indeed. The collection can be accessed by entering *géorgien* in the 'Google-like' query field on the start page ('search in all collections'); however, in the query result, the 97 codices in question are arranged without any ordering rule being discernible, beginning with Sin.georg. 6, 8, 11, 16, 15 (<http://www.e-corpus.org/search/search.php?search=search&page=1&q=g%C3%A9orgien&search=Search>). Another result will be achieved by selecting *Bibliothèque de l'Université Catholique de Louvain, Institut orientaliste* as the 'Location' and *Georgian* as the 'Language' in the (main) search form (<http://www.e-corpus.org/search/index.php>): this, however, yields only 21 items, again starting with Sin.georg. 6 but continuing with Sin.grec 230 and 566. Searching for *Georgian* instead of *géorgien* via the 'Google-like' form yields no results from the collection at Louvain at all but, among others (of a total of 74 'hits'), a quotation from Tommaso Vallauri's *Latinae exercitationes grammaticae et rhetoricae studiosis propositae* (1869) about Virgil's *Bucolica et Georgica.* Note that a more or less numerical arrangement of the 97 items can be accessed via <http://www.e-corpus.org/eng/ref/96559/Sinai_Mf_UCL_Georgiens/> (last updated 7 September 2011), but this is not searchable.

h) Authorship and authors' rights

As with all other kinds of digital publications that are accessible online, compilers of electronic catalogues may be concerned about their authorship being protected well enough to prevent theft or misuse of their work. As everyone knows, not every change in a database is correct, and there are cases where the modified data is less correct than the previous one. Therefore it is very important that the name of the person who enters a given item of information into the database and who takes the 'scientific responsibility' for it to be secured, even across several stages of development of the database; in other words, if the compilers want to keep their author's rights guaranteed when being read and quoted by others, they should take care to place their authorship 'seal' on every single description that might be accessed and displayed separately (for example via a search function); depending on the retrieval engine used, this might also be generated automatically. This implies that regulations must be agreed upon between the compilers of electronic catalogues and the institutions hosting and publishing them concerning the preservation of the former's rights and concerning the question of whether, how and to what extent the institution may have the data modified or altered by others. And users of electronic catalogues should be sure to name the authors of the catalogued information they refer to, provided this is correctly 'signed'.

In addition, authors of electronic catalogues may have to face problems with 'scholarly referencing'. If, for example, in an article, someone refers to information found in a printed catalogue, the information is easily verifiable in the sense that anyone can check whether the person referring to it did, or did not, quote it correctly. When referring to information given in an electronic catalogue, there may be a discrepancy between a given quotation and what is found in the catalogue online at the time someone else accesses it; in this case it remains unclear if the quoting person did not excerpt it correctly or if the catalogue (output) was changed after the quotation was executed. It is therefore essential that quotations from online catalogues contain an indication of the exact date when the information was retrieved (in quite the same way as we should do with other online publications). It would further be desirable that future generations of databases to be used for electronic cataloguing provide a function for 'tracking changes' (in a similar way as Wikipedia does).

The safeguarding of authors' rights may also be crucial for the compilers of electronic catalogues themselves. In general, authors' rights are much harder to maintain in the globalized digital world than in the universe of printed matters. One reason is that the rights differ considerably from country to country, a fact that can easily be illustrated by the policy of the 'Google Books' project, which aims at digitizing all printed books of all times and places. Users of the project web site (<http://books.google.com/>) will realize easily that it is mostly older books that are accessible to them for full download (in PDF form), in accordance with copyright regulations. However, the terms of accessibility are different for users from the

USA and users from Europe: for US citizens (or, rather, users with a US-American IP address), Google will provide free access to books that were published before 1923; for Europeans (i.e. users with a European IP address), the borderline is the year 1871. This implies, for example, that the *Catalogue of the Hebrew Manuscripts Preserved in the University Library, Cambridge* (I) published by Salomon Marcus Schiller-Szinessy in 1876 is freely downloadable from the USA but not from Europe (<http://books.google.de/books?id=GEMPAAAAIAAJ>). This procedure is not only disturbing but also far from being legally exact, for no European country has a copyright regulation that would determine 1871 as a borderline year. Instead, copyright regulations usually prescribe that a given work be protected for a certain amount of time after the death of the author(s); in Germany, this is a period of 70 years. Obviously, Google deems it unnecessary to investigate authors' lives in order to determine the exact end of the protection period of a given work. I may quote here from an e-mail by Mr Jon Orwant (Google Inc.) of 2 May 2011: 'Each nation has their own copyright rules. Within the US, we are usually able to use 1923 as a cutoff date for determining whether books are in copyright, and so some of the seven books you identified are fully readable and downloadable inside the US. Outside the US we have to use the rules of the appropriate country. ... We are able to make the PDFs available within a country when the books are out of copyright in that country, and when we do they're available directly from Google Book Search; if you had a US IP address you could just visit Google Book Search and download the PDF with no involvement from us. But because copyright status is often hard to determine, we have settled on the following rule for countries that don't have a cutoff like the US: either the book must have been published before 1871, or there must be clear and convincing evidence that all authors of the book died more than 70 years ago...' (in the given example, this would have been as early as 1960 as Salomon Marcus Schiller-Szinessy died in 1890, cf. <http://en.wikipedia.org/wiki/Solomon_Marcus_Schiller-Szinessy>, last access May 2014; by the way, the book can be freely downloaded from the 'Internet Archive' at <http://www.archive.org>, a Canadian site that does not block European users, see < https://archive.org/details/cataloguehebrew01schigoog>, last access October 2014).

Be that as it may, compilers of electronic catalogues who wish to include data from other works, either as quotations or via links to online resources, should treat these in the same way as they would do with quotations in a printed book.

c) Maintenance and longevity of data

In contrast to printed books, digital media are often regarded as unstable and therefore uncertain. It is true, for example, that most data carriers of today (for example, CDs, DVDs, hard disks) have only a limited 'lifetime' during which the data they contain remain both unaltered and retrievable, and the question whether data compiled and stored today will still be interpretable in, say, fifty years' time also depends on the availability of matching software. The developers of electronic catalogues should therefore consider thoroughly how and where to publish them, and they should be aware of the necessity to maintain the data by regularly adapting them to upgraded soft- and hardware and the like.

One important prerequisite for this is the usage of international standards. In the field of oriental languages, this is first of all a matter of the encoding of scripts and characters. We are in the lucky position today to be able to apply the Unicode standard for this (<http://www.unicode.org>; cf. General introduction § 2.1), which comprises nearly all scripts and characters of the languages involved, both modern and ancient, thus enabling us even to present original scripts and Roman transcriptions side by side in one document. In comparison with the chaos produced by the mapping of proprietary fonts in the 1980s and 1990s, this is a huge achievement leading towards long-time interpretability of our data.

Another important issue is the standards to be applied in the structure of databases and their output. Here, too, proprietary formats should be avoided right from the beginning. Any solution that is based upon XML structures will be preferable to relational databases as they provide greater flexibility and, what is more, transformability into usual output schemes, for example as HTML-based web pages; however, relational databases still tend to be more homogeneous than XML bases, and the quality of XML bases largely depends on the skills of the person who tags the data. Given the huge amount of data that is already available online, it is anything but probable that the basic features of web output will change dramatically in the future; in other words, both the use of Unicode character encoding and of 'markup languages' of the HMTL / XML type are likely to survive long enough so that electronic catalogues of today should build upon them.

References

Andrist 2010, 2014; Nosnitsin 2012b; Raschmann 2012. Web sources: CERL <http://www.cerl.org>, last access November 2014; Dublin Core <http://dublincore.org/documents/dcmi-terms>, last access November 2014; *e-codices* <http://www.e-codices.unifr.ch>, last access November 2014; *e-corpus* <http://www.e-corpus.org>, last access November 2014; Google Books <http://books.google.com/>, last access November 2014; Handschriftencensus <http://www.handschriftencensus.de/>, last access November 2014; Internet Archive <https://archive.org/>; Palaeography Training <http://palaeography_training.bangor.ac.uk/paleo.php>, last access November 2014; *Pinakes* <http://pinakes.irht.cnrs.fr>, last access November 2014; *SfarData* <http://sfardata.nli.org.il>, last access November 2014; TEI; TITUS <http://titus.fkidg1.uni-frankfurt.de/curric/comst/links.htm>, last access November 2014; Verbundkatalog Handschriften – Archive – Nachlässe (HAN) <http://aleph.unibas.ch/F?con_lng=GER&func=file&local_base=DSV05&file_name=verbund-han>, last access November 2014; Unicode <http://www.unicode.org>, last access November 2014.

Chapter 5. Conservation and preservation

edited by Laura E. Parodi

1. Introduction and definitions (KS)

1.1. Introduction

Scholars and students in the field of manuscript studies, cataloguers, collection keepers and staff of digitization studios, all working with original manuscripts, have to rely on the physical condition of the materials, and their activities also have to affect it. Thus they are involved with conservation and preservation issues. It is evident that without conservation and preservation strategies, the availability and accessibility of the materials is at stake. But what exactly is the scope of conservation, what is the role of a conservator and what can be expected of him or her? In this chapter the different aspects of conservation and preservation will be discussed. It is not a concise manual for conservators to be, it contains no instructions for hands-on treatment, nor any in-depth analysis of deterioration problems or overview of treatment options. It rather aims to explain what conservation entails and how conservation can be best deployed by those individuals or institutions concerned with the safeguarding, accessibility and use of manuscript material. Indeed, conservation in the broadest sense is subservient to cultural heritage itself. In the field of written and printed heritage, conservation specialists not only actively intervene to preserve deteriorated documents; preservation responsibilities also concern storage and handling issues, awareness-raising and training of staff. Furthermore, conservators—because of their specialist knowledge of the physical aspects of documents—may advise on material and technical analysis and description of manuscripts.

'Conservation' and 'preservation' are umbrella terms under which the whole range of activities and responsibilities can be subsumed. The conservator's vocabulary developed while the field was emerging as a separate and identifiable profession, in fact, only quite recently. Thus this chapter begins with an introduction to the terminology and history of conservation. With the vocabulary, it will become clear that the field of conservation is defined by a widely accepted set of standards and approaches. They form the point of departure for all conservation-related decisions, a description of which will follow, providing first an overview of the current situation in Europe and the Orient and subsequently exploring the possibilities of material research in relation to condition problems and conservation treatments, and explaining contemporary techniques and practices. Preceding this description of conservation and preservation issues, measures and actions, context is provided by a description of the agents of damage and types of decay, for it is necessary to be aware of the factors that have an impact on the preservation of manuscripts.

To set preservation priorities or decide on a preferred intervention often is a delicate task; it depends not only on the condition and value of the object, but on a range of factors concerning, among other things, time, budget, the skills of the available professionals, and the circumstances of the item or the collection that it is kept in. Additionally, old repairs as well as material evidence of former use or users are part of the history of the artefact. Examining ethical considerations will shed light on the complexity of decision-making.

The final topic considered is digitization, as its development is so closely connected with the accessibility and preservation of textual material, whether it concerns the imaging of a single manuscript or a whole collection. Technical aspects, current standards and consequences of image management, including future accessibility, will be considered.

This chapter can only give an outline of the intricacy of conservation practice. Conservators are not only dexterous people who know how to treat damaged documents; they also assess conservation needs, undertake research, advise and organize conservation projects. Every conservation treatment and every conservation project requires tailor-made solutions; it is therefore useless to give recipes and treatment proposals. A professional conservator is trained to assess the situation and judge any needs and options. There are levels of complexity in different objects, but also in different circumstances. For example, certain types of inks and pigments may add to the complexity of the treatment approach, necessitating testing and literature research. For some decorated manuscripts it will be advisable to interleave the pages with miniatures or ornaments with thin protective leaves whereas in other instances the manuscript is best left without interleaving. On a different plane, unfavourable environmental conditions and a peripheral location may hinder straightforward preservation actions, in which case a well trained conservator will approach the situation accordingly. That means we do have accepted standards for conservation and preservation, but they need to be contextualized, which is part of the conservator's job. In other words: *best practice* is dependent on context and circumstances.

1.2. Definitions

From a glance at the terminology it becomes clear how wide the spectrum of conservation actually is. A lot of terms are needed to cover the full scope of the field. Traditionally, it is associated with physical interference in the condition of the object, involving terms like repair, mending, restoration, often implying the addition or replacement of materials to improve the object's function and/or visual appearance. More recently, conservation is felt also to encompass measures taken to stabilize or consolidate the object's condition, without directly intervening and altering the original object. Authenticity has become an important value and a key concept in conservation. To differentiate between the active and passive approaches, another term was introduced to address the latter: preservation. Presently, conservation and preservation are the most frequent terms in the field. Confusingly, when the digital copy became an established means to replace the original, conservation was also used as an equivalent for 'preserving the content' and, although not preferred by conservationists, restoration is a term still used by some. To differentiate between the terms it is helpful to explore their use over the decades, by consulting previous discussions in conservation literature as well as some official documents used by professional conservation organizations: the American Institute for Conservation (AIC); the European Confederation of Conservator-Restorers' Organizations (ECCO); and the International Institute for Conservation of Historic and Artistic Works (ICON). The following definitions reflect their common application.

Restoration is interventive treatment, aiming at improving the condition and aesthetic value of a damaged or deteriorated object. Although codes of ethics refer to 'bringing back to a former condition, fixed prior to the treatment', the term has the connotation of restoring the original condition. Precisely this association disqualifies the term among conservation specialists, because the 'original' condition is a state we cannot be certain of, and the attempt to return the object to its 'original' state would therefore always remain an interpretation. Even more importantly, it would by definition imply that traces of the object's history have to be disguised or removed. That in itself is against the accepted standards.

Preservation (*Preventive conservation, Passive conservation*) comprises all actions and measures that positively influence the condition of objects of cultural heritage. Such are: environmental monitoring and improvement of the climatic conditions in which the objects are stored, used or presented; integrated pest management; risk analysis; optimizing storage conditions with respect to shelving, boxing and hygiene; data collation and analysis. Furthermore, it also includes awareness-raising, staff training, setup of protocols for the handling, transport and exhibition of materials, and the implementation of reproduction techniques such as digitization with the purpose of preventing or at least limiting further consultation of the original. Thus, preservation consists of a whole range of measures and actions that are not necessarily part of a conservator's daily tasks, but are key to safeguarding cultural heritage, and a prerequisite to making interventive conservation treatments meaningful.

Conservation (*Active conservation*) comprises all actions and measures directly intervening in the object's condition, aiming to stabilize it and prevent further deterioration. It involves consolidation of the condition with or without enhancing the aesthetic value and it often aims to improve the condition of the object with the purpose of enabling access.

Minimal conservation is an approach that aims to consolidate the object's condition without disturbing its authenticity. With book conservation this involves the greatest respect for the book-archaeological qualities of the artefact.

Stabilization stands for the implementation of preventive measures that affect the process of natural decline and risk of further dilapidation in a positive way.

Consolidation means making the object physically stronger or more stable, and less prone to losing nearly loose parts, by applying minimal intervention techniques.

Repair is a generic term that can both include conservation treatments as well as old mends, carried out to restore the object's functionality.

References

AIC 1994a, 1994b, 2008, 2013; ECCO 2002; ICON 2011; IIC 2010; Newman [Walter] – Quandt 1994.

2. Core principles of conservation (KS)

2.1. Reversibility

Conservation and preservation are allied in their purpose to maintain or restore access to artefacts and documents. However, conservation can be distinguished from preventive measures as it involves a physical intervention on individual items, even if this is done to prevent further damage. Because the action involves actual physical interference with the object, the profession of conservator is not without risks, and much harm can be done when objects are treated by non-experts. Therefore, a set of guidelines is agreed on by the professional community and conservation specialists are required to respect these principles.

The first rule in conservation is that any treatment and alteration to the object should be reversible. For example, when adhesive is used, it should not change the chemical composition of the original material and future reactivation and removal of the adhesive layer should remain possible. However, reversibility in the strictest sense is not always feasible: for example, when dust and dirt have to be removed prior to applying an adhesive, it will not be possible to return the object to the soiled state, should removal of the adhesive layer in the future be necessary. Another instance of this is the consolidation of flaking paint: it is not possible to remove a consolidant from the paint layers in decoration, and it is unlikely it will become feasible in the future. Although the irreversibility of a dilapidated condition may not seem disadvantageous, we cannot predict what material issues may be crucial for future research and readings of the objects. As a consequence, we have to accept that the principle of reversibility is impracticable to a certain extent, and that the practice of conservation sometimes involves uncomfortable compromises. On the one hand, this highlights the urgency for continuing research to ensure that we are using the best possible materials in our treatments. It also argues for continuing education of staff to be aware of new developments in preservation and conservation issues. Conservation ethics require us to be responsible for striving to be perfect in our conservation treatments even though perfection cannot be achieved in the strictest sense; we have to acknowledge the risk/benefit analysis that underlies treatment choices. For example: there is no excuse for using PVA (polyvinyl acetate, an acidic, irreversible adhesive) on a binding when other reversible adhesives are well-known and readily available; however, there is no known reversible paint consolidant and sometimes it is not the best option to let damage continue unchecked. Conservators will then have to weigh the options and choose the best defensible treatment.

This situation underlies one of the core arguments for documentation: besides an accurate object and condition description, documentation contains the reasoning behind an intervention. Careful documentation is also a prerequisite should future use, research or damage require the removal of added materials in order to return the object to its untreated condition at the time of the intervention, within the limits of the 'reversibility compromise'.

2.2. Integrity of the object

Secondly, conservators have to respect the integrity of the object, which means that they will try to stay as close as possible to the character the artefact has at the moment in time of the necessary treatment. However, there is a range of 'acceptable' treatment approaches available and, indeed, it is widely encountered today in various institutions that consider themselves to be maintaining the highest conservation standards. Institutions which hold manuscript collections use them in different ways: an art museum tries to instruct the public about the artistic values of a particular culture, while libraries may be more concerned with textual analysis or codicology. Moreover, a research university that allows and even encourages users to examine the real manuscript is quite different from one that only provides digital copies. Consequently, although it is widely accepted that traces of the object's history have become an integral part of it, dealing with the material evidence may take different directions. For example, an art museum may place greater emphasis on aesthetics in its treatment decisions: an unsightly repair is likely to be removed if it makes the object difficult to appreciate as a work of art, while in a research library historic repairs are to remain unless they cause harm to the object or form a threat to its preservation. Again, this issue highlights the importance of documentation, which may be the only way for a record of some previous repairs to survive.

2.3. Retraceability

Another essential notion is that the intervention should remain visible and retraceable. That does not mean that materials added to strengthen and support original material or fill losses are not to be toned in the colour of the original. Quite the contrary: for the repairs to blend in with the original object visually it will be necessary to dye or retouch the new materials; this will help the user of the artefact to appreciate the object's authenticity. However, such treatment should not hamper the possibility to perceive the object's age, use and purpose. In general, it is thought that an exact matching of the old and new materials in both colour and structure and texture is to be avoided, for when the intervention is not visually detectable, the history of the object is in a sense obscured. Moreover, such treatments would be close to falsification and could support fraudulent practices.

2.4. Compatibility

The last principle supports the above rules: the compatibility of methods and materials, in a technical and visual sense. In general, the original methods and adhesives are reversible. Organic adhesives are water-soluble and can be reactivated with moisture; sewing structures are reversible by nature. If diverging materials are chosen, it should be for reasons of functionality: flexibility or strength for example. It is self-evident that all the materials used should be durable and not affect the original materials in any negative way.

2.5. A holistic approach

Although not a principle specified in existing Ethical Codes (AIC, ECCO, ICON, see also General introduction § 4.1), a conservation specialist will weigh his decisions starting from a sound perspective of feasibility and sensibility. In the first place, this implies that the object must be stored in a safe and appropriate place after treatment. If the conditions for preservation are not reached, one should question the purpose and rationale of conservation treatments. As much time and expense will be involved when setting up and carrying out conservation programmes, a conservator feels the responsibility for this effort to be well invested. But, without concern for the objects' storage conditions, careful handling or display, the effect of conservation treatment is less valuable. Indeed, preservation is the foundation of the long-term safeguarding of cultural heritage. For that reason, professional conservators are equally concerned with the training of staff, providing guidelines for use, transport and storage, and advising on digitization procedures and equipment or exhibition guidelines.

Objects are also not to be conserved simply because they are damaged and someone is available to take on the job; there should be a reason for interfering. This could be a progressive deterioration process or the inaccessibility or unsuitability of the current condition for certain uses such as digitization or exhibiting. It is the conservator's job to ask for the context of a certain object within a collection and its anticipated use, in order to be able to propose a conservation treatment.

These guidelines indicate the main reasons for conservation. Books are objects to be used, so conservation measures aim to make or keep the object accessible. However, the intervention will be limited to treatment that does not interfere with traces of the object's history and that will allow (future) material research or future treatment. It aims to facilitate the object's perception and appreciation. From these guidelines the profile of a conservator also becomes clear: he is a sort of a book surgeon and archaeologist, and he needs a wide background in cultural history, a knowledge of organic matter and an understanding of chemical processes.

2.6. Book archaeology

Ever since manuscripts were made they were valued for their intellectual content, and the relative scarcity of texts or the evident value a manuscript represented in terms of an economic entity—it would require time and materials to replace it—has led to a long tradition of repair. These actions were undertaken for obvious reasons: people wanted to safeguard and preserve manuscripts, make them accessible and ensure future use. A relatively recent development in the field of manuscript studies is material research (see Ch. 1). It is based on the assumption that documents contain much more information than their intellectual content only; all aspects of manufacturing, technical details and choices of material can provide clues about the socio-cultural context and history of the artefact (Szirmai 1999; Maniaci 2002a; Pearson 2008; Scheper 2014, forthcoming).

The growing awareness of the importance of the physical aspects of a book also affects the development of the conservator's profession, for conservation specialists are not only actively involved in the safeguarding of manuscript collections and the stabilization of the objects' condition, therewith enabling their accessibility. They also, and probably increasingly so, play a role in the understanding of the object as an artefact. The very nature of the work—getting inside the structure of the object—allows for examination of the materials and construction in a way no other specialist can, and because of the specialist understanding of materials and their characteristics, a conservator has insights into the use of techniques or changes in traditions that will add to the framework of codicological knowledge, necessary for a full understanding of a manuscript culture.

With that, one of the most important factors for conservation is explained. Notwithstanding the value of digitization or other means of creating surrogates (and we may expect the technical possibilities to develop further in the near future), the safekeeping of the original artefacts will remain essential.

References

Maniaci 2002a; Pearson 2008; Scheper 2014, forthcoming; Szirmai 1999.

3. Defining the need for conservation (PH)

In general there are four parts to a manuscript: the support used for the text block, the media with which the text block is written and decorated, the sewing to hold the text block together and the binding with which the text block is covered. The basic principles that guide all conservation treatment—such as preserving the original artefact and using reversible methods and materials—are the same for each of these parts. Still, the parts are quite distinct in terms of the different materials with which they were made and their different functions, and all are aspects of the manuscript which the conservator must understand well. For repair materials to be appropriate and effective, their chemical nature must be compatible with those of the manuscript's original materials. Similarly, when treatment is necessary, methods must be chosen which do not change how each part of the manuscript functions.

Damage and loss to the support may not always require treatment. Those that do not compromise the stability of the manuscript or increase the risk of further damage when it is handled can be left untreated. If intervention is necessary, however, repair materials must be used that do not significantly alter how the original support behaves. When a manuscript leaf is turned or moves in response to changes in humidity and temperature, it will tend to fold and bend where it is weakest. Repairs that are too heavy and stiff will restrict movement where they have been applied and instead shift associated stresses to the weaker adjacent areas of the original support. These formerly undamaged areas may then crack or break. On the other hand, if a repair is too light or weak it will not sufficiently support a damaged area. The stresses associated with any movement of the leaf will then be focused on these still weakened areas, exacerbating the earlier damage that exists there.

The written text and any illumination or illustration present in the manuscript are not to be changed during treatment. There is no justification for the removal or obliteration of original media. The inks and paints used in different manuscript traditions are highly varied and their components are still not well known. When they are flaking or friable, careful testing is required to find an appropriate consolidant and method of application.

The sewing associated with a particular manuscript tradition often strongly affected how a manuscript was used. Most commonly then, a repair sewing should ensure that the manuscript can be opened and used as originally intended. Value judgments during treatment that equate stronger sewing with better sewing are neither appropriate nor correct. Some manuscripts were intended by their makers to be opened more easily and fully than those in other traditions. So adding sewing supports, for example, to manuscripts that originally had unsupported sewing may have the consequence of greatly restricting the flexing of the leaves and cause damage to the support and media in the text block. In some instances, however, the historical sewing present on a manuscript can be the source of considerable damage to it and an alternative method of sewing must be considered during treatment.

Historical bindings are not to be replaced during treatment with ones that are considered more attractive or in some other preferred style. Nor is it always necessary or desirable to reconstruct bindings for manuscripts that come to the conservator unbound. New bindings compromise the historical integrity of manuscripts to which they are applied. So in collections where unbound manuscripts are expected to be handled little if at all, individual boxes for each of these manuscripts can adequately protect them without necessitating any changes to their structure.

4. Types of decay in manuscripts (PH)

As a carrier of information and vector for the expression of cultural values and aesthetics, a manuscript was made to be used. Accordingly, its functional purpose often exposed it to many potentially damaging conditions. As a manuscript is a complex structure with many moving parts, damage can occur in different places and vary widely in degree of severity. A manuscript is also a composite structure, made from several different materials, each of which can vary in its susceptibility to a particular damaging influence and its chemical and physical response to that influence.

An understanding of these agents of deterioration is critical for effective manuscript preservation and conservation. For the safekeeping of manuscripts, deleterious conditions must be identified and ameliorated. Any conservation treatment must depend on accurately assessing the issues manifest in the condition of an individual manuscript and determining how properly to address them (see also Ch. 5 §§ 1, 2, 3 and 5).

With almost everything in the immediate environment of a manuscript a possible source of damage, manuscript custodians face a great challenge in trying to limit harm to their collections. Circumstances must be defined, be they in institutional or personal settings, in which legitimate use of manuscripts for research and display is balanced with safeguards appropriate for their long-term survival (see also Ch. 5 § 2).

The enormous array of influences which are potentially damaging to manuscripts can be usefully grouped into general categories. For the purposes of this discussion these are: damages caused by Natural Ageing; Human Agency; Biological Factors; Chemical Factors; Environmental Factors; and Disaster (another categorization and description of these agents of deterioration is given in CCI 2009). It should be emphasized that these groupings are not mutually exclusive and that the sources of the damage observed in a manuscript will usually come from several different categories. For example, high humidity (an Environmental Factor) is a necessary precursor to mould attack (a Biological Factor), and the severity of the attack may be exacerbated by elevated temperature (another Environmental Factor). Similarly, if inks or paints used in a manuscript cause deterioration of the paper support (Chemical Factors), weakening of the paper often promotes tearing, losses and other physical damage when the manuscript is handled during reading (Human Agency).

The condition of a manuscript, whether damaged or not, may be stable or the damage may be ongoing, which can have immediate repercussions for how that manuscript is stored or when treatment is undertaken. Active infestation by mould or insects, for example, must be addressed quickly and effectively to prevent it from spreading. Damage may be limited to a particular area in a manuscript or more generally distributed, which can give useful information about the history of the object—how it was used in the past and under what conditions. Tears and heavy soiling restricted to a few particular leaves, for example, may indicate that generations of previous readers focused their attention for some reason on these pages in the manuscript. Finally, it is the holistic analysis and understanding of the damage in manuscripts, both individually and collectively, which underlies effective policies for preservation and conservation (see also Ch. 5 § 5). Poor outcomes can be expected, for example, from preservation efforts which limit human handling in a manuscript collection but ignore insect infestation. By the same token, conservation treatments which focus exclusively on one aspect of a manuscript can lead to the severe and irreversible damage of other aspects. For example, in order to make a text block support easily accessible for treatment, original sewing and endbands are frequently cut and discarded and historical bindings permanently altered or removed.

4.1. Manuscript damage caused by natural ageing

Even if a manuscript has been stored and used under ideal conditions, simply with the passage of time, the ageing of the organic materials from which it is made causes them to weaken and become more vulnerable to other types of damage.

4.2. Manuscript damage caused by human agency

Manuscripts are made by and for human beings. They were intended to be read, looked at, admired, traded and transported. So the various kinds of damage caused to manuscripts by human use and misuse are probably the most common and pervasive form of damage they exhibit. As this is also one of the forms of damage most readily amenable to control, proper handling is a cornerstone of good preservation.

Humans can be extremely negligent when using manuscripts, as evinced by a wide variety of stains, soiling, tears, splits, folds, creases, gouges, scratches, ink marks and losses to be found in them (fig. 5.4.1). Without user guidelines and proper care, it is demonstrably apparent that people will eat and drink over manuscripts, use sharp objects in their vicinity, write in them, remove pages, lift and hold them carelessly and, in extreme instances, even vandalize them. Although some institutions try to solve this problem by entirely eliminating outside readership, human agency can never be entirely eliminated as a danger to manuscripts: manuscript custodians—owners, librarians, curators and conservators—will have access to them and must also be trained in proper handling. Common sense policies must be established, communicated and enforced which do not permit the use of pens, sharp objects, food or drink around manuscripts by anyone at any time. When manuscripts are consulted or displayed they always need to be supported at an angle of opening that does not stress either their bindings or sewing structures. When removed from or returned to shelves, the person handling the manuscript must be conscious of the potential for abrasion caused by sliding the book across the shelf or against adjacent volumes. A manuscript transported more than a short distance should be on a cart or supported in a container in case the mover stumbles or trips.

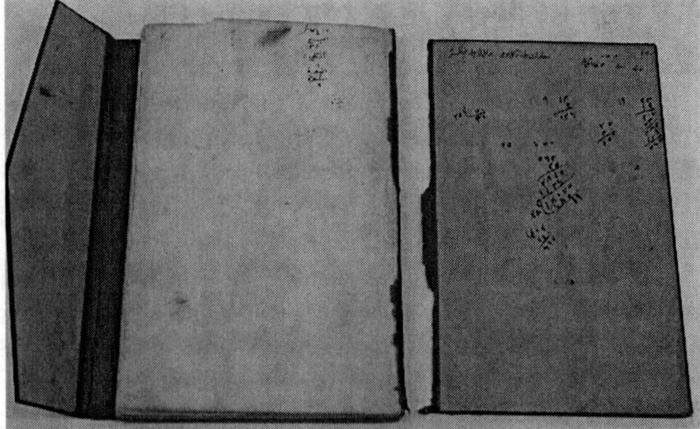

Fig. 5.4.1 Detached cover: Use and misuse of manuscripts can cause the joints of the binding to split. This often results in the detachment of a cover from the rest of the book, as shown here. Leiden University Library, Or. 194, photograph by KS.

A special type of damage to manuscripts caused by human agency can be the result of the process of digitization. Often one goal of digitization is to allow readers access to the information in manuscripts while limiting their physical contact with the objects, thereby reducing damage through reader handling. But a digitization process in which the manuscript is opened flat and pressed down to take the image, a process repeated for every opening in the book, places maximal stress on the binding and sewing structures and areas of the text block weakened by paint or ink deterioration. Such stress, compounded during the entire period of digitization, can ironically cause more damage than it was intended to forestall. When sewing structures are broken, for example, loose leaves become vulnerable to being lost and tend to slide past the edges of the text block where they can be easily crushed and torn (for prevention see also Ch. 5 § 7).

In this regard, another ironic type of damage to manuscripts is caused by improper conservation treatment. Conservators without adequate training may learn a few repair techniques which then get applied, whether necessary and appropriate or not, to every manuscript that comes to them. Or they may use chemically harmful and irreversible materials in their treatments, such as PVA glues (see also Ch. 5 § 2.1), laminating substances, or poisonous pesticides. Finally, there may be an institutional imperative to return manuscripts to some kind of idealized state, so that old bindings are removed and invasive repairs are made which destroy original materials and remove evidence about how the manuscripts were actually made and changed over time. The goals and purposes of conservation and preservation must be understood by everyone who works with the manuscripts.

The types of damage caused by human agency discussed in this section are largely controlled by education and oversight. Those with access to the manuscripts must know how to handle them properly and be expected to do so. Digitization and conservation treatment must be based on a clear understanding of the purposes for these activities and employ methods that do not cause further damage (see Ch. 5 §§ 6, 7).

4.3. Manuscript damage caused by biological factors

Mould, insects and vermin, in particular rodents, such as rats and mice, are biological agents which threaten manuscripts. For mould and insects the manuscripts themselves are a food source. For the larger vermin, manuscripts may sometimes be a source of nutrition but also provide nesting materials. The degree of the threat depends in part on climatic conditions in the location of the manuscript collection, with hot, damp places that support larger and more varied pest populations being more vulnerable to attack. Vulnerability also depends on custodial care—how frequently the manuscripts are monitored for an attack and how quickly and effectively a response to such an attack is marshalled.

Mould damage (fig. 5.4.2) can often be identified visually as lightly coloured, powdery residues—white, green, purple or black in association with an area that is or was damp, as evinced by a stain in that vicinity. If a manuscript is wet, for example, due to a water leak or a damp wall, mould can begin to grow quickly and will spread from there to other manuscripts, especially if environmental humidity levels are high. As active mould fluoresces under UV light, this can be a method then for determining if the danger is a present one. In cases of doubt, a sample taken with a cotton swab can be sent to a biolaboratory to ascertain whether it is active or not.

Insect damage (fig. 5.4.3) is readily apparent as holes and channels in manuscript supports and bindings. Also insect frass, whitish powdery material on the shelves near manuscripts, or such material falling out of a manuscript when it is picked up or handled, may indicate insect activity. Insect traps put in the manuscript storage area may catch live specimens and show that they are present and active, but many insects are small and hard to see in a manuscript.

Bite marks on bindings and text blocks (fig. 5.4.4) indicate vermin activity. Rodents' excrement is also detrimental to manuscripts; faeces and urine may dissolve parchment leaving irreparable damage.

Effective control of these forms of damage depends first on maintaining a clean, well-regulated space and a stable environment for the storage of manuscripts. Then, in the event of a biological threat, early detection and rapid response is critical.

Responsible staff need to regularly monitor a collection, be familiar with the signs that indicate infestation and know what to do if an outbreak occurs. Active mould on manuscripts can be disinfected with alcohol solutions, but spores will always be present and potentially able to grow again when conditions are favourable. Insect attacks are preferably given an anoxic treatment: infested manuscripts are placed in a sealed environment from which oxygen is removed and replaced with an inert gas, thereby killing the insects who need oxygen for their survival. An alternative method of treatment is freezing. But insecticides and poisons which leave chemical residues on the manuscripts, pose a health hazard to humans, and harm the environment should not be used.

4.4. Manuscript damage caused by chemical factors

One of the most problematic sources of damage to manuscripts are materials which are intrinsically part of the manuscripts and are themselves chemically deleterious. These may include poor quality papers (often made from wood pulps), iron gall inks (fig. 5.4.5), and copper-containing pigments in paints used for illumination or illustration (fig. 5.4.6). Such materials contain acids and catalytic ions which often lead to darkening, embrittlement, losses in strength and flexibility and other forms of deterioration in adjacent materials. In general, this damage cannot be stopped so much as slowed down both by treatment protocols and control of the manuscript environment. However, by the same token, inappropriate treatments may exacerbate the deleterious effects of these materials. For example, aqueous repair treatments of a text block may accelerate the deterioration caused by iron gall inks or copper-containing pigments on the paper. So treatment choices must be based on a good understanding of the materials a manuscript contains and their chemical behaviour.

Pollutants in urban areas can also adversely affect manuscripts. Sulphurous gases are involved in the darkening of lead white paints, for example. Additionally, poor quality and inappropriate materials in the immediate environment of manuscripts can also produce acidic gases which cause deterioration of the materials from which the manuscripts are made. These harmful materials may be, for example, in the boxes in which the manuscripts are stored, or in the exhibition cases in which they are displayed. To control such damage, collection custodians must be able to test for and identify materials that should be kept out of the manuscripts' environment.

4.5. Manuscript damage caused by environmental factors

Levels of light, humidity and temperature are important in creating an environment that promotes manuscript preservation. High exposure to light can lead to embrittlement and fading of some materials. High levels of humidity promote mould growth while very low levels can lead to desiccation, embrittlement and cracking in some materials. The different materials from which a manuscript is made expand as tempera-

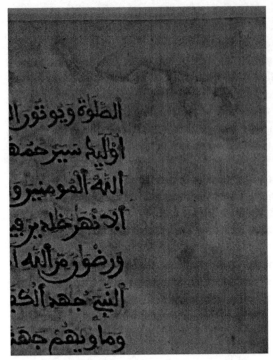

Fig. 5.4.2 Mould: The stain on the paper indicates that it was once wet in this area, and the associated purplish colour is the result of mould attack. Private collection, Istanbul, photograph by PH.

Fig. 5.4.3 Insects: The visible channels and holes in the text block are created by insects as they eat their way through the support. Private collection, Istanbul, photograph by PH.

Fig. 5.4.4 Rodent damage in an Ethiopic manuscript. Bite marks on parchment are clearly visible; the leaves have been partially destroyed. Northern Ethiopia, 2011, photograph by EBW.

Fig. 5.4.5 Iron gall ink: Characteristic browning of the support behind where ink was applied on the other side of the leaf indicates the deterioration of the paper in these areas. When the manuscript is used, cracks and breaks can occur in the weakened and brittle support and result in losses over time. Private collection, Istanbul, photograph by PH.

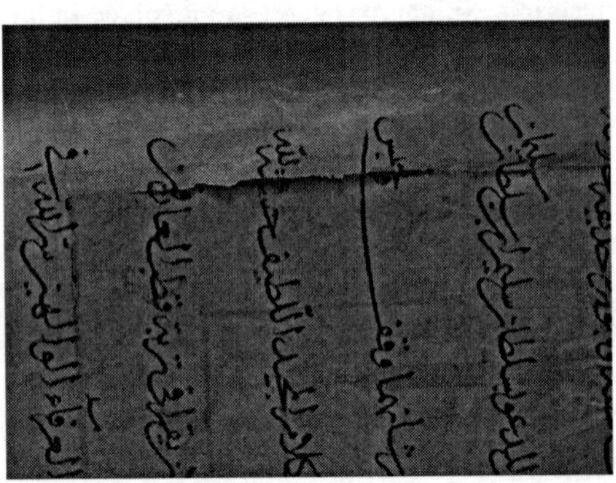

Fig. 5.4.6 Copper corrosion: Browning of the support is visible behind a framing line drawn on the other side of the leaf with copper-containing paint. When the leaf was turned, the paper cracked along this weakened line. Small losses have been sustained along the edge of the break and eventually the whole section framed by the painted line may break out of the leaf and be lost. Private collection, Istanbul, photograph by PH.

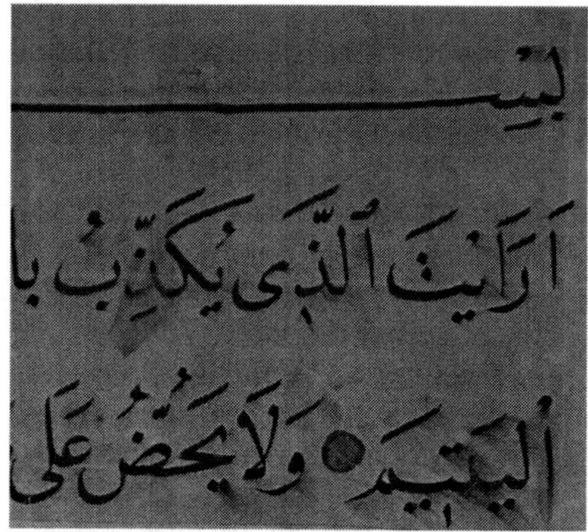

Fig. 5.4.7 Bleed: Many inks or paints can be reactivated by water in liquid form or high environmental humidity which causes them to spread across the support. Private collection, Istanbul, photograph by PH.

Fig. 5.4.8 Transfer: The binder which causes ink or paint to adhere to the support can be softened by high environmental humidity, causing it to adhere to another object when it is pressed against the softened media. In this case, the painted red circle across some of the letters was transferred from an illumination on the facing page in the manuscript. Private collection, Istanbul, photograph by PH.

Fig. 5.4.9 Flaking media: Ink (and paint) made with insufficient binder or binder that has weakened with age is prone to flaking losses, as can be seen in the letters in this sample of calligraphy. Private collection, Istanbul, photograph by PH.

Fig. 5.4.10 Multiple damage: As is typical, a single page in a manuscript often shows many different types of damage. In this case, from a manuscript on a paper support, some of the damage that is apparent includes water and mould stains, transfer of ink from the opposite page, and insect damage and old repairs near the gutter. Leiden, Leiden University Library, Or. 107, photograph by KS.

ture rises and contract as it cools, but have different rates of expansion and contraction (see table 5.1.2 for the hygroscopic differences); so, rapidly fluctuating temperatures may cause them to exert large stresses on each other. Additionally, corrosive processes caused by inks or paints containing iron or copper are accelerated by the presence of moisture and high temperatures, so climatic fluctuations can also promote this chemical deterioration (figs. 5.4.7–9).

Control of the manuscript environment is a basic way to limit these types of damage. Light levels should be kept as low as possible for adequate viewing. In general, cooler temperatures are preferred for manuscript exhibition and storage because the chemical reactions which cause deterioration are accelerated as temperature increases. Ideally, levels for relative humidity in a collection should fall within the range of approximately 35% to 60% RH, but there are exceptions (see Ch. 5 § 5.1). But the most crucial aspect of environmental control is the avoidance of rapid fluctuations in the levels of temperature and relative humidity, since during such fluctuations the different materials in manuscripts expand (or contract) both rapidly and differentially. It is recommended, therefore, that changes in relative humidity and temperature during a 24-hour cycle as well as seasonally be as slow as possible (as is the case in many thick-walled historic buildings), so that the manuscript materials can adjust gradually to their environmental conditions (NPS 1999; ICON 2011).

4.6. Manuscript damage caused by disaster

Fire, flood, earthquake, war and terrorism are all potential sources of catastrophic damage to manuscript collections. These cannot be controlled, but their effect can be minimized by sound planning and preparation. Collection custodians need to be trained in how to respond to different emergencies. Much of this planning is common sense: Who has the keys to the storage areas if they need to be accessed quickly? Where are the fire extinguishers and do staff know how to use them? Where is the power box in case the electrical supply needs to be shut off? Who should be contacted in an emergency?

4.7. Damage control

In conclusion, much of the damage to be seen in manuscripts could have been prevented. For this reason, reducing future damage depends on creating proper controls for their use and storage (see Ch. 5 § 5.5). The success collection custodians have in establishing and using such controls will depend in turn on the education and support they receive (see Ch. 5 § 5.11). Supervisors need a thorough understanding of what constitutes proper conservation and preservation so as to be able to make effective policy. Then those responsible for the day-to-day care of the collections—librarians, curators and conservators—need fully to understand and carry out these policies consistently. The viewpoint must be a holistic one. The sources of damage to manuscripts are highly interrelated and cannot effectively be addressed in isolation. However well-intentioned, the misguided focus on one problem in a manuscript collection can worsen others (see also Ch. 5 § 5 for more guidance).

References

AIC 2013; CCI 2002, 2009; NPS 1999; ICON 2011; Michalski 2009; Newman [Walter] – Quandt 1994; Pinninger 2001.

5. Preservation: a comparative overview (AR–FV)

Oriental manuscripts are found in large numbers worldwide, with many collected in major libraries and institutions in the west (Europe and North America), but also in their nation of origin, whether housed in national, public or private museums or libraries, or dispersed in private collections, churches, in cities and small villages (see also General introduction § 3 and Ch. 4 for the particular oriental traditions). It is very difficult to locate and record all oriental manuscripts; some joint programmes (sponsored by national institutions, private foundations and generous donors) aim at systematically recording and assessing the preservation condition of large collections. Such programmes include the EU-sponsored MANUMED (<http://www.manumed.org/en/presentation.htm>), which aims at enhancing the written and intangible heritage of the Euro-Mediterranean region and has made possible, among others, the conservation of Syrian manuscripts in the monastery of Charfet, in Lebanon (communication by Vinourd 2010). Another example that can be quoted here is the cooperation, which started in 2005 between the Universities of Toronto and Uppsala (supported by different European and American Institutions, amongst which is the British Library), that allowed the study and digitization of Ethiopian manuscripts (notably the collection held in the remote monastery of Gunda Gundē, survey supported by the Hill Museum and Manuscript Library), putting them online, therefore promoting and making knowledge accessible to the general public (Balicka-Witakowska 2010c). The European Research Council-sponsored project Ethio-SPaRe project led by Denis Nosnitsin, Hamburg has equally conducted extensive study digitization of numerous Ethiopian manuscripts, in addition to making possible the conservation of several valuable mediaeval codices (Di Bella – Sarris 2014).

In the Orient, collections are often privately held (by families or religious communities), making access to them for research purposes rather difficult or in some cases even impossible, despite the fact that the benefits of opening private collections to the public are remarkable (Parodi 2012). This condition must not be mistaken for a lack of interest in their preservation, nor is it due to bad organization, but more likely to a sense of private guarding and a lack of trust (in some cases justified). In the west we often speak of 'unsuitable conditions' and deterioration problems that, in many instances, are often the result of very old damage, ascribable to past periods of negligence, or due to periods of extreme political or natural turmoil (Ipert 2005).

Although nowadays the use of manuscripts is not for reading purposes in the way it used to be, manuscripts are a necessary aid to scholars, who need to access the original material in order to study it, record it and make it public. Besides, by recording a manuscript in a database and making the information or a reproduction accessible to the general public, not only do we promote research but we also protect the objects from a possible theft: a secure identification is created, and the object, if stolen, cannot be easily sold (Ipert 2005, Briquel-Chatonnet 2012, Moukarzel 2012). Therefore the documentation and preservation of large and small collections alike remains of prime importance.

5.1. Preservation from environmental factors

The main factors that may contribute to the deterioration of manuscripts are presented in Ch. 5 § 4.5. An important aspect to consider here is the geographic location of a given collection. The climatic conditions, temperature or humidity, the air quality and other circumstances largely depend on whether the location is near the sea or in the mountains, in the city or in the country.

In humid areas of the world, where relative humidity (RH) never falls below 65%, it is very difficult to drastically lower the RH percentage of the collection area, unless with an extensive (and expensive) use of air conditioning, which is not suitable in all cases. On the other hand, in very arid climates, where the RH often falls below 45%, it will prove extremely difficult and costly to achieve those rates. If however, a stable environmental condition is secured, which does not allow for sudden fluctuations and which will take into consideration the most sensitive materials such as parchment (trying to keep the humidity rates as specific as possible), mostly likely no serious problems will be encountered.

Besides, the locations in the east may be in secluded sites, difficult to reach (such as the St Catherine's Monastery on Mount Sinai, 1,000 m up in the mountains), with possibly communication difficulties (in areas where a local dialect is the norm) and with traditional, cultural, religious barriers, that create sometimes a sense of mistrust, or even hostile attitude (in some instances as a result of acts of destruction or theft in the past, Ipert 2005, or of religious reservations, see General introduction § 4.1). All these issues must be approached with patience, open-mindedness and mostly with a diplomatic attitude, bearing in mind that the main goal is to cooperate, learning from each civilization, without prejudice, with an aim to expanding and highlighting cultural knowledge and historical treasures, beyond the limitations posed by any national, political or personal approach.

Conservation plans should be called into life wherever manuscripts are in danger. This is possible also in the orient, as illustrated by various projects focusing on condition surveys, digital recording of the treasures, while assessing risks and creating strategic planning for future actions. Many such projects are the product of multi-national cooperation and most of the times are presented on line through a thorough research network, a great tool for scholars and conservators alike. Such projects include: the digital library *e-corpus* (<http://www.e-corpus.org/>), the Syriac manuscript database *e-ktobe* (<www.mss-syriaques.org>), or the database of Byzantine bindings *Studite* (<www.studite.org>). The St Catherine's Library Conservation Programme, undertaken by The University of the Arts, Camberwell College of Arts, London and supported by the Saint Catherine Foundation, has aimed since 1998 at setting up a conservation-preservation plan for repairing damaged manuscripts and ensuring their preservation in the future (Pickwoad 2004).

Even more important than the geographic location is the type of building that houses the collection. In many instances the actual building was originally constructed for a completely different use, therefore not always presenting ideal housing conditions for the objects. Buildings used for manuscript storage can be divided into three major groups.

The first comprises modern buildings which were conceived and designed from the very beginning as libraries or museums, therefore taking into account all proper technical and environmental requirements (air conditioning, humidity control, and so forth).

A very good example of a modern library, complying with all conservation standards, living up to its historical 'legend' is the new Alexandria Library (Bibliotheca Alexandrina): all windows have UV protective filters, the RH rate is kept between 45%-55%, the temperature is 18°C in the storage areas, 20°C in the reading rooms and 23°C in the offices, the air conditioning functions all day every day, while the air is constantly monitored with special sensors that can detect gas leaks and pollutants (Di Bella 2002a). Another example of a success in the Orient is the library of the Dayr al-Suryān monastery in Egypt, which made part of the network of the Coptic desert monasteries of Scetis (Wādī al-Naṭrūn) as early as since the fifth or early sixth century and passed, in the eighth century, to a Syriac Orthodox community. Within the framework of a joint project between the Levantine Foundation and the Dayr al-Suryān Monastic Council, a new building was built from scratch, providing high standard environmental conditions, reading rooms and exhibition facilities (with a rotating display of the collection's treasures) and a conservation laboratory, open to a wide range of professionals (Sobczynski – Antonia 2013).

A second group includes buildings that, while having been conceived as libraries, lack proper installations for environmental control.

Finally, a third group are buildings that were initially designed for some other use (churches, historic houses, storehouses) and were eventually transformed into libraries, collection houses or storage premises for the collection.

In some cases, where space is limited, certain rooms have a double function (for example, reading room and simultaneously storage/conservation area). Then, temperature, humidity and light levels are usually less ideal. In other situations, the climate may be controlled in storage areas but not in the reading rooms. Technical problems with the air conditioning or humidity control (due to a temporary malfunction) even in cases with stable, controlled environmental conditions may lead to the development of microorganisms.

Infestations due to external factors include both incoming infestations from adjacent areas (for instance through the ventilation channels), and the introduction of contaminated material to the collection without prior check. Usually, in historic buildings or traditional libraries, the shelves may be made of wood, which could be subject to insect migration.

Buildings constructed in or after the twentieth century were usually made (according to the fashion of the time) of concrete, with large windows, which allow the external light to penetrate (the use of filters is not always standard). In buildings with no air conditioning, the time of the year (winter or spring and of course summer), the geographical area, the hour of the day, the floor level, the presence of windows, are all factors that may play a major role in the conservation conditions of the objects.

Whatever the climate and the type of building, the core issues that need to be considered in preservation are, first and foremost, what affects manuscripts and what needs to be monitored (De Tapol 2000, Méric 2000, see also Ch. 5 § 4), and, finally, what the ideal actions and conditions are. It is necessary to develop a knowledge and understanding of the deterioration agents in order to prevent them from occurring, and to control the environmental conditions insofar as possible, always keeping in mind the specific requirements and conditions of each collection (Gallo 2000)

Common problems as a result of poor environmental conditions (Gallo 2000; Montanari 1999) include: bad, insufficient ventilation, as well as insufficient housekeeping (accumulation of dust and dirt), which can produce ideal conditions for insect or mould infestations, both of which are encouraged by certain temperature and humidity rates; the poor condition of storage rooms and facilities, of reading aids in reading rooms and supports in exhibition rooms; and environmental disasters and natural catastrophes, such as earthquakes or floods.

Building maintenance is crucial, since the moisture present in walls may lead to a rise of the RH. Holes and cracks may allow insects, rodents and superficial dirt to enter (Le Guen 1995; see also Ch. 5 § 4 above and §§ 5.2 and 5.3 below). Table 5.5.1 synthesizes the recommended conditions in which manuscripts should be kept (see also Gallo 2000; Ipert 1995; Montanari 1999; Thomson [G.] 1997); following is a more detailed list of the most common problems that may affect manuscripts, along with suggested preventive measures. It must be noted that, even if not ideal in terms of museum standards, local conditions can nevertheless be acceptable for the objects, which have adapted to them (for example to the extreme dryness of a desert area; see Thomson 1997). There is no 'ideal' conditioning, but only what is best for the specific needs of the objects in each collection, which may vary considerably.

Light—The main damage caused by light is discolouration and a weakening of materials (De Moncy 1995; Ipert 1995; Thomson [G.] 1997). According to the wavelength of light, we can divide it into three separate groups: visible light (380-740nm), ultraviolet (400-10nm: UV) and infrared (700-1nm: IR). Each radiation can cause different types of damage to the objects (CCI). Visible light fades colours: depending on the sensitivity of the object to light, it is a process which can either be extremely rapid (the discolouration may take just a few hours under direct sunlight), or take a few years at low museum lighting. UV causes the most severe damage, resulting in yellowing, chalking, weakening, and/or disintegration of materials. IR heats the surface of objects (with an increase in temperature), resulting in structural weakening.

Objects can be divided into two major groups: those which can be adapted to steady, artificial light of 50Lux and a general light of the environment at ±200Lux, and those which are very sensitive to light, which must be kept clear of daylight at all times.

The chemical reactions initiated by light exposure continue even after the light source is removed and may lead to irreversible damage to the objects. It must also be noted that light damage is accumulative (Adcock – Varlamoff 1998).

Preventive measures include: avoiding direct sunlight by means of shades or filters on the windows; avoiding long periods of lighting, and reducing the intensity and duration of exposure where possible. Artificial light must be clear of UV radiation (or at least UV must be reduced to a minimum); especially during the brightest times of the year, the general lighting of the environment should not exceed 200Lux (achievable through the use of blinds and artificial lights).

Temperature—most deterioration agents (insects and microorganisms) develop between 20°C-30°C, though sometimes it may occur with temperatures above 30°C or below 0°C. Additionally, temperature may often act as a catalyst for many chemical reactions (see also De Tapol 2000; Méric 2000).

Relative humidity—In general, it is advised to keep RH below 60% (preferably below 55%), because above 60% chances of a microbiological attack are high, especially in combination with high temperatures. Insects seem to be less dependant on RH; their infestations are largely related to opportunity of access and favourable circumstances such as bad housekeeping, food in storage rooms or offices and so forth. By keeping the RH at 50-60% we also minimize the risk of mechanical damage. At RH below 40% most materials may suffer shrinkage, stiffness, cracking, or embrittlement. Conditions should be as stable as possible all year round, and when changing the conditions, variations must be introduced gently and with great care. Abrupt changes in RH can cause very serious damage to the objects (Méric 2000; Thomson [G.] 1997).

RH stands in a direct relationship to the hygroscopicity, or hygroscopic capacity of materials: their water consistency, or readiness to take up and retain moisture. Different materials may have different

Table 5.5.1 Summary of the key parameters for proper manuscript storage

Light	Temperature	Relative humidity
Avoid direct sunlight Artificial light UV-free 50Lux acceptable level for most objects	Between 16°C-20°C. It is important that the temperature is similar in storage and in reading rooms as abrupt changes in conditions may damage the objects.	Between 55%-65% Use of controlled air conditioning Use a buffer if needed (especially within display cases) Changes must be avoided

Table 5.5.2 Hygroscopic capacity of the main manuscript materials

Leather	Parchment	Adhesives	Iron gall inks	Green pigments
RH above 60% with a highly acidic pH may cause a structural loss. If leather is moistened the tannins may dissolve and leave the surface. However they will function as a protective barrier compared to the semi-tanned leathers.	Highly hygroscopic material: very sensitive to humidity variations. In a dry environment runs the risk of shrinkage-dryness. In a humid environment the parchment will react and expand, however the painted decorations will not, resulting in a cracking of the painted surface (Meric 2000)	Highly hygroscopic and may lose their adhesive capacity in cases of extreme humidity loss or raise (Meric 2000)	Iron sulphates may react chemically in the presence of humidity, producing a very acidic substance, extremely corrosive for both paper and parchment support (Meric 2000)	High humidity levels may accelerate chemical reactions of the (acidic) green pigments (for example, verdigris) contained in the paintings that can migrate to parchment pores, oxidize and damage the support (Madani 2002, Meric 2000)

needs: for example, paper can be preserved at a lower RH rate (30%-40%), while parchment needs more moisture in order to stay flexible. Since there is not a single ideal condition for all materials, careful consideration must be given to the choice of environmental values (Adcock – Varlamoff 1998).

Dust and dirt are very hygroscopic, posing a major threat to collections for that very reason, besides providing nourishment to insects and bacteria. In a decreasing order of hygroscopic capacity are leather, wood, cardboard, paper, cotton, as further detailed in Table 5.5.2.

5.2. Preservation from superficial dirt and pollution

Air pollutants and dust collected on the surface pose a serious threat to objects, since they may cause degradation and increase the risk of microbiological contamination. Basic prevention of damage from superficial dirt involves regular mechanical dry cleaning of the objects' surfaces; but air filtering may also be necessary.

Air quality depends on the presence of indoor and outdoor polluters and air exchange rates (most indoor/outdoor exchange occur during warm seasons, when windows and doors remain open for prolonged periods of time). As a rule, the concentration of pollutants is higher in the outside air; though has been observed that sometimes the concentration of indoor pollutants is higher, particularly in the presence of a strong indoor source, and when there is a low air exchange rate, especially in confined spaces, such as display cases.

Indoor pollutants may result from various sources such as display or building materials, or even the objects themselves.

Indoor air quality is a relatively young research field and acceptable pollution levels are still widely debated. Air quality tests and proper equipment have not yet been standardized. There is no consensus as to whether closed areas such as storage rooms should be kept airtight. Though it would reduce influx of external pollutants, this strategy would not offer protection against the internally generated ones. In such case, re-circulation of air through chemical filters would become a necessity. It has been agreed, however, that one should at least limit the mass flow of air towards the objects. To this effect it has been suggested to use a ventilation system capable of blocking outdoor pollutants and removing indoor pollutants through the ventilation exhaust. Studies have shown that a considerable decrease in the level of indoor air pollution can be achieved by chemical air filtration, for instance with the use of activated carbon. Ventilation intensity, high or low, may interfere with human comfort demands which are particularly relevant in reading and consultation areas. Paradoxically, old buildings sometimes have a better performance with respect to blocking external pollutants and controlling indoor climate as compared to modern ones (made of relatively inert materials such as glass, metal and polymers). In instances where the infiltration of air pollutants is mainly driven by free air movement, passive insulation control may offer a satisfactory solution allowing a reduction in the use of air conditioning. However full documentation of the results produced by this strategy is not available yet. The key outdoor pollutants are sulphur dioxide, nitrogen dioxide, ozone; the main indoor pollutant is acetic acid (see also Ch. 5 § 4.4). Therefore, in polluted urban areas one should minimize the external air influx.

For more details see Adcock – Varlamoff 1998; De Moncy 1995; Ryhl-Svendsen 2006; Thomson [G.] 1997.

5.3. Prevention of damage from biological factors

Microorganisms and insects may badly damage and in several cases irreversibly destroy manuscripts (see figs. 5.4.1 and 5.4.2). A warm and humid environment makes it easier for microorganisms to develop (mould usually appears at temperatures between 20° and 30°C and at RH above 65%): even a small wet spot or location can cause the initial activity. Additionally, since mould spores can be easily carried away with the air, an affected object may easily infect the others. Extended mould damage in certain cases can also lead to irreparable loss of the support, generally causing colour stains, the weakening of the support and generating an increased vulnerability to bacterial attack. Recommended prevention consists in guaranteeing a steadily controlled environment. Humidity leaks must be avoided; contaminated objects must be first isolated and then cleaned and treated (for treatment options see Ch. 5 § 4.4.3).

The presence of insects (appearing at temperatures between 20°C and 30°C) is usually caused by insufficient cleaning (unused, dirty rooms or storage areas where debris and dirt offer ideal food for insects) and can also be encountered if an already affected object is introduced into the collection without prior disinfestation, spreading thereby the insect attack to the other objects. The main damage caused by insects are losses, corrosion of the surface due to the excrement, the creation of galleries, all resulting in the object's structural weakening and in some cases to its partial or complete destruction. Recommended prevention consists in regular cleaning of all areas and systematic checks for any signs of contamination, including close control of any new objects that are introduced to the collection (with a quarantine period if needed). For more see Adcock – Varlamoff 1998, Bülow et al. 2002.

5.4. Monitoring conditions

Monitoring environmental conditions and pests on a regular basis is essential. Measurements must be taken for at least one year, in order to get characteristic readings. It is advisable to take monthly measurements, rather than daily or weekly ones, and to take detailed notes of the results, in particular if there is any variation in the condition of the objects. Systematic control is much more efficient than sporadic checks (Pinniger 2001).

The measurements inside the premises should be compared with the external ones, in order to check the inertia of the building, thereby pinpointing any problem zones. The building can also be divided into separate climatic zones, according to its orientation, the heating system, the type of construction, and so forth (Ipert 1995).

Monitoring instruments should *never* be placed close to doors, windows, ventilation panels, or radiators. They must be regularly calibrated, and their position should not be changed. If adequate instruments are lacking, prioritize the storage areas and especially those where the manuscripts and the most valuable items are kept. Insect traps, placed in corners, under shelves and in storage areas, must be checked at least four times per year. Trapped insects must be cleared at all times, since they constitute potential food for pests.

Regular, consistent feedback among the groups involved is crucial to good communication (Pinniger 2001). Maintenance, cleaning and security staff must regularly check for poor environment and unsuitable conditions. The same rules apply to temporary or permanent exhibitions, with an aim to achieve controlled, stable environmental conditions.

5.5. Storage

The aim of any conservation approach, regardless of the type of object (whether it is flat, rolled, or bound, on paper, parchment, or some other writing support), is to preserve its original condition insofar as possible, limiting conservation treatments to only those which are essential in order to prolong its longevity and, ideally, prevent it from further decay. In many instances by simply improving the environmental conditions and those of storage and handling, optimum preservation of the objects is achieved without the need for any further, more drastic, treatment, which can be postponed for a future time.

Proper storage involves not only shelves and cabinets, but also the use of appropriate boxes to house the objects, as well as other means of packaging and safekeeping (Brown et al. 1982). It is also important to remember that not all practices are adapted to the special needs of each object: for instance the use of acid-free tissue as a barrier between a painting and the adjacent page should be avoided in most cases, because it may cause worse damage to the pigments than the protection it affords: they may stick to the interleaving page and become detached from the illumination.

Both wooden and metallic shelves can be appropriate. Each has advantages and disadvantages; however, as a general rule, books should ideally not come into contact with unsealed wood, which can release organic acid vapours. In order to avoid this problem it is recommended to line shelves with archival board (acid-free; see Adcock – Varlamoff 1998; Gallo – Regni 2000; ICON 2011; Montanari 1999). Wooden shelves have a greater hygroscopic power compared to paper and absorb the excess humidity in the environment, but are more easily attacked by insects. On the other hand, metallic shelves, ideally made of steel with a baked enamel finish, do not run the risk of insect or rodent infestation, but can sometimes create a 'cold barrier' on their surface, increasing the possibility of condensation in a humid environment.

A further distinction should be made between open shelves, with no front protection whatsoever, and either hermetically closed ones (compact shelving) or bookshelves with wooden, glass, or wire-net front panels. In the first case, free air circulation represents an advantage, but conversely dirt, dust and airborne pollutants will easily affect the objects, while in the case of closed panels the main disadvantage lies in the fact that if humidity penetrates, it will be locked in, creating much greater damage in terms of micro-organism development.

A wire-net front window panel represents a compromise between protection from dust and free air circulation. When using glass or wooden front panels, which tend to seal up the contents, ventilation must be ensured. It is very important to make use of large shelves, in order to prevent book edges from extending beyond the shelves (with a risk of mechanical damage), while when employing moving shelves, special attention must be given in order to prevent objects from being crushed or falling.

Shelves should not be placed close to radiators, walls, windows, or ventilation panels. Books should be at least 10 cm off the floor, as a protective measure in case of water leaks and minor floods, and also from damage caused by passers-by.

It is also recommended not to place books too tightly on shelves (which might cause abrasion, or other superficial damage), to avoid placing large books close to small ones (which cannot provide sufficient support), and to use bookends where needed. Paper and cloth bindings should not come into direct contact with leather covers, because in case of degradation, the acidity and oils in the leather tend to migrate, soiling and deteriorating paper and cloth bindings (Adcock – Varlamoff 1998).

Boxes (or other forms of protective casing, such as folders) provide the ideal storage solution protecting the objects both from light exposure and from external conditions (water leaking, dust, possible pest or mould infestations), particularly in the case of very environmentally sensitive material like parchment, or when the storage conditions are far from ideal, acting as a safety barrier against environmental variations and pollution, dust or any other form of external hazard. They also provide an ideal solution for temporary (short- or long-term) protection, in situations where a specific active conservation programme is not immediately possible (due to a lack of financial support, specialized personnel, or any other reasons), protecting the object(s) from further damage.

Usually two types of boxes are recommended. The less expensive phase box is suitable in the case of structurally steady books or as a temporary solution for objects waiting for conservation treatments. The drop-spine box provides a better support as well as better protection. Boxes and folders should only be made from durable and archival-quality materials (Adcock – Varlamoff 1998; Brown et al. 1982).

While most books are stored vertically, for some types of books, a horizontal arrangement may be more suitable. This is the case of Byzantine and Islamic bindings, or of large volumes, with a maximum of three volumes one on top of the other (where applicable). Flat storage should also be considered in the case of damaged, heavy, or structurally weak volumes (Porterie 1995). When volumes with decorated bindings are stacked on top of one another in the absence of proper boxing, placing a custom-size sheet of acid-free cardboard between them is recommended, with holes corresponding to the metallic decoration of the book boards in order to compensate for the difference in thickness. The use of acid-free tissue (or other types of protective wrappers) is another alternative for the protection of heavily decorated bindings (with metal clasps, nails, and the like).

Finally, loose leaves must at all times be housed in appropriate envelopes or boxes (Brown et al. 1982; Porterie 1995).

Boxes should preferably be sized to fit the dimensions of the books and leaves. Too tight a structure may cause damage to the edges of the cover, if the book is forced into the box (Adcock – Varlamoff 1998). If the boxes are too large, when they are stacked perpendicularly, the objects will sag into the box, risking permanent deformation (Bülow 2010). In case of a limited budget, larger boxes should be preferred, and acid-free tissue can be used to accommodate books in boxes or housing that are not exactly of the correct size (Bendix et al. 2003). Alternatively, soft foam may be used to compensate for the extra space.

Dusting should be carried out at least once a year, preferably in the spring, using special vacuum cleaners and soft brushes (for very sensitive, fragile objects). Before replacing the objects it is imperative to carefully clean the storage areas, shelves and cases, either with a vacuum cleaner or with a soft cloth and where possible, a damp one, making sure that no humidity remains afterwards. During cleaning, safety rules need to be followed (using gloves, masks, and so forth: Porterie 1995).

Regular monitoring of the environmental conditions is essential. Good ventilation should be maintained, air conditioning should be stable and filters regularly checked. The walls must be regularly checked for humidity leaks. Within badly ventilated and warm enclosures (especially in seasons such as the Mediterranean spring, when temperatures may rise above 20°C and the weather may still be humid), the risk of RH raising above 70%-75% is eminent (Gallo – Regni 2000). In storage areas, low temperatures (around 10°C) can be beneficial for archival materials (Thomson [G.] 1997).

5.6. Exhibitions

First and foremost it is essential to select only the items that are fit for display, according to the conservator who is responsible for them. Secondly it is important to maintain a controlled and steady environment, regularly monitored, preferably before exhibiting the objects as well (Bendix et al. 2003). All the materials used for display (book cradles, supports, cases, mounting materials) should be chemically stable, of archival quality, and pose no potential damage to the objects. Finally, for security purposes, it is crucial to employ locks for the display cases, shutter-proof windows, alarm systems, and to have a surveillance system in place at all times (Adcock – Varlamoff 1998, McCormick – Whitford 2003; Regni 1995).

As mentioned, environment and lighting are a crucial factor. In many instances it may be not possible to maintain a controlled environment, since the exhibitions are held in buildings or rooms which were not originally conceived as exhibition spaces (such as churches or historic buildings). In such instances, where additional air conditioning is not always possible, a reasonable solution is the use of a buffer (a moisture-containing solid which can exchange moisture with the environment, like silica gel and art-sorb and pro-sorb products), which will be helpful in maintaining a fairly constant humidity level (McCormick – Whitford 2003; Regni 1995; Thomson [G.] 1997).

It is recommended to reduce the light exposure of sensitive objects to no more than 50Lux for a maximum of eight hours a day and a total exposure up to three months (ninety days, according to Thomson [G.] 1997), or according to other sources for no more than forty days per year (Regni 1995). The above recommendations are general and may in fact differ from country to country: for example in the Netherlands it is advised to differentiate between types of objects/materials, and the 'three-months' rule' is observed in the case of yearly or two-year exhibits, while it is equally possible to exhibit an item for a year if it is agreed that afterwards it will be kept in storage for four or five years (ICON 2005). Special attention must be given to the 'glare' effect when lighting an object on display in a cabinet. The visitors' adaptation to light needs to be considered carefully, especially when they walk in from an external, well-lit surrounding to a dark exhibition area (Thomson [G.] 1997). Consideration must also be given to the control of UV radiation, keeping it at no more than 75 microwatts/lumen (Adcock – Varlamoff 1998; Regni 1995; Thomson [G.] 1997).

In order to reduce the light exposure (especially with the more sensitive objects), it is possible to turn the lights on only during the opening hours of the exhibition, or in some cases to illuminate the displays only when on view (with the use of light sensors, or other similar devices: Regni 1995; Thomson [G.] 1997).

Over-bright spotlights and lamps produce heat in showcases; tungsten lamps also emit IR radiation and must therefore be banned. It is also preferable to keep the light sources outside the display cases (Regni 1995; Thomson [G.] 1997).

Cradles and supports are another element to consider. When displaying open books, it must always be remembered that very few can be opened flat (at a 180° angle) without being damaged; therefore, ideally, books should never be opened at an angle greater than 120°, and in the case of tight bindings at no more than 90°. Acrylic sized-to-fit cradles or cradle-supports, tailor-made from museum-quality board (for open books) or supports (for flat objects or closed books), must be used at all times (Adcock – Varlamoff 1998). The cradles should fully support the boards and the spine, with melinex strips to keep the pages open in place, being careful however of not to stress the object too much (Regni 1995). Mirrors can be employed to show the binding, as well as the context of the book on display (Bendix et al. 2003). In the case of particularly sensitive material, it is recommended to turn the display pages at regular intervals during the exhibition period (McCormick – Whitford 2003). Sometimes, for instance in the case of multi-site exhibitions, it is possible to vary supports/cradles as long as the conservation standards are respected (compare the experience of the exhibition of the Aga Khan Collection of Islamic Art, Junod 2010).

Similar cradles, made of soft foam wedges and of adjustable sizes, can be used as reading supports for books, along with strips of weighted fabric that will keep the pages open, while the same rules for opening apply (Adcock – Varlamoff 1998; see fig. 5.7.1 below for an illustration). A variety of cushions is often available for reading room use. Pillows can be an alternative.

There is no uniform opinion on the question of the use of gloves. It is often recommended to provide readers and staff alike with soft white cotton gloves. They reduce the risk of staining the leaves with the superficial dirt and natural oil and salts of human hands. Hand sweat may corrode metal bosses and clasps of the binding. However, gloves also reduce the sensitivity, especially when browsing through the text block, and may transfer additional germs and dirt from one object to another. It is therefore often better to simply wash and carefully dry one's hands before consultation and handling, and the International Federation of Library Associations (IFLA) advises against the use of gloves (Adcock – Varlamoff 1998). Another practical solution to this problem could be the use of disposable latex gloves (CCI 2002; ICON 2011; NPS 1996; NPO 2000; UNESCO 2006).

5.7. Documentation

Within any preservation plan of any type of collection, whether private or public, large or small-scale, it is essential to document at least once the condition of each individual object, using specifically designed forms, which will form a database of the collection's preservation state at a specific time. Such survey makes it possible to assess potential damage which may occur to the objects and to identify its causes, as well as the potential risks that may endanger the objects' stability.

Similarly, prior to any conservation treatment, it is essential to fill in specially conceived condition reports, complete with a photographic documentation, in order to record the exact condition of the object prior to any intervention. This assessment shall lead the conservation treatment and be used for future reference (cf. Fani 2011).

Depending on the size of the collection, the budget available for conservation treatments, time limitations or any other specific problem connected to the collection, the type of documentation—its length, the detailed information included, its format (multiple choice, or text filling spaces)—may vary. However, there are certain fields that should always be included in any type of record in order to readily identify the object and to report the minimal essential information needed before any treatment can be considered. The basic information should at all times include the catalogue/archive/collection number of the item, as well as the reference number given to the object by the conservation department, the date of recording, the name of the person who is compiling the form, the object's name or title, its dimensions, the language(s) in which the text is written, its dating, its writer, whether it is a book or flat object and the type of writing support. Additional information regarding the type of binding, its material(s), the presence of painted decoration, provenance, types of inks, numbering, etc. can be added, depending on the specific requirements of the survey. For each item an assessment of its preservation condition must be provided which can be roughly categorized into bad, average or good, that is in immediate need for treatment, for future action or in no need of any treatment at all, respectively. This elementary type of record, which can be used when time is limited or when the collection's scale is very large, can work as an indicator of the general condition of the collection and what goals must be achieved in order to maintain or improve its preservation. In the case of documentation preceding a particular treatment, conservation or also digitization (see Ch. 5 §§ 7.2 and 7.3), the conservator in charge of the object usually records a more detailed version of the above basic elements: this should include more information regarding the object's structural elements, including any missing parts (for example: presence or absence of boards in a bound volume, missing pages, and so on), with particular emphasis on damage (causes, location, type and extent) and any other element that may be significant in order to assess the object's state.

A condition survey is an essential step to take, even when collections are so large that a conservation project may take up to several decades to complete, in order to establish a prioritized conservation plan, identifying what is in need of immediate repair and what may wait (Fani 2011; Revithi 2010, 2011; Scheper 2011). It also gives researchers the possibility of obtaining important, and otherwise inaccessible or unclear, information regarding the structural details of the objects: see for example the manuscripts of St Catherine's Monastery on Mount Sinai, Egypt (Pickwoad 2004; Velios 2011; Vnouček 1998). The ten-page condition survey template created for the needs of the manuscripts of the St Catherine's collection and the database drawn upon the collected data are part of the *Ligatus* project (<http://www.ligatus.org.uk/stcatherines/>, last access June 2014).

Depending on the type of objects found in the collection, there might be the need for a different type of form each time: if a very detailed record is needed, obviously it might not be applicable to all the styles of objects (for example a description form for Byzantine bindings does not apply to Islamic ones); therefore the conservator, in close collaboration with the curator, needs to categorize the collection and create multiple forms (Pickwoad 2004).

The key question before creating any type of form is: what is the main goal of the survey? Is it to record detailed information about each object, both structurally and in terms of damages? Is it to create a priority plan in order to facilitate any future conservation programme? Is it a reference for future use? By answering the above questions (or any other relevant question) the type of condition report should be fairly easy to determine, in terms of extent, content and form (Vnouček 1998). Whatever the style of the record, it is always useful to leave a blank space at the end of the form for any additional notes that may be of importance depending on the object.

If possible, it is useful to include recommendations about the future storage of the objects, such as environmental conditions, type of storage, need for housing, and instructions or recommendations for curators about the possibility of access to each item by scholars (Vnouček 1998). Secondly it is very important to keep the text as clear and as objective as possible, therefore allowing for very little personal interpretation that may result in misleading readings. For this purpose, ideally, working in pairs could be the optimal solution to increase objectivity (Pickwoad 2004).

The photographic documentation that will accompany the forms is essential, not only as additional means of presenting an overall idea of each item, but also as indisputable proof of the condition of the object at the time of the survey (while a condition report may always be subject to multiple interpretations). It is also a more direct way of showing details that may otherwise be difficult to describe concisely in a documentation form (Vnouček 1998).

If conservation work on an item is required, then the conservator(s) in charge must complete another report for the duration of the treatments (together with photographs taken during significant steps of the treatments, such as washing or filling in of losses for instance). This will accompany the object, together with the initial condition report, as part of its record. It is imperative always to note the name(s) of the person(s) who undertook the work, together with its exact duration (beginning and end of treatment dates).

Once the documentation is completed, it is always useful, if possible, to gather all the information into a database, which will allow easy access (with the use of keywords) to all interested parties (conservators, curators, possibly readers if made available online, as in the above example of the St Catherine's collection). Although it may take up more space than a digital copy, it is always recommended to keep the original paper copy of any documentation form, complete with the date and the name of the person(s) who did the assessment, as a reference record for each object. It is also a good idea for the conservator to keep a second copy for his/her personal record, as a reference of the work done, which can also be helpful as a guideline for similar future cases. Whether we are concerned with museums or institutions with a conservation department for their collections that will keep records for everything, or in the case of private collectors or smaller institutions and museums, it is imperative for conservators to provide a full report of the initial condition of each object, along with the conservation treatments that have been carried out.

A more detailed documentation form, focusing on the major points of interest depending on each case, could also be of significant use for insurance purposes (in which case it is most likely to be compulsory) in the case of an exhibition (whether *in situ* or on loan elsewhere). This should record the condition of the object before and after its display in order to note any damage caused, especially in the case of object(s) on loan abroad, when the items are inevitably subject to a lot more handling and travelling. The documentation in those instances must at all times include specific requirements and instructions prior to the loan on the part of the lenders as to the environmental conditions, the particular needs or any other important detail concerning the object (Cross – Flynn 2003; McCornick – Whitford 2003).

On the other hand, a detailed condition report should at all times be checked in conjunction with the courier of the object upon arrival at the exhibition venue, in order to establish its condition prior to display. Similarly, at the end of the exhibition, another report must be compiled, before departure. In the instances where objects are travelling unaccompanied, a completed condition report (with joint photographs) becomes imperative (McCornick – Whitford 2003).

5.8. Transport

No matter how careful the travelling conditions, there is always a risk percentage that must be considered; therefore it is crucial to assess all possible dangers, establishing specific guidelines each time specific to the object(s) and taking special precautions for those object(s) that are more fragile and most susceptible to potential damage (Cross – Flynn 2003).

It is vital to make sure that the travelling conditions of the objects will be as steady and as similar to those of the exhibition as possible. It is useful to make sure that the cases and the materials used for the transport of the objects are pre-conditioned to the desired values and that before being re-used (for example shortly before returning the object in the case of a loan) they are re-adapted to those chosen conditions (Cross – Flynn 2003; Montanari 1999; Regni 1995). Ideally, the conservator(s) responsible for the object(s) should at all times evaluate their condition, deciding if the item is suitable for travelling, and proceed to (at least minimum) conservation treatment, if necessary. A condition report should accompany the object(s) at all times, specifying conditions and (if applicable) problems that might occur or have already occurred, as well as any record of previous travelling arrangements, to serve as guidelines (Cross – Flynn 2003). It must also be taken into account that the (sometimes excessive) amount of handling and travelling may result in damage to otherwise fairly stable objects, for example in the case of a multi-tour exhibition. It is therefore very important to provide travelling conditions that will protect the objects against any mechanical damage (Regni 1995).

As a general rule, allowing for at least a twenty-four-hour adjustment before unpacking is advisable. Reports of the condition of the object prior to travelling, complete with photographic documentation, and a record of how it was packed are also recommended (McCormick – Whitford 2003). In the case of very long journeys to exotic climates (or at least very different from the one where the object belongs originally), it might be useful to use a hermetically sealed case.

5.9. Security

Human-induced damage to manuscripts may be unintentional, or caused by intentional acts of vandalism (Montanari 1999, Madan 2002).

Unintentional damage may be caused by inexperience or negligence on the part of personnel or readers, leading to incorrect or careless handling, tears, soiling and staining, excessive flexing of books or album pages, dropping of object(s). Unintentional damage unfortunately also comprises bad conservation treatments: something that could have been avoided if in case of uncertainty the person in charge of the conservation work had chosen to seek professional advice, refraining from unknown or uncertain treatment(s).

Intentional damage includes theft (of individual pages, illustrations, or of the entire volume or manuscript), and acts of vandalism. Unfortunately there have been instances of theft not by readers but by the actual institutions' staff. The problem can be solved or at least limited to a great extent by better controlling the access to the original objects (in some cases, providing high-quality digital copies instead of originals may represent a solution), by reducing scanning and limiting access to the storage facilities to fewer selected personnel. Online access to consultation is a very good alternative that should be promoted as a key strategic aim (Marzo 2012; Bülow 2010).

Another key security measure, especially during exhibitions or loans off-site or to another institution, is to have a very specific knowledge of the main entrance and service entrances to the display, storage and consulting areas, and possibly have only a single designated entrance, with designated personnel-only access (Cross – Flynn 2003; McCormick – Whitford 2003).

5.10. Disaster planning

It is of vital importance for any collection, regardless of size, to adopt every possible safety precaution in order to prevent the outbreak of a disaster and in the unfortunate case of such an event, whether human-induced (acts of vandalism, fires, water leaks, explosions, and so forth) or a natural catastrophe (earthquakes, hurricanes, floods, sandstorms, biological agents, volcanic eruptions), to have at hand a functional disaster plan that will take immediate effect. It is also advisable to make special arrangements to ensure the safety of library or archival material when it is exhibited and to provide security copies of vital records such as collection inventories, and store these off-site (UNESCO 1999).

General guidelines for effective disaster planning can be divided into five main sections, which can be further developed according to the specific needs of each collection. Guidelines include a risk assessment of all potential hazards that may endanger the collection, followed by a prevention plan, aiming to minimize all possible risks, taking specific actions and precautions. A written preparedness plan must be set up, including the procedures that need to be followed when disaster strikes, as well as a recovery strategic plan that will focus on the actions to be taken during the recovery of damaged material (Adcock – Varlamoff 1998; Skepastianu 1995). In the risk assessment, special attention must be given to all potential internal and external environmental threats concerning the building in which the collection is housed, such as water pipes, electronic appliances, potential natural hazards like rivers, and so on; and protective measures must be listed, including effective fire protection systems (fire detection and extinguishing), routine building inspections and maintenance, security systems, insurance policies and so on.

One responsible person, who will be the main coordinator, together with a select group of people, who will act as the support team in an emergency (emergency response team), must be appointed and subsequently trained in emergency response procedures. Those persons, including their contact details, must be known to all personnel, in order immediately to alert them in the event of an emergency. Regular participation of the emergency response team to disaster workshops, where different emergency situations can be simulated, is an excellent way of rehearsing on how to move material and automatically making the correct decisions during a crisis.

A written preparedness plan must be set up, to be regularly edited, reviewed and updated and should include an evacuation plan together with the floor plans of the building (indicating entrances and exits, storage areas, windows, fire extinguishers and all other information that is considered useful in the event of an emergency), a priority rescue list of the objects, detailed instructions on the actions to be undertaken depending on the type of disaster (for instance in the case of fire the response will be different than in the case of pest infection) and the names and contact details of all the parties involved in a rescue situation (Adcock – Varlamoff 1998, Milheirão 1995, Neirinck 1999, Skepastianu 1995, Thouin 1999).

It is also useful to have a ready and easy-to-access 'first aid kit' of all essential materials and tools that will be needed in an emergency and that may not be easily reached at that time (for example in the middle of the night or during weekends). It must be remembered at all times that a successful response strategy aims at two things: to try and stabilize the damage (for instance, in a flood, freezing the objects prevents the appearance of mould); and to save as much material as possible (Neirinck 1999).

Finally, a recovery plan must be established, which will determine the priorities to be covered (restore the disaster site, evaluate and prioritize damaged material), how and where the conservation treatments will take place (development of a phased conservation programme), and also take care of some legal and technical aspects (insurance coverage, auditing as to the causes of the disaster and ways of preventing them in the future: Adcock – Varlamoff 1998; Skepastianu 1995).

Whether the emergency plan concerns a small private collection or a large institution or museum, it should comprise a written priority rescue list, compiled by each department, stating which object(s) are to be salvaged from each room (irreplaceable and important material for priority salvage), including those in the storage areas. This list is of vital importance, since during an emergency evacuation, time is extremely limited and only the designated personnel will be granted access (if possible) for a short time and only for salvaging purposes. During an emergency, it is also essential to be able to assess the situation in order to ensure correct and safe response actions noting: the source of the disaster, primarily establishing whether it may endanger human lives (as in the event of fire or earthquakes), which are obviously prioritized over any artefact, regardless of its value; and secondly if the collection material is affected and whether the collection area is safe (NLA 2013). Depending on the type of disaster, it is not always recommended to remove the objects from the site (for example in the case of mould outbreak, a strategic plan may include quarantining the affected items, without however removing them from the building or the storage facilities, but simply isolating them in another storage area). In the event of any object's removal (to be carried out only by the designated personnel), it is essential to have been granted authorization from the person in charge (typically, the library's or museum's director) and to compile a full inventory of the items removed; all stages of the disaster response and recovery procedures should be documented so that no object can get lost, go astray, or be subject to theft. When recording a rescue procedure, the time constraints and the quantity of material involved should be taken into account, trying to keep documentation brief but accurate. The purpose is to keep a record of what has been damaged and where it has been relocated (NLA 2013).

A recovery area must be established, where all salvaged material will be moved and possibly treated (at least initially, with first aid procedures); in the event of water damage it is crucial to set up an area for recording and packing material which requires freezing, and an area for air-drying slightly wet material and providing other minor treatment (UNESCO 1999).

During the creation of a disaster plan, external help from other institutions and private conservators/specialists (preferably with previous experience in salvaging objects from disaster conditions) is recommended, in order to create beforehand a network of specialists that, in the unfortunate event of a calamity, will be contacted to assist in salvaging the collection. This way it will be possible to deal more rapidly and efficiently with the damaged material, limiting the risk of further endangering the rest of the collection.

5.11. Training and human resources

Training encompasses any form of education, whether aimed at students or professionals. As mentioned, human misuse, unsuitable storage and incorrect handling are among the main causes of deterioration for manuscripts, as well as historic artefacts and works of art in general. Much severe damage is typically caused by improper use, and the damage can easily be avoided if a few simple but effective rules of proper manipulation and preservation are followed. A code of ethics should indicate the standards of behaviour expected of a member of a group. It is intended to protect the profession, the practitioner, the client and the collections/works of art (see Genadry 2010 and General introduction § 4).

It is therefore crucial to raise the awareness of proper handling and caring for the objects, not only among the personnel involved, but also among the general public, explaining the importance of preservation and the extent of (sometimes irreversible) damage that could be avoided, if proper attention were given during handling and conditioning. Small leaflets or strategically placed information stands, with easy-to-follow, basic instructions on the correct manipulation of the items, the use of acid-free bookmarks and support cradles, together with a ban on any food or drink near the objects, as well as the use of pencils instead of pens, are just a few, simple solutions, that will reduce the risk of damage to a minimum and will create over time a correct attitude among readers, scholars and the general public towards preservation and conservation issues (CCI 2002; Bülow 2010; ICON 2011). The persons responsible for a collection must make sure to give proper attention to correct conservation and preservation, by taking into serious consideration all preservation issues and by properly training the personnel in charge of the objects (Bülow 2010; Montanari 1999).

For Integrated Pest Management (IPM) strategies it is crucial that all involved parties (curators, conservators, those responsible for cleaning, and support staff) cooperate and have good communication (with regular, consistent feedback among the groups involved).

Since best practice evolves over time, it is important to keep the personnel updated, through seminars, specialized books, and leaflets and handouts from various companies and governmental institutions. Professional exchanges and consultations with other collections, museums and libraries should be sought when possible (Bülow 2010).

When objects are loaned, displayed or moved from one site to another, highly trained couriers should be employed, with a full understanding of the particularities of manuscripts and the importance of applying strict preservation and security regulations (Cross – Flynn 2003).

Many universities, national or international organizations, institutes and academies offer preservation/conservation programmes, either as part or full-time academic courses at various levels (undergraduate, postgraduate, research), or as short or long-term internships, fellowships, or even short-training professional development courses (varying from daily to weekly or even monthly duration), many of which have scholarships or grants attached to them to cover their costs. Important international organizations, like UNESCO, sponsor and promote cooperation between countries, aiming at protecting, conserving and highlighting national cultural treasures, allowing them to be made accessible and known to a wider public. One such project, just to give an example, is *Euromed Heritage,* launched in 1998, aiming amongst other things at safeguarding cultural heritage and providing professional training in order to alert the public to a new mentality about cultural heritage and at the same time establishing new preservation/conservation standards and activities (Ipert 2005).

References

Adcock – Varlamoff 1998; Balicka-Witakowska 2010c; Bendix et al. 2003; Briquel-Chatonnet 2012; Brown et al. 1982; Bülow 2010; Bülow et al. 2002; CCI 2002; Cross – Flynn 2003; De Moncy 1995; De Tapol 2000; Di Bella 2002a, 2002b; Di Bella – Sarris 2014; Fani 2011; Gallo 2000; Gallo – Regni 2000; Genadry 2010; ICON 2011; Ipert 1995, 2005; Junod 2010; Le Guen 1995; Madani 2002; McCormick – Whitford 2003; Méric 2000; Milheirão 1995 ; Montanari 1999; Moukarzel 2012; Neirinck 1999; NLA 2013; NPO 2000; NPS 1999; Ogden 1999; Parodi 2012; Pickwoad 2004; Pinniger 2001; Porterie 1995; Regni 1995; Regni – Tordella 1996; Revithi 2010, 2011; Ryhl-Svendsen 2006; Scheper 2011; Skepastianu 1995; Sobczynski – Antonia 2013; Thomson [G.] 1997; Thouin 1999; UNESCO 1999, 2006; Velios 2011; Vinourd 2010; Vnouček 1998. Web sources: Euromed Heritage, <http://www.euromedheritage.net>, last access October 2014; LIGATUS, *Saint Catherine's Project*, <http://www.ligatus.org.uk/stcatherines/>, last access October 2014.

6. Conservation: main contemporary techniques and practices (NS)

In order to understand the role of the conservator in the care of manuscripts, books, paper artefacts and archival material, it is necessary to follow how the evolution of the science of conservation has matured up to the present day. The philosophy around the multi-disciplinary field of conservation has evolved as the natural sciences and bibliographical studies have developed, providing the conservator with more options with regard to materials, equipment and techniques, as our understanding of the physical and chemical properties of the materials present in manuscript cultures deepens and at the same time as we learn from our past experiences and mistakes.

6.1. Basic principles

The same basic principles direct the conservator and his decisions on how best to preserve and conserve an object. The integrity of an object, the evidence of its history and its archaeological significance must be preserved above all. The conservator's role is to prolong the life of an object in its entirety, which in the case of manuscripts means that all parts of the object, not only the text or the text block but also its binding, its sewing, its boards and endbands, the covering materials and their decoration, are of equal importance and must be preserved.

A fundamental change in the concept of carrying out treatments on bound manuscripts over the last few decades has redefined what conservation is, with a shift from 'restoration' work, which aimed at remodelling and rebinding manuscripts entirely in order to create aesthetically pleasing results, towards a more moderate and reflective approach towards the history of the object, which conceives manuscripts also as archaeological objects. Thus the structural elements of books are respected and preserved. What is more, over the last three decades the science of conservation has experienced a gradual shift towards what is known as *minimal intervention* (or *minimal conservation*, see Ch. 5 § 1.2) giving more ground to the application of preventive conservation measures. It is now widely perceived that minimizing intervention with a greater concern for the historical and archaeological aspects of collections is the most effective way to approach collections, and many institutions and conservation professionals are following entirely a minimal intervention policy.

The concept of minimal intervention since its first appearance relied greatly on the fundamental growth of preventive conservation science and the concept that conservation treatments must be fully reversible. Nevertheless, full reversibility of treatments is gradually re-evaluated as its feasibility is questioned, since most conservation treatments will inevitably alter even in the smallest amount the structural and physical properties of objects.

Minimal intervention is still a driving concept in the area of the conservation of manuscripts. However, there are limitations to its benefits, which relate to the requirements of the accessibility of manuscripts and the need to display them for exhibition purposes. What is more, minimal intervention may not deal with certain types of decay on specific objects which may require a more interventive approach to address immediate threats.

The decision on what should be the most appropriate conservation treatment depends on the conservator's critical thinking and his examination, evaluation and appreciation of the condition of the object and the requirements of the manuscript he is called upon to take care of. Interventive treatments may be deemed more necessary on certain occasions and, guided by professional principles and practices, the trained conservator must make intelligent and realistic decisions on each manuscript individually.

The conservator is also called upon to take decisions on what treatment is most appropriate for an object judging by the possible implications of his actions on the evidence of the object's history, the possibility that his interventions may interfere with parts of the structure that will be excessively disturbed, and the necessity to stop or delay any form of decay or damage that is a risk for the manuscript. Conservation treatment may also be decided on for specific reasons. The display of manuscripts in exhibitions and their digitization may also dictate that specific treatments are required, while financial and time perspectives are also fundamental in the decision-making process, and different conservation plans and priorities are therefore formulated.

Treatments may thus generally be categorized as either minimal or interventive. This fact has significance for projections on the types of treatment that are considered acceptable and respectful for manuscripts in each case, as well as for the materials that conservators may apply to them. The materials that are selected for conservation work, particularly those materials that will be used and will become part of the object, must be as reversible as possible and should leave the smallest possible deposits, remnants and influence on the integrity of the manuscript, should they need to be removed in the future for any reason. The quality and availability of materials is a fundamental part in the equation to justify whether conservation treatments are possible. Inappropriate materials, such as acidic repair papers and acidic boards, synthetic adhesives and poor quality leathers are only some examples of materials that have been used in the repair process of oriental manuscripts primarily in areas where conservation standard materials are not always available, or due to inadequate understanding of their possible negative effects. It is vital to stress that introducing poor quality materials into manuscripts may be severely damaging and conservation treatments are best not executed unless good quality materials are available.

The conservator is equipped with the training to have an understanding of materials in manuscript cultures, the knowledge of the historical evidence contained in the structural features of bindings and the processes of degradation. His critical thinking and evaluation of what is the best way to approach a damaged manuscript on a case by case basis is the most effective way to address its problems. These constitute the principal guidelines for state-of-the-art conservation.

6.2. Conservation of text blocks

Mechanical damage to the leaves of the text block, flaking pigments of painted decoration and areas that present imminent threats of further mechanical damage are often types of damage that may be resolved by localized minimal treatments, with the aim of stabilizing them and preventing losses. The justification for their employment lies in the expected use of the manuscript, its possible digitization or display and the estimated benefits to the overall condition of the manuscript with localized stabilization.

– *Washing and deacidification*

The processes of washing and deacidification of paper text blocks have been practised extensively over the last decades, with the aim of reducing the discolouration and acidity of objects, and there are several studies to demonstrate both their disadvantages and advantages. In many cases, institutions have prompted the application of these treatments as a standardized practice of 'conservation', regardless of whether these treatments would be beneficial for the manuscripts in the long term, without looking at each manuscript and its problems individually and often without appropriate analytical testing. Washing and deacidification are not entirely inappropriate treatments, provided there is a good justification for their application, and there are certain cases where they might prove necessary. However, aqueous treatments require that text blocks are completely dismantled in order for them to be carried out, which is a severely destructive process, which interferes considerably with the historical integrity of the manuscripts and the archaeological evidence of bindings. In another respect, examinations and research on the effects of washing have shown that the primary objective of this treatment, which is to remove acidic products in the paper and to strengthen and return flexibility to the fibre matrix of the paper, is not always realistic or possible. The problems that washing aims to address may not always be possible to resolve, since it is vital to understand the source of acidity in the paper. Acidity may derive from products used in the paper-making process, in which case the acidity will be entirely irreversible, regardless of any washing or deacidification treatment. In other cases, where acidity is the result of external materials adjacent to our objects, preventive measures may be deemed much more effective, realistic and sympathetic to the overall state of the manuscript.

It is important to weigh the consequences of such drastic treatments, when substantial results may be achieved by the correct housing of manuscripts, which would slow down the process of oxidization or hydrolysis of the cellulose polymer of paper. Overall, the damage-benefit aspect of these treatments is often not in favour of their execution and it is seldom justifiable to dismantle a manuscript with the sole purpose of carrying out these treatments.

– *Paper and parchment repairs*

The materials and techniques used for the repair of tears, lacunae and mechanical damage to paper have developed significantly during the last decades, relying considerably on a range of suitable, traditional Japanese papers that are still produced in adequate qualities and quantities for the conservation market. Japanese papers offer excellent options with which the reinforcement and infilling of damaged paper and parchment can be performed. Pulp repairs have also been used by conservators and institutions around the world; these offer very good aesthetic results and can appear outstanding. Unfortunately, these pulp repairs have very low tensile strength and very short fibres, which result in weak repairs with low stability that are often in need of extra tissue lining or extra adhesive, so that it is debatable whether they will last in time. What is more, in order to carry out pulp repairs it is necessary to work on individual leaves and not on bound manuscripts; therefore these repairs cannot be performed unless manuscripts are disbound. In comparison with Japanese paper repairs (using good quality, pH-neutral, long-fibre papers) pulp repairs may be easier and quicker to carry out, with good aesthetic results, but are significantly inferior in their mechanical properties and more restricting in the conditions under which they can be performed. This is also the case with leafcasting (an apparatus used for infilling large areas of losses with paper pulp): although good aesthetic results can be produced, the unavoidable aqueous environment in which this treatment has to take place, along with the low tensile strength of the pulp fibres, have made leafcasting a less preferred method.

– *Ink corrosion treatments*

For many years it was believed that the cure for the problem of ink corrosion from iron-gall inks, a common problem for manuscripts across the oriental manuscript traditions, was a deacidification treatment where the acidity of the ink could be counterbalanced by an alkaline solution, thereby arresting corrosion. Recent research has raised doubts as to the efficacy of this approach. One of the main disadvantages of alkaline treatments is that they must be performed in aqueous solutions, otherwise the alkaline solutions would act only superficially and not on the whole matrix of the paper. Water, however, acts as a vector for the soluble ferrous irons, enhancing the corrosion process (Hahn et al. 2008a). The use of chelating agents (such as EDTA) is considered equally unsatisfactory, since the iron-EDTA complex can still react with hydrogen peroxide and result in active free iron ions (Fe^{++}) that will catalyse the oxidization process and lead to the degradation of the cellulose polymer. Alternative treatments such as the *calcium phytate treatment* in water-alcohol solutions (Neevel 1995, Botti et al. 2005) have shown better results in recent research; however the costs involved with these treatments are generally high, and for many institutions and conservation laboratories it may be a prohibiting factor. Low relative humidity (RH < 50%) slows down the oxidization process and is one of the most significant measures to take.

Parchment manuscripts on the other hand do not always present ink corrosion problems and are thus not equally in need of ink treatments. This is mainly related to the process of preparation of medieval parchment, which involved treatment with lime thus supplying an alkaline reserve.

– *Adhesives*

Numerous adhesives have traditionally been used in the *restoration* and *conservation* of manuscripts. Most frequently we encounter organic adhesives such as wheat starches, gelatin (animal glue or fish glue), isinglass (used for parchment repairs) and in the last few decades the laboratory-produced methyl cellulose. Local variants, such as the *bamia* paste (a derivative of okra), found in Middle Eastern countries, are occasionally found and traditionally used but in most cases are not tested for their conservation quality properties. The most frequently encountered synthetic adhesives are PVA (polyvinyl acetate) and EVA (ethylene vinyl acetate).

Depending on the type of work to be carried out—whether paper repairs, leatherwork, parchment repairs or box-making—different adhesives may be selected and considered appropriate. The most significant recommendation that conservators can provide today is that synthetic adhesives, such as PVA and EVA, should never be used in direct contact with any part of the object, for two main reasons: a) they are irreversible, particularly as they lose their elasticity over time, b) off-gassing acetates produced from these adhesives are damaging to the manuscripts (see also Ch. 5 §§ 2.1 and 4.2). It is therefore recommended to avoid using synthetic adhesives entirely, reserving them only for the production of boxes and containers for the safe-keeping of manuscripts, in which case EVA is preferable over PVA, and again it should be kept away from areas in contact with the manuscript as much as possible.

There has been a long debate over the use of methyl cellulose versus wheat starch in the last decades, with equally strong arguments from both sides. Wheat starch is a traditional adhesive that has been used for centuries across most manuscript cultures and which has proved in time to have excellent properties and not to be harmful to objects in any way. Its strength may often be partly lost in time, depending on the quality of the wheat used and the manufacturing of the adhesive, but particularly for use on paper repairs it is an excellent option, with very good flexibility characteristics that work very well with paper. But on the other hand, wheat starches are believed to attract insects, even though there is no systematic research to demonstrate that they are more attractive than the paper, wood, leather or other organic materials or even other adhesives that constitute the manuscript itself. The same is believed of animal glue, which was often used as a bookbinding adhesive in many oriental binding traditions, particularly at the spine and spine lining of bindings. The alleged insect-attracting properties of wheat starch and gelatin may perhaps originate in a confusion with the properties of the area in which they are most frequently applied. The spine of the book is an area most suitable for insects to lay their eggs and for the larvae to develop, as it is a dark, inaccessible, and safe place for them to act. It is reasonable that this would be the first area to suffer insect damage. Methyl cellulose appeared as an alternative to wheat starch particularly for this reason, and it has indeed very good conservation properties. However, it is less strong than wheat starch, which makes it unsuitable for bookbinding purposes, but only adequate for paper repairs, and it is also less tested over time. Its applications in other processes in conservation, such as adhesive removal, paper sizing and the making of pre-coated Japanese tissues, make methyl cellulose nonetheless a very useful adhesive. It is evident that more research is required in the field, to determine if indeed the excellent properties of adhesives such as wheat starch are counterbalanced by their supposed insect-attracting characteristics. Many conservators over the years preferred to use insect repellents and insecticides such as formaldehyde and bromide mixed with wheat starch or methyl cellulose to prevent insect damage. This approach is objectionable in several respects. Primarily, the protection of a manuscript from insect damage is a preservation measure that should be considered in a more holistic and effective way, by improving the environmental and storage/ housing conditions of an item, as there are several other parts of a book that are prone to insect damage besides the adhesives. What is more, the application of insecticides is severely damaging for the paper or parchment substrates, and they also entail considerable risks for the health of the conservators applying them.

Parchment repairs require stronger adhesives than wheat starch or methyl-cellulose. Tests and the experiences of conservators over the years have demonstrated that isinglass, gelatin, or a mixture of gelatin with wheat starch are strong, flexible and sympathetic to parchment (Di Bella – Sarris 2014).

As an alternative to using adhesives directly on water or humidity-sensitive media or substrates, such as certain pigments, iron gall inks or substrates such as papyrus, it is often advised to use Japanese tissues pre-coated with an adhesive, such as methyl-cellulose or wheat starch, which can be activated with minor humidity or solvents (Rouchon et al. 2009).

– Adhesive tapes

Repairs made with adhesive tapes are one of the most common and most damaging habits of book readers and librarians, and have been used throughout the twentieth century. Either as an easy repair method for torn and damaged leaves or as a means of labelling, they pose an immediate problem to manuscripts.

These adhesive tapes are composed of two parts: the paper or synthetic tape and the adhesive, the latter being the most difficult to remove and the tapes' most damaging part. There are numerous varieties of tape and the adhesives applied on them are equally numerous, depending on the different producers, but the vast majority have severely damaging effects on paper and parchment substrates, which escalate with time as the adhesive penetrates deeper into the manuscript substrate and becomes less flexible and soluble. The most effective method to remove the adhesive and the tape is with the use of organic solvents, such as ethanol or acetone, but even so it is often inevitable that part of the adhesive will have crystallized and irreversibly penetrated the matrix of the substrate, and little can be done about it without disturbing the substrate too much. The presence of adhesive tapes is often flagged as an emergency risk for manuscripts and calls for the immediate attention of the conservator, since it is a type of damage that becomes more and more difficult to resolve with the passage of time.

– Lamination of leaves

The lamination of fragile manuscript leaves is a technique that was developed long ago and has been used for many decades, in order to improve the handling of these materials and stabilize them against further losses. In previous decades, particularly between the 1950s and 1970s, many libraries and archives around the world embarked largely on lamination projects, looking for quick, cheap and effective methods for mass lamination of documents and book leaves. Soluble, machine or hand lamination with nylon and heat set tissues were the most common techniques adopted, but unfortunately the ageing properties of these materials and the impossibility of reversing them raised great concerns for conservators from early on. Nowadays, lamination of manuscript leaves is considered an inappropriate and destructive method: research now aims to find solutions to reverse the damage it has caused. Alternatives to lamination should be sought by conservators needing to reinforce a fragile manuscript, such as using a facing technique with pre-coated Japanese tissues with wheat starch paste or methyl cellulose, or making ordinary paper repairs and paper bridges (Pataki 2009; Lau-Lamb 2007).

6.3. Sewing

Broken or damaged sewing is most often a result of handling and mechanical damage, or pest damage when infestation occurs at the spine of the book. The failed sewing may result in bifolia or quires coming loose from the text block and weakened opening and mechanical properties of the structure are observed. The conservator is often called upon to repair damaged sewing structures to restore the mechanics and functionality of the book. The decision on if and how to repair the book's sewing may be deeply complicated, depending on how accessible the spine area of the book is, how much the book will be used, what disturbance will occur to other areas of the structure in order to repair the sewing, how feasible it is to achieve a stable sewing judging from the condition of the leaves of the text block and how beneficial the repair of the sewing will be for the structure overall.

In situ minimal repairs of sewing are a possibility depending on these factors, without the need to dismantle a manuscript; adequate sewing techniques have been developed that aid the conservator with this choice, which can be less invasive and more respectful to the object. Disbinding bound manuscripts is widely regarded as an unnecessary procedure, except as a last resort. Inevitably, when dismantling a binding, much of the history of the structure and of the manuscript itself will be irreversibly lost.

In those cases where the conservator reaches the decision to re-sew a text block entirely, the style of the original structure, its history of repairs and the strength of the text block leaves are some of the variables that the conservator needs to consider in deciding what style and materials he will use, as well as how best to apply these to minimize the interference with the manuscript and to provide an aesthetic and functional result that will not be foreign to the earlier sewing.

6.4. Binding

Minimal or more interventive treatments may be employed on binding elements such as the end-leaves, the spine lining, the endbands and the boards, following the general concept of minimal intervention. The intention would be to consolidate, repair locally and *in situ* areas of damage that need to be secured before leading to further damage, which will help the manuscript to be used, digitized or displayed with greater safety. None of these treatments should have the sole goal of restoring the book to a perfect state and the utmost care should be taken of those elements of its history that are disturbed by the choices the conservator makes.

– Leather repairs and the choice of leather

The repair of broken, torn and damaged leather covers is a type of damage the conservator frequently faces. The conservator's task is not that of removing damaged covers and replacing them with stronger and better functioning ones; he must attempt to consolidate, repair and strengthen the original leather, in order to prevent further losses and damages and to stabilize it so as to return the book to a functional state, in case it needs to be used. This is done with little less than mechanical applications of either Japanese paper linings and/or infills, toned appropriately to the shades of the leather, or with the addition of new pieces of leather, which are used to fill in the missing parts, to strengthen and replace the functionality of the cover.

One of the most important parts of this process—and most difficult to achieve, apart from having sufficient manual dexterity to complete good infills and repairs, is the choice of the additional materials to be used: the leather and the adhesive. It is unfortunate that good-quality leather, prepared with a natural vegetable tanning process as it has been traditionally used for many centuries on bookbindings, is not easily acquired nowadays. Research has shown that chrome tanning, which has dominated the leather manufacturing process over the last century, should be avoided for use on historical objects due to its unfavourable ageing properties and the reduced durability of the grain (Barlee 2001). Archival-quality, vegetable-tanned (semi-aluminium) skins should be preferred. Chrome-tanned leather is also found to be less workable by bookbinders. Care should be taken also of the dyes that have been used to colour or tone the leather, which must not be colour-fast or water-soluble, and of finishing skin lubricants with unknown and aesthetically inappropriate properties. Such lubricants should be applied with great care, as they can affect the long-term condition of leather: their incorrect application will form a barrier that can trap humidity within the collagen of the skin, leading to the growth of microorganisms and preventing the skin from reaching an equilibrium with the surrounding environment.

– *Board attachment repairs and consolidation*

Like the sewing of a text block, board-attachments may be repaired either *in situ*, by reinforcing the damaged attachment or by introducing a new board-attachment system. In the latter case many considerations will need to be made to evaluate the implications on the other components of the binding that may be affected by this process and to avoid disturbing, removing or altering them as much as possible.

– *Old repairs*

Old repairs, either in the text block or in parts of the sewing and binding of a manuscript, offer valuable evidence on the history of the manuscript and its previous conditions, its past owners, and may lead to significant information about its provenance. The history of repairs in parallel to the history of bookbinding is at the same time a topic for systematic research as it may contribute substantially to what we know about individual manuscripts and about book producing cultures as a whole.

It is recognized however that certain repairs of the past often pose problems to the present conditions of manuscripts and are a cause of further damage. The conservator may be faced with a dilemma between removing historical evidence, which may nevertheless be jeopardizing the very safety of the original manuscript. Unless threatening to the object, these pieces of evidence should be regarded as part of the manuscript and not removed or disturbed. Decisions must be weighed, justified and most importantly documented meticulously to provide the historical evidence in the event that they have to be disturbed.

References

Barlee 2001; Botti et al. 2005; Di Bella – Sarris 2014; Hahn et al. 2008a; Lau-Lamb 2007; Neevel 1995; Pataki 2009; Rouchon et al. 2009.

7. Digitization for access and preservation (MMy–JM–EBW)

7.1. Introduction (MMy)

The digitization of historical written heritage began around 1990, at a time when the first digital cameras came on the market at affordable prices. Whilst at the very beginning digitization focused on individual objects, such as the Gutenberg Bible and other outstanding manuscripts and books of intrinsic value, it soon became clear that only the digitization of entire groups of records would play an important role for research. Technology improved step by step and nowadays the problem of increasing storage capacity is negligible. At the same time, the quality of scanners and cameras has improved significantly, so that some collections could be re-digitized (examples include the TITUS project: <http://titus.fkidg1.uni-frankfurt.de/texte/tocharic/tht.htm>, and manuscript digitization project at the University Library in Graz). Besides, the software operability as well as the computer memory have seen a drastic development. Today, the technical prerequisites easily allow the presentation of entire collections on the web with international accessibility.

From the very beginning the target group consisted of researchers and students, but also scientifically interested laymen. Digitization opened up as yet unprecedented opportunities to virtually visit collections, for example to compare and edit scattered groups of manuscripts, scriptoria, printed books and documents. However, digitization alone is of less value if the objects are not described in a catalogue to make them searchable and discoverable. Therefore the creation of descriptive metadata grew in the same proportion as the number of digitized books and today plays an extremely important role alongside the practical creation of digital images (see General introduction § 2.1.4).

The challenge for the future will be to ensure the readability and accessibility of electronic data. Each technical process has its own dynamics and for the maintenance of a data unit, either by format migration or emulation, accessibility is and will remain a constant concern. Format migration means reformatting the data to the current standard, while emulation is a process to make old data readable by using special software. Both procedures for ensuring the readability of data will become a basic task of libraries and archives. Most probably, any solution to this challenge will be of limited time duration, and regular updates will always be necessary.

7.2. Digitization for preservation (MMy)

The unrestricted use of written sources is often associated with the human right to freedom of information and opinion. The provision of digital data is a prerequisite, although it cannot replace the preservation of the originals. The originals—manuscripts, documents and archival material, artistic graphics and so forth—are likely analogous to master files, whose preservation is a top priority. In fact, some people erroneously think digital copies will totally replace protection of the originals, as if they virtually replaced the analogue object. Undoubtedly, digitization allows virtually worldwide access to much-demanded collection items. This allows a certain protection of vulnerable objects as the necessity of physical access seemingly decreases. In practice, however, it has been shown quite often that due to the digitization of certain codices these objects gain a popularity that leads to an increasing demand for consultation of the originals. This effect could already be observed before digitization with high-quality facsimile editions. An important point is also the risk for the original, which arises in the digitization of sensitive objects. For this reason, digitization should be carried out only by trained staff and after a carefully coordinated workflow (see below). Even the best digital copy is only a copy of the surface of a document that contains possibly visible and invisible information. A digitized version preserves neither the material substance of the object nor its condition. Therefore, while satisfying certain conservation-based aspects, digitization is not a measure for the permanent preservation of cultural heritage.

The long-term preservation of data is still an unsolved problem. It challenges research and development on the basis of international cooperation, which will have to be reflected in practice and appropriate guidelines and also best-practice models (see Ch. 4 § 6). It is particularly desirable to always associate future digitized objects with conservational securing of the originals.

7.3. Preparing for digitization (MMy)

The digitization workflow can be divided into the following main parts: first, transport of the book from the shelf to the photographer followed by autopsy and decision-making; the actual digitization followed by return transport; the creation of metadata, control and processing.

Presumably, codices spend 99% of their lifetime on the shelf. For the purpose of digitization, individual books are picked and must first undergo an assessment of their suitability for risk-free digitization. After a survey of their physical condition (see also Ch. 5 § 5), books in a risky condition are labelled to warn the photographer against risk of damage. Photographers often act under time pressure and are also affected by the monotony of the work, which leads to a certain dullness in dealing with the objects. They should undergo some training in handling sensitive books, preferably under the supervision of a conservator. Ideally, photographers and conservators should work closely together.

First, the condition of the binding is examined. The focus lies here on defining the degree at which the book can be opened without causing any harm or stress to the binding. To do this the book is placed on a v-shaped cradle (as described in Ch. 5 § 5.6; see there also for the discussion on the use of gloves). The text block must then be opened in the middle, carefully pressing the two halves of the book block apart while feeling and observing the resistance against opening (fig. 5.7.1). The book should be opened to an angle of 120°–140° without violence. Now the book rests in an open position on the cradle and one can browse forward and backward to consider if other areas allow a violence-free opening of the book as well. During this process the book is also examined for damage to the pages of all kinds, particularly tears, loose or partially loose sheets, mould and inserted parts, slips, and similar (see also Ch. 5 § 4).

If irregularities of any kind are discovered, they must be documented in a condition report or survey protocol (see Ch. 5 § 5.7). In any case inserted loose slips or documents should be included in the digitization process based on their importance. Depending on the case, a decision will have to be made on whether the images of these documents are inserted into the sequence of the captured pages or stored in a separate file.

Depending on the results of the survey, one may have to consider a conservation process for damaged books before digitization. Only in the rarest cases will a complete restoration be carried out, as there is often a lack of human and financial resources. Interestingly, on the other hand, a weakened binding with a partly loose backing even promotes a digitization of the text block, since due to the open joint the text block opens wide without resistance (fig. 5.7.2). The conservator or experienced photographer will decide from case to case if a scanning process can be carried out before conservation treatment.

Fig. 5.7.1 Opening a manuscript on a support created from soft foam cushions, photograph by MMy.

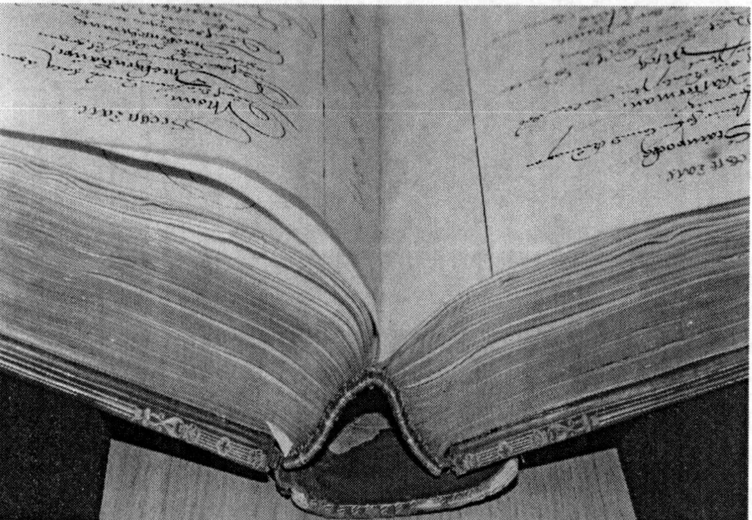

Fig. 5.7.2 Opening a manuscript with a damaged spine, photograph by MMy.

It is always recommended to remount loose sections or sheets before digitization. The risk of more detachment is too great, and confusion is likely to occur when re-inserting the loose parts.

Cracked or torn pages run a risk of further tearing, often during the process of turning the pages. A temporary fixing must precede the digitization. If mould is discovered, consultation from a professional conservator is mandatory in order not to endanger the health of the photographers. Books with mould growth should be isolated in order not to infest other books.

If microbiological attack or dust, moisture, or similar damage is registered, a special treatment should be started, not only to ensure protection of the staff (recommended: use masks, gloves, disinfectant liquids), but also to enhance the quality of the images. Treatment can involve the mechanical cleaning of pages, and unfolding of corners or curled edges. The importance of such more or less 'cosmetic' treatment also depends on the importance of the original and the aim of the reproducing process.

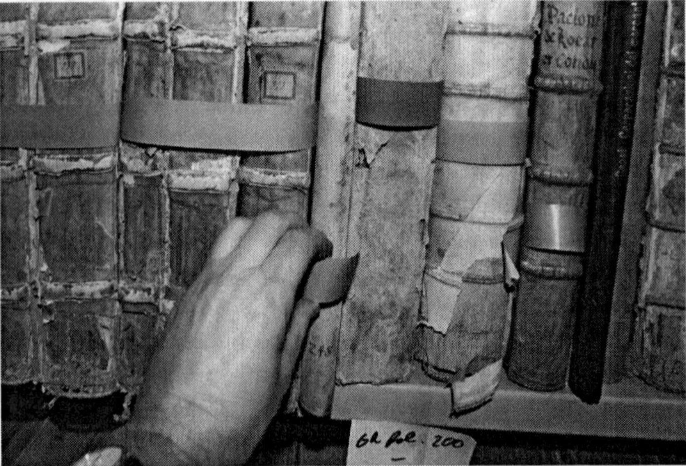

Fig. 5.7.3 Coding the preservation state of manuscripts by signal stripes, photograph by MMy.

Iron gall ink damage and copper green damage are not so prominent in parchment as in paper manuscripts, yet in certain cases they are highly problematic and prohibit normal use, including handling for digitization. The same goes for loose or flaking paint layers (see Ch. 5 § 4 for examples and illustrations): a consolidation here will depend on the degree of the damage and must be carried out by an expert.

If the photographer faces the problem of having to digitize a large collection of books, which is very often the case, it is recommended to start with medium-sized, risk-free books. This allows the photographer to familiarize him or herself with the particular features of the collection and with the digitization equipment used.

As discussed above, the condition report should contain at least: signature (shelf-mark), book specifications (author, title, place of origin); material of text carrier, writing material, binding description, cover type, details of folia, additions, ownership history and generally any specific abnormalities.

Finally, the introduction of a practical three-level grading is recommended. In a protocol, it can be easily represented with the 'traffic light' system to identify the individual cases quickly: green means good condition, no risk; yellow means average condition, some risk exists, digitization feasible at low risk, minimal conservation treatment required; red means bad condition, high risk of damage, conservation treatment necessary. The same colours can be used to mark the manuscripts themselves: for example, with a paper-strip wrapped around the binding (fig. 5.7.3).

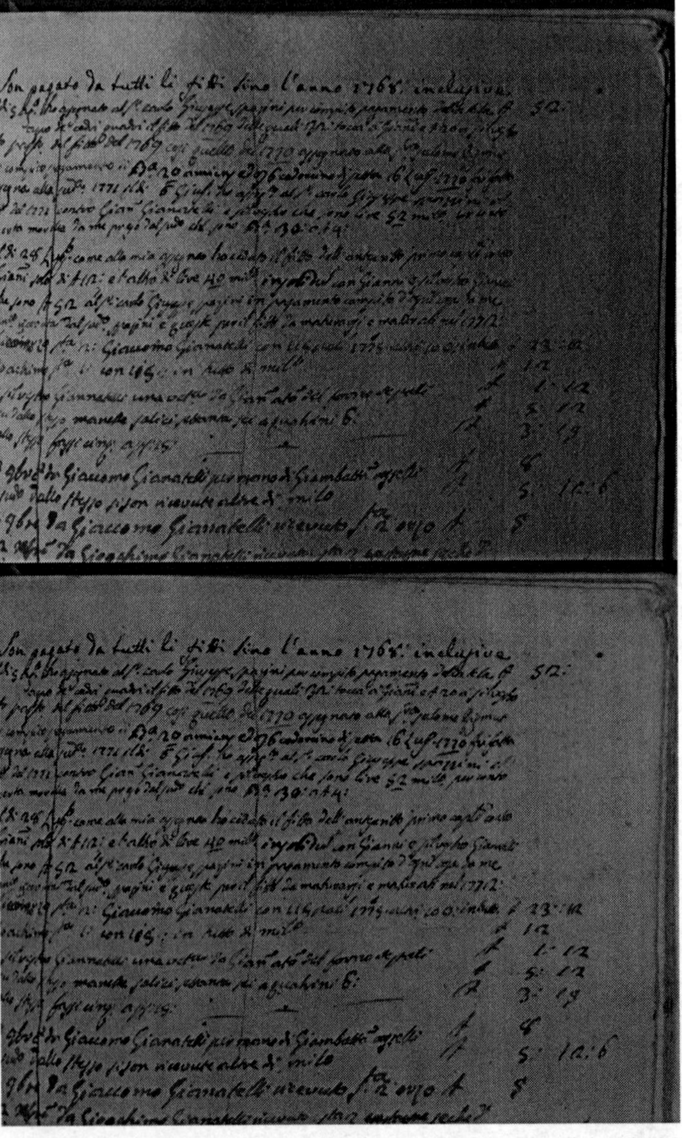

Fig. 5.7.4 One and the same page photographed with raking light (above) and balanced light (below), photograph by MMy.

7.4. Digitization: handling and equipment (MMy)

For gentle and safe handling of the object during the imaging process, the following conditions can be identified. Book cradles (see above) must be used at all times to ensure that the book will not open fully to 180° and the binding is protected against breakage. No glass plates may be used, either for holding down the sheets or for holding the text block in an open shape. Glass plates are electrostatic, albeit to a lesser extent, but principally they create a certain vacuum due to adhesion when lifting off from the page. This creates the risk that particles are pulled up. Last but not least the use of a glass plate implicates a certain risk because of its weight and risk of glass breakage. Lighting without infrared (IR) and ultraviolet (UV) emissions is obligatory (compare also Ch. 5 § 5.1 and § 7.4.1). Modern LED-lights (see below) do not emit IR- or UV-rays. On the contrary light bulbs, and fluorescent tubes do emit a certain amount of IR- and UV-rays. If possible, digitization should be undertaken in an air-conditioned room with no ambient light influence, since ambient light impacts on the exposure of the sheets. The tripod used must be mechanically stable, to ensure that it cannot accidentally fall on the book. Secure mounting of the camera and the lights to the tripod to obtain images under reproducible conditions are equally essential.

7.4.1. Light sources

Due to the required reproducibility, light sources with a constant light emission must be used. Fluorescent tubes with daylight emission have been used widely so far. However, they age and continuously lose luminance; their average life-span is given at 2000 hours. A certain amount of ultraviolet radiation cannot be excluded, and should be eliminated through the application of UV-filters. Nowadays fluorescent lamps will be replaced by high-quality LEDs (light emitting diodes). These light sources have the advantage of an extremely long lifetime (at least 20,000 hours) and, as mentioned, they emit neither IR nor UV radiation.

Flash may also be used from a technical standpoint, but there is an open discussion among experts about the harm it may do to illuminated manuscripts. The scientific community is not quite sure about the harmful effects of flash, and many collecting institutions prohibit its use. The physiological effect of flash on the photographer is not negligible either, since on an average workday the photographer is exposed to 2000–3000 flashes. Besides that, flashes emit a significant amount of UV radiation and therefore the use of UV filters is essential.

Even greater attention than to the selection of light sources itself should be given to the alignment of the lamps in relation to the sheet to be digitized. A perfectly symmetrical illumination, as repro stands ideally provide, leads to excellent illuminated templates. This means that the image is photographed virtually shadow-free and all parts of the sheet receive uniform illumination. Perfectly symmetrical illumination may lead to photographs of excellent quality for catalogues, research purposes and for text studies, but they lack a certain vitality in the reproduction. For example, paper and parchment structures, surface irregularities, blind-ruled lines, or wrinkles in the manuscript or print are only poorly, if at all, reproduced under balanced lighting. To some extent this is a disadvantage for codicological research. For this reason, one should consider the additional digital capturing of the same page under raking light, as the information content of such an image is much higher than that of a perfectly lit one. A good example of this double capturing is the digitization of the *Codex Sinaiticus* (<http://www.codexsinaiticus.org>). Raking light recordings can easily be accomplished, for example by covering or shading one of the two or more light sources. The imbalanced lighting can easily be compensated for by software. As a result, one has a more realistic, vivid image of the original (fig. 5.7.4).

In addition to reflected light images, transmitted light images may be helpful, as long as they do not burden the text block and the sheet. Transmitted light photographs allow for significantly better recognition of the structure of the paper and the watermarks. Digitization with invisible radiation, such as infrared and ultraviolet radiation, contributes further evidence. If invisible radiation is used, the duration and intensity of IR- and UV-radiation must be strictly limited to the minimum necessary level. As for these cases special equipment and a photographer with specific knowledge are needed, details of this procedure are not included in this publication. Digitization under UV and IR light (multispectral imaging) is nowadays a standard tool for palimpsest research (see General introduction § 2.3).

A prism 3/3/3cm × 30cm (or longer), made of acrylic or glass, can be useful to capture the full text block in tightly bound volumes or the writing on the guard strips added sometimes in the middle of a quire in order to strengthen the sewing. Larger prisms are less practical because, being very heavy, they may damage the binding; thus they require a special holding device. Moreover their thickness may cause Newton's rings in the image (fig. 5.7.5).

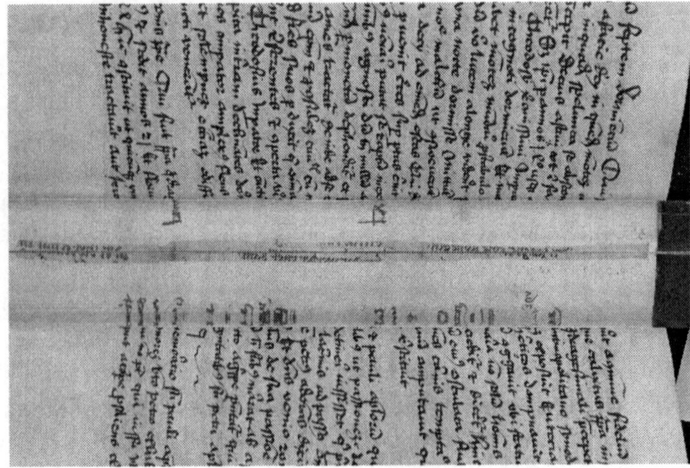

Fig. 5.7.5 The prism effect, photograph by MMy.

7.4.2. Choosing the image section

It is important for the captured image of a page to contain as much information as possible. Therefore, it is imperative to photograph the entire sheet, including the edges and preferably the inner margin. These elements, although they are outside the text, often include important codicological information. For example, the position and proportion of the written or printed area in respect to the whole page plays an important role when studying the layout of a page. If edges and margins are cropped in the image, information about layout and design of a page is lost.

If there are missing parts in the sheet, holes and similar losses, a sheet of grey or black paper should be placed underneath. Otherwise, the text of the page underneath cannot be separated by the viewer from the text on the upper sheet, which can lead to confusion.

7.4.3. Camera settings

Due to the limited space available in this handbook, we shall abstain from discussing the settings of exposure time, shutter speed, ISO and other such technical specifications; instead we recommend consulting publications such as Warda 2008 which holds all the necessary information (see also Ch. 5 § 7.6.5). Most European and American libraries regularly issue digitization guidelines that can be consulted in the libraries and online (e.g., University of Massachusetts at Amherst, <http://www.library.umass.edu/assets/aboutus/attachments/UMass-Amherst-Libraries-Best-Practice-Guidelines-for-Digitization-20110523-templated.pdf>; Library of Congress, <http://memory.loc.gov/ammem/about/techIn.html> and <http://www.loc.gov/preservation/care/scan.html>; University of Manchester, <http://www.library.manchester.ac.uk/ourservices/serviceweprovide/digitisation/_files/DigitisationStrategyfinal.pdf>, last access October 2014).

References

Federal Agencies Digitization Initiative 2010; ICN 2005; NARA 2004; *Technical Guidelines* 2004, 2010; Warda 2008.

7.5. Data format, storage and conservation challenges (JM)

7.5.1. Digitization for distribution

The digitization of a manuscript should be done in both RAW and TIFF formats; JPEG can later be derived. RAW is the most comprehensive format and always uncompressed. Concerning JPEG and TIFF one can say that there are very different compression rates possible in this format, with higher compression rates causing greater loss of information. Images with higher compression may be usable for distribution but not for long-time storage and maintenance.

One must be careful not to miss any page, and pay attention to the camera's focus (or every ten pages by autofocus), to the manuscript, and the colour management QP card position. The data should be checked by another person to spot blurred images or missing pages, adjust any detected problem, separate and number the different images.

7.5.2. Storage and security

For secure storage, one must keep at least one RAW copy and one uncompressed TIFF copy. Images may be stored at Storage Area Networks (SANs) to reduce the percentage of data loss and protect digitized copies of the manuscripts. SANs are not the only possible storage facilities for our purposes. Any data

Signature:			
Title:			
Location / Collection:			
Height:	Width:	Thickness:	

Condition:		
□ excellent	□ loose or torn sheets	□ microbiological attacked
□ good	□ adhesive tapes, sticky paper	□ ink/copper corroded
□ good but tight bound	□ detached cover(s)	□ brittle paper / parchment

Camera model:			
Type	Lens:		
Camera Settings:			
Exp. Time:	Aperture:	ISO:	ColTemp: Kelvin

Lights:	
Type:	Flash:
Position of lights vs. Object: symmetrical / Raking light / Direction	

Equipment Settings:			
Distance Camera-Object (mm):			
Other:			

Fig. 5.7.6 Digitization protocol.

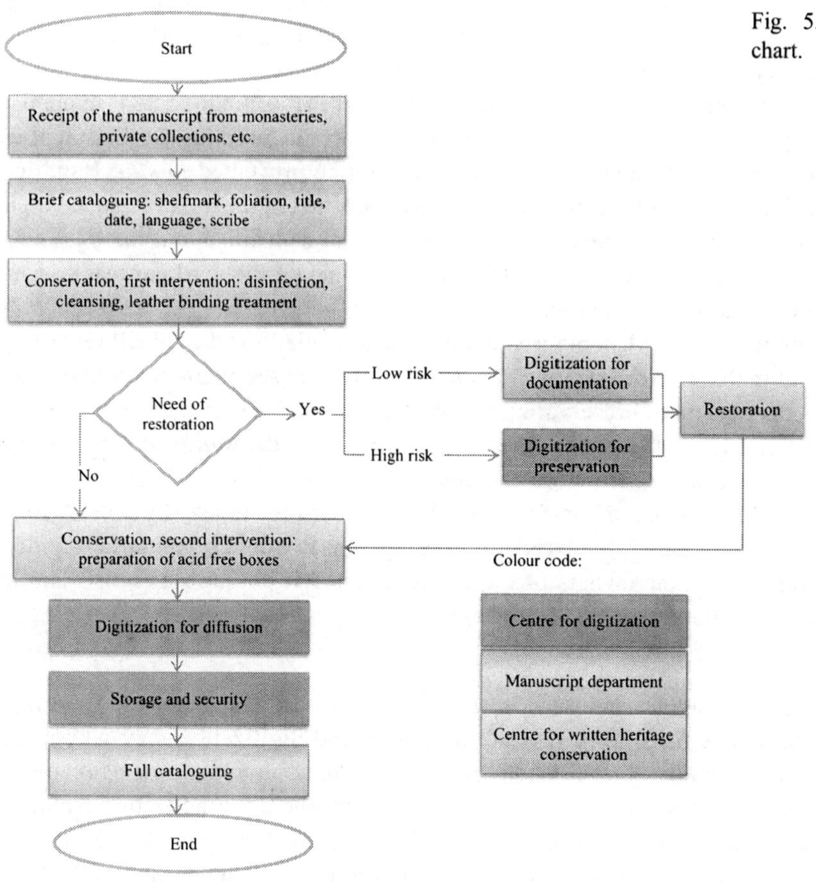

Start

Receipt of the manuscript from monasteries, private collections, etc.

Brief cataloguing: shelfmark, foliation, title, date, language, scribe

Conservation, first intervention: disinfection, cleansing, leather binding treatment

Need of restoration

Yes

Low risk

Digitization for documentation

High risk

Digitization for preservation

Restoration

No

Conservation, second intervention: preparation of acid free boxes

Digitization for diffusion

Storage and security

Full cataloguing

End

Colour code:

Centre for digitization

Manuscript department

Centre for written heritage conservation

Fig. 5.7.7 Digitization workflow chart.

storage centre that is equipped for the long-term maintenance of data can be used. Finally, a full cataloguing of the manuscript must be performed. Data Leakage Protection (DLP) is a possible solution to reduce the Data Leakage.

References

Library of Congress 2007; see also Ch. 5 §§ 7.4, 7.6.

7.6. Recording manuscripts in the field (EBW)

The question of how best to record a manuscript is particularly important when the examination and imaging process is not performed in the modern, fully supportive western institutions but concerns collections belonging to communities (often religious), families or individuals in remote parts of the world, where work is carried out under challenging conditions, and undisturbed access to the books is seldom guaranteed. In some cases the collection can be examined only once and for a very short time.

Although some general guidelines, based on the experience of several professionals of digitization, will be provided below, it should be kept in mind that every campaign requires flexibility and compromises. Nevertheless, estimating the possible disturbing factors and possible ways of dealing with them in advance makes the task easier.

For collections that are difficult of access, it is desirable to decide for whom the data are being collected: the text users, the codicologists or the conservators. In cases where both text and form or context of the manuscripts have to be taken in consideration, it should be decided how much information has to be collected by digitization and how much is left to the description following the physical examination of the books. Generally one should not spend time on registering data which can be elicited from the photographs. An objective judgement of the work conditions, estimation of the equipment's efficiency and the time available to accomplish the task influence the decisions in these matters. Obviously it would not be possible to gather data for the recently recommended description of manuscript bindings that lists over one hundred categories (Miller 2010). It would not be realistic, either, to take a dozen or so images of each damaged manuscript leaf, resulting in data counted in terabytes for a single manuscript as was the case with the Archimedes palimpsest project (Emery et al. 2011; Toth – Emery 2011).

Despite difficult work conditions, one must ensure the preservation of the original and consequently the rules established for such an approach (see also Ch. 5 §§ 7.3 and 7.4) have to be followed. This applies even to manuscripts in a state of progressive deterioration which cannot be prevented *in situ*. Handling routines could be less strict if such a manuscript were unique, which means that in the near future the digitized material may be the only witness of the original. In any case the final decision about the treatment of each manuscript should be left to the conservator—an obligatory member of the working team—who supervises the whole examination and digitization process.

The possibility of finding compromises with some treatments recommended for the 'ideal' recording conditions is particularly pertinent in the case of manuscripts permanently exposed to unintentional damage, i.e. manuscripts that are not the objects of preservation but are still in use. The book collections kept in Ethiopian churches and monasteries that, at least partly, are read daily during the liturgical services and used for educational purposes, can be recalled here as an example.

In some remote parts of the world the storage conditions of the manuscripts are usually not satisfactory, but can often be improved in connexion with the recording campaign. It would be important to discuss basic rules of book preservation with the owners of the collection, and if possible, to help them to organize or reorganize the space where the manuscripts are kept.

7.6.1. Equipment

The whole equipment should be as light as possible, and take up little space in a luggage, which in turn should be easy to lift and transport. The possibility that the recording and digitization may take place in the open air should be taken into consideration. Besides the photographic equipment itself (camera, tripod, lamp ...) one should carry the accessories necessary to handle (baseboard, cradles or cushions), examine (microscope, measurement band, etc.) and preserve manuscripts (acid-free paper and/or boxes). The choice of comfortable equipment to sit and work on also has its importance when working in the field for prolonged periods. Carrying reliable folding chairs and tables is worth considering.

7.6.2. Baseboard

A baseboard suitable for manuscripts of different sizes can be made of light plywood or foam core and coated with fabric. The fabric, preferably dark, because it creates the manuscript's background caught on every picture, should be easy to clean, i.e. not electrostatic, for instance velour. A brush for cleaning should not be forgotten.

7.6.3. Book cradle

A stable but light cradle (see Ch. 5 §§ 5.6 and 7.3) can be set up from triangular foam segments, preferably in the same colour as the baseboard. It is practical to have several sets of different sizes. The pieces may be supplied with crochet tape to fasten them to the baseboard in order to prevent them from moving when the pages of the manuscript are turned.

Another type of cradle was patented by Wayne Torborg, Collegeville (see <http://www.html.org/wtorborg/downloads/downloads.htm>). It is constructed of joined triangular apexes made of folded hard cardboard pieces (alternatively of foam core or plywood) with the crochet tapes allowing the triangles to be fastened onto the baseboard and for their angles to be changed. The advantage of this device is that the triangles can be flattened for transport, but they are less resistant to damage than sponge supports.

Manuscripts which open easily, instead of being placed in a cradle, can have an adjustable support, for instance a cushion filled with Styrofoam pellets or rolls of polyester felt.

For books fragmented from damage or with deteriorated leather covers, smooth paper or plastic should be placed over the cradle or foam support to reduce rubbing.

7.6.4. Photography kit

The best device to keep the pages of a book open in place and at the same time cover the minimum space on the page are transparent round sticks with rounded ends. Several sets of different length and diameter, thus fitting diverse sizes of manuscripts, are recommended.

Acrylic glass narrow strips with rounded corners held by the 'robot arms' (see below) may be an alternative, but are applicable only for those manuscripts which open easily. The strips and the arms are not strong enough to hold large and tightly bound books. The best practice to handle them safely is to press the page corners gently with the transparent stick. If only one page at once is photographed two people should be engaged, if two pages—four. Similar precautions should be taken when the digitization takes place in the open air during a windy day. The long sticks have one more advantage—the hands holding them will not be visible in the picture. The strips of weighted fabric often used in the libraries to keep the pages in place (also known as book snakes) are not recommended because they screen off too much space on the photographed page, but they are useful for an examination of the manuscript.

Adjustable robot arms (also known as dual helping arms) are usually used to hold the greyscale/metric scale/signum mark bar, in case these need to be photographed with every page of the manuscript. The arms are particularly useful for broad and thick manuscripts requiring several adjustments of the bar or bars during the photographic process.

*7.6.5. Choosing your camera**

Any digital SLR camera (with display monitor), which can save the images in either uncompressed TIFF format, or in uncompressed RAW format with a megapixel (MP) capacity of 14 and higher can be used. Full-frame cameras are preferable to the current half-frame standard as they provide a greater focal plane, which is of particular advantage when working with a fixed lens on a tripod. As a last resort, point-and-shoot cameras with even higher MP capacity may be used as an alternative, but there will be a greater tendency for blurring around the edges of the image. A 50 mm fixed lens on a full-frame camera will work well, but for a half-frame a wider angle will be necessary when shooting large folia or pages.

Choosing a lens always entails a compromise between optical quality, price, weight and focus length. Zoom lenses which cover a wider area are more practicable, but the images will show some distortion, especially on the limits of the zoom (wide-angle–tele). Nor is the optical quality of most zoom-lenses fully satisfactory. However the distortions on wide-angle lenses may often be corrected by software (some cameras like Canon do this automatically, if the option is selected in the settings).

Professional and semi-professional cameras usually come with software allowing the unit to be 'tethered' to a computer. Shooting through the computer greatly reduces the problem of camera shake and ena-

* I am grateful to Michael Gervers for his help in writing this paragraph.

bles the images to be stored temporarily on the computer. The downside is that one needs a regular supply of electricity to power both the computer and the camera together. In the absence thereof, one can achieve the same results using batteries and flash memory cards, but they too need to be recharged at the end of the day. If necessary, all images can be temporarily stored on these cards.

Fig. 5.7.8 Digitization studio set up in a cave. Northern Ethiopia, 2011, photograph by EBW.

The tripods should be very stable, especially if one anticipates digitization in the open air. Unfortunately such tripods are heavy, so the alternative would be to use light ones, but with a stabilizing device (for instance allowing a weight to be attached).

In every case, a tripod with a cross bar enabling the camera to shoot straight down should be used. The heavier the tripod, the greater the stability and the smaller the problem of camera shake. The weight of such an instrument will, however, cancel any advantages if it has to be carried on foot over long distances. An alternative is to use a more expensive lightweight carbon fibre magnesium unit and weigh it down on site.

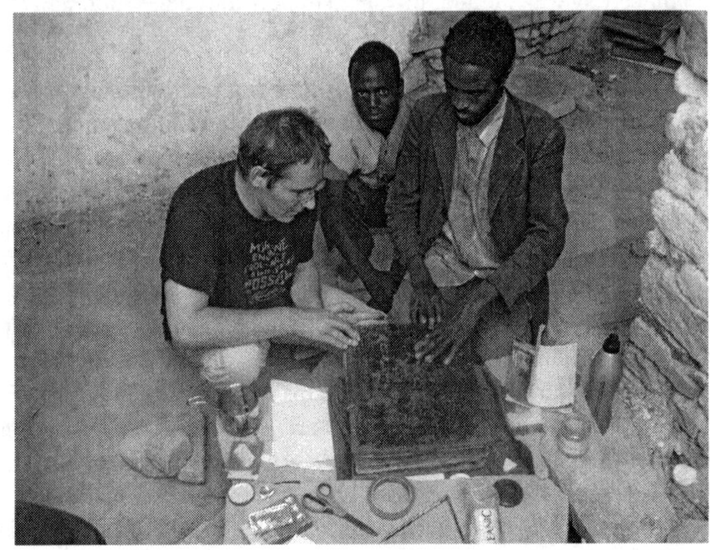

Fig. 5.7.9 Keeper of a church's manuscript collection instructed by a book conservator. Northern Ethiopia, 2013, photograph by EBW.

The pictures should be stored in RAW and TIFF (see also Ch. 5 § 7.5.1); they should preferably be transferred immediately to the computer and later to external storage. Storing the pictures on CF-cards is not recommended, because they are sensitive and may destroy the camera if not slotted in correctly. It is further advisable to divide the data between several smaller discs resistant to bumps and drops with at least 2.5 internal anti-shock mechanism.

For every piece of equipment at least one replacement should be brought. The cameras and computers, independently of the ordinary cases, should be wrapped in protective tissues to shelter them from dust and humidity and transported in containers which minimize damage caused by shaking and dropping onto the ground.

7.6.6. Microscope, lamps

The microscope features of choice depend on what kind of surface inspection is required. The following optical parameters were found satisfactory: 5.0 megapixel sensor, removable plastic caps to get close-ups for a wider focusing range, optical magnifier adjustable from 20x (for basic PCB inspection) to 220x (for detailed inspection); eight white adjustable LEDs.

The edge of the lenses and the foot of the stand should be covered with smooth fabric or paper to prevent rubbing of the surface to be photographed. For every manuscript a new set must be used to avoid transferring microorganisms from one manuscript to another.

For lamps, the guidelines given in Ch. 5 § 7.4.1 can be followed.

7.6.7. Source of energy

Although it is often believed that solar panels can be used in places without electricity but with intense sun exposure, this source of energy is not recommended for an intensive digitization process. The power generation performed by a set of easily transportable panels does not suffice. The set is not able to serve two photographic stations with one camera and one computer in each for longer than five hours and it recharges slowly. Moreover it cannot be used after sunset when the daily work result is being checked (see below). A portable gasoline-fuelled generator is a much better solution, but electricity has to be transferred via a voltage stabilizer, a precaution which prevents burning of electric equipment.

7.6.8. Waterproof tarpaulin

Large tarpaulin sheets are very useful to put on the ground before the digitization station is set up. They can also be arranged as a roof to provide shade in places fully exposed to the sun and to protect equipment from rain. When shade is provided by an artificial roof, the colour and type of fabric have to be chosen according to the light requirements. Bluish and beige seem to provide the best light conditions.

7.6.9. Materials for preservation of the manuscripts

Boxes or folders (of acid-free materials: see Ch. 5 § 5.5) should be provided for vulnerable manuscripts and manuscript fragments (loose folia and quires). If the collection and its condition cannot be checked in advance, it is difficult to estimate how many containers will be needed and of what size. Envelopes of the required size can be made on the spot from paper brought in rolls. The boxes (if they are too large; boxes that are too small should be avoided at all times) can be adjusted as described in Ch. 5 § 5.5.

7.6.10. Metadata

Customarily each manuscript is accompanied by two forms, both prepared in advance. The first is a survey form used for manuscript examination before digitization and includes keywords to facilitate matching the survey record with the physical book. The keywords should be based on what one wishes most to record in the collection (for example: binding, decoration, codicological details), and preferably listed by a specialist who can evaluate the collection. In case this person cannot oversee or conduct the survey he should give travelling team members treatment recommendations in anticipation of possible damage assessments and the like. The form may be completed with a series of photographs (close-ups, digital microscope images and so on).

The second digitization form contains basic information about the manuscript and its identification number, and is to be photographed with the manuscript, customarily when the photographing of the manuscript is completed (last shot). Since data from this form usually accompany the manuscript when it is put online, the form should be modelled on a short catalogue entry.

7.6.11. Examination and digitization of the manuscript

The effectiveness of work carried under challenging work conditions depends on how well the members of the team cooperate. It is important to assign precise tasks to each member of the group from the start, and that beginners get precise instructions. The process of digitization should be rehearsed by the team before it starts in the open-air and all equipment needs to be carefully checked.

It is important to find a space suitable for the whole day's activities because moving the equipment interrupts work flow and may cause mistakes. To make communication between the team's members easier, their working places should not be far from each other's.

Foliation of the manuscripts facilitates both examination and the digitization process. It should be done after the conservator's preliminary survey. One uses a pencil and writes the page/folium number always in the same place (for instance, in the middle of the bottom margin, or in the top outer corner) in every manuscript belonging to the collection being recorded. The correctness of the numbering should be checked at least twice.

The process of a manuscript's examination starts with the condition survey done by the conservator, who presents the manuscript to the team, pointing out the problems and damage that may occur during the further examination and digitization. After a general cleaning of the manuscript (with the removal of dust, dirt, candle-grease), some preliminary repairs may be executed, such as: joining of broken boards, gluing on the cover leather, sewing of the text block using existing holes and tunnels, temporary connexion of loose parts and folia, clearing of existing book boxes. Vulnerable miniatures and large ornamentations may be protected with Japanese paper or thin cotton tissue. Acid-free boxes for particularly vulnerable manuscripts and folders for loose quires and folia should be provided. The condition of the manuscript before any kind of intervention and before digitization should be documented (description and photographs).

The study of the manuscripts, which follows the tasks specified in the survey form, may include, if possible, non-invasive examination of the materials: colours, parchment, inks, leather and so forth.

The digitization staff must follow the instructions given by the conservator who decides what kind of support is to be used and the angle at which the book can be opened. Based on the opening angle, it may or may not be possible to photograph two pages at once. If this proves impossible, first all recto or all verso pages are photographed, then the remainder, in order to avoid moving the manuscript with its support. The correct order of the pages is to be arranged once the files are on a computer.

The digitizer always works with one or more helpers who turn the manuscript's folia, keep them open, and adjust the manuscript with its support. It is desirable to rotate the support with the manuscript on it, rather than to drag the book around for a different vantage point. It is also important to pay attention to and support the changing profile of the book as one moves through it, because its spine is deformed as the text block is opened at different locations.

Periodical washing or cleaning of hands is recommended. On the use of gloves see Ch. 5 § 5.6.

Checking the digitized material after daily work gives opportunity to re-photograph the wrongly recorded pages, which is particularly important if the collection is difficult of access.

References

Emery et al. 2011; Miller 2010; Toth – Emery 2011.

8. Conclusions (LEP)

The conservator's profile has considerably changed over the past decade, raising from that of a practitioner to, increasingly, that of a scholar actively engaged in research during the very process of conservation. Self-reflection on the profession may now build on over two centuries of debate on restoration, and more specifically on over half a century of technologically advanced and scientifically-minded engagement in the stabilization and repair of manuscripts. We may now reflect back on the past century's breakthroughs as well as its mistakes, from the careless application of adhesive tape to the well-meaning use of materials that have over time proved unstable or damaging.

It is a great and positive paradox that the manuscript as a physical object and the profession of those in charge of stabilizing it and preserving it for future generations have never been so much in focus as in this digital era. On the one hand, technological advancements have made the scientific analysis of materials more and more affordable for institutions and even private patrons. On the other hand, digital photography in particular has made it virtually inexpensive to acquire and share high-quality reproductions of the objects' details—an essential basis for the cataloguing and philological analysis of manuscripts, and a significant aid in the codicological and art-historical study thereof. Digital imaging has vastly expanded our range of inquiry by getting where the human eye cannot, in a manner that was conceivable yet not wholly feasible with pre-digital technology—from the optical correction of visual angles and colour palettes to the virtual unwinding of scrolls. The affordability of digital images has also made it possible to share a vast body of information widely and fast, accelerating the pace of research and increasing the opportunity for cross-disciplinary teamwork (as is testified by this very volume, cp. also Parodi et al. 2010). At the same time, nothing can replace the actual physical autopsy of a manuscript, and here is where the conservator's expertise comes into play, not only as the one in charge of assessing the object's condition and its suitability for examination, digitization, or exhibition, but as a scholar actively contributing to the study of its material aspects as an index of its making in the broader sense.

Last but not least, online repositories, virtual exhibitions and online publications have been strengthening the public perception of manuscripts as a significant portion of the world's cultural heritage, which it is our responsibility to document, interpret, and physically preserve for future generations.

References

Parodi et al. 2010.

References*

A2 Technologies, <http://www.a2technologies.com/exoscan_handheld.html>, cached copy 2011; see <http://www.chem.agilent.com/en-US/products-services/Instruments-Systems/Molecular-Spectroscopy/4100-ExoScan-Series-FTIR-(handheld)/Pages/default.aspx>, last access November 2014.

d'Abbadie, Antoine (1859), *Catalogue raisonné de manuscrits éthiopiens appartenant à Antoine d'Abbadie*, Paris: Imprimerie Impériale.

ʿAbd al-Qādir Mammā Ḥaydara – Ayman Fuʾād Sayyid (2000–2003), فهرس مخطوطات مكتبة مماحيدرة للمخطوطات والوثائق (*Fihris maḫṭūṭāt maktabat Mammā Ḥaydara li-ʾl-maḫṭūṭāt wa-ʾl-waṯāʾiq*, 'Catalogue of Manuscripts in Mamma Haidara Library – Mali'), I–IV, London: Al-Furqān (Silsilat Fahāris al-maḫṭūṭāt al-Islāmiyya / Handlists of Islamic Manuscripts 34-36, 46).

Abełyan, Manuk (1941), Կորյուն, Վարք Մաշտոցի (*Koryun, Varkʿ Maštocʿi*, 'Koriun, The Life of Maštocʿ'), Erevan: Haypethrat.

al-Abnūdī, ʿAbd ar-Raḥmān (1988), السيرة الهلالية (*Al-Sīra al-Hilālīya*, 'The deeds of the [Banu] Hilal'), Al-Qāhira: Aḫbār al-yawm.

Abrahamyan, Ašot G. (1947), Հայկական պալեոգրաֆիա (*Haykakan paleografia*, 'Armenian Paleography'), Erevan: Aredit.

Abrahamyan, Ašot G. (1973), Հայոց գիր եւ գրչություն (*Hayocʿ gir ew grčʿutʿyun*, 'The Letters and Writing of the Armenians'), Erevan.

Abramišvili, Guram (1976), 'ატენის სიონის უცნობი წარწერები' (*Aṭenis Sionis ucnobi çarçerebi*, 'Unknown inscriptions from the Sioni of Aṭeni'), *Macne. Isṭoriisa da arkeologiis seria*, 2, 170–176.

Abramišvili, Guram – Zaza Aleksiʒe (1978), 'მხედრული დამწერლობის სათავეებთან' (*Mxedruli damçerlobis sataveebtan*, 'At the origins of the mxedruli script'), *Cisḳari*, 5, 134–144; 6, 128–137.

Abrams, Daniel (2012), *Kabbalistic Manuscripts and Textual Theory: Methodologies of Textual Scholarship and Editorial Practice in the Study of Jewish Mysticism*, Jerusalem: The Hebrew University Magnes Press (Sources and Studies in the Literature of Jewish Mysticism).

Abū ʿAlī, A. (1926–1929), فهرس مخطوطات المكتبة البلدية في الاسكندرية (*Fihris maḫṭūṭāt al-maktaba al-baladīya fī al-Iskandariyya*, 'Catalogue of Manuscripts in the Municipal Library of Alexandria'), I–VI, Alexandria.

Abulaʒe, Ilia (1938), 'К открытию алфавита кавказских албанцев' (*K otkrytiju alfavita kavkazskich albancev*, 'On the discovery of the alphabet of the Caucasian Albanians'), *Aḳad. N. Maris saxelobis Enis, Isṭoriisa da Maṭerialuri Ḳulṭuris Insṭiṭuṭis Moambe / Bulletin de l'Institut Marr de Langues, d'Histoire et de Culture Matérielle / Izvestija Instituta Jazyka, Istorii i Material'noj Kul'tury imeni Akademika N. Ja Marra*, 4, 69–71.

Abulaʒe, Ilia (1949), ქართული წერის ნიმუშები. პალეოგრაფიული ალბომი (*Kartuli çeris nimušebi. Ṗaleograpiuli albomi*, 'Examples of Georgian writing. A paleographical album'), Tbilisi: Tbilisis Saxelmçipo Universiṭeṭis Gamomcemloba.

Abulaʒe, Ilia (1967), ძველი ქართული აგიოგრაფიული ლიტერატურის ძეგლები / *Памятники древнегрузинской агиографической литературы* (*Ʒveli kartuli agiograpiuli ʒeglebi. Pamjatniki drevnegruzinskoj agiografičeskoj literatury*, 'Old Georgian hagiographical monuments'), II, Tbilisi: Mecniereba.

Abulaʒe, Ilia (1973), ქართული წერის ნიმუშები. პალეოგრაფიული ალბომი (*Kartuli çeris nimušebi. Ṗaleograpiuli albomi*, 'Examples of Georgian writing. A paleographical album'). Second enlarged edition, Tbilisi: Mecniereba.

Abulaʒe, Ilia et al. (1987) {I.A. – Mixeil Kavtaria – Caca Čanḳievi}, ივ. ჯავახიშვილის სახელობის სამცხე-ჯავახეთის ისტორიულ-ეთნოგრაფიული მუზეუმის ხელნაწერთა აღწერილობა (= ახალციხის მუზეუმის ხელნაწერთა აღწერილობა) (*Iv. Ǯavaxišvilis saxelobis Samcxe-Ǯavaxetis Isṭoriul-Etnograpiuli Muzeumis xelnaçerta aġçeriloba* [= *Axalcixis muzeumis xelnaçerta aġçeriloba*], 'Catalogue of the manuscripts of the Ivane Javakhishvili Historical-Ethnographical Museum of Samtskhe-Javakheti [= Description of the manuscripts from Axalcixe museum]'), Tbilisi: Mecniereba.

Adamova, Adel (1996), *Персидская живопись и рисунок XV–XIX веков в собрании Ермитажа* (*Persidskaja živopis' i risunok XV–XIX vekov v sobranii Ermitaža*, 'Persian painting and drawing of the 15th–19th centuries in the Hermitage collection'), St Petersburg: Slavija.

Adamova, Adel (2012), *Persian Manuscripts, Paintings and Drawings: From the 15th to the Early 20th Century in the Hermitage Collection*, Oxbow: Azimuth.

Adcock, Edward P. – Marie-Thérèse Varlamoff (eds) (1998), *IFLA Principles for the care and handling of library material*, Paris: IFLA – Washington: CLIR (International Preservation Issues, 1).

Adler, Jacob Georg Christian (1780), *Descriptio codicum quorundam Cuficorum – partes corani exhibentium – in Bibliotheca Regia Hafniensi et ex iisdem De scriptura cufica arabum observationes novae. Praemittitur disquisitio generalis De arte scribendi apud arabes ex ipsis auctoribus arabicis iisque adhuc ineditis sumta*, Altonae: Ex Officina Eckhardiana.

Adler, Jacob Georg Christian (1782), *Museum Cuficum Borgianum Velitris*, I, Romae: Apud Antonium Fulgonium.

Adler, Jacob Georg Christian (1792), *Museum Cuficum Borgianum Velitris*, II, Hafniae: Excudebat Fridericus Wilhelmus Thiele (Collectio nova numorum cuficorum seu arabicorum veterum, CXVI continens numos plerosque ineditos e museis Borgiano et Adleriano).

Agapētos, Panagiotēs A. (2006), *Ἀφήγησις Λιβίστρου καὶ Ροδάμνης. Κριτικὴ ἔκδοση της διασκευής α´*, Athens: MIET - Μορφωτικό Ίδρυμα Εθνικής Τραπέζης (Byzantinē kai neoellēnikē bibliothēkē, 9).

Agati, Maria Luisa (1992), *La minuscola 'bouletée'*, I–II, Città del Vaticano: Scuola Vaticana di Paleografia, Diplomatica e Archivistica (Littera Antiqua, 9).

Agati, Maria Luisa (2003), *Il libro manoscritto. Introduzione alla codicologia*, Roma: L'Erma di Bretschneider (Studia archaeologica, 124).

Agati, Maria Luisa (2009), *Il libro manoscritto da Oriente a Occidente. Per una codicologia comparata*, Roma: L'Erma di Bretschneider (Studia archaeologica, 166).

Agati, Maria Luisa (2012), 'Codicologia. Osservazioni e riflessioni', in: *Storie di cultura scritta. Studi per Francesco Magistrale*, ed. by Paolo Fioretti, Spoleto: Fondazione Centro italiano di studi sull'alto medioevo (Collectanea, 28), 1–14.

Agemian, Sylvia (1991), *Manuscrits arméniens enluminés du Catholicossat de Cilicie*, Antélias: Catholicossat arménien de Cilicie.

Aggoula, Basile (2005), 'Les inscriptions 'édesséniennes' et la naissance de l'écriture et de la langue syriaque', in: *Nos sources. Arts et Littérature syriaques*, Antélias: Centre d'études et de recherches orientales (Sources syriaques, 1), 543–579.

Ahlwardt, Wilhelm (1887–1899), *Verzeichniß der arabischen Handschriften der Königlichen Bibliothek zu Berlin*, I–X, Berlin: Ascher u. Co.

* Only works cited in this volume are listed here. For a comprehensive updated bibliography on all subjects related to the comparative oriental manuscript studies visit http://www1.uni-hamburg.de/COMST.

Aḥmad Muḫtār ʿUmar – ʿAbd al-ʿĀl Sālim Makram (1402–1408 AH/1982–1988 CE), معجم القراءات القرآنية : مع مقدمة في القراءات وأشهر القراء (*Muʿǧam al-qirāʾāt al-qurʾāniyya: maʿa muqaddima fī ʾl-qirāʾāt wa-ašhar al-qurrā*ʾ, 'Lexicon of Qurʾānic Variant Readings, with an introduction into variant readings and the most famous readers'), I–VIII, Kuwait: Ǧāmiʿat Kuwayt.

AIC (American Institute for Conservation of Historic and Artistic Works) (1994a), *Code of Ethics*, <http://www.conservation-us.org/about-us/core-documents/code-of-ethics>, Washington, DC: AIC.

AIC (American Institute for Conservation of Historic and Artistic Works) (1994b), *Guidelines for Practice*, <http://www.conservation-us.org/about-us/core-documents/guidelines-for-practice>, Washington, DC: AIC.

AIC (American Institute for Conservation of Historic and Artistic Works) (2008), *The AIC Guide to Digital Photography and Conservation Documentation*, <http://www.jiscdigitalmedia.ac.uk/digitisation/>, Washington, DC: AIC.

AIC (American Institute for Conservation of Historic and Artistic Works) (2013), *Caring for your Treasures. Books*, <http://www.conservation-us.org/about-conservation/caring-for-your-treasures/books>, Washington, DC: AIC.

Albert, Micheline et al. (1993) {M.A. – Robert Beylot – René-Georges Coquin – Antoine Guillaumont – Bernard Outtier – Charles Renoux}, *Christianismes orientaux: introduction à l'étude des langues et des littératures*, Paris: Cerf (Initiations au christianisme ancien).

Alberti, Giovan Battista (1979), *Problemi di critica testuale*, Firenze: La Nuova Italia (Paideia, 23).

Albiero, Laura (2011), 'Le trappole della codifica. Osservazioni intorno ai sistemi di notazione dei tipi di rigatura', *Scrineum. Saggi e materiali on line di scienze del documento e del libro medievali*, 8.

Albrecht, Felix (2010), 'Codex Ephraemi Syri rescriptus. Neue Lesarten zum Septuagintatext des Koheletbuches', *Zeitschrift für die Alttestamentliche Wissenschaft*, 122, 272–279.

Albrecht, Felix (2012), 'Between boon and bane. The use of chemical reagents in palimpsest research in the nineteenth century', in: *Care and Conservation of Manuscripts 13. Proceedings of the thirteenth international seminar held at the University of Copenhagen* 13th*-*15th *April 2011*, ed. by Matthew James Driscoll, Copenhagen: Museum Tusculanum Press, 147–165.

Albrecht, Felix (2014), 'A new portable system for multispectral and full spectral imaging', in: *Care and Conservation of Manuscripts 14. Proceedings of the fourteenth international seminar held at the University of Copenhagen* 17th*-*19th *October 2012*, ed. by Matthew James Driscoll, Copenhagen: Museum Tusculanum Press, 237–252.

Album 2002 see Stone et al. (2002).

Aleksiʒe [Aleksidze], Zaza et al. (2005) {Z.A. – Mzekala Šaniʒe [Shanidze] – Lili Xevsuriani [Khevsuriani] – Mixeil Kavtaria}, *Κατάλογος γεωργιανῶν χειρογράφων εὑρεθέντων κατὰ τὸ 1975 εἰς τὴν ἱερὰν μονὴν τοῦ θεοβαδίστου ὄρους Σινᾶ τῆς Ἁγίας Αἰκατερίνης* / სინის მთაზე წმ. ეკატერინეს მონასტერში 1975 წელს აღმოჩენილ ქართულ ხელნაწერთა აღწერილობა / *Catalogue of Georgian Manuscripts discovered in 1975 at St Catherine's Monastery on Mount Sinai*, Athens: Greek Ministery of Culture / Mt. Sinai Foundation.

Aleksiʒe [Aleksidzé], Zaza – Jean-Pierre Mahé (1997), 'Découverte d'un texte albanien: une langue ancienne du Caucase retrouvée', *Comptes rendus de l'Académie des inscriptions et belles-lettres*, 517–532.

Alhussein Alhaidary, Ali Abd [ʿAlī ʿAbd al-Ḥusayn Ḥaydarī] – Stig T. Rasmussen (1995), *Catalogue of Arabic Manuscripts. Codices Arabici Additamenta & Codices Simonseniani Arabici*, Copenhagen: The Royal Library & Munksgaard (Catalogue of Oriental Manuscripts in Danish Collections (COMDC), 5.1).

Ališan, Łewond (1901), Հայապատում (*Hayapatum*, 'Armenian History'), I–II, Venice.

Allen, John Willoughby Tarleton (1970), *The Swahili and Arabic manuscripts and tapes in the Library of the University College, Dar-es-Salaam: a catalogue*, Leiden: Brill.

Allony, Nehemiah (2006), *The Jewish Library in the Middle Ages: Book Lists from the Cairo Genizah*, ed. by Miriam Frenkel – Haggai Ben-Shammai, Jerusalem: Ben Zvi Institute for the Study of Jewish Communities in the East (Oriens Judaicus, 1/3).

Altıkulaç, Tayyar (1428 AH/2007 CE), المصحف الشريف المنسوب إلى عثمان بن عفّان : نسخة طوپ قاپي سرايى (*al-Muṣḥaf al-Šarīf: al-mansūb ilā ʿUṯmān b. ʿAffān, nusḫat mutḥaf Ṭūb Qābī Sarāyī) / Al-Muṣḥaf al-Sharīf attributed to ʿUthmān b. ʿAffān. The copy of Topkapı Palace Museum*, translated into Arabic by Salih Sadawi and into English by Semiramis Çavoşoğlu; preface by Ekmeleddin İhsanoğlu; foreword by Halit Eren, Istanbul: Munaẓẓamat al-Muʾtamar al-Islāmī, Markaz al-Abḥāṯ lil-Tārīḫ wa-ʾl-Funūn wa-ʾl-Ṯaqāfa al-Islāmiyya bi-Istānbūl (Silsilat nuṣūṣ muḥaqqaqa, 2).

Altıkulaç, Tayyar (1430 AH/2009 CE), المصحف الشريف المنسوب الى عثمان بن عفان : نسخة المشهد الحسيني بالقاهرة (*al-Muṣḥaf al-Šarīf: al-mansūb ilā ʿUṯmān b. ʿAffān: nusḫat al-Mašhad al-Ḥusaynī bi-ʾl-Qāhira) /Al-Muṣḥaf al-Sharīf attributed to ʿUthmān b. ʿAffān. The copy at Mashhad Imam Husaini in Cairo*, foreword by Halit Eren, I–II, Istanbul: Munaẓẓamat al-Muʾtamar al-Islāmī, Markaz al-Abḥāt lil-Tārīḫ wa-ʾl-Funūn wa-ʾl-Ṯaqāfa al-Islāmiyya bi-Istānbūl / Organisation of the Islamic Conference Research Centre for Islamic History, Art and Culture (IRCICA) (Silsilat nuṣūṣ muḥaqqaqa, 4).

Altıkulaç, Tayyar (1432 AH/2011 CE), المصحف الشريف المنسوب الى علي بن ابي طالب : نسخة صنعاء (*al-Muṣḥaf al-Šarīf: al-mansūb ilā ʿAlī ibn Abī Ṭālib: nusḫat Ṣanʿāʾ) / Hz. Ali'ye Nisbet Edilen Mushaf-i Şerîf: San'â Nüshası / Al-Muṣḥaf al-Sharīf attributed to ʿAlī b. Abī Ṭālib. The copy of Sanaa*, foreword by Halit Eren, Istanbul: Munaẓẓamat al-Muʾtamar al-Islāmī, Markaz al-Abḥāt lil-Tārīḫ wa-ʾl-Funūn wa-ʾl-Ṯaqāfa al-Islāmiyya bi-Istānbūl / Organisation of the Islamic Conference Research Centre for Islamic History, Art and Culture (IRCICA) (Silsilat nuṣūṣ muḥaqqaqa, 6).

Amand de Mendieta, Emmanuel (1987), 'Un problème d'ecdotique. Comment manier la tradition manuscrite surabondante d'un ouvrage patristique', in: *Texte und Textkritik. Eine Aufsatzsammlung*, ed. by Jürgen Dummer, Berlin: Akademie-Verlag (Texte und Untersuchungen zur Geschichte der altkirchlichen Literatur, 133), 29–42.

Ambrosiani, Per – Antoaneta Granberg (2010), 'Slavonica Glagolitica and Cyrillica in Swedish Repositories. The project Digitalised Descriptions of Slavic Cyrillic Manuscripts and Early Printed Books in Swedish Libraries and Archives', *Slovo* (*Uppsala*), 51, 107–113.

Amélineau, Émile (1907–1914), *Œuvres de Schenoudi. Texte copte et traduction française*, I–II, Paris: Leroux.

Amiaud, Arthur (1889), 'La légende syriaque de Saint Alexis l'Homme de Dieu', Paris: F. Vieweg, Librairie-Éditeur Émile Bouillon (Bibliothèque de l'École des Hautes Études, 69).

Andreas, Friedrich Carl – Walter Bruno Henning (1934), 'Mitteliranische Manichaica aus Chinesisch-Turkestan. III', *Sitzungsberichte der Preußischen Akademie der Wissenschaften*, 848–912.

Andrés-Toledo, Miguel Ángel – Alberto Cantera (2012), 'Manuscripts of the Wīdēwdād', in: *The transmission of the Avesta*, ed. by Alberto Cantera, Wiesbaden: Harrassowitz (Iranica, 20), 207–243.

Andrews, Tara L. (2009), *Prolegomena to a Critical Edition of the Chronicle of Matthew of Edessa, with a Discussion of Computer-Aided Methods Used to Edit the Text*, <http://ora.ouls.ox.ac.uk/objects/uuid:67ea 947c-e3fc-4363-a289-c345e61eb2eb.>, Oxford: Oxford University [diss.].

Andrews, Tara L. – Caroline Macé (2013), 'Beyond the Tree of Texts: Building an Empirical Model of Scribal Variation Through Graph Analysis of Texts and Stemmata', *Literary and Linguistic Computing*, 28, 504–521.

Andrews, Tara L. – Caroline Macé (eds) (2014), *Analysis of Ancient and Medieval Texts and Manuscripts: Digital Approaches*, Turnhout: Brepols (Lectio Studies in the Transmission of Texts and Ideas, 1).

Andrisano, Angela Maria (2007), *Biblioteche del mondo antico. Dalla tradizione orale alla cultura dell'Impero*, Roma: Carocci.

Andrist, Patrick (2003), *Catalogus codicum graecorum Helveticorum. Règles de catalogage, élaborées sous le patronage du Kuratorium «Katalogisierung der mittelalterlichen und frühneuzeitlichen Handschriften der Schweiz». Version 2.0*, <http://www.codices.ch/catalogi/leges_2003.pdf>, Bern: Burgerbibliothek Bern.

Andrist, Patrick (2004), 'Formule de description des signatures, réclames et autres marques de cahiers', *Gazette du livre médiéval*, 44, 25–38.

Andrist, Patrick (2006), 'La descrizione scientifica dei manoscritti complessi: fra teoria e pratica', *Segno e Testo*, 4, 299–356.

Andrist, Patrick (2007a), *Les manuscrits grecs conservés à la Bibliothèque de la Bourgeoisie de Berne – Burgerbibliothek Bern. Catalogue et histoire de la collection*, Zurich: Dietikon (Règles de catalogage).

Andrist, Patrick (2007b), *Catalogus codicum graecorum Helveticorum. Règles de catalogage, élaborées sous le patronage du Kuratorium «Katalogisierung der mittelalterlichen und frühneuzeitlichen Handschriften der Schweiz». Version 3.0*, <http://www.codices.ch/catalogi/leges_2007.pdf>, Bern: Burgerbibliothek Bern.

Andrist, Patrick (2008), 'Purposes and methods of a modern catalogue of ancient manuscripts: some reader's notes on the recent catalogue of Greek Manuscripts at St John's College, Oxford', *Medium Aevum*, 77, 293–305.

Andrist, Patrick (2010), 'La description des manuscrits médiévaux sur Internet: un regard critique', in: *La descrizione dei manoscritti: esperienze a confronto*, ed. by Edoardo Crisci – Marilena Maniaci, Cassino: Università degli studi di Cassino, Dipartimento di filologia e storia (Studi e ricerche del Dipartimento di Filologia e Storia, 1), 19–45.

Andrist, Patrick (2014), 'Going online is not enough! ... Electronic descriptions of ancient manuscripts, and the needs of manuscript studies', in: *Analysis of Ancient and Medieval Texts and Manuscripts: Digital Approaches*, ed. by Tara Andrews – Caroline Macé, Turnhout: Brepols (Lectio Studies in the Transmission of Texts and Ideas, 1), 309–334.

Andrist, Patrick et al. (2010) {P.A. – Paul Canart – Marilena Maniaci}, 'L'analyse structurelle du codex, clef de sa genèse et de son histoire', in: *The Legacy of Bernard de Montfaucon: Three Hundred Years of Studies on Greek Handwriting. Proceedings of the Seventh International Colloquium of Greek Palaeography (Madrid – Salamanca, 15-20 September 2008)*, I, ed. by Antonio Bravo García – Inmaculada Pérez Martín, Turnhout: Brepols (Bibliologia: Elementa ad Librorum Studia Pertinentia, 31A), 289–299.

Andrist, Patrick et al. (2013) {P.A. – Paul Canart – Marilena Maniaci}, *La syntaxe du codex. Essai de codicologie structurale*, Turnhout: Brepols (Bibliologia: Elementa ad Librorum Studia Pertinentia, 34).

Andrzejewski, Bogumił W. – Ioan Myrrhdin Lewis (1994), 'New Arabic Documents from Somalia', *Sudanic Africa*, 5, 39–54.

Andrzejewski, Bogumił W. – Ioan Myrrhdin Lewis (1998), 'New Arabic Documents from Somalia', in: *Saints and Somalis. Popular Islam in a Clan-based Society*, ed. by Ioan Myrrhdin Lewis, Lawrenceville – Asmara: Red Sea Press.

Annequin, Guy (1972), 'L'illustration des Ta'amra Maryam de 1630 à 1730. Quelques remarques sur le premier style de Gondar', *Annales d'Éthiopie*, 9, 193–219.

Appleyard, David (1993), *Ethiopian Manuscripts*, London: Jed Press.

Āqā Bozorg Ṭehrānī (1403 AH / 1983 CE), الذريعة الى تصانيف الشيعة (*al-Ḏarīʿa ilā taṣānīf al-šīʿa*, 'Access to the writings of the Šīʿa'), I–XXVI, 3rd print, Bayrūt: Dār al-Aḍwāʾ.

Aṙakʿelyan, Babgen (1958), 'Կազմերի զարդարման արվեստը միջնադարյան Հայաստանում (*Kazmeri zardarman arvestə mijnadaryan Hayastanum*, 'The Art of Bookbinding Decoration in Medieval Armenia')', *Banber Matenadarani*, 4, 183–203.

Arberry, Arthur John (1967), *The Koran Illuminated. A Handlist of Korans in the Chester Beatty Library*, Dublin: Hodges, Figgis and Co.

Arberry, Arthur John et al. (1959–1962) {A.A. – M. Minovi – E. Blochet – J.V.S. Wilkinson – B.W. Robinson}, *The Chester Beatty Library. A Catalogue of the Persian Manuscripts and Miniatures*, I: *Mss. 101-150*, II: *Mss 150-220*, III: *Mss 221-398*, Dublin: The Chester Beatty Library.

Arif, Aida S. – Ahmed M. Abu Hakima (1965), *Descriptive Catalogue of Arabic Manuscripts in Nigeria: Jos Museum and Lugard Hall Library, Kaduna*, London: Luzac and Co (Silsilat fahāris al-maktabāt al-haṭṭiyya an-nādira, 23).

Arranz, Miguel (1969), *Le typicon du monastère du Saint-Sauveur à Messine: Codex Messinensis Gr 115, a.D. 1131*, Roma: Pontificio Istituto Orientale (Orientalia Christiana Analecta, 185).

Aslanian, Sebouh David (2011), *From the Indian Ocean to the Mediterranean. The Global Trade Networks of Armenian Merchants from New Julfa*, Berkeley – New York – London: University of California Press (California World History Library).

Assefa Liban (1958), 'Preparation of Parchment Manuscripts', *University College of Addis Ababa Ethnological Society Bulletin*, 8, 5–21.

Assemani, Giuseppe Simone (1719–1728), *Bibliotheca Orientalis Clementino-Vaticana: In qua manuscriptos codices Syriacos, Arabicos, Persicos, Turcicos, Hebraicos, Samaritanos, Armenicos, Aethiopicos, Graecos, Aegyptiacos, Ibericos, & Malabaricos, jussu et munificentia Clementis XI. Pontificis Maximi ex Oriente conquisitos, comparatos, avectos, & Bibliothecae Vaticanae addictos*, Romae: Typis Sacræ Congregationis de Propaganda Fide.

Assemani, Giuseppe Simone (1721), *Bibliotheca Orientalis Clementino-Vaticana* II. *De scriptoribus Syris Monophysitis*, Romae: Typis Sacræ Congregationis de Propaganda Fide.

Assemani, Stefano Evodio (1742), *Bibliothecae Mediceae Laurentianae et Palatinae codicum mms. Orientalium catalogus*, Florentiae: Ex Typographio Albiziniano.

Assemani, [Giuseppe] Simone (1787), *Catalogo de' codici manoscritti orientali della Biblioteca Naniana*, I, Padova: Stamperia del Seminario.

Assemani, Stefano Evodio – Giuseppe Simone Assemani (1758–1759), *Biblioteca apostolica vaticana. Bibliothecae Apostolicae Vaticanae codicum manuscriptorum catalogus in tres partes distributus...*, Romae (reprint Paris: Maisonneuve 1926).

Assfalg, Julius (1963a), *Georgische Handschriften*, Wiesbaden: Franz Steiner (Verzeichnis der orientalischen Handschriften in Deutschland, 3).

Assfalg, Julius (1963b), *Syrische Handschriften: syrische, karšunische, christlich-palästinische, neusyrische und mandäische Handschriften*, Wiesbaden: Franz Steiner (Verzeichnis der orientalischen Handschriften in Deutschland, 5).

Assfalg, Julius – Paul Krüger (eds) (1975), *Kleines Wörterbuch des Christlichen Orients*, Wiesbaden: Harrassowitz.

Assfalg, Julius – Paul Krüger (eds) (1991), *Petit dictionnaire de l'Orient Chrétien*, Turnhout: Brepols.

Assfalg, Julius – Joseph Molitor (1962), *Armenische Handschriften*, Wiesbaden: Franz Steiner (Verzeichnis der orientalischen Handschriften in Deutschland, 4).

Astruc, Charles (1981), 'L'inventaire dressé en septembre 1200 du trésor et de la bibliothèque de Patmos', *Travaux et mémoires*, 8, 15–30.

Astruc, Charles (ed.) (1989), *Les manuscrits grecs datés des XIIIe et XIVe siècles conservés dans les bibliothèques de France*, I: *XIIIe siècle*, Paris: Centre national de la recherche scientifique.

Atalla, Nabil Selim (2000), *Illustrations from Coptic Manuscripts*, Cairo: Lehnert and Landrock.

Atiya, Aziz S. – Joseph N. Youssef (1970), *Catalogue raisonné of the Mount Sinai Arabic Manuscripts*, الفهارس التحليلية لمخطوطات طور سينا العربية (*al-Fahāris al-taḥlīliyya li-maḫṭūṭāt Ṭūr Sīnā al-ʿarabiyya*), I, Alexandria: Galal Hazzi.

Attridge, Harold W. – George W. MacRae (1985), 'The Gospel of Truth', in: *Nag Hammadi Codex I* (*The Jung codex*): *Introductions, Texts, Translations, Indices*, ed. by Harold W. Attridge, Leiden: Brill (Nag Hammadi Studies, 22), 55–117.

Avestan Digital Archive, <http://www.avesta-archive.com>, last access October 2014.

Axobaʒe, L[ia] et al. (1986) {L.A. – Rusudan Gvaramia – Nargiza Goguaʒe – Manana Dvali – Manana Dolakiʒe – Manana Ḳvačaʒe – Gulnaz Ḳiḳnaʒe – G. Ninua – Ciala Kurciḳiʒe -- Lela Šatirišvili -- Mzekala Šaniʒe -- Nesṭan Čxiḳvaʒe}, ქართულ ხელნაწერთა აღწერილობა. ათონური კოლექცია (*Kartul xelnaçerta aǧçeriloba. Atonuri ḳolekcia*, 'Description of Georgian manuscripts. Athonite collection'), I, Tbilisi: Mecniereba.

Ayoub, Abderrahman (1978), 'À propos des manuscrits de la geste des Banû Hilâl conservés à Berlin', in: *Proceedings of the Second International Congress on Studies on Cultures of the Western Mediterranean*, ed. by Micheline Galley, Algiers: Société nationale d'édtion et de diffusion, 347–363.

Babenko, Vitaly (1988), translated by Lemyel Amirian, 'Vordan Karmir, or Armenian Cochineal', *Oriental Rug Review*, 8/5, 40–42.

Babinger, Franz (1931), 'Papierhandel und Papierbereitung in der Levante', *Wochenblatt für Papierfabrikation*, 62, 1215–1217.

Bady, Guillaume (2008), review of J. Mossay, *Sancti Gregorii Nazianzeni Opera. Versio Graeca*. I. *Orationes X et XII*, Turnhout: Brepols (Corpus Christianorum. Series Graeca, 64; Corpus Nazianzenum, 22), 2006, *Le Muséon*, 121, 463–470.

Baer, Eva (1998), *Islamic ornament*, Edinburgh: Edinburgh University Press.

Baethgen, Friedrich (1890), 'Die syrische Handschrift 'Sachau 302' aus der Kgl. Bibliothek zu Berlin', *Zeitschrift für Kirchengeschichte*, 11, 442–447.

Bagnall, Roger S. (1996), *Egypt in Late Antiquity*, Princeton: Princeton University Press.

Bagnall, Roger S. (2009), *Early Christian Books in Egypt*, Princeton: Princeton University Press. French version: Bagnall, Roger S. (2009), *Livres chrétiens antiques d'Égypte*, Genève: Droz.

Bagnall, Roger S. – Dominic W. Rathbone (eds) (2004), *Egypt from Alexander to the Early Christians. An Archeological and Historical Guide*, Los Angeles: J. Paul Getty Museum.

Bagnall, Roger S. – Klaas A. Worp (2004), *Chronological systems of Byzantine Egypt*, 2nd edition, Leiden: Brill.

Baillet, Maurice (1963), 'Un livret magique en christo-palestinien à l'Université de Louvain', *Le Muséon*, 76, 375–401.

Baissari, Francis (1999), *Catalogue raisonné des manuscrits de la bibliothèque de la résidence patriarcale maronite* (*Bkerké*). *Deuxième Fonds Bkerké*, Beyrouth: Fondation René Moawad (Textes et Documents Historiques).

Baissari, Francis (2001), *Catalogue raisonné des manuscrits de Cannoubine*, Kaslik: Institut de liturgie à l'Université Saint-Esprit de Kaslik.

Baker, Don (1991), 'Arab Papermaking', *The Paper Conservator*, 15, 28—35.

Bakraʒe, Ana et al. (1961) {A.B. – Tamar Bregaʒe – Mzekala Šaniʒe – Elene Meṭreveli}, ქართულ ხელნაწერთა აღწერილობა ყოფილი ქართველთა შორის წერა-კითხვის გამავრცელებელი საზოგადოების (S) კოლექციისა. *Описание грузинских рукописей коллекции* (*S*) *– бывшего Общества Распространении Грамотности среди Грузинского Населения* (*Kartul xelnaçerta aǧçeriloba q̇opili kartvelta šoris çera-ḳitxvis gamavrcelebeli sazogadoebis* (*S*) *ḳolekciisa / Opisanie gruzinskich rukopisej kollekcii* (*S*) *– byvšego Obščestva Rasprostranenii Gramotnosti sredi Gruzinskogo Naselenija* 'Description of the Georgian manuscripts of the collection (S) of the former Society for the Promotion of Literacy among the Georgians'), II, Tbilisi: Sakartvelos SSR Mecnierebata Aḳademiis Gamomcemloba.

Balageorgos, Demetrius – Flora Crete (2008), *Τα χειρόγραφα βυζαντινής μουσικής – Σινά*, I, Athens: Ἵδρυμα Βυζαντινης Μουσικολογίας.

Balduino, Armando (1979), *Manuale di filologia italiana*, Firenze: Sansoni (Manuali Sansoni).

Balić, Smail (2006), *Katalog der türkischen Handschriften der Österreichischen Nationalbibliothek*: *Neuerwerbungen 1864-1994*, *mit einem Anhang*: *Bosnische Aljamiado-Handschriften*, Ankara: Türk Tarih Kurumu (Museion., nf, 4. Reihe: Veröffentlichungen der Handschriftensammlung, 5. Bd. = Atatürk Kültür, Dil ve Tarih Yüksek Kurumu – Türk Tarih Kurumu yayınları, XII. Dizi, Sayı. 13).

Balicka-Witakowska, Ewa (1983), 'Le psautier illustré de Belēn Sägäd', in: *Imagines Medievales. Studier i medeltida ikonografi, arkitektur, skulptur, måleri och konstverk*, ed. by Rudolf Zeitler – Jan O. Karlsson, Uppsala: Uppsala University Press (Acta Universitatis Upsaliensis. Ars Suetica, 7), 1–46.

Balicka-Witakowska, Ewa (1984–1986), 'Un psautier éthiopien illustré inconnu', *Orientalia Suecana*, 33-35 (= *On the Dignity of Man. Oriental and Classical Studies in Honour of Frithiof Rundgren*, ed. by T. Kronholm – E. Riad et al.), 17–48.

Balicka-Witakowska, Ewa (1997), *La crucifixion sans crucifié dans l'art éthiopien*: *recherches sur la survie de l'iconographie chrétienne de l'antiquité tardive*, Warszawa – Wiesbaden: ZAS PAN (Bibliotheca nubica et aethiopica. Schriftenreiche zur Kulturgeschichte um das Rote Meer, 4).

Balicka-Witakowska, Ewa (1998), 'Remarks on the Decoration and Iconography of the Syriac Gospels, British Library, Add. 7174', in: *Symposium Syriacum VII. Uppsala University, Department of Asian and African Languages, 11–14 August 1996*, ed. by René Lavenant, Roma: Pontificio Istituto Orientale (Orientalia Christiana Analecta, 256), 641–659.

Balicka-Witakowska, Ewa (2005a), 'Gundä Gunde: art and architecture', in: *Encyclopaedia Aethiopica*, II: D–Ha , ed. by Siegbert Uhlig et al., Wiesbaden: Harrassowitz, 919–921.

Balicka-Witakowska, Ewa (2005b), 'Haräg', in: *Encyclopaedia Aethiopica*, II: D–Ha, ed. by Siegbert Uhlig et al., Wiesbaden: Harrassowitz, 1009–1010.

Balicka-Witakowska, Ewa (2006), ''Against Thirty and Twenty-Five Devils': Two Ethiopian Painted Amulets in the British Museum Collection', in: *Wälättä Yohanna. Ethiopian Studies in Honour of Joanna Mantel-Niecko on the Occasion of the 50th Year of her Work at the Institute of Oriental Studies, Warsaw University*, ed. by Witold Witakowski – Laura Lykowska, Warszawa: Elipsa (Rocznik Orientalistyczny, 59), 33–46.

Balicka-Witakowska, Ewa (2008), 'Illustrating Charms: a Syriac Manuscript with Magic Drawings in the Collection of the British Library', in: *Malphono w-Rabo d-Malphone. Studies in Honor of Sebastian P. Brock*, ed. by George A. Kiraz, Piscataway, NJ: Gorgias Press, 779–804.

Balicka-Witakowska, Ewa (2010a), 'Sənsul', in: *Encyclopaedia Aethiopica*, IV: O–W, ed. by Siegbert Uhlig – Alessandro Bausi et al., Wiesbaden: Harrassowitz, 625–626.

Balicka-Witakowska, Ewa (2010b), 'Tä'ammərä Maryam in art', in: *Encyclopaedia Aethiopica*, IV: O-W, ed. by Siegbert Uhlig – Alessandro Bausi et al., Wiesbaden: Harrassowitz, 789–795.

Balicka-Witakowska, Ewa (2010c), 'Successful Experiences in the Recording and Preservation of Oriental Manuscripts', paper presented at the COMSt workshop *Conservation Studies on Oriental Manuscripts*, Istanbul.

Balicka-Witakowska, Ewa (2014), 'Nägärä Maryam in art', in: *Encyclopaedia Aethiopica*, V, ed. by Alessandro Bausi, Wiesbaden: Harrassowitz, 457–458.

Balicka-Witakowska, Ewa (forthcoming a), 'The Illuminated 'Golden Gospel' of Agwäza and its Historical Documents', in: *Festschrift Getatchew Haile*, ed. by Adam McCollum, Wiesbaden: Harrassowitz.

Balicka-Witakowska, Ewa (forthcoming b), 'Syriac Decorated and Illuminated Manuscripts: a Codicological Approach', in: *Manuscripta syriaca. Des sources de première main*, ed. by Françoise Briquel-Chatonnet – Muriel Debié, Paris: Geuthner.

Balog, Paul (1949), 'Apparition prématurée de l'écriture naskhy sur un dinar de l'imam fatimite al-Moustaly-billah', *Bulletin de l'Institut d'Égypte*, 31, 181–185.

Bandini, Angelo Maria (1764, 1768, 1770), *Catalogus codicum manuscriptorum Bibliothecae Mediceae Laurentianae varia continens Opera Graecorum Patrum*, I, Florentiae: Typis Caesareis; II, III, Florentiae: Typis Regiis.

Bar-Asher, Moshe (1977), *Palestinian-Syriac Studies. Source-Texts, Tradition and Grammatical Problems*, Jerusalem [diss.].

Baraldi, Pietro et al. (2009) {P.B. – Giulia Moscardi – Paolo Bensi – Maurizio Aceto – Lorenzo Tassi}, 'An Investigation of the Palette and Techniques of Some High Medieval Codices by Raman Microscopy', *e-PreservationScience*, 6, 163–168.

Barbi, Michele (1938), *La nuova filologia e l'edizione dei nostri scrittori da Dante al Manzoni*, Firenze: Sansoni.

Barbieri, Giuseppe – Gianfranco Fiaccadori (eds) (2009), *Nigra sum sed formosa. Sacro e bellezza dell'Etiopia cristiana*, Vicenza: Terra Ferma.

Barc, Bernard – Louis Painchaud (1999), 'La réécriture de l'Apocryphon de Jean à la lumière de l'hymne final de la version longue', *Le Muséon*, 112, 317–333.

Baret, Philippe et al. (2006) {P.B. – Caroline Macé – Peter Robinson}, 'Testing Methods on an Artificially Created Textual Tradition', in: *The evolution of texts: confronting stemmatological and genetical methods. Proceedings of the International Workshop held in Louvain-la-Neuve (Septembre 1-2, 2004)*, ed. by Caroline Macé – Philippe Baret, Pisa – Roma: IEPI (Linguistica computazionale, 24-25), 255–283.

Barkeshli, Mandana (2008), 'Historical and scientific analysis of materials used in Iranian paper dyeing process with special reference to henna', in: *Preprints to the 15th Triennial Meeting of ICOM-CC, New Delhi*, ed. by J. Bridgland, London: James & James, 255–263.

Barlee, Roger (2001), 'Development of Archival Quality Leather', *Skin Deep*, 12, 3–8 .

Barone, Francesca Prometea (2008), *Iohannis Chrysostomi De Davide et Saule homiliae tres*, Turnhout: Brepols (Corpus Christianorum. Series Graeca, 70).

Barrett, David (1973), *Catalogue of the Wardrop Collection and of other Georgian Books and Manuscripts in the Bodleian Library*, Oxford: Oxford University Press.

Barṣawm, Ignatius Afrem (2008), I. مخطوطات طور عبدين / ܡܟܬܒܢܘܬܐ ܕܛܘܪ ܥܒܕܝܢ (*Maḫṭūṭāt Ṭūr ʿAbdīn*, 'Tur ʿAbdin Manuscripts'). II. مخطوطات دير الزعفران / ܡܟܬܒܢܘܬܐ ܕܕܝܪܐ ܕܟܘܪܟܡܐ (*Maḫṭūṭāt Dayr al-Za'farān*) / *Deyrul-Zafaran Manuscripts*. III. مخطوطات آمد وماردين / ܡܟܬܒܢܘܬܐ ܕܐܡܝܕ ܘܡܪܕܝܢ (*Maḫṭūṭāt Amid wa-Mardīn*) / *Omid & Mardin Manuscripts*, Damascus: Maʿarrat Saydnaya.

Barthélémy, Pascale (2002), *La Sedacina ou l'Œuvre au crible: l'alchimie de Guillaume Sedacer, carme catalan de la fin du XIVe siècle*, Milano: Arche (Textes et Travaux de Chrysopœia, 8).

Barthes, Roland (1984), 'La mort de l'auteur [1968]', in: *Le Bruissement de la langue. Essais critiques IV*, Paris: Seuil (Collection 'Points Essais'), 63–69.

Bartoll, Jens et al. (2008) {J.B. – Oliver Hahn – Ulrich Schade}, 'Application of Synchrotron Infrared Radiation in the Study of Organic Coatings in Cross Sections', *Studies in Conservation*, 53, 1–8.

Bastianini, Guido – Guglielmo Cavallo (2011), 'Un nuovo frammento di lettera festale (PSI inv. 3779)', in: *I papiri letterari cristiani. Atti del Convegno internazionale di studi in memoria di Mario Naldini. Firenze 10-11 giugno 2010*, ed. by Guido Bastianini – Angelo Casanova, Firenze: Istituto Papirologico 'G. Vitelli' (Studi e Testi di Papirologia, n.s. 13), 31–45.

Battista, Antonio – Bellarmino Bagatti (1979), *La Caverna dei Tesori*: testo arabo con traduzione italiana e commento, Jerusalem: Franciscan Printing Press (Collectio minor (Studium Biblicum Franciscanum), 26).

Baumeister, Theofried (2006), 'Geschichte und Historiographie des ägyptischen Christentums: Studien und Darstellungen der letzten Jahre', in: *Huitième congrés international d'Études coptes (Paris 2004)*, I: *Bilans et perspectives 2000-2004*, ed. by Anne Boud'hors – Denyse Vaillancourt, Paris: De Boccard (Cahiers de la Bibliothèque copte, 15), 37–67.

Bausi, Alessandro (1993), 'I manoscritti arabo-cristiani: la catalogazione', *Bulletin de l'AELAC*, 3, 17–21.

Bausi, Alessandro (1994 [1996]), 'Su alcuni manoscritti presso comunità monastiche dell'Eritrea. I. Dabra Māryām', *Rassegna di studi etiopici*, 38, 13–69.

Bausi, Alessandro (1995a [1997]), 'Su alcuni manoscritti presso comunità monastiche dell'Eritrea. II. Dabra Bizan', *Rassegna di studi etiopici*, 39, 25–48.

Bausi, Alessandro (1995b), *Il Sēnodos etiopico. Canoni pseudoapostolici*: *Canoni dopo l'Ascensione*, *Canoni di Simone il Cananeo*, *Canoni Apostolici*, *Lettera di Pietro*, Lovanii: Peeters (Corpus Scriptorum Christianorum Orientalium, 552, 553, Scriptores Aethiopici, 101, 102).

Bausi, Alessandro (1997 [1998]), 'Su alcuni manoscritti presso comunità monastiche dell'Eritrea. III. Dabra Libānos. Dabra Abuna Beṣuʿa Amlāk. Dabra Marqorēwos', *Rassegna di studi etiopici*, 41, 13–56.

Bausi, Alessandro (1998), 'L'Epistola 70 di Cipriano di Cartagine in versione etiopica', *Aethiopica*, 1, 101–130.

Bausi, Alessandro (2002a), 'New Egyptian texts in Ethiopia', *Adamantius*, 8, 146–151.

Bausi, Alessandro (2002b), *La versione etiopica degli Acta Phileae nel Gadla samāʿtāt*, Napoli: Istituto Universitario Orientale (Annali dell'Istituto Universitario Orientale. Supplemento, 92).

Bausi, Alessandro (2003a), 'San Clemente e le tradizioni clementine nella letteratura etiopica canonico-liturgica', in: *Studi su Clemente romano. Atti degli Incontri di Roma, 29 marzo e 22 novembre 2001*, ed. by Philippe Luisier, Roma: Pontificio Istituto Orientale (Orientalia Christiana Analecta, 268), 13–55.

Bausi, Alessandro (2003b), *La «Vita» e i «Miracoli» di Libānos*, Louvain: Peeters (Corpus Scriptorum Christianorum Orientalium, 595, 596, Scriptores Aethiopici, 105, 106).

Bausi, Alessandro (2004a), 'Il testo, il supporto e la funzione. Alcune osservazioni sul caso dell'Etiopia', in: *Studia Aethiopica in Honour of Siegbert Uhlig on the Occasion of his 65th Birthday*, ed. by Verena Böll – Denis Nosnitsin – Evgenia Sokolinskaia, Wiesbaden: Harrassowitz, 7–22.

Bausi, Alessandro (2004b), 'La versione etiopica della Didascalia dei 318 niceni sulla retta fede e la vita monastica', in: *Ægyptus Christiana. Mélanges d'hagiographie égyptienne et orientale dédiés à la mémoire du P. Paul Devos bollandiste*, ed. by Ugo Zanetti – Enzo Lucchesi, Genève: Cramer (Cahiers d'Orientalisme, 25), 225–248.

Bausi, Alessandro (2005a), 'Note aggiuntive sull'Epistola 70 di Cipriano: versione etiopica e versione siriaca', in: *Scritti in onore de Giovanni M. d'Erme. Saggi di colleghi e amici in occasione del suo compleanno*, I, ed. by Michele Bernardini – Natalia L. Tornesello, Napoli: Università degli Studi di Napoli 'L'Orientale'. Dipartimento di Studi Asiatici (Series minor, 67), 99–109.

Bausi, Alessandro (2005b), 'Ancient features of Ancient Ethiopic', *Aethiopica*, 8, 149–169.

Bausi, Alessandro (2006a), 'Current Trends in Ethiopian Studies: Philology', in: *Proceedings of the XVth International Conference of Ethiopian Studies. Hamburg July 20-25, 2003*, ed. by Siegbert Uhlig – Maria Bulakh – Denis Nosnitsin, Wiesbaden: Harrassowitz (Aethiopistische Forschungen, 65), 542–551.

Bausi, Alessandro (2006b), 'La Collezione aksumita canonico-liturgica', *Adamantius*, 12 (= *Il Patriarcato di Alessandria nella tarda antichità e nel Medioevo*, ed. by Alberto Camplani), 43–70.

Bausi, Alessandro (2006c), 'The Aksumite background of the Ethiopic 'Corpus canonum'', in: *Proceedings of the XVth International Conference of Ethiopian Studies. Hamburg July 20–25, 2003*, ed. by Siegbert Uhlig – Maria Bulakh – Denis Nosnitsin, Wiesbaden: Harrassowitz (Aethiopistische Forschungen, 65), 532–541.

Bausi, Alessandro (2007), 'La catalogazione come base della ricerca. Il caso dell'Etiopia', in: *Zenit e Nadir* II. *I manoscritti dell'area del Mediterraneo: la catalogazione come base della ricerca. Atti del Seminario internazionale. Montepulciano, 6-8 luglio 2007*, ed. by Benedetta Cenni – Chiara Maria Francesca Lalli: Collana di studi promossa dal CISLAB [Centro Interdipartimentale di Studi sui Beni Librari e Archivistici] e dal Dottorato in Scienze del Libro (Medieval Writing. Settimane poliziane di studi superiori sulla cultura scritta in età medievale e moderna), 87–108.

Bausi, Alessandro (2008a), 'La tradizione scrittoria etiopica', *Segno e testo*, 6, 507–557.

Bausi, Alessandro (2008b), 'Philology as Textual Criticism: 'Normalization' of Ethiopian Studies', *Bulletin of Philological Society of Ethiopia*, 1, 13–46.

Bausi, Alessandro (2009), 'The 'so-called Traditio apostolica': preliminary observations on the new Ethiopic evidence', in: *Volksglaube im antiken Christentum. Prof. Dr. Theofried Baumeister OFM zur Emeritierung*, ed. by Heike Grieser – Andreas Merkt, Darmstadt: Wissenschaftliche Buchgesellschaft, 291–321.

Bausi, Alessandro (2010a), 'Philology', in: *Encyclopaedia Aethiopica*, IV: O–X, ed. by Siegbert Uhlig – Alessandro Bausi et al., Wiesbaden: Harrassowitz, 142–144.

Bausi, Alessandro (2010b), 'Senodos', in: *Encyclopaedia Aethiopica*, IV: O–X, ed. by Siegbert Uhlig – Alessandro Bausi et al., Wiesbaden: Harrassowitz, 623–625.

Bausi, Alessandro (2010c), 'Traditio apostolica', in: *Encyclopaedia Aethiopica*, IV: O–X, ed. by Siegbert Uhlig – Alessandro Bausi et al., Wiesbaden: Harrassowitz, 980–981.

Bausi, Alessandro (2010d), 'Wängelä wärq', in: *Encyclopaedia Aethiopica*, IV: O–X, ed. by Siegbert Uhlig – Alessandro Bausi et al., Wiesbaden: Harrassowitz, 1130–1132.

Bausi, Alessandro (2010e), 'A Case for Multiple Text Manuscripts being 'Corpus-Organizers'', *Manuscript Cultures Newsletter*, 3, 34–36.

Bausi, Alessandro (2011a), 'The 'True Story' of the Abba Gärima Gospels', *Comparative Oriental Manuscript Studies Newsletter*, 1, 17–20.

Bausi, Alessandro (2011b), 'La 'nuova' versione etiopica della Traditio apostolica: edizione e traduzione preliminare', in: *Christianity in Egypt: Literary Production and Intellectual Trends in Late Antiquity. Studies in Honor of Tito Orlandi*, ed. by Paola Buzi – Alberto Camplani, Roma: Institutum Patristicum Augustinianum (Studia Ephemeridis Augustinianum, 125), 19–69.

Bausi, Alessandro (2012), 'Una 'lista' etiopica di apostoli e discepoli', in: *Æthiopica et Orientalia. Studi in onore di Yaqob Beyene*, ed. by Alessandro Bausi – Antonella Brita – Ersilia Francesca, Napoli: Dipartimento Asia, Africa e Mediterraneo (Studi Africanistici. Serie Etiopica, 9), 43–67.

Bausi, Alessandro (2013a), 'Liste etiopiche di vescovi niceni', in: *Orientalia Christiana. Festschrift für Hubert Kaufhold zum 70. Geburtstag*, ed. by Peter Bruns – Heinz Otto Luthe, Wiesbaden: Harrassowitz, 33–73.

Bausi, Alessandro (2013b), 'Kings and Saints: Founders of Dynasties, Monasteries and Churches in Christian Ethiopia', in: *Stifter und Mäzene und ihre Rolle in der Religion: Von Königen, Mönchen, Vordenkern und Laien in Indien, China und anderen Kulturen*, ed. by Barbara Schuler, Wiesbaden: Harrassowitz, 161–186.

Bausi, Alessandro (2014), 'Copying, Writing, Translating: Ethiopia as a Manuscript Culture', in: *Manuscript Cultures: Mapping the Field*, ed. by Jörg Quenzer – Dmitry Bondarev – Jan-Ulrich Sobisch, Berlin – New York: De Gruyter (Studies in Manuscript Cultures, 1), 37–77.

Bausi, Alessandro (forthcoming a), 'Composite and Multiple Text Manuscripts: The Ethiopian Evidence', in: *'One-Volume Libraries': Composite Manuscripts and Multiple Text Manuscripts. Proceedings of the International Conference, Asien-Afrika-Institut, Universität Hamburg, October 7–10, 2010*, ed. by Michael Friedrich – Jörg Quenzer, Berlin – New York: De Gruyter (Studies in Manuscript Cultures).

Bausi, Alessandro (forthcoming b), 'I colofoni e le sottoscrizioni dei manoscritti etiopici', in: *Atti della conferenza 'Colofoni armeni a confronto: Le sottoscrizioni dei manoscritti in ambito armeno e nelle altre tradizioni scrittorie del mondo mediterraneo', Alma Mater Studiorum, Università degli Studi di Bologna, Dipartimento di Medievistica e Paleografia, 12–13 ottobre 2012*, ed. by Paola Buzi – Anna Sirinian, Roma: Pontificio Istituto Orientale (In Oriente Scripta, 1).

Bausi, Alessandro – Alberto Camplani (2013), 'New Ethiopic Documents for the History of Christian Egypt', *Zeitschrift für antikes Christentum. Journal of Ancient Christianity*, 17/2-3, 195–227.

Bausi, Alessandro – Alessandro Gori (2006), *Tradizioni orientali del «Martirio di Areta». La prima recensione araba e la versione etiopica: edizione critica e traduzione*, Firenze: Dipartimento di Linguistica – Università di Firenze (Quaderni di Semitistica, 27).

Bayani, Manijeh et al. (1999) {M.B. – Anna Contadini – Tim Stanley}, *The decorated word: Qur'ans of the 17th to the 19th centuries AD*, London: Azimuth (The Nasser D. Khalili collection of Islamic art, 4/1).

Bayerische Staatsbibliothek (2007), *Katalogisierung mittelalterlicher Handschriften in internationaler Perspektive: Vorträge der Handschriftenbearbeitertagung vom 24. bis 27. Oktober 2005 in München*, Wiesbaden: Harrassowitz (Beiträge zum Buch- und Bibliothekswesen, 5).

Bayraktar, Nimet – Mihin Lugal (1995), *Bibliography on manuscript libraries in Turkey and the publications on the manuscripts located in these libraries*, ed. by Ekmeleddin İhsanoğlu, Istanbul: Research Centre for Islamic History, Art, and Culture (Bibliographical series, 4).

Bdinski zbornik. Ghent Slavonic Ms 408, A.D. 1360. Facsimile edition, introduction by Ivan Dujčev, London: Variorum Reprints, 1972.

Beach, Milo Cleveland (2004), 'Jahangir's Album: Some Clarifications', in: *Arts of Mughal India: Studies in Honour of Robert Skelton*, ed. by Rosemary Crill – Susan Stronge, London: Victoria and Albert Museum, 111-118.

Beal, Peter (2008), *A dictionary of English manuscript terminology: 1450 to 2000*, Oxford: Oxford University Press.

Beck, Edmund (1955), *Des heiligen Ephraem des Syrers Hymnen de Fide*, Louvain: Peeters (Corpus Scriptorum Christianorum Orientalium, 154, 155, Scriptores Syri, 73, 74).

Beck, Edmund (1957), *Des heiligen Ephraem des Syrers Hymnen contra Haereses*, Louvain: Peeters (Corpus Scriptorum Christianorum Orientalium, 169, 170, Scriptores Syri, 76, 77).

Beck, Edmund (1960), *Des heiligen Ephraem des Syrers Hymnen de Ecclesia*, Louvain: Peeters (Corpus Scriptorum Christianorum Orientalium, 198, 199, Scriptores Syri, 84, 85).

Beck, Edmund (1961), *Des heiligen Ephraem des Syrers Carmina Nisibena*, I, Louvain: Peeters (Corpus Scriptorum Christianorum Orientalium, 218, 219, Scriptores Syri, 92, 93).

Beck, Edmund (1963), *Des heiligen Ephraem des Syrers Carmina Nisibena*, II, Louvain: Peeters (Corpus Scriptorum Christianorum Orientalium, 240, 241, Scriptores Syri, 102, 103).

Beck, Edmund (1972), *Des heiligen Ephraem des Syrers Hymnen auf Abraham Kidunaya und Julianos Saba*, Louvain: Peeters (Corpus Scriptorum Christianorum Orientalium, 322, 323, Scriptores Syri, 140, 141).

Beck, Edmund (1979), *Ephraem Syrus. Sermones in Hebdomadam Sanctam*, Louvain: Peeters (Corpus Scriptorum Christianorum Orientalium, 412, 413, Scriptores Syri, 181, 182).

Bedjan, Paul (1897), *Acta martyrum et sanctorum*, VII, Paris – Leipzig: Harrassowitz.

Bedjan, Paul (1898), *Ethicon, seu Moralia Gregorii Barhebraei*, Paris – Leipzig: Harrassowitz.

Bedjan, Paul (1902), *S. Martyrii, qui et Sahdona, quæ supersunt omnia*, Paris – Leipzig: Harrassowitz.

Bedjan, Paul (1909), *Mar Isaacus Ninivita. De perfectione religiosa*, Paris – Leipzig: Harrassowitz.

Beit-Arié, Malachi (1967–1968), 'פאלימפססט מינכן: שרידי מגילה מלפני המאה השמינית / The Munich Palimpsest: A Hebrew Scroll Written Before the Eighth Century', *Kiryat Sefer* 43, 411–428.

Beit-Arié, Malachi (1977), *Hebrew Codicology: Tentative Typology of Technical Practices Employed in Hebrew Dated Medieval Manuscripts*, Paris: Institut de recherche et d'histoire des textes.

Beit-Arié, Malachi (1981), *Hebrew Codicology*, Jerusalem: The Israel Academy of Sciences and Humanities.

Beit-Arié, Malachi (1993), *Hebrew Manuscripts of East and West: Towards a Comparative Codicology*, London: British Library (The Panizzi Lectures, 1992).

Beit-Arié, Malachi (1996), 'The Oriental Arabic Paper', *Gazette du livre médiéval*, 28, 9–12.

Beit-Arié, Malachi (1999), 'Quantitative Typology of Oriental Paper Patterns', in: *Le papier au Moyen Âge: histoire et techniques*, ed. by Monique Zerdoun Bat-Yehouda, Turnhout: Brepols (Bibliologia: Elementa ad Librorum Studia Pertinentia, 19), 41–53.

Beit-Arié, Malachi (2000), 'Publication and Reproduction of Literary Texts in Jewish Medieval Civilization: Jewish Scribality and its Impact on the Texts Transmitted', in: *Transmitting Jewish Traditions: Orality, Textuality, and Cultural Diffusion*, ed. by Yaakov Elman – Israel Gershoni, New Haven – London: Yale University Press, 225–247.

Beit-Arié, Malachi (2006), 'How Scribes Disclosed their Names in Hebrew Manuscripts', in: *Omnia in Eo: Studies on Jewish Books and Libraries in Honour of Adri Offenberg Celebrating the 125th Anniversary of the Bibliotheca Rosenthaliana in Amsterdam*, ed. by Irene Zwiep, Louvain: Peeters (Studia Rosenthaliana, 38/39), 144–157.

Beit-Arié, Malachi (2014), *Hebrew Codicology: Historical and Comparative Typology of Medieval Hebrew Codices based on the Documentation of the Extant Dated Manuscripts in Quantitative Approach. Version 3.0*, <http://web.nli.org.il/sites/NLI/Hebrew/collections/manuscripts/hebrewcodicology/Documents/Hebrew-Codicology-continuously-updated-online-version.pdf>, Jerusalem: The Israel Academy of Sciences and Humanities.

Beit-Arié, Malachi et al. (1979) {M.B. – Colette Sirat – Arlette Attali}, *Manuscrits médiévaux en caractères hébraïques portant des indications de date jusqu'à 1540*, II: *Bibliothèque de France et d'Israël: Manuscrits de petit format jusqu'à 1470*, Paris: Centre national de la recherche scientifique.

Beit-Arié, Malachi et al. (1987) {M.B. – Edna Engel – Ada Yardeni}, *Specimens of medieval Hebrew scripts*. I: *Oriental and Yemenite Scripts*, Jerusalem: The Israel Academy of Sciences and Humanities (The Hebrew Paleography Project).

Beit-Arié, Malachi et al. (1997) {M.B. – Colette Sirat – Mordechai Glatzer}, *Codices hebraicis litteris exarati quo tempore scripti fuerint exhibentes*, I: *jusqu'à 1020*, Turnhout: Brepols (Monumenta Palaeographica Medii Aevi, Series Hebraica, 1).

Beit-Arié, Malachi et al. (2006) {M.B. – Colette Sirat – Mordechai Glatzer}, *Codices hebraicis litteris exarati quo tempore scripti fuerint exhibentes*, IV: *1144 -1200*, Turnhout: Brepols (Monumenta Palaeographica Medii Aevi, Series Hebraica, 5).

Beit-Arié, Malachi – Edna Engel (2002), *Specimens of Mediaeval Hebrew Scripts*, II: *Sefardic Script*, Jerusalem: The Israel Academy of Sciences and Humanities (The Hebrew Paleography Project).

Beit-Arié, Malachi – R.A. May (1994), *Catalogue of the Hebrew Manuscripts in the Bodleian Library: Supplement of Addenda and Corrigenda to Volume I (A. Neubauer's Catalogue)*, New York: Oxford University Press.

Beltz, Walter (1978, 1980), 'Katalog der koptischen Handschriften der Papyrus-Sammlung der Staatlichen Museen zu Berlin', *Archiv für Papyrusforschung*, (I) 26, 57–119; (II) 27, 121–222.

Ben Azzouna, Nourane (forthcoming), 'La question des niveaux de production à travers trois études de codicologie comparée: les dimensions du papier, les formats des feuillets et l'emploi de papiers teintés dans les manuscrits de l'Iraq et de l'Iran occidental à l'époque mongole (XIIIe-XIVe siècles)', *Journal of Islamic manuscripts*.

Ben Cheneb, Mohammed (1909), *Catalogue des manuscrits arabes conservés dans les principales bibliothèques algériennes* [...] *Grande Mosquée d'Alger*, Algier: Jourdan.

Bendix, Caroline et al. (2003) {C.B. – Christopher Calnan – Sarah Hickey}, 'An unfolding exhibition – conservation and registrar perspectives', *The Paper Conservator*, 27, 87–95.

Benedetti, Lisa (2010), 'L'autonomia del calamo', in: *The Legacy of Bernard de Montfaucon: Three Hundred Years of Studies on Greek Handwriting. Proceedings of the Seventh International Colloquium of Greek Palaeography (Madrid – Salamanca, 15-20 September 2008)*, ed. by Antonio Bravo García – Inmaculada Pérez Martín, Turnhout: Brepols (Bibliologia: Elementa ad Librorum Studia Pertinentia, 31A), 347–352.

Bensly, Robert Lubbock et al. (1894) {R.B. – James Rendel Harris – Francis Crawford Burkitt}, *The Four Gospels in Syriac*, Cambridge: Cambridge University Press.

Benton, John F. et al. (1979) {J.B. – Alan R. Gillespie – James M. Soha}, 'Digital Image-Processing Applied to the Photography of Manuscripts: with Examples Drawn from the Pincus MS of Arnald of Villanova', *Scriptorium*, 33, 40–55.

Bergmann, Uwe (2011), 'Synchrotron Rapid-Scan X–ray Fluorescence Imaging of Ancient Documents', in: *EIKONOPOIIA. Digital Imaging of Ancient Textual Heritage. Proceedings of the international conference Helsinki, 28-29 November, 2010*, ed. by Vesa Vahtikari – Mika Hakkarainen – Antti Nurminen, Helsinki: Societas scientiarum Fennica (Commentationes Humanarum Litterarums, 129), 39–50.

Bernabé, Alberto – Felipe G. Hernández Muñoz (2010), *Manual de crítica textual y edición de textos griegos* (2[a] ed. corrigida y aumentada), Madrid: Akal (Textos, 33).

Bernard, Étienne et al. (1991–2000) {È.B. – Abraham Johannes Drewes – Roger Schneider}, *Recueil des Inscriptions de l'Éthiopie des périodes pré-axoumite et axoumite*, avec introduction de Fr. Anfrais, I: *Les documents*; II: *Les Planches*; III: *Traductions et commentaires*, A: *Les inscriptions grecques*, Paris: Diffusion de Boccard (=*RIÉ*).

Bernus-Taylor, Marthe – Thérèse Bittar (2001), 'Décors', in: *L'art du livre arabe: du manuscrit au livre d'artiste*, ed. by Marie-Geneviève Guesdon – Annie Vernay-Nouri, Paris: Bibliothèque nationale de France, 85–97.

Berthelot, Marcellin (1893), *La chimie au Moyen Âge* II, Paris.

Berti, Vittorio (2009), *Vita e studi di Timoteo I patriarca cristiano di Baghdad. Ricerche sull'epistolario e sulle fonti contigue*, Paris: Association pour l'avancement des études iraniennes.

Bertotti, Filippo (1991), *L'opera dello storico persiano Bayhaqī*, Napoli: Istituto universitario orientale, Seminario di studi asiatici (Series minor, 37).

Bettini, Lidia – Paolo La Spisa (eds) (2012), *Au-delà de l'arabe standard. Moyen arabe et arabe mixte dans les sources médiévales, modernes et contemporaines*, Firenze: Dipartimento di Linguistica – Università di Firenze (Quaderni di Semitistica, 28).

Beylot, Robert – Maxime Rodinson (1995), *Répertoire des bibliothèques et des catalogues de manuscrits éthiopiens*, Paris: Centre national de la recherche scientifique (Documents, études et répertoires publiés par l'Institut de recherches et d'histoire des textes, 46).

Bežanov, Semjon – Michail Bežanov (1902), *Господа нашего Iисуса Христа Святое Евангелiе отъ Матөея, Марка, Луки и Iоанна на русскомъ и удинскомъ языкахъ* (*Gospoda našego Iisusa Christa Svjatoe Evangelie ot" Mattheja, Marka, Luki i Ioanna na russkom" i udinskom" jazykach"*, 'The Holy Gospel of Our Lord Jesus Christ by Matthew, Mark, Luke, and John, in the Russian and Udi language'), Tiflis (*Sbornik materialov dlja opisanija mestnostej i plemen Kavkaza*, 30). New edition in: Schulze (2001).

Bianchi, Francesco et al. (1993) {F.B. – Paul Canart – Carlo Federici – Denis Muzerelle – Ezio Ornato – Giancarlo Prato}, 'La structure matérielle du codex dans les principales aires culturelles de l'Italie du XIe siècle', in: *Ancient and Medieval Book Materials and Techniques* (*Erice, 18-25 September 1992*), II, ed. by Marilena Maniaci – Paola F. Munafò, Città del Vaticano: Biblioteca Apostolica Vaticana (Studi e Testi, 358), 363–452.

Bianchi Bandinelli, Ranuccio (1955), *Hellenistic-Byzantine Miniatures of the Iliad* (*Ilias Ambrosiana*), Olten – Lausanne: Urs Graf.

Bianconi, Daniele (2010), 'Età comnena e cultura scritta. Materiali e considerazioni alle origini di una ricerca', in: *The Legacy of Bernard de Montfaucon: Three Hundred Years of Studies on Greek Handwriting. Proceedings of the Seventh International Colloquium of Greek Palaeography (Madrid – Salamanca, 15-20 September 2008)*, I, ed. by Antonio Bravo García – Inmaculada Pérez Martín, Turnhout: Brepols (Bibliologia: Elementa ad Librorum Studia Pertinentia, 31A), 75–96.

Bianconi, Daniele (2012), '«Duplici scribendi forma». Commentare Bernard de Montfaucon', *Medioevo e Rinascimento*, n.s. 23, 299–317.

Bianconi, Daniele (2014), 'Paleografia: riflessioni su concetto e ruolo', in: *Storia della scrittura e altre storie*, ed. by Daniele Bianconi, Roma: Accademia nazionale dei Lincei (Supplemento al 'Bollettino dei Classici', 29), 7–29.

Bibliographie annotée de vieux manuscrits arabes collectés dans l'île de Zanzibar. Annotated bibliography of old Arabic manuscripts collected in Zanzibar island, Zanzibar: EACROTANAL (Collection: Vieux Manuscrits, 2-4), 1986–1988.

Библиотека Фронтистеса (*Biblioteka Frontistesa*), <http://ksana-k.narod.ru>, last access May 2014.

Bibliothèque nationale de France (1975), *Catalogue général des manuscrits latins*. Tome VI. (*Nos 3536 à 3775B*), Paris: Bibliothèque nationale.

Bibliothèque nationale de France, *Archives et manuscrits* <http://archivesetmanuscrits.bnf.fr/cdc.html>, last access October 2014.

Bicchieri, Marina et al. (2008) {M.B. – Michela Monti – Giovanna Piantanida – Armida Sodo}, 'All that is iron-ink is not always iron-gall!', *Journal of Raman Spectroscopy*, 39, 1074–1078.

Bigoul El-Souriany – Lucas Van Rompay (2001), 'Syriac Papyrus Fragments Recently Discovered in Deir al-Surian (Egypt)', *Hugoye*, 4/1, 93–101.

Birnbaum, Solomon Asher (1954–1971), *The Hebrew scripts*, I–II, Leiden: E.J. Brill.

Birnbaum, Eleazar (1967), 'The Transliteration of Ottoman Turkish for Library and General Purposes', *Journal of the American Oriental Society*, 87/2, 122–156.

Birnbaum, Eleazar (1983a), 'Turkish Manuscripts: Cataloguing since 1960 and Manuscripts Still Uncatalogued, Part 1. The Berlin Catalogue', *Journal of the American Oriental Society*, 103/2, 413–420.

Birnbaum, Eleazar (1983b), 'Turkish Manuscripts: Cataloguing since 1960 and Manuscripts Still Uncatalogued, Part 2. Yugoslavia, Bulgaria, Romania', *Journal of the American Oriental Society*, 103/3, 515–532.

Birnbaum, Eleazar (1983c), 'Turkish Manuscripts: Cataloguing since 1960 and Manuscripts Still Uncatalogued, Part 3. U.S.S.R., Iran, Afghanistan, Arab Lands (Except Palestine), Israel and Palestine, India and Pakistan, China', *Journal of the American Oriental Society*, 103/4, 691–707.

Birnbaum, Eleazar (1984a), 'Turkish Manuscripts: Cataloguing since 1960 and Manuscripts Still Uncatalogued, Part 4. Hungary, Czechoslovakia, Poland, Great Britain, Ireland, The Netherlands, Belgium, France, Germany, Switzerland, Austria, Italy, Finland, United States, Canada', *Journal of the American Oriental Society*, 104/2, 303–314.

Birnbaum, Eleazar (1984b), 'Turkish Manuscripts: Cataloguing since 1960 and Manuscripts Still Uncatalogued, Part 5. Turkey and Cyprus', *Journal of the American Oriental Society*, 104/3, 465–503.

Birnbaum, David J. (1996), 'Standardizing characters, glyphs and SGML entities for encoding early Cyrillic writing', *Computer Standards & Interfaces*, 18, 201–252.

Birnbaum, David J. (2003), 'Computer-assisted analysis and study of the structure of mixed-content miscellanies', *Scripta & e-Scripta*, 1, 15–54.

Birnbaum, David J. et al. (2008) {D.B. – Ralph Cleminson – Sebastian Kempgen – Kiril Ribarov}, 'Character Set Standardization for Early Cyrillic Writing after Unicode 5.1', paper prepared for the *XIV International Congress of Slavists, Ohrid 10–16 September.*

Bischoff, Bernard (1985), *Paléographie de l'antiquité romaine et du Moyen Âge occidental*, introduction by Jean Vezin, Paris: Picard.

Bischoff, Frank Michael (1992), 'Methoden der Lagenbeschreibung', *Scriptorium*, 46, 3–27.

Bischoff, Frank Michael (1993), 'Observations sur l'emploi de différentes qualités de parchemin dans les manuscrits médiévaux', in: *Ancient and Medieval Book Materials and Techniques (Erice, 18-25 September 1992)*, I, ed. by Marilena Maniaci – Paola F. Munafò, Città del Vaticano: Biblioteca Apostolica Vaticana (Studi e Testi, 357), 57–94.

Biscioni, Antonio Maria (1752), *Bibliothecae Mediceo-Laurentianae catalogus*, Firenze: ex Imperiali typographio.

Blachère, Regis – Jean Sauvaget (1945), *Règles pour éditions et traductions de textes arabes*, Paris: Belles Lettres.

Black, Matthew (1954), *A Christian Palestinian Syriac Horologion (Berlin MS. Or. Oct. 1019)*, Cambridge: Cambridge University Press.

Blair, Sheila S. – Jonathan M. Bloom (eds) (2009), *The Grove Encyclopaedia of Islamic art and architecture*, I–III, Oxford: Oxford University Press.

Blake, Robert Pierpont (1922–1923), 'Catalogue des manuscripts géorgiens de la Bibliothèque patriarcale grecque à Jérusalem [I]', *Revue de l'Orient Chrétien*, 3/23, 315–413.

Blake, Robert Pierpont (1924), 'Catalogue des manuscripts géorgiens de la Bibliothèque patriarcale grecque à Jérusalem [II–III]', *Revue de l'Orient Chrétien*, 4/24, 190–210, 387–429.

Blake, Robert Pierpont (1925–1926), 'Catalogue des manuscripts géorgiens de la Bibliothèque patriarcale grecque à Jérusalem [IV]', *Revue de l'Orient Chrétien*, 5/25, 132–155.

Blake, Robert Pierpont (1932a), 'Catalogue des manuscrits géorgiens de la bibliothèque de la Laure d'Iviron au Mont Athos [1]', *Revue de l'Orient Chrétien*, 3 ser. 8=28, 289–361.

Blake, Robert Pierpont (1932b), 'Catalogue of the Georgian Manuscripts in the Cambridge University Library', *The Harvard Theological Review*, 25/3, 207–224.

Blake, Robert Pierpont (1933), 'Catalogue des manuscrits géorgiens de la bibliothèque de la Laure d'Iviron au Mont Athos [2] [3]', *Revue de l'Orient Chrétien*, 3 ser. 9=29, 114–159, 225–271.

Blake, Robert Pierpont – Maurice Brière (1961–1963), *The Old Georgian version of the Prophets. Critical edition with a Latin translation*, I–V, Paris: Firmin-Didot (Patrologia Orientalis, 29, 2-5/30, 3).

Blau, Joshua (1965), *The Emergence and Linguistic Background of Judaeo-Arabic. A Study of the Origins of Middle Arabic*, Oxford: Oxford University Press.

Blau, Joshua (1966–1967), *A Grammar of Christian Arabic Based Mainly on South-Palestinian Texts from the First Millennium*, Louvain: Peeters (Corpus Scriptorum Christianorum Orientalium, 267, 276, 279, Subsidia 27, 28, 29).

Blau, Joshua (1986), 'On Two Works in Middle Arabic Literary Standard', in: *Studies in Islamic Civilisation in Honour of Professor David Ayalon*, ed. by Moše Šārôn, Jerusalem: Cana – Leiden: Brill, 447–473.

Blau, Joshua (1988), 'The Beginnings of the Arabic Diglossia', in: *Studies in Middle Arabic and its Judeo-Arabic Variety*, ed. by Joshua Blau, Jerusalem: The Magnes Press-The Hebrew University Press, 1–38.

Blau, Joshua (1999), 'The Status and Linguistic Structure of Middle Arabic', *Jerusalem Studies in Arabic and Islam*, 23, 221–227.

Blau, Joshua (2002), *A Handbook of Early Middle Arabic*, Jerusalem: The Magnes Press-The Hebrew University Press.

Blau, Joshua (2003), 'The Importance of Middle Arabic for the Understanding of the History of Neo-Arabic', in: *Mélanges David Cohen présentés à l'occasion de son quatre-vingtième anniversaire*, ed. by Jérôme Lentin – Antoine Lonnet, Paris: Maisonneuve-Larose, 111–117.

Blochet, Edgar (1900), *Catalogue de la collection de manuscrits orientaux arabes, persans et turcs formée par M. Charles Schefer et acquis par l'état*, Paris: Imprimerie nationale.

Blochet, Edgar (1925), *Catalogue des manuscrits arabes des nouvelles acquisitions (1884-1924)*, Paris: Ernest Leroux.

Blochet, Edgar (1926), *Les enluminures des manuscrits orientaux turcs, arabes, persans de la Bibliothèque nationale*, Paris: Éditions de la Gazette des beaux-arts.

de Blois, François (1992–1997), *Persian Literature, A Bio-bibliographical Survey*, V/1-3, Oxford: Royal Asiatic Society.

Bloom, Jonathan (1989), 'The Blue Koran. An early Fatimid Kufic manuscript from the Maghrib', in: *Les manuscrits du Moyen Orient. Essais de codicologie et de paléographie. Actes du Colloque d'Istanbul, Istanbul 26-29 mai, 1986*, ed. by François Déroche, Istanbul: I.F.E.A. – Paris: Bibliothèque nationale (Varia turcica, 8), 95–99.

Bloom, Jonathan (2001), *Paper before Print: The History and Impact of Paper in the Islamic World*, New Haven – London: Yale University Press.

Bober, Harry (1967), 'On the Illumination of the Glazier Codex: A Contribution to Early Coptic Art and Its Relation to Hiberno-Saxon Interlace', in: *Homage to a Bookman: Essays on Manuscripts, Books and Printing Written for Hans P. Kraus on His Sixtieth Birthday, Oct. 12, 1967*, ed. by Hellmut Lehmann-Haupt, Berlin: Mann, 30–49.

Bobichon, Philippe (2008), *Bibliothèque nationale de France. Hébreu 669 à 703. Manuscrits de théologie*, Turnhout: Brepols (Manuscrits en caractères hébreux conservés dans les bibliothèques de France. Catalogues, 1).

Bobichon, Philippe (2014), *Bibliothèque nationale de France. Hébreu 704 à 733, Manuscrits de théologie*, Turnhout: Brepols (Manuscrits en caractères hébreux conservés dans les bibliothèques de France. Catalogues, 5).

Boeder, Winfried (1987), 'Versuch einer sprachwissenschaftlichen Interpretation der altgeorgischen Abkürzungen', *Revue des études géorgiennes et caucasiennes*, 3, 33–81.

Bogdan, Damian P. (1978), *Paleografia româno-slavă: Tratat şi album*, Bucharest: Direcţia Generală a Arhivelor Statului din Republica Socialistă România.

Bogdanović, Dimitrije (1978), *Каталог ћирилских рукописа манастира Хиландара* (*Katalog ćirilskih rukopisa manastira Hilandara*, 'Catalogue of the Cyrillic Manuscripts of Hilandar Monastery'), I–II, Belgrade: Srpska akademija nauka i umetnosti – Narodna biblioteka SR Srbije.

Bohak, Gideon (2011), 'The Magical Rotuli from the Cairo Genizah', in: *Continuity and Innovation in the Magical Tradition*, ed. by Gideon Bohak – Yuval Harari, Leiden: Brill (Jerusalem Studies in Religion and Culture, 15), 321–340.

Bohas, George [Ğūrğ Būhās] – Kātyā Zaḫariyyā – Salām Diyāb (2000–2011), سيرة الملك الظاهر بيبرص حسب الرواية الشامية (*Sīrat al-malik al-Ẓāhir Baybarṣ ḥasab al-riwāya al-Šāmiyya*, 'The *Sīra* of King Ẓāhir Baybars according to the Syrian Tradition'), I–IX, Damas: Institut français du Proche-Orient (Publications de l'institut français de Damas 182, 192, 201, 207, 212, 229, 239, 242, 268).

Bompaire, Jacques (1979), 'Les catalogues de livres-manuscrits d'époque byzantine (XIe-XVe s.)', in: *Byzance et les Slaves, Études de civilisation: Mélanges Ivan Dujčev*, Paris, 59–81.

Bonmariage, Cécile – Sébastien Moureau (2011), '*Corpus Dionysiacum Arabicum*: Étude, édition critique et traduction des Noms Divins IV, §1-9, Partie I', *Le Muséon*, 124, 181–227.

Books within Books, <http://www.hebrewmanuscript.com>, last access October 2014.

Borbone, Pier Giorgio (2003), 'I Vangeli per la principessa Sara. Un manoscritto siriaco crisografato, gli Öngüt cristiani e il principe Giorgio', *Egitto e Vicino Oriente*, 26, 63–82.

Borbone, Pier Giorgio (2013), 'More on the Priest Särgis in the White Pagoda. The Syro-Turkic Inscriptions of the White Pagoda, Hohhot', in: *From the Oxus River to the Chinese Shores: Studies on East Syriac Christianity in China and Central Asia*, ed. by Li Tang – Dietmar W. Winkler, Berlin: LIT, 49–63.

Bornert, René (1966), 'Les commentaires byzantins de la Divine Liturgie du VIIe au XVe siècle', Paris: Institut d'Études Byzantines (Archives de l'Orient chrétien, 6).

Bosc-Tiessé, Claire (2008), *Les îles de la mémoire. Fabrique des images et écriture de l'histoire dans les églises du lac Tana, Éthiopie, XVIIe-XVIIIe siècle*, Paris : Publications de la Sorbonne.

Bosc-Tiessé, Claire (2009), 'Gouverner et définir un territoire. Géopolitique, art et production manuscrite au Lāstā entre 1667 et 1768', *Annales d'Éthiopie*, 24, 87–148.

Bosc-Tiessé, Claire (2010a), 'La tête qui fume de l'église de Nārgā. Histoire des mœurs et histoire politique du royaume d'Éthiopie du XVIe au XIXe siècle', *Afriques. Débats, méthodes et terrains d'histoire*, 1 <http://afriques.revues.org/414>.

Bosc-Tiessé, Claire (2010b), 'Sainteté et intervention royale au monastère Saint-Étienne de Ḥayq au tournant du XIIIe et du XIVe siècle. L'image de Iyasus Mo'a dans son Évangile', *Oriens Christianus*, 94, 199–227.

Bosc-Tiessé, Claire – Anais Wion (2010), 'Les manuscrits éthiopiens d'Antoine d'Abbadie à la Bibliothèque Nationale de France. Collecte, copie et étude', in: *Antoine d'Abbadie (1810–1897). De l'Abyssinie au Pays basque: voyage d'une vie*, ed. by Jean Delcourt, Biarritz: Atlantica, 77–116.

Bosch, Gulnar et al. (1981) {G.B. – John Carswell – Guy Petherbridge}, *Islamic Bindings and Bookmaking. A Catalogue of an Exhibition. The Oriental Institute of Chicago*, Chicago: University of Chicago Press.

Bosson, Nathalie – Sydney Aufrère (eds) (1999), *Égyptes... L'égyptien et le copte*, Lattes: Musée archéologique Henri Prades (Association Imago).

Bosworth, Clifford Edmund (2011), *The History of Beyhaqi* (*The History of Sultan Mas'ud of Ghazna, 1030–1041*), revision by Mohsen Ashtiany, I–III, Boston: Ilex Foundation – Washington, DC: Center for Hellenic Studies, Trustees for Harvard University (Ilex Foundation Series, 6).

von Bothmer, Hans-Caspar (1986), 'Frühislamische Koran-Illuminationen', *Kunst und Antiquitäten*, 1, 22–33.

von Bothmer, Hans-Caspar (1995), 'Architekturbilder im Koran: eine Prachthandschrift der Umayyadenzeit aus dem Yemen', *Pantheon*, 45, 4–20.

Botte, Bernard (1955), 'Le texte de la Tradition apostolique', *Recherches de théologie ancienne et médiévale*, 22, 161–172.

Botte, Bernard (1966), 'À propos de la «Tradition apostolique»', *Recherches de théologie ancienne et médiévale*, 33, 177–186.

Botti, Lorena et al. (2005) {L.B. – Orietta Mantovani – Daniele Ruggiero}, 'Calciumphytat zur Behandlung von Tintenfraß: Wirkungen auf das Papier', *Restaurator. International Journal for the Preservation of Library and Archival Material*, 26, 44–62.

Boud'hors, Anne (1987), *Catalogue des fragments coptes*. 1. *Fragments bibliques nouvellement identifiés*, Paris: Bibliothèque Nationale.

Boud'hors, Anne (1998), *Catalogue des fragments coptes de la Bibliothèque Nationale et Universitaire de Strasbourg*. I. *Fragments bibliques*, Louvain: Peeters (Corpus Scriptorum Christianorum Orientalium, 571, Subsidia, 99).

Boud'hors, Anne (1999a), 'Manuscrits coptes de papier (XIe–XIVe siècle): quelques éléments de caractérisation', in: *Le papier au Moyen Âge: histoire et techniques*, ed. by Monique Zerdoun Bat-Yehouda, Turnhout: Brepols (Bibliologia: Elementa ad Librorum Studia Pertinentia, 19), 75–84.

Boud'hors, Anne (1999b), 'Le catalogage des textes coptes du Louvre', in: *Ägypten und Nubien in spätantiker und christlicher Zeit. Akten des 6. Internationalen Koptologenkongresses. Münster, 20.—26. Juli 1996*, II: *Schrifttum, Sprache und Gedankenwelt*, ed. by Stephen Emmel – Martin Krause, Wiesbaden: Reichert (Sprachen und Kulturen des Christlichen Orients, 6.2), 257–267.

Boud'hors, Anne (2000), 'L'écriture, la langue et le livre', in: *L'art copte en Égypte. 2000 ans de christianisme*, ed. by Marie-Hélène Rutschowskaya, Paris: Institut du monde arabe – Éditions Gallimard, 52–91.

Boud'hors, Anne (2004), *Pages chrétiennes d'Égypte: les manuscrits des Coptes*, Paris: Bibliothèque nationale de France.

Boud'hors, Anne (2006), 'Paléographie et codicologie coptes: progrès et perspectives (1996–2004)', in: *Huitième congrés international d'études coptes (Paris 2004)*, I: *Bilans et perspectives 2000–2004*, ed. by Anne Boud'hors – Denyse Vaillancourt, Paris: De Boccard (Cahiers de la Bibliothèque copte, 15), 95–110.

Boud'hors, Anne (2008), 'Copie et circulation des livres dans la région thébaine (7e-8e siècles)', in: *'Et maintenant ce ne sont plus que des villages': Thèbes et sa région aux époques hellénistique, romaine et byzantine. Actes du colloque tenu à Bruxelles les 2 et 3 décembre 2005*, ed. by Alain Delattre – Paul Heilporn, Bruxelles: Association Égyptologique Reine Élisabeth (Papyrologica Bruxellensia, 34), 149–161, pls. 14–15.

Boud'hors, Anne (2011), 'L'Allocutio ad monachos d'Athanase d'Alexandrie (CPG 2186): nouveaux fragments coptes', in: *Christianity in Egypt: Literary Production and Intellectual Trends. Studies in Honor of Tito Orlandi*, ed. by Paola Buzi – Alberto Camplani, Roma: Institutum Patristicum Augustinianum (Studia Ephemeridis Augustinianum, 125), 101–158.

Boud'hors, Anne (2013), *Le Canon 8 de Chénouté d'après le manuscrit Ifao Copte 2 et les fragments complémentaires*, I–II, Cairo: Institut français d'archéologie orientale (Bibliothèque d'études coptes, 21).

Bourdeau, Louis (1888), *L'Histoire et les historiens. Essai critique sur l'histoire considérée comme science positive*, Paris: Alcan.

Bower, Mim A. et al. (2010) {M.B. – Michael G. Campana – Caroline Checkley-Scott – Barry Knight – Christopher J. Howe}, 'The potential for extraction and exploitation of DNA from parchment: a review of the opportunities and hurdles', *Journal of the Institute of Conservation*, 33/1, 1–11.

Boyo, Osman E. et al. (1962) {O.B. – Thomas Hodgkin – Ivor Wilks}, *Check List of Arabic Works from Ghana*, Legon: Institute of African Studies.

Bozzacchi, Giampiero ([2000]), *Censimento dei dati materiali dei codici etiopici della Sezione Orientale della Biblioteca dell'Accademia Nazionale dei Lincei e Corsiniana*, [Roma] [typewritten].

Bozzolo, Carla – Ezio Ornato (eds) (1980), *Pour une histoire du livre manuscrit au Moyen Âge. Trois essais de codicologie quantitative*, Paris: Centre national de la recherche scientifique.

Bradshaw, Paul F. (1993), 'Liturgy and 'Living Literature'', in: *Liturgy in Dialogue: Essays in Memory of Ronald Jasper*, ed. by Paul F. Bradshaw – Bryan Spinks, London: SPCK, 138–153.

Bradshaw, Paul F. (2002), *The Search for the Origins of Christian Worship: Sources and Methods for the Study of Early Liturgy*, 2nd rev. edition, London: SPCK.

Bradshaw, Paul F. et al. (2002) {P.B. – Maxwell E. Johnson – L. Edward Phillips}, *The apostolic tradition: a commentary*, Minneapolis, MN: Fortress Press (Hermeneia).

Brakmann, Heinzgerd (2004), 'Fragmenta Graeco-Copto-Thebaica. Zu Jutta Henners Veröffentlichung alter und neuer Dokumente südägyptischer Liturgie', *Oriens christianus*, 88, 117–172.

Brakmann, Heinzgerd (2011), 'Der Gottesdienst der östlichen Kirchen', *Archiv für Liturgiewissenschaft*, 53, 138–270.

Brambilla Ageno, Franca (1984), *L'edizione critica dei testi volgari.* Seconda edizione riveduta e ampliata, Padova: Antenore (Medioevo e Umanesimo, 22).

Brashear, William (1998), 'Syriaca', *Archiv für Papyrusforschung und verwandte Gebiete*, 44/1, 86–127 (pl. XIII).

Braun, Jan (1958), 'Rękopisy gruzińskie', in: *Katalog rękopisów ormiańskich i gruzińskich*, Warszawa: Państwowe wydawnictwo naukowe (Katalog rękopisów orientalnych ze zbiorów polskich, 3), 51–55.

Bregaʒe, Tamar et al. (1958) {T.B. – Tina Enukiʒe – N. Ḳasraʒe – Elene Meṭreveli – Lili Kutatelaʒe – Krisṭine Šarašiʒe}, ქართულ ხელნაწერთა აღწერილობა ახალი (*Q*) კოლექციისა. *Описание грузинских рукописей новой* (*Q*) *коллекции* (*Kartul xelnaçerta aǧçeriloba axali* (*Q*) *ḳolekciisa. Opisanie gruzinskich rukopisej novoj* (*Q*) *kollekcii*, 'Description of the Georgian manuscripts of the new (Q) Collection'), II, Tbilisi: Sakartvelos SSR Mecnierebata Aḳademiis Gamomcemloba.

Bregaʒe, Tamar et al. (1959) {T.B. – Tina Enukiʒe – N. Ḳasraʒe – Elene Meṭreveli – Lili Kutatelaʒe – Krisṭine Šarašiʒe }, ქართულ ხელნაწერთა აღწერილობა ყოფილი ქართველთა შორის წერა-კითხვის გამავრცელებელი საზოგადოების (*S*) კოლექციისა. *Описание грузинских рукописей коллекции* (*S*) *– бывшего Общества Распространении Грамотности среди Грузинского Населения* (*Kartul xelnaçerta aǧçeriloba q̇opili kartvelta šoris çera-ḳitxvis gamavrcelebeli sazogadoebis* (*S*) *ḳolekciisa / Opisanie gruzinskich rukopisej kollekcii* (*S*) *– byvšego Obščestva Rasprostranenii Gramotnosti sredi Gruzinskogo Naselenija*, 'Description of the Georgian manuscripts of the collection (S) of the former Society for the Promotion of Literacy among the Georgians'), I, Tbilisi: Sakartvelos SSR Mecnierebata Aḳademiis Gamomcemloba.

Bregaʒe, Tamar et al. (1965) {T.B. – Lia Ḳiḳnaʒe – Mixeil Kavtaria – Lamara Kaǯaia – Mzekala Šaniʒe – Krisṭine Šarašiʒe – Caca Çanḳievi}, ქართულ ხელნაწერთა აღწერილობა ყოფილი ქართველთა შორის წერა-კითხვის გამავრცელებელი საზოგადოების (*S*) კოლექციისა. *Описание грузинских рукописей коллекции* (*S*) *– бывшего Общества Распространении Грамотности среди Грузинского Населения* (*Kartul xelnaçerta aǧçeriloba q̇opili kartvelta šoris çera-ḳitxvis gamavrcelebeli sazogadoebis* (*S*) *ḳolekciisa / Opisanie gruzinskich rukopisej kollekcii* (*S*) *– byvšego Obščestva Rasprostranenii Gramotnosti sredi Gruzinskogo Naselenija*, 'Description of the Georgian manuscripts of the collection (S) of the former Society for the Promotion of Literacy among the Georgians'), IV, Tbilisi: Sakartvelos SSR Mecnierebata Aḳademiis Gamomcemloba.

Bregaʒe, Tamar et al. (1967) {T.B. – Tina Enukiʒe – Lia Ḳiḳnaʒe – Mzekala Šaniʒe – Caca Çanḳievi}, ქართულ ხელნაწერთა აღწერილობა ყოფილი ქართველთა შორის წერა-კითხვის გამავრცელებელი საზოგადოების (*S*) კოლექციისა. *Описание грузинских рукописей коллекции* (*S*) *– бывшего Общества Распространении Грамотности среди Грузинского Населения* (*Kartul xelnaçerta aǧçeriloba q̇opili kartvelta šoris çera-ḳitxvis gamavrcelebeli sazogadoebis* (*S*) *ḳolekciisa / Opisanie gruzinskich rukopisej kollekcii* (*S*) *– byvšego Obščestva Rasprostranenii Gramotnosti sredi Gruzinskogo Naselenija*, 'Description of the Georgian manuscripts of the collection (S) of the former Society for the Promotion of Literacy among the Georgians'), V, Tbilisi: Sakartvelos SSR Mecnierebata Aḳademiis Gamomcemloba.

Bregaʒe, Tamar et al. (1969) {T.B. – Lamara Kaǯaia – Lili Kutatelaʒe – Mzekala Šaniʒe – Caca Çanḳievi}, ქართულ ხელნაწერთა აღწერილობა ყოფილი ქართველთა შორის წერა-კითხვის გამავრცელებელი საზოგადოების (*S*) კოლექციისა. *Описание грузинских рукописей коллекции* (*S*) *– бывшего Общества Распространении Грамотности среди Грузинского Населения* (*Kartul xelnaçerta aǧçeriloba q̇opili kartvelta šoris çera-ḳitxvis gamavrcelebeli sazogadoebis* (*S*) *ḳolekciisa / Opisanie gruzinskich rukopisej kollekcii* (*S*) *– byvšego Obščestva Rasprostranenii Gramotnosti sredi Gruzinskogo Naselenija*, 'Description of the Georgian manuscripts of the collection (S) of the former Society for the Promotion of Literacy among the Georgians'), VI, Tbilisi: Mecniereba.

Bregaʒe, Tamar et al. (1973a) {T.B. – Mixeil Kavtaria – Lamara Kaǯaia – Lili Kutatelaʒe – Caca Čanḳievi}, ქართულ ხელნაწერთა აღწერილობა ყოფილი ქართველთა შორის წერა-კითხვის გამავრცელებელი საზოგადოების (*S*) კოლექციისა. *Описание грузинских рукописей коллекции* (*S*) *– бывшего Общества Распространении Грамотности среди Грузинского Населения* (*Kartul xelnaçerta ağçeriloba q̇opili kartvelta šoris çera-ḳitxvis gamavrcelebeli sazogadoebis* (*S*) *ḳolekciisa / Opisanie gruzinskich rukopisej kollekcii* (*S*) *– byvšego Obščestva Rasprostranenii Gramotnosti sredi Gruzinskogo Naselenija* 'Description of the Georgian manuscripts of the collection (S) of the former Society for the Promotion of Literacy among the Georgians'), VII, Tbilisi: Sakartvelos SSR Mecnierebata Aḳademiis Gamomcemloba.

Bregaʒe, Tamar et al. (1973b) {T.B. – Mixeil Kavtaria – Lili Kutatelaʒe}, ქართულ ხელნაწერთა აღწერილობა ყოფილი საეკლესიო მუზეუმის (*A*) კოლექციისა (*Kartul xelnaçerta ağçeriloba q̇opili saeḳlesio muzeumis* (*A*) *ḳolekciisa*, 'Description of the Georgian manuscripts of the collection of the former Ecclesiastical Museum (A)'), I/1, Tbilisi: Mecniereba.

Bregaʒe, Tamar et al. (1976) {T.B. – Ciala Ḳaxabrišvili – Tamila Mgaloblišvili – Mixeil Kavtaria – Lili Kutatelaʒe – Ciala Ǯġamaia}, ქართულ ხელნაწერთა აღწერილობა ყოფილი საეკლესიო მუზეუმის (*A*) კოლექციისა (*Kartul xelnaçerta ağçeriloba q̇opili saeḳlesio muzeumis* (*A*) *ḳolekciisa*, 'Description of the Georgian manuscripts of the collection of the former Ecclesiastical Museum (A)'), I/2, Tbilisi: Sakartvelos SSR Mecnierebata Aḳademiis Gamomcemloba.

Bregaʒe, Tamar et al. (1980) {T.B. – Mixeil Kavtaria – Lili Kutatelaʒe}, ქართულ ხელნაწერთა აღწერილობა ყოფილი საეკლესიო მუზეუმის (*A*) კოლექციისა (*Kartul xelnaçerta ağçeriloba q̇opili saeḳlesio muzeumis* (*A*) *ḳolekciisa*, 'Description of the Georgian manuscripts of the collection of the former Ecclesiastical Museum (A)'), I/3, Tbilisi: Mecniereba.

Bregaʒe, Tamar et al. (1985) {T.B. – Mixeil Kavtaria – Lili Kutatelaʒe}, ქართულ ხელნაწერთა აღწერილობა ყოფილი საეკლესიო მუზეუმის (*A*) კოლექციისა (*Kartul xelnaçerta ağçeriloba q̇opili saeḳlesio muzeumis* (*A*) *ḳolekciisa*, 'Description of the Georgian manuscripts of the collection of the former Ecclesiastical Museum (A)'), I/4, Tbilisi: Sakartvelos SSR Mecnierebata Aḳademiis Gamomcemloba.

Bregaʒe, Tamar et al. (1986) {T.B. – Ciala Ḳaxabrišvili – Mixeil Kavtaria – Caca Čanḳievi – Lili Xevsuriani}, ქართულ ხელნაწერთა აღწერილობა ყოფილი საეკლესიო მუზეუმის (*A*) კოლექციისა (*Kartul xelnaçerta ağçeriloba q̇opili saeḳlesio muzeumis* (*A*) *ḳolekciisa*, 'Description of the Georgian manuscripts of the collection of the former Ecclesiastical Museum (A)'), II/1, Tbilisi: Sakartvelos SSR Mecnierebata Aḳademiis Gamomcemloba.

Bregaʒe, Tamar et al. (2004), ქართულ ხელნაწერთა აღწერილობა ყოფილი საეკლესიო მუზეუმის (*A*) კოლექციისა (*Kartul xelnaçerta ağçeriloba q̇opili saeḳlesio muzeumis* (*A*) *ḳolekciisa*, 'Description of the Georgian manuscripts of the collection of the former Ecclesiastical Museum (A)'), II/2, Tbilisi: Sakartvelos SSR Mecnierebata Aḳademiis Gamomcemloba.

Bregaʒe, Tamar – Ciala Ḳaxabrišvili (2002), გორის სახელმწიფო ისტორიულ-ეთნოგრაფიული მუზეუმის ქართულ ხელნაწერთა აღწერილობა (*Goris saxelmçipo isṭoriul-etnograpiuli muzeumis kartul xelnaçerta ağçeriloba*, 'Description of the Georgian Manuscripts of the historical-ethnographical Museum of Gori'), Tbilisi: Mecniereba.

Bregel, Yuri (2005), 'Storey, Charles Ambrose – British orientalist, author of the bio-bibliographical survey of Persian literature (1888-1968)', *Encyclopaedia Iranica* online, <http://www.iranicaonline.org/articles/storey-charles-ambrose>.

Brinkmann, Stephanie – Beate Wiesmüller (eds) (2009), *From Codicology to Technology – Islamic Manuscripts and their Place in Scholarship*, Berlin: Frank & Timme.

Briquel-Chatonnet, Françoise (1997), *Manuscrits syriaques de la Bibliothèque nationale de France* (*n°s 356-435, entrés depuis 1911*), *de la bibliothèque Méjanes d'Aix-en-Provence, de la Bibliothèque municipale de Lyon et de la Bibliothèque nationale et universitaire de Strasbourg. Catalogue*, Paris: Bibliothèque nationale de France.

Briquel-Chatonnet, Françoise (1998a), 'Le temps du copiste. Notations chronologiques dans les colophons de manuscrits syriaques', in: *Proche-Orient ancien. Temps vécu, temps passé. Actes de la table ronde du 15 novembre 1997 organisée par l'URA 1062, 'Études Sémitiques'*, ed. by Françoise Briquel-Chatonnet – Hélène Lozachmeur, Paris: Jean Maisonneuve (Antiquités sémitiques, 3).

Briquel-Chatonnet, Françoise (1998b), 'Cahiers et signatures dans les manuscrits syriaques. Remarques sur les manuscrits de la Bibliothèque nationale de France', in: *Recherches de codicologie comparée*: *la composition du codex au Moyen Âge en Orient et en Occident*, ed. by Philippe Hoffmann, Paris: Presses de l'École normale supérieure (Collection bibliologie), 153–169.

Briquel-Chatonnet, Françoise (2000), 'De l'écriture édessénienne à l'esṭrangelā et au serṭō', *Semitica*, 50, 81–90.

Briquel-Chatonnet, Françoise (2003), 'La mise en page dans les manuscrits syriaques d'après les plus anciens manuscrits', *Manuscripta Orientalia*, 9, 3–13.

Briquel-Chatonnet, Françoise (2005), 'Some Reflections about the Origin of the Serto Script', *The Harp*, 18, 173–177.

Briquel-Chatonnet, Françoise (2012), 'Trafficking of counterfeit Syriac manuscripts', paper presented at the COMSt workshop *Legal and illegal circulation of library collections*: *a study for a better conservation*, Paris.

Briquel-Chatonnet, Françoise (2013a), 'Le contexte de la diffusion de l'écriture édessénienne en Antiochène', paper read at the colloquium *Le contexte de naissance de l'écriture arabe*: *écrit et écritures araméennes et arabes au 1er millénaire après J.-C.*, Paris.

Briquel-Chatonnet, Françoise (ed.) (2013b), *Les églises en monde syriaque*, Paris: Geuthner (Études syriaques, 10).

Briquel-Chatonnet, Françoise (forthcoming), 'De l'usage du parchemin à celui du papier dans les manuscrits syriaques', in: *Manuscripta syriaca. Des sources de première main*, ed. by Françoise Briquel-Chatonnet – Muriel Debié, Paris: Geuthner.

Briquel-Chatonnet, Françoise et al. (2006) {F.B. – Alain Desreumaux – André Binggeli}, 'Un cas très ancien de garshouni? Quelques réflexions sur le manuscrit BL Add. 14644', in: *Loquentes Linguis. Studi linguistici e orientali in onore di Fabrizio A. Pennacchietti*, ed. by Pier Giorgio Borbone – Alessandro Mengozzi, Wiesbaden: Harrassowitz, 141–147.

Briquel-Chatonnet, Françoise – Muriel Debié (eds) (forthcoming), *Manuscripta syriaca. Des sources de première main*, Paris: Geuthner (Cahiers d'études syriaques, 3).

Briquel-Chatonnet, Françoise – Alain Desreumaux (2010), 'A Study and Characterization of the Syro-Malabar script', *Journal of Semitic Studies*, 55/2, 407–421.

Briquel-Chatonnet, Françoise – Alain Desreumaux (2011), 'Syriac Inscriptions in Syria', *Hugoye*, 14, 27–44.

Briquet, Charles Moïse (1907), *Les filigranes. Dictionnaire historique des marques du papier dès leur apparition vers 1282 jusqu'en 1600*, Paris: Picard – Genève: Jullien.

Brock, Sebastian P. (1965), 'An Early Armenian Palimpsest Fragment of Hebrews', *Revue des études arméniennes*, new ser. 2, 129–134.

Brock, Sebastian P. (1982), *Soghyatha Mgabbyatha*, Glane: St Ephrem the Syrian Monastery.

Brock, Sebastian P. (1983), 'Dialogue Hymns of the Syriac Churches', *Sobornost. Eastern Churches Review*, 5/1, 35–45.

Brock, Sebastian P. (1984), 'Syriac Dialogue Poems: Marginalia to a Recent Edition', *Le Muséon*, 97, 29–58.

Brock, Sebastian P. (1985a), 'Syriac and Greek Hymnography: Problems of Origin', in: *Studia Patristica XVI - Monastica et Ascetica, Orientalia, E Saeculo Secundo, Origen, Athanasius, Cappadocian Fathers, Chrysostom, Augustine*, ed. by Elizabeth A. Livingstone, Leuven: Peeters (Studia patristica, 16).

Brock, Sebastian P. (1985b), 'A Dispute of the Months and Some Related Syriac Texts', *Journal of Semitic Studies*, 30/2, 181–211.

Brock, Sebastian P. (1986), 'The Syriac Tradition', in: Cheslyn Jones – Geoffrey Wainwright – Edward Yarnold (eds.), *The Study of Spirituality*, London: SPCK, 199–215.

Brock, Sebastian P. (1987a), *Soghiatha: Syriac Dialogue Hymns*, Kottayam: St Joseph's Press (The Syrian Churches Series, 11).

Brock, Sebastian P. (1987b), 'Dramatic Dialogue Poems', in: *IV Symposium Syriacum 1984. Literary Genres in Syriac Literature (Groningen-Oosterhesselen, 10-12 September)*, ed. by Hans J.W. Drijvers – R. Lavenant, Roma: Pontificium Institutum Studiorum Orientalium (Orientalia Christiana Analecta, 229), 135–147.

Brock, Sebastian P. (1988), 'The Sinful Woman and Satan: Two Syriac Dialogue Poems', *Oriens Christianus*, 72, 21–62.

Brock, Sebastian P. (1989), 'Three Thousand Years of Aramaic Literature', *ARAM*, 1/1, 11–23.

Brock, Sebastian P. (1991a), 'Some New Syriac Documents from the Third Century AD', *ARAM*, 3/2, 259–267.

Brock, Sebastian P. (1991b), 'Syriac Dispute Poems: The Various Types', in: *Dispute Poems and Dialogues in the Ancient and Mediaeval Near East: Forms and Types of Literary Debates in Semitic and Related Literatures*, ed. by Gerrit J. Reinink – Herman L.J. Vanstiphout, Leuven: Peeters (Orientalia Lovaniensia Analecta, 42), 109–119.

Brock, Sebastian P. (1992), 'A dialogue between Joseph and Mary from the Christian Orient', *Logos: the Welsh Theological Review*, 1/3, 4–11.

Brock, Sebastian P. (1995a), *Catalogue of Syriac Fragments (New Finds) in the Library of the Monastery of Saint Catherine, Mount Sinai*, Athens: Mount Sinai Foundation.

Brock, Sebastian P. (1995b), *Isaac of Nineveh (Isaac the Syrian). 'The Second Part', chapters IV–XLI*, Louvain: Peeters (Corpus Scriptorum Christianorum Orientalium, 554, 555, Scriptores Syri, 224, 225).

Brock, Sebastian P. (1998), 'A Monastic Anthology from Twelfth-century Edessa', in: *Symposium Syriacum VII. Uppsala University, Department of Asian and African Languages 11 14 August 1996*, ed. by René Lavenant, Roma: Pontificio Istituto Orientale (Orientalia Christiana Analecta, 256), 221–231.

Brock, Sebastian P. (2001), 'The Dispute Poem: From Sumer to Syriac', *Journal of the Canadian Society for Syriac Studies*, 1, 3–10.

Brock, Sebastian P. (2004), 'Crossing the Boundaries: An Ecumenical Role Played by Syriac Monastic Literature', in: *Il monachesimo tra Eredità e Aperture. Atti del simposio «Testi e temi nella tradizione del monachesimo cristiano» per il 50° anniversario dell'Istituto monastico di Sant'Anselmo, Roma, 28 maggio - 1° giugno 2002*, ed. by Maciej Bielawski – Daniël Hombergen, Roma: Istituto monastico di Sant'Anselmo (Studia Anselmiana, 140, Analecta monastica, 8), 221–238.

Brock, Sebastian P. (2005), 'The Use of Hijra Dating in Syriac Manuscripts. A Preliminary Investigation', in: *Redefining Christian Identity: cultural interaction in the Middle East since the rise of Islam*, ed. by Jan Jacob van Ginkel – Heleen Murre-van den Berg, Leuven – Paris – Dudley: Peeters (Orientalia Lovaniensia Analecta, 134), 275–290.

Brock, Sebastian P. (2008), 'Poetry and Hymnography: Syriac', in: *The Oxford Handbook of Early Christian Studies*, ed. by Susan Ashbrook Harvey – David G. Hunter, Oxford: Oxford University Press, 657–671.

Brock, Sebastian P. (2010a), 'Les signatures en chiffres arithmétiques dans les manuscrits syriaques de la British Library', in: *Sur le pas des araméens chrétiens. Mélanges offertes à Alain Desreumaux*, ed. by Françoise Briquel-Chatonnet – Muriel Debié, Paris: Geuthner, 159–167.

Brock, Sebastian P. (2010b), *Bride of Light: Hymns on Mary from the Syriac Churches*, Piscataway, NJ: Gorgias Press.

Brock, Sebastian (2012a), 'A Tentative Check List of Syriac Dated Manuscripts up to 1300', *Hugoye*, 15/1, 21–48.

Brock, Sebastian (2012b), 'Abbot Mushe of Nisibis, Collector of Syriac Manuscripts', in: *Gli studi orientalistici in Ambrosiana nella cornice del IV centenario (1609-2009)*, ed. by Carmela Baffioni – Rosa Bianca Finazzi, Roma: Bulzoni, 15–32.

Brock, Sebastian P. et al. (1973) {S.B. – Charles T. Fritsch – Sidney Jellicoe}, *A Classified Bibliography of the Septuagint*, Leiden – Boston: Brill.

Brock, Sebastian et al. (eds) (2001) {S.B. – David G. Taylor – Ewa Balicka-Witakowska – Witold Witakowski}, *The Hidden Pearl. The Syriac Orthodox Church and its ancient Aramaic heritage*. II: *The Heirs of the Ancient Aramaic Heritage*, Roma: Trans World Film.

Brock, Sebastian et al. (eds) (2011) {S.B. – Aaron Butts – George Kiraz – Lucas Van Rompay}, *Gorgias Encyclopedic Dictionary of the Syriac Heritage*, Piscataway, NJ: Gorgias Press.

Brock, Sebastian – Lucas Van Rompay (2014), *Catalogue of the Syriac Manuscripts and Fragments in the Library of Deir al-Surian, Wadi al-Natrun*, Louvain: Peeters (Orientalia Lovaniensia Analecta, 227).

Brockelmann, Carl (1899–1902), *Geschichte der Arabischen Litteratur*, I–II, Berlin: Felber; reprint Leipzig: Amelang, 1909 (Die Litteraturen des Ostens in Einzeldarstellungen, 6/2).

Brockelmann, Carl (1937–1942), *Geschichte der Arabischen Litteratur Supplementband*, I–III, Leiden: Brill.

Brockelmann, Carl (1943–1949), *Geschichte der Arabischen Litteratur*. 2nd Edition, I–II, Leiden: Brill; new edition with a foreword by Jan-Just Witkam, Leiden: Brill, 2012.

van den Broek, Roelof (1978), 'Four Coptic Fragments of a Greek Theosophy', *Vigiliae Christianae*, 32, 118–142.

Bronk, Heike et al. (2001) {H.B. – Stefan Röhrs – Aniouar Bjeoumikhov – Norbert Langhoff – Jürgen Schmalz – Reiner Wedell – Hans-Eberhard Gorny – Alexander Herold – Ulrich Waldschläger}, 'ArtTAX®: A New Mobile Spectrometer for Energy Dispersive Micro X-Ray Fluorescence Spectrometry on Art and Archaeological Objects', *Fresenius' Journal of Analytical Chemistry*, 371, 307–316.

Brosset, Marie-Félicité (1833), 'Notice des manuscrits géorgiens envoyés en France par le prince Théimouraz, membre de la Société Asiatique', *Nouveau journal asiatique*, 12, 155–162.

Brosset, Marie-Félicité (1840), *Каталогъ книгамъ Эчмядзинской библиотеки (Katalog" knigam" Ėčmjadzinskoj biblioteki). Catalogue de la bibliothèque d'Edchmiadzin*, St Petersburg: Tipografija Imperatorskoj Akademii Nauk.

Brown, Katherine L. – Robin J.H. Clark (2004), 'The Lindisfarne Gospels and two other 8th century Anglo-Saxon/Insular manuscripts: pigment identification by Raman microscopy', *Journal of Raman Spectroscopy*, 35, 4–12.

Brown, Margaret R. et al. (1982) {M.B. – Don Etherington – Linda K. Ogden}, *Boxes for the Protection of Rare Books: their Design and Construction*, Washington, DC: Library of Congress.

Brussels Coptic Database, <http://dev.ulb.ac.be/philo/bad/copte/baseuk.php?page=accueiluk.php>, last access May 2014.

Bryant, John (2002), *The Fluid Text. A Theory of Revision and Editing for Book and Screen*, Ann Arbor, MI: University of Michigan Press.

Bryant, John (2007), 'Witness and Access: The Uses of the Fluid Text', *Textual Cultures*, 2, 16–42.

Buberl, Paul (1937), *Die byzantinischen Handschriften*. I: *Der Wiener Dioskurides und die Wiener Genesis*, Leipzig: Hiersemann (Beschreibendes Verzeichnis der Illuminierten Handschriften in Österreich, 8/4).

Buchthal, Hugo – Otto Kurz (1942), *A Hand List of Illuminated Oriental Christian Manuscripts*, London: Warburg Institute (Studies of the Warburg Institute, 12).

Bucossi, Alessandra (2014), *Andronici Camateri 'Sacrum Armamentarium'*, Turnhout: Brepols (Corpus Christianorum. Series Graeca, 75).

Budde, Achim (2004), *Die ägyptische Basilios-Anaphora. Text – Kommentar – Geschichte*, Münster: Aschendorff Verlag (Jerusalemer Theologisches Forum, 7).

Budge, Ernest Albert [Thompson] Wallis (1894), *The Discourses of Philoxenus, Bishop of Mabbôgh, A.D. 485-519*, London: Asher.

Budge, Ernest Albert [Thompson] Wallis (1904), *The Book of Paradise Being the Histories and Sayings of the Monks and Ascetics of the Egyptian Desert by Palladius, Hieronimus and Others. The Syriac Text According to the Recension of 'Anân-Îshô' of Bêth 'Âbhê*, I–II, London: Drugulin.

Budge, Ernest Albert [Thompson] Wallis (1912), *Coptic Biblical Texts in the Dialect of Upper Egypt*, London: British Museum.

Budge, Ernest Albert [Thompson] Wallis (1923), *One hundred and ten miracles of Our Lady Mary*, London: Medici Society.

Bülow, Anna E. (2010), 'Collection management using preservation risk assessment', *Journal of the Institute of Conservation*, 33/1, 65–78.

Bülow, Anna E. et al. (2002) {A.B. – Belinda J. Colston – David S. Watt}, 'Preventive conservation of paper-based collections within historic buildings', in: *Contributions to the Baltimore Congress, 2-6 September 2002: Works of Art on Paper: Books, Documents and Photographs. Techniques and Conservation*, ed. by Vincent Daniels – Alan Donnithorne, London: The International Institute for Conservation, 27–31.

Burčulaʒe, Nana (ed.) (2012), შუა საუკუნეების ქართული საეკლესიო ხელოვნება საქართველოს ეროვნულ მუზეუმში (*Šua sauḳuneebis kartuli saeḳlesio xelovneba sakartvelos erovnul muzeumši*, 'Medieval Georgian Ecclesiastical Art in The Georgian National Museum'), Tbilisi: Sakartvelos Erovnuli Muzeumi.

Burmester, Oswald H. E. (1975), *Koptische Handschriften* 1: *Die Handschriftenfragmente der Staats- und Universitätsbibliothek Hamburg*. Teil 1. *Coptic manuscript fragments from the Monastery of Abba Pisoi*, Wiesbaden: Franz Steiner (Verzeichnis der Orientalischen Handschriften in Deutschland, 21/1).

Burnett, Charles (1997), 'Translating from Arabic into Latin in the Middle Ages, Theory, Practice, and Criticism', in: *Éditer, traduire, interpréter: essais de méthodologie philosophique*, ed. by Steve G. Lofts – Philipp W. Rosemann, Louvain-la-Neuve: Éditions de l'Institut supérieur de philosophie – Louvain/Paris: Peeters (Philosophes Médiévaux, 36), 57–78.

Burnett, Charles – Danielle Jacquart (eds) (1994), *Constantine the African and ʿAlī Ibn Al-ʿAbbās Al-Majūsī: The Pantegni and Related Texts*, Leiden: Brill (Studies in Ancient Medicine, 10).

Busby, Keith (1993), 'Variance and the Politics of Textual Criticism', in: *Towards a Synthesis? Essays on the New Philology*, ed. by Keith Busby, Amsterdam: Rodopi, 29–45.

Buschhausen, Heide et al. (1976) {H.B. – Helmut Buschhausen, mit hilfe von Eva Zimmermann}, *Die Illuminierten Armenischen Handschriften der Mechitaristen-Congregation in Wien*, Wien: Mechitharisten-Buchdruckerei.

Butts, Aaron M. (2011), 'Papyri, Syriac', in: *Gorgias Encyclopedic Dictionary of the Syriac Heritage*, ed. by Sebastian Brock, Piscataway, NJ: Gorgias Press, 320–322.

Buzi, Paola (2005), *Titoli ed autori nella tradizione copta. Studio storico e tipologico*, Pisa: Giardini Editori e Stampatori (Biblioteca degli Studi di Egittologia e di Papirologia, 2).

Buzi, Paola (2009), *Catalogo dei manoscritti copti Borgiani conservati presso la Biblioteca Nazionale 'Vittorio Emanuele III' di Napoli, con un profilo scientifico di Stefano Borgia e Georg Zoega e una breve storia della formazione della collezione Borgiana*, Roma: Scienze e Lettere (Atti della Accademia Nazionale dei Lincei: Memorie, classe di scienze morali, storiche e filologiche, ser. 9^{a}, 25.1).

Buzi, Paola (2011a), 'Miscellanee e florilegi. Osservazioni preliminari per uno studio dei codici copti pluritestuali: il caso delle raccolte di excerpta', in: *Christianity in Egypt: Literary Production and Intellectual Trends. Studies in Honor of Tito Orlandi*, ed. by Paola Buzi – Alberto Camplani, Roma: Institutum Patristicum Augustinianum (Studia Ephemeridis Augustinianum, 125), 177–203.

Buzi, Paola (2011b), 'Giovanni Luigi Mingarelli e il 'primo tentennare per vie nuove'. Gli studi copti a Bologna e in Italia nella seconda metà del XVIII secolo e la nuova stagione dei caratteri tipografici copti', in: *Aegyptiaca et Coptica. Studi in onore di Sergio Pernigotti*, ed. by Paola Buzi – Daniela Picchi, Oxford: Archaeopress (BAR Series, 2264), 33–57.

Buzi, Paola – Delio Vania Proverbio (eds) (2012), *Coptic Treasures from the Vatican Library: A Selection of Coptic, Copto-Arabic and Ethiopic Manuscripts. Papers Collected on the Occasion of the Tenth International Congress of Coptic Studies (Rome, September 17th–22nd, 2012)*, Città del Vaticano: Biblioteca Apostolica Vaticana (Studi e testi, 472).

<http://www.c14dating.com/>, last access October 2013.

Čaev, Nikolaj Sergeevič – Lev Vladimirovič Čerepnin (1946), *Русская палеография* (*Russkaja paleografija*, 'Russian palaeography'), Moskva: Glavnoe archivnoe upravlenie.

Cagareli, Aleksandre [Aleksandr Antonovič] (1886), 'Каталогъ грузинскихъ рукописей и старопечатных книгъ Иверскаго монастыря на Афонѣ, составленъ въ іюнѣ мѣсяцѣ 1883 года (*Katalog" gruzinskich" rukopisej i staropečatnych" knig" Iverskago monastyrja na Afonĕ, sostavlen" v ïjunĕ mĕsjacĕ 1883 goda*, 'Catalogue of the Georgian manuscripts and ancient printed books of the Iveron Monastery on Mt. Athos, compiled in June, 1883')', in: *Свѣдѣнія о памятникахъ грузинской письменности* (*Svĕdĕnija o pamjatnikach" gruzinskoj pis'mennosti*, 'Information on monuments of Georgian antiquity'), I/1, St Petersburg, 69–96.

Cagareli, Aleksandre [Aleksandr Antonovič] (1888a), 'Каталогъ грузинскихъ рукописей монастыря св. Креста, близъ Іерусалима (*Katalog" gruzinskich" rukopisej monastyrja sv. Kresta, bliz" Ïerusalima*, 'Catalogue of the Georgian manuscripts of the Monastery of the Holy Cross near Jerusalem')', in: *Памятники грузинской старины въ святой землѣ и на Синаѣ* (*Pamjatniki gruzinskoj stariny v" Svjatoj Zemlĕ i na*

Sinaě, 'Monuments of Georgian antiquity in the Holy Land and on Mt. Sinai'), St Petersburg (Pravoslavnyj Palestinskij sbornik, IV/1 = 10), 143–192. Also in: Cagareli 1889.

Cagareli, Aleksandre [Aleksandr Antonovič] (1888b), 'Каталогъ грузинскихъ рукописей Синайскаго монастыря (*Katalog" gruzinskich" rukopisej Sinajskago monastyrja*, 'Catalogue of the Georgian manuscripts of the Sinai Monastery')', in: *Памятники грузинской старины въ святой землѣ и на Синаѣ* (*Pamjatniki gruzinskoj stariny v" Svjatoj Zemlě i na Sinaě*, 'Monuments of Georgian antiquity in the Holy Land and on Mt. Sinai'), St Petersburg (Pravoslavnyj Palestinskij sbornik, IV/1 = 10), 193–240. Also in: Cagareli 1889.

Cagareli, Aleksandre [Aleksandr Antonovič] (1889), *Свѣдѣнія о памятникахъ грузинской письменности* (*Svěděnija o pamjatnikach" gruzinskoj pis'mennosti*, 'Information on monuments of Georgian antiquity'), I/2, Sanktpeterburg: Imperatorskaja Akademija Nauk.

Cagareli, Aleksandre [Aleksandr Antonovič] (1894), *Свѣдѣнія о памятникахъ грузинской письменности* (*Svěděnija o pamjatnikach" gruzinskoj pis'mennosti*, 'Information on monuments of Georgian antiquity'), I/3, Sanktpeterburg: Imperatorskaja Akademija Nauk.

Calderini, Aristide et al. (eds) (1953) {A.C. – Antonio Maria Ceriani – Angelo Mai}, *Ilias Ambrosiana. Cod. F.205 P.Inf. Bibliothecae Ambrosianae Mediolanensis*, Olten – Lausanne: Urs Graf (Fontes Ambrosiani in lucem editi cura et studio Bibliothecae Ambrosianae, 28).

Calzolari, Valentina (2004), 'Il rapporto della versione armena del 'Martirio di Paolo' con l'originale greco: nuovi contributi sulla base di undici testimoni armeni inediti', in: *Bnagirk' yišatakac' / Documenta memoriae. Dall'Italia e dall'Armenia studi in onore di Gabriella Uluhogian*, ed. by Valentina Calzolari – Anna Sirinian – Boghos Levon Zekiyan, Bologna: Dipartimento di Paleografia e Medievistica, 23–43.

Calzolari, Valentina (2007), 'La transmission des textes apocryphes chrétiens ou de l''excès joyeux de la variance': variantes, transformations et problèmes d'édition (L'exemple du Martyre de Paul arménien)', in: *Poussières de christianisme et de judaïsme antiques. Études réunies en l'honneur de Jean-Daniel Kaestli et Éric Junod*, ed. by Albert Frey – Rémi Gounelle, Lausanne: Zèbre (Publications de l'Institut romand des sciences bibliques, 5), 129–160.

Calzolari, Valentina (2011), 'Les récits apocryphes de l'enfance dans la tradition arménienne', in: *Infancy Gospels. Stories and Identities*, ed. by Claire Clivaz – Andreas Dettwiler – Benjamin Bertho, Tübingen: Mohr Siebeck (Wissenschaftliche Untersuchungen zum Neuen Testament, I, 281), 560–587.

Calzolari, Valentina (2013), 'La version arménienne du *Martyre de Philippe* grec. Passages encratites et manuscrits inédits', *Apocrypha*, 24, 111–137.

Calzolari, Valentina (2014a), 'The Editing of Christian Apocrypha in Armenian: Should We Turn Over a New Leaf?', in: *Armenian Philology in the Modern Era: From Manuscript to Digital Text*, ed. by Valentina Calzolari, with collaboration of Michael E. Stone, Leiden: Brill (Handbook of Oriental Studies / Handbuch der Orientalistik, VIII, 23/1), 264–291.

Calzolari, Valentina (ed.) (2014b), with the collaboration of Michael E. Stone, *Armenian Philology in the Modern Era. From Manuscript to Digital Text*, Leiden: Brill (Handbook of Oriental Studies / Handbuch der Orientalistik, VIII, 23/1).

Calzolari, Valentina (forthcoming), *Apocrypha Armeniaca. Acta Pauli et Theclae – Prodigia Theclae – Martyrium Pauli*, Turnhout: Brepols (Corpus Christianorum. Series Apocryphorum).

Camplani, Alberto (1999), 'La prima lettera festale di Cirillo di Alessandria e la testimonianza di *P. Vindob.* K 10157', *Augustinianum*, 39, 129–138.

Camplani, Alberto (2003a), *Atanasio di Alessandria. Lettere festali. Anonimo. Indice delle lettere festali*, Milano: Paoline (Letture cristiane del primo millennio, 34).

Camplani, Alberto (2003b), 'Momenti di interazione religiosa ad Alessandria e la nascita dell'élite egiziana cristiana', in: *Origeniana Octava. Origen and the Alexandrian Tradition. Origene e la tradizione alessandrina. Papers of the 8th International Origen Congress. Pisa, 27-31 August 2001*, ed. by Lorenzo Perrone, Leuven: Leuven University Press (Bibliotheca Ephemeridum Theologicarum Lovaniensium, 164), 32–42.

Camplani, Alberto (2006), 'Lettere episcopali, storiografia patriarcale e letteratura canonica. A proposito del Codex Veronensis LX (58)', *Rivista di storia del cristianesimo*, 3/1, 117–164.

Camplani, Alberto (2007), 'L'*Historia ecclesiastica* en copte et l'historiographie du siège épiscopal d'Alexandrie. À propos d'un passage sur Mélitios de Lycopolis', *Actes du huitième Congrès international d'études coptes Paris, 28 juin-3 juillet 2004*, II.1, 417–424.

Camplani, Alberto (2008), 'La funzione religiosa del vescovo di Alessandria: a proposito di alcune recenti prospettive di ricerca', in: *Sacerdozio e società civile nell'Egitto antico. Atti del terzo Colloquio. Bologna - 30/31 maggio 2007*, ed. by Sergio Pernigotti – Marco Zecchi, Bologna: La Mandragora (Università di Bologna - Dipartimento di Archeologia. Archeologia e Storia della Civiltà Egiziana e del Vicino Oriente Antico - Materiali e Studi, 14), 149–165.

Camplani, Alberto (2009), 'Pietro di Alessandria tra documentazione d'archivio e agiografia popolare', in: *Volksglaube im antiken Christentum. Prof. Dr. Theofried Baumeister OFM zur Emeritierung*, ed. by Heike Grieser – Andreas Merkt, Darmstadt: Wissenschaftliche Buchgesellschaft, 138–156.

Camplani, Alberto (2011a), 'Un'antica teoria della successione patriarcale in Alessandria', in: *Aegyptiaca et Coptica. Studi in onore di Sergio Pernigotti*, ed. by Paola Buzi – Daniela Picchi, Oxford: Archaeopress (BAR Series, 2264), 59–68.

Camplani, Alberto (2011b), 'A Syriac fragment from the *Liber Historiarum* by Timothy Aelurus (CPG 5486), the *Coptic Church History*, and the Archives of the Bishopric of Alexandria', in: *Christianity in Egypt: Literary Production and Intellectual Trends in Late Antiquity. Studies in Honor of Tito Orlandi*, ed. by Paola Buzi – Alberto Camplani, Roma: Institutum Patristicum Augustinianum (Studia Ephemeridis Augustinianum, 125), 205–226.

Canart, Paul (1970), *Codices Vaticani Graeci - Codices 1745-1962*, I, Città del Vaticano: Biblioteca Apostolica Vaticana (Bibliothecae Apostolicae Vaticanae codices manu scripti recensiti).

Canart, Paul (1980), 'De la catalographie à l'histoire du livre. Vingt ans de recherches sur les manuscrits grecs', *Byzantion*, 50, 563–616.

Canart, Paul (1982), 'À propos du Vaticanus graecus 207. Le recueil scientifique d'un érudit constantinopolitain du XIIIe siècle et l'emploi du papier 'à zig-zag' dans la capitale', *Illinois Classical Studies*, 7, 271–298.

Canart, Paul (1992), 'Postilla', in: *Studi su codici e papiri filosofici: Platone, Aristotele, Ierocle*, Firenze: Olschki (Accademia Toscana di Scienze e Lettere 'La Colombaria'. Studi, 129; Studi e Testi per il 'Corpus dei Papiri Filosofici Greci e Latini', 6), 137–146.

Canart, Paul (1998), 'Quelques exemples de division du travail chez les copistes byzantins', in: *Recherches de codicologie comparée: la composition du codex au Moyen Âge en Orient et en Occident*, ed. by Philippe Hoffmann, Paris: Presses de l'École normale supérieure (Collection bibliologie), 49–67.

Canart, Paul (2005), 'L'ornamentazione nei manoscritti greci del Rinascimento: un criterio d'attribuzione da sfruttare?', *Rivista di studi bizantini e neoellenici*, n.s. 42, 203–222.

Canart, Paul (2006), 'La paléographie est-elle un art ou une science?', *Scriptorium*, 60, 159–185.

Canart, Paul (2010), 'La descrizione dei manoscritti greci: riflessioni di un catalogatore 'tradizionalista'', in: *La descrizione dei manoscritti: esperienze a confronto*, ed. by Edoardo Crisci – Marilena Maniaci, Cassino: Università degli studi di Cassino, Dipartimento di filologia e storia (Studi e ricerche del Dipartimento di Filologia e Storia, 1), 71–90.

Canfora, Luciano (1974), *Conservazione e perdita dei classici*, Padova: Antenore (Miscellanea erudita, 25).

Çanķievi, Caca – Lamara Ǯġamaia (1979), ქართულ ხელნაწერთა აღწერილობა. სინური კოლექცია (*Kartul xelnaçerta aġçeriloba. Sinuri ķolekcia*, 'Description of Georgian manuscripts. Sinai collection'), II, Tbilisi: Sakartvelos SSR Mecnierebata Aķademiis Gamomcemloba.

Cantera, Alberto (2004), *Studien zur Pahlavi-Übersetzung des Avesta*, Wiesbaden: Harrassowitz (Iranica, 7).

Cantera, Alberto (2010), 'Rituales, manuscritos y ediciones del Avesta: Hacia una nueva edición de los textos avésticos de la liturgia larga', *Boletín de la Sociedad española de Iranología*, 1, 28–42.

Cantera, Alberto (2011), 'Breve tipología e historia de los manuscritos avésticos de la liturgia larga', *Aula Orientalis*, 29, 199–238.

Cantera, Alberto (2012a), 'Building Trees: Genealogical Relations between the Manuscripts of Wīdēwdād', in: *The transmission of the Avesta*, ed. by Alberto Cantera, Wiesbaden: Harrassowitz (Iranica, 20), 279–346.

Cantera, Alberto (2012b), 'Why do we Really Need a New Edition of the Zoroastrian Long Liturgy?', in: *The transmission of the Avesta*, ed. by Alberto Cantera, Wiesbaden: Harrassowitz (Iranica, 20), 439–475.

Cantera, Alberto (2013a), 'Die Manuskriptologie der Avesta-Handschriften', in: *Handbuch der Iranistik*, ed. by Ludwig Paul, Wiesbaden: Reichert, 345–351.

Cantera, Alberto (2013b), 'Los manuscritos de Yasna con traducción pahlaví e instrucciones rituales (abāg zand ud nērang)', in: *Séptimo Centenario de los Estudios Orientales en Salamanca*, ed. by A. Agud – A. Cantera, Salamanca: Ediciones Universidad de Salamanca (Estudios filológicos, 337), 503–521.

Cantera, Alberto (forthcoming), 'On Avestan text criticism (2): the accusative singular of the ū̆- and u̯a- stems in the long liturgy', *Faventia*, 34 (= *Florilegium Indogermanicum, Palaeohispanicum et Eurasiaticum in Memoriam José Fortes Fortes*, ed. by A. Alemany, N. Olaya, M. Vernet).

Cantera, Alberto – Michiel Arnoud Cor de Vaan (2005), 'The colophon of the Avestan manuscripts Pt4 and Mf4', *Studia Iranica*, 34, 31–42.

Capon, Lester (2008), 'Extreme Bookbinding – a fascinating preservation project in Ethiopia', *Skin Deep*, 26, 2–11.

Capron, Laurent (2013), *Codex hagiographiques du Louvre sur papyrus*, Paris: PUPS (Papyrologica Parisina, 11).

Careri, Maria (1998), 'Interpunzione in codici romanzi: filologia e interpretazione', in: *Filologia classica e filologia romanza: esperienze ecdotiche a confronto. Atti del Convegno Roma 25-27 maggio 1995*, ed. by Anna Ferrari, Spoleto: Centro Italiano di Studi sull'Alto Medioevo (Incontri di Studio, 2), 367–386.

<http://www.carlroth.com>, last access December 2014.

Casamassima, Emanuele (1963), 'Note sul metodo della descrizione dei codici', *Rassegna degli Archivi di Stato*, 23, 181–205.

Casamassima, Emanuele (1988), *Tradizione corsiva e tradizione libraria nella scrittura latina del Medioevo*, Roma: Gela.

Casamassima, Emanuele – Elena Staraz (1977), 'Varianti e cambio grafico nella scrittura dei papiri latini. Note paleografiche', *Scrittura e Civiltà*, 1, 9–110.

Casiri, Miguel [Michael] (1760–1770), *Bibliotheca Arabico-Hispana Escurialensis sive Librorum omnium Mss., quos Arabice ab auctoribus magnam partem Arabo-Hispanis compositos Bibliotheca Coenobii Escurialensis complectitur*, I–II, Matriti: Antonius Perez de Soto.

Cavallo, Guglielmo (1967), *Ricerche sulla maiuscola biblica*, Firenze: Le Monnier (Studi e Testi di Papirologia editi dall'Istituto Papirologico «Girolamo Vitelli» dell'Università di Firenze, 2).

Cavallo, Guglielmo (1975), 'Grammata Alexandrina', *Jahrbuch der Österreichischen Byzantinistik*, 24, 23–54.

Cavallo, Guglielmo (ed.) (1982), *Libri e lettori nel mondo bizantino. Guida storica e critica*, Roma – Bari: Laterza (Universale Laterza, 612).

Cavallo, Guglielmo (1983), *Libri, scritture, scribi a Ercolano. Introduzione allo studio dei materiali greci*, Napoli: Gaetano Macchiaroli (Cronache Ercolanesi, Supplemento 1, 13).

Cavallo, Guglielmo (1988), 'Cultura scritta e conservazione del sapere: dalla Grecia Antica all'occidente medievale', in: *La memoria del sapere. Forme di conservazione e strutture organizzative dall'antichità ad oggi*, ed. by Pietro Rossi, Bari: Laterza (Storia e società), 29–67.

Cavallo, Guglielmo (1996), 'Iniziali, scritture distintive, fregi. Morfologie e funzioni', in: *Libri e documenti d'Italia: dai Longobardi alla rinascita delle città. Atti del Convegno nazionale dell'Associazione Italiana Paleografi e Diplomatisti (Cividale del Friuli, 5-7 ottobre 1994)*, ed. by Cesare Scalon, Udine: Arti grafiche friulane (Libri e Biblioteche, 4), 15–33.

Cavallo, Guglielmo (1999), 'Methoden der Schriftbeschreibung in der griechischen Paläographie', in: *Methoden der Schriftbeschreibung*, ed. by Peter Rück, Stuttgart: Thorbecke (Historische Hilfswissenschaften, 4), 17–20.

Cavallo, Guglielmo (2001a), 'Le rossignol et l'hirondelle. Lire et écrire à Byzance, en Occident', *Annales. Histoire Sciences Sociales*, 56, 849–861.

Cavallo, Guglielmo (2001b), 'L'immagine ritrovata. In margine ai palinsesti', *Quinio*, 3, 5–16.

Cavallo, Guglielmo (2004a), *Le biblioteche nel mondo antico e medievale*, 7. ed., Bari: Laterza (Biblioteca universale Laterza, 250).

Cavallo, Guglielmo (2004b), *Libri, editori e pubblico nel mondo antico. Guida storica e critica*, 4. ed. aggiornata, Bari: Laterza (Biblioteca universale Laterza, 297).

Cavallo, Guglielmo (2004c), 'Sodalizi eruditi e pratiche di scrittura a Bisanzio', in: *Bilan et perspectives des études médiévales (1993-1998). Euroconférence (Barcelone, 8-12 juin 1999)*, ed. by Jacqueline Hamesse, Turnhout: Brepols (Textes et études du Moyen Âge, 22), 649–669.

Cavallo, Guglielmo (2006), 'Libri in scena', in: *Proceedings of the 21st International Congress of Byzantine Studies (London, 21–26 August 2006)*, I. *Plenary Papers*, Aldershot: Ashgate, 345–364.

Cavallo, Guglielmo (2007), *Leggere a Bisanzio*, Milano: Sylvestre Bonnard.

Cavallo, Guglielmo (2012), 'Ricerche e iniziative promosse dalla Sapienza per lo studio delle scritture greche antiche e bizantine nell'ultimo trentennio', in: *La Sapienza bizantina. Un secolo di ricerche sulla civiltà di Bisanzio all'Università di Roma. Atti della Giornata di Studi. Sapienza Università di Roma, 10 ottobre 2008*, ed. by Augusta Acconcia Longo – Guglielmo Cavallo, Roma: Campisano, 285–293.

Cavallo, Guglielmo et al. (eds) (1991) {G.C. – Giuseppe De Gregorio – Marilena Maniaci}, *Scritture, libri e testi nelle aree provinciali di Bisanzio. Atti del seminario di Erice (TP) (18-25 settembre 1988)*, Spoleto: Centro italiano di studi sull'alto medioevo (Biblioteca del 'Centro per il Collegamento degli Studi Medievali e Umanistici nell'Università di Perugia', 5).

Cavallo, Guglielmo – Herwig Maehler (1987), *Greek Bookhands of the Early Byzantine Period: A.D. 300-800*, London: Institute of Classical Studies (Bulletin Supplement – Institute of Classical Studies, 47).

Cavallo, Guglielmo – Herwig Maehler (2008), *Hellenistic Bookhands*, Berlin – New York: De Gruyter.

CCI (Canadian Conservation Institute) (2002), *How to Care for Books*, <http://www.cci-icc.gc.ca/caringfor-prendresoindes/articles/419-eng.aspx>, Ottawa: CCI.

CCI (Canadian Conservation Institute) (2009), *Ten Agents of Deterioration*, <http://www.cci-icc.gc.ca/caringfor-prendresoindes/articles/10agents/index-eng.aspx>, Ottawa: CCI.

Cecchelli, Carlo – Giuseppe Furlani (1959), *Evangelarii syriaci, vulgo rabbulae, in bibliotheca medicea-laurentiana (Plut. I, 56) adservati ornamenta edenda notisque instruenda = The Rabbula Gospels: facsimile edition of the miniatures of the Syriac manuscript Plut. I, 56 in the Medicaean-Laurentian Library*, Olten – Lausanne: Urs Graf.

Celsi, Mino (1572), *Artis chemicae principes, Avicenna atque Geber, hoc volumine continentur. Quorum alter nunquam hactenus in lucem prodiit: alter vero vetustis exemplaribus collatus, atque elegantioribus et pluribus figuris quam antehac illustratus, doctrinæ huius professoribus, hac nostra editione tum iucundior, tum vtilior euasit. Adiecto Indice rerum et verborum copioso*, Basileae: Per Petrum Pernam.

Ceraʒe [Ceradze], Tinatin (forthcoming), *Каталог грузинских рукописей Института Востоковедения Российской Академии Наук*, выпуск III: *Рукописи духовного содержания* (*Katalog gruzinskich rukopisej Instituta Vostokovedenija Rossijskoj Akademii Nauk.* III: *Rukopisi duchovnogo soderžanija*, 'Catalogue of the Georgian Manuscripts of the Oriental Institute of the Russian Academy of Sciences. III. Manuscripts of Spiritual Content'), Moskva: Vostočnaja Literatura.

Ceraʒe, Tinatin – Lela Xoperia (2009), 'პეტერბურგის აღმოსავლეთმცოდნეობის ინსტიტუტის ქართულ ხელნაწერთა კოლექცია: ისტორია და ახალი მიგნებები (*Peṭerburgis aġmosavletmcodneobis insṭiṭuṭis kartul xelnaçerta ḳolekcia: isṭoria da mignebebi*, 'Collection of the Georgian manuscripts of the Oriental Institute in St Petersburg: history and new finds')', *Inṭelekṭi*, 1 (33), 281–284.

Çereteli, Giorgi [Cereteli, Georgij Vasil'evič; Tseretheli, George] (1941), არმაზის ბილინგვა. მცხეთა-არმაზის არქეოლოგიური გათხრების დროს აღმოჩენილი ორენოვანი წარწერა / *Армазская билингва. Двуязычная надпись, найденная при археологических раскопках в Мцхета-Армази* (Armazis bilingva. Mcxeta-Armazis arkeologiuri gatxrebis dros aġmočenili orenovani çarçera / *Armazskaja bilingva. Dvujazyčnaja nadpis', najdennaja pri archeologičeskich raskopkach v Mcxeta-Armazi*) / *A Bilingual Inscription from Armazi near Mthskheta in Georgia*, Tbilisi: Sakartvelos SSR Mecnierebata Aḳademiis Gamomcemloba.

Çereteli, Giorgi [Cereteli, Georgij Vasil'evič; Tseretheli, George] (1960), უძველესი ქართული წარწერები პალესტინიდან / *Древнейшие грузинские надписи из Палестины* (*Uʒvelesi kartuli çarçerebi ṗalesṭinidan / Drevnejšie gruzinskie nadpisi iz Palestiny*) / *The Most Ancient Georgian Inscriptions from Palestine*, Tbilisi: Sakartvelos SSR Mecnierebata Aḳademiis Gamomcemloba.

Cereti, Carlo G. (2008), 'On the Pahlavi cursive script and the Sasanian Avesta', *Studia Iranica*, 37, 175–195.

Cerquiglini, Bernard (1989), *Éloge de la variante. Histoire critique de la philologie*, Paris: Seuil.

Cerquiglini, Bernard (1999), *In Praise of the Variant: A Critical History of Philology*, translated by B. Wing, Baltimore, ML: Johns Hopkins University Press.

Cerulli, Enrico (1943), *Il libro etiopico dei Miracoli di Maria e le sue fonti nelle letterature del Medio Evo latino*, Roma: Dott. Giovanni Bardi Editore (Studi orientali pubblicati a cura della Scuola Orientale, 1).

Cerulli, Enrico (1965), 'I manoscritti etiopici della Chester Beatty Library in Dublino', *Atti della Accademia Nazionale dei Lincei, Classe di Scienze morali, storiche e filologiche: Memorie*, serie 8, volume 11, fascicolo 6, 277–324.

Cerulli, Enrico (2004), *Inventario dei manoscritti Cerulli Etiopici*, ed. by Osvaldo Raineri, Città del Vaticano: Biblioteca Apostolica Vaticana (Studi e Testi, 420).

Chabot, Jean-Baptiste (1899, 1901, 1905, 1910), *Chronique de Michel de Syrien, patriarche jacobite d'Antioche (1166–1199)*, I–IV, Paris: Ernest Leroux; Supplement to volume I, Paris: Ernest Leroux, 1924.

Chabot, Jean-Baptiste (1954), *Anonymi auctoris Chronicon ad annum Christi 1234 pertinens*, Louvain: Peeters (Corpus scriptorum Christianorum Orientalium, 82, Scriptores Syri 37).

Chaîne, Marius (1912), *Catalogue des manuscrits éthiopiens de la collection Antoine d'Abbadie*, Paris: Imprimerie nationale.

Chaldaiaki, Achilleos (2004), *Τα χειρόγραφα βυζαντινής μουσικής – Νησιωτική Ελλάδα*, I, Athens: Ἵδρυμα Βυζαντινης Μουσικολογίας.

Checkley-Scott, Caroline (2008), 'The Syriac Book', in: *Contributions to the Symposium on the Care and Conservation of Middle Eastern Manuscripts*, Melbourne: Centre for Cultural Materials Conservation, 49–54.

Chernetsov, Sevir (2007), 'Magic Scrolls', in: *Encyclopaedia Aethiopica*, III: He-N, ed. by Siegbert Uhlig, Wiesbaden: Harrassowitz, 642–643.

Chabot, Jean-Baptiste (1920), *Chronicon ad A.C. 1234 pertinens*, I. *Praemissum est Chronicon anonymum ad A.D. 819 pertinens curante Aphram Barsaum*, Parisiis: E Typographeo republicae – Louvain: Peeters (Corpus Scriptorum Christianorum Orientalium, 81, Scriptores Syri, 36).

Chaplin, Tracey D. et al. (2006) {T.C. – Robin J. H. Clark – Alison McKay – Sabina Pugh}, 'Raman spectroscopic analysis of selected astronomical and cartographic folios from the early 13th century Islamic *Book of Curiosities of the Sciences and Marvels for the Eyes*', *Journal of Raman Spectroscopy*, 37/8, 865–877.

Chiesa, Bruno (1992), 'Textual History and Textual Criticism of the Hebrew Old Testament', in: *The Madrid Qumran Congress: Proceedings of the International Congress on the Dead Sea Scrolls, Madrid 18-21 March, 1991*, ed. by Luis Trebolle Barrera, Julio Vegas Montaner, Leiden: Brill (Accademia Nazionale dei Lincei. Atti dei Convegni lincei, 151), 257–272.

Chiesa, Bruno (2000–2002), *Filologia storica della Bibbia ebraica*, I–II, Brescia: Paideia.

Chraïbi, Aboubakr (1996), *Contes nouveaux des 1001 Nuits: étude du manuscrit Reinhardt*, Paris: Jean Maisonneuve Successeur.

Christens-Barry, William A. et al. (2011) {W.C. – Ken Boydston – Roger L. Easton}, 'Some Properties of Textual Heritage Materials of Importance in Spectral Imaging Projects', in: *EIKONOPOIIA. Digital Imaging of Ancient Textual Heritage. Proceedings of the international conference Helsinki, 28–29 November*, ed. by Vesa Vahtikari, Helsinki: Ekenäs (Commentationes Humanarum Litterarum, 129), 35–50.

Ciasca, Agostino – Giuseppe Balestri (1885–1904), *Sacrorum Bibliorum fragmenta copto-sahidica Musei Borgiani, iussu et sumptibus S. Congregationis de Propaganda Fide*, I–III, Roma: typis eiusdem S. Congregationis.

Çiçek, Julius (1985), ܡܪܬܝܢܘܬܐ ܕܐܒܗܬܐ ܕܥܕܬܐ (*Martyānūtā d-abāhātā d-ʿe(d)tā*, 'Admonition of the Church Fathers'), Glane/Losser: Bar-Hebraeus Verlag.

Čikobava, Arnold (1927–1930), სავარჯიშო ქართულ პალეოგრაფიაში (*Savarǯišo kartul ṗaleograpiaši*, 'Exercises in Georgian Palaeography'), I–II, Tbilisi: Saxelmçipo P̣edagogiuri Insṭiṭuṭi.

Čiḳvašvili, C. (1964), კ. მარქსის სახელობის საქართველოს სსრ სახელმწიფო რესპუბლიკის ბიბლიოთეკაში დაცული ხელნაწერებისა და საარქივო მასალების კატალოგი (*Ḳ. Marksis saxelobis Sakartvelos SSR saxelmçipo resṗubliḳur biblioteḳaši daculi xelnaçerebisa da saarkivo masalebis ḳaṭalogi* 'Catalogue of the manuscript and archive materials kept in the K. Marx State Republic Library of Georgia'), Tbilisi: Sakartvelos SSR Mecnierebata Aḳademiis Gamomcemloba.

Cisḳarišvili, V. (1954), 'წარწერები ასპინძის რაიონიდან (*Çarçerebi asṗinʒis raionidan*, 'Inscriptions from the district of Asṗinʒa')', *Masalebi Sakartvelosa da Ḳavḳasiis isṭoriidan*, 30, 167–180.

Ciucu, Cristina (2014), *Bibliothèque nationale de France. Hébreu 763 à 777. Manuscrits de Kabbale*, Turnhout: Brepols (Manuscrits en caractères hébreux conservés dans les bibliothèques de France. Catalogues, 6).

Clackson, James (2000), 'A Greek Papyrus in Armenian Script', *Zeitschrift für Papyrologie und Epigraphik*, 129, 223–258.

Clark, Robin – Peter Gibbs (1998), 'Raman Microscopy of a 13th-century Illuminated Text: a Study of a Rare Manuscript Demonstrates a Promising Technique for the Non-destructive, *in situ* Analysis of Historical Artifacts', *Analytical Chemistry*, 70/3, 99A–104A.

Clemens, Raymond – Timothy Graham (2007), *Introduction to Manuscript Studies*, Ithaca – London: Cornell University Press.

Cleminson, Ralph et al. (2007) {R.C. – Elissaveta Moussakova – Nina Voutova}, *Catalogue of the Slavonic Cyrillic Manuscripts of the National Széchényi Library*, Budapest: Central European University Press (CEU Medievalia, 9).

Coakley, James F. (1993), 'A Catalogue of the Syriac Manuscripts in the John Rylands Library', *Bulletin of the John Rylands Library*, 78/2, 105–257.

Coakley, James F. (2011), 'When were the five Greek vowel signs introduced into Syriac writing?', *Journal of Semitic Studies*, 56/2, 307–325.

Cockerell, Douglas (1932), 'The Development of Bookbinding Methods – Coptic Influence', *The Library*, ser. 4, 13/1, 1–19, pls. 1–6.

Cody, Aelred (1991), 'Calendar, Coptic', in: *The Coptic Encyclopedia*, II, ed. by Aziz S. Atiya, New York: Macmillan, 433–436.

Colini, Claudia (2008), 'Carte di manoscritti islamici', in: *Libri islamici in controluce: ricerche, modelli, esperienze conservative*, ed. by Valentina Sagaria Rossi, Roma: Università degli studi di Roma 'Tor Vergata', 73–117.

Colini, Claudia (2011), *Un unicum arabo dallo Yemen. Dialogo tra conservazione, restauro e archeologia*, Roma: Università degli studi di Roma 'Tor Vergata' [Master diss.].

Coll, Emma – Isabelle de Conihout (eds) (2003), *Reliures médiévales et premières reliures à décor doré. 22 reliures choisies dans les collections de la Bibliothèque Mazarine* (*catalogue d'exposition*), Paris: CNRS-IRHT.

Colless, Brian (1966), 'A Pot-Pourri of Eastern Mysticism: Mingana Syriac Ms: no. 86', *Milla wa-Milla. The Australian Bulletin of Comparative Religion*, 6, 34–43.

Compagnon, Antoine (1998), *Le démon de la théorie. Littérature et sens commun*, Paris: Seuil.

Compagnon, Antoine (2000), 'Un monde sans auteurs?', in: *Où va le livre?*, ed. by Jean-Yves Mollier, Paris: La Dispute, 229–246.

Condello, Emma – Giuseppe De Gregorio (eds) (1995), *Scribi e colofoni. Le sottoscrizioni di copisti dalle origini all'avvento della stampa. Atti del seminario di Erice, X Colloquio del Comité international de paléographie latine* (*23-28 ottobre 1993*), Spoleto: Centro Italiano di Studi sull'Alto Medioevo (Biblioteca del «Centro per il collegamento degli studi medievali e umanistici in Umbria», 14).

Conti Rossini, Carlo (1901), 'L'evangelo d'oro di Dabra Libānos', *Rendiconti della Reale Accademia dei Lincei, Classe di scienze morali, storiche e filologiche*, ser. 5a, 10, 177–219.

Conti Rossini, Carlo (1914), *Notice sur les manuscrits éthiopiens de la Collection d'Abbadie*, Paris: Imprimerie nationale.

Contini, Gianfranco (1986), *Breviario di ecdotica*, Milano – Napoli: Riccardo Ricciardi.

Contini, Gianfranco (1992), *Breviario di ecdotica*, Second edition, Torino: Einaudi.

Conybeare, Frederick Cornwallis (1913), *A Catalogue of the Armenian Manuscripts in the British Museum*, London: British Museum.

Coquin, René-Georges (1991), 'Tutūn', in: *The Coptic Encyclopedia*, VII, ed. by Aziz S. Atiya, New York: Macmillan, 2283.

Coquin, René-Georges (2001), 'Le traité de Šenoute 'Du salut de l'âme humaine'', *Journal of Coptic Studies*, 3, 1–43, pls. 1–2.

Corpus dei Manoscritti Copti Letterari, <http://cmcl.aai.uni-hamburg.de/>, last access October 2014.

Corpus der arabischen und syrischen Gnomologien, <http://casg.orientphil.uni-halle.de/?lang=en>, last access May 2014.

Coulie, Bernard (1992), *Répertoire des bibliothèques et des catalogues de manuscrits arméniens*, Turnhout: Brepols (Corpus Christianorum).

Coulie, Bernard (1995), 'Répertoire des bibliothèques et des catalogues de manuscrits arméniens. Supplément I', *Le Muséon*, 108/1-2, 115–130.

Coulie, Bernard (2000a), 'Répertoire des bibliothèques et des catalogues de manuscrits arméniens. Supplément II', *Le Muséon*, 113/1-2, 149–176.

Coulie, Bernard (2000b), *Studia Nazianzenica*, Turnhout: Brepols (Corpus Christianorum. Series Graeca, 41; Corpus Nazianzenum, 8).

Coulie, Bernard (2004), 'Répertoire des bibliothèques et des catalogues de manuscrits arméniens. Supplément III', *Le Muséon*, 117/3-4, 473–496.

Coulie, Bernard (2014), 'Collections and catalogues of Armenian manuscripts', in: *Armenian Philology in the Modern Era: From Manuscript to Digital Text*, ed. by Valentina Calzolari, with collaboration of Michael E. Stone, Leiden: Brill (Handbook of Oriental Studies / Handbuch der Orientalistik, VIII, 23/1), 23–64.

Coupry, Claude (2004), 'Analyse de pigments de deux manuscrits coptes', in: *Pages chrétiennes d'Égypte, les manuscrits des Coptes*, ed. by Anne Boud'hors, Paris: Bibliothèque nationale de France, 28–29.

Coupry, Claude (2007), 'Approche analytique du décor de deux manuscrits coptes', in: *Actes du huitième Congrès international d'études coptes Paris, 28 juin-3 juillet 2004*, II.1, ed. by Nathalie Bosson – Anne Boud'hors, Leuven etc.: Peeters – Departement Oosterse Studies (Orientalia Lovaniensia Analecta, 163.1), 199–208.

Č'rak'ean, Kerovbē (1904), Անկանոն գիրք Առաքելական (*Ankanon girk' aṙak'elakank'*, 'Non-canonical Books of the Apostles'), Venetik: S. Łazar (T'angaran haykakan hin ew nor dprut'eanc', 3).

Cramer, Maria (1964a), *Koptische Buchmalerei. Illumination in Manuskripten des christlich-koptischen Ägypten von 4. bis 19. Jahrhundert*, Recklinghausen: Aurel Bongers (Beiträge zur Kunst des christlichen Ostens, 2).

Cramer, Maria (1964b), *Koptische Paläographie*, Wiesbaden: Harrassowitz.

Cramer, Maria (1964c), 'Illuminationen aus koptischen und koptisch-arabischen Tetraevangelien als Typen koptischer Buchmalerei', *Oriens Christianus*, 48, 77–83, with 12 pls. between pp. 82 and 83.

Čremošnik, Gregor (1959), 'Die serbische diplomatische Minuskel', in: *Studien zur älteren Geschichte Osteuropas*. II: *Festgabe zur 50-Jahr-Feier Instituts für Osteuropäische Geschichte und Südostforschung der Universität Wien*, ed. by Heinrich Felix Schmid, Graz – Cologne: Böhlau (Wiener Archiv für Geschichte des Slawentums und Osteuropas, 3), 103–115.

Čremošnik, Gregor (1963), 'Srpska diplomatska minuskula ('Serbian Diplomatic Minuscule')', *Slovo*, 13, 119–136.

Crisci, Edoardo (1990), *I palinsesti di Grottaferrata. Studio codicologico e paleografico*, I–II, Napoli: ESI (Pubblicazioni dell'Università degli studi di Cassino. Sezione di studi filologici, letterari, storici, artistici e geografici, 2).

Crisci, Edoardo (2008), 'Riflessioni paleografiche (e non solo) sui più antichi manoscritti greci del Nuovo Testamento', in: *Oltre la scrittura. Variazioni sul tema per Guglielmo Cavallo*, ed. by Daniele Bianconi – Lucio Del Corso, Paris: École des Hautes Études en Sciences Sociales – Centre d'Études Byzantines, Néo-Helléniques et Sud-Est Européennes (Dossiers byzantins, 8), 53–93.

Crisci, Edoardo (2012), 'Esperienze grafiche sinaitico-palestinesi (secoli VIII–IX). Qualche riflessione', in: *Sit liber gratus, quem servulus est operatus. Studi in onore di Alessandro Pratesi per il suo 90° compleanno*, I, ed. by Paolo Cherubini – Giovanna Nicolaj, Città del Vaticano: Scuola Vaticana di Paleografia, Diplomatica e Archivistica (Littera antiqua, 19), 43–63.

Crisci, Edoardo et al. (2007) {E.C. – Christoph Eggenberger – Robert Fuchs – Doris Oltrogge}, 'Il Salterio Purpureo Zentralbibliothek Zürich, RP 1', *Segno e testo*, 5, 31–98.

Crisci, Edoardo – Paola Degni (eds) (2011), *La scrittura greca dall'antichità all'epoca della stampa. Una introduzione*, Roma: Carocci (Beni culturali, 35).

Crisci, Edoardo – Marilena Maniaci (eds) (2010), *La descrizione dei manoscritti*: *esperienze a confronto*, Cassino: Università degli studi di Cassino, Dipartimento di filologia e storia (Studi e ricerche del Dipartimento di Filologia e Storia, 1).

Crisci, Edoardo – Oronzo Pecere (eds) (2004), *Il codice miscellaneo, tipologia e funzioni. Atti del convegno internazionale* (*Cassino, 14-17 maggio 2003*), Cassino: Università degli studi di Cassino (Segno e testo, 2).

Cronier, Marie (2006), 'Quelques aspects de l'histoire du texte du *De materia medica* de Dioscoride: forme originelle, remaniements et révisions à Constantinople aux Xe-XIe siècles', in: *Ecdotica e ricezione dei testi medici greci. Atti del V Convegno Internazionale, Napoli 1–2 ottobre 2004*, ed. by Véronique Boudon-Millot – Antonio Garzya – Amneris Roselli – Jacques Jouanna, Napoli: M. D'Auria (Collectanea, 24), 43–65.

Cronier, Marie (2012), 'Un manuscrit méconnu du *De materia medica* de Dioscoride: New York, Pierpont Morgan Library, M. 652', *Revue des études grecques*, 125, 95–130.

Cronier, Marie – Brigitte Mondrain (forthcoming), 'Georges Chrysococcès, copiste et éditeur de textes médicaux au XIVe siècle. L'exemple de Dioscoride', in: *Atti del VII Colloquio internazionale sull'ecdotica dei testi medici greci* (*Procida, 11-13 giugno 2013*), ed. by Amneris Roselli, Napoli: M. D'Auria.

Cross, Maureen – Kathleen Flynn (2003), 'From sausage rolls to sushi and back again: Lessons for successful travelling block-buster loans', *The Paper Conservator*, 27, 59–68.

Crown, Alan D. (1998), *A Catalogue of the Samaritan manuscripts in the British Library*, London: The British Library.

Crum, Walter Ewing (1893), *Coptic Manuscripts Brought from the Fayyum by W.M. Flinder Petrie ... Together with a Papyrus in the Bodleian Library*, London: David Nutt.

Crum, Walter Ewing (1905a), 'A Coptic Recipe for the Preparation of Parchment', *Proceedings of the Society of Biblical Archaeology*, 27, 166–171.

Crum, Walter Ewing (1905b), *Catalogue of the Coptic Manuscripts in the British Museum*, London: The British Museum.

Crum, Walter Ewing (1909), *Catalogue of the Coptic Manuscripts in the Collection of the John Rylands Library*, Manchester: Manchester University Press.

Crum, Walter Ewing (1926), 'Writing Materials', in: *The Monastery of Epiphanius at Thebes*, I, ed. by H.E. Winlock – Walter E. Crum, New York: Metropolitan Museum of Art (Publications of the Metropolitan Museum of Art Egyptian Expedition, 3), 186–195.

Crum, Walter Ewing et al. (1922) {W.C. – Harold Idris Bell – R. Campbell Thompson}, *Wadi Sarga. Coptic and Greek Texts from the Excavations Undertaken by the Byzantine Research Account*, Copenhagen: Gyldendal (Coptica, 3).

Čubinašvili, Niḳo [Čubinov, N.] (1894), 'Описанiе Крестнаго монастыря, близъ Iерусалима, и нѣкоторыхъ Грузинскихъ рукописей, хранищихся въ немъ, сдѣланное Н. Чубиновымъ съ 3-4 по конецъ мая 1845 г. (*Opisanïe Krestnago monastyrja, bliz" Ïerusalima, i někotorych" Gruzinskich" rukopisej, chraniščichsja v" nem", sdělannoe N. Čubinovym" s" 3-4 po konec" maja 1845 g.*, 'Description of the Monastery of the Holy Cross near Jerusalem, and of some Georgian manuscripts preserved in it, provided by N. Čubinov in May, 1845')', in: Cagareli 1894, 44–52.

Cureton, William (1846), *Catalogus codicum manuscriptorum orientalium qui in Museo Britannico asservantur.* Pars secunda codices Arabicos amplectens, London: The British Museum.

Cutler, Anthony (1981), 'The Social Status of Byzantine Scribes, 800-1500. A Statistical Analysis based on Vogel-Gardthausen', *Byzantinische Zeitschrift*, 74, 328–332.

Daccache, Jimmy – Alain Desreumaux (forthcoming), 'Les textes des recettes d'encre en syriaque et en garshouni', in: *Manuscripta syriaca. Des sources de première main*, ed. by Françoise Briquel-Chatonnet – Muriel Debié, Paris: Geuthner.

Dahlström, Mats (2010), 'Critical Editing and Critical Digitisation', in: *Text Comparison and Digital Creativity. The Production of Presence and Meaning in Digital Text Scholarship*, ed. by Wido Th. van Peursen – Ernst D. Thoutenhoofd, Leiden: Brill (Scholarly Communication, 1), 79–97.

Dain, Alphonse (1949), *Les manuscrits*, Paris: Les Belles-Lettres (Collection d'Études Anciennes).

Dain, Alphonse (1975), *Les manuscrits.* 3e éd. revue et augmentée d'un index, Paris: Les Belles-Lettres.

D'Aiuto, Francesco (2003), 'Graeca in codici orientali della Biblioteca Vaticana (con i resti di un manoscritto tardoantico delle commedie di Menandro)', in: *Tra Oriente e Occidente*: *scritture e libri greci fra le regioni orientali di Bisanzio e l'Italia*, ed. by Lidia Perria, Roma: Dipartimento di filologia greca e latina, Sezione bizantino-neoellenica (Testi e studi bizantino-neoellenici, 14), 227–296.

Dammann, Ernst (1993), *Afrikanische Handschriften.* I: *Handschriften in Swahili und anderen Sprachen Afrikas*, Stuttgart: Steiner (Verzeichnis der orientalischen Handschriften in Deutschland, 24/1).

Danelia, Ḳorneli (2009), 'ქართული ანბანის განვითარების საფეხურები (*Kartuli anbanis ganvitarebis sapexurebi*, 'Stages of the development of the Georgian alphabet')', in: ქართული ენა და ლიტერატურა (*Kartuli ena da liṭeraṭura*, 'Georgian language and literature'), I, Tbilisi, 38–40.

Danelia, Ḳorneli – Zurab Sarǯvelaʒe (1997), ქართული პალეოგრაფია (*Kartuli ṗaleograpia*, 'Georgian Palaeography'), Tbilisi: Neḳeri.

Daskalova, Angelina – Marija Rajkova (2005), *Грамоти на българските царе* (*Gramoti na bălgarskite care*, 'Charters of the Bulgarian Tsars'), Sofia: Marin Drinov.

Davidsson, Carin (1975a), 'Собрание славянских рукописей в Библиотеке Университета в Уппсале (*Sobranie slavjanskich rukopisej v Biblioteke Universiteta v Uppsale*, 'The Collection of Slavonic Manuscripts in Uppsala University Library')', *Slavica Lundensia*, 3r, 57–85.

Davidsson, Carin (1975b), 'Den slaviska handskriftssamlingen i Uppsala universitetsbibliotek', *Slavica Lundensia*, 3, 53–82.

Davis, Edward – Jill Norgren (1969), *Preliminary Index of Shah-nameh Illustrations*, Ann Arbor, MI.

De Beul, Geertje et al. (1965) {G.B. – Jan L. Scharpé – Frans Vyncke}, 'Slovo blaženago Avramia', *Orientalia Gandensia*, 2, 315–349.

De Groote, Marc (2012), *Christophori Mitylenaii 'Versuum variorum collectio cryptensis'*, Turnhout: Brepols (Corpus Christianorum. Series Graeca, 74).

De Moncy, Birgit (1995), 'Les causes de dégradation des documents', <http://1.static.e-corpus.org/download/ notice_file/178244/b-les_causes_de_dadations.pdf>, *Conservation préventive du patrimoine documentaire. Archives-livres-photographies-arts graphiques*, fiche 1.

De Robertis, Teresa et al. (2007) {T.D.R. – Nicoletta Giovè Marchioli – Rosanna Miriello – Marco Palma – Stefano Zamponi}, *Norme per i collaboratori dei manoscritti datati d'Italia.* Seconda edizione rivista ed ampliata, Firenze: Cleup.

De Rossi, Giovanni Bernardo (1803–1804), *Manuscripti codices Hebraici bibliothecae J.B. De-Rossi, accurate ab eodem descripti et illustrati: accedit appendix quâ continentur manuscripti codices reliqui aliarum linguarum*, I–III, Parma: Ex publico typographeo.

De Tapol, Benoît (2000), 'L'impact des publications scientifiques et de vulgarisation sur les comportements en conservation préventive dans les archives et les bibliothèques', in: *La climatologie dans les archives et les bibliothèques: actes des troisièmes Journées sur la conservation préventive, 2-3 décembre, 1998*, Arles: Centre de Conservation du Livre, 13–24.

De Vos, Ilse et al. (2010) {I.D.V. – Erika Gielen – Caroline Macé – Peter Van Deun}, 'La lettre β du Florilège Coislin: édition princeps', *Byzantion*, 80, 72–120.

Dearing, Vinton A. (1968), 'Abaco-Textual Criticism', *The Papers of the Bibliographical Society of America*, 62/4, 547–578.

Deckers, Daniel – Leif Glaser (2011), 'Imaging Palimpsest Manuscripts Using High-Flux Micro X-ray Fluorescence', in: *EIKONOPOIIA. Digital Imaging of Ancient Textual Heritage. Proceedings of the international conference Helsinki, 28-29 November, 2010*, ed. by Vesa Vahtikari – Mika Hakkarainen – Antti Nurminen, Helsinki: Societas scientiarum Fennica (Commentationes Humanarum Litterarums, 129), 161–171.

Deckers, Daniel – Jana Grusková (2010), 'Zum Einsatz verschiedener digitaler Verfahren in der Palimpsestforschung', in: *The Legacy of Bernard de Montfaucon: Three Hundred Years of Studies on Greek Handwriting. Proceedings of the Seventh International Colloquium of Greek Palaeography (Madrid – Salamanca, 15–20 September 2008)*, I, ed. by Antonio Bravo García – Inmaculada Pérez Martín, Turnhout: Brepols (Bibliologia: Elementa ad Librorum Studia Pertinentia, 31A), 353–362.

Declich, Lorenzo (2006), *The Arabic Manuscripts of the Zanzibar National Archives: a Checklist*, Pisa – Roma: Istituti Editoriali e Poligrafici Internazionali (Rivista degli Studi Orientali, n.s. 78, suppl. 2).

Dédéyan, Gérard (1998), 'Les colophons de manuscrits arméniens comme sources pour l'histoire des Croisades', in: *The Crusades and Their Sources: Essays Presented to Bernard Hamilton*, ed. by John France – William Zajac, Brookfield, VT: Ashgate, 89–110.

Degni, Paola (2008), 'I manoscritti dello 'scriptorium' di Gioannicio', *Segno e Testo*, 6, 179–248.

Del Barco, Francisco Javier (2003–2006), *Catálogo de Manuscritos Hebreos de la Comunidad de Madrid*, I–III, Madrid: Consejo Superior de Investigaciones Científicas, Instituto de Filología.

Del Barco, [Francisco] Javier (2011), *Bibliothèque nationale de France. Hébreu 1 à 32. Manuscrits de la Bible hébraïque*, Turnhout: Brepols (Manuscrits en caractères hébreux conservés dans les bibliothèques de France. Catalogues, 4).

Delamarter, Steven – Demeke Berhane (2007), *A Catalogue of Previously Uncatalogued Ethiopic Manuscripts in England. Twenty-three Manuscripts in the Bodleian, Cambridge University and John Rylands University Libraries and in a Private Collection*, Oxford: Oxford University Press (Journal of Semitic Studies Supplement, 21).

Delange, Élisabeth et al. (1990) {É.D. – M. Grange – Bruce Kusko – Eve Menei}, 'Apparition de l'encre métallogallique en Égypte à partir de la collection de papyrus du Louvre', *Revue de l'Égyptologie*, 41, 213–217.

Delaporte, Louis Joseph (1909, 1910, 1911, 1912, 1913), 'Catalogue sommaire des manuscrits coptes de la bibliothèque Nationale', *Revue de l'Orient Chrétien*, 14, 417–423; 15, 85–96, 133–156, 392–397; 16, 85–99, 155–160, 239–248, 368–395; 17, 390–394; 18, 84–91.

Delatte, Armand (1926), *Les manuscrits à miniatures et à ornements des Bibliothèques d'Athènes*, Liége: Imp. H. Vaillant-Carmanne – Paris: É. Champion (Bibliothèque de la Faculté de Philosophie et Lettres de l'Université de Liège, 34).

Delatte, Armand et al. (1938) {A.D. – Albert Severyns – Joseph Bidez – Anders Bjorn Drachmann}, *Emploi des signes critiques, disposition de l'apparat dans les éditions savantes des textes grecs et latins. Conseils et recommandations*, Bruxelles: Union académique internationale. Secrétariat administratif; Les Belles Lettres.

Delattre, Alain (2007), *Papyrus coptes et grecs du monastère d'apa Apollô de Baouît conservés aux Musées Royaux d'Art et d'Histoire de Bruxelles*, Bruxelles: Académie royale de Belgique (Mémoires de la Classe des Lettres et des Sciences morales et politiques de l'Académie royale de Belgique. Collection in-8°.).

Delavault, Bernard et al. (2010) {B.D. – Pierre Petitmengin – Françoise Briquel-Chatonnet}, 'Épigraphie sémitique', in: *Guide de l'épigraphiste: Bibliographie choisie des épigraphies antiques et médiévales*, ed. by François Bérard – Denis Feissel, Paris: Éditions ENS, 306–321.

Deleva, Antoaneta (1997), 'Кънигы – произход и значение на думата (*K"nigy - proizhod i značenie na dumata*, 'Kn"igy – the origin and meaning of the word')', *Preslavska knižovna škola*, 2, 31–40.

den Heijer, Johannes (2012a), 'On Language and Religious Identity: the Case of Middle Arabic, with Special Reference to the Christian Arab Communities in the medieval Middle East', in: *High vs. Low and Mixed Varieties - Domains, Status, and Functions across Time and Languages*, ed. by Gunvor Mejdell – Lutz Edzard, Wiesbaden: Harrassowitz (Abhandlungen für die Kunde des Morgenlandes, 77), 53–87.

den Heijer, Johannes (2012b), 'Introduction: Middle and Mixed Arabic, a New Trend in Arabic Studies', in: *Middle Arabic and Mixed Arabic: Diachrony and Synchrony*, ed. by Liesbeth Zack – Arie Schippers, Leiden – Boston: Brill (Studies in Semitic Languages and Linguistics, 64), 1–25.

den Heijer, Johannes et al. (eds) (2014) {J.d.H. – Andrea Schmidt – Tamara Pataridze}, *Scripts Beyond Borders. A Survey of Allographic Traditions in the Euro-Mediterranean World*, Louvain: Peeters (Publications de l'Institut Orientaliste de Louvain, 62).

den Heijer, Johannes – Andrea Schmidt (2014), 'Scripts Beyond Borders: Allographic Traditions and their Social, Cultural and Philological Aspects. An Analytical Introduction', in: *Scripts Beyond Borders. A Survey of Allographic Traditions in the Euro-Mediterranean World*, ed. by Johannes den Heijer – Andrea Schmidt – Tamara Pataridze, Louvain: Peeters (Publications de l'Institut Orientaliste de Louvain, 62), 1–63.

Dendrinos, Charalambos (2011), 'Palaiologan scholars at work: Makarios Makres and Joseph Bryennios' autograph', in: *From Manuscripts to Books. Proceedings of the International Workshop on Textual Criticism and Editorial Practice for Byzantine Texts (Vienna 10-11 December 2009)*, ed. by Antonia Giannouli – Elisabeth Schiffer, Wien: Verlag der Österreichischen Akademie der Wissenschaften (Denkschriften der philosophisch-historischen Klasse, 431, Veröffentlichungen zur Byzanzforschung, 29), 25–54.

Denker, Andrea et al. (eds) (2006) {A.D. – Annemie Adriaens – Mark Dowsett – Alessandra Giumlia-Mair}, *COST Action G8: Non-destructive Testing and Analysis of Museum Objects*, Stuttgart: Fraunhofer IRB Verlag.

Depuydt, Leo (1993), *Catalogue of Coptic Manuscripts in the Pierpont Morgan Library*, I–II, Leuven: Peeters (Corpus of Illuminated Manuscripts, 4-5; Oriental series, 1-2).

Der Nersessian, Sirarpie (1936–1937), *Manuscrits arméniens illustrès des XIIe, XIIIe et XIVe siècles de la Bibliothèque des Pères Mekhitaristes de Venise*, I–II, Venice: S. Lazar.

Der Nersessian, Sirarpie (1958), *The Chester Beatty Library, A Catalogue of the Armenian Manuscripts*, I–II, Dublin: Hodges Figgis & Co.

Der Nersessian, Sirarpie (1964), 'La peinture arménienne au VIIe siècle et les miniatures de l'Évangile d'Etchmiadzin', in: *Actes du XIIe Congrès international des études byzantines*, III, Belgrade, 49–57.

Der Nersessian, Sirarpie (1973a), *Études byzantines et arméniennes*, I–II, Lisbon: Calouste Gulbenkian Foundation.

Der Nersessian, Sirarpie (1973b), *Armenian Manuscripts in the Walters Art Gallery*, Baltimore.

Der Nersessian, Sirarpie (1993), *Miniature Painting in the Armenian Kingdom of Cilicia from the Twelfth to the Fourteenth Century*, I–II, Washington, D.C.: Dumbarton Oaks.

Derat, Marie Laure (2005), 'Les homélies du roi Zar'a Ya'eqob: la communication d'un souverain éthiopien du XVe siècle', in: *L'écriture publique du pouvoir*, ed. by Alain Bresson, Anne-Marie Cocula, Christophe Pebarthe, Bordeaux: Ausonius, 45–57.

Derat, Marie-Laure (2010), 'Les donations du roi Lālibalā. Éléments pour une géographie du royaume chrétien d'Éthiopie au tournant du XIIe et du XIIIe siècle', *Annales d'Éthiopie*, 25, 19–42.

Dergham, Youssef – François Vinourd (forthcoming), 'Les reliures syriaques: essai de caractérisation par comparaison avec les reliures byzantines et arméniennes', in: *Manuscripta syriaca. Des sources de première main*, ed. by Françoise Briquel-Chatonnet – Muriel Debié, Paris: Geuthner.

Déroche, François (1980), 'Les écritures coraniques anciennes. Bilan et perspectives', *Revue des études islamiques*, 48, 207–224.

Déroche, François (1983, 1985), *Catalogue des manuscrits arabes.* 2ème partie. I: *Les manuscrits du Coran.* 1. *Aux origines de la calligraphie coranique*, 2. *Du Maghreb à l'Insulinde*, Paris: Bibliothèque nationale de France.

Déroche, François (ed.) (1989), *Les Manuscrits du Moyen-Orient. Essais de codicologie et de paléographie. Actes du Colloque d'Istanbul (Istanbul, 26–29 mai 1986)*, Istanbul: I.F.E.A – Paris: Bibliothèque nationale (Varia turcica, 8).

Déroche, François (1992), *The Abbasid tradition. Qur'ans of the 8th to the 10th centuries AD*, London: The Nour Foundation in association with Azimuth Editions and Oxford University Press (The Nasser D. Khalili collection of Islamic art, 1).

Déroche, François (ed.) (1993–2000), *Nouvelles des manuscrits du Moyen-Orient*, <http://www.manumo.org/>

Déroche, François (1998), 'Les études de paléographie des écritures livresques arabes: quelques observations', *Al-Qanṭara*, 19, 365–381.

Déroche, François (1999), 'Un critère de datation des écritures coraniques anciennes. Le kāf final ou isolé', *Damaszener Mitteilungen*, 11, 87–94, pl. XV– XVI.

Déroche, François (2003), 'Analyser l'écriture arabe. Remarques sur la 'cursivité'', *Manuscripta Orientalia*, 9/3, 4–7.

Déroche, François (2005), *Le livre manuscrit arabe: préludes à une histoire*, Paris: Bibliothèque nationale de France.

Déroche, François (2006), *Islamic codicology. An introduction to the study of manuscripts in Arabic script*, ed. by Muhammad Isa Waley, London: Al-Furqān.

Déroche, François (2007), 'La biblioteca medievale della moschea grande di Kairouan', in: *Le mille e una cultura. Scrittura e libri fra Oriente e Occidente*, ed. by Maria Cristina Misiti, Bari: Edipuglia (Il futuro del passato, 2), 141–151.

Déroche, François (2009), *La transmission écrite du Coran dans les débuts de l'islam*, Leiden – Boston: Brill (Texts and Studies on the Qur'ān, 5).

Déroche, François (2012), 'Contrôler l'écriture. Sur quelques caractéristiques de manuscrits coraniques omeyyades', in: Le Coran: Nouvelles Approches, ed. by Mehdi Azaiez – Sabrina Mervin, Paris: CNRS Editions, 39–56.

Déroche, François (forthcoming), 'Of volumes and skins. II. The Qur'anic manuscripts of al-Mahdi', in: *In Memoriam Professor Iraj Afshar*, London: Al-Furqān.

Déroche, François et al. (2000) {F.D., with contribution of Annie Berthier – Marie-Geneviève Guesdon – Bernard Guineau}, *Manuel de codicologie des manuscrits en écriture arabe*, Paris: Bibliothèque nationale de France.

Déroche, François – Sergio Noja Noseda (eds) (1998), *Les manuscrits de style ḥiǧāzī*, I: *Le manuscrit arabe 328 (a) de la Bibliothèque nationale de France*, Lesa (Novara): Fondazione Ferni Noja Noseda (Sources de la transmission manuscrite du texte coranique, 1, Projet Amari, 1).

Déroche, François – Francis Richard (eds) (1997), *Scribes et manuscrits du Moyen-Orient*, Paris: Bibliothèque nationale de France.

Déroche, François – Francis Richard (1998), 'Du parchemin au papier: Remarques sur quelques manuscrits du Proche-Orient', in: *Recherches de codicologie comparée: la composition du codex au Moyen Âge en Orient et en Occident*, ed. by Philippe Hoffmann, Paris: Presses de l'École normale supérieure (Collection bibliologie), 192–197.

Déroche, François – Valentina Sagaria Rossi (2012), *I manoscritti in caratteri arabi*, Roma: Viella (Scritture e libri del Medioevo, 9).

Derolez, Albert (1974a), 'Les nouvelles instructions pour le catalogue des manuscrits en République Fédérale allemande', *Scriptorium*, 28, 299–300.

Derolez, Albert (1974b), 'Quelques problèmes méthodologiques posés par les manuscrits autographes: le cas du Liber Floridus de Lambert de Saint-Omer', in: *La paléographie hébraïque médiévale*, ed. by Jean Glénisson – Colette Sirat, Paris (Colloques internationaux du Centre national de la recherche scientifique, 547), 29–36.

Derolez, Albert (1979), *Les Catalogues de bibliothèques*, Turnhout: Brepols (Typologie des sources du Moyen âge occidental, 31).

Derolez, Albert (1984), *Codicologie des manuscrits en écriture humanistique sur parchemin*, Turnhout: Brepols (Bibliologia: Elementa ad Librorum Studia Pertinentia, 5-6).

Derolez, Albert (1988), 'Catalogues codicologiques', *Gazette du livre médiéval*, 12, 4–6.

Desreumaux, Alain (1979), *Les matériaux du syro-palestinien. Pour une étude théorique des documents d'un dialecte. Thesis*, Paris: Paris X–Nanterre [diss.].

Desreumaux, Alain (1983a), 'Les manuscrits syro-palestiniens: propositions pour des comparaisons', *Orientalia christiana periodica*, 221, 341–347.

Desreumaux, Alain (1983b), 'Les recherches à Khirbet es-Samra (Jordanie) et la question du syro-palestinien', *Comptes rendus de l'Académie des inscriptions et belles-lettres*, avril-juin, 316–329.

Desreumaux, Alain [as A. Jacques] (1987a), 'A Palestinian-Syriac Inscription in the Mosaic Pavement at 'Evron', *Eretz-Israel*: *Archaeological, Historical and Geographical Studies*, 19 (Michael Avi-Yonah Memorial Volume), 54–56.

Desreumaux, Alain (1987b), 'La naissance d'une nouvelle écriture araméenne à l'époque byzantine', *Semitica*, 37, 95–107.

Desreumaux, Alain (1989a), 'Les araméens melkites. Vie et mort d'une communauté chrétienne à l'époque byzantine. Quelques réflexions à propos d'un programme de recherche', *Canal-infos*, 6, 9–32.

Desreumaux, Alain (1989b), 'The Birth of a New Aramaic Script in Bilad al-Sham at the End of the Byzantine Period', in: *The Fourth International Conference on the History of Bilād al-Shām during the Umayyad Period. Proceedings of the third Symposium 2-7 Rabīʿ 1408 A.H./24-29 October 1987*, ed. by Muhammad Adnan al-Bakhit – Robert Schick, Amman – Damascus: History of Bilād al-Shām Committee, 26–36.

Desreumaux, Alain (1990–1991), 'Populations araméennes chrétiennes du Proche-Orient à l'époque byzantine: textes et vestiges archéologiques', *Annuaire de l'EPHE*, 99, 297–300.

Desreumaux, Alain (1991), with Françoise Briquel Chatonnet, *Répertoire des bibliothèques et des catalogues de manuscrits syriaques*, Paris: Éditions du Centre national de la recherche scientifique (Documents, études et répertoires).

Desreumaux, Alain (1992), 'Identification du texte araméen', in: *La peinture copte* (*Musée du Louvre. Département des Antiquités Égyptiennes*), ed. by Marie-Hélène Rutschowscaya, Paris: Réunion des Musées nationaux, 60–62.

Desreumaux, Alain (1996a), 'Une inscription araméenne melkite sous une peinture copte du Musée du Louvre. Le texte araméen melkite', *Oriens Christianus*, 80, 82–97.

Desreumaux, Alain (1996b), 'Les lectionnaires syro-palestiniens', in: *La lecture liturgique des Épîtres catholiques dans l'Église ancienne*, ed. by Christian Amphoux – J.-P. Bouhot, Lausanne: Éditions du Zèbre (Histoire du texte biblique, 1), 87–103.

Desreumaux, Alain (1998a), *Codex sinaiticus Zosimi rescriptus. Description codicologique des feuillets araméens melkites des manuscrits Schøyen 35, 36 et 37* (*Londres – Oslo*) *comprenant l'édition de nouveaux passages des Évangiles et des Catéchèses de Cyrille*, Lausanne: Éditions du Zébre (Histoire du texte biblique, 3).

Desreumaux, Alain (1998b), 'Saint Ephraim in Christian Palestinian Aramaic', *Hugoye*, 1/2 (= Andrew Palmer [ed.], *St Ephraim the Syrian* I), 221–226.

Desreumaux, Alain (1998c), 'Introduction à l'histoire des documents araméens melkites: l'invention du christo-palestinien', in: *Khirbet es-Samra* (*Jordanie*). I. *La voie romaine, le cimetière, les documents épigraphiques*, ed. by Jean-Baptiste Humbert – Alain Desreumaux, Turnhout (Bibliothèque de l'Antiquité tardive, 1), 3–18.

Desreumaux, Alain (1998d), 'L'onomastique des stèles de Samra et les populations de Haditha à l'époque byzantin', in: *Khirbet es-Samra* (*Jordanie*). I. *La voie romaine, le cimetière, les documents épigraphiques*, ed. by Jean-Baptiste Humbert – Alain Desreumaux, Turnhout: Brepols (Bibliothèque de l'Antiquité tardive, 1), 547–554.

Desreumaux, Alain (1999), 'Marc en araméen christo-palestinien', *Mélanges de science religieuse*, juillet-septembre, 73–84.

Desreumaux, Alain (1999 [2001]), 'Les œuvres de la littérature apocryphe chrétienne en araméen christo-palestinien', *Bulletin de l'AELAC*, 9, 9–14.

Desreumaux, Alain (2002), 'Les types de texte de la version araméenne de l'Évangile selon Marc', in: *The New Testament Text in Early Christianity. Proceedings of the Lille colloquium, July 2000 / Le texte du Nouveau Testament au début du christianisme. Actes du colloque de Lille, juillet 2000*, ed. by Christian Amphoux, Lausanne: Éditions du Zèbre (Histoire du texte biblique, 1), 201–214.

Desreumaux, Alain (2004), 'La paléographie des manuscrits syriaques et araméens melkites: le rôle d'Antioche', *Topoi*, Suppl. 5, 555–571.

Desreumaux, Alain (2008), 'Les manuscrits christo-palestiniens M11N/B; SP41N; SP42N; M52N/C; M56N/3; SP1N à SP9N', in: *Nouveaux manuscrits syriaques du Sinaï*, ed. by Philothée du Sinai, Athens: Mount Sinai Foundation, 300–305; 440–447; 449–463; 520; 533–537; 635–643.

Desreumaux, Alain (2009), 'L'apport des palimpsestes araméens christo-palestiniens: le cas du Codex sinaiticus Zosimi rescriptus et du Codex Climaci rescriptus', in: *Palimpsestes et éditions de textes*: *les textes littéraires. Actes du colloque tenu à Louvain-la-Neuve* (*septembre 2003*), ed. by Véronique Somers, Louvain: Université catholique de Louvain, Institut orientaliste (Publications de l'Institut Orientaliste de Louvain, 56), 201–211.

Desreumaux, Alain (forthcoming), 'Des couleurs et des encres dans les manuscrits syriaques', in: *Manuscripta syriaca. Des sources de première main*, ed. by Françoise Briquel-Chatonnet – Muriel Debié, Paris: Geuthner.

Desreumaux, Alain – Maria Gorea (2003), 'Rouleau magique chrétien syriaque', in: *Manuscrits chrétiens du Proche-Orient*, Arles: Centre de Conservation du Livre, 16–17.

Desreumaux, Alain – Francis Schmidt (1989), 'Notes sur le rapport 'Langues et littératures orientales (hébreu et syriaque)'', in: *Rapports à l'Empereur sur le progrès des sciences, des lettres et des arts depuis 1789*. IV: *Histoire et littérature ancienne par Bon-Joseph Dacier*, ed. by F. Hartog, Paris – Berlin: Librairie du bicentenaire de la Révolution française, 293–297.

Deutsche Forschungsgemeinschaft, Unterausschuß für Handschriftenkatalogisierung (1973), *Richtlinien Handschriftenkatalogisierung*, Bonn: DFG.

Deutsche Forschungsgemeinschaft, Unterausschuß für Handschriftenkatalogisierung (1992), *Richtlinien Handschriftenkatalogisierung*. 5. erw. Auflage, Bonn: DFG.

Devreesse, Robert (1954), *Introduction à l'étude des manuscrits grecs*, Paris: Klincksieck.

Di Bella, Marco (2002a), 'La Bibliotheca Alexandrina', *Cabnewsletter*, 3–6, 12–15.

Di Bella, Marco (2002b), 'Note sulla legatura islamica', *Cabnewsletter*, 3–6, 16–17.

Di Bella, Marco (2011), 'An Attempt at a Reconstruction of Early Islamic Bookbinding: The Box Binding', in: *Care and Conservation of Manuscripts 12. Proceedings of the Twelfth international seminar held at the University of Copenhagen 14th-16th October 2009*, ed. by Matthew James Driscoll, Copenhagen: Museum Tusculanum Press, 99–115.

Di Bella, Marco – Nicolas Sarris (2014), 'Field Conservation in East Tigray, Ethiopia', in: *Care and Conservation of Manuscripts 14. Proceedings of the fourteenth international seminar held at the University of Copenhagen 17th-19th October 2012*, ed. by Matthew James Driscoll, Copenhagen: Museum Tusculanum Press, 271–307.

Di Donato, Silvia (2011), *Bibliothèque nationale de France. Hébreu 214 à 259. Commentaires bibliques*, Turnhout: Brepols (Manuscrits en caractères hébreux conservés dans les bibliothèques de France. Catalogues, 3).

Diallo, Thierno et al. (1966) {T.D. – Mame Bara M'Backé – Mirjana Trifkovic – Boubacar Barry}, *Catalogue des manuscrits de l' I.F.A.N.*, Dakar: Institut Fondamental d'Afrique Noire.

Diebner, Bernd Jørg – Rodolphe Kasser (1989), *Hamburg Papyrus Bil. 1. Die alttestamentlischen Texte des Papyrus Bilinguis 1 der Staats- und Universitätbibliothek Hamburg. Canticum Canticorum (coptice), Lamentationes Ieremiae (coptice), Ecclesiastes (graece et coptice)*, Genève: Cramer (Cahiers d'Orientalisme, 18).

Diehl, Charles (1905), *Études byzantines: introduction à l'histoire de Byzance; les études d'histoire byzantine en 1905; la civilisation byzantine; l'empire grec sous les Paléologues; les mosaïques de Nicée, Saint-Luc, Kahrié-Djami, etc*, Paris: Alphonse Picard et fils, éditeurs.

Digitale Sammlungen, <http://www.digitale-sammlungen.de/>, last access October 2014.

Dillmann, [Christian Friedrich] August (1847), *Catalogus codicum manuscriptorum orientalium qui in Museo Britannico asservantur*, Pars tertia: *Codices Aethiopicos amplectens*, London: British Museum.

Dillmann, [Christian Friedrich] August (1848), *Catalogus codicum manuscriptorum Bibliothecae Bodleianae Oxoniensis*, Pars VII: *Codices Aethiopici*, Oxford: E Typographeo Academico.

Dillmann, [Christian Friedrich] August (1857), *Grammatik der äthiopischen Sprache*, Leipzig: T.O. Weigel.

Dillmann, [Christian Friedrich] August (1865), *Lexicon linguae aethiopicae*, Lipsiae: T.O. Weigel.

Dillmann, [Christian Friedrich] August (1878), *Verzeichnis der abessinischen Handschriften*, Berlin: Buchdruckerei der Königlichen Akademie der Wissenschaften (G. Vogt) (Die Handschriften-Verzeichnisse der Königlichen Bibliothek zu Berlin).

Dillmann, [Christian Friedrich] August (1899), *Grammatik der äthiopischen Sprache*, zweite verbesserte und vermehrte Auflage, ed. by Carl Bezold, Leipzig: Tauchnitz.

Dillmann, [Christian Friedrich] August (1907), *Ethiopic Grammar*, Second Edition, enlarged and improved, translated by James A. Crichton, ed. by Carl Bezold, London: Williams & Norgate.

Doborǯiniʒe, Nino (2011), ლინგვისტურ-ჰერმენევტიკული მეტატექსტები. პრაქტიკული გრამატიკა და ჰერმენევტიკა *X–XIII* საუკუნეების ქართულ წყაროებში (*Lingvisṭur-hermenevṭiḳuli meṭaṭeksṭebi. Ṗrakṭiḳuli gramaṭiḳa da hermenevṭiḳa X–XIII sauḳuneebis kartul c̣q̇aroebši*, 'Linguistic and Hermeneutic Metatexts. Practical Grammar and Hermeneutics in Georgian Sources of the 10th-13th Centuries'), Tbilisi: Ilias Saxelmc̣ipo Universiṭeṭi.

Dobronravin, Nikolay (2006), 'Gumilev's Manuscript Collections (Harar and Jimma)', in: *Proceedings of the XVth International Conference of Ethiopian Studies. Hamburg July 20–25, 2003*, ed. by Siegbert Uhlig et al., Wiesbaden: Harrassowitz (Aethiopistische Forschungen, 65), 569–571.

Doerfer, Gerhard (1993), *Versuch einer linguistischen Datierung älterer osttürkischer Texte*, Wiesbaden: Harrassowitz (Turcologica, 14).

Dogniez, Cécile (1995), *Bibliography of the Septuagint. Bibliographie de la Septante (1970–1993)*, Leiden – Boston: Brill (Supplements to Vetus Testamentum, 60).

Dolabani, Filoksinos Yuhanna (1994a), *Catalogue of Syriac Manuscripts in St Mark's Monastery (Dairo dmor Marqos)*, Damascus: Mardin (Syriac Patrimony, 8), reprint, with an introduction by Gregorios Ibrahim, Piscataway, NJ: Gorgias Press, 2009 (Dar Mardin: Christian Arabic and Syriac Studies from the Middle East, 26).

Dolabani, Filoksinos Yuhanna (1994b), *Catalogue of Syriac Manuscripts in Za'faran Monastery (Dairo dmor Ḥananyo)*, Damascus: Mardin (Syriac Patrimony, 9), reprint, with an introduction by Gregorios Ibrahim, Piscataway, NJ: Gorgias Press, 2009 (Dar Mardin: Christian Arabic and Syriac Studies from the Middle East, 27).

Dolabani, Filoksinos Yuhanna (1994c), *Catalogue of Syriac Manuscripts in Syrian Churches and Monasteries (Dairotho w'idotho suryoyotho)*, Damascus: Mardin (Syriac Patrimony, 10), reprint, with an introduction by Gregorios Ibrahim, Piscataway, NJ: Gorgias Press, 2010 (Dar Mardin: Christian Arabic and Syriac Studies from the Middle East, 28).

Dolabani, Filoksinos Yuhanna et al. (1994) {Y.D. – René Lavenant – Sebastian Brock}, 'Catalogue des manuscrits de la bibliothèque du Patriarcat syrien Orthodoxe à Ḥomṣ (aujourd'hui à Damas)', *Parole de l'Orient*, 19, 555–661.

Dolbeau, François (2012), *Prophètes, apôtres et disciples dans les traditions chrétiennes d'Occident. Vies brèves et listes en latin*, Bruxelles: Société des Bollandistes (Subsidia Hagiographica, 92).

Дом живоначальной Троицы. Славянские рукописи (*Dom živonačal'noj Troicy. Slavjanskie rukopisi*, 'The house of life-giving Trinity. Slavonic manuscripts'), <http://www.stsl.ru/manuscripts/index.php>, last access May 2014.

Dorandi, Tiziano (2007), review of D. Searby, *The Corpus Parisinum. A Critical Edition of the Greek Text with Commentary and English Translation. A Medieval Anthology of Greek Texts from the Pre-Socratics to the Church Fathers, 600 B.C. - 700 A.D.*, I–II, Lewiston, NY: Edwin Mellen Press, 2007, *Elenchos*, 28, 482–486.

Đorđić, Petar (1971), *Историја српске ћирилице* (*Istorija srpske ćirilice*, 'History of Serbian Cyrillic Alphabet'), Beograd: Zavod za izdavanje udžbenika SR Srbije.

Dorfmann-Lazarev, Igor (2010), 'La transmission de l'apocryphe de l'Enfance de Jésus en Arménie', in: *Jesus in apokryphen Evangelienüberlieferungen: Beiträge zu ausserkanonischen Jesusüberlieferungen aus verschiedenen Sprach- und Kulturtraditionen*, ed. by Jörg Frey – Jens Schröter, Tübingen: Mohr Siebeck (Wissenschaftliche Untersuchungen zum Neuen Testament, 254), 557–582.

Dorival, Gilles et al. (1988) {G.D. – Marguerite Harl – Olivier Munnich}, *La Bible grecque des Septante*, Paris: Cerf.

D'Ottone, Arianna (2006), *I manoscritti arabi dello Yemen: una ricerca codicologica*, Roma: Università degli Studi di Roma 'La Sapienza' – Facoltà di Studi Orientali (La Sapienza Orientale. Ricerche).

D'Ottone, Arianna (2007), 'Some Remarks on Yemeni Medieval Bookbindings', in: *Arabica 2007*, ed. by Angelo Arioli, Roma: Università degli Studi di Roma 'La Sapienza', Facoltà di Studi Orientali (La Sapienza Orientale. Miscellanee), 49–66.

D'Ottone, Arianna (2013), '*Al-ḫaṭṭ al-maġribī* et le fragment bilingue latin-arabe Vat.lat. 12900. Quelques observations', in: *Les écritures des manuscrits de l'Occident musulman. Journée d'études tenue à Rabat le 29 novembre 2012*, ed. by Mustapha Jaouhari, Rabat: Centre Jacques Berque (Les Rencontres du Centre Jacques Berque, 5), 7–18.

D'Ottone, Arianna (2014), 'Un'altra lezione negata. Paleografia araba e altre paleografie', *Rivista degli Studi Orientali*, 87, 213–221.

Doufikar-Aerts, Faustina (2010), *Alexander Magnus Arabicus. A Survey of the Alexander Tradition through Seven Centuries. From Pseudo-Calisthenes to Ṣūrī*, Leuven: Peeters (Mediaevalia Groningana, n.s., 13).

Dournovo, Lydia (1953), *Армянская набойка* (*Armjanskaja nabojka*, 'Armenian tooling'), Moskva: Izobrazitel'noe iskusstvo.

Draguet, René (1973), *Commentaire anonyme du Livre d'abba Isaïe*, Louvain: Peeters (Corpus Scriptorum Christianorum Orientalium, 336, 337, Scriptores Syri, 150, 151).

Draguet, René (1977), 'Une méthode d'édition des textes syriaques', in: *A Tribute to Arthur Vööbus. Studies in Early Christian Literature and its Environment, Primarily in the Syrian East*, ed. by Robert H. Fischer, Chicago: The Lutheran School of Theology, 13–18.

Drampian, Irina (2004), *Lectionary of King Hetum II* (*Armenian Illustrated Codex of 1286 A.D.*), Erevan: Nairi.

Dreibholz, Ursula (1991), 'Der Fund von Sanaa. Frühislamische Handschriften auf Pergament', in: *Pergament, Geschichte – Struktur – Restaurierung – Herstellung*, ed. by Peter Rück, Sigmaringen: J. Thorbecke (Historische Hilfswissenschaften, 2), 299–313.

Drijvers, Han J.W. – John Healey (1999), *The Old Syriac Inscriptions of Edessa and Osrhoene. Texts, Translations and Commentary*, Leiden: Brill (Handbuch der Orientalistik, I, 42).

Driscoll, Matthew J. (2010), 'The Words on the Page: Thoughts on Philology, Old and New', in: *Creating the Medieval Saga: Versions, Variability, and Editorial Interpretations of Old Norse Saga Literature*, ed. by Judy Quinn – Emily Lethbridge, Odense: University Press of Southern Denmark, 87–104.

Du Bourguet, Pierre (1985), 'Signes de ponctuation dans un manuscrit de l'œuvre de Chenoute', in: *Acts of the Second International Congress of Coptic Studies*, ed. by Tito Orlandi – Friedrich Wisse, Roma: CIM, 13–26.

Du Feu, V.M. – John Simon Gabriel Simmons (1970), 'Early Russian Abecedaria in Oxford and London', *Oxford Slavonic Papers*, n.s. 3, 119–133.

Duan Qing (2000), '敦煌新 出土叙利亚文文书释读报告' (*Dunhuang xin chutu Xuliyawen wenshu shidu baogao*, 'Report about the new Syriac manuscript discovered at Dunhuang'), in: 敦煌莫高窟北区石窟 (*Dunhuang Mogaoku beiqu shiku*, 'Northern Grottoes of Mogaoku, Dunhuang'), ed. by Peng Jinzhang – Wang Jianjun, I, Beijing: Wenwu chubanshe, 382–389.

Duan Qing (2001), 'Bericht über ein neuentdecktes syrisches Dokument aus Dunhuang/Cina', *Oriens Christianus*, 85, 84–93.

Dubuisson, Marc – Caroline Macé (2003), 'L'apport des traductions anciennes à l'histoire du texte de Grégoire de Nazianze. Application au Discours 2', *Orientalia Christiana Periodica*, 69, 287–340.

Dubuisson, Marc – Caroline Macé (2006), 'Handling a large manuscript tradition with a computer', translated by Caroline Macé, in: *The evolution of texts: confronting stemmatological and genetical methods. Proceedings of the International Workshop held in Louvain-la-Neuve (Septembre 1-2, 2004)*, ed. by Philippe Baret – Andrea Bozzi, Pisa – Roma: Istituti Editoriali e Poligrafici Internazionali (Linguistica computazionale, 24-25), 25–37.

Duda, Dorothea (1983), *Islamische Handschriften* I: *Persische Handschriften*, Wien: Verlag der Österreichischen Akademie der Wissenschaften (Denkschriften der philosophisch-historischen Klasse, 167; Veröffentlichungen der Kommission für Schrift- und Buchwesen, Reihe 1, Die illuminierten Handschriften und Inkunabeln der österreichischen Nationalbibliothek, 4/1–2).

Duda, Dorothea (1992), *Islamische Handschriften* II. Teil 1: *Die Handschriften in arabischer Sprache*, Wien: Verlag der Österreichischen Akademie der Wissenschaften (Denkschriften der philosophisch-historischen Klasse, 229; Veröffentlichungen der Kommission für Schrift- und Buchwesen, Reihe 1, Die illuminierten Handschriften und Inkunabeln der österreichischen Nationalbibliothek, 5/1).

Duda, Dorothea (2008), *Islamische Handschriften* II. Teil 2: *Die handschriften in türkischer Sprache*, Wien: Verlag der Österreichischen Akademie der Wissenschaften (Denkschriften der philosophisch-historischen Klasse, 229; Veröffentlichungen der Kommission für Schrift- und Buchwesen, Reihe 1, Die illuminierten Handschriften und Inkunabeln der österreichischen Nationalbibliothek, 5/2).

Dukan, Michèle (1988), *La réglure des manuscrits hébreux au Moyen Âge*, I-II, Paris: Éditions du Centre national de la recherche scientifique.

Dukan, Michèle (2006), *La Bible hébraïque. Les codices copiés en Orient et dans la zone séfarade avant 1280*, Turnhout: Brepols – Paris: Institut de recherche et d'histoire des textes (Bibliologia: Elementa ad Librorum Studia Pertinentia, 22).

Dukan, Michèle (2008), *Bibliothèque de l'Alliance Israélite Universelle. Fragments bibliques en hébreu provenant de guenizot*, Turnhout: Brepols (Manuscrits en caractères hébreux conservés dans les bibliothèques de France. Catalogues, 2).

Dummer, Jürgen (ed.) (1987), *Texte und Textkritik. Eine Aufsatzsammlung*, Berlin: Akademie-Verlag (Texte und Untersuchungen zur Geschichte der altkirchlichen Literatur, 133).

Durand, Jannic (2007), 'Reliure d'un livre des Évangiles', in: *Armenia sacra. Mémoire chrétienne des Arméniens (IVe-XVIIIe siècle)*, ed. by Jannic Durand – Dorota Giovannoni, Paris: Somogy, Éditions d'art, 266–267.

Durand, Jannic – Zepyur Tarayan (2007), 'Évangile de Grégoire de Tatev et sa reliure', in: *Armenia sacra. Mémoire chrétienne des Arméniens (IVe-XVIIIe siècle)*, ed. by Jannic Durand – Dorota Giovannoni, Paris: Somogy, Éditions d'art, 338–339.

Durkin-Meisterernst, Desmond (2004), 'The Parthian mwqr'nyg b'š'ẖ (Turfan Collection, Berlin, M4a I V 3-16)', *ARAM*, 16, 95–107.

Dutton, Yasin (2004), 'Some Notes on the British Library's 'Oldest Qur'an Manuscript' (Or. 2165)', *Journal of Qur'anic Studies*, 6/1, 43–71.

Duval, Rubens (1881), *Traité de grammaire syriaque*, Paris: F. Vieweg.

Džurova, Aksinia (1997), *Въведение в славянската кодикология: византийският кодекс и рецепцията му сред славяните* (*Văvedenie v slavjanskata kodikologija. Vizantijskijat kodeks i recepcijata mu sred slavjanite*, 'Introduction into Slavonic Codicology. The Byzantine codex and its reception among the Slavs'), Sofia: CIBAL (Studia Slavico-Byzantina et Mediaevalia Europensia).

Džurova, Aksinia [Axinia] (2006), *Répertoire des manuscrits grecs enluminés IXe-Xe s. Centre de recherches slavo-byzantines «Ivan Dujčev». Université de Sofia «St Clément d'Ohrid»*, I, Sofia: Universitecko izdatelstvo 'Sv. Kliment Ohridski'.

Džurova, Aksinia [Axinia] (2008), 'La décoration des manuscrits grecs et slaves (IXe–XIe siècles)', *Scripta. An International Journal of Codicology and Palaeography*, 1, 45–59.

e-codices, <http://www.e-codices.unifr.ch>, last access October 2014.

e-corpus, <http://www.e-corpus.org>, last access October 2014.

e-ktobe: manuscrits syriaques, <http://mss-syriaques.org>, last access May 2014.

EAE = Siegbert Uhlig (I–IV) – Alessandro Bausi (IV–V) (eds) (2003, 2005, 2007, 2010, 2014), *Encyclopaedia Aethiopica*, I: *A-C*; II: *D-Ha*; III: *He-N*; IV: *O-X*; V: *Y-Z. Addenda. Corrigenda. Maps. Index*, Wiesbaden: Harrassowitz.

EAP466: The manuscripts of the Riyadh Mosque of Lamu, Kenya, <http://eap.bl.uk/database/overview_project.a4d? projID=EAP466;r=13064>, 2012.

ECCO (European Confederation of Conservator-Restorers' Organisations) (2002), *Professional guidelines*, <http://www.ecco-eu.org/about-e.c.c.o./professional-guidelines.html>, Brussels.

Eckhardt, Thorvi (1955), 'Ustav: Glossen zur paläographischen Terminologie', *Wiener Slavistisches Jahrbuch*, 4, 130–146.

Eckhardt, Thorvi (1989), *Azbuka: Versuch einer Einführung in das Studium der slavischen Paläographie*, Vienna – Cologne: Böhlau (Wiener Archiv für Geschichte des Slawentums und Osteuropas, 14).

Edelby, Néophytos (1986), سليمان الغزي : المقالات اللهوتية النثرية (*Sulaymān al-Ġazzī, al-Maqālāt al-lāhūtiyya al-naṯriyya*, 'Sulaymān al-Ġazzī, Theological Treatises in Prose'), Jūniya: al-Maktaba al-Būlusīya / Librairie Saint Paul – Roma: Pontificio Istituto Orientale (Turāṯ al-'Arabī al-Masīḥī / Patrimoine Arabe Chrétien, 9).

Eganyan, Ōnnik et al. (1965, 1970, 2007) {Ō.E. – Andranik Zeyt'unyan – P'. Ant'abyan (I–II); Armen Malxasyan – A. Tēr-Stepanyan (III)}, Ցուցակ ձեռագրաց Մաշտոցի անուան մատենադարանի (*C'uc'ak jeṙagrac' Maštoc'i anowan matenadarani*, 'Catalogue of Manuscripts of the Matenadaran Named Maštoc''), I–III, Erevan: Haykakan SSH Gitut'yunneri Akademia.

Eganyan, Ōnnik et al. (1984, 2004, 2007, 2008, 2009, 2012, 2013, 2013) {Ō.E. – Andranik Zeyt'unyan – P'. Ant'abyan – A. K'eōškeryan et al.}, Մայր ցուցակ հայերէն ձեռագրաց Մաշտոցի անուան մատենադարանի (*Mayr c'uc'ak jeṙagrac' Maštoc'i anowan matenadarani*, 'Grand catalogue of the Armenian manuscripts of Maštoc' Matenadaran'), I–VIII, Erevan: Nairi.

Ehrman, Bart D. – Michael W. Holmes (eds) (2013), *The text of the New Testament in contemporary research: essays on the status quaestionis*, Leiden: Brill (New Testament tools, studies, and documents, 42).

Eldin, Munir Fakken (2013), 'A Historian's Task: Make Sure the Object Does Not Turn Against Itself in the Museum', in: *Islamic Art and the Museum: Approaches to Art and Archaeology of the Muslim World in the Twenty-First Century*, ed. by Benoît Junod – Georges Khalil, London: Saqi Books, 135–138.

Электронная библиотека по палеославистике (*Èlektronnaja biblioteka po paleoslavistike*, 'Electronic library on Palaeo-Slavistics'), <http://byzantinorossica.org.ru/paleoslavistics.html>, last access May 2014.

Eleuteri, Paolo (1993), *I manoscritti greci della Biblioteca Palatina di Parma*, Milano: Edizioni Il Polifilo di Paolo Vigevani e C. S.a.s (Documenti sulle arti del libro, 17).

Elkin, Zeev – Dan Shapira (2003), 'The Firkovich Collection: Historical Origins and Background', in: *Karaite Judaism: A Guide to Its History and Literary Sources*, ed. by Meira Polliack, Leiden: Brill (Handbook of Oriental Studies / Handbuch der Orientalistik, I/73).

Emery, Douglas et al. (2011) {D.E. – Alex Lee – Michael B. Toth}, 'The Palimpsest Data Set', in: *The Archimedes Palimpsest* I. *Catalogue and Commentary*, Cambridge: Cambridge University Press, 222–239.

Emmel, Stephen (1984), *Nag Hammadi Codex III, 5: The Dialogue of the Savior*, Leiden: Brill (Nag Hammadi and Manichaean Studies, 26).

Emmel, Stephen (1990), 'Coptic Biblical Texts in the Beinecke Library', *Journal of Coptic Studies*, 1, 13–28, pls. 1–4.

Emmel, Stephen (1993), 'Recent Progress in Coptic Codicology and Paleography (1988–1992)', in: *Acts of the Fifth International Congress of Coptic Studies, Washington, 12–15 August 1992*, ed. by Tito Orlandi – David W. Johnson, I–II, Rome: Centro Italiano Microfisches, I, 33–49.

Emmel, Stephen (1996), 'Greek Biblical Papyri in the Beinecke Library', *Zeitschrift für Papyrologie und Epigraphik*, 112, 289–294, pls. 2–3.

Emmel, Stephen (1997), 'Religious Tradition, Textual Transmission, and the Nag Hammadi Codices', in: *The Nag Hammadi Library after Fifty Years: Proceedings of the 1995 Society of Biblical Literature Commemoration*, ed. by John D. Turner – Anne McGuire, Leiden etc.: Brill (Nag Hammadi and Manichaean Studies, 44), 34–43.

Emmel, Stephen (1998), 'The Christian Book in Egypt: Innovation and the Coptic Tradition', in: *The Bible as Book. The Manuscript Tradition*, ed. by John Lawrence III Sharpe – Kimberly Van Kampen, London: The British Library – New Castle, Delaware: Oak Knoll Press, 35–43.

Emmel, Stephen (1999), 'Recent Progress in Coptic Codicology and Paleography (1992–1996)', in: *Ägypten und Nubien in spätantiker und christlicher Zeit. Akten des 6. Internationalen Koptologenkongresses. Münster, 20.—26. Juli 1996*, II: *Schrifttum, Sprache und Gedankenwelt*, ed. by Stephen Emmel – Martin Krause, Wiesbaden: Reichert (Sprachen und Kulturen des Christlichen Orients, 6.2), 65–78.

Emmel, Stephen (2003), 'A Question of Codicological Terminology: Revisiting GB-BL Or. 7594 to Find the Meaning of 'Papyrus Fiber Pattern'', in: *Sprache und Geist. Peter Nagel zum 65. Geburtstag*, ed. by Walter Beltz – Ute Pietruschka, Halle/ Saale: Druckerei der Martin-Luther-Universität Halle-Wittenberg (Hallesche Beiträge zur Orientwissenschaft, 35), 83–111.

Emmel, Stephen (2004), *Shenoute's Literary Corpus*, I–II, Leuven: Peeters (Corpus Scriptorum Christianorum Orientalium, 599, 600, Subsidia, 111, 112).

Emmel, Stephen (2005), 'The Library of the Monastery of the Archangel Michael at Phantoou (al-Hamuli)', in: *Christianity and Monasticism in the Fayyum Oasis. Essays from the 2004 International Symposium of the Saint Mark Foundation and the Saint Shenouda the Archimandrite Coptic Society in Honor of Martin Krause*, ed. by Gawdat Gabra, Cairo – New York: The American University in Cairo Press, 63–70.

Emmel, Stephen (2007), 'Coptic Literature in the Byzantine and Early Islamic World', in: *Egypt in the Byzantine World, 300-700*, ed. by Roger S. Bagnall, Cambridge – New York: Cambridge University Press, 83–102.

Emmel, Stephen (2008), 'The Coptic Gnostic Texts as Witnesses to the Production and Transmission of Gnostic (and Other) Traditions', in: *Das Thomasevangelium. Entstehung - Rezeption - Theologie*, ed. by Jörg Frey – Enno Edzard Popkes, Berlin – New York: De Gruyter (Beihefte zur Zeitschrift für die neutestamentliche Wissenschaft, 157), 33–49.

EMML = *Ethiopian Manuscript Microfilm Library*, Addis Ababa – Collegeville, MN, <http://www.hmml.org/ emml.html>, last access October 2014.

Endangered Archives Programme, Project 340, <http://eap.bl.uk/database/all_projects.a4de>, last access October 2013.

Engel, Edna (1999), 'The Analysis of Letter – a New Palaeographical Method', in: *Methoden der Schriftbeschreibung*, ed. by Peter Rück, Stuttgart: Thorbecke (Historische Hilfswissenschaften, 4), 43–50.

Engel, Edna (2013), 'The Development of Hebrew Script', in: *Encyclopedia of Hebrew Language and Linguistics*, III, ed. by Geoffrey Khan, Leiden: Brill, 485–502.

Engel, Edna – Malachi Beit-Arié ([2015]), *Specimens of Mediaeval Hebrew Scripts*, III: *Ashkenazic Script*, Jerusalem: Israel Academy of Sciences and Humanities (The Hebrew Paleography Project).

Enukiʒe, Tina et al. (1963) {T.E. – Elene Meṭreveli – Mixeil Kavtaria – Lili Kutatelaʒe – Mzekala Šaniʒe – Krisṭine Šarašiʒe}, ქართულ ხელნაწერთა აღწერილობა ყოფილი ქართველთა შორის წერა-კითხვის გამავრცელებელი საზოგადოების (*S*) კოლექციისა / *Описание грузинских рукописей коллекции* (*S*) *– бывшего Общества Распространении Грамотности среди Грузинского Населения* (*Kartul xelnaçerta aġçeriloba q̇opili kartvelta šoris çera-ḳitxvis gamavrcelebeli sazogadoebis* (*S*) *ḳolekciisa / Opisanie gruzinskich rukopisej kollekcii* (*S*) *– byvšego Obščestva Rasprostranenii Gramotnosti sredi Gruzinskogo Naselenija*, 'Description of the Georgian manuscripts of the collection (S) of the former Society for the Promotion of Literacy among the Georgians'), III, Tbilisi.

Espejo Arias, Teresa et al. (2008) {T.E. – Ana López Montes – Ana García Bueno – Adrián Durán Benito – Rosario Blanc García}, 'A Study about Colourants in the Arabic Manuscript Collection of the Sacromonte Abbey, Granada, Spain. A New Methodology for Chemical Analysis', *Restaurator. International Journal for the Preservation of Library and Archival Material*, 29, 76–106.

Estève, Jean-Louis (2001), 'Le zig-zag dans les papiers arabes', *Gazette du livre médiéval*, 38, 40–49.

Euromed Heritage, <http://www.euromedheritage.net>, last access October 2014.

Evans, Helen C. – William D. Wixom (eds) (1997), *The Glory of Byzantium. Art and Culture of the Middle Byzantine Era A.D. 843–1260*, New York: The Metropolitan Museum of Art.

Evelyn-White, Hugh G. (1926), *The Monasteries of the Wadi 'n Natrûn*, I, New York: Metropolitan Museum of Art (Publications of the Metropolitan Museum of Art Egyptian Expedition, 2).

Ewald, Heinrich von (1844), 'Ueber die Aethiopischen Handschriften in Tübingen', *Zeitschrift für die Kunde des Morgenlandes*, 6, 164–201.

Ewald, Heinrich von (1847), 'Ueber eine zweite Sammlung Aethiopischer Handschriften in Tübingen', *Zeitschrift der Deutschen Morgenländischen Gesellschaft*, 1, 1–43.

Fabian, Claudia – Bettina Wagner (eds) (2007), *Katalogisierung mittelalterlicher Handschriften in internationaler Perspektive. Vorträge der Handschriftenbearbeitertagung vom 24. bis 27. Oktober 2005 in München*, Wiesbaden: Harrassowitz.

von Falck, Martin et al. (1996), *Ägypten. Schätze aus dem Wüstensand*: *Kunst und Kultur der Christen am Nil*, Wiesbaden: Reichert.

Fani, Sara (2011), 'A conservative census of the Arabic manuscripts in the Central National Library of Florence', *Comparative Oriental Manuscript Studies Newsletter*, 2, 5–6.

Faqāda Śellāsē Tafarrā (2002 AM / 2010 CE), **ጥንታዊ የብራና መጻሕፍት አዘጋጃጀት** (*Ṭentāwi yaberānnā maṣāḥeft azzagāǧāǧat*, 'The ancient manner of preparing parchment books'), Addis Ababa: Addis Ababā Yunivarsiti Prēss.

Federal Agencies Digitization Initiative Still Image Working Group (August 2010), *Technical Guidelines for Digitizing Cultural Heritage Materials: Creation of Raster Image Master Files*, <http://www.digitizationguidelines.gov/guidelines/FADGI_Still_Image-Tech_Guidelines_2010-08-24.pdf>.

Federici, Carlo – Kostantinos Houlis (1988), *Legature bizantine vaticane*, Roma: Palombi: Istituto centrale per la patologia del libro Alfonso Gallo.

Fernández Marcos, Natalio (1998), *Introducción a las versiones griegas de la Biblia*, Madrid: Consejo Superior de Investigaciones Científicas (Textos y estudios 'Cardenal Cisneros', 23).

Feydit, Frédéric (1986), *Amulettes de l'Arménie chrétienne*, Venise: St. Lazare (Bibliothèque arménienne de la fondation Calouste Gulbenkian).

Fiaccadori, Gianfranco (1993), 'Bisanzio e il regno di 'Aksum. Sul manoscritto Martini etiop. 5 della Biblioteca Forteguerriana di Pistoia', *Bollettino del Museo Bodoniano di Parma*, 7, 161–199.

Fiaccadori, Gianfranco (2001), 'Album di pittore etiopico (Ms. Parm. 3853)', *Cum picturis ystoriatum. Codici devozionali e liturgici della Biblioteca Palatina*, 280–285.

Fiaccadori, Gianfranco (2011), 'Orientalistica', in: *La Biblioteca Apostolica Vaticana come luogo di ricerca al servizio degli studi. Atti del convegno Roma, 11–13 novembre 2010*, ed. by Marco Buonocore – Ambrogio M. Piazzoni, Città del Vaticano: Biblioteca Apostolica Vaticana (Studi e testi, 468), 299–336.

Fiaccadori, Gianfranco (2011 [2012]), 'Per la cronologia di un atto «feudale» del neguś Lālibalā', *Crisopoli. Bollettino del Museo Bodoniano di Parma*, 14 (2), 201–204.

Fiaccadori, Gianfranco (2014), 'Archives', in: *Encyclopaedia Aethiopica*, V, ed. by Alessandro Bausi, Wiesbaden: Harrassowitz, 244–248.

Fiddyment, Sarah et al. (2014) {S.F. – Caroline Checkley-Scott – M. Garrison et al.}, 'My library and other animals: How non-invasive techniques can uncover the secrets hidden in parchment', paper presented at the workshop *Natural Sciences and Technology in Manuscript Analysis, December 4-6, 2014*, Hamburg: Centre for the Studies of Manuscript Cultures.

Fiesoli, Giovanni – Elena Somigli (2009), *RICABIM. Repertorio di inventari e cataloghi di biblioteche medievali dal secolo VI al 1520*, I, Firenze: SISMEL Edizioni del Galluzzo (Biblioteche e archivi, 24).

FiMMOD = *Fichier des Manuscrits Moyen-Orientaux datés*, ed. by F. Déroche et alii, 1993–2000, <http://www.maxvanberchem.org/en/scientific-activities/projets/?a=79>, last access October 2014.

Finck, Franz Nikolaus – Levon Gjandschezian (1907), *Verzeichnis der armenischen Handschriften der königlichen Universitätsbibliothek*, Tübingen: Universitätsbibliothek (Systematisch-alphabetischer Hauptkatalog der Königl. Universitätsbibliothek zu Tübingen, 13).

Fingernagel, Andreas (2007), 'Die Beschreibung des Buchschmucks in Handschriftenkatalogen', in: *Katalogisierung mittelalterlicher Handschriften in internationaler Perspektive. Vorträge der Handschriftenbearbeitertagung vom 24. bis 27. Oktober 2005 in München*, Wiesbaden: Harrassowitz (Beiträge zum Buch- und Bibliothekswesen, 53), 89–98.

Finney, Timothy John (1999), *The Ancient Witnesses of the Epistle to the Hebrews: A Computer-Assisted Analysis of the Papyrus and Uncial Manuscripts of PROS EBRAIOUS*, Murdoch University [diss.].

Fischer, Franz (2013), 'All texts are equal, but... Textual plurality and the critical text in digital scholarly editions', *Variants: The Journal of the European Society for Textual scholarship*, 10, 77–91.

Fischer, Franz et al. (eds) (2010) {F.F. – Christiane Fritze – Georg Vogeler }, *Kodikologie und Paläographie im digitalen Zeitalter 2 - Codicology and Palaeography in the Digital Age 2*, Norderstedt: BOD (Schriften des Instituts für Dokumentologie und Editorik, 3).

Fischer, Wolfdietrich (1982), *Grundriß der arabischen Philologie. I. Sprachwissenschaft*, Wiesbaden: Reichert.

Fischer, Wolfdietrich (1991), 'What is Middle Arabic?', in: *Semitic Studies in honour of Wolf Leslau on the occasion of his eighty-fifth birthday*, I, ed. by Alan S. Kaye, Wiesbaden: Harrassowitz, 430–436.

Fleisch, Henri (1990), *Traité de philologie arabe*, II, Beyrouth: Dar al-Machreq (Recherches, 16).

Flemming, Barbara (1986), 'The Union Catalogue of Manuscripts in Turkey. Türkiye Yazmaları Toplu Kataloğu (TÜYATOK)', *Manuscripts of the Middle East*, 1, 109–110.

Foehr-Janssens, Yasmina – Olivier Collet (eds) (2010), *Le recueil au Moyen Âge. Le Moyen Âge central*, Turnhout: Brepols (Texte, Codex et Contexte, 8).

Fogg, Sam (ed.) (1991), *Medieval Manuscripts Catalogue 14*, London: Sam Fogg Rare Books and Manuscripts.

Ford, Helen – Jonathan Rhys-Lewis (eds) (2013), *Preserving Archives*, Second Edition, London: Facet Publishing (Principles and Practice in Records Management and Archives).

Foucault, Michel (1994), 'Qu'est-ce qu'un auteur? [Paris 1969]', in: *Dits et Écrits*, I, ed. by Michel Foucault, Paris: Gallimard (Quarto Gallimard), 820–821.

Foumia, Khairy (2013), 'The Manuscripts of the Church of Telkeppe', *Journal of the Canadian Society of Syriac Studies*, 13, 66–76.

Frankenberg, Wilhelm (1937), *Die syrischen Clementinen mit griechischem Paralleltext: eine Vorarbeit zu dem literargeschichtlichen Problem der Sammlung*, Leipzig: Hinrichs (Texte und Untersuchungen zur Geschichte der altchristlichen Literatur, 48, 3).

Franklin, Simon (2002), *Writing, Society and Culture in Early Rus, c. 950-1300*, Cambridge – New York: Cambridge University Press.

Frantsouzoff [Francuzov], Serguei [Sergej] (2005), 'Matres lectionis в раннем геэзе (*Matres lectionis v rannem geėze*, 'Matres lectionis in early Ge'ez')', *Scrinium*, 1 (= *Varia Aethiopica. In Memory of Sevir B. Chernetsov (1943-2005)*, ed. Denis Nosnitsin et al.), 50–57.

Frantsouzoff, Serguei (2010), 'Script, Ethiopic', in: *Encyclopaedia Aethiopica*, IV: O–X, ed. by Siegbert Uhlig – Alessandro Bausi, Wiesbaden: Harrassowitz, 580–585.

Franzmann, Majella (1999), 'P. Kell. Addenda & Corrigenda: Syriac texts', in: *Coptic Documentary Texts from Kellis, Vol. 1: P. Kell. V (P. Kell. Copt. 10-52; O. Kell. Copt. 1-2)*, ed. by Iain Gardner – Anthony Alcock – Wolf-Peter Funk, Oxford: Oxbow Press (Dakhleh Oasis Project Monographs, 9), 303–323.

Franzmann, Majella – Iain Gardner (1996), 'Syriac Texts', in: *Kellis Literary Texts*, I, ed. by Iain Gardner – Sarah Clackson – Majella Franzmann, Oxford: Oxbow Press (Dakhleh Oasis Project Monographs, 4 = Oxbow Monographs, 69), 101–131, pls. 17–20.

The Friedberg Jewish Manuscript Society <http://www.jewishmanuscripts.org/>, last access October 2014.

Friedman, Florence D. et al. (1989), *Beyond the Pharaohs: Egypt and the Copts in the Second to Seventh Centuries A.D.*, Providence: Rhode Island School of Design Museum of Art.

Froger, Jacques (1968), *La critique des textes et son automatisation*, Paris: Dunod (Initiation aux nouveautés de la science, 7).

Froschauer, Harald – Cornelia Eva Römer (eds) (2008), *Spätantike Bibliotheken: Leben und Lesen in den frühen Klöstern Ägyptens*, Wien: Phoibos Verlag (Nilus. Studien zur Kultur Ägyptens und des Vorderen Orients, 14).

Fuchs, Robert (2003), 'The History of Chemical Reinforcement of Texts in Manuscripts. What Should We Do Now?', in: *Care and Conservation of Manuscripts 7: Proceedings of the Seventh International Seminar Held at the Royal Library, Copenhagen 18th-19th April 2002*, ed. by Matthew James Driscoll, Copenhagen: Museum Tusculanum Press, 159–170.

Funk, Wolf-Peter (1988), 'Dialects Wanting Homes: A Numerical Approach to the Early Varieties of Coptic', in: *Historical Dialectology: Regional and Social*, ed. by Jacek Fisiak, Berlin etc.: Mouton de Gruyter, 149–192.

Funk, Wolf-Peter (1990), 'Zur Faksimileausgabe der koptischen Manichaica in der Chester-Beatty-Sammlung, I', *Orientalia*, ser. 2, 59, 524–541.

Funk, Wolf-Peter (2012), 'Coptic Dialects and the Vatican Library', in: *Coptic Treasures from the Vatican Library: A Selection of Coptic, Copto-Arabic and Ethiopic Manuscripts. Papers Collected on the Occasion of the Tenth International Congress of Coptic Studies (Rome, September 17th–22nd, 2012)*, ed. by Paola Buzi – Delio Vania Proverbio, Città del Vaticano: Biblioteca Apostolica Vaticana (Studi e Testi, 472), 47–51.

Furlan, Italo (1978–1997), *Codici greci illustrati della Biblioteca Marciana*, I–VII, Milano: La Garangola (Studi sull'arte paleocristiana e bizantina).

Gabra, Gawdat (ed.) (2014), *Coptic Civilization: Two Thousand Years of Christianity in Egypt*, Cairo – New York: The American University in Cairo Press.

Gabra, Gawdat – Marianne Eaton-Krauss (2006), *The Treasures of Coptic Art in the Coptic Museum and Churches of Old Cairo*, Cairo – New York: The American University in Cairo Press.

Gacek, Adam (2001), *The Arabic Manuscript Tradition. A Glossary of Technical Terms and Bibliography*, Leiden: Brill (Handbook of Oriental Studies / Handbuch der Orientalistik, I/58).

Gacek, Adam (2002), 'On the Making of Local Paper: A Thirteenth Century Yemeni Recipe', in: *La tradition manuscrite en écriture arabe*, ed. by Geneviève Humbert, Paris (Revue des Mondes Musulmans et de la Méditerranée, 99-100), 79–93.

Gacek, Adam (2007), 'Taxonomy of scribal errors and corrections in Arabic manuscripts', in: *Theoretical Approaches to the Transmission and Edition of Oriental Manuscripts. Proceedings of a symposium held in Istanbul March 28–30, 2001*, ed. by Judith Pfeiffer – Manfred Kropp, Beirut: Ergon Verlag Würzburg in Kommission (Beiruter Texte und Studien, 111), 217–235.

Gacek, Adam (2008), *The Arabic Manuscript Tradition. A Glossary of Technical Terms and Bibliography. Supplement*, Leiden: Brill (Handbook of Oriental Studies / Handbuch der Orientalistik, I/95).

Gacek, Adam (2009), *Arabic manuscripts. A vademecum for readers*, Leiden: Brill (Handbook of Oriental Studies / Handbuch der Orientalistik, I/98).

Gaetani, Maria Carolina et al. (2004) {M.G. – Claudio Seccaroni – Ulderico Santamaria}, 'The Use of Egyptian Blue and Lapis Lazuli in the Middle Ages: The Wall Paintings of the San Saba Church in Rome', *Studies in Conservation*, 49, 13–22.

Gaffino Moeri, Sarah et al. (eds) (2010), *Les papyrus de Genève. 4, Nos 147-205: textes littéraires, semi-littéraires et documentaires*, Genève: Bibliothèque publique et universitaire.

Ǧahānpūr [Jahanpour], Farhang (1376–1377 Šamsī / 1997–1998 CE), 'وندیداد آستان قدس' (*Vandidād-e Āstān-e Qods*, 'The Vandīdād of Āstān-e Qods [Library]', *Nāme-ye Bahārestān*, ser. 8/9, 13–14, 379–400.

Galavaris, George (1969), *The Illustrations of the Liturgical Homilies of Gregory Nazianzenus*, Princeton: Princeton University Press (Studies in Manuscript Illumination, 6).

Galēmk'earean [Kalemkiar], Grigoris (1892), Ցուցակ հայերէն ձեռագրաց արքունի մատենադարանի ի Միւնխեն (*C'uc'ak hayerēn jeṙagrac' ark'uni matenadaranin i Miunxen) / Catalog der armenischen Handschriften in der königlichen Hof- und Staatsbibliothek zu München*, Wien: Mechitaristen-Buchdruckerei (Haupt-Catalog der armenischen Handschriften, 2/1).

Galfajan, Ch. K. (1975a), 'Технология изготовления пергамента по рецептам армянских мастеров (*Technologija izgotovlenija pergamenta po receptam armjanskich masterov*, 'Technology of Parchment Production in the Recepies of Armenian Craftsmen')', *Chudožestvennoe nasledie*, 1/31, 74–79.

Galfajan, Ch. K. (1975b), 'История изготовления железогалловых чернил в древней Армении (*Istorija izgotovlenija železogallovych černil v drevnej Armenii*, 'History of the Production of Iron Gall Ink in Ancient Armenia')', *Soobščenija Vsesojuznoj central'noj naučno-issledovatel'skoj laboratorii po konservacii i restavracii muzejnych chudožestvennych cennostej*, 30, 57–69.

Galfajan, Ch. K. (1975c), 'Влияние средневековых красок и чернил на бумагу (*Vlijanie srednevekovych krasok i černil na bumagu*, 'Influence of Medieval Pigments and Inks on Paper')', *Soobščenija Vsesojuznoj central'noj naučno-issledovatel'skoj laboratorii po konservacii i restavracii muzejnych chudožestvennych cennostej*, 29, 62–71.

Galletti, Mirella (2013), 'Studi orientalistici in Italia', in: *Orientalisti Italiani e aspetti dell'Orientalismo in Italia. In memoria di Mirella Galletti*, ed. by Angela Spina, Benevento: AIC – Edizioni Labrys, 31–49.

Gallo, Fausta (2000), 'Rapport entre le climat et la biologie', in: *La climatologie dans les archives et les bibliothèques: actes des troisièmes Journées sur la conservation préventive, 2-3 décembre, 1998*, Arles: Centre de Conservation du Livre, 39–68.

Gallo, Fausta – Marina Regni (2000), 'Conditions microclimatiques dans les bibliothèques italiennes', in: *La climatologie dans les archives et les bibliothèques: actes des troisièmes Journées sur la conservation préventive, 2-3 décembre, 1998*, Arles: Centre de Conservation du Livre, 69–83.

Gamillscheg, Ernst et al. (1981) {E.G. – Dieter Harlfinger – Herbert Hunger}, *Repertorium der griechischen Kopisten 800-1600.* 1.Teil: *Handschriften aus Bibliotheken Großbritanniens.* Fasz. A: *Verzeichnis der Kopisten.* Fasz. B: *Paläographische Charakteristika.* Fasz. C: *Tafeln*, Wien: Verlag der Österreichischen Akademie der Wissenschaften (Veröffentlichungen der Kommission für Byzantinistik, 3/1).

Gamillscheg, Ernst et al. (1989) {E.G. – Dieter Harlfinger – Herbert Hunger}, *Repertorium der griechischen Kopisten 800-1600.* 2.Teil: *Handschriften aus Bibliotheken Frankreichs und Nachträge zu den Bibliotheken Großbritanniens.* Fasz .A: *Verzeichnis der Kopisten.* Fasz. B: *Paläographische Charakteristika.* Fasz. C: *Tafeln*, Wien: Verlag der Österreichischen Akademie der Wissenschaften (Veröffentlichungen der Kommission für Byzantinistik, 3/2).

Gamillscheg, Ernst et al. (1997) {E.G. – Dieter Harlfinger – Herbert Hunger}, *Repertorium der griechischen Kopisten 800 - 1600.* 3.Teil: *Handschriften aus Bibliotheken Roms mit dem Vatikan.* Fasz. A: *Verzeichnis der Kopisten.* Fasz. B: *Paläographische Charakteristika.* Fasz. C: *Tafeln*, Wien: Verlag der Österreichischen Akademie der Wissenschaften (Veröffentlichungen der Kommission für Byzantinistik, 3/3).

Gamq̇relize, Tamaz [Gamkrelidze, Tamaz Valerianovič; Gamkrelidze, Thomas V.] (1990), წერის ანბანური სისტემა და ძველი ქართული დამწერლობა: ანბანური წერის ტიპოლოგია და წარმომავლობა / Алфавитное письмо и древнегрузинская письменность. Типология и происхождение алфавитных систем письма (*Çeris anbanuri sisṭema da ʒveli kartuli damçerloba: anbanuri çeris ṭipologia da çarmomavloba / Alfavitnoe pis'mo i drevnegruzinskaja pis'mennost'. Tipologija i proisxoždenie alfavitnych sistem pis'ma*) / *Alphabetic writing and the Old Georgian script: a typology and provenience of alphabetic writing systems*, Tbilisi: Tbilisis Universiṭeṭis Gamomcemloba.

Ġanī, Qāsim – 'Alī Akbar Fayyāḍ (1324 Š./1945 CE), تاریخ بیهقی (*Tārīḫ-i Bayhaqī*, 'The *History* of Bayhaqī'), Tehran: Čāpḫāna-yi Bānk-i Millī-i Īrān.

Ġanī, Qāsim – 'Alī Akbar Fayyāḍ (1350 Š./1971 CE; [2]1355 AH /1976 CE), تاریخ بیهقی (*Tārīḫ-i Bayhaqī*, 'The *History* of Bayhaqī'), Mashhad.

Garbini, Giovanni (1979), *Storia e problemi dell'epigrafia semitica*, Napoli: Istituto Universitario Orientale (Annali dell'Istituto Orientale di Napoli. Supplemento, 19).

Gardner, Iain et al. (1996), *Kellis Literary Texts*, I, Oxford: Oxbow Press (Dakhleh Oasis Project Monographs, 4; Oxbow Monographs, 69).

Gardner, Iain (2007), *Kellis Literary Texts*, II, Oxford: Oxbow Press (Dakhleh Oasis Project Monographs, 15).

Gardner, Iain – Malcolm Choat (2004), 'Towards a palaeography of fourth century documentary Coptic', in: *Coptic Studies on the Threshold of a New Millennium: Proceedings of the Seventh International Congress of Coptic Studies, Leiden, August 27-September 2, 2000*, ed. by Mat Immerzeel – Jacques Van Der Vliet, Leuven: Peeters (Orientalia Lovaniensia Analecta, 133), 495–504.

Gardthausen, Viktor Emil (1911), *Griechische Paläographie. Band 1: Das Buchwesen im Altertum und im byzantinischen Mittelalter*, Leipzig.

Garitte, Gérard (1956), *Catalogue des manuscrits géorgiens littéraires du Mont Sinai*, Louvain: Peeters (Corpus Scriptorum Christianorum Orientalium, 165, Subsidia 9).

Garitte, Gérard (1958), *Le calendrier palestino-géorgien du Sinaiticus 34 (Xe siècle)*, Bruxelles: Société des Bollandistes (Subsidia Hagiographica, 30).

Garitte, Gérard (1960), 'Les feuillets géorgiens de la collection Mingana à Selly Oak (Birmingham)', *Le Muséon*, 73, 239–259.

Gascou, Jean (1989), 'Les codices documentaires égyptiens', in: *Les débuts du codex. Actes de la journée d'étude organisée à Paris les 3 et 4 juillet 1985 par l'Institut de papyrologie de la Sorbonne et l'Institut de recherche et d'histoire des textes*, ed. by Alain Blanchard, Turnhout: Brepols (Bibliologia: Elementa ad Librorum Studia Pertinentia, 9), 71–101.

Gavillet Matar, Marguerite (2003), 'Situation narrative et fonctions de l'extra-narratif dans les manuscrits des conteurs', in: *Studies on Arabic Epics*, ed. by Giovanni Canova, Roma: Istituto per l'Oriente C. A. Nallino (Oriente Moderno, n.s., 2), 377–397.

Gavillet Matar, Marguerite (2005), *La Geste de Zīr Sālim d'après un manuscrit syrien*, Damas: Institut français du Proche-Orient.

Géhin, Paul (ed.) (2005), *Lire le manuscrit médiéval: observer et décrire*, Paris: Colin (Collection U. Histoire).

Géhin, Paul (2009), 'Fragments patristiques syriaques des nouvelles découvertes du Sinaï', *Collectanea Christiana Analecta*, 6, 67–93.

Géhin, Paul et al. (2005) {P.G. – Michel Cacouros – Christian Förstel – Marie-Odile Germain – Philippe Hoffmann, Corinne Jouanno – Brigitte Mondrain}, *Les manuscrits grecs datés des XIIIe et XIVe siècles conservés dans les bibliothèques municipales de France*, II: *XIVe siècle (première moitié)*, Turnhout: Brepols (Monumenta Palaeographica Medii Aevi, Series Graeca, 1).

Geldner, Karl Friedrich (1885–1896), *Avesta. The sacred books of the Parsis*, I–III, Stuttgart: Kohlhammer.

Geldner, Karl Friedrich (1896), 'Prolegomena', in: *Avesta. The sacred books of the Parsis*, ed. by Karl Friedrich Geldner, III, Stuttgart: Kohlhammer, i–liv.

Genadry, Zeina (2010), 'Conservation Challenges and ethics', paper presented at the COMSt workshop *Conservation Studies on Oriental Manuscripts*, Istanbul.

Gengaro, Maria Luisa et al. (1959) {M.G. – Francesca Leoni – Gemma Villa}, *Codici decorati e miniati dell'Ambrosiana ebraici e greci*, Milano: Ceschina (Fontes ambrosiani, 33-A).

George, Alain (2011), 'Le palimpseste Lewis-Mingana de Cambridge, témoin ancien de l'histoire du Coran', *Comptes rendus de l'Académie des inscriptions et belles-lettres*, 1 (janvier-mars), 377–429.

George, Alain (2012), 'Orality, writing and the image in the Maqamat: Arabic illustrated books in context', *Art history*, 35/1, 10–37.

Gēorgyan, Astłik (1973), Արհեստներն ու կենցաղը հայկական մանրանկարներում (*Arhestnern u kenc'alə haykakan manrankarnerum*, 'The Crafts and Mode of Life in Armenian Miniatures'), Erevan: Hayastan.

Gēorgyan, Astłik [Guévorkian, Astghik] (1978), *Les portraits dans les miniatures arméniennes*, Erevan: Academy of Sciences.

Gēorgyan, Astłik (1982), Հայկական մանրանկարչություն. Դիմանկար (*Haykakan manrankarč'ut'yun. Dimankar*, 'Portraits in Armenian Miniatures'), Erevan: Sovetakan Groł.

Gēorgyan, Astłik (1996), Կենդանազարդեր: Հայկական մանրանկարչություն (*Kendanazarder: Haykakan manrankarč'ut'yun*, 'Animal Decorations: Armenian Miniature Painting'), Erevan: Anahit.

Gēorgyan, Astłik (1998), Հայ մանրանկարիչներ մատենագիտուտիւն, Թ-Ժ դդ. (*Hay manrankarič'ner matenagitut'iwn, IX–XIX dd.*, 'Bibliography of Armenian Miniaturists, IXth–XIXth Centuries'), Cairo.

Gēorgyan, Astłik (2005), Անանուն Հայ մանրանկարիչներ մատենագիտուտիւն, Թ-ԺԷ դդ. (*Ananun Hay manrankarič'ner matenagitut'iwn, IX–XVII dd.*, 'Bibliography of Anonymous Armenian Miniaturists, IXth–XVIIth Centuries'), Cairo.

Gerlach, Jens (2008a), *Gnomica Democritea: Studien zur Gnomologischen Tradition der Ethik Demokrits und zum Corpus Parisinum mit einer Edition der Democritea des Corpus Parisinum*, Wiesbaden: Harrassowitz (Serta Graeca. Beiträge zur Erforschung griechischer Texte, 26).

Gerlach, Jens (2008b), 'Die kompositorische Einheit des Corpus Parisinum. Eine methodologische Stellungnahme zu Searbys Gesamtedition', *Medioevo Greco*, 8, 201–254.

Getatchew Haile (1993), *A Catalogue of Ethiopian manuscripts microfilmed for the Ethiopian Manuscript Microfilm Library, Addis Ababa, and for the Hill Monastic Manuscript Library, Collegeville, Vol. X: Project Numbers 4001-5000*, Collegeville, MN: HMML.

Getatchew Haile (2011), *A History of the First Əsṭifanosite Monks*, I. Text, II. Translation, Louvain: Peeters (Corpus Scriptorum Christianorum Orientalium, 635-636, Scriptores Aethiopici 112-113).

Getatchew Haile et al. (2009) {G.H. – Melaku Terefe – Roger M. Rundell – Daniel Alemu – Steve Delamarter}, *Catalogue of the Ethiopic Manuscript Imaging Project*. Volume 1: *Codices 1–105, Magic Scrolls 1–134*, Eugene, OR: Pickwick Publications (Ethiopic Manuscripts, Texts and Studies Series, 1).

Ghali, Noureddine et al. (1985) {N.Gh. – Mohamed Mahibou – Louis Brenner}, *Inventaire de la Bibliothèque 'Umarienne de Ségou (conservée à la Bibliothèque Nationale – Paris)*, Paris: Centre national de la recherche scientifique (Documents, études et répertoires. Fontes historiae Africanae, 2).

Giannopoulos, Emmanuel (2008), *Τα χειρόγραφα βυζαντινής μουσικής – Αγγλία. Περιγραφικός κατάλογος των χειρογράφων ψαλτικής τέχνης των αποκειμένων στις βιβλιοθήκες του Ηνωμένου Βασιλείου*, Athens: Ιδρυμα Βυζαντινησ Μουσικολογιασ.

Giannouli, Antonia (2014), 'Byzantine punctuation and orthography. Between normalisation and respect of the manuscripts. Introductory remarks', *Comparative Oriental Manuscript Studies Newsletter* 8, 2014, 18–22.

Gibson, Margareth Dunlop (1901), *Apocrypha Arabica. 1 Kitāb al-Mağall or the Book of the Rolls*, London: C. J. Clay – New York: Macmillan (Studia Sinaitica, 8).

Gigineišvili, Bakar – Elguǯa Giunašvili (1979), შატბერდის კრებული *X* საუკუნისა / *Шатбердский сборник X века* (*Šaṭberdis ḳrebuli X sauḳunisa / Šatberdskij sbornik X veka*, 'The Šaṭberd miscellany of the tenth century'), Tbilisi: Mecniereba (Ʒveli kartuli mçerlobis ʒeglebi, 1).

Gignoux, Philippe (1987), *Incantations magiques syriaques*, Louvain: Peeters (Collection de la Revue des études juives, 4).

Gippert, Jost (1988), 'Die altgeorgischen Monatsnamen', in: *Proceedings of the 3rd Caucasian Colloquium, Oslo, July 1986*, ed. by Fridrik Thordarson, Oslo: Norwegian University Press / Institute for Comparative Research in Human Culture (Studia Caucasologica, 1), 87–154.

Gippert, Jost (2007), 'The Application of Multispectral Imaging in the Study of Caucasian Palimpsests', *Bulletin of the Georgian National Academy of Sciences / Sakartvelos mecnierebata erovnuli aḳademiis moambe*, 175/1, 168–179.

Gippert, Jost (2010a), *The Caucasian Albanian Palimpsests of Mount Sinai*. III: *The Armenian Layer*, Turnhout: Brepols (Monumenta Palaeographica Medii Aevi, Series Ibero-Caucasica, 3).

Gippert, Jost (2010b), 'Towards a Typology of The Use of Coloured Inks in Old Georgian Manuscripts', *Manuscript cultures* [*Newsletter*], 3, 2–13.

Gippert, Jost (2012), 'The Albanian Gospel Manuscript – New Findings', in: *Research Papers of the International scientific conference 'The Place and Role of Caucasian Albania in the History of Azerbaijan and Caucasus'*, Baku: Nacional'naja Akademija Aviacii, 55–64.

Gippert, Jost (2013), 'The Gospel Manuscript of Kurashi. A preliminary account', *Le Muséon*, 126, 83–160.

Gippert, Jost (2014a), 'Nochmals zur Bauinschrift von Bolnisi', in: *Kaukasiologie heute – Festschrift für Heinz Fähnrich zum 70. Geburtstag*, ed. by Natia Reineck – Ute Rieger, Greiz: König.

Gippert, Jost (2014b), 'O en arši anarxos logos – Greek Verses in Georgian Disguise', in: *Scripts Beyond Borders. A Survey of Allographic Traditions in the Euro-Mediterranean World*, ed. by Johannes Den Heijer – Andrea Schmidt – Tamara Pataridze, Louvain: Peeters (Publications de l'Institut Orientaliste de Louvain, 62), 481–527.

Gippert, Jost (forthcoming), 'Mravaltavi – Old Georgian Multi-Text Manuscripts', in: *'One-Volume Libraries': Composite Manuscripts and Multiple Text Manuscripts. Proceedings of the International Conference, Asien-Afrika-Institut, Universität Hamburg, October 7–10, 2010*, ed. by Michael Friedrich – Jörg Quenzer, Berlin – New York: De Gruyter (Studies in Manuscript Cultures).

Gippert, Jost et al. (2007a) {J.G. – Zurab Sarǯvelaʒe [Sarjveladze] – Lamara Kaǯaia [Kajaia]}, *The Old Georgian Palimpsest Codex Vindobonensis georgicus 2*, Turnhout: Brepols (Monumenta Palaeographica Medii Aevi, Series Ibero-Caucasica, 1).

Gippert, Jost et al. (2007b) {J.G. – Vaxṭang [Vakhtang] Imnaišvili [Imnaishvili] – Zurab Sarǯvelaʒe [Sarjveladze]}, *Lectionarium Gracense. Codex Chanmeticus*. Online edition, <http://titus.uni-frankfurt.de/texte/etcs/cauc/ageo/xanmeti/grlekt/grlek.htm>, Frankfurt.

Gippert, Jost et al. (2009) {J.G. – Wolfgang Schulze – Zaza Aleksiʒe [Aleksidze] – Jean-Pierre Mahé}, *The Caucasian Albanian Palimpsests of Mount Sinai*, I–II, Turnhout: Brepols (Monumenta Palaeographica Medii Aevi, Series Ibero-Caucasica, 2).

Gippert, Jost – Vaxṭang Imnaišvili (2009a), *Iohannes Chrysostomus, Liturgia e codice Gracensi*. Online edition, <http://titus.uni-frankfurt.de/texte/etcs/cauc/ageo/johchrys/chryslit/chrys.htm>, Frankfurt.

Gippert, Jost – Vaxṭang Imnaišvili (2009b), *Psalterium et Odae e codice palimpsesto Gracensi*. Online edition, <http://titus.uni-frankfurt.de/texte/etcs/cauc/ageo//at/psgraz/psgra.htm>, Frankfurt.

Gippert, Jost – Bernard Outtier (2009), 'Fragments de l'Evangile de Luc dans le Maténadaran', in: ისტორიანი. სამეცნიერო კრებული მიძღვნილი როინ მეტრეველის დაბადების *70* წლისთავისადმი (*Isṭoriani. Samecniero ḳrebuli, miʒġvnili Roin Meṭrevelis dabadebis 70 çlistavisadmi*, 'Histories. Scientific works dedicated to the 70th anniversary of Roin Metreveli'), Tbilisi: Arṭanuǯi, 584–603.

Gippert, Jost – Manana Tandaschwili (1999), *Die Armazi-Bilingue (1. Jh. n.Chr.) / The Bilingual Inscription from Armazi (1st century A.D.)*. Online edition, <http://armazi.uni-frankfurt.de/armazibl.htm#bilingva>, Frankfurt.

Gippert, Jost – Manana Tandaschwili (1999–2002), *Die Bolnisi-Inschriften / The Bolnisi Inscriptions*. Online edition, <http://armazi.uni-frankfurt.de/armazibo.htm#bolnisi1>, Frankfurt.

Gippert, Jost – Manana Tandaschwili (2002), *Die Jerusalemer Inschriften / The Jerusalem Inscriptions*. Online edition, <http://armazi.uni-frankfurt.de/armazijm.htm#inscr>, Frankfurt.

Gippert, Jost – Manana Tandaschwili (2014), 'Šota Rustaveli und sein Epos', in: Schota Rusthaweli, *Der Recke im Tigerfell. Altgeorgisches Poem*. Deutsche Nachdichtung von Hugo Huppert, Wiesbaden: Reichert, 5–17.

Glatzer, Mordechai et al. (1997) {M.G. – Colette Sirat – Malachi Beit-Arié}, *Codices hebraicis litteris exarati quo tempore scripti fuerint exhibentes*, II: *de 1021 à 1079*, Turnhout: Brepols (Monumenta Palaeographica Medii Aevi, Series Hebraica).

Gleßgen, Martin-Dietrich – Franz Lebsanft (1997), 'Von alter und neuer Philologie. Oder: Neuer Streit über Prinzipen und Praxis der Textkritik', in: *Alte und neue Philologie*, ed. by Martin-Dietrich Gleßgen – Franz Lebsanft, Tübingen: Max Niemeyer (Beihefte zu editio, 8), 1–14.

Glubokovskij, N.N. (1918), *Описание славянских рукописей хранящихся въ Королевской библиотеке Упсальскаго Университета* (*Opisanie slavjanskich rukopisej chranjaščichsja v Korolevskoj biblioteke Upsal'skago Universiteta*, 'Description of Slavonic Manuscripts in the Royal Library of Uppsala University') [manuscript].

Glubokovskij, N.N. (1919), *Les manuscrits slaves de la Bibliothèque de l'Université d'Upsal*, translated by Alexandre de Roubetz [manuscript].

Godet, Éric (1980–1982), 'La préparation du parchemin en Éthiopie', *Abbay*, 11, 203–210.

Goehring, James (1990), *The Crosby-Schøyen Code MS 193 in the Schøyen Collection*, Louvain: Peeters (Corpus Scriptorum Christianorum Orientalium, 521, Subsidia, 85).

Gogašvili, Dareǯan (2003), 'ეტრატი – საწერი მასალა და მისი დამზადების წესი (*Eṭraṭi – saçeri masala da misi damzadebis çesi*, 'Parchment as a writing material and the method of its preparation')', *Mravaltavi*, 20, 405–411.

Gogašvili, Dareǯan (2004), საწერი მასალების დამზადების ისტორია ქართულ ხელნაწერებში დაცული ცნობების მიხედვით (*Saçeri masalebis damzadebis isṭoria kartul xelnaçerebši daculi cnobebis mixedvit*, 'The history of writing materials according to the information given in Georgian manuscripts'), Tbilisi: Xelnaçerta insṭiṭuṭi [diss.].

Gogašvili, Dareǯan (2006), 'ხელნაწერი წიგნის დამზადება და მასთან დაკავშირებული ზოგიერთი ტერმინი (*Xelnaçeri çignis damzadeba da mastan daḳavširebuli zogierti ṭermini*, 'The making of the manuscript book and some terms related to this')', *Sakartvelos siʒveleni*, 9, 77–88.

Gollancz, Hermann (1912), *The Book of Protection, being a collection of charms now edited for the first time from Syriac mss*, London: Oxford University Press.

Gorgaʒe, S. (1927), 'სვანეთის მრავალთავი (*Svanetis mravaltavi*, 'The Polykephalion of Svanetia')', *Sakartvelos arkivi*, 3, 1–35.

Gori, Alessandro (1999), review of E. Wagner, *Afrikanische Handschriften*. II: *Islamische Handschriften aus Äthiopien*, Stuttgart: Steiner, 1997, *Aethiopica*, 2, 250–257.

Gori, Alessandro (2007), 'Manuscripts: Arabic manuscripts', in: *Encyclopaedia Aethiopica*, III: He-N, ed. by Siegbert Uhlig, Wiesbaden: Harrassowitz, 744–749.

Gori, Alessandro (2009), 'Italy in the Horn of Africa and the Ethiopian Islamic literary tradition: L. Robecchi Bricchetti and his collection of manuscripts', *Manuscripta Orientalia*, 15/2, 25–37.

Gori, Alessandro (2014) {with contributions from Anne Regourd – Jeremy R. Brown – Steve Delamarter}, *A Handlist of the Manuscripts in the Institute of Ethiopian Studies, Volume Two: The Arabic Materials of the Ethiopian Islamic Tradition*, Eugene, OR: Pickwick Publications (Ethiopic Manuscripts, Texts, and Studies, 20).

Gorskij, Aleksandr – Kapiton Nevostruev (1855–1869), *Описанiе славянскихъ рукописей Московской Синодальной библiотеки* (*Opisanïe slavjanskich" rukopisej Moskovskoj Sinodal'noj biblïoteki*, 'Description of Slavonic Manuscripts of Moscow Synod Library'), I–III, Moskva.

Goshen-Gottstein, Moshe H. (1979), *Syriac Manuscripts in the Harvard College Library. A Catalogue*, Harvard: Harvard University Press.

Götze, Albrecht (1922), *Die Schatzhöhle. Überlieferung und Quellen*, Heidelberg (Sitzungsberichte der Heidelberger Akademie der Wissenschaften. Philos.-histor. Klasse, 1922/4).

Grabar, André (1972), *Les manuscrits grecs enluminés de provenance italienne IXe-XIe siècle*, Paris: Klincksieck (Bibliothèque des Cahiers archéologiques, 8).

Grabar, Oleg (1970), 'The Illustrated Maqamat of the Thirteenth Century: the Bourgeoisie and the Arts', in: *The Islamic City. A Colloquium*, ed. by Albert Hourani, Oxford: University of Pennsylvania Press, 207–222.

Grabar, Oleg (1984), *The illustrations of the Maqamat*, Chicago–London: University of Chicago Press (Chicago visual library text-fiche, 45).

Grabar, Oleg (2006), *Dome of the Rock*, Harvard: Harvard University Press.

Graf, Georg (1934), *Catalogue des manuscrits arabes chrétiens conservés au Caire*, Città del Vaticano: Biblioteca Apostolica Vaticana (Studi e Testi, 63).

Graf, Georg (1944–1953), *Geschichte der christlichen arabischen Literatur*, I–V, Città del Vaticano: Biblioteca Apostolica Vaticana (Studi e Testi, 118, 133, 146, 147, 172).

Graffin, François (1963), 'Un inédit de l'abbé Isaïe sur les étapes de la vie monastique', *Orientalia Christiana Periodica*, 29, 449–454.

Granberg, Antoaneta (2005), 'On Deciphering Mediaeval Runic Scripts from the Balkans', in: *Културните текстове на миналото: знаци, текстове, носители* (*Kulturnite tekstove na minaloto: znaci, tekstove, nositeli*, 'Cultural Texts of the Past: Signs, Texts, Mediators), III, Sofia: St Kliment Ohridski UP, 128–139.

Grébaut, Sylvain (1938), *Catalogue des manuscrits éthiopiens de la Collection Griaule*, I: *sections I–VI*, Paris: Institut d'ethnologie (Université de Paris: Travaux et mémoires de l'Institut d'ethnologie, 29).

Grébaut, Sylvain (1941), *Catalogue des manuscrits éthiopiens de la Collection Griaule*, II: *sections VII–IX*, Paris: Librairie Orientaliste P. Geuthner (Miscellanea Africana Lebaudy, 3).

Grébaut, Sylvain (1944), *Catalogue des manuscrits éthiopiens de la Collection Griaule*, III: *sections X–XI*, Paris: Institut d'ethnologie (Travaux et mémoires de l'Institut d'ethnologie, 30).

Grébaut, Sylvain – Eugène Tisserant (1935, 1936), *Bybliothecae apostolicae Vaticanae codices manu scripti recensiti iussu Pii XI Pontificis maximi. Codices Aethiopici Vaticani et Borgiani, Barberinianus orientalis 2, Rossianus 865*, I: *Enarratio codicum*; II: *Prolegomena, Indices, Tabulae*, Città del Vaticano: In Bybliotheca Vaticana.

Greek Manuscripts in Sweden, <http://www.manuscripta.se>, last access May 2014.

Greene, Belle Da Costa et al. (1934) {B.G. – Meta P. Harrsen – Charles Rufus Morey}, *The Pierpont Morgan Library Exhibition of Illuminated Manuscripts Held at the New York Public Library, November 1933 to April 1934*, New York: New York Public Library.

Greenfield, Jane (1991), 'Bookbinding', in: *The Coptic Encyclopedia*, II, ed. by Aziz S. Atiya, New York: Macmillan, 407–409.

Greetham, David C. (ed.) (1995), *Scholarly Editing: A Guide to Research*, New York: Modern Language Association of America.

Greg, Walter Wilson (1927), *The Calculus of Variants. An Essay in Textual Criticism*, Oxford: Clarendon Press.

Gregorios Y. Ibrahim (2009), *Text and Translations of the Chronicle of Michael the Great. The Edessa-Aleppo Syriac Codex of the Chronicle of Michael the Great*, I, Piscataway, NJ: Gorgias Press.

Griaule, Marcel (1930), *Le livre de recettes d'un dabtara abyssin*, Paris: Institut d'Ethnologie (Travaux et mémoires de l'Institut d'Ethnologie, 12).

Grier, James (1988), 'Lachmann, Bédier and the bipartite stemma: towards a responsible application of the common-error method', *Revue d'Histoire des Textes*, 18, 263–277.

Griffith, John G. (1968), 'A Taxonomic Study on the Manuscript Tradition of Juvenal', *Museum Helveticum*, 25/2, 101–138.

Griffith, Sydney H. (1997), 'From Aramaic to Arabic: The Languages of the Monasteries of Palestine in the Byzantine and Early Islamic Periods', *Dumbarton Oaks Papers*, 51, 11–31.

Griffith, Sydney H. (2010), *The church in the shadow of the mosque. Christians and Muslims in the world of Islam*, 4th edition, Princeton – Oxford: Princeton University Press.

Grob, Eva Mira (2010), *Documentary Arabic Private and Business Letters on Papyrus: Form and Function, Content and Context*, Berlin – New York: De Gruyter (Archiv für Papyrusforschung, Beihefte, 29).

Grob, Eva Mira (2013), 'A Catalogue of Dating Criteria for Undated Arabic Papyri with 'Cursive' Features', in: *Documents et histoire. Islam, VIIe-XVIe s. Actes des premières Journées d'étude internationales. École pratique des hautes études, IVe section, Musée du Louvre, département des Arts de l'Islam. Paris, 16 et 17 mai 2008*, ed. by Anne Regourd, Genève: Droz (École pratique des hautes études, Sciences historiques et philologiques II, Hautes études orientales – Moyen et Proche-Orient, 5/51), 123–143.

Grohmann, Adolf (1952), *From the World of Arabic Papyri*, Cairo: al-Maaref.

Grohmann, Adolf (1958), 'The problem of dating early Qur'āns', *Der Islam*, 33, 213–231.

Grohmann, Adolf (1967), *Arabische Paläographie*, 1. Teil, Vienna: Hermann Böhlaus Nachf. (Denkschriften der philosophisch-historischen Klasse, 94/1).

Grosdidier de Matons, Dominique – François Vinourd (2010), 'Description d'une reliure byzantine: techniques et matériaux', in: *The Legacy of Bernard de Montfaucon: Three Hundred Years of Studies on Greek Handwriting. Proceedings of the Seventh International Colloquium of Greek Palaeography (Madrid – Salamanca, 15-20 September 2008)*, ed. by Antonio Bravo García – Inmaculada Pérez Martín, Turnhout (Bibliologia: Elementa ad Librorum Studia Pertinentia, 31A), 363–371.

Grotzfeld, Heinz (2006), 'The Age of the Galland Manuscript of the Nights: Numismatic Evidence for Dating a Manuscript?', in: *The Arabian Nights Reader*, ed. by Ulrich Marzolph, Detroit: Wayne State University Press, 105–121.

Gruendler, Beatrice (1993), *The development of the Arabic scripts from the Nabatean to the first Islamic century according to dated texts*, Atlanta, GA: Scholars Press (Harvard Semitic Series, 43).

Gruendler, Beatrice (2006), 'Arabic Alphabet: Origin', in: *Encyclopedia of Arabic Language and Linguistics*, I, Leiden: Brill, 148–155.

Grünbart, Michael (2004), 'Byzantium – a Bibliophile Society?', *Basilissa. Byzantium, Belfast and Beyond*, 1, 113–121.

Grünberg, Karsten (1996), *Die kirchenslavische Überlieferung der Johannes-Apokalypse*, Frankfurt am Main: Peter Lang (Heidelberger Publikationen zur Slavistik A. Linguistische Reihe, 9).

Grusková, Jana (2010), *Untersuchungen zu den griechischen Palimpsesten der Österreichischen Nationalbibliothek. Codices historici, Codices philosophici et philologici, Codices iuridici*, Wien: Österreichische Akademie der Wissenschaften (Denkschriften der philosophisch-historischen Klasse, 401, Veröffentlichungen zur Byzanzforschung, 20).

Guesdon, Marie-Geneviève (1997), 'Les réclames dans les manuscrits arabes datés antérieurs à 1450', in: *Scribes et manuscrits du Moyen-Orient*, ed. by François Déroche – Francis Richard, Paris: Bibliothèque nationale de France, 66–75.

Guesdon, Marie-Geneviève (2002), 'La numérotation des cahiers et la foliotation dans les manuscrits arabes datés jusqu'à 1450', *Revue des mondes musulmans et de la Méditerranée*, 99-100, 101–115.

Guidi, Ignazio (1901), *Vocabolario amarico-italiano*, Roma: Istituto per l'Oriente.

Guidi, Ignazio (1907), 'Historia gentis Galla', in: *Historia regis Sarsa Dengel (Malak Sagad)*, ed. by Ignazio Guidi – Carlo Conti Rossini, Parisiis: E Typographeo republicae (Corpus Scriptorum Christianorum Orientalium, Scriptores Aethiopici, II/3), 223–231 (text), 193–208 (tr.).

Guidi, Vincenzo – Paolo Trovato (2004), 'Sugli stemmi bipartiti. Decimazione, asimmetria e calcolo delle probabilità', *Filologia italiana*, 1, 9–48.

Gulácsi, Zsuzsanna (2005), *Mediaeval Manichaean Book Art. A Codicological Study of Iranian and Turkic Illuminated Fragments from 8th-11th Century East Central Asia*, Leiden: Brill (Nag Hammadi and Manichaean studies, 57).

Gullath, Brigitte (2003), 'Handschriftenkunde', in: *Lebendiges Büchererbe. Säkularisation, Mediatisierung und die Bayerische Staatsbibliothek*, ed. by Comelia Jahn – Dieter Kudorfer, München: Bayerische Staatsbibliothek, 80–85.

Gullick, Michael (1995), 'How Fast Did Scribes Write? Evidence from Romanesque Manuscripts', in: *Making the Medieval Book: Techniques of Production. Proceedings of the fourth conference of the Seminar in the History of the Book to 1500, Oxford, July 1992*, ed. by Linda L. Brownrigg, Los Altos Hills: Anderson – London: Lovelace, 39–58.

Gullino, Giuseppe – Cesare Preti (2007), 'Marsili (Marsigli), Luigi Ferdinando', in: *Dizionario Biografico degli Italiani*, 70, 771b–781b.

Gumbert, Johann Peter (1984), 'Inventaire illustré de manuscrits médiévaux', *Gazette du livre médiéval*, 5, 11–15.

Gumbert, Johann Peter (1995a), 'C Catalogue and Codicology. Some Reader's Notes', in: *A Catalogue and Its Users. A Symposium on the Uppsala C Collection of Medieval Manuscripts*, ed. by Monica Hedlund, Uppsala: Acta universitatis Upsaliensis (Acta Bibliothecae R. Universitatis Upsaliensis, 34), 57–70.

Gumbert, Johann Peter (1995b), 'The Speed of Scribes', in: *Scribi e colofoni. Le sottoscrizioni di copisti dalle origini all'avvento della stampa. Atti del seminario di Erice, X Colloquio del Comité international de paléographie latine (23-28 ottobre 1993)*, ed. by Emma Condello – Giuseppe De Gregorio, Spoleto: Centro Italiano di Studi sull'Alto Medioevo (Biblioteca del «Centro per il collegamento degli studi medievali e umanistici in Umbria», 14), 57–69.

Gumbert, Johann Peter (2004), 'Codicological Units: Towards a Terminology for the Stratigraphy of the Non-Homogeneous Codex', in: *Il codice miscellaneo, tipologia e funzioni. Atti del convegno internazionale (Cassino, 14-17 maggio 2003)*, ed. by Edoardo Crisci – Oronzo Pecere, Cassino (Segno e testo, 2), 17–42.

Gumbert, Johann Peter (2008), 'Old and New Style. Terminology, and Ruling Systems and Methods', *Gazette du livre medieval*, 52–53, 25–33.

Gumbert, Johann Peter (2009a), 'IIMM – A completely new Type of Manuscript Inventory', *Gazette du livre médieval*, 55, 43–46.

Gumbert, Johann Peter (2009b), *IIMM. Illustrated Inventory of Medieval Manuscripts / Inventaire Illustré de Manuscrits Médiévaux / Illustriertes Inventar Mittelalterlicher Manuskripte. 2. Leiden, Universiteitsbibliotheek, BPL*, Hilversum: Verloren.

Gumbert, Johann Peter (2010a), 'Zur Kodikologie und Katalographie der zusammengesetzten Handschrift', in: *La descrizione dei manoscritti: esperienze a confronto*, ed. by Edoardo Crisci – Marilena Maniaci, Cassino: Università degli studi di Cassino, Dipartimento di filologia e storia (Studi e ricerche del Dipartimento di Filologia e Storia, 1), 1–18.

Gumbert, Johann Peter ([2010b]), *Words for Codices: A Codicological Terminology in English (online)*, <http://www.cei.lmu.de/extern/VocCod/WOR10-1.pdf>; <http://www.cei.lmu.de/extern/VocCod/WOR10-2.pdf>; <http://www.cei.lmu.de/extern/VocCod/WOR10-3.pdf>

Gumbert, Johann Peter (2011), 'The Tacketed Quire: an Exercise in Comparative Codicology', *Scriptorium*, 44/2, 299–320, pl. 50–54.

Gumbrecht, Hans Ulrich (2003), *The Powers of Philology. Dynamics of Textual Scholarship*, Urbana – Chicago, IL: University of Illinois Press.

Gutas, Dimitri (1975), *Greek Wisdom Literature in Arabic Translation. A Study of the Graeco-Arabic Gnomologia*, New Haven: American Oriental Society (American Oriental Series, 60).

Gutman, Ariel – Wido Th. van Peursen (2011), *The Two Syriac Versions of the Prayer of Manasseh*, Piscataway, NJ: Gorgias Press.

Gvaramia, Rusudan et al. (1987) {R.G. – Elene Meṭreveli – Caca Çanḳievi – Lili Xevsuriani – Lamara Ǯġamaia}, ქართულ ხელნაწერთა აღწერილობა. სინური კოლექცია (*Kartul xelnaçerta aġçeriloba. Sinuri ḳolekcia*, 'Description of Georgian manuscripts. Sinai collection'), III, Tbilisi: Sakartvelos SSR Mecnierebata Aḳademiis Gamomcemloba.

Gwilliam, George Henry et al. (1896) {G.G. – Francis Crawford Burkitt – John F. Stenning}, *Biblical and Patristic Relics of the Palestinian Syriac Literature from mss. in the Bodleian Library and in the Library of Saint Catherine on Mount Sinai*, Oxford: Clarendon Press (Anecdota Oxoniensia. Texts, Documents, and Extracts chiefly from Manuscripts in the Bodleian and other Oxford Libraries. Semitic Series, I/9).

ter Haar Romeny, B. (2006), 'The Greek vs. The Peshitta in a West Syrian Exegetical Collection (BL Add. 12168)', in: *The Peshitta: Its Use in Literature and Liturgy. Proceedings of the Third Peshitta Symposium Held at Leiden University, 12–15 August 2001*, ed. by B. ter Haar Romeny, Leiden: Brill (Monographs of the Peshitta Institute Leiden, 15), 297–310.

Ḥaddād, Buṭrus [Petros] – Ǧāk Isḥāq [Jacques Isaac] (1998), المخطوطات السريانية والعربية في خزانة الرهبانية الكلدانية في بغداد (*Al-maḫṭūṭāt al-suryāniyya wa-'l-'arabiyya fī ḫazānat al-rahbāniyyat al-Kaldāniyya fī Baġdād*, 'Syriac and Arabic manuscripts in the Treasure of the Chaldean Monastery in Baghdad'), I–II, Baghdad: al-Maǧma' al-'Ilmī al-'Irāqī.

Haentjens Dekker, Ronald – Gregor Middell (2011), 'Computer-Supported Collation with CollateX: Managing Textual Variance in an Environment with Varying Requirements', in: *Supporting Digital Humanities 2011. University of Copenhagen, Denmark, 17–18 November 2011*, Copenhagen.

Ḥaǧǧī Ḫalīfa (1835–1858), كشف الظنون عن اسامى الكتب والفنون (*Kašf al-ẓunūn 'an asāmī al-kutub wa-'l-funūn*). *Lexicon biblographicum et encyclopaedicum a Mustafa ben Abdallah Katib Jelebi dicto et nomine Haji Khalfa celebrato compositum*, I–VII, ed. by Gustav Fluegel, Leipzig: Oriental Translation Fund of Great Britain and Ireland.

Hahn, Oliver et al. (2004) {O.H. – Wolfgang Malzer – Birgit Kanngießer – Burkhard Beckhoff}, 'Characterization of Iron Gall Inks in Historical Manuscripts Using X-Ray Fluorescence Spectrometry', *X-Ray Spectrometry*, 33, 234–239.

Hahn, Oliver (2008a) {O.H. – Max Wilke – Timo Wolff}, 'Influence of aqueous calcium phytate/calcium hydrogen carbonate treatment on the chemical composition of iron gall inks', *Restaurator. International Journal for the Preservation of Library and Archival Material*, 29, 235–250.

Hahn, Oliver (2008b) {O.H. – Timo Wolff – Hartmut-Ortwin Feistel – Ira Rabin – Malachi Beit-Arié}, 'The Erfurt Hebrew Giant Bible and the Experimental XRF Analysis of Ink and Plummet Composition', *Gazette du livre médiéval*, 51, 16–29.

Haile Gabriel Dagne (1989), 'The Scriptorium at the Imperial Palace and the Manuscripts of Addis Ababa Churches', in: *Proceedings of the Eighth International conference of Ethiopian Studies. University of Addis Ababa, 1984*, II, ed. by Tadesse Beyene, Addis Ababa, 215–223.

Hajdú, Kerstin (2002), *Katalog der griechischen Handschriften der Bayerischen Staatsbibliothek München*, Bd. 10, 1: *Die Sammlung griechischer Handschriften in der Münchener Hofbibliothek bis zum Jahr 1803. Eine Bestandsgeschichte der Codices graeci Monacenses 1–323 mit Signaturenkonkordanzen und Beschreibung des Stephanus-Katalogs* (*Cbm Cat. 48*), Wiesbaden: Harrassowitz (Catalogus codicum manu scriptorum Bibliothecae Monacensis, 10/1).

Hajdú, Kerstin (2003), *Katalog der griechischen Handschriften der Bayerischen Staatsbibliothek München*, Bd. 3, *Codices graeci Monacenses 110-180*, Wiesbaden: Harrassowitz (Catalogus codicum manu scriptorum Bibliothecae Monacensis, 2/3).

Hajdú, Kerstin (2012), *Katalog der griechischen Handschriften der Bayerischen Staatsbibliothek München*. Bd. 4: *Codices graeci Monacenses 181–265*, Wiesbaden: Harrassowitz (Catalogus codicum manu scriptorum Bibliothecae Monacensis, 2/4).

Hakobyan, Vazgen – Ašot Hovhannisyan (1974, 1978, 1984), Հայերեն ձեռագրերի ԺԷ դարի հիշատակարաններ (*Hayeren jeṙagreri XVII dari hišatakaranner*, 'Colophons of the Seventeenth-Century Armenian Manuscripts'), I (*1601-1620*), II (*1621-1640*), III (*1641-1660*), Erevan: Haykakan SSH Gitut'yunneri Akademia.

Haldane, Duncan (1983), *Islamic Bookbindings in the Victoria and Albert Museum*, London: The World of Islam Festival Trust.

Halflants, Bruno (2007), *Le conte du Portefaix et des Trois Jeunes Femmes dans le manuscrit de Galland* (*XIV*[e] *– XV*[e] *siècles*): *édition, traduction et étude du Moyen Arabe d'un conte des Mille et une nuits*, Louvain-la-Neuve: Université Catholique de Louvain, Institut Orientaliste (Publications de l'Institut orientaliste de Louvain, 55).

Halflants, Bruno (2012), 'Présentation du livre Le Conte du Portefaix et des Trois Jeunes Femmes, dans le Manuscrit de Galland (XIVe–XVe siècles)', in: *Middle Arabic and Mixed Arabic: Diachrony and Synchrony*, ed. by Liesbeth Zack – Arie Schippers, Leiden – Boston: Brill (Studies in Semitic Languages and Linguistics, 64), 113–123.

Hall, Isaac H. (1886), *Williams Manuscript. The Syrian Antilegomena Epistles. 2 Peter, 2 and 3 John, and Jude, written A.D. 1471 by Suleimân of Husn Keifa*, Baltimore, ML: Publication Agency of the John Hopkins University.

Hammerschmidt, Ernst (1973), *Äthiopische Handschriften vom Ṭānāsee* 1: *Reisebericht und Beschreibung der Handschriften in dem Kloster der Heiligen Gabriel auf der Insel Kebrān*, Wiesbaden: Steiner (Verzeichnis der orientalischen Handschriften in Deutschland, 20/1).

Hammerschmidt, Ernst (1977a), *Äthiopische Handschriften vom Ṭānāsee* 2: *Die Handschriften von Dabra Māryām und von Rēmā*, Wiesbaden: Steiner (Verzeichnis der orientalischen Handschriften in Deutschland, 20/2).

Hammerschmidt, Ernst (1977b), *Illuminierte Handschriften der Staatsbibliothek Presussischer Kulturbesitz und Handschriften vom Ṭānāsee*, Graz: Akad. Druck- u. Verlag-Anst. (Codices Aethiopici, 1).

Hammerschmidt, Ernst – Otto, A. Jäger (1968), *Illuminierte äthiopische Handschriften*, Wiesbaden: Steiner (Verzeichnis der orientalischen Handschriften in Deutschland, 15).

Hammerschmidt, Ernst – Veronika Six (1983), *Äthiopische Handschriften* 1: *Die Handschriften der Staatsbibliothek Preussischer Kulturbesitz*, Wiesbaden: Steiner (Verzeichnis der orientalischen Handschriften in Deutschland, 20/4).

Hamzaoui, Rachad (1965), *L'Académie Arabe de Damas et le problème de la modernisation de la langue arabe*, Leiden: Brill.

Haran, Menahem (1985), 'Bible Scrolls in Eastern and Western Jewish Communities from Qumran to the High Middle Ages', *Hebrew Union College Annual*, 56, 21–62.

Haran, Menahem (1991), 'Technological Heritage in the Preparation of Skins for Biblical Texts in Medieval Oriental Jewry', in: *Pergament, Geschichte – Struktur – Restaurierung – Herstellung*, ed. by Peter Rück, Sigmaringen: J. Thorbecke (Historische Hilfswissenschaften, 2), 35–43.

Hārīn, 'Abd al-Salām Muḥammad (1965), تحقيق النصوص ونشرها اول كتاب عربي في هذا الفن يوضح مناهجه ويعالج مشكلاته (*Taḥqīq al-nuṣūṣ wa-našruhā: awwal kitāb 'arabī fī hāḏā al-fann yuwaḍḍiḥu manāhiğahu wa-yu'āliğu muškilātahu*, 'Editing and publishing Arabic texts: first Arabic book in this subject explaining its methods and treating its problems'), Cairo: Mu'assasat al-Ḥalabī li-'l-Našr wa-'l-Tawzī'.

Harlfinger, Dieter (ed.) (1980a), *Griechische Kodikologie und Textüberlieferung*, Darmstadt: Wissenschaftliche Buchgesellschaft.

Harlfinger, Dieter (1980b), 'Zur Datierung von Handschriften mit Hilfe von Wasserzeichen', in: *Griechische Kodikologie und Textüberlieferung*, ed. by Dieter Harlfinger, Darmstadt: Wissenschaftliche Buchgesellschaft, 144–169.

Harlfinger, Dieter – Johanna Harlfinger (1974, 1980), *Wasserzeichen aus griechischen Handschriften*, I–II, Berlin: Mielke.

Harrak, Amir (2011), *Catalogue of Syriac and Garshuni Manuscripts owned by the Iraqi Department of Antiquities and Heritage*, Louvain: Peeters (Corpus Scriptorum Christianorum Orientalium, 693, Subsidia 126).

Harut'yunyan, A. (1941), Ներկերի եւ թանակների գործածությունը հին հայկական ձեռագրերում / *Краски и чернила по древне-армянским рукописям* (*Nerkeri ew t'anakneri gorcacut'yunə hin haykakan jeṙagrerum / Kraski i černila po drevne-armjanskim rukopisjam*, 'The Use of Pigments and Inks in Old Armenian Manuscripts'), Erevan: Haykakan SSH Żołkomsovetin kic' jeṙagreri Usumnasirut'yan Institut (Matenadaran).

Ḥasan Mawlāy – Ayman Fu'ād Sayyid (2004),فهرس المخطوطات الإسلامية الموجودة بمعهد الأبحاث في العلوم الإنسانية، النيجر (*Fihris al-maḫṭūṭāt al-Islāmiyya al-mawğūda bi-Ma'had al-Abḥāṯ fī al-'Ulūm al-Insāniyya, al-Nīğar*) / *Catalogue of Islamic Manuscripts at the Institut des Recherches en Sciences Humaines (IRSH), Niger*, I–II, London: Al-Furqān (Silsilat Fahāris al-maḫṭūṭāt al-Islāmiyya / Handlists of Islamic Manuscripts, 48).

Hasznos, Andrea (2006–2007), 'A Shenoute Homily Found in Theban Tomb 65', *Enchoria*, 30, 7–9, pls. 1–3.

Hatch, William Henry Payne (1931), *Greek and Syrian miniatures in Jerusalem, with an introduction and a description of each of the seventy-one miniatures reproduced*, Cambridge, MA: Medieval Academy of America.

Hatch, William Henry Payne (1946), *An Album of Dated Syriac Manuscripts*, Boston: The American Academy of Arts and Sciences.

Hatch, William Henry Payne (2002), *An Album of Dated Syriac Manuscripts*, introduction by Lucas Van Rompay, Piscataway: Gorgias Press.

Haugen, Odd Einar (ed.), *Parvum Lexicon Stemmatologicum. A wiki hosted by the University of Helsinki*, <https://wiki.hiit.fi/display/stemmatology>, last access 2014.

Havet, Louis (1911), *Manuel de critique verbale appliquée aux textes latins*, Paris: Librairie Hachette.

Hazai, György – Andreas Tietze (2006), *Ferec ba'd eş-şidde* (*Ein frühosmanisches Geschichtenbuch*): *‚Freud nach Leid'*, 1. *Text*, 2. *Faksimiles*, Berlin: Klaus Schwarz (Studien zur Sprache, Geschichte und Kultur der Türkvölker, 5/2).

Heal, Kristian S. (2012), 'Corpora, eLibraries and Databases: Locating Syriac Studies in the 21st Century', *Hugoye*, 15/1, 65–78.

Healey, John F. (2000), 'The Early History of the Syriac Script. A Reassessment', *Journal of Semitic Studies*, 45, 55–67.

Heath, Peter (2004), 'Sīra Sha'biyya', in: *Encyclopaedia of Islam, Second Edition*, Leiden: Brill Online <http://referenceworks.brillonline.com/entries/encyclopaedia-of-islam-2/si-ra-s-h-a-biyya-SIM_7058?s.num= 543&s.rows=100&s.start=500>.

Hebbelynck, Adolphe (1900, 1901), 'Les mystères des lettres grecques d'après un manuscrit copte-arabe de la bibliothèque Bodléienne d'Oxford', I–III: *Le Muséon*, 19, 5–36, 105–136, 269–300, IV–V: *Le Muséon*, 20, 5–333, 369–414.

Hebbelynck, Adolphe – Arnold van Lantschoot (1937), *Codices coptici Vaticani Barberiniani Borgiani Rossiani*, 1. *Codices vaticani*, Città del Vaticano: Biblioteca Vaticana.

van der Heide, Albert (1977), *Hebrew Manuscripts of Leiden University Library*, Leiden: Universitaire Pers Leiden (Codices manuscripti, 18).

Heidemann, Stefan (2010), 'Calligraphy on Islamic coins', in: *The aura of Alif. The art of writing in Islam*, ed. by Jurgen Wasim Frembgen, Munich: Prestel Publishing, 161–171.

Heinen, Anton (1994), 'Vatican City State', in: *The World Survey of Islamic Manuscripts*, IV, ed. by Geoffrey Roper, London: Al-Furqān, 629–642.

Heldman, Marilyn (1989), 'An Ewostathian style and the Gunda Gunde style in 15th-century Ethiopian manuscript illumination', in: *Proceedings of the First International Conference of the History of Ethiopian Art, Held at the Warburg Institute, 21-22 October 1986*, London, 5–14, 135–139.

Heldman, Marilyn (1993), 'The Early Solomonic Period 1270–1527', in: *African Zion. The sacred art of Ethiopia. Catalog*, ed. by Marilyn Heldman – Stuart Munro-Hay, New Haven: Yale University Press, 141–197.

Heldman, Marilyn (2003), 'Canon Tables', in: *Encyclopaedia Aethiopica*, I: *A–C*, ed. by Siegbert Uhlig et al., Wiesbaden: Harrassowitz, 680–681.

Heldman, Marilyn (2007), 'Metropolitan Bishops as Agents of Artistic Interaction between Egypt and Ethiopia during the Thirteenth and Fourteenth Centuries', in: *Interactions. Artistic Interchange between the Eastern and Western Worlds in the Medieval Period*, ed. by Colum Hourihane, Princeton: Princeton University in association with Penn State University Press (The Index of Christian Art. Occasional Papers), 84–105.

Hemmerdinger-Iliadou, Démocratie (1965), 'Étude comparative des versions grecque, latine et slave de la Vita Abrahamii (BHG 5, 6, et 7)', *Études balkaniques*, 2-3, 301–308.

Hendel, Ronald S. (2010), 'Assessing the Text-Critical Theories of the Hebrew Bible after Qumran', in: *The Oxford Handbook of the Dead Sea Scrolls*, ed. by Timothy H. Lim – John J. Collins, Oxford: Oxford University Press, 281–302.

Herskovits Library of African Studies at Northwestern University <http://digital.library.northwestern.edu/ arbmss/index.html>, last access October 2014.

Herzog, Thomas (2006), *Geschichte und Imaginaire. Entstehung, Überlieferung und Bedeutung der Sīrat Baibars in ihrem sozio-politischen Kontext*, Wiesbaden: Harrassowitz (Diskurse der Arabistik, 8).

Herzog, Thomas (2012), 'Orality and the Tradition of Arabic Storytelling', in: *Medieval Oral Literature*, ed. by Karl Reichl, Berlin – New York: De Gruyter (De Gruyter Lexikon), 629–651.

Heurtel, Chantal (2007), 'Marc le prêtre de Saint-Marc', in: *Actes du Huitième Congrès International d'Études Coptes, Paris 28 Juin – 3 Juillet 2004*, II.2, ed. by Nathalie Bosson – Anne Boud'hors, Leuven: Peeters (Orientalia Lovaniensia Analecta, 163.2), 727–749.

Heyworth, Peter L. (1981), 'The Punctuation of Middle English Texts', in: *Medieval Studies for J. A. W. Bennet*, ed. by Peter L. Heyworth, Oxford: Clarendon Press, 139–157.

Hinterberger, Martin (2014), 'Between Simplification and Elaboration: Byzantine Metaphraseis Compared', in: *Textual Transmission in Byzantium: between Textual Criticism and Quellenforschung*, ed. by Juan Signes Codoñer – Inmaculada Pérez Martín, Turnhout: Brepols (Lectio Studies in the Transmission of Texts and Ideas, 2), 33–60.

Hintze, Almut (2012a), 'Manuscripts of the Yasna and Yasna ī Rapithwin', in: *The transmission of the Avesta*, ed. by Alberto Cantera, Wiesbaden: Harrassowitz (Iranica, 20), 244–278.

Hintze, Almut (2012b), 'On Editing the Avesta', in: *The transmission of the Avesta*, ed. by Alberto Cantera, Wiesbaden: Harrassowitz (Iranica, 20), 419–432.

Hirschler, Konrad (2012), *The Written Word in the Medieval Arabic Lands: A Social and Cultural History of Reading Practices*, Edinburgh: Edinburgh University Press.

Hobson, Geoffrey Dudley (1938), 'Some Early Bindings and Binders' tools', *The Library*, ser. 4, 19, 202–249, pls. 1–7.

Hofenk de Graaff, Judith H. et al. (2004) {J.H.G. – Wilma G. Roelofs – Maarten van Bommel}, *The Colourful Past: Origins, Chemistry and Identification of Natural Dyestuffs*, London: Abegg-Stiftung, Riggisberg and Archetype Publications Ltd.

Hoffman, Adina – Peter Cole (2011), *Sacred Trash: The Lost and Found World of the Cairo Geniza*, New York: Schocken.

Hoffmann, Karl (1969), 'Zur Yasna-Überlieferung', *Münchener Studien zur Sprachwissenschaft*, 26, 35–38.

Hoffmann, Karl (1971), 'Zum Zeicheninventar der Avesta-Schrift', in: *Festgabe Deutscher Iranisten zur 2500 Jahrfeier Irans*, Stuttgart: Hochwacht Druck, 64–73.

Hoffmann, Karl (1986), 'Avestisch ṣ̌', in: *Studia grammatica iranica. Festschrift für Helmut Humbach*, ed. by Rüdiger Schmitt – Prods Oktor Skjaervø, München: Kitzinger (Münchener Studien zur Sprachwissenschaft. Beiheft. Neue Folge, 13), 168–183.

Hoffmann, Karl – Johanna Narten (1989), *Der Sasanidische Archetypus. Untersuchungen zu Schreibung und Lautgestalt des Avestischen*, Wiesbaden: Reichert.

Hoffmann, Philippe (ed.) (1998), *Recherches de codicologie comparée: la composition du codex au Moyen Âge en Orient et en Occident*, Paris: Presses de l'École normale supérieure (Collection bibliologie).

Höfler, Karl Adolph Constantin – Paul Joseph Šafařík (1857), *Glagolitische Fragmente*, Prag: Haase.

Hollerweger, Hans (1999), *Lebendiges Kulturerbe - Living Cultural Heritage - Canlı Kültür Mirası. Turabdin: Wo die Sprache Jesu gesprochen wird - Where Jesus language is spoken - İsa Mesih dilinin konuşulduğu yer*, Linz: Freunde des Turabdin.

Holman, Susan et al. (2012) {S.H. – Caroline Macé – Brian Matz}, 'De Beneficentia: A Homily on Social Action attributed to Basil of Caesarea', *Vigiliae Christianae*, 66, 457–481.

Holovata, Larisa V. – Marija M. Kol'buch (eds) (2007), *Кириличні рукописні книги у фондах Львівської наукової бібліотеки ім. В. Стефаника НАН України. Каталог* (*Kyrylyčni rukopysni knyhy u fondach L'vivskoji naukovoji biblioteky im. V. Stefanyka NAN Ukrajiny. Kataloh*, 'Cyrillic Manuscripts in the Collections of the Stefanik Lviv National Library'), I: *XI-XVI вв.* (*XI–XVI vv.*, '11th–16th cent.'), Lviv: Oriyana-Nova.

Hortin, Samuel (1634), *Clavis Bibliothecae Bongarsianae*, Bern.

Ḥosaynī, Sayyed Aḥmad et al. (1354–1395 š. / 1975–2010 CE), فهرست نسخه های خطی کتابخانهٔ عمومی حضرت آیة الله العظمی نجفی مرعشی (*Fehrest-e nosxeh-hā-ye xaṭṭī ketābxāneh-ye ʿomūmī-ye haẓrat-e Āyatollāh al-ʿOzmā Nağafī Marʿašī*, 'Catalogue of the Manuscripts in the Public Library of Grand Ayatollah Nağafī Marʿašī'), I–XXXVIII, index I–III, Qom: Ketābxāneh-ye ʿomūmī-ye Āyatollāh al-ʿOzmā Nağafī Marʿašī.

Houdas, Octave (1886), 'Essai sur l'écriture maghrébine', in: *Nouveaux mélanges orientaux*; *mémoires, textes et traductions publiés par les professeurs de l'École spéciale des langues orientales vivantes, à l'occasion du Septième Congrès international des orientalistes réuni à Vienne* (*septembre 1886*), Paris: Leroux, 85–112.

Hoyland, Robert (2010), 'Mount Nebo, Jabal Ramm, and the status of Christian Palestinian Aramaic and old Arabic in the Late Roman Palestine and Arabia', in: *The Development of Arabic as a Written Language*, ed. by Michael C.A. Macdonald, Oxford: Archaeopress (Supplement to the Proceedings of the Seminar for Arabian Studies, 40), 29–46.

Hristova, Borjana et al. (2003, 2004) {B.H. – Darinka Karadžova – Elena Uzunova}, *Бележки на българските книжовници*: *X–XVIII век* (*Beležki na bălgarskite knižovnici X–XVIII vek*, 'Notes on Bulgarian Writers of the 10th–18th centuries'), I: *X–XV век* (*X–XV vek*, '10th–15th centuries'); II: *XVI–XVIII век* (*XVI–XVIII vek*, '16th–18th centuries'), Sofia: NBKM.

Huisman, August Jan Willem (1967), *Les manuscrits arabes dans le monde*: *une bibliographie des catalogues*, Leiden: E.J. Brill.

Humbach, Helmut (1973), 'Beobachtungen zur Überlieferungsgeschichte des Awesta', *Münchener Studien zur Sprachwissenschaft*, 31, 109–122.

Humbert, Geneviève (1998), 'Papiers non filigranés utilisés au Proche-Orient jusqu'en 1450. Essai de typologie', *Journal Asiatique*, 286, 1–54.

Humbert, Geneviève (1999), 'Un papier fabriqué vers 1350 en Égypte', in: *Le papier au Moyen Âge*: *histoire et techniques*, ed. by Monique Zerdoun Bat-Yehouda, Turnhout: Brepols (Bibliologia: Elementa ad Librorum Studia Pertinentia, 19), 61–73.

Humbert, Geneviève (2002), 'Le manuscrit arabe et ses papiers', in: *La tradition manuscrite en écriture arabe*, ed. by Geneviève Humbert, Paris (Revue des Mondes Musulmans et de la Méditerranée, 99-100), 55–77.

Humbert, Jean-Baptiste – Alain Desreumaux (eds) (1998), *Khirbet es-Samra* (*Jordanie*). I. *La voie romaine, le cimetière, les documents épigraphiques*, Turnhout: Brepols (Bibliothèque de l'Antiquité tardive, 1).

Hunger, Herbert (1961), *Katalog der griechischen Handschriften der Österreichischen Nationalbibliothek* 1: *Codices historici, codices philosophici et philologici*, Wien: Prachner – Hollinek (Museion N.F. 4, Bd. 1, T. 1).

Hunger, Herbert (1989), *Schreiben und Lesen im Byzanz*: *die byzantinische Buchkultur*, München: C. H. Beck (Beck's archäologische Bibliothek).

Hunger, Herbert et al. (1984) {H.H. – Otto Kresten – Christian Hannick}, *Katalog der griechischen Handschriften der Österreichischen Nationalbibliothek* 3,2: *Codices theologici 101-200*, Wien: Hollinek (Museion N.F. 4, Bd. 1, T. 3,2).

Hunger, Herbert – Otto Kresten (1969), *Katalog der griechischen Handschriften der Österreichischen Nationalbibliothek* 2: *Codices juridici, codices medici*, Wien: Hollinek (Museion N.F. 4, Bd. 1, T. 2).

Hunger, Herbert – Otto Kresten (1976), *Katalog der griechischen Handschriften der Österreichischen Nationalbibliothek* 3,1: *Codices theologici 1-100*, Wien: Prachner (Museion N.F. 4, Bd. 1, T. 3,1).

Hunger, Herbert – Wolfgang Lackner (1992), *Katalog der griechischen Handschriften der Österreichischen Nationalbibliothek* 3,3: *Codices theologici 201-337*, Wien: Hollinek (Museion N.F. 4, Bd. 1, T. 3,3).

Hunt, Lucy-Anne (2001), 'Leaves from an Illustrated Syriac Lectionary', in: *Syrian Christians under Islam. The First Thousand Years*, ed. by David Thomas, Leiden – Boston – Köln: Brill, 185–202.

Hunter, Erica C. (1998), 'Syriac Ostraca from Mesopotamia', in: *Symposium Syriacum VII. Uppsala University, Department of Asian and African Languages 11-14 August 1996*, ed. by René Lavenant, Roma: Pontificio Istituto Orientale (Orientalia Christiana Analecta, 256), 617–639.

Hunter, Erica C. (1999), 'Another Scroll Amulet from Kurdistan', in: *After Bardaisan. Studies on Continuity and Change in Syriac Christianity in Honour of Prof. Han J W Drijvers*, ed. by G. Reinink – A. Klugkist, Leuven: Peeters (Orientalia Lovaniensia Analecta, 89), 161–172.

Hunwick, John O. – Rex Sean O'Fahey (1995–), *Arabic Literature of Africa*: *The Writings of Central Sudanic Africa*, I–VI, Leiden: Brill (Handbuch der Orientalistik, 1: The Near and Middle East, 13/1–6).

Hurtado, Larry W. (2006), *The Earliest Christian Artifacts*: *Manuscripts and Christian Origins*, Grand Rapids: Eerdmans.

Hussein Ahmed (1994), 'Ethiopia', in: *The World Survey of Islamic Manuscripts*, IV, ed. by Geoffrey Roper, London: Al-Furqān, 128–130.

Hutter, Irmgard (1977–1997), *Corpus der byzantinischen Miniaturen-handschriften*, I–III: *Oxford Bodleian Library*, IV: *Oxford Christ Church*, V: *Oxford college libraries*, Stuttgart: Hiersemann (Denkmäler der Buchkunst, 2, 3, 5, 9).

Hyvernat, Henri (1888), *Album de Paléographie copte pour servir à l'introduction paléographique des Actes des Martyrs de l'Égypte*, Paris: E. Leroux.

ICN (Instituut Collectie Nederland) (2005), *Het beperken van lichtschade aan museale objecten*: *lichtlijnen*, <http://www.cultureelerfgoed.nl/sites/default/files/documenten/info13.pdf>, Amersfoort: ICN.

ICOM (International Council of Museums) (2004), *Code of Ethics*, <http://icom.museum/the-vision/code-of-ethics/?p=ethics>, Paris: ICOM.

ICON (The Institute of Conservation) (2011), *Care and conservation of books*, <http://www.icon.org.uk/images/leaflets/careconbooksa4version.pdf>, London: ICON.

ICSU (International Council for Science) (last access 2013), *Freedom and Responsibility Portal*, <http://www.icsu.org/freedom-responsibility>, Paris: ICSU.

IFLA (International Federation of Library Associations and Institutions (1979), *The Principles of Conservation and Restoration of the Collections in the Libraries*, Edinburgh: IFLA.

Iḥsānī, ʿAlī (1358 š./1979 CE), تاریخ بیهقی (*Tārīḫ-i Bayhaqī*, 'The *History* of Bayhaqī'), Tehran: Čāpḫāna-yi Dānišgāh.

İhsanoğlu, Ekmeleddin (ed) (1984), *Catalogue of Islamic Medical Manuscripts in Arabic, Turkish & Persian in the libraries of Turkey*, with contributions by Ramazan Şeşen – Cemil Akpinar – Cevad Izgi, Istanbul: Research Centre for Islamic History, Art, and Culture (Studies and Sources on the History of Science).

İhsanoğlu, Ekmeleddin – Ramazan Şeşen (eds) (2008), *Osmanlı Tıbbi Bilimler Literatürü Tarihi*, I–IV, Istanbul: IRCICA.

IIC (International Institute for Conservation of Historic and Artistic Works) (2010), *The Plus/Minus Dilemma*: *The Way Forward in Environmental Guidelines. Conference transcript*, <https://www.iiconservation. org/sites/default/files/dialogues/plus-minus-en.pdf>, Milwakee: International Institute for Conservation of Historic and Artistic Works (Dialogues for the New Century. Discussions on the conservation of cultural heritage in a changing world).

Imbert, Frédéric (2013), 'Le coran des pierres: statistiques et premières analyses', in: *Le Coran, nouvelles approches*, ed. by Mehdi Azaiez – Sabrina Mervin, Paris: Centre national de la recherche scientifique, 99–124.

Imnaišvili, Ivane (1961), იოვანეს გამოცხადება და მისი თარგმანება: ძველი ქართული ვერსია (*Ioanes gamocxadeba da misi targmaneba. Ʒveli kartuli versia*, 'St John's Revalation and its Explanation. The Old Georgian version'), Tbilisi: Saxelmçipo Universiṭeṭi (Ʒveli kartuli enis ḳatedris šromebi, 7).

Imnaišvili, Vaxṭang (2004), უძველესი ქართული ხელნაწერები ავსტრიაში (*Uʒvelesi kartuli xelnaçerebi avsṭriaši*, 'The oldest Georgian manuscripts in Austria'), Tbilisi: Sakartvelos Saṗaṭriarko.

Indian National Mission for Manuscripts, <http:// www.namami.org/pdatabase.aspx>, last access October 2014.

Institut de recherche et d'histoire des textes (1977), *Guide pour l'élaboration d'une notice de manuscrit*, *Bibliographies*, *colloques*, *travaux préparatoires*, Paris: Institut de recherche et d'histoire des textes (Informatique et documentation textuelle).

Inventario general de manuscritos de la Biblioteca National, I–XIII, Madrid, 1953–1995.

Ipert, Stéphane (1995), 'L'environnement dans les bâtiments', *Conservation préventive du patrimoine documentaire. Archives-livres-photographies-arts graphiques*, fiche 2.

Ipert, Stéphane (2005), 'Les programmes de préservation', in: *Les trésors manuscrits de la Méditerranée*, Dijon: Faton, 294–307.

Irigoin, Jean (1950), 'Les premiers manuscrits grecs écrits sur papier et le problème du bombycin', *Scriptorium*, 4, 194–204.

Irigoin, Jean (1954), 'Stemmas bifides et états de manuscrits', *Revue de Philologie*, 3/28, 211–217.

Irigoin, Jean (1968), 'La datation des papiers italiens des XIIIe et XIVe siècles', *Papiergeschichte*, 18, 49–52, 76.

Irigoin, Jean (1972), *Règles et recommandations pour les éditions critiques* (*Série grecque*), Paris: Les Belles Lettres.

Irigoin, Jean (1979), 'Sélection et utilisation des variantes', in: *La pratique des ordinateurs dans la critique des textes*, Paris: Centre national de la recherche scientifique (Colloques internationaux du Centre national de la recherche scientifique, 579), 265–271.

Irigoin, Jean (1981a), 'La critique des textes doit être historique', in: *La critica testuale greco-latina, oggi. Metodi e problemi. Atti del Convegno Internazionale* (*Napoli 29-31 ottobre 1979*), ed. by Enrico Flores, Roma: Edizioni dell'Ateneo, 27–43.

Irigoin, Jean (1981b), 'Une écriture d'imitation: le Palatinus Vaticanus Graecus 186', *Illinois Classical Studies*, 6/2, 416–430.

Irigoin, Jean (1988), 'Papiers orientaux et papiers occidentaux. Les techniques de confection de la feuille', *Bollettino dell'Istituto Centrale per la Patologia del Libro*, 42, 57–80.

Irigoin, Jean (1991), 'Typologie et description codicologique des manuscrits de papier', in: *Paleografia e codicologia greca. Atti del II Colloquio internazionale di paleografia greca* (*Berlino-Wolfenbüttel, 17-21 ottobre 1983*), I, ed. by Dieter Harlfinger – Giancarlo Prato, Alessandria: Edizioni dell'Orso, 275–303.

Irigoin, Jean (1993), 'Les papiers non filigranés. État présent des recherches et perspectives d'avenir', in: *Ancient and Medieval Book Materials and Techniques* (*Erice, 18-25 September 1992*), I, ed. by Marilena Maniaci – Paola F. Munafò, Città del Vaticano: Biblioteca Apostolica Vaticana (Studi e Testi, 357), 265–312.

Irigoin, Jean (1996), 'Dom Bernard de Montfaucon', in: *L'Académie des inscriptions et belles-lettres et l'Académie des beaux-arts face au message de la Grèce ancienne*, ed. by Jean Leclant – Bernard Zehrfuss, Paris: Académie des inscriptions et belles-lettres (Cahiers de la Villa Kérylos, 6), 71–85.

Irigoin, Jean (1998), 'Dom Bernard de Montfaucon et la *Palaeographia graeca*', in: *Dom Bernard de Montfaucon. Actes du Colloque de Carcassonne. Octobre 1996*, ed. by Daniel-Odon Hurel – Raymond Rogé, Saint-Wandrille: Éditions de Fontenelle (Bibliothèque Bénédictine, 4), I, 211–223.

Irigoin, Jean (2000), 'Deux servantes maîtresses en alternance: paléographie et philologie', in: *I manoscritti greci tra riflessione e dibattito. Atti del V Colloquio Internazionale di Paleografia Greca. Cremona, 4-10 ottobre 1998*, II, ed. by Giancarlo Prato, Firenze: Edizioni Gonnelli (Papyrologica Florentina, 31), 589–600.

Irwin, Robert G. (2006), *For Lust of Knowing: The Orientalists and their Enemies*, London: Allen Lane.

Isḥāq, Ğāk [Isaac, Jacques] (2005), فهرس المخطوطات السريانية في خزانة مطرانية أربيل الكلدانية، عينكاوا (*Fihris al-maḫṭūṭāt al-suryāniyya fī Ḫazānat Muṭrāniyyat Irbīl al-Kaldāniyya* (*'Aynkāwā*), 'Catalogue of Syro-Chaldaean manuscripts in the library of the Chaldaean Archbishopric of Erbil, at Ainkawa'), Baghdad: Nağm al-Mašriq (L'étoile de l'Orient, 9).

Islamic Manuscript Collection, University of Michigan, Ann Arbor, <http://www.lib.umich.edu/islamic/>, last access 2013.

Ivanova-Mavrodinova, Vera – Aksinija Džurova (1981), *Асеманиевото Евангелие*: *Старобългарски глаголически паметник от X век* (*Asemanievoto evangelie. Starobălgarski glagoličeski pametnik ot X vek*, 'The Assemani Gospel. An Old Bulgarian Glagolitic Document from the Tenth Century'), Sofia: Nauka i Izkustvo.

Ivanow, Wladimir – M. Hidayat Hosein (1939), *Catalogue of the Arabic manuscripts in the collection of the Royal Asiatic Society of Bengal*, Calcutta: The Royal Asiatic Society.

Jacob, André (1976), 'Deux formules d'immixtion syro-palestiniennes et leur utilisation dans le rite byzantin de l'Italie méridionale', *Vetera christianorum*, 13, 29–64.

Jäger, Otto (1957), *Äthiopische Miniaturen*, Berlin: Gebr. Mann.

James, David (1992a), *Master scribes. Qur'ans from the 11th to the 14th centuries*, London: Azimuth (The Nasser D. Khalili collection of Islamic art, 2).

James, David (1992b), *After Timur. Qur'ans of the 15th and 16th centuries*, London: Azimuth (The Nasser D. Khalili collection of Islamic art, 3).

James, Montague Rhodes (1906–1907), *Catalogue of manuscripts and early printed books from the libraries of William Morris, Richard Bennett, Bertram fourth earl of Ashburnham, and other sources, now forming portion of the library of J. Pierpont Morgan*, I-IV, London, Chiswick Press.

Janc, Zagorka (1974), *Кожни повези српске ћирилске књиге од XII до XIX века* (*Kožni povezi srpske ćirilske knjige od XII do XIX veka*, 'Leather Bindings of Serbian Cyrillic Books from the 12th to 19th Centuries'), Beograd: Srbija.

Janeras, Sebastià (2005), 'Les lectionnaires de l'ancienne liturgie de Jérusalem', *Collectanea Christiana Orientalia*, 2, 71–92.

Jaouhari, Mustapha (2009), 'Notes et documents sur la ponctuation dans les manuscrits arabes', *Arabica*, 56, 315–359.

Jaouhari, Mustapha (ed.) (2013), *Les écritures des manuscrits de l'Occident musulman. Journée d'études tenue à Rabat le 29 novembre 2012*, Rabat: Centre Jacques Berque (Les Rencontres du Centre Jacques Berque, 5).

Jeffreys, Elizabeth – Michael Jeffreys (eds) (2009), *Iacobi monachi Epistulae*, Turnhout: Brepols (Corpus Christianorum. Series Graeca, 68).

Jellicoe, Sidney (1968), *The Septuagint and Modern Study*, Oxford: Clarendon Press.

Jemolo, Viviana – Mirella Morelli (1990), *Guida a una descrizione uniforme dei manoscritti e al loro censimento*, Roma: Arti grafiche moderne.

Jenkins, Marilyn (ed.) (1983), *Islamic art in the Kuwait National Museum: the al-Sabah Collection*, London: Sotheby.

Jenkins, R. Jeoffrey (1987), 'The Text of P Antinoopolis 8/210', in: *VI Congress of the IOSCS*, ed. by Claude E. Cox, Atlanta, GA: Scholars Press, 65–77.

Jenner, Konrad D. et al. (2006) {K.J. – Wido Th. van Peursen – Eep Talstra}, 'CALAP: An Interdisciplinary Debate between Textual Criticism, Textual History and Computer-Assisted Linguistic Analysis', in: *Corpus Linguistics and Textual History. A Computer-Assisted Interdisciplinary Approach to the Peshitta*, ed. by P[ercy] S.F. van Keulen – W[ido] Th. van Peursen, Assen: Van Gorcum (Studia Semitica Neerlandica, 48), 13–44.

Jerković, Vera et al. (1988–2009), *Ћириласке рукописне књиге Библиотеке Матице српске* (*Ćirilske rukopisne knjige Biblioteke Matice srpske*, 'The Cyrillic manuscript books of Matica Srpska Library'), I–XV, Novi Sad: Biblioteka Matice srpske.

Jerphanion, Guillaume de (1940), *Les miniatures du manuscrit syriaque N° 559 de la Bibliothèque Vaticane*, Città del Vaticano (Codices e Vaticanis selecti, 25).

Jobes, Karen H. – Moisés Silva (2000), *Invitation to the Septuagint*, Carlisle – Grand Rapids: Paternoster - Baker Academic.

Jocham, Tobias J. – Michael Marx (forthcoming), 'Radiocarbon and manuscripts of the Qur'ān'.

Johnson, William A. (1993), 'Column Layout in Oxyrhynchus Literary Papyri: Maas's Law, Ruling and Alignment Dots', *Zeitschrift für Papyrologie und Epigraphik*, 96, 211–215.

Johnson, William A. (2004), *Bookrolls and Scribes in Oxyrhynchus*, Toronto – Buffalo – London: University of Toronto Press.

Johnson, William A. (2009), 'The Ancient Book', in: *The Oxford Handbook of Papyrology*, ed. by Roger S. Bagnall, Oxford: Oxford University Press, 256–281.

Jomier, Jacques (1967), 'Note sur quelques manuscrits arabes se trouvant en Éthiopie', *Mélanges de l'Institut Dominicain d'Études Orientales*, 9, 287–293.

Jones, Leslie Weber (1941), 'Pricking Manuscripts: the Instruments and their Significance', *Speculum*, 21, 389–403.

Junod, Éric (1992), ''Apocryphes du Nouveau Testament': une appellation erronée et une collection artificielle. Discussion de la nouvelle définition proposée par W. Schneemelcher', *Apocrypha*, 3, 17–46.

Junod, Benoit (2010), 'Conservation supports for manuscripts exhibitions: a challenge for between conservation and aesthetic', paper presented at the COMSt workshop *Conservation Studies on Oriental Manuscripts*, Istanbul.

Ḳaḳabaʒe, Sargis – P̣eṭre Gagošiʒe (1949–1950), ქართულ ხელნაწერთა კოლექციის აღწერილობა (*Kartul xelnaçerta ḳolekciis aġçeriloba*, 'Description of the collection of Georgian manuscripts'), I–II, Tbilisi.

Kakridis, Ioannis (2004), 'Barlaam von Kalabrien. Gegen die Lateiner: Edition der serbisch-kirchenslavischen Übersetzung nach der Handschrift Dečani 88', *Hilandarski zbornik*, 11, 181–226.

Kamil, Murad (1957), 'Ein syrisches Ostrakon aus dem V. Jahrhundert', *Rivista degli Studi Orientali*, 57 (= *Scritti in Onore di Giuseppe Furlani* I), 411–413.

Kaplan, Ayda (2008), *Paléographie syriaque. Développement d'une méthode d'expertise sur base des manuscrits syriaques de la British Library* (*V^e-Xe siècles*), Louvain-la-Neuve: Oriental Institute [diss.].

Kaplan, Ayda (2013), *Le lectionnaire de Dioscoros Théodoros* (*Mardin Syr. 41/2*). *Calligraphie, ornementation et iconographie figurée*, Bruxelles: Éditions d'Antioche.

Kaplony, Andreas (2008), 'What are those few dots for? Thoughts on the orthography of the Qurra papyri (709-710), the Khurasan parchments (755-777) and the inscription of the Jerusalem Dome of the rock (692)', *Arabica*, 55, 91–112.

von Karabacek, Joseph (1888), 'Neue Quellen zur Papiergeschichte', *Mittheilungen aus der Sammlung der Papyrus Erzherzog Rainer* 4, 75–122.

von Karabacek, Joseph (2001), *Arab paper*, ed. by Don Baker – Suzy Dittmar, London: Archetype Publ.

Karamianz, N. (1888), *Verzeichniss der armenischen Handschriften*, Berlin: Asher (Die Handschriften-verzeichnisse der Königlichen Bibliothek zu Berlin, 10).

Ḳaranaʒe, Maia (2002), ქართული წიგნის ყდის ისტორია (*Kartuli çignis q̇dis isṭoria*, 'History of bookbinding in Georgia'), Tbilisi: Xelnaçerta insṭiṭuṭi.

Ḳaranaʒe, Maia et al. (2010) {M.Ḳ. – Lela Šatirišvili – Nesṭan Čxiḳvaʒe – Tamar Abulaʒe}, ქართული ხელნაწერი წიგნი. *V–XIX* სს. ელექტრონული ალბომი (*Kartuli xelnaçeri çigni. V–XIX ss. Elekṭronuli albomi*, 'The Georgian Manuscript Book. 5th – 19th centuries. Online Album'), ed. by Nesṭan Čxiḳvaʒe, Tbilisi: Xelnaçerta Erovnuli Çenṭri, <http://geomanuscript.ge/Kartuli_Khelnaweri_Albomi.pdf>; <http://dspace.nplg.gov.ge/handle/1234/ 8834>.

Ḳaričašvili, David (1905), კატალოგი ქართველთა შორის წერა-კითხვის გამავრცელებელის საზოგადოების წიგნთ-საცავისა (*Ḳaṭalogi kartvelta šoris çera-ḳitxvis gamavrcelebelis sazogadoebis çignt-sacavisa*, 'Catalogue of the library of the Society for the Promotion of Literacy among the Georgians'), Tbilisi (Kartvelta šoris çera-ḳitxvis gamavrcelebelis sazogadoebis gamocema, [Edition of the Society for the Promotion of Literacy among the Georgians], 67).

Karskij, Evfimij Fjodorovič (1928), *Славянская кирилловская палеография* (*Slavjanskaja kirillovskaja paleografija*, 'Slavic Cyrillian Palaeography'), Leningrad: Izdatelstvo Akademii nauk SSSR.

Ḳasraʒe, N. et al. (1953) {N.Ḳ. – Elene Meṭreveli – Luba Meparišvili – Lili Kutatelaʒe – Krisṭine Šarašiʒe}, საქართველოს სახელმწიფო მუზეუმის ქართულ ხელნაწერთა აღწერილობა. საქართველოს საისტორიო და საეთნოგრაფიო საზოგადოების ყოფილი მუზეუმის ხელნაწერები (*H* კოლექცია). *Описание грузинских рукописей государственного музея Грузии. Рукописи бывшего Музея Грузинского Общества Истории и Этнографии* (*коллекция H*) (*Sakartvelos saxelmçipo muzeumis kartul xelnaçerta aġçeriloba. Sakartvelos saisṭorio da saetnograpio sazogadoebis q̇opili muzeumis xelnaçerebi* (*H ḳolekcia*) / *Opisanie gruzinskich rukopisej Gosudarstvennogo muzeja Gruzii. Rukopisi byvšego Muzeja Gruzinskogo Obščestva Istorii i Ėtnografii* (*kollekcija H*), 'Description of Georgian Manuscripts of the State Museum of Georgia. Manuscripts of the former Museum of the Society of History and Ethnography of Georgia (collection H)'), VI, ed. by A. Baramiʒe, Tbilisi.

Kasser, Rodolphe (1960), *Papyrus Bodmer VI*: *Livre des Proverbes*, Louvain: Peeters (Corpus Scriptorum Christianorum Orientalium, 194, Scriptores Coptici, 27).

Kasser, Rodolphe (1991a), 'Alphabet in Coptic, Greek', in: *The Coptic Encyclopedia*, VIII, ed. by Aziz S. Atiya, New York: Macmillan, 30–32.

Kasser, Rodolphe (1991b), 'Alphabet, Coptic', in: *The Coptic Encyclopedia*, VIII, ed. by Aziz S. Atiya, New York: Macmillan, 32–41.

Kasser, Rodolphe (1991c), 'Paleography', in: *The Coptic Encyclopedia*, VIII, ed. by Aziz S. Atiya, New York: Macmillan, 175–184.

Kasser, Rodolphe (2001), 'Le Papyrus Bodmer III réexaminé: amélioration de sa transcription', *Journal of Coptic Studies*, 2, 81–112.

Kaufhold, Hubert (2007), *Kleines Lexikon des Christlichen Orients*, Wiesbaden: Harrassowitz.

Kaufhold, Hubert (2008), 'Zur Datierung nach christlicher Ära in den syrischen Kirchen', in: *Malphono w-Rabo d-Malphone. Studies in Honor of Sebastian P. Brock*, ed. by George A. Kiraz, Piscataway, NJ: Gorgias Press (Gorgias Eastern Christian Studies, 3), 283–337.

Kaǯaia, Lamara (1963), 'პუნქტუაცია ძველ ქართულ ხელნაწერებში (*Punkṭuacia ʒvel kartul xelnaçerebši*, 'Punctuation in Old Georgian manuscripts')', *Xelnaçerta insṭiṭuṭis moambe*, 5, 67–83.

Kaǯaia, Lamara (1965), 'განკვეთილობის ნიშნები ძველ ქართულ ხელნაწერებში, VII–X საუკუნეები (*Ganḳvetilobis nišnebi ʒvel kartul xelnaçerebši, VII–X saukuneebi*, 'Separation marks in Old Georgian manuscripts, 7th-10th centuries')', *Ṗaleograpiuli ʒiebani*, 1, 33–44.

Kaǯaia, Lamara (1969a), 'ორი ტექნიკური ნიშანი ძველ ქართულ ხელნაწერებში (*Ori ṭekniḳuri nišani ʒvel kartul xelnaçerebši*, 'Two technical signs in Old Georgian manuscripts')', *Ṗaleograpiuli ʒiebani*, 2, 103–107.

Kaǯaia, Lamara (1969b), 'პირობითი ნიშნები ქართულ კომენტარებიან ხელნაწერებში (*Ṗirobiti nišnebi kartul ḳomenṭarebian xelnaçerebši*, 'Conventional signs in Georgian manuscripts with commentaries')', *Ṗaleograpiuli ʒiebani*, 2, 32–50.

Kaǯaia, Lamara (1969c), პუნქტუაცია *V–XII* საუკუნეების ქართულ ხელნაწერებში (*Ṗunkṭuacia V–XII sauḳuneebis kartul xelnaçerebši*, 'Punctuation in Georgian manuscripts of the 5th–12th centuries'), Tbilisi: Sakartvelos SSR Mecnierebata Aḳademia, Xelnaçerta Insṭiṭuṭi [diss.].

Kaǯaia [Kadžaia], Lamara (1974), 'Ханмэтные палимпсесты (*Chanmètnye palimpsesty*, 'Khanmeti Palimpsests')', in: *Проблемы палеографии и кодикологии в СССР* (*Problemy paleografii i kodikologii v SSSR*, 'Problems of palaeography and codicology in the USSR'), ed. by A.D. Ljubinskaja, 409–427.

Kaǯaia [Kajaia], Lamara – Maia Maçavariani [Matchavariani] (2009), 'The History of the Georgian Palimpsests', in: *Palimpsestes et éditions de textes, Les textes littéraires. Actes du colloque tenu à Louvain-la-Neuve, Septembre 2003*, ed. by Véronique Somers, Louvain-la-Neuve: Université catholique de Louvain, Institut orientaliste (Publications de l'Institut Orientaliste de Louvain, 56), 245–259.

Keenan, Edward L. (1971), 'Paper for the Tsar: A Letter of Ivan IV of 1570', *Oxford Slavonic Papers*, n.s. 4, 21–29.

Keipert, Helmut (1975), 'Zur Parallelüberlieferung des 'Bdinski zbornik' (Cod. Gand. 408)', *Analecta Bollandiana*, 93, 269–286.

Kellens, Jean (1998), 'Considérations sur l'histoire de l'Avesta', *Journal Asiatique*, 286, 415–519.

Kellens, Jean (2012), 'Contre l'idée platonicienne d'Avesta ou les Considérations revisitées', in: *The transmission of the Avesta*, ed. by Alberto Cantera, Wiesbaden: Harrassowitz (Iranica, 20), 49–58.

Kellermann, Andreas (1995), 'Die 'Mündlichkeit' des Koran. Ein forschungsgeschichtliches Problem der Arabistik', *Beiträge zur Geschichte der Sprachwissenschaft*, 5, 1–34.

Kensdale, William Elliott Norwood (1955–1958), *Catalogue of the Arabic Manuscripts Preserved in the University Library, Ibadan*, Ibadan: Ibadan University Press.

Keshavarz, Fateme (1986), *A descriptive and analytical catalogue of Persian manuscripts in the Library of the Wellcome Institute for the History of Medicine*, London: The Wellcome Institute for the History of Medicine.

Kessel, Grigory (2009), 'Letter of Thomas the Monk. A Study of the Syriac Text and its Author', *The Journal of Eastern Christian Studies*, 61, 43–100.

Kessel, Grigory – Karl Pinggéra (2011), *A Bibliography of Syriac Ascetic and Mystical Literature*, Leuven: Peeters (Eastern Christian Studies, 11).

Kévorkian, Raymond (1986), *Catalogue des 'Incunables' arméniens (1511/1695) ou chronique de l'imprimerie arménienne*, Genève: Cramer (Cahiers d'orientalisme, 9).

Kévorkian, Raymond et al. (1998) {R.K. – Armèn Ter-Stépanian – Bernard Outtier – Guévorg Ter-Vardanian}, *Manuscrits arméniens de la Bibliothèque nationale de France. Catalogue*, Paris: Bibliothèque nationale de France – Fondation Calouste Goulbenkian.

Khachatrian, Žores (1996), 'The Archives of Sealings Found at Artashat (Artaxata)', in: *Archives et sceaux du monde hellénistique / Archivi e sigilli nel mondo ellenistico*, ed. by Marie-Françoise Boussac – Antonio Invernizzi, Paris: Diffusion de Boccard (Bulletin de Correspondance Hellénique, Supplément, 29), 365–370.

Khafaji, Rasoul (2001), 'Punctuation Marks in Original Arabic Texts', *Zeitschrift für arabische Linguistik*, 40, 7–24.

Khalili, Nasser D. et al. (1996) {N.K. – Basil W. Robinson – Tim Stanley}, *Lacquer of the Islamic lands*, I, London: Azimuth (The Nasser D. Khalili collection of Islamic art, 22).

Khan, Geoffrey (1992), *Arabic Papyri. Selected Material from the Khalili Collection*, London: The Nour Foundation – Azimuth Editions – Oxford: Oxford University Press (Studies in the Khalili Collection, 1).

Khan, Yasmeen – Sophie Lewincamp (2008), 'Characterization and analysis of early Qur'ān fragments at the Library of Congress', in: *Contributions to the Symposium on the Care and Conservation of Middle Eastern Manuscripts*, Melbourne: Centre for Cultural Materials Conservation, 55–65.

Khouzam, A. Fouad (1999), 'Le manuscrit copte 44 de Paris de la Bibliothèque nationale de France', in: *Ägypten und Nubien in spätantiker und christlicher Zeit. Akten des 6. Internationalen Koptologenkongresses. Münster, 20.—26. Juli 1996*, II: *Schrifttum, Sprache und Gedankenwelt*, ed. by Stephen Emmel – Martin Krause, Wiesbaden: Reichert (Sprachen und Kulturen des Christlichen Orients, 6.2), 131–143.

King, Karen L. (1997), 'Approaching the Variants of the Apocryphon of John', in: *The Nag Hammadi Library After Fifty Years: Proceedings of the 1995 Society of Biblical Literature Commemoration*, ed. by John D. Turner – Anne McGuire, Leiden: Brill (Nag Hammadi and Manichaean Studies, 44), 105–137.

King, Karen L. (2006), *The Secret Revelation of John*, Cambridge, MA: Harvard University Press.

Kiraz, George A. (2012), 'Old Syriac Graphotactics', *Journal of Semitic Studies*, 57/2, 231–264.

Kireeva, Vilena N. (1997), 'Русский пергамент (Russkij pergament, 'Russian Parchment')', in: *Консервация и реставрация памятников истории и культуры. Экспресс-информация* (*Konservacija i restavracija pamjatnikov istorii i kul'tury: èkspress-informacija*, 'Conservation and restauration of historical and cultural monuments: express information'), Moskva: Rossijskaja gosudarstvennaja biblioteka (Konservacija i restavracija pamjatnikov istorii i kul'tury, 2), 1–21.

Kireeva [Kireyeva], Vilena (1999), 'Examination of Parchment in Byzantine Manuscripts', *Restaurator. International Journal for the Preservation of Library and Archival Material*, 20/1, 39–47.

Kloppenborg, John S. – Judith H. Newman (eds) (2012), *Editing the Bible: Assessing the Task Past and Present*, Atlanta, GA: Society of Biblical Literature (Resources for biblical study, 69).

Koceva, Elena (1972), 'Първопечатната и ръкописна книга' (*Părvopečatnata i răkopisna kniga*, 'The early printed and manuscript book'), *Izkustvo*, 4, 10–16.

Kögel, Raphael (1912), 'Die Photographie unleserlicher und unsichtbarer Schriften der Palimpseste', *Studien und Mitteilungen zur Geschichte des Benediktinerordens und seiner Zweige*, 33, 309–315.

Kokowzoff, P. (ed.) (1906), *Nouveaux fragments syropalestiniens de la Bibliothèque impériale publique de Saint-Pétersbourg*, St Petersburg: Académie impériale des sciences.

Kolmodin, Johannes (1916), 'Abessinische Bücherverzeichnisse (aus den Inventaren der Zion von Aksum und einiger anderen Kirchen)', *Le Monde Oriental*, 10, 241–255.

Kopitarjeva zbirka slovanskih kodeksov (*The collection of Slavic manuscripts in Kopitar*), <http://www.nuk.uni-lj.si/kopitarjevazbirka>, last access May 2014.

Korxmazyan, Emma [Korchmazjan, Ėmma / Korkhmazian, Emma] et al. (1984) {E.K. – Irina Drambyan [Drapjan, Drapian] – Hravard [Gravard] Hakobyan [Akopjan, Hakopian]}, *Армянская миниатюра XIII–XIV веков из собрания Матенадарана, Ереван* (*Armjanskaja miniatjura XIII–XIV vekov iz sobranija Matenadarana, Erevan*) / *Armenian Miniatures of the 13th and 14th Centuries from the Matenadaran Collection, Yerevan*, Leningrad: Aurora.

Kostjuchina, L.M. (1999), *Палеография русских рукописных книг XV–XVII вв.: русский полуустав* (*Paleografija russkich rukopisnych knig XV–XVII vv.: russkij poluustav*, 'The palaeography of Russian manuscript books of the 15th-17th centuries: Russian semi-uncial'), Moskva: Gosudarstvennyj istoričeskij muzej (Trudy Gosudarstvennogo istoričeskogo muzeja, 108).

Kotsifou, Chrysi (2007), 'Books and Book Production in the Monastic Communities of Byzantine Egypt', in: *The Early Christian Book*, ed. by William E. Klingshirn – Linda Safran, Washington: The Catholic University of America Press (Catholic University of American Studies in Early Christianity), 48–66.

Kotsifou, Chrysi (2011), 'Bookbinding and Manuscript Illumination in Late Antique and Early Medieval Monastic Circles in Egypt', in: *Eastern Christians and their Written Heritage: Manuscripts, Scribes and Context*, ed. by Juan Pedro Monferrer Sala – Sofía Torallas Tovar, Leuven etc.: Peeters (Eastern Christian Studies, 14), 213–244.

Kotzampasē [Kotzabassi], Sophia (2004), *Βυζαντινά χειρόγραφα από τα μοναστήρια της Μικράς Ασίας*, Athens: Ephesos.

Kouroupou, Matoula – Paul Géhin (2008), *Catalogue des manuscrits conservés dans la Bibliothèque du Patriarcat Œcuménique: les manuscrits du monastère de la Panaghia de Chalki*, I–II, Turnhout: Brepols.

Kouymjian, Dickran (1977, 1979), *Index of Armenian Art* (*IAA*), fascicle I. *Armenian Manuscript Illumination to the Year 1000 A.D.*; fascicle II. *Illuminated Armenian Manuscripts of the 11th Century, Preliminary Report and Checklist*, <http://armenianstudies.csufresno.edu/iaa_miniatures/index.htm>, Fresno.

Kouymjian, Dickran (1982), 'Sous le joug des Turcomans et des Turcs ottomans (XVe-XVIe siècles)', in: *Histoire des Arméniens*, ed. by Gérard Dédéyan, Toulouse: Privat, 341–376.

Kouymjian, Dickran (1983), 'Dated Armenian Manuscripts as a Statistical Tool for Armenian History', in: *Medieval Armenian Culture*, ed. by Thomas J. Samuelian – Michael Stone, Chico, CA: Scholars Press (University of Pennsylvania Armenian Texts and Studies, VI), 425–439.

Kouymjian, Dickran (1992a), *The Arts of Armenia* (*Accompanied by a Collection of 300 Slides in Color*), Lisbon: Calouste Gulbenkian Foundation.

Kouymjian, Dickran (1992b), 'Dated Armenian Manuscript Bindings from the Mekhitarist Library, Venice', in: *Atti del Quinto Simposio Internazionale di Arte Armena - Venezia, Milano, Bologna, Firenze, 25 maggio - 5 giugno 1988*, Venezia: San Lazzaro, 403–412.

Kouymjian, Dickran (1993a), 'Inscribed Armenian Manuscript Bindings: A Preliminary General Survey', in: *Armenian Texts: Tasks and Tools*, ed. by Henning J. Lehmann – J.J.S. Weitenberg, Aarhus: Aarhus University Press (Acta Jutlandica, 69, 1, Humanities series, 68), 101–109.

Kouymjian, Dickran (1993b), 'The Evolution of Armenian Gospel Illumination: The Formative Period (9th-11th Centuries)', in: *Armenia and the Bible: Papers Presented to the International Symposium Held at Heidelberg, July 16-19, 1990*, ed. by Christoph Burchard, Atlanta: Scholars Press (University of Pennsylvania Armenian Texts and Studies, 12), 125–142.

Kouymjian, Dickran (1994), 'From Disintegration to Reintegration: Armenians at the Start of the Modern Era, XVIth-XVIIth Centuries', *Revue du monde aménien*, 1, 9–18.

Kouymjian, Dickran (1995 [1997]), 'The New Julfa Style of Armenian Manuscript Binding', *Journal of the Society for Armenian Studies*, 8, 13–36.

Kouymjian, Dickran (1996a), 'Armenian Manuscript Illumination in the Formative Period: Text Groups, Eusebian Apparatus, Evangelists' Portraits', in: *Il Caucaso. Cerniera fra culture dal Mediterraneo alla Persia, secoli IV–XI*, Spoleto: Centro italiano di studi sull'alto medioevo (Settimane di studio del Centro italiano di studi sull'alto medioevo, 43), 1015–1051, 20 plates.

Kouymjian, Dickran (1996b), 'Unique Armenian Papyrus', in: *Proceedings of the Fifth International Conference on Armenian Linguistics, McGill University, Montreal, Quebec, Canada, May 1-5, 1995*, ed. by Dora Sakayan, Delmar, NY: Caravan Books, 381–386.

Kouymjian, Dickran (1997), 'Armenia from the Fall of the Cilician Kingdom (1375) to the Forced Emigration under Shah Abbas (1604)', in: *The Armenian People from Ancient to Modern Times*, II. *Foreign Dominion to Statehood: The Fifteenth Century to the Twentieth Century*, ed. by Richard Hovannisian, New York: St Martin Press, 1–50.

Kouymjian, Dickran (1998a), 'A Unique Armeno-Greek Papyrus', in: *Études Coptes V*, ed. by M. Rassart-Debergh, Louvain: Peeters, 165–169.

Kouymjian, Dickran (1998b), 'Les reliures de manuscrits arméniens à inscriptions', in: *Recherches de codicologie comparée: la composition du codex au Moyen Âge en Orient et en Occident*, ed. by Philippe Hoffmann, Paris: Presses de l'École normale supérieure (Collection bibliologie), 259–274.

Kouymjian, Dickran (1999), 'L'iconographie de l'Histoire d'Alexandre le Grand dans les manuscrits arméniens', in: *Alexandre le Grand dans les littératures occidentales et proche-orientales. Actes du Colloque de Paris, 27-29 novembre 1997*, ed. by Laurence Harf-Lancner – Claire Kappler – François Suard, Nanterre: Université Paris X, 95–112.

Kouymjian, Dickran (2002a), 'The Armeno-Greek Papyrus', in: *Album of Armenian Paleography*, ed. by Michael Stone – Dickran Kouymjian – Henning Lehmann, Aarhus: Aarhus University Press, 59–63.

Kouymjian, Dickran (2002b), 'History of Armenian Paleography', in: *Album of Armenian Paleography*, ed. by Michael Stone – Dickran Kouymjian – Henning Lehmann, Aarhus: Aarhus University Press, 5–75.

Kouymjian, Dickran (2006), 'Armenian Binding from Manuscript to Printed Book (16th–19th cent.)', *Gazette du livre médiéval*, 49, 1–14.

Kouymjian, Dickran (2007a), 'La structure et l'illustration des manuscrits arméniens', in: *Illuminations d'Arménie. Arts du livre et de la pierre dans l'Arménie ancienne et médiévale (Fondation Martin Bodmer, Genève, 15 septembre–30 decembre 2007)*, ed. by Valentina Calzolari, Genève: Fondation Martin Bodmer, 41–59.

Kouymjian, Dickran (2007b), 'Recueil de textes sur la fondation et l'histoire de l'Église arménienne', in: *Illuminations d'Arménie. Arts du livre et de la pierre dans l'Arménie ancienne et médiévale (Fondation Martin Bodmer, Genève, 15 septembre–30 decembre 2007)*, ed. by Valentina Calzolari, Genève: Fondation Martin Bodmer, 164–171.

Kouymjian, Dickran (2007c), 'Recueil (zodiaque, astronomie)', in: *Illuminations d'Arménie. Arts du livre et de la pierre dans l'Arménie ancienne et médiévale (Fondation Martin Bodmer, Genève, 15 septembre–30 decembre 2007)*, ed. by Valentina Calzolari, Genève: Fondation Martin Bodmer, 226–229.

Kouymjian, Dickran (2007d), 'Les illustrations du Roman d'Alexandre et autres textes profanes', in: *Arménie: la magie de l'écrit (Marseille, Centre de la Vieille Charité, 27 avril-22 juillet 2007)*, ed. by Claude Mutafian, Paris – Marseille: Somogy, 164–172.

Kouymjian, Dickran (2007e), 'Les reliures à inscriptions des manuscrits arméniens', in: *Arménie: la magie de l'écrit (Marseille, Centre de la Vieille Charité, 27 avril-22 juillet 2007)*, ed. by Claude Mutafian, Paris – Marseille: Somogy, 236–247.

Kouymjian, Dickran (2007f), 'Évolution de la Paléographie arménienne', in: *Illuminations d'Arménie. Arts du livre et de la pierre dans l'Arménie ancienne et médiévale (Fondation Martin Bodmer, Genève, 15 septembre–30 decembre 2007)*, ed. by Valentina Calzolari, Genève: Fondation Martin Bodmer, 27–33.

Kouymjian, Dickran (2008a), 'Post-Byzantine Armenian Bookbinding and its Relationship to the Greek Tradition', in: *Το βιβλίο στο Βυζάντιο. Βυζαντινή και μεταβυζαντινή βιβλιοδεσία. Πρακτικά διεθνούς συνεδρίου, Αθήνα, 13-16 Οκτωβρίου 2005 (To biblio sto Byzantio. Byzantinē kai metabyzantinē bibliodesia. Praktika diethnous synedriou, Athēna, 13-16 Oktōbriou 2005*, 'The Book in Byzantium: Byzantine and Post-Byzantine Bookbinding'), ed. by Niki Tsironi, Athens: Ellēnikē Etaireia Bibliodesias – Institouto Byzantinōn Ereunōn – Ethniko Idryma Ereunōn – Byzantino kai Christianiko Mouseio (Biblioamphiastēs, 3), 163–176.

Kouymjian, Dickran (2008b), 'From Manuscript to Printed Book: Armenian Bookbinding from the Sixteenth to the Nineteenth Century', in: *History of Printing and Publishing in the Languages and Countries of the Middle East*, ed. by Philip Sadgrove, Oxford: Oxford University Press (Journal of Semitic Studies Supplement, 15), 13–21, plates pp. 276–297.

Kouymjian, Dickran (2008c), 'The Decoration of Medieval Armenian Manuscript Bindings', in: *La reliure médiévale: pour une description normalisée. Actes du colloque international (Paris, 22 - 24 mai 2003)*, ed. by Guy Lanoë, Turnhout: Brepols (Reliures médiévales des bibliothèques de France), 209–218.

Kouymjian, Dickran (2011a), 'L'art de l'enluminure. The Art of Miniature Painting', in: *Artsakh-Karabagh. Jardin des arts et des traditions arméniens. Garden of Armenian Arts and Traditions*, ed. by Dickran Kouymjian – Claude Mutafian, Paris: Somogy, 104–137.

Kouymjian, Dickran (2011b), 'Armenian Medieval Illumination', in: *Armenia. Imprints of a Civilization. Exhibition on the Occasion of the Fifth Centenary of Armenian Printing, Venice, Correr, 14 Dec-10 April 2012*, ed. by Gabriella Uluhogian – Boghos Levon Zekiyan, Milan: Skira, 91–97.

Kouymjian, Dickran (2012a), 'Notes on Armenian Codicology. Part 1: Statistics Based on Surveys of Armenian Manuscripts', *Comparative Oriental Manuscript Studies Newsletter*, 4, 18–23.

Kouymjian, Dickran (2012b), 'Did Byzantine Iconography Influence the Large Cycle of the Life of Alexander the Great in Armenian Manuscripts?', in: *Bizancjum a renesansy: dialog kultur, dziedzictwo antyku: tradycja i współczesność / Byzantium and Renaissances. Dialogue of Cultures, Heritage of Antiquity – Tradition and Modernity*, ed. by Michał Janocha, Warsaw: Instytut Badań Interdyscyplinarnych 'Artes Liberales' UW, 209–216, figures 61–70.

Kouymjian, Dickran (2013), 'Notes on Armenian Codicology. Part 2. Armenian Palaeography: Dating the Major Scripts', *Comparative Oriental Manuscript Studies Newsletter*, 6, 22–28.

Kouymjian, Dickran (2014), 'The Archaeology of the Armenian Manuscript: Codicology, Paleography and Beyond', in: *Armenian Philology in the Modern Era: From Manuscript to Digital Text*, ed. by Valentina Calzolari, with collaboration of Michael E. Stone, Leiden: Brill (Handbook of Oriental Studies / Handbuch der Orientalistik, VIII, 23/1), 5–22.

Kouymjian, Dickran (forthcoming a), 'Liturgical Metalwork from the Cilician Museum', in: *The Armenian Catholicosate of Cilicia and its Treasures*, ed. by Seta Dadoyan, Antelias: Armenian Catholicosate.

Kouymjian, Dickran (forthcoming b), 'Jerusalem Manuscript J473, History of Alexander the Great Dated 1536: Remarks on its Iconography', paper presented at the conference *Armenian Art History and Culture (10th – 20th Century)*, Jerusalem 2011, forthcoming in the proceedings.

Krätli, Graziano (2011), 'Camel to Kilobytes: Preserving the Cultural Heritage of Trans-Saharan Book Trade', in: *The Trans-Saharan Book Trade: Manuscript Culture, Arabic Literacy and Intellectual History in Muslim Africa*, ed. by Graziano Krätli – Ghislaine Lydon, Leiden: Brill (Library of the Written Word, 8, The Manuscript World, 3), 319–358.

Krause, Martin (1981), 'Der Erlassbrief Theodors', in: *Studies Presented to Hans Jakob Polotsky*, ed. by Dwight Wayne Young, East Gloucester: Pirtle and Polson, 220–238, pl. 6 facing p. 220.

Krekel, Christoph (1999), 'Chemische Struktur historischer Eisengallustinten', in: *Tintenfraßschäden und ihre Behandlung*, ed. by Gerhard Banik – Hartmut Weber, Stuttgart: Kohlhammer (Werkhefte der staatlichen Archivverwaltung Baden-Württemberg, Serie A Landesarchivdirektion, 10), 25–36.

Kresten, Otto – Giancarlo Prato (1985), 'Die Miniatur des Evangelisten Markus im Codex Purpureus Rossanensis. Eine spätere Einfügung', *Römische Historische Mitteilungen*, 27, 381–399.

Krikorian, Mesrob K. (1997), 'Nerses Akinian (1883-1963). Ein grosser Philologe und Armenologe', in: *Das Lemberger Evangeliar. Eine wiederentdeckte armenische Bilderhandschrift des 12. Jahrhunderts*, ed. by Günter Pritzing – Andrea Schmidt, Wiesbaden: Harrassowitz (Sprachen und Kulturen des christlichen Orients, 2), 171–177.

Kropf, Evyn – Cathleen A. Baker (2013), 'A Conservative Tradition? Arab Papers of the 12th-17th Centuries from the Islamic Manuscripts Collection at the University of Michigan', *Journal of Islamic Manuscripts* 4/1, 1–48.

Kropp, Manfred (1988), 'The Ser'atä gebr: a mirror view of daily life at the Ethiopian Royal Court in the Middle Ages', *Northeast African Studies*, 10/2-3, 51–87.

Krutzsch, Myriam – Günter Poethke (1984), 'Der Einband des koptisch-gnostischen Kodex Papyrus Berolinensis 8502', *Forschungen und Berichte [der Staatlichen Museen zu Berlin, Archäologische Beiträge]*, 24, 37–40, pls. 5–6.

Kühn, Hermann (1988), 'Farbmaterialien', in: *Reclams Handbuch der künstlerischen Techniken*, 2nd edition, I, Stuttgart: Reclam, 31.

Kukuškina, Margarita V. (1977), *Монастырские библиотеки русского севера* (*Monastyrskie biblioteki russkogo severa*, 'Monastic Libraries of the Russian North'), Leningrad: Nauka.

Kunze, Gerhard (1947), *Die gottesdienstliche Schriftlesung*. Teil I: *Stand und Aufgaben der Perikopenforschung*, Göttingen: Vandenhoeck & Ruprecht (Veröffentlichungen der Evangelischen Gesellschaft für Liturgieforschung, 1).

K'urdyan, H. (1948), 'Կեսարիոյ ոսկերչական դպրոցին արծաթ կազմերը (*Kesarioy oskerč'akan dproc'in arcat' kazmerə*, 'The Silver Bindings of the Goldsmith School of Caesarea')', *Hask hayagitakan taregirk'*, 1, 51–61.

Kurz, Josef – Zoe Hauptová (1958–1997), *Slovník jazyka staroslověnského. Lexicon linguae Palaeoslovenicae*, I–IV, Praha: Academia.

Kut, Turgut (1972), 'Türkçe Yazma Eserler Katalogları Repertuvarı', *Türk Dili Araştırmaları Yıllığı – Belleten* [*TDAY-B*], 183–240.

Kut, Günay (1988), 'Some aspects of the cataloguing of Turkish manuscripts', *Manuscripts of the Middle East*, 3, 58–68.

Kut, Günay (2003), *Supplementary catalogue of Turkish Manuscripts in the Bodleian Library, with reprint of the 1930 catalogue by H. Ethé*, Oxford: Oxford University Press.

Kut, Günay (2010), *Supplementary catalogue of Turkish Manuscripts in the Bodleian Library*, 2nd edition, Oxford: Oxford University Press.

Kutatelaʒe, Lili (1951), საქართველოს სახელმწიფო მუზეუმის ქართულ ხელნაწერთა აღწერილობა. საქართველოს საისტორიო და საეთნოგრაფიო საზოგადოების ყოფილი მუზეუმის ხელნაწერები (*H* კოლექცია). *Описание грузинских рукописей государственного музея Грузии. Рукописи бывшего Музея Грузинского Общества Истории и Этнографии* (*коллекция H*) (*Sakartvelos saxelmçipo muzeumis kartul xelnaçerta aġçeriloba. Sakartvelos saisṭorio da saetnograpio sazogadoebis q̇opili muzeumis xelnaçerebi* (*H ḳolekcia*) / *Opisanie gruzinskich rukopisej Gosudarstvennogo muzeja Gruzii. Rukopisi byvšego Muzeja Gruzinskogo Obščestva Istorii i Ėtnografii* (*kollekcija H*), 'Description of Georgian Manuscripts of the State Museum of Georgia. Manuscripts of the former Museum of the Society of History and Ethnography of Georgia (collection H)'), II, Tbilisi: Sakartvelos SSR Mecnierebata Aḳademiis Gamomcemloba.

Kutatelaʒe, Lili – N. Ḳasraʒe (1946), საქართველოს სახელმწიფო მუზეუმის ქართულ ხელნაწერთა აღწერილობა. საქართველოს საისტორიო და საეთნოგრაფიო საზოგადოების ყოფილი მუზეუმის ხელნაწერები (*H* კოლექცია). *Описание грузинских рукописей государственного музея Грузии. Рукописи бывшего Музея Грузинского Общества Истории и Этнографии* (*коллекция H*) (*Sakartvelos saxelmçipo muzeumis kartul xelnaçerta aġçeriloba. Sakartvelos saisṭorio da saetnograpio sazogadoebis q̇opili muzeumis xelnaçerebi* (*H ḳolekcia*) / *Opisanie gruzinskich rukopisej Gosudarstvennogo muzeja Gruzii. Rukopisi byvšego Muzeja Gruzinskogo Obščestva Istorii i Ėtnografii* (*kollekcija H*), 'Description of Georgian Manuscripts of the State Museum of Georgia. Manuscripts of the former Museum of the Society of History and Ethnography of Georgia (collection H)'), I, Tbilisi: Sakartvelos SSR Mecnierebata Aḳademiis Gamomcemloba.

La Chapelle, Ariane de – André Le Prat (1996), *Les relevés de filigranes. Watermark records. I rilievi di filigrane*, translated by Geoffrey Capner – Giovanna Bertazzoni, Paris: La Documentation française (Service culturel).

La Spisa, Paolo (2012), 'Perspectives ecdotiques pour textes en moyen arabe: l'exemple des traités théologiques de Sulaymān al-Ġazzī', in: *Middle Arabic and Mixed Arabic*: *Diachrony and Synchrony*, ed. by Liesbeth Zack – Arie Schippers, Leiden: Brill (Studies in Semitic Languages and Linguistics, 64), 187–208.

La Spisa, Paolo (2013), *I trattati teologici di Sulaymān Ibn Ḥasan Al-Ġazzī*, I–II, Louvain: Peeters (Corpus Scriptorum Christianorum Orientalium, 648-649, Scriptores Arabici, 52-53).

La Spisa, Paolo (2014), 'Contamination, conflation and 'fluid' tradition in the Martyrdom of Aretha and his companions in Najran', *Comparative Oriental Manuscript Studies Newsletter*, 7, 23–26.

Lacau, Pierre (1911), 'Textes coptes en dialectes akhmimique et sahidique', *Bulletin de l'Institut français d'archéologie orientale*, 8, 43–109.

Lacau, Pierre (1946), 'Fragments de l'Ascension d'Isaïe en copte', *Le Muséon*, 59, 453–467.

Łafadaryan, Karo (1939), Հայկական գրի սկզբնական տեսակները, հնագրական-բանասիրական ուսումնասիրության (*Haykakan gri skzbnakan tesaknerə, hnagrakan-banasirakan usumnasirut'yan*, 'The Original Types of Armenian Letters, Paleographic-Philological Study'), Erevan: ArmFAN.

Lagrange, Marie-Joseph (1925), 'L'origine de la version syro-palestinienne des évangiles', *Revue biblique*, 34, 481–504.

Lake, Kirsopp – Silva Lake (1934–1945), *Dated Greek Minuscule Manuscripts to the Year 1200*, I–XI, Boston: The American Academy of Arts and Sciences.

Lalayan, Ervand (1915), Ցուցակ հայերէն ձեռագրաց Վասպուրականի (*C'uc'ak hayerēn jeṙagrac' Vaspurakani*, 'Catalogue of the Armenian manuscripts of Vaspurakan'), I, T'iflis: Tparan 'Ēsperantō'.

Lalou, Elisabeth (ed.) (1992), *Les tablettes à écrire de l'Antiquité à l'époque moderne. Actes du colloque international du Centre national de la recherche scientifique, Paris, Institut de France, 10–11 octobre 1990*, Turnhout: Brepols (Bibliologia: Elementa ad Librorum Studia Pertinentia, 12).

Lamacraft, Charles T. (1940), 'Early Book-bindings from a Coptic Monastery', *The Library*, ser. 4, 20, 214–233, pls. 1–[5].

Lameï, Mahmoud (2000), 'Les manuscrits illustrés orientaux dans les institutions publiques en Suisse. I, Les bibliothèques universitaires de Lausanne et de Genève', *Asiatische Studien*: *Zeitschrift der Schweizerischen Asiengesellschaft* = *Études asiatiques*: *revue de la Société Suisse-Asie*, 54/3, 499–595.

Lameï, Mahmoud (2002), 'Les manuscrits illustrés orientaux dans les institutions publiques en Suisse. II, Les manuscrits de la Bibliothèque de la Bourgeoisie de Berne', *Asiatische Studien*: *Zeitschrift der Schweizerischen Asiengesellschaft* = *Études asiatiques*: *revue de la Société Suisse-Asie*, 56/2, 273–406.

Lameï, Mahmoud (2005), 'Les manuscrits illustrés orientaux dans les institutions publiques en Suisse. III, Les manuscrits du musée historique de Berne 1: le livre des rois (Šāhnāme)', *Asiatische Studien*: *Zeitschrift der Schweizerischen Asiengesellschaft* = *Études asiatiques*: *revue de la Société Suisse-Asie*, 59/3, 697–794.

Lameï, Mahmoud (2013), 'Les manuscrits illustrés orientaux dans les institutions publiques en Suisse. IV, Bibliothèque Universitaire de Bâle', *Asiatische Studien: Zeitschrift der Schweizerischen Asiengesellschaft = Études asiatiques: revue de la Société Suisse-Asie*, 67/1, 207–340.

Land, Jan Pieter Nicolaas (1862, 1868, 1870, 1875), *Anecdota Syriaca*, I–IV, Lugduni Batavorum: Brill.

van Lantschoot, Arnold (1929), *Recueil des colophons des manuscrits chrétiens d'Égypte*, I: *Le colophons coptes de manuscrits sahidiques*, Louvain: Istas (Bibliothèque du Muséon, 1).

van Lantschoot, Arnold (1965), *Inventaire des manuscrits syriaques des fonds Vatican (490–631), Barberini oriental et Neofiti*, Città del Vaticano: Biblioteca Apostolica Vaticana (Studi e testi, 243).

Lau-Lamb, Leyla (2007), 'A New Material for the Conservation of Papyrus', *The Book and Paper Group Annual Annual* 26, 187–188.

Lavrov, P.A. (1914), *Палеографическое обозрѣніе кирилловскаго письма* (*Paleografičeskoe obozrěnïe kirillovskago pis'ma*, 'Palaeographic Review of the Cyrillic Script'), Petrograd: Imperatorskaja Akademija Nauk (Enciklopedija slavjanskoj filologii, 4/1).

Law, T. Michael (2013), *When God Spoke Greek: The Septuagint and the Making of the Christian Bible*, Oxford: Oxford University Press.

Layton, Bentley (1979), *The Gnostic Treatise on Resurrection from Nag Hammadi*, Missoula: Scholars Press (Harvard Dissertations in Religion, 12).

Layton, Bentley (1981), 'The Recovery of Gnosticism: The Philologist's Task in the Investigation of Nag Hammadi', *Second Century: A Journal of Early Christian Studies*, 1, 85–99.

Layton, Bentley (1985), 'Towards a New Coptic Palaeography', in: *Acts of the Second International Congress of Coptic Studies: Roma, 22–26 September 1980*, ed. by Tito Orlandi – Frederik Wisse, Roma: Centro Italiano Microfiches, 149–158.

Layton, Bentley (1987), *Catalogue of Coptic Literary Manuscripts in the British Library Acquired since the Year 1906*, London: British Library.

Lazard, Gilbert (1963), *La langue des plus anciens monuments de la prose persane*, Paris: C. Klincksieck (Études linguistiques, 2).

Lazard, Gilbert (1974), 'Un mémorialiste persan du XIe siècle: Beyhaqi', in: *Études de civilisation médiévale (IXe-XIIe siècles). Mélanges offerts à Edmond-René Labande ...*, Poitiers: C.E.S.C.M., 471–478.

Łazaryan, Viken (1995), Խորանների մեկնություններ (*Xoranneri Meknut'yunner*, 'Commentaries on Canon Tables', Erevan: Sargis Xač'enc'.

LDAB: Leuven Database of Ancient Books, <http://www.trismegistos.org/ldab/>, last access October 2014.

Le Guen, Gilbert (1995), 'Les problèmes biologiques', *Conservation préventive du patrimoine documentaire. Archives-livres-photographies-arts graphiques*, fiche 3.

Le Léannec-Bavavéas, Marie-Thérèse (1998), *Les papiers non filigranés médiévaux de la Perse à l'Espagne. Bibliographie 1950-1995*, Paris: Institut de recherche et d'histoire des textes (Documents, études et répertoires).

Le Léannec-Bavavéas, Marie-Thèrèse – Geneviève Humbert (1990), 'Une méthode de description du papier non filigrané (dit 'oriental')', *Gazette du livre médiéval*, 17, 24–30.

Lee, Alana et al. (2008) {A.L. – Vincent Otieno-Alego – Dudley Creagh}, 'Identification of iron-gall inks with near-infrared Raman microspectroscopy', *Journal of Raman Spectroscopy*, 39, 1079–1084.

Lefort, Louis-Théophile (1939), 'Fragments d'apocryphes en copte-akhmîmique', *Le Muséon*, 52, 1–10.

Leloir, Louis (1986–1992), *Écrits apocryphes sur les apôtres*, Turnhout: Brepols (Corpus Christianorum. Series Apocryphorum, 3-4).

Lentin, Jérôme (1997), *Recherches sur l'histoire de la langue arabe à l'époque moderne*, II, Université de Lille – Université de la Sorbonne Nouvelle Paris III [diss.].

Lentin, Jérôme (2004), 'La langue des manuscrits de Galland et la typologie du moyen arabe', in: *Les Milles et Une Nuits en partage*, ed. by Aboubakr Chraïbi, Paris: Sindbad, 434–455.

Lentin, Jérôme (2008), 'Middle Arabic', in: *Encyclopedia of Arabic Language and Linguistics*, III, ed. by Kees Versteegh et al., Leiden – Boston: Brill, 215–224.

Lentin, Jérôme (2012a), 'Normes orthographiques en moyen arabe: sur la notation du vocalisme bref', in: *Middle Arabic and Mixed Arabic: Diachrony and Synchrony*, ed. by Liesbeth Zack – Arie Schippers, Leiden – Boston: Brill (Studies in Semitic Languages and Linguistics, 64), 209–234.

Lentin, Jérôme (2012b), 'Reflections on Middle Arabic', in: *High vs. Low and Mixed Varieties - Domains, Status, and Functions across Time and Languages*, ed. by Gunvor Mejdell – Lutz Edzard, Wiesbaden: Harrassowitz (Abhandlungen für die Kunde des Morgenlandes, 77), 32–52.

Lentin, Jérôme (2012c), 'Du malheur de ne parler ni araméen ni kurde: une complainte en moyen arabe de l'evêque chaldéen de Siirt en 1766', in: *Autour de la langue arabe. Études présentées à Jacques Grand'Henry à l'occasion de son 70e anniversaire*, ed. by Johannes den Heijer – Paolo La Spisa – Laurence Tuerlinckx, Louvain-la-Neuve: Université catholique de Louvain-Institut Orientaliste (Publications de l'Institut Orientaliste de Louvain, 61), 229–251.

Lentin, Jérôme – Jacques Grand'Henry (eds) (2008), *Moyen arabe et variétés mixtes de l'arabe à travers l'histoire. Actes du Premier Colloque International (Louvain-la-Neuve, 10-14 mai 2004)*, Louvain-la-Neuve: Université catholique de Louvain, Institut Orientaliste (Publications de l'Institut Orientaliste de Louvain, 58).

Lepage, Claude (1987), 'Reconstruction d'un cycle protobyzantin à partir des miniatures de deux manuscrits éthiopiens du XIVe siècle', *Cahiers archéologiques*, 35, 159–196.

Lepage, Claude – Jacques Mercier (2011-2012), 'Un tétraévangile illustré éthiopien à cycle long du XVe siècle. Codicologie et iconographie', *Cahiers archéologiques*, 54, 99–174.

Leroy, Jules (1960), ' L'évangéliaire éthiopien du couvent d'Abba Garima et ses attaches avec l'ancien art chrétien de Syrie', *Cahiers archéologiques*, 11, 131–143.

Leroy, Jules (1961), 'L'évangéliaire éthiopien illustré du British Museum (Or. 510) et ses sources iconographiques', *Annales d'Éthiopie*, 4, 155–168.

Leroy, Jules (1962), 'Recherches sur la tradition iconographique des canons d'Eusèbe en Éthiopie', *Cahiers archéologiques*, 12, 173–204.

Leroy, Jules (1964), *Les manuscrits syriaques à peintures conservés dans les bibliothèques d'Europe et d'Orient*, I–II, Paris: Librarie orientaliste Paul Geuthner (Institut français d'archéologie de Beyrouth, Bibliothèque archéologique et historique, 77).

Leroy, Jules (1974), *Les manuscrits coptes et coptes-arabes illustrés*, Paris: Librarie orientaliste Paul Geuthner (Institut français d'archéologie de Beyrouth, Bibliothèque archéologique et historique, 96).

Leroy, Jules et al. (1961) {J.L. – Stephen Wright – Otto Jäger}, *Ethiopia. Illuminated manuscript*, New York: New York Graphic Society (UNESCO World art series).

Leroy, Julien (1976), *Les types de réglure des manuscrits grecs*, Paris: Éditions du Centre national de la recherche scientifique (Institut de recherche et d'histoire des textes. Bibliographies, colloques, travaux préparatoires).

Leroy, Maurice (1938), 'Un papyrus arméno-grec', *Byzantion*, 13/2, 513–537.

Lessing, Gotthold Ephraim (1802), *Du Laocoon, ou des limites respectives de la poésie et de la peinture*, Paris: Renouard.

Leveen, Jacob (1935), *Supplementary volume (vol. 4) to G. Margoliouth's Catalogue*, London: British Museum.

Levey, Martin (1962), '[al-Mu'izz ibn Badis] Mediaeval Arabic bookmaking and its relation to early chemistry and pharmacology (= *Umdat al-kuttâb*)', *Transactions of American philosophical society* n.s. 3/4, 3–79.

Levi Della Vida, Giorgio (1947), *Frammenti coranici in carattere cufico nella Biblioteca Vaticana (codici arabi 1605 e 1606)*, Città del Vaticano: Biblioteca Apostolica Vaticana (Studi e Testi, 132).

Levi Della Vida, Giorgio (1962), 'Assemani, Stefano Evodio', in: *Dizionario Biografico degli Italiani*, 4, 441a–442a.

Levi Della Vida, Giorgio (1965), *Secondo elenco dei manoscritti arabi islamici della Biblioteca Vaticana*, Città del Vaticano: Biblioteca Apostolica Vaticana (Studi e Testi, 242).

Lévi-Provençal, Évariste (1921), *Les manuscrits arabes de Rabat*, Paris: Leroux (Institut des hautes-études marocaines, 8).

Lewis, Agnes Smith (1894), *Catalogue of the Syriac Mss. in the Convent of S. Catherine on Mount Sinai*, Cambdridge: Cambridge University Press (Studia Sinaitica, 1).

Lewis, Agnes Smith (1897), *A Palestinian Syriac Lectionary. Containing Lessons from the Pentateuch, Job, Proverbs, Prophets, Acts, and Epistles*, London: Clay and Sons.

Lewis, Agnes Smith (1912), *The Forty Martyrs of the Sinai Desert and the Story of Eulogios from a Palestinian Syriac and Arabic Palimpsest*, Cambridge: Cambridge University Press (Horae Semiticae, 9).

Lewis, Agnes Smith – Alphonse Mingana (1914), *Leaves from three ancient Qur'âns, possibly pre-'Othmânic, with a list of their variants*, Cambridge: Cambridge University Press.

Libby, Willard F. (1946), 'Atmospheric Helium Three and Radiocarbon from Cosmic Radiation', *Physical Review*, 69, 671–672.

Library of Congress (2007), *Technical Standards for Digital Conversion of Text and Graphic Materials*, <http://memory.loc.gov/ammem/about/techStandards.pdf>, Washington, DC: Library of Congress.

Lichačev, Dmitrij S. (2001), *Текстология. На материале русской литературы X–XVII веков.* Издание третье, переработанное и дополненное (*Tekstologija. Na materiale russkoj literatury X–XVII vekov.* Izdanie tret'e, pererabotannoe i dopolnennoe, 'Textology. On the basis of material from Russian literature, X–XVII centuries, Third edition, revised and supplemented'), St Petersburg: Aleteja.

Lichačev, Nikolaj P. (1891), *Бумага и древнейшія бумажныя мельницы въ Московскомъ государствѣ* (*Bumaga i drevnejšija bumažnyja mel'nicy v" moskovskom" gosudarstvě*, 'Paper and the oldest paper mills in the Muscovite state'), St Petersburg: Imperatorskaja Akademija Nauk.

Lichačev, Nikolaj P. (1899), *Палеографическое значѣніе бумажныхъ водяныхъ знаковъ* (*Paleografičeskoe značěnïe bumažnych" vodjanych" znakov*, 'The Palaeographical Significance of Watermarks'), I–III, St Petersburg: Imperatorskaja Akademija Nauk.

Lichačev [Likhachev], Nikolaj P. (1994), *Likhachev's watermarks: an English-language version*, I–II, ed. by John Simon Gabriel Simmons – Bé van Ginneken, Amsterdam: Paper Publications Society (Monumenta chartae papyraceae historiam illustrantia, 15).

Lichačeva, Vera (1977), *Византийская миниатюра: памятники византийской миниатюры IX–XV веков в собраниях Советского Союза* (*Vizantijskaja miniatjura: pamjatniki vizantijskoj miniatjury IX–XV vekov v sobranijach Sovetskogo Sojuza*, 'Byzantine miniature: monuments of Byzantine miniature of the 9th-15th centuries in the collections of the Soviet Union'), Moskva: Iskusstvo.

LIGATUS, *Saint Catherine's Project*, <http://www.ligatus.org.uk/stcatherines/>, last access October 2014.

Liszewska, Weronika (2012), 'The problems concerning the use of new parchment leafcasting methods in the case of conservation treatment of highly gelatinised Ethiopian scrolls', in: *Conservation of Historical Parchments. New Methods of Leafcasting with the Use of Parchment Fibres*, Warszawa: Akademia Sztuk Pięknych w Warszawie, 379–399.

Liu, Guanghua (2005), 'Chinese Cinnabar', *The Mineralogical Record*, 36, 69–80.

Lo Monaco, Francesco (1996), 'In codicibus … qui Bobienses inscribuntur. Scoperte e studio di palinsesti Bobbiesi in Ambrosiana dalla fine del settecento ad Angelo Mai (1819)', *Aevum*, 70, 657–719.

Löfgren, Oscar – Renato Traini (1975, 1981, 1995), *Catalogue of the Arabic Manuscripts in the Biblioteca Ambrosiana.* I: *Antico Fondo and Medio Fondo*, II: *Nuovo Fondo: series A-D (Nos. 1-830)*, III: *Nuovo Fondo: series E (Nos. 831-1295)*, Vicenza: Neri Pozza (Fontes Ambrosiani, 51, 66, N.s. 2).

Lomagistro, Barbara (2008a), 'La genesi della scrittura cirillica: osservazioni paleografiche', *Nea Rhōmē*, 5, 147–167.

Lomagistro, Barbara (2008b), 'La scrittura cirillica minuscola: genesi ed evoluzione', in: *Contributi italiani al XIV Congresso Internazionale degli Slavisti (Ohrid, 10-16 settembre 2008)*, ed. by Alberto Alberti – Stefano Garzonio – Nicoletta Marcialis, Firenze (Biblioteca di Studi slavistici, 7), 111–148.

Loopstra, Jonathan A. (2009), *Patristic Selections in the 'Masoretic' Handbooks of the Qarqapā Tradition*, Catholic University of America [diss.].

Love, Harold (1984), 'The Ranking of Variants in the Analysis of Moderately Contaminated Manuscript Traditions', *Studies in Bibliography*, 37, 39–57.

Loveday, Helen (2001), Islamic Paper. A Study of an Ancient Craft, London: Archetype Books.

Lowry, Glenn D. – Susan Nemazee (1988), *A Jeweller's Eye: Islamic Art of the Book from Vever Collection*, Washington, DC: University of Washington Press.

Lucas, Alfred (1922), 'The Inks of Ancient and Modern Egypt', *The Analyst*, 47, 9–15.

Lucas, Alfred (1962), *Ancient Egyptian materials and Industries*, edited by John Richard Harris, 4th edition, London: Edward Arnold Publishers.

Lucchesi, Enzo (1981), *Répertoire des manuscrits coptes (sahidiques) publiés de la Bibliothèque nationale de Paris*, Genève: Cramer (Cahiers d'Orientalisme, 1).

Luffin, Xavier (2014), 'Tatruli: writing a Turkish language in Georgian alphabet', in: *Scripts Beyond Borders. A Survey of Allographic Traditions in the Euro-Mediterranean World*, ed. by Johannes den Heijer – Andrea Schmidt – Tamara Pataridze, Louvain: Peeters (Publications de l'Institut Orientaliste de Louvain, 62), 603–608.

Lundhaug, Hugo (2010), *Images of Rebirth: Cognitive Poetics and Transformational Soteriology in the Gospel of Philip and the Exegesis on the Soul*, Leiden: Brill (Nag Hammadi and Manichaean Studies, 73).

Lusini, Gianfrancesco (1996), *Il 'Gadla Absādi' (Dabra Māryām, Sarā'ē)*, I–II, Louvain: Peeters (Corpus Scriptorum Christianorum Orientalium, 557, 558, Scriptores Aethiopici, 103, 104).

Lusini, Gianfrancesco (2001), 'L'Église axoumite et ses traditions historiographiques (IVe-VIIe siècle)', in: *L'historiographie de l'Église des premiers siècles [Actes du Colloque de Tours Septembre 2000 organisé par l'Université de Tours et l'Institut Catholique de Paris]*, introduction by Michel Quesnel, ed. by Bertrand Pouderon – Yves-Marie Duval, Paris: Beauchesne (Théologie historique, 114), 541–557.

Lusini, Gianfrancesco (2002), 'I codici etiopici del fondo Martini nella Biblioteca Forteguerriana di Pistoia', *Aethiopica*, 5, 156–176.

Lusini, Gianfrancesco (2004), 'Copisti e filologi dell'Etiopia medievale. Lo Scriptorium di Dabra Māryām del Sarā'ē (Eritrea)', *La Parola del Passato*, 59/3 (336), 230–237.

Lusini, Gianfrancesco (2005), 'Philology and the Reconstruction of the Ethiopian Past', in: *Afrikas Horn. Akten der Ersten Internationalen Littmann-Konferenz 2. bis 5. Mai 2002 in München*, ed. by Walter Raunig – Steffen Wenig, Wiesbaden: Harrassowitz (Meroitica, 22), 91–106.

Lusini, Gianfrancesco (2006), 'I manoscritti etiopici dell'Università di Napoli 'L'Orientale'', in: *Studi berberi e mediterranei. Miscellanea offerta in onore di Luigi Serra*, II, ed. by A. M. Di Tolla, Napoli (Studi magrebini, n.s. 4), 85–90.

Luzatto, Aldo – Luisa Mortara Ottolenghi (1972), *Hebraica Ambrosiana*. I: *Catalogue of Undescribed Hebrew Manuscripts in the Ambrosiana Library*. II: *Description of Decorated and Illuminated Hebrew Manuscripts in the Ambrosiana Library*, Milano: Il Polifilo (Fontes Ambrosiani, 45).

Maas, Paul (1957), *Textkritik*, 3., verbesserte und vermehrte Auflage, Leipzig: Teubner.

Mabillon, Jean (1681), *De re diplomatica libri VI*, Paris: J.B.Coignard.

MacArthur, Duncan (1995), 'AGLAE et l'étude des encres et des colorants de manuscrits', *Techne: la science au service de l'histoire de l'art et des civilisations*, 2, 68–75.

Mačavariani [Machavariani], Elene [Helen] (1970), ქართული ხელნაწერები[: ალბომი] / *Грузинские рукописи*: *альбом* / *Georgian manuscripts*: *album* (*Kartuli xelnaçerebi*[: *albomi*] / *Gruzinskie rukopisi*: *al'bom*), Tbilisi: Xelovneba.

Mačavariani, Elene (1973), 'ასომთავრული დამწერლობის მხატვრული თავისებურებანი ქართული ხელნაწერების მიხედვით V–XII სს. (*Asomtavruli damçerlobis mxaṭvruli taviseburebani kartuli xelnaçerebis mixedvit*, 'Some peculiarities of the Asomtavruli script according to Georgian manuscripts of the 5th-12th centuries')', *Mravaltavi*, 2, 236–260.

Mačavariani, Elene (2008), ქართული დამწერლობა (*Kartuli damçerloba*, 'Georgian writing'), Tbilisi: Xelovneba.

Mačavariani, Elene (2012), ქართული ხელნაწერები: დამწერლობისა და შემკულობის საკითხები (*Kartuli xelnaçerebi*: *damçerlobisa da šemḳulobis saḳitxebi*, 'Georgian manuscripts: questions of paleography and decoration'), Tbilisi: Xelnaçerta erovnuli cenṭri.

Macdonald, Duncan Black (1910), '*Ali Baba and The Forty Thieves* in Arabic from a Bodlean MS', *Journal of the Royal Asiatic Society*, 42, 327–386.

Macdonald, Duncan Black (1913), 'Further Notes on *Ali Baba and the Forty Thieves*', *The Journal of the Royal Asiatic Society*, 45/1, 41–53.

Macé, Caroline (2004), 'Note sur la tradition manuscrite d'un passage disputé du Discours 38 de Grégoire de Nazianze (BHG 1938)', *Analecta Bollandiana*, 122, 51–68.

Macé, Caroline (2008), 'À propos d'une édition récente de Grégoire de Nazianze', *L'Antiquité Classique*, 77, 243–256.

Macé, Caroline (2011), 'Latin and Armenian translations and the prehistory of the Homilies of St Gregory of Nazianzus', *Comparative Oriental Manuscript Studies Newsletter*, 1, 21–23.

Macé, Caroline (forthcoming), 'Rules and guidelines in book series and their impact on scholarly editions', in: *Ars edendi Casebook*, ed. by Elisabet Göransson, Toronto: Pontifical Institute of Medieval Studies.

Macé, Caroline et al. (2001) {C.M. – Thomas Schmidt – Jean-François Weiler}, 'Le classement des manuscrits par la statistique et la phylogénétique: les cas de Grégoire de Nazianze et de Basile le Minime', *Revue d'Histoire des Textes*, 31, 243–276.

Macé, Caroline et al. (2004) {C.M. – Philippe Baret – Anne-Catherine Lantin}, 'Philologie et phylogénétique: regards croisés en vue d'une édition critique d'une homélie de Grégoire de Nazianze', in: *Digital Technology and Philological Disciplines*, ed. by Andrea Bozzi – Laura Cignoni, Pisa – Roma: Istituti Editoriali e Poligrafici Internazionali (Linguistica Computazionale, 20-21), 305–341.

Macé, Caroline et al. (2012) {C.M. – Ilse De Vos – Koen Geuten}, 'Comparison of stemmatological and phylogenetic methods to understand the copying history of the 'Florilegium Coislinianum'', in: *Ars edendi lectures Series*, II, ed. by Alessandra Bucossi – Erika Kihlman, Stockholm: Stockholm University Press, 107–129.

Mackeprang, Mouritz et al. (1921) {M.M. – Victor Madsen – Carl S[ophus] Petersen – Axel Anthon Björnbo – Ellen Jørgensen}, *Greek and Latin illuminated manuscripts, X–XIII centuries, in Danish collections*, Copenhagen: Levin & Munksgaard.

Macler, Frédéric (1908), *Catalogue des manuscrits arméniens et géorgiens de la bibliothèque Nationale*, Paris: Geuthner.

Macler, Frédéric (1920), *L'Évangile arménien. Édition phototypique du manuscrit n° 229 de la Bibliothèque d'Etchmiadzin*, Paris: Geuthner.

Macler, Frédéric (1924), *Documents d'art arméniens*: *De arte illustrandi, collections diverses*, I–II, Paris: Geuthner.

Macler, Frédéric (1928), *L'enluminure arménienne profane*, Paris: Geuthner.

Macomber, William F. (1978), *A catalogue of Ethiopian manuscripts microfilmed for the Ethiopian Manuscript Microfilm Library, Addis Ababa and for the Hill Monastic Manuscript Microfilm Library, Collegeville.* Vol. III: *Project Numbers 701–1100*, Collegeville, MN: Hill Monastic Manuscript Library.

MacRobert, Catherine Mary (2002), 'The linguistic basis of textual segmentation in Serbian Church Slavonic sources of the 14th-15th centuries', *Oxford University Working Papers in Linguistics, Philology & Phonetics*, 7, 207–224.

Madan, Falconer et al. (1895–1953), *A summary catalogue of western manuscripts in the Bodleian Library at Oxford which have not hitherto been catalogued in the Quarto series*, I–VII, Oxford: Clarendon Press.

Madani, Zubair Ahmed (2002), 'The development of a conservation treatment approach for Islamic miniatures', in: *Contributions to the Baltimore Congress, 2-6 September 2002*: *Works of Art on Paper*: *Books, Documents and Photographs. Techniques and Conservation*, ed. by Vincent Daniels – Alan Donnithorne, London: The International Institute for Conservation, 144–148.

Madden, Frederic (1850), *Catalogue of additions to the manuscripts in the British Museum in the years 1841-1845*, London: British Museum.

Mahdi, Muhsin S. (1984, 1984, 1994), *The Thousand and One Nights. (Alf Layla wa-Layla) from the Earliest Known Sources*, I–III, Leiden: Brill.

Mahdi, Muhsin S. (2014), *The Thousand and One Nights. (Alf Layla wa-Layla). The Classic Edition (1984–1994)*, I–II, Leiden: Brill.

Mahé, Jean-Pierre (1986–1987), review of Ō. Eganyan et al., *C'uc'ak jeṙagrac' Maštoc'i anuan matenadarani*, I–II, Yerevan, 1965, 1970, *Révue des études arméniennes*, 20, 583.

Mahé, Jean-Pierre (2005–2007), 'Koriun, la Vie de Maštoc'', *Revue des études arméniennes*, n.s. 30, 59–97.

Mairinger, Franz (1981), 'Physikalische Methoden zur Sichtbarmachung verblasster oder getilgter Tinten', *Restaurator. International Journal for the Preservation of Library and Archival Material*, 5, 45–56.

Mairinger, Franz (2000), 'The Ultraviolet and Fluorescence Study of Paintings and Manuscripts, ', in: *Radiation in Art and Archeometry*, ed. by D.C. Creagh – D.A. Bradley, Amsterdam: Elsevier Science, 56–75.

Mairinger, Franz (2004), 'UV-, IR- and X-ray imaging', in: *Non-Destructive Microanalysis of Cultural Heritage Materials*, ed. by Koen H. A. Janssens – René Van Grieken, Amsterdam: Elsevier Science (Wilson & Wilson's Comprehensive Analytical Chemistry, 42), 15–72.

Malak, Hanna (1964), 'Les livres liturgiques de l'Église Copte', in: *Mélanges Eugène Tisserant*, III: *Orient chrétien*, Città del Vaticano: Biblioteca Apostolica Vaticana (Studi e Testi, 233), 1–35.

Mallette, Karla (2010), *European Modernity and the Arab Mediterranean. Toward a New Philology and a Counter-Orientalism*, Philadelphia, PA: University of Pennsylvania Press.

Mallon, Jean (1952), *Paléographie romaine*, Madrid: Consejo Superior de Investigaciones Científicas (Scripturae Monumenta et Studia, 3).

Malxasyan, Armen (1996), 'Կեսարահայ կազմարվեստի պատմությունից (ԺԷ-ԺԸ դարեր)' (*Kesarahay kazmarvesti patmut'yunic' (XVII–XVIII darer)*, 'From the History of the Art of Bookbinding in Armenian Caesarea (17th–18th Centuries)'), *Ējmiacin*, 53, 174–190.

Mandosio, Jean-Marc (2010), 'Humanisme ou Barbarie? Formes de la latinité et mémoire de l'Antiquité dans quelques traductions médiévales de textes philosophiques arabes', in: *Écritures latines de la mémoire de l'antiquité au XVIe siècle*, ed. by Hélène Casanova-Robin – Perrine Galand, Paris: Classiques Garnier, 227–263.

Mandosio, Jean-Marc – Carla Di Martino (2006), 'La 'Météorologie' d'Avicenne (Kitāb Al-Shifā' V) et sa diffusion dans le monde latin', in: *Wissen über Grenzen: arabisches Wissen und Lateinisches Mittelalter*, Berlin: De Gruyter (Miscellanea mediaevalia, 33), 404–425.

Maniaci, Marilena (1995), 'Ricette di costruzione della pagina nei manoscritti greci e latini', *Scriptorium*, 49, 16–41.

Maniaci, Marilena (1996), *Terminologia del libro manoscritto*, Milano: Bibliografica (Addenda. Studi sulla conoscenza, la conservazione e il restauro del libro, 3).

Maniaci, Marilena (1997), 'Alla fine della riga. Divisione delle parole e continuità del testo nel manoscritto bizantino', *Scriptorium*, 51, 189–203.

Maniaci, Marilena (1999a), 'Suddivisione delle pelli e allestimento dei fascicoli nel manoscritto bizantino', *Quinio*, 1, 83–122.

Maniaci, Marilena (1999b), 'L'art de ne pas couper les peaux en quatre: les techniques de découpage des bifeuillets dans les manuscrits byzantins', *Gazette du livre médiéval*, 34, 1–12.

Maniaci, Marilena (2000a), 'La pergamena nel manoscritto bizantino dei secoli XI e XII: caratteristiche e modalità d'uso', *Quinio*, 2, 63–92.

Maniaci, Marilena (2000b), 'Stratégies de juxtaposition du texte et du commentaire dans quelques manuscrits d'Homère', in: *Le commentaire entre tradition et innovation. Actes du colloque international de l'Institut des traditions textuelles (Paris et Villejuif, 22-25 septembre 1999)*, ed. by Marie-Odile Goulet-Cazé – Tiziano Dorandi – Alain Le Boulluec – Ezio Ornato, Paris: Vrin (Bibliothèque d'histoire de la philosophie. Nouvelle série), 65–78.

Maniaci, Marilena (2002a), *Archeologia del manoscritto. Metodi, problemi, bibliografia recente. Con contributi di Carlo Federici e di Ezio Ornato*, Roma: Viella (I libri di Viella, 34).

Maniaci, Marilena (2002b), *Costruzione e gestione della pagina nel manoscritto bizantino (secoli IX–XII)*, Cassino: Università degli studi di Cassino.

Maniaci, Marilena (2004), 'Il codice greco 'non unitario'. Tipologie e terminologia', in: *Il codice miscellaneo, tipologia e funzioni. Atti del convegno internazionale (Cassino, 14-17 maggio 2003)*, ed. by Edoardo Crisci – Oronzo Pecere, Cassino (Segno e testo, 2), 75–107.

Maniaci, Marilena (2006a), 'Problemi di mise en page dei manoscritti con commento 'a cornice'. L'esempio di alcuni testimoni dell'Iliade', *Segno e testo*, 4, 211–298.

Maniaci, Marilena (2006b), 'Words within Words: Layout Strategies in some Glossed Manuscripts of the Iliad', *Manuscripta*, 50/2, 241–268.

Maniaci, Marilena (2008), 'Terminologia, manualistica, bibliografia: nuove possibilità di interazione fra risorse nello spazio della Rete', in: *Oltre la scrittura. Variazioni sul tema per Guglielmo Cavallo*, ed. by Daniele Bianconi – Lucio Del Corso, Paris: École des Hautes Études en Sciences Sociales – Centre d'Études Byzantines, Néo-Helléniques et Sud-Est Européennes (Dossiers byzantins, 8), 167–212.

Maniaci, Marilena (2011), 'Il libro manoscritto greco. Materiali e tecniche di confezione', in: *La scrittura greca dall'antichità all'epoca della stampa. Una introduzione*, ed. by Edoardo Crisci – Paola Degni, Roma: Carocci (Beni culturali, 35), 239–280.

Maniaci, Marilena (2013), 'Ricette e canoni di impaginazione del libro medievale. Nuove osservazioni e verifiche', *Scrineum*, 10, 1–48.

Maniaci, Marilena (forthcoming), 'The Mediaeval Codex as a Complex Contaner: the Greek and Latin Traditions', in: *'One-Volume Libraries': Composite Manuscripts and Multiple Text Manuscripts. Proceedings of the International Conference, Asien-Afrika-Institut, Universität Hamburg, October 7–10, 2010*, ed. by Michael Friedrich – Jörg Quenzer, Berlin – New York: De Gruyter (Studies in Manuscript Cultures).

Maniaci, Marilena – Paola Franca Munafò (eds) (1993), *Ancient and Medieval Book Materials and Techniques (Erice, 18-25 September 1992)*, I–II, Città del Vaticano (Studi e Testi, 357, 358).

Maniaci, Marilena – Giulia Orofino (2012), 'Les 'rouleaux d'Exultet' du Mont Cassin (techniques de fabrication, caractéristiques matérielles, décoration, rapports avec les rouleaux grecs', *Les Cahiers de Saint-Michel de Cuxa*, 43 (= *Gestes et techniques de l'artiste à l'époque romane. Actes de XLIIIes Journées romanes de Cuxa, 6-13 juillet 2011*), 71–82.

Manoscritti Greci d'Italia, <http://www.nuovabibliotecamanoscritta.it/MaGI/index.html>, last access May 2014.

Manoukian, Hasmik (1996), 'Les empreintes d'Artachate (antique Artaxata)', in: *Archives et sceaux du monde hellénistique / Archivi e sigilli nel mondo ellenistico*, ed. by Marie-Françoise Boussac – Antonio Invernizzi, Paris: Diffusion de Boccard (Bulletin de Correspondence Hellénique, Supplément 29), 371–373.

Манускриптъ (*Manuskript"*, 'Manuscript'), <http://manuscripts.ru>, last access May 2014.

Manuscripta medievalia, <http://www.manuscripta-mediaevalia.de>, last access May 2014.

Maqamat Al-Hariri. Illustrated by Yahya ibn Mahmud al-Wasiti [*facsim. BnF, Arabe 5847*], introduction by Oleg Grabar, New York: OMI, 2003.

Marava-Chatznicolaou, Anna – Christina Toufexi-Paschou (1978, 1985, 1997), *Catalogue of the Illuminated Byzantine Manuscripts of the National Library of Greece*, I: *Manuscripts of New Testament: Texts 10th -12th Century*; II: *Manuscripts of New Testament: Texts 13th-15th Century*; III: *Homilies of the Church Fathers and Menologia 9th -12th Century*, Athens: Publications Bureau of the Academy of Athens.

Maravela-Solbakk, Anastasia (2008), 'Monastic Book Production in Christian Egypt', in: *Spätantike Bibliotheken: Leben und Lesen in den frühen Klöstern Ägyptens*, ed. by Harald Froschauer – Cornelia Eva Römer, Wien: Phoibos Verlag (Nilus. Studien zur Kultur Ägyptens und des Vorderen Orients, 14), 25–37.

Marc multilingue, <http://www.safran.be/marcmultilingue/>, last access May 2014.

Marçais, Georges – Louis Poinssot (1948), *Objets kairouanais, IXe au XIIIe s. Reliures, verreries, cuivres et bronzes, bijoux*, I, Tunis – Paris: Direction des Antiquités et Arts (Notes et Documents, 9).

Marcel, Jean-Joseph (1828), *Palaeographie arabe ou recueil de mémoires sur différens monumens lapidairies, numismatiques, glyptiques et manuscrits*, Paris: Imprimerie royale.

Marchand, Suzanne (2009), *German Orientalism in the Age of Empire. Religion, Race, and Scholarship*, Washington, DC – Cambridge: German Historical Institute – Cambridge University Press (Publications of the German Historical Institute).

Marengo, Emilio et al. (2005) {E.M. – Maria Cristina Liparota – Elisa Robotti – Marco Bobba}, 'Monitoring of Paintings under Exposure to UV Light by ATR-FT-IR Spectroscopy and Multivariate Control Charts', *Vibrational Spectroscopy*, 40, 225–234.

Margoliouth, George (1899–1915), *Catalogue of the Hebrew and Samaritan Manuscripts in the British Museum*, I–III, London: British Museum.

Marr, Nikolaj Jakovlevič (1892), *Списокъ рукописей Севанского монастыря. Изъ лѣтней* (*1890*) *поѣздки въ Арменію* / Ցուցակ համառօտ ձեռագրաց Վանուց Սևանայ (*Spisok" rukopisei Sevanskago monastyrja. Iz" lětnej (1890) poězdki v Armeniïu / C'uc'ak hamarōt jeṙagrac' Vanuc' Sewanay*, 'Catalogue of the Armenian manuscripts in the Monastery of Sevan. From a summer (1890) journey to Armenia'), Moskva: Barchudarjan.

Marr, Nikolaj Jakovlevič (1901), 'Агіографическіе матеріалы по грузинскимъ рукописямъ Ивера (*Agïografičeskïe materïaly po gruzinskim" rukopisjam" Ivera*, 'Hagiographical materials according to Georgian manuscripts of the Iviron')', *Zapiski Vostočnago Otdělenïja Russkago Archeologičeskago Obščestva*, 13, 1–144.

Marr, Nikolaj Jakovlevič (1940), *Описание грузинских рукописей Синайского монастыря* (*Opisanie gruzinskich rukopisej Sinajskogo monastyrja*, 'Description of the Georgian manuscripts of the Sinai monastery'), Moskva – Leningrad: Izdatel'stvo Akademii Nauk SSSR.

Marr, Nikolaj [Niḳo] Jakovlevič (1955), იერუსალიმის ბერძნული საპატრიარქო წიგნსაცავის ქართული ხელნაწერების მოკლე აღწერილობა / *Краткое описание грузинских рукописей библиотеки греческого патриархата в Иерусалиме* (*Ierusalimis berʒnuli saṗaṭriarko çignsacavis kartuli xelnaçerebis moḳle aġçeriloba / Kratkoe opisanie gruzinskich rukopisej biblioteki grečeskogo patriarchata v Ierusalime*, 'A short description of the Georgian manuscripts in the library of the Greek Patriarchate in Jerusalem', Tbilisi: Sakartvelos SSR Mecnierebata Aḳademiis Gamomcemloba.

Marrassini, Paolo (1987), 'L'edizione critica dei testi etiopici: problemi di metodo e reperti linguistici', in: *Linguistica e filologia. Atti del VII Convegno Internazionale di Linguisti tenuto a Milano nei giorni 12-14 settembre 1984*, ed. by Giancarlo Bolognesi – Vittore Pisani, Brescia: Paideia (Sodalizio Glottologico Milanese - Istituto Lombardo di Scienze e Lettere), 347–356.

Marrassini, Paolo (1987–1988), 'I manoscritti etiopici della Biblioteca Medicea Laurenziana di Firenze', *Rassegna di Studi Etiopici*, 30; 31, 81–116; 69–110.

Marrassini, Paolo (1992), 'Interpunzione e fenomeni demarcativi nelle lingue semitiche', in: *Storia e teoria dell'interpunzione. Atti del Convegno Internazionale di Studi, Firenze, 19-21 maggio 1988*, ed. by Emanuela Cresti – Nicoletta Maraschio, Roma: Bulzoni, 501–520.

Marrassini, Paolo (1993), *Lo scettro e la croce. La campagna di ʿAmda Ṣeyon contro l'Ifāt* (*1332*), Napoli: Università degli Studi di Napoli l''Orientale' (Studi Africanistici. Serie Etiopica, 4).

Marrassini, Paolo (1996), 'Problems of Gəʿəz philology', in: *Studies in Near Eastern Languages and Literatures. Memorial volume of Karel Petráček*, ed. by Petr Zemánek, Prague: Academy of Sciences of the Czech Republic. Oriental Institute, 371–378.

Marrassini, Paolo (2003), *«Vita», «Omelia», «Miracoli» del santo Gabra Manfas Qeddus*, Louvain: Peeters (Corpus Scriptorum Christianorum Orientalium, 597-598, Scriptores Aethiopici, 107-108).

Marrassini, Paolo (2008a), 'Salient Features of Philology: The Science of Establishing Primary Sources', *Bulletin of Philological Society of Ethiopia*, 1, 4–12.

Marrassini, Paolo (2008b), review of R. Voigt, *Die äthiopischen Studien im 20. Jahrhundert / Ethiopian Studies in the 20th Century. Akten der internationalen äthiopischen Tagung Berlin 22. bis 24. Juli 2000*. Semitica et Semitohamitica Berolinensia 2. Aachen: Shaker Verlag, 2003, *Bibliotheca Orientalis*, 65/1-2, 267–274.

Marrassini, Paolo (2009), 'Problems in Critical Edition and the State of Ethiopian Philology', *Journal of Ethiopian Studies*, 42, 25–68.

Martinelli Tempesta, Stefano (2010), review of D. Searby, *The Corpus Parisinum. A Critical Edition of the Greek Text with Commentary and English Translation. A Medieval Anthology of Greek Texts from the Pre-Socratics to the Church Fathers, 600 B.C. - 700 A.D.*, I–II, Lewiston, NY: Edwin Mellen Press, 2007, *Bryn Mawr Classical Review*, 02.02. <http://bmcr.brynmawr.edu/2010/2010-02-02.html>.

Martínez Porro, Jaime (2013), 'La ceremonia zoroástrica de Vīštāsp Yašt y sus manuscritos', *Boletín de la Sociedad Española de Iranología*, 2, 69–80.

Marx, Michael (2012), 'Der Koran das erste arabische Buch', *Rottenburger Jahrbuch zur Kirchengeschichte*, 31, 25–48.

Marzo, Flavio (2012), 'The creation of a custom-made cradle to minimise risk during the digitisation process', *ICON news*, 41, 30–34.

Marzolph, Ulrich (1999), *Das Buch der wundersamen Geschichten. Erzählungen aus der Welt von Tausendundeiner Nacht*, München: C.H. Beck.

Marzolph, Ulrich (2004), 'Narrative Strategies in Popular Literature: Ideology and Ethics in Tales from the Arabian Nights and Other Collections', *Middle Eastern Literatures*, 7/2, 171–182.

Masai, François (1950), 'Paléographie et codicologie', *Scriptorium*, 4, 279–293.

Masai, François (1956), 'La paléographie gréco-latine, ses tâches, ses méthodes', *Scriptorium*, 10, 281–302.

Massignon, Louis (1909), 'Une bibliothèque saharienne: la bibliothèque de Cheikh Sidia au Sahara', *Revue du Monde Musulman*, 8, 409–418.

Mastruzzo, Antonio (1995), 'Ductus, corsività, storia della scrittura. Alcune considerazioni', *Scrittura e civiltà*, 19, 403–464.

Matejic, Mateja (1983), *Slavic Manuscripts from the Fekula Collection. A Description*, Columbus, OH: Ohio State University.

Matejic, Predrag – Hannah Thomas (1992), *Manuscripts on Microform of the Hilandar Research Library* (*The Ohio State University*), Columbus, OH: Resource Center for Medieval Slavic Studies (Ohio State University) – Sofia: 'Ivan Dujchev' Research Centre for Slavo-Byzantine Studies (Resources in medieval Slavic studies, 1).

Matenadaran manuscripts, <http://www.matenadaran.am/v2_2/>, last access October 2014.

Mat'evosyan, Artašes (1969), 'Երբ և որտեղ է գրվել Մշո Տօնական-Ճառընտիրը (*Erb ew orteł ē grvel Mšo Tōnakan-čaṙəntirə*, 'When and Where was the Muš Saintday-Homiliary Copied?')', *Banber Matenadarani*, 9, 137–162.

Mat'evosyan, Artašes (1984), Հայերեն ձեռագրերի հիշատակարաններ ԺԳ դար (*Hayeren jeṙagreri hišatakaranner XIII dar*, 'Colophons of Armenian Manuscripts, 13th Century'), Erevan: Nairi.

Mat'evosyan, Artašes (1988), Հայերեն ձեռագրերի հիշատակարաններ Ե-ԺԲ դդ. (*Hayeren jeṙagreri hišatakaranner V–XII dd.*, 'Colophons of Armenian Manuscripts, 5th-12th Centuries'), Erevan: Nairi.

Mat'evosyan, Artašes [Mathevossian, Artashes] – Tatyana Izmaylova [Tatiana Izmailova] (2000), Վազգեն Վեհափառի Աւետարանը Ժ դար. Նմանահանություն (*Vazgen Vehapaṙi Avetaranə, X dar. Nmanahanut'yun*) / *The Gospel of Catholicos Vasgen, Tenth Century. Facsimile*, Erevan: Nairi.

Mathews, Thomas F. – Mary Virginia Orna (1992–1993), 'Four Manuscripts at San Lazzaro, Venice', *Revue des études arméniennes*, n.s. 22, 471–486.

Mathews, Thomas F. – Avedis K. Sanjian (1991), *Armenian Gospel Iconography. The Tradition of the Glajor Gospel*, Washington, D.C.: Dumbarton Oaks (Dumbarton Oaks Studies, 29).

Mathews, Thomas – Roger S. Wieck (eds) (1994), *Treasures in Heaven*: *Armenian Illuminated Manuscripts*, New York: Pierpont Morgan Library.

Matthew of Edessa (Matt'ēos Uṙhayec'i) (1869), Մատթէոսի Ուռհայեցւոյ Պատմութիւն (*Matt'ēosi Uṙhayec'woy Patmut'iwn*, 'Matthew of Edessa's History'), Jerusalem.

Matthew of Edessa (Matt'ēos Uṙhayec'i) (1898), Ժամանակագրութիւն (*Žamanakagrut'iwn*, 'Chronicle'), Vałaršapat.

Maue, Dieter (1996), *Alttürkische Handschriften*. I: *Dokumente in Brāhmī und Tibetischer Schrift*, Stuttgart: Steiner (Verzeichnis der orientalischen Handschriften in Deutschland, 13/9).

Mazdāpūr, Katayūn (1378 Šamsī / 1999 CE), 'چند دستنويس نويافتهٔ أوستا' (*Čand dastnevīs-e nouyāfte-ye avestā*, 'Some newly found Avestan manuscripts'), *Me-ye Irān bāstān*, 8, 3–19.

Mazdāpūr [Mazdapour], Katayūn [Katayoun] (2012), 'Twelve Newly Found Avestan Manuscripts in Iran', in: *The transmission of the Avesta*, ed. by Alberto Cantera, Wiesbaden: Harrassowitz (Iranica, 20), 165–172.

Mazzucchi, Carlo Maria (2005), 'Inchiostri bizantini del XII secolo', in: *Ricordo di Lidia Perria*, I, Roma: Dipartimento di Filologia Greca e Latina, Sezione Bizantino-Neoellenica (Rivista di Studi Bizantini e Neoellenici, n.s. 42), 157–162.

McCormick, Sarah – Ros Whitford (2003), ''The Story of Time': Managing a major loans-in exhibition at the National Maritime Museum', *The Paper Conservator*, 27, 79–86.

McEwan, Robin (2006), *Picturing Apocalypse at Gondär. A Study of the Two Known Sets of Ethiopian Illuminations of the Revelation of St John and the Life and Death of John*, ed. by Dorothea McEwan, Torino: Nino Aragno.

Mefod'eva, V.S. (2009), 'Из истории производства пергамента в России в первой половине XVIII века (*Iz istorii proizvodstva pergamenta v Rossii v pervoj polovine XVIII veka*, 'From the history of parchment manufacture in Russia in the first half of the eighteenth century')', *Chrizograf*, 3, 517–525.

Meghapart Project, <http://www.nla.am/arm/meghapart/index.htm>, last access 2013.

Meisami, Julie Scott (1999), *Persian historiography to the end of the twelfth century*, Edinburgh: Edinburgh University Press.

Mellors, John – Anne Parsons (2002a), *Bookmaking in Rural Ethiopia in the Twenty-First Century*: *Ethiopian Bookmaking*, London: New Cross Books.

Mellors, John – Anne Parsons (2002b), *Bookmaking in Rural Ethiopia in the Twenty-First Century*: *Scribes of South Gondar*, London: New Cross Books.

Melot, Amicet (1739), *Catalogus codicum manuscriptorum Bibliothecæ regiæ*, I, Parisiis: E Typographia regia.

Ménard, Philippe (1997), 'Réflexions sur la 'nouvelle philologie'', in: *Alte und neue Philologie*, ed. by Martin-Dietrich Gleßgen – Franz Lebsanft, Tübingen: Max Niemeyer (Beihefte zu editio, 8), 17–33.

Meparišvili, Luba (1949), საქართველოს სახელმწიფო მუზეუმის ქართულ ხელნაწერთა აღწერილობა. საქართველოს საისტორიო და საეთნოგრაფიო საზოგადოების ყოფილი მუზეუმის ხელნაწერები (*H კოლექცია*). *Описание грузинских рукописей государственного музея Грузии. Рукописи бывшего Музея Грузинского Общества Истории и Этнографии* (*коллекция H*) (*Sakartvelos saxelmçipo muzeumis kartul xelnaçerta aġçeriloba. Sakartvelos saisṭorio da saetnograpio sazogadoebis q̇opili muzeumis xelnaçerebi* (*H ḳolekcia*) / *Opisanie gruzinskich rukopisej Gosudarstvennogo muzeja Gruzii. Rukopisi byvšego Muzeja Gruzinskogo Obščestva Istorii i Ėtnografii* (*kollekcija H*), 'Description of Georgian Manuscripts of the State Museum of Georgia. Manuscripts of the former Museum of the Society of History and Ethnography of Georgia (collection H)'), V, Tbilisi: Sakartvelos SSR Mecnierebata Aḳademiis Gamomcemloba.

Mercati, Giovanni – Pio Franchi de' Cavalieri (1923), *Codices Vaticani Graeci* – Tomus I. *Codices 1–329*, Città del Vaticano: Biblioteca Apostolica Vaticana (Bibliothecae Apostolicae Vaticanae codices manu scripti recensiti).

Mercier, Charles (1978–1979), 'Notes de paléographie arménienne', *Revue des études arméniennes*, n.s. 13, 51–58.

Mercier, Jacques (1979), *Rouleaux magiques éthiopiens*, Paris: Éditions du Seuil.

Mercier, Jacques (1992), *Le Roi Salomon et les maîtres du regard. Art et médecine en Éthiopie*, Paris: Réunion des Musées Nationaux.

Mercier, Jacques (2000), 'La peinture éthiopienne à l'époque axoumite et au XVIIIe siècle', *Comptes Rendus de l'Académie des inscriptions et belles-lettres*, 35–71.

Mercier, Jacques (ed.) (2001), *L'arche éthiopienne*: *Art chretien d'Éthiopie. 27 septembre 2000-7 janvier 2001, Paris, Pavilion des Arts*, Paris: Paris-Musées.

Mercier, Jacques (2004), *Vierges d'Éthiopie*, Montpellier: Archange Minotaure.

Mercier, Jacques – Daniel Seifemichael (eds) (2009), *Ethiopian Church. Treasures & Faith*, Montpellier: Archange Minotaure.

Merian, Sylvie (1993), *The Structure of Armenian Bookbinding and its Relation to Near Eastern Bookmaking Traditions. Ph.D. dissertation*, Columbia University.

Merian, Sylvie (1994), 'Silver Covers', in: *Treasures in Heaven: Armenian Illuminated Manuscripts*, ed. by Thomas F. Mathews – Roger S. Wieck, New York: Pierpont Morgan Library, 115–123.

Merian, Sylvie (1995), 'Cilicia as the Locus of European Influence on Armenian Medieval Book Production', *Armenian Review*, 45, no. 4 /180, 61–72.

Merian, Sylvie (1996), 'From Venice to Isfahan and Back: The Making of an Armenian Manuscript in Early 18th-Century Persia', in: *The Compleat Binder: Studies in Book Making and Conservation in Honour of Roger Powell*, ed. by John L. Sharpe, Turnhout: Brepols (Bibliologia. Elementa ad librorum studia pertinentia, 14), 280–291.

Merian, Sylvie (1998), 'The Armenian Bookmaking Tradition in the Christian East. A Comparison with the Syriac and Greek Traditions', in: *The Bible as Book. The Manuscript Tradition*, ed. by John L. Sharpe – Kimberly van Kampen, London: The British Library – New Castle, Delaware: Oak Knoll Press, 205–214.

Merian, Sylvie (2008), 'The characteristics of Armenian medieval bindings', in: *Care and Conservation of Manuscripts 10. Proceedings of the tenth international seminar held at the University of Copenhagen, 19th-20th October 2006*, ed. by Gillian Fellows-Jensen – Peter Springborg, Copenhagen: Museum Tusculanum Press, 89–107.

Merian, Sylvie (2013), 'The Armenian Silversmiths of Kesaria/Kayseri in the Seventeenth and Eighteenth Centuries', in: *Armenian Kesaria/Kayseri and Cappadocia*, ed. by Richard Hovannisian, Costa Mesa: Mazda, 117–185.

Merian, Sylvie et al. (1994a) {S.M. – Thomas F. Mathews – Mary Virginia Orna}, 'The Making of an Armenian Manuscript', in: *Treasures in Heaven: Armenian Illuminated Manuscripts*, ed. by Thomas F. Mathews – Roger S. Wieck, New York: Pierpont Morgan Library, 124–134.

Merian, Sylvie et al. (1994b) {S.M. – Thomas F. Mathews – Mary Virginia Orna}, 'Pigment Analysis of Armenian, Byzantine, Iranian, Indian, and Persian Manuscripts', in: *Treasures in Heaven: Armenian Illuminated Manuscripts*, ed. by Thomas F. Mathews – Roger S. Wieck, New York: Pierpont Morgan Library, 135–142.

Méric, Laure (2000), 'L'eau dans les livres', in: *La climatologie dans les archives et les bibliothèques: actes des troisièmes Journées sur la conservation préventive, 2-3 décembre, 1998*, Arles: Centre de Conservation du Livre, 25–38.

Merk, Augustin (1957), *Novum Testamentum graece et latine apparatu critico instructum edidit…*, 8th ed., Roma: Pontificii instituti biblici.

Mersha Alehegne (2011), 'Towards a Glossary of Ethiopian Manuscript Culture and Practice', *Aethiopica*, 14, 145–162.

Meščerskaja, E.N. (1987), 'Сирийская рукописная книга (Sirijskaja rukopisnaja kniga, 'The Syriac Manuscript Book')', in: *Рукописная книга в культуре народов Востока* (*Rukopisnaja kniga v kul'ture narodov Vostoka*, 'The manuscript book in the culture of the peoples of the orient'), I, Moskva: Nauka - Glavnaja redakcija vostočnoj literatury, 104–144.

Messina, Giuseppe (1951), *Diatessaron persiano*. I. *Introduzione*, II. *Testo e traduzione*, Roma: Pontificio Istituto Biblico.

Meṭreveli, Elene (1950), საქართველოს სახელმწიფო მუზეუმის ქართულ ხელნაწერთა აღწერილობა. საქართველოს საისტორიო და საეთნოგრაფიო საზოგადოების ყოფილი მუზეუმის ხელნაწერები (*H* კოლექცია). *Описание грузинских рукописей государственного музея Грузии. Рукописи бывшего Музея Грузинского Общества Истории и Этнографии* (*коллекция H*) (*Sakartvelos saxelmçipo muzeumis kartul xelnaçerta aġçeriloba. Sakartvelos saisṭorio da saetnograpio sazogadoebis q̇opili muzeumis xelnaçerebi* (*H ḳolekcia*) / *Opisanie gruzinskich rukopisej Gosudarstvennogo muzeja Gruzii. Rukopisi byvšego Muzeja Gruzinskogo Obščestva Istorii i Ėtnografii* (*kollekcija H*), 'Description of Georgian Manuscripts of the State Museum of Georgia. Manuscripts of the former Museum of the Society of History and Ethnography of Georgia (collection H)'), IV, Tbilisi: Sakartvelos SSR Mecnierebata Aḳademiis Gamomcemloba.

Meṭreveli, Elene et al. (1957) {E.M. – Krisṭine Šarašiʒe}, საქართველოს სახელმწიფო მუზეუმის ქართულ ხელნაწერთა აღწერილობა. მუზეუმის ხელნაწერთა ახალი (*Q*) კოლექცია. *Описание грузинских рукописей государственного музея Грузии. Рукописи новой* (*Q*) *коллекции музея* (*Sakartvelos saxelmçipo muzeumis kartul xelnaçerta aġçeriloba. Muzeumis xelnaçerta axali* (*Q*) *ḳolekcia / Opisanie gruzinskich rukopisej Gosudarstvennogo muzeja Gruzii. Rukopisi novoj* (*Q*) *kollekcii muzeja*, 'Description of Georgian Manuscripts of the State Museum of Georgia. Manuscripts of the New (Q) Collection'), I, Tbilisi: Sakartvelos SSR Mecnierebata Aḳademiis Gamomcemloba.

Meṭreveli, Elene et al. (1978) {E.M. – Caca Čanḳievi – Lili Xevsuriani – Lamara Ǯġamaia}, ქართულ ხელნაწერთა აღწერილობა. სინური კოლექცია (*Kartul xelnaçerta aġçeriloba. Sinuri ḳolekcia*, 'Description of Georgian manuscripts. Sinai collection'), I, Tbilisi: Sakartvelos SSR Mecnierebata Aḳademiis Gamomcemloba.

Meṭreveli, Roin (2008), ქართლის ცხოვრება (*Kartlis cxovreba*, 'The Life of Kartli'), Tbilisi: Meridiani / Arṭanuǯi.

Metzger, Bruce M. (1977), *The Early Versions of the New Testament. Their Origin, Transmission, and Limitations*, Oxford: Clarendon.

Michalski, Stefan (2009), 'Agent of Deterioration: Light, Ultraviolet and Infrared', in: *Ten Agents of Deterioration*, ed. by Canadian Conservation Institute, Ottawa: CCI, Chapter 8, <http://www.cci-icc.gc.ca/caringfor-prendresoindes/articles/10agents/chap08-eng.aspx>.

Miklas, Heinz et al. (2008), *Standard of the Old Slavic Cyrillic Script*, <http://www.sanu.ac.rs/Cirilica/Prilozi/ StandardOld.pdf>, Beograd [manuscript].

Milheirão, Victor (1995), *Conservation préventive du patrimoine documentaire. Archives-livres-photographies-arts graphiques*, Arles: Centre de Conservation du Livre.

Miliani, Costanza et al. (2007) {C.M. – Francesca Rosi – Ilaria Borgia – Pier A. Benedetti – Brunetto Giovanni Brunetti – Antonio Sgamellotti}, 'Fiber-optic Fourier Transform Mid-infrared Reflectance Spectroscopy: A Suitable Technique for in situ Studies of Mural Paintings', *Applied Spectroscopy*, 61, 293–299.

Milik, Jozef Tadeusz (1953), 'Une inscription et une lettre en araméen christo-palestinien', *Revue biblique*, 60, 526–539.

Milikowsky, Chaim (1988), 'The Status Quaestionis of Research in Rabbinic Literature', *Journal of Jewish Studies*, 39, 201–211.

Miller, Julia (2010), *Books will Speak Plain. A Handbook for Identifying and Describing Historical Bindings*, Ann Arbor, Michigan: The Legacy Press.

Milne, H.J.M. (1927), *Catalogue of the Literary Papyri in the British Museum*, London: British Museum.

Miltenova, Anisava L. (2013), 'Intertextuality in the Orthodox Slavic Tradition. The case of Mixed-Content Miscellanies', in: *Between Text and Text: International Symposium on Intertextuality in Ancient Near Eastern, Ancient Mediterranean, and Early Medieval Literatures*, Göttingen: Vandenhoeck & Ruprecht (Journal of Ancient Judaism. Supplements, 6), 314–327.

Minasyan, Lewon (1972), Նոր Ջուղայի տպարանն ու իր տպագրած գրքերը (*Nor Jułayi tparann u ir tpagrac grkʿerə*, 'The Press of New Julfa and its Published Books'), New Julfa: Holy Saviour Monastery.

Mingana, Alphonse (1933), *Catalogue of the Mingana collection of manuscripts. Now in the possession of the Trustees of the Woodbrooke settlement, Selly Oak, Birmingham*, Cambridge: Heffer and Sons.

Mingana, Alphonse (1934a), *Catalogue of the Arabic Manuscripts in the John Rylands Library*, Manchester: Manchester University Library.

Mingana, Alphonse (1934b), *Early Christian Mystics. Christian Documents in Syriac, Arabic, and Garshuni*, Cambridge: Heffer and Sons (Woodbrooke studies, 7).

Mingana, Alphonse – Agnes Smith-Lewis (1914), *Leaves from three ancient Qurâns possibly pre-'Othmânic, with a list of their variants*, Cambridge: Cambridge University Press.

Mingarelli, Giovanni Luigi (1785), *Aegyptiorum codicum reliquiae Venetiis in Bibliotheca Naniana asservatae …*, Bologna: Laelii a Vulpe.

Minorski, V. (1958), *A Catalogue of the Turkish Manuscripts and Miniatures. The Chester Beatty Library*, introduction by J.V.S. Wilkinson, Dublin: Hodges Figgis.

Misk'č'ean, Y. (1892), 'Ցուցակ հայերէն ձեռագրաց Քահանայապետական Մատենադարանին Վատիկանու (*C'uc'ak hayerēn jeṙagrac' K'ahanayapetakan Matenadaranin Vatikanu*, 'Catalogue of the Armenian Manuscripts in the Papal Library of the Vatican')', *Handēs Amsōrya*, 6, 211–214, 244–247, 273–275, 339–343.

Mkelle, Mohamed Burhan (1981), *Résumés de vieux manuscrits arabes collectés dans l'île de Zanzibar par M. B. Mkelle. Summary of old Arabic manuscripts collected in Zanzibar Island*, Zanzibar: EACROTANAL.

Moberg, Axel (1924), *The Book of Himyarites. Fragments of a Hitherto Unknown Syriac Work*, Lund: Gleerup (Acta Regiae Societatis Humaniorum Litterarum Lundensis, 7).

Mokretsova, Inna (1995), 'Russian Medieval Book Bindings', *Restaurator. International Journal for the Preservation of Library and Archival Material*, 16, 100–102.

Molin Pradel, Marina (2013), *Katalog der griechischen Handschriften der Bayerischen Staatsbibliothek München*. Bd. 2: *Codices graeci Monacenses 56–109*, Wiesbaden: Harrassowitz (Catalogus codicum manu scriptorum Bibliothecae Monacensis, 2/2).

Mondrain, Brigitte (1998), 'Les signatures des cahiers dans les manuscrits grecs', in: *Recherches de codicologie comparée: la composition du codex au Moyen Âge en Orient et en Occident*, ed. by Philippe Hoffmann, Paris: Presses de l'École normale supérieure (Collection bibliologie), 21–48.

Mondrain, Brigitte (2012a), 'Bernard de Montfaucon et l'étude des manuscrits grecs', *Scriptorium*, 66, 281–316.

Mondrain, Brigitte (2012b), 'La lecture et la copie de textes scientifiques à Byzance pendant l'époque Paléologue', in: *La produzione scritta tecnica e scientifica nel medioevo: libro e documento tra scuole e professioni*, ed. by Giuseppe De Gregorio, Spoleto: Centro Italiano di Studi sull'Alto Medioevo (Studi e ricerche del Dipartimento di Filologia e Storia, 5), 607–632.

Monferrer-Sala, Juan Pedro (2010), 'Once again on the early Christian Arabic Apology: remarks on a palaeographic singularity', *Journal of Near Eastern Studies*, 69/2, 195–197.

Montanari, Mariasanta (1999), 'Biodétérioration: considérations sur les conditions à garder dans les dépôts et pendant les expositions', in: *Biodétérioration et désinfection des collections d'archives et des bibliothèques: actes des deuxièmes Journées sur la conservation préventive, 18-19 novembre, 1996*, Arles: Centre de Conservation du Livre, 95–111.

Montfaucon, Bernard de (1708), *Paleografia graeca, sive, De ortu et progressu literarum graecarum*, Parisiis: L. Guerin, veuve J. Boudot & C. Robustel.

Montfaucon, Bernard de (1715), *Bibliotheca Coisliniana, olim Segueriana sive manuscriptorum omnium Graecorum quae in ea continentur, accurata descriptio, ubi operum singulorum notitia datur, aetas cujusque Manuscripti indicatur, vetustiorum specimina exhibentur, aliaque multa annotantur, quae ad Palaeographiam Graecam pertinent*, Parisiis: L. Guerin et Ch. Robustel.

Moraux, Paul (1976), *Aristoteles Graecus. Die Griechischen Manuskripte des Aristoteles* I: *Alexandrien-London*, Berlin – New York: De Gruyter (Peripatoi, 8).

Morley, William H. (1862), *The Táríkh-i Baihaki containing the life of Masaúd, son of Sultán Mahmúd of Ghaznín…*, Calcutta: The College Press (Bibliotheca Indica, 37).

Morozov, D.A. (1994), 'Древнерусская рукопись на среднеазиатской бумаге (*Drevnerusskaja rukopis' na sredneaziatskoj bumage*, 'An Old Russian Manuscript on Central Asian Paper')', *Archiv russkoj istorii*, 5, 123–200.

Mortley, Raoul (1992), 'The Name of the Father is the Son' (Gospel of Truth 38) [with afterword by Michel Tardieu]', in: *Neoplatonism and Gnosticism*, ed. by Richard T. Wallis – Jay Bregman, Albany, NY: State University of New York Press, 239–252.

Mošin, Vladimir (1965), 'Metodološke bilješke o tipovima pisma u ćirilici ('Methodological remarks on the types of Cyrillic script')', *Slovo*, 15-16, 150–182.

Mošin, Vladimir – Seid M. Traljić (1957), *Filigranes des XIIIe et XIVe siècles / Vodeni znakovi XIII. i XIV. vijeka*, I–II, Zagreb: Jugoslavenska Akademija Znanosti I Umjetnosti. Historijski Institut.

Mossay, Justin (2006), *Sancti Gregorii Nazianzeni Opera. Versio Graeca* I. *Orationes X et XII*, Turnhout: Brepols (Corpus Christianorum. Series Graeca, 64; Corpus Nazianzenum, 22).

Mossay, Justin et al. (1981–1998), *Repertorium Nazianzenum. Orationes. Textus Graecus*, I–VI, Paderborn: Ferdinand Schöningh (Studien zur Geschichte und Kultur des Altertums, Neue Folge, 2. Reihe: Forschungen zu Gregor von Nazianz, 1, 5, 10, 11, 12, 14).

Mostafa, Mohamed (1960), *Miniatures of the School of Behzad in Cairo collections*, Baden-Baden: W. Klein (Der Silberne Quell).

Moukarzel, Joseph (2012), 'The situation of Near Eastern Libraries', paper presented at the COMSt workshop *Legal and illegal circulation of library collections: a study for a better conservation*, Paris.

Mouraviev, Serge (2010), *ERKATAGUIR* ԵՐԿԱԹԱԳԻՐ *ou Comment naquit l'alphabet arménien. Les trois secrets de Mesrop Machtots. Avec, en supplément: une Paléographie arménienne des Ve-VIe/VIIe siècles et un choix de sources historiques*, introduction by Dickran Kouymjian, Sankt Augustin: Academia.

Moureau, Sébastien (2010a), 'Questions of Methodology about Pseudo-Avicenna's *De Anima in Arte Alchemiae*', in: *Chymia: Science and Nature in Early Modern Science (1450-1750)*, ed. by Miguel López-Pérez – Didier Kahn, Newcastle: Cambridge Scholars Publishing, 1–19.

Moureau, Sébastien (2010b), *Le 'De anima in arte alchemiae' du Pseudo-Avicenne. Édition critique, traduction et étude*, Louvain-la-Neuve: Université catholique de Louvain, Institut orientaliste [diss.].

Moureau, Sébastien (2013a), 'Physics in the Twelfth Century: The 'Porta Elementorum' of Pseudo-Avicenna's Alchemical 'De Anima' and Marius' 'De Elementis'', *Archives d'Histoire Doctrinale et Littéraire Du Moyen Âge*, 80, 147–221.

Moureau, Sébastien (2013b), 'Elixir Atque Fermentum'. New Investigations About The Link Between Pseudo-Avicenna's Alchemical 'De Anima' and Roger Bacon: Alchemical and Medical Doctrines', *Traditio*, 68, 277–325.

Moureau, Sébastien (forthcoming), *Le De anima alchimique du Pseudo-Avicenne. Édition critique, traduction annotée et étude*, Florence: Sismel-Edizioni del Galluzzo (Micrologus' Library 74, 75).

Mouren, Raphaële (ed.) (2013), *La description des reliures orientales: conservation, aspects juridiques et prise de vue*, London: Archetype Publications.

Müller, Friedrich Wilhelm Carl (1904), *Handschriften-Reste in Estrangelo-Schrift aus Turfan, Chinesisch-Turkistan*, II Teil, Berlin: Reimer (Abhandlungen der Preußischen Akademie der Wissenschaften, Anhang 2).

Müller, Rudolf Wolfgang (1964), *Rhetorische und syntaktische Interpunktion: Untersuchungen zur Pausenbezeichnung im antiken Latein*, Tübingen: Eberhard-Karl-Universität [diss.].

Müller-Kessler, Christa (1991), *Grammatik des Christlich-Palästinisch-Araméischen*. 1. *Schriftlehre, Lautlehre, Formenlehre*, Hildesheim: Georg Olms (Texte und Studien zur Orientalistik).

Müller-Kessler, Christa – Michael Sokoloff (1996a), *The forty martyrs of the Sinai Desert, Eulogios, the stone-cutter, and Anastasia*, Groningen: Styx (A Corpus of Christian Palestinian Aramaic, 3).

Müller-Kessler, Christa – Michael Sokoloff (1996b), *The Christian Palestinian Aramaic New Testament version from the early period*, I–II, Groningen: Styx (A Corpus of Christian Palestinian Aramaic, 2A-B).

Müller-Kessler, Christa – Michael Sokoloff (1997), *The Christian Palestinian Aramaic Old Testament and Apocrypha version from the early period*, Groningen: Styx (A Corpus of Christian Palestinian Aramaic, 1).

Müller-Kessler, Christa – Michael Sokoloff (1999), *The catechism of Cyril of Jerusalem in the christian palestinian aramaic version*, Groningen: Styx (A Corpus of Christian Palestinian Aramaic, 5).

Mumin, Meikal – Kees Versteegh (eds) (2014), *The Arabic Script in Africa: Studies in the Use of a Writing System*, Leiden: Brill (Studies in Semitic Languages and Linguistics, 71).

al-Munajjid, Salāh al-Din (1956), 'Règles pour l'édition des textes arabes', *Mélanges de l'Institut dominicain d'études orientales du Caire*, 3, 359–374.

Mundell Mango, M. (1991), 'The Production of Syriac Manuscripts, 400-700 AD', in: *Scritture, libri e testi nelle aree provinciali di Bisanzio. Atti del seminario di Erice (TP) (18-25 settembre 1988)*, I, ed. by Guglielmo Cavallo – Giuseppe De Gregorio, Spoleto: Centro italiano di studi sull'alto medioevo (Biblioteca del 'Centro per il Collegamento degli Studi Medievali e Umanistici nell'Università di Perugia', 5), 161–179.

Munk Olsen, Birger (1998), 'L'élément codicologique', in: *Recherches de codicologie comparée: la composition du codex au Moyen Âge en Orient et en Occident*, ed. by Philippe Hoffmann, Paris: Presses de l'École normale supérieure (Collection bibliologie), 105–129.

Musakova, Elisaveta (1996), 'Илюстрираните глаголически евангелия (*Ilustriranite glagoličeski evangelija*, 'The Illustrated Glagolitic Gospels')', *Izkustvo / Art in Bulgaria*, 33-34, 6–12.

Musxelišvili, L. (1938), 'ბოლნისი (*Bolnisi*)', *Akad. N. Maris saxelobis enis, isṭoriisa da maṭerialuri ḳulṭuris insṭiṭuṭis moambe*, 3, 311–382.

Mutafian, Claude (ed.) (2007a), *Arménie: la magie de l'écrit (Marseille, Centre de la Vieille Charité, 27 avril-22 juillet 2007)*, Paris – Marseille: Somogy.

Mutafian, Claude (2007b), 'Les documents officiels arméniens jusqu'au XIVe siècle', in: *Arménie: la magie de l'écrit (Marseille, Centre de la Vieille Charité, 27 avril-22 juillet 2007)*, ed. by Claude Mutafian, Paris – Marseille: Somogy, 149–152.

Muto, Shinichi (2013), 'The Triune God in the Tripartite World in a Syriac Manuscript found at Khara-Khoto', in: *From the Oxus River to the Chinese Shores: Studies on East Syriac Christianity in China and Central Asia*, ed. by Li Tang – Dietmar W. Winkler, Wien: LIT (Orientalia – patristica – oecumenica, 5), 381–386.

Muzerelle, Denis (1985), *Vocabulaire codicologique. Repertoire methodique des termes français relatifs aux manuscrits*, <http://vocabulaire.irht.cnrs.fr/vocab.htm>, Paris: Centre national de la recherche scientifique (Rubricae, 1).

Muzerelle, Denis (1991), 'Évolution et tendances actuelles de la recherche codicologique', *Historia, instituciones, documentos*, 18, 347–374.

Muzerelle, Denis (1994), *Analyse des schémas de réglure. Formule symbolique universelle*, Paris: Institut de recherche et d'histoire des textes, <http://www.palaeographia.org/muzerelle/reglure.htm>.

Muzerelle, Denis (1999), 'Pour décrire les schémas de réglure. Une méthode de notation symbolique applicable aux manuscrits latins (et autres)', *Quinio: International Journal on the History and Conservation of the Book*, 1, 123–170.

Muzerelle, Denis et al. (2005) {D.M. – Paul Géhin – Colette Sirat – Marc Geoffroy}, 'L'écriture', in: *Lire le manuscrit médiéval: observer et décrire*, ed. by Paul Géhin, Paris: Colin (Collection U. Histoire), 85–121.

Nabhani, Ahmad Shaykh et al. (1993) {A.N. – Yahya Ali Omar – David Colton Sperling}, 'Kenya', in: *The World Survey of Islamic Manuscripts*, II, ed. by Geoffrey Roper, London: Al-Furqān, 152–162.

Nabhani, Ahmad Shaykh – David Colton Sperling (1994), 'Comoros', in: *The World Survey of Islamic Manuscripts*, IV, ed. by Geoffrey Roper, London: Al-Furqān, 118–125.

Nafīsī, Sa'īd (1319–1332 Š./1940–1953 CE), تاريخ مسعودي معروف به تاريخ بيهقي ... با مقابله و تصحيح و حواشي و تعليقات سعيد نفيسي (*Tārīḫ-i Mas'ūdī ma'rūf ba Tārīḫ-i Bayhaqī … bā muqābala wa taṣḥīḥ wa ḥawāšī wa ta'līqāt-i Sa'īd Nafīsī*, 'The *History* of Mas'ūd known as the *History* of Bayhaqī … with a comparison, corrections, notes and annotations by Sa'īd Nafīsī'), I–III, Tehran: Širkat-i Kitābfurūšī-yi Adab – Intishārāt-i Kitābḫānah-'i Sanā'ī – Čāpḫāna-yi Dānišgāh.

Nafīsī, Sa'īd [Naficy, Said] (1957), 'Bayhaḳī, Abu 'l-Faḍl Muḥammad b. Ḥusayn Kātib', in: *The Encyclopaedia of Islam*, New Edition, I, Leiden: Brill, 1130–1131.

Nafīsī, Sa'īd (1342–1343 Š./1963–1964 CE), در پيرامون تاريخ بيهقي: شامل آثار گمشدهء ابو الفضل بيهقى و تاريخ غزنويان (*Dar pīrāmūn-i tārīḫ-i Bayhaqī, šāmil-i āṯār-i gumšuda-yi Abū al-Faḍl Bayhaqī wa Tārīḫ-i Ġaznavīyān*, 'Around the *History* of Bayhaqī, including lost works by Abū al-Faḍl Bayhaqī and the History of the Ghaznavids'), I–II, Tehran: Kitābfurūšī-yi Furūghī.

Nagel, Peter (1994), 'Aufbau und Komposition des Papyruskodex BL Or. 7594 der British Library', in: *Coptology, Past, Present, and Future: Studies in Honour of Rodolphe Kasser*, ed. by Søren Giversen – Martin Krause, Leuven: Peeters (Orientalia Lovaniensia Analecta, 61), 347–355.

Nanobašvili, I. (1973), ტყავის დამუშავების ხალხური წესები საქართველოში (*Ṭq̇avis damušavebis xalxuri çesebi sakartveloši*, 'Popular methods of the treatment of animal hides in Georgia'), Tbilisi: Mecniereba.

NARA (U.S. National Archives and Records Administration), *Technical Guidelines for Digitizing Archival Materials for Electronic Access: Creation of Production Master Files – Raster Images*, <http://www.archives.gov/preservation/technical/guidelines.pdf>, last access June 2004.

Narkiss, Bezalel (1982), *Hebrew Illuminated Manuscripts in the British Isles: A Catalogue Raisonné*, vol. 1:1-2: *The Spanish and Portuguese Manuscripts*, Jerusalem – London: The Israel Academy of Sciences and Humanities - The British Academy.

Narkiss, Bezalel – Gabrielle Sed-Rajna (1976), *Iconographical Index of Hebrew Illuminated Manuscripts*, I: *Four Haggadot*, Jerusalem: The Israel Academy of Sciences and Humanities – Paris: IRHT (Index of Jewish Art).

Narkiss, Bezalel – Gabrielle Sed-Rajna (1981), *Iconographical Index of Hebrew Illuminated Manuscripts*, II: *Three Haggadot*, Jerusalem: The Israel Academy of Sciences and Humanities – Munich: Saur (Index of Jewish Art).

Narkiss, Bezalel – Gabrielle Sed-Rajna (1983), *Iconographical Index of Hebrew Illuminated Manuscripts*, III: *The Rothschild Miscellany*, Jerusalem: The Israel Academy of Sciences and Humanities (Index of Jewish Art).

Narkiss, Bezalel – Gabrielle Sed-Rajna (1990), *Iconographical Index of Hebrew Illuminated Manuscripts*, IV: *Illuminated manuscripts of the Kaufmann collection at the Library of the Hungarian Academy of Sciences*, Jerusalem: The Israel Academy of Sciences and Humanities – Budapest: The Library of the Hungarian Academy of Sciences (Index of Jewish Art).

Narkiss, Bezalel – Gabrielle Sed-Rajna (1994), *Iconographical Index of Hebrew Illuminated Manuscripts*, V: *Illuminated Manuscripts of the Copenhagen Collection at the Royal Library*, Jerusalem: The Israel Academy of Sciences and Humanities (Index of Jewish Art).

Narkiss, Bezalel – Michael Stone (eds) (1979), *Armenian Art Treasures of Jerusalem*, New Rochelle, NY: Caratzas Bros – Jerusalem: Masada Press.

Nau, François (1912a), *Un martyrologe et douze ménologes syriaques*, Paris: Firmin-Didot (Patrologia orientalis, 10, 1 = 46).

Nau, François (1912b), *Les ménologes des Évangéliaires copto-arabes*, Paris: Firmin-Didot (Patrologia orientalis, 10, 2 = 47).

Naumow, Aleksander – Andrzej Kaszlej (2004), *Rękopisy cerkiewnosłowiańskie w Polsce. Katalog*, Kraków: Scriptum.

Nebbiai-Dalla Guarda, Donatella (1992), *I documenti per la storia delle biblioteche medievali (secoli IX–XV)*, Roma: Jouvence (Materiali e ricerche. Nuova serie. Sezione di studi storici, 15, 8).

Neevel, Johan G. (1995), 'Phytate: A Potential Conservation Agent for the Treatment of Ink Corrosion caused by Iron Gall Inks', *Restaurator. International Journal for the Preservation of Library and Archival Material*, 16, 143–160.

Neirinck, Danièle (1999), 'L'établissement d'un plan d'urgence pour les services d'archives en cas de sinistres', in: *La prévention et l'intervention en cas de sinistre dans les archives et les bibliothèques: actes des premières Journées sur la conservation préventive, 15-16 mai, 1995*, Arles: Centre de Conservation du Livre, 85–102.

Nersessian, Vrej (1987), *Armenian Illuminated Gospel Books [in the collection of the British Library]*, London: The British Library.

Nersessian, Vrej (2002), *A Catalogue of the Armenian Manuscripts in the British Library acquired since the year 1913 and of Collections in other Libraries in the United Kingdom*, I–II, London: The British Library.

Neubauer, Adolf (1886), *Catalogue of the Hebrew manuscripts in the Bodleian Library and in the college libraries of Oxford: including mss. in other languages, which are written with Hebrew characters, or relating to the Hebrew language or literature, and a few Samaritan mss*, I, Oxford: Clarendon Press.

Neubauer, Adolf – Arthur Ernest Cowley (1906), *Catalogue of the Hebrew manuscripts in the Bodleian Library and in the college libraries of Oxford: including mss. in other languages, which are written with Hebrew characters, or relating to the Hebrew language or literature, and a few Samaritan mss*, II, Oxford: Clarendon Press.

Newman, Walter – Abigail Quandt (1994), '18: Parchment Treatments', in: *Paper Conservation Catalog*, ed. by AIC (American Institute for Conservation of Historic and Artistic Works). Book and paper group, Washington, DC: AIC.

Newman, William R. (1991), *The* Summa Perfectionis *of Pseudo-Geber*, Leiden: Brill (Travaux de l'Académie Internationale d'Histoire des Sciences, 35).

Nichols, Stephen G. (1990), 'The New Philology: Introduction: Philology in a Manuscript Culture', *Speculum*, 65, 1–10.

Niḳolaʒe, E[vsebi] (1953–1964), ხელნაწერთა აღწერილობა / *Описание рукописей* (*Xelnaçerta aġçeriloba / Opisanie rukopisej*, 'Description of manuscripts'), I–II, Tbilisi: Mecniereba.

Nir-El, Yoram – Magen Broshi (1996), 'The black ink of the Qumran Scrolls', *Dead Sea Discoveries*, 3, 158–167.

NLA (National Library of Australia), *Collection disaster plan. Part 1: Disaster preparedness and prevention policy*, <http://www.nla.gov.au/collection-disaster-plan/disaster-preparedness-and-prevention>, Canberra: NLA, last access 2013.

Nobili, Mauro (2011), 'Manuscript culture of West Africa. Part 1: The disqualification of a heritage', *Comparative Oriental Manuscript Studies Newsletter*, 2, 21–24.

Nobili, Mauro (2012), 'Manuscript culture of West Africa. Part 2: A survey of the scholarly production', *Comparative Oriental Manuscript Studies Newsletter*, 3, 11–17.

Nobili, Mauro (2012/2013), 'Manuscript culture of West Africa', *manuscript cultures*, 5, 42–51 (Revised reprint of Nobili 2011, 2012).

Nobili, Mauro (2013), *Catalogue des manuscrits arabes du fonds de Gironcourt (Afrique de l'Ouest) de l'Institut de France*, Roma: Istituto per l'Oriente 'C. A. Nallino' (Series Catalogorum, IV).

Nordenfalk, Carl (1938), *Die spätantiken Kanontafeln*, I–II, Göteborg: Oscar Isacson.

Norelli, Enrico (ed.) (2004), *Recueils normatifs et canons dans l'Antiquité: perspectives nouvelles sur la formation des canons juif et chrétien dans leur contexte culturel: Actes du colloque organisé dans le cadre du programma plurifacultaire 'La Bible à la croisée des saviors' de l'Université de Genève 11-12 avril 2002*, Prahins: Éditions du Zèbre (Publications de l'Institut romand des sciences bibliques, 3).

Nosnitsin, Denis (2012a), 'Ethiopian Manuscripts and Ethiopian manuscript studies. A brief overview and evaluation', *Gazette du livre médiéval*, 58, 2–16.

Nosnitsin, Denis (2012b), 'DomLib/Ethio-SPARE Manuscript Cataloguing Database', paper presented at the COMSt workshop *The electronic revolution? The impact of the digital on cataloguing*, Copenhagen.

Nosnitsin, Denis (2013a), *Churches and Monasteries of Təgray. A Survey of Manuscript Collections*, Wiesbaden: Harrassowitz (Supplement to Aethiopica, 1).

Nosnitsin, Denis (2013b), 'The Four Gospel Book of Däbrä Maʿṣo and its Marginal Notes. Part 2. An Exercise in Ethiopian Palaeography', *Comparative Oriental Manuscript Studies Newsletter*, 6, 29–33.

Nosnitsin, Denis (2013c), 'Ehio-SPaRe: Cultural Heritage of Christian Ethiopia: Salvation, Preservation and Research', *Comparative Oriental Manuscript Studies Newsletter*, 5, 3–4.

Nosnitsin, Denis et al. (2014) {D.N. – Emanuel Kindzorra – Oliver Hahn – Ira Rabin}, 'A 'Study Manuscript' from Qäqäma (Təgray, Ethiopia): Attempts at Ink and Parchment Analysis', *COMSt Newsletter*, 7, 28–31.

NPO (National Preservation Office) (2000), *Guidance for exhibiting archive and library materials*, <http:// www.bl.uk/blpac/pdf/exhibition.pdf>, London: British Library.

NPS (National Park Service) (1996), *Conserve O Gram*, 19/17, <http://www.nps.gov/history/museum/ publications/conserveogram/19-17.pdf>.

NPS (National Park Service) (1999), *The Museum Handbook*. Part 1: *Museum Collections*, Washington, DC: National Park Service Museum Management Program, <http://www.nps.gov/history/ museum/publications/ MHI/CHAPTER4.pdf>.

O'Fahey, Rex Séan (1994), 'Somali', in: *The World Survey of Islamic Manuscripts*, III, ed. by Geoffrey Roper, London: Al-Furqān, 88–90.

Obbink, H.W. (1968), *Godsdienst en Alphabet, valedictory lecture*, Utrecht University.

Obshtezhitie. The World Wide Web portal for the study of Cyrillic and Glagolitic manuscripts and early printed books, <http://www.obshtezhitie.net/>, last access October 2014.

Ogden, Sherelyn (1999), *Storage Methods and Handling Practices for Library and Archival Materials*, <http://www.nedcc.org/free-resources/preservation-leaflets/4.-storage-and-handling/4.1-storage-methods-and-handling-practices>, Andover, MA (Northeast Document Conservation Center Preservation Leaflets, 4.1).

Olivier, Jean-Marie (1995), *Répertoire des bibliothèques et des catalogues de manuscrits grecs de Marcel Richard*, 3. éd. entièrement refondue, Turnhout: Brepols.

Olszowy-Schlanger, Judith (2003), *Les manuscrits hébreux dans l'Angleterre médiévale: étude historique et paléographique*, Paris: Peeters (Collection de la Revue des Études Juives, 29).

Oltrogge, Doris – Oliver Hahn (1999), 'Über die Verwendung mineralischer Pigmente in der mittelalterlichen Buchmalerei', *Aufschluss*, 50, 383–390.

Omar, Hamad – Tigiti S.Y. Sengo (1994), 'Tanzania', in: *The World Survey of Islamic Manuscripts*, III, ed. by Geoffrey Roper, London: Al-Furqān, 226–229.

Omidsalar, Mahmoud (2004), 'The State of Persian Manuscripts: A Call to Action', <http://www.payvand.com/ news/04/oct/1004.html>, *Payvand News [online]*, October 1, 2004.

Omont, Henri (1889), *Catalogues des manuscrits grecs de Fontainebleau sous François Ier et Henri II*, Paris: Imprimerie nationale.

Omont, Henri (1929), *Miniatures les plus anciens manuscrits grecs de la Bibliothèque Nationale du VIe au XIVe siècle*, Paris: Champion.

Orbeli, R[usudana] R[ubenovna] (1956), *Грузинские рукописи Института Востоковедения АН СССР*, вып. I: *История, география, путешествия, археология, законодательство, философия, языкознание, библиография* (*Gruzinskie rukopisi Instituta Vostokovedenija AN SSSR*, vyp. I: *Istorija, geografija, putešestvija, archeologija, zakonodatel'stvo, filosofija, jazykoznanie, bibliografija*, 'Georgian Manuscripts of the Oriental Institute of the Academy of Sciences of the USSR, issue 1: History, geography, travels, archaeology, law, philosophy, linguistics, bibliography'), Moskva – Leningrad: Izdatelstvo Akademii Nauk SSSR.

Orbélian, Stéphannos (1864), *Histoire de la Siounie*, translated by Marie-Felicité Brosset, St Petersburg: Académie impériale des sciences.

Oriental Manuscript Resource, Tübingen <http://omar.ub.uni-freiburg.de>, last access October 2014.

Orlandi, Giovanni (2008), 'Perché non possiamo non dirci lachmanniani', in *Giovanni Orlandi. Scritti di filologia mediolatina*, ed. by Paolo Chiesa – Anna Maria Fagnoni – Rossana E. Guglielmetti – Giovanni Paolo Maggioni, Firenze: SISMEL – Edizioni del Galluzzo, 95–130.

Orlandi, Tito (1974), 'Les papyrus coptes du Musée égyptien de Turin', *Le Muséon*, 87, 115–127.

Orlandi, Tito (1991), 'Literature, Coptic', in: *The Coptic Encyclopedia*, V, ed. by Aziz S. Atiya, New York: Macmillan, 1450–1460.

Orlandi, Tito (1995), 'La documentation patristique copte. Bilan et prospectives', in: *La documentation patristique. Bilan et prospective*, ed. by Jean-Claude Fredouille – René-Michel Roberge, Québec: Les Presses de l'Université Laval – Paris: Les Presses de l'Université de Paris-Sorbonne, 121–147.

Orlandi, Tito (1999), 'Il sistema ortografico copto', in: *Sesh: lingue e scritture nell'antico Egitto. Inediti dal Museo archeologico di Milano*, ed. by Francesco Tiradritti, Milano: Electa, 81–86.

Orlandi, Tito (2010), *Informatica testuale. Teoria e prassi*, Bari: Laterza (Manuali Laterza, 308).

Orna, Mary Virginia – Thomas F. Mathews (1981), 'Pigment Analysis of the Glajor Gospel Book of U.C.L.A.', *Studies in Conservation*, 26, 57–72.

Ornato, Ezio (1997), 'L'histoire du livre et les méthodes quantitatives. Bilan de vingt ans de recherche', in: *La fache cachée du livre médiéval. L'histoire du livre vue par Ezio Ornato ses amis et ses collègues*, Roma: Viella (I libri di Viella, 10), 607–679.

Orsatti, Paola (1989), 'Épigraphes poétiques dans des manuscrits persans du XVe et XVIe siècle et exergue du Sahnama de Firdawsi', in: *Les manuscrits du Moyen-Orient. Essais de codicologie et de paléographie. Actes du Colloque d'Istanbul* (*Istanbul, 26-29 mai, 1986*), ed. by Francois Déroche, Istanbul: I.F.E.A – Paris: Bibliothèque nationale (Varia turcica, 8), 69–75.

Orsatti, Paola (1993), 'Le manuscrit islamique: caractéristiques matérielles et typologie', in: *Ancient and Medieval Book Materials and Techniques* (*Erice, 18-25 September 1992*), II, ed. by Marilena Maniaci – Paola Franca Munafò, Città del Vaticano: Biblioteca Apostolica Vaticana (Studi e Testi, 358), 269–331.

Orsatti, Paola (1994), 'Il manoscritto come specchio di una cultura: il caso dell'Islam', *Gazette du livre médiéval*, 24, 1–7.

Orsatti, Paola (1997), 'L'innamoramento di Ḫusraw va Šīrīn nel poema di Niẓāmī e il potere psicagogico della parola', in: *In memoria di Francesco Gabrieli (1904-1996)*, Roma: Bardi (Rivista degli Studi Orientali, 71, Supplemento, 2), 129–145.

Orsini, Pasquale (2005), *Manoscritti in maiuscola biblica. Materiali per un aggiornamento*, Cassino: Università di Cassino (Studi archeologici, artistici, filologici e storici, 7).

Orsini, Pasquale (2008a), 'Le scritture dei codici di Nag Hammadi. Il punto di vista paleografico', in: *Oltre la scrittura. Variazioni sul tema per Guglielmo Cavallo*, ed. by Daniele Bianconi – Lucio Del Corso, Paris: École des Hautes Études en Sciences Sociales – Centre d'Études Byzantines, Néo-Helléniques et Sud-Est Européennes (Dossiers byzantins, 8), 95–121, 2 tabl. et pll. 11–17.

Orsini, Pasquale (2008b), 'La maiuscola biblica copta', *Segno e Testo 6*, 121–150, figg. et 8 pll.

Orsini, Pasquale (2013), *Scrittura come immagine. Morfologia e storia della maiuscola liturgica bizantina*, Roma: Viella (Scritture e libri del medioevo, 12).

Orsini, Pasquale (forthcoming), 'Il contributo dei Codices Graeci Antiquiores allo studio delle scritture copte', in: *Proceedings of the Tenth International Congress of Coptic Studies*, ed. by Paola Buzi – Alberto Camplani, Louvain: Peeters.

Ostos, Pilar et al. (1997) {P.O. – M. Luisa Pardo – Elena E. Rodríguez}, *Vocabulario de codicología. Versión española revisada y aumentada del 'Vocabulaire codicologique' de Denis Muzerelle*, Madrid: Arco-Libros (Instrumenta bibliologica).

Остромирово евангелие (*Ostromirovo evangelie*, 'The Ostromir Gospels'), <http://www.nlr.ru/exib/Gospel/ ostr>, last access May 2014.

Ostrowski, Donald (2003), *The Pověst' vremennykh lět. An Interlinear Collation and Paradosis*, I–III, Harvard: Harvard University Press (Harvard library of early Ukrainian literature, 10).

Ott, Claudia (2003a), *Metamorphosen des Epos: Sīrat al-Muǧāhidīn* (*Sīrat al-Amīra Dāt al-Himma*) *zwischen Mündlichkeit und Schriftlichkeit*, Amsterdam: Amsterdam University Press (Contributions by the Nederlands-Vlaams Instituut in Cairo, 6).

Ott, Claudia (2003b), 'From the Coffeehouse into the Manuscript: The Storyteller and his Audience in the Manuscripts of an Arabic Epic', *Oriente Moderno*, 83/2, 443–451.

Outtier, Bernard (1972), 'Un feuillet du lectionnaire géorgien ḫanmeti à Paris', *Le Muséon*, 85, 399–402.

Outtier, Bernard (1986), 'Les feuilles de garde géorgiennes des manuscrits du Patriarcat arménien Saint-Jacques de Jérusalem: Rapport préliminaire', *Revue des études géorgiennes et caucasiennes*, 2, 67–73.

Outtier, Bernard (1999–2000), 'Guillaume de Villefroy, un arméniste méconnu', *Revue du monde arménien moderne et contemporain*, 5, 45–54.

Outtier, Bernard (2010), 'The Armenian and Georgian Versions of the 'Evangelium Nicodemi'', *Apocrypha*, 21, 49–55.

Outtier, Bernard (2013), 'Les feuilles de garde géorgiennes des manuscrits arméniens de Nor-Djoulfa (Ispahan)', *Pro Georgia*, 23, 7–22.

Ovčinnikova-Pelin, Valentina S. (1989), *Сводный каталог молдавских рукописей, хранящихся в СССР. Коллекция Ново-Нямецкого монастыря* (*XIV–XIX вв.*) (*Svodnyj katalog moldavskich rukopisej, chranjaščichsja v SSSR. Kollekcija Novo-Njameckogo monastyrja XIV–XIX vv.*, 'General catalogue of Moldavian manuscripts preserved in the USSR. The collection of the Noul Neamţ Monastery, fourteenth–nineteenth centuries'), Kišinev: Štiinca.

Overwien, Oliver (2005), *Die Sprüche des Kynikers Diogenes in der griechischen und arabischen Überlieferung*, Stuttgart: Steiner.

The Oxyrhynchus Papyri, I–IC, London: Egypt Exploration Society (Graeco-Roman Memoirs), 1898–2012.

Pächt, Otto – Jonathan James Graham Alexander (1966, 1970, 1973), *Illuminated Manuscripts in the Bodleian Library, Oxford*, I–III, Oxford: Clarendon Press.

Painchaud, Louis (1995), 'La classification des textes de Nag Hammadi et le phénomène des réécritures', in: *Les textes de Nag Hammadi et le problème de leur classification: Actes du colloque tenu à Québec du 15 au 19 Septembre 1993*, ed. by Louis Painchaud – Anne Pasquier, Québec: Les presses de l'Université Laval (Bibliothèque copte de Nag Hammadi, Études, 3), 51–85.

Painchaud, Louis – Timothy Janz (1997), 'The 'Kingless Generation' and the Polemical Rewriting of Certain Nag Hammadi Texts', in: *The Nag Hammadi Library After Fifty Years: Proceedings of the 1995 Society of Biblical Literature Commemoration*, ed. by John D. Turner – Anne McGuire, Leiden: Brill (Nag Hammadi and Manichaean Studies, 44), 439–460.

Pajkova [Paykova], A. (1979), 'The Syrian Ostracon from Panjikant', *Le Muséon*, 92, 159–169.

Pajkova, A.V. – Boris I. Maršak (1976), 'Сирийская надпись из Пенджикента (Sirijskaja nadpis' iz Pendžikenta, 'A Syriac Inscription from Panjakent')', *Kratkie soobščenija Instituta archeologii*, 147, 34–38.

Panaino, Antonio (1999), 'Avesta', in: *Religion in Geschichte und Gegenwart. Handwörterbuch für Theologie und Religionswissenschaft*, I, Tübingen: Mohr Siebeck, 1024–1026.

Panaino, Antonio (2012), 'The Age of the Avestan Canon and the Origins of the Ritual Written Texts', in: *The transmission of the Avesta*, ed. by Alberto Cantera, Wiesbaden: Harrassowitz (Iranica, 20), 70–97.

Pankhurst, Richard (1980), 'Imported Textiles in Ethiopian Sixteenth and Seventeenth Century Manuscripts in Britain', *Azania*, 15, 43–55.

Pankhurst, Richard (1981), 'Imported Textiles in Ethiopian Eighteenth Century Manuscripts in Britain', *Azania*, 16, 131–150.

Pankhurst, Richard (1983–1984), 'Ethiopian manuscript bindings and their decoration', *Abbay*, 12, 205–257.

Pankhurst, Richard (1984), 'Ethiopian Manuscripts Illumination. Some Aspects of the Artist's Craft as Revealed in the Seventeenth- and Eighteenth-century Manuscripts in the British Library', *Azania*, 19, 105–114.

Pankhurst, Richard (1985–1986), 'Imported cloth in early 19th century Ethiopian bindings', *Quaderni di Studi Etiopici*, 6-7, 105–114.

Pankhurst, Richard (1999), 'An Ethiopian Binding with Silver Plaques, Crosses and Pins', *The Book Collector*, 48, 101–109.

Pankhurst, Rita (1973), 'The Library of Emperor Tewodros II at Mäqdäla (Magdala)', *Bulletin of the School of Oriental and African Studies*, 36, 14–42.

Pankhurst, Rita (1990), 'The Mäqdäla Library of Tewodros', in: *Kasa and Kasa: Papers on the Lives, Times and Images of Téwodros II and Yohannes IV (1855–1889)*, ed. by Tadesse Beyene – Richard Pankhurst, Addis Ababa: Institute of Ethiopian Studies, 223–230.

Panzer, Baldur (1991), 'Zur Edition kirchenslavischer Texte', *Die Slawischen Sprachen*, 28, 83–102.

Paret, Rudi (1927), *Der Ritter-Roman von 'Umar an-Nu'mān und seine Stellung zur Sammlung von tausendundeiner Nacht: ein Beitrag zur arabischen Literaturgeschichte*, Tübingen: Mohr.

Paret, Rudi (1981), *Schriften zum Islam. Volksroman, Frauenfrage, Bilderverbot*, ed. by Joseph van Ess, Stuttgart: W. Kohlhammer.

Paris, Gaston – Léopold Pannier (1872), *La vie de saint Alexis, poème du XIe siècle et renouvellements des XIIe, XIIIe et XIVe siècles*, Paris: Librairie A. Franck (Bibliothèque de l'École des Hautes Études, 7).

Parker, David C. (2007), 'Textual Criticism and Theology', *Expository Times*, 118:12, 583–589.

Parkes, Malcolm B. (1998), 'Medieval Punctuation and the Modern Editor', in: *Filologia classica e filologia romanza: esperienze ecdotiche a confronto. Atti del Convegno Roma 25-27 maggio 1995*, ed. by Anna Ferrari, Spoleto: Centro Italiano di Studi sull'Alto Medioevo (Incontri di Studio, 2), 337–349.

Parodi, Laura E. (2010), 'Portraits and Albums', in: *Treasures of the Aga Khan Museum – Arts of the Book and Calligraphy in the Islamic World*, Istanbul: AKTC, 308–315.

Parodi, Laura E. (2011), 'Two Pages from the Late Shahjahan Album', *Ars Orientalis*, 40, 267–294.

Parodi, Laura E. (2012), 'Historic Cases in Persian and Islamic Iconographic Heritage', paper presented at the COMSt workshop *Legal and illegal circulation of library collections: a study for a better conservation*, Paris.

Parodi, Laura E. et al. (2010) {L.P. – Frank D. Preusser – Jennifer M. Porter – Yosi Pozeilov}, 'Tracing the History of a Mughal Album Page in the Collection of the Los Angeles County Museum of Art', *Asianart.com*, March 2010.

Parodi, Laura E. – Bruce Wannell (2011), 'The Earliest Datable Mughal Painting: an Allegory of the Celebrations for Akbar's Circumcision at the Sacred Spring of Khwaja Seh Yaran near Kabul (1546 AD) [Staatsbibliothek zu Berlin – Preussischer Kulturbesitz, Libr. Pict. A117, fol. 15A]', *Asianart.com*, November 2011.

Pasquali, Giorgio (1931), 'Paleografia quale scienza dello spirito', *Nuova Antologia*, 7/277, 342–354.

Pasquali, Giorgio (1934, ^{2}1952), *Storia della tradizione e critica del testo*, Firenze: Le Monnier.

Pataki, Andrea (2009), 'Remoistenable Tissue Preparation and its Practical Aspects', *Restaurator* 30, 1–19.

Ṗaṭariʒe, Ramaz (1965a), 'ქაღალდის დამუშავების საკითხისათვის ფეოდალურ საქართველოში (*Kaġaldis damušavebis saḳitxisatvis peodalur sakartveloši*, 'On the treatment of paper in feudal Georgia')', *Ṗaleograṗiuli ʒiebani*, 1, 45–56.

Ṗaṭariʒe, Ramaz (1965b), 'XIV–XV საუკუნეების ქართული ხელნაწერების ჭვირნიშნები (*XIV–XV sauḳuneebis kartuli xelnaçerebis čvirnišnebi*, 'Watermarks of Georgian manuscripts of the 14th–15th centuries')', *Ṗaleograṗiuli ʒiebani*, 1, 109–130.

Ṗaṭariʒe, Ramaz (1968), 'ქართული ხელნაწერების სპარსული ქაღალდის შესახებ (*Kartuli xelnaçerebis sṗarsuli kaġaldis šesaxeb*, 'On Persian paper used in Georgian manuscripts')', *Macne*: *enisa da liṭeraṭuris seria*, 2, 165–178.

Peacock, Andrew (2007), 'The Medieval Manuscript Tradition of Bal'amī's Version of al-Ṭabarī's History', in: *Theoretical Approaches to the Transmission and Edition of Oriental Manuscripts. Proceedings of a symposium held in Istanbul March 28-30, 2001*, ed. by Judith Pfeiffer – Manfred Kropp, Beirut: Ergon Verlag Würzburg in Kommission (Beiruter Texte und Studien, 111), 93–105.

Pearson, James Douglas (1971), *Oriental Manuscripts in Europe and North America*: *A Survey*, Zug: Inter Documentation Company (Bibliotheca Asiatica, 7).

Pearson, David (2008), *Books as History*: *The importance of books beyond their texts*, London: The British Library – New Castle, Delaware: Oak Knoll Press.

Pedersen, Johannes (1984), *The Arabic book*, Princeton, NJ: Princeton University Press.

Peeters, Paul (1912), 'De codice hiberico Bibliothecae Bodleianae Oxoniensis', *Analecta Bollandiana*, 31, 301–318.

Peeters, Paul (1917–1919), 'Histoires monastiques géorgiennes', *Analecta Bollandiana*, 36–37, 5–317.

Pelikanidis, S[tylianos] M. et al. (1974–1991) {S.P. – P.C. Christou – Ch. Tsioumi – S.N. Kadas}, *The Treasures of Mount Athos - Illuminated Manuscripts*: *Miniatures – Headpieces – Initial Letters*, I–IV, Athens: Ekdotike Athenon.

Pelzer, Auguste (1936), Review of E. C. Richardson, *A union world catalog of manuscript books*, New York: H.W.Wilson, 1933–1937, *Revue d'histoire ecclésiastique*, 32, 621–630.

Peradze, Gregor (1940), 'Über die georgischen Handschriften in Österreich', *Wiener Zeitschrift für die Kunde des Morgenlandes*, 47, 219–232.

Perho, Irmeli (2003), *Catalogue of Arabic Manuscripts. Codices Arabici Arthur Christenseniani*, Copenhagen: The Royal Library & NIAS Press (Catalogue of Oriental manuscripts, xylographs etc. in Danish collections, 5/2).

Perho, Irmeli (2007), *Catalogue of Arabic Manuscripts. Codices Arabici & Codices Arabici Additamenta*, Copenhagen: The Royal Library & NIAS Press (Catalogue of Oriental manuscripts, xylographs etc. in Danish collections, 5/3).

Perria, Lidia (1983–1984), 'Il Vat. Gr. 2200. Note codicologiche e paleografiche', *Rivista di studi bizantini e neoellenici*, n. s. 20-21, 25–68.

Perria, Lidia (1992), 'A proposito del codice L di Platone. Problemi di datazione e attribuzione', in: *Studi su codici e papiri filosofici*: *Platone, Aristotele, Ierocle*, Firenze: Olschki (Accademia Toscana di Scienze e Lettere 'La Colombaria'. Studi, 129; Studi e Testi per il 'Corpus dei Papiri Filosofici Greci e Latini', 6), 103–136.

Perria, Lidia (2011), *Graphis. Per una storia della scrittura greca libraria* (*secoli IV a.C. - XVI d.C.*), Roma: Università degli studi 'Tor Vergata' – Città del Vaticano: Biblioteca Apostolica Vaticana (Quaderni di Nea Rome, 1).

Perrot, Charles (1963), 'Un fragment christo-palestinien découvert à Khirbet Mird', *Revue biblique*, 70, 506–555.

Petersen, Theodore C. (1954a), 'The Paragraph Mark in Coptic Illuminated Ornament', in: *Studies in Art and Literature for Belle da Costa Greene*, ed. by Dorothy Eugenia Miner, Princeton, NJ: Princeton University Press, 295–330.

Petersen, Theodore C. (1954b), 'Early Islamic Bookbindings and their Coptic Relations', *Ars Orientalis*: *The Arts of Islam and the East*, 1, 41–64.

Pétrof, D[mitrij] K[onstantinovič] (1914), *Abû-Muhammed-Alî-Ibn-Hazm al-Andalusî, Ṭauḳ-al-Ḥamâma.* Publié d'après l'unique manuscrit de la bibliothèque de l'université de Leide, Leiden: Brill.

Petrova, Maya (2001), 'The Ghent Manuscript of the Bdinski Zbornik: The Original or a Copy?', *Slavica Gandensia*, 28, 115–144.

Petrova, Maya (2003), *The Bdinski Sbornik*: *A study of a medieval Bulgarian book*, Budapest: Central European University [diss.].

Petrova, N. – Ju. Sadovskaja (2009), 'Особенности раскроя листов из пергамена при создании древнерусских рукописей (на примере манускриптов, прошедших реставрацию в ВХНРЦ им. академика И. Э. Грабаря)' (*Osobennosti raskroja listov iz pergamena pri sozdanii drevnerusskich rukopisej* [*na primere manuskriptov, prošedšich restavraciju v VChNRC im. akademika I. Ė. Grabarja*], 'Features peculiar to parchment cutting for mediaeval Russian manuscripts [based on codices restored at the Grabar Art Conservation Centre]'), *Chrizograf*, 3, 492–506.

Petrucci, Armando (1969a), 'Alle origini del libro moderno. Libri da banco, libri da bisaccia, libretti da mano', *Italia Medioevale e Umanistica*, 12, 295–313.

Petrucci, Armando (1969b), 'Scrittura e libro nell'Italia altomedievale. Il sesto secolo', *Studi Medievali*, 3/10, 157–213.

Petrucci, Armando (1972), 'Libro, scrittura e scuola', in: *La scuola nell'Occidente latino dell'alto medioevo. 15-21 aprile 1971*, I, Spoleto: Centro Italiano di Studi sull'Alto Medioevo (Settimane di Studio del Centro Italiano di Studi sull'Alto Medioevo, 19), 313–337, 363–381 (discussione).

Petrucci, Armando (1973), 'Scrittura e libro nell'Italia altomedievale. La concezione Cristiana del libro fra VI e VII secolo', *Studi Medievali*, 3/14, 961–1002.

Petrucci, Armando (1977), *Catalogo sommario dei manoscritti del Fondo Rossi. Sezione Corsiniana*, Roma: Accademia Nazionale dei Lincei.

Petrucci, Armando (1978), 'Per la storia dell'alfabetismo e della cultura scritta: metodi – materiali – quesiti', in: *Alfabetismo e cultura scritta nella storia della società italiana. Atti del Seminario tenutosi a Perugia il 29-30 marzo 1977*, Perugia: Università degli Studi, 33–47.

Petrucci, Armando (1979), 'Funzione della scrittura e terminologia paleografica', in: *Palaeographica, diplomatica et archivistica. Studi in onore di Giulio Battelli*, I, Roma: Edizioni di Storia e Letteratura (Storia e Letteratura, 140), 1–30.

Petrucci, Armando (1986a), 'Dal libro unitario al libro miscellaneo', in: *Società romana e impero tardoantico.* IV: *Tradizione dei classici, trasformazioni della cultura*, ed. by Andrea Giardina, Roma – Bari: Editori Laterza (Collezione storica), 173–187.

Petrucci, Armando (1986b), *La scrittura. Ideologia e rappresentazione*, Torino: Einaudi (Piccola biblioteca Einaudi, 473).

Petrucci, Armando (1996), 'Au-delà de la paléographie: histoire de l'écriture, histoire de l'écrit, histoire de l'écrire', *Bulletin de la Classe des lettres et des sciences morales et politiques de l'Académie royale de Belgique*, 6/7, 123–135.

Petrucci, Armando (1999), 'Die beschreibene Schrift', in: *Methoden der Schriftbeschreibung*, ed. by Peter Rück, Stuttgart: Thorbecke (Historische Hilfswissenschaften, 4), 9–15.

Petrucci, Armando (2001), *La descrizione del manoscritto. Storia, problemi, modelli*, 2nd edition, Roma: Carocci (Beni culturali, 2).

Petrucci, Armando (2002, [6]2011), *Prima lezione di paleografia*, Roma – Bari: Laterza (Universale Laterza, 811).

Petrucci, Armando (2005), 'Leggere nel Medioevo', in: *La lettura spirituale. Scrittori cristiani tra Medioevo ed età moderna*, ed. by Lucio Coco, Milano: Edizioni Sylvestre Bonnard, 5–25.

van Peursen, Wido Th. (2008a), 'La diffusion des manuscrits bibliques conservés: typologie, organisation, nombre et époques de copie', in: *L'Ancient Testament en syriaque*, ed. by Françoise Briquel Chatonnet – Philippe Le Moigne, Paris: Geuthner (Études Syriaques, 5), 193–214.

van Peursen, Wido Th. (2008b), 'Language Variation, Language Development and the Textual History of the Peshitta', in: *Aramaic in its Historical and Linguistic Setting*, ed. by Holger Gzella – M.L. Folmer, Wiesbaden: Harrassowitz (Veröffentlichungen der Orientalischen Kommission, 50), 231–256.

van Peursen, Wido Th. (2010), 'Text Comparison and Digital Creativity. An Introduction', in: *Text Comparison and Digital Creativity. The Production of Presence and Meaning in Digital Text Scholarship*, ed. by Wido Th. van Peursen – Ernst D. Thoutenhoofd, Leiden: Brill (Scholarly Communication, 1), 1–27.

van Peursen, Wido Th. (2011), 'The Book of Ben Sira in the Syriac Tradition', in: *The Texts and Versions of the Book of Ben Sira. Transmission and Interpretation*, ed. by Jean-Sébastien Rey – Jan Joosten, Leiden: Brill (Supplements to the Journal for the Study of Judaism, 150), 143–165.

Pfeiffer, Judith – Manfred Kropp (eds) (2007), *Theoretical Approaches to the Transmission and Edition of Oriental Manuscripts. Proceedings of a symposium held in Istanbul March 28-30, 2001*, Beirut: Ergon Verlag Würzburg in Kommission (Beiruter Texte und Studien, 111).

Phillipson, Laurel (2013), 'Parchment Production in the First Millennium BC at Seglamen, Northern Ethiopia', *African Archaeological Review*, August.

Philothée du Sinai (ed.) (2008), *Nouveaux manuscrits syriaques du Sinaï*, Athens: Mount Sinai Foundation.

Piccard, Gerhard (1961–1997), *Die Wasserzeichenkartei Piccard im Hauptstaatsarchiv Stuttgart*, I–XVII, Stuttgart. (See also *Wasserzeichensammlung Piccard* online).

Pickwoad, Nicholas (2004), 'The condition survey of the manuscripts in the Monastery of Saint Catherine on Mount Sinai', *The Paper Conservator*, 28, 33–61.

Piemontese, Angelo Michele (1989), 'Devises et vers traditionnels des copistes entre explicit et colophon des manuscrits persans', in: *Les manuscrits du Moyen Orient. Essais de codicologie et de paléographie. Actes du Colloque d'Istanbul, Istanbul 26-29 mai, 1986*, ed. by François Déroche, Istanbul: I.F.E.A. – Paris: Bibliothèque nationale (Varia turcica, 8), 77–87.

Piemontese, Angelo Michele (1994), 'Paleografia araba', in: *Enciclopedia Italiana di scienze, lettere e arti, 1979-1992 Appendice*, V, Roma, 23b–24a.

Pierazzo, Elena (2011), 'A Rationale of Digital Documentary Editions', *Literary and Linguist Computing*, 26, 463–477.

Pietersma, Albert – Susan Turner Comstock (2011), 'Two More Pages of Crosby-Schøyen Codex MS 193: A Pachomian Lectionary?', *Bulletin of the American Society of Papyrologists*, 48, 27–46.

Pietersma, Albert – Benjamin G. Wright (eds) (2007), *A New English Translation of the Septuagint*, Oxford: Oxford University Press.

Pigulevskaja, Nina V. (1960), 'Каталог сирийских рукописей Ленинграда (*Katalog sirijskich rukopisej Leningrada*, 'Catalogue of the Syriac Manuscripts of Leningrad')', *Palestinskij Sbornik*, 6/69, 3–230.

Pinakes, <http://pinakes.irht.cnrs.fr>, last access May 2014.

Pinninger, David (2001), *Pest Management in Museums, Archives and Historic Houses*, London: Archetype.

Pirenne, Jacqueline (1963), 'Aux origines de la graphie syrienne', *Syria*, 40, 101–137.

Pīšāwarī, Aḥmad Adīb (1307 AH/1889–1890 CE), تاريخ بيهقى (*Tārīḫ-i Bayhaqī*, 'The *History* of Bayhaqī'), Tehran [lithograph edition].

Platt, Thomas Pell (1823), *A Catalogue of the Ethiopic Biblical Manuscripts in the Royal Library of Paris and in the Library of the British and Foreign Bible Society*, London: Richard Watts.

Platti, Emilio (1981), *La grande polémique antinestorienne de Yaḥyā b. ʿAdī*, I–II, Louvain: Peeters (Corpus Scriptorum Christianorum Orientalium, 427, 437, Scriptores Arabici 36, 38).

Platti, Emilio (1987), *Abū ʿĪsā al-Warrāq Yaḥyā ibn ʿAdī: de l'incarnation*, I–II, Louvain: Peeters (Corpus Scriptorum Christianorum Orientalium, 490, 491, Scriptores Arabici 46, 47).

Plumley, J. Martin (1975), *The Scrolls of Bishop Timotheos: Two Documents from Medieval Nubia*, London: Egypt Exploration Society (Texts from Excavations, 1).

Plummer, John (1968), *The Glazier Collection of Illuminated Manuscripts*, New York: The Pierpont Morgan Library.

Pöhlmann, Egert – Martin L. West (2012), 'The Oldest Greek Papyrus and Writing Tablets. Fifth-Century Documents from the 'Tomb of the Musician' in Attica', *Zeitschrift für Papyrologie und Epigraphik*, 180, 1–16.

Poirel, Dominique (2006), 'L'édition des textes médiolatins', in: *Pratiques philologiques en Europe. Actes de la journée d'étude organisée à l'École des chartes le 23 septembre 2005*, ed. by Frédéric Duval, Paris: École des Chartes (Études et rencontres de l'École des chartes, 21), 151–173.

Połarian [Bogharyan], Norayr (Norair) (1966–1991), Մայր ցուցակ ձեռագրաց Սրբոց Յակոբեանց (*Mayr cʻucʻak jeṙagracʻ Srbocʻ Yakobeancʻ* 'Grand Catalogue of St James Manuscripts [Armenian Patriarchate of Jerusalem]'), I–XI, Jerusalem: Trapan Srbocʻ Yakobeancʻ.

Polidori, Valerio (2013), 'L'edizione delle fonti liturgiche greche: una questione di metodo', *Bollettino della Badia Greca di Grottaferrata*, 3/10, 173–197.

Ponthot, Joseph (1981), 'In memoriam René Draguet', *Revue théologique de Louvain*, 12, 137–141.

Popkonstantinov, Kazimir – Rossina Kostova (2010), 'Architecture of Conversion: Provincial Monasteries in the 9th – 10th Centuries. Bulgaria', in: *Архитектура Византии и Древней Руси IX–XII вв.* (*Architektura Vizantii i Drevnej Rusi IX–XII vv.*, 'The Architecture of Byzantium and Ancient Rus, 9th-12th cent.'), St Petersburg: Gosudarstvennyj Ermitaž (Trudy Gosudarstvennogo Ermitaža, 53), 116–129.

Popova, Olga S. (1975), *Les miniatures russes du XIe au XVe siècle / Russian miniatures of the 11th to the 15th centuries*, Leningrad: Aurora.

Popova, Olga S. (1984), *Les miniatures russes XIe – debut du XVIe siecle*, Leningrad: Aurora.

Porter, Venetia (2011), *Arabic and Persian Seals and Amulets in the British Museum*, London: British Museum (British Museum Research Publication, 106).

Porter, Venetia (2012), *The Art of Hajj*, London: British Museum.

Porter, Yves (1992), *Peinture et arts du livre. Essai sur la littérature technique indo-persane*, Paris – Téhéran: Institut français de recherche en Iran.

Porter, Yves (2003), 'La réglure (mastar). De la 'formule d'atelier' aux jeux de l'esprit', *Studia islamica*, 96, 55–74.

Porter, Stanley E. – Wendy J. Porter (2008), *New Testament Greek Papyri and Parchments. New editions: Texts*, Berlin – New York: De Gruyter (Mitteilungen aus der Papyrussammlung der Österreichischen Nationalbibliothek [Papyrus Erzherzog Rainer], 29).

Porterie, Mireille (1995), 'Rangement et conditionnement des documents', *Conservation préventive du patrimoine documentaire. Archives-livres-photographies-arts graphiques*, fiche 4.

Posse, Otto (ed.) (1899), *Handschriften-Konservierung: nach der St Gallener Konferenz 1898 sowie der Dresdener Konferenz 1899*, Dresden: Verlag des Apollo.

Poulakakis, Nikos et al. (2007) {N.P. – Agamemnon Tselikas – Moysis Mylonas – Petros Lymberakis}, 'Ancient DNA and the genetic signature of ancient Greek manuscripts', *Journal of Archaeological Science*, 34/5, 675–680.

Pratesi, Alessandro (1979), 'Paleografia in crisi?', *Scrittura e Civiltà*, 3, 329–337.

Prato, Giancarlo (1979), 'Scritture librarie arcaizzanti della prima età dei Paleologi e loro modelli', *Scrittura e Civiltà*, 3, 151–193.

Prato, Giancarlo (1984), 'La presentazione del testo nei manoscritti tardobizantini', in: *Il libro e il testo. Atti del convegno internazionale (Urbino, 20-23 settembre 1982)*, ed. by Cesare Questa – Renato Raffaelli, Urbino: Università degli studi di Urbino (Pubblicazioni dell'Università di Urbino. Scienze umane, atti di congressi, 1), 69–84.

Proverbio, Delio Vania (2000), 'Inventario sommario dei manoscritti arabi, ebraici, etiopici – con notizia dei turchi – conservati presso la Biblioteca della Badia di Grottaferrata', *Atti della Accademia Nazionale dei Lincei. Classe di scienze morali, storiche e filologiche. Memorie*, ser. 9[a], 12/4, 468–570.

Proverbio, Delio Vania (2008), 'Historical Introduction', in: *Hebrew manuscripts in the Vatican Library. Catalogue*, ed. by Benjamin Richler, Città del Vaticano: Biblioteca Apostolica Vaticana (Studi e Testi, 438), xv–xxiv.

Proverbio, Delio Vania (2010), *Turcica Vaticana*, Città del Vaticano: Biblioteca Apostolica Vaticana (Studi e Testi, 461).

Proverbio, Delio Vania (2012a), 'Barb. or. 2 (Psalterium pentaglottum)', in: *Coptic Treasures from the Vatican Library: A Selection of Coptic, Copto-Arabic and Ethiopic Manuscripts. Papers Collected on the Occasion of the Tenth International Congress of Coptic Studies (Rome, September 17th–22nd, 2012)*, ed. by Paola Buzi – Delio Vania Proverbio, Città del Vaticano: Biblioteca Apostolica Vaticana (Studi e Testi, 472), 163–174.

Proverbio, Delio Vania (2012b), 'On subject of transliterating Ottoman and other Turkic texts written in Arabic script for philological purposes', *Turcica*, 44, 317–332.

Proverbio, Delio Vania – Gianfranco Fiaccadori (2004), 'Un nuovo testimone etiopico della Rivelazione di Pietro a Clemente: il ms.121 del Monumento Nazionale di Casamari (Veroli)', *Atti della Accademia nazionale dei Lincei. Rendiconti Classe di scienze morali storiche e filologiche*, ser. 9a, 15/4, 665–693.

Qauxčišvili, Simon (1955–1959), ქართლის ცხოვრება (*Kartlis cxovreba*, 'The Life of Kartli'), I–II, Tbilisi: Saxelgami.

قواعد تحقيق المخطوطات الإسلامية ومناهجها (*Qawā'id taḥqīq al-maḫṭūṭāt al-Islāmiyya wa-minhāǧuhā*, 'Rules and Methods of Editing Islamic Manuscripts'), London: Al-Furqān, 2013.

Quecke, Hans (1975), 'Ein Brief von einem Nachfolger Pachoms (Chester Beatty Library Ms. Ac. 1486)', *Orientalia*, ser. 2, 44, 426–433, pl. 42.

Quentin, Henri (1926), *Essais de critique textuelle* (*Ecdotique*), Paris: Picard.

Rabb, Intisar (2006), 'Non-Canonical Readings of the Qur'an: Recognition and Authenticity (The Ḥimṣī Reading)', *Journal of Qur'anic Studies*, 8/2, 84–127.

Rabin, Ira (2014), 'Ink Identification to Accompany Digitization of the Manuscripts', in: *Analysis of Ancient and Medieval Texts and Manuscripts: Digital Approaches*, ed. by Tara L. Andrews – Caroline Macé, Turnhout: Brepols (Lectio Studies in the Transmission of Texts and Ideas, 1), 293–307.

Rabin, Ira et al. (2012) {I.R. – Roman Schütz – Anka Kohl – Timo Wolff – Roald Tagle – Simone Pentzien – Oliver Hahn – Stephen Emmel}, 'Identification and classification of historical writing inks in spectroscopy: a methodological overview', *Comparative Oriental Manuscript Studies Newsletter*, 3, 26–30.

Raby, Julian – Zeren Tanındı (1993), *Turkish bookbinding in the 15th century. The foundation of an Ottoman court style*, London: Azimuth.

Rafti, Patrizia (1988), 'L'interpunzione nel libro manoscritto: mezzo secolo di studi', *Scrittura e civiltà*, 12, 239–298.

Rahbar, Ḫalīl Ḫaṭīb (1373 Š./1994 CE), تاريخ بيهقي با معنى واژها و شرح بيتها و جملها دشوار و امثال و حكم و برخي نكتها دستوري و ادبي (*Tārīḫ-i Bayhaqī, bā ma'nā-yi wāžahā wa šarḥ-i baithā wa ǧumlahā-yi dušwār wa amṯāl wa ḥikam wa barḫī nuktahā-yi dastūrī wa adabī*, 'The *History* of Bayhaqī, with the meanings of the words, a commentary of the verses and difficult phrases, proverbs, sayings, and some notes on grammar and literature'), 3rd edition, I–III, Tehran: Mahtāb.

Rahlfs, Alfred – Robert Hanhart (eds) (2006), *Septuaginta*, Stuttgart: Deutsche Bibelgesellschaft.

Ramazanova, N.V. (2010), 'Остромирово Евангелие и древнерусские нотированные рукописи (Ostromirovo evangelie i drevnerusskie notirovannye rukopisi, 'The Ostromir Gospels and Old Russian Musical Manuscripts')', in: *Остромирово Евангелие и современные исследования рукописной традиции новозаветных текстов* (*Ostromirovo Evangelie i sovremennye issledovanija rukopisnoj tradicii novozavetnych tekstov*, 'The Ostromir Gospels and Current Research in Manuscript Tradition of New Testament Texts'), ed. by E.V. Krušel'nickaja, St Petersburg: Rossijskaja Nacionalnaja Biblioteka, 221–238.

Raschmann, Simone-Christiane (2012), 'The Union Catalogue of Oriental Manuscripts in German Collections. The manuscripts and block prints preserved in the Berlin Turfan collection', paper presented at the COMSt workshop *The electronic revolution? The impact of the digital on cataloguing*, Copenhagen.

Rayfield, Donald (2010), *The Literature of Georgia. A History*. Third, revised and expanded edition, London: Garnett Press.

Rāġib, Yūsuf (1990), 'L'écriture des papyrus arabes aux premiers siècles de l'Islam', *Revue des Mondes Musulmans et de la Méditerranée*, 58/4, 14–29.

Rebstock, Ulrich (1989), *Sammlung arabischer Handschriften aus Mauretanien: Kurzbeschreibung von 2239 Handschrifteneinheiten mit Indices*, Wiesbaden: Harrassowitz.

van Reenen, Pieter – Margot van Mulken (eds) (1996), *Studies in stemmatology*, Amsterdam – Philadelphia: John Benjamins.

van Reenen, Pieter et al. (eds) (2004) {P.R. – August den Hollander – Margot van Mulken}, *Studies in stemmatology* II, Amsterdam – Philadelphia: John Benjamins.

Reeve, Michael D. (1998), 'Shared innovations, dichotomies, and evolution', in: *Filologia classica e filologia romanza: esperienze ecdotiche a confronto. Atti del Convegno Roma 25-27 maggio 1995*, ed. by Anna Ferrari, Spoleto: Centro Italiano di Studi sull'Alto Medioevo (Incontri di Studio, 2), 445–505.

Reeve, Michael D. (2011), *Manuscripts and Methods: Essays on Editing and Transmission*, Roma: Edizioni di storia e letteratura (Raccolta di studi e testi, 270).

van Regemorter, Berthe (1953), 'La reliure arménienne', *Bazmavēp*, 8-10, 200–204.

van Regemorter, Berthe (1967), 'La reliure byzantine', *Revue belge d'archéologie et d'histoire de l'art*, 36, 99–142.

Regni, Marina (1995), 'L'exposition des documents', *Conservation préventive du patrimoine documentaire. Archives-livres-photographies-arts graphiques*, fiche 9.

Regni, Marina – Piera Giovanna Tordella (eds) (1996), *Conservazione dei materiali librari archivistici e grafici*, Torino: Umberto Allemandi & C. (Documenti).

Regourd, Anne (2002), 'Les manuscrits des bibliothèques privées de Zabīd (Yémen): enjeu d'un catalogage', *Seminar for Arabian Studies*, 32, 247–257.

Regourd, Anne (ed.) (2006), *Catalogue cumulé des bibliothèques des manuscrits de Zabid, fascicule* I, *Bibliothèque 'Abd al-Rahman al-Hadhrami*, Sanaa: Centre français d'archéologie et de sciences sociales – Fonds social de développement.

Rehbein, Malte et al. (eds) (2009) {M.L. – Patrick Sahle – Thorsten Schaßan}, *Kodikologie und Paläographie im digitalen Zeitalter / Codicology and Palaeography in the Digital Age*, Norderstedt: BOD (Schriften des Instituts für Dokumentologie und Editorik, 1).

Reif, Stefan C. (2000), *A Jewish Archive from Old Cairo: The History of Cambridge University's Genizah Collection*, Richmond, Surrey: Curzon Press (Culture and Civilization in the Middle East).

Renhart, Erich (2009), 'Le Caucase. Eine Armenische Palimpsesthandschrift an der Universitätsbibliothek Graz (UBG, ms. 2058/2)', in: *Palimpsestes et éditions de textes, Les textes littéraires. Actes du colloque tenu à Louvain-la-Neuve, Septembre 2003*, ed. by Véronique Somers, Louvain-la-Neuve: Université catholique de Louvain, Institut orientaliste (Publications de l'Institut Orientaliste de Louvain, 56), 215–232.

Renoux, Charles (2003), 'Un bilan provisoire sur l'héritage grec du rite arménien', *Le Muséon*, 116, 53–69.

Revithi, Anna-Arietta (2010), 'Condition Survey of the Manuscript Collection of the Hellenic Parliament Library: Present evaluation and future planning', paper presented at the COMSt workshop *Conservation Studies on Oriental Manuscripts*, Istanbul.

Revithi, Anna-Arietta (2011), 'Digitization project of the Hellenic Parliament Library', paper presented at the COMSt workshop *Preservation of Middle Eastern Manuscripts - Restoration and digitization process: what should be done first?*, Leiden.

Reynolds, Dwight Fletcher (2006), 'Sīrat Banī Hilāl', in: *Arabic Literature in the Post-Classical Period*, ed. by Roger Allen – D.S. Richards, Cambridge: Cambridge University Press, 307–318.

Reynolds, Leighton D. – Nigel G. Wilson (1991), *Scribes and Scholars: A Guide to the Transmission of Greek and Latin Literature*, 3rd edition, Oxford: Oxford University Press.

Rezaei, Siamak (2008), 'Punctuation', in: *Encyclopedia of Arabic Language and Linguistics*, III, Leiden: Brill, 740–742.

Rezvan, Efim (2004), *The 'Qur'ān of 'Uthmān' (St Petersburg, Kattar-Langar, Bukhara, Tashkent)*, I, St Petersburg: St Petersburg Centre of Oriental Studies.

Richard, Francis (1989), *Catalogue des manuscrits persans*, I, *Ancien fonds*, Paris: Bibliothèque nationale.

Richard, Jean (2001), 'Les précurseurs de l'orientalisme', *Comptes-rendus des séances de l'Académie des inscriptions et belle-lettres*, 145/4, 1639–1644.

Richard, Marcel (1948, 1958[2]), *Répertoire des bibliothèques et des catalogues de manuscrits grecs*, Paris: Institut de recherche et d'histoire des textes.

Richard, Marcel (1954), *Règles à suivre pour la confection des catalogues de manuscrits grecs*, Bruxelles: Union Académique Internationale, Commission des Éditions Savantes.

Richard, Marcel (1980), 'La recherche des textes hier et demain', in: *Griechische Kodikologie und Textüberlieferung*, ed. by Dieter Harlfinger, Darmstadt: Wissenschaftliche Buchgesellschaft, 3–13.

Richardin, Pascale et al. (2006), 'Les rouleaux protecteurs éthiopiens d'une donation au Musée du quai Branly. Étude historique, scientifique et interventions de conservation-restauration', *Technè*, 23, 79–84.

Richardson, Ernest C. (1933–1937), *A union world catalog of manuscript books*, New York: H.W.Wilson.

Richler, Benjamin (1994), *Guide to Hebrew Manuscript Collections*, Jerusalem: The Israel Academy of Sciences and Humanities.

Richler, Benjamin et al. (ed.) (2008) {B.R., palaeographical and codicological descriptions by Malachi Beit-Arié, in collaboration with Nurit Pasternak}, *Hebrew manuscripts in the Vatican Library. Catalogue*, Città del Vaticano: Biblioteca Apostolica Vaticana (Studi e Testi, 438).

Richler, Benjamin – Malachi Beit-Arié (eds) (2001), *Hebrew manuscripts in the Biblioteca Palatina in Parma: Catalogue*, Jerusalem: Hebrew University of Jerusalem, Jewish National and University Library.

Richter, Siegfried G. (1998), *The Manichaean Coptic Papyri in the Chester Beatty Library: Psalm Book*. II.2: *Die Herakleides-Psalmen*, Turnhout: Brepols (Corpus Fontium Manichaeorum, Series Coptica, 1.2.2).

Richter, Siegfried G. (2005), 'The Coptic Manichaean Library from Madinat Madi in the Fayoum', in: *Christianity and Monasticism in the Fayoum Oasis: Essays from the 2004 International Symposium of the Saint Mark Foundation and the Saint Shenouda the Archimandrite Coptic Society in Honor of Martin Krause*, ed. by Gawdat Gabra, Cairo – New York: The American University in Cairo Press, 71–78.

Riddle, John M. (1984), 'Byzantine Commentaries on Dioscorides', *Dumbarton Oaks Papers*, 38, 95–102.

RIÉ see Bernard et al. 1991–2000.

Riecke, Anne-Beate (2009), *Die Erstellung von Handschriftenbeschreibungen nach den Richtlinien der DFG mit Hilfe von Manuscriptum XML, Version 1.1*, <http://www.manuscripta-mediaevalia.de/hs/handbuch.pdf>, Berlin: Staatsbibliothek zu Berlin – Preußischer Kulturbesitz.

Riederer, Josef (1977), *Technik und Farbstoffe der frühmittelalterlichen Wandmalereien Ostturkestans*, Berlin: Museum für Indische Kunst (Veröffentlichungen des Museums für Indische Kunst, 4).

Rieu, Charles (1879–1883), *Catalogue of the Persian Manuscripts in the British Museum*, I–III, London: British Museum.

Rieu, Charles (1894), *Supplement to the Catalogue of the Arabic Manuscripts in the British Museum*, London: British Museum.

Rieu, Charles (1895), *Supplement to the Catalogue of the Persian Manuscripts in the British Museum*, London: British Museum.

Rilliet, Frédéric (1986), *Jacques de Saroug, Six homélies festales en prose*, Turnhout: Brepols (Patrologia Orientalis, 43, 4).

Rinascimento virtuale. Digitale Palimpsestforschung (virtual exhibition), <http://www.bml.firenze.sbn.it/rinascimentovirtuale/pannello01a.shtm>, 2002.

Río Sánchez, Francisco del (2011), *Manuscrits en arabe karšūnī conservés dans la bibliothèque des Maronites d'Alep (Syrie)*, Piscataway, NJ: Gorgias Press (Gorgias Eastern Christian Studies, 23).

Río Sánchez, Francisco del – Amalia Zomeño (2012), *Catálogo de los manuscritos siríacos, árabes karšūnī y copto-árabes de Montserrat*, Barcelona: Consejo Superior de Investigaciones Científicas (Orientalia montserratensia, 6).

Roberts, Colin H. – Theodor C. Skeat (1983), *The Birth of the Codex*, London: Oxford University Press.

Robin, Christian Julien (2001), 'Les inscriptions de l'arabe antique et les études arabes', *Arabica*, 48, 509–577.

Robin, Christian Julien (2006), 'La réforme de l'écriture arabe à l'époque du califat médinois', *Mélanges de l'Université Saint-Joseph*, 59, 319–364.

Robinson, Basil William (1958), *Descriptive Catalogue of the Persian Paintings in the Bodleian Library*, Oxford: Oxford University Press.

Robinson, Basil William – Robert W. Skelton (1978), *Islamic Art in the Keir Collection*, London: Faber and Faber.

Robinson, James M. (1975), 'The Construction of the Nag Hammadi Codices', in: *Essays on the Nag Hammadi Texts in Honour of Pahor Labib*, ed. by Martin Krause, Leiden: Brill (Nag Hammadi Studies, 6), 170–190.

Robinson, James M. (1978), 'The Future of Papyrus Codicology', in: *The Future of Coptic Studies*, ed. by Robert McLachlan Wilson, Leiden: Brill (Coptic Studies, 1), 23–70.

Robinson, James M. (1979), 'Codicological Analysis of Nag Hammadi Codices V and VI and Papyrus Berolinensis 8502', in: *Nag Hammadi Codices V, 2–5 and VI with Papyrus Berolinensis 8502, 1 and 4*, ed. by Douglas M. Parrott, Leiden: Brill (Nag Hammadi Studies, 11), 9–45.

Robinson, James M. (1984), 'Introduction', in: *The Facsimile Edition of the Nag Hammadi Codices: Introduction, published under the auspices of the Department of Antiquities of the Arab Republic of Egypt in conjunction with the United Nations Educational, Scientific and Cultural Organization*, ed. by James M. Robinson, Leiden: Brill, 1–102.

Robinson, James M. (1990a), *The Pachomian Monastic Library at the Chester Beatty Library and the Bibliothèque Bodmer*, Claremont: Institute for Antiquity and Christianity (Occasional Papers of the Institute for Antiquity and Christianity, 19).

Robinson, James M. (1990b), 'The Manuscript's History and Codicology', in: *The Crosby-Schøyen Codex MS 193 in the Schøyen Collection*, ed. by James E. Goehring, Louvain: Peeters (Corpus Scriptorum Christianorum Orientalium, 521, Subsidia, 85), xvii–xlvii.

Robinson, James M. (1990–1991), 'The Pachomian Monastic Library at the Chester Beatty Library and the Bibliothèque Bodmer', *Manuscripts of the Middle East*, 5, 26–40.

Robinson, James M. et al. (1972), *The Facsimile Edition of the Nag Hammadi Codices: Codex VII*, Leiden: Brill.

Robinson, Pamela R. (1980), 'The 'Booklet': A Self-Contained Unit in Composite Manuscripts', in: *Codicologica 3, Essais typologiques*, ed. by Albert Gruys – Peter Gumbert, Leiden: Brill (Litterae textuales), 46–69.

Robinson, Peter (1989), 'The Collation and Textual Criticism of Icelandic Manuscripts', *Literary and Linguistic Computing*, 4, 99–105, 174–181.

Robinson, Peter (1994), 'Textual Criticism, Publication, and the Computer', *Text*, 7, 77–94.

Robinson, Peter (2004), 'Making Electronic Editions and the Fascination of What is Difficult', in: *Digital Technology and Philological Disciplines*, ed. by Andrea Bozzi – Laura Cignoni, Pisa – Roma: Istituti Editoriali e Poligrafici Internazionali (Linguistica Computazionale, 20-21), 415–437.

Rodríguez Adrados, Francisco (2009), *Greek Wisdom Literature and the Middle Ages. The Lost Greek Models and Their Arabic and Castilian Translations*, translated by Joyce Greer, Bern: Peter Lang (Sapheneia: Contributions to Classical Philology, 14).

Roger, Patricia et al. (2004) {P.R. – Serghini Malika – François Déroche}, 'Les matériaux de la couleur dans les manuscrits arabes de l'Occident musulman. Recherches sur la collection de la Bibliothèque générale et archives de Rabat et de la Bibliothèque nationale de France (note d'information)', *Comptes rendus des séances de l'Académie des inscriptions et belles-lettres*, 148/2, 799–830.

Roman, Agathe – Paul-Hubert Poirier (eds) (2013), *Titus Bostrensis, Contra Manichaeos Libri IV Graece et Syriace, cum excerptis e Sacris Parallelis Iohanni Damasceno attributis*, Turnhout: Brepols (Corpus Christianorum. Series Graeca, 82).

Ronconi, Filippo (2007), *I manoscritti greci miscellanei: ricerche su esemplari dei secoli IX–XII*, Spoleto: Centro Italiano di Studi sull'Alto Medioevo (Testi, studi, strumenti, 21).

Ronconi, Filippo (2012), 'La main insaisissable. Rôle et fonctions des copistes byzantins entre réalité et imaginaire', in: *Scrivere e leggere nell'Alto Medioevo (Spoleto 28 aprile – 4 maggio 2011)*, II, Spoleto: Centro Italiano di Studi sull'Alto Medioevo (Settimane di studio della Fondazione Centro italiano di studi sull'alto Medioevo, 59), 627–664.

Roper, Geoffrey (ed.) (1992–1994), *The World Survey of Islamic Manuscripts*, I–IV, London: Al-Furqān.

Rosenthal, Erwin (1967), 'Some Observations on Coptic Influence in Western Early Medieval Manuscripts', in: *Homage to a Bookman: Essays on Manuscripts, Books and Printing Written for Hans P. Kraus on His Sixtieth Birthday, Oct. 12, 1967*, ed. by Hellmut Lehmann-Haupt, Berlin: Mann, 51–74.

Rosenthal, Franz (1947), *The technique and approach of Muslim scholarship*, Roma: Pontificium Institutum Biblicum (Analecta Orientalia, 24).

Rosselli Del Turco, Roberto (2007), 'La digitalizzazione di testi letterari di area germanica: problemi e proposte', in: *Digital Philology and Medieval Texts*, ed. by Arianna Ciula – Francesco Stella, Pisa: Pacini (Arti Spazi Scritture, 4), 187–213.

Roubetz, Alexandre de (1919), *Les manuscrits slaves de la Bibliothèque Royale de Stockholm* (*section russe*), Stockholm [manuscript].

Rouchon, Véronique et al. (2009) {V.R. – Julie Stordiau-Pallot – Blandine Durocher – Eleonora Pellizzi}, 'The water sensitivity of iron gall ink and its risk assessment', *Studies in Conservation* 54, 236–254.

Roxburgh, David J. (1995), 'Heinrich Friedrich von Diez and his Eponymous Albums: Mss. Diez a. Fols. 70-74', *Muqarnas*, 12, 112–136.

Roxburgh, David J. (2001), *Prefacing the Image: the Writing of Art History in Sixteenth-Century Iran, Studies and Sources in Islamic Art and Architecture*, Leiden: Brill (Supplements to Muqarnas, 9).

Roxburgh, David J. (2005), *The Persian Album, 1400-1600. From Dispersal to Collection*, New Haven – London: Yale University Press.

Rück, Peter (ed.) (1999), *Methoden der Schriftbeschreibung*, Stuttgart: Thorbecke (Historische Hilfswissenschaften, 4).

Rückert, Peter et al. (eds) (2009) {P.R. – Sandra Hodeček – Emanuel Wenger}, *Bull's Head and Mermaid. The History of Paper and Watermarks from the Middle Ages to the Modern Period. Booklet and catalogue of the exhibition presented by the Landesarchiv Baden-Württemberg, Hauptstaatsarchiv Stuttgart and the Austrian Academy of Sciences, Kommission für Schrift- und Buchwesen des Mittelalters, Vienna*, 3rd edition, Wien: Österreichische Akademie der Wissenschaften – Stuttgart: Landesarchiv Baden-Württemberg, Hauptstaatsarchiv.

Ruska, Julius (1934), 'Die Alchemie des Avicenna', *Isis*, 21, 13–51.

Russell, James (1991), 'Two Interpretations of the Ten Canon Tables', in: *Armenian Gospel Iconography. The Tradition of the Glajor Gospel*, ed. by Thomas F. Mathews – Avedis K. Sanjian, Washington, D.C.: Dumbarton Oaks (Dumbarton Oaks Studies, 29), 206–211.

Russo, Joseph (1997), 'Prose Genres for the Performance of Traditional Wisdom in Ancient Greece: Proverb, Maxim, Apothegm', in: *Poet, Public and Performance in Ancient Greece*, ed. by Lowell Edmunds – Robert W. Wallace, Baltimore, ML: Johns Hopkins University Press, 49–64.

Rutschowskaya [Rutschowscaya], Marie-Hélène et al. (2000) {M.R. – Dominique Bénazeth et al.}, *L'art copte en Égypte. 2000 ans de christianisme*, Paris: Institut du monde arabe – Éditions Gallimard.

Rutschowskaya, Marie-Hélène – Alain Desreumaux (1992), 'Une peinture copte sur un bois inscrit en araméen christo-palestinien au musée du Louvre. II – Le texte araméen de la plaquette d'origine', *Comptes rendus de l'Académie des inscriptions et belles-lettres*, janvier-mars, 83–92.

Ryder, Michael L. (1991), 'The biology and history of parchment', in: *Pergament, Geschichte – Struktur – Restaurierung – Herstellung*, ed. by Peter Rück, Sigmaringen: J. Thorbecke (Historische Hilfswissenschaften, 2), 25–34.

Ryhl-Svendsen, Morten (2006), 'Indoor air pollution in museums: prediction models and control strategies', *Reviews in Conservation*, 7, 27–41.

Šabbūḥ, Ibrāhīm (1376/1956), 'سجل قديم لمكتبة جامع القيروان' (*Siğill qadīm li-maktabat Ǧāmi' al-Qayrawān*, 'An antique inventory of the library of the mosque of al-Qayrawān'), *Maǧallat Maʿhad al-maḫṭūṭāt al-ʿarabiyya*, I/2, 339–372.

Šabbūḥ [Chabbouh], Ibrāhīm (1995), 'Two new sources on the art of mixing ink', in: *The Codicology of Islamic Manuscripts: Proceedings of the second Conference of al-Furqân Islamic Heritage Foundation (4-5 December 1993)*, ed. by Yasin Dutton, 59–76.

Sachau, Eduard (1899), *Verzeichniss der syrischen Handschriften*, I–II, Berlin: A. Asher (Handschriften-Verzeichnisse der königlichen Bibliothek zu Berlin, 23).

Sahle, Patrick (2013), *Digitale Editionsformen, Zum Umgang mit der Überlieferung unter den Bedingungen des Medienwandels*, I–III, Norderstedt: Book on Demand (Schriften des Instituts für Dokumentologie und Editorik, 7-9).

Said, Edward W. (1978), *Orientalism*, New York: Pantheon Books.

Sakisian, Arménag (1927a, 1927b), 'La reliure turque du XVe au XIXe siècle', *Revue de l'art ancien et moderne*, [I] 51, 277–284; [II] 52, 141–154, 286–298.

Sakisian, Arménag (1934), 'La reliure persane au XVe siècle sous les Timourides', *Revue de l'art ancien et moderne*, 66, 145–168.

Salemann, Carl (1901), 'Mittelpersisch', in: *Grundriss der Iranischen Philologie*, I/1, ed. by Wilhelm Geiger – Ernst Kuhn, Strassburg: Trübner, 249–332.

Salemann, Carl (1908), *Manichäische Studien* I. *Die mittelpersischen Texte in revidierter Transcription, mit Glossar und grammatischen Bemerkungen*, St Petersburg: Imperatorskaja Akademija Nauk (Zapiski imperatorskoj Akademiï nauk". Mémoires de l'Acad. imp. des Sciences de St-Pétersbourg, 8e sér., cl. Hist-phil. 8, 10).

Salvadó, Nati et al. (2005) {N.S. – Salvador Butí – Mark J. Tobin – Emmanuel Pantos – A. John N. W. Prag – Trinitat Pradell}, 'Advantages of the Use of SR-FT-IR Microspectroscopy: Applications to Cultural Heritage', *Analytical Chemistry*, 77, 3444–3451.

al-Sāmarrāʾī, Qāsim (2013a), التحقيق النقدي للمخطوطات: التاريخ، القواعد والمشكلات (*al-Taḥqīq al-naqdī li-ʾl-maḫṭūṭāt: al-taʾrīḫ, al-qawāʿid wa-ʾl-muškilāt*, 'The Critical Edition of Manuscripts: History, Rules and Problems'), London: Al-Furqān.

al-Sāmarrāʾī, Qāsim (2013b), *The Critical Edition of Manuscripts: Past, Present and Future*, London: Al-Furqān.

Samir Khalil Samir (1980), *Le Traité de l'Unité de Yahya ibn ʿAdī (893-974). Etude et édition critique*, Junieh – Roma: Pontificio Istituto Orientale (Patrimoine arabe chrétien, 2).

Samir Khalil Samir (1982), 'La tradition arabe chrétienne. État de la question, problèmes et besoins', in: *Actes du Premier Congrès International d'Études Arabes Chrétiennes* (*Goslar, septembre 1980*), ed. by Samir Khalil Samir, Roma: Pontificium Institutum Studiorum Orientalium (Orientalia Christiana Analecta, 218), 21–120.

Šaniʒe, A[ḳaḳi] (1924), თარგმანი ქებათა ქებათაჲსაჲ. პალეოგრაფიული რვეული (*Targmani kebata kebataysay. Ṗaleograpiuli rveuli*, 'Explanation of the Song of Songs. A palaeographic booklet'), Tbilisi: Ṭpilisis universiṭeṭis sṭudenṭta ḳavširis gamocema, Universiṭeṭis litograpia.

Šaniʒe, A[ḳaḳi] (1929), 'ქართული ხელნაწერები გრაცში (*Kartuli xelnaçerebi gracši*, 'Georgian manuscripts in Graz')', *Ṭpilisis Universiṭeṭis moambe*, 9, 310–353.

Šaniʒe, Aḳaḳi (1938), 'Новооткрытый алфавит кавказских албанцев и его значение для науки (*Novootkrytyj alfavit kavkazskich albancev i ego značenie dlja nauki*, 'The newly discovered alphabet of the Caucasian Albanians and its scientific importance')', *Aḳad. N. Maris saxelobis Enis, Isṭoriisa da Maṭerialuri Ḳulṭuris Insṭiṭuṭis Moambe / Bulletin de l'Institut Marr de Langues, d'Histoire et de Culture Matérielle / Izvestija Instituta Jazyka, Istorii i Material'noj Kul'tury im. Akad. N. Ja Marra*, 4/1, 1–68.

Šaniʒe, Aḳaḳi (1944), ხანმეტი ლექციონარი. ფოტოტიპიური რეპროდუქცია / *Грузинский ханмэтный лекционарий. Фототипическая репродукция* (*Xanmeṭi lekcionari. Poṭoṭiṗiuri reṗrodukcia / Gruzinskij chanmėtnyj lekcionarij. Fototipičeskaja reprodukcija*, 'The Georgian Khanmeti Lectionary. Phototypic Reproduction'), Tbilisi: Sakartvelos SSR Mecnierebata Aḳademiis Gamomcemloba.

Šaniȝe, Aḳaḳi (1959), სინური მრავალთავი *864 წლისა. Синайский многоглав 864-го года* (*Sinuri mravaltavi 864 çlisa. Sinajskij mnogoglav 864-go goda*, 'The Sinai mravaltavi of the year 864'), Tbilisi: Saxelmçipo Universiṭeṭi (Ʒveli kartuli enis ḳatedris šromebi, 5).

Šaniȝe, Aḳaḳi – Aram Marṭirosovi (1977), ჭილ-ეტრატის იადგარი / *Папирусно-пергаментная минея* (*Čil-eṭraṭis iadgari / Papirusno-pergamentnaja mineja*, 'The hymnary on papyrus and parchment'), Tbilisi: Mecniereba (Ʒveli kartuli enis ȝeglebi, 15).

Sanjian, Avedis K. (1968), 'The Historical Significance of the Colophons of Armenian Manuscripts', *Le Muséon*, 81, 181–195.

Sanjian, Avedis K. (1969), *Colophons of Armenian Manuscripts, 1300-1480. A Source for Middle Eastern History*, Cambridge, MA: Harvard University Press.

Sarab'janov, V[ladimir] D[mitrievič] – Ė[ngelina] S[ergeevna] Smirnova (2007), *История древнерусской живописи* (*Istorija drevnerusskoj živopisi*, 'History of Ancient Russian Art'), Moskva: Izdatelstvo Svjato-Tichonovskogo gumanitarnogo universiteta.

Šarašiȝe, Krisṭine (1948), საქართველოს სახელმწიფო მუზეუმის ქართულ ხელნაწერთა აღწერილობა. საქართველოს საისტორიო და საეთნოგრაფიო საზოგადოების ყოფილი მუზეუმის ხელნაწერები (*H* კოლექცია). *Описание грузинских рукописей государственного музея Грузии. Рукописи бывшего Музея Грузинского Общества Истории и Этнографии* (*коллекция H*) (*Sakartvelos saxelmçipo muzeumis kartul xelnaçerta aġçeriloba. Sakartvelos saisṭorio da saetnograpio sazogadoebis q̇opili muzeumis xelnaçerebi* (*H ḳolekcia*) / *Opisanie gruzinskich rukopisej Gosudarstvennogo muzeja Gruzii. Rukopisi byvšego Muzeja Gruzinskogo Obščestva Istorii i Ėtnografii* (*kollekcija H*), 'Description of Georgian Manuscripts of the State Museum of Georgia. Manuscripts of the former Museum of the Society of History and Ethnography of Georgia (collection H)'), III, Tiflis.

Sargisyan [Sargisean, Sarghissian], Barseł [Basile] (I-III) – Sahak Čemčemyan [Čemčemean] (IV-VIII) (1914, 1924, 1966, 1993–1998), Մայր ցուցակ ձեռագրաց Մատենադարանի Մխիթարեանց ի Վենետիկ (*Mayr c'uc'ak hayerēn jeṙagrac' matenadarani Mxit'areanc' i Venetik*, 'Grand Catalogue of the Armenian Manuscripts in the Library of the Mekhitarist Brotherhood in Venice'), I–VIII, Venetik: S. Łazar.

Sauget, Joseph-Marie (1962), *Bibliographie des liturgies orientales* (*1900-1960*), Roma: Pontificio Istituto Orientale.

Sauget, Joseph-Marie (1985), 'Le fragment de papyrus syriaque conservé à Florence', *Annali dell'Istituto Orientale di Napoli*, 45/1, 1–16.

Sautel, Jacques-Hubert (1995), *Répertoire de réglures dans les manuscrits grecs sur parchemin.* Base de données établie par Jacques-Hubert Sautel à l'aide du fichier Leroy et des catalogues récents, Turnhout: Brepols (Bibliologia: Elementa ad Librorum Studia Pertinentia, 13).

Sautel, Jacques-Hubert (2000), 'Aspects de la mise en page des manuscrits grecs à chaînes exégétiques (Paris, BnF, Fonds Coislin)', in: *Le commentaire entre tradition et innovation. Actes du colloque international de l'Institut des traditions textuelles* (*Paris et Villejuif, 22-25 septembre 1999*), ed. by Marie-Odile Goulet-Cazé – Tiziano Dorandi, Paris: Vrin (Bibliothèque d'histoire de la philosophie. Nouvelle série), 89–98.

Sautel, Jacques-Hubert (2001), 'Trois Tétraévangiles jumeaux entourés de la chaîne de Pierre de Laodicée. Étude de la mise en page et de la réglure', *Quinio*, 3, 113–135.

Sautel, Jacques-Hubert (2012), 'Le choix du type de réglure dans les manuscrits byzantins: les 'Homélies sur la Genèse' de saint Jean Chrysostome conservées à la BnF (Paris, BnF, gr. 602–605)', *Scriptorium*, 66, 221–280.

Sayyid, Fu'ād Ayman (2009), كتاب الفهرست لأبي الفرج محمد بن إسحاق النديم (*Kitāb al-fihrist li-Abī 'l-Farağ Muḥammad ibn Isḥāq al-Nadīm*, 'Ibn al-Nadim's Catalogue of Books'), London: Al-Furqān.

Ščepkin, Vjačeslav [Wenceslaus Stschepkin] (1903), 'Cyrillische Ligaturschrift', *Archiv für Slavische Philologie*, 25, 109–129.

Ščepkin, Vjačeslav (1918), *Учебникъ русской палеографіи* (*Učebnik" russkoj paleografii*, 'Textbook on Russian palaeography'), Moskva: Obščestvo Istorii i Drevnostej Rossijskih" pri Moskovskom" Universitetě.

Schäfer, Peter (1986), 'Research into Rabbinic Literature: An Attempt to Define the Status Quaestionis', *Journal of Jewish Studies*, 37, 139–152.

Schäfer, Peter (1989), 'Once again the Status Quaestionis of Research in Rabbinic Literature: An Answer to Chaim Milikowsky', *Journal of Jewish Studies*, 40, 89–94.

Schäfer, Peter – Chaim Milikowski (2010), 'Current Views on the Editing of the Rabbinic Texts of late Antiquity: Reflections on a Debate after Twenty Years', in: *Rabbinic Texts and the History of Late-Roman Palestine*, ed. by Martin Goorman – Philip Alexander, Oxford: British Academy (Proceedings of the British Academy, 165), 79–90.

Scharpé, Jan L. – Frans Vyncke (eds) (1973), *Bdinski zbornik. An Old-Slavonic Menologium of Women Saints* (*Ghent University Library Ms. 408, A.D. 1360*), Brugge: De Tempel (Werken uitgegeven door de Faculteit van de Letteren en Wijsbegeerte, 155).

Schen, Isaac (1972, 1973), 'Usama ibn Munqidh's Memoirs: some further light on Muslim Middle Arabic', *Journal of Semitic Studies*, 17, 218–216; 18, 64–97.

Schenke, Hans-Martin (1981), *Das Matthäus-Evangelium im mittelägyptischen Dialekt des Koptischen* (*Codex Scheide*), Berlin: Akademie-Verlag (Texte und Untersuchungen zur Geschichte der altchristlichen Literatur, 127).

Schenke, Hans-Martin (1991), *Apostelgeschichte 1, 1–15, 3 im mittelägyptischen Dialekt des Koptischen* (*Codex Glazier*), Berlin: Akademie-Verlag (Texte und Untersuchungen zur Geschichte der altchristlichen Literatur, 137).

Schenke, Hans-Martin (2001), 'Evangelium Veritatis (NHC II, 3/XII, 2)', in: *Nag Hammadi Deutsch*, I, ed. by Hans-Martin Schenke – Hans-Gebhard Bethge, Berlin: De Gruyter (Die Griechischen Christlichen Schriftsteller der ersten Jahrhunderte, Neue Folge 8, Koptisch-Gnostische Schriften, 2), 27–44.

Schenker, Alexander M. (1995), *The Dawn of Slavic. An Introduction to Slavic Philology*, New Haven: Yale University Press.

Scheper, Karin (2011), 'Examples of repairs and conservation treatments prior to digitalization', paper presented at the COMSt workshop *Preservation of Middle Eastern Manuscripts - Restoration and digitization process: what should be done first?*, Leiden.

Scheper, Karin (2014), *The Islamic Bookbinding Tradition. A Book Archaeological Study*, Leiden University [diss.].

Scheper, Karin (forthcoming), *The Technique of Islamic Bookbinding. Methods, Materials and Regional Varieties*, Leiden: Brill.

Schiaparelli, Luigi et al. (1935), 'Paleografia', in: *Enciclopedia Italiana*, XXVI, Roma: Enciclopedia Italiana Treccani, 34.

Schiller-Szinessy, Salomon Marcus (1876), *Catalogue of the Hebrew Manuscripts Preserved in the University Library, Cambridge*, I, Cambridge: Cambridge University Press.

Schmidt, Andrea (2009), 'Syriac palimpsests in the British Library', in: *Palimpsestes et éditions de textes: les textes littéraires. Actes du colloque tenu à Louvain-la-Neuve* (*septembre 2003*), ed. by Véronique Somers, Louvain-la-Neuve: Université catholique de Louvain, Institut orientaliste (Publications de l'Institut Orientaliste de Louvain, 56), 161–186.

Schmidt, Carl – Wilhelm Schubart (1936), *Acta Pauli nach dem Papyrus der Hamburger Staats- und Universitäts-Bibliothek*, Glückstadt – Hamburg: J. J. Augustin (Veröffentlichungen aus der Hamburger Staats- und Universitäts-Bibliothek, 2).

Schmidt, Desmond (2010), 'The inadequacy of embedded markup for cultural heritage texts', *Literary and Linguistic Computing*, 25/3, 337–356.

Schmidt, Desmond – Robert Robert Colomb (2009), 'A data structure for representing multi-version texts online', *International Journal of Human-Computer Studies*, 67/6, 497–514.

Schmidt, Jan (2000), *Catalogue of Turkish manuscripts in the Library of Leiden University and other collections in the Netherlands*, I. *Comprising the acquisitions of Turkish manuscripts in the seventeenth and eighteenth centuries*, Leiden: Legatum Warnerianum, Leiden University Library (Bibliotheca Universitatis Leidensis Codices manuscripti, 30).

Schmidt, Jan (2002), *Catalogue of Turkish manuscripts in the Central Library of the University of Leiden and other Collections in the Netherlands*, II, Leiden: Legatum Warnerianum, Leiden University Library (Bibliotheca Universitatis Leidensis Codices manuscripti, 34).

Schmidt, Jan (2006), *Catalogue of Turkish manuscripts in the Library of Leiden University and other collections in the Netherlands*, III. *Comprising the acquisitions of Turkish manuscripts in Leiden University Library between 1970 and 2003*, Leiden: Legatum Warnerianum, Leiden University Library (Bibliotheca Universitatis Leidensis Codices manuscripti, 39).

Schmidt, Jan (2011), *A Catalogue of the Turkish Manuscripts in the John Rylands University Library at Manchester*, Leiden: Brill (Islamic Manuscripts and Books, 2).

Schmidt, Thomas S. (2001), *Basilii Minimi in Gregorii Nazianzeni orationem XXXVIII commentarii*, Turnhout: Brepols (Corpus Christianorum. Series Graeca, 46; Corpus Nazianzenum 13).

Schmitz, Barbara (ed.) (1992), *Islamic Manuscripts in the New York Public Library*, I, New York: Oxford University Press.

Schneider, Roger (1995), 'À propos de la vocalisation de l'écriture éthiopienne', *Groupe linguistique d'études chamito-sémitique. Compte-rendus des séances*, 31, 107–108.

Schopen, Armin (2006), *Tinten und Tuschen des arabisch-islamischen Mittelalters. Dokumentation – Analyse – Rekonstruktion. Ein Beitrag zur materiellen Kultur des Vorderen Orients*, Göttingen: Vandenhoeck & Ruprecht (Abhandlungen der Akademie der Wissenschaften zu Göttingen, Philologisch-Historische Klasse, 3. Folge, 269).

Schreiner, Peter (1983), 'Zur Pergamentherstellung in byzantinischen Osten', *Codices manuscripti*, 9, 122–127.

Schreiner, Peter – Doris Oltrogge (2011), *Byzantinische Tinten-, Tuschen- und Farbrezepte*, Wien: Verlag der Österreichischen Akademie der Wissenschaften (Denkschriften der philosophisch-historischen Klasse, 419, Veröffentlichungen der Kommission für Schrift- und Buchwesen des Mittelalters, 4).

Schubert, Paul (1996), *Les papyrus de Genève. 3, Nos 118-146: textes littéraires et documentaires*, Genève: Bibliothèque publique et universitaire.

Schubert, Paul (2009), 'Editing a papyrus', in: *The Oxford Handbook of Papyrology*, ed. by Roger S. Bagnall, Oxford: Oxford University Press, 197–215.

Schulthess, Friedrich (1903), *Lexicon Syropalaestinum*, Berlin.

Schulthess, Friedrich (1905), *Christlich-Palästinische Fragmente aus der Omajjaden-Moschee zu Damaskus*, Berlin: Weidmansche Buchhandlung (Abhandlungen der königlichen Gesellschaft der Wissenschaften zu Göttingen. Philologisch-Historische Klasse, N.F., 8, 3).

Schulthess, Friedrich (1924), *Grammatik des christlich-palästinischen aramäisch*, Tübingen.

Schüssler, Karlheinz (forthcoming), 'Zur 14C-Datierung der koptischen Pergamenthandschriften sa 11, sa 615 und sa 924', in: *Proceedings of the Tenth International Congress of Coptic Studies*, ed. by Paola Buzi – Alberto Camplani, Louvain: Peeters.

Scripta & e-Scripta, <http://www.ceeol.com/aspx/publicationdetails.aspx?publicationid=f7af099a-3b1c-477b-989f-cad8aa2d485e>, last access October 2014.

Searby, Denis M. (2007), *The Corpus Parisinum. A Critical Edition of the Greek Text with Commentary and English Translation. A Medieval Anthology of Greek Texts from the Pre-Socratics to the Church Fathers, 600 B.C. - 700 A.D.*, I–II, Lewiston, NY: Edwin Mellen Press.

Searby, Denis M. (2011), 'Intertitles in Stobaeus', in: *Thinking through Excerpts. Studies on Stobaeus*, ed. by Gretchen Reydam Schils, Turnhout: Brepols (Monothéismes et philosophie, 14), 23–70.

Sed-Rajna, Gabrielle (1970), *Les manuscrits hébreux de Lisbonne: un atelier de copistes et d'enlumineurs au XVe siècle*, Paris: Centre national de la recherche scientifique (Documents, études et répertoires, 16).

Sed-Rajna, Gabrielle (1994), *Les manuscrits hébreux enluminés des bibliothèques de France*, Louvain: Peeters (Corpus of Illuminated Manuscripts, 7, Oriental Series, 3).

Segre, Cesare (1976), 'Critique textuelle, théorie des ensembles et dyasistème', *Bulletin de la Classe des lettres et des sciences morales et politiques de l'Académie royale de Belgique*, 62, 279–292.

Segre, Cesare (1979), *Semiotica filologica. Testo e modelli culturali*, Torino: Einaudi (Einaudi Paperbacks, 100).

Sels, Lara (2009), *Gregory of Nyssa, De hominis opificio. O obrazě člověka. The Fourteenth-Century Slavonic Translation. A Critical Edition with Greek Parallel and Commentary*, Köln: Böhlau (Bausteine zur slavischen Philologie und Kulturgeschichte. Neue Folge. Reihe B: Editionen, 21).

Sels, Lara (2013), 'Early Slavic Hagiography Translation in the Vidin Miscellany', *Comparative Oriental Manuscript Studies Newsletter*, 5, 37–40.

Sels, Lara – Dieter Stern (2012), 'Preparing a Digital Edition of the Bdinski Sbornik', in: *Преоткриване: Супрасълски сборник, старобългарски паметник от X век* (*Preotkrivane: Suprasălski sbornik, starobălgarski pametnik ot X vek*, 'Rediscovering: Codex Suprasliensis, a Slavonic monument of the tenth century'), ed. by Anisava Miltenova, Sofia: East West Publisher, 355–367.

Senguerdius, Wolferdus et al. (1716–1741) {W.F. – Jacobus Gronovius – Johannes Heyman}, *Catalogus Librorum tam impressorum quam manuscriptorum Bibliothecae publicae Universitatis Lugduno-Batavae*, Leiden: Vander.

Sergew Hable Selassie (1981), *Bookmaking in Ethiopia*, Leiden: Karstens Drukkers.

Sergew Hable Selassie (1987–1988), 'An Early Ethiopian Manuscript EMML 8509 (Ethiopian Manuscript Microfilm Library)', *Quaderni di Studi Etiopici*, 8-9, 5–27.

Sergew Hable Selassie (1991), 'An Early Ethiopian Manuscript EMML 8509 (Ethiopian Manuscript Microfilm Library)', *Ostkirchliche Studien* 40, 64–80.

Şeşen, Ramazan (1997), 'Esquisse d'une histoire du développement des colophons dans les manuscrits musulmans', in: *Scribes et manuscrits du Moyen-Orient*, ed. by François Déroche – Francis Richard, Paris: Bibliothèque nationale de France, 189–221.

Ševčenko, Nancy Patterson (1990), *Illustrated manuscripts of the Metaphrastian Menologion*, Chicago: The University of Chicago Press (Studies in medieval manuscript illumination).

Sezgin, Fuat (1967–2010), *Geschichte des arabischen Schrifttums*, I–XV, Leiden – Frankfurt: Brill - Universität Frankfurt.

SfarData. The Codicological Data-Base of the Hebrew Palaeography Project, <http://sfardata.nli.org.il/>, last access May 2014.

Shailor, Barbara A. (1988), *The Medieval Book. Illustrated from the Beinecke Rare Book and Manuscript Library*, New Haven, Yale University: Beineke Rare Book and Manuscript Library (Medieval Academy Reprints for Teaching, 28).

Shailor, Barbara A. (1996), 'A Cataloger's View', in: *The Whole Book. Cultural Perspectives on the Medieval Miscellany*, ed. by Stephen G. Nichols – Siegfried Wenzel, Ann Arbor, MI: University of Michigan Press, 153–167.

Sharing Ancient Wisdoms, <http://www.ancientwisdoms.ac.uk/library/arabicphilos>, last access May 2014.

Sharpe, John Lawrence (1996), 'The Earliest Bindings with Wooden Board Covers: The Coptic Contribution to Binding Construction', in: *Erice 96, International Conference on Conservation and Restoration of Archive and Library Materials, Erice (Italy), CCSEM, 22nd–29th April 1996: Pre-prints*, II, ed. by Piero Colaizzi – Daniela Costanini, Roma: Istituto centrale per la patologia del libro, 381–400.

Sīdī ʿUmar b. ʿAlī [Sidi Amar] et al. (1995–1998), فهرس مخطوطات مركز أحمد بابا للتوثيق والبحوث التاريخية بتنبكتو (*Fihris maḫṭūṭāt Markaz Aḥmad Bābā li-ʾl-Tawṯīq wa-ʾl-Buḥūṯ al-Tārīḫiyya bi-Tunbuktū*) / *Handlist of Manuscripts in the Centre de Documentation et de Recherches Historiques Ahmed Baba, Timbuktu, Mali*, I–V, London: Al-Furqān (Handlists of Islamic Manuscripts).

Signes Codoñer, Juan (2014), 'Towards a vocabulary for rewriting in Byzantium', in: *Textual Transmission in Byzantium: between Textual Criticism and Quellenforschung*, ed. by Juan Signes Codoñer – Inmaculada Pérez Martín, Turnhout: Brepols (Lectio Studies in the Transmission of Texts and Ideas, 2), 61–92.

Sijpesteijn, Petra M. (2008), 'Palaeography', in: *Encyclopedia of Arabic Language and Linguistics*, III, Leiden: Brill, 513–524.

Silbergeld, Jerome (1982), *Chinese Painting Style: Media, Methods, and Principles of Form*, Seattle: University of Washington Press.

Silogava, Valeri (1986), სვანეთის წერილობითი ძეგლები. I: ისტორიული საბუთები და სულთა მატიანეები (*Svanetis çerilobiti ʒeglebi.* I: *Isṭoriuli sabutebi da sulta maṭianebi*, 'Written Monuments of Svanetia. I: Historical Documents and Lists of Parishioners'), Tbilisi: Mecniereba.

Simonet, Jean-Marie (2010), 'Les variantes communes des versions syriaques, arméniennes et latines dans le Discours 41 de Grégoire de Nazianze', in: *Studia Nazianzenica II*, ed. by Andrea Schmidt, Turnhout: Brepols (Corpus Christianorum. Series Graeca, 73; Corpus Nazianzenum, 24), 585–604.

Simoni, Pavel Konstantinovič (1903), *Опытъ сборника свѣдѣній по исторіи и техникѣ книгопереплетнаго художества на Руси* (*Opyt" sbornika svěděnïj po istorïi i technikě knigoperepletnago chudožestva na Rusi*, 'An attempt at a collection of information about the art of bookbinding in Russia'), St Petersburg: Imperatorskoe Obščestvo lubitelej drevnej pis′mennosti (Pamjatniki drevnej pis′mennosti i iskusstva, 122).

Simoni, Pavel Konstantinovič (1906), *Къ исторіи обихода книгописца, переплетчика и иконнаго писца при книжномъ и иконномъ строеніи* (*K" istorii obichoda knigopisca, perepletčika i ikonnago pisca pri knižnom" i ikonnom" stroenïi*, 'Towards the history of the practice of the scribe, binder and icon-painter in the making of books and icons'), St Petersburg: Imperatorskoe Obščestvo lubitelej drevnej pis′mennosti (Pamjatniki drevnej pis′mennosti i iskusstva, 161).

Simpson, Marianna Shreve (1980), *Arab and Persian Painting in the Fogg Art Museum*, Cambridge, MA: Fogg Art Museum – Harvard University.

Sims-Williams, Nicholas (1976), 'The Sogdian fragments of the British library', *Indo-Iranian Journal*, 18, 43–82.

Sinko, Taddeus (1917), *De traditione orationum Gregorii Nazianzeni*, Cracoviae: Gebethner et Wolff (Meletemata Patristica, 2).

Sirat, Colette (1989), 'Le codex de bois', in: *Les débuts du codex. Actes de la journée d'étude organisée à Paris les 3 et 4 juillet 1985 par l'Institut de papyrologie de la Sorbonne et l'Institut de recherche et d'histoire des textes*, ed. by Alain Blanchard, Turnhout: Brepols (Bibliologia: Elementa ad Librorum Studia Pertinentia, 9), 37–40.

Sirat, Colette (1992), 'Les éditions critiques: un mythe?', in: *Les problèmes posés par l'édition critique des textes anciens et médiévaux*, ed. by Jacqueline Hamesse, Louvain-la-Neuve: Brepols (Université Catholique de Louvain. Publications de l'Institut d'Études Médiévales. Textes, Études, Congrès, 13), 159–171.

Sirat, Colette (2002), *Hebrew Manuscripts of the Middle Ages*, Cambridge: Cambridge University Press.

Sirat, Colette et al. (1972) {C.S. – Malachi Beit-Arié – Annie Genevois – Mordechai Glatzer et al.}, *Manuscrits médiévaux en caractères hébraïques portant des indications de date jusqu'à 1540*, I: *Bibliothèque de France et d'Israël*: *Manuscrits de grand format*, Paris: Centre national de la recherche scientifique.

Sirat, Colette et al. (1985) {C.S. – Malachi Beit-Arié – Michèle Dukan – Felix Klein-Franke – Hermann Harrauer – Ada Yardeni}, *Les papyrus en caractères hébraïques trouvés en Égypte*, Paris: Éditions du Centre national de la recherche scientifique (Manuscrits médiévaux en caractères hébraïques).

Sirat, Colette et al. (2002) {C.S. – Malachi Beit-Arié – Mordechai Glatzer}, *Codices hebraicis litteris exarati quo tempore scripti fuerint exhibentes*, III: *de 1085 à 1140*, Turnhout: Brepols (Monumenta Palaeographica Medii Aevi, Series Hebraica).

Sirat, Colette – Malachi Beit-Arié (1986), *Manuscrits médiévaux en caractères hébraïques portant des indications de date jusqu'à 1540*, III: *Bibliothèques de France et d'Israël*: *Manuscrits de petit format de 1471-1540*, Paris: Centre national de la recherche scientifique.

Sirinian, Anna (2014), 'On the Historical and Literary Value of the Colophons in Armenian Manuscripts', in: *Armenian Philology in the Modern Era*: *From Manuscript to Digital Text*, ed. by Valentina Calzolari, with collaboration of Michael E. Stone, Leiden: Brill (Handbook of Oriental Studies / Handbuch der Orientalistik, VIII, 23/1), 65–100.

Six, Veronika (1989), *Äthiopische Handschriften* 2: *Die Handschriften der Bayerischen Staatsbibliothek*, Wiesbaden: Steiner (Verzeichnis der orientalischen Handschriften in Deutschland, 20/5).

Six, Veronika (1994), *Äthiopische Handschriften* 3: *Handschriften deutscher Bibliotheken, Museen, und aus Privatbesitz*, Wiesbaden: Steiner (Verzeichnis der orientalischen Handschriften in Deutschland, 20/6).

Six, Veronika (1999), *Äthiopische Handschriften vom Ṭānāsee* 3: *nebst einem Nachtrag zum Katalog der äthiopischen Handschriften Deutscher Bibliotheken und Museen*, Stuttgart: Steiner (Verzeichnis der orientalischen Handschriften in Deutschland, 20/3).

Siyāqī, Muḥammad Dabīr (1348 Š./1969 CE), گزیدهٔ تاریخ بیهقی : متن فارسی از قرن پنجم هجری (*Guzīda-yi Tārīḫ-i Bayhaqī: matn-i Fārsī az qarn-i panǧum-i Hiǧrī*, 'A Selection from the History of Bayhaqī: the Persian text from the Fifth Century Hegira'), Tehran: Širkat-i Sahamī-yi kitābḫā-yi Ǧībī.

Skepastianu, Maria (1995), *Library Disaster Planning* (*prepared for the IFLA Section on Conservation and Preservation*), The Hague: International Federation of Library Associations and Institutions.

Sklare, David (2003), 'A Guide to Collections of Karaite Manuscripts', in: *Karaite Judaism: A Guide to Its History and Literary Sources*, ed. by Meira Polliack, Leiden: Brill (Handbook of Oriental Studies / Handbuch der Orientalistik, I/73), 893–924.

Sloggett, Robyn (2008), 'Raman Analysis of Pigments Found in Middle Eastern Manuscripts in the University of Melbourne Collection', in: *Contributions to the Symposium on the Care and Conservation of Middle Eastern manuscripts. The University of Melbourne, Australia, 26-28 November 2007*, ed. by Robyn Sloggett, Melbourne: Centre for Cultural Materials Conservation, 89–99.

Slovo. Towards a Digital Library of South Slavic Manuscripts, <http://slovo-aso.cl.bas.bg>, last access October 2014.

Smbat Sparapet (1980), *La Chronique attribuée au Connétable Smbat*, translated by Gerard Dédéyan, Paris: Geuthner (Documents relatifs à l'histoire des croisades publiés par l'Académie des inscriptions et belles-lettres, 13).

Smelik, Willem (2007), 'Code-switching: The Public Reading of the Bible in Hebrew, Aramaic and Greek', in: *Was ist ein Text? Alttestamentliche, ägyptologische und altorientalistische Perspektiven*, ed. by Ludwig Morenz – Stefan Schorch, Berlin: De Gruyter (Beihefte zur Zeitschrift für die Alttestamentliche Wissenschaft, 362), 123–151.

Šmidt, S. O. et al. (eds) (1984), *Сводный каталог славяно-русских рукописных книг, хранящихся в СССР, XI–XIII вв.* (*Svodnyj katalog slavjano-russkich rukopisnych knig, chranjaščichsja v SSSR, XI–XIII vv.*, 'General catalogue of Slavonic-Russian manuscripts kept in the USSR, eleventh-thirteenth centuries'), Moskva: Nauka.

Smith, Margit J. (2012), 'Die erste internationale Konferenz zur Erhaltung und Ausbesserung alter Handschriften', in: *Care and Conservation of Manuscripts 13. Proceedings of the thirteenth international seminar held at the University of Copenhagen* 13th*–*15th *April 2011*, ed. by Matthew James Driscoll, Copenhagen: Museum Tusculanum Press, 33–47.

Sobczynski, Elisabeth – nun Antonia (2013), 'The new Deir al-Surian Library and Conservation Centre', *ICON news*, 46, 20–23.

Soldati, Agostino (2014), 'Papyrus', in: *Encyclopaedia Aethiopica*, V, ed. by Siegbert Uhlig, 476.

Somers, Véronique (1997), *Histoire des collections complètes des Discours de Grégoire de Nazianze*, Louvain-la-Neuve: Peeters (Publications de l'Institut Orientaliste de Louvain, 48).

Somers, Véronique (2001), 'Description des collections complètes des Orationes de Grégoire de Nazianze: quelques compléments', *Byzantion*, 71, 462–504.

Somers, Véronique (2002), 'Les collections byzantines de XVI discours de Grégoire de Nazianze', *Byzantinische Zeitschrift*, 95, 102–135.

Somers, Véronique (2009), 'Les palimpsestes de Grégoire de Nazianze. Heuristique', in: *Palimpsestes et éditions de textes: les textes littéraires. Actes du colloque tenu à Louvain-la-Neuve* (*septembre 2003*), ed. by Véronique Somers, Louvain-la-Neuve: Université catholique de Louvain, Institut orientaliste (Publications de l'Institut Orientaliste de Louvain, 56), 53–69.

Sony, Behnam (1993), *Le catalogue des manuscrits du Patriarcat au Couvent de Charfet - Liban*, Beyrouth: The Convent.

Sony, Behnam (1997),فهرس مخطوطات دير الآباء الدومنيكان في الموصل / *Le catalogue des manuscrits du couvent des Dominicains, Mossoul* (*Fihris maḫṭūṭāt Dayr al-Ābā' al-Dūminīkān fī 'l-Mawṣil*), Mosul: Imprimerie des Pères dominicains.

Sony, Behnam (2005), فهرس مخطوطات دير مار بهنام الشهيد (*Fihris maḫṭūṭāt Dayr Mār Bahnām al-Šahīd*, 'Catalogue of manuscrips of the Monastery of Mar Behnam the Martyr'), Baghdad.

Sosower, Mark (2004), *Signa officinarum chartariarum in codicibus graecis saeculo sexto decimo fabricatis in bibliothecis Hispaniae*, Amsterdam: A.M. Hakkert.

Sotheby's Catalogue of Important Oriental Manuscripts and Miniatures: the Property of the Hagop Kevorkian Found, 2 May 1977, London: Sotheby's, 1977.

Soudavar, Abolalla (1992), *Art of the Persian courts: Selections from the Art and History Trust Collection*, New York: Rizzoli.

Spanheim, Friedrich (1674), *Catalogus Bibliothecae publicae Lugduno Batavae*, Leiden: apud viduam & heredes Johannis Elsevirii.

Spatharakis, Johannis (1981), *Corpus of Dated Illuminated Greek Manuscripts to the Year 1453*, Leiden: Brill (Byzantina Neederlandica, 8).

Spencer, Diana (1967), 'Trip to Wag and Northern Wällo', *Journal of Ethiopian Studies*, 5/1, 95–108.

Spina, Angela (ed.) (2013), *Orientalisti italiani e aspetti dell'Orientalismo in Italia. In memoria di Mirella Galletti*, Benevento: AIC – Edizioni Labrys.

Spitaler, Anton (1935), *Die Verszählung des Koran nach islamischer Überlieferung*, mit Vorwort von Otto Pretzl, München: Verlag der Bayerischen Akademie der Wissenschaften, in Kommission bei der C. H. Beck'schen Verlagsbuchhandlung (Sitzungsberichte der Bayerischen Akademie der Wissenschaften. Philosophisch-Historische Abteilung, 1935/11).

Spitaler, Anton (1960), 'Die Schreibung des Typus ṣlwh im Koran. Ein Beitrag zur Erklärung der koranischen Orthographie', *Wiener Zeitschrift für die Kunde des Morgenlandes*, 56, 212–226.

Spitaler, Anton (1994), 'Bemerkungen zu Hans Wehr's Ausgabe der Wunderbaren Erzählungen und Seltsamen Geschichten', *Oriens*, 34, 387–403.

Средновековни словенски ракописи во Македонија (*Srednovekovni slovenski rakopisi vo Makedonija*, 'Mediaeval Slavonic Manuscripts in Macedonia'), <http://staroslovenski.nubsk.edu.mk>, last access May 2014.

Sreznevskij, Izmail I. (1885), *Славяно-русская палеография XI–XIV вв.* (*Slavjano-russkaja paleografija XI–XIV vv.*, 'Slavonic-Russian palaeography of the 11th–14th centuries'), St Petersburg: Balašev.

Standaert, Benoît (1976), 'L'Évangile de Vérité: Critique et Lecture', *New Testament Studies*, 22, 243–275.

Stathis, Gr. (1975, 1976, 1993), *Τα χειρόγραφα βυζαντινής μουσικής – Άγιον Όρος. Κατάλογος περιγραφικός των χειρογράφων κωδίκων βυζαντινής μουσικής, των αποκειμένων εν ταις βιβλιοθήκαις των ιερών μονών και σκήτεων του Αγίου Όρους*, I–III, Athens: Ίδρυμα Βυζαντινης Μουσικολογίας.

Stathis, Gr. (2006), *Τα χειρόγραφα βυζαντινής μουσικής – Μετέωρα. Κατάλογος περιγραφικός των χειρογράφων της ελληνικής ψαλτικής τέχνης, βυζαντινής και μεταβυζαντινής, των αποκειμένων εις τας βιβλιοθήκας των ιερών μονών των Μετεώρων*, Athens: Ίδρυμα Βυζαντινης Μουσικολογίας.

Stchoukine, Ivan et al. (1971) {I.S. – Barbara Flemming – Paul Luft – Hanna Sohrweide}, *Illuminierte Islamische Handschriften*, Wiesbaden: Steiner (Verzeichnis der Orientalischen Handschriften in Deutschland, 16).

Steel, Carlos et al. (eds) (2007) {C.S. – Pieter d'Hoine – Caroline Macé}, *Procli In Parmenidem commentaria*, t. I: *books I–III*, Oxford: Clarendon Press (Oxford Classical Texts).

Steensland, Lars (2005), 'Trash and Treasure. Russian Parchment Fragments in Swedish Archives', in: *Medieval Book Fragments in Sweden. An International Seminar in Stockholm 13–16 November 2003*, ed. by Jan Brunius, Stockholm: Almqvist & Wiksell International (Kungliga Vitterhets Historie och Antikvitets Akademien / Kungliga Vitterhets Historie och Antikvitets Akademien Stockholm: Konferenser, 58), 210–225.

Stegemann, Viktor (1936), *Koptische Paläographie*, Heidelberg: F. Bilabel (Quellen und Studien, 1).

Stein, Peter (2010), *Die altsüdarabischen Minuskelinschriften auf Holzstäbchen aus der Bayerischen Staatsbibliothek in München. I. Die Inschriften der mittel- und spätsabäischen Periode.* 1. Teil: *Text*, 2. Teil: *Verzeichnisse und Tafeln*, Tübingen: Ernst Wasmuth Verlag (Deutsches Archäologisches Institut, Epigraphische Forschungen auf der Arabischen Halbinsel, 5).

Steinschneider, Moritz (1852–1860), *Catalogus librorum hebraeorum in bibliotheca Bodleiana*, I–II, Berlin: Friedlaender.

Steinschneider, Moritz (1858), *Catalogus codicum hebraeorum Bibliothecae Academiae Lugduno-Batavae*, Leiden: Brill.

Steinschneider, Moritz (1875), *Die hebräischen Handschriften der K. Hof- und Staatsbibliothek in München*, München: Palm'sche Buchhandlung.

Steinschneider, Moritz (1878), *Catalog der hebräischen Handschriften in der Staats- und Universitätsbibliothek zu Hamburg und der sich anschließenden in anderen Sprachen*, Hamburg: Meissner (Katalog der Handschriften der Staats- und Universitätsbibliothek Hamburg, 1).

Steinschneider, Moritz (1897), *Verzeichniss der hebräischen Handschriften*, I–II, Berlin: Asher (Die Handschriften-verzeichnisse der Königlichen Bibliothek zu Berlin, 2/1-2).

Stemberger, Günter (2004), 'La formation et la conception du canon dans la pensée rabbinique', in: *Recueils normatifs et canons dans l'Antiquité: perspectives nouvelles sur la formation des canons juif et chrétien dans leur contexte culturel: Actes du colloque organisé dans le cadre du programma plurifacultaire 'La Bible à la croisée des saviors' de l'Université de Genève 11-12 avril 2002*, ed. by Enrico Norelli, Prahins: Éditions du Zèbre (Publications de l'Institut romand des sciences bibliques, 3), 113–131.

Sterligova, I.A. (ed.) (2013), *Byzantine Antiquities. Works of Art from the Fourth to Fifteenth Centuries in the Collection of the Moscow Kremlin Museums*, Moscow: Pinakothēkē.

Stern, S.M. (1969), 'A manuscript from the library of the Ghaznawid Amir ʿAbd al-Rashīd', in: *Paintings from Islamic lands*, ed. by Ralph H. Pinder-Wilson, Columbia, SC: University of South Carolina Press, 7–31.

Stern, Dieter (2013), 'Изучая источники Бдинского сборника: слово об Авраамии Кидунском и его племяннице Марии (*Izučaja istočniki bdinskogo sbornika: Slovo ob Avramii Kidunskom i ego plemjannice Marii*, 'In Search of the Sources of the Bdinski Sbornik: The Story of Abraham of Qidun and His Niece Mary')', *Starobălgarska literatura*, 47/1, 74–91.

Sternbach, Leo (1887, 1888, 1889), 'Gnomologium Vaticanum e codice Vaticano graeco 743', *Wiener Studien*, 9, 175–206; 10, 1–49, 211–260; 11, 43–64, 192–242.

Stojanović, Ljubomir (1903), *Katalog Narodne biblioteke u Beogradu*, Beograd: Izd. i štampa Kralj.-srpske državne štamparije.

Stone, Michael E. (1982), *The Armenian Inscriptions from the Sinai. With Appendices on the Georgian and Latin Inscriptions by Michel van Esbroeck and William Adler*, Cambridge, MA: Harvard University Press (Harvard Armenian Texts and Studies, 6).

Stone, Michael E. (1995), 'Colophons in Armenian Manuscripts', *Scribi e colofoni. Le sottoscrizioni di copisti dalle origini all'avvento della stampa. Atti del seminario di Erice, X Colloquio del Comité international de paléographie latine (23-28 ottobre 1993)*, 463–471.

Stone, Michael E. (1998), 'The Mixed Erkatʿagir-Bolorgir Script in Armenian Manuscripts', *Le Muséon*, 111, 293–317.

Stone, Michael et al. (eds) (2002) {M.S. – Dickran Kouymjian – Henning Lehmann}, *Album of Armenian Paleography*, Aarhus: Aarhus University Press. Armenian translation: Erevan–Holy Ējmiacin: Mecn Tigran Press, 2006.

Storey, Charles Ambrose (1927–1958), *Persian Literature, A Bio-bibliographical Survey*, I–II:1, London: Luzac.

Storey, Charles Ambrose (1971–1977), *Persian Literature, A Bio-bibliographical Survey*, II:2-3, Oxford: Royal Asiatic Society.

Störk, Lothar (1995), *Koptische Handschriften.* 2: *Die Handschriften der Staats- und Universitätsbibliothek Hamburg.* Teil 2: *Die Handschriften aus Dair Anba Maqar*, Stuttgart: Franz Steiner (Verzeichnis der orientalischen Handschriften in Deutschland, 21/2).

Störk, Lothar (1996), *Koptische Handschriften.* 3: *Die Handschriften der Staats- und Universitätsbibliothek Hamburg.* Teil 3: *Addenda und Corrigenda zu Teil 1*, Stuttgart: Franz Steiner (Verzeichnis der orientalischen Handschriften in Deutschland, 21/3).

Störk, Lothar (2002), *Koptische Handschriften.* 4: *Die Handschriften der Staatsbibliothek zu Berlin.* 1, *Liturgische Handschriften* 1, Stuttgard: Franz Steiner (Verzeichnis der orientalischen Handschriften in Deutschland, 21/4).

Strelcyn, Stefan (1954), *Catalogue des manuscrits éthiopiens* (*Collection Griaule*), IV, Paris: Imprimerie nationale.

Strelcyn, Stefan (1976), *Catalogue des manuscrits éthiopiens de l'Accademia Nazionale dei Lincei. Fonds Conti Rossini et Fonds Caetani 209, 375, 376, 377, 378*, Roma: Accademia Nazionale dei Lincei (Indici e Sussidi Bibliografici della Biblioteca, 9).

Strelcyn, Stefan (1978), *Catalogue of Ethiopian Manuscripts in the British Library acquired since the Year 1877*, London: British Museum.

Strothmann, Werner (1978), *Codex syriacus secundus. Bibel-Palimpsest aus dem 6./7. Jh.* (*Katalog Hiersemann 500/3*), Wiesbaden: Harrassowitz (Göttinger Orientforschungen. Reihe 1, Syriaca, 13).

Studi 1992 = *Studi su codici e papiri filosofici*: *Platone, Aristotele, Ierocle*, Firenze: Olschki, 1992 (Accademia Toscana di Scienze e Lettere 'La Colombaria'. Studi, 129; Studi e Testi per il 'Corpus dei Papiri Filosofici Greci e Latini', 6).

Stussi, Alfredo (2002), *Breve avviamento alla filologia italiana*, Bologna: Il Mulino.

Stussi, Alfredo (2004), 'Forme e Sostanze: 'Il Cortigiano' di Amedeo Quondam', *Ecdotica*, 1, 157–209.

Stussi, Alfredo (2006), *Fondamenti di critica testuale*, Bologna: Il Mulino.

Stutzmann, Dominique – Piotr Tylus (2007), *Les manuscrits médievaux français et occitans de la Preussische Staatsbibliothek et de la Staatsbibliothek zu Berlin - Preussischer Kulturbesitz*, Wiesbaden: Harrassowitz (Staatsbibliothek Preussischer Kulturbesitz. Kataloge der Handschriftenabteilung: Reihe 1. Handschriften, 5).

Šul'gina, E.V. (2000), *Русская книжная скоропись* (*Russkaja knižnaja skoropis'*, 'Russian book cursive'), St Petersburg: Bulanin.

Sundermann, Werner (1981), *Mitteliranische manichäische Texte kirchengeschichtlichen Inhalts*, Berlin: Akademie-Verlag (Berliner Turfantexte, 11).

Sundermann, Werner (1992), *Der Sermon vom Licht-Nous. Eine Lehrschrift des östlichen Manichäismus. Edition der parthischen und sogdischen Version*, Berlin: Akademie-Verlag (Berliner Turfantexte, 17).

Supino Martini, Paola (1995), 'Sul metodo paleografico: formulazione di problemi per una discussione', *Scrittura e Civiltà*, 19, 5–29.

Surgulaʒe, Mzia (1978), ძველი ქართული პალეოგრაფიული ტერმინები (*Ʒveli kartuli ṗaleograpiuli ṭerminebi*, 'Ancient Georgian paleographical terminology'), Tbilisi: Mecniereba.

Swahili manuscripts at the School of Oriental and African Studies, London <http://www.swahilimanuscripts. soas.ac.uk>, last access October 2014.

Swete, Henry B. (1914), *An Introduction to the Old Testament in Greek revised by R.R. Ottley*, Cambridge: Cambridge University Press.

Szirmai, Janos A. (1999), *The Archaeology of Medieval Bookbinding*, Aldershot – Brookfield: Ashgate.

Taddesse Tamrat (1970), 'The Abbots of Däbrä-Hayq, 1248-1535', *Journal of Ethiopian Studies*, 8, 87–117.

Taft, Robert F. (1990), 'The Authenticity of the Chrysostom Anaphora Revisited. Determining the Authorship of Liturgical Texts by Computer', *Orientalia Christiana Periodica*, 56, 5–51.

Tahom, Ilana (2007), *Hebrew Manuscripts. The Power of Script and Image*, London: British Library.

Talman, Michael (1702), *Elenchus librorum Orientalium manuscriptorum, videlicet Græcorum, Arabicorum, Persicorum, Turcicorum* [...] *a domino comite Aloysio Ferdinando Marsigli* [...] *collectorum*, Wien: Cosmerovy.

Tanselle, George Thomas (1983), 'Classical, Biblical, and Medieval Textual Criticism and Modern Editing', *Studies in Bibliography*, 36, 21–68.

Tanselle, George Thomas (1995), 'The Varieties of Scholarly Editing', in: *Scholarly Editing: A Guide to Research*, ed. by David C. Greetham, New York: Modern Language Association of America, 9–32.

Taqaišvili [Takajšvili], Ekvtime (1902; 1903; 1904; 1905; 1907; 1908; 1909; 1910; 1911; 1912), 'Описаніе рукописей библіотеки Общества распространенія грамотности среди грузинского населенія (*Opisanïe rukopisej biblïoteki Obščestva rasprostranenïja gramotnosti sredi gruzinskogo naselenïja*, 'Description of the manuscripts of the library of the Society for the Promotion of Literacy among the Georgian population') [1-10]', *Sbornik materialov dlja opisanija městnostej i plemen Kavkaza*, 31, 1–202; 32, 15–232; 33, 1–134; 34, 1–162; 36, 1–132; 37, 1–224; 39, 1–199; 40, 1–64; 41,1–96; 42, 1–64.

Taqaišvili [Takajšvili], Ekvtime (1916), *Адышское эвангеліе. 200 фототипическихъ таблицъ* (*Adysškoe ėvangelïe. 200 fototipičeskich" tablic"*, 'The Adysh evangeliary. 200 phototypic tables'), Moskva: Imperatorskoe Moskovskoe archeologičeskoe obščestvo (Materialy po archeologii Kavkaza, 14).

Taqaišvili [Takaïchvili], Ekvtime (1933), პარიზის ნაციონალური ბიბლიოთეკის ქართული ხელნაწერები და ოცი ქართული საიდუმლო დამწერლობის ნიშანი (*Ṗarizis nacionaluri biblioteḳis kartuli xelnaçerebi da oci kartuli saidumlo damçerlobis nišani*) / *Les manuscrits Géorgiens de la Bibliothèque Nationale de Paris et les vingt alphabets secrets Géorgiens*, Paris.

Tarayan, Zemfira R. (1978), *Набойка в Армении* (*Nabojka v Armenii*, 'Stamping in Armenia'), Erevan: Academy of Sciences.

Tašyan [Tašean, Dashian], Yakovbos [Jacob] (1891–1895), Ցուցակ հայերէն ձեռագրաց Մատենադարանին Մխիթարեանց ի Վիեննա (*C'uc'ak hayerēn jeṙagrac' Matenadaranin Mxit'areanc' i Vienna*). *Catalog der Armenischen Handschriften in der Mechitharisten-Bibliothek zu Wien*, I–II, Wien: Mechitharisten-Buchdruckerei (Haupt-Catalog der armenischen Handschriften, 1-2).

Tašyan [Tašean, Dashian], Yakovbos [Jacob] (1898), Ակնարկ մը հայ հնագրութեան վրայ. Ուսմնասիրութիւն Հայոց գրչութեան արուեստին (*Aknark mə hay hnagrut'ean vray. Usmnasirut'iwn Hayoc' grč'ut'ean aruestin*, 'An Overview of Armenian Palaeography: A Study of the Art of Armenian Writing'), Wien: Mechitharisten-Buchdruckerei (Azgayin matenadaran (National Library), 28).

Tattam, Henry (1853), 'A Catalogue of the Rev. H. Tattam's Coptic and Sahidic Manuscripts Purchased or Copied in Egypt', *Zeitschrift der Deutschen Morgenländischen Gesellschaft*, 7, 94–97.

Taye Wolde Medhin (1980-1982), 'La préparation traditionnelle des couleurs en Éthiopie', *Abbay*, 11, 219–224.

Tayec'i, Esayi (1898), Անկանոն գիրք նոր կտակարանաց (*Ankanon girk' nor ktakaranac'*, 'Non-canonical Books of the New Testament'), Venetik: S. Łazar (T'angaran haykakan hin ew nor dprut'eanc', 2).

Tbilisi, National Centre of Manuscripts / ხელნაწერთა ეროვნული ცენტრი (*Xelnaçerta Erovnuli Cenṭri*), <http://www.manuscript.ge/index.php?m=73&ln=eng>, last access 29 November 2014.

Technical Guidelines for Digitizing Archival Materials for Electronic Access: Creation of Production Master Files – Raster Images, <http://www.archives.gov/preservation/technical/guidelines.pdf>, June 2004.

Technical Guidelines for Digitizing Cultural Heritage Materials: Creation of Raster Image Master Files, <http://www.digitizationguidelines.gov/guidelines/FADGI_Still_Image-Tech_Guidelines_2010-08-24.pdf>, August 2010.

TEI. Text encoding initiative, <http://www.tei-c.org/>, last access October 2014.

Teixidor, Javier (1990), 'Deux documents syriaques du IIIe siècle après J.-C. provenant du Moyen-Euphrate', *Comptes-rendus des séances de l'Académie des inscriptions et belles-lettres*, 134/1, 144–166.

Terian, Abraham (2008), *The Armenian Gospel of the Infancy with three early versions of the Protevangelium of James*, Oxford: Oxford University Press.

TEUCHOS, <http://beta.teuchos.uni-hamburg.de/projekt>, last access May 2014.

Teule, Herman (1997), 'A Fifteenth-century Spiritual Anthology from the Monastery of Mar Ḥannanyā', *Het Christelijk Oosten*, 49, 79–102.

Teule, Herman (1998), 'Les compilations monastiques syriaques', in: *Symposium Syriacum VII. Uppsala University, Department of Asian and African Languages 11-14 August 1996*, ed. by René Lavenant, Roma: Pontificio Istituto Orientale (Orientalia Christiana Analecta, 256), 249–262.

Teule, Herman (2008), 'Christian Spiritual Sources in the Ethicon of Barhebraeus', *Journal of Eastern Christian Studies*, 60, 242–264.

Thackeray, Henry StJohn (1909), *A Grammar of the Old Testament in Greek According to the Septuagint*, I, Cambridge: Cambridge University Press.

Thomassen, Einar (2006), *The Spiritual Seed: The Church of the 'Valentinians'*, Leiden: Brill (Nag Hammadi and Manichaean Studies, 60).

Thompson, Herbert (1908), *The Coptic (Sahidic) Version of Certain Books of the Old Testament from a Papyrus in the British Museum*, London: Henry Frowde – Oxford University Press.

Thompson, Herbert (1911), *A Coptic Palimpsest Containing Joshua, Judges, Ruth, Judith and Esther in the Sahidic Dialect*, London: Henry Frowde – Oxford University Press.

Thomson, Francis (1998), 'The Slavonic Translation of the Old Testament', in: *Interpretation of the Bible*, ed. by Jože Krašovec, Ljubljana & Sheffield: Slovenska akademija znanosti in umetnosti & Sheffield Academic Press, 605–920.

Thomson, Garry (1997), *The Museum Environment*, Oxford: Butterworth-Heinemann.

Thomson, Robert W. (1965), *Athanasiana Syriaca*, I. 1. *De Incarnatione*. 2. *Epistula ad Epicteum*, Louvain: Peeters (Corpus Scriptorum Christianorum Orientalium, 257, Scriptores Syri, 114).

Thomson, Robert W. (1995), *The Syriac Version of the Hexaemeron by Basil of Caesarea*, Louvain: Peeters (Corpus Scriptorum Christianorum Orientalium, 550, Scriptores Syri, 222).

Thorndike, Lynn (1946), 'The Problem of the Composite Manuscript', in: *Miscellanea Giovanni Mercati*. VI: *Paleografia, Bibliografia, Varia*, Città del Vaticano: Biblioteca Apostolica Vaticana (Studi e Testi, 126), 93–104.

Thouin, Richard (1999), 'Une approche pratique de la prévention et de l'intervention en cas de sinistre', in: *La prévention et l'intervention en cas de sinistre dans les archives et les bibliothèques: actes des premières Journées sur la conservation préventive, 15-16 mai, 1995*, Arles: Centre de Conservation du Livre, 13–32.

Tiftixoglu, Victor (2004), *Katalog der griechischen Handschriften der Bayerischen Staatsbibliothek München*. Bd. 1. *Codices graeci Monacenses 1-55*, Wiesbaden: Harrassowitz (Catalogus codicum manu scriptorum Bibliothecae Monacensis, 2/1).

Till, Walter Curt (1931), *Osterbrief und Predigt in achmimischem Dialekt*, Leipzig: Dieterich'sche Verlagsbuchhandlung (Studien zur Epigraphik und Papyruskunde, 2.1).

Till, Walter Curt (1940), 'Papyrussammlung der Nationalbibliothek in Wien. Katalog der koptischen Bibelbruchstücke. Die Pergamente', *Zeitschrift für die Neutestamentliche Wissenschaft*, 39, 1–57.

Till, Walter Curt (1958), *Die koptischen Rechtsurkunden der Papyrussammlung der Österreichischen Nationalbibliothek*, Wien: Adolf Holzhausens Nachfolger (Corpus Papyrorum Raineri, 4).

Timoṭe, archbishop (1852), მოხილუჳა წმინდათა და სხუჳათა ადგილთა ტიმოთესგან ქართლისა მთავარ-ეპისკოპოსისა (*Moxilûa çmindata da sxûata adgilta Ṭimotesgan Kartlisa mtavar-episḳoṗosisa*, 'Examination of holy and other places by Timothy, archbishop of Kartli'), Tbilisi: Ḳavḳasiis namesṭniḳis ḳancelaria.

Timpanaro, Sebastiano (1963), *La genesi del metodo del Lachmann*, Firenze: Le Monnier.

Timpanaro, Sebastiano (1973), 'Il contrasto tra i fratelli Schlegel e Franz Bopp sulla struttura e la genesi delle lingue indeuropee', *Critica storica*, 10, 553–590.

Timpanaro, Sebastiano (1985), 'Recentiores e deteriores, codices descripti e codices inutiles', *Filologia e critica*, 10, 164–192.

Timpanaro, Sebastiano (2003), *La genesi del metodo del Lachmann. Con una Presentazione e una Postilla di* Elio Montanari, Torino: UTET (UTET Libreria).

Timpanaro, Sebastiano (2005), *The genesis of Lachmann's method*, translated by Glenn W. Most, Chicago: The University of Chicago Press.

Tischendorf, Constantin von (1855), *Anecdota sacra et profana ex oriente et occidente allata, sive, Notitia codicum Graecorum, Arabicorum, Syriacorum, Copticorum, Hebraicorum, Aethiopicorum, Latinorum, cum excerptis multis maximam partem Graecis et triginta quinque scripturarum antiquissimarum exemplis*, Lipsiae: Apud Emilium Graul.

Tischendorf, Constantin von (1861), *Anecdota sacra et profana ex oriente et occidente allata, sive, Notitia codicum Graecorum, Arabicorum, Syriacorum, Copticorum, Hebraicorum, Aethiopicorum, Latinorum, cum excerptis multis maximam partem Graecis et triginta quinque scripturarum antiquissimarum exemplis*, 2nd edition, Lipsiae: Fries.

Tisserant, Eugène (1911), 'Le plus ancien manuscrit biblique daté. Notes sur trois palimpsestes syriaques des Prophètes', *Revue Biblique*, N.S. 9, 85–95.

Tisserant, Eugène (1912), *Le Calendrier d'Abou'l-Barakat*, Paris: Firmin-Didot (Patrologia orientalis, 48 [10.3]), 245–286.

Tisserant, Eugène (1914), *Specimina Codicum Orientalium*, Bonn: Marcus et Weber (Tabulae in usum scholarum, 8).

Tisserant, Eugène (1932), 'Notes pour servir à la biographie d'Étienne Évode Assémani', *Oriens Christianus*, 7, 264–276.

Titley, Norah M. (1977), *Miniatures from Persian Manuscripts: A Catalogue and Subject Index of Paintings from Persia, India and Turkey in the British Library and the British Museum*, London: British Library.

Titley, Norah M. (1981), *Miniatures from Turkish Manuscripts: A Catalogue and Subject Index of Paintings in the British Library and British Museum*, London: British Library.

TITUS. Thesaurus Indogermanischer Text- und Sprachmaterialien, <http://titus.uni-frankfurt.de/indexe.htm>, last access December 2014.

Tomaszewski, Jacek et al. (forthcoming) {J.T. – Ewa Balicka-Witakowska – Zofia Żukowska}, 'Ethiopian Manuscript Maywäyni 041 with Added Miniature: Codicological and Technological Analysis', *Annales d'Éthiopie*, 29.

Tomaszewski, Jacek – Michael Gervers (forthcoming 2015), 'Technological aspects of the monastic manuscript collection at May Wayni, Ethiopia', in: *From Dust to Digital. Ten Years of the Endangered Archives Programme*, ed. by Maja Kominko, Cambridge: Open Book Publishers, 89–134.

Toomer, Gerald James (1996), *Eastern Wisdom and Learning. The Study of Arabic in Seventeenth-Century England*, Oxford: Oxford University Press.

Toth, Michael – Doug Emery (2011), 'Are Digital Images Really All that Matters? Preserving the Archimedes Palimpsest in Digital Form as a Research Tool', in: *Care and Conservation of Manuscript 12. Proceedings of the Twelfth International Seminar Held at the University of Copenhagen 14th-16th October 2009*, ed. by Matthew J. Driscoll, Copenhagen: Museum Tusculanum Press 2011, 307–319.

Tournerie, Patricia Irwin (1986), *Colour and Dye: Recipes of Ethiopia*, London [private publication]. Reprint London: New Cross Books, 2010.

Touwaide, Alain (2006), 'The development of Paleologan Renaissance. An analysis based on Dioscorides' *De materia medica*', in: *Philosophie et sciences à Byzance de 1204 à 1453. Actes de la Table Ronde organisée au XXe Congrès International d'Études Byzantines (Paris, 2001)*, ed. by Michel Cacouros – Marie-Hélène Congourdeau, Leuven: Peeters (Orientalia Lovaniensia Analecta, 146), 189–224.

Tov, Emanuel (1981), *The Text-Critical Use of the Septuagint in Biblical Research*, Jerusalem: Simor.

Tov, Emanuel (2001), *Textual Criticism of the Hebrew Bible*. Second revised edition, Assen: Van Gorcum.

Tov, Emanuel (2004), *Scribal Practices and Approaches Reflected in the Texts Found in the Judean Desert*, Leiden – Boston: Brill (Studies on the Texts of the Desert of Judah, 54).

Traina, Giusto et al. (2003) {G.T. – Carlo Franco – Dickran Kouymjian – Cecilia Veronese Arslan}, *La Storia di Alessandro il Macedone, Codice miniato armeno del secolo XIV*. I: *Introduction, study of the miniatures, translation, bibliography, index*. II: *Le miniature, facsimile*, Padova: Bottega d'Erasmo ('Helios'. Collana editoriale del Centro Veneto Studi e Ricerche sulle Civiltà Classiche e Orientali, 5).

Traini, Renato (1973), 'I manoscritti arabi esistenti nelle biblioteche di Pavia (Collezione Robecchi Bricchetti)', *Atti dell'Accademia Nazionale dei Lincei – Rendiconti, Classe di Scienze morali, storiche e filologiche*, ser. 8[a], 28, 7-12, 841–865.

Traini, Renato (1975), 'Considerazioni preliminari allo studio dei manoscritti arabi', in: *Onomasticon Arabicum. Sussidi didattici*, I, Roma: IpO – Paris: Centre national de la recherche scientifique, 1–13.

Traini, Renato (2011), *Catalogue of the Arabic Manuscripts in the Biblioteca Ambrosiana*. IV: *Nuovo Fondo: series F-H (Nos. 1296-1778)*, Vicenza: Neri Pozza (Fontes Ambrosiani, n.s. 4).

Les tranchefiles brodées. Étude historique et technique, Paris: Bibliothèque nationale, 1989.

Traube, Ludwig (1909), *Vorlesungen und Abhandlungen. Bd. 1. Zur Paläographie und Handschriftenkunde*, München: C.H. Beck'sche Verlagsbuchhandlung-O. Beck.

Tremblay, Xavier (2012), 'Ibant obscuri uaria sub nocte: Les textes avestiques et leurs recensions des Sassanides au XIIIe s. ad en particulier d'après l'alphabet avestique. Notes de lecture avestiques VIII', in: *The transmission of the Avesta*, ed. by Alberto Cantera, Wiesbaden: Harrassowitz (Iranica, 20), 98–135.

Treu, Kurt (1980), 'Überlieferungs- und Editionsprobleme der Patristik', in: *Griechische Kodikologie und Textüberliefering*, ed. by Dieter Harlfinger, Darmstadt: Wissenschaftliche Buchgesellschaft, 613–628.

Tromonin, Kornelij Jakovlevič – Sokrat A. Klepikov (1844), *Изъясненія знаковъ, видимыхъ въ писчей бумагѣ, посредствомъ которыхъ можно узнавать, когда написаны или напечатаны какіе-либо книги, грамоты, рисунки, картинки и другіе старинныя и не старинныя дела, на которыхъ не означено годовъ* (*Izjasnenïja znakov", vidimych" v pisčej bumagě, posredstvom" kotorych" možno uznavat', kogda napisany ili napečatany kakïe-libo knigi, gramoty, risunki, kartinki i drugïe starinnye i ne starinnye dela, na kotorych" ne označeno godov*, 'An explanation of the signs visible in writing paper, whereby it is possible to discover when any books, documents, drawings, pictures or other items, ancient or not, on which no year is indicated, were written or printed'), Moskva: Tipografija Aleksandra Semena.

Tromp, Johannes (2005), *The Life of Adam and Eve in Greek. A Critical Edition*, Leiden: Brill (Pseudepigrapha Veteris Testamenti Graece, 6).

Troupeau, Gérard (1972–1974), *Catalogue des manuscrits arabes*, Première partie: *Manuscrits chrétiens*, I–II, Paris: Bibliothèque nationale de France.

Troupeau, Gérard (1997), 'Les colophons des manuscrits arabes chrétiens', in: *Scribes et manuscrits du Moyen-Orient*, ed. by François Déroche – Francis Richard, Paris: Bibliothèque nationale de France, 223–231.

Trovato, Paolo (2005), 'Archetipo, stemma codicum e albero reale', *Filologia italiana*, 2, 9–18.

Trovato, Paolo (2013), 'La tradizione manoscritta del Lai de l'ombre. Riflessioni sulle tecniche d'edizione primonovecentesche', *Romania*, 131, 338–380.

Trovato, Paolo (2014), *Everything you Always Wanted to Know about Lachmann's Method. A Non-Standard Handbook of Genealogical Textual Criticism in the Age of Post-Structuralism, Cladistics, and Copy-Text*, introduction by Michael D. Reeve, Padova: Libreria universitaria (Storie e linguaggi).

Türkiye Yazmaları, <http://www.yazmalar.gov.tr/>, last access May 2014.

Türkmen, Hüseyin (2010), *Türkiye Kütüphaneleri Yazma Eserler Katalogları, 1923-2006* (*Catalogues of manuscripts in Turkish libraries, 1923-2006*), İstanbul: Kitabevi Yayınları (Kitabevi, 425).

Turner, Eric G. (1971), *Greek Manuscripts of the Ancient World*, Oxford: Clarendon Press.

Turner, Eric G. (1977), *The Typology of the Early Codex*, Philadelphia: University of Pennsylvania Press (Haney Foundation Series, 18).

Turner, Eric G. (1980), *Greek Papyri. An Introduction*, Oxford: University of Pennsylvania Press.

Turner, Eric G. (1984), *Papiri greci*, Firenze: La Nuova Italia Scientifica.

Uchanova, Elena V. (2007), 'Византийский унциал и славянский устав: проблемы источников и эволюции (*Vizantijskij uncial i slavjanskij ustav: problemy istočnikov i ėvoljucii*, 'Byzantine uncial and Slavonic ustav: problems of origins and evolution')', *Monfokon*, 1, 19–88.

Uchanova, Elena V. (2008), 'Об одном Киевском скриптории последней четверти XI–начала XII в (*Ob odnom Kievskom skriptorii poslednej četverti XI – načala XII v.*, 'On a Kievan scriptorium of the last quarter of the 11th – beginning of the 12th century')', in: *Палеография и кодикология: 300 лет после Монфокона: материалы международной научной конференции, Москва, 14-16 мая 2008 г.* (*Paleografija i kodikologija: 300 let posle Monfokona. Materialy meždunarodnoj naučnoj konferencii, Moskva, 14-16 maja 2008 g.*, 'Paleography and codicology: 300 hundred years after Montfaucon. Materials from the International Scientific Conference, Moscow, 14-16 May 2008'), Moskva: Institut vseobščej istorii RAN, 225–229.

Uchova, T. B. (1960), *Каталог миниатюр, орнамента и гравюр собраний Троице-Сергиевой лавры и Московской Духовной Академии* (*Katalog miniatjur, ornamenta i gravjur sobranij Troice-Sergievoj lavry i Moskovskoj Duchovnoj Akademii*, 'Catalogue of miniatures, ornaments and engravings from the collection of the Trinity Lavra of St Sergius and Moscow Spiritual Academy'), Moskva: Gosudarstvennaja biblioteka (Zapiski otdela rukopisej, 22).

Uhlig, Siegbert (1988), *Äthiopische Paläographie*, Stuttgart: Franz Steiner (Äthiopistische Forschungen, 22).

Uhlig, Siegbert (1989), 'Grundfragen äthiopischer Kodikologie', in: *Les manuscrits du Moyen-Orient. Essais de codicologie et de paléographie. Actes du Colloque d'Istanbul (Istanbul, 26-29 mai, 1986)*, ed. by François Déroche, Istanbul: I.F.E.A – Paris: Bibliothèque nationale (Varia turcica, 8), 35–38.

Uhlig, Siegbert (1990), *Introduction to Ethiopian Paleography*, Stuttgart: Franz Steiner (Äthiopistische Forschungen, 28).

Uhlig, Siegbert (2003), 'Chronography', in: *Encyclopaedia Aethiopica*, I: A-C, ed. by Siegbert Uhlig, Wiesbaden: Harrassowitz, 733–737.

Uhlig, Siegbert – Alessandro Bausi (2007), 'Manuscripts', in: *Encyclopaedia Aethiopica*, III: He–N, ed. by Siegbert Uhlig, Wiesbaden: Harrassowitz, 738–744.

Uhlig, Siegbert – Alessandro Bausi (2010), 'Palaeography', in: *Encyclopaedia Aethiopica*, IV: O–X, ed. by Siegbert Uhlig – Alessandro Bausi, Wiesbaden: Harrassowitz, 101–104.

Ullendorff, Edward (1951), 'Studies in the Ethiopic Syllabary', *Africa*, 21, 207–217.

Uluhogian, Gabriella (2010), *Catalogo dei manoscritti armeni delle biblioteche d'Italia*, Roma: Istituto Poligrafico dello Stato (Indici e cataloghi, nuova serie, 20).

UNESCO (1999), *Disaster Planning: prevention, preparedness, response, recovery*, <http://webworld.unesco.org/safeguarding/en/pdf/txt_sini.pdf>, Paris: UNESCO (Safeguarding our documentary heritage).

UNESCO (2006), *Care and Handling of Manuscripts*, <http://unesdoc.unesco.org/images/0014/001484/ 148463e.pdf>, Paris: UNESCO (Cultural Heritage Protection Handbook, 2).

UNESCO, *Memory of the World Programme* <http://www.unesco.org/new/en/communication-and-information/flagship-project-activities/memory-of-the-world/about-the-programme/objectives/>, last accessed June 2014.

UNIDROIT Convention 1995 <http://www.unidroit.org/instruments/cultural-property/1995-convention>, last accessed June 2014.

Uri, Joannes (1787), *Bibliothecae Bodleianae codicum manuscriptorum Orientalium videlicet Hebraicorum, Chaldaicorum, Syriacorum, Aethiopicorum, Arabicorum, Persicorum, Turcicorum, Copticorumque catalogus...*, I, Oxford: Clarendon Press.

Uthemann, Karl-Heinz (1996), 'Which Variants are Useful in Discovering the Deep Structure of the Manuscript Tradition of a Text?', in: *Studies in stemmatology*, ed. by Pieter van Reenen – Margot van Mulken, Amsterdam – Philadelphia: John Benjamins, 249–261.

ʿUṯmān Kan [Ousmane Kane] (1997), فهرس مخطوطات مكتبة الشيخ مورمباي سيسي و مكتبة الحاج مالك سه و مكتبة الشيخ إبراهيم نياس في السنغال (*Fihris maḫṭūṭāt maktabat al-šayḫ Mūr Mbāi Sīsī wa-maktabat al-ḥāǧǧ Mālik Sīh wa-maktabat al-šayḫ Ibrāhīm Niyās fi 'l-Siniġāl*) / *Handlist of Manuscripts in the Libraries of Shaykh S. M. Cisse al-Ḥājj Malick Sy and Ibrāhīm Niasse in Senegal*, London: Al-Furqān (Silsilat Fahāris al-maḫṭūṭāt al-Islāmiyya / Handlists of Islamic Manuscripts, 8).

de Vaan, Michiel Arnoud Cor (2003), *The Avestan vowels*, Amsterdam: Rodopi (Leiden Studies in Indo-European, 12).

Vaganay, Léon (1934), *Initiation à la critique textuelle du Nouveau Testament*, Paris: Bloud et Gay. (Revised English Edition: L.V. – C.B. Amphoux, *An Introduction to New Testament Textual Criticism*, translated by Jenny Heimerdinger, foreword by Keith Elliott, Cambridge: Cambridge University Press, 2004).

Vajda, Georges – Madeleine Durantet (1949), *Répertoire des catalogues et inventaires de manuscrits arabes*, Paris: Centre national de la recherche scientifique (Institut de recherche et d'histoire des textes, 2).

Vajs, Josef (1932), *Rukověť hlaholské paleografie: Uvedeni do knižniho pisma hlaholského ('Handbook of Glagolitic Palaeography. Introduction to Glagolitic Writing')*, Praha: Orbis (Rukověti Slovanského Ústavu, 2).

Vallauri, Tommaso (1869), *Latinae exercitationes grammaticae et rhetoricae studiosis propositae*, Augustae Taurinorum: A. Salesiani.

Van den Eynde, Ceslas (1955), *Commentaire d'Iso'dad de Merv sur l'Ancien Testament*, I. *Genèse* (Corpus Scriptorum Christianorum Orientalium, 156, Scriptores Syri, 75).

Van den Eynde, Ceslas (1958), *Commentaire d'Iso'dad de Merv sur l'Ancien Testament*, II. *Exode-Deutéronome* (Corpus Scriptorum Christianorum Orientalium, 176, 179, Scriptores Syri, 80, 81).

Van den Eynde, Ceslas (1963), *Commentaire d'Iso'dad de Merv sur l'Ancien Testament*, III. *Livre des Sessions* (Corpus Scriptorum Christianorum Orientalium, 229, 230, Scriptores Syri, 96, 97).

Van den Eynde, Ceslas (1969), *Commentaire d'Iso'dad de Merv sur l'Ancien Testament*, IV. *Isaïe et les Douze* (Corpus Scriptorum Christianorum Orientalium, 303, 304, Scriptores Syri, 128, 129).

Van den Eynde, Ceslas (1972), *Commentaire d'Iso'dad de Merv sur l'Ancien Testament*, V. *Jérémie, Ezéchiel, Daniel* (Corpus Scriptorum Christianorum Orientalium, 328, 329, Scriptores Syri, 146, 147).

Van den Eynde, Ceslas (1981), *Commentaire d'Iso'dad de Merv sur l'Ancien Testament*, VI. *Psaumes* (Corpus Scriptorum Christianorum Orientalium, 433, 434, Scriptores Syri, 185, 186).

Van den Eynde, Ceslas – Vosté, Jaques Marie (1950), *Commentaire d'Iso'dad de Merv sur l'Ancien Testament*, I. *Genèse* (Corpus Scriptorum Christianorum Orientalium, 126, Scriptores Syri, 67).

Van Haelst, Joseph (1989), 'Les origines du codex', in: *Les débuts du codex. Actes de la journée d'études organisée à Paris les 3 et 4 juillet 1985*, ed. by Alain Blanchard, Turnhout: Brepols (Bibliologia: Elementa ad Librorum Studia Pertinentia, 9), 12–35.

Van Hemelryck, Tania – Stefania Marzano (eds) (2010), *Le recueil au Moyen Âge. La fin du Moyen Âge*, Turnhout: Brepols (Texte, Codex et Contexte, 9).

Van Rompay, Lucas (forthcoming), 'L'histoire du Couvent des Syriens (Wadi al-Natrun, Égypte) à la lumière des colophons de la Bibliothèque nationale de France', in: *Manuscripta syriaca. Des sources de première main*, ed. by Françoise Briquel-Chatonnet – Muriel Debié, Paris: Geuthner.

Varvaro, Alberto (1999), translated by Marcello Cherchi, 'The 'New Philology' from an Italian Perspective', *Text*, 12, 49–58.

Vasilyeva, O. (2009), 'Gilt-stamped Bindings of the Last Quarter of the 16th Century and the Qazwin Workshop', *Manuscripta Orientalia* 15/2, 38–56.

Vasmer, Max (1953–1958), *Russisches etymologisches Wörterbuch*, I–III, Heidelberg: Winter.

Veder, William R. (1999), *Utrum in alterum abiturum erat? A Study of the Beginnings of Text Transmission in Church Slavic. The Prologue to the Gospel Homiliary by Constantine of Preslav, the Text* On the Script *and the Treatise* On the Letters *by Anonymous Authors*, Bloomington, IN: Slavica.

Velios, Athanasios (2011), 'The experience of St Catherine of Sinaï and the digitalization project', paper presented at the COMSt workshop *Preservation of Middle Eastern Manuscripts – Restoration and digitization process: what should be done first?*, Leiden University.

Vergote, Joseph – George M. Parássoglou (1974), 'Les Psaumes 76 et 77 en copte-sahidique d'après le P. Yale Inv. 1779', *Le Muséon*, 87, 531–541.

Vernay-Nouri, Annie (2002), 'Marges, gloses et décor dans une série de manuscrits arabo-islamiques', in: *La tradition manuscrite en écriture arabe*, Paris: Edisud (Revue des mondes musulmans et de la Méditerranée, 99, 100), 117–131.

Vernay-Nouri, Annie (2011), *Enluminures d'Islam entre abstraction et figuration*, Paris: Bibliothèque nationale de France.

Vetter, Paul (1906), 'Die armenische apokryphen Apostelgeschichten. I. Die Petrus- und Paulus-Akten', *Theologische Quartalschrift*, 88, 161–186.

Vianès, Laurence (2000), 'Aspects de la mise en page des manuscrits dans les manuscrits des chaînes sur Ézéchiel', in: *Le commentaire entre tradition et innovation. Actes du colloque international de l'Institut des traditions textuelles (Paris et Villejuif, 22-25 septembre 1999)*, ed. by Marie-Odile Goulet-Cazé – Tiziano Dorandi, Paris: Vrin (Bibliothèque d'histoire de la philosophie. Nouvelle série), 79–88.

Vicini, Donata (1987), 'Luigi Robecchi Bricchetti, la nascita del museo etnografico pavese', *Pavia Econo*, 3, 113–123.

Vikan, Gary (ed.) (1973), *Illuminated Greek Manuscripts from American Collections. An Exhibition in Honor of Kurt Weitzman*, Princeton: The Art Museum.

Viktorov, Aleksej E. (1879), *Собранie рукописей В.И. Григоровiча* (*Sobranïe rukopisej V.I. Grigorovič̈a*, 'V.I. Grigorovič's manuscript collection'), Moskva: Lavrov.

Villefroy, Guillaume de (1735), *Discours préliminaire de la notice des manuscrits arméniens de la Bibliothèque du Roy apportés de Constantinople en l'année 1730*, Parisiis.

Villefroy, Guillaume de (1739), 'Catalogue des manuscrits arméniens de la bibliothèque du Roy, dressé en 1735', in: *Bibliotheca bibliothecarum manuscriptorum nova: ubi, quae innumeris pene manuscriptorum bibliothecis continentur, ad quodvis literaturae genus spectantia & notatu digna, describuntur & indicantur*, II, ed. by Bernard de Montfaucon, Paris: apud Briasson via Jacobaea ad insigne scientiae, 1015–1027.

Vinourd, François (2010), 'The Conservation of Syriac Manuscripts in the monastery of Charfet, Lebanon', paper presented at the COMSt workshop *Conservation Studies on Oriental Manuscripts*, Istanbul.

Viola, Natalia (2007), 'Les décors des Corans 'soudanais'', *Studi magrebini*, n.s. 5, 211–223.

Vnouček, Jiří (1998), 'Short History of Preservation at the National Library of the Czech Republic', *International Preservation News*, 16, 19–20.

Voguet, Elise (2003), 'L'inventaire des manuscrits de la bibliothèque de la grande mosquée de Kairouan (693/1293-4). Une contribution à l'histoire du mālikisme kairouannais', *Arabica*, 50/4, 532–544.

Voicu, Sever J. (2013), 'John Chrysostom in the Oriental Literatures', *Comparative Oriental Manuscript Studies Newsletter*, 5, 41–46.

Voigt, Rainer (1997), 'Das Vokalsystem des Syrischen nach Barhebraeus', *Oriens Christianus*, 81, 36–72.

Vööbus, Arthur (1978), 'Die Entdeckung eines Florilegiums der asketischen und mystischen Schriften im Syrischen', in: *Erkenntnisse und Meinungen*, II, ed. by Gernot Wiessner, Wiesbaden: Harrassowitz (Göttinger Orientforschungen, I. Reihe: Syriaca, 17), 263–271.

Voordeckers, Edmond (1964), 'Une vie slave de sainte Thaïs', *Analecta Bollandiana*, 82, 182–188.

Voskanyan, Ninel et al. (1988) {N.V. – K'narik Korkotyan – Ant'aṙam Savalyan}, Հայ գիրքը *1512-1800* թվականներին. Հայ հնատիպ գրքի մատենագիտություն (*Hay girk'ə 1512–1800 t'vakannerin. Hay hnatip grk'i matenagitut'yun*, 'The Armenian Book in 1512-1800. The Old-Print Books [Bibliography]'), Erevan: Haypethrat.

Vosté, Jacques-Marie (1929), 'Recueil d'auteurs ascétiques nestoriens du VIIe et VIIIe siècle', *Angelicum*, 6, 143–206.

Wachsmuth, Curt (1882), 'Die Wiener Apophthegmen-Sammlung', in: *Festschrift zur Begrüssung der in Karlsruhe vom 27.-30. Sept. 1882 tagenden XXXVI. Philologen-Versammlung, verfasst von den philologischen Collegen an der Heidelberger Universität*, Tübingen: Mohr, 1–36.

Wachtel, Klaus – Michael W. Holmes (eds) (2011), *Textual History of the Greek New Testament: Changing Views in Contemporary Research*, Atlanta, GA: Society of Biblical Literature (Text-critical studies, 8).

Wagner, Ewald (1976–2010), *Arabische Handschriften*, I–X, Wiesbaden: Steiner (Verzeichnis der Orientalischen Handschriften in Deutschland, 17B).

Wagner, Ewald (1997), *Afrikanische Handschriften*, II: *Islamische Handschriften aus Äthiopien*, Stuttgart: Steiner (Verzeichnis der orientalischen Handschriften in Deutschland, 24/2).

Waldman, Marilyn Robinson (1980), *Toward a theory of historical narrative. A case-study in Perso-Islamicate historiography*, Columbus, OH: Ohio State University Press.

Waldstein, Michael – Frederik Wisse (eds) (1995), *The Apocryphon of John: Synopsis of Nag Hammadi Codices II, 1; III, 1; and IV, 1 with BG 8502, 2*, Leiden: Brill (Nag Hammadi and Manichaean Studies, 33).

Walter, Donald (2001), 'Multidimensional Scaling (Mapping) of Peshitta Manuscripts of Numbers and Deuteronomy', in: *Biblical Hebrew, Biblical texts: Essays in memory of Michael P. Weitzman*, ed. by Ada Rapoport-Albert – Gillian Greenberg, Sheffield: Sheffield Academic Press, 178–198.

Warda, Jeffrey (2008), The AIC Guide to Digital Photography and Conservation Documentation, <http://www.jiscdigitalmedia.ac.uk/digitisation>, Washington, DC: AIC.

Waring, Judith (2010), 'Byzantine Book Culture', in: *A Companion to Byzantium*, ed. by Liz James, Malden – Oxford – Chichester: Wiley–Blackwell (Blackwell Companions to the Ancient World), 275–288.

Warner, George (1920), *Descriptive Catalogue of Illuminated Manuscripts in the Library of C.W. Dyson Perrins*, I–II, London: Oxford University Press.

Wasserzeichensammlung Piccard, <http://www.piccard-online.de>, last access October 2014 (See also Piccard 1961–1997).

Wattenbach, Wilhelm (1896), *Das Schriftwesen im Mittelalter*, Leipzig: Hirzel.

Wehr, Hans (1956), *Das Buch der wunderbaren Erzählungen und seltsamen Geschichten*, Wiesbaden: Harrassowitz (Bibliotheca Islamica, 18).

Weisweiler, Max (1962), *Der islamische Bucheinband des Mittelalters*, Wiesbaden: Harrassowitz (Beiträge zum Buch- und Bibliothekswesen, 10).

Weitzman, Michael P. (1985), 'The Analysis of Open Traditions', *Studies in Bibliography*, 38, 82–120.

Weitzman, Michael P. (1987), 'The Evolution of Manuscript Traditions', *Journal of the Royal Statistical Society. Series A*, 150, 287–308.

Weitzmann, Kurt (1960), 'Aristocratic Psalter and Lectionary', *Record of the Art Museum, Princeton University* 19 (= *Special Number in Honor of the Director Ernest Theodore DeWald on the Occasion of His Retirement*), 98–107.

Weitzmann, Kurt (1977), *Late Antique and Early Christian Book Illumination*, London: George Braziller.

Weitzmann, Kurt – George Galavaris (1990), *The Monastery of Saint Catherine at Mount Sinai: the Illuminated Greek Manuscripts*. I: *From the Ninth to the Twelfth Century*, Princeton: Princeton University Press.

Welch, Anthony (1972–1978), *Collection of Islamic Art*, I–IV, Geneva: Château de Bellerive - Prince Sadruddin Aga Khan.

Welch, Stuart Cary et al. (1987) {S.W. – Annemarie Schimmel – Marie L. Swietochowski – Wheeler M. Thackston}, *The Emperors' Album: Images of Mughal India*, New York: The Metropolitan Museum of Art.

Wellcome Arabic Manuscripts Online, <http://wamcp.bibalex.org/home>, last access October 2014.

Wellmann, Max (1906–1914), *Pedanii Dioscuridis Anazarbei, De materia medica libri quinque*, I–III, Berlin: Weidmann.

Werner, John (1920), *Descriptive Catalogue of Illuminated Manuscripts in the Library of C.W. Dyson Perrins*, I–II, Oxford: Oxford University Press.

Werner, Petra (ed.) (2002), *Jüdische Handschriften. Restaurieren. Bewahren. Präsentieren*, I, Berlin: Staatsbibliothek.

West, Martin L. (1973), *Textual Criticism and Editorial Technique: applicable to Greek and Latin texts*, Stuttgart: Teubner (Teubner Studienbücher: Philologie).

West, Martin L. (2008), 'On editing the Gāthās', *Iran*, 46, 121–134.

West, Stephanie (1963), 'Reclamantes in Greek Papyri', *Scriptorium*, 17, 314–315.

West African Arabic Manuscripts Database <http://www.westafricanmanuscripts.org>, last access October 2014.

Westergaard, Niels Ludvig (1852–1854), *Zendavesta, or The religious books of the Zoroastrians*, Copenhagen: Berling Brothers.

Weyl Carr, Annemarie (1980), 'Diminutive Byzantine Manuscripts', *Codices Manuscripti*, 6, 130–136.

Whelan, Estelle (n.d.), 'The Phantom of Ḥiǧāzī Script. A Note on Palaeographic Method' [manuscript].

Whitfield, Philip et al. (eds) (2010), *Coptic Art Revealed*, Cairo: Supreme Council of Antiquities.

Whittaker, John (1991), 'The Practice of Manuscript Collation', *Text*, 5, 121–130.

Wilkinson, Robert J. (2007a), *Orientalism, Aramaic and Kabbalah in the Catholic Reformation. The First Printing of the Syriac New Testament*, Leiden: Brill (Studies in the history of Christian thought, 138).

Wilkinson, Robert J. (2007b), *The Kabbalistic Scholars of the Antwerp Polyglot Bible*, Leiden: Brill.

Williams, Jacqueline A. (1988), *Biblical Interpretation in the Gnostic Gospel of Truth from Nag Hammadi*, Atlanta, GA: Scholars Press (Society of Biblical Literature Dissertation Series, 79).

Williams, Michael A. (1997), 'Response to the papers of Karen King, Frederik Wisse, Michael Waldstein and Sergio La Porta', in: *The Nag Hammadi Library After Fifty Years: Proceedings of the 1995 Society of Biblical Literature Commemoration*, ed. by John D. Turner – Anne McGuire, Leiden: Brill (Nag Hammadi and Manichaean Studies, 44), 208–220.

Wilson, Nigel Guy (1983), *Scholars of Byzantinum*, London: Gerald Duckworth – Baltimore: Johns Hopkins University Press.

Wilson, Nigel Guy (1992), *From Byzantium to Italy: Greek Studies in the Italian Renaissance*, London: Gerald Duckworth – Baltimore: Johns Hopkins University Press.

Wilson, Nigel Guy (2011), *A Descriptive Catalogue of the Greek Manuscripts of Corpus Christi College*, Cambridge: Brewer.

Wilson, Robert McL. (1975), 'The Trials of a Translator: Some Translation Problems in the Nag Hammadi Texts', in: *Les Textes de Nag Hammadi: Colloque du Centre d'Histoire des Religions (Strasbourg, 23–25 octobre 1974)*, ed. by Jacques-É. Ménard, Leiden: Brill (Nag Hammadi Studies, 7), 32–40.

Winkler, Gabriele (2005a), *Die Basilius-Anaphora. Edition der beiden armenischen Redaktionen und der relevanten Fragmente. Übersetzung und Zusammenschau aller Versionen im Licht der orientalischen Überlieferungen*, Roma: Pontificio Istituto Orientale (Anaphorae orientales, 2, Anaphorae armenicae, 2).

Winkler, Gabriele (2005b), review of A. Budde, *Die ägyptische Basilios-Anaphora. Text – Kommentar – Geschichte*, Münster: Aschendorff Verlag (Jerusalemer Theologisches Forum, 7), 2004, *Oriens christianus*, 89, 264–275.

Winlock, Herbert E. et al. (1926) {H.W. – Walter E. Crum [I]; H.W. – Hugh Gerard Evelyn White [II]}, *The Monastery of Epiphanius at Thebes*, I–II, New York: Metropolitan Museum of Art (Publications of the Metropolitan Museum of Art Egyptian Expedition, 3–4).

Wion, Anaïs (2004), 'An Analysis of 17th-Century Ethiopian Paintings', in: *The Indigenous and the Foreign in Christian Ethiopian Art. On Portuguese-Ethiopian Contacts in the 16th-17th Centuries. Papers from the Fifth International Conference on the History of Ethiopian Art (Arrábida, 26–30 November 1999)*, ed. by Manuel João Ramos – Isabel Boavida, Aldershot: Ashgate, 103–112.

Wion, Anaïs et al. (2006) {A.W. – Marie-Laure Derat – Claire Bosc-Tiessé}, *Inventaire des bibliothèques et des catalogues de manuscrits éthiopiens*, <http://www.menestrel.fr/spip.php?rubrique694>.

Wisse, Frederik (1990), 'NHC XII, 2: The Gospel of Truth', in: *Nag Hammadi Codices XI, XII, XIII*, ed. by Charles W. Hedrick, Leiden: Brill (Nag Hammadi Studies, 28), 329–347.

Wisse, Frederik (1997), 'After the Synopsis: Prospects and Problems in Establishing a Critical Text of the Apocryphon of John and in Defining its Historical Location', in: *The Nag Hammadi Library After Fifty Years: Proceedings of the 1995 Society of Biblical Literature Commemoration*, ed. by John D. Turner – Anne McGuire, Leiden: Brill (Nag Hammadi and Manichaean Studies, 44), 138–153.

Witakowski, Witold (2012), 'Coptic and Ethiopic Historical Writing', in: *The Oxford Handbook of Historiography*, II: 400-1400, ed. by Sarah Foot – Chase F. Robinson, Oxford: Oxford University Press, 138–154.

Witkam, Jan Just (1983–1986), *Catalogue of Arabic Manuscripts in the Library of the University of Leiden and other collections in the Netherlands*, I–IV, Leiden: Brill (Codices manuscripti).

Witkam, Jan Just (1988), 'Establishing the stemma: fact or fiction?', *Manuscripts of the Middle East*, 3, 88–101.

Witkam, Jan Just (2007), *Inventory of the Oriental Manuscripts of the Library of the University of Leiden*, I–XXV, Leiden: Ter Lugt Press.

Witkam, Jan-Just (2013), 'The Philologist's Stone. The Continuing Search for the Stemma', *Comparative Oriental Manuscript Studies Newsletter*, 6, 34–38.

World Intellectual Property Organization, *Berne Convention 1886* <http://www.wipo.int/treaties/en/text.jsp? file_id=283698>, last accessed June 2014.

World Trade Organization, *General Agreement on Tariffs and Trade* <http://www.wto.org/english/ docs_e/legal_e/06-gatt.pdf>, last accessed June 2014.

World Trade Organization, *Trade-Related Aspects of Intellectual Property Rights* <http://www.wto.org/english/tratop_e/trips_e/t_agm0_e.htm>, last accessed June 2014.

Worp, Klaas Anthony (2012), *A New Survey of Greek, Coptic, Demotic and Latin Tabulae Preserved from Classical Antiquity, version 1.0*, <http://www.trismegistos.org/top.php>, Leiden – Leuven: Trismegistos (Trismegistos Online Publications, 6).

Worp, Klaas Anthony – Albert Rijksbaron (1997), *The Kellis Isocrates Codex*, Oxford: Oxbow (Dakhleh Oasis Project, 5 = Oxbow Monograph, 88).

Worrell, William H. (1923), *The Coptic Manuscripts in the Freer Collection*, New York – London: Macmillan (University of Michigan Studies, Humanistic Series, 10).

Worthington, Martin (2012), *Principles of Akkadian Textual Criticism*, Berlin: De Gruyter (Studies in Ancient Near Eastern Records, 1).

Wright, Elaine – Stronge, Susan (2008), *Muraqqaʿ: Imperial Mughal Albums from the Chester Beatty Library*, Alexandria, VA: Art Services International.

Wright, William (1870–1872), *Catalogue of Syriac Manuscripts in the British Museum, acquired since the year 1838*, I–III, London: The British Museum.

Wright, William (1877), *Catalogue of the Ethiopic Manuscripts in the British Museum, acquired since the year 1847*, London: Gilbert and Rivington.

Wright, William (1896), *A Grammar of the Arabic Language*, I–II, Cambridge: Cambridge University Press.

Wright, William (1901), *A catalogue of the Syriac manuscripts preserved in the library of the University of Cambridge*, I–II, Cambridge: Cambridge University Press.

Wurst, Gregor (1996), *The Manichaean Coptic Papyri in the Chester Beatty Library*: *Psalm Book*, *II.1*: *Die Bēma-Psalmen*, Turnhout: Brepols (Corpus Fontium Manichaeorum, Series Coptica, 1.2.1).

Xačʿikyan, Levon S. (1950), ԺԴ դարի Հայերեն ձեռագրերի հիշատակարաններ (*XIV dari hayeren jeṙagreri hišatakaranner*, ʻColophons of Fourteenth-Century Armenian Manuscripts'), Erevan: Haykakan SSH Gitutʿyunneri Akademia.

Xačʿikyan, Levon S. (1955, 1958, 1967), ԺԵ դարի Հայերեն ձեռագրերի հիշատակարաններ (*XV dari hayeren jeṙagreri hišatakaranner*, ʻColophons of Fifteenth-Century Armenian Manuscripts'), I: *1401-1450*; II: *1451-1480*; III: *1480-1500*, Erevan: Haykakan SSH Gitutʿyunneri Akademia.

Xalatʿeancʿ, Grigor (1899), Աւետարան ըստ թարգմանութեան նախնեաց մերոց գրեալ ՅԼԶ թ. հայոց եւ յամի տեառն *887*. Լուսատիպ հրատարակութիւն գրչագիր Լազարեան Ճեմարանի Արեւեան լեզուաց / *Евангелiе въ древне-армянскомъ переводѣ, написанное въ 887 году. Фототипическое изданiе рукописи Лазаревскаго института восточныхъ языковъ / Évangile traduit en langue arménienne ancienne et écrit en l'an 887. Édition phototypique du manuscript de l'Institut Lazareff des langues Orientales* (*Awetaran əst tʿargmanutʿean naxneacʿ merocʿ greal YLZ tʿ. hayocʿ ew yami teaṙn 887. Lusatip hratarakutʿyun grčʿagir Lazarean Čemarani Arewelean lezuacʿ / Evangelie v" drevne-armjanskom" perevodě, napisannoe v 887 godu*: *fototipičeskoe izdanïe rukopisi Lazarevskago instituta vostochnych" jazykov"*), Moskva: Lazarevskij institut vostočnych jazykov.

Xažakyan, Levon (1984), ʻX–XIV դարերի թղթյա ձեռագրերի պատառիկների ֆիզիկաքիմիական վերլուծության արդյունքները (*X–XIV dareri tʿltʿya jeṙagreri pataṙikneri fizikakʿimiakan verlucutʿyan ardyunkʿnerə*, ʻPhysical-chemical Study of Tenth to Fourteenth Century Paper Manuscript Fragments')', *Banber Matenadarani*, 14, 163–170.

Yāḥaqqī, Muḥammad Ǧaʿfar – Mahdī Sayyidī (1388 š./2009 CE), تاريخ بيهقي (*Tārīḫ-i Bayhaqī*, ʻThe *History* of Bayhaqī'), I–II, Tihrān: Suḫan.

Yaqṭīn, Saʿīd (1994), قال الراوي، البنية الحكائية في السيرة الشعبية (*Qāla ʾl-rāwī. Al-Binya al-ḥikāʾīya fī ʾs-sīra al-šaʿbīya*,ʻThe storyteller said, narratological structure of Arab popular epic'), Bayrūt: al-Markaz al-ṯaqāfī ʾl-ʿarabī.

Yardeni, Ada (2002), *The Book of Hebrew Script*: *History*, *Palaeography*, *Script Styles*, *Calligraphy and Design*, London: The London Library.

Yarshater, Ehsan (2011), ʻForeword', in: *The ʻHistory' of Beyhaqi* (*The History of Sultan Masʿud of Ghazna*, *1030–1041*) *by Abu ʾl-Fażl Beyhaqi*, 1: *Introduction and Translation of Years 421–423 A.H = 1030–1032 A.D.*, ed. by Clifford Edmund Bosworth, Boston: Ilex Foundation – Washington, DC: Center for Hellenic Studies, Trustees for Harvard University (Ilex Foundation Series, 6), xiii–xx.

Yoshida, Jun'ichi – Chimeddorji (eds) (2008), ハラホト出土モンゴル文書の研究 (*Harahoto shutsudo mongoru monjo no kenkyū*, ʻStudy on the Mongolian Documents Found at Qaraqota'), Tokyo: Yūzankaku.

Young, Dwight Wayne (2001), ʻShenute's Fifth Canon in Three Folios at the National Library in Vienna', *Journal of Juristic Papyrology*, 31, 187–208, pls. 1–6.

Yovsēpʻeancʿ, Sargis (1896), Անկանոն գիրք Հին Կտակարանաց (*Ankanon girkʿ Hin Ktakaranacʿ*, ʻNon-canonical Books of the Old Testament'), Venetik: S. Łazar (Tʿangaran haykakan hin ew nor dprutʿeancʿ, 1).

Yovsēpʻyan [Hovsēpʻean], Garegin (1913), ʻՔարտէզ հայ հնագրութեան (*Kʿartez hay hnagrutʿean*, ʻAlbum of Armenian Palaeography')', *Šołakatʿ*, 1, 170–214, v, 70 plates.

Yovsēpʻyan [Hovsēpʻean], Garegin (1951), Յիշատակարանք ձեռագրաց. I: Ե. դարից մինչեւ 1250 թ. (*Yišatakarankʿ jeṙagracʿ*, I. *V daricʿ minčew 1250 tʿ*., ʻColophons of Manuscripts. I. From the Fifth Century to 1250'), Antelias: Cilician Catholicosate.

Yusofi, Gholām-Ḥoseyn (1988), ʻBayhaqī, Abu'l Fażl', in: *Encyclopaedia Iranica*, III/8, London, 889–894 (= *Encyclopaedia Iranica online*, <http://www.iranicaonline.org/articles/bayhaqi-abul-fazl-mohammad-b>, last updated December 15, 1988, last access November 2014.

Yūsuf ʿAlī Ṭawīl (2002), كتاب الفهرست لأبي الفرج محمد بن إسحاق النديم (*Kitāb al-fihrist li-Abī ʾl-Farağ Muḥammad b. Isḥāq al-Nadīm*, ʻIbn al-Nadim's Catalogue of Books'), Bayrūt: Dār al-kutub al-ʿilmiyya.

Zabelin, Ivan E[gorovič] (1915), *Домашнiй бытъ русскихъ царей въ XVI и XVII столетияхъ* (*Domašnij byt" russkich" carej v" XVI i XVII stoletijach"*, ʻThe domestic life of the Russian tsars in the 16th and 17th centuries'), II, Moskva: Sinodal'naja tipografija.

Zaborski, Andrzej (1995), ʻSome Greek, Latin and Coptic loanwords in Ethiopic', in: *Analecta Indoeuropaea Cracoviensia I. Safarewicz memoriae dicata*, ed. by Wojciech Smoczyński, Cracoviae: In officina cuius nomen Universitas, 537–543.

Zack, Liesbeth – Arie Schippers (eds) (2012), *Middle Arabic and Mixed Arabic*: *Diachrony and Synchrony*, Leiden – Boston: Brill (Studies in Semitic Languages and Linguistics, 64).

Zagrebin, Vjačeslav Michajlovič – Žanna Leonidovna Levšina (2009), ʻО предполагаемых миниатюрах Зографского Евангелия' (*O predpolagaemych miniatjurach Zografskogo Evangelija*, ʻOn the supposed miniatures of the Zographou Gospels'), *Chrizograf*, 3, 478–491.

Zakharia, Katia (2010), ʻLe patrimoine littéraire oral et les paradoxes de sa conservation écrite, l'exemple de la littérature arabe populaire', paper presented at the conference *Patrimoines Culturels en Méditerranée orientale*: *recherche scientifique et enjeux identitaires. 4. atelier* (*25. novembre 2010*): *Patrimoine institutionnel et patrimoine populaire. L'accession au statut patrimonial en Méditerranée orientale*, Rencontres scientifiques en ligne de la Maison de l'Orient et de la Méditerranée, Lyon, 18 pp., <http://www.mom.fr/ressources-numeriques/documents-numerises/colloques-texte-integral/patrimoines-culturels-en-mediterranee-orientale/4eme-atelier>, last access October 2014.

Zanetti, Ugo (1985), *Les lectionnaires coptes annuels*: *Basse-Égypte*, Louvain: Peeters (Publications de l'Institut Orientaliste de Louvain, 33).

Zanetti, Ugo (1986a), ʻFiligranes vénitiens en Égypte', in: *Studi albanologici, balcanici, bizantini e orientali in onore di Giuseppe Valentini, S. J.*, Firenze: Leo S. Olschki, 437–499.

Zanetti, Ugo (1986b), *Les manuscrits de Dair Abû Maqâr. Inventaire*, Genève: Cramer (Cahiers d'Orientalisme, 11).

Zanetti, Ugo (1987), ʻEsquisse d'une typologie des euchologes coptes bohaïriques', *Le Muséon*, 100, 407–418.

Zanetti, Ugo (1995), ʻBohairic Liturgical Manuscripts', *Orientalia Christiana Periodica*, 61, 65–94.

Zanetti, Ugo (1998), 'Les manuscrits de Saint-Macaire. Observations codicologiques', in: *Recherches de codicologie comparée: la composition du codex au Moyen Âge en Orient et en Occident*, ed. by Philippe Hoffmann, Paris: Presses de l'École normale supérieure (Collection bibliologie), 171–182.

Zanetti, Ugo (2007), 'Leçons liturgiques au Monastère Blanc', *Bulletin de la Société d'archéologie copte*, 46, 205–304.

Zanetti, Ugo (forthcoming), 'La liturgie dans les monastères de Shenoute', *Bulletin de la Société d'archéologie copte*, 53.

Zarri, Gian Piero (1971), 'L'automazione delle procedure di critica testuale. Problemi e prospettive', *Lingua e Stile*, 6, 397–414.

Ǯavaxišvili, Ivane (1947), სინის მთის ქართულ ხელნაწერთა აღწერილობა (*Sinis mtis kartul xelnaçerta aġçeriloba*, 'Description of the Georgian manuscripts of the Sinai'), Tbilisi: Sakartvelos SSR Mecnierebata Aḳademiis Gamomcemloba.

Zaydān, Yūsuf (1996–1997), فهرس مخطوطات مكتبة رفاعة رافع الطهطاوى (*Fihris maḫṭūṭāt maktabat Rifāʿat Rāfiʿ al-Ṭahṭāwī*, 'Catalogue of Rifāʿat Rāfiʿ aṭ-Ṭahṭāwī Manuscripts'), I–III, Cairo: Institute of Arabic Manuscripts.

Zerdoun Bat-Yehouda, Monique (1983), *Les encres noires au Moyen Âge (jusqu'à 1600)*, Paris: Centre national de la recherche scientifique.

Zerdoun Bat-Yehouda, Monique (1997), *Les papiers filigranés des manuscrits hébreux datés jusqu'à 1450 conservés en France et en Israël*, I–II, Turnhout: Brepols (Bibliologia: Elementa ad Librorum Studia Pertinentia, 16–17).

Zoëga, Georg (1810), *Catalogus codicum Copticorum manuscriptorum qui in Museo Borgiano Velitris adservantur*, Roma: Sacra Congregatio de Propaganda Fide.

Žordania [Žordanija], Th[eodor] D[avidovič] – M[ose] G[eorgievič] Ǯanašvili [Džanašvili] (1902–1908), *Описание рукописей Тифлисскаго Церковнаго Музея Карталино-Кахетинскаго духовенства* (*Opisanïe rukopisej Tiflisskago Cerkovnago Muzeja Kartalino-Kachetinskago duchovenstva*, 'Description of the manuscripts of the Ecclesiastical Museum of the Clergy of Kartli-Kakheti in Tiflis'), I–III, Tiflis: Gutenberg (Izdanie Cerkovnago Muzeja, 12, 9, 13).

Zotenberg, Hermann (1866), *Catalogues des manuscrits hébreux et samaritains de la Bibliothèque Impériale*, Paris: Imprimerie imperiale.

Zotenberg, Hermann (1877), *Catalogue des manuscrits éthiopiens (gheez et amharique) de la Bibliothèque Nationale*, Paris: Imprimerie nationale (Manuscrits Orientaux).

Zuurmond, Rochus (1989), *Novum Testamentum Aethiopice: The Synoptic Gospels*. I. *General Introduction*. II. *Edition of the Gospel of Mark*, Stuttgart: Steiner (Äthiopistische Forschungen, 27).

Indexes

The indexes include (1) languages and traditions; (2) place names, excluding those associated with manuscript collections that are indexed separately; (3) names of persons (whether ancient writers, literary figures, or modern scholars) and titles of literary works mentioned in the text of the handbook (the titles appear under the names of the respective authors when known); (4) institutions and projects; (5) index of manuscript collections and manuscripts quoted, with an additional sublist of papyri (even if these are already listed as manuscripts); and (6) general index.

The indexes are supposed to help the users to find the information that cannot be directly deduced from the Table of Contents. Thus, the keywords already clearly and fully indexed by the Table of Contents do not necessarily reappear in the Indices, and when they do, they tend to supply additional page references. This is in particular relevant for the General Index.

The entries are alphabetized word-by-word; abbreviated forms are treated as if they were written out (e.g. St as if it were spelled Saint). In compound names, articles and prepositions are disregarded for the purposes of alphabetization (e.g. John the Baptist comes before John Chrysostom).

Languages and traditions

Place names

For the sites of collections see Collections and manuscripts below. The maps in the General introduction have not been indexed.

Persons and works

All personal names, whether historical, literary, or modern, are listed here. Works appear under the name of the author whenever known. The index also includes titles of academic series. For particular manuscripts (e.g. *Ilias picta*) or text genres (e.g. homilies, hagiography) see General index.

Institutions and projects

Collections and manuscripts

Papyri

General index

Lightning Source UK Ltd.
Milton Keynes UK
UKOW01f1939270115

245240UK00011B/137/P